The Nature of this Book

This book is designed as a working tool. It is a concise, highly practical guide to the leading cases which shape European competition law.

Cases in this book include judgments of the Court of Justice of the European Union and General Court as well as leading decisions of the European Commission. Reference is also made to a number of cases from the United States and from EU Member States. The book includes over 500 case entries. It covers the leading cases taught in universities across Europe, as well as many additional cases which shape the scope and application of European competition law.

The book is divided into 13 chapters, focusing on Article 101 TFEU, Article 102 TFEU and the European Merger Regulation. In addition it explores the public and private enforcement of competition law, the intersection between intellectual property rights and competition law, the application of competition law to state action and state aid laws.

A short introduction at the beginning of each chapter summarises the relevant regulations and guidelines and provides an analytical framework for the cases covered in the chapter. All case entries are accompanied by commentary which adds further context by, among other things, analysing the case in relation to other cases, regulations and guidelines.

In line with the functional approach at the heart of this book, case entries are concise. They include a mixture of quotes and summaries, extracting the main points of each case that are relevant to the chapter in which the case appears. The reader will not find long extracts from regulations or guidelines in this book. These are easily accessible in print or electronic form.

References in decisions or judgments to the old numbering of the Treaty of Amsterdam have been updated throughout this book to include the renumbering following the Treaty of Lisbon (Treaty on the functioning of the European Union). Thus, references in earlier cases to Articles 81, 82 and 86 EC are represented as Article 101 TFEU, Article 102 TFEU and Article 106 TFEU respectively.

Following the coming into force of the Treaty of Lisbon, the European courts have been renamed. Article 19 TEU stipulates that the Court of Justice of the European Union (CJEU) shall include the Court of Justice (formerly abbreviated 'ECJ') and the General Court (formerly the Court of First Instance). References throughout this book have been updated accordingly.

Outline Contents

Contents

b. One-way Substitution

c. Markets for Spare Parts/Aftermarkets

d. Narrow Markets

Including the following summary references:

e. Switching Costs

f. Markets for Raw Materials

g. Data markets

h. Judicial review

3.   Article 101 TFEU   56

a. Agreement between Undertakings

Including the following summary references:

b. Concerted Practice

Including the following summary references:

c. Joint Classification and Single Overall Agreement

Including the following summary references:

d. Decision by an Association

Including the following summary references:

e. Authorised representatives

f. Object or Effect

Including the following summary references:

g. Scope of Analysis under Article 101(1) TFEU and the 'Rule of Reason'

Including the following summary references:

h. Ancillary Restraints

i. Appreciable Effect (de minimis)

j. Appreciable Effect on Trade between Member States

Including the following summary reference:

k. Article 101(2) TFEU

Including the following summary references:

l. Article 101(3) TFEU

Including the following summary references:

m. The range of goals and values in Article 101 TFEU

4.   Horizontal and Vertical Agreements   145

a. Cartel Agreements

Including the following summary references:

b. Price Fixing

Including the following summary references:

c. Purchase Price Fixing

Including the following summary references:

d. Collusive Tendering

Including the following summary references:

e. Market Sharing and Non-compete Agreements

Including the following summary references:

f. Collective Boycott

Including the following summary references:

g. Information Exchange Arrangements

Including the following summary references:

h. Hub and Spoke Information Exchange

Including the following summary references:

i. Export Bans

Including the following summary references:

o. Resale Price Maintenance

p. Most Favoured Nation Clauses

q. Agency Agreements

a. Dominance

Including the following summary references:

b. Dominant Position within the Internal Market or in a Substantial Part of it

c. Abuse and the Goals of Article 102 TFEU

d. Predatory Pricing

Including the following summary references:

e. Selective Price Cuts

Including the following summary references:

f. Price Alignment

Including the following summary references:

g. Price Discrimination

Including the following summary references:

h. Rebates

Including the following summary references:

i. Margin Squeeze

Including the following summary references:

j. Excessive Pricing

Including the following summary references:

k. Refusal to Supply

Including the following summary references:

l. Tying and Bundling

Including the following summary references:

m. Other forms of Exclusion

Including the following summary references:

n. Objective Justification and Efficiency Defence

Including the following summary references:

o. Effect on Trade between Member States

p. Nullity and Severance

a. Article 102 TFEU

Including the following summary references:

b. The European Merger Regulation

Including the following summary reference:

c. Conscious Parallelism vis-à-vis Concerted Practice

7.   Competition Law and the State   334

a. Article 4(3) Treaty on European Union (TEU)

Including the following summary references:

b. State Compulsion Defence

Including the following summary references:

c. Article 106(1) TFEU

| 8. | **Competition Law and Intellectual Property Rights** | 361 |

a. Article 101 TFEU and Licensing of Intellectual Property Rights

Including the following summary references:

e. Investigation

Including the following summary references:

f. Horizontal Mergers

Including the following summary references:

g. Vertical Mergers

Including the following summary references:

h. Conglomerate Mergers

Including the following summary references:

i. Buyer Power

Including the following summary references:

j. Countervailing Buyer Power

k. Efficiencies

l. Failing Firm Defence

m. Remedies

b. Inspection Powers

c. Obstruction during inspection

d. Request for Information

Including the following summary reference:

e. Statement of Objections and Access to File

Including the following summary references:

f. Professional Secrecy

Including the following summary references:

g. Limited Right against Self-incrimination

Including the following summary references:

h. Professional Legal Privilege

Including the following summary references:

i. Interim Measures

Including the following summary references:

j. Finding and Termination of Infringement—Remedies

Including the following summary reference:

k. Commitments

l. Fines

m. Liability of a parent company to a fine

n. Recovery of fine from employees and directors

o. Limitation Periods

Including the following summary references:

p. Full and Effective Judicial Review

g. Burden and Standard of Proof in Competition Cases

h. Standing and Passing on Defence

Including the following summary reference:

i. Uniform Application of Competition Laws

Including the following summary references:

j. Cooperation between National Courts and Commission

Including the following summary references:

k. Jurisdiction and Applicable Law

12.   Extraterritoriality

a. The Implementation Doctrine

Including the following summary references:

b. The Single Economic Entity Doctrine

13. State Aid 639

a. Condition 1—By the State *and* through State Resources

Including the following summary references:

b. Condition 2—Conferral of an Advantage

Including the following summary references:

c. Condition 3—Selectivity

Including the following summary references:

d. Condition 4—Distortion of Competition and Effect on Trade

Including the following summary references:

Table of Cases

Introductory Note

This Table of Cases is divided into four sections: Court of Justice, General Court, European Commission, and Other Cases (which contains all national court rulings and rulings by non-European Union courts). References such as '178–9' indicate (not necessarily continuous) discussion of a case across a range of pages. Page numbers in bold denote full discussion of the case in question.

Court of Justice

General Court

European Commission

Other Cases

1

The Concept of Undertaking

The term 'undertaking' identifies the addressees of the European competition provisions. As such, it is central to the analysis of Article 101 TFEU, Article 102 TFEU and the European Merger Regulation, as only 'undertakings' may be subjected to these regulatory instruments.

The Functional Approach

The Treaty on the Functioning of the European Union (TFEU) is silent on the meaning of the term 'undertaking', leaving it to the European Courts to develop and establish its content and realm. To ensure the full effectiveness of the competition provisions the Courts adopted a functional approach, applying the term to entities engaged in economic activities regardless of their legal status and the way in which they are financed. This functional approach focuses on the commercial nature of activities and not on the type of entity engaged in them. Consequently, it may capture individuals, trade associations, partnerships, clubs, companies and public authorities. See for example:

IV/33.384 etc	*FIFA—distribution of package tours during the 1990 World Cup*	4

The Relativity of the Concept

The notion of undertaking is a relative one. The functional approach and the corresponding focus on the activity, rather than the form of the entity may result in an entity being considered an undertaking when it engages in some activities, but not when it engages in others. The relativity of the concept is most evident when considering activities carried out by non-profit-making organisations or public bodies. These entities may at times operate in their charitable or public capacity but may be considered as undertakings when they engage in commercial activities. The economic nature of an activity is often apparent when the entities offer goods and services in the marketplace and when the activity could, potentially, yield profits.

The following cases highlight the way in which the European Courts and the Commission assess the nature of activities:

C-41/90	*Höfner and Elser v Macrotron GmbH*	5
C-364/92	*SAT Fluggesellschaft v Eurocontrol*	6
C-159/91 etc	*Poucet v Assurances Générales de France*	7
C-343/95	*Cali & Figli v Servizi ecologici porto di Genova SpA*	8
T-319/99	*FENIN v Commission*	9
C-205/03P	*FENIN v Commission*	10
C-309/99	*Wouters*	12
C-264/01 etc	*AOK-Bundesverband*	13
C-67/96	*Albany v Stichting Bedriifspensioenfonds Textielindustrie*	15
C-113/07	*SELEX Sistemi Integrati SpA v Commission*	16
C-138/11	*Compass-Datenbank GmbH v Republik Österreich*	19

See also summary references to:

Single Economic Entity

Moving away from the functional assessment of the activity, another question related to the term 'undertaking' is raised in the application of Article 101 TFEU. The Article applies to, among other things, agreements between undertakings. It therefore does not cover internal activities within an undertaking.

The concept of undertaking may encompass several legal entities or natural persons. Subsequently, the corporate principle of separate legal personality gives way in the area of competition law to the economic concept of undertaking.

The scope given to the term undertakings may affect the application of competition laws to groups of companies. On one hand it may exclude agreements between separate legal entities within a single economic unit from the application of competition law and view them as an internal allocation of functions. On the other hand, it may link separate legal entities by viewing them as a single undertaking, thus holding the group of entities responsible for an anticompetitive activity carried out by one of them. See for example:

See also summary references to:

Pure financial investor defence

When a parent company exercises decisive influence over a subsidiary, it can be held liable for the activities of the subsidiary. Where a parent company has a 100 per cent shareholding in its subsidiary there is a rebuttable presumption that that parent company exercises a decisive influence over the conduct of its subsidiary. The presumption of decisive influence may be rebutted by demonstrating that in practice the parent company exercised restraint and did not influence the market conduct of its subsidiary. Such may be the case, for example, when the parent company is a pure financial investor.

See also summary references to:

FIFA—distribution of package tours during the 1990 World Cup Cases IV/33.384 and IV/33.378 European Commission, [1992] OJ L326/31	**Undertaking** Functional Approach

Facts

The European Commission considered a complaint regarding the ticket distribution system endorsed by the International Federation of Football Associations (FIFA) during the FIFA World Cup, held in Italy in 1990. The organisation of the event and the distribution of tickets were managed through a 'local organising committee' which was set up jointly by FIFA and the National Italian Football Association (FIGC). The ticket distribution system operated through various sports associations yet it included a restriction on sales to travel agencies. This restriction enabled the exclusive grant of the world wide distribution rights of tickets as part of package tours to an Italian joint venture '90 Tour Italia SpA'. This exclusivity arrangement prevented other travel agencies from offering combined package tours with tickets for the 1990 World Cup. In its decision the Commission considered the compatibility of the exclusive distribution agreement with Article 101 TFEU. A preliminary question concerned the nature of the entities involved and whether they constituted an undertaking within the meaning of Article 101 TFEU.

Held

Any entity, regardless of its legal form, which engages in economic activity, constitutes an undertaking within the meaning of Articles 101 and 102 TFEU. An economic activity includes any activity, whether or not profit-making, that involves economic trade. (para 43)

The World Cup is indisputably a major sporting event yet it also involves activities of an economic nature. These activities include the sale of package tours comprising hotel accommodation, transport and sight-seeing, the conclusion of contracts for advertising, the conclusion of television broadcasting contracts and more. (para 44)

FIFA is a federation of sports associations and accordingly carries out sports activities, yet it also carries out activities of an economic nature. These include, among other things, the conclusion of advertising contracts and television broadcasting rights which account for around 65 per cent of total World Cup revenue. Consequently, FIFA is an entity carrying on activities of an economic nature and constitutes an undertaking within the meaning of Article 101 TFEU. (paras 47–9)

Similarly, the National Italian Football Association (FIGC) carries on activities of an economic nature and is consequently an undertaking within the meaning of Article 101 TFEU. (paras 50–3)

The 'local organizing committee' was set up jointly by FIFA and the FIGC for the purpose of carrying on activities relating to the technical and logistical organisation of the World Cup and the establishment and implementation of the ticket distribution arrangements. The local organizing committee's revenue derived from, among other things, television rights, advertising rights and the sale of tickets. The exclusive rights granted to the Italian joint venture '90 Tour Italia' resulted in remuneration for the local organizing committee. Subsequently, the local organizing committee carried on activities of an economic nature and constituted an undertaking within the meaning of Article 101 TFEU.

Comment

Note that the fact that an organisation lacks profit motive or economic purpose does not in itself bring it outside the concept of undertakings.

On the functional approach, see also the following cases below (pages 5–19), which focus on the distinction between economic activity and public or charitable activities which fall outside the competition prohibitions.

Höfner and Elser v Macrotron GmbH	**Undertaking**
Case C-41/90	The Relativity of the Concept
Court of Justice, [1991] ECR I-1979, [1993] 4 CMLR 306	Employment Procurement

Facts

A preliminary reference to the Court of Justice by the German court seeking advice on, among other things, whether a monopoly of employment procurement granted to a public employment agency constituted an abuse of a dominant position within the meaning of Article 102 TFEU.

In its ruling the Court of Justice examined the exclusive rights in light of both Article 102 TFEU and Article 106 TFEU. The latter concerned the conditions that a Member State must observe when it grants special or exclusive rights. The former examines whether an undertaking abused its dominant position and thus required the Court of Justice to establish whether the public employment agency may be classified as an undertaking.

Held

In the context of competition law, the concept of an undertaking encompasses every entity engaged in an economic activity, regardless of the legal status of the entity and the way in which it is financed. (para 21)

'The fact that employment procurement activities are normally entrusted to public agencies cannot affect the economic nature of such activities. Employment procurement has not always been, and is not necessarily, carried out by public entities. That finding applies in particular to executive recruitment.' (para 22)

It follows that an entity such as a public employment agency engaged in the business of employment procurement may be classified as an undertaking for the purpose of applying the Union competition rules. (paras 21–3)

Comment

In defining the scope of the Union rules on competition, the Court of Justice gave priority to considerations of an economic nature rather than to stricter classification of a legal entity. The functional benchmark relies on the nature of the activity rather than on the form of the entity. This functional approach widens the group of entities which may be classified as undertakings and thereby subjected to the competition provisions. These may include, among other things, individuals, trade associations, clubs, societies, partnerships and companies.

Examples of entities being found not to constitute an undertaking may be found in Case C-364/92 *SAT v Eurocontrol* (page 6 below), Case C-159/91 etc *Poucet v Assurances Générales de France* (page 7 below), Case C-343/95 *Cali & Figli Srl* (page 8 below), Case T-319/99 and C-205/03P *FENIN v Commission* (pages 9–10 below), and Cases C-264 /01 etc *AOK-Bundesverband* (page 13 below).

Note that the application of Article 102 TFEU to public bodies or undertakings entrusted with the operation of services of general economic interest may be limited by the provisions of Article 106(2) TFEU. Subsequently, a public employment agency such as the one in this case, which is classified as an undertaking, is subjected to the prohibition contained in Article 102 TFEU, so long as the application of that provision does not obstruct the performance of the particular task assigned to it. A Member State which has conferred an exclusive right to carry on that activity upon the public employment agency may be in breach of Article 106(1) TFEU where it creates a situation in which that agency cannot avoid infringing Article 102 TFEU. On the application and interpretation of Article 106 TFEU, see Chapter 7 'Competition Law and the State'.

SAT Fluggesellschaft mbH v Eurocontrol	**Undertaking**
Case C-364/92	The Relativity of the Concept
Court of Justice, [1994] ECR I-43, [1994] 5 CMLR 208	Public Tasks

Facts

Eurocontrol is a regionally oriented international organisation which was founded by a multinational agreement between several Member States to strengthen cooperation between them in the field of air navigation and provide a common system for establishing and collecting route charges for flights within their airspace.

The dispute in question came before the Belgian court and concerned the refusal of the air navigation company SAT Fluggesellschaft mbH (SAT) to pay Eurocontrol the route charges for flights made between September 1981 and December 1985. SAT alleged, among other things, that the procedure followed by Eurocontrol in fixing variable rates for equivalent services constituted an abuse of a dominant position.

In a reference made by the Belgian 'Cour de cassation', the Court of Justice was asked whether Eurocontrol was an undertaking within the meaning of Articles 102 and 106 TFEU.

Held

In Union competition law, the concept of an undertaking encompasses every entity engaged in an economic activity, regardless of the legal status of the entity and the way in which it is financed. Subsequently, in order to determine whether Eurocontrol's activities are those of an undertaking within the meaning of Articles 102 and 106 TFEU, it is necessary to establish the nature of those activities. (paras 18, 19)

The Convention establishing Eurocontrol outlines its tasks which are chiefly concerned with research, planning, coordination of national policies and the establishment and collection of route charges levied on users of airspace. Eurocontrol also provides air space control for the Benelux countries and the northern part of the Federal Republic of Germany from its Maastricht centre. For the purposes of such control, Eurocontrol is vested with rights and powers of coercion which derogate from ordinary law and which affect users of airspace. With respect to this operational exercise Eurocontrol is required to provide navigation control in that airspace for the benefit of any aircraft travelling through it, even where the owner of the aircraft has not paid the route charges owed to Eurocontrol. Finally, Eurocontrol's activities are financed by the contributions of the Member States which established it. (paras 20–6)

Eurocontrol carries out, on behalf of the Contracting States, tasks in the public interest aimed at contributing to the maintenance and improvement of air navigation safety. Eurocontrol's collection of route charges cannot be separated from its other activities. The charges are set by, and collected on behalf of, the Member States and are merely the consideration, payable by users, for the obligatory and exclusive use of air navigation control facilities and services. (paras 27–9)

'Taken as a whole, Eurocontrol's activities, by their nature, their aim and the rules to which they are subject, are connected with the exercise of powers relating to the control and supervision of air space which are typically those of a public authority. They are not of an economic nature justifying the application of the Treaty rules of competition.' (para 30)

Comment

Eurocontrol was found not to constitute an undertaking. The collection of the route charges was held by the Court of Justice to be inseparable from Eurocontrol's other activities, thus making its operation, as a whole, one that is connected with the performance of a public/state task.

Poucet v Assurances Générales de France	**Undertaking**
Joined Cases C-159/91 and C-160/91	The Relativity of the Concept
Court of Justice, [1993] ECR I-637	Sickness Funds

Facts

Mr Poucet and Mr Pistre sought the annulment of orders served on them to pay social security contributions to French social security organisations which manage the sickness and maternity insurance scheme for self-employed persons in non-agricultural occupations. The proceedings, which took place in the French Tribunal des Affaires de Securité Sociale de l'Herault, were stayed while the French tribunal referred to the Court of Justice for a preliminary ruling two questions, one of them on whether an organization charged with managing a special social security scheme is an undertaking for the purposes of Articles 101 and 102 TFEU.

Held

The social security systems at issue subject self-employed persons in non-agricultural occupations to compulsory social protection. They are intended to provide cover for all the persons to whom they apply against the risks of sickness, old age, death and invalidity, regardless of their financial status and their state of health at the time of affiliation. (paras 7–9)

The systems pursue a social objective and embody the principle of solidarity. The compulsory contribution to such system is indispensable for application of the principle of solidarity and entails paying statutory benefits which bear no relation to the amount of the contributions received. (paras 8–13)

The schemes at issue are entrusted by statute to social security funds whose activities are subject to control by the State. The funds thus cannot influence the amount of the contributions, the use of assets and the fixing of the level of benefits. (paras 14, 15)

The concept of an undertaking, within the meaning of Articles 101 and 102 TFEU, encompasses all entities engaged in an economic activity. It does not include, therefore, sickness funds and organisations involved in the management of the public social security system. These organisations fulfil a social function exclusively which is based on the principle of national solidarity and is entirely non-profit-making. Accordingly, the organisations to which this non-economic activity is entrusted are not undertakings. (paras 17–20)

Comment

Solidarity was used in this case as the benchmark which distinguishes between commercial and non-commercial activities. Its impact on the nature of the scheme was apparent at different levels: first, 'solidarity in time' in that the contributions paid by active workers were directly used to finance benefits paid to pensioners; secondly, 'financial solidarity', balancing the compulsory schemes in surplus and those in deficit; and thirdly 'solidarity in relation to the least well-off', who are entitled to certain minimum benefits even in the absence of adequate contributions paid by them. (See analysis by AG Tesauro in Case C-244/94 *Fédération Française des Sociétés d'Assurance v Ministère de l'Agriculture et de la Peche* [1995] ECR I-4013).

Contrast the facts in *Poucet v Assurances Générales de France* with those in Case C-244/94 *Fédération Française des Sociétés d'Assurance*. There, the scheme in question was based on the principle of capitalisation and paid benefits to persons insured in proportion to their contributions and the financial results of the investments made by the insurance provider. The scheme established a direct link between the amount of contributions and the amount of benefits and followed the principle of solidarity only to a minimal extent, in so far as it provided for a limited balancing mechanism between insured persons.

Note references to both of these judgments in Cases C-264/01 etc, *AOK-Bundesverband*, page 13 below.

Cali & Figli v Servizi ecologici porto di Genova SpA	**Undertaking**
Case C-343/95	The Relativity of the Concept
Court of Justice, [1997] ECR I-1547, [1997] 5 CMLR 484	Task of a Public Nature

Facts

A dispute between Cali & Figli and Servizi Ecologici Porto di Genova SpA (SEPG) regarding the payment to be made by Cali & Figli for preventive anti-pollution services performed by SEPG in the oil port of Genoa. The proceedings which took place in the Italian Tribunale di Genova were stayed while the Italian tribunal referred to the Court of Justice for a preliminary ruling several questions concerning the application of Article 102 TFEU, one of them being whether SEPG could qualify as an undertaking.

Held

'As regards the possible application of the competition rules of the Treaty, a distinction must be drawn between a situation where the State acts in the exercise of official authority and that where it carries on economic activities of an industrial or commercial nature by offering goods or services on the market (Case 118/85 *Commission v Italy* [1987] ECR 2599, paragraph 7).' (para 16)

'In that connection, it is of no importance that the State is acting directly through a body forming part of the State administration or by way of a body on which it has conferred special or exclusive rights ...' (para 17)

'In order to make the distinction between the two situations referred to in paragraph 16 above, it is necessary to consider the nature of the activities carried on by the public undertaking or body on which the State has conferred special or exclusive rights (Case 118/85 *Commission v Italy*, cited above, paragraph 7).' (para 18)

SEPG activities are carried on under an exclusive concession granted to it by a public body. The anti-pollution surveillance for which SEPG was responsible in the oil port of Genoa is a task in the public interest which forms part of the essential functions of the State as regards protection of the environment in maritime areas. Such surveillance is connected by its nature, its aim and the rules to which it is subject with the exercise of powers relating to the protection of the environment which are typically those of a public authority. It is not of an economic nature justifying the application of the Treaty rules on competition. (paras 15, 22, 23)

Comment

Note that the public task in this case was performed by SEPG, which was not a state entity. Despite this, SEPG was held not to act as an undertaking as it exercised official authority. SEPG's position was not pertinent to the analysis since the public nature of the task performed was not questionable.

In many instances, doubts may be raised as to the public nature of the task performed. See for example Case C-475/99 *Ambulanz Glöckner v Landkreis Sudwestpflaz* [2001] ECR I-8089 where health organisations, to which the public authorities delegated the task of providing the public ambulance service, were held to be undertakings. The court focused on the nature of the activity and noted that 'any activity consisting in offering goods and services on a given market is an economic activity' (para 19). It held that 'the medical aid organisations provide services, for remuneration from users, on the market for emergency transport services and patient transport services. Such activities have not always been, and are not necessarily, carried on by such organisations or by public authorities. ... The provision of such services therefore constitutes an economic activity for the purposes of the application of the competition rules laid down by the Treaty' (para 20). The activities in question were carried on under market conditions, albeit facing limited competition. As such they resemble schemes operating under the principle of capitalisation (see for example Cases C-244/94, C-159/91 etc, page 7 above) and are distinguishable from those operating under the principle of solidarity.

FENIN v Commission	**Undertaking**
Case T-319/99	The Relativity of the Concept
General Court, [2003] ECR II-357, [2003] 5 CMLR 1	Purchasing Goods

Facts

FENIN is an association of undertakings which markets medical goods and equipment used in Spanish hospitals. It submitted to the Commission a complaint alleging an abuse of a dominant position, within the meaning of Article 102 TFEU, by various bodies or organizations responsible for the operation of the Spanish national health system (SNS). The Commission rejected FENIN's complaint on the ground that the alleged bodies were not acting as undertakings when they purchased medical goods and equipment from the members of the association (Decision SG(99) D/7.040). FENIN launched an action for annulment.

Held

It is a well established principle that the concept of an undertaking covers any entity engaged in an economic activity, regardless of its legal status and the way in which it is financed. (para 35)

Whereas the offering of goods and services on a given market were the characteristic feature of an economic activity, purchasing, as such, was not. Therefore, in deciding whether an activity is economic, it was incorrect to dissociate the activity of purchasing goods from their subsequent use. The nature of the purchasing activity had to be determined according to whether or not the subsequent use of the purchased goods amounted to an economic activity. (para 36)

'Consequently, an organisation which purchases goods—even in great quantity—not for the purpose of offering goods and services as part of an economic activity, but in order to use them in the context of a different activity, such as one of a purely social nature, does not act as an undertaking simply because it is a purchaser in a given market. Whilst an entity may wield very considerable economic power, even giving rise to a monopsony, it nevertheless remains the case that, if the activity for which that entity purchases goods is not an economic activity, it is not acting as an undertaking for the purposes of [Union] competition law and is therefore not subject to the prohibitions laid down in Articles [101(1) TFEU] and [102 TFEU].' (para 37)

Consequently, SNS did not act as an undertaking. This conclusion relies on SNS operating according to the principle of solidarity in that it was funded from social security contributions and other State funding and in that it provided services free of charge to its members on the basis of universal cover. Consequently SNS did not act as an undertaking when purchasing from FENIN. (paras 38–40)

Comment

FENIN challenged the Commission's reliance on Cases C-159/91 etc *Poucet v Assurances Générales de France* (page 7 above), arguing that whereas in *Poucet* the question before the Court was whether such bodies acted as undertakings in their dealings with their members, in this case the question centred on whether SNS acted as undertaking when purchasing from third parties goods which they needed in order to provide services to their members. FENIN thus favoured a functional approach which focused on the nature of the activity rather than the nature of the body. Accordingly, FENIN deemed irrelevant the principle of solidarity relied upon in *Poucet*. The General Court impliedly rejected this argument when in its decision it based its conclusion that SNS did not act as an undertaking on the fact that it operated according to the principle of solidarity.

The consequences of dual, public and private, characteristics were not explored in this case. FENIN argued that SNS, on occasion, provided private care in addition to State-sponsored healthcare and consequently in those circumstances should be regarded as an undertaking. The Court did not decide on this point as it was not raised in the original complaint to the Commission.

FENIN appealed against the judgment of the General Court (see page 10 below).

FENIN v Commission	**Undertaking**
Case C-205/03P	The Relativity of the Concept
Court of Justice, [2006] ECR I-6295, [2006] 5 CMLR 7	Purchasing Goods

Facts

FENIN appealed against the judgment of the General Court (Case T-319/99 (page 9 above)) in which the General Court dismissed its action for annulment against the Commission's decision. In its appeal to the Court of Justice, FENIN alleged that the General Court misinterpreted the definition of 'undertaking' by either [1] wrongfully omitting to consider whether a purchasing activity is in itself an economic activity which may be dissociated from the service subsequently provided or, [2] failing to consider whether the provision of medical treatment, is itself economic in nature and therefore makes the purchasing activity an economic activity subject to the competition rules.

Held

FENIN's allegations, on which the second part of the plea is based, were not raised at first instance and are submitted for the first time at the appeal stage. 'It follows that the second part of the single plea relied on by FENIN must be dismissed as inadmissible.' (paras 22, 20–22)

With respect to the first part of the plea, the General Court rightly held in paragraph 36 of its judgment 'that it is the activity consisting in offering goods and services on a given market that is the characteristic feature of an economic activity (Case C-35/96 *Commission v Italy* [1998] ECR I-3851, paragraph 36).' (para 25)

The General Court rightly deduced that 'there is no need to dissociate the activity of purchasing goods from the subsequent use to which they are put in order to determine the nature of that purchasing activity, and that the nature of the purchasing activity must be determined according to whether or not the subsequent use of the purchased goods amounts to an economic activity.' (para 26)

FENIN's plea, according to which the purchasing activity of the SNS management bodies constitutes an economic activity in itself, must therefore be dismissed as unfounded. Appeal dismissed.

Comment

In his opinion AG Maduro provided an excellent overview of the concept of undertaking. The opinion is interesting, not the least since the AG proposed that the Court of Justice uphold the second part of the appeal and refer the case back to the General Court. AG Maduro was of the opinion that the General Court should have distinguished between SNS activities and roles. In this respect, the compulsory membership of a sickness or insurance fund should have been distinguished from the activity in this case, being that of the provision of healthcare. 'Accordingly, the degree of solidarity which exists in that sector must be assessed in the light of factors other than those which apply to the activity of a sickness or insurance fund' (paras 30, 31, 46, 47, AG opinion). 'In the present case, it does not appear that the activity of providing health care to its members carried on by the SNS is of a different kind from that which was carried on by the public hospitals in *Smits and Peerbooms* [Case C-157/99 [2001] ECR I-5473]. While it does not comprise only hospital care, it none the less includes such care. Similarly, if patients do not pay medical practitioners the amount owing in respect of treatment provided to them, those practitioners are nevertheless remunerated. However, in order to determine whether that activity should be subject to competition law, it is necessary to establish whether the State, with a view to adopting a policy of redistribution by entrusting that activity exclusively to State bodies which would be guided solely by considerations of solidarity, intended to exclude it from all market considerations' (para 52, AG opinion). 'The judgment under appeal shows that the SNS is obliged to guarantee universal cover to all its members free of charge. However, the [General Court] did not state whether the requirements of the market are entirely satisfied by public bodies or whether private organisations having the characteristics of an undertaking take part in it as well. The essential information for concluding that the activity of providing health care of the SNS is of a non-economic nature is therefore not available' (para 53, AG Opinion). 'In any event, were it to be concluded that the SNS carries on an economic activity, that would not call into question the social objectives pursued by the SNS, because such a conclusion does not preclude the implementation of the principle of solidarity, whether in relation to the method of financing by social security and other State contributions or in relation to the provision of services provided to members free of charge on the basis of universal cover. The application of competition law and a recognition that certain sectors must be subject to special rules are not mutually incompatible. On the contrary, the purpose of Article [106(2) TFEU] is precisely to provide a basis for conferring exclusive rights on undertakings entrusted with the operation of services of general interest [Case C-475/99 *Ambulanz Glöckner v Landkreis Sudwestpflaz* [2001] ECR I-8089]. The likely effects of making certain activities carried on by undertakings entrusted with the operation of services of general interest subject to competition law do not lead to a reduction in social protection any more than do those which arise from the application of the principle of freedom of movement to the health sector. In both cases, [Union] law seeks to incorporate principles of openness and transparency into health systems originally conceived on a national scale ...' (para 55, AG Opinion). He concluded that the case should be referred back to the General Court 'for it to make the necessary findings in fact in order to determine whether public and private health sectors coexist in Spain or whether the solidarity which exists in the provision of free health care is predominant' (paras 54, 57, AG Opinion).

It is interesting to contrast the Court of Justice and General Court approach in *FENIN* with the judgment of the English Competition Commission Appeal Tribunal (CCAT) in *BetterCare v The Director General of Fair Trading* [Case No 1006/2/1/01 [2002] Competition Appeal Reports 299]. There, the CCAT considered an alleged abuse by a Trust which was entrusted, under the law, to provide nursing home and residential care services for elderly persons. The trust was accused by BetterCare, a UK provider of residential and nursing home care, of abusing its dominant position by forcing it to agree to unduly low prices. The CCAT considered whether the Trust may be considered as an undertaking and concluded that it was acting as an undertaking, both in the purchasing of services from BetterCare and the direct provision of elderly care by its own statutory homes. The CCAT decision differs from the European courts' approach in *FENIN* in terms of the test used to establish economic activity and the finding of solidarity. According to the CCAT, the decisive factor was the Trust being in a position to generate effects which the competition rules seek to prevent. The CCAT also distinguished the facts in *BetterCare* from those in previous European cases and found little to support the application of the principle of solidarity in this case.

In December 2011, the UK Office of Fair Trading (OFT) issued a policy note on 'Public Bodies and Competition' (OFT 1389), which replaced the initial note published in August 2004 (OFT 443). The OFT's policy note on public bodies has been adopted by the Competition and Markets Authority (CMA). According to the publication, 'Where the nature of the activity is such that profitable private sector involvement is impossible, no "market" for the activity exists. Market forces do not (and could not) therefore play any part in the activity and, as such, that activity would not be capable of having anti-competitive effects. The fact that a public body's conduct was capable of having anti-competitive effects in the market has been taken by the UK Competition Appeal Tribunal as evidence that that conduct was economic (see BetterCare II). To the extent that that judgment focused on purchasing conduct, it must now be considered in the light of the principles subsequently endorsed by the Court of Justice in *FENIN* and *SELEX*' (para 2.23, OFT 1389).

The narrow definition of the term undertaking in the case of National Health Services, as advocated in *FENIN*, may be viewed and understood from a political perspective. It reflects a policy choice embedded in constitutional reasoning and affected by the division of powers between the Union and its Member States. The application of EU competition law in this case would have intruded into the national social sphere. The narrow approach to the term 'undertaking' safeguards the state's sovereignty as national health provider and shields it from the application of European competition, despite possible anticompetitive effects.

Wouters v Algemene Raad van de Nederlandse Orde van Advocaten **Undertaking**
Case C-309/99 Relative Concept
Court of Justice, [2002] ECR I-1577, [2002] 4 CMLR 27

Facts

The case arose out of a dispute between Mr Wouters and the Dutch Bar which under its regulations prohibited its members from practising in full partnership with accountants. Mr Wouters argued that the prohibition is incompatible with Union rules on competition and freedom of establishment. The Dutch court referred the case to the Court of Justice, asking, among other things, whether a regulation concerning partnerships between members of the Bar and other professionals is to be regarded as a decision taken by an association of undertakings within the meaning of Article 101(1) TFEU.

Held

'In order to establish whether a regulation such as the 1993 Regulation is to be regarded as a decision of an association of undertakings within the meaning of [Article 101(1) TFEU], the first matter to be considered is whether members of the Bar are undertakings for the purposes of [Union] competition law.' (para 45)

The concept of an undertaking covers any entity engaged in an economic activity, regardless of its legal status and the way in which it is financed. It is also settled case-law that any activity consisting of offering goods and services on a given market is an economic activity. Members of the Bar offer, for a fee, services in the form of legal assistance and bear the financial risks attached to the performance of those activities. That being so, members of the Bar carry on an economic activity and are undertakings for the purposes of Article 101 TFEU. The complexity and technical nature of the services they provide and the fact that the practice of their profession is regulated cannot alter that conclusion. (paras 46–9)

A second question is whether when it adopts a regulation concerning partnerships between members of the Bar and members of other professions, the Bar is to be regarded as an association of undertakings, or on the contrary, as a public authority. 'According to the case-law of the Court, the Treaty rules on competition do not apply to activity which, by its nature, its aim and the rules to which it is subject does not belong to the sphere of economic activity (see to that effect, Joined Cases C-159/91, C-160/91 *Poucet and Pistre* [1993] ECR I-637, paragraphs 18 and 19, concerning the management of the public social security system), or which is connected with the exercise of the powers of a public authority (see to that effect, Case C-364/92 *Sat Fluggesellschaft* [1994] ECR I-43, paragraph 30, concerning the control and supervision of air space, and Case C-343/95 *Diego Cali & Figli* [1997] ECR I-1547, paragraphs 22 and 23, concerning anti-pollution surveillance of the maritime environment).' (para 57)

The Netherlands Bar is not fulfilling a social function based on the principle of solidarity, unlike certain social security bodies (*Poucet and Pistre*), nor does it exercise powers which are typically those of a public authority (*Sat Fluggesellschaft*). It acts as the regulatory body of a profession, the practice of which constitutes an economic activity. Its governing bodies are composed exclusively of members of the Bar elected solely by members of the profession. In addition, when it adopts measures such as the Regulation in question, the Bar is not required to do so by reference to specified public-interest criteria. Subsequently, the Netherlands Bar must be regarded as an association of undertakings within the meaning of Article 101(1) TFEU. (paras 58–64).

Comment

The Bar was held to be an association of undertakings when it adopts a regulation such as the 1993 Regulation which regulates the member's economic activities. Note, however, that the Bar was held not to constitute an undertaking or group of undertakings for the purposes of Article 102 TFEU, since it does not carry on any economic activity and because its members are not sufficiently linked to each other to be able adopt the same conduct and limit competition between them. (paras 112–14)

AOK-Bundesverband and others v Ichthyol-Gesellschaft Cordes
Joined Cases C-264, 306, 354 and 355/01
Court of Justice, [2004] ECR I-2493, [2004] 4 CMLR 22

Undertaking
Relative Concept
Sickness Funds

Facts

Reference from the German courts for a preliminary ruling, concerning the classification of German 'associations of sickness funds' as undertakings. According to the statutory health insurance scheme in Germany, employees are obliged, subject to some exceptions, to be insured by statutory sickness funds. These funds, which are governed by German law and financed through contributions levied on insured persons and their employers, based on their income, operate under the principle of solidarity. They compete, to a limited extent, with each other and with private funds when providing services to those people for whom insurance is voluntary. In the proceedings at the German courts the question arose whether these funds, when operating according to the law and setting the maximum level of contribution for medicines and medical products are operating as undertakings.

Held

'The concept of an undertaking in competition law covers any entity engaged in economic activity, regardless of the legal status of the entity or the way in which it is financed (Case C-41/90 *Höfner and Elser* [1991] ECR I-1979, paragraph 21, and Case C-218/00 *Cisal* [2002] ECR I-691, paragraph 22).' (para 46)

'In the field of social security, the Court has held that certain bodies entrusted with the management of statutory health insurance and old-age insurance schemes pursue an exclusively social objective and do not engage in economic activity. The Court has found that to be so in the case of sickness funds which merely apply the law and cannot influence the amount of the contributions, the use of assets and the fixing of the level of benefits. Their activity, based on the principle of national solidarity, is entirely non-profit-making and the benefits paid are statutory benefits bearing no relation to the amount of the contributions (Joined Cases C-159/91 and C-160/91 *Poucet and Pistre* [1993] ECR I-637, paragraphs 15 and 18).' (para 47)

'The fact that the amount of benefits and of contributions was, in the last resort, fixed by the State led the Court to hold, similarly, that a body entrusted by law with a scheme providing insurance against accidents at work and occupational diseases, such as the Istituto nazionale per l'assicurazione contro gli infortuni sul lavoro (the Italian National Institute for Insurance against Accidents at Work), was not an undertaking for the purpose of the Treaty competition rules (see *Cisal*, cited above, paragraphs 43 to 46).' (para 48)

'On the other hand, other bodies managing statutory social security systems and displaying some of the characteristics referred to in paragraph 47 of the present judgment, namely being non-profit-making and engaging in activity of a social character which is subject to State rules that include solidarity requirements in particular, have been considered to be undertakings engaging in economic activity (see Case C-244/94 *Fédération Française des Sociétés d'Assurance and others* [1995] ECR I-4013, paragraph 22, and Case C-67/96 *Albany* [1999] ECR I-5751, paragraphs 84 to 87).' (para 49)

'Thus, in *Fédération Française des Sociétés d'Assurance and others*, at paragraph 17, the Court held that the body in question managing a supplementary old-age insurance scheme, engaged in an economic activity in competition with life assurance companies and that the persons concerned could opt for the solution which guaranteed the better investment. In paragraphs 81 and 84 of *Albany*, concerning a supplementary pension fund based on a system of compulsory affiliation and applying a solidarity mechanism for determination of the amount of contributions and the level of benefits, the Court noted however that the fund itself determined the amount of the contributions and benefits and operated in accordance with the principle of capitalisation. It deduced therefrom that such a fund engaged in an economic activity in competition with insurance companies.' (para 50)

Sickness funds in the German statutory health insurance scheme are involved in the management of the social security system and fulfil an exclusively non-profit making social function, which is founded on the principle of national solidarity. The funds are compelled by law to offer their members benefits which do not depend on the amount of the contributions. The funds are not in competition with one another or with private institutions as regards grant of the obligatory statutory benefits in respect of treatment or medicinal products which constitutes their main function. (paras 51–4)

'It follows from those characteristics that the sickness funds are similar to the bodies at issue in *Poucet and Pistre* and *Cisal* and that their activity must be regarded as being non-economic in nature.' Subsequently, the funds do not constitute undertakings within the meaning of Articles [101 TFEU] and [102 TFEU]. (paras 55, 57)

'The latitude available to the sickness funds when setting the contribution rate and their freedom to engage in some competition with one another is meant to encourage the sickness funds to operate in accordance with principles of sound management and does not call this analysis into question.' (para 56)

When the fund associations determine the fixed maximum amounts they merely perform an obligation which is imposed upon them by the law. This action is linked to the exclusively social objective of the sickness funds and does not constitute an activity of an economic nature. (paras 58–64)

Comment

In paragraph 58 the Court noted that there is a possibility that, 'besides their functions of an exclusively social nature within the framework of management of the German social security system, the sickness funds ... engage in operations which have a purpose that is not social and is economic in nature. In that case the decisions which they would be led to adopt could perhaps be regarded as decisions of undertakings or of associations of undertakings.' The court then concluded that the fixing of maximum amounts in this particular case is linked to the social objectives of the funds (paras 58–64). The statement of principle is interesting as the court considered it possible for the funds to be classified as undertakings if they would engage in operations which are not social in nature.

Note that the Court of Justice did not follow the opinion of Advocate General Jacobs. In his opinion, AG Jacobs stated that 'compulsory state social security schemes such as those at issue in *Cisal* [Case C-218/00 *Cisal di Battistello Venanzio & Co Sas v Istituto Nazionale Per L'Assicurazione Contro Gli Infortuni Sul Lavoro*, [2002] ECR I-691, [2002] 4 CMLR 24,] and *Poucet and Pistre* [Joined cases C-159/91 and C-160/91, page 7 above] are not classified as economic activities because they are incompatible, even in principle, with the possibility of a private undertaking carrying them on' (paras 30–2, AG opinion). 'By contrast, pension schemes which are funded through the administration of a capital fund, into which contributions are paid, and in which benefits are directly related to contributions, have been held in *FFSA* and *Albany* to be subject to the [Union] competition rules, despite the existence of certain elements of solidarity. In such schemes, the redistributive element is not such as to entail a suppression of the types of activity habitually provided by private insurance and pension companies, such as actuarial assessment and the management of investments.' (para 34, AG opinion). He subsequently distinguished between this case and *Cisal* and *Poucet and Pistre* as in the present case there was potential for the funds to compete with one another and with private undertakings in the provision of health insurance services, a fact which demonstrates that the system's redistributive element is not such as to preclude economic activity. The Advocate General added that the fact that the level of benefits provided under a scheme is determined by law cannot in itself rule out the application of the competition rules. Given the existence of such competition, he concluded that European competition rules should be applicable. In addition he concluded that the setting of fixed amounts, which is the alleged anti-competitive conduct, falls within the sphere of the economic activity which the sickness funds perform.

Albany International BV v Stichting Bedriifspensioenfonds Textielindustrie	**Undertaking**
Case C-67/96	The Relativity of the Concept
Court of Justice, [1999] ECR I-5751, [2000] 4 CMLR 446	Employees and Trade Unions

Facts

A preliminary reference to the Court of Justice which originated in proceedings in the Netherlands Hoge Raad that reviewed Albany's refusal to make contribution to 'State endorsed' pension funds, while arguing that these acted in violation of competition law. In its judgment the Court of Justice considered, among other things, whether a non-profit-making pension fund which has been entrusted with the management of a supplementary pension scheme, which has been set up by a collective agreement between organisations representing management and labour, constitutes an undertaking. The Court of Justice made references to *Höfner and Elser* (page 5 above), *Poucet Pistre* (page 7 above), and *Fédération française des sociétés d'assurance* (page 7 above). It noted that the sectoral pension fund in this case engaged in an economic activity in competition with insurance companies. It held that the fact that the fund was non-profit-making and that its operation was based on the principle of solidarity were not sufficient to deprive the sectoral pension fund of its status as an undertaking.

Comment

The judgment is consistent with earlier case-law. Noteworthy are comments made by AG Jacobs on the status of employees and trade unions.

The AG confirmed in his opinion that it is generally accepted that employees fall outside the prohibition of Article 101(1) TFEU. As for trade unions, he commented that: 'Since employees cannot be qualified as undertakings for the purposes of [Article 101 TFEU], trade unions, or other associations representing employees, are not "associations of undertakings". However, are trade unions themselves "undertakings"? The mere fact that a trade union is a non-profit-making body does not automatically deprive the activities which it carries on of their economic character. A trade union is an association of employees. It is established that associations may also be regarded as 'undertakings' in so far as they themselves engage in an economic activity. It must be borne in mind that an association can act either in its own right, independent to a certain extent of the will of its members, or merely as an executive organ of an agreement between its members. In the former case its behaviour is attributable to the association itself, in the latter case the members are responsible for the activity. With regard to ordinary trade associations, the result of that delimitation is often not important, since [Article 101 TFEU] applies in the same way to agreements between undertakings and to decisions by associations of undertakings. It maybe relevant when the Commission has to decide to whom to address its decision and whom to fine. However, in the case of trade unions that delimitation becomes decisive, since, if the trade union is merely acting as agent, it is solely an executive organ of an agreement between its members, who themselves—as seen above—are not addressees of the prohibition of [Article 101(1) TFEU]. With regard to trade union activities one has therefore to proceed in two steps: first, one has to ask whether a certain activity is attributable to the trade union itself and if so, secondly, whether that activity is of an economic nature. There are certainly circumstances where activities of trade unions fulfil both conditions. Some trade unions may for example run in their own right supermarkets, savings banks, travel agencies or other businesses. When they are acting in that capacity the competition rules apply. However in the present cases the trade unions are engaged in collective bargaining with employers on pensions for employees of the sector. In that respect the trade unions are acting merely as agent for employees belonging to a certain sector and not in their own right. That alone suffices to show that in the present cases they are not acting as undertakings for the purposes of competition law.' (paras 218–27, AG opinion)

In Case C-22/98 *Jean Claude Becu* [2001] ECR I-5665, [2001] 4 CMLR 968, the Court of Justice noted that in performance of dock work for their employers, recognised dockers operate as workers and are incorporated into their employer's economic unit and do not therefore in themselves constitute 'undertakings' within the meaning of Union competition law. (para 26)

SELEX Sistemi Integrati SpA v Commission   **Undertaking**
Case C-113/07P   Relative Concept
Court of Justice, [2009] ECR I-2207, [2009] 4 CMLR 24

Facts

An appeal on the General Court judgment in Case T-155/04 *SELEX Sistemi Integrati v Commission* [2006] ECR II-4797.

In its judgment the General Court dismissed an application for annulment of a Commission's decision in which it rejected a complaint concerning an alleged infringement of Article 102 TFEU by the European Organisation for the Safety of Air Navigation (Eurocontrol) on the basis that Eurocontrol did not constitute an undertaking within the meaning of Article 102 TFEU.

The General Court held that the European Commission was wrong to rely on its decision in a previous Court of Justice judgment in which Eurocontrol was held not to constitute an undertaking. (Case C-364/92 *SAT Fluggesellschaft*, page 6 above) It stated that, 'since the Treaty provisions on competition are applicable to the activities of an entity which can be severed from those in which it engages as a public authority, ... the various activities of an entity must be considered individually.' (para 54, General Court judgment) It therefore held that that judgment did not preclude Eurocontrol from being regarded as an undertaking in relation to other activities than those referred to in Case C-364/92.

The General Court examined Eurocontrol's activity of technical standardisation and found it not to constitute an economic activity as it did not consist of offering goods or services on a given market. (paras 56–62, General Court) Citing the *FENIN* judgment (pages 9 and 10 above) the General Court stated, that the fact that Eurocontrol's standardisation activity is not an economic activity implies that the acquisition of prototypes in the context of that standardisation is also not an economic activity and, in any event, is ancillary to the promotion of technical development. (paras 65–77, General Court) The General Court noted that Eurocontrol's activity of assisting the national administrations was separable from its tasks of airspace management and involved the offering of services in a market in which private undertakings operate. It concluded that the activity whereby Eurocontrol provides assistance to the national administrations is an economic activity and that, consequently, Eurocontrol, in the exercise of that activity, is an undertaking within the meaning of Article 102 TFEU. (paras 86–90, General Court) It nonetheless did not find this activity to infringe Article 102 TFEU.

Held

Did the assistance provided by Eurocontrol constitute an economic activity?

'It should be borne in mind in this regard, as the [General Court] observed at paragraph 87 of the judgment under appeal, that any activity consisting in offering goods or services on a given market is an economic activity (Case 118/85 *Commission v Italy* [1987] ECR 2599, paragraph 7; Joined Cases C-180/98 to C-184/98 *Pavlov and Others* [2000] ECR I-6451, paragraph 75; and Case C-49/07 *MOTOE* [2008] ECR I-4863, paragraph 22).' (para 69)

'It should also be borne in mind that, according to the case-law of the Court of Justice, activities which fall within the exercise of public powers are not of an economic nature justifying the application of the Treaty rules of competition (see, to that effect, Case 107/84 *Commission v Germany* [1985] ECR 2655, paragraphs 14 and 15; *SAT Fluggesellschaft*, paragraph 30; and *MOTOE*, paragraph 24).' (para 70)

'In *SAT Fluggesellschaft*, the Court, while not specifically ruling on Eurocontrol's activity of assisting the national administrations, considered at paragraph 30 of that judgment that, taken as a whole, Eurocontrol's activities, by their nature, their aim and the rules to which they are subject, are connected with the exercise of powers relating to the control and supervision of air space, which are typically those of a public authority and are not of an economic nature. The Court therefore held that [Articles 102 and 106 TFEU] must be interpreted as meaning that an international organisation such as Eurocontrol is not an undertaking for the purposes of those provisions.' (para 71)

'Contrary to what Selex maintains, that conclusion also applies with regard to the assistance which Eurocontrol provides to the national administrations, when so requested by them, in connection with tendering procedures carried out by those administrations for the acquisition, in particular, of equipment and systems in the field of air traffic management.' (para 72)

'It can be inferred from the Convention on the Safety of Air Navigation that the activity of providing assistance is one of the instruments of cooperation entrusted to Eurocontrol by that convention and plays a direct role in the attainment of the objective of technical harmonisation and integration in the field of air traffic with a view to contributing to the maintenance of and improvement in the safety of air navigation. That activity takes the form, inter alia, of providing assistance to the national administrations in the implementation of tendering procedures for the acquisition of air traffic management systems or equipment and is intended to ensure that the common technical specifications and standards drawn up and adopted by Eurocontrol for the purpose of achieving a harmonised European air traffic management system are included in the tendering specifications for those procedures. It is therefore closely linked to the task of technical standardisation entrusted to Eurocontrol by the contracting parties in the context of cooperation among States with a view to maintaining and developing the safety of air navigation and is thus connected with the exercise of public powers.' (para 76)

'The [General Court] therefore made an assessment that was erroneous in law in finding that the activity of assisting the national administrations was separable from Eurocontrol's tasks of air space management and development of air safety by considering that that activity had an indirect relationship with air navigation safety, on the ground that the assistance provided by Eurocontrol covered only technical specifications in the implementation of tendering procedures and therefore affected air navigation safety only as a result of those procedures.' (para 77)

'It follows from all the foregoing considerations that the [General Court] erred in law by regarding Eurocontrol's activity of assisting the national administrations as an economic activity and, as a consequence, on the basis of grounds that were erroneous in law, considering that Eurocontrol was, in the exercise of that activity, an undertaking within the meaning of Article [102 TFEU]. Consequently, it erred in upholding, to that extent, the first plea in law expounded before it by the appellant alleging a manifest error of assessment as to the applicability of Article [102 TFEU] to Eurocontrol.' (para 80)

This error in law in the grounds of the judgment under appeal does not affect its operative part and subsequently does not mean that it must be set aside. (para 83)

The activity of technical standardisation

'In order to draw the distinction complained of, the [General Court] first of all stated, at paragraph 59 of the judgment under appeal, that the adoption by the Council of Eurocontrol of standards drawn up by the executive organ of that organisation is a legislative activity, since the Council of Eurocontrol is made up of directors of the civil aviation administration of each contracting Member State, appointed by their respective States for the purpose of adopting technical specifications which will be binding in all those States. According to the grounds of the judgment under appeal, that activity is directly connected with the exercise by those States of their powers of public authority, Eurocontrol's role thus being akin to that of a minister who, at national level, prepares legislative or regulatory measures which are then adopted by the government. This activity therefore falls within the public tasks of Eurocontrol.' (para 89)

'The [General Court] then stated, at paragraph 60 of the judgment under appeal, that the preparation and production of technical standards by Eurocontrol could, conversely, be separated from its tasks of managing air space and developing air safety. As justification for that assessment, it considered that the arguments advanced by the Commission to prove that Eurocontrol's standardisation activities were connected with that organisation's public service mission related, in fact, only to the adoption of those standards and not to the production of them, since the need to adopt standards at international level does not necessarily mean that the body which sets those standards must also be the one which subsequently adopts them.' (para 90)

'However, Article 2(1)(f) of the Convention on the Safety of Air Navigation provides that Eurocontrol is responsible for developing, adopting and keeping under review common standards, specifications and practices for air traffic management systems and services. It is therefore clear that the contracting States entrusted Eurocontrol with both the preparation and production of standards and with their adoption, without separating those functions.' (para 91)

'Moreover, the preparation and production of technical standards plays a direct role in the attainment of Eurocontrol's objective, defined in Article 1 of the Convention on the Safety of Air Navigation and referred to at paragraph 73 above, which is to achieve harmonisation and integration with the aim of establishing a uniform European air traffic management system. Those activities form an integral part of the task of technical standardisation entrusted to Eurocontrol by the contracting parties in the context of cooperation among States with a view to maintaining and developing the safety of air navigation, which constitute public powers.' (para 92)

'It follows that the judgment under appeal is vitiated by an error in law in that it states that the preparation and production of technical standards by Eurocontrol can be separated from its task of managing air space and developing air safety. However, that error does not affect the [General Court's] conclusion, which is based on other grounds, that the Commission did not make a manifest error of assessment in taking the view that Eurocontrol's technical standardisation activities were not economic activities and that the competition rules of the Treaty did not apply therefore to them. It must therefore be held once again that the fact that there is an error of law in the grounds of the judgment under appeal does not mean that that judgment must be set aside.' (para 93)

The EU case-law on social benefits

The General Court did not err when it held 'that it would be incorrect, when determining whether or not a given activity is economic, to dissociate the activity of purchasing goods from the subsequent use to which they are put and that the nature of the purchasing activity must therefore be determined according to whether or not the subsequent use of the purchased goods amounts to an economic activity (see Case C-205/03P *FENIN v Commission* [2006] ECR I-6295, paragraph 26). The [General Court] correctly concluded from this that the fact that technical standardisation is not an economic activity means that the acquisition of prototypes in connection with that standardisation is not an economic activity either…That reasoning can obviously be applied to activities other than those that are social in nature or are based on solidarity, since those factors do not constitute conditions for the purpose of determining that an activity is not of an economic nature …' (paras 102, 103)

Appeal dismissed.

Comment

The company in these proceedings is the same company as that in Case C-364/92 (page 6 above) which was held in those proceedings not to be an undertaking. Note, however, that the functional approach requires each activity to be evaluated in context and subsequently led the General Court to reject the Commission's reliance on the previous judgment by the Court of Justice. (para 54, General Court judgment)

The Court of Justice rejected the General Court's finding that the activity of assisting the national administrations was separable from Eurocontrol's tasks of air space management. (paras 69–83)

Note the application of the reasoning laid down in *FENIN* according to which the nature of the purchasing activity is determined according to the nature of the subsequent use of the purchased goods. (paras 102, 103 Court of Justice judgment; paras 65–77, General Court judgment)

Compass-Datenbank GmbH v Republik Österreich	**Undertaking**
Case C-138/11	The Relativity of the Concept
Court of Justice, [2012] 5 CMLR 13, [2013] All ER (EC) 920	Public Tasks

Facts

A reference for a preliminary ruling concerning activities of a public authority operating the 'companies register', which collects information that undertakings have a statutory obligation to submit to it, and which provides access to that information and searches in its database in return for payment. The referring Court asked whether this constitutes an economic activity, as a result of which the public authority is considered an undertaking and therefore may be subjected to the provisions of Article 102 TFEU.

Held

An undertaking is any entity engaged in an economic activity, irrespective of its legal status and the way in which it is financed. Offering goods and services amounts to an economic activity. Accordingly, the state, or a state entity may act as an undertaking, in relation to part of its activities, and be subjected to the competition provisions. (paras 35–7)

'In so far as a public entity exercises an economic activity which can be separated from the exercise of its public powers, that entity, in relation to that activity, acts as an undertaking, while, if that economic activity cannot be separated from the exercise of its public powers, the activities exercised by that entity as a whole remain activities connected with the exercise of those public powers (see, to that effect, Case C-113/07P *SELEX Sistemi Integrati v Commission* [2009] ECR I-2207, paragraph 72 et seq).' (para 38)

'In addition, the fact that a product or a service supplied by a public entity and connected to the exercise by it of public powers is provided in return for remuneration laid down by law and not determined, directly or indirectly, by that entity, is not alone sufficient for the activity carried out to be classified as an economic activity and the entity which carries it out as an undertaking (see, to that effect, *SAT Fluggesellschaft*, paragraph 28 et seq and *Diego Calì & Figli*, paragraphs 22 to 25).' (para 39)

The data collection activity in this case, which is based on a statutory obligation on undertakings to submit information, falls within the exercise of public powers and is not an economic activity. Maintaining the database, making that data available to the public and allowing searches cannot be separated from the activity of collection of the data and therefore do not constitute economic activities. (paras 40–41)

Access to the data in this case is subjected to payment. '[T]o the extent that the fees or payments due for the making available to the public of such information are not laid down directly or indirectly by the entity concerned but are provided for by law, the charging of such remuneration can be regarded as inseparable from that making available of data. Thus, the charging … of fees or payments due for the making available to the public of that information cannot change the legal classification of that activity, meaning that it does not constitute an economic activity.' (para 42)

Comment

The judgment reflects the Court's jurisprudence, as developed in *FENIN* (pages 9 and 10 above) and *SELEX* (page 16 above), and maintains a narrow interpretation of the concept of 'economic activity'.

The Court held that it is impossible to separate the activity of collecting data submitted by undertakings in accordance with a statutory obligation (that activity was held not to amount to an economic activity) from the activity of making that data available to the public against payment. The Court did not elaborate on the reason which ties the profitmaking utilisation of the data to the regulatory harvesting of the data.

AEG-Telefunken v Commission	**Undertaking**
Case 107/82	Single Economic Entity
Court of Justice, [1983] ECR 3151, [1984] 3 CMLR 325	

Facts

AEG–Telefunken (AEG), a German company which manufactures and markets consumer electronic products, notified the Commission of a selective distribution system (SDS) for its branded products. The Commission did not object to the SDS, yet later found that the actual application of the SDS by AEG and its subsidiaries did not correspond to the scheme notified to it. Subsequently, the Commission found that AEG had infringed Article 101 TFEU and improperly applied its SDS by discriminating against certain distributors and by influencing dealers' resale prices. AEG appealed to the Court of Justice, arguing, among other things, that it cannot be held liable for activities and individual infringements alleged by the Commission to have been committed by its subsidiaries (TFR, ATF, ATBG).

Held

The fact that a subsidiary has separate legal personality is not sufficient to exclude the possibility of imputing its conduct to the parent company. This is particularly so where the subsidiary, although having separate legal personality, does not decide independently upon its own conduct on the market, but carries out, in all material respects, the instructions given to it by the parent company. (para 49)

'As AEG has not disputed that it was in a position to exert a decisive influence on the distribution and pricing policy of its subsidiaries, consideration must still be given to the question whether it actually made use of this power. However, such a check appears superfluous in the case of TFR which, as a wholly-owned subsidiary of AEG, necessarily follows a policy laid down by the same bodies as, under its statutes, determine AEG's policy.' (para 50)

'AEG's influence on ATF emerges indirectly from an internal memorandum of ATF dated 30 June 1978, where it is stated that a distributor with whom ATF was negotiating with a view to his acceptance was aware of "Telefunken's policy, which succeeds in keeping retail prices stable and thus in maintaining an appropriate profit margin for retailers". The word "Telefunken" shows that in fact ATF was referring to commercial policy perceived as being the result of an initiative on the part of AEG which alone was in a position to draw up a unitary policy to be followed by its various subsidiaries responsible for distributing Telefunken products.' (para 51)

'As to ATBG, it may be seen from the documents relating to the case of the Belgian wholesaler Diederichs that ATBG constantly informed TFR about its negotiations with Diederichs. … Furthermore, it emerges from those documents that TFR made direct contact with Diederichs to consider the possibility of regularizing his activities, although they did not involve the German market …, that it raised within its organization problems raised by Diederichs's application for admission… and that it finally stated that: "at present there is no reason to pursue the discussions initiated with Mr Diederichs". … These matters show clearly that there was no question of ATBG's having any independent power of decision-making as against AEG and TFR.' (para 52)

'It must therefore be concluded that the conduct of TFR, ATF and ATBG in restraint of competition are to be ascribed to AEG.' (para 53)

Comment

In Case C-286/98P *Stora Kopparbergs Bergslags v Commission* [2000] ECR I-9925, the Court of Justice held that when a subsidiary is wholly owned it is legitimate to assume 'that the parent company in fact exercised decisive influence over its subsidiary's conduct.' This was particularly so since in that case 'the appellant had presented itself as being, as regards companies in the Stora Group, the Commission's sole interlocutor concerning the infringement in question.' (para 29)

Viho Europe BV v Commission	**Undertaking**
Case C-73/95P	Single Economic Entity
Court of Justice, [1996] ECR I-5457, [1997] 4 CMLR 419	

Facts

Parker Pen Ltd operated a distribution system in Europe which was partially based on wholly owned subsidiaries. The sales and marketing activities of these subsidiaries were directed and controlled by Parker Pen. One of the main characteristics of the system was the prohibitions imposed on Parker Pen's subsidiaries from supplying Parker products to customers established in Member States other than that of the subsidiary.

Viho Europe BV challenged Parker's practice in a complaint to the European Commission alleging, among other things, that Parker infringed Article 101 TFEU by restricting the distribution of Parker products to allocated territories, consequently dividing the internal market into national markets. The Commission rejected the complaint on the ground that Parker's subsidiary companies were wholly dependent on Parker Pen UK and enjoyed no real autonomy in determining their course of action. Subsequently the implementation of Parker's policies was regarded as a normal allocation of tasks within a group of undertakings which is not subjected to Article 101 TFEU.

Viho Europe BV appealed to the General Court for annulment of the Commission's decision. The General Court dismissed the appeal and held that in the absence of an agreement between economically independent entities, relations within an economic unit cannot amount to an agreement or concerted practice between undertakings which restricts competition within the meaning of Article 101 TFEU (Case T-102/92 *Viho v Commission* [1995] ECR II-17).

Viho appealed to the Court of Justice.

Held

'Parker and its fully owned subsidiaries form a single economic unit within which the subsidiaries do not enjoy real autonomy in determining their course of action in the market, but carry out the instructions issued to them by the parent company controlling them.' (para 16)

As the subsidiaries do not enjoy real autonomy in determining their course of action in the market, activities within the Parker unit, even if affecting the competitive position of third parties, cannot make Article 101 TFEU applicable. Such activities are unilateral and could in principle only fall under Article 102 TFEU if the conditions for its application were fulfilled. Appeal dismissed. (paras 17, 18)

Comment

Note the Court of Justice ruling in Case 170/83 *Hydrotherm v Compact* [1984] ECR 2999, where it held that 'in competition law, the term "undertaking" must be understood as designating an economic unit for the purpose of the subject-matter of the agreement in question even if in law that economic unit consists of several persons, natural or legal'. (para 11).

Also note the General Court judgment in Joined Cases T-68/89, T-77/89 and T-78/89 *SIV and others v Commission* [1992] ECR II-1403, where it was held that Article 101 TFEU refers only to relations between economic entities which are capable of competing with one another and does not cover agreements or concerted practices between undertakings belonging to the same economic unit (paragraph 357). See also the Court of Justice ruling in Case 22/71 *Beguelin Import Co v SAGL Import Export* [1971] ECR 949, which focused on the lack of economic independence.

In *ArcelorMittal Luxembourg SA v Commission* (Joined Cases C-201/09P and C-216/09P [2011] 4 CMLR 21) AG Bot noted that this 'interpretation of the concept of undertaking has the consequence of excluding the application of Article 101(1) TFEU to agreements between a subsidiary and its parent company, since there is no agreement "between undertakings".' (para 178).

IJsselcentrale and others	**Undertaking**
Case IV/32.732	Single Economic Entity
European Commission, [1991] OJ L28/32	

Facts

The Commission considered a complaint which alleged that four electricity-generating companies in the Netherlands, and a joint venture (SEP) established by them to facilitate cooperation between the electricity generators, infringed Article 101 TFEU. As part of the assessment of the complaint the Commission considered the competitiveness of a cooperation agreement concluded between the four electricity companies and SEP. It especially focused on Article 21 of the cooperation agreement which prohibited the importation and exportation of electricity by undertakings other than SEP.

SEP argued that Article 101 TFEU is not applicable to the cooperation agreement as it was not concluded between independent undertakings. It submitted that the participating companies formed an economic unit, because they were components in 'one indivisible public electricity supply system'. Accordingly, Article 21 of the cooperation agreement secured an internal allocation of tasks within the group and is not subjected to competition laws.

Held

Article 101 TFEU 'is not concerned with agreements between undertakings belonging to the same group of companies, and having the status of parent company and subsidiary, if the undertakings form an economic unit within which the subsidiary has no real freedom to determine its course of action on the market, and if the agreements are concerned merely with the internal allocation of tasks as between the undertakings.' (para 23)

In this case, however, 'the four participants do not belong to a single group of companies. They are separate legal persons, and are not controlled by a single person, natural or legal. Each generating company determines its own conduct independently. … The fact that the generators all form part of one indivisible system of public supply changes nothing here. The distributors likewise form part of the same system, but there is no reason to suppose that they form an economic unit with the generators on that ground alone. Finally, it cannot be said that SEP itself forms an economic unit with one or more of the generating companies. SEP is a joint venture controlled by its parent companies together.' (para 24)

Comment

The Commission's finding that the companies do not form part of the same undertaking paved the way for the application of Article 101 TFEU to the agreements between them.

Note that SEP's argument raises an interesting question as to the level of control which would be deemed to deprive companies from 'real autonomy in determining their course of action in the market' (*Viho Europe BV v Commission*, page 21 above). Whereas in *Viho* the holding structure of the Parker Pen group gave rise to clear control and dependence, it is difficult to identify clearly which lower levels of control might suffice to bring different companies under the umbrella of a single undertaking. On this issue note references to *Sepia Logistics v OFT* and *Suretrack Rail Services Limited v Infraco JNP Limited*, page 25 below.

In merger cases control is defined by Article 3(2) of the Merger Regulation (Regulation (EC) No 139/2004) as the possibility of exercising decisive influence. The Commission Consolidated Jurisdictional Notice on the control of concentrations between undertakings ([2008] OJ C95/1) elaborates on that concept. Note that the Merger Regulation benchmark for control, 'possible decisive influence', is lower than the *Viho* benchmark which requires 'actual control'. (See *Viho*, para 16, contrast with the Jurisdictional Notice, paras 23, 11–35.)

Dansk Rørindustri A/S and others v Commission	**Undertaking**
Joined Cases C-189, 205–8, 213/02P	Single Economic Entity
Court of Justice, [2005] ECR I-5425, [2005] 5 CMLR 17	

Facts

Joined appeals on several General Court judgments in which the General Court dismissed the appellants' actions for annulment of Commission decisions in which various undertakings, and in particular certain of the appellants, were found to participate in a series of agreements and concerted practices within the meaning of Article 101(1) TFEU (Case IV/35.691/E-4 *Pre-insulated pipes*) ([1999] OJ L24/1). One of the issues raised on appeal concerned the General Court finding that a group of companies constituted a single undertaking for the purpose of European competition law.

Held

'[T]he anti-competitive conduct of an undertaking can be attributed to another undertaking where it has not decided independently upon its own conduct on the market but carried out, in all material respects, the instructions given to it by that other undertaking, having regard in particular to the economic and legal links between them (see, in particular, Case C-294/98P *Metsa-Serla and others v Commission* [2000] ECR I-10065, paragraph 27).' (para 117)

'It is true that the mere fact that the share capital of two separate commercial companies is held by the same person or the same family is insufficient, in itself, to establish that those companies are a single economic unit with the result that, under [Union] competition law, the actions of one company can be attributed to the other and that one can be held liable to pay the fine for the other (see Case C-196/99P *Aristrain v Commission* [2003] ECR I-11005, paragraph 99).' (para 118)

In the present case the General Court did not infer the existence of the economic unit constituting the Henss/Isoplus group solely from the fact that the undertakings concerned were controlled from the viewpoint of their share capital by a single person, but considered a series of additional elements. These established that the companies were controlled by one individual who held key functions within the management boards of those companies and represented them in various meetings. (paras 119, 120)

'In those circumstances, the [General Court] cannot be criticised for having held, following an overall and, in principle, sovereign assessment of a range of facts, that the various undertakings constituting the Henss/Isoplus group must, for that purpose, be regarded as belonging to a single economic entity.' (para 130)

Comment

Note the Court of Justice decision in Case C-286/98P *Stora Kopparbergs Bergslags v Commission* [2000] ECR I-9925, [2001] 4 CMLR 12. There, while dealing with a claim contesting the General Court finding that two entities formed one single undertaking, the Court noted that 'the fact that a subsidiary has separate legal personality is not sufficient to exclude the possibility of its conduct being imputed to the parent company, especially where the subsidiary does not independently decide its own conduct on the market, but carries out, in all material respects, the instructions given to it by the parent company (see, in particular, *ICI v Commission*, cited above, paragraphs 132 and 133); Case 52/69 *Geigy v Commission* [1972] ECR 787, paragraph 44, and Case 6/72 *Europemballage and Continental Can v Commission* [1973] ECR 215, paragraph 15).' (para 26)

In Case T-301/04 *Clearstream v Commission* the General Court noted that when a parent company holds 100 per cent of the capital of a subsidiary which has committed an infringement, there is a rebuttable presumption that the parent company exercises decisive influence over the conduct of its subsidiary and that they therefore constitute a single undertaking for the purposes of competition law. It is for the parent company to rebut that presumption by adducing evidence to establish that its subsidiary was independent. (para 199) See also Case T-314/01 *Avebe v Commission* [2006] ECR II-3085, para 136.

Provimi Ltd v Aventis Animal Nutrition SA and others	**Undertaking**
2002/470	Single Economic Entity
High Court (Queen's Bench Division), [2003] 2 All ER 683	

Facts

Following an investigation into the vitamin and pigment markets in Europe, the Commission found that various manufacturers of vitamins, among them Hoffmann-La Roche and Aventis SA, had operated price-fixing and market-sharing cartels contrary to Article 101 TFEU (Commission decision in Case COMP/E-1/37.512—*Vitamins*). The claimants, who had purchased vitamins from the Roche and Aventis groups during the existence of the cartels, brought proceedings in the English court for damages against a number of the cartel members and subsidiaries of the cartel members.

In the applications before the court, the defendants' aim was to strike out and/or set aside part of the proceedings. One of the issues raised by the applicants was that there is no infringement of Article 101 TFEU if the implementation of the agreement by the subsidiary company consisted simply of obeying the orders of the parent company to sell at cartel prices that have been agreed by the parent company without the knowledge of the subsidiary.

Held

It is arguable that where two corporate entities are part of the same undertaking and one of those corporate entities has entered into a cartel agreement with a third independent undertaking, then if the first corporate entity, which was not part of the agreement and lacks knowledge of it, implements that infringing agreement, it is also infringing Article 101 TFEU. 'In my view it is arguable that it is not necessary to plead or prove any particular "concurrence of wills" between the two legal entities within Undertaking A. The EU competition law concept of an "undertaking" is that it is one economic unit. The legal entities that are a part of the one undertaking, by definition of the concept, have no independence of mind or action or will. They are to be regarded as all one. Therefore, so it seems to me, the mind and will of one legal entity is, for the purposes of Article 101 TFEU, to be treated as the mind and will of the other entity. There is no question of having to "impute" the knowledge or will of one entity to another, because they are one and the same.'

'In my view the fact that, in the Decision, the Commission identifies only one particular legal entity as the "infringing undertaking" does not detract from my conclusion. EU competition law has to bow to the practical fact that in national laws it is legal entities that exist; and it is legal entities that own the funds from which fines are paid. So particular entities need to be identified in order to enforce the Decision. But those practical considerations cannot determine a prior question which is whether, if one entity of an undertaking is an infringer by agreeing to fix prices, another entity that has implemented the same infringing agreement, is also an infringer.' (paras 31, 32)

Comment

Note that in this motion the Court aimed to establish whether claims brought by the claimants were arguable. The weight attributed to the holding of the Court should reflect this lower yardstick.

In *Cooper Tire and Rubber Company v Shell Chemicals UK* Case No A3/2009/2487 [2010] EWCA Civ 864, the English Court of Appeal noted that 'Although one can see that a parent company should be liable for what its subsidiary has done on the basis that a parent company is presumed to be able to exercise (and actually exercise) decisive influence over a subsidiary, it is by no means obvious even in an [Article 101] context that a subsidiary should be liable for what its parent does, let alone for what another subsidiary does. Nor does the Provimi point sit comfortably with the apparent practice of the Commission, when it exercises its power to fine, to single out those who are primarily responsible or their parent companies rather than to impose a fine on all the entities of the relevant undertaking. If, moreover, liability can extend to any subsidiary company which is part of an undertaking, would such liability accrue to a subsidiary which did not deal in rubber at all, but another product entirely? ...' (para 45)

Sepia Logistics Ltd and another v Office of Fair Trading
Case No 1072/1/1/06
Competition Appeal Tribunal, [2007] CAT 13

Undertaking
Single Economic Entity

Facts

Sepia Logistics Ltd (formerly known as Double Quick Supplyline Ltd (DQS)) appealed to the Competition Appeal Tribunal against a decision taken by the Office of Fair Trading (OFT) in which the OFT concluded that, together with a number of suppliers of aluminium double-glazing spacer bars, it participated in an anti-competitive agreement and/or concerted practice and infringed the Chapter I prohibition of the UK Competition Act 1998. The OFT decision addressed not only DQS but also its parent company, Precision Concepts Ltd (PC), on the basis that PC formed part of the same undertaking as DQS, and was equally liable for its participation in the infringement. On appeal, DQS and PC challenged, among other things, the OFT's conclusion that DQS and PC form part of the same undertaking.

Held

'It is well established that an undertaking does not correspond to the commonly understood notion of a legal entity under, for example, English commercial or tax law; and that a single undertaking may comprise one or more legal or natural persons.' (para 70)

'The European Court of Justice in *Hydrotherm*, [Case 170/83 *Hydrotherm Gerätebau GmbH v Compact de Dott Ing Mario Andreoli & CSAS* [1984] ECR 2999, [1985] 3 CMLR 224] said at paragraph [11]: "In competition law, the term 'undertaking' must be understood as designating an economic unit for the purpose of the subject-matter of the agreement in question even if in law that economic unit consists of several persons, natural or legal."' (para 72)

Crucial to this question is the matter of control as highlighted in Case C-73/95P *Viho v Commission*. The issue of control was also considered in Case C-286/98 *Stora Kopparbergs Bergslag AB*, where the Court of Justice held that the fact that a subsidiary has separate legal personality does not exclude the possibility of its conduct being imputed to the parent company, especially where it does not independently decide its own conduct on the market. Similarly, in Cases C-189/02P etc *Dansk Rørindustri and others v European Commission*, the Court of Justice held that conduct of one undertaking can be attributed to a controlling undertaking. (paras 73–6)

In this case DQS was a wholly-owned subsidiary of PBM of which 80 per cent were held by SGH, which was a wholly-owned subsidiary of PC. PC therefore owned indirectly 80 per cent of the shares in DQS. Mr Sander, a director of both DQC and PC had direct involvement in the infringement. Consequently, PC, through Mr Sander, was both aware of DQS' involvement in the infringement and capable of exercising control over DQS. (paras 77–80)

Comment

Note the English High Court of Justice (Chancery Division) decision in *Suretrack Rail Services Limited v Infraco JNP Limited* [2002] EWHC 1316 (Ch), where as part of an application for interim relief the Honourable Mr Justice Laddie commented that 'The fact that subsidiaries take their own decisions does not, of itself, indicate whether those subsidiaries are either independent of each other or independent of the parent. … If the fact that directors of a subsidiary take their own decisions and make their own assessment of the risks and profitability of the decisions from the viewpoint of that subsidiary were enough to prevent the subsidiary from being considered as part of a single economic unit for competition law purposes, then all subsidiaries would be treated as being separate undertakings' (para 18). Chapter I of the UK Competition Act 1998 was held not to be applicable as the three companies concerned were subsidiaries of the same parent company and subsequently an 'agreement between undertakings' did not exist.

Also note Case IV/32.732 *IJsselcentrale and others*, and the commentary on page 22 above.

Akzo Nobel and others v Commission	**Undertaking**
Case C-97/08P	Single Economic Entity
Court of Justice, [2009] ECR I-8237, [2005] 5 CMLR 23	Liability of Parent Company

Facts

An appeal by Akzo Nobel NV against the General Court's judgment in Case T-112/05 *Akzo Nobel and others v Commission* [2007] ECR II-5049, by which the General Court dismissed an action for annulment of Commission decision in Case No C-37.533—*Choline Chloride* ([2005] OJ L190, 22).

The Commission's decision followed an investigation into cartel activity in which several subsidiaries of Akzo Nobel NV were involved. In its decision the Commission concluded that the subsidiaries lacked commercial autonomy and were controlled by their parent company, Akzo Nobel NV. Together, these companies formed a single economic unit and constituted a single undertaking. The Commission subsequently addressed the contested decision to Akzo Nobel, notwithstanding the fact that it had not itself participated in the cartel.

Held

The concept of an undertaking covers any entity engaged in an economic activity, regardless of its legal status and the way in which it is financed. That concept must be understood as designating an economic unit even if in law that economic unit consists of several persons, natural or legal. (paras 54–55)

'It is clear from settled case-law that the conduct of a subsidiary may be imputed to the parent company in particular where, although having a separate legal personality, that subsidiary does not decide independently upon its own conduct on the market, but carries out, in all material respects, the instructions given to it by the parent company, … having regard in particular to the economic, organisational and legal links between those two legal entities. … That is the case because, in such a situation, the parent company and its subsidiary form a single economic unit and therefore form a single undertaking. … Thus, the fact that a parent company and its subsidiary constitute a single undertaking within the meaning of [Article 101 TFEU] enables the Commission to address a decision imposing fines to the parent company, without having to establish the personal involvement of the latter in the infringement.' (paras 58, 59)

Where a parent company has a 100 per cent shareholding in a subsidiary which has infringed competition rules, there is a rebuttable presumption that the parent company exercised a decisive influence over the conduct of its subsidiary. The Commission is able to regard the parent company as jointly and severally liable for the payment of the fine imposed on its subsidiary, unless the parent company, which has the burden of rebutting that presumption, show that its subsidiary acts independently on the market. (paras 61–65) Appeal dismissed.

Comment

The concept of a single economic unit implies that a parent company may be held liable for the anticompetitive activity of its wholly owned subsidiary even if the parent company was not party to the anticompetitive activity. The Commission can subsequently address a decision imposing fines to the parent company, without having to establish the personal involvement of the latter in the infringement.

In its judgment the Court of Justice clarified that where a parent company has a 100 per cent shareholding in its subsidiary there is a rebuttable presumption that that parent company exercises a decisive influence over the conduct of its subsidiary. That presumption may also be applied in cases of partial ownership which entail control. See, for example, Case T-168/05 *Arkema SA v Commission*, in which the General Court held that holding of 'almost entirety of the capital of a subsidiary' will give rise to a rebuttable presumption that the parent company exercises a decisive influence. (para 70) On appeal, the Court of Justice upheld the General Court's judgment (Case C-520/09P).

Alliance One International and Others v Commission	**Undertaking**
Case C-628/10P	Single Economic Entity
Court of Justice, [2012] 5 CMLR 14	Liability of Parent Company

Facts

An application for annulment of Commission Decision (Case COMP/C.38.238.B-2—Raw tobacco) in which the Commission found that a number of undertakings had infringed Article 101 TFEU by fixing the price of raw tobacco. One of the undertakings involved in the cartel was World Wide Tobacco España, SA ('WWTE'). In its decision the Commission attributed the unlawful conduct of WWTE to three companies which directly or indirectly held controlling shares in WWTE. These were (1) Trans-Continental Leaf Tobacco Corp Ltd ('TCLT'), a wholly owned subsidiary of (2) Standard Commercial Tobacco Co, Inc ('SCTC'), a wholly owned subsidiary of (3) American Multinational Standard Commercial Corp ('SCC'). The Commission found WWTE and its parent companies jointly responsible for the infringement.

The parties applied to the General Court for annulment of the Commission's decision. Case T-24/05 [2011] 4 CMLR 9. The General Court held that the conduct of a subsidiary may be attributed to the parent company in particular where that subsidiary does not decide independently upon its own conduct on the market, but carries out the instructions the parent company gives it. The Court noted that the fact that a subsidiary has a dedicated local management and its own resources does not prove, in itself, that the subsidiary is independent of its parent companies. It clarified that the Commission is able to address a decision imposing fines on the parent company not because of an alleged liability of the parent company due to its participation in the infringement, but because the parent company and the subsidiary constitute a single undertaking for the purposes of Article 101 TFEU. The Court added that the Commission has to establish (1) that the parent company is in a position to exercise decisive influence over the conduct of its subsidiary, and (2) that that influence was actually exercised. Decisive influence may be exercised through sole or joint control. Where a parent company has, directly or indirectly, 100% shareholding in a subsidiary there is a rebuttable presumption that the parent company exercises decisive influence over the conduct of its subsidiary. The fact that a subsidiary has a dedicated local management and its own resources does not prove, in itself, that that company decides upon its conduct on the market independently of its parent companies. The General Court partially annulled the Commission's decision with respect to TCLT's liability. The judgment had no effect on the fine for which the other two parent companies, SCC and SCTC, remained jointly and severally liable. The undertakings and Commission appealed to the Court of Justice. Appeals dismissed.

Held

When a parent company has a 100% shareholding in a subsidiary, there is a rebuttable presumption that the parent company exercises decisive influence over the conduct of its subsidiary. In those circumstances, it is sufficient for the Commission to prove that the entire capital of the subsidiary is held by its parent company in order for it to be presumed that the parent exercises decisive influence over the commercial policy of that subsidiary. In its decision, the Commission is not bound to rely exclusively on that presumption. There is nothing to prevent the Commission from establishing that a parent company actually exercises decisive influence over its subsidiary by means of other evidence or by a combination of such evidence and that presumption. (paras 47–49)

Comment

In its decision, the Commission found the parent companies liable only where there was evidence to support actual exercise of decisive influence by the parent companies holding the entire share capital of the subsidiaries. The Court of Justice held that the Commission was justified to use the 'dual basis' approach, considering the uncertainty as to the case law at the time of the decision. The General Court and Court of Justice noted that in choosing that method, the Commission imposed upon itself a standard of proof of the actual exercise of decisive influence which was more onerous than that under the presumption of decisive influence.

EI du Pont de Nemours v Commission	**Undertaking**
Case C-172/12P	Liability of Parent Company
Court of Justice, [2014] 4 CMLR 7	Joint Venture

Facts

An appeal against the General Court's judgment in Case T-76/08 in which the General Court dismissed the application to annul a Commission decision which found EI du Pont de Nemours and the Dow Chemical Company to be liable for cartel activity carried out by their joint venture, DuPont Dow Elastomers LLC, which was held, at that time, in equal shares by both companies.

In its judgment the General Court considered the economic, legal and organisational links between the parent companies and the joint venture. It noted the parent companies' ability to supervise the strategic direction of the joint venture, their power to appoint and dismiss officers of the joint venture, and to approve capital expenditure and borrowing above certain levels. The fact that the parent companies held equal shares in the joint venture meant that each could block the joint venture's strategic decisions. The General Court held that:

'It is clear from settled case-law that the conduct of a subsidiary may be imputed to the parent company in particular where that subsidiary, despite having a separate legal personality, does not decide independently upon its own conduct on the market, but carries out, in all material respects, the instructions given to it by the parent company, regard being had in particular to the economic, organisational and legal links between those two legal entities... in such a situation, the parent company and its subsidiary form a single economic unit and therefore form a single undertaking.' (para 59, General Court Judgment, Case T-76/08)

EI du Pont de Nemours appealed to the Court of Justice, asking to set aside the General Court' judgment.

Held

The conduct of a subsidiary can be imputed to its parent company where that subsidiary, although it has separate legal personality, does not operate independently but carries out, in all material respects, the instructions given to it by the parent company. In such case, the parent company and its subsidiary form a single economic unit and therefore a single undertaking for the purposes of Article 101 TFEU. Subsequently, 'the Commission may address a decision imposing fines to the parent company, without having to establish the personal involvement of the latter in the infringement (see *Akzo Nobel and Others v Commission*, paragraph 59, and *Alliance One International and Standard Commercial Tobacco v Commission* and *Commission v Alliance One International and Others*, paragraph 44).' (paras 41, 42)

'[I]n order to be able to impute the conduct of a subsidiary to the parent company, the Commission cannot merely find that the parent company is in a position to exercise decisive influence over the conduct of its subsidiary, but must also check whether that influence was actually exercised (see, to that effect, Case 107/82 *AEG-Telefunken v Commission* [1983] ECR 3151, paragraph 50).' (para 44)

'It should be noted in that regard that the rule that it is necessary to check whether the parent company actually exercised decisive influence over its subsidiary applies only where the subsidiary is not wholly owned by its parent company. According to the settled case-law of the Court of Justice, where the entire capital of the subsidiary is owned, there is no longer any requirement to carry out such a check since, in those circumstances, there is a presumption of decisive influence on the part of the parent company, which has the burden of rebutting that presumption (see *Alliance One International and Standard Commercial Tobacco v Commission* and *Commission v Alliance One International and Others*, paragraphs 46 and 47 and the case-law cited).' (para 45)

'Where two parent companies each have a 50% shareholding in the joint venture which committed an infringement of the rules of competition law, it is only for the purposes of establishing liability for participation in the infringement of that law and only in so far as the Commission has demonstrated, on the basis of factual evidence, that both parent companies did in fact exercise decisive influence over the joint venture, that those three entities can be considered to form a single economic unit and therefore form a single undertaking for the purposes of [Article 101 TFEU].' (para 47)

'It must therefore be held that, as regards the verification process of the assessment carried out by the Commission, the General Court did not misconstrue the term "a single undertaking". ' (para 48)

The autonomy which a joint venture enjoys within the meaning of Article 3(4) of the EC Merger Regulation does not mean that that joint venture also enjoys autonomy in relation to adopting strategic decisions and that it is not under the decisive influence of its parent companies for the purposes of Article 101 TFEU. (paras 51–53)

Appeal dismissed.

Comment

When a parent company holds the entire capital of the subsidiary, there is a rebuttable presumption of decisive influence on the part of the parent company. The two entities form a single economic unit and therefore a single undertaking for the purposes of Article 101 TFEU. Unless the parent company rebuts the presumption of decisive influence, the conduct of its subsidiary can be imputed to it and the Commission may address a decision imposing fines to the parent company, without establishing its involvement in the infringement.

When a parent company does not hold the entire capital of the subsidiary, the Commission must show that influence was actually exercised in order to impute the conduct of a subsidiary to a parent company. To do so, the Commission needs to take account of all the relevant factors relating to the economic, organisational and legal links which tie the subsidiary to the parent company.

The fact that a joint venture forms a separate legal personality from that of the parent companies, and is an 'autonomous economic entity' in the context of the European Merger Regulation, does not preclude the possibility that it does not enjoy autonomy in strategic decision-making, and that it is therefore under the decisive influence of its parent companies for the purposes of Article 101 TFEU.

The fact that a parent company is liable for the activities of a joint venture under Article 101 TFEU does not necessarily lead to the conclusion that the companies form a single undertaking. Agreements between the parent company and the joint venture may constitute an agreement 'between undertakings' and be subjected to Article 101 TFEU if the two companies do not form a 'single economic entity'.

In Case C-408/12P *YKK v Commission*, the Court held that: 'A company cannot be held to be responsible for infringements committed independently by its subsidiaries before the date of their acquisition, since the latter must themselves answer for their unlawful conduct prior to that acquisition, and the company which has acquired them cannot be held to be responsible (see the judgment in *Cascades v Commission*, C-279/98 P, …, paragraphs 77 to 79).' (para 65) For a full review of this case, see the discussion on fines in Chapter 10.

In Case C-279/98P, *Cascades SA v Commission*, the Court held that: 'It falls, in principle, to the legal or natural person managing the undertaking in question when the infringement was committed to answer for that infringement, even if, when the Decision finding the infringement was adopted, another person had assumed responsibility for operating the undertaking.' (para 78)

Koninklijke Grolsch v Commission	**Undertaking**
Case T-234/07	Liability of Parent Company
General Court, [2011] ECR 11-6169	Right of Defence

Koninklijke Grolsch NV (Grolsch), and its fully owned subsidiary were found by the Commission to have taken part in an anticompetitive cartel between brewing companies in the Netherlands. Grolsch brought an action of annulment against the decision and denied direct involvement in the infringement to which its subsidiary was part.

The General Court held that the Commission had not established Grolsch's direct involvement in the agreement. The Court repeated the case law on parent liability and noted that the conduct of a subsidiary may be imputed to the parent company especially when, despite having a distinct legal personality, the subsidiary does not decide independently upon its own conduct in the market. In such a situation, the parent company and its subsidiary form a single economic unit and are treated as a single undertaking within the meaning of Article 101 TFEU. This allows the Commission to issue a decision imposing fines on the parent company, without any requirement to establish its personal involvement in the offence. Where a parent company owns 100% interest in a subsidiary, there is a rebuttable presumption that the parent company actually exercises decisive influence. (paras 80–2)

However, in this case the Commission failed to state clearly the reasons why it attributes the infringement carried out by the subsidiary to the parent company, Grolsch. The Commission's decision makes no reference to the economic, organisational and legal relationship between the parent company and its subsidiary. By omitting to state clearly that Grolsch's liability was imputed based on its full ownership and control of the subsidiary, the Commission deprived Grolsch of its right of defence and of an opportunity to rebut the presumption of influence. (paras 76–94). The Commission's decision was annulled.

L'Air Liquide and others v Commission	**Undertaking**
Case T-185/06	Liability of Parent Company
General Court, [2011] ECR 11-2809	Obligation to State Reasons

Application for partial annulment of Commission decision (Case COMP/F/38.620—Hydrogen peroxide and perborate), in which the Commission found Air Liquide to be liable for the unlawful conduct of its subsidiary, Chemoxal. In its decision the Commission noted that where a parent company owns 100% interest in a subsidiary there is a rebuttable presumption that the parent company effectively exercises a decisive influence on the conduct of its subsidiary. In those circumstances, it is sufficient that the Commission shows that the entire capital of a subsidiary is owned by its parent to assume that the latter has a decisive influence on trade policy of the subsidiary. Air Liquide attempted to rebut the presumption by demonstrating, among other things, the lack of overlap between the companies in terms of management and staff, the broad powers of Chemoxal's officers to run the company, Chemoxal's autonomy in the development of strategic projects, and the fact that it had its own services to implement its commercial activities. The Commission considered that evidence presented by Air Liquide was insufficient to rebut the presumption. Air Liquide brought an action of annulment against the decision.

The General Court did not comment directly on the arguments put forward by Air Liquide to demonstrate the independence of Chemoxal. It held, however, that the nature of the rebuttable presumption at issue required the Commission to examine whether Air Liquide had demonstrated that its subsidiary was acting independently. However, the Commission did not adequately examine the arguments put forward by Air Liquid, in light of all relevant factors relating to economic, organisational and legal issues between the companies concerned. In doing so the Commission failed to state reasons for the attribution of the infringement at issue to Air Liquide. Decision annulled. (paras 66–84)

Toshiba Carrier UK Ltd v KME Yorkshire Ltd	**Undertaking**
HC09C04733	Single Economic Entity
High Court of Justice, [2011] EWHC 2665 (Ch)	Liability of a Subsidiary to Parent's Conduct

Facts

The European Commission found a number of companies to have infringed Article 101 TFEU by taking part in an international cartel in the supply of industrial copper tubing. Following the Commission decision, Toshiba Carrier and other companies launched a damage action in the English court against the infringing companies. The action targeted the companies identified in the Commission's decision, as well as their UK subsidiaries, even though those companies were not the subject of Commission findings. In a summary judgment the Court was required to consider whether the claims were arguable. It dismissed the defendant's application for orders striking out the claims.

Held

In *Provimi v Roche Products Ltd* Aikens J considered it arguable that where two corporate entities are part of an undertaking and one of those entities has entered into an infringing agreement, then if the other corporate entity implements that infringing agreement, it is also infringing Article 101 TFEU. He added that the fact that the Commission identifies in its decision only one particular legal entity as the infringing undertaking does not detract from that conclusion. (para 27)

In *Cooper Tire and Rubber Company v Shell Chemicals UK* the Court of Appeal made reference to the Provimi judgment and noted that it does not sit comfortably with the apparent practice of the Commission, when it exercises its power to fine, to single out those who are primarily responsible, rather than to impose a fine on all the entities of the relevant undertakings. It is therefore by no means obvious that a subsidiary should be liable for what its parent does, let alone for what another subsidiary does. The Court concluded by stating that if it had been necessary to address the *Provimi* point, it would have been inclined to make a reference to the Court of Justice before coming to a conclusion on jurisdiction. (paras 28–30)

'I have, of course, noted and carefully considered what the Court of Appeal there said about making a reference to the Court of the European Union. In my view it would not be appropriate to make a reference at this stage.' (para 43)

'If the Commission has investigated certain trade practices pursued by specified undertakings and reached the conclusion that they infringed Article 101 that will bind the addressee. If a national court concludes on evidence adduced before it that X Ltd was a part of the same undertaking and involved in the same trade practices as that addressee it would be contrary to Article 16 to conclude that X Ltd or that undertaking had not infringed Article 101 in pursuing those same trade practices. And if the national court is precluded by Article 16 from reaching a conflicting decision why should it undertake the task of re-investigating the same matters …' (para 44)

Comment

The judgment adds to a number of cases in which as part of a private action before national courts, purchasers bring proceedings against the subsidiaries of addressees of a Commission decision (the undertaking). These subsidiaries are used as 'Anchor defendants' to bring the claim within the jurisdiction of the national court, in line with the provisions of Regulation 44/2001 and as of January 2015 with Regulation 1215/2012 on jurisdiction and the recognition and enforcement of judgments in civil and commercial matters.

In the context of the discussion of the notion of undertaking, these cases raise a difficult question as to whether the competition law notion of undertaking is sufficient in order to impute liability to a company which was not addressed directly in the Commission's decision, yet forms part of the single economic entity.

For a discussion of *Cooper Tire & Rubber Company Europe Ltd v Dow Deutschland Inc*, see page 24 above.

Power Cables	**Public Enforcement**
Case COMP/39610	Liability of a Parent Company
European Commission, [2014] OJ C319/10	Pure Financial Investor Defence

Facts

On 2 April 2014, the European Commission adopted a decision condemning a number of undertakings for their participation in a cartel activity in the market for underground and submarine high-voltage power cables. One of the undertakings, Prysmian, which participated in the cartel, was owned by the private equity fund Goldman Sachs Group, Inc, during part of the cartel operation period. Having established that Prysmian infringed the competition laws, the Commission subsequently found both Prysmian and its former owner, Goldman Sachs, to be jointly and severally liable for the fine.

In a press release Commissioner Almunia noted that the investment bank Goldman Sachs had acquired decisive influence over Prysmian—the same as that of industrial owners. The bank had several managers and directors on Prysmian's board and took part in strategic decision-making. He noted that investment companies have a responsibility to ensure a compliance culture.

Goldman Sachs applied for annulment of the decision: Case T-419/14 *The Goldman Sachs Group v Commission*. Judgment pending.

Comment

The pure financial investor defence reflects the understanding that such an investor would not acquire decisive influence over the target company. In her opinion in Case C-97/08P *Akzo Nobel*, Advocate General Kokott noted that the presumption of decisive influence may be rebutted by demonstrating that in practice the parent company exercised restraint and did not influence the market conduct of its subsidiary. Such may be the case, for example, when the parent company is a pure financial investor.

The scope of the pure financial investor defence was later explored by the General Court in Case T-392/09 *1. Garantovaná as. v Commission*. There, the Court held that 'a "pure financial investor" must therefore be understood as referring to the case of an investor who holds shares in a company in order to make a profit, but who refrains from any involvement in its management and in its control.' (para 52)

In Case T-395/09 *Gigaset AG v Commission* the General Court considered the activities of an investment company specialising in restructuring. That company was held liable for the activities of the target company, SKW, which participated in a cartel activity. Gigaset argued that it is not liable for the activities of SKW as it acted as a 'pure financial investor'. The Court rejected this argument. It noted that as part of the restructuring Gigaset had the ability to make strategic decisions with regard to SKW, received on an ongoing basis information on the economic performance of SKW and established a taskforce dedicated to the implementation of the restructuring. The General Court found these actions to form evidence of actual exercise of influence. It held that: '[T]he person responsible within the applicant, for the acquisition of SKW, was appointed to lead SKW Holding. This person would report regularly on behalf of that company, the applicant, in particular the progress of the restructuring of SKW. Assuming these reports disclose any difficulty in the implementation of the restructuring strategy, the applicant stood ready to intervene with the task force to the restructuring. All these elements show that the applicant had implemented, through SKW Holding, a specific strategy SKW restructuring and that it was closely following its implementation, in order to intervene at the slightest indication of trouble in the achievement of objectives, including financial, of this strategy. This is the effective exercise of decisive influence on the behaviour of SKW Holding, namely the management of the single element of its assets (SKW, SKW Holding which owned the entire share capital).' (para 54, unofficial translation)

2

Market Definition

Market Definition

The definition of the market is an important step in the identification of boundaries of competition between firms. The main purpose of market definition as laid down in the Commission Notice on the Definition of the Relevant Market for the Purposes of Community Competition Law ([1997] OJ C372) 'is to identify in a systematic way the competitive constraints that the undertakings involved face. The objective of defining a market in both its product and geographic dimension is to identify the actual competitors of the undertakings involved that are capable of constraining their behaviour and preventing them from behaving independently of an effective competitive pressure. It is from this perspective, that the market definition makes it possible, inter alia, to calculate market shares that would convey meaningful information regarding market power for the purpose of assessing dominance or for the purpose of applying [Article 101 TFEU]' (para 2).

The Commission Notice on the Definition of the Relevant Market provides valuable insight into the methodology applied by the Commission when defining the product and geographic markets. The product market is generally defined in the Notice as one which 'comprises all those products and/or services which are regarded as interchangeable or substitutable by the consumer, by reason of the products' characteristics, their prices and their intended use' (para 7). The geographic market is defined in the Notice as one which 'comprises the area in which the undertakings concerned are involved in the supply and demand of products or services, in which the conditions of competition are sufficiently homogeneous and which can be distinguished from neighbouring areas because the conditions of competition are appreciably different in those areas' (para 8).

The process of market definition is also referred to in some detail in the Commission's Guidelines on the Assessment of Horizontal Mergers ([2004] OJ C31/5), and the Commission's Discussion Paper on the Application of [Article 102 TFEU] to Exclusionary Abuses (December 2005).

Although the process of market definition is primarily an economic exercise, European case law provides a useful reflection of the methodology used in the analysis. The following cases highlight various aspects of market definition.

Product and Geographic Markets

See also summary reference to:

One-way Substitution

Markets for Spare Parts/Aftermarkets

Narrow Markets

See also summary references to:

Switching Costs/Technology Markets

Markets for Raw Materials

Data markets

Market Definition in Article 102 TFEU Cases

The SSNIP test which is used to define the market is based on the assumption that prevailing prices on the market are competitive. However, in the context of Article 102 cases, it is often the case that the price on the market is likely to be above competitive levels. Failure to take this into account may give rise to the 'cellophane fallacy' and lead to the market being defined too widely. Consequently, in cases of dominance it is appropriate to rely on a wider range of methods to assess the market and eliminate false substitutes. See the Commission Notice on the Definition of the Relevant Market (para 25) and the Commission's Discussion Paper on the Application of [Article 102 TFEU] to Exclusionary Abuses (December 2005) (paras 11–19).

The 'cellophane fallacy' highlights a significant shortcoming in the process of market definition. The risk of distortion in the analysis may arise even below the levels of dominance, when more limited levels of market power are present. Subsequently, conclusions as to the elasticity of demand should be treated with caution when used to delineate the market. It is prudent to treat the defined market as a valuable analytical framework but refrain from attributing rigid boundaries to it.

Barriers to Expansion or Entry, and Potential Competition

The methodology used to define the market primarily focuses on demand and supply substitutability. As such, it does not provide the complete picture of the competitive pressures faced by the undertakings. For example, potential competition is a major competitive restraint on undertakings, but does not feature in assessments of market definition. An analysis of the wider picture is called for where the position of the undertakings involved in the relevant market raises concerns from a competition point of view.

On potential competition and barriers to expansion or entry see discussion in Chapter 5 herein. Also note the 'Guidance on the Commission's enforcement priorities in applying [Article 102 TFEU] to abusive exclusionary conduct by dominant undertakings' [2009] OJ C45/7.

Judicial Review

In so far as the definition of the product market involves complex economic assessments on the part of the Commission, it is subject to limited review by the Court. The Court will assess whether the Commission based its assessment on accurate, reliable and coherent evidence which contains all relevant data and is capable of substantiating the conclusions drawn from it. See:

T-301/04	*Clearstream v Commission*	55

The Limitations of Market Definition

Market definition serves as an important preliminary instrument to identify the boundaries of competition and provide a framework in which the effects on competition may be analysed. It is important to note, however, that market realities are often complex and comprise of differentiated products, various levels of substitution and multiproduct firms. As a result, a clear-cut market boundary may not always exist and the process of market definition should not lead to the false assumption of a 'sealed market environment'.

Some areas of analysis, and in particular ex ante merger control, have been characterised by a process of de-emphasis on market definition. While market definition is considered as part of the competitive assessment, it may be left open when the proposed transaction does not raise competitive concerns under the contemplated alternative market definitions. One may observe greater focus on the competitive pressures to which the undertakings will be subjected. This approach aims to approximate more closely the competitive environment post-transaction and avoid over-reliance on artificial market boundaries.

United Brands v Commission	**Market Definition**
Case 27/76	Product and Geographic Markets
Court of Justice, [1978] ECR 207, [1978] 1 CMLR 429	

Facts

In a Commission decision United Brands was found to infringe Article 102 TFEU by abusing its dominant position in the market for bananas (IV/26.699 *Chiquita*). United Brands (UBC) appealed to the ECJ and challenged, among other things, the Commission's conclusions with respect to the market definition.

Held

'In order to determine whether UBC has a dominant position on the banana market it is necessary to define this market both from the standpoint of the product and from the geographic point of view.' (para 10)

'As far as the product market is concerned it is first of all necessary to ascertain whether, as the applicant maintains, bananas are an integral part of the fresh fruit market, because they are reasonably interchangeable by consumers with other kinds of fresh fruit such as apples, oranges, grapes, peaches, strawberries, etc. Or whether the relevant market consists solely of the banana market which includes both branded bananas and unlabelled bananas and is a market sufficiently homogeneous and distinct from the market of other fresh fruit.' (para 12)

'For the banana to be regarded as forming a market which is sufficiently differentiated from other fruit markets it must be possible for it to be singled out by such special features distinguishing it from other fruits that it is only to a limited extent interchangeable with them and is only exposed to their competition in a way that is hardly perceptible.' (para 22)

'The ripening of bananas takes place the whole year round without any season having to be taken into account. Throughout the year production exceeds demand and can satisfy it at any time. Owing to this particular feature the banana is a privileged fruit and its production and marketing can be adapted to the seasonal fluctuations of other fresh fruit which are known and can be computed.' (paras 23–5)

'There is no unavoidable seasonal substitution since the consumer can obtain this fruit all the year round. Since the banana is a fruit which is always available in sufficient quantities the question whether it can be replaced by other fruits must be determined over the whole of the year for the purpose of ascertaining the degree of competition between it and other fresh fruit.' (paras 26, 27)

'The studies of the banana market on the court's file show that on the latter market there is no significant long term cross-elasticity any more than—as has been mentioned—there is any seasonal substitutability in general between the banana and all the seasonal fruits, as this only exists between the banana and two fruits (peaches and table grapes) in one of the countries (west Germany) of the relevant geographic market.' (para 28)

'As far as concerns the two fruits available throughout the year (oranges and apples) the first are not interchangeable and in the case of the second there is only a relative degree of substitutability. This small degree of substitutability is accounted for by the specific features of the banana and all the factors which influence consumer choice.' (paras 29, 30)

'The banana has certain characteristics, appearance, taste, softness, seedlessness, easy handling, a constant level of production which enables it to satisfy the constant needs of an important section of the population consisting of the very young, the old and the sick.' (para 31)

'As far as prices are concerned two FAO studies show that the banana is only affected by the prices—falling prices—of other fruits (and only of peaches and table grapes) during the summer months and mainly in July and then by an amount not exceeding 20%. Although it cannot be denied that during these months and some weeks at the end of the year this product is exposed to competition from other fruits, the flexible way in which the volume of imports and their marketing on the relevant geographic market is adjusted means that the conditions of competition are extremely limited and that its price adapts without any serious difficulties to this situation where supplies of fruit are plentiful.' (paras 32, 33)

'It follows from all these considerations that a very large number of consumers having a constant need for bananas are not noticeably or even appreciably enticed away from the consumption of this product by the arrival of other fresh fruit on the market and that even the personal peak periods only affect it for a limited period of time and to a very limited extent from the point of view of substitutability.' (para 34)

Geographic market: the French, UK and Italian markets are organised nationally and subsequently display different market conditions. The effect of this is that UBC's bananas do not compete on equal terms with the other bananas sold in these states, which benefit from a preferential system. The Commission was right to exclude these three national markets from the geographic market under consideration. On the other hand, the Federal Republic of Germany, Denmark, Ireland and the Netherlands form an area that is sufficiently homogeneous to be considered in its entirety as one geographic market. (paras 36–57)

'It follows from all these considerations that the geographic market as determined by the Commission which constitutes a substantial part of the common market must be regarded as the relevant market for the purpose of determining whether the applicant may be in a dominant position.' (para 57)

Comment

The decision centres on the characteristics of bananas that single them out from other fruits (para 31). These unique features arguably indicate low substitutability. To prove substitutability one need not show that all customers would seek substitutions when faced with an increase in price, but that a sufficiently large number of customers would do so. It is therefore important to assess the size of the marginal consumer group which would react to a change in price. When this group is large enough the increase in price would be deemed unprofitable.

In para 31 the Court commented that a large group which consists of the very young, the old and the sick especially values the special characteristics of bananas and is 'locked in' due to its inelastic demand. A similar statement is repeated on para 34. Note, however, that in order to assess substitutability the analysis should have not centred only on the 'captive consumers' but rather on whether a sufficient number of non-captive consumers would seek substitution when faced with an increase in price. If this marginal group is large enough, the increase in price would be unprofitable. On this point also note *France Télécom SA v Commission* and *FTC v Whole Foods Market* (page 45 below).

Examples of captive consumers may be found when considering the market for spare parts (Case 22/78 *Hugin v Commission* (page 48 below)), Case T-427/08 *CEAHR v Commission* (page 50 below) or the secondary market for computer games (COMP/35.587 *Nintendo* (page 52 below)).

Note that a monopolist may be able to isolate the captive group by using price discrimination, thus charging higher prices from those with inelastic demand. In this respect, note paragraph 43 of the Commission Notice on the Definition of the Relevant Market: 'The extent of the product market might be narrowed in the presence of distinct groups of customers. A distinct group of customers for the relevant product may constitute a narrower, distinct market when such a group could be subject to price discrimination. This will usually be the case when two conditions are met: (a) it is possible to identify clearly which group an individual customer belongs to at the moment of selling the relevant products to him, and (b) trade among customers or arbitrage by third parties should not be feasible.'

Note the Court of Justice's short reference to the absence of a temporal dimension to the market in question (paras 28–30). Evidence on seasonal changes to cross elasticity of demand was considered in the Commission investigation (IV/26.699 *Chiquita*) but not dealt with by the Court of Justice in its judgment.

Hoffmann-La Roche & Co v Commission	**Market Definition**
Case 85/76	Product and Geographic Markets
Court of Justice, [1979] ECR 461, [1979] 3 CMLR 211	

Facts

Hoffmann-La Roche (Roche) applied for the annulment of a Commission decision (IV/29.020—*Vitamins*) which found Roche to have abused its dominant position in the market for vitamins A, B2, B3, B6, C, E and H. Roche challenged the Commission's decision on several points, including the definition of the market.

Held

'The contested Decision refers to bulk vitamins belonging to 13 groups. … The Commission found that there was a dominant position in the case of seven of the eight groups of vitamins manufactured by Roche. … The parties are agreed, on the one hand, that each of these groups has specific metabolizing functions and for this reason is not interchangeable with the others and, on the other hand, that in the case of the possible uses which these three groups have in common, namely for food, animal feed and for pharmaceutical purposes, the vitamins in question do not encounter the competition of other products.' (para 23)

The Commission considered that each group of vitamins constitutes a separate market. Roche accepted this point of view but argued that the C and E group of vitamins, as far as each of them is concerned, together with other products, form part of a wider market. (para 24)

'It is an established fact that vitamins C and E apart from their uses in the pharmaceutical industry and in food and animal feed … are also sold, inter alia, as antioxidants, fermentation agents and additives …' (para 25)

'If a product could be used for different purposes and if these different uses are in accordance with economic needs, which are themselves also different, there are good grounds for accepting that this product may, according to the circumstances, belong to separate markets which may present specific features which differ from the standpoint both of the structure and of the conditions of competition. However this finding does not justify the conclusion that such a product together with all the other products which can replace it as far as concerns the various uses to which it may be put and with which it may compete, forms one single market. The concept of the relevant market in fact implies that there can be effective competition between the products which form part of it and this presupposes that there is a sufficient degree of interchangeability between all the products forming part of the same market in so far as a specific use of such products is concerned. There was no such interchangeability, at any rate during the period under consideration, between all the vitamins of each of the groups c and e and all the products which, according to the circumstances, may be substituted for one or other of these groups of vitamins for technological uses which are themselves extremely varied.' (para 28)

'On the other hand there may be some doubt whether, for the purpose of delimit the respective markets of the C and E groups of vitamins, it is necessary to include all the vitamins of each of these groups in a market corresponding to that group, or whether, on the contrary, each of these groups must be placed in a separate market, one comprising vitamins for bio-nutritive use and the other vitamins for technological purposes.' (para 29)

Comment

Following the consideration of demand substitutability, each group of vitamins was held to constitute a separate market. Note that vitamins C and E could be used for different purposes, for some of which they did act as substitutes. Nonetheless, this limited substitution seemed insufficient to establish interchangeability.

Europemballage Corp & Continental Can v Commission	**Market Definition**
Case 6/72	Substitution
Court of Justice, [1973] ECR 215, [1973] CMLR 199	

Facts

An action for annulment of the Commission's Decision which found Continental Can Company Inc to infringe Article 102 TFEU by acquiring, through the Europemballage Corporation, approximately 80 per cent of the shares of Thomassen and Drijver-Verbliva NV. On appeal the Court of Justice commented on the definition of the relevant market.

Held

For the appraisal of a dominant position the definition of the relevant market is of essential significance, 'for the possibilities of competition can only be judged in relation to those characteristics of the products in question by virtue of which those products are particularly apt to satisfy an inelastic need and are only to a limited extent interchangeable with other products.' (para 32)

The Commission's decision deals with three markets: the market for light containers for canned meat products, the market for light containers for canned seafood, and the market for metal closures for the food packing industry, other than crown corks. 'The Decision does not, however, give any details of how these three markets differ from each other, and must therefore be considered separately. Similarly, nothing is said about how these three markets differ from the general market for light metal containers, namely the market for metal containers for fruit and vegetables, condensed milk, olive oil, fruit juices and chemico-technical products. In order to be regarded as constituting a distinct market, the products in question must be individualized, not only by the mere fact that they are used for packing certain products, but by particular characteristics of production which make them specifically suitable for this purpose. Consequently, a dominant position on the market for light metal containers for meat and fish cannot be decisive, as long as it has not been proved that competitors from other sectors of the market for light metal containers are not in a position to enter this market, by a simple adaptation, with sufficient strength to create a serious counterweight.' (para 33)

'Besides, there are in the Decision itself indications which make one doubt whether the three markets are to be considered separately from other markets for light metal containers, indications which rather lead one to conclude that they are parts of a larger market.' (para 34)

'As regards in particular competition by other manufacturers of metal containers, the … argument put forward … that the plants of certain manufacturers in the countries bordering on Germany were located too far away from most German consumers to enable the latter to decide to use them as a permanent source of supply, has not been substantiated…. In addition, it is uncontested that transport costs are of no essential significance in the case of metal closures.' (para 35)

'All this leads to the conclusion that the Decision has not, as a matter of law, sufficiently shown the facts and the assessments on which it is based. It must therefore be annulled.' (para 37)

Comment

The Commission decision preceded the coming into force of the European Merger Regulation and was an attempt, by the Commission, to monitor such transactions while applying Article 102 TFEU. See discussion in Chapter 9 below.

As evident from the above, the Commission's market analysis was not embedded in facts and, among other things, failed to take into account possible entry by other competitors which could have provided substitution by simple adaptation to their products. (para 33)

Nederlandsche Banden Industrie Michelin v Commission	**Market Definition**
Case 322/81	Product and Geographic Markets
Court of Justice, [1983] ECR 3461, [1985] 1 CMLR 282	

Facts

Michelin NV, the Dutch subsidiary of the Michelin group, was responsible for the production and sale of Michelin tyres in the Netherlands. Michelin NV was found by the European Commission to abuse its dominant position on the market for new replacement tyres for lorries, buses and similar vehicles by operating anticompetitive target-based discount schemes (IV/29.491 *Michelin*). On appeal, Michelin NV challenged, among other things, the Commission's definition of the market.

Held

'The applicant claims that the definition of the relevant market on which the Commission based its decision is too wide, inasmuch as in the eyes of the consumer different types and sizes of tyres for heavy vehicles are not interchangeable, and at the same time too narrow inasmuch as car and van tyres are excluded from it although they occupy similar positions on the market. …' (para 35)

'The Commission defends the definition of the relevant product market used in its decision by pointing out that with a technically homogeneous product it is not possible to distinguish different markets depending on the dimensions, size or specific types of products: in that connection the elasticity of supply between different types and dimensions of tyre must be taken into account. On the other hand the criteria of interchangeability and elasticity of demand allow a distinction to be drawn between the market in tyres for heavy vehicles and the market in car tyres owing to the particular structure of demand, which, in the case of tyres for heavy vehicles, is characterized by the presence above all of experienced trade buyers.' (para 36)

'As the court has repeatedly emphasized … for the purposes of investigating the possible dominant position of an undertaking on a given market, the possibilities of competition must be judged in the context of the market comprising the totality of the products which, with respect to their characteristics, are particularly suitable for satisfying constant needs and are only to a limited extent interchangeable with other products. However, it must be noted that the determination of the relevant market is useful in assessing whether the undertaking concerned is in a position to prevent effective competition from being maintained and behaves to an appreciable extent independently of its competitors and customers and consumers. For this purpose, therefore, an examination limited to the objective characteristics only of the relevant products cannot be sufficient: the competitive conditions and the structure of supply and demand on the market must also be taken into consideration.' (para 37)

'Moreover, it was for that reason that the Commission and Michelin NV agreed that new, original-equipment tyres should not be taken into consideration in the assessment of market shares. Owing to the particular structure of demand for such tyres characterized by direct orders from car manufacturers, competition in this sphere is in fact governed by completely different factors and rules.' (para 38)

'As far as replacement tyres are concerned, the first point … is that at the user level there is no interchangeability between car and van tyres, on the one hand, and heavy-vehicle tyres on the other. Car and van tyres therefore have no influence at all on competition on the market in heavy-vehicle tyres.' (para 39)

'Furthermore, the structure of demand for each of those groups of products is different. Most buyers of heavy-vehicle tyres are trade users, particularly haulage undertakings, for whom, as the Commission explained, the purchase of replacement tyres represents an item of considerable expenditure and who constantly ask their tyre dealers for advice and for long-term specialized services adapted to their specific needs. On the other hand, for the average buyer of car or van tyres the purchase of tyres is an occasional event and even if the buyer operates a business he does not expect such specialized advice and service adapted to specific needs. Hence the sale of heavy-vehicle tyres requires a particularly specialized distribution network which is not the case with the distribution of car and van tyres.' (para 40)

'The final point which must be made is that there is no elasticity of supply between tyres for heavy vehicles and car tyres owing to significant differences in production techniques and in the plant and tools needed for their manufacture. The fact that time and considerable investment are required in order to modify production plant for the manufacture of light-vehicle tyres instead of heavy-vehicle tyres or vice versa means that there is no discernible relationship between the two categories of tyre enabling production to be adapted to demand on the market ...' (para 41)

'The Commission rightly examined the structure of the market and demand primarily at the level of dealers to whom Michelin NV applied the practice in question. Michelin NV has itself stated, although in another context, that it was compelled to change its discount system to take account of the tendency towards specialization amongst its dealers, some of whom ... no longer sold tyres for heavy vehicles and vans. This confirms the differences existing in the structure of demand between different groups of dealers.' (para 42)

The applicant also contends that the Commission arbitrarily excluded retreads from the relevant market while these offer consumers a genuine alternative as regards both quality and price. 'In this regard it must first be recalled that although the existence of a competitive relationship between two products does not presuppose complete interchangeability for a specific purpose, it is not a pre-condition for a finding that a dominant position exists in the case of a given product, that there should be a complete absence of competition from other partially interchangeable products as long as such competition does not affect the undertaking's ability to influence appreciably the conditions in which that competition may be exerted or at any rate to conduct itself to a large extent without having to take account of that competition and without suffering any adverse effects as a result of its attitude.' (paras 48, 46–52)

With respect to the geographic market definition, 'The Commission's allegation concerns Michelin NV's conduct towards tyre dealers and more particularly its discount policy. In this regard the commercial policy of the various subsidiaries of the groups competing at the European or even the world level is generally adapted to the specific conditions existing on each market. In practice dealers established in the Netherlands obtain their supplies only from suppliers operating in the Netherlands. The Commission was therefore right to take the view that the competition facing Michelin NV is mainly on the Netherlands market and that it is at that level that the objective conditions of competition are alike for traders.' (paras 26, 23–8)

Comment

The Court of Justice confirmed the Commission's definition of the product market which stemmed from examination of substitutability at the dealer level. It also accepted the exclusion of retreads from the relevant market as these were only partially interchangeable (para 48). It explained that although Michelin 'produced calculations to show that the price and quality of retreads are comparable to those of new tyres and that a number of users do in fact consider the two groups of products interchangeable for their purposes, it has nevertheless admitted that in terms of safety and reliability a retread's value may be less than that of a new tyre and, what is more, the Commission has shown that a number of users have certain reservations, which may or may not be justified, regarding the use of a retread, particularly on a vehicle's front axle.' (para 49, see further paras 50–2).

The Commission identified the Netherlands as the relevant geographical market. The Court of Justice accepted this analysis. It noted that the Commission decision addressed Michelin NV which is active in the Netherlands (rather than the Michelin group as a whole) and its abusive discount policy and conduct in that country. The court noted that 'in practice dealers established in the Netherlands obtain their supplies only from suppliers operating in the Netherlands' (para 26). Several commentators argued that this reasoning overly focuses on the alleged abusive behaviour to define the geographical market, instead of on the conditions of competition and the national dealers' possible reaction to increase in price.

Note the similar market analysis in *Michelin II* (Commission Decision 2002/405/EC ([2002] OJ L143/1)), as well as the General Court judgment on appeal (Case T-203/01 *Michelin v Commission* [2003] ECR II-4071).

British Airways v Commission	**Market Definition**
Case T-219/99	Product and Geographic Markets
General Court, [2003] ECR II-5917, [2004] 4 CMLR 19	

Facts

British Airways (BA) operated a range of target incentives which were offered to travel agents. These commission schemes had one notable feature in common: in each case meeting the targets for sales growth lead to an increase in the commission paid on all tickets sold by the travel agent, not just on the tickets sold after the target was reached. The Commission found that this practice amounted to an abuse of BA's dominant position (IV/D-2/34.780 *Virgin/British Airways*). For the purpose of establishing dominance, the Commission took the view that the relevant market was the UK market, comprised of the services which airlines purchase from travel agents for the purposes of marketing and distributing their airline tickets (recital 72). BA challenged that analysis by the Commission, arguing that even if it exists, the market for services supplied by travel agents to airlines cannot constitute the relevant product market in the circumstances of this case.

Held

'According to settled case-law (Case 322/81 *Michelin v Commission* [1983] ECR 3461, paragraph 37; Case T-65/96 *Kish Glass v Commission* [2000] ECR II-1885, paragraph 62, confirmed on appeal by order of the Court of Justice in Case C-241/00P *Kish Glass v Commission* [2001] ECR I-7759), for the purposes of investigating the possible dominant position of an undertaking on a given product market, the possibilities of competition must be judged in the context of the market comprising the totality of the products or services which, with respect to their characteristics, are particularly suitable for satisfying constant needs and are only to a limited extent interchangeable with other products or services. Moreover, since the determination of the relevant market is useful in assessing whether the undertaking concerned is in a position to prevent effective competition from being maintained and behave to an appreciable extent independently of its competitors and, in this case, its service providers, an examination to that end cannot be limited to the objective characteristics only of the relevant services, but the competitive conditions and the structure of supply and demand on the market must also be taken into consideration.' (para 91)

'It is clear from BA's pleadings that it itself acknowledges the existence of an independent market for air travel agency services, since it states in … its application that travel agents themselves operate in a competitive market, competing with each other to provide the best possible service to their customers.' (para 92)

'In that regard, although travel agents act on behalf of the airlines, which assume all the risks and advantages connected with the transport service itself and which conclude contracts for transport directly with travellers, they nevertheless constitute independent intermediaries carrying on an independent business of providing services.' (para 93)

'As the Commission states in recital 31 of the contested decision, that specific business of travel agents consists, on the one hand, in advising potential travellers, reserving and issuing airline tickets, (and) collecting the price of the transport and remitting it to the airlines, and, on the other hand, in providing those airlines with advertising and commercial promotion services.' (para 94)

'In that regard, BA itself states that travel agents are and will remain, in the short term at least, a vital distribution channel for airlines, allowing them efficiently to sell seats on the flights they offer, and that there is a mutual dependence between travel agents and airlines which are not in themselves in a position to market their air transport services effectively. As BA has also stated, travel agents offer a wider range of air routes, departure times and arrival times than any airline could. Travel agents filter information concerning various flights for the benefit of travellers faced with the proliferation of different air transport fare structures, which arise from the real-time pricing systems operated by airlines.' (paras 95, 96)

'The Court therefore considers that the services of air travel agencies represent an economic activity for which, at the time of the contested decision, airlines could not substitute another form of distribution of their tickets, and that they therefore constitute a market for services distinct from the air transport market.' (para 100)

Article 102 TFEU applies 'both to undertakings whose possible dominant position is established, as in this case, in relation to their suppliers and to those which are capable of being in the same position in relation to their customers.' (para 101)

'BA cannot therefore validly argue that, in order to define the product market in question, with a view to assessing the effects on competition of the financial advantages which it allows to travel agents established in the United Kingdom, it is necessary to determine whether a single supplier of air transportation services on a particular route can profitably increase its prices. Such a parameter, which might be relevant in relation to each airline, is not of such a kind as to enable measurement of BA's economic strength in its capacity not as provider of air transport services but as purchaser of travel agency services, on all routes to and from United Kingdom airports, either in relation to all other airlines regarded in the same capacity as purchasers of air travel agency services or in relation to travel agents established in the United Kingdom.' (paras 103, 104)

The Commission did not make any error of assessment in defining the relevant product market. (para 107)

'As for the geographic market to be taken into consideration, consistent case-law shows that it may be defined as the territory in which all traders operate in the same or sufficiently homogeneous conditions of competition in so far as concerns specifically the relevant products or services, without it being necessary for those conditions to be perfectly homogeneous (Case T-83/91 *Tetra Pak v Commission* [1994] ECR II-755, paragraph 91, confirmed on appeal by judgment in Case C-333/94P *Tetra Pak v Commission* (Tetra Pak II) [1996] ECR I-5951).' (para 108)

In the overwhelming majority of cases, travellers reserve airline tickets in their country of residence. Moreover, IATA's rules on the order of using the coupons in airline tickets prevent tickets sold outside the territory of the UK from being used for flights departing from UK airports. (paras 109, 110)

'Since the distribution of airline tickets takes place at national level, it follows that airlines normally purchase the services for distributing those tickets on a national basis, as is shown by the agreements signed to that end by BA with travel agents established in the United Kingdom.' (para 111)

'Contrary to what BA maintains, the fact that BA concludes global agreements with certain travel agents is not capable of establishing that the latter increasingly deal with airlines on the international level. As is shown in recital 20 of the contested decision, which BA has not challenged, those global agreements were signed with only three travel agents and only for the winter season 1992/1993. Moreover, those agreements were merely added to local agreements made in the countries concerned.' (para 115)

The Commission did not make any error of assessment in defining the relevant geographic market. (para 116)

Comment

Note how the product market definition stemmed from the market in which BA's alleged anticompetitive activity took place. Subsequently, in paragraphs 103 and 104 the General Court rejected BA's argument that the market should be defined based on whether a single supplier of air transportation services on a particular route can profitably increase its prices. The General Court noted that such an approach would not allow measurement of BA's economic strength in its capacity as purchaser of travel agency services.

BA lodged an appeal against the General Court judgment. Appeal dismissed (Case C-95/04P [2007] ECR I-2331).

France Télécom SA v Commission	**Market Definition**
Case T-340/03	The SSNIP Test
General Court, [2007] ECR II-107	

Facts

Wanadoo Interactive (WIN), a subsidiary of France Télécom, was fined by the Commission for abusing its dominant position in the market for ADSL-based internet access services for the general public by charging predatory prices for its Pack eXtense and Wanadoo ADSL services. (Case COMP/38.233 *Wanadoo Interactive*). WIN applied to the General Court for annulment of the Commission's decision and contested, among other things, the definition of the market. It argued that the Commission's distinction between low-speed and high-speed internet access for residential customers is based on a seriously flawed and contradictory analysis. In its view, there is only one market for internet access, which takes the form of a continuum from low-speed to high-speed.

Held

'According to settled case-law (Case 322/81 *Michelin v Commission* [1983] ECR 3461, paragraph 37; Case T-65/96 *Kish Glass v Commission* [2000] ECR II-1885, paragraph 62; and Case T-219/99 *British Airways v Commission* [2003] ECR II-5917, paragraph 91), for the purposes of investigating the possibly dominant position of an undertaking on a given product market, the possibilities of competition must be judged in the context of the market comprising the totality of the products or services which, with respect to their characteristics, are particularly suitable for satisfying constant needs and are only to a limited extent interchangeable with other products or services. Moreover, since the determination of the relevant market is useful in assessing whether the undertaking concerned is in a position to prevent effective competition from being maintained and to behave to an appreciable extent independently of its competitors and, in this case, of its service providers, an examination to that end cannot be limited solely to the objective characteristics of the relevant services, but the competitive conditions and the structure of supply and demand on the market must also be taken into consideration.' (para 78)

'If a product could be used for different purposes and if these different uses are in accordance with economic needs, which are themselves also different, there are good grounds for accepting that this product may, according to the circumstances, belong to separate markets which may present specific features which differ from the standpoint both of the structure and of the conditions of competition. However, this finding does not justify the conclusion that such a product, together with all the other products which can replace it as far as concerns the various uses to which it may be put and with which it may compete, forms one single market.' (para 79)

'The concept of the relevant market in fact implies that there can be effective competition between the products which form part of it and this presupposes that there is a sufficient degree of interchangeability between all the products forming part of the same market in so far as a specific use of such products is concerned (Case 85/76 *Hoffmann-La Roche v Commission* [1979] ECR 461, paragraph 28).' (para 80)

'It is also apparent from the Commission Notice on the definition of the relevant market for the purposes of Community competition law (OJ 1997 C 372, p 5, paragraph 7) that "[a] relevant product market comprises all those products and/or services which are regarded as interchangeable or substitutable by the consumer, by reason of the products' characteristics, their prices and their intended use".' (para 81)

There are several differences in comfort or quality between high-and low-speed access. Some applications available with high-speed access are not feasible with low-speed access, including, the downloading of very voluminous video files or interactive network games. As regards the differences in technical features and performances, an important technical feature of high-speed internet access is the specific nature of the modems used. There is also a significant price differential between the two technologies. In addition, in the French market, there was a considerable difference in performance between the two technologies during the period investigated.' (paras 82–5)

According to the Notice on the definition of the relevant market 'the assessment of demand substitution entails a determination of the range of products which are viewed as substitutes by the consumer. One way of making this determination can be viewed as a speculative experiment, postulating a hypothetical small but lasting change in relative prices and evaluating the likely reactions of customers to that increase. In paragraph 17 of the Notice, the Commission states '[t]he question to be answered is whether the parties' customers would switch to readily available substitutes … in response to a hypothetical small (in the range 5 to 10%) but permanent relative price increase in the products and areas being considered'. (para 87)

'In recital 193 of the decision, the Commission admits that low-speed and high-speed access indeed present some degree of substitutability. It adds in recital 194, however, that the operation of such substitutability is extremely asymmetrical, the migrations of customers from offers of high-speed to low-speed access being negligible compared with the migrations in the other direction. However, according to the Commission, if the products were perfectly substitutable from the point of view of demand, the rates of migration should be identical or at least comparable.' (para 88)

'It should be pointed out, … that, first of all, it is clear from the information gathered by WIN and reproduced in Table 7 of the decision that the migration rates of high-speed subscribers to integral low-speed offers were very low during the period covered, in spite of the difference in price between those services, which should have prompted numerous internet users to turn to low-speed access. This large discrepancy in the rates of migration between low-speed and high-speed access and between high-speed and low-speed access does not lend credence to the argument that those services are interchangeable in the eyes of consumers. In the application, WIN also failed to adduce any evidence to cast doubt on that analysis.' (para 89)

'Secondly, it transpires that, according to a survey carried out on behalf of the Commission and presented by WIN in an annex to its application, 80% of subscribers would maintain their subscription in response to a price increase in the range 5 to 10%. According to paragraph 17 of the Notice on the definition of the relevant market for the purposes of Community competition law (see paragraph 87 above), this high percentage of subscribers who would not abandon high-speed access in response to a price increase of 5 to 10% provides a strong indication of the absence of demand-side substitution.' (para 90)

Consequently, the Commission correctly defined the market in question. (para 91)

Comment

The General Court considered the product characteristics (paras 82–5) before applying the SSNIP test (paras 87–9). Note the asymmetric substitution between the two services—the migrations of customers from high-speed to low-speed service being negligible compared with the migrations in the other direction. (para 88)

In para 90 the General Court noted the high percentage of subscribers (80 per cent) who would not abandon high-speed access in response to a price increase and held that this provided a strong indication of the absence of demand-side substitution. In its statement the General Court focused on the core customer and not the marginal one. Arguably, from an economic perspective and in line with the SSNIP test, when defining the market the focus should not be on the core customer but on the marginal group. The question to be asked is whether the marginal group (in this case 20 per cent), which would switch products when faced with an increase in price, would make that increase in price unprofitable. See additional comments in *United Brands*, pages 34–5 above.

The locked-in group may be relevant when it comprises a significant proportion of existing customers. Note the US Court of Appeal ruling in *FTC v Whole Foods Market* (23 April 2008, No 07-5276). There the Appeal Court found the District Court had committed a legal error in assuming that market definition must depend on marginal consumer. Indeed, when a company loses market shares, the identity of its core customers changes (since those with elastic demand leave) and subsequently the proportion of locked-in customers increases. This in turn may allow the company to further increase its prices on account of the core (locked-in) customers.

Aberdeen Journals v Director General of Fair Trading	**Market Definition**
1005/1/1/01	Other Indicators
Competition Appeal Tribunal, [2002] CAT 4 [2002] Comp AR 167	The Undertaking's View

'[T]he relevant product market is to be defined by reference to the facts in any given case, taking into account the whole economic context, which may include notably (i) the objective characteristics of the products; (ii) the degree of substitutability or interchangeability between the products, having regard to their relative prices and intended use; (iii) the competitive conditions; (iv) the structure of the supply and demand; and (v) the attitudes of consumers and users.' (para 96)

'However, this checklist is neither fixed, nor exhaustive, nor is every element mentioned in the case law necessarily mandatory in every case. Each case will depend on its own facts, and it is necessary to examine the particular circumstances in order to answer what, at the end of the day, are relatively straightforward questions: do the products concerned sufficiently compete with each other to be sensibly regarded as being in the same market? The key idea is that of a competitive constraint: do the other products alleged to form part of the same market act as a competitive constraint on the conduct of the allegedly dominant firm?' (para 97)

'In general, evidence as to how the undertakings in question themselves see the market is likely to be particularly significant. As the Director points out at paragraph 2.6 of OFT 403: "The idea of a market is familiar. Annual reports, business plans and other documents often refer to the market in which the undertaking operates. This will normally include other undertakings which the undertaking views as its competitors."' (para 103)

'In the Tribunal's view, contemporary evidence as to how the allegedly dominant undertaking itself views its competitors, and vice versa, may, depending on the particular circumstances, be of decisive importance when it comes to defining the market in any given case.' (para 104)

Genzyme Limited v Office of Fair Trading	**Market Definition**
1016/1/1/03	Other Indicators
Competition Appeal Tribunal, [2004] CAT 4, [2004] Comp AR 358	The Undertaking's View

Genzyme supplies a drug called Cerezyme for the treatment of Gaucher disease. Gaucher disease is a rare enzyme deficiency disorder. The OFT found, in the decision, that Genzyme has a dominant position in the 'upstream' market for the supply of drugs for the treatment of Gaucher disease.

'In simple terms, an undertaking's market power will depend on whether the consumers or users of the product have any alternatives available to them. It is thus the market in which substitutes are, or are not, available that is the *relevant* market for the purpose of addressing the issue of dominance. In the present case sufferers from Gaucher disease have no other alternatives available to them. That remains true irrespective of whether there is in some looser, non technical, sense a wider "market" for [Lysosomal storage disorders] in general. It follows that in this case the *relevant* upstream market for the purposes of the Chapter II prohibition is the market for drugs for the treatment of Gaucher disease.' (para 216)

'Although, as the Tribunal said in *Aberdeen Journals (No 1)*, ... contemporary documents showing how an undertaking views its competitors may constitute important evidence on the question of market definition, each case depends on its own factual circumstances. In that case the internal documents evidencing predatory conduct by Aberdeen Journals were relevant on the facts. In this case, however, we do not think the rather general comments on the ... website undermine our conclusions that in this case the specific *relevant* market for the purpose of assessing dominance is that of drugs for the treatment of Gaucher disease.' (para 217)

Mitsui/CVRD/Caemi	**Market Definition**
Case COMP/M.2420	One-way Product Substitution
European Commission, [2004] OJ L92/50	

The Commission appraised under the European Merger Regulation a proposed acquisition of joint control of Caemi, a Brazilian iron ore mining company by CVRD and Mitsui, another Brazilian iron ore producer and a Japanese trading company, respectively. Following the Commission assessment the transaction was cleared subject to conditions.

As part of the assessment the Commission examined the market for the supply of iron ore. In doing so it considered the substitutability between DR lump and pellets, on the one hand, and BOF lump and pellets, on the other. It noted that 'this is a one-way substitution process: the latter are replaceable by the former but not vice versa, principally on account of the higher iron content and lower level of impurities of DR ore. However, in view of the higher price of DR iron ore, this substitutability of DR ore for BOF ore is of a theoretical nature' (para 134). Additionally, the Commission found there to be 'a one-way substitutability between DR lump and DR pellets, in that DR lump cannot replace DR pellets over a certain proportion of the burden (for technical reasons) but DR pellets can fully replace DR lump' (para 135). This provided indication for the existence of a market for 'DR pellets' and a separate market for 'DR lump and pellets'. (paras 136, 140)

Bertelsmann/Springer/JV	**Market Definition**
Case COMP/M.3178	One-way Geographic Substitution
European Commission, [2006] OJ L61/17	

Following an appraisal under the European Merger Regulation, the Commission cleared the creation of the 'Rotogravure printing joint venture' by German media companies Bertelsmann AG and Axel Springer AG.

In its decision the Commission identified a distinct product market for high-volume rotogravure printing of magazines. With respect to the geographical market definition, the Commission noted that 'the structure of supply and demand for rotogravure printing services in Germany differs considerably from the situation in most other European countries. Owing to the large rotogravure printing capacity available in Germany which accounts for almost 50% of the total capacity installed in the EU, there are considerable exports of printing services, in particular to France and the UK. By contrast, German customers purchase rotogravure printing services abroad only to a rather limited extent. However, the number and volume of print jobs handled by foreign rotogravure printers for German customers varies among the different product markets described above' (para 59). This finding contributed to the conclusion that German consumers faced a domestic market consisting of German suppliers, and to the Commission noting the possibility that the market for magazines in other Member States might be wider and include Germany: 'As to the other countries, such as France and UK, the market investigation has shown that imports of rotogravure magazine printing services from Germany are significantly higher than the other way around. The reason for this is the historically larger capacity located in Germany. This apparently led, to some extent, to differing preferences and a higher readiness of magazine publishers in the other countries to print abroad than is the case with German publishers. However, the exact definitions of the geographic market for these countries with the exception of Germany can be left open in this respect since even the narrowest possible delineation of the geographic markets as national markets does not raise any competition concerns in these countries'. (para 70)

Hugin v Commission	**Market Definition**
Case 22/78	Narrow Markets
Court of Justice, [1979] ECR 1869, [1979] 3 CMLR 345	Aftermarket—Spare Parts

Facts

Hugin was fined by the European Commission for refusing to supply spare parts for its cash registers to Liptons, an independent company which operated outside the Hugin distribution system. The Commission found Hugin's refusal to supply to constitute an abuse of a dominant position (IV/29.132 *Hugin/Liptons*). Hugin applied for the annulment of the decision and challenged, among other things, the Commission's definition of the market.

Held

'[I]t is necessary, first, to determine the relevant market. In this respect account must be taken of the fact that the conduct alleged against Hugin consists in the refusal to supply spare parts to Liptons and, generally, to any independent undertaking outside its distribution network. The question is, therefore, whether the supply of spare parts constitutes a specific market or whether it forms part of a wider market. To answer that question it is necessary to determine the category of clients who require such parts.' (para 5)

'In this respect it is established, on the one hand, that cash registers are of such a technical nature that the user cannot fit the spare parts into the machine but requires the services of a specialized technician and, on the other, that the value of the spare parts is of little significance in relation to the cost of maintenance and repairs. That being the case, users of cash registers do not operate on the market as purchasers of spare parts, however they have their machines maintained and repaired. Whether they avail themselves of Hugin's after-sales service or whether they rely on independent undertakings engaged in maintenance and repair work, their spare part requirements are not manifested directly and independently on the market. While there certainly exists amongst users a market for maintenance and repairs which is distinct from the market in new cash registers, it is essentially a market for the provision of services and not for the sale of a product such as spare parts, the refusal to supply in which forms the subject-matter of the Commission's Decision.' (para 6)

'On the other hand, there exists a separate market for Hugin spare parts at another level, namely that of independent undertakings which specialize in the maintenance and repair of cash registers, in the reconditioning of used machines and in the sale of used machines and the renting out of machines. The role of those undertakings on the market is that of businesses which require spare parts for their various activities. They need such parts in order to provide services for cash register users in the form of maintenance and repairs and for the reconditioning of used machines intended for re-sale or renting out. Finally, they require spare parts for the maintenance and repair of new or used machines belonging to them which are rented out to their clients. It is, moreover, established that there is a specific demand for Hugin spare parts, since those parts are not interchangeable with spare parts for cash registers of other makes.' (para 7)

'Consequently the market thus constituted by Hugin's spare parts required by independent undertakings must be regarded as the relevant market for the purposes of the application of [Article 102 TFEU] to the facts of the case. It is in fact the market on which the alleged abuse was committed.' (para 8)

Comment

The Court of Justice distinguished between the demand characteristics at consumer level and at maintenance level. In the latter, where Liptons operated, the lack of interchangeability between Hugin spare parts and spare parts produced by other makers led to a finding of a narrow market for 'Hugin spare parts'.

Where customers in the aftermarket, that is the market for replacement parts, accessories, or service for a product, are captive and unable to use other brands to service the product, that market may constitute a separate product market. Note the *Nintendo* decision (page 52 below) and the *CEAHR* judgment (page 50 below), which further highlight the considerations relevant to aftermarkets and 'locked in customers'.

Hilti AG v Commission	**Market Definition**
Case T-30/89	Narrow Markets
General Court, [1991] ECR II-1439, [1992] 4 CMLR 16	Aftermarket

Facts

The Commission fined Hilti AG for abusing its dominant position by tying the sale of nails to the sale of cartridge strips. The finding of dominance stemmed from the Commission's narrow market definition. In its decision the Commission identified three separate product markets which were (a) the market for nail guns, (b) the market for Hilti-compatible cartridge strips and (c) the market for Hilti-compatible nails. On appeal, Hilti contested, among other things, the Commission's definition of the product market and asserted that the three markets comprise one single product market.

Held

'The Court takes the view that nail guns, cartridge strips and nails constitute three specific markets. Since cartridge strips and nails are specifically manufactured, and purchased by users, for a single brand of gun, it must be concluded that there are separate markets for Hilti-compatible cartridge strips and nails, as the Commission found in its decision (paragraph 55).' (para 66)

'With particular regard to the nails whose use in Hilti tools is an essential element of the dispute, it is common ground that since the 1960s there have been independent producers, including the interveners, making nails intended for use in nail guns. Some of those producers are specialized and produce only nails, and indeed some make only nails specifically designed for Hilti tools. That fact in itself is sound evidence that there is a specific market for Hilti-compatible nails.' (para 67)

'Hilti's contention that guns, cartridge strips and nails should be regarded as forming an indivisible whole, 'a powder-actuated fastening system' is in practice tantamount to permitting producers of nail guns to exclude the use of consumables other than their own branded products in their tools. However, in the absence of general and binding standards or rules, any independent producer is quite free, as far as [Union] competition law is concerned, to manufacture consumables intended for use in equipment manufactured by others, unless in doing so it infringes a patent or some other industrial or intellectual property right. Even on the assumption that, as the applicant has argued, components of different makes cannot be interchanged without the system characteristics being influenced, the solution should lie in the adoption of appropriate laws and regulations, not in unilateral measures taken by nail gun producers which have the effect of preventing independent producers from pursuing the bulk of their business.' (para 68)

'The conclusion must be that the relevant product market in relation to which Hilti's market position must be appraised is the market for nails designed for Hilti nail guns.' (para 77)

As far as the definition of the geographic market is concerned, there appear to be large price differences for Hilti products between the Member States. In addition the transport costs for nails are low. Subsequently, parallel trading is highly likely between the national markets and the Commission was right in taking the view that the relevant geographic market in this case is the Union as a whole. (paras 79–81)

Comment

For another example of a finding of a distinct market for consumables, see Case C-333/94P *Tetra Pak International SA v Commission* [1996] ECR I-5951, [1997] 4 CMLR 662 (an appeal on the General Court judgment in Case T-83/91, [1994] ECR II-755, [1997] 4 CMLR 726). In paragraph 83 of its judgment the General Court noted that 'any independent producer is … [free] to manufacture consumables intended for use in equipment manufactured by others …' (the Court of Justice confirmed this finding in paragraph 36 of its judgment). Tetra Pak was not alone in being able to manufacture cartons for use in its machines. That finding of a separate market for consumables led to finding of abusive tying of sales of cartons and filling machines. See detailed discussion on page 298 below.

CEAHR v Commission	**Market Definition**
Case T-427/08	Aftermarkets
General Court, [2010] ECR II-5865, [2011] 4 CMLR 14	

Facts

The European Confederation for Watch Repairer Associations (CEAHR) lodged a complaint with the European Commission against several watch manufacturers, alleging the existence of anticompetitive agreements and the abuse of a dominant position resulting from their refusal to continue to supply spare parts to independent watch repairers. The Commission rejected the complaint due to insufficient Community interest. CEAHR applied for the annulment of the decision and challenged the Commission's finding of a single luxury watch market with no separate market for repair and maintenance services.

Held

Spare parts

When considering spare parts for prestige watches, the definition of the relevant market raises two distinct questions: (1) Do all spare parts for luxury/prestige watches form a single market, or do they constitute numerous brand-specific markets. To answer this question one needs to consider whether there is a sufficient degree of substitutability between the spare parts manufactured by the various producers. (2) Is the market for spare parts (or the numerous markets for spare parts) separated from the primary market for luxury/prestige watches. The markets would be regarded as a single market if consumers are able to switch to another primary product in order to avoid a price increase for the spare parts of a particular producer. (paras 82–4)

As for the first question, the Commission did not consider substitutability in detail and noted that CEAHR did not provide clear-cut evidence of the impossibility for the consumer to switch to spare parts manufactured by other producers in order to avoid a price increase by a particular producer. The Commission's approach stands in contrast to its initial position which stated explicitly that there is no substitutability between spare parts belonging to different brands because of the differences in size, design and other factors. It is also inconsistent with evidence presented to the Commission which supported the conclusion of separate market for specific spare parts belonging to each brand. (paras 85–8)

'The possibility for the consumer to switch to spare parts manufactured by another producer in order to avoid an increase in the price of spare parts was in no way established in the contested decision. Consequently, the Commission was not entitled to base its decision on that hypothesis when defining the relevant market in the present case.' (para 89)

As for the second question, 'it is necessary to examine the Commission's finding that consumers may avoid price increases for spare parts by switching to another primary product. First, according to the contested decision, such a possibility exists even if the consumer already owns a luxury/prestige watch, since that watch may have a high residual value on the second-hand market. … It should be noted that, due to the complexity involved in repairing and maintaining watches, the demand for spare parts does not, in principle, come from watch users, but from specialists who provide those services. Therefore, from the point of view of the consumer, a price increase for spare parts is normally included in the price of those services.' (paras 91–3)

'Next, in its analysis which led to its conclusion that it was possible for the consumer to switch to another primary product, the Commission takes no account of its finding … that the cost of after-sales services over the life time of a watch is minor in comparison with the initial cost of a luxury/prestige watch itself, and that the consumer will consider such costs as a relatively minor element in the price of the overall package … a moderate price increase for spare parts remains a negligible sum in comparison to the price of a new luxury/prestige watch. That factor is capable, in itself, of undermining the validity of the Commission's finding concerning the possibility for the consumer to switch to another primary product … The Commission's reference to the existence of a market for second-hand watches cannot compensate for that omission in its assessment.' (paras 94–7)

'Finally, the Commission considers, in point 26 of the contested decision, that the cost of switching to another primary product does not involve any investment such as training, changing routines, installations or software, which makes such a switch even easier. It should be noted, in that regard, that the Commission chose to consider the market for spare-parts from the point of view of the final consumer (the user of the watch). The use of such an item of consumer goods does not typically involve any investment in training, changing routines, installations or software. Thus, the Commission cannot validly claim that the fact that such investments are not necessary facilitates the switch to another primary product.' (paras 100–1)

To be able to treat the primary market and the after markets jointly, as a single unified market (system market), it must be shown that a sufficient number of consumers would switch to other primary products when faced with a moderate price increase for the products or services on the after markets, thus rendering such increase unprofitable. The mere fact that consumers may choose from several brands on the primary market is not sufficient to conclude the presence of such single unified market, unless it is established that that choice is made, among others, on the basis of the competitive conditions on the secondary market. In its decision, the Commission did not establish presence of a 'system market' and therefore should not have examined the two markets together as forming part of a single relevant market. (paras 103–9)

Repair and maintenance

The Commission concluded that the market for repair and maintenance should not be treated as a separate relevant market. It noted in its decision that most manufacturers allow maintenance and repair only within their selective distribution system and that these aftersales services are ancillary to the distribution of watches. (paras 110–11)

The Commission, however, failed to take account of the fact that some independent watchmakers are not active on the watch market, but solely on the market for watch repair and maintenance services. This serves as a strong indicator which suggests the existence of a separate market. The Commission did not consider the most relevant question in relation to the presence of after-market services, which is whether consumers may avoid a price increase for repair and maintenance services by switching to primary products from other manufacturers. Consequently, the Commission was not entitled to conclude that the market for watch repair and maintenance services did not constitute a separate relevant market. (paras 112–20)

Comment

The Court annulled the Commission's Decision.

The General Court discussed the conditions needed to find a unified 'system market' (ie a market comprising both the primary market and the aftermarkets), namely that following a moderate price increase for products in the aftermarket, enough consumers would switch to other primary products to render the price increase unprofitable. While the General Court accepted the Commission's principal approach to market definition and aftermarkets it criticised the lack of market analysis in the decision. The Commission's flawed assessment led to the finding of a single market for luxury watches and aftermarket services, and the subsequent conclusion that there is a low probability of an infringement of competition rules.

PO Video Games, PO Nintendo Distribution, Omega-Nintendo	**Market Definition**
COMP/35.587, 35.706, 36.321	Switching Costs
European Commission, [2003] OJ L255/33	Technology Markets

Facts

The European Commission found that Nintendo, a Japanese video games maker, and seven of its official distributors in Europe, infringed Article 101 TFEU by colluding to maintain artificially high price differences for play consoles and games in the EU. According to the arrangements, distributors prevented parallel trade from their territories, thus hindering exports to high-priced from low-priced territories.

Held

Game consoles are not substitutable with personal computers. They may be divided into two distinct markets: static game consoles and portable, hand-held game consoles. Each of these comprises products intended to fulfil different user needs, and displaying different technical capabilities and price range. (paras 19–34)

Game cartridges are purchased by the users separately and are used with the game consoles. Due to different technical specifications, a cartridge with a game designed for a specific console cannot be used with any other console and, once a particular game console is chosen, only game cartridges compatible with the chosen console can be used. (paras 35, 36)

'As a result, in the event of a small, permanent increase in the price of a particular game cartridge, a user of a given game console is unlikely to switch to a game cartridge compatible with a different console. This is due to the fact that the user has to bear the cost not only of the new cartridge, but also that of buying a new console able to interoperate with that cartridge. It is uncontested that the number of game cartridges that need to be purchased to make switching worthwhile is far in excess of the average number of game cartridges owned by the average game console owner …' (para 37)

'[C]urrent owners of a game console would face substantial switching costs if they switched to different game cartridges, and are generally "locked in" for a period of at least three to four years, usually until their current game console becomes obsolete. For them, competition took place at the time of deciding what console to buy. Their reaction to a small, permanent price increase in game cartridges compatible with their console would be limited because buying an incompatible game only makes sense if the console associated with that new game is bought at the same time.' (para 46)

'For consumers who do not yet own a console … prices for game cartridges may be one of the competitive variables used by console manufacturers to compete in that market. However, there are no indications in the file to support that prices of games are more or less important than other elements such as the price of the console itself, its technical capabilities … the availability and types of games …' (para 48)

Subsequently, 'contrary to Nintendo's argument about system's competition, game cartridges compatible with a particular game console belong to a different market than those compatible with another.' (para 51)

Comment

The analysis shares similarities with the approach taken in Case 22/78 *Hugin v Commission* (page 48 above) where the finding of a group of locked-in customers led to a narrow market definition.

The market definition in this case raises interesting questions with respect to 'whole-life costing'. Do consumers take into account the prices of the secondary product (video games) when making a decision to purchase the main platform? If they do, then changes at the secondary market are likely to affect the competitiveness of the primary market (para 48). The consumers' ability to whole-life cost depends on the price difference between the secondary and primary products, the availability of information on the cost of spare parts and the frequency with which they are required.

Commercial Solvents v Commission	**Market Definition**
Case 6/73	Market for Raw Materials
Court of Justice, [1974] ECR 223, [1974] 1 CMLR 309	

Facts

Commercial Solvents Corporation (CSC) was the main supplier of the chemical amino-butanol, which can be used as raw material for the production of other chemicals. One of CSC's customers, Zoja, purchased large quantities of this raw material and used it for the manufacturing of another chemical, ethambutol. CSC informed Zoja that it would stop supplying it with the raw material necessary for the production of ethambutol. This decision coincided with CSC's decision to engage itself in the production of ethambutol. The Commission found this refusal to supply to constitute an infringement of Article 102 TFEU. CSC applied for the annulment of the Commission's decision.

Held

CSC disputes the Commission's finding according to which it has a dominant position in the common market for the raw material necessary for the manufacture of ethambutol. For this purpose it argues, among other things, that ethambutol can be produced from other raw materials and not only from the chemicals produced by CSC. However, according to an expert opinion presented by the Commission, these processes would be possible only at considerable expense and at some risk. (paras 9–14)

'This dispute is of no great practical importance since it relates mainly to processes of an experimental nature, which have not been tested on an industrial scale and which have resulted in only a modest production. The question is not whether Zoja, by adapting its installations and its manufacturing processes, would have been able to continue its production of ethambutol based on other raw materials, but whether CSC had a dominant position in the market in raw material for the manufacture of ethambutol. It is only the presence on the market of a raw material which could be substituted without difficulty for nitropropane or aminobutanol for the manufacture of ethambutol which could invalidate the argument that CSC has a dominant position within the meaning of [Article 102 TFEU]. On the other hand reference to possible alternative processes of an experimental nature or which are practiced on a small scale is not sufficient to refute the grounds of the decision in dispute.' (para 15)

CSC further challenges the Commission's conclusion that the relevant market for determining the dominant position is the one of ethambutol. Such a market, it argues, does not exist since ethambutol is only a part of a larger market in anti-tuberculosis drugs, where it is in competition with other drugs which are to a large extent interchangeable. 'Contrary to the arguments of the applicants it is in fact possible to distinguish the market in raw material necessary for the manufacture of a product, from the market on which the product is sold. An abuse of a dominant position on the market in raw materials may thus have effects restricting competition in the market on which the derivatives of the raw material are sold and these effects must be taken into account in considering the effects of an infringement, even if the market for the derivative does not constitute a self-contained market.' (paras 22, 19–22)

Comment

The product market definition stemmed from the market in which CSC's alleged anticompetitive activity took place. The Court therefore focused on Zoja's inability to use other raw materials to produce the final derivative.

The fact that the derivative did not constitute a self-contained market did not affect the Court of Justice finding of two distinct markets, an upstream market for raw materials and a downstream for the derivatives of the raw material. This finding facilitated the conclusion regarding refusal to supply (see below Chapter 5). An interesting extension to this analysis of a downstream market may be found in Case C-418/01 *IMS Health*, where the Court of Justice identified a hypothetical downstream market (see below Chapter 5).

TomTom/Tele Atlas	**Market Definition**
COMP/M.4854	Data Markets
European Commission, [2008] OJ C237/8	One-sided Supply Substitution

Facts

TomTom, a leading manufacturer of portable navigation devices and a supplier of navigation software, sought to acquire Tele Atlas, one of two main suppliers, both in Europe and North America, of digital map databases for navigation and other end-uses. The vertical merger would have enabled TomTom to control a key input, namely Tele Atlas' navigable digital map data. Following its investigation, the Commission cleared the transaction. In its decision the Commission considered whether or not digital map databases for navigation purposes and non-navigation purposes constitute separate markets.

Held

'The degree of demand-side substitutability between digital map databases for navigation purposes and for non-navigation purposes must be regarded as limited, because the quality requirements are very different. In order to be used for navigation, a digital map database must be sufficiently detailed, accurate and updated and must contain the necessary attributes and add-on layers, whereas a more basic database will suffice to provide simpler services such as route planning and address location. A navigation device will not function (… properly) if used with a basic digital map database of inferior quality.' (para 22)

'The degree of supply-side substitutability must be regarded as one-sided, because a provider of the higher quality digital map databases for navigation purposes may also easily provide the simpler database used for non-navigation purposes. The core databases used for the two types of applications are very similar (in fact, the basic map is the same). However, there is no supply-side substitution in the other direction due to the substantial costs and time required to upgrade a basic database to navigable quality. Whereas it is possible to produce a basic digital map database for many territories relatively quickly and at limited cost by compiling data from various public sources, producing a navigable digital map database is costly and very resource-intensive.' (para 23)

'Compiling and processing the data necessary for a navigable digital map database is a very time-consuming process. Upgrading in this manner a basic digital map database covering the European Union, is likely to take several years' (para 26)

Comment

Given the lack of demand-side as well as supply-side substitutability the Commission concluded that digital map databases for navigation and non-navigation applications constitute separate product markets.

In its decision, the Commission considered the possibility of other companies entering the market. It noted that Google and Microsoft, which were customers of Tele Atlas and provided map services over the Internet, would find it difficult and costly to upgrade their map databases to navigable quality by using feedback from their user communities.

Recent advances in technology and analytics increased the significance of data and subsequently the scrutiny of mergers involving Big Data. When analysing the effects of data one commonly considers the four "V"s: the volume of data; the velocity at which data is collected, used and disseminated; the variety of information aggregated; and finally the value of the data.

The usability of data has significant implications on the way one may define the market. Here, the role of advanced analytics may play a significant role. Analytics and data have a mutual reinforcing relationship, as data would have less value if companies couldn't rapidly analyse and act upon it.

Clearstream v Commission	**Market Definition**
Case T-301/04	Judicial Review
General Court, [2009] ECR II-3155,[2009] 5 CMLR 24	Fresh Analysis

Facts

An application for annulment of Commission decision in Case COMP/38.096—*Clearstream*, in which the Commission found Clearstream Banking AG ('CBF') and its parent company, Clearstream International SA ('CI'), to have abused their dominant position by, among other things, refusing to provide cross-border clearing and settlement services to Euroclear Bank SA ('EB') for more than two years, and by applying discriminatory prices to EB. One of the claims made by CBF and CI was that the Commission erred in its market definition.

Held

'It should be noted, at the outset, that in so far as the definition of the product market involves complex economic assessments on the part of the Commission, it is subject to only limited review by the [Union] judicature. However, this does not prevent the [Union] judicature from examining the Commission's assessment of economic data. It is required to decide whether the Commission based its assessment on accurate, reliable and coherent evidence which contains all the relevant data that must be taken into consideration in appraising a complex situation and is capable of substantiating the conclusions drawn from it (see Case T-201/04 *Microsoft v Commission* [2007] ECR II-3601, paragraph 482, …).' (para 47)

'[F]or the purposes of investigating the possibly dominant position of an undertaking on a given product market, the possibilities of competition must be judged in the context of the market comprising the totality of the products or services which, with respect to their characteristics, are particularly suitable for satisfying constant needs and are only to a limited extent interchangeable with other products or services. Moreover, since the determination of the relevant market is useful in assessing whether the undertaking concerned is in a position to prevent effective competition from being maintained and to behave to an appreciable extent independently of its competitors and its customers, an examination to that end cannot be limited solely to the objective characteristics of the relevant services, but the competitive conditions and the structure of supply and demand on the market must also be taken into consideration.' (para 48)

'The concept of the relevant market implies that there can be effective competition between the products or services which form part of it and this presupposes that there is a sufficient degree of interchangeability between all the products or services forming part of the same market in so far as a specific use of such products or services is concerned (Case 85/76 *Hoffmann-La Roche v Commission* [1979] ECR 461, paragraph 28).' (para 49)

'The applicants' claim that viewing matters from the point of view of the intermediary depositories conflicts with some earlier Commission decisions is irrelevant. The present case can be distinguished from the facts of the cases relied upon by the applicants. In any case, it must be noted that the Commission is required to carry out an individual appraisal of the circumstances of each case, without being bound by previous decisions concerning other undertakings, other product and service markets or other geographic markets at different times (Joined Cases T-346/02 and T-347/02 *Cableuropa and Others v Commission* [2003] ECR II-4251, paragraph 191).' (para 55)

In the present case the Commission did not make a manifest error of assessment when holding that the relevant market was the provision by CBF, to intermediaries, of primary clearing and settlement services in respect of securities issued under German law, over which CBF has a de facto monopoly and is therefore an indispensable commercial partner. (paras 50–73)

Comment

On the framework for judicial review and its limitations, see discussion in Chapter 10.

3

Article 101 TFEU

Article 101 TFEU

1. The following shall be prohibited as incompatible with the internal market: all agreements between undertakings, decisions by associations of undertakings and concerted practices which may affect trade between Member States and which have as their object or effect the prevention, restriction or distortion of competition within the internal market, and in particular those which:

   (a) directly or indirectly fix purchase or selling prices or any other trading conditions;
   (b) limit or control production, markets, technical development, or investment;
   (c) share markets or sources of supply;
   (d) apply dissimilar conditions to equivalent transactions with other trading parties, thereby placing them at a competitive disadvantage;
   (e) make the conclusion of contracts subject to acceptance by the other parties of supplementary obligations which, by their nature or according to commercial usage, have no connection with the subject of such contracts.

2. Any agreements or decisions prohibited pursuant to this Article shall be automatically void.

3. The provisions of paragraph 1 may, however, be declared inapplicable in the case of:
   – any agreement or category of agreements between undertakings;
   – any decision or category of decisions by associations of undertakings;
   – any concerted practice or category of concerted practices,
   which contributes to improving the production or distribution of goods or to promoting technical or economic progress, while allowing consumers a fair share of the resulting benefit, and which does not:

   (a) impose on the undertakings concerned restrictions which are not indispensable to the attainment of these objectives;
   (b) afford such undertakings the possibility of eliminating competition in respect of a substantial part of the products in question.

The application of Article 101 TFEU depends on a series of distinct conditions being satisfied. For ease of analysis Article 101 TFEU may be divided into four main questions:

1. Is there an agreement between undertakings, decisions by associations of undertakings or concerted practices?
2. Is its object or effect the prevention, restriction or distortion of competition within the Internal Market?

3. Does it affect trade between Member States?
4. Could it benefit from an exemption under Article 101(3) TFEU?

Agreement between Undertakings

The concept of 'undertaking' is discussed in Chapter 1 above. The following section is concerned with the criteria for establishing the existence of an agreement between undertakings.

Generally, in order for there to be an agreement caught under Article 101 TFEU, it is sufficient that at least two undertakings have expressed their joint intention to conduct themselves in a specific way on the market. The concept of an agreement centres on the existence of a concurrence of wills between the parties, the form in which it is manifested being insignificant. The following cases provide a good illustration of the notion of agreement and the distinction between agreements and unilateral actions:

107/82	*AEG–Telefunken v Commission*	65
25 & 26/84	*Ford v Commission*	66
T-41/96	*Bayer v Commission*	67
T-208/01	*Volkswagen v Commission*	69
C-74/04P	*Volkswagen v Commission*	70

See also summary references to:

277/87	*Sandoz Prodotti Farmaceutici SpA v Commission*	65, 68
41/69	*ACF Chemiefarma NV v Commission*	66
C-279/87	*Tipp-Ex v Commission*	68
C-338/00P	*Volkswagen v Commission*	69

Concerted Practice

At times it is possible for some form of cooperation between undertakings to take place without giving rise to an agreement. To ensure the effectiveness of the competition provisions, Article 101 TFEU is also applicable to 'concerted practices'. The concept of 'concerted practice' refers to forms of coordination between companies, which, without reaching the level of an agreement, have nevertheless established practical cooperation between them. This cooperation substitutes the risks of competition to the detriment of consumers.

Concerted practice is commonly proven by showing parallel conduct between companies, which cannot be explained by any other reason but cooperation. It is therefore of major importance to distinguish between anticompetitive parallel conduct and similarity of conduct which results from the competitive process. Accordingly, concerted practice will not be established when market conditions provide an explanation to the parallel conduct or where companies adapt themselves intelligently and unilaterally to the existing and anticipated conduct of their competitors.

In its Guidelines on Horizontal Co-operation Agreements ([2011] OJ C11/01) the Commission notes that '[w]here a company makes a unilateral announcement that is also genuinely public, for example through a newspaper, this generally does not constitute a concerted practice within the meaning of Article 101(1) (52). However, depending on the facts underlying the case at hand, the possibility of finding a concerted practice cannot be excluded, for example in a situation where such an announcement was followed by public announcements by other competitors, not least because strategic responses of competitors to each other's public announcements (which, to take one instance, might involve readjustments of their own earlier announcements to announcements made by competitors) could prove to be a strategy for reaching a common understanding about the terms of coordination.' (para 63)

On the concept of concerted practice, see:

48/69	*ICI v Commission (Dyestuffs)*	71
40/73 etc	*Suiker Unie and others v Commission*	72
89/85 etc	*A Ahlström Osakeyhtiö and others v Commission (Wood Pulp II)*	74
C-199/92P	*Hüls AG v Commission*	75
C-204/00P etc	*Aalborg Portland A/S and others v Commission*	77
T-442/08	*CISAC v Commission*	78

See also summary reference to:

IV/37.614/F3	*PO/Interbrew and Alken-Maes*	76
T-25/95 etc	*Cimenteries CBR SA v Commission*	76
T-186/06	*Solvay SA v Commission*	73
T-305/94 etc	*PVC II*	78
92-466	*Brooke Group Ltd v Brown & Williamson Tobacco Corp*	80
82-914	*Monsanto Co v Spray-Rite Service Corp*	80
No 14-2301	*Aircraft Check Services Co v Verizon Wireless*	80

Joint Classification and Single Overall Agreement

When dealing with complex cartel arrangements that involve different levels of cooperation, one can use a joint classification to establish coordination without distinguishing between agreements or concerted practices. In addition, in such circumstances the Commission is not required to establish the exact level of participation of each cartel member and may rely on the concept of a 'single overall agreement'.

C-204/00P etc	*Aalborg Portland A/S and others v Commission*	77
T-305/94 etc	*Limburgse Vinyl Maatschappij NV and others v Commission*	81, 82
T-101/05 etc	*BASF AG and UCB SA v Commission*	83
C-441/11P	*Commission v Verhuizingen Coppens NV*	85

See also summary reference to:

C-49/92P	*Commission v Anic Partecipazioni SpA*	81
IV/37.614/F3	*PO/Interbrew and Alken-Maes*	81
C-238/99	*Limburgse Vinyl Maatschappij NV v Commission*	81, 82
T-210/08	*Verhuizingen Coppens NV v Commission*	85

An undertaking may be liable for taking part in a cartel even when it is not active on the market on which the restriction of competition materialised, but nonetheless, in its action it contributed to the implementation of the cartel.

T-99/04	*AC-Treuhand AG v Commission*	86

Decision by an Association

Article 101 TFEU also applies to decisions by associations of undertakings, thus preventing the use of associations as a vehicle to coordinate and promote anticompetitive activities.

T-325/01	*Daimler Chrysler AG v Commission*	88
96/82	*IAZ International Belgium NV v Commission*	89
C-382/12P	*MasterCard Inc v Commission*	90

See also summary reference to:

209/78 etc	*Van Landewyck and others v Commission*	88
8/72	*Cementhandelaren v Commission*	89
45/85	*Verband der Sachversicherer v Commission*	89

Authorised representatives

An agreement or concerted practice, in violation of Article 101 TFEU, may be established when concluded by a person who is authorised to act on behalf of the undertaking, even if that person or representative is not authorised to engage in the illicit conduct. Action or knowledge by the principals of the undertaking is not required.

100/80 to 103/80	*Musique Diffusion française v Commission*	91
C-68/12	*Protimonopolný úrad Slovenskej republiky v Slovenská sporiteľňa*	91

Object or Effect

Agreements, concerted practices or decisions of associations of undertakings are caught under Article 101 TFEU when they have the object or effect of preventing, restricting or distorting competition within the Internal Market. Anti-competitive object and anti-competitive effects constitute alternative conditions and are distinguishable by the fact that certain forms of collusion between undertakings can be regarded, by their very nature, as being injurious to the proper functioning of normal competition.

The dividing line between object and effect is not always clear. Recent case law seems to reflect a lowering of the threshold for the finding an anticompetitive object (see for example *T-Mobile* and *Allianz Hungária*). The following cases illustrate the distinction between object and effect and the depth of analysis called for when assessing anticompetitive effect:

56/65	*Société Technique Minière v Maschinenbau Ulm GmbH*	92
56/64 etc	*Consten & Grundig v Commission*	93
23/67	*SA Brasserie de Haecht v Consorts Wilkin-Janssen*	96
T-374/94 etc	*European Night Services v Commission*	97
C-234/89	*Stergios Delimitis v Henninger Bräu AG*	98
C-209/07	*Competition Authority v Beef Industry Development Society*	100
C-8/08	*T-Mobile Netherlands and Others*	101
C-501/06P etc	*GlaxoSmithKline Services Unlimited v Commission*	103
T-328/03	*O2 (Germany) GmbH & Co OHG v Commission*	105
C-32/11	*Allianz Hungária Biztosító Zrt*	107
C-68/12	*Protimonopolný úrad Slovenskej republiky v Slovenská sporiteľňa a.s*	109
C-63/13P	*Groupement des Cartes Bancaires (CB) v Commission*	110

See also summary reference to:

On the distinction between restrictions by object and restrictions by effect and their assessment, see also paragraphs 17–27, Commission Guidelines on the Application of [Article 101(3) TFEU], [2004] OJ C101/94.

Scope of Analysis under Article 101(1) TFEU and the 'Rule of Reason'

Whilst the evaluation of the effect an agreement may generate under Article 101(1) TFEU takes account of its economic context, it does not encompass a balancing exercise of the competitive benefits and harm. Such balancing exercise is confined to the analysis under Article 101(3) TFEU.

Subsequently, Article 101(1) TFEU does not encompass a 'rule of reason' consideration and is limited in its scope in so much that it does not overlap with the Article 101(3) TFEU analysis.

See also summary references to:

Ancillary Restraints

The concept of ancillary restraints covers restrictions of competition which are directly related to and necessary for the implementation of a main non-restrictive transaction and proportionate to it. Accordingly, a restriction which is ancillary to an agreement that does not infringe Article 101(1) TFEU, or is exempted under Article 101(3) TFEU, will be allowed as long as it is objectively necessary for the operation of the agreement and is proportionate to it.

The application of the ancillary restraint concept differs from the balancing exercise under Article 101(3) TFEU and does not involve weighing of procompetitive and anticompetitive effects. It should also not be mistaken to constitute a 'Rule of Reason' analysis under Article 101(1) TFEU.

On ancillary restraints also note paragraphs 28–31, Commission Guidelines on the Application of [Article 101(3) TFEU], [2004] OJ C101/94.

Appreciable Effect (de minimis)

The de minimis doctrine excludes from the application of Article 101 TFEU agreements that do not have an appreciable effect on competition or on trade between Member States.

Early case law suggested that the de minimis doctrine may be applicable to agreements with either an anticompetitive object or effect. The more recent *Expedia* judgment (C-226/11) limits the availability of the de minimis safe harbour and presumes that agreements which restrict competition by object will have an appreciable effect on competition.

In June 2014, the Commission published a revised notice which clarified the scope of the doctrine. See the Commission Notice on Agreements of Minor Importance which do not Appreciably Restrict Competition under Article 101(1) TFEU (de minimis), C(2014) 4136 final. Also note the Commission's 'Guidance on restrictions of competition "by object" for the purpose of defining which agreements may benefit from the De Minimis Notice', SWD(2014) 198 final. The Commission's notice excludes from its scope agreements which have as their object the prevention, restriction or distortion of competition within the internal market.

The market share thresholds in the Notice are neither absolute nor binding. They reflect the Commission's view on which agreements are not likely to have an appreciable effect on competition or trade between Member States. It is therefore possible to find agreements which exceed the thresholds yet do not have an appreciable effect on competition, and vice versa.

5/69	*Franz Völk v SPRL Est J Vervaecke*	124
T-7 /93	*Langnese-Iglo GmbH v Commission*	124
T-374/94 etc	*European Night Services Ltd and others v Commission*	124
C-226/11	*Expedia Inc v Autorité de la concurrence and Others*	125

Appreciable Effect on Trade between Member States

Article 101(1) TFEU applies only to agreements between undertakings, decisions by associations of undertakings and concerted practices which may appreciably affect trade between Member States. In general, an agreement may be found to appreciably affect trade between Member States when it has an actual or potential, direct or indirect, positive or negative influence on patterns of trade between Member States. See the following cases which illustrate the European Courts' broad interpretation of 'effect on trade':

56/65	*Société Technique Minière v Maschinenbau Ulm GmbH*	126
56/64 etc	*Consten & Grundig v Commission*	126
8/72	*Vereeniging van Cementhandelaren v Commission*	126
23/67	*SA Brasserie de Haecht v Consorts Wilkin-Janssen*	127
107/82	*AEG–Telefunken v Commission*	127
T-199/08	*Ziegler SA v Commission*	128

With summary reference to:

174/84 etc	*Bulk Oil v Sun International Limited*	128

For additional discussion on 'effect on trade', see the Commission Guidelines on the Effect on Trade Concept Contained in [Articles 101 and 102 TFEU], [2004] OJ C101/81.

Article 101(2) TFEU

Article 101(2) TFEU provides that any agreement or decision prohibited under Article 101(1) TFEU and not exempted under Article 101(3) TFEU are automatically void. The automatic nullity under Article 101(2) TFEU only applies to those parts of the agreement affected by the prohibition, or to the agreement as a whole when those parts are not severable from the agreement itself.

| 56/64 etc | *Consten and Grundig v Commission* | 129 |

See also summary references to:

56/65	*Société Technique Minière v Maschinenbau Ulm GmbH*	129
T-9/99	*HFB Holding and others v Commission*	129
English CA	*David John Passmore v Morland and others*	129

Note also the discussion in Chapter 10 below on the Euro defence and the use of Article 101 TFEU before the National Court.

Article 101(3) TFEU

Article 101(3) TFEU provides a possible exemption route for agreements, concerted practices or decisions by associations of undertakings which were found to restrict competition by their effect or object. Accordingly it stipulates that the provisions of Article 101(1) TFEU may be declared inapplicable in the case of an agreement, decision or concerted practice 'which contributes to improving the production or distribution of goods or to promoting technical or economic progress, while allowing consumers a fair share of the resulting benefit, and which does not: (a) impose on the undertakings concerned restrictions which are not indispensable to the attainment of these objectives; (b) afford such undertakings the possibility of eliminating competition in respect of a substantial part of the products in question.'

Exemptions under Article 101(3) may take one of two forms:

(a)   Block Exemptions apply Article 101(3) to categories of agreements. Agreements covered by block exemptions are presumed to fulfil the conditions laid down in Article 101(3), thus relieving the parties to these agreements from the burden under Article 2 of Regulation 1/2003 of establishing that the agreement satisfies the conditions of Article 101(3) TFEU. A complete list of block exemption regulations may be found on the European Commission competition website (www.europa.eu.int/comm/dgs/competition). Agreements which are covered by one of the block exemption regulations are 'legally valid and enforceable even if they are restrictive of competition within the meaning of [Article 101(1)]. Such agreements can only be prohibited for the future and only upon formal withdrawal of the block exemption by the Commission or a national competition authority. Block exempted agreements cannot be held invalid by national courts in the context of private litigation' (para 2, Guidelines on the Application of [Article 101(3) TFEU], [2004] OJ C101/97).

(b)   In individual cases, the European Commission, National Competition Agencies or National Courts may disapply Article 101(1) TFEU, when an agreement, although found to infringe Article 101(1) TFEU, satisfies the cumulative conditions in Article 101(3) TFEU. In such cases, it is for the party seeking to defend the validity of the agreement to satisfy the cumulative conditions of Article 101(3) TFEU by showing that the agreement:

1.   contributes to improving the production or distribution of goods or to promoting technical or economic progress;
2.   allows consumers a fair share of the resulting benefit;
3.   does not impose restrictions which are not indispensable to the attainment of these objectives;
4.   does not eliminate competition in respect of a substantial part of the products in question.

Many of the cases concerning the realm of Article 101(3) TFEU date back to Regulation 17/62, which preceded Regulation 1/2003. Needless to say, the change in the enforcement regime and the abolition of the notification system did not affect the substantive analysis of Article 101(3) TFEU. As part of the modernisation package which accompanied the coming into force of Regulation 1/2003, the European Commission published a set of Guidelines on the Application of [Article 101(3) TFEU] ([2004] OJ C101/97). These Guidelines, although not binding on National Courts and National Competition Authorities, embody the European case-law and establish an analytical framework for the application of Article 101(3) TFEU.

The following cases illustrate the scope and nature of analysis under Article 101(3) TFEU.

On consideration of the first two (positive) conditions, namely the improvement of production or distribution of goods, the promotion of technical or economic progress and consumers' fair share of the resulting benefits, see:

56/64 etc	*Consten and Grundig v Commission*	130
26/76	*Metro SB-Großmarkte GmbH & Co KG v Commission*	131
C-360/92P	*Publishers Association v Commission*	132
IV.F.1/36.718	*CECED*	133
T-168/01	*GlaxoSmithKline Services Unlimited v Commission*	134
COMP/29.373	*Visa International—Multilateral Interchange Fee*	136
T-111/08	*MasterCard v European Commission*	138

See also summary references to:

T-528/93 etc	*Métropole télévision SA and others v Commission*	131
T-17/93	*Matra Hachette SA v Commission*	130, 131
T-131/99	*Michael Hamilton Shaw and others v Commission*	132
C-501/06P etc	*GlaxoSmithKline Services Unlimited v Commission*	135
T-86/95	*Compagnie Générale Maritime and others*	139

On consideration of the last two (negative) conditions, namely the requirement for indispensability and the need to avoid substantial elimination to competition, see:

56/64 etc	*Consten and Grundig v Commission*	130
IV.F.1/36.718	*CECED*	133
T-168/01	*GlaxoSmithKline Services Unlimited v Commission*	134
COMP/29.373	*Visa International—Multilateral Interchange Fee*	136
T-111/08	*MasterCard v European Commission*	138

See also summary references to:

T-17/93	*Matra Hachette SA v Commission*	137
IV/36.748	*Reims II*	137

On the scope of judicial review on decisions concerning exemption under Article 101(3) TFEU, see:

T-168/01	*GlaxoSmithKline Services Unlimited v Commission*	140

See also summary references to:

26/76	*Metro SB-Großmarkte GmbH & Co KG v Commission*	141
T-528/93 etc	*Métropole télévision SA and others v Commission*	141

Article 101 TFEU—goals and values

The European Commission has long stated that: 'competition policy cannot be pursued in isolation, as an end in itself, without reference to the legal, economic, political and social context.' (European Commission (EC), XXII Report on Competition Policy 1992, 13) An assessment of the anticompetitive object or effect of an agreement, concerted practice or a decision of an association of undertakings is influenced by the stated goals of EU competition law. The nature of these goals affects the scope of legality and the level of antitrust intervention.

A number of cases provide indication of the objectives of Article 101 TFEU and the interests taken into account in its application—from consumer welfare, innovation and market integration, to the competitive process, the structure of the market, and other social and environmental goals:

T-213/01, T-214/01	*Österreichische Postsparkasse v Commission*	142
C-8/08	*T-Mobile Netherlands BV*	142
C-52/09	*Konkurrensverket v TeliaSonera AB*	142
56/64, 58/64	*Consten and Grundig v Commission*	142
C-403/08, C-429/08	*Football Association Premier League Ltd*	143
IV.F.1/36.718	*CECED*	143
COMP/34493	*DSD*	144
IV/34.252	*Philips-Osram*	143
IV/33.814	*Ford/Volkswagen*	144
67/96	*Albany International BV v Stichting Bedrijspensioenfonds Textielindustrie*	144

AEG–Telefunken v Commission	**Article 101 TFEU**
Case 107/82	Agreement
Court of Justice, [1983] ECR 3151, [1984] 3 CMLR 325	Selective Distribution System

Facts

AEG–Telefunken (AEG), a German company which manufactures and markets consumer electronic products, notified the Commission of a selective distribution system (SDS) for its branded products. The Commission did not object to the SDS, yet later found that the actual application of the SDS by AEG and its subsidiaries did not correspond to the scheme notified to it. Subsequently, the Commission found that AEG had infringed Article101 TFEU and improperly applied its SDS by discriminating against certain distributors and by influencing dealers' resale prices. AEG appealed to the Court of Justice, arguing, among other things, that its actions were unilateral and did not constitute an agreement under Article 101 TFEU. The Court of Justice dismissed the appeal.

Held

A selective distribution system (SDS) may include acceptable limitations leading to a reduction of price competition in favour of competition relating to factors other than price. This would be the case, for example, when an SDS is used to attain legitimate goals such as the maintenance of a specialist trade capable of providing specific services as regards high-quality and high-technology products. The criteria for permissible SDS were laid down by the Court in *Metro v Commission* and were not met in this case. (paras 33–7, 40–3)

A refusal by AEG to approve distributors who satisfy the qualitative criteria of the SDS, with a view to maintaining a high level of prices, is unlawful. Such refusal does not constitute unilateral conduct on the part of AEG and therefore does not exempt it from the prohibition contained in Article 101(1) TFEU. 'On the contrary, it forms part of the contractual relations between the undertaking and resellers. Indeed, in the case of the admission of a distributor, approval is based on the acceptance, tacit or express, by the contracting parties of the policy pursued by AEG which requires inter alia the exclusion from the network of all distributors who are qualified for admission but are not prepared to adhere to that policy.' (para 38)

'The view must therefore be taken that even refusals of approval are acts performed in the context of the contractual relations with authorised distributors inasmuch as their purpose is to guarantee observance of the agreements in restraint of competition which form the basis of contracts between manufacturers and approved distributors. Refusals to approve distributors who satisfy the qualitative criteria mentioned above therefore supply proof of an unlawful application of the system if their number is sufficient to preclude the possibility that they are isolated cases not forming part of systematic conduct.' (para 39)

Comment

The refusal by AEG to approve distributors that did not accept its price policy arose out of the agreement between AEG and its existing distributors. Those existing distributors accepted, tacitly or expressly, the policy pursued by AEG. The refusal formed an agreement, the provisions of which are subjected to Article 101(1) TFEU.

See Case C-277/87 *Sandoz Prodotti Farmaceutici SpA v Commission* [1990] ECR I-45, in which Sandoz attempted to deter parallel imports to countries where prices of its pharmaceutical products were not controlled. It did so by adding the words 'export prohibited' to invoices sent to its distributors. The Court of Justice rejected Sandoz's claim that this was unilateral conduct and found this to form part of an agreement between Sandoz and its distributors. The distributors tacitly accepted Sandoz's wish by placing repeated orders without contesting the restrictive conditions. The tacit acceptance constituted an agreement subject to Article 101 TFEU, despite it not constituting a valid and binding contract under national law.

Ford Werke AG, Ford Europe Inc v Commission	**Article 101 TFEU**
Joined Cases 25/84 & 26/84	Agreement
Court of Justice, [1985] ECR 2725, [1985] 3 CMLR 528	Selective Distribution System

Facts

In the early 1980s prices for Ford's right-hand-drive cars sold in Germany were considerably lower than those sold on the British market. Subsequently, a growing number of British customers were buying those vehicles from German dealers. Ford Werke AG (Ford AG) was concerned about the effects of such sales on the position of Ford Britain and its distribution network. Consequently, in April 1982 it notified the German Ford dealers who were part of its selective distribution system that it would no longer accept their orders for right-hand-drive cars. All such cars would have to be purchased either from a Ford dealer established in the United Kingdom or from a subsidiary of Ford Britain. The Commission found that Ford AG's conduct constituted an anticompetitive agreement between Ford AG and its distributors. Ford appealed to the Court of Justice, arguing that, among other things, its decision to stop supplies was unilateral, did not form part of an agreement and was therefore not subjected to Article 101 TFEU. Ford's appeal was dismissed.

Held

'It must be observed in this regard that agreements which constitute a selective distribution system and which, as in this case, seek to maintain a specialized trade capable of providing specific services for high-technology products are normally concluded in order to govern the distribution of those products for a certain number of years. Because technological developments are not always foreseeable over such a period of time, those agreements necessarily have to leave certain matters to be decided later by the manufacturer.' Such later decisions were provided for in 'schedule 1' of the Ford AG selective distribution agreement, as far as the models to be delivered under the terms of that agreement were concerned. (para 20)

'Such a decision on the part of the manufacturer does not constitute, on the part of the undertaking, a unilateral act which, as the applicants claim, would be exempt from the prohibition contained in [Article 101(1) TFEU]. On the contrary, it forms part of the contractual relations between the undertaking and its dealers. Indeed, admission to the Ford AG dealer network implies acceptance by the contracting parties of the policy pursued by Ford with regard to the models to be delivered to the German market.' (para 21)

The applicants' argument based on the unilateral nature of the withdrawal of right-hand-drive cars from Ford AG's model range must be rejected.

Comment

Similarly to *AEG* (page 65 above) the Court found that the activity formed part of an ongoing relationship between the appellants and the distributors. The two cases are distinguished by the fact that AEG's policies benefited its own distributors, whereas Ford AG's change of policy did not benefit its German distributors.

Ford AG v Commission can be regarded as an extension of the AEG ruling, since despite the conduct not operating to the distributors' advantage it was found to form part of the agreement between the manufacturer and distributor.

Note generally that in order for there to be 'agreement' within the meaning of Article 101(1) TFEU it is sufficient that the undertakings in question have expressed their joint intention to conduct themselves on the market in a specific way. (Case 41/69 *ACF Chemiefarma NV v Commission* [1970] ECR 661 (paras 106–13)).

Bayer v Commission	**Article 101 TFEU**
Case T-41/96	Agreement
General Court, [2000] ECR II-3383, [2001] 4 CMLR 4	Export Ban/Parallel Imports

Facts

Bayer AG (Bayer), the parent company of one of the main European chemical and pharmaceutical groups, manufactures and markets a range of medicinal products under the trade name 'Adalat'. The price of Adalat is fixed by the national health authorities in most Member States. Between 1989 and 1993, the prices for Adalat in Spain and France were, on average, 40 per cent lower than prices in the United Kingdom. These price differences provided a business opportunity to wholesalers in Spain and France that started exporting Adalat to the United Kingdom.

The parallel imports lead to a sharp drop in sales of Adalat and loss of revenue by Bayer's British subsidiary. In an attempt to stop the parallel imports the Bayer group began to cease fulfilling all of the increasingly large orders placed by wholesalers in Spain and France with its Spanish and French subsidiaries.

Some of the wholesalers concerned complained to the Commission. Following its investigation, the Commission found that Bayer France and Bayer Spain identified wholesalers who engaged in export to the United Kingdom and applied successive reductions in the volumes delivered to them. The two subsidiaries imposed an export ban as part of their continuous commercial relations with their customers and were therefore found to enter an agreement contrary to Article 101(1) TFEU.

Bayer appealed to the General Court, claiming, among other things, that its conduct was unilateral.

Held

'[I]n order for there to be an agreement within the meaning of [Article 101(1) TFEU] it is sufficient that the undertakings in question should have expressed their joint intention to conduct themselves on the market in a specific way (Case 41/69 *ACF Chemiefarma v Commission* [1970] ECR 661, paragraph 112).' (para 67)

'As regards the form in which that common intention is expressed, it is sufficient for a stipulation to be the expression of the parties' intention to behave on the market in accordance with its terms (see, in particular, *ACF Chemiefarma*, paragraph 112, and *Van Landewyck*, paragraph 86), without its having to constitute a valid and binding contract under national law (*Sandoz*, paragraph 13).' (para 68)

The concept of an agreement within the meaning of Article 101(1) TFEU 'as interpreted by the case-law, centres around the existence of a concurrence of wills between at least two parties, the form in which it is manifested being unimportant so long as it constitutes the faithful expression of the parties' intention.' (para 69)

'[A] distinction should be drawn between cases in which an undertaking has adopted a genuinely unilateral measure, and thus without the express or implied participation of another undertaking, and those in which the unilateral character of the measure is merely apparent. Whilst the former do not fall within [Article 101(1) TFEU] the latter must be regarded as revealing an agreement between undertakings and may therefore fall within the scope of that article. That is the case, in particular, with practices and measures in restraint of competition which, though apparently adopted unilaterally by the manufacturer in the context of its contractual relations with its dealers, nevertheless receive at least the tacit acquiescence of those dealers.' (para 71)

The Commission cannot hold that apparently unilateral conduct on the part of a manufacturer, adopted in the context of the contractual relations which it maintains with his dealers, forms the basis of an agreement between the parties unless it establishes the existence of an acquiescence by the other partners, express or implied, in the attitude adopted by the manufacturer. (para 72)

In this case, in the absence of evidence of the conclusion of an agreement between the parties concerning the limitation of exports, the Commission has relied on the conduct of the applicant and the wholesalers to establish the concurrence of wills. It therefore found the unilateral decision as to the export ban, to form the subject-matter of an agreement between the applicant and the wholesalers as the latter adopted an implicit acquiescence in the export ban. (paras 73–6)

'In those circumstances, in order to determine whether the Commission has established to the requisite legal standard the existence of a concurrence of wills between the parties concerning the limitation of parallel exports, it is necessary to consider whether, as the applicant maintains, the Commission wrongly assessed the respective intentions of Bayer and the wholesalers.' (para 77)

The Commission has not proven to the requisite legal standard either that the subsidiaries imposed an export ban on their respective wholesalers, or that Bayer systematically monitored the export of Adalat, or that it applied a policy of threats and sanctions against exporting wholesalers, or that it made supplies of this product conditional on compliance with the alleged export ban. (paras 81–109)

The Commission did not prove the intention of the wholesalers to adhere to the export ban and cannot view the reduction in orders as a sign that the wholesalers had accepted Bayer's requirements. On the contrary, the wholesalers continued to try to obtain extra quantities of Adalat for export and demonstrated a firm intention to continue carrying on parallel exports of Adalat. The Commission was therefore wrong in holding that the actual conduct of the wholesalers constitutes sufficient proof in law of their acquiescence in the applicant's policy designed to prevent parallel imports. (paras 110–57)

Comment

The clear lack of concurrence of wills led the Court to view the activity as unilateral in nature and bring it outside the scope of Article 101 TFEU.

The case was appealed to the Court of Justice (Joined Cases C-2/01P, C-3/01P *Bundesverband der Arzneimittel-Importeure v Bayer and Commission*). The Court of Justice dismissed the appeal.

Both the General Court and the Court of Justice referred in their decisions to the case law relied on by the Commission in its decision and distinguished between those cases and the circumstances in the present case. Note in particular the Courts' references to the following two cases.

In Case C-277/87 *Sandoz Prodotti Farmaceutici SpA v Commission* [1990] ECR I-45, the manufacturer had sent invoices to its suppliers carrying the express words 'export prohibited', which had been tacitly accepted by the suppliers. The Court of Justice found the repeated orders of the products and the successive payments without protest by the customer of the words 'export prohibited' to constitute a tacit acquiescence. It therefore held that the whole of the continuous commercial relations, of which the 'export prohibited' clause formed an integral part, established between Sandoz PF and its customers, were governed by a pre-established general agreement applicable to the innumerable individual orders for Sandoz products. The facts in Sandoz are distinguishable from the present case as in Bayer there was no formal clause prohibiting export and no conduct of non-contention or acquiescence, either in form or in reality.

Bayer v Commission is also distinguishable from Case C-279/87 *Tipp-Ex v Commission* [1990] ECR I-261, which concerned an exclusive distribution agreement between Tipp-Ex and its French distributor, DMI. The latter had complied with the manufacturer's demand that the prices charged to a customer should be raised so far as was necessary to eliminate any economic interest on its part in parallel export. In *Tipp-Ex*, unlike the situation in the Bayer case, there was no doubt as to the fact that the policy of preventing parallel exports was established by the manufacturer with the cooperation of the distributors. That intention was manifested in the oral and written contracts between the two parties.

Volkswagen AG v Commission	**Article 101 TFEU**
Case T-208/01	Agreement
General Court, [2003] ECR II-5141, [2004] 4 CMLR 14	Selective Distribution System

Facts

Volkswagen AG (VW) produces motor vehicles and sells them throughout the EU via a system of selective and exclusive distribution agreements signed with authorised dealers. The dealership agreements stipulate, among other things, that that the dealers will comply with all instructions issued by VW for the purposes of the agreement regarding the distribution of new cars and that VW will issue non-binding price recommendations concerning retail prices and discounts.

Between 1996 and 1998 VW issued several calls to its distributors in Germany requiring them to comply with a strict price discipline for the sale of its Passat model. The Commission found this to infringe Article 101 TFEU. VW appealed to the General Court.

Held

'[T]he concept of "agreement" within the meaning of [Article 101(1) TFEU], as interpreted by the case-law, centres around the existence of a concurrence of wills between at least two parties, the form in which it is manifested being unimportant so long as it constitutes the faithful expression of the parties' intention (the *Bayer* judgment, paragraph 69).' (para 32)

A distinction should be drawn between cases in which an undertaking has adopted a genuinely unilateral measure, and those in which the unilateral character of the measure is merely apparent. (para 35)

The Commission's argument, according to which a dealer who has signed a dealership agreement which complies with competition law is deemed to have accepted in advance a later unlawful variation of that contract, even though, by virtue of its compliance with competition law, that contract could not enable the dealer to foresee such a variation, cannot succeed. (paras 43, 44)

'[A] contractual variation could be regarded as having been accepted in advance, upon and by the signature of a lawful dealership agreement, where it is a lawful contractual variation which is foreseen by the contract, or is a variation which, having regard to commercial usage or legislation, the dealer could not refuse. By contrast, it cannot be accepted that an unlawful contractual variation could be regarded as having been accepted in advance, upon and by the signature of a lawful distribution agreement. In that case, acquiescence in the unlawful contractual variation can occur only after the dealer has become aware of the variation desired by the manufacturer.' (para 45)

Comment

The Commission did not establish in its decision that the dealers followed and implemented VW's pricing policy. The facts in this case are distinguishable from Case C-338/00P *Volkswagen v Commission* [2003] ECR I-9189, [2004] 4 CMLR 7, where VW's anti-competitive initiatives were accepted by its dealers and put into effect. It was this implementation of initiatives in that case which led the General Court (Case T-62/98) and the Court of Justice (Case C-338/00P) to reject the plea for annulment of the Commission's decision based on Volkswagen's allegedly unilateral initiatives.

In its judgment, the General Court distinguished between the facts in this case and the *AEG* judgment (page 65 above). In *AEG* in order to establish agreement the Court of Justice relied on tacit or express acceptance by the distributors of the policy pursued by AEG. The Court of Justice did not suggest that the distributors' consent to AEG's anticompetitive policy was given in advance, upon signature of the contract, to an as of yet unknown policy of the manufacturer. (paras 47–50)

The General Court judgment was appealed to the Court of Justice. On appeal, the Court of Justice held that the General Court erred in law in finding, in paras 45 and 46, that clauses which comply with the competition rules may not be regarded as authorising calls which are contrary to those rules. See page 70 below.

Volkswagen AG v Commission	**Article 101 TFEU**
Case C-74/04P	Agreement
Court of Justice, [2006] ECR I-06585	Selective Distribution System

Facts

An appeal by the Commission on the General Court ruling in Case T-208/01 (page 69 above). The Commission asked the Court of Justice to set aside the judgment of the General Court, alleging that the General Court misconstrued Article 101(1) TFEU in finding that the call by the motor vehicle manufacturer to its authorised dealers did not constitute an agreement, despite it being part of continuous business relations governed by a general agreement drawn up in advance.

Held

'[T]he case-law to which the Commission refers does not imply that any call by a motor vehicle manufacturer to dealers constitutes an agreement within the meaning of [Article 101(1) TFEU] and does not relieve the Commission of its obligation to prove that there was a concurrence of wills on the part of the parties to the dealership agreement in each specific case.' (para 36)

The General Court rightly noted, in paras 30–4 of its judgment that in order to constitute an agreement 'it is sufficient that an act or conduct which is apparently unilateral be the expression of the concurrence of wills of at least two parties, the form in which that concurrence is expressed not being by itself decisive.' (para 37)

As stated by VW 'to find otherwise would have the effect of reversing the burden of proof of the existence of a breach of the competition rules and contravening the principle of presumption of innocence.' (para 38)

'The will of the parties may result from both the clauses of the dealership agreement in question and from the conduct of the parties, and in particular from the possibility of there being tacit acquiescence by the dealers in a call from the manufacturer (Case C-338/00P *Volkswagen v Commission*, paragraphs 61 to 68).' (para 39)

In the present case the Commission inferred the concurrence of wills solely on the basis of the clauses of the dealership agreement. The General Court then had to proceed, 'as it did, to consider whether those calls were explicitly contained in the dealership agreement or, at the very least, whether the clauses of that agreement authorised motor vehicle manufacturers to make such calls.' (para 40)

'In that context, this Court notes that its case-law does not indicate that the compliance or non-compliance of the contractual clauses in question with the competition rules is necessarily decisive in that examination. It follows that the [General Court] erred in law in finding, in paragraphs 45 and 46 of the judgment under appeal, that clauses which comply with the competition rules may not be regarded as authorising calls which are contrary to those rules. The possibility that a call which is contrary to the competition rules may be regarded as being authorised by seemingly neutral clauses of a dealership agreement cannot be automatically excluded. Consequently, the [General Court] could not, without making an error of law, refrain from examining the clauses of the dealership agreement individually, taking account, where applicable, of all other relevant factors, such as the aims pursued by that agreement in the light of the economic and legal context in which it was signed.' (paras 43–5)

For it to determine whether the calls were part of the overall commercial relationship the General Court should have considered 'whether they were provided for or authorised by the clauses of the dealership agreement, taking account of the aims pursued by that agreement per se, in the light of the economic and legal context in which the agreement was signed.' (para 48)

Comment

The General Court made an error of law in its reasoning in finding that clauses which comply with the competition rules may not be regarded as authorising calls which are contrary to those rules. The Court of Justice held, however, that this error did not affect the soundness of the General Court's judgment as the non-binding calls from VW to its dealers did not constitute an agreement within the meaning of Article 101(1) TFEU. Appeal dismissed.

Imperial Chemical Industries (ICI) v Commission (Dyestuffs)	**Article 101 TFEU**
Case 48/69	Concerted Practice
Court of Justice, [1972] ECR 619, [1972] CMLR 557	Price Announcements

Facts

Following uniform increases in the prices of dyestuffs in the Union, the Commission found several producers of dyestuffs had infringed Article 101 TFEU by taking part in a concerted practice which led to the price increase. On appeal to the Court of Justice, Imperial Chemical Industries (ICI) challenged the Commission's finding of concerted practice.

Held

'By its very nature ... a concerted practice does not have all the elements of a contract but may inter alia arise out of coordination which becomes apparent from the behaviour of the participants.' (para 65)

'Although parallel behaviour may not by itself be identified with a concerted practice, it may however amount to strong evidence of such a practice if it leads to conditions of competition which do not correspond to the normal conditions of the market, having regard to the nature of the products, the size and number of the undertakings, and the volume of the said market.' (para 66)

'This is especially the case if the parallel conduct is such as to enable those concerned to attempt to stabilize prices at a level different from that to which competition would have led, and to consolidate established positions to the detriment of effective freedom of movement of the products in the [internal] market and of the freedom of consumers to choose their suppliers.' (para 67)

The finding of concerted practice can only be correctly determined when considering the evidence of price increase while taking account of the specific market features in this case, including the market concentration, the production patterns and cost structures of the manufacturers, the demand for dyestuffs and the geographical markets for dyestuffs. In this context the simultaneous increases in price and price announcements reveal progressive cooperation between the undertakings concerned with the common intention to adjust the level of prices and avoid the risks of competition. (paras 68–119)

Advance price announcements by some of the undertakings concerned allowed the undertakings to observe each other's reactions on the different markets, and to adapt accordingly.

By means of these advance announcements the various undertakings eliminated all uncertainty between them as to their future conduct and, in doing so, also eliminated a large part of the risk usually inherent in any independent change of conduct on one or several markets.' They therefore temporarily eliminated with respect to prices some of the preconditions for competition on the market. (paras 101, 100–03)

'The function of price competition is to keep prices down to the lowest possible level and to encourage the movement of goods between the Member States, thereby permitting the most efficient possible distribution of activities in the matter of productivity and the capacity of undertakings to adapt themselves to change.' (para 115)

Comment

Note the weight attributed to price announcements in this case (paras 100–03). Contrast this approach with the Court of Justice judgment in *Ahlström Osakeyhtiö and others v Commission* (Wood Pulp Cartel). There, while considering the pulp market conditions, the Court of Justice held that a system of quarterly price announcements did not eliminate uncertainty as to the future conduct of the others and therefore was not to be regarded as constituting in itself an infringement of Article 101 TFEU. (See page 74 below.)

Suiker Unie and others v Commission	**Article 101 TFEU**
Joined Cases 40, 48, 50, 54–56, 111, 113,114/73	Concerted Practice
Court of Justice, [1975] ECR 1663, [1976] 1 CMLR 295	

Facts

A Commission investigation into the sugar market led to a decision (IV/26.918—*European sugar industry*) finding a number of undertakings to have infringed Article 101 TFEU. A central part of the decision referred to the existence of concerted practices in the market for sugar which led to price alignment, control of deliveries of sugar and other limitations on sales. On appeal, nine undertakings argued, among other things, that the common organisation of the sugar market, the involvement of Member States in setting the prices for sugar, and fixing basic and maximum quotas for sugar eliminated any effective competition.

On appeal, the Court considered separately each of the nine applications for the annulment. The following analysis focuses on the Italian and Netherlands markets as the court's analysis of these two is most illustrative.

Held

'The concept of a "concerted practice" refers to a form of coordination between undertakings, which, without having been taken to the stage where an agreement properly so-called has been concluded, knowingly substitutes for the risks of competition, practical cooperation between them which leads to conditions of competition which do not correspond to the normal conditions of the market, having regard to the nature of the products, the importance and number of the undertakings as well as the size and nature of the said market.' (para 26)

'Such practical cooperation amounts to a concerted practice, particularly if it enables the persons concerned to consolidate established positions to the detriment of effective freedom of movement of the products in the [internal] market and of the freedom of consumers to choose their suppliers.' (para 27)

'In a case of this kind the question whether there has been a concerted practice can only be properly evaluated if the facts relied on by the Commission are considered not separately but as a whole, after taking into account the characteristics of the market in question.' (para 28)

The Italian market

With respect to the Commission's finding of a concerted practice having as its object and effect the control of deliveries of sugar on the Italian market, it is necessary to consider whether Union rules together with the measures taken by national authorities left opportunity for competition on the market. From examination of the market it emerges that Italian regulations and the way in which they have been implemented had a determinative effect on some of the most important aspects of the course of conduct of the undertakings concerned, so that it appears that, had it not been for these Regulations and their implementation, the cooperation, which is the subject-matter of these proceedings, either would not have taken place or would have assumed a form different from that found to have existed by the Commission. The Commission has not made sufficient allowance for the effect of those regulations and has consequently overlooked a crucial factor in the evaluation of the infringements which it alleges. (paras 29–73)

The Netherlands market

'The criteria of coordination and cooperation laid down by the case-law of the court, which in no way requires the working out of an actual plan, must be understood in the light of the concept inherent in the provisions of the Treaty relating to competition that each economic operator must determine independently the policy which he intends to adopt on the [internal] market including the choice of the persons and undertakings to which he makes offers or sells.' (para 173)

'Although it is correct to say that this requirement of independence does not deprive economic operators of the right to adapt themselves intelligently to the existing and anticipated conduct of their competitors, it does however strictly preclude any direct or indirect contact between such operators, the object or effect whereof is either to influence the conduct on the market of an actual or potential competitor or to disclose to such a competitor the course of conduct which they themselves have decided to adopt or contemplate adopting on the market.' (para 174)

'The documents quoted show that the applicants contacted each other and that they in fact pursued the aim of removing in advance any uncertainty as to the future conduct of their competitors.' (para 175)

The evidence in this case supports the Commission finding of coordination and cooperation in the Netherlands to the detriment of the effective freedom of movement of the products in the internal market and of the freedom enjoyed by consumers to choose their suppliers. The practices to which the Commission refers to in its decision were not the natural consequence of market conditions. These practices intended to ward off the risk of competition to which the undertakings could by no means be certain that they would not be exposed, if there was no concerted action. The concerted action in question and the practices whereby it was implemented were likely to remove any doubts the Netherlands producers had as to their chances of maintaining the position which they had established. (paras 74–180)

Comment

The concept of 'concerted practice' subjects to the competition rules forms of communication between undertakings which do not amount to an agreement. The Commission is not required to distinguish between concerted practice and agreement and may rely on 'joint classification' to catch any form of communication between undertakings, the result of which is the restriction of competition. On joint classification see page 81 below.

The concept of a concerted practice, 'as it results from the actual terms of [Article 101(1) TFEU], implies, besides undertakings' concerting with each other, subsequent conduct on the market, and a relationship of cause and effect between the two.' Case C-199/92P *Hüls AG v Commission* (para 161), page 75 below.

A possible lack of mutual trust between competitors does not rule out the possibility of the existence of a concerted practice. In Case T-186/06 *Solvay SA v Commission*, the General Court held that Solvay had taken part in a concerted practice with an anticompetitive object. The Court added that 'that finding is not called into question by the applicant's argument that, given the lack of mutual trust between the competitors, it was inconceivable that they could have engaged in concerted practices.' (para 152)

Parallel conduct cannot be regarded as furnishing proof of concerted practice unless it constitutes the only plausible explanation for such conduct. The undertakings may therefore be able to disprove the existence of concerted practice if they can provide an alternative explanation for their parallel behaviour in the market. Such an explanation might, for example, include evidence on changes in the market which affected all undertakings and led to alignment of price, or evidence concerning the market structure and the undertakings' rational and independent operation in the market.

Some oligopolistic markets may, under certain conditions, enable undertakings to sustain joint policies without entering into agreement or concerted practice. In such markets the rational and independent behaviour of the undertakings may lead to parallel behaviour without entering into cooperation. This phenomenon is often referred to by economists as 'tacit collusion' or 'conscious parallelism' and is discussed in Chapter 6 below. Note that tacit collusion falls outside the realm of Article 101 EU which is only applicable to agreements, concerted practices or decisions of associations of undertakings.

A Ahlström Osakeyhtiö and others v Commission (Wood Pulp II) Joined Cases 89, 104, 114, 116, 117, 125, 129/85 Court of Justice, [1993] ECR I-1307, [1993] 4 CMLR 407	**Article 101 TFEU** Concerted Practice Price Announcements

Facts

The Commission found forty wood pulp producers and three of their trade associations to have infringed Article 101 TFEU by forming a price-fixing cartel. The market for pulp was characterised by long-term supply contracts and by 'quarterly price announcements' by which producers communicated to their customers the prices of pulp. The Commission found the practice of price announcement to facilitate collusion between the undertakings on the transaction prices for pulp (IV/29.725—*Woodpulp*). On appeal to the Court of Justice, the undertakings contested, among other things, the Commission's finding of concerted practice.

Held

A concerted practice refers to a form of coordination between undertakings which, without having been taken to the stage where an agreement properly so-called has been concluded, knowingly substitutes for the risks of competition. In this case, the communications arising from the price announcements did not lessen each undertaking's uncertainty as to the future attitude of its competitors. The system of quarterly price announcements did not eliminate uncertainty as to the future conduct of the others and therefore is not to be regarded as constituting in itself an infringement of Article 101 TFEU. (paras 59–65)

The system of price announcements could, however, constitute evidence of concertation at an earlier stage. In its decision, the Commission stated that, as proof of such concertation, it relied on the parallel conduct of the pulp producers, the simultaneous price announcements and similarity in price and on different kinds of direct or indirect exchange of information. (paras 66–9)

'Since the Commission has no documents which directly establish the existence of concertation between the producers concerned, it is necessary to ascertain whether the system of quarterly price announcements, the simultaneity or near-simultaneity of the price announcements and the parallelism of price announcements … constitute a firm, precise and consistent body of evidence of prior concertation.' (para 70)

'In determining the probative value of those different factors, it must be noted that parallel conduct cannot be regarded as furnishing proof of concertation unless concertation constitutes the only plausible explanation for such conduct … [Article 101 TFEU] does not deprive economic operators of the right to adapt themselves intelligently to the existing and anticipated conduct of their competitors'. (para 71)

'In this case, concertation is not the only plausible explanation for the parallel conduct. To begin with, the system of price announcements may be regarded as constituting a rational response to the fact that the pulp market constituted a long-term market and to the need felt by both buyers and sellers to limit commercial risks. Further, the similarity in the dates of price announcements may be regarded as a direct result of the high degree of market transparency, which does not have to be described as artificial. Finally, the parallelism of prices and the price trends may be satisfactorily explained by the oligopolistic tendencies of the market and by the specific circumstances prevailing in certain periods. Accordingly, the parallel conduct established by the Commission does not constitute evidence of concertation.' (paras 126, 72–126)

Comment

Contrast the treatment of price announcements in this case with the Court's approach in Case 48/69 *Imperial Chemical Industries (ICI) v Commission* (Dyestuffs), page 71 above.

Hüls AG v Commission	**Article 101 TFEU**
Case C-199/92P	Concerted Practice
Court of Justice, [1999] ECR I-4287, [1999] 5 CMLR 1016	Burden of Proof/Cartel Meetings

Facts

This case arose out of the Commission's Polypropylene decision (IV/31.149—*Polypropylene*) in which it found Hüls AG (Hüls) to have infringed Article 101(1) TFEU by participating with other undertakings in an agreement and concerted practice aimed at coordinating their commercial practices and fixing the prices of polypropylene. Hüls appealed unsuccessfully to the General Court (Case T-9/89 *Hüls v Commission*). On appeal to the Court of Justice, it argued, among other things, that the Commission and General Court decisions were based on insufficient evidence as to its regular participation in the producers' meetings and did not establish the evidential requirements in respect of concerted practices within the meaning of Article 101(1) TFEU.

Held

On the burden of proof and the presumption of innocence

The presumption of innocence resulting in particular from Article 6(2) of the ECHR is one of the fundamental rights which are protected in the Union legal order. In this case the Commission successfully established that Hüls had participated in meetings between undertakings of a manifestly anticompetitive nature. Subsequently the burden of proof reversed and it was for Hüls to put forward evidence to establish that its participation was without any anticompetitive intention by demonstrating that it had indicated to its competitors that it was participating in those meetings in a spirit that was different from theirs. (paras 141–55)

On concerted practice

'The Court of Justice has consistently held that a concerted practice refers to a form of coordination between undertakings which, without having been taken to a stage where an agreement properly so-called has been concluded, knowingly substitutes for the risks of competition practical cooperation between them (see Joined Cases 40/73 etc *Suiker Unie and others v Commission* [1975] ECR 1663, paragraph 26, and Joined Cases C-89/85 etc *Ahlström Osakeyhtiö and others v Commission* [1993] ECR I-1307, paragraph 63).' (para 158)

Each economic operator must determine independently the policy it adopts on the market. 'Although that requirement of independence does not deprive economic operators of the right to adapt themselves intelligently to the existing and anticipated conduct of their competitors, it does however strictly preclude any direct or indirect contact between such operators, the object or effect whereof is either to influence the conduct on the market of an actual or potential competitor or to disclose to such a competitor the course of conduct which they themselves have decided to adopt or contemplate adopting on the market, where the object or effect of such contact is to create conditions of competition which do not correspond to the normal conditions of the market in question, regard being had to the nature of the products or services offered, the size and number of the undertakings and the volume of the said market. (See, to that effect, *Suiker Unie and others v Commission*, paragraph 174).' (paras 159, 160)

'It follows, first, that the concept of a concerted practice, as it results from the actual terms of [Article 101(1) TFEU], implies, besides undertakings' concerting with each other, subsequent conduct on the market, and a relationship of cause and effect between the two.' (para 161)

'However, subject to proof to the contrary, which the economic operators concerned must adduce, the presumption must be that the undertakings taking part in the concerted action and remaining active on the market take account of the information exchanged with their competitors for the purposes of determining their conduct on that market. That is all the more true where the undertakings concert together on a regular basis over a long period, as was the case here, according to the findings of the [General Court].' (para 162)

Although the concept of a concerted practice presupposes conduct by the participating undertakings on the market, it does not necessarily mean that such conduct should produce the specific effect of restricting, preventing or distorting competition. A concerted practice is therefore caught by [Article 101(1) TFEU], even in the absence of anticompetitive effects on the market and is prohibited, regardless of its effect, when it has an anticompetitive object. (paras 163–6)

'Consequently, contrary to Hüls's argument, the [General Court] was not in breach of the rules applying to the burden of proof when it considered that, since the Commission had established to the requisite legal standard that Hüls had taken part in polypropylene producers' concerting together for the purpose of restricting competition, it did not have to adduce evidence that their concerting together had manifested itself in conduct on the market or that it had had effects restrictive of competition; on the contrary, it was for Hüls to prove that that did not have any influence whatsoever on its own conduct on the market.' (para 167)

Since none of the pleas in law put forward by Hüls have been upheld, the appeal must be dismissed in its entirety.

Comment

The courts laid down the elements constituting concerted practice. These include (1) undertakings concerting with each other, (2) subsequent conduct on the market, and (3) a relationship of cause and effect between the two. (para 161)

Note that the above elements do not include a requirement for effect on the market. The Court held in paragraph 163 of its decision that 'a concerted practice as defined above is caught by Article 101(1) TFEU, even in the absence of anti-competitive effects on the market.' Accordingly, 'as in the case of agreements between undertakings and decisions by associations of undertakings, concerted practices are prohibited, regardless of their effect, when they have an anti-competitive object. … Although the very concept of a concerted practice presupposes conduct by the participating undertakings on the market, it does not necessarily mean that that conduct should produce the specific effect of restricting, preventing or distorting competition.' (paras 164, 165)

See Commission decision in Case IV/37.614/F3 *PO/Interbrew and Alken-Maes* [2003] OJ L200/1, where the Commission noted that 'behaviour can be regarded as a "concerted practice" where the parties have not reached agreement in advance on a common plan defining their action on the market but have adopted or adhered to collusive devices which facilitate the coordination of their commercial behaviour'. (para 221) 'Although it is clear from the actual terms of [Article 101(1) TFEU] … that the concept of a concerted practice implies, besides undertakings consulting with each other, subsequent conduct on the market, and a relationship of cause and effect between the two, the presumption must be, subject to proof to the contrary which the economic operators concerned must adduce, that the undertakings taking part in the consultation and remaining active on the market take account of the information exchanged with their competitors for the purposes of determining their conduct on that market. That is all the more true where the undertakings consult together on a regular basis over a long period. A concerted practice is caught by [Article 101(1) TFEU] even in the absence of anti-competitive effects on the market'. (para 222)

With regard to the participation in meetings (paras 141–55), note Joined Cases T-25/95 etc *Cimenteries CBR SA v Commission*, where the General Court held that in the absence of positive evidence disassociating the undertakings from the anticompetitive objectives of the meetings, producers in attendance at the meetings were participants in concerted practice. Those who did not attend the meetings, but aligned their behaviour at a later stage to give effect to the objective of the meetings, were also liable. However, their liability ran only from the dates of the action of alignment and not from the date of the meeting. Also note Joined Cases C-204/00 *Aalborg Portland A/S and others v Commission*, page 77 below.

Aalborg Portland A/S and others v Commission	**Article 101 TFEU**
Joined Cases C-204, 205, 211, 213, 217, 219/00P	Concerted Practice
Court of Justice, [2004] ECR I-123, [2005] 4 CMLR 4	Cartel Meetings—Single Agreement

Facts

Following an investigation into the European cement market, the Commission uncovered a series of anticompetitive agreements and concerted practices which facilitated, among other things, exchange of information on prices, supply and demand, and the regulation of cement transfers. The Commission adopted a decision that found producers and trade associations in this sector to have participated in a cartel contrary to Article 101 TFEU (Cases IV/33.126 and 33.322 *Cement*). On appeal to the General Court, the Court confirmed most of the infringements found in the Commission decision. On appeal to the Court of Justice, the undertakings disputed, among other things, the General Court's findings concerning their participation in the cartel.

Held

'According to settled case-law, it is sufficient for the Commission to show that the undertaking concerned participated in meetings at which anti-competitive agreements were concluded, without manifestly opposing them, to prove to the requisite standard that the undertaking participated in the cartel. Where participation in such meetings has been established, it is for that undertaking to put forward evidence to establish that its participation in those meetings was without any anti-competitive intention by demonstrating that it had indicated to its competitors that it was participating in those meetings in a spirit that was different from theirs (see Case C-199/92P *Hüls v Commission* [1999] ECR I-4287, paragraph 155, and Case C-49/92P *Commission v Anic* [1999] ECR I-4125, paragraph 96).' (para 81)

'The reason underlying that principle of law is that, having participated in the meeting without publicly distancing itself from what was discussed, the undertaking has given the other participants to believe that it subscribed to what was decided there and would comply with it.' (para 82)

That principle of law also applies to participation in the implementation of a single agreement. 'In order to establish that an undertaking has participated in such an agreement, the Commission must show that the undertaking intended to contribute by its own conduct to the common objectives pursued by all the participants and that it was aware of the actual conduct planned or put into effect by other undertakings in pursuit of the same objectives or that it could reasonably have foreseen it and that it was prepared to take the risk' (*Commission v Anic*, paragraph 87). (para 83)

'In that regard, a party which tacitly approves of an unlawful initiative, without publicly distancing itself from its content or reporting it to the administrative authorities, effectively encourages the continuation of the infringement and compromises its discovery. That complicity constitutes a passive mode of participation in the infringement which is therefore capable of rendering the undertaking liable in the context of a single agreement.' (para 84)

The fact that an undertaking does not act on the outcome of a meeting with an anticompetitive purpose does not relieve it of responsibility for participation in a cartel, unless it has publicly distanced itself from what was agreed in the meeting. Similarly, it is immaterial for the establishment of infringement that an undertaking has not taken part in all aspects of an anticompetitive scheme or that it played only a minor role in it. Those factors are taken into consideration only when the gravity of the infringement is assessed and if and when it comes to determining the fine. (paras 85, 86)

Comment

On participation in cartel meetings see also Case C-199/92P page 75 above, Joined Cases T-25/95 etc page 76 above, and Joined Cases T-305/94 etc, pages 78, 79 below.

CISAC v Commission	**Article 101 TFEU**
Cases T-442/08	Concerted Practice
General Court, [2013] 5 CMLR 15	Conscious Parallelism

Facts

The International Confederation of Societies of Authors and Composers (CISAC) is a non-profit umbrella organisation representing collecting societies and managing authors' rights in over 100 countries. As part of its activities, CISAC has drawn up a non-binding model contract on which the collecting societies rely when they enter into reciprocal representation agreements (RRAs). The Commission raised concerns as to the territorial segmentation fostered by the RRAs and the agreements were subsequently amended to exclude territorial segmentation. Despite the removal of the territorial exclusivity clause, the collecting societies continued to operate with territorial segmentation. The Commission pointed out that as the collecting societies differ in terms of efficiency, administrative costs and their repertoires, they should have had an interest in granting licences covering wider territories or mandating more than one collecting society in some regions, in order to increase the distribution of their repertoire and thereby the remuneration of their authors. Accordingly, the retention of territorial segmentation did not correspond to normal market conditions, and therefore the parallel conduct of the collecting societies indicated the presence of a concerted practice contrary to Article 101 TFEU.

In an application for annulment of the Commission decision, the collecting societies and the CISAC contested the finding of concerted practice.

Held

Burden of proof

Article 2 of Regulation No 1/2003 and settled case-law establish that it is for the Commission to prove any infringements it finds. In that context, any doubt of the Court must benefit the undertaking to which the decision finding an infringement was addressed. It is necessary to take into account the presumption of innocence resulting in particular from Article 6(2) of the European Convention for the Protection of Human Rights and Fundamental Freedoms. The presumption of innocence is one of the fundamental rights which, according to the case-law of the Court of Justice, constitute general principles of the Union's legal order. That case-law, developed in cases where the Commission had imposed a fine, is also applicable where, as in the present case, the decision finding an infringement is ultimately not accompanied by the imposition of a fine. (paras 91–4)

'The Commission must show precise and consistent evidence in order to establish the existence of the infringement (*Dresdner Bank and Others v Commission*, paragraph 62) and to support the firm conviction that the alleged infringement constitutes a restriction of competition within the meaning of [Article 101 TFEU] (Joined Cases T 185/96, T 189/96 and T 190/96 *Riviera Auto Service and Others v Commission* [1999] ECR II 93, paragraph 47, and *Romana Tabacchi v Commission*, paragraph 129). However, it is not necessary for every item of evidence produced by the Commission to satisfy those criteria in relation to every aspect of the infringement. It is sufficient if the set of indicia relied on by the Commission, viewed as a whole, meets that requirement (see *Dresdner Bank and Others v Commission*, paragraph 63, and *Romana Tabacchi v Commission*, paragraph 130).' (paras 96, 97)

'In most cases, the existence of an anti-competitive practice or agreement must be inferred from a number of coincidences and indicia which, taken together, may, in the absence of another plausible explanation, constitute evidence of an infringement of the competition rules (see Case C 407/08P *Knauf Gips v Commission* [2010] ECR I 6375, paragraphs 48 and 49 and the case-law cited).' (para 98)

In PVC II (Joined Cases T-305/94 etc *Limburgse Vinyl Maatschappij and others v Commission* [1999] ECR II-931) the Court held that 'where the Commission's reasoning is based on the supposition that the facts established in its decision cannot be explained other than by concertation between the undertakings, it is sufficient for the applicants to prove circumstances which cast the facts established by the Commission in a different light and thus allow another explanation of the facts to be substituted for the one adopted by the Commission. However, the Court specified that that case-law was not applicable where the proof of concertation between the undertakings is based not on a mere finding of parallel market conduct but on documents which show that the practices were the result of concertation. In those circumstances, the burden is on the applicants not merely to submit another explanation for the facts found by the Commission but to challenge the existence of those facts established on the basis of the documents produced by the Commission (*PVC II*, paragraphs 725 to 728; see also, to that effect, Joined Cases 29/83 and 30/83 *Compagnie royale asturienne des mines and Rheinzink v Commission* [1984] ECR 1679, paragraph 16, and Joined Cases C 89/85, C 104/85, C 114/85, C 116/85, C 117/85 and C 125/85 to C 129/85 *Ahlström Osakeyhtiö and Others v Commission* [1993] ECR I 1307, paragraphs 71 and 126).' (para 99)

Documents establishing concerted practice

The evidential value of the elements put forward by the Commission in its decision, to prove the existence of the concerted practice, is insufficient in order to establish the existence of an infringement in relation to the national territorial limitations by evidence other than the mere finding of parallel conduct. (paras 102–31)

Parallel behaviour establishing concerted practice

As the Commission did not establish, to the requisite legal standard, the existence of a concerted practice between the collecting societies to fix the national territorial limitations, it is necessary to examine whether the Commission provided sufficient evidence to render implausible the explanations of the collecting societies' parallel conduct, put forward by the applicant, other than the existence of concertation. (paras 132, 133)

The evidence relied on by the Commission is not sufficient to render implausible the explanation provided by the applicant according to which the national territorial limitations are the result of individual, carefully considered and rational decisions on a practical and economic level, given the specific conditions of the market, and not the result of a concerted practice. (paras 134–81)

Comment

The *CISAC* judgment is one of several judgments dealing with the Commission's finding of a concerted practice between collecting societies. The Court annulled the Commission decision addressed to CISAC and the collecting societies concerned, in respect of the finding of a concerted practice.

When the parallel behaviour cannot be explained other than by a concerted practice between the undertakings, it is sufficient for the undertaking to prove circumstances which provide an alternative explanation and cast the facts established by the Commission in a different light. (*PVC II*, para 99 above)

Where proof of a concerted practice is based on documents which show that the practices were the result of collusion, the undertakings cannot merely submit another explanation for the parallel behaviour, but will have to challenge the existence of those facts. (*PVC II*, para 99 above)

In the present case the Commission has not proven the existence of a concerted practice by factors other than the parallel conduct. It was therefore sufficient for the undertakings to provide alternative explanations of that parallel behaviour.

When the economic actions and outcomes do not correspond to the normal conditions of the market, they may serve as strong evidence of the presence of collusion. One should explore the presence of 'plus factors'— evidence which is inconsistent with unilateral action. Such evidence, may include for example, increase in market price despite industry overcapacity, firms not fighting for market share, despite ability to do so, the sharing of sensitive information or unexplainable inter-firm transactions and transfers between undertakings.

Noteworthy is the fact that the Court set a high burden of proof in this case and held that 'any doubt ... must benefit the undertaking' regardless of whether the decision finding an infringement is accompanied by the imposition of a fine. (paras 91–4)

In *Brooke Group Ltd v Brown & Williamson Tobacco Corp* the Supreme Court of the United States held that 'Tacit collusion, sometimes called oligopolistic price coordination or conscious parallelism, describes the process, not in itself unlawful, by which firms in a concentrated market might in effect share monopoly power, setting their prices at a profit-maximizing, supracompetitive level by recognizing their shared economic interests and their interdependence with respect to price and output decisions. See Areeda & Turner ¶ 404; Scherer & Ross 199–208.' (509 US 209 (1993), page 227)

In *Monsanto Co v Spray-Rite Service Corp* the Supreme Court of the United States held that 'there is a basic distinction between concerted and independent action—a distinction not always clearly drawn by parties and courts. Section 1 of the Sherman Act requires that there be a "contract, combination … or conspiracy" between the manufacturer and other distributors in order to establish a violation … [to prove concerted action] the correct standard is that there must be evidence that tends to exclude the possibility of independent action by the [parties]. That is, there must be direct or circumstantial evidence that reasonably tends to prove that the [parties] had a conscious commitment to a common scheme designed to achieve an unlawful objective.' (page 465)

In *Aircraft Check Services Co v Verizon Wireless* the United States Court of Appeal held that:

'The Sherman Act imposes no duty on firms to compete vigorously, or for that matter at all, in price. This troubles some antitrust experts, such as Harvard Law School Professor Louis Kaplow, whose book Competition Policy and Price Fixing (2013) argues that tacit collusion should be deemed a violation of the Sherman Act. That of course is not the law, and probably shouldn't be. A seller must decide on a price; and if tacit collusion is forbidden, how does a seller in a market in which conditions (such as few sellers, many buyers, and a homogeneous product, which may preclude non-price competition) favor convergence by the sellers on a joint profit-maximizing price without their actually agreeing to charge that price, decide what price to charge? If the seller charges the profit-maximizing price (and its "competitors" do so as well), and tacit collusion is illegal, it is in trouble. But how is it to avoid getting into trouble? Would it have to adopt cost-plus pricing and prove that its price just covered its costs (where cost includes a "reasonable return" to invested capital)? Such a requirement would convert antitrust law into a scheme resembling public utility price regulation, now largely abolished.'

'And might not entry into concentrated markets be deterred because an entrant who, having successfully entered such a market, charged the prevailing market price would be a tacit colluder and could be prosecuted as such, if tacit collusion were deemed to violate the Sherman Act? What could be more perverse than an antitrust doctrine that discouraged new entry into highly concentrated markets? Prices might fall if the new entrant's output increased the market's total output, but then again it might not fall; the existing firms in the market might reduce their output in order to prevent the output of the new entrant from depressing the market price. If as a result the new entrant found itself charging the same price as the incumbent firms, it would be tacitly colluding with them and likewise even if it set its price below that of those firms in order to maximize its profit from entry yet above the price that would prevail were there no tacit collusion.'

'Further illustrating the danger of the law's treating tacit collusion as if it were express collusion, suppose that the firms in an oligopolistic market don't try to sell to each other's sleepers, "sleepers" being a term for a seller's customers who out of indolence or ignorance don't shop but instead are loyal to whichever seller they've been accustomed to buy from. Each firm may be reluctant to "awaken" any of the other firms' sleepers by offering them discounts, fearing retaliation. To avoid punishment under antitrust law for such forbearance (which would be a form of tacit collusion, aimed at keeping prices high), would firms be required to raid each other's sleepers? It is one thing to prohibit competitors from agreeing not to compete; it is another to order them to compete. How is a court to decide how vigorously they must compete in order to avoid being found to have tacitly colluded in violation of antitrust law? Such liability would, to repeat, give antitrust agencies a public-utility style regulatory role.'

Limburgse Vinyl Maatschappij NV and others v Commission	**Article 101 TFEU**
Joined Cases T-305–7, 313–318, 325, 328–9, 335/94	Joint Classification
General Court, [1999] ECR II-931, [1999] 5 CMLR 303	

Facts

A Commission investigation into the polypropylene sector led to a decision finding several polyvinyl chloride (PVC) producers to have infringed Article 101 TFEU by taking part in cartel activities (IV/31.865 *PVC*). The Commission decision stated that the undertakings infringed the Treaty provision by participating in an agreement and/or concerted practice by which the producers supplying PVC in the Union took part in regular meetings in order to fix target prices and quotas and plan concerted initiatives to raise price levels. On appeal to the General Court, some of the appellants argued, among other things, that the Commission was wrong to allege an alternative in relation to Article 101 TFEU in the relevant part of the decision in that the undertakings had participated in an agreement 'and/or' a concerted practice.

Held

'In the context of a complex infringement which involves many producers seeking over a number of years to regulate the market between them the Commission cannot be expected to classify the infringement precisely, for each undertaking and for any given moment, as in any event both those forms of infringement are covered by [Article 101 TFEU].' (para 696)

'The Commission is therefore entitled to classify that type of complex infringement as an agreement "and/or" concerted practice, inasmuch as the infringement includes elements which are to be classified as an "agreement" and elements which are to be classified as a "concerted practice".' (para 697)

'In such a situation, the dual classification must be understood not as requiring simultaneous and cumulative proof that every one of those factual elements reveals the factors constituting an agreement and a concerted practice, but rather as designating a complex whole that includes factual elements of which some have been classified as an agreement and others as a concerted practice within the meaning on [Article 101 TFEU], which does not provide for any specific classification in respect of that type of complex infringement.' (para 698)

Comment

An appeal on the judgment was dismissed—Case C-238/99, *Limburgse Vinyl Maatschappij NV v Commission*.

In Case C-49/92P, *Commission v Anic Partecipazioni SpA*, the Court of Justice held that 'whilst the concepts of an agreement and of a concerted practice have particularly different elements, they are not mutually incompatible … the [General Court] did not therefore have to require the Commission to categorise either as an agreement or as a concerted practice each form of conduct found but was right to hold that the Commission had been entitled to characterise some of those forms of conduct as principally "agreements" and others as "concerted practices" … it must be pointed out that this interpretation is not incompatible with the restrictive nature of the prohibition laid down in [Article 101 TFEU]. … Far from creating a new form of infringement, the arrival at that interpretation merely entails acceptance of the fact that, in the case of an infringement involving different forms of conduct, these may meet different definitions whilst being caught by the same provision and being all equally prohibited.' (paras 132, 133)

In Case IV/37.614/F3 *PO/Interbrew and Alken-Maes*, [2003] OJ L200/1, the Commission noted that 'The concepts of "agreement" and "concerted practice" are variable and may overlap. Realistically, it may even be impossible to make such a distinction, since an infringement may simultaneously have the characteristics of both forms of prohibited behaviour, whereas, taken separately, some of its elements may correctly be regarded as one rather than the other form. It would also be artificial from an analytical point of view to split what is clearly a continuous, collective enterprise with a single objective into several forms of infringement. A cartel may for instance constitute an agreement and a concerted practice at the same time …' (para 223)

Limburgse Vinyl Maatschappij NV and others v Commission	**Article 101 TFEU**
Joined Cases T-305–7, 313–318, 325, 328–9, 335/94	Single Overall Agreement
General Court, [1999] ECR II-931, [1999] 5 CMLR 303	

Facts

A Commission investigation into the polypropylene sector led to a decision finding several polyvinyl chloride (PVC) producers to have infringed Article 101 TFEU by taking part in cartel activities (IV/31.865—*PVC*). The Commission in its decision stated that it was not necessary for it to prove that each participant had taken part in every manifestation of the infringement, but only that it had participated in the cartel as a whole: 'In the present case it has not been possible, given the absence of pricing documentation, to prove the actual participation of every producer in concerted price initiatives. The Commission has therefore considered in relation to each suspected participant whether there is sufficient reliable evidence to prove its adherence to the cartel as a whole rather than proof of its participation in every manifestation thereof' (point 25 of the decision). 'The essence of the present case is the combination of the producers over a long period toward a common unlawful end, and each participant must not only take responsibility for its own direct role as an individual, but also share responsibility for the operation of the cartel as a whole' (point 31 of the decision). The appellants challenged the Commission's approach and its alleged reliance on collective responsibility.

Held

In its decision the Commission was aware of the need to prove the participation of each undertaking in the cartel. 'For that purpose, it referred to the concept of the cartel considered "as a whole". That does not justify the conclusion, however, that the Commission applied the principle of collective responsibility, in the sense that it deemed certain undertakings to have participated in actions with which they were not concerned simply because the participation of other undertakings in those actions was established.' (paras 769–71)

'The concept of the cartel considered "as a whole" is indissociable from the nature of the infringement in question. That consisted, as the examination of the facts shows, in the regular organisation over the years of meetings of rival producers, the aim of which was to establish illicit practices intended to organise artificially the functioning of the PVC market.' (para 772)

'An undertaking may be held responsible for an overall cartel even though it is shown to have participated directly only in one or some of its constituent elements if it is shown that it knew, or must have known, that the collusion in which it participated, especially by means of regular meetings organised over several years, was part of an overall plan intended to distort competition and that the overall plan included all the constituent elements of the cartel.' (para 773)

'In this case, even if in the absence of documentation the Commission was not able to prove the participation of every undertaking in the implementation of the price initiatives, such implementation being one of the manifestations of the cartel, it nevertheless considered itself able to demonstrate that each undertaking had in any event participated in the producer meetings, the purpose of which was, *inter alia*, to fix prices in common.' (para 774)

'The Commission did not impute collective responsibility to each undertaking, or responsibility in respect of a manifestation of the cartel in which that undertaking did not become involved, but responsibility for the actions in which each had participated.' (para 778)

Comment

The General Court annulled part of the Commission's decision for failure to establish infringement of Article 101 TFEU with respect to one of the undertakings involved. The fines imposed on three of the appellants were reduced. The remainder of the action was dismissed.

A subsequent appeal to the Court of Justice was dismissed—Case C-238/99, *Limburgse Vinyl Maatschappij NV v Commission*.

BASF AG and UCB SA v Commission	**Article 101 TFEU**
Case T-101/05 and T-111/05	Single Overall Agreement
General Court, [2007] ECR II-4949, [2008] 4 CMLR 13	Limitation rule

Facts

An appeal over a Commission decision under which a number of undertakings were held to infringe Article 101 TFEU by participating in a complex agreement and concerted practices consisting of price fixing, market sharing and agreed actions against competitors in the Choline Chloride market (Case COMP/E-2/37.533—*Choline Chloride*). On appeal, the appellants challenged, among other things, the Commission's characterisation of the global and European cartels as one single and continuous infringement. They argued that the two separate cartels were characterised as one to avoid the limitation rule on the global cartel which was time-barred.

Held

'The characterisation of certain unlawful actions as constituting one and the same infringement affects the penalty that may be imposed, since a finding that a number of infringements exist may entail the imposition of several distinct fines.... However, a finding of a number of infringements may be advantageous to those responsible when some of the infringements are time-barred.' (para 158)

'[A] case of infringement of [Article 101(1) TFEU] could result from a series of acts or from continuous conduct which formed part of an "overall plan" because they had the same object of distorting competition within the [internal] market. In such a case, the Commission is entitled to attribute liability for those actions on the basis of participation in the infringement considered as a whole (*Aalborg Portland and Others v Commission*, paragraph 66 above, paragraph 258), even if it is established that the undertaking concerned directly participated in only one or some of the constituent elements of the infringement (PVC II, paragraph 159 above, paragraph 773). Likewise, the fact that different undertakings played different roles in the pursuit of a common objective does not mean that there was no identity of anti- competitive object and, accordingly, of infringement, provided that each undertaking contributed, at its own level, to the pursuit of the common objective (*Cement*, paragraph 157 above, paragraph 4123, and *JFE Engineering and Others v Commission*, paragraph 139 above, paragraph 370).' (para 161)

The anti-competitive cartel activities at the global level and the European levels, each constitutes a single and continuous infringement. 'However, it does not automatically follow ... that the arrangements at the global and European levels, taken together, form a single and continuous infringement. It appears that, in the cases which the case-law envisages, the existence of a common objective consisting in distorting the normal development of prices provides a ground for characterising the various agreements and concerted practices as the constituent elements of a single infringement. In that regard, it cannot be overlooked that those actions were complementary in nature, since each of them was intended to deal with one or more consequences of the normal pattern of competition and, by interacting, contributed to the realisation of the set of anti-competitive effects intended by those responsible, within the framework of a global plan having a single objective.' (paras 197, 177–9)

'In that connection, it must be made clear that the concept of single objective cannot be determined by a general reference to the distortion of competition in the choline chloride market, since an impact on competition, whether it is the object or the effect of the conduct in question, constitutes a consubstantial element of any conduct covered by [Article 101(1) TFEU]. Such a definition of the concept of a single objective is likely to deprive the concept of a single and continuous infringement of a part of its meaning, since it would have the consequence that different types of conduct which relate to a particular economic sector and are prohibited by [Article 101(1) TFEU] would have to be systematically characterised as constituent elements of a single infringement.' (para 180)

'The Court must therefore ascertain whether the two sets of agreements and concerted practices penalised by the Commission in the Decision as a single and continuous infringement are complementary in the way described at paragraph 179 above. The Commission itself bases its theory on the fact that the global and European arrangements were "closely linked".… In that regard, it will be necessary to take into account any circumstance capable of establishing or casting doubt on that link, such as the period of application, the content (including the methods used) and, correlatively, the objective of the various agreements and concerted practices in question.' (para 181)

As regards the period of application of the cartel agreements it is noted that the agreements on the sharing of the European market were implemented without there being any agreement prohibiting exports from the United States. Subsequently, the Commission's argument that the sharing of the global and European markets are interlinked, cannot be accepted. (paras 182, 183)

Similarly, the Commission's assertion that the agreements at the European level constituted the continuation and the implementation of the global agreements by merely substituting the allocation of the European markets for the global allocation cannot be accepted. 'An anti-competitive agreement cannot, in principle, be regarded as a means of implementing another agreement which has already come to an end.' (para 191)

'As regards the objective pursued by each of the two sets of arrangements, it follows from … the Decision that the Commission invoked the existence of a single anti-competitive objective, consisting in arriving at artificially high prices. However, while it is true that the global agreement specified minimum prices to be charged by producers … the fact remains that the sole objective of that measure was to protect the key element of that agreement, namely to avoid exports from Europe to North America and vice versa, and not to bring about a division of the European market between European producers. If the producers had decided to sell to converters and to European distributors at prices that were too low (because of excess capacity), that, according to recital 151 to the Decision, would have allowed those converters and distributors to export choline chloride to the United States at competitive prices. Clearly, the North American producers would, in return, have had to adopt appropriate conduct within the meaning of the agreement vis-à-vis their customers (converters and distributors) in the United States.' (para 192)

'It must also be emphasised that there is nothing in the Decision to demonstrate that the European producers had entered into an agreement on the allocation (even at a later stage) of the EEA market at the meetings relating to the global cartel or that they intended to use the global arrangements in order to facilitate a subsequent allocation of the EEA market. The Commission acknowledges, moreover, at recital 151 to the Decision that it is not in a position to prove that. Had that been the case, there would have been no reason not to put the beginning of the arrangements relating to the allocation of the EEA before 14 March 1994, the date of the first meeting among the European producers. However, that was not the case.' (para 203)

'In light of the consequences drawn from the absence of any temporal overlap between the implementation of the global and European arrangements (see paragraphs 182 to 191 above), from the fact that the mutual withdrawal from the European and North American markets and the sharing of the EEA market by the allocation of customers constitute different objectives implemented by dissimilar methods (see paragraphs 192 to 202 above) and, last, from the absence of evidence that the European producers intended to adhere to the global arrangements in order to divide the EEA market (see paragraph 203 above), it must be concluded that the European producers committed two separate infringements of [Article 101(1) TFEU] and not a single and continuous infringement.' (para 209) The Commission decision must therefore be annulled.

Comment

The judgment clarifies the limits of the principle of single overall agreement. In doing so it stresses that the rhetoric of single agreement cannot be used as a substitute for careful factual and economic analysis. The lack of single agreement in this case meant that the global cartel was time-barred.

On limitation periods see discussion in Chapter 10.

Commission v Verhuizingen Coppens NV	**Article 101 TFEU**
Case C-441/11P	Single and Continuous Infringement
Court of Justice, [2013] 4 CMLR 8	Article 264 TFEU

Facts

The European Commission found a number of companies to infringe Article 101 TFEU by participating in a cartel in the Belgian international removal services. Cartel members engaged in (1) price fixing, (2) cover bidding and (3) the establishment of an illegal commission system (COMP/38.543– International Removal Services). Verhuizingen Coppens NV (Coppens), one of the companies accused of participation in the cartel agreement, contested the decision and argued that the Commission should have accused it only of issuing cover quotes and not for participation in the agreement on commissions since the Commission did not establish its knowledge of that agreement (Case T-210/08, [2011] 5 CMLR 11).

On appeal, the General Court held that in order to hold a company liable for a single and continuous infringement, 'awareness (proved or presumed) of the offending conduct of the other participants in the cartel is required' (para 29), and that 'the mere fact that there is identity of object between an agreement in which an undertaking participated and a global cartel does not suffice to render that undertaking responsible for the global cartel. It is only if the undertaking knew or should have known when it participated in the agreement that in doing so it was joining in the global cartel that its participation in the agreement concerned can constitute the expression of its accession to that global cartel (Case T-28/99 *Sigma Tecnologie v Commission*).' (para 30) The Court concluded that the Commission failed to establish that when the applicant participated in the agreement on cover quotes, it was aware of the other companies' anticompetitive conduct, or could reasonably have foreseen such conduct. The Commission's failure to establish Coppens' awareness of the anticompetitive commission system meant that it did not discharge the burden of proof required to establish a single infringement. The Commission appealed to the Court of Justice.

Held

If an undertaking took part in one or more forms of anticompetitive conduct comprising a single continuous infringement, but did not intend to contribute to all of the cartel's common objectives, the undertaking is only liable for the conduct in which it directly participated, and the conduct other cartel members engaged in to achieve the same objectives that the undertaking itself pursued. The undertaking is only liable for other cartel members' anticompetitive conduct where it is aware of their conduct or can reasonably foresee it. An undertaking intends to contribute to a cartel objective if its conduct furthers that objective, or it can reasonably foresee that other cartel members will engage in conduct that furthers that objective. (para 44)

'That cannot, however, relieve the undertaking of liability for conduct in which it has undeniably taken part or for conduct for which it can undeniably be held responsible. Nor is the fact that an undertaking did not take part in all aspects of an anticompetitive arrangement or that it played only a minor role in the aspects in which it did participate material for the purposes of establishing the existence of an infringement on its part, given that those factors need to be taken into consideration only when the gravity of the infringement is assessed and only if and when it comes to determining the fine (*Commission v Anic Partecipazioni*, paragraph 90, and *Aalborg Portland and Others v Commission*, paragraph 86).' (para 45)

Comment

The Court of Justice held that the General Court erred when it annulled the contested decision in its entirety in relation to Coppens, even though it had not called in question Coppens' participation in the agreement on cover quotes. It noted that the only circumstances in which the General Court would have been justified, under the first paragraph of Article 264 TFEU, in annulling the contested decision in its entirety in respect of Coppens would have been if the partial annulment of that decision would have altered the substance of the decision. As the Commission did prove Coppens participation in part of the conduct, that part of the decision should not have been annulled.

AC-Treuhand AG v Commission	**Article 101 TFEU**
Case T-99/04	Liability for Cartel Activity
General Court, [2008] ECR II-1501, [2008] 5 CMLR 13	

Facts

The Commission found a number of companies had infringed Article 101 TFEU by forming a cartel in the European market for organic peroxides (Case COMP/E-2/37.857—*Organic peroxides* [2005] OJ L110, 44). Although Treuhand AG, a consultancy firm, was not active in the market for organic peroxides, it facilitated the cartel activity. Among other things, it organised meetings and covered up evidence of the infringement. Treuhand AG appealed to the General Court and argued that it has not infringed Article 101 TFEU since its relationship with the cartel members was merely one of non-punishable complicity.

Held

Literal interpretation of the term 'agreements between undertakings'

With respect to the term 'agreements between undertakings' in Article 101 TFEU, 'it should be noted, first, that the [Union] judicature has yet to give an explicit ruling on the question whether the notions of agreement and undertaking as used in [Article 101(1) TFEU] are conceived in accordance with a "unitary" perspective, so as to cover any undertaking which has contributed to the committing of an infringement, irrespective of the economic sector in which that undertaking is normally active or—as the applicant submits—in accordance with a "bipolar" perspective, so that a distinction is drawn between undertakings which "perpetrate" an infringement and those whose role is one of "complicity" in the infringement. It should also be noted that, according to the applicant, there is a lacuna in the wording of [Article 101(1) TFEU], in that, in referring to the "undertaking" which is the perpetrator of the infringement and to its participation in the "agreement", that provision covers only certain undertakings with particular characteristics and refers only to certain forms of participation. Consequently, it is only on the assumption that the notions of undertaking and agreement fall to be so narrowly construed, and that the scope of [Article 101(1) TFEU] is accordingly so limited, that the principle of nullum crimen, nulla poena sine lege could be applied in such a way as to preclude a broad interpretation of the wording of that provision.' (para 117)

'In the present case, the question arises whether, as claimed by the applicant, the cartel must concern a specific sector of activity, or even the same market for goods or services, so that only undertakings which are active in such a sector or market as competitors, or on the side of supply or demand, are capable of coordinating their conduct as undertakings which are the (co) perpetrators of an infringement.' (para 119)

In that regard, it should be noted that Article 101(1) TFEU applies to both horizontal and vertical agreements, and that 'to fall within the ambit of the prohibition laid down in [Article 101(1) TFEU] it is sufficient that the agreement at issue restricts competition on the neighbouring and/or emerging markets on which at least one of the participating undertakings is not (yet) present (see, to that effect, Case T-328/03 *O2 (Germany) v Commission* [2006] ECR II-1231, paragraphs 65 et seq; see also, as regards the application of [Article 102 TFEU], Case C-333/94P *Tetra Pak v Commission* [1996] ECR I-5951).' (paras 120, 121)

'In that regard, the formulations used in the caselaw—the "joint intention of conducting themselves on the market in a specific way" (*Bayer v Commission*, cited in paragraph 118 above, paragraph 67) or "expression of the joint intention of the parties to the agreement with regard to their conduct in the [internal] market" (*ACF Chemiefarma v Commission*, cited in paragraph 23 above, paragraph 112)—stress the element of "joint intention" and do not require the relevant market on which the undertaking which is the "perpetrator" of the restriction of competition is active to be exactly the same as the one on which that restriction is deemed to materialise. It follows that any restriction of competition within the [internal] market may be classed as an "agreement between undertakings" within the meaning of [Article 101(1) TFEU]. That conclusion is confirmed by the criterion of the existence of an agreement whose object is to restrict competition within the [internal] market. That criterion implies that an undertaking may infringe the prohibition laid down in [Article 101(1) TFEU] where the purpose of its conduct, as coordinated with that of other undertakings, is to restrict competition on a specific relevant market within the [internal] market, and that does not mean that the undertaking has to be active on that relevant market itself.' (para 122)

The contextual notion of restriction of competition

As regard to the contextual notion of restriction of competition, 'it is not therefore to be ruled out that an undertaking may participate in the implementation of such a restriction even if it does not restrict its own freedom of action on the market on which it is primarily active. Any other interpretation might restrict the scope of the prohibition laid down in [Article 101(1) TFEU] to an extent incompatible with its useful effect and its main objective, as read in the light of Article 3(1)(g) EC [repealed following the ratification of the Lisbon Treaty], which is to ensure that competition in the internal market is not distorted, since proceedings against an undertaking for actively contributing to a restriction of competition could be blocked simply on the ground that that contribution does not come from an economic activity forming part of the relevant market on which that restriction materialises or on which it is intended to materialise. It should be pointed out that, as submitted by the Commission, it is only by making all "undertakings" within the meaning of [Article 101(1) TEFU] subject to liability that that useful effect can be fully guaranteed, since that makes it possible to penalise and to prevent the creation of new forms of collusion with the assistance of undertakings which are not active on the markets concerned by the restriction of competition, with the aim of circumventing the prohibition laid down in [Article 101(1) TFEU].' (para 127)

Conditions to establish that an undertaking is liable as a co-perpetrator of the infringement

In order to establish that an undertaking that participated in the cartel is liable as a co-perpetrator of the infringement, it is sufficient to show that it attended meetings at which anticompetitive agreements were concluded, without manifesting its opposition to such meetings. The Commission must prove that that undertaking intended to contribute to the activity and was aware of the substantive conduct planned or implemented by other undertakings, or that it could reasonably have foreseen that conduct and that it was ready to accept the attendant risk. (paras 129, 130)

'[A]s regards the determination of the individual liability of an undertaking whose participation in the cartel is not as extensive or intense as that of the other undertakings, ... the mere fact that each undertaking takes part in the infringement in ways particular to it does not suffice to rule out its liability for the entire infringement, including conduct put into effect by other participating undertakings but sharing the same anticompetitive object or effect (*Commission v Anic Partecipazioni*, ..., paragraphs 78 to 80).' (para 131)

The fact that an undertaking did not take part in all aspects of an anti-competitive scheme, or played a minor role in it, or only passively contributed to its implementation, is not material to the establishment of an infringement and does not call into question the undertaking's individual liability for the infringement as a whole. That fact, none the less has an influence on the assessment of the extent of that liability and thus on the severity of the penalty. (para 132, 133) Appeal dismissed.

Comment

The fact that an undertaking is not active on the market in which the cartel takes place does not rule out its liability for participating in the implementation of a cartel.

To ensure the effectiveness of Article 101 TFEU, the court held that an undertaking may be responsible for the implementation of the anticompetitive activity even if it does not restrict its own freedom of action on the market on which it is primarily active. (para 127)

Treuhand AG played an accessory role as coperpetrator of the infringement and was therefore found jointly liable for the infringement of Article 101 TFEU.

On the liability of a parent company for cartel activity carried by its subsidiary, see Chapter 1 (Undertaking) and in particular: Case C-97/08 *Akzo Nobel and others v Commission* (page 26 above), Case T-24/05 *Alliance One International and Others v Commission* (page 27 above).

Daimler Chrysler AG v Commission	**Article 101 TFEU**
Case T-325/01	Association of Undertakings
General Court, [2005] ECR II-3319, [2007] 4 CMLR 15	Cartel Meetings

Facts

An action for the annulment of a Commission Decision (Case COMP/36.264—*Mercedes-Benz*) in which the Commission found Mercedes-Benz and two of its subsidiaries to have infringed Article 101(1) TFEU by engaging in various anticompetitive agreements in connection with the retailing of its passenger cars. Part of the Commission's decision referred to an agreement between Mercedes-Benz Belgium SA (MBBel) and the Belgian Mercedes-Benz dealers' association, which limited discounts on vehicles and had as its object the restriction of price competition in Belgium. The appellants challenged the Commission's finding and argued that the Belgian dealers' association had no power to take a decision which would bind its members and enter them into an anticompetitive agreement.

Held

'[W]here it has been established that an undertaking has participated in meetings between undertakings of a manifestly anticompetitive nature, it is for that undertaking to put forward evidence to establish that its participation in those meetings was without any anti-competitive intention, by demonstrating that it had indicated to its competitors that it was participating in those meetings in a spirit that was different from theirs. ... In the absence of evidence of that distancing, the fact that an undertaking does not abide by the outcome of those meetings is not such as to relieve it of full responsibility for the fact that it participated in the concerted practice (Case T-347/94 *MayrMelnhof v Commission* [1998] ECR II-1751, paragraph 135, and Joined Cases T-25/95, [...] *Cimenteries CBR and others v Commission* [2000] ECR II-491, paragraph 1389).' (para 202)

It is not disputed that MBBel was present at the meeting of the dealers' association in which price slashing and the intention to take steps to detect and prevent various discounts were referred to. MBBel did not publicly distance itself from the discussions and led the other participants to believe that it accepted the decisions taken at the meeting and that it intended to contribute by its own conduct to the common objectives of the meeting. (paras 203–07)

'As regards the applicant's argument that the dealers' association did not have the authority to take decisions binding its members, but only to formulate recommendations, it is settled case-law that a measure may be categorised as a decision of an association of undertakings for the purposes of [Article 101(1) TFEU] even if it is not binding on the members concerned, at least to the extent that the members to whom the decision applies comply with its terms (see, by way of analogy, Joined Cases 96/82 [...] *IAZ and others v Commission* [1983] ECR 3369, paragraph 20; [Joined Cases 209/78 [...] *Van Landewyck and others v Commission* [1980] ECR 3125, at paragraphs 88 and 89]; and Case T-136/94 *Eurofer v Commission* [1999] ECR II-263, paragraph 15). That requirement is sufficiently established in this case by the fact that the members of the dealers' association in Belgium and MBBel decided at the meeting of 20 April 2005 to monitor, using ghost purchasing by members of an outside agency, the level of discounts given for the W 210 vehicle model and that ghost shoppers did indeed make visits to dealers. That information shows that the course of action decided upon at the meeting of 20 April 1995 was implemented.' (para 210)

Comment

In Joined Cases 209/78 etc *Van Landewyck and others v Commission* the Court of Justice held that Article 101(1) TFEU also applies to non-profit-making associations 'in so far as their own activities or those of the undertakings belonging to them are calculated to produce the results which it aims to suppress' (para 88). The Court rejected an argument that the decisions of the association in question were not binding and pointed to the compliance with the recommendation by several of the undertakings involved. (para 89)

IAZ International Belgium NV v Commission	**Article 101 TFEU**
Case 96/82	Association of Undertakings
Court of Justice, [1983] ECR 3369, [1984] 3 CMLR 276	Non Binding Recommendation

Facts

An agreement between an association of producers and the national association of water supplies (ANSEAU), according to which members of the latter will only connect washing machines and dishwashers which have a conformity label issued by the former. The Commission found the agreement and the use of conformity label to foreclose the market. On appeal ANSEAU argued that as an association of undertakings which does not carry any economic activity, it is not subjected to Article 101 TFEU.

Held

'As the court has already held, in its judgments of 15 May 1975 in case 71/74 (*Frubo* (1975) ECR 563) and of 29 October 1980 in joined cases 209 to 215 and 218/78 *Van Landewyck* (1980) ECR 3125, [Article 101(1) TFEU] applies also to associations of undertakings in so far as their own activities or those of the undertakings affiliated to them are calculated to produce the results which it aims to suppress. It is clear particularly from the latter judgment that a recommendation, even if it has no binding effect, cannot escape [Article 101(1) TFEU] where compliance with the recommendation by the undertakings to which it is addressed has an appreciable influence on competition in the market in question.' (para 20)

'In the light of that case-law, it must be emphasized, as the Commission has pertinently stated, that the recommendations made by ANSEAU under the agreement to the effect that its member undertakings were to take account of the terms and of the purpose of the agreement and were to inform consumers thereof, in fact produced a situation in which the water-supply undertakings in the built-up areas of Brussels, Antwerp and Ghent carried out checks on consumers' premises to determine whether machines connected to the water-supply system were provided with a conformity label. Those recommendations therefore determined the conduct of a large number of ANSEAU's members and consequently exerted an appreciable influence on competition.' (para 21)

Comment

A mere recommendation from a non-profit making trade association is sufficient to bring it within the scope of Article 101 TFEU.

In Case 8/72 *Cementhandelaren v Commission* [1972] ECR 977 the Court of Justice held that Article 101 TFEU applies also to non-binding recommendations of an association. In that case the association issued recommended target prices which were rarely adhered to in practice by the members of the association. The court held that 'the fixing of a price, even one which merely constitutes a target, affects competition because it enables all the participants to predict with a reasonable degree of certainty what the pricing policy pursued by their competitors will be.' (para 21) it concluded there to be a 'coherent and strictly organized system the object of which is to restrict competition between the members of the association.' (para 25)

In Case 45/85 *Verband der Sachversicherer v Commission* [1987] ECR-405, [1988] 4 CMLR 264, the Court held that a recommendation by an association of undertakings, 'regardless of what its precise legal status may be, constituted the faithful reflection of the applicant's resolve to coordinate the conduct of its members on the German insurance market in accordance with the terms of the recommendation. It must therefore be concluded that it amounts to a decision of an association of undertakings within the meaning of [Article 101 TFEU].' (para 32)

The UK OFT guidelines on 'Trade associations, professions and self-regulating bodies' (OFT 408) stipulate that 'a recommendation of an association of undertakings may also be a decision, as may an oral exhortation which it is intended that members should follow. This will be the case even if the recommendation is not binding on the members or has not been fully complied with.' (para 2.4)

MasterCard Inc v Commission	**Article 101 TFEU**
Case C-382/12P	Association of Undertakings
Court of Justice, [2014] 5 CMLR 23	

Facts

The European Commission found MasterCard to have infringed Article 101 TFEU by establishing a system of multilateral interchange fees (MIFs) for cross-border bank card payments. That system led to a restriction of competition between participating banks providing merchants with services enabling them to accept MasterCard charge and credit cards. In its decision, the Commission found the MIF to constitute a decision by an association of undertakings. MasterCard's action for annulment was dismissed (Case T-111/08). It subsequently appealed to the Court of Justice, challenging, among other things, the classification of the MIF as association of undertakings. Relevant to its argument was the fact that whereas before May 2006 MasterCard was wholly owned by the participating financial institutions, it was later the subject of an initial public offering (IPO) on the New York Stock Exchange which modified its structure and governance. MasterCard argued that after the IPO, the banks no longer controlled MasterCard and MasterCard determined the MIF unilaterally

Held

'[A]lthough [Article 101 TFEU] distinguishes between "concerted practice", "agreements between undertakings" and "decisions by associations of undertakings", the aim is to have the prohibitions of that article catch different forms of coordination between undertakings of their conduct on the market ... and thus to prevent undertakings from being able to evade the rules on competition on account simply of the form in which they coordinate that conduct.' (para 63)

It is undisputed that before the IPO MasterCard could be considered to be an 'association of undertakings'. The question is whether that remains the case following the IPO. In its judgment, the General Court relied on (1) the retention of the banks' decision-making power within MasterCard, and (2) the existence of a commonality of interests between that organisation and the banks on the issue of the MIF. The General Court subsequently rejected the arguments that following the IPO MasterCard could no longer be considered to be an 'association of undertakings'. (paras 64–67)

The General Court found that even though the MasterCard member banks were no longer taking part in the decision-making process within the bodies of that organisation in relation to the MIF, MasterCard was continuing to operate in Europe as an association of undertakings, in which the banks participated collectively in all essential elements of the decision-making power. The General Court also found that the Commission had been able properly to conclude that the MIF reflected the banks' interests, because there was, on that point, a commonality of interests between MasterCard, its shareholders and the banks. In its consideration of the commonality of interests, the General Court took into account specific factual circumstances. indicating that that MIF, in reality, was continuing to take into account concrete banks' interests in setting the level of the MIF. (paras 68–71)

'In those circumstances, it was open to the General Court to find, ... that both the banks' residual decision-making powers after the IPO on matters other than the MIF, and the commonality of interests between MasterCard and the banks, were both relevant and sufficient for the purposes of assessing whether, after the IPO, MasterCard could still be considered to be an 'association of undertakings.' (para 72)

Comment

The finding of communality of interest was case specific and stemmed from the unique relationship between the banks and Mastercard, which reflected a commonality of interests.

While the relationship between the banks and MasterCard seems vertical, it had, in practice, horizontal features. The IPO, while changing the legal relationship, included conditions which retained part of the structure of the previous association of undertakings.

Musique Diffusion française v Commission	**Article 101 TFEU**
Cases 100/80 to 103/80	Authorised Representative
Court of Justice, [1983] ECR 1825, [1983] 3 CMLR 221	No Knowledge Required

The Commission is empowered to 'impose on undertakings or associations of undertakings fines where, intentionally or negligently, they have been guilty of infringements. For that provision to apply it is not necessary for there to have been action by, or even knowledge on the part of, the partners or principal managers of the undertaking concerned; action by a person who is authorized to act on behalf of the undertaking suffices.' (para 97)

Protimonopolný úrad Slovenskej republiky v Slovenská sporiteľňa	**Article 101 TFEU**
Case C-68/12	Authorised Representative
Court of Justice, [2013] 4 CMLR 16	

'In the present case, Slovenská sporiteľňa has maintained that its employee who took part in the meeting of the representatives of the banks concerned on 10 May 2007 had not been given authority to that effect; nor had it been shown that he had endorsed the conclusions of that meeting.' (para 24)

'The Court observes in that regard that, for Article 101 TFEU to apply, it is not necessary for there to have been action by, or even knowledge on the part of, the partners or principal managers of the undertaking concerned; action by a person who is authorised to act on behalf of the undertaking suffices (Joined Cases 100/80 to 103/80 *Musique Diffusion française and Others v Commission* [1983] ECR 1825, paragraph 97). Furthermore, as the Commission has pointed out, participation in agreements that are prohibited by the FEU Treaty is more often than not clandestine and is not governed by any formal rules. It is rarely the case that an undertaking's representative attends a meeting with a mandate to commit an infringement.' (paras 25–26)

'Moreover, it is settled case-law that when it is established that an undertaking has participated in anti-competitive meetings between competing undertakings, it is for that undertaking to put forward evidence to establish that its participation in those meeting was without any anti-competitive intention by demonstrating that it had indicated to its competitors that it was participating in those meetings in a spirit that was different from theirs. If an undertaking's participation in such a meeting is not to be regarded as tacit approval of an unlawful initiative or as subscribing to what is decided there, the undertaking must publicly distance itself from that initiative in such a way that the other participants will think that it is putting an end to its participation, or it must report the initiative to the administrative authorities (judgment of 3 May 2012 in Case C-290/11 P *Comap v Commission*, not published in the ECR, paragraphs 74 and 75 and the case-law cited).' (para 27)

Société Technique Minière v Maschinenbau Ulm GmbH	**Article 101 TFEU**
Case 56/65	Object or Effect
Court of Justice, [1966] ECR 235, [1966] CMLR 357	Distribution Agreement

Facts

The French Cour d'appel de Paris made an application for a preliminary ruling concerning the interpretation of Article 101 TFEU and its application to exclusive distribution agreements. According to the agreement in question, a German manufacturer granted exclusive right of sale to a French distributor, yet did not prohibit it from selling to other territories, nor did it prohibit dealers in other territories from selling the products in the territory which was the primary responsibility of the distributor with whom the agreement was made. A dispute between the parties led to legal proceedings in which the French distributor argued that the agreement infringed Article 101(1) TFEU and was void under Article 101(2) TFEU.

Held

'For the agreement at issue to be caught by the prohibition contained in [Article 101(1)] it must have as its object or effect the prevention, restriction or distortion of competition within the [internal] market.' (p 249)

'The fact that these are not cumulative but alternative requirements, indicated by the conjunction "or", leads first to the need to consider the precise purpose of the agreement, in the economic context in which it is to be applied. This interference with competition referred to in [Article 101(1) TFEU] must result from all or some of the clauses of the agreement itself. Where, however, an analysis of the said clauses does not reveal the effect on competition to be sufficiently deleterious, the consequences of the agreement should then be considered and for it to be caught by the prohibition it is then necessary to find that those factors are present which show that competition has in fact been prevented or restricted or distorted to an appreciable extent.' (p 249)

'The competition in question must be understood within the actual context in which it would occur in the absence of the agreement in dispute. In particular it may be doubted whether there is an interference with competition if the said agreement seems really necessary for the penetration of a new area by an undertaking. Therefore, in order to decide whether an agreement containing a clause "granting an exclusive right of sale" is to be considered as prohibited by reason of its object or of its effect, it is appropriate to take into account in particular the nature and quantity, limited or otherwise, of the products covered by the agreement, the position and importance of the grantor and the concessionaire on the market for the products concerned, the isolated nature of the disputed agreement or, alternatively, its position in a series of agreements, the severity of the clauses intended to protect the exclusive dealership or, alternatively, the opportunities allowed for other commercial competitors in the same products by way of parallel re-exportation and importation.' (p 250)

Comment

The agreement was found not to infringe Article 101 TFEU. Contrast the nature of the agreement in this case with the distribution agreement in *Consten and Grundig* (page 93 below). There, the distribution agreement was found to infringe Article 101 TFEU as it resulted in absolute territorial protection.

Note the 2010 Commission Guidelines on Vertical Restraints, SEC (2010) 411, which outline the principles for the assessment of vertical agreements under Article 101 TFEU. Paragraphs 151–67 lay down the analytical framework for the analysis of exclusive distribution agreements. Also note the Vertical Block Exemption Regulation (Regulation 330/2010 (20 April 2010)) under which an exclusive distribution agreement is exempted when (1) the market share held by the supplier does not exceed 30 per cent of the relevant market on which it sells the contract goods or services, (2) the market share held by the buyer does not exceed 30 per cent of the relevant market on which it purchases the contract goods or services, and (3) the agreement does not contain hard-core restrictions.

Consten SaRL and Grundig-Verkaufs-GmbH v Commission	**Article 101 TFEU**
Joined Cases 56 and 58/64	Object or Effect
Court of Justice, [1966] ECR 299, [1966] CMLR 418	Distribution Agreement

Facts

The case concerned an exclusive distribution agreement between Consten and Grundig under which the former received exclusive rights to sell Grundig products in France in return for its promise not to handle competing brands. Under the agreement Grundig agreed to impose restrictions on its distributors in other Member States to prevent parallel import into Consten's exclusive territory. In addition, the Grundig trademark 'Gint' was registered in France under Consten's name, thus providing it with absolute territorial protection. The Commission found the agreement to infringe Article 101 TFEU. The companies appealed to the Court of Justice.

Held

Article 101 TFEU does not lay down any distinction between horizontal and vertical agreements and applies to all agreements which distort competition within the internal market. (p 339)

'[A]n agreement between producer and distributor which might tend to restore the national divisions in trade between Member States might be such as to frustrate the most fundamental objections of the [Union]. The Treaty, whose preamble and content aim at abolishing the barriers between states, and which in several provisions gives evidence of a stern attitude with regard to their reappearance, could not allow undertakings to reconstruct such barriers. [Article 101(1) TFEU] is designed to pursue this aim, even in the case of agreements between undertakings placed at different levels in the economic process.' (p 340)

'For the purpose of applying [Article 101(1)TFEU], there is no need to take account of the concrete effects of an agreement once it appears that it has as its object the prevention, restriction or distortion of competition.' (p. 342)

The court needs to consider whether in this case the agreement in question had the object of restricting competition. 'The infringement which was found to exist by the contested Decision results from the absolute territorial protection created the said contract in favour of Consten on the basis of French law. The applicants thus wished to eliminate any possibility of competition at the wholesale level in Grundig products in the territory specified in the contract essentially by two methods.' (p 342)

'First, Grundig undertook not to deliver even indirectly to third parties products intended for the area covered by the contract. The restrictive nature of that undertaking is obvious if it is considered in the light of the prohibition on exporting which was imposed not only on Consten but also on all the other sole concessionaires of Grundig, as well as the German wholesalers. Secondly, the registration in France by Consten of the Gint trade mark, which Grundig affixes to all its products, is intended to increase the protection inherent in the disputed agreement, against the risk of parallel imports into France of Grundig products, by adding the protection deriving from the law on industrial property rights. Thus no third party could import Grundig products from other Member States of the [Union] for resale in France without running serious risks.' (p 343)

'The defendant properly took into account the whole distribution system thus set up by Grundig. In order to arrive at a true representation of the contractual position the contract must be placed in the economic and legal context in the light of which it was concluded by the parties ...' (p 343)

'The situation as ascertained above results in the isolation of the French market and makes it possible to charge for the products in question prices which are sheltered from all effective competition. In addition, the more producers succeed in their efforts to render their own makes of product individually distinct in the eyes of the consumer, the more the effectiveness of competition between producers tends to diminish. Because of the considerable impact of distribution costs on the aggregate cost price, it seems important that competition between dealers should also be stimulated. The efforts of the dealer are stimulated by competition between distributors of products of the same make. Since the agreement thus aims at isolating the French market for Grundig products and maintaining artificially, for products of a very well-known brand, separate national markets within the [Union], it is therefore such as to distort competition in the [internal] market.' (p 343)

'It was therefore proper for the contested Decision to hold that the agreement constitutes an infringement of [Article 101(1) TFEU]. No further considerations, whether of economic data (price differences between France and Germany, representative character of the type of appliance considered, level of overheads borne by Consten) or of the correction of the criteria upon which the Commission relied in its comparisons between the situations of the French and German markets, and no possible favourable effects of the agreement in other respects, can in any way lead, in the face of the abovementioned restrictions, to a different solution under [Article 101(1) TFEU].' (p 343)

'Consten's right under the contract to the exclusive use in France of the Gint trade mark, which may be used in a similar manner in other countries, is intended to make it possible to keep under surveillance and to place an obstacle in the way of parallel imports. Thus, the agreement by which Grundig, as the holder of the trademark by virtue of an inter-national registration, authorized Consten to register it in France in its own name tends to restrict competition.' (p 345)

'That agreement therefore is one which may be caught by the prohibition in [Article 101(1) TFEU]. The prohibition would be ineffective if Consten could continue to use the trade-mark to achieve the same object as that pursued by the agreement which has been held to be unlawful.' (p 345)

Comment

The Consten and Grundig distribution agreement led to absolute territorial protection by prohibiting parallel export and using trademark law to seal the market. Such an agreement was considered by the Court of Justice as having the object of restricting competition.

In Joined Cases C-403/08, C-429/08 *FA Premier League and others v QC Leisure and others* [2011] ECR I-9083 the Court of Justice considered the legality of a broadcasting agreement which included an exclusive territorial licence. The Court took an expansive approach as to what constitutes a violation by object and held that an agreement which restores the divisions between national markets is liable to frustrate the Treaty's objective of integration through the establishment of a single market. Accordingly, where a licence agreement is designed to prohibit or limit the cross-border provision of broadcasting services, it is deemed to have as its object the restriction of competition. The obligation on the broadcasters not to supply decoding devices enabling access to the protected subject-matter with a view to their use outside the territory covered by the licence agreement results in absolute territorial exclusivity in the area covered by its licence and, thus, all competition between broadcasters in the field of those services to be eliminated. (paras 139–42)

A proof of intention is not necessary when determining whether an agreement restricts competition by object. Nonetheless, although intention is not a necessary factor in determining the restrictive character of an agreement, the Commission and European Court may take the presence of intention into account. Case C-551/03P *General Motors v Commission* [2006] ECR I-3173. (77–78)

Note the opinion of Advocate General Roemer who disagreed with the Commission's object-based analysis and considered the case to require the examination of effects. The opinion is interesting, not the least as the Court of Justice did not follow it, and analysed the agreement as having the object of restricting competition. The following extracts from the AG's opinion are illustrative:

'[T]he Commission was content to find that the agreement in question *has as its object* an adverse effect upon competition, because it has the aim of freeing Consten from the competition of other wholesalers in the sale of *Grundig equipment.* ... I consider that there are several reasons why that point of view is invalid. ... I have already indicated in another case that American law ... requires for situations of the type before us a comprehensive examination of their economic repercussions. Clearly I do not mean to say that we should imitate in all respects the principles of American procedure in the field of cartels. This would not in fact be justified by reason of the essential differences between the systems. ... But such a reference is useful nevertheless in so far as it shows that in respect of [Article 101(1) TFEU] also it is not possible to dispense with observing the market in concreto. It seems to me wrong to have regard to such observation only for the application of paragraph (3) of [Article 101 TFEU], because that paragraph requires an examination from other points of view which are special and different. But in particular (as is shown by *Société Technique Minière v Maschinenbau Ulm GmbH*) it would be artificial to apply [Article 101(1) TFEU], on the basis of purely theoretical considerations, to situations which upon closer inspection would reveal no appreciable adverse effects on competition, in order then to grant exemption on the basis of [Article 101(3) TFEU].

Properly understood, therefore, [Article 101(1) TFEU] requires a comparison between two market situations: that which arises after the making of an agreement and that which would have arisen had there been no agreement. This concrete examination may show that it is not possible for a manufacturer to find an outlet in a particular part of the market unless he concentrates supply in the hands of a sole concessionnaire. That would signify that in a given situation an exclusive distributorship agreement has effects which are likely only to *promote* competition. Such a situation can in particular appear when what is at issue is gaining access to and penetrating a market. It is clear that the Commission did not take considerations of this type into account as regards the relationship between Grundig and Consten, although they must have come to the fore as regards the problem of gaining access to the market, in view of the fact that the measures for liberalization of the French import trade were taken only during the years 1960–1961. The possibility cannot be excluded that such an examination of the market might have led to a finding that in the Grundig-Consten case the *suppression* of the sole distributorship might involve a noticeable reduction in the supply of Grundig products on the French market and consequently an unfavourable influence on the conditions of competition existing there.

A second point is even more important … it is perfectly possible that there exists between different products or rather between different producers such sharp competition that there remains no appreciable margin for what is called internal competition in a product (for example, in relation to price and servicing). The Commission considers that it does not have to take into consideration this competition between different manufacturers except for simple mass-produced articles. That does not seem to be correct, if it is desired to judge economic phenomena realistically. … So in reality it was necessary to require from the Commission a judgment on the whole of the competitive conditions, … It is possible that such observation of the effects on the market … would have led to a conclusion favourable to the appliants. It might have been so for example because of the fairly small share of the French market for tape-recorders and dictaphones held by Grundig (about 17%) (we know that the Commission did not make any inquiry in respect of other products) or because of the applicants' assertion that the market for television sets (in which for technical reasons there were no parallel imports of Grundig models) and the transistor market were subject to such strong competition from various producers (some of whom were very powerful) in the Union and from third countries that the price of the Grundig models had to be reduced considerably several times.

Since an examination of the market of this kind did not take place because of the Commission's narrow view of the concept of "restriction on competition", and as the Court of Justice cannot be required to carry out such an examination itself during the course of the proceedings, it only remains for me to say that the conclusions reached by the Commission in examining the criterion of "adverse effect upon competition" must be considered as insufficiently based and consequently must be rejected.' (AG Roemer)

Note also the Commission Guidelines on the Application of [Article 101(3) TFEU], [2004] OJ C101/94), where the Commission states: 'The assessment of whether or not an agreement has as its object the restriction of competition is based on a number of factors. These factors include, in particular, the content of the agreement and the objective aims pursued by it. It may also be necessary to consider the context in which it is (to be) applied and the actual conduct and behaviour of the parties on the market. In other words, an examination of the facts underlying the agreement and the specific circumstances in which it operates may be required before it can be concluded whether a particular restriction constitutes a restriction of competition by object. The way in which an agreement is actually implemented may reveal a restriction by object even where the formal agreement does not contain an express provision to that effect. Evidence of subjective intent on the part of the parties to restrict competition is a relevant factor but not a necessary condition. (para 22)

SA Brasserie de Haecht v Consorts Wilkin-Janssen	**Article 101 TFEU**
Case 23/67	Object or Effect
Court of Justice, [1967] ECR 407, [1968] CMLR 26	Exclusive Distribution Agreement

Facts

A reference for a preliminary ruling from the Belgian Tribunal de Commerce de Liège. The Belgian court requested the Court of Justice to clarify whether when assessing the possible anticompetitive effects of an exclusive distribution agreement which forms part of a large number of similar agreements it should review the agreement in isolation or take account of the existence of a network of distribution agreements.

Held

'Agreements whereby an undertaking agrees to obtain its supplies from one undertaking to the exclusion of all others do not by their very nature necessarily include all the elements constituting incompatibility with the [internal] market as referred to in [Article 101(1)TFEU]. Such agreements may, however, exhibit such elements where, taken either in isolation or together with others, and in the economic and legal context in which they are made on the basis of a set of objective factors of law or of fact, they may affect trade between Member States and where they have either as their object or effect the prevention, restriction or distortion of competition.' (p 416)

Article 101(1) TFEU implies that regard must be had to the effects an agreement may have on competition in the economic and legal context in which they occur. 'In fact, it would be pointless to consider an agreement, decision or practice by reason of its effects if those effects were to be taken distinct from the market in which they are seen to operate and could only be examined apart from the body of effects, whether convergent or not, surrounding their implementation. Thus in order to examine whether it is caught by [Article 101(1) TFEU] an agreement cannot be examined in isolation from the above context, that is, from the factual or legal circumstances causing it to prevent, restrict or distort competition. The existence of similar contracts may be taken into consideration for this objective to the extent to which the general body of contracts of this type is capable of restricting the freedom of trade.' (p 415)

Comment

'If an agreement is not restrictive of competition by object it must be examined whether it has restrictive effects on competition. Account must be taken of both actual and potential effects. In other words the agreement must have likely anti-competitive effects. In the case of restrictions of competition by effect there is no presumption of anti-competitive effects. For an agreement to be restrictive by effect it must affect actual or potential competition to such an extent that on the relevant market negative effects on prices, output, innovation or the variety or quality of goods and services can be expected with a reasonable degree of probability. Such negative effects must be appreciable. The prohibition rule of [Article 101(1) TFEU] does not apply when the identified anti-competitive effects are insignificant. This test reflects the economic approach which the Commission is applying. The prohibition of Article 81(1) only applies where on the basis of proper market analysis it can be concluded that the agreement has likely anti-competitive effects on the market. It is insufficient for such a finding that the market shares of the parties exceed the thresholds set out in the Commission's de minimis notice. Agreements falling within safe harbours of Block Exemption regulations may be caught by [Article 101(1) TFEU] but this is not necessarily so. Moreover, the fact that due to the market shares of the parties, an agreement falls outside the safe harbour of a Block Exemption is in itself an insufficient basis for finding that the agreement is caught by [Article 101(1) TFEU] or that it does not fulfil the conditions of [Article 101(3) TFEU]. Individual assessment of the likely effects produced by the agreement is required.' (para 24, Commission Guidelines on the Application of [Article 101(3) TFEU], [2004] OJ C101/94)

For a detailed evaluation of effect, see for example Case C-234/89 *Stergios Delimitis v Henninger Bräu AG* (page 98 below), Case C-501/06P etc *GlaxoSmithKline Services Unlimited v Commission* (page 103 below).

European Night Services Ltd v Commission	**Article 101 TFEU**
Joined Cases T-374, 375, 384 and 388/94	Object or Effect
General Court, [1998] ECR II-3141, [1998] 5 CMLR 718	

Facts

European Night Services Ltd (ENS), a cooperative joint venture, intended to operate, in conjunction with several railway companies, night passenger services through the Channel Tunnel. Following notification of the agreement, the Commission concluded that the ENS agreements restricted competition among the ENS parent companies, and between the parent companies, ENS and third parties, and that it restricted competition as a result of the presence of networks of joint ventures on the market for rail transport. The Commission found, nonetheless, that the agreements qualified for an exemption under Article 101(3) TFEU, on condition that the railway companies who were party to the ENS agreements should supply the same necessary rail services as they have agreed to supply to ENS to third parties. (IV/34.600—*Night Services*). On appeal ENS challenged, among other things, the Commission's analysis as regards restrictions of competition under Article 101(1) TFEU.

Held

When assessing an agreement under Article 101(1) TFEU, 'account should be taken of the actual conditions in which it functions, in particular the economic context in which the undertakings operate, the products or services covered by the agreement and the actual structure of the market concerned, ... unless it is an agreement containing obvious restrictions of competition such as price-fixing, market-sharing or the control of outlets. ... In the latter case, such restrictions may be weighed against their claimed pro-competitive effects only in the context of [Article 101(3) TFEU], with a view to granting an exemption from the prohibition in [Article 101(1) TFEU].' (para 136)

'It must also be stressed that the examination of conditions of competition is based not only on existing competition between undertakings already present on the relevant market but also on potential competition, in order to ascertain whether, in the light of the structure of the market and the economic and legal context within which it functions, there are real concrete possibilities for the undertakings concerned to compete among themselves or for a new competitor to penetrate the relevant market and compete with the undertakings already established.' (para 137)

In this case the Commission failed to make a correct and adequate assessment of the economic and legal context in which the ENS agreements were concluded. It therefore did not demonstrate that the agreements restrict competition within the meaning of Article 101(1) TFEU and therefore need to be exempted under Article 101(3) TFEU. (paras 138–60)

Commission decision annulled.

Comment

The agreements in this case did not contain restrictions which by their nature are regarded as having the object of restricting competition; therefore the Commission was expected to conduct a more thorough evaluation and take into consideration the economic and legal context in which the ENS agreements were concluded.

In its judgment the General Court provided a few examples of agreements which by their nature can be regarded as having the object of restricting competition. These include 'price-fixing, market-sharing or the control of outlets' (para 136). Note, however, that the object 'tag' is not absolute and in some instances the courts and Commission may find a seemingly 'hard-core' restriction not to amount to 'object'. See for example Case C-306/96 *Javico v Yves St Laurent* (page 180 below), and Case COMP/29.373 *Visa International—Multilateral Interchange Fee* (page 136 below). Also note paragraphs 21–3, Commission Guidelines on the Application of [Article 101(3) TFEU] [2004] OJ C101/97 which discuss restrictions of competition by object.

Stergios Delimitis v Henninger Bräu AG	**Article 101 TFEU**
Case C-234/89	Object or Effect
Court of Justice, [1991] ECR I-935, [1992] 5 CMLR 210	Beer Supply Agreements

Facts

A reference for a preliminary ruling to the Court of Justice by the Higher Regional Court in Frankfurt concerning the legality of a beer supply agreement. The case concerned a financial dispute between Delimitis, a former licensee of a public house, and the brewery, Henninger Bräu AG. The agreement between the parties required Delimitis to obtain a minimum quantity of beer and soft drinks from the brewery and its subsidiaries. Failure to reach the minimum quantity resulted in a penalty for non-performance. On termination of the agreement the brewery refused to return the full deposit to Delimitis and deducted sums of money it considered owed to it. Delimitis challenged the deduction made by the brewery and brought proceedings against it before the Regional Court. In support of its claim, it contended, among other things, that the contract was void by virtue of Article 101(2) TFEU. Following an appeal, the case reached the Higher Regional Court, which referred it to the Court of Justice for a preliminary ruling on the compatibility of the beer supply agreements with Union competition rules.

Held

The beer supply agreements in this case do not have as their object the restriction of competition within the meaning of Article 101(1) TFEU. Subsequently it is for the Court to consider whether they have the effect of preventing, restricting or distorting competition. (paras 10–13)

The effects of the beer supply agreement have to be assessed in the context in which they occur. When the agreement is part of a larger web of similar contracts the cumulative effect on competition needs to be considered. Consequently, it is necessary to analyse the effects of the cumulative effect on the opportunities of national competitors or those from other Member States, to gain access to the market for beer consumption or to increase their market share and, accordingly, the effects on the range of products offered to consumers. (paras 14, 15)

In order to ascertain the effects of the agreement one first needs to define the relevant market on the basis of the nature of the economic activity in question, in this case the sale of beer. In this case the market is the one for the distribution of beer in premises for the sale and consumption of drinks in Germany. (paras 16–18)

Following the definition of the market, one needs to assess whether the existence of several beer supply agreements impedes access to the market. 'The effect of those networks of contracts on access to the market depends specifically on the number of outlets thus tied to national producers in relation to the number of public houses which are not so tied, the duration of the commitments entered into, the quantities of beer to which those commitments relate, and on the proportion between those quantities and the quantities sold by free distributors.' (para 19)

The existence of a web of similar contracts, even if it has a considerable effect on the access to the market, is only one of the factors that needs to be taken into account and cannot in itself support a finding that the relevant market is inaccessible. (para 20)

One factor to be taken into account is the opportunity for access. The court needs to consider whether a new competitor could enter the market by acquiring a brewery already established on the market or by opening new public houses. 'For that purpose it is necessary to have regard to the legal rules and agreements on the acquisition of companies and the establishment of outlets, and to the minimum number of outlets necessary for the economic operation of a distribution system. The presence of beer wholesalers not tied to producers who are active on the market is also a factor capable of facilitating a new producer's access to that market since he can make use of those wholesalers' sales networks to distribute his own beer.' (para 21)

Another factor to be taken into account is the conditions under which competitive forces operate on the relevant market. For this purpose it is necessary to consider the number and size of the competitors, the level of market concentration and customer fidelity to existing brands. (para 22)

'If an examination of all similar contracts entered into on the relevant market and the other factors relevant to the economic and legal context in which the contract must be examined shows that those agreements do not have the cumulative effect of denying access to that market to new national and foreign competitors, the individual agreements comprising the bundle of agreements cannot be held to restrict competition within the meaning of [Article 101(1) TFEU]. They do not, therefore, fall under the prohibition laid down in that provision.' (para 23)

'If, on the other hand, such examination reveals that it is difficult to gain access to the relevant market, it is necessary to assess the extent to which the agreements entered into by the brewery in question contribute to the cumulative effect produced in that respect by the totality of the similar contracts found on that market. Under the [Union] rules on competition, responsibility for such an effect of closing off the market must be attributed to the breweries which make an appreciable contribution thereto. Beer supply agreements entered into by breweries whose contribution to the cumulative effect is insignificant do not therefore fall under the prohibition under [Article 101(1) TFEU].' (para 24)

The contribution of the individual agreement in question to the cumulative sealing-off effect depends on several factors, including the market position of the contracting parties, the number of outlets tied to the brewery in relation to the total number of public houses in the relevant market and the duration of the agreement in relation to the average duration of other beer supply agreements. 'A brewery with a relatively small market share which ties its sales outlets for many years may make as significant a contribution to a sealing-off of the market as a brewery in a relatively strong market position which regularly releases sales outlets at shorter intervals.' (paras 25, 26)

Comment

The analysis in this case was influenced by the characteristics of the beer supply market. It was therefore divided into two stages; first, the Court considered the sealing-off effect brought about by the totality of the beer distribution agreements. Following this, the contribution of the agreement to the foreclosure of the market was considered.

The Court of Justice was concerned with the sealing-off effect the agreement might generate. The Commission Guidelines on Vertical Restraints, [2010] OJ C130/1, elaborate on the potential negative effects of vertical restraints (paras 100–05). Of main concern is the risk that the vertical agreement would lead to market foreclosure by raising barriers to entry and reducing inter-brand competition.

Note that '[f]or most vertical restraints, competition concerns can only arise if there is insufficient competition at one or more levels of trade, that is, if there is some degree of market power at the level of the supplier or the buyer or at both levels. Vertical restraints are generally less harmful than horizontal restraints and may provide substantial scope for efficiencies.' (para 6, Guidelines on Vertical Restraints)

Contrast the analysis in this case with the one in *Consten and Grundig* in terms of both the finding of object and the focus on inter- or intra-brand competition (page 93 above). Note that there, the distribution agreement led to absolute territorial protection and was held to have the object of restricting competition.

Competition Authority v Beef Industry Development Society	**Article 101 TFEU**
Case C-209/07	Object or Effect
Court of Justice, [2008] ECR I-8637, [2009] 4 CMLR 6	Crisis Cartel

Facts

A reference for a preliminary ruling from the Irish Supreme Court concerning the interpretation of the notion of restriction of competition by object. The question arose in the context of overcapacity in the Irish beef industry and the alleged illegality of agreements which aimed to address this overcapacity.

Held

'In deciding whether an agreement is prohibited by [Article 101(1) TFEU], there is therefore no need to take account of its actual effects once it appears that its object is to prevent, restrict or distort competition within the [internal] market (Joined Cases 56/64 and 58/64 *Consten and Grundig v Commission* [1966] ECR 299, 342, and Case C-105/04P *Nederlandse Federatieve Vereniging voor de Groothandel op Elektrotechnisch Gebied v Commission* [2006] ECR I-8725, paragraph 125). That examination must be made in the light of the agreement's content and economic context (Joined Cases 29/83 and 30/83 *Compagnie royale asturienne des mines and Rheinzink v Commission* [1984] ECR 1679, paragraph 26, and Case C-551/03P *General Motors v Commission* [2006] ECR I-3173, paragraph 66).' (para 16)

'The distinction between "infringements by object" and "infringements by effect" arises from the fact that certain forms of collusion between undertakings can be regarded, by their very nature, as being injurious to the proper functioning of normal competition.' (para 17)

'[T]o determine whether an agreement comes within the prohibition laid down in [Article 101(1) TFEU], close regard must be paid to the wording of its provisions and to the objectives which it is intended to attain. In that regard, even supposing it to be established that the parties to an agreement acted without any subjective intention of restricting competition, but with the object of remedying the effects of a crisis in their sector, such considerations are irrelevant for the purposes of applying that provision. Indeed, an agreement may be regarded as having a restrictive object even if it does not have the restriction of competition as its sole aim but also pursues other legitimate objectives (*General Motors v Commission*, paragraph 64 and the case-law cited). It is only in connection with [Article 101(3) TFEU] that matters such as those relied upon by BIDS may, if appropriate, be taken into consideration for the purposes of obtaining an exemption from the prohibition laid down in [Article 101(1) TFEU].' (para 21)

Comment

The Court of Justice concluded that the agreement in question, between the ten principal beef and veal processors in Ireland, which included provisions for the reduction of 25 per cent in processing capacity, had as its object the prevention, restriction or distortion of competition.

In her opinion, Advocate General Trstenjak, noted the open-ended nature of the 'object category': 'It follows from the alternative relationship between the object and the effect of restrictions of competition … and from the fact that [Article 101(1) TFEU], as regards the alternative of restriction of competition by object, is designed as a form of inchoate offence that regard is to be had not solely to the necessary consequences of an agreement. The intentions of the parties to an agreement may also be taken into account. … In the light of the foregoing, it is clear that the category of restrictions of competition by object cannot be reduced to agreements which obviously restrict competition. If not only the content of an agreement but also its legal and economic context must be taken into account, classification as a restriction of competition by object cannot depend on whether that object is clear at first sight or becomes evident only on closer examination of the circumstances and the intentions of the parties. In my view, the notion of restriction of competition by object cannot be reduced to an exhaustive list either. … Nor can the notion of restriction of competition by object be reduced to price-fixing, market-sharing or the control of outlets.' (paras 46–49)

T-Mobile Netherlands and Others	**Article 101 TFEU**
Case C-8/08	Object or Effect
Court of Justice, [2009] ECR I-4529, [2009] 5 CMLR 11	Exchange of Information

Facts

A reference for a preliminary ruling which was made in proceedings between T-Mobile Netherlands BV ('T-Mobile') and the Netherlands competition authority concerning fines imposed on T-Mobile and other undertakings for infringing Article 101 TFEU by exchanging confidential information and coordinating their market conduct. In its reference to the Court of Justice, the national court requested clarification as to the criteria which apply when assessing whether a concerted practice has as its object the prevention, restriction or distortion of competition within the internal market.

Held

The criteria for establishing whether conduct has as its object or effect the prevention, restriction or distortion of competition are applicable irrespective of whether the case entails an agreement, a decision or a concerted practice. (para 24)

An anti-competitive object and anti-competitive effects constitute alternative conditions. The distinction between 'infringements by object' and 'infringements by effect' arises from the fact that certain forms of collusion between undertakings can be regarded, by their very nature, as being injurious to the proper functioning of normal competition. There is no need to consider the actual effects of a concerted practice where its anti-competitive object is established. (paras 26–30)

As pointed out by the Advocate General at point 46 of her Opinion, 'in order for a concerted practice to be regarded as having an anti-competitive object, it is sufficient that it has the potential to have a negative impact on competition. In other words, the concerted practice must simply be capable in an individual case, having regard to the specific legal and economic context, of resulting in the prevention, restriction or distortion of competition within the [internal] market. Whether and to what extent, in fact, such anti-competitive effects result can only be of relevance for determining the amount of any fine and assessing any claim for damages.' (para 31)

With regard to the exchange of information between competitors, as was in this case, 'it should be recalled that the criteria of coordination and cooperation necessary for determining the existence of a concerted practice are to be understood in the light of the notion inherent in the Treaty provisions on competition, according to which each economic operator must determine independently the policy which he intends to adopt on the [internal] market (see *Suiker Unie and Others v Commission*, paragraph 173; Case 172/80 *Züchner* [1981] ECR 2021, paragraph 13; *Ahlström Osakeyhtiö and Others v Commission*, paragraph 63; and Case C-7/95 P *Deere v Commission* [1998] ECR I-3111, paragraph 86).' (para 32)

'While it is correct to say that this requirement of independence does not deprive economic operators of the right to adapt themselves intelligently to the existing or anticipated conduct of their competitors, it does, none the less, strictly preclude any direct or indirect contact between such operators by which an undertaking may influence the conduct on the market of its actual or potential competitors or disclose to them its decisions or intentions concerning its own conduct on the market where the object or effect of such contact is to create conditions of competition which do not correspond to the normal conditions of the market in question, regard being had to the nature of the products or services offered, the size and number of the undertakings involved and the volume of that market (see, to that effect, *Suiker Unie and Others v Commission*, paragraph 174; *Züchner*, paragraph 14; and *Deere v Commission*, paragraph 87).' (para 33)

'At paragraphs 88 et seq. of *Deere v Commission*, the Court therefore held that on a highly concentrated oligopolistic market, such as the market in the main proceedings, the exchange of information was such as to enable traders to know the market positions and strategies of their competitors and thus to impair appreciably the competition which exists between traders.' (para 34)

'It follows that the exchange of information between competitors is liable to be incompatible with the competition rules if it reduces or removes the degree of uncertainty as to the operation of the market in question, with the result that competition between undertakings is restricted (see *Deere v Commission*, paragraph 90, and Case C-194/99P *Thyssen Stahl v Commission* [2003] ECR I-10821, paragraph 81).' (para 35)

'As to whether a concerted practice may be regarded as having an anti-competitive object even though there is no direct connection between that practice and consumer prices, it is not possible on the basis of the wording of [Article 101(1) TFEU] to conclude that only concerted practices which have a direct effect on the prices paid by end users are prohibited.' (para 36)

'On the contrary, it is apparent from [Article 101(1)(a) TFEU] that concerted practices may have an anti-competitive object if they "directly or indirectly fix purchase or selling prices or any other trading conditions". In the present case, as the Netherlands Government submitted in its written observations, as far as concerns postpaid subscriptions, the remuneration paid to dealers is evidently a decisive factor in fixing the price to be paid by the end user.'

'In any event, … [Article 101 TFEU] like the other competition rules of the Treaty, is designed to protect not only the immediate interests of individual competitors or consumers but also to protect the structure of the market and thus competition as such.' (paras 37–8)

Comment

In order to find that a concerted practice has an anti-competitive object, there does not need to be a direct link between that practice and consumer prices. The Court held that for a finding of 'object' it is sufficient that the practice 'has the potential to have a negative impact on competition.' (para 31) Contrast this approach with the more restrictive approach in Case C-67/13P *Groupement des Cartes Bancaires (CB) v Commission* (page 110 below), where the Court emphasised the need to establish a 'sufficient degree of harm'.

An exchange of information between competitors is tainted with an anti-competitive object if it is capable of removing uncertainties concerning the intended conduct of the participating undertakings. See further discussion in Chapter 4 below.

In her opinion, Advocate General Kokott noted that 'the criteria from which to develop a presumption of an anti-competitive object are the content and objectives of the concerted practice, subject to the proviso that the subjective intentions of the parties are at best indicative but not decisive in the matter. Account must be taken also of the economic and legal context in which the concerted practice arises.' (para 39) She then added that 'it goes too far to make the finding of an anti-competitive object dependent on an actual determination of the presence or absence of an anti-competitive impact in an individual case, irrespective of whether that impact relates to competitors, consumers or the general public. Instead, for the prohibition of [Article 101(1) TFEU] to be triggered it is sufficient that a concerted practice has the potential—on the basis of existing experience— to produce a negative impact on competition. In other words, the concerted practice must simply be *capable in an individual case*, that is, having regard to the specific legal and economic context, of resulting in the prevention, restriction or distortion of competition within the [internal] market. Whether and to what extent, in fact, such anti-competitive effects result can at most be of relevance for determining the amount of any fine and in relation to claims for damages.' (para 46) 'Ultimately, therefore, the prohibition on "infringements of competition by object" resulting from [Article 101(1) TFEU] is comparable to the risk offences (*Gefährdungsdelikte*) known in criminal law: in most legal systems, a person who drives a vehicle when significantly under the influence of alcohol or drugs is liable to a criminal or administrative penalty, wholly irrespective of whether, in fact, he endangered another road user or was even responsible for an accident. In the same vein, undertakings infringe European competition law and may be subject to a fine if they engage in concerted practices with an anti-competitive object; whether in an individual case, in fact, particular market participants or the general public suffer harm is irrelevant.' (para 47) 'The correct position, as I set out above, is that a finding of an anti-competitive object does not depend on an assessment of the actual impact of a concerted practice but simply the *capacity in an individual case* for that concerted practice to produce an anti-competitive impact.' (para 49)

GlaxoSmithKline Services Unlimited v Commission	**Article 101 TFEU**
Case C-501/06P etc	Object or Effect
Court of Justice, [2009] ECR I-9291, [2010] 4 CMLR 2	Parallel Trade

Facts

GlaxoSmithKline (GSK), formerly Glaxo Wellcome, SA (GW), a producer of pharmaceutical products, notified the Commission of a 'General Sales Conditions' document it issued to its Spanish wholesalers. The document included in Clause 4 a 'dual pricing mechanism' which resulted in a distinction between prices charged from wholesalers for medicines sold domestically and higher prices charged in the case of exports to other Member States. The Commission found the document to constitute an agreement. In addition it observed that the Court of Justice and the General Court always have qualified agreements containing export bans, dual-pricing systems or other limitations of parallel trade as restricting competition 'by object'. It therefore found Clause 4 to have both the object and the effect of restricting competition by limiting parallel trade between Spain and other Member States.

GSK appealed to the General Court, challenging, among other things, the finding of an agreement between undertakings, the existence of anticompetitive object and effect, and the Commission's refusal to exempt the agreement under Article 101(3) TFEU. (Case T-168/01, General Court, [2006] ECR II-2969 5 CMLR 29) On appeal the General Court took account of the exceptional characteristics of the pharmaceuticals sector which meant that prices of medicines were to a large extent shielded from the free forces of supply and demand due to state regulations. In such circumstances the General Court considered it impossible to infer merely from a reading of the terms of the agreement that it has the object of restricting competition.

The General Court subsequently held that agreements which ultimately seek to prohibit parallel trade must in principle be regarded as having the restriction of competition as their object. Similarly, agreements that clearly intend to treat parallel trade unfavourably must in principle be regarded as having the restriction of competition as their object. Yet, in this case, having regard to the legal and economic context, 'the Commission could not rely on the mere fact that Clause 4 of the General Sales Conditions established a system of differentiated price intended to limit parallel trade as the basis for its conclusion that that provision had as its object the restriction of competition.' (paras 115–17) 'Consequently, while it is accepted that an agreement intended to limit parallel trade must in principle be considered to have as its object the restriction of competition, that applies in so far as the agreement may be presumed to deprive final consumers of those advantages.' (para 121)

The Commission and GSK appealed to the Court of Justice.

Held

'[I]t must be borne in mind that the anti-competitive object and effect of an agreement are not cumulative but alternative conditions for assessing whether such an agreement comes within the scope of the prohibition laid down in [Article 101(1) TFEU]. According to settled case-law since the judgment in Case 56/65 *LTM* [1966] ECR 235, the alternative nature of that condition, indicated by the conjunction "or", leads first to the need to consider the precise purpose of the agreement, in the economic context in which it is to be applied. Where, however, the analysis of the content of the agreement does not reveal a sufficient degree of harm to competition, the consequences of the agreement should then be considered and for it to be caught by the prohibition it is necessary to find that those factors are present which show that competition has in fact been prevented, restricted or distorted to an appreciable extent. It is also apparent from the case-law that it is not necessary to examine the effects of an agreement once its anti-competitive object has been established (see, to that effect, Case C-8/08 *T-Mobile Netherlands and Others* [2009] ECR I-0000, paragraphs 28 and 30).' (para 55)

'According to settled case-law, in order to assess the anti-competitive nature of an agreement, regard must be had inter alia to the content of its provisions, the objectives it seeks to attain and the economic and legal context of which it forms a part (see, to that effect, Joined Cases 96/82 to 102/82, 104/82, 105/82, 108/82 and 110/82 *IAZ International Belgium and Others v Commission* [1983] ECR 3369, paragraph 25, and Case C-209/07 *Beef Industry Development Society and Barry Brothers* [2008] ECR I-0000, paragraphs 16 and 21).

In addition, although the parties' intention is not a necessary factor in determining whether an agreement is restrictive, there is nothing prohibiting the Commission or the [Union] judicature from taking that aspect into account (see, to that effect, *IAZ International Belgium and Others v Commission*, cited above, paragraphs 23 to 25).' (para 58)

With respect to parallel trade, the court has already held that, in principle, agreements aimed at prohibiting or limiting parallel trade have as their object the prevention of competition. On a number of occasions the court has held agreements aimed at partitioning national markets according to national borders or making the interpenetration of national markets more difficult, in particular those aimed at preventing or restricting parallel exports, to be agreements whose object is to restrict competition (Joined Cases C-468/06 to C-478/06 *Sot Lélos kai Sia and Others* [2008] ECR I-7139). (paras 59–61)

'With respect to the [General Court's] statement that, while it is accepted that an agreement intended to limit parallel trade must in principle be considered to have as its object the restriction of competition, that applies in so far as it may be presumed to deprive final consumers of the advantages of effective competition in terms of supply or price, the Court notes that neither the wording of [Article 101(1) TFEU] nor the case-law lend support to such a position.' (para 62)

'First of all, there is nothing in that provision to indicate that only those agreements which deprive consumers of certain advantages may have an anti-competitive object. Secondly, it must be borne in mind that the Court has held that, like other competition rules laid down in the Treaty, [Article 101 TFEU] aims to protect not only the interests of competitors or of consumers, but also the structure of the market and, in so doing, competition as such. Consequently, for a finding that an agreement has an anti-competitive object, it is not necessary that final consumers be deprived of the advantages of effective competition in terms of supply or price (see, by analogy, *T-Mobile Netherlands and Others*, cited above, paragraphs 38 and 39).' (para 63)

'It follows that, by requiring proof that the agreement entails disadvantages for final consumers as a prerequisite for a finding of anti-competitive object and by not finding that that agreement had such an object, the [General Court] committed an error of law.' (para 64) However, in this instance the operative part of the General Court judgment appears to be well founded on other legal grounds and it therefore need not be set aside. Accordingly, GSK's appeal must be dismissed as unfounded in so far as it seeks to establish that the agreement was compatible with Article 101(1) TFEU. (paras 65–7)

Comment

The Court of Justice held that for a finding that an agreement has an anti-competitive object, it is not necessary that final consumers be deprived of the advantages of effective competition in terms of supply or price. It therefore found the General Court committed an error in law by requiring proof that the agreement entails disadvantages for final consumers as a prerequisite for a finding of anti-competitive object. The judgment aims to bring back the concept of 'object' to its former scope, as it was before the General Court decision. Accordingly, the Court of Justice held that there is no requirement of proof of disadvantage to final consumer in order to establish anticompetitive object. Unfortunately, in its attempt to correct the scope of 'object', the Court of Justice judgment makes vague references to the 'interests of competitors' and to the protection of the 'structure of the market' under Article 101 TFEU. (para 63) In doing so the Court seems to have 'over-corrected' and triggered uncertainties as to the notion of 'object'.

The Court of Justice's approach as highlighted in para 63 is formalistic. It differs from the General Court's approach which reviewed the economic effect when considering the 'object' of an agreement. Some may view this formalism as a step back in the sophistication of competition law enforcement.

Note, that as a matter of principle, any agreement, having an object or effect, may be exempted under Article 101(3) TFEU. See Case T-17/93 *Matra Hachette SA v Commission* [1994] ECR II-595.

O2 (Germany) GmbH & Co OHG v Commission	**Article 101 TFEU**
Case T-328/03	Object or Effect
General Court, [2006] ECR II-1231, [2006] 5 CMLR 5	Rule of Reason

Facts

O2 (Germany) GmbH & Co OHG (O2) and T-Mobile Deutschland GmbH (T-Mobile), two operators of digital mobile telecommunications networks, entered into an infrastructure sharing agreement in Germany for third-generation GSM mobile telecommunications. Following the notification of the agreement, the Commission found no grounds for action with respect to the site sharing agreement between the parties but raised concerns as to the compatibility of the provisions relating to national roaming between network operators with Article 101(1) TFEU. In its decision the Commission granted exemption to the provisions for limited periods under Article 101(3) TFEU. O2 appealed the decision to the General Court, contesting, among other things, the finding that the provisions relating to national roaming restricted competition between the operators.

Held

'In order to assess whether an agreement is compatible with the [internal] market in the light of the prohibition laid down in [Article 101(1) TFEU], it is necessary to examine the economic and legal context in which the agreement was concluded (Case 22/71 *Beguelin Import* [1971] ECR 949, paragraph 13), its object, its effects, and whether it affects intra-[Union] trade taking into account in particular the economic context in which the undertakings operate, the products or services covered by the agreement, and the structure of the market concerned and the actual conditions in which it functions (Case C-399/93 *Oude Luttikhuis and others* [1995] ECR I-4515, paragraph 10).' (para 66)

'That method of analysis is of general application and is not confined to a category of agreements (see, as regards different types of agreements, Case 56/65 *Société Technique Minière* [1966] ECR 235, at 249–250; Case C-250/92 *DLG* [1994] ECR I5641, paragraph 31; Case T-35/92 *John Deere v Commission* [1994] ECR I-957, paragraphs 51 and 52; and Joined Cases T-374/94, T-375/94, T-384/94 and T-388/94 *European Night Services and others v Commission* [1998] ECR II-3141, paragraphs 136 and 137).' (para 67)

'Moreover, in a case such as this, where it is accepted that the agreement does not have as its object a restriction of competition, the effects of the agreement should be considered, and for it to be caught by the prohibition it is necessary to find that those factors are present which show that competition has in fact been prevented or restricted or distorted to an appreciable extent. The competition in question must be understood within the actual context in which it would occur in the absence of the agreement in dispute; the interference with competition may in particular be doubted if the agreement seems really necessary for the penetration of a new area by an undertaking (*Société Technique Minière* at 249–250).' (para 68)

'Such a method of analysis, as regards in particular the taking into account of the competition situation that would exist in the absence of the agreement, does not amount to carrying out an assessment of the pro- and anti-competitive effects of the agreement and thus to applying a rule of reason, which the [Union] judicature has not deemed to have its place under [Article 101(1) TFEU] (Case C-235/92P *Montecatini v Commission* [1999] ECR I-4539, paragraph 133; *M6 and others v Commission*, paragraphs 72 to 77; and Case T-65/98 *Van den Bergh Foods v Commission* [2002] ECR II-4653, paragraphs 106 and 107).' (para 69)

'In this respect, to submit, as the applicant does, that the Commission failed to carry out a full analysis by not examining what the competitive situation would have been in the absence of the agreement does not mean that an assessment of the positive and negative effects of the agreement from the point of view of competition must be carried out at the stage of [Article 101(1) TFEU]. Contrary to the defendant's interpretation of the applicant's arguments, the applicant relies only on the method of analysis required by settled case-law.' (para 70)

'The examination required in the light of [Article 101(1) TFEU] consists essentially in taking account of the impact of the agreement on existing and potential competition (see, to that effect, Case C-234/89 *Delimitis* [1991] ECR I-935, paragraph 21) and the competition situation in the absence of the agreement (*Société Technique Minière* at 249–250), those two factors being intrinsically linked.' (para 71)

'The examination of competition in the absence of an agreement appears to be particularly necessary as regards markets undergoing liberalisation or emerging markets, as in the case of the 3G mobile communications market here at issue, where effective competition may be problematic owing, for example, to the presence of a dominant operator, the concentrated nature of the market structure or the existence of significant barriers to entry—factors referred to, in the present case, in the Decision.' (para 72)

'In order to take account of the two parts which this plea actually contains, it is therefore necessary to examine, first, whether the Commission did in fact consider what the competition situation would have been in the absence of the agreement and, second, whether the conclusions which it drew from its examination of the impact of the agreement on competition are sufficiently substantiated.' (para 73)

'It follows from the foregoing that the [Commission's Decision], in so far as it concerns the application of [Article 101(1) TFEU] and Article 53(1) of the EEA Agreement, suffers from insufficient analysis, first, in that it contains no objective discussion of what the competition situation would have been in the absence of the agreement, which distorts the assessment of the actual and potential effects of the agreement on competition and, second, in that it does not demonstrate, in concrete terms, in the context of the relevant emerging market, that the provisions of the agreement on roaming have restrictive effects on competition, but is confined, in this respect, to a "petitio principii" and to broad and general statements.' (para 116)

Comment

Note the General Court's clear comment in paragraph 69 regarding the scope of analysis under Article 101(1) TFEU. The court held that the examination of effect under Article 101(1) TFEU 'as regards in particular the taking into account of the competition situation that would exist in the absence of the agreement, does not amount to carrying out an assessment of the pro-and anti-competitive effects of the agreement and thus to applying a rule of reason, which the [Union] judicature has not deemed to have its place under Article 101(1) TFEU.'

Allianz Hungária Biztosító Zrt and others v Gazdasági Versenyhivatal	**Article 101 TFEU**
Case C-32/11	Object or Effect
Court of Justice, [2013] 4 CMLR 25	Vertical Agreements

Facts

A request for a preliminary ruling concerning the interpretation of Article 101 TFEU and its application to agreements between Hungarian insurance companies and authorised dealers operating auto repair shops. Under the agreements in question (1) the parties agreed in advance on the rates applicable to repair services payable by the insurer in the case of accidents involving insured vehicles, and (2) the parties agreed that the dealers would act as intermediaries for the insurers by offering car insurance to their customers. According to the agreement, the hourly repair charge was linked to the number of insurance policies signed, thus incentivising the dealers to increase the sale efforts to their clients.

The Hungarian competition authority found that the agreements, considered together and individually, had the object of restricting competition in the car insurance contracts market and the car repair services market. That finding was contested and the proceedings eventually reached the Hungarian Supreme Court. In its preliminary reference to the Court of Justice the Court asked whether bilateral agreements between an insurance company and individual car repairers under which the hourly repair charge paid by the insurance company depends, among other things, on the number and percentage of insurance policies sold by the repairer, acting as the insurance broker for the insurance company, are anticompetitive by object.

Held

'The distinction between "infringements by object" and "infringements by effect" arises from the fact that certain forms of collusion between undertakings can be regarded, by their very nature, as being injurious to the proper functioning of normal competition.' (para 33)

'In order to determine whether an agreement involves a restriction of competition "by object" regard must be had to the content of its provisions, its objectives and the economic and legal context of which it forms a part (see *GlaxoSmithKline Services and Others v Commission and Others*, paragraph 58; *Football Association Premier League and Others*, paragraph 136; and *Pierre Fabre Dermo-Cosmétique*, paragraph 35). When determining that context, it is also appropriate to take into consideration the nature of the goods or services affected, as well as the real conditions of the functioning and structure of the market or markets in question (see *Expedia*, paragraph 21 and the case-law cited).' (para 36)

'[I]n order for the agreement to be regarded as having an anti-competitive object, it is sufficient that it has the potential to have a negative impact on competition, that is to say, that it be capable in an individual case of resulting in the prevention, restriction or distortion of competition within the internal market. Whether and to what extent, in fact, such an effect results can only be of relevance for determining the amount of any fine and assessing any claim for damages (see *T-Mobile Netherlands and Others*, paragraph 31).' (para 38)

The agreements referred to in the question submitted provide that the hourly charge will increase in accordance with the number and percentage of insurance contracts sold by the dealer. The agreements link the remuneration for the car repair service to that for the car insurance brokerage. That link does not automatically mean that the agreement concerned has as its object the restriction of competition. It can nevertheless constitute an important factor in determining the object of the agreement. It is also necessary to take account of the fact that such an agreement is likely to affect two markets—the car insurance and car repair services—and that its object must be determined with respect to the two markets concerned. In addition, the fact that the agreements are meant to maintain or increase the market shares of the insurance companies should be noted. (paras 39–43)

The fact that the agreements in this case are vertical in nature, does not exclude the possibility of them having the object of restricting competition. (paras 44–46)

'That could in particular be the case where, as is claimed by the Hungarian Government, domestic law requires that dealers acting as intermediaries or insurance brokers must be independent from the insurance companies. That government claims, in that regard, that those dealers do not act on behalf of an insurer, but on behalf of the policyholder and it is their job to offer the policyholder the insurance which is the most suitable for him amongst the offers of various insurance companies. It is for the referring court to determine whether, in those circumstances and in light of the expectations of those policyholders, the proper functioning of the car insurance market is likely to be significantly disrupted by the agreements at issue in the main proceedings.' (para 47)

'Furthermore, those agreements would also amount to a restriction of competition by object in the event that the referring court found that it is likely that, having regard to the economic context, competition on that market would be eliminated or seriously weakened following the conclusion of those agreements. In order to determine the likelihood of such a result, that court should in particular take into consideration the structure of that market, the existence of alternative distribution channels and their respective importance and the market power of the companies concerned.' (para 48)

'Finally, with regard to determining the object of the agreements at issue in the main proceedings with respect to the car repair service market, it is necessary to take account of the fact that those agreements appear to have been concluded on the basis of 'recommended prices' established in the three decisions taken by GÉMOSZ from 2003 to 2005. In that context, it is for the referring court to determine the exact nature and scope of those decisions (see, to that effect, Case C 260/07 *Pedro IV Servicios* [2009] ECR I 2437, paragraphs 78 and 79).' (para 49)

Comment

While the judgment begins with the traditional approach to establishing object restrictions (paras 33–8), it then suggests a hybrid analysis which results in de facto widening of the object category and the blurring of the dividing line between object and effect analysis (paras 48–51).

The origins of this widening approach may be traced to paragraph 36 of the judgment where the Court, when discussing the object analysis, makes reference to the *Expedia* judgment (page 116 below) and states that when determining the object of the agreement 'it is also appropriate to take into consideration the nature of the goods or services affected, as well as the real conditions of the functioning and structure of the market or markets in question.' The reference to the *Expedia* judgment and the analysis of the 'real functioning and structure of the market' is odd and misplaced. That judgment deals with the de minimis doctrine and as such should not have been used to establish the nature of object analysis. Despite this, the Court's reference to the *Expedia* judgment enabled it to adopt a liberal reading of the *T-Mobile* judgment, according to which it is sufficient to establish a potential to have a negative impact on competition for the finding of anticompetitive object. Following this, in paragraph 48 the Court puts forward its new formula and suggests that when the anticompetitive object is not apparent, one should take into consideration 'the structure of that market, the existence of alternative distribution channels and their respective importance and the market power of the companies concerned.' Worryingly, that proposition blurs the distinction between object and effect analysis. It calls for an effects analysis in order to establish the presence of object.

In paragraph 47, the Court links the finding of an anticompetitive object to the possible illegality of a conduct under national legislation that requires insurance brokers to be independent from the insurance companies. That statement is controversial as it suggests that illegality under competition law is affected by the infringement of non-competition related provisions. That approach, if followed, is likely to increase the likelihood of finding of object violations in regulated markets.

In Case C-67/13P, *CB v Commission* (page 110 below) Advocate General Wahl discussed how *Allianz* blurs the distinction between restrictions by object and by effect, and called for greater clarity. In its judgment, the Court held that the concept of object is narrow in nature and must be interpreted restrictively, when a 'sufficient degree of harm' to competition is revealed, following consideration of the economic and legal context.

Protimonopolný úrad Slovenskej republiky v Slovenská sporiteľňa as	Article 101 TFEU
Case C-68/12	Object or Effect
Court of Justice, [2013] 4 CMLR 16	Illegality

Facts

Request for a preliminary ruling from the Supreme Court of the Slovak Republic, concerning three banks which the Competition Council found had infringed Article 101 TFEU by entering into an agreement to terminate contracts with one of their customers—Akcenta CZ as—a non-bank financial institution. In its decision, the Council found that the banks agreed to terminate their separate agreements with Akcenta as the latter competed with them and provided services to their customers on the market for cashless foreign-exchange operations. In their investigation and on appeal, the banks argued that since Akcenta operated illegally, their decision to terminate their contract with it cannot be condemned. The preliminary reference addressed, among other things, the validity of that defence argument.

Held

'Article 101 TFEU is intended to protect not only the interests of competitors or consumers but also the structure of the market and thus competition as such (Joined Cases C-501/06P, C-513/06P, C-515/06P and C-519/06P *GlaxoSmithKline Services and Others v Commission and Others* [2009] ECR I-9291, paragraph 63).' (para 18)

The alleged illegality of Akcenta's situation is irrelevant for the purpose of determining whether the conditions for an infringement of the competition rules are met. It is apparent from the order for reference that the agreement between the banks had as its object the restriction of competition and that none of the banks challenged the legality of Akcenta's business before they were investigated in the case giving rise to the main proceedings. (para 19)

'Moreover, it is for public authorities and not private undertakings or associations of undertakings to ensure compliance with statutory requirements. The Czech Government's description of Akcenta's situation is evidence enough of the fact that the application of statutory provisions may call for complex assessments which are not within the area of responsibility of those private undertakings or associations of undertakings.' (para 20)

Comment

An agreement to exclude a customer which operates illegally may infringe Article 101 TFEU. The illegality of the customer's activities does not play a mitigating role in the assessment of the anticompetitiveness of the exclusionary agreement.

It is for the state to address such illegality and for the undertaking to report it.

Note by analogy the *Hilti* judgment (page 308 below) where the Court rejected Hilti's argument that it did not abuse its dominant position by refusing to supply products. Hilti claimed that the refusal is objectively justified and stems from safety concerns. The Court held that Hilti should have approached the competent authorities which would have dealt with its concerns. It emphasised that it was not the task of an undertaking to take steps on its own initiative to eliminate products which it regards as dangerous or inferior in quality. (para 118)

Note that whereas (in this case) the illegality of a third party's conduct did not mitigate an anticompetitive agreement to exclude that third party, the illegality of an agreement under national law (other than national competition law), may increase the likelihood that the agreement infringes competition by object (see *Allianz Hungária*, page 107 above).

Groupement des Cartes Bancaires (CB) v Commission	**Article 101 TFEU**
Case C-67/13P	Object or Effect
Court of Justice	Payment Card Scheme

Facts

Groupement des Cartes Bancaires (CB) was a consortium managed by several leading French banks. The group adopted several price measures which included membership fees and charges on the use of payment cards. The tariffs were applied in a way that distinguished between the major banks which managed the CB and other banks and new members. The scheme also included 'sleeper member fees' charged to members that did not develop significant payment card business. In October 2007 the Commission reached a decision finding that the measures were anticompetitive by object and effect. They resulted in discriminatory high payments by small operators, which in turn undermined their ability to issue cards at competitive rates in France. CB applied for annulment of the Commission's decision and contested, among other things, the finding that the tariff measures were anticompetitive by object. The group argued that the measure had a legitimate objective of combating free riding. (Case T-491/07)

In its judgment, the General Court held that 'the concept of infringement by object should not be given a strict interpretation'. It further held that 'it is sufficient that the agreement or the decision of an association of undertakings has the potential to have a negative impact on competition. In other words, the agreement or decision must simply be capable in the particular case, having regard to the specific legal and economic context, of preventing, restricting or distorting competition within the common market. It is not necessary for there to be actual prevention, restriction or distortion of competition or a direct link between [that agreement or decision] and consumer prices.' (paras 124, 125)

CB appealed to the Court of Justice. In his opinion, Advocate General M Nils Wahl underlined the need to instil more clarity in the distinction between object and effect infringements, following *Allianz* (see page 107 above), and noted that object infringements should form a narrow category reserved for cases that in accordance with economic theory are always restrictive of competition. (paras 50, 52, 55, 58, AG opinion)

Held

'Certain types of coordination between undertakings can be regarded, by their very nature, as being harmful to the proper functioning of normal competition. … Consequently, it is established that certain collusive behaviour, such as that leading to horizontal price-fixing by cartels, may be considered so likely to have negative effects, in particular on the price, quantity or quality of the goods and services, that it may be considered redundant, for the purposes of applying [Article 101(1) TFEU], to prove that they have actual effects on the market. … Experience shows that such behaviour leads to falls in production and price increases, resulting in poor allocation of resources to the detriment, in particular, of consumers.' (paras 50–1)

'According to the case-law of the Court, in order to determine whether an agreement between undertakings or a decision by an association of undertakings reveals a sufficient degree of harm to competition that it may be considered a restriction of competition "by object" within the meaning of Article 81(1) EC, regard must be had to the content of its provisions, its objectives and the economic and legal context of which it forms a part. When determining that context, it is also necessary to take into consideration the nature of the goods or services affected, as well as the real conditions of the functioning and structure of the market or markets in question (see, to that effect, judgment in *Allianz Hungária Biztosító and Others* …, paragraph 36 …).' (para 53)

'In addition, although the parties' intention is not a necessary factor in determining whether an agreement between undertakings is restrictive, there is nothing prohibiting the competition authorities, the national courts or the Courts of the European Union from taking that factor into account (see judgment in *Allianz Hungária Biztosító and Others* …, paragraph 37…).' (para 54)

In defining the criteria to be taken into account to ascertain whether there was a restriction of competition 'by object' the General Court in part failed to have regard to the case-law of the Court of Justice and, therefore, erred in law. First, the General Court failed 'to have regard to the fact that the essential legal criterion for ascertaining whether coordination between undertakings involves such a restriction of competition "by object" is the finding that such coordination reveals in itself a sufficient degree of harm to competition.' (paras 56, 57)

Secondly, the General Court erred in finding, 'that the concept of restriction of competition by "object" must not be interpreted "restrictively". The concept of restriction of competition "by object" can be applied only to certain types of coordination between undertakings which reveal a sufficient degree of harm to competition that it may be found that there is no need to examine their effects, otherwise the Commission would be exempted from the obligation to prove the actual effects on the market of agreements which are in no way established to be, by their very nature, harmful to the proper functioning of normal competition. The fact that the types of agreements covered by [Article 101(1) TFEU] do not constitute an exhaustive list of prohibited collusion is, in that regard, irrelevant.' (para 58)

Although the General Court set out the reasons why the measures at issue are capable of restricting competition, it did not explain—contrary to the requirements of the case-law—how they reveal a sufficient degree of harm and amount to a restriction 'by object'. (para 60) The judgment of the General Court is set aside. The case is referred back to that court for judgment.

Comment

The Court sent a clear signal that the concept of object is narrow in nature and must be interpreted restrictively, when a 'sufficient degree of harm' to competition is revealed following consideration of the economic and legal context.

Interestingly, the judgment includes several references to Case C-32/11 *Allianz Hungária Biztosító* which arguably significantly blurred the distinction between restrictions by object and by effect. Despite this odd referencing, the *Groupement des Cartes Bancaires* judgment puts forward a more restrictive approach to the scope of the 'object' concept.

Similarly, the judgment advances a more restrictive approach than that found in *T-Mobile*, where the Court held that for a finding of 'object' it is sufficient that the practice 'has the potential to have a negative impact on competition.' (page 101 above)

That narrow approach was later reaffirmed in Case C-345/14, *SIA 'Maxima Latvija' v Konkurences padome* where the Court of Justice referred to its judgment in *CB v Commission*, holding that 'the essential legal criterion for ascertaining whether an agreement involves a restriction of competition "by object" is therefore the finding that such an agreement reveals in itself a sufficient degree of harm to competition for it to be considered that it is not appropriate to assess its effects.' (para 20) It subsequently held that restrictions in land agreements which grant the lessee the right to oppose the letting by the lessor do not amount to a restriction of competition by object. (para 24)

In its 'Guidance on restrictions of competition "by object" for the purpose of defining which agreements may benefit from the De Minimis Notice' (revised version June 2015) the Commission makes reference to the *CB v Commission* judgment and notes: 'The distinction between "restrictions by object" and "restrictions by effect" arises from the fact that certain forms of collusion between undertakings reveal such a sufficient degree of harm to competition that there is no need to examine their actual or potential effects. Such types of coordination between undertakings can be regarded, by their very nature, as being harmful to the proper functioning of normal competition. These are restrictions which in the light of the objectives pursued by the Union competition rules are so likely to have negative effects on competition, in particular on the price, quantity or quality of goods or services, that it is unnecessary to demonstrate any actual or likely anti-competitive effects on the market. This is due to the serious nature of the restriction and experience showing that such restrictions are likely to produce negative effects on the market and to jeopardise the objectives pursued by the EU Union competition rules.' (pages 3–4)

Métropole Télévision (M6) and others v Commission	**Article 101 TFEU**
Case T-112/99	Scope of Analysis
General Court, [2001] ECR II-2459, [2001] 5 CMLR 33	Rule of Reason

Facts

'Télévision Par Satellite' (TPS) was set up as a partnership by six major companies active in the television sector. Its aim was to devise, develop and broadcast a range of television programmes, against payment, to French-speaking television viewers in Europe. The agreements forming the TPS partnership were notified to the Commission in order to obtain negative clearance and/or exemption. In its decision the Commission did not object to the creation of TPS. However, the Commission raised concerns with respects to the impact of non-competition, exclusivity and other clauses in the agreement and subsequently granted limited negative clearance and exemption.

With reference to the non-competition clause the Commission held that there were no grounds for action in respect of that clause for a period of three years. With regard to an exclusivity clause and the clause relating to special-interest channels, the Commission held that those provisions could benefit from an exemption under Article 101(3) TFEU for a period of three years. (Case No IV/36.237—*TPS*)

The applicants challenged the Commission's decision and the limited period for which negative clearance and exemption were granted. Among other things, the applicants argued that the Commission failed to apply a rule of reason when considering the agreements under Article 101(1) TFEU.

Held

'[Article 101 TFEU] expressly provides, in its third paragraph, for the possibility of exempting agreements that restrict competition where they satisfy a number of conditions, in particular where they are indispensable to the attainment of certain objectives and do not afford undertakings the possibility of eliminating competition in respect of a substantial part of the products in question. It is only in the precise framework of that provision that the pro and anti-competitive aspects of a restriction may be weighed (see, to that effect, Case 161/84 *Pronuptia* [1986] ECR 353, paragraph 24, and Case T-17/93 *Matra Hachette v Commission* [1994] ECR II-595, paragraph 48, and *European Night Services and others v Commission*, [[1998] ECR II-3141], paragraph 136). [Article 101(3) TFEU] of the Treaty would lose much of its effectiveness if such an examination had to be carried out already under [Article 101(1) TFEU].' (para 74)

'It is true that in a number of judgments the Court of Justice and the [General Court] have favoured a more flexible interpretation of the prohibition laid down in [Article 101(1) TFEU] (see, in particular, *Société technique minière* and *Oude Luttikhuis and others*, [[1995] ECR I-4515, paragraph 10], *Nungesser and Eisele v Commission* and *Coditel and others*, [[1982] ECR 3381], *Pronuptia*, cited in paragraph 74 above, and *European Night Services and others v Commission*, cited in paragraph [74] above, as well as the judgment in Case C-250/92 *DLG* [1994] ECR I-5641, paragraphs 31 to 35).' (para 75)

'Those judgments cannot, however, be interpreted as establishing the existence of a rule of reason in [Union] competition law. They are, rather, part of a broader trend in the case-law according to which it is not necessary to hold, wholly abstractly and without drawing any distinction, that any agreement restricting the freedom of action of one or more of the parties is necessarily caught by the prohibition laid down in [Article 101(1) TFEU]. In assessing the applicability of [Article 101(1) TFEU] to an agreement, account should be taken of the actual conditions in which it functions, in particular the economic context in which the undertakings operate, the products or services covered by the agreement and the actual structure of the market concerned (see, in particular, *European Night Services and others v Commission*, paragraph 136, *Oude Luttikhuis*, paragraph 10, and *VGB and others v Commission*, paragraph 140, …).' (para 76)

'That interpretation, while observing the substantive scheme of [Article 101 TFEU] and, in particular, preserving the effectiveness of [Article 101(3) TFEU], makes it possible to prevent the prohibition in [Article 101(1) TFEU] from extending wholly abstractly and without distinction to all agreements whose effect is to restrict the freedom of action of one or more of the parties. It must, however, be emphasised that such an approach does not mean that it is necessary to weigh the pro and anti-competitive effects of an agreement when determining whether the prohibition laid down in [Article 101(1) TFEU] applies.' (para 77)

In this case the Commission correctly applied Article 101(1) TFEU to the exclusivity clause and the clause relating to the special-interest channels inasmuch as it was not obliged to weigh the pro- and anticompetitive aspects of those agreements outside the specific framework of Article 101(3) TFEU. (paras 78, 79)

Comment

In paragraphs 75 and 76 the General Court explained that the analysis under Article 101(1) may include some evaluation of the agreement so to avoid the conclusion that 'any agreement restricting the freedom of action of one or more of the parties is necessarily caught by the prohibition laid down in [Article 101(1) TFEU].' Such approach does not amount to a rule of reason, and is aimed at enabling the courts to apply a more flexible analysis grounded in facts rather than a wholly abstract analysis.

Note the General Court comment in Case T-17/93 *Matra Hachette SA v Commission*, [1994] ECR II-595, where it held that 'the assessment of the extent of the anti-competitive effect of an agreement for which an exemption is requested is entirely unconnected with the assessment of the substantive scope of [Article 101(1) TFEU] and must be carried out by the Commission not under [Article 101(1) TFEU] but under [Article 101(3) TFEU], in relation, in particular, to the indispensability of the restrictions of competition.' (para 48)

Note that following the coming into force of Regulation 1/2003, the national courts and national competition agencies may apply Article 101 TFEU in its entirety. Subsequently, the rule of reason debate lost much of its significance following the abolition of notifications. However, the debate is still relevant for two purposes. First, due to the shift in the burden of proof when considering Article 101(3) provisions. Secondly, as to the nature of the considerations used to counterbalance anticompetitive effects. In this respect, whereas Article 101(3) TFEU provides for a structured framework of analysis based on competitive variables, Article 101(1) TFEU does not. The latter thus allows for a more flexible framework in which a balancing exercise may take place. See for example the *Wouters* decision, page 113 below, where the Court of Justice balanced between public interest and anticompetitive effect within the framework of Article 101 TFEU.

Note Case T-328/03 *O2 (Germany) GmbH & Co OHG v Commission* (page 105 above) in which the General Court held that the analysis under Article 101(1) TFEU 'does not amount to carrying out an assessment of the pro-and anti-competitive effects of the agreement and thus to applying a rule of reason.' (para 69)

See also the discussion of ancillary restraints which includes additional references to the scope of analysis under Article 101 TFEU (pages 116–23 below).

Competition Authority v Beef Industry Development Society (BIDS)	**Article 101 TFEU**
Case C-209/07	Object or Effect
Court of Justice, [2008] ECR I-8637, [2009] 4 CMLR 6	Rule of Reason

Facts

A reference for a preliminary ruling from the Irish Supreme Court concerning the interpretation of the notion of restriction of competition by object. The question arose in the context of overcapacity in the Irish beef industry and the alleged illegality of agreements which aimed to address this overcapacity. The Court of Justice concluded that the agreement in question was anticompetitive by object (see page 100 above). The Court and the Advocate General also commented on the scope of analysis under Article 101(1) and (3) TFEU.

Held

'To determine whether an agreement comes within the prohibition laid down in [Article 101(1) TFEU], close regard must be paid to the wording of its provisions and to the objectives which it is intended to attain. In that regard, even supposing it to be established that the parties to an agreement acted without any subjective intention of restricting competition, but with the object of remedying the effects of a crisis in their sector, such considerations are irrelevant for the purposes of applying that provision. Indeed, an agreement may be regarded as having a restrictive object even if it does not have the restriction of competition as its sole aim but also pursues other legitimate objectives (*General Motors* v *Commission*, paragraph 64 and the case-law cited). It is only in connection with [Article 101(3) TFEU] that matters such [as the need to rationalise the beef industry in order to make it more competitive by reducing production overcapacity] … may, if appropriate, be taken into consideration.' (para 21)

Comment

Advocate General Trstenjak elaborated in his opinion on the scope of analysis under Articles 101(1) and 101(3) TFEU: 'It follows from the scheme of [Article 101 TFEU] that account is to be taken under [Article 101(1) TFEU] only of the elements of the legal and economic context which could cast doubt on the existence of a restriction of competition.' (para 50) 'Factors which are not capable of casting doubt on the existence of a restriction of competition, such as improvements in the production of goods as a result of economies of scale, may not be taken into account in the context of [Article 101(1) TFEU], but only in the context of [Article 101(3) TFEU], even where they are ultimately to be assessed positively in terms of an agreement's compatibility with [Article 101 TFEU]. This distinction is apparent already from the wording of [Article 101(3) TFEU], which makes clear that these kinds of effects of an agreement are to be taken into account under [Article 101(3) TFEU]. The distinction is based on the following idea: the general conception of [Article 101 TFEU] is to ensure the optimal supply of consumers. However, *different aspects* of consumer welfare are taken into account under [Article 101(1) TFEU] and under [Article 101(3) TFEU]. Under [Article 101(1) TFEU], agreements which restrict competition between market participants and thus its function of supplying consumers optimally with a product at the lowest possible price or with innovative products are prohibited in principle. Such agreements directly affect consumer welfare and as such are prohibited in principle. Nevertheless, [Article 101(3) TFEU] recognises that agreements which restrict competition between market participants result in particular in a reduction in production costs, and the reduction in production costs can contribute indirectly to consumer welfare. However, because first and foremost the reduction in production costs directly benefits producers, the compatibility of such an agreement with the common market under [Article 101(3) TFEU] is subject in particular to the condition that consumers are allowed a share of the resulting benefit. The Community legislature implemented this idea in the rules on evidence by providing that it is for the parties to an anti-competitive agreement to prove that the conditions under [Article 101(3) TFEU] are satisfied, in particular that consumers share in the benefit. For these reasons, factors which are not capable of casting doubt on the existence of a restriction of competition, in particular efficiencies in production as a result of economies of scale, may not be taken into account in the context of [Article 101(1) TFEU], but only in the context of [Article 101(3) TFEU], even where they ultimately have to be assessed positively in terms of an agreement's compatibility with [Article 101 TFEU].' (paras 55–8)

Meca-Medina and Majcen v Commission	**Article 101 TFEU**
Case C-519/04P	Scope of Analysis
Court of Justice, [2006] ECR I-6991, [2006] 5 CMLR 18	Rule of Reason/Ancillary Restraints

Facts

Mr Meca-Medina and Mr Majcen, two professional athletes, were suspended by the International Olympic Committee (IOC) for a period of four years following a positive anti-doping test for Nandrolone. The two athletes lodged a complaint with the Commission alleging that certain rules adopted by the IOC and certain practices relating to doping control were in breach of EC competition law and freedom of movement provisions. The Commission rejected their complaint. On appeal, the General Court dismissed their action for annulment of the Commission's decision (Case T-313/02) and held, with reference to competition law, that Articles 101 TFEU and 102 TFEU do not apply to purely sporting rules. An appeal to the Court of Justice raised important questions as to the application of the Treaty provisions to sports bodies' rules and with respect to exemption on the grounds of legitimate objectives.

Held

The general objective of the anti-doping rules is to combat doping in order for competitive sport to be conducted fairly. The rules safeguard equal chances for athletes, athletes' health, the integrity and objectivity of competitive sport, and ethical values in sport. (paras 43, 44)

Subsequently, 'even if the anti-doping rules at issue are to be regarded as a decision of an association of undertakings limiting the appellants' freedom of action, they do not, for all that, necessarily constitute a restriction of competition incompatible with the [internal] market, within the meaning of [Article 101 TFEU], since they are justified by a legitimate objective. Such a limitation is inherent in the organisation and proper conduct of competitive sport and its very purpose is to ensure healthy rivalry between athletes.' (para 45)

'It must be acknowledged that the penal nature of the anti-doping rules at issue and the magnitude of the penalties applicable if they are breached are capable of producing adverse effects on competition because they could, if penalties were ultimately proven to be unjustified, result in an athlete's unwarranted exclusion from sporting events, and thus in impairment of the conditions under which the activity at issue is engaged in. It follows that, in order not to be covered by the prohibition laid down in [Article 101(1) TFEU], the restrictions thus imposed by those rules must be limited to what is necessary to ensure the proper conduct of competitive sport.' (para 47) In this case the appellant failed to establish that the Commission made a manifest error of assessment in finding those rules to be justified.

The current restrictions imposed on professional sportsmen do not appear to go beyond what is necessary in order to ensure that sporting events take place and function properly. (paras 48–55)

Comment

Some commentators view this decision as one that introduces a rule of reason element to Article 101(1) TFEU, as the Court of Justice in paragraph 45 balances between the legitimate objectives of the provision and the restriction of competition. Accordingly, the decision shares similarities with Case C-309/99 *Wouters* (page 121 below), and on the other hand stands at odds with the General Court approach in Case T-112/99 *Métropole* (page 112 above) and Case T-328/03 *O2* (page 105 above).

On the other hand, one can read paragraph 45 as one which merely distinguishes between a restriction on the freedom of action and a restriction of competition, holding that the former would not necessarily result in the latter. The possible restriction of competition may then be regarded as ancillary, objectively necessary and proportionate to the anti-doping rules. (See further discussion on ancillary restraints on pages 116–23 below and in particular Case C-309/99 *Wouters*, page 121 below.)

Remia BV and Nv Verenigde Bedrijven Nutricia v Commission	**Article 101 TFEU**
Case 42/84	Ancillary Restraints
Court of Justice, [1985] ECR 2545, [1987] 1 CMLR 1	Non-Compete Obligation

Facts

Nv Verenigde Bedrijven Nutricia (Nutricia), a manufacturer of health and baby foods, transferred two of its subsidiaries, Remia and Luycks, to third parties. The agreements contained non-competition clauses intended to protect the purchasers from competition from the vendor (Nutricia) in the same market immediately after the transfers. Following the notification of the transfer agreements to the Commission, it found that the duration and scope of the restrictions were excessive, that they constituted a restriction on competition and that they were not eligible for exemption under Article 101(3) TFEU. On appeal to the Court of Justice the parties contested the decision.

Held

'It should be stated at the outset that the Commission has rightly submitted—and the applicants have not contradicted it on that point—that the fact that non-competition clauses are included in an agreement for the sale of an undertaking is not of itself sufficient to remove such clauses from the scope of [Article 101(1) TFEU].' (para 17)

'In order to determine whether or not such clauses come within the prohibition in [Article 81(1) EC], it is necessary to examine what would be the state of competition if those clauses did not exist.' (para 18)

'If that were the case, and should the vendor and the purchaser remain competitors after the transfer, it is clear that the agreement for the transfer of the undertaking could not be given effect. The vendor, with his particularly detailed knowledge of the transferred undertaking, would still be in a position to win back his former customers immediately after the transfer and thereby drive the undertaking out of business. Against that background non-competition clauses incorporated in an agreement for the transfer of an undertaking in principle have the merit of ensuring that the transfer has the effect intended. By virtue of that very fact they contribute to the promotion of competition because they lead to an increase in the number of undertakings in the market in question.' (para 19)

'Nevertheless, in order to have that beneficial effect on competition, such clauses must be necessary to the transfer of the undertaking concerned and their duration and scope must be strictly limited to that purpose. The Commission was therefore right in holding that where those conditions are satisfied such clauses are free of the prohibition laid down in [Article 101(1) EC].' (para 20)

The Commission correctly assessed the facts of the case before coming to the conclusion that the period of the prohibition agreed upon between the parties was excessive and that a shorter duration of four years was objectively justified. (paras 21–36)

The Commission did not err in its decision to refuse exemption under Article 101(3) TFEU. (paras 37–48)

Comment

The Court accepted that a non-compete clause is necessary in order to ensure the viability of the transaction and as such is procompetitive. It did, however, hold that the duration and scope of the non-compete clause need not go beyond what is necessary to facilitate the transaction.

Note also Case T-112/99 *Métropole Télévision* where the Court assessed the Commission decision concerning the creation of the Joint venture 'Television Par Satellite' (Case No IV/36.237—*TPS*) (page 119 below).

Gøttrup-Klim v Dansk Landbrugs Grovvareselskab AmbA	**Article 101 TFEU**
Case C-250/92	Ancillary Restraints
Court of Justice, [1994] ECR I-5641, [1996] 4 CMLR 191	Non-Compete Obligation

Facts

Dansk Landbrugs Grovvareselskab AmbA (DLG), a Danish cooperative association distributing farm supplies, was established to provide its members with farm supplies, including fertilisers and plant protection products, at the lowest prices. In 1975 a group of DLG members formed a national union of cooperative associations (LAG) which specialised in the distribution of farm supplies. In 1988 DLG amended its statutes because of increasing competition from LAG and excluded from its membership members who were also part of LAG. The amendment was intended to induce LAG members to stop purchasing fertilisers and plant protection products from anyone other than DLG, so that within the cooperative sector in Denmark there would be just one large association purchasing supplies on behalf of Danish farmers. This, it was hoped, would enable DLG to obtain better prices for its members. By March 1989, 37 local associations who continued their participation in LAG were excluded from DLG. These associations brought an action against DLG before the Danish court for the annulment of the amendments to the statutes. They claimed that the object or effect of the amendments to the statutes was to restrict competition, as it aimed at putting an end to members' purchasing through LAG in competition with DLG.

The Danish court referred the matter to the Court of Justice, asking, among other things, whether a provision in the statutes of a cooperative purchasing association, the effect of which is to forbid its members from participating in other forms of organised cooperation which are in direct competition with it, is caught by the prohibition in Article 101(1) TFEU.

Held

A cooperative purchasing association is a voluntary association established in order to pursue common commercial objectives. The compatibility of the statutes of such an association with the Union rules on competition cannot be assessed in the abstract. It depends on the particular clauses in the statutes and the economic conditions prevailing on the markets concerned. (paras 30, 31)

'In a market where product prices vary according to the volume of orders, the activities of cooperative purchasing associations may, depending on the size of their membership, constitute a significant counterweight to the contractual power of large producers and make way for more effective competition.' (para 32)

'Where some members of two competing cooperative purchasing associations belong to both at the same time, the result is to make each association less capable of pursuing its objectives for the benefit of the rest of its members, especially where the members concerned, as in the case in point, are themselves cooperative associations with a large number of individual members.' (para 33)

'It follows that such dual membership would jeopardize both the proper functioning of the cooperative and its contractual power in relation to producers. Prohibition of dual membership does not, therefore, necessarily constitute a restriction of competition within the meaning of [Article 101 TFEU] and may even have beneficial effects on competition.' (para 34)

'Nevertheless, a provision in the statutes of a cooperative purchasing association, restricting the opportunity for members to join other types of competing cooperatives and thus discouraging them from obtaining supplies elsewhere, may have adverse effects on competition. So, in order to escape the prohibition laid down in [Article 101 TFEU], the restrictions imposed on members by the statutes of cooperative purchasing associations must be limited to what is necessary to ensure that the cooperative functions properly and maintains its contractual power in relation to producers.' (para 35)

'The particular features of the case at issue in the main proceedings, which are referred to in the questions submitted by the national court, must be assessed in the light of the foregoing considerations. In addition, it is necessary to establish whether the penalties for non-compliance with the statutes are disproportionate to the objective they pursue and whether the minimum period of membership is unreasonable.' (para 36)

'First of all, the amendment of DLG's statutes is restricted so as to cover only fertilizers and plant protection products, the only farm supplies in respect of which a direct relationship exists between sales volume and price.' (para 37)

'Furthermore, even after DLG has amended its statutes and excluded the plaintiffs, it is open to "non-members" of the association, including the plaintiffs, to buy from it the whole range of products which it sells, including fertilizers and plant protection products, on the same commercial terms and at the same prices as members, except that "non-members" are obviously not entitled to receive a yearly discount on the amount of the transactions carried out.' (para 38)

'Finally, DLG's statutes authorize its members to buy fertilizers and plant protection products without using DLG as an intermediary, provided that such transactions are carried out otherwise than through an organized consortium. In that context, each member acts individually or in association with others but, in the latter case, only in making a one-off common purchase of a particular consignment or shipload.' (para 39)

'Taking all those factors into account, it would not seem that restrictions laid down in the statutes, of the kind imposed on DLG members, go beyond what is necessary to ensure that the cooperative functions properly and maintains its contractual power in relation to producers.' (para 40)

'As regards the penalties imposed on the plaintiffs as a result of their exclusion for infringing DLG's rules, these would not appear to be disproportionate, since DLG has treated the plaintiffs as if they were members exercising their right to withdraw.' (para 41)

'The answer to the second set of questions referred by the national court must therefore be that a provision in the statutes of a cooperative purchasing association, forbidding its members to participate in other forms of organized cooperation which are in direct competition with it, is not caught by the prohibition in Article [Article 101 TFEU], so long as the abovementioned provision is restricted to what is necessary to ensure that the cooperative functions properly and maintains its contractual power in relation to producers.' (para 45)

Comment

'The application of the ancillary restraint concept does not involve any weighing of pro-competitive and anti-competitive effects. Such balancing is reserved for [Article 101(3) TFEU]. The assessment of ancillary restraints is limited to determining whether, in the specific context of the main non-restrictive transaction or activity, a particular restriction is necessary for the implementation of that transaction or activity and proportionate to it. If on the basis of objective factors it can be concluded that without the restriction the main non-restrictive transaction would be difficult or impossible to implement, the restriction may be regarded as objectively necessary for its implementation and proportionate to it. If, for example, the main object of a franchise agreement does not restrict competition, then restrictions, which are necessary for the proper functioning of the agreement, such as obligations aimed at protecting the uniformity and reputation of the franchise system, also fall outside [Article 101(1)]. Similarly, if a joint venture is not in itself restrictive of competition, then restrictions that are necessary for the functioning of the agreement are deemed to be ancillary to the main transaction and are therefore not caught by [Article 101(1)] …' (paras 30, 31, Commission Guidelines on the Application of [Article 81(3) TFEU], [2004] OJ C101/94)

Métropole Télévision (M6) and others v Commission	**Article 101 TFEU**
Case T-112/99	Ancillary Restraints
General Court, [2001] ECR II-2459, [2001] 5 CMLR 33	

Facts

'Télévision Par Satellite' (TPS), was set up as a partnership by six major companies active in the television sector. Its aim was to devise, develop and broadcast a range of television programmes, against payment, to French-speaking television viewers in Europe. The agreements forming the TPS partnership were notified to the Commission in order to obtain negative clearance and/or exemption. In its decision the Commission did not object to the creation of TPS. The Commission raised concerns with respects to some of the provisions in the agreement and granted limited negative clearance and exemption. With reference to the non-competition clause which formed part of the agreement, the Commission held that there were no grounds for action in respect of that clause for a period of three years. With regard to an exclusivity clause which formed part of the agreement, and the clause relating to special-interest channels, the Commission held that those provisions could benefit from an exemption under Article 101(3) TFEU for a period of three years (Case No IV/36.237—TPS). The applicants challenged the Commission's decision and argued, among other things, that the exclusivity clause and the clause relating to the special-interest channels are ancillary restrictions.

Held

The concept of an ancillary restriction covers any restriction which is directly related and necessary to the implementation of a main operation. To establish that a restriction is necessary a twofold examination is required, first, assessing whether the restriction is objectively necessary for the implementation of the main operation and, second, whether it is proportionate to it. (paras 104–06)

'As regards the objective necessity of a restriction … it would be wrong, when classifying ancillary restrictions, to interpret the requirement for objective necessity as implying a need to weigh the pro and anti-competitive effects of an agreement. Such an analysis can take place only in the specific framework of [Article 101(3) TFEU]. … That approach is justified not merely so as to preserve the effectiveness of [Article 101(3) TFEU] of the Treaty, but also on grounds of consistency. As [Article 101(1) TFEU] of the Treaty does not require an analysis of the positive and negative effects on competition of a principal restriction, the same finding is necessary with regard to the analysis of accompanying restrictions.' (paras 107, 108)

'Consequently, as the Commission has correctly asserted, examination of the objective necessity of a restriction in relation to the main operation cannot but be relatively abstract. It is not a question of analysing whether, in the light of the competitive situation on the relevant market, the restriction is indispensable to the commercial success of the main operation but of determining whether, in the specific context of the main operation, the restriction is necessary to implement that operation. If, without the restriction, the main operation is difficult or even impossible to implement, the restriction may be regarded as objectively necessary for its implementation.' (para 109)

'Where a restriction is objectively necessary to implement a main operation, it is still necessary to verify whether its duration and its material and geographic scope do not exceed what is necessary to implement that operation. If the duration or the scope of the restriction exceed what is necessary in order to implement the operation, it must be assessed separately under [Article 101(3)TFEU] (see, to that effect, Case T-61/89 *Dansk Pelsdyravlerforening v Commission* [1992] ECR II-1931, paragraph 78).' (para 113)

'Lastly, it must be observed that, inasmuch as the assessment of the ancillary nature of a particular agreement in relation to a main operation entails complex economic assessments by the Commission, judicial review of that assessment is limited to verifying whether the relevant procedural rules have been complied with, whether the statement of the reasons for the decision is adequate, whether the facts have been accurately stated and whether there has been a manifest error of appraisal or misuse of powers (see, to that effect, with regard to assessing the permissible duration of a non-competition clause, *Remia v Commission*, … paragraph 34).' (para 114)

As a consequence of classification as an ancillary restriction, the compatibility of that restriction with the competition rules must be examined with that of the main operation. If the main operation does not infringe Article 101(1) TFEU, the same holds for the restrictions directly related and necessary for that operation. Similarly, if the main operation benefits from an exemption under Article 101(3) TFEU, that exemption also covers those ancillary restrictions. (para 116)

Exclusivity clause

It is necessary to examine, whether in the present case the Commission committed a manifest error of assessment in not classifying the exclusivity clause as a restriction that was ancillary to the creation of TPS. The applicants submit that the exclusivity clause is ancillary to the creation of TPS as the clause is indispensable to allow TPS to penetrate the pay-TV market in France. Yet, it must, however, be observed that the fact that the exclusivity clause would be necessary to allow TPS to establish itself on a long-term basis on that market, it is not relevant to the classification of that clause as an ancillary restriction. 'Such considerations, relating to the indispensable nature of the restriction in light of the competitive situation on the relevant market, are not part of an analysis of the ancillary nature of the restrictions. They can be taken into account only in the framework of [Article 101(3) TFEU].' (paras 108–21)

'Next, it must be observed that although, in the present case, the applicants have been able to establish to the requisite legal standard that the exclusivity clause was directly related to the establishment of TPS, they have not, on the other hand, shown that the exclusive broadcasting of the general-interest channels was objectively necessary for that operation. As the Commission has rightly stated, a company in the pay-TV sector can be launched in France without having exclusive rights to the general-interest channels. That is the situation for CanalSatellite and AB-Sat, the two other operators on that market.' (para 122)

'Even if the exclusivity clause was objectively necessary for the creation of TPS, the Commission did not commit a manifest error of assessment in taking the view that this restriction was not proportionate to that objective.' The exclusivity clause is for an initial period of ten years which is excessive as TPS has to establish itself on the market before the end of that period. Moreover, the exclusivity clause is disproportionate in so far as its effect is to deprive TPS's actual and potential competitors of any access to the programmes that are considered attractive by a large number of French television viewers. (paras 123–25)

Special-interest clause

Similarly, the Commission did not commit a manifest error of assessment in not classifying the clause relating to the special-interest channels as a restriction that was ancillary to the creation of TPS. The Commission rightly refused to classify the clause as an ancillary restriction as it limited the supply of special-interest channels and television services and had a negative impact on the situation of third parties over a long period of ten years which exceeded what was necessary for the creation of TPS. (paras 126–35)

Comment

The Court accepted the Commission's conclusion that the exclusivity clause and the clause relating to the special-interest channels were not ancillary to the creation of TPS. The Court noted that even when the clause is directly related to the main operation it needs to be objectively necessary for that operation and proportionate to it.

Wouters v Algemene Raad van de Nederlandse Orde van Advocaten	**Article 101 TFEU**
Case C-309/99	Ancillary Restraints
Court of Justice, [2002] ECR I-1577, [2002] 4 CMLR 27	

Facts

The case arose out of a dispute between Mr Wouters and the Dutch Bar on the basis that the Bar's regulations prohibited its members from practising in full partnership with accountants. Mr Wouters argued that the prohibition was incompatible with Union rules on competition and freedom of establishment. The Dutch court referred the case to the Court of Justice, asking, among other things, whether a regulation which, in order to guarantee the independence and loyalty to the client of members of the Bar who provide legal assistance in conjunction with members of other liberal professions, adopts universally binding rules governing the formation of multi-disciplinary partnerships, has the object or effect of restricting competition within the internal market.

Held

'The prohibition at issue ... prohibits all contractual arrangements between members of the Bar and accountants which provide in any way for shared decision-making, profit-sharing or for the use of a common name, and this makes any form of effective partnership difficult.' (para 84)

'It appears to the Court that the national legislation at issue in the main proceedings has an adverse effect on competition and may affect trade between Member States.' (para 85)

'As regards the adverse effect on competition, the areas of expertise of members of the Bar and of accountants may be complementary. Since legal services, especially in business law, more and more frequently require recourse to an accountant, a multi-disciplinary partnership of members of the Bar and accountants would make it possible to offer a wider range of services, and indeed to propose new ones. Clients would thus be able to turn to a single structure for a large part of the services necessary for the organisation, management and operation of their business (the one-stop shop advantage).' (para 87)

Furthermore, a multi-disciplinary partnership of members of the Bar and accountants would satisfy the needs created by the increasing interpenetration of national markets and might have positive effects on the cost of services. (paras 88, 89)

A prohibition of such multi-disciplinary partnerships 'is therefore liable to limit production and technical development within the meaning of [Article 101(1)(b) TFEU].' (para 90)

On the other hand, it is true that the accountancy market is highly concentrated, to the extent that the firms dominating it are at present known as the Big Five. 'The prohibition of conflicts of interest with which members of the Bar in all Member States are required to comply with may constitute a structural limit to extensive concentration of law-firms and so reduce their opportunities of benefiting from economies of scale or of entering into structural associations with practitioners of highly concentrated professions.' (paras 91, 92)

'In those circumstances, unreserved and unlimited authorisation of multi-disciplinary partnerships between the legal profession, the generally decentralised nature of which is closely linked to some of its fundamental features, and a profession as concentrated as accountancy, could lead to an overall decrease in the degree of competition prevailing on the market in legal services, as a result of the substantial reduction in the number of undertakings present on that market.' (para 93)

'Nevertheless, in so far as the preservation of a sufficient degree of competition on the market in legal services could be guaranteed by less extreme measures than national rules such as the 1993 Regulation, which prohibits absolutely any form of multi-disciplinary partnership, whatever the respective sizes of the firms of lawyers and accountants concerned, those rules restrict competition.' (para 94)

'However, not every agreement between undertakings or every decision of an association of undertakings which restricts the freedom of action of the parties or of one of them necessarily falls within the prohibition laid down in [Article 101(1) TFEU]. For the purposes of application of that provision to a particular case, account must first of all be taken of the overall context in which the decision of the association of undertakings was taken or produces its effects. More particularly, account must be taken of its objectives, which are here connected with the need to make rules relating to organisation, qualifications, professional ethics, supervision and liability, in order to ensure that the ultimate consumers of legal services and the sound administration of justice are provided with the necessary guarantees in relation to integrity and experience (see, to that effect, Case C-3/95 *Reiseburo Broede* [1996] ECR I-6511, paragraph 38). It has then to be considered whether the consequential effects restrictive of competition are inherent in the pursuit of those objectives.' (para 97)

Account should be taken of the legal framework applicable in the Netherlands to members of the Bar, including the obligation of the Bar to ensure the proper practice of the profession, the duty to act for clients in complete independence and in their sole interest, and the duty to avoid all risk of conflict of interest and to observe strict professional secrecy. (paras 98–102)

No comparable requirements of professional conduct are imposed on accountants in the Netherlands. In addition, there may be a degree of incompatibility between the advisory activities carried out by a member of the Bar and the supervisory activities carried out by an accountant. The Bar was entitled to consider that its members might not be in a position to advise and represent their clients independently and in strict professional secrecy if they belonged to a multi-disciplinary partnership. (paras 103–05)

The Regulation in question could therefore reasonably be considered to be necessary in order to ensure the proper practice of the legal profession. To that extent even if multi-disciplinary partnerships of lawyers and accountants are allowed in other Member States, the Bar is entitled to consider that the objectives pursued by the Regulation cannot be attained by less restrictive means. (paras 106–10)

Comment

Paragraphs 84–90 highlight the anticompetitive effect of the Regulation. From paragraph 91 onwards the Court of Justice treats the Regulation and the anticompetitive effects it generates as restraints necessary in order to fulfil the legal obligations of the Bar. In this respect the analysis resembles an ancillary restraint argument, although the restraint here does not facilitate a commercial agreement but rather a regulatory based obligation.

In its decision the Court of Justice balanced in paragraphs 91–110 between public interest and anticompetitive effect. This exercise raises two main difficulties. First, the anticompetitive effects of the Regulation were counterbalanced by reference to non-economic variables. Second, this exercise was conducted under Article 101(1) TFEU and resembles a rule of reason analysis. One would have expected the balancing exercise to take place under Article 101(3) TFEU. Yet, it is questionable whether non-economic variables such as public interest could have been integrated into the framework of Article 101(3) TFEU. It is possible that Article 101(1) TFEU provided the court with a more flexible framework to consider non-qualifying elements such as public interest.

Following *Wouters*, it may be possible to argue that a 'public interest arguments' can be heard as part of the Article 101(1) analysis. Such balancing exercise will not necessarily overlap with the Article 101(3) analysis as most public interest arguments are external to Article 101(3) TFEU. It is therefore best viewed as a widening of the variables considered under Article 101(1); a tool allowing the Court to balance anticompetitive effects against a range of non-qualifying policy variables. Although attractive in its ability to protect national public interests, the risk associated with such a flexible approach in a decentralised enforcement regime is clear.

Note the Court of Justice decision in Case C-519/04P *Meca-Medina and Majcen v Commission*, page 115 above.

MasterCard Inc v Commission	**Article 101 TFEU**
Case C-382/12 P	Ancillary Restraints
Court of Justice	'Objective Necessity'

Facts

The European Commission found MasterCard to have infringed Article 101 TFEU by establishing a system of multilateral interchange fees (MIFs) for cross-border bank card payments. That system led to a restriction of competition between participating banks providing merchants with services enabling them to accept MasterCard charge and credit cards. MasterCard's action for annulment was dismissed (Case T-111/08). It subsequently appealed to the Court of Justice, arguing, among other things, that the MIF system was objectively necessary and as such should escape the prohibition laid down in Article 101 TFEU.

Held

'Where it is a matter of determining whether an anti-competitive restriction can escape the prohibition laid down in [Article 101(1) TFEU] because it is ancillary to a main operation that is not anti-competitive in nature, it is necessary to inquire whether that operation would be impossible to carry out in the absence of the restriction in question. Contrary to what the appellants claim, the fact that that operation is simply more difficult to implement or even less profitable without the restriction concerned cannot be deemed to give that restriction the "objective necessity" required in order for it to be classified as ancillary. Such an interpretation would effectively extend that concept to restrictions which are not strictly indispensable to the implementation of the main operation. Such an outcome would undermine the effectiveness of the prohibition laid down in [Article 101(1) TFEU].' (para 91)

'However, that interpretation does not mean that there has been an amalgamation of, on the one hand, the conditions laid down by the case-law for the classification—for the purposes of the application of [Article 101(1) TFEU]—of a restriction as ancillary, and, on the other hand, the criterion of the indispensability required under [Article 101(3) TFEU] in order for a prohibited restriction to be exempted.' (para 92)

Those two provisions have different objectives. Article 101(3) TFEU provides that coordination which infringes Article 101(1) TFEU can none the less 'be considered indispensable to the improvement of production or distribution or to the promotion of technical or economic progress, while allowing consumers a fair share of the resulting benefits'. By contrast, the objective necessity test 'concerns the question whether, in the absence of a given restriction of commercial autonomy, a main operation or activity which is not caught by the prohibition laid down in [Article 101(1) TFEU]' and to which that restriction is secondary, is likely not to be implemented or not to proceed.' (para 93)

When considering the ancillary nature of a restriction, one should consider not only its 'objective necessity' but also that the restriction is proportionate to the underlying objectives of that operation or activity. To make that assessment, the Commission may rely on the existence of realistic alternatives that are less restrictive of competition than the restriction at issue. Importantly, the alternatives on which the Commission may rely are not limited to the situation that would arise in the absence of the restriction in question but may also extend to other counterfactual hypotheses based, inter alia, on realistic situations that might arise in the absence of that restriction. (paras 107–11)

Comment

The Court endorsed the General Court's holding that the fact that the absence of the MIF MasterCard system would have been more difficult and costly to implement does not lead to a conclusion that the MIF is objectively necessary to the system, as long as the MasterCard system is still capable of functioning without it.

The counterfactual hypothesis put forward in the examination of the objective necessity is not limited to the situation that would arise in the absence of the restriction in question. One may consider other plausible realistic scenarios under which the MasterCard system would be economically viable.

Franz Völk v SPRL Est J Vervaecke	**Article 101 TFEU**
Case 5/69	Appreciable Effect (de minimis)
Court of Justice, [1969] ECR 295, [1969] CMLR 273	

'[T]he prohibition in [Article 101(1) TFEU] is applicable only if the agreement in question also has as its object or effect the prevention, restriction or distortion of competition within the [internal] market. Those conditions must be understood by reference to the actual circumstances of the agreement. Consequently an agreement falls outside the prohibition in [Article 101(1) TFEU] when it has only an insignificant effect on the markets, taking into account the weak position which the persons concerned have on the market of the product in question. Thus an exclusive dealing agreement, even with absolute territorial protection, may, having regard to the weak position of the persons concerned on the market in the products in question in the area covered by the absolute protection, escape the prohibition laid down in [Article 101(1) TFEU].' (para 7)

Langnese-Iglo GmbH v Commission	**Article 101 TFEU**
Case T-7 /93	Appreciable Effect (de minimis)
General Court, [1995] ECR II-1533, [1995] 5 CMLR 602	

'It must be borne in mind that [the Commission Notice on Agreements of Minor Importance] is intended only to define those agreements which, in the Commission's view, do not have an appreciable effect on competition or trade between Member States. The Court considers that it cannot however be inferred with certainty that a network of exclusive purchasing agreements is automatically liable to prevent, restrict or distort competition appreciably merely because the ceilings laid down in it are exceeded. Moreover, it is apparent from the actual wording of paragraph 3 of that notice that it is entirely possible, in the present case, that agreements concluded between undertakings which exceed the ceilings indicated, affect trade between Member States or competition only to an insignificant extent and consequently are not caught by [Article 101(1) TFEU].' (para 98)

European Night Services Ltd and others v Commission	**Article 101 TFEU**
Joined Cases T-374, 375, 384, 388/94	Appreciable Effect (de minimis)
Court of Justice, [1998] ECR II-3141, [1998] 5 CMLR 718	

'[I]t must be borne in mind that, according to the case-law, an agreement may fall outside the prohibition in [Article 101(1) TFEU] if it has only an insignificant effect on the market, taking into account the weak position which the parties concerned have on the product or service market in question…. With regard to the quantitative effect on the market, the Commission has argued that, in accordance with its notice on agreements of minor importance, cited above, [Article 101(1) TFEU] applies to an agreement when the market share of the parties to the agreement amounts to. … However, the mere fact that that threshold may be reached and even exceeded does not make it possible to conclude with certainty that an agreement is caught by [Article 101(1) TFEU]. Point 3 of that [N]otice itself states that the quantitative definition of "appreciable" given by the Commission is, however, no absolute yardstick' and that 'in individual cases … agreements between undertakings which exceed these limits may … have only a negligible effect on trade between Member States or on competition, and are therefore not caught by [Article 101(1) TFEU]…. It is noteworthy, moreover, if only as an indication, that that analysis is corroborated by the Commission's 1997 notice on agreements of minor importance (OJ 1997 C 372, p 13) replacing the [N]otice of 3 September 1986, cited above, according to which even agreements which are not of minor importance can escape the prohibition on agreements on account of their exclusively favourable impact on competition.' (para 102)

Expedia Inc v Autorité de la concurrence and Others	**Article 101 TFEU**
Case C-226/11	The De Minimis Notice
Court of Justice, [2013] 4 CMLR 14	Appreciable Effect

Facts

Reference for a preliminary ruling concerning the legality of an agreement between Expedia Inc, which specialises in the sale of travel over the internet, and a French train operator (SNCF), which operated a website dealing with train travel. The agreement in question concerned the creation of a joint subsidiary (Agence VSC) for the marketing of train travel online. The French Competition Authority found that Expedia and SNCF were competitors in the market for online travel agency services and that the creation of Agence VSC infringed competition law. The Competition Authority found that the market shares of the two companies exceeded 10% and that, consequently, the de minimis notice was not applicable. Following two appeals, the case reached the French Cour de cassation which referred a question to the Court of Justice on the applicability of the European de minimis notice in national proceedings.

Held

'The de minimis doctrine establishes that an agreement would fall outside the competition provisions if it has only an insignificant effect on the market. ... Accordingly, if it is to fall within the scope of the prohibition under Article 101(1) TFEU, an agreement of undertakings must have the object or effect of perceptibly restricting competition within the common market and be capable of affecting trade between Member States.' (paras 16–17)

In its de minimis Notice the Commission intends to quantify, with the help of market share thresholds, what is not an appreciable restriction of competition. The Commission further notes that the negative definition of the appreciability of such a restriction does not imply that agreements of undertakings which exceed those thresholds appreciably restrict competition. (paras 18–25)

The Notice outlines the manner in which the Commission will itself apply Article 101 TFEU. The competition authorities and the courts of the Member States are not bound by the Notice, but may take into account the thresholds established in it in their decision making. Accordingly, as the notice is not binding at national level there can be no legitimate expectation that the national authorities will follow it. (paras 26–33)

'An agreement that may affect trade between Member States and that has an anticompetitive object constitutes, by its nature and independently of any concrete effect that it may have, an appreciable restriction on competition.' (para 37)

Comment

The Court's statement in paragraph 37 is controversial. It stands in contrast to earlier case-law which applied the de minimis concept to agreements with either object or effect. In paragraph 37, the Court of Justice held that by its nature an agreement which has the object of restricting competition will have an appreciable effect on competition. That holding limits the role of the de minimis doctrine and the usefulness of the safe harbour it provides.

To fully understand the effect of the linkage between object and the unavailability of the de minimis safe harbour, one should take into account the recent widening of the object category as manifested in Case C-8/08 and Case C-32/11 (pages 100 and 107 above).

Following the judgment, the European Commission amended its de minimis Notice and clarified that agreements containing a restriction by object result in appreciable restriction of competition. That change will limit the application of the Notice, which prior to the change assumed that only hard core restrictions were always outside its scope. (C(2014) 4136 final)

Société Technique Minière v Maschinenbau Ulm GmbH	**Article 101 TFEU**
Case 56/65	Appreciable Effect on Trade
Court of Justice, [1966] ECR 235, [1966] CMLR 357	

'It is in fact to the extent that the agreement may affect trade between Member States that the interference with competition caused by that agreement is caught by the prohibitions in [Union] law found in [Article 101 TFEU], whilst in the converse case it escapes those prohibitions. For this requirement to be fulfilled it must be possible to foresee with a sufficient degree of probability on the basis of a set of objective factors of law or of fact that the agreement in question may have an influence, direct or indirect, actual or potential, on the pattern of trade between Member States. Therefore, in order to determine whether an agreement which contains a clause "granting an exclusive right of sale" comes within the field of application of [Article 101 TFEU], it is necessary to consider in particular whether it is capable of bringing about a partitioning of the market in certain products between Member States and thus rendering more difficult the interpenetration of trade which the Treaty is intended to create.' (para 249)

Consten SaRL and Grundig-Verkaufs-GmbH v Commission	**Article 101 TFEU**
Joined Cases 56 and 58/64	Appreciable Effect on Trade
Court of Justice, [1966] ECR 299, [1966] CMLR 418	

'The concept of an agreement "which may affect trade between Member States" is intended to define, in the law governing cartels, the boundary between the areas respectively covered by [Union] law and national law. It is only to the extent to which the agreement may affect trade between Member States that the deterioration in competition caused by the agreement falls under the prohibition of [Union] law contained in [Article 101 TFEU] otherwise it escapes the prohibition.'

'In this connection, what is particularly important is whether the agreement is capable of constituting a threat, either direct or indirect, actual or potential, to freedom of trade between Member States in a manner which might harm the attainment of the objectives of a single market between states. Thus the fact that an agreement encourages an increase, even a large one, in the volume of trade between states is not sufficient to exclude the possibility that the agreement may "affect" such trade in the abovementioned manner. In the present case, the contract between Grundig and Consten, on the one hand by preventing undertakings other than Consten from importing Grundig products into France, and on the other hand by prohibiting Consten from re-exporting those products to other countries of the [internal] market, indisputably affects trade between Member States. These limitations on the freedom of trade, as well as those which might ensue for third parties from the registration in France by Consten of the Gint trade mark, which Grundig places on all its products, are enough to satisfy the requirement in question.' (p 341)

Vereeniging van Cementhandelaren v Commission	**Article 101 TFEU**
Case 8/72	Appreciable Effect on Trade
Court of Justice, [1972] ECR 977, [1973] CMLR 7	

'An agreement extending over the whole of the territory of a Member State by its very nature has the effect of reinforcing the compartmentalization of markets on a national basis, thereby holding up the economic interpenetration which the Treaty is designed to bring about and protecting domestic production.' (para 29)

'In particular, the provisions of the agreement which are mutually binding on the members of the applicant association and the prohibition by the association on all sales to resellers who are not authorized by it make it more difficult for producers or sellers from other Member States to be active in or penetrate the Netherlands market.' (para 30)

SA Brasserie de Haecht v Consorts Wilkin-Janssen	**Article 101 TFEU**
Case 23/67	Appreciable Effect on Trade
Court of Justice, [1967] ECR 407, [1968] CMLR 26	

'[I]t is only to the extent to which agreements, Decisions or practices are capable of affecting trade between Member States that the alteration of competition comes under [Union] prohibitions. In order to satisfy this condition, it must be possible for the agreement, Decision or practice, when viewed in the light of a combination of the objective, factual or legal circumstances, to appear to be capable of having some influence, direct or indirect, on trade between Member States, of being conducive to a partitioning of the market and of hampering the economic interpenetration sought by the Treaty. When this point is considered the agreement, Decision or practice cannot therefore be isolated from all the others of which it is one.'

'The existence of similar contracts is a circumstance which, together with others, is capable of being a factor in the economic and legal context within which the contract must be judged. Accordingly, whilst such a situation must be taken into account it should not be considered as decisive by itself, but merely as one among others in judging whether trade between Member States is capable of being affected through any alteration in competition.' (p 416)

AEG–Telefunken AG v Commission	**Article 101 TFEU**
Case 107/82	Appreciable Effect on Trade
Court of Justice, [1983] ECR 3151, [1984] 3 CMLR 325	

'As regards the second argument put forward by AEG, it must be pointed out that the risk of obstacles to potential trade cannot be ruled out on the basis of a mere allegation that the traders did not or were not in a position to carry on trade between Member States. In that connection it is important to stress that several of the undertakings mentioned in the Decision (for example, Diederichs in Belgium and the Auchan, Darty, Fnac and Conforama shops in France) actually undertook or were prepared to undertake parallel imports. The Ratio chain of stores in the Federal Republic of Germany on several occasions effected re-imports of Telefunken products from Austria and would no doubt have done so from Member States of the [Union] if the re-importation from those states had brought it the same advantages.' (para 59)

'In any case it must be recalled that, according to the Miller judgment [Case 19/77 *Miller International Schallplatten GmbH v Commission*, [1978] ECR 131, [1978] 2 CMLR 334,] …, the mere fact that at a certain time traders applying for admission to a distribution network or who have already been admitted are not engaged in intra-[Union] trade cannot suffice to exclude the possibility that restrictions on their freedom of action may impede intra-[Union] trade, since the situation may change from one year to another in terms of alterations in the conditions or composition of the market both in the [internal] market as a whole and in the individual national markets.' (para 60)

Ziegler SA v Commission	**Article 101 TFEU**
Case T-199/08	Appreciable Effect on Trade
General Court, [2011] ECR II-3507, [2011] 5 CMLR 9	

Facts

The European Commission found a number of companies to infringe Article 101 TFEU by participating in a cartel in the Belgian international removal services. Cartel members engaged in price fixing, cover bidding and established an illegal commission system (COMP/38.543– International Removal Services). On appeal the applicant argued, among other things, that the Commission failed to prove that trade between Member States was appreciably affected.

Held

The Commission argues that since the object of the cartel was to restrict competition, it was not necessary for it to define the relevant market. That argument cannot be accepted. (paras 41, 42)

'Admittedly, for the purpose of the application of [Article 101(1) TFEU], the Commission is not required to show the actual anti-competitive effects of agreements or practices which have as their object the prevention, restriction or distortion of competition.' (para 43)

'Nevertheless, in accordance with settled case-law, [Article 101(1) TFEU] is not applicable if the effect of a restrictive practice on intra-Community trade or on competition is not 'appreciable'. An agreement escapes the prohibition laid down in [Article 101(1) TFEU] if it restricts competition or affects trade between Member States only insignificantly (Case 56/65 *LTM* [1966] ECR 235, 249; Case 5/69 *Völk* [1969] ECR 295, paragraph 7; Case C-306/96 *Javico* [1998] ECR I-1983, paragraphs 12 and 17; and Case T-213/00 *CMA CGM and Others v Commission* [2003] ECR II-913, paragraph 207).' (para 44)

'Consequently, there is an obligation on the Commission to define the market in a decision applying [Article 101 TFEU] where it is impossible, without such a definition, to determine whether the agreement or concerted practice at issue is liable to affect trade between Member States and has as its object or effect the prevention, restriction or distortion of competition (Case T-62/98 *Volkswagen v Commission* [2000] ECR II-2707, paragraph 230).' (para 45)

Comment

An appeal to the Court of Justice was dismissed—Case C-439/11P *Ziegler SA v Commission* [2013] 5 CMLR 36.

In cases where the agreement that has the object of restricting competition does not clearly affect trade between Member States, the Commission is required to define the relevant market in order to establish an appreciable effect on intra-Union trade.

The Commission Guidelines on the Effect on Trade Concept elaborate on the notion of appreciability. The Commission notes that 'Appreciability can be appraised in particular by reference to the position and the importance of the relevant undertakings on the market for the products concerned … The stronger the market position of the undertakings concerned, the more likely it is that an agreement or practice capable of affecting trade between Member States can be held to do so appreciably … Appreciability [can be] measured both in absolute terms (turnover) and in relative terms, comparing the position of the undertaking(s) concerned to that of other players on the market (market share).' (paras 44–8)

In Case 174/84 *Bulk Oil (Zug) AG and Sun International Limited and Sun Oil Trading Company* [1986] ECR 559, the Court of Justice referred to the effect generated by an export activity. It held that a measure 'which is specifically directed at exports of oil to a non-member country is not in itself likely to restrict or distort competition within the common market. It cannot therefore affect trade within the community and infringe … [Article 101 TFEU].' (para 44)

Consten SaRL and Grundig-Verkaufs-GmbH v Commission
Joined Cases 56 and 58/64
Court of Justice, [1966] ECR 299, [1966] CMLR 418

Article 101(2) TFEU
Severability
Temporaneous Nullity

Facts

An exclusive distribution agreement between Consten and Grundig under which the former received exclusive rights to sell Grundig products in France in return for its promise not to handle competing brands. The agreement led to absolute territorial protection and was found by the Commission to infringe Article 101 TFEU. On appeal to the Court of Justice, the companies argued that, among other things, the Commission did not exclude from the prohibition those clauses of the contract in respect of which there was found no effect capable of restricting competition.

Held

'The provision in [Article 101(2) TFEU] that agreements prohibited pursuant to [Article 101 TFEU] shall be automatically void applies only to those parts of the agreement which are subject to the prohibition, or to the agreement as a whole if those parts do not appear to be severable from the agreement itself. The Commission should, therefore, either have confined itself in the operative part of the contested Decision to declaring that an infringement lay in those parts only of the agreement which came within the prohibition, or else it should have set out in the preamble to the Decision the reasons why those parts did not appear to it to be severable from the whole agreement.' (p 344)

'It follows, however, from Article 1 of the Decision that the infringement was found to lie in the agreement as a whole, although the Commission did not adequately state the reasons why it was necessary to render the whole of the agreement void when it is not established that all the clauses infringed the provisions of [Article 101(1) TFEU]. The state of affairs found to be incompatible with [Article 101(1) TFEU] stems from certain specific clauses of the contract of 1 April 1957 concerning absolute territorial protection and from the additional agreement on the Gint trade mark rather than from the combined operation of all clauses of the agreement, that is to say, from the aggregate of its effects. Article 1 of the contested Decision must therefore be annulled in so far as it renders void, without any valid reason, all the clauses of the agreement by virtue of [Article 101(2) TFEU].' (p 344)

Comment

In *Société Technique Minière v Maschinenbau Ulm GmbH* (page 92 above) the Court of Justice held similarly that the automatic nullity under Article 101(2) TFEU only applies to those parts of the agreement affected by the prohibition, or to the agreement as a whole if it appears that those parts are not severable from the agreement itself.

'The fact that only binding agreements can, by their nature, be rendered void [under Article 101(2) TFEU] does not mean that non-binding agreements must escape the prohibition laid down in [Article 101(1) TFEU].' (Case T-9/99 *HFB Holding and others v Commission*, para 101, [2002] ECR II-1487)

In *David John Passmore v Morland and others* [1999] 1 CMLR 1129, the English Court of Appeal held that an agreement which falls outside Article 101(1) TFEU at the time when it is entered, may nonetheless be prohibited under the Article when, for example, a change in market conditions influences the economic effects generated by it. The same is true for agreements which were prohibited under Article 101(1) TFEU, but do to changes in circumstances, no longer have anticompetitive effects. (paras 26, 27) Subsequently, Article 101(2) TFEU 'has to be construed in light of an appreciation that the prohibition in [Article 101(1)] is not an absolute prohibition. ... The prohibition is temporaneous (or transient) rather than absolute; in the sense that it endures for a finite period of time–the period of time for which it is needed–rather than for all time ...' (para 28) '[T]he nullity imposed by [Article 101(2) TFEU] is an exact reflection of the prohibition imposed by [Article 101(1) TFEU]. If the prohibition is temporaneous (or transient) then so is the nullity.' (para 34)

Consten SaRL and Grundig-Verkaufs-GmbH v Commission	**Article 101(3) TFEU**
Joined Cases 56 and 58/64	First and Third Conditions
Court of Justice, [1966] ECR 299, [1966] CMLR 418	

Facts

An exclusive distribution agreement between Consten and Grundig under which the former received exclusive rights to sell Grundig products in France in return for its promise not to handle competing brands. The agreement led to absolute territorial protection and was found by the Commission to infringe Article 101 TFEU. On appeal to the Court of Justice the possibility for Article 101(3) TFEU exemption was considered.

Held

When assessing the conditions for exemption under Article 101(3) TFEU 'the Commission may not confine itself to requiring from undertakings proof of the fulfilment of the requirements for the grant of the exemption but must, as a matter of good administration, play its part, using the means available to it, in ascertaining the relevant facts and circumstances. Furthermore, the exercise of the Commission's powers necessarily implies complex evaluations on economic matters. A judicial review of these evaluations must take account of their nature by confining itself to an examination of the relevance of the facts and of the legal consequences which the Commission deduces therefrom. This review must in the first place be carried out in respect of the reasons given for the Decisions which must set out the facts and considerations on which the said evaluations are based.' (p 347)

'The question whether there is an improvement in the production or distribution of the goods in question, which is required for the grant of exemption, is to be answered in accordance with the spirit of [Article 101 TFEU]. First, this improvement cannot be identified with all the advantages which the parties to the agreement obtain from it in their production or distribution activities. These advantages are generally indisputable and show the agreement as in all respects indispensable to an improvement as understood in this sense. This subjective method, which makes the content of the concept of "improvement" depend upon the special features of the contractual relationships in question, is not consistent with the aims of [Article 101 TFEU]. Furthermore, the very fact that the Treaty provides that the restriction of competition must be "indispensable" to the improvement in question clearly indicates the importance which the latter must have. This improvement must in particular show appreciable objective advantages of such a character as to compensate for the disadvantages which [are caused] in the field of competition.' (p 348)

'In its evaluation of the relative importance of the various factors submitted for its consideration, the Commission … had to judge their effectiveness by reference to an objectively ascertainable improvement in the production and distribution of the goods, and to decide whether the resulting benefit would suffice to support the conclusion that the consequent restrictions upon competition were indispensable. The argument based on the necessity to maintain intact all arrangements of the parties in so far as they are capable of contributing to the improvement sought cannot be reconciled with the view propounded in the last sentence …' (p 348)

Comment

The Court emphasised that when considering the benefits stemming from the agreement, under the first condition in Article 101(3) TFEU, account should only be taken of objective benefits which generate value to the Union as a whole and not to subjective benefit which the parties obtain from the agreement (see p 348).

For a detailed account of the different categories of efficiencies, see paragraphs 48–72, the Commission Guidelines on the Application of [Article 101(3) TFEU], [2004] OJ C101/97.

Note, that as a matter of principle, any agreement, having an anti competitive object or effect, may be exempted under Article 101(3) TFEU. See Case T-17/93 *Matra Hachette SA v Commission* [1994] ECR II-595.

Metro SB-Großmarkte GmbH & Co KG v Commission	**Article 101(3) TFEU**
Case 26/76	First Condition
Court of Justice, [1977] ECR 1875, [1978] 2 CMLR 1	Policy Considerations

Facts

Following a complaint submitted by Metro, the Commission started an investigation into a selective distribution system for electric goods, operated by SABA. The Commission concluded that the distribution system did infringe Article 101 TFEU. It found that the conditions of sale for the domestic market as laid down in the distribution system did not fall within the prohibition in Article 101(1) TFEU and that the other provisions in the distribution agreement qualified for an exemption under Article 101(3) TFEU. Metro applied for annulment of the Commission decision. On appeal the Court of Justice considered, among other things, the Commission's evaluation of the distribution system under Article 101(3). Application was dismissed.

Held

The Court needs to consider whether the supply contracts which form part of the selective distribution system satisfy the conditions under Article 101(3) TFEU. With regard to the first condition in Article 101(3) TFEU, 'the conclusion of supply contracts for six months, taking account of the probable growth of the market, should make it possible to ensure both a certain stability in the supply of the relevant products, which should allow the requirements of persons obtaining supplies from the wholesaler to be more fully satisfied, and, since such supply contracts are of relatively short duration, a certain flexibility, enabling production to be adapted to the changing requirements of the market. Thus a more regular distribution is ensured, to the benefit both of the producer, who takes his share of the planned expansion of the market in the relevant product, of the wholesaler, whose supplies are secured, and, finally, of the undertakings which obtain supplies from the wholesaler, in that the variety of available products is increased. … Furthermore, the establishment of supply forecasts for a reasonable period constitutes a stabilizing factor with regard to the provision of employment which, since it improves the general conditions of production, especially when market conditions are unfavourable, comes within the framework of the objectives to which reference may be had pursuant to [Article 101(3) TFEU].' (para 43)

Comment

The Court of Justice considered that employment was a relevant factor under the first condition of Article 101(3) TFEU. Employment considerations constitute a non-efficiency variable which the court considered relevant in balancing the anticompetitive effects of the agreement under Article 101(3) TFEU.

This broad approach opens the door to variables that are not directly linked to efficiencies. In Case T-528/93 etc *Métropole télévision SA and others v Commission* [1996] ECR II-649, [1996] 5 CMLR 386, the General Court held that: 'Admittedly, in the context of an overall assessment, the Commission is entitled to base itself on considerations connected with the pursuit of the public interest in order to grant exemption under [Article 101(3) TFEU] of the Treaty …' (para 118)

Contrast with the General Court comment in Case T-17/93 *Matra Hachette SA v Commission* [1994] ECR II-595, where in paragraph 139 it seems to suggest that considerations as to public infrastructures, employment and European integration were external to the analysis of Article 101(3) TFEU.

Also note the restrictive attitude as indicated in the (post-modernisation) Guidelines on [Article 101(3) TFEU]. The Guidelines, in line with the new decentralised enforcement regime, seem to foster a rather restrictive approach and focus primarily on cost and qualitative efficiencies. This restrictive approach is aimed at minimising divergence between national courts and competition authorities when considering individual exemptions. Note, however, that the Guidelines are not binding, and national courts and competition authorities are free to follow the more permissive case-law if they wish to do so.

Publishers Association v Commission	**Article 101(3) TFEU**
Case C-360/92P	First Condition
Court of Justice, [1995] ECR I-23, [1995] 5 CMLR 33	Externalities of Effect

Facts

The Publishers Association (PA) brought an appeal against the General Court judgment in Case T-66/89 ([1992] ECR II-1995), in which the Court dismissed its application for annulment of the Commission Decision. The case concerned the lawfulness of two agreements which were concluded in the United Kingdom under the aegis of the PA and established a 'net price system' for books. The system included provisions for fixing prices and sale conditions for books. It was established, among other things, in order to avoid the decline in stock levels and to prevent an increase in book prices. The Commission found the agreements to constitute an infringement of Article 101(1) TFEU and rejected the PA's application for an exemption under Article 101(3) TFEU on the ground that the restrictions imposed by the agreements were not indispensable to the attainment of its stated objectives.

Held

In its review of the lawfulness of the Commission's refusal to grant an exemption under Article 101(3) TFEU for the 'net price system for books', the General Court failed to consider the existence of a single language area forming a single market for books in Ireland and the United Kingdom. 'Having regard to the single language area, the objectives pursued by the agreements and the restrictions of competition arising therefrom, and the relationship between the objectives and the restrictions were to be assessed in the same way or differently, depending on whether the assessment related to the national territory alone or to the [internal] market.' (paras 24–7)

'In paragraph 84 of the judgment under appeal, the Court then held that "the PA, which is an association consisting of publishers established in the United Kingdom, is not entitled to rely on any negative effects which might be felt on the Irish market, even though that market belongs to the same language area". That finding is vitiated by an error of law. Nothing in the wording or the spirit of [Article 101(3) TFEU] allows that provision to be interpreted as meaning that the possibility for which it provides, of declaring the provisions of paragraph 1 inapplicable in the case of certain agreements which contribute to improving the production or distribution of goods or to promoting technical or economical progress, is subject to the condition that those benefits should occur only on the territory of the Member State or States in which the undertakings who are parties to the agreement are established and not in the territory of other Member States. Such an interpretation is incompatible with the fundamental objectives of the [Union] and with the very concepts of [internal] market and single market.' (paras 28, 29)

Comment

In Case T-131/99 *Michael Hamilton Shaw and others v Commission* [2002] ECR II-2023, the General Court reached a similar conclusion, holding that examination of the grant of an individual exemption had to be made within the same analytical framework as that used for assessing the restrictive effects. (para 163)

See also para 43, Guidelines on [Article 101(3) TFEU] according to which 'the conditions that consumers must receive a fair share of the benefits implies in general that efficiencies generated by the restrictive agreement within the relevant market must be sufficient to outweigh the anti-competitive effects produced by the agreement within the same relevant market. Negative effects on consumers in one geographic market or product market cannot normally be balanced against and compensated by positive effects for consumers in another unrelated geographic market or product market. However, where two markets are related, efficiencies achieved on separate markets can be taken into account provided that the group of consumers affected by the restriction and benefiting from the efficiency gains are substantially the same. Indeed, in some cases only consumers in a downstream market are affected by the agreement in which case the impact of the agreement on such consumers must be assessed. This is for instance so in the case of purchasing agreements.'

CECED	**Article 101(3) TFEU**
Case IV.F.1/36.718	The Four Conditions
European Commission, [2000] OJ L187/47	Object of Restricting Competition

Facts

The Conseil Européen de la Construction d'Appareils Domestiques (CECED) is an association which comprises manufacturers of domestic appliances and national trade associations. It notified an agreement to the Commission under the provisions of Regulation 17/62, for negative clearance or exemption. The agreement in question included provisions under which the parties agreed to cease producing and/or importing into the Community certain categories of washing machines. The agreement also included provisions for the joint dissemination of information on the environmentally conscious use of washing machines.

Held

The agreement in question sets a standard of energy efficiency, with which all the washing machines that the parties manufacture or import have to comply. It restricts the parties' autonomy in producing or importing washing machines thereby restricting competition between the parties. That agreement has the object of restricting or distorting competition within the meaning of Article 101(1) TFEU. (paras 30–7)

The agreement may be exempted under Article 101(3) TFEU if it satisfies the cumulative conditions in Article 101(3) TFEU:

Contribution to economic or technical progress and conferment of benefits on the consumer: 'The agreement is designed to reduce the potential energy consumption of new washing machines. ... Washing machines which, other factors being constant, consume less electricity are objectively more technically efficient. Reduced electricity consumption indirectly leads to reduced pollution from electricity generation.' The agreement will yield individual economic benefits as well as collective environmental benefits. (paras 47–57)

Indispensability of the restrictions: 'The agreement does not impose on the parties restrictions that are unrelated or unnecessary to the fulfilment of its objective benefits.' (para 58)

No elimination of competition: 'Major distributors agree that other factors like price, brand image, and technical performance may have more weight in purchase decisions than energy efficiency. ... Moreover, whilst not imposing unnecessary restrictions de jure, the agreement does not de facto impose any particular means of improving energy efficiency. The technology needed to produce machines under categories A to C is available to all manufacturers. The parties have therefore a wide variety of technical choices, on which they can effectively compete, to meet the minimum energy efficiency standard. ... Since third parties remain free to produce and to import machines below such categories, the agreement does not appreciably raise barriers to entry into the EEA market.' (paras 64–6)

'The cumulative conditions of Articles 101(3) TFEU are fulfilled.' (para 67)

Comment

The agreement in question was notified to the European Commission under the regime as set by Regulation 17/62. The change in the enforcement regime following the entry into force of Regulation 1/2003 and the abolition of the notification system did not affect the substantive analysis of Article 101(3) TFEU.

The agreement in question was found to have an anticompetitive object. Nonetheless it was subsequently exempted under Article 101(3) TFEU. Note in this respect Case T-17/93 *Matra Hachette SA v Commission*, where the General Court held that 'in principle, no anti-competitive practice can exist which, whatever the extent of its effects on a given market, cannot be exempted, provided that all the conditions laid down in [Article 101(3)] of the Treaty are satisfied.'

Facts

GlaxoSmithKline (GSK) (formerly Glaxo Wellcome, SA (GW)), a producer of pharmaceutical products, notified the Commission of a 'General Sales Conditions' document it issued to its Spanish wholesalers. The document included in Clause 4 a 'dual pricing mechanism' which resulted in a distinction between prices charged from wholesalers for medicines sold domestically and higher prices charged in the case of exports to other Member State. The Commission found Clause 4 to have both the object and the effect of restricting competition by limiting parallel trade between Spain and other Member States. The Commission rejected GW's request for exemption under Article 101(3) TFEU. GSK appealed the decision, and contested among other things the Commission refusal to grant an exemption under Article 101(3) TFEU.

Held

'Any agreement which restricts competition, whether by its effects or by its object, may in principle benefit from an exemption ...' (para 233)

A person who relies on Article 101(3) TFEU must demonstrate that the four conditions in that Article are satisfied. The Commission, for its part, must adequately examine the arguments and evidence. 'In certain cases, those arguments and that evidence may be of such a kind as to require the Commission to provide an explanation or justification, failing which it is permissible to conclude that the burden of proof borne by the person who relies on Article 101(3) TFEI has been discharged.... As the Commission agrees in its written submissions, in such a case it must refute those arguments and that evidence.' (paras 236, 234–36)

'[T]he Court dealing with an application for annulment of a decision applying [Article 101(3) TFEU] carries out, in so far as it is faced with complex economic assessments, a review confined, as regards the merits, to verifying whether the facts have been accurately stated, whether there has been any manifest error of appraisal and whether the legal consequences deduced from those facts were accurate (*Consten and Grundig v Commission*, ... p. 347; Case 26/76 *Metro v Commission*, paragraph 25; *Remia and others v Commission*, ... paragraph 34; and *Aalborg Portland and others v Commission*, [Joined Cases C-204/00 etc, [2004] ECR I-123, paragraph 279).' (para 241)

Under the first condition in Article 101(3) TFEU, an agreement must be found to yield appreciable objective advantages. The Commission is required first to 'examine whether the factual arguments and the evidence submitted to it show, in a convincing manner, that the agreement in question must enable appreciable objective advantages to be obtained ... it being understood that these advantages may arise not only on the relevant market but also on other markets (Case T-86/95 *Compagnie Générale Maritime and others v Commission* [2002] ECR II-1011, paragraph 343).' (paras 247–8)

'In the affirmative, it is for the Commission, in the second place, to evaluate whether those appreciable objective advantages are of such a kind as to offset the disadvantages identified for competition in the context of the examination carried out under [Article 101(1) TFEU] (see, to that effect, [Case 209/78] *Van Landewyck and others v Commission*, [1980] ECR 3125, paragraphs 183 to 185).' (para 250)

In the present case, 'the Commission did not validly take into account all the factual arguments and the evidence pertinently submitted by GSK, did not refute certain of those arguments even though they were sufficiently relevant and substantiated to require a response, and did not substantiate to the requisite legal standard its conclusion that it was not proved, first, that parallel trade was apt to lead to a loss in efficiency by appreciably altering GSK's capacity for innovation and, second, that Clause 4 of the General Sales Conditions was apt to enable a gain in efficiency to be achieved by improving innovation.' (paras 303, 251–306)

'After concluding its examination of the factual arguments and the evidence submitted by GSK and finding that they did not demonstrate the existence of an appreciable objective advantage, the Commission did not carry out the complex assessment (see paragraph 241 above) which would have been involved by the exercise seeking to balance that advantage against the disadvantage for competition identified in the part of the Decision devoted to the application of [Article 101(1) TFEU], as it stated on a number of occasions at the hearing.' (paras 304, 251–306)

The Commission's conclusions regarding the advantages being passed on to the consumer, the indispensability of Clause 4 of the General Sales Conditions and the absence of the elimination of competition were based on its conclusion relating to the lack of efficiency gain. Insofar as that conclusion is vitiated by illegality, those conclusions are themselves invalid. (paras 309, 310)

Comment

The Court upheld the plea alleging infringement of Article 101(3) TFEU. Note that this does not amount to clearance of the distribution system but only to rejection of the Commission's analysis.

In paragraph 248 the General Court noted that it is possible to balance between advantages in one market and detriment in another. Contrast this statement with paragraph 43, Guidelines on [Article 101(3) TFEU] and with Case C-360/92P *Publishers Association v Commission* (page 132 above).

GSK argued, among other things, that in the unique condition of the pharmaceutical market parallel trade leads to free riding, loss of efficiency and income. To address this, Clause 4 of the GSK General Sales Conditions optimised income and neutralised parallel trade. According to GSK, a rational producer is likely to reinvest those additional profits, made due to the restriction on parallel trade, in innovation. (paras 269–74) The Court noted that although parallel trade seems not to be the main factor underlying decisions on R&D it was for the Commission to conduct a more thorough examination of this point. (para 277)

In paragraph 273 the General Court refers to the final consumer, noting that 'The legitimacy of that transfer of wealth from producer to intermediary is not in itself of interest to competition law, which is concerned only with its impact on the welfare of the final consumer. In so far as the intermediary participates in intrabrand competition, parallel trade may have a pro-competitive effect …'. Contrast this with paragraph 84, Guidelines on [Article 101(3) TFEU] which states that 'consumers within the meaning of [Article 101(3) TFEU] are the customers of the parties to the agreement and subsequent purchasers.'

In paragraph 313 the General Court noted that due to the special characteristics of the pharmaceutical market, in terms of innovation and competition, GSK's market position and market shares 'do not in itself make it possible to conclude, in a convincing manner, that competition would be eliminated for a substantial part of the relevant products.' On this point note the Court of Justice judgment on appeal, page 103 above.

The Commission and GSK requested the Court of Justice to set aside in part the judgment of the General Court (Case C-501/06P). With respect to Article 101(3) TFEU, the Court of Justice rejected the Commission's claim of its incorrect application. The Court of Justice noted that: 'the examination of an agreement for the purposes of determining whether it contributes to the improvement of the production or distribution of goods or to the promotion of technical or economic progress, and whether that agreement generates appreciable objective advantages, must be undertaken in the light of the factual arguments and evidence provided in connection with the request for exemption under [Article 101(3) TFEU].' (para 102) 'Such an examination may require the nature and specific features of the sector concerned by the agreement to be taken into account if its nature and those specific features are decisive for the outcome of the analysis. Taking those matters into account, moreover, does not mean that the burden of proof is reversed, but merely ensures that the examination of the request for exemption is conducted in the light of the appropriate factual arguments and evidence provided by the party requesting the exemption.' (para 103) 'In holding, in paragraphs 276 and 303 of the judgment under appeal, that the Commission had erroneously failed to take into account certain aspects highlighted by GSK in its request, including in particular the specific structural features of the pharmaceuticals sector in question, and that such an omission vitiated the examination of GSK's request for exemption, the [General Court] did not err in law.' (para 104)

Visa International—Multilateral Interchange Fee	Article 101(3) TFEU
Case No COMP/29.373	The Four Conditions
European Commission, [2002] OJ L318/17	Price Fixing

Facts

The Commission reviewed various rules and regulations governing the Visa association and its members. In particular the Commission focused on a proposed, modified, Visa EU intra-regional interchange reimbursement fee scheme which sets the inter-bank payments made for each transaction carried out with a Visa payment card. The Commission found the scheme to appreciably restrict competition within the meaning of Article 101(1) TFEU by creating an agreement between competitors which restrict the freedom of banks individually to decide their own pricing policies and distorts the conditions of competition on the Visa issuing and acquiring markets. Following its finding, the Commission considered whether the scheme may be exempted under Article 101(3) TFEU. It concluded, subject to certain obligations, that the scheme fulfils the conditions for an exemption under Article 101(3) TFEU.

Held

First condition

The Commission accepted Visa's view that the multilateral interchange fee scheme (MIF) generates positive network effects and promotes the wider distribution and acceptance of Visa cards and all the services they provide. In the absence of the scheme there would be fewer Visa cardholders and fewer merchants accepting Visa cards. The Commission concluded that the Visa International Rules meet the first condition in Article 101(3) as they contribute to the existence of a large-scale international payment system with positive network externalities. (paras 79–91)

Second condition

'[F]our-party payment card schemes like that of Visa are networks with two distinct and interdependent types of consumers, merchants and cardholders. Each type of consumer would prefer the costs of the system to be paid by the other user. ... The Visa network, like any network characterized by network externalities, will provide greater utility to each type of user, the greater the number of users of the other type: the more merchants in the system, the greater the utility to cardholders and vice versa. The maximum number of users in the system will be achieved if the cost to each category of user is as closely as possible equivalent to the average marginal utility of the system to that category of user.' (paras 82, 83)

The proposed MIF is based on objective criteria and is transparent for users of the Visa scheme who end up paying the MIF in whole or in part. It can be said to provide a fair share of the benefits to each category of user of the Visa system. (paras 84–92)

Third condition

The Commission considered the indispensability of the proposed MIF scheme for the achievement of the benefits identified under the first and second conditions of Article 101(3), in particular, the positive network externalities. It found that 'without some kind of multilateral interchange fee arrangement, it would not be possible for issuers to recover from merchants the costs of services which are provided ultimately to the benefit of merchants, and this would lead to negative consequences, to the detriment of the entire system and all of its users.' (para 98)

The Commission was content that the proposed MIF, based as it was on objective criteria and being transparent is the least restrictive of competition out of all the possible types of MIF and satisfies the condition of indispensability. (paras 96–103)

Fourth condition

'The MIF does not eliminate competition between issuers, which remain free to set their respective client fees. Moreover, although it sets de facto a floor in the merchant fees it does not eliminate competition between acquirers either, since acquiring banks remain free to set the merchant fees and can still compete on the other components of the merchant fee apart from the MIF. Nor does it eliminate competition between Visa and its competitors ...' (para 106)

Comment

Although exceptional, as a matter of law, any agreement, including a price fixing agreement, could benefit from exemption under Article 101(3). In Case T-17/93 *Matra Hachette v Commission*, [1994] ECR II-595, the General Court held that 'In principle, no anti-competitive practice can exist which, whatever the extent of its effects on a given market, cannot be exempted, provided that all the conditions laid down in [Article 101(3)] of the Treaty are satisfied ...' See similarly *Consten and Grundig v Commission*, page 130 above, paragraph 110, *GlaxoSmithKline Services Unlimited v Commission*, page 134 above, paragraph 233.

In *Reims II* (Case IV/36.748) ([1999] OJ L275/17, [2000] 4 CMLR 704) the Commission granted exemption under Article 101(3) TFEU to an agreement between sixteen European postal operators on the fixing of fees for the costs of delivering cross-border mail. Although the agreement was found to be a price-fixing agreement and led to price increases for some customers, these negative effects were offset by the elimination of cross-subsidies and the improvement in service. The agreement was exempted subject to conditions.

Note that the MIF scheme in the Visa International case is not a 'classic' price-fixing agreement. The scheme does not set a price which is charged from a customer but establishes a remuneration mechanism between banks. Therefore although it restricted the freedom of the banks involved it did not result in subsequent restriction on competition. The scheme may be viewed as an example of a price-fixing mechanism which does not have as its object the restriction of competition.

With respect to the third condition under Article 101(3) TFEU (indispensability), note that 'the decisive factor is whether or not the restrictive agreement and individual restrictions make it possible to perform the activity in question more efficiently than would likely have been the case in the absence of the agreement or the restriction concerned. The question is not whether in the absence of the restriction the agreement would not have been concluded, but whether more efficiencies are produced with the agreement or restriction than in the absence of the agreement or restriction.' (para 74, Guidelines on [Article 101(3) TFEU])

With respect to the fourth condition under Article 101(3) TFEU (no elimination of competition), note that 'Whether competition is being eliminated within the meaning of the last condition of [Article 101(3) TFEU] depends on the degree of competition existing prior to the agreement and on the impact of the restrictive agreement on competition, i.e. the reduction in competition that the agreement brings about. The more competition is already weakened in the market concerned, the slighter the further reduction required for competition to be eliminated within the meaning of [Article 101(3)]. Moreover, the greater the reduction of competition caused by the agreement, the greater the likelihood that competition in respect of a substantial part of the products concerned risks being eliminated.' (para 107, Guidelines on [Article 101(3) TFEU])

On multilateral interchange fee arrangements and the application of Article 101(3) TFEU, note also the General Court's judgment in Case T-111/08 *MasterCard v European Commission* (below).

MasterCard v European Commission	**Article 101(3) TFEU**
Case T-111/08	The Four Conditions
General Court, [2009] 4 CMLR 17	Price Fixing

Facts

In 2007 the Commission adopted a decision on 'multilateral fallback interchange fees' (MIF) which concerned the relationship between the issuing and the acquiring bank on settlement of card transactions (COMP/34.579—*MasterCard*, COMP/36.518—*EuroCommerce*, COMP/38.580—*Commercial Cards*). In its decision the Commission found that the decisions of the MasterCard payment organisation in relation to the setting of the MIF constitute decisions by an association of undertakings that had the effect of inflating merchant service charges and restricted price competition between acquiring banks. In its decision, the Commission took the view that MIFs could not be regarded as ancillary restrictions as they were not objectively necessary for an open payment card scheme or for MasterCard's operation. In addition, the Commission did not accept MasterCard's argument that the MIFs should be exempted under Article 101(3) TFEU. MasterCard brought an action for the annulment of the Commission decision. Action dismissed.

Held (on exemption criteria)

When dealing with an application for annulment of a decision applying Article 101(3) TFEU the Court will carry, 'in so far as it is faced with complex economic assessments, a review confined, as regards the merits, to verifying whether the facts have been accurately stated, whether there has been any manifest error of appraisal and whether the legal consequences deduced from those facts were accurate (see *GlaxoSmithKline Services v Commission*, cited in paragraph 196 above, paragraph 241 and the case-law cited). ... It is nevertheless for the Court to establish not only whether the evidence relied on is factually accurate, reliable and consistent, but also whether it contains all the information which must be taken into account for the purpose of assessing a complex situation and whether it is capable of substantiating the conclusions drawn from it. On the other hand, it is not for the Court to substitute its own economic assessment for that of the institution which adopted the decision the legality of which it is requested to review (*GlaxoSmithKline Services v Commission*, cited in paragraph 196 above, paragraphs 242 and 243).' (paras 201, 202)

'Under the first condition laid down under [Article 101(3) TFEU], agreements that may be exempted must '[contribute] to improving the production or distribution of goods or to promoting technical or economic progress'. It is clear from the case-law of the Court of Justice and of the General Court that the improvement cannot be identified with all the advantages which the parties obtain from the agreement in their production or distribution activities. The improvement must in particular display appreciable objective advantages of such a character as to compensate for the disadvantages which they cause in the field of competition (see *Van den Bergh Foods v Commission* ...).' (para 206)

The fact that the Commission admits that payment card schemes such as the MasterCard system represent technical and economic progress is of no relevance to whether the MIF satisfies the first condition laid down under [Article 101(3) TFEU]. To satisfy that condition, it is for the parties to demonstrate that there were appreciable objective advantages arising specifically from the MIF. (para 207)

'[E]ven on the assumption that ... MIF contributes to increasing the output of the MasterCard system, that is not sufficient to establish that it satisfies the first condition laid down under [Article 101(3) TFEU].' (para 220)

'It must be observed that the primary beneficiaries of an increase in MasterCard system output are the MasterCard payment organisation and participating banks. However, as the case-law cited in paragraph 206 above shows, the improvement, within the meaning of the first condition of [Article 101(3) TFEU], cannot be identified with all the advantages which the parties obtain from the agreement in their production or distribution activities.' (para 221)

'As regards merchants, while an increase in the number of cards in circulation may increase the utility of the MasterCard system as far as they are concerned, it also has the effect of reducing their ability to constrain the level of the MIF and, therefore, of increasing the applicants' market power. It is reasonable to conclude that the risk of adverse effects on merchants' custom of a refusal to accept this method of payment, or of discrimination in that respect, is higher the greater the number of cards in circulation.' (para 222)

'[I]n the absence of proof of a sufficiently close link between the MIF and the objective advantages enjoyed by merchants, the fact that the MIF may contribute to the increase in MasterCard system output is not, in itself, capable of establishing that the first condition laid down under [Article 101(3)] is satisfied.' (para 226)

'The appreciable objective advantages to which the first condition of [Article 101(3) TFEU] relates may arise not only for the relevant market but also for every other market on which the agreement in question might have beneficial effects, and even, in a more general sense, for any service the quality or efficiency of which might be improved by the existence of that agreement (Case T-86/95 *Compagnie Générale Maritime* ..., paragraph 343, and *GlaxoSmithKline Services* ... paragraph 248). However, as merchants constitute one of the two groups of users affected by payment cards, the very existence of the second condition of [Article 101(3) TFEU] necessarily means that the existence of appreciable objective advantages attributable to the MIF must also be established in regard to them.' (para 228)

Comment

The applicants had not established that the conditions for the application of Article 101(3) TFEU were fulfilled. To satisfy the first condition of Article 101(3) TFEU it was not sufficient to show an increase in the output of the MasterCard system. The undertakings have to establish the presence of appreciable objective advantages, which compensate for the disadvantages which they cause in the field of competition, and which benefit not only the parties involved. (paras 206, 220, 221).

In paragraph 228 the Court held that the appreciable objective advantages may arise not only for the relevant market but also for every other market on which the agreement in question might have beneficial effects. Contrast this 'wide' approach with the Commission's more cautious view as manifested in its Guidelines on the application of Article 101(3) TFEU. There the Commission states that 'the assessment under [Article 101(3) TFEU] of benefits flowing from restrictive agreements is in principle made within the confines of each relevant market to which the agreement relates. ... Negative effects on consumers in one geographic market or product market cannot normally be balanced against and compensated by positive effects for consumers in another unrelated geographic market or product market.' (para 43) The Commission refers to Case T-86/95 *Compagnie Générale Maritime* [2002] ECR II-1011 in which the General Court held that Article 101(3) does not require that the benefits are linked to a specific market. The Commission notes however the limited application of this case as the affected group of consumers was the same. It subsequently states that 'where two markets are related, efficiencies achieved on separate markets can be taken into account provided that the group of consumers affected by the restriction and benefiting from the efficiency gains are substantially the same.' (para 43)

Note that in the *MasterCard* decision, as well as the *Visa* decision (COMP/29.373—*Visa International* (page 136 above)) the Commission concluded that the MIFs restricted competition, in particular, between acquirers and that they were not objectively necessary for the operation of the MasterCard and Visa schemes. The Commission's decisions differ on the application of Article 101(3) TFEU, as it took the view that Visa's MIF qualified for an exemption, whereas MasterCard's MIF did not. The Court noted on this matter that 'the Commission cannot be accused of having departed without explanation from the position it adopted in the *Visa II* decision regarding the analysis of MIFs for the purposes of [Article 101(3) TFEU], since the exemption in the *Visa II* decision was granted on the basis of a method of calculation that limited the level of the MIF to certain specific advantages for merchants, which distinguishes the circumstances in which that decision was adopted from those of the present case.' (para 235)

MasterCard appealed to the Court of Justice in Case C-382/12P *MasterCard and others v Commission*. Appeal dismissed.

GlaxoSmithKline Services Unlimited v Commission	**Article 101(3) TFEU**
Case T-168/01	Judicial Review
General Court, [2006] ECR II-2969 5 CMLR 29	Third Party Rights

Facts

GlaxoSmithKline (GSK) (formerly Glaxo Wellcome, SA (GW)), a producer of pharmaceutical products, notified the Commission of a selective distribution agreement. The Commission found Clause 4 of the agreement to have both the object and the effect of restricting competition by limiting parallel trade between Member States and rejected GW request for exemption under Article 101(3) TFEU. GSK appealed the decision, and contested the Commission's refusal to grant an exemption under Article 101(3) TFEU.

Held

'In that regard, the Court dealing with an application for annulment of a decision applying [Article 101(3) TFEU] carries out, in so far as it is faced with complex economic assessments, a review confined, as regards the merits, to verifying whether the facts have been accurately stated, whether there has been any manifest error of appraisal and whether the legal consequences deduced from those facts were accurate (*Consten and Grundig v Commission*, [Joined Cases 56/64 etc, [1966] ECR 299], p 347; *Metro I*, [Case 26/76, [1977] ECR 1875], paragraph 25; *Remia and others v Commission*, [Case 42/84, [1985] ECR 2545], paragraph 34; and *Aalborg Portland and others v Commission*, [Joined Cases C-204/00P etc, [2004] ECR I-123] paragraph 279).' (para 241)

'It is for the Court to establish not only whether the evidence relied on is factually accurate, reliable and consistent, but also whether it contains all the information which must be taken into account for the purpose of assessing a complex situation and whether it is capable of substantiating the conclusions drawn from it (Case C-12/03P *Commission v Tetra Laval* [2005] ECR I-987, paragraph 39, and Case T-210/01 *General Electric v Commission* [2005] ECR II-5575, paragraphs 62 and 63).' (para 242)

'On the other hand, it is not for the Court to substitute its own economic assessment for that of the institution which adopted the decision the legality of which it is requested to review.' (para 243)

'The Commission has, in particular, a margin of discretion which is subject to a restricted judicial review, in the operation consisting, once it has been ascertained that one of the criteria on which [Article 101(3) TFEU] makes provision for an exemption was satisfied, in weighing up the advantages expected from the implementation of the agreement and the disadvantages which the agreement entails for the final consumer owing to its impact on competition, which takes the form of a balancing exercise carried out in the light of the general interest appraised at [Union] level.' (para 244)

'Furthermore, review of the Commission's decision is carried out solely by reference to the elements of fact and of law existing on the date of adoption of the contested decision, without prejudice to the possibility afforded to the parties, in the exercise of their rights of defence, to supplement them by evidence established after that date but for the specific purpose of contesting or defending that decision ...' (para 245)

Comment

The Court adopted a non-interventionist approach and did not substitute its own economic assessment for that of the Commission. The court noted especially the Commission's margin of discretion in weighing up the advantages and disadvantages which the agreement entails.

Note that, according to Regulation 1/2003, National Competition Authorities and National Courts may exempt under Article 101(3) TFEU agreements, decisions and concerted practices caught by Article 101(1) TFEU. These decisions at the national level, when appealed, will be heard by the relevant appeal court within the national jurisdiction. One would expect to see a similar non-interventionist approach at the national level when judicial authorities review decisions of the national competition agency or lower courts concerning exemptions under Article 101(3) TFEU.

Under Article 263 TFEU, a natural or legal person may institute proceedings against a decision addressed to another person if the decision in question is of direct and individual concern to the former. In the context of Article 101(3) TFEU this provision opens the door to third parties who can contest the Commission's decision to clear an agreement under Article 101(3) TFEU. In Case 26/76 *Metro SB-Großmarkte GmbH & Co KG v Commission*, page 131 above, the court accepted an application for annulment of the Commission's decision granting exemption under Article 101(3) TFEU, from a third party (Metro) which was held to be directly and individually concerned by the contested Decision.

Similarly, in Case T-528/93 etc *Métropole Télévision SA and others v Commission*, [1996] ECR II-649, [1996] 5 CMLR 386, the Court noted in para 60 that the 'provisions of the Treaty concerning the right of interested persons to bring an action must not be interpreted restrictively, and hence, where the Treaty makes no provision, a limitation in that respect cannot be presumed to exist. Persons other than those to whom a decision is addressed may only claim to be individually concerned if that decision affects them by reason of certain attributes which are peculiar to them or by reason of circumstances in which they are differentiated from all other persons and by virtue of these factors distinguishes them individually just as in the case of the person addressed …' The Court then concluded that 'Antena 3' and 'RTI' were individually concerned by the Decision within the meaning of Article 263 TFEU. (paras 61–5, 78)

Österreichische Postsparkasse and Bank für Arbeit und Wirtschaft v Commission	**Article 101 TFEU**
Cases T 213/01 and T 214/01	Goals and Values
Court of Justice, [2006] ECR II-1601; [2007] 4 CMLR 14	Consumer Welfare

'It should be pointed out in this respect that the ultimate purpose of the rules that seek to ensure that competition is not distorted in the internal market is to increase the well-being of consumers. That purpose can be seen in particular from the wording of [Article 101 TFEU]. Whilst the prohibition laid down in [Article 101(1) TFEU] may be declared inapplicable in the case of cartels which contribute to improving the production or distribution of the goods in question or to promoting technical or economic progress, that possibility, for which provision is made in [Article 101(3) TFEU], is inter alia subject to the condition that a fair share of the resulting benefit is allowed for users of those products. Competition law and competition policy therefore have an undeniable impact on the specific economic interests of final customers who purchase goods or services. Recognition that such customers—who show that they have suffered economic damage as a result of an agreement or conduct liable to restrict or distort competition—have a legitimate interest in seeking from the Commission a declaration that [Articles 101 TFEU and 102 TFEU] have been infringed contributes to the attainment of the objectives of competition law.' (para 115)

T-Mobile Netherlands BV v Raad van bestuur van de Nederlandse Mededingingsautoriteit	**Article 101 TFEU**
	Goals and Values
Case C-8/08	Structure of the Market
Court of Justice, [2009] ECR I-4529; [2009] 5 CMLR 11	

'[Article 101 TFEU], like the other competition rules of the Treaty, is designed to protect not only the immediate interests of individual competitors or consumers but also to protect the structure of the market and thus competition as such.' (para 38)

'Therefore, contrary to what the referring court would appear to believe, in order to find that a concerted practice has an anti competitive object, there does not need to be a direct link between that practice and consumer prices.' (para 39)

Konkurrensverket v TeliaSonera AB	**Articles 101, 102 TFEU**
Case C-52/09	Goals and Values
Court of Justice, [2011] OJ C103/3	Internal Market

'[I]t must be observed at the outset that Article 3(3) TEU states that the European Union is to establish an internal market, which, in accordance with Protocol No 27 on the internal market and competition, annexed to the Treaty of Lisbon (OJ 2010 C 83, p 309), is to include a system ensuring that competition is not distorted.' (para 20)

Consten and Grundig v Commission	**Article 101 TFEU**
Joined Cases 56/64 and 58/64	Goals and Values
Court of Justice, [1966] ECR 299, 340	Internal Market

'[T]he Treaty, whose preamble and content aim at abolishing the barriers between States ... could not allow undertakings to reconstruct such barriers. [Article 101 TFEU] is designed to pursue this aim.'

Football Association Premier League Ltd	**Article 101 TFEU**
Joined Cases C-403/08 and C-429/08	Goals and Values
Court of Justice, [2011] ECR I-9083	Internal Market

'None the less, regarding the territorial limitations upon exercise of such a right, it is to be pointed out that, in accordance with the Court's case-law, an agreement which might tend to restore the divisions between national markets is liable to frustrate the Treaty's objective of achieving the integration of those markets through the establishment of a single market. Thus, agreements which are aimed at partitioning national markets according to national borders or make the interpenetration of national markets more difficult must be regarded, in principle, as agreements whose object is to restrict competition within the meaning of Article 101(1) TFEU (see, by analogy, in the field of medicinal products, Joined Cases C-468/06 to C-478/06 *Sot Lélos kai Sia and Others* [2008] ECR I-7139, paragraph 65, and *GlaxoSmithKline Services and Others v Commission and Others*, paragraphs 59 and 61).' (para 139)

CECED	**Article 101 TFEU**
Case IV.F.1/36.718	Goals and Values
European Commission, [2000] OJ L187/47	Environmental Considerations

'CECED members agree no longer to manufacture or to import washing machines that do not meet the criteria that they have agreed upon. The agreement sets a standard of energy efficiency, with which all the washing machines that the parties manufacture or import have to comply. By this obligation, the parties are no longer free to produce or to import machines under categories D to G, as they were free to do, and actually did, before the agreement.' (para 30)

'Washing machines which, other factors being constant, consume less electricity are objectively more technically efficient. Reduced electricity consumption indirectly leads to reduced pollution from electricity generation. The future operation of the total of installed machines providing the same service with less indirect pollution is more economically efficient than without the agreement.' (para 48)

'According to [Article 191 TFEU], environmental damage should be rectified at source. The Community pursues the objective of a rational utilisation of natural resources, taking into account the potential benefits and costs of action. Agreements like CECED's must yield economic benefits outweighing their costs and be compatible with competition rules. Although electricity is not a scarce resource and consumption reductions do not tackle emissions at source, account can also be taken of the costs of pollution.' (para 55)

'[T]he benefits to society brought about by the CECED agreement appear to be more than seven times greater than the increased purchase costs of more energy-efficient washing machines. Such environmental results for society would adequately allow consumers a fair share of the benefits even if no benefits accrued to individual purchasers of machines.' (para 56)

'The expected contribution to furthering energy efficiency both within the current technological limits of categories A to C and beyond the limits of category A, the cost–benefit ratio of the standard and the return on investment for individual users point to the conclusion that the agreement is likely to contribute significantly to technical and economic progress whilst allowing users a fair share of the benefits.' (para 57)

Philips-Osram	**Article 101 TFEU**
Case IV/34.252	Goals and Values
European Commission, [1994] OJ L378/37	Environmental Considerations

'The use of cleaner facilities will result in less air pollution, and consequently in direct and indirect benefits for consumers from reduced negative externalities. This positive effect will be substantially reinforced when R&D in the field produces lead-free materials.' (para 27)

DSD	**Article 101 TFEU**
Case COMP/34493	Goals and Values
European Commission, [2001] OJ L319/1	Environmental Considerations

'DSD is currently the only extensive take-back and exemption system for used sales packaging; according to its objects, it seeks to give effect to national and Community environmental policy with regard to the prevention, recycling and recovery of waste packaging. The Service Agreement is therefore intended to implement the objectives of the German Packaging Ordinance and of Parliament and Council Directive 94/62/EC of 20 December 1994 on packaging and packaging waste. This legislation is aimed at preventing or reducing the impact of waste packaging on the environment, thus providing a high level of environmental protection.' (para 143)

'The Service Agreements concluded by DSD and the collectors provide for practical steps to implement these environmental objectives in the collection and sorting of used sales packaging collected from households and equivalent collection points. Such agreements are essential if DSD is to meet the targets and obligations it has assumed in connection with the operation of the system. To this end the Service Agreements require the establishment of logistical arrangements for collection and sorting which involve substantial investment (see recital 53). Regular collection from private final consumers of used sales packaging differentiated into specified reusable materials, and subsequent sorting or preparation for full recovery, gives direct practical effect to environmental objectives.' (para 144)

Ford/Volkswagen	**Article 101 TFEU**
Case IV/33.814	Goals and Values
European Commission, [1993] OJ L20/14	Employment

'[The project] will have extremely positive effects on the infrastructure and employment in one of the poorest regions in the Community.' (para 23)

'In the assessment of this case, the Commission also takes note of the fact that the project constitutes the largest ever single foreign investment in Portugal. It is estimated to lead, inter alia, to the creation of about 5000 jobs and indirectly create up to another 10000 jobs, as well as attracting other investment in the supply industry. It therefore contributes to the promotion of the harmonious development of the Community and the reduction of regional disparities which is one of the basic aims of the Treaty.' (para 36)

Albany International BV v Stichting Bedrijspensioenfonds Textielindustrie	**Article 101 TFEU**
Case 67/96	Goals and Values
Court of Justice, [1999] ECR I-5751	Social Goals and Employment

'Next, it is important to bear in mind that, ... the activities of the Community are to include not only a "system ensuring that competition in the internal market is not distorted" but also "a policy in the social sphere".' (para 54)

'[C]ertain restrictions of competition are inherent in collective agreements between organisations representing employees and workers. However, the social policy objectives pursued by such agreements would be seriously undermined if management and labour were subject to [Article 101(1) TFEU] when seeking jointly to adopt a measure to improve conditions of work and employment.' (para 59)

4

Horizontal and Vertical Agreements

This chapter supplements Chapter 3 by providing a (non-exhaustive) review of different categories of agreements which may raise competitive concerns.

Horizontal Agreements

Horizontal agreements are those concluded between undertakings operating at the same level of production or distribution. These agreements may reduce competition when they involve price fixing, sharing of markets or other restrictions on business operations. They may also reduce competition when they involve softer forms of cooperation which increase the transparency in the market and reduce uncertainty concerning the competitors' conduct. On the other hand, they may at times yield substantial efficiencies and economic benefits, allowing companies to cope better with changing market realities, when they deal, for example, with research and development, production, purchasing, commercialisation, standardisation and environmental matters.

Cartel Agreements

The term 'cartel' usually refers to practices such as market sharing (Case IV/30.907), price fixing (Case C-199/92, 40/73, 2005/1071) and bid rigging (Case T-9/99) which have as their object the restriction of competition. When putting their case forward, competition authorities are not required to distinguish between agreements or concerted practice to establish the infringement (Case T-305/94) and may rely on the concept of single overall agreement to prove membership in the cartel (Case T-305/94, C-204/00, T-325/01). Undertakings that take part in cartel meetings may be responsible for the conduct of other cartel members (Case T-8/99). To limit their responsibility they must publicly distance themselves from the collusive discussions (T-303/02). An undertaking which did not take part in the cartel activity, may still be liable for it, if found to have contributed to its implementation (T-99/04). See:

On the enforcement powers of the European Commission, the European leniency programme, administrative fines and the Commission's inspection powers, see Chapter 10 below.

Price Fixing

Price fixing shields cartel members from price competition and transfers wealth from consumers to the conspiring undertakings. Article 101(1) TFEU provides that agreements, decisions or concerted practices which have as their object or effect the direct or indirect fixing of selling price would be prohibited. The European courts and Commission have generally treated price-fixing arrangements as having the object of restricting competition (above, Case C-199/92, 40/73). Such arrangements may be caught in cases of indirect communication between undertakings (Case 2005/1071 etc) and would rarely benefit from exemption under Article 101(3) (Case COMP/29.373).

With summary references to:

Purchase Price Fixing

In an effort to improve bargaining position and extract greater value in negotiation with suppliers, undertakings may join forces and form buying alliances. Joint purchasing may yield efficiencies and enhance welfare by creating economies of scale and reducing transaction costs. However, when members of the alliance engage in the fixing of input price, that activity falls foul of Article 101 TFEU, which condemns the direct or indirect fixing of purchase price.

The European Commission and the Court of Justice have generally condemned purchase price fixing as being anti-competitive by object (COMP/C.38.238/B.2, 123/83, C-209/07, C-264/01, C-8/08, C-501/06). Nonetheless, in instances where the fixing of purchase price formed part of an otherwise legitimate and transparent activity of a buying alliance, that activity has been analysed in light of its effect on the market (IV/27.958).

See also summary references to:

Collusive Tendering

A system of tendering relies on the absence of coordination or communication between the bidders to achieve a competitive result in areas where it might otherwise be absent. When tenders submitted by bidders are not the result of individual economic calculation, but of knowledge of the submissions of the other participants, competition is prevented, or at least restricted.

1061/1/1/06	*Makers UK Ltd v Office of Fair Trading*	166
1114/1/1/09	*Kier Group PLC and others v Office of Fair Trading*	167

With summary reference to:

2005/1071 etc	*Argos, Littlewoods and others v Office of Fair Trading*	166
IV/26 918	*European Sugar Industry*	166
IV/35.691.E-4	*Pre-Insulated Pipe Cartel*	166
1032/1/1/04	*Apex Asphalt and Paving Co Ltd v Office of Fair Trading*	167
C-209/07	*Competition Authority v Beef Industry Development Society Ltd*	167

Market Sharing and Non-compete Agreements

Article 101(1) TFEU, subsections (b) and (c) specifically refer to the limitation or control of markets and the sharing of markets. Market sharing allows competitors to shield themselves from the pressures of competition by dividing the market between them, thereby allowing them to exercise a large degree of market power within their exclusive territory. Note that whereas an agreement to fix price might still allow for residual competition between undertakings, for example on quality of service, market sharing, at its extreme, eliminates all forms of competition between undertakings.

IV/30.907	*Peroxygen products*	168
41/69	*ACF Chemie farma NV v Commission*	169
C-468/06 etc	*Sot Lélos kai Sia EE and Others v GlaxoSmithKline AEVE*	169

See also summary references to:

COMP/37.978	*Methylglucamine*	168
COMP/39.839	*Telefónica and Portugal Telecom*	168

At times, an agreement between undertakings to refrain from competition may form part of a wider permissible transaction. When such a non-compete agreement is directly related, proportionate and objectively necessary to the implementation of a main non-restrictive transaction, it may be classified as ancillary restraint and fall outside the scope of Article 101(1) TFEU. See Commission Guidelines on the Application of Article 101(3) TFEU, paragraphs 28–31. Also note the following cases, discussed in Chapter 3 above, under 'ancillary restraints':

42/84	*Remia BV v Commission*	116
C-250/92	*Gøttrup-Klim v Dansk Landbrugs Grovvareselskab AmbA*	117
T-112/99	*Metropole Télévision (M6) v Commission*	119

Collective Boycott

A collective boycott concerns an agreement between a group of competitors to exclude an actual or potential competitor by refusing to supply or acquire goods or services from it. This practice generally constitutes a restriction by object. See for example:

C-68/12	*Protimonopolný úrad Slovenskej republiky v Slovenská sporiteľňa*	170

With summary reference to:

T-21/99	*Dansk Rorindustri v Commission*	170
IV/35.691	*Pre-insulated pipes*	170
No. 537	*Fashion Originators Guild of Am v Federal Trade Commission*	170

Horizontal Cooperation Agreements

By contrast to the anticompetitive horizontal agreements discussed above, it is important to note that horizontal agreements can lead to efficiency gains, allowing medium and small sized companies to achieve greater efficiencies and cope with dynamic markets. The European Commission published Guidelines on the Applicability of Article 101 TFEU to Horizontal Cooperation Agreements [20011] OJ C11/1. The Guidelines provide an analytical framework for the most common types of horizontal cooperation, including agreements on research and development, production, purchasing, information exchange, commercialisation, and standardisation.

Also note the two Block Exemption Regulations which cover specialisation and research and development agreements:

• Commission Regulation No 1218/2010 on the Application of Article 101(3) TFEU to Certain Categories of Specialisation Agreements [2010] OJ L335/43
• Commission Regulation No 1217/2010 on the Application of Article 101(3) TFEU to Certain Categories of Research and Development Agreements [2010] L335/36

The Guidelines and Block Exemptions are avilable on the European Commission's website.

Information Exchange Arrangements

Information exchange, even between competitors, may serve legitimate goals when it concerns, for example, general information, standardisation or developments of new technologies. 'The exchange of information may however have an adverse effect on competition where it serves to reduce or remove uncertainties inherent in the process of competition. … Whether or not exchange of information has an appreciable effect on competition will depend on the circumstances of each individual case: the market characteristics, the type of information and the way in which it is exchanged…' (see UK OFT Guidelines on Agreements and Concerted Practices, OFT 401, 3.17–3.23)

The following cases illustrate the Courts' and Commission's approach toward information exchange, and its analysis as infringement by effect (T-34/92, T-35/92, C-89/85) or object (C-8/08, C-286/13P).

T-34/92	*Fiatagri v Commission (UK Agricultural Tractor Registration Exchange)*	171
T-35/92	*John Deere v Commission*	172
C-89/85	*A Ahlström Osakeyhtiö and others v Commission (Wood Pulp II)*	173
C-8/08	*T-Mobile Netherlands BV and others*	174
C-286/13P	*Dole Food Company*	175

With summary reference to:

T-141/94	*Thyssen Stahl AG v Commission*	172
T-25/95	*Cimenteries CBR and others v Commission*	172

The Guidelines on the Applicability of Article 101 TFEU to Horizontal Cooperation Agreements, [2011] OJ C11/1, provide a detailed outline of the Commission's approach to information exchange (paras 55–110).

Hub and Spoke Information Exchange

Hub and Spoke, also known as A–B–C information exchange, concerns the use of vertical information flow from a competing undertaking to a third party, which often operates upstream. The third party serves as the hub, through which information is disseminated back to the competing undertakings. The analysis of A–B–C information exchange, which has both horizontal and vertical elements, is divided to two phases, each comprising a conduct element and a mental element. See:

With summary reference to:

<u>Vertical Agreements</u>

Vertical agreements are agreements entered into between companies operating at different levels of the production or distribution chain. These agreements differ in their potential anticompetitive effect from horizontal agreements. Whereas the latter may eliminate competition between competing undertakings, the former concerns the relationship between upstream operator and downstream distributor or retailer. As a result, vertical agreements often generate positive effects and would raise concerns predominantly when there is some degree of market power at the upstream and/or downstream levels.

Of major significance to the application of Article 101 TFEU to vertical agreements are the Vertical Block Exemption and Vertical Guidelines.

The 2010 Vertical Guidelines set out the principles for the assessment of vertical agreements under Article 101(1) and 101(3) TFEU. See Commission Notice—Guidelines on Vertical Restraints, [2010] OJ C130/1.

The Vertical Block Exemption identifies categories of agreements which can be regarded as normally satisfying the conditions laid down in Article 101(3) TFEU. It provides exemption to vertical agreements when the market share held by each of the parties to the agreement on the relevant market does not exceed 30 per cent, and the agreement does not contain hard core or excluded restrictions (Article 4, 5, Vertical Block Exemption). See: Regulation 330/2010 on the application of Article 101(3) of the Treaty on the Functioning of the European Union to categories of vertical agreements and concerted practices ([2010] OJ L102/1).

Export Bans

Distribution agreements which include restrictions on export from one territory to another are generally regarded as having the object of restricting competition. The Vertical Block Exemption makes a direct reference to these restrictions in Article 4, treating them as hard-core restrictions which do not benefit from exemption. In line with this, export bans are unlikely to benefit from an individual exemption under Article 101(3) TFEU.

On export bans, see:

19/77	*Miller International Schallplatten GmbH v Commission*	179
31/85	*ETA Fabriques d'Ebauches v SA DK Investment and others*	181

With summary reference to:

56/64 etc	*Consten and Grundig v Commission*	179
C-279/87	*Tipp-Ex v Commission*	179
COMP/35.587	*PO Video Games (Nintendo)*	180
C-468/06 etc	*Sot Lélos kai Sia EE and others v GlaxoSmithKline AEVE*	180
C-501/06P etc	*GlaxoSmithKline Services Unlimited v Commission*	180
C-306/96	*Javico v Yves St Laurent*	180

Exclusive Distribution Agreements

Exclusive distribution agreements generally involve a supplier's commitment to sell his products to a single distributor in a designated territory, in return for a commitment from the distributor not to engage in active sales in other exclusively allocated territories. Such agreements are exempted by the Vertical Block Exemption when the market share held by each of the undertakings party to the agreement on the relevant market does not exceed 30 per cent, and the agreement does not contain hard-core restrictions (Article 4, Vertical Block Exemption). When combined with selective distribution, these agreements are exempted if active selling in other territories is not restricted. On exclusive distribution agreements, see for example:

03/2005	*Sarl Kitch Moto v SA Suzuki France*	182

With summary reference to:

56/64 etc	*Consten and Grundig v Commission*	182
56/65	*Société Technique Minière v Maschinenbau Ulm GmbH*	182
23/67	*SA Brasserie de Haecht v Consorts Wilkin-Janssen*	182

On the analysis of exclusive distribution agreements see also paragraphs 151–67, Vertical Guidelines.

Selective Distribution Agreements

Selective distribution agreements restrict the number of distributors by applying selection criteria for admission as an authorised distributor. These systems are commonly used to maintain a specialist distribution chain capable of providing specific services to branded high-quality or high-technology products. Purely qualitative selective distribution systems are in general considered to fall outside Article 101(1) for lack of anticompetitive effects (Case 26/76). Both qualitative and quantitative selective distribution systems are exempted by the Vertical Block Exemption when the market shares of the supplier and buyer do not exceed 30 per cent, provided active selling by the authorised distributors to each other and to end users is not restricted. On selective distribution systems, see:

26/76	*Metro SB-Großmarkte GmbH & Co KG v Commission*	183
C-439/09	*Pierre Fabre v Président de l'Autorité de la concurrence*	185

With summary reference to:

31/85	*ETA Fabriques d'Ebauches v SA DK Investment and others*	184
243/85	*SA Binon & Cie v SA Agence et Messageries de la Presse*	184
75/84	*Metro SB-Großmarkte GmbH & Co KG v Commission*	184

T-88/92	*Groupement d'achat Edouard Leclerc v Commission*	184
IV/33.542	*Parfums Givenchy system of selective distribution*	184

On the analysis of selective distribution agreements see also paras 174–88, Vertical Guidelines.

Online Sales Restrictions

The use of online sales enables retailers and producers to reach a large number and wide variety of customers. As such, it supports the creation of an open and competitive environment, to the benefit of consumers. By contrast, a ban on online sales may significantly limit competition and has been treated by the Commission and Court of Justice as having the object of restricting competition.

C-439/09	*Pierre Fabre v Président de l'Autorité de la concurrence*	185
COMP/37.975	*PO/Yamaha*	187

On the Commission's approach to online sales restrictions see paras 50–4, Vertical Guidelines.

Single Branding Agreements

A non-compete arrangement is based on a buyer's obligation to purchase all or most of his requirements of a particular group of products from one supplier. These agreements are exempted under the Vertical Block Exemption as long as the market share of both supplier and buyer each do not exceed 30 per cent, and subject to a limitation in time of five years for the non-compete obligation.

T-65/98	*Van den Bergh Foods Ltd v Commission*	188

With summary references to:

T-7/93	*Langnese-Iglo v Commission*	188
C-234/89	*Stergios Delimitis v Henninger Bräu AG*	189

On the analysis of single branding agreements see also paras 129–50, Vertical Guidelines.

Franchise Agreements

A franchise agreement allows the franchisor to expand his brand without investing its own capital and allows the franchisee to benefit from the reputation and experience of the franchisor. Under a franchise agreement, the franchisor which has established itself on a given market licenses trademarks, business systems and know-how to independent traders (franchisee) in exchange for a fee. On the analysis of these agreements under Article 101 TFEU, see:

161/84	*Pronuptia de Paris GmbH v Pronuptia de Paris Irmgard Schillgallis*	190

With summary reference to:

56/64 etc	*Consten and Grundig v Commission*	191
IV/31.697	*Charles Jourdan*	191
IV/31.428 etc	*Yves Rocher*	191

On the analysis of franchise agreements see also paragraphs 189–91, Vertical Guidelines.

Licensing of Intellectual Property Rights

Licensing concerns the grant by the holder of an intellectual properly right (the licensor) of such right to a third party (the licensee), allowing it to use the licensed materials. Such agreements may concern patented goods, copyrights, trademarks or brand licensing.

Of major significance to licensing agreements is the Technology Transfer Block Exemption (TTBER) which provides exemptions to a range of technology transfer agreements. The Commission elaborates on the application of the TTBER in its Guidelines on the application of Article 101 TFEU to technology transfer agreements.

Where the intellectual property provisions in an agreement do not constitute its primary object, the Vertical Block Exemption may be applicable (Article 2(3), Regulation 330/2010). Note however that the Vertical Block Exemption does not apply to vertical agreements the subject matter of which falls within the scope of any other block exemption regulation (Article 2(5), Regulation 330/2010).

See Chapter 8 for an in-depth analysis of licensing agreements.

Resale Price Maintenance

Restriction of the buyer's ability to determine its sale price is generally regarded as having the object of restricting competition. Such restriction on pricing policies should be distinguished from recommended and maximum resale prices which may have the effect of restricting competition but are not considered as having the object of restricting competition.

The Vertical Block Exemption blacklists restrictions of the buyer's ability to determine the sale price (Article 4(a)). The Vertical Guidelines note that while Resale Price Maintenance is presumed to restrict competition and thus to fall within Article 101(1), undertakings have the possibility to plead an efficiency defence under Article 101(3) in an individual case. (Vertical Guidelines, paras 223–9)

Indeed, economic literature suggests that, at times, the fixing of resale price in vertical agreements may be pro-competitive. This insight led the US Supreme Court to overturn the per se rule which previously deemed such activity as categorically illegal. See: *Leegin judgment* (06-480).

243/83	*SA Binon & Cie v SA Agence et Messageries de la Presse*	192

See also summary references to:

161/84	*Pronuptia de Paris GmbH v Pronuptia de Paris Irmgard Schillgallis*	193
26/76	*Metro SB-Großmarkte GmbH & Co KG v Commission*	193
IV/30.658	*Polistil/Arbois*	193
06–480	*Leegin Creative Leather Products, Inc v PSKS, Inc*	193

On resale price maintenance note also paragraphs 223–9, Vertical Guidelines.

Most-Favoured Nation Clauses

Most-favoured-nation clauses (MFNs), also known as Parity Clauses, aim to provide assurance to the downstream distributor that it has received goods or services from the upstream supplier, at terms that are at least as favourable as those offered to any other distributors. MFNs help resolve the hold-up problem, often manifested in vertical relationships, by removing the risk of the supplier, or other sellers, free-riding on the downstream distributor's investment in promoting the supplier's products and services. MFNs may be narrow or wide in scope and may adopt an agency or wholesale distribution model.

MFNs combined with agency distribution models have played an increasingly significant role in the relationship between price comparison websites (PCWs) and their suppliers and led to several investigations into their pro, and possible anticompetitive effects. In general, while wide MFNs have been condemned as restricting competition, narrow MFNs have been more positively accepted as pro-competitive. See:

VI—Kart 1 /14 (V)	*HRS-Hotel Reservation Service v Bundeskartellamt*	194
596/2013	*Booking.com BV*	196

See also summary references to:

COMP/AT-39.847	*E-Books*	195
No 13-3741	*United States v Apple, Inc*	195
No 14155-4	*United States v Blue Cross Blue Shield of Michigan*	195

Agency Agreements

An agent is vested with the power to negotiate and conclude an agreement on behalf of the principal. Agreements entered into between agent and principal will not be subjected to the prohibitions laid down under Article 101(1) TFEU where an agent, although having separate legal personality, does not independently determine his own conduct on the market, but carries out the instructions given to him by his principal. In such circumstances the agreement between the two parties will not amount to an agreement between undertakings. See:

T-325/01	*DaimlerChrysler AG v Commission*	198
C-217/05	*Confederación Española de Empresarios de Staciones de Servicio v Compañia de Petróleos SA*	200

See also summary references to:

40/73 etc	*Suiker Unie and others v Commission*	199
C-266/93	*Bundeskartellamt v Volkswagen AG and VAG Leasing GmbH*	199

On agency agreements note also paragraphs 12–21, Vertical Guidelines.

Tate & Lyle plc and others v Commission
Joined Cases T-202, 204, 207/98
General Court, [2001] ECR II-2035, [2001] 5 CMLR 22

Horizontal Agreements
Cartel Agreement

Facts

Application for annulment of Commission decision in which a number of undertakings which took part in various meetings with other sugar producers were found to have infringed Article 101(1) TFEU by engaging in anticompetitive agreements or concerted practice on the industrial and retail sugar markets. (Case IV/F-3/33.708 *British Sugar plc*, Case IV/F-3/33.709 *Tate & Lyle plc*, Case IV/F-3/33.710 *Napier Brown & Company Ltd*, Case IV/F-3/33.711 *James Budgett Sugars Ltd*) ([1999] OJ L76/1).

Held

The undertakings involved do not deny their participation in meetings but challenge the Commission finding that such meetings had an anticompetitive purpose. In particular they argue that the nature of the EU sugar market and the Union sugar scheme do not allow producers the freedom to determine themselves the price of products. This argument cannot be accepted. Price competition is still possible between the minimum price offered by the Union sugar scheme and the prices decided upon by the undertakings. The Commission was therefore right to take the view that the purpose of those meetings was to restrict competition by the coordination of pricing policies. (paras 42–3)

'[T]he fact that only one of the participants at the meetings in question reveals its intentions is not sufficient to exclude the possibility of an agreement or concerted practice. The criteria of coordination and cooperation laid down by the case-law on restrictive practices, far from requiring the working out of an actual plan, must be understood in the light of the concept inherent in the provisions of the Treaty relating to competition that each economic operator must determine independently the policy which he intends to adopt on the [internal] market (40/73 etc *Suiker Unie* [1975] ECR 1663, paragraph 173).' (paras 54, 55)

'Although it is correct to say that that requirement of independence does not deprive economic operators of the right to adapt intelligently to the existing and anticipated conduct of their competitors, it does however strictly preclude any direct or indirect contact between such operators, the object or effect whereof is either to influence the conduct on the market of an actual or potential competitor or to disclose to such a competitor the course of conduct which they themselves have decided to adopt or contemplate adopting on the market (*Suiker Unie*, paragraph 174).' (paras 56)

'In the present case, it is undisputed that there were direct contacts between the three applicants, whereby British Sugar informed its competitors, Tate & Lyle and Napier Brown, of the conduct which it intended to adopt on the sugar market in Great Britain. In Case T-1/89 *Rhône-Poulenc v Commission* [1991] ECR II-867, in which the applicant had been accused of taking part in meetings at which information was exchanged amongst competitors concerning, inter alia, the prices which they intended to adopt on the market, the [General Court] held that an undertaking, by its participation in a meeting with an anti-competitive purpose, not only pursued the aim of eliminating in advance uncertainty about the future conduct of its competitors but could not fail to take into account, directly or indirectly, the information obtained in the course of those meetings in order to determine the policy which it intended to pursue on the market (*Rhône-Poulenc*, paragraphs 122 and 123). This Court considers that that conclusion also applies where, as in this case, the participation of one or more undertakings in meetings with an anti-competitive purpose is limited to the mere receipt of information concerning the future conduct of their market competitors.' (paras 57, 58)

Comment

Note paragraph 58 in which the General Court condemned not only the exchange of information but also the receipt of information in a meeting, as both have the same impact of eliminating in advance uncertainty about the competitors' future conduct. See also Case T-8/99 and commentary on pages 155 and 156 below.

Sigma Tecnologie di Rivestimento Srl v Commission	**Horizontal Agreements**
Case T-28/99	Cartel Agreement
General Court, [2002] ECR II-1845	

Facts

An application for annulment of Commission decision in Case No IV/35.691/E-4 *Pre-Insulated Pipe* Cartel ([1999] OJ L24/1) in which the Commission found that various undertakings and, in particular, Sigma Tecnologie di Rivestimento Srl (STR), had participated in a European-wide cartel agreement, fixed quotes and shared with others the market for heating pipes. In addition the Commission found that STR had participated in an Italian cartel in which members fixed quotes between them. STR contested the findings and argued, among other things, that it did not take part in all the cartel meetings and did not know of or take part in the European cartel agreements.

Held

'It is settled case-law that an undertaking which has participated in a multiform infringement of the competition rules by its own conduct, which met the definition of an agreement or concerted practice having an anti-competitive object within the meaning of [Article 101(1) TFEU] and was intended to help bring about the infringement as a whole, may also be responsible for the conduct of other undertakings followed in the context of the same infringement throughout the period of its participation in the infringement, where it is proved that the undertaking in question was aware of the unlawful conduct of the other participants, or could reasonably foresee such conduct, and was prepared to accept the risk (Case C-49/92 P *Commission v Anic Partecipazioni* [1999] ECR I-4125, paragraph 203).' (para 40)

The Commission established that STR participated in cartel meetings concerning the Italian market. Since STR accepts that it participated, at least in some of the cartels meetings, it must be concluded that the Commission properly established its participation in an agreement on the Italian market. (paras 41–3)

'However, the Commission did not show that [STR], when participating in the agreement on the Italian market, was aware of the anti-competitive conduct at the European level of the other undertakings, or that it could reasonably have foreseen such conduct.' (para 44)

'The mere fact that there is identity of object between an agreement in which an undertaking participated and a global cartel does not suffice to render that undertaking responsible for the global cartel. It is only if the undertaking knew or should have known when it participated in the cartel that in doing so it was joining in the global cartel that its participation in the agreement concerned can constitute the expression of its accession to that global cartel.' (para 45)

'It follows from all the foregoing that the Commission has failed to adduce evidence sufficiently precise and consistent to found the firm conviction that [STR] knew or should have known that by participating in the agreement on the Italian market it was joining the European cartel. Accordingly, the decision must be annulled in so far as the applicant is alleged, in addition to participating in an agreement on the Italian market, to have participated in the cartel covering the whole of the [internal] market.' (paras 51, 52)

Comment

In C-204/00P etc *Aalborg Portland A/S and others v Commission* the Court of Justice held that to prove membership in a cartel, 'it is sufficient for the Commission to show that the undertaking concerned participated in meetings at which anti-competitive agreements were concluded, without manifestly opposing them, to prove to the requisite standard that the undertaking participated in the cartel. Where participation in such meetings has been established, it is for that undertaking to put forward evidence to establish that its participation in those meetings was without any anti-competitive intention by demonstrating that it had indicated to its competitors that it was participating in those meetings in a spirit that was different from theirs.' (para 81) For detailed analysis of this case see page 77 above, Chapter 3.

In Case T-113/07 *Toshiba Corp v Commission*, the General Court noted that when establishing the existence of a cartel, 'the Commission cannot be required to produce documents expressly attesting to contacts between the traders concerned. The fragmentary and sporadic items of evidence which may be available to the Commission should, in any event, be capable of being supplemented by inferences which allow the relevant circumstances to be reconstituted. The existence of an anti-competitive practice or agreement may therefore be inferred from a number of coincidences and indicia which, taken together, can, in the absence of another plausible explanation, constitute evidence of an infringement.' (para 82)

In Joined Cases T-305/94 etc *LVM and others v Commission*, the General Court held that an undertaking may be held responsible for an overall cartel even though it is shown to have participated directly only in one or some of its constituent elements. For detailed analysis of this case see pages 81, 82 above.

In T-325/01 *Daimler Chrysler AG v Commission* the General Court held that where it has been established that an undertaking has participated in cartel meetings 'it is for that undertaking to put forward evidence to establish that its participation in those meetings was without any anti-competitive intention, by demonstrating that it had indicated to its competitors that it was participating in those meetings in a spirit that was different from theirs. … In the absence of evidence of that distancing, the fact that an undertaking does not abide by the outcome of those meetings is not such as to relieve it of full responsibility for the fact that it participated in the concerted practice (Case T-347/94 *MayrMelnhof v Commission* [1998] ECR II-1751, paragraph 135, and Joined Cases T-25/95, […] *Cimenteries CBR and others v Commission* [2000] ECR II-491, paragraph 1389).' (para 202). For detailed analysis of this case see page 88 above, Chapter 3.

In Case C-199/92 *Hüls AG v Commission* the Court of Justice considered the Commission's Polypropylene decision (IV/31.149—*Polypropylene*) in which it found Hüls AG to have infringed Article 101(1) TFEU by participating in an agreement and concerted practice aimed at coordinating their commercial practices and fixing the prices of polypropylene. For detailed analysis see page 75 above, Chapter 3.

In Case 40/73 etc *Suiker Unie and others v Commission*, the Court of Justice considered a Commission decision (IV/26.918—*European sugar industry*) finding a number of undertakings to collude in the market for sugar by aligning prices, control deliveries of sugar and applying other limitations on sales. For detailed analysis of this case, see page 72 above, Chapter 3.

In Case T-99/04 *AC-Treuhand AG v Commission* the General Court held that an undertaking may be liable for taking part in a cartel even when it is not active on the market on which the restriction of competition materialised, but nonetheless, in its action it contributed to the implementation of the cartel. For detailed analysis of this case, see page 86 above, Chapter 3, and page 156 below.

In Case C-97/08P *Akzo Nobel and others v Commission* [2009] 5 CMLR 23, the Court of Justice held that a parent company can be held liable for cartel activity in which its wholly owned subsidiary participated even if the parent company was not party to the anticompetitive activity. When the two form a single undertaking, the Commission can address a decision imposing fines to the parent company, without having to establish the personal involvement of the latter in the infringement. The Court of Justice clarified that where a parent company has a 100 per cent shareholding in its subsidiary, there is a rebuttable presumption that that parent company exercises a decisive influence over the conduct of its subsidiary. That presumption may also be applied in cases of partial ownership which entail control.

In Case T-303/02 *Westfalen Gassen Nederland v Commission* [2006] ECR II-4567, [2007] 4 CMLR 334, the General Court held that the notion of public distancing from the cartel agreement, as a means of excluding liability, 'must be interpreted narrowly'. (para 103) In this case the undertaking did not express a view which would have left the other undertakings in no doubt that it was distancing itself from the agreement. Its conduct was akin to tacit approval which effectively encouraged the continuation of the infringement and compromised its discovery. (para 84) If the undertaking 'wanted to disassociate itself from the collusive discussions, it could easily have written to its competitors … to say that it did not in any way want to be considered to be a member of the cartel.' (para 103)

AC-Treuhand AG v Commission (AC-Treuhand I)	**Article 101 TFEU**
Case T-99/04	Liability for Cartel Activity
General Court, [2008] ECR II-1501	Cartel Facilitator

Facts

The Commission found a number of companies to have infringed Article 101 TFEU by forming a cartel in the European market for organic peroxides (Case COMP/E-2/37.857—*Organic peroxides* [2005] OJ L110, 44). Although Treuhand AG, a consultancy firm, was not active in the market for organic peroxides, it facilitated the cartel activity. Among other things, it organised meetings and covered up evidence of the infringement. Treuhand AG appealed to the General Court and argued that it has not infringed Article 101 TFEU since its relationship to the cartel members was merely one of non-punishable complicity.

Held

An undertaking may participate in the implementation of a restriction of competition even if it does not restrict its own freedom of action on the market on which it is primarily active. (para 127)

In order to establish that an undertaking that participated in the cartel is liable as a co-perpetrator of the infringement it is sufficient to show that it attended meetings at which anticompetitive agreements were concluded, without manifesting its opposition to such meetings. The Commission must prove that that undertaking intended to contribute to the activity and was aware of the substantive conduct planned or implemented by other undertakings, or that it could reasonably have foreseen that conduct and that it was ready to accept the attendant risk. (paras 129, 130)

'In addition, as regards the determination of the individual liability of an undertaking whose participation in the cartel is not as extensive or intense as that of the other undertakings, it is apparent from the caselaw that, although the agreements and concerted practices referred to in Article 101(1) TFEU necessarily result from collaboration by several undertakings, all of whom are co-perpetrators of the infringement but whose participation can take different forms—according to, inter alia, the characteristics of the market concerned and the position of each undertaking on that market, the aims pursued and the means of implementation chosen or envisaged—the mere fact that each undertaking takes part in the infringement in ways particular to it does not suffice to rule out its liability for the entire infringement, including conduct put into effect by other participating undertakings but sharing the same anticompetitive object or effect (*Commission v Anic Partecipazioni*, …, paragraphs 78 to 80).' (para 131)

The fact that an undertaking did not take part in all aspects of an anticompetitive scheme, or played a minor role in it, or only passively contributed to its implementation, is not material to the establishment of an infringement and does not call into question the undertaking's individual liability for the infringement as a whole. That fact, none the less has an influence on the assessment of the extent of that liability and thus on the severity of the penalty. (paras 132, 133)

Appeal dismissed.

Comment

To ensure the effectiveness of Article 101 TFEU the court held that an undertaking may be responsible for the implementation of the anticompetitive activity even if it does not restrict its own freedom of action on the market on which it is primarily active. (para 127)

Treuhand AG played an accessory role as coperpetrator of the infringement and was therefore found jointly liable for the infringement of Article 101 TFEU.

On a parent company's liability for its subsidiary's cartel activity, see Chapter 1 (Undertakings) and in particular: Case C-97/08P *Akzo Nobel and others v Commission* (page 26 above), Case C-628/10P *Alliance One International and Others v Commission* (page 27 above), Case C-172/12P *EI du Pont v Commission* (page 28 above).

AC-Treuhand AG v Commission (AC-Treuhand II)	**Article 101 TFEU**
Case C-194/14	Liability for Cartel Activity
Court of Justice, [2015] CMLR 26	Cartel Facilitator

Facts

The Commission found a number of companies to have infringed Article 101 TFEU by participating in a set of anti-competitive agreements and concerted practices relating to heat stabilisers (COMP/38589—Heat Stabilisers). AC-Treuhand, a consultancy firm not active on the relevant markets, was found to have played an essential role in the infringements by organising meetings, collecting and supplying data, and offering to act as a moderator between the parties. An action for annulment of the Commission decision was dismissed by the General Court (Case T-27/10). The company subsequently appealed to the Court of Justice.

Held

There is nothing in the wording of Article 101 TFEU that indicates that it is directed only at the parties to agreements or concerted practices who are active on the markets affected by those agreements or practices. In order to be able to find that an undertaking participated in and is liable for an infringement, the Commission must show that the undertaking intended to contribute by its own conduct to the common objectives pursued by all the participants and was aware of the actual conduct planned. (paras 27–30)

'[P]assive participation in the infringement, such as the presence of an undertaking in meetings at which anti-competitive agreements were concluded, without that undertaking clearly opposing them, are indicative of collusion capable of rendering the undertaking liable under Article 81(1) EC, since a party which tacitly approves of an unlawful initiative, without publicly distancing itself from its content or reporting it to the administrative authorities, encourages the continuation of the infringement and compromises its discovery (see, to that effect, judgment in *Dansk Rørindustri and Others* v *Commission*, C-189/02 P, C-202/02 P, C-205/02 P to C-208/02 P and C-213/02 P, EU:C:2005:408, paragraphs 142 and 143 and the case-law cited).' (para 31)

The terms 'agreement' and 'concerted practice' in Article 101 TFEU do not presuppose a mutual restriction of freedom of action on one and the same market on which all the parties are present. Article 101 TFEU refers generally to all agreements and concerted practices which, in either horizontal or vertical relationships, distort competition on the common market, irrespective of the market on which the parties operate. (paras 33–5)

In the present case AC-Treuhand played an essential role in the infringements at issue by organising meetings and actively participating in them, by collecting and supplying data on sales on the relevant markets, and by offering to act as a moderator. The action taken by AC-Treuhand did not constitute mere peripheral services but was directly linked to the anticompetitive efforts made by the producers of heat stabilisers. (paras 37–9)

Comment

Appeal dismissed. A facilitator is liable for cartel activity, irrespective of whether the facilitator operates on the relevant market as long as it is aware of the anticompetitive efforts of the cartel members.

Note the Commission decision in Case AT.39861—*Yen Interest Rate Derivatives* (COM(2015) 432 final), where ICAP was found to have facilitated the exchange of information between the banks, leading to manipulation of the yen LIBOR. Appeal pending: Case T-180/15 *ICAP AO v Commission*.

Also note the discussion on hub-and-spoke on pages 176–8 below.

Argos, Littlewoods and others v Office of Fair Trading	**Horizontal Agreements**
Case No 2005/1071, 1074 and 1623	Price Fixing
Court of Appeal, [2006] EWCA Civ 1318	Indirect Price Fixing

Facts

The appeals arose of two distinct investigations by the UK Office of Fair Trading (OFT) under the UK Competition Act 1998. In the first decision the OFT found a price-fixing agreement in the toys and games market between Hasbro UK Ltd, Argos Ltd and Littlewoods Ltd. In the second decision the OFT found that a number of companies fixed the prices of replica football kits. Both decisions were appealed (separately) to the UK Competition Appeal Tribunal (the Tribunal) (Football Shirts decision, Toys and Games decision). The Tribunal's decisions were appealed to the Court of Appeal (CA). In both cases the appellants challenged the OFT and Tribunal holding that there was a horizontal agreement between competitors (the appellants accepted the OFT's finding of an anticompetitive vertical agreement).

The CA judgment is long and detailed, not least because it concerns two different sets of facts. The analysis includes very interesting comments on indirect price fixing. Extracts of the analysis concerning the football shirt cartel are given below.

Held

'Although the concept of a concerted practice implies the existence of reciprocal contacts, that requirement may be met where one competitor discloses its future intentions or conduct on the market to another when the latter requests it or, at the very least, accepts it.' (para 21(V))

'It is not in dispute that there could be a trilateral or multilateral agreement or concerted practice between two or more customers and their common supplier, nor that this might come about by virtue of indirect contact between the customers via that supplier. Equally it is clear that there could be a series of bilateral vertical agreements between one supplier and several of its customers, none of the customers being aware of the fact or nature of the agreements between the supplier and other customers, such that there would be no horizontal element to the customers' agreements. If, on the other hand, each customer did know of the other agreements, it could be equivalent to a multilateral agreement between the supplier and each of the customers.' (para 31)

'Mr Lasok QC, for JJB, criticised as too general paragraph 664 of the [Tribunal] judgment, as follows: "The cases about complaints cited above, notably *Suiker Unie* … and the Commission's decision in *Hasselblad* …, show that if a competitor (A) complains to a supplier (B) about the market activities of another competitor (C), and the supplier B acts on A's complaint in a way which limits the competitive activity of C, then A, B and C are all parties to a concerted practice to prevent, restrict or distort competition. We can see the sense of that case law. Were it otherwise, established customers would always be able to exert pressure on suppliers not to supply new and more competitive outlets, free of any risk of infringing the Chapter I prohibition. A competitor who complains to a supplier about the activities of another competitor should not in our view be absolved of responsibility under the Act if the supplier chooses to act on the complaint."' (para 33)

'Mr Lasok submitted that the law as to complaints does not permit a conclusion that, merely by complaining, the complainer is party to an agreement or concerted practice with the undertaking to which the complaint is made, let alone with the party complained about. Of course there is and could be no general rule on the point. There can be complaints of all sorts, by no means all of which are made in the expectation that anything will be done about the matter complained about, still less something that might amount to a breach of the Chapter I prohibition. In the present case, however, as the Tribunal pointed out at paragraph 667, the complaints were vigorous and repeated, they were made at the highest levels, and they were backed up by an implicit threat arising from the strength of JJB's commercial position in relation to Umbro.' (para 72)

'Mr Lasok submitted that, for an undertaking to be involved in an anti-competitive arrangement reached between others, it must know of the arrangement, not merely of the possibility that there might be such an arrangement. He cited passages from the judgment of the General Court in *Cimenteries v Commission*, Cases T-25/95 etc [2000] ECR II-491 for this proposition, where the General Court considered whether one undertaking … was aware that the others with whom it was dealing were themselves part of a much wider and more serious agreement or concerted practice, and concluded that it was not, and was therefore not to be penalised on the basis that it was a participant in the more serious breach of [Article 101 TFEU].' (para 87) 'In general that is no doubt the case, but it seems to us that, where the first undertaking, in effect, asks the second to do something in relation to a third which would be an anti-competitive agreement or concerted practice, and the second does do so, the first cannot rely on the fact that it may not have known whether the second and third did enter into such an agreement or concerted practice in order to assert that it was not involved as a participant in what they did. No doubt Umbro's staff did not perceive JJB's conduct as "asking" Umbro to act in relation to Sports Soccer, but it did amount to a particularly forceful form of request or demand.' (para 88)

'[W]e do not need to decide … whether Mr Lasok's criticism … is justified. But it does seem to us that the Tribunal may have gone too far, in that paragraph, insofar as it suggests that if one retailer (A) privately discloses to a supplier (B) its future pricing intentions "in circumstances where it is reasonably foreseeable that B might make use of that information to influence market conditions" and B then passes that pricing information on to a competing retailer (C) then A, B and C are all to be regarded as parties to a concerted practice having as its object or effect the prevention, restriction or distortion of competition. The Tribunal may have gone too far if it intended that suggestion to extend to cases in which A did not, in fact, foresee that B would make use of the pricing information to influence market conditions or in which C did not, in fact, appreciate that the information was being passed to him with A's concurrence. This is not such a case on the facts.' (para 91)

'[T]he Tribunal was entitled to find that (1) JJB provided confidential price information to Umbro in circumstances in which it was obvious that it would or might be passed on to Sports Soccer in support of Umbro's attempt to persuade Sports Soccer to raise its prices … (2) Umbro did use the information in relation to Sports Soccer in that way, (3) Sports Soccer did agree to raise its prices in reliance on this information … and (4) Umbro did tell JJB of this, thereby making it clear to JJB that it would be able to maintain its prices at their current level, as it did. It also seems to us that the Tribunal was right to hold that this sequence of events amounted to a concerted practice.' (paras 102, 103)

Comment

Indirect communication in which a retailer discloses commercial information to its supplier with the intention that this information will be communicated to its competitor would amount to concerted practice when the competitor acted on that information. On the other hand, communication between retailer and supplier of commercial information which is not intended to be passed to the competitor, does not amount to concerted practice. The same would apply to a complaint to a supplier concerning business terms.

In paragraph 91 of the judgment the CA held that in order to prove concerted practice one must show that the retailer foresaw that the supplier would make use of the information to influence market conditions and that the competitor appreciated that the information was being passed to him with the retailer's concurrence.

In paragraphs 72–80 the CA referred to the facts in *Camera Care v Victor Hasselblad AB* [1982] 2 CMLR 233. There, the Commission found undertakings to rely on a complaint mechanism to affect their actions on the market. This enabled the undertakings involved to indirectly raise concerns regarding the sales by other undertakings in some territories and obtain their commitment to withdraw from those markets.

Note generally Case No COMP/29.373 *Visa International—Multilateral Interchange Fee*, where a banking system which restricted the freedom of banks to decide their own pricing policies was exempted under Article 101(3) TFEU (page 136 above).

Vereeniging Van Cementhandelaren v Commission	**Horizontal Agreements**
Case 8/72	Price Fixing
Court of Justice, [1972] ECR 977, [1973] CMLR 7	

'[T]he fixing of a price, even one which merely constitutes a target, affects competition because it enables all the participants to predict with a reasonable degree of certainty what the pricing policy pursued by their competitors will be.' (para 21)

BELASCO SC v Commission (Roofing Felt)	**Horizontal Agreements**
Case 246/86	Price Fixing
Court of Justice, [1989] ECR 2117, [1990] 4 CMLR 96	

'The applicants maintain that a common price list for Belasco products was adopted not in order to distort competition but only for the purpose of submitting, as recommended by the Belgian administration itself, collective applications for price rises so as to obtain the requisite authorizations more rapidly than would have been the case if applications had been submitted individually. They claim that in any case the common price list did not have the effect of distorting competition since, on the one hand, the prices charged on the market varied in practice from one undertaking to another and, on the other, the price lists in question were notified to undertakings that were not members of Belasco, which thus had an opportunity to adjust their prices in such a way as to improve their position on the market by comparison with that of the members of Belasco.' (para 10)

'It is apparent from the file on the case that, first, the applicants did not confine themselves to submitting joint applications for price increases but also acted in concert regarding the apportionment of the authorized increases as between the various products and the best time at which to put them into effect. The common price list was supplemented by measures concerning the discount rates to be granted. The adoption of the common price list was thus intended to restrict price competition.' (para 12)

'It must also be stated that the notification to undertakings that were not Belasco members of draft applications for price increases to be submitted to the administrative authorities and of draft price lists implementing the increases allowed was intended to encourage those undertakings to align their prices with those of the members in order to reinforce the effects of the cartel beyond its membership. It has been established that the draft documents in question were notified to the non-member undertakings as part of arrangements between them and Belasco intended to associate them with the pricing policies, price discounts and other measures agreed by the members of Belasco and to induce them to adopt the same conduct on the market.' (para 13)

'Finally, it must be pointed out that, although the prices fixed for new products may not have been observed in practice, the decisions of the general meeting fixing them were intended to restrict competition.' (para 15)

Raw Tobacco Italy	**Purchase Price Fixing**
COMP/C.38.281/B.2	Buyer Cartel
European Commission [2006] OJ L353/45	Object Analysis

Facts

The European Commission found a number of Italian processors of raw tobacco to infringe Article 101 TFEU by entering into agreements aimed at fixing the trading conditions for the purchase of raw tobacco in Italy. Among other things, the agreements in question set common purchase prices which processors would pay on the delivery of tobacco.

Held

'The agreements between processors mainly had the objective of setting average price or maximum prices per kilo of tobacco to be paid at delivery as well as average prices paid to third packers. ... The impact of this aspect of the infringement on competition was significant as purchase price is a fundamental aspect of the competitive conduct of any undertaking operating in a processing business and is also, by definition, capable of affecting the behaviour of the same companies in any other market in which they compete, including downstream markets. This is particularly so in cases like this, where the product affected by the buying cartel (raw tobacco) constitutes a substantial input of the activities carried out by participants downstream (the first processing and sale of processed tobacco in this case).' (para 280)

Comment

In *AOK Bundesverband v Ichthyol-Gesellschaft Cordes* Advocate General Jacobs voiced a clear opinion as to the treatment of purchase price fixing: '[A]n agreement or decision on the part of buyers to fix the purchase price on a given market must be understood to have as its object to restrict competition, without the need, at that stage of the analysis, for any investigation of its competitive effects. Purchasing cartels are expressly identified in [Article 101(1)(a)TFEU] as falling within the mischief of [Article 101]. The special attention which they receive can be understood in the light of their potential to suppress the price of purchased products to below the competitive level, with negative consequences for the supply side of the relevant market. In my view, therefore, they should be subject to the same strict control applied by [Union] competition law to supply cartels.' (para 69). (Joined Cases C-264/01, C-306/01, C-354/01 and C-355/01 *AOK Bundesverband and others v Ichthyol-Gesellschaft Cordes and others* [2004] ECR I-2493 (page 12))

In *Bureau National Interprofessionnel du Cognac v Guy Clair*, Case 123/83, [1985] ECR 391, the Court of Justice considered provisions of a trade organisation which fix the purchase of potable spirits. The Court of Justice held that 'It must be pointed out in that respect that for the purposes of [Article 101(1)] it is unnecessary to take account of the actual effects of an agreement where its object is to restrict, prevent or distort competition. By its very nature, an agreement fixing a minimum price for a product which is submitted to the public authorities for the purpose of obtaining approval for that minimum price, so that it becomes binding on all traders on the market in question, is intended to distort competition on that market.' (para 22)

In *T-Mobile* the Court considered an exchange of confidential information between mobile operators and their agreement to reduce dealer remunerations for post paid mobile subscriptions. In essence, the agreement in question concerned the fixing of input prices for services supplied by dealers. The Court held, in line with AG Kokott's opinion, that in order to establish anti-competitive object, it is sufficient that the conduct in question has the potential to have a negative impact on competition. A finding of an anti-competitive object depends on an assessment of the *capacity in an individual case* for that concerted practice to produce an anti-competitive impact. (para 31) The Court added that: 'A concerted practice may be regarded as having an anti-competitive object even though there is no direct connection between that practice and consumer prices ... it is apparent from [Article 101(1)(a) TFEU] that concerted practices may have an anti-competitive object if they "directly or indirectly fix purchase or selling prices or any other trading conditions".' (paras 36, 37, Case C-8/08 *T-Mobile Netherlands and Others* [2009] 5 CMLR 11 (page 160))

It is worth noting that the object approach to purchase price fixing is independent of the presence of buyer power. In other words, collusive input price fixing is condemned under Article 101 TFEU, regardless of the joint entity occupying a significant market position. Accordingly, the presence of collusive monopsony or bargaining power is not necessary for a finding of anticompetitive object. It is the act of input price fixing which triggers the 'object assumption', regardless of the effect on the market. As a result, an object approach under Article 101 TFEU subjects the buying alliance to a stricter regime than would have apply under Article 102 TFEU, to the extent that it would capture activities which give rise to collusion, even absent buying power.

In the Horizontal Cooperation Guidelines, the Commission outlines its approach to joint purchasing arrangements and the dividing line between object and effects analysis. It states that 'Joint purchasing arrangements restrict competition by object if they do not truly concern joint purchasing, but serve as a tool to engage in a disguised cartel, that is to say, otherwise prohibited price fixing, output limitation or market allocation.' (para 205)

The fixing of a lower purchase price by intermediate operators may at times lead to lower sale prices by those operators, to the benefit of consumers. Note, however, that the object approach condemns purchase price fixing regardless of the effect on consumer. It is the act of purchase price fixing which triggers the object approach. The view of purchase price fixing as objectively anti-competitive arguably receives support from the Court of Justice's recent widening of the approach toward 'object'. To illustrate, note for example an opinion by Advocate General Trstenjak, who noted the open ended nature of the 'object category'. The AG stated that: 'it is clear that the category of restrictions of competition by object cannot be reduced to agreements which obviously restrict competition. If not only the content of an agreement but also its legal and economic context must be taken into account, classification as a restriction of competition by object cannot depend on whether that object is clear at first sight or becomes evident only on closer examination of the circumstances and the intentions of the parties. In my view, the notion of restriction of competition by object cannot be reduced to an exhaustive list either.' (paras 47–8) (Case C-209/07 *Competition Authority v Beef Industry Development Society* [2008] ECR I-8637, [2009] 4 CMLR 6 (page 93))

In general terms, the distinction between 'object' and 'effect' violations arises from the fact that certain forms of collusion can be regarded, by their very nature, as being injurious to the proper functioning of normal competition. (Case C-209/07 *Competition Authority v Beef Industry Development Society Ltd*, para 17)

In *GlaxoSmithKline Services Unlimited v Commission* (Case C-501/06P [2010] 4 CMLR 2) the Court of Justice held that Article 101 TFEU 'aims to protect not only the interests of competitors or of consumers, but also the structure of the market and, in so doing, competition as such.' (para 63) Consequently, the Court held that in order to find that an agreement has an anti-competitive object, it is not necessary that final consumers be deprived of the advantages of effective competition in terms of supply or price. In the context of input price fixing, the *GlaxoSmithKline* judgment supports a shift in focus from the downstream market to the upstream one, and a closer look at the effects on suppliers and other competitors. According to this approach, for input price fixing to be found anti-competitive by object there is no need to consider harm to final consumers. It is therefore irrelevant if the saving obtained through input price fixing is passed on to consumers, as the act of price fixing and the distortion of competition upstream are sufficient to justify a finding of violation by object (page 96).

National Sulphuric Acid Association	**Purchase Price Fixing**
IV/27.958	Buying Alliance
European Commission, [1980] OJ L260/24	Effects Analysis

Facts

The Rules governing the National Sulphuric Acid Association's purchasing pool granted the association the power to negotiate and purchase sulphur for its members. The rules deprived members of the Association of the choice to negotiate independently terms of supply and rebates. Members, to the extent that they were tied to the pool, were also prevented from purchasing input when prices became lower than those paid by the pool. The Commission reviewed the rules of the Association following their notification under Regulation 17/62.

Held

The members of the Association have agreed to be bound by the rules of the purchasing pool. These rules have the effect of restricting competition between the members of the Pool. 'Each member of the Pool, to the extent he is committed to purchasing through the Pool, is prevented from competing with other Pool members to obtain more fabourable terms from the suppliers than those obtained by the management committee.' Paras (30–2)

'Individual members, to the extent that they are tied to the Pool, cannot purchase sulphur should prices become lower than those paid by the Pool or benefit from a particularly advantageous situation, e.g. where a supplier may have encountered contractual difficulties with another user or where a user wishes to sell surplus stocks.' (para 34)

'About 30% of the sulphuric acid manufactured by the Pool members is sold commercially to third parties and since sulphur accounts for up to 80% of the production cost of sulphuric acid, the equalising effect the Pool Rules have on the price of sulphur paid by the acid producers is felt in the price of sulphuric acid itself and, at least to some extent, in the prices of the numerous products which require, to a greater or lesser degree, sulphuric acid as a constituent chemical. This is true whether these acid-based products are manufactured by Pool members or by those to whom sulphuric acid is sold. Thus price competition… is largely eliminated between Pool members selling sulphuric acid, a homogeneous product for which little other competition is possible.' (para 35)

Despite the above, the Pool's operation allows for a range of benefits to its members. The result of these benefits in cost, flexibility in distribution and supply is that members of the Pool are assured of obtaining adequate supplies of the raw material. The consumer benefit from the activities of the Pool through regular supplies at a cost which reflects the price obtained by the Pool for the raw sulphur. The pool satisfies the conditions of Article 101(3) TFEU and is accordingly exempted. (paras 38–57)

Comment

The Commission assessed the effects the purchasing pool will have on competition. Following the finding of anti-competitive effect under Article 101(1) TFEU, the provisions of the purchasing pool were exempted under Article 101(3) TFEU.

In the Horizontal Cooperation Guidelines, the Commission notes that while the fixing of purchase prices can have the object of restricting competition, 'this does not apply where the parties to a joint purchasing arrangement agree on the purchasing prices [that] the joint purchasing arrangement may pay to its suppliers for the products subject to the supply contract. In that case an assessment is required as to whether the agreement is likely to give rise to restrictive effects on competition within the meaning of Article 101(1). In both scenarios the agreement on purchase prices will not be assessed separately, but in the light of the overall effects of the purchasing agreement on the market.' (para 206)

The object and effects doctrines respectively represent two opposite assumptions as to the effects generated by purchase price fixing. The latter more readily assumes efficiencies flowing out of the buying alliance which outweigh the expected social costs of collusive input price fixing. The former treats the mere act of input price fixing as sufficiently harmful for establishing an assumption of illegality.

The reading of the Horizontal Cooperation Guidelines together with the Commission's previous practice suggest that an effect-based approach would be called for in the case of transparent buying consortia which include provisions which set the purchase price. In such cases the Commission will examine the actual effects on two markets: the upstream input market for competing uses of the seller's output and the downstream output market, where members of the alliance act as sellers.

In *P&H/MAKRO Joint Purchasing Agreement* the OFT released a short-form Opinion in which it assessed a joint purchase agreement which included provisions for joint negotiation of discounts and overall promotional contributions. The OFT noted that in the absence of parallel networks of similar agreements in the relevant market, and where the parties have no downstream market power, such agreements are unlikely to cause harm and that the price benefits attained by the alliance will generally be passed on to consumers. The OFT added that cost commonality will give rise to concern, when it leads to coordination between alliance members that would significantly reduce competition downstream. The OFT made reference to the EU Horizontal Guidelines and noted that: 'Although a joint purchasing agreement is an agreement between competing undertakings, it would be unlikely to have as its "object" the restriction of competition. However, it may constitute an object restriction where it facilitates a cartel among the parties to the agreement (and, potentially, upstream suppliers). An object restriction of this sort might take the form of output limitation (demand withholding), market sharing/allocation (for example, through purchasing quotas), price fixing or "rent sharing" with upstream suppliers. Based on the information supplied by the Parties, the OFT has no reason to believe that the agreement in this case would constitute an object infringement.' (para 6.1) *P&H/MAKRO Joint Purchasing Agreement* (Short-form Opinion 27 April 2010)

In general, joint purchasing agreements are unlikely to be restrictive of competition where the parties' combined market share is under 15 per cent in both the upstream and downstream markets. (EU Horizontal Cooperation Guidelines, para 208)

It is important to note that under both object and effects approaches, parties to an agreement for the fixing of purchase price may seek exemption under Article 101(3) TFEU. Accordingly, an object approach which allows for adequate consideration of exemption may result in a similar conclusion as that reached under an effect based approach.

Makers UK Ltd v Office of Fair Trading	**Horizontal Agreements**
Case 1061/1/1/06	Collusive Tendering
Competition Appeal Tribunal, [2007] CAT 11	Cover Pricing

Facts

Makers UK Limited (Makers) appealed to the Tribunal against the Office of Fair Trading (OFT) Decision in which various roofing contractors, including Makers, were found to collude in the making of bids tendered for flat roof and car park surfacing contracts. The collusion at issue was that of 'cover bidding' which occurs when a contractor that is not intending to win the contract submits a price for it after communicating and agreeing the price with the designated winner. The OFT's case against Makers rested on the fact that the figures submitted in Makers' tender bid were identical to figures submitted by another undertaking (Asphaltic). Makers argued that it had made speculative contacts with Asphaltic and requested a subcontractor quotation. Accordingly, it asserted that the figures used in its bid did not amount to collusive tendering but rather constituted a quotation from Asphaltic for carrying out the work as a subcontractor.

Held

'Cover pricing gives the impression of competitive bidding but, in reality, contractors agree to submit token bids that are higher than the bid of the contractor that is seeking the cover. The issue in this case is whether Makers had been involved in cover pricing with either or both of Asphaltic and Rock.' (para 14)

'In *Apex Asphalt and Paving Co Limited v Office of Fair Trading* [2005] CAT 4 ("Apex"), the Tribunal noted that when an undertaking (which for whatever reason does not wish to win the tender) opts to put in a cover bid rather than declining to bid, it deprives a bidder with the genuine intention to win the tender of the opportunity to take its place and put in a competitive bid. The CAT said: "the tendering process provides for the tenderee to receive independent bids following the acceptance of an invitation to tender, alternatively for the invited tenderer to decline the invitation to bid so that the tenderee has the opportunity to replace that undertaking with another competitor. ... The effect of the conduct ... was to deprive the tenderee of a similar opportunity. In this respect also the concerted practice has as its object or effect the prevention, restriction or distortion of competition." (para 15)

The burden of proof in this case lies on the OFT and the standard of proof is the balance of probabilities, taking into account the gravity of what is alleged. The Tribunal has to consider whether the evidence before it provides a 'plausible' explanation for the events other than collusion. (paras 45–50)

Maker failed to provide a plausible explanation for the identical bid. Its explanation regarding the subcontractor quote lacks commercial sense. 'We agree with the inference drawn by the OFT that Maker knew when they incorporated the figures into their own bid to AKS, that the figures represented a cover price for another bidder.' Even if Makers' explanation was true, Makers submitted a bid which was influenced by the figures provided by Asphaltic and thus infringed the Chapter I prohibition. (paras 93, 54–110)

Comment

In paragraphs 99–100, the Tribunal distinguished between this case and *Argos & Littlewoods* (page 159 above) where an undertaking operating at the retail level of the market disclosed information to an undertaking operating at the supplier level of the market, followed by the subsequent disclosure of that information by that supplier to a different retailer.

Note the Commission's decision in IV/26.918—*European Sugar Industry* [1973] OJ L140/17, where the Commission noted that in a system of tendering, competition is of the essence and that it would be restricted if tenders were not the result of individual economic calculation. Also note Commission decision Case No IV/35.691.E-4 *Pre-Insulated Pipe Cartel* in which several producers of heating pipes were found to have participated in a cartel involved price fixing, market sharing and bid-rigging arrangements [1999] OJ L24/1.

Kier Group PLC and others v Office of Fair Trading	**Horizontal Agreements**
Case 1114/1/1/09	Cover Pricing
Competition Appeal Tribunal, [2011] CAT 3	Level of Fine

Facts

An appeal on a decision of the UK Office of Fair Trading which found 103 construction companies in England to engage in bid rigging, the object of which was to restrict competition. The majority of companies engaged in 'cover pricing'. On appeal the companies argued that the OFT's analysis of cover pricing overemphasised the anticompetitive impact of that infringement. Notwithstanding that cover pricing forms an infringements 'by object', the lack of likely impact on competition should have been relevant when assessing seriousness of the infringement and setting the fine.

Held

There is no doubt that cover pricing constitutes an infringement of Article 101 TFEU/Chapter I prohibition. 'but in our view the practice is materially distinct from "bid rigging" as ordinarily understood. Bid rigging implies an agreement or arrangement which determines, or assists in the determination of, the price which will actually be charged to the purchaser. Cover pricing is less serious than conduct of that kind.' (para 94)

Cover pricing is certainly not an innocuous activity. 'It is an unlawful practice which at the very least may deceive the customer about the source and extent of the competition which exists for the work in question, and which is capable of having anti-competitive effects on the particular tendering exercise and on future exercises.' (para 99)

'All that being said, it also needs to be recognised that "simple" cover pricing is a bilateral arrangement in the context of a multi-partite tendering exercise. Its purpose is not (as in a conventional price-fixing cartel) to prevent competition by agreeing the price which it is intended the client should pay. Indeed, its purpose is quite the reverse, namely to identify a price which the client will *not* be willing to pay. Nor is its purpose to reach an agreement that the recipient of the cover price will cease to be a contender—it is strongly argued by the Present Appellants, and not disputed by the OFT, that in a case of "simple" cover pricing the recipient has already made its own unilateral decision not to compete for the work before the request for a cover price is made.' (para 100)

Although the endemic nature of simple cover pricing in the construction industry may sometimes have raised prices and harmed clients, the harm is likely to be small by comparison with hard-core cartels. The small profit margins in the construction industry do not support the existence of substantial overcharges. We therefore consider the final penalties imposed by the OFT to be excessive. (paras 101–18)

'The characterisation of the infringement as "by object" means that effects need not be proved in order to establish the breach, this does not render irrelevant the likely effects to *penalty*. It is clearly necessary to take into account the effects (actual or potential) of an infringement when considering its seriousness.' (para 133)

Comment

While accepting that cover pricing is anti-competitive by object, the CAT significantly reduced the total fine imposed by the OFT, by more than 87 per cent. This, one would argue, sends a mixed signal as to the severity of cover pricing and the justification for treating it as an infringement by object. On that point, recall that the distinction between 'object' and 'effect' arises from the fact that some forms of collusion are regarded, by their very nature, as being injurious to the proper functioning of normal competition. (Case C-209/07 *Competition Authority v Beef Industry Development Society Ltd*, para 17)

On the way in which cover pricing is capable of distorting competition in relation to a tendering see also *Apex Asphalt and Paving Co Ltd v Office of Fair Trading* [2005] CAT 4, cited in *Makers UK Ltd v Office of Fair Trading*, page 166 above.

Peroxygen products	**Horizontal Agreements**
IV/30.907	Market Sharing
European Commission, [1985] OJ L35/1	

Facts

A Commission investigation into the 'hydrogen peroxide and sodium perborate' market led to a finding of several anticompetitive agreements or concerted practices between several undertakings under which they agreed that each national market was to be reserved for those producers which manufacture inside the territory in question (the 'home market rule').

Decision

'The [Union] markets for both hydrogen peroxide and sodium perborate are strictly divided on national lines. Each producer limits its sales to end-users in those Member States where it possesses production facilities. … The strict separation of the national markets and the absence of intra-[Union] exchanges is all the more remarkable given the very considerable price differences, particularly as between France and the neighbouring Member States.' (para 10) 'A similar market division is apparent in sodium perborate …' (para 11)

'The Commission does not accept that the strict market separation on national lines, which is a characteristic of both the hydrogen peroxide and sodium perborate sectors in the [Union], results from natural market forces or the independent commercial judgment of the producers. It considers that the market separation is the result of an arrangement or understanding of long duration (from at least 1961) between the producers, originally based on an acceptance of the "home market principle", i.e. that the national markets would be reserved for domestic producers …' (para 23)

'It is not necessary, for the establishment of a concerted practice, for the parties to have agreed a precise or detailed plan in advance. … The criteria of coordination and cooperation laid down in the case law of the Court must be understood in the light of the concept inherent in the provisions of the Treaty relating to competition that each economic operator must determine independently the policy which he intends to adopt on the [internal] market. … The documents show that the decision by each producer of its markets and customers was not the subject of independent commercial judgment. The "home market rule" is expressly and consistently mentioned as the basis on which they conducted their activities …' (para 45)

'The overall market division and sharing arrangement, and the individual agreements covering particular geographical areas and products, together regulate almost all trade in the products concerned in a major part of the [internal] market, and involved all the principal producers in the European market for a major industrial sector. The "home market" arrangement … delineated the territories in which each producer was to supply and consolidated the established positions of those producers to the detriment of effective freedom of movement in the [internal] market …' (para 50)

Comment

In the EU, market sharing raises concerns not only due to its anticompetitive effects but also as it undermines the goal of achieving market integration.

Note the Commission decision in Case COMP/E-2/37.978 *Methylglucamine* [2004] OJ L38/18, where the Commission exposed a cartel between producers of methylglucamine, which lasted nine years and eliminated competition through market sharing and price fixing.

Note the Commission investigation into the non-compete agreement between Telefónica and Portugal Telecom. The two companies agreed not to compete in their respective telecommunication home markets. When issuing the Statement of Objections the Commission noted that 'Non-compete clauses are one of the most serious violations of fair and healthy competition.' See Commission opening proceedings statement, Case Comp 39.839 and press release IP/11/1241.

ACF Chemie farma NV v Commission Case 41/69 Court of Justice, [1970] ECR 661	**Horizontal Agreements** Market Sharing

'The gentlemen's agreement guaranteed protection of each domestic market for the producers in the various Member States.' (para 117)

'The applicant maintains that owing in particular to the shortage of raw materials the sharing out of domestic markets, as emerges from the exchange of letters of October and November 1963, had no effect on competition in the [internal] market.' (para 125)

'Despite the scarcity of raw materials and an increase in the demand for the products in question, as the contested Decision finds, a serious threat of shortage nevertheless emerged only in 1964 as a result of the interruption of Nedchem' s supplies from the American general service administration.' (para 126)

'On the other hand such a situation cannot render lawful an agreement the object of which is to restrict competition in the [internal] market and which affects trade between the Member States.' (para 127)

'The sharing out of domestic markets has as its object the restriction of competition and trade within the [internal] market.' (para 128)

'The fact that, if there were a threatened shortage of raw materials, such an agreement might in practice have had less influence on competition and on international trade than in a normal period in no way alters the fact that the parties did not terminate their activities.' (para 129)

Sot Lélos kai Sia EE and Others v GlaxoSmithKline AEVE C-468/06 to C-478/06 Court of Justice, [2008] ECR I-7139	**Horizontal Agreements** Market Sharing Vertical Agreement, Dominance

'In relation to the application of [Article 101 TFEU], the Court has held that an agreement between producer and distributor which might tend to restore the national divisions in trade between Member States might be such as to frustrate the objective of the Treaty to achieve the integration of national markets through the establishment of a single market. Thus on a number of occasions the Court has held agreements aimed at partitioning national markets according to national borders or making the interpenetration of national markets more difficult, in particular those aimed at preventing or restricting parallel exports, to be agreements whose object is to restrict competition within the meaning of that Treaty article (see, for example, Joined Cases 96/82 to 102/82, 104/82, 105/82, 108/82 and 110/82 *IAZ International Belgium and Others v Commission* [1983] ECR 3369, paragraphs 23 to 27; Case C-306/96 *Javico* [1998] ECR II 983, paragraphs 13 and 14; and Case C-551/03 P *General Motors v Commission* [2006] ECR I 3173, paragraphs 67 to 69).' (para 65)

'In the light of the abovementioned Treaty objective as well as that of ensuring that competition in the internal market is not distorted, there can be no escape from the prohibition laid down in [Article 102 TFEU] for the practices of an undertaking in a dominant position which are aimed at avoiding all parallel exports from a Member State to other Member States, practices which, by partitioning the national markets, neutralise the benefits of effective competition in terms of the supply and the prices that those exports would obtain for final consumers in the other Member States.' (para 66)

Protimonopolný úrad Slovenskej republiky v Slovenská sporiteľňa	**Horizontal Agreements**
Case C-68/12	Collective Boycott
Court of Justice, [2013] 4 CMLR 16	Illegality of Target's Action

Facts

The Competition Authority of the Slovak Republic found three major banks to have infringed Article 101 TFEU by entering into an agreement to terminate contracts and refrain from concluding new contracts with Akcenta, a non-bank financial institution that provided services to customers in competition with the three banks. The banks argued that they jointly terminated the agreement as Akcenta was operating illegally. The case reached the appellant court which stayed the proceedings and referred several questions to the Court of Justice, one of which concerned whether an alleged illegality of Akcenta's activities is relevant for the assessment of the collective boycott under Article 101 TFEU.

Held

Article 101 TFEU protects not only the interests of competitors or consumers but also the structure of the market and thus competition as such. The agreement entered into by the banks had as its object the restriction of competition. 'None of the banks had challenged the legality of Akcenta's business before they were investigated in the case giving rise to the main proceedings. The alleged illegality of Akcenta's situation is therefore irrelevant for the purpose of determining whether the conditions for an infringement of the competition rules are met. Moreover, it is for public authorities and not private undertakings or associations of undertakings to ensure compliance with statutory requirements.' (paras18–20)

Comment

The illegally of the 'target' company's activities is of no relevance to the question of whether a collective boycott of that company infringed Article 101 TFEU. It is for the public authorities, not private parties, to deal with such illegality.

In Case No IV/35.691.E-4—*Pre-Insulated Pipe Cartel* ([1999] OJ L24/1) the European Commission found several undertakings to have participated in cartel agreements to fix prices and quotes. The illicit activity also included a decision by some of the undertakings operating on the German market to eliminate the only competitor which was not part of the agreement. To do so, the parties agreed to organise a collective boycott of the competitor's customers and suppliers. The Commission held that: 'A boycott may be attributed to an undertaking without there being any need for it actually to participate, or even be capable of participating, in its implementation. Were that not so, an undertaking which approved a boycott but did not have the opportunity to adopt a measure to implement it would avoid any form of liability for its participation in the agreement.' (para 157) An application for annulment of the decision was partially upheld due to lack of evidence that the applicant attended some of the cartel meetings (Case T-21/99, *Dansk Rørindustri A/S v Commission*).

In *Fashion Originators Guild of America v FTC* (312 US 457 (1941)) the US Supreme Court condemned members of the Guild for the design, manufacturing and sale of women's clothing for engaging in a group boycott of retailers that sold clothing which other manufacturers had copied from Guild members. The Court held that the aim of the boycott was 'the intentional destruction of one type of manufacture and sale which competed with Guild members. The purpose and object of this combination, its potential power, its tendency to monopoly, the coercion it could and did practice upon a rival method of competition, all brought it within the policy of the prohibition.' It further held that the boycott cannot be justified 'upon the argument that systematic copying of dress designs is itself tortious. … [E]ven if copying were an acknowledged tort under the law of every state, that situation would not justify petitioners in combining together to regulate and restrain interstate commerce in violation of federal law.' (page 312 US 467, 468)

Fiatagri UK Ltd and New Holland Ford Ltd v Commission	**Horizontal Agreements**
(UK Agricultural Tractor Registration Exchange)	Information Exchange
Case T-34/92	
General Court, [1994] ECR II-905	

Facts

The UK Agricultural Engineers Trade Association (AEA) notified to the Commission an information exchange agreement concerning data on the registrations of agricultural tractors. In its decision the Commission held that the agreement, which was open to all and not confined to members of the AEA, infringed Article 101 TFEU as it facilitated exchange of information identifying sales of individual competitors, as well as information on dealer sales and imports of own products. The decision in this case was the first one in which the Commission prohibited an information exchange system which did not directly concern prices or underpin any other anti-competitive arrangement (IV/31.370 and 31.446—*UK Agricultural Tractor Registration Exchange*, [1992] OJ L68/19). The Commission's decision was challenged before the General Court.

Held

'As the applicants correctly argue, in a truly competitive market transparency between traders is in principle likely to lead to the intensification of competition between suppliers, since in such a situation the fact that a trader takes into account information made available to him in order to adjust his conduct on the market is not likely, having regard to the atomized nature of the supply, to reduce or remove for the other traders any uncertainty about the foreseeable nature of its competitors' conduct. On the other hand, the Court considers that, as the Commission argues this time, general use, as between main suppliers, of exchanges of precise information at short intervals, identifying registered vehicles and the place of their registration is, on a highly concentrated oligopolistic market such as the market in question ... and on which competition is as a result already greatly reduced and exchange of information facilitated, likely to impair considerably the competition which exists between traders. In such circumstances, the sharing, on a regular and frequent basis, of information concerning the operation of the market has the effect of periodically revealing to all the competitors the market positions and strategies of the various individual competitors.' (para 91)

The exchange of information presupposes an agreement, or tacit agreement, between the traders to define the boundaries of dealer sales territories by reference to the United Kingdom postcode system, as well as a framework for information exchange between traders through the trade association to which they belong. The information agreement is also disadvantageous for a trader wishing to penetrate the United Kingdom agricultural tractor market. If the trader does not join the information exchange agreement it will not benefit from the information and market knowledge which is available to its competitors under the information exchange. On the other hand, if it decides to become a member of the agreement, its business strategy is then immediately revealed to all its competitors by means of the information which they receive. (para 92)

'It follows that the applicants are wrong in arguing that the information exchange agreement at issue is likely to intensify competition on the market and that the Commission has not established to the requisite legal standard the anti-competitive nature of the agreement at issue. The fact that the Commission is not able to demonstrate the existence of an actual effect on the market ... has no bearing on the outcome of this case since [Article 101(1) TFEU] prohibits both actual anti-competitive effects and purely potential effects, provided that these are sufficiently appreciable, as they are in this case, having regard to the characteristics of the market as described above.' (para 93)

Comment

The parties appealed to the Court of Justice, Case C-8/95P *New Holland Ford Ltd v Commission* [1998] ECR I-3175. Appeal dismissed. See the comments below in Case T-35/92 *John Deere Ltd v Commission* which dealt with the same information exchange arrangement (page 172).

John Deere Ltd v Commission	**Horizontal Agreements**
Case T-35/92	Information Exchange
General Court, [1994] ECR II-957	

Facts

The UK Agricultural Engineers Trade Association (AEA) notified to the Commission an agreement relating to an information system based on data held by the United Kingdom Department of Transport relating to registrations of agricultural tractors, called the 'UK Agricultural Tractor Registration Exchange'. Membership of the notified agreement was open to all manufacturers or importers of agricultural tractors in the United Kingdom, whether or not they are members of the AEA. The AEA provides the secretariat for the agreement. In its decision the Commission held that the agreement infringed Article 101 TFEU as it facilitated exchange of information identifying sales of individual competitors, as well as information on dealer sales. The Commission refused to grant exemption under Article 101(3) TFEU.

This is the same information agreement considered by the General Court in Case T-34/92 *Fiatagri UK Ltd and New Holland Ford Ltd v Commission* (*Fiatagri*) (above, page 171). The General Court analysis in paragraphs 51 and 52 of this decision is identical to its analysis in paragraphs 91 and 92 in *Fiatagri* and is therefore not repeated below.

Held

'[W]ith regard to the type of information exchanged, the Court considers that, contrary to the applicant's contention, the information concerned, which relates in particular to sales made in the territory of each of the dealerships in the distribution network, is in the nature of business secrets. Indeed, this is admitted by the members of the agreement themselves, who strictly defined the conditions under which the information received could be disseminated to third parties, especially to members of their distribution network. The Court also observes that, as stated above (in paragraph 51), having regard to its frequency and systematic nature, the exchange of information in question makes the conduct of a given trader's competitors all the more foreseeable for it in view of the characteristics of the relevant market as analysed above, since it reduces, or even removes, the degree of uncertainty regarding the operation of the market, which would have existed in the absence of such an exchange of information, and in this regard the applicant cannot profitably rely on the fact that the information exchanged does not concern prices or relate to past sales. Accordingly, the first part of the plea, to the effect that there is no restriction of competition as a result of alleged "prevention of hidden competition", must be dismissed.' (para 81)

Comment

The Court of Justice dismissed the parties' appeal—C-7/95P *John Deere Ltd v Commission* [1998] ECR I-3111).

Note Case T-141/94 *Thyssen Stahl AG v Commission* [1999] ECR II-347, where the General Court held that it is not necessary, to demonstrate that exchanges of information led to a specific result or were put into effect on the market in order to establish the existence of concerted practice. (General Court judgment upheld on appeal in Case C-194/99P)

Note Case T-25/95 *Cimenteries CBR and others v Commission* [2000] ECR II-491, [2000] 5 CMLR 204, where the General Court considered that exchange of price information has as its object the restriction of competition. (para 1531)

'Whether or not exchange of information has an appreciable effect on competition will depend on the circumstances of each individual case: the market characteristics, the type of information and the way in which it is exchanged.' See the OFT Guidelines (401) on Agreements and Concerted Practices which consider the pro and anticompetitive effects of information exchange. (paras 3.17–3.23)

In its Guidelines on Horizontal Cooperation Agreements the Commission discusses in length the assessment of information exchange under Article 101 TFEU (paras 55–110).

Ahlström Osakeyhtiö and others v Commission (Wood Pulp II)	**Horizontal Agreements**
Joined Cases C-89, 104, 114, 116, 117, 125, 129/85	Information Exchange
Court of Justice, [1993] ECR I-1307, [1993] 4 CMLR 407	Price Announcements

Facts

The Commission found forty wood pulp producers and three of their trade associations to have infringed Article 101 TFEU by forming a price-fixing cartel. The market for pulp was characterised by long-term supply contracts and by 'quarterly price announcements' by which producers communicated to their customers the prices of pulp.

According to the Commission's hypothesis, the system of quarterly price announcements constitutes in itself an infringement of Article 101 TFEU and was deliberately introduced by the pulp producers in order to enable them to ascertain the prices charged by their competitors in the following quarters. The disclosure of prices to third parties well before their application at the beginning of a new quarter had the effect of making the market artificially transparent and gave the producers sufficient time to adjust their own prices before that quarter and to apply them from the commencement of that quarter. In addition the Commission put forward a second hypothesis according to which the system of price announcements constitutes evidence of concentration.

Held

'According to the Court's judgment in *Suiker Unie* ... a concerted practice refers to a form of coordination between undertakings which, without having been taken to the stage where an agreement properly so-called has been concluded, knowingly substitutes for the risks of competition practical cooperation between them. ... the Court added that the criteria of coordination and cooperation must be understood in the light of the concept inherent in the provisions of the Treaty relating to competition that each economic operator must determine independently the policy which he intends to adopt on the [Internal] Market.' (para 63)

'In this case, the communications arise from the price announcements made to users. They constitute in themselves market behaviour which does not lessen each undertaking's uncertainty as to the future attitude of its competitors. At the time when each undertaking engages in such behaviour, it cannot be sure of the future conduct of the others.' (para 64)

'Accordingly, the system of quarterly price announcements on the pulp market is not to be regarded as constituting in itself an infringement of [Article 101(1) TFEU].' (para 65)

As for the Commission's second hypothesis; in this case, the system of price announcements does not provide sufficient evidence of concentration as such concentration is not the only plausible explanation for the parallel conduct of the undertakings. (paras 66–126)

Comment

On price announcements note Case 48/69 *Imperial Chemical Industries v Commission* where the Court held that advance price announcements eliminated all uncertainty between the undertakings as to their future conduct and, in doing so, also eliminated a large part of the risk usually inherent in any independent change of conduct on one or several markets. For detailed analysis of this case see page 71 above.

'The exchange of information on prices may lead to price co-ordination and therefore diminish competition which would otherwise be present between the undertakings. This will be the case whether the information exchanged relates directly to the prices charged or to the elements of a pricing policy, for example discounts, costs, terms of trade and rates and dates of change. The more recent or current the information exchanged, the more likely it is that exchange will have an appreciable effect on competition ...' (OFT Guidelines (401) on Agreements and Concerted Practices, paras 3.20–3.21)

T-Mobile Netherlands BV and others v Raad van bestuur van de Nederlandse Mededingingsautoriteit Case C-8/08 Court of Justice, [2009] ECR I-4529, [2009] 5 CMLR 11	**Horizontal Agreements** Information Exchange Concerted Practice

Facts

A reference for a preliminary ruling which was made in proceedings between T-Mobile Netherlands BV and the Netherlands competition authority. The proceedings at national level concerned a decision by the Netherlands competition authority in which five mobile operators were fined for exchanging confidential information at a single meeting with the aim of restricting competition.

Held

With regard to the exchange of information between competitors, it should be recalled that each economic operator must determine independently the policy which he intends to adopt on the internal market. Undertakings are strictly precluded from direct or indirect contact which can influence the conduct on the market of its actual or potential competitors or disclose decisions or intentions concerning conduct on the market where the object or effect of such contact is to create conditions of competition which do not correspond to the normal conditions of the market in question. (paras 32–3)

'At paragraphs 88 et seq of *Deere v Commission*, the Court therefore held that on a highly concentrated oligopolistic market, such as the market in the main proceedings, the exchange of information was such as to enable traders to know the market positions and strategies of their competitors and thus to impair appreciably the competition which exists between traders. It follows that the exchange of information between competitors is liable to be incompatible with the competition rules if it reduces or removes the degree of uncertainty as to the operation of the market in question, with the result that competition between undertakings is restricted.' (paras 34, 35)

'While not all parallel conduct of competitors on the market can be traced to the fact that they have adopted a concerted action with an anti-competitive object, an exchange of information which is capable of removing uncertainties between participants as regards the timing, extent and details of the modifications to be adopted by the undertaking concerned must be regarded as pursuing an anti-competitive object, and that extends to situations, such as that in the present case, in which the modification relates to the reduction in the standard commission paid to dealers.' (para 41)

Comment

Note that the Court of Justice discussed the treatment of information exchange within the context of a price fixing agreement/concerted practice. This context presumably contributed to what may be seen as a harsh formalistic approach to information exchange. See in particular the statement in paragraph 41 which states that 'an exchange of information which is capable of removing uncertainties between participants as regards the timing, extent and details of the modifications to be adopted by the undertaking concerned must be regarded as pursuing an anti-competitive object.' This overreaching statement creates uncertainty as to treatment of information exchange. In this respect it would have been prudent to unbundle the legal treatment of information exchange and the price fixing activity. On 'object' see further pages 85–103, Chapter 3.

On this point, note AG Kokkot's opinion, which makes reference to Case C-238/05 *Asnef-Equifax v Ausbanc* [2006] ECR I-11125 and states that 'Not every exchange of information between competitors necessarily has as its object the prevention, restriction or distortion of competition.' (para 37) In that case the Court held that the credit information exchange systems did not have, by their very nature, the object of restricting competition.

In its Guidelines on Horizontal Cooperation Agreements the Commission makes reference to the T-Mobile case and notes that an isolated exchange of information may constitute sufficient basis for the participating undertakings to concert their market conduct. (para 91)

Dole Food Company	**Horizontal Agreements**
Case C-286/13P	Information Exchange
Court of Justice, [2015] 4 CMLR 16	Concerted Practice

Facts

An appeal on a judgment of the General Court in case T-588/08 by which that court dismissed Dole Food's action for annulment of Commission Decision in case COMP/39 188—*Bananas*. In its decision the Commission found Dole Food to have participated in a concerted practice consisting of coordination of quotation prices for bananas marketed in several European Member States. On appeal, Dole Food challenged, among other things, the Court finding that pre-pricing communications with other competitors constituted a restriction of competition by object. Appeal dismissed.

Held

'[A]n exchange of information which is capable of removing uncertainty between participants as regards the timing, extent and details of the modifications to be adopted by the undertakings concerned in their conduct on the market must be regarded as pursuing an anticompetitive object (… *T-Mobile* …). Moreover, a concerted practice may have an anticompetitive object even though there is no direct connection between that practice and consumer prices. Indeed, it is not possible on the basis of the wording of [Article 101(1) TFEU] to conclude that only concerted practices which have a direct effect on the prices paid by end users are prohibited. … [Article 101 TFEU], like the other competition rules of the Treaty, is designed to protect not only the immediate interests of individual competitors or consumers but also to protect the structure of the market and thus competition as such. Therefore, in order to find that a concerted practice has an anticompetitive object, there does not need to be a direct link between that practice and consumer prices (judgment in *T-Mobile Netherlands and Others*, …, paragraphs 38 and 39).' (paras 122–5)

'[S]ubject to proof to the contrary, … it must be presumed that the undertakings taking part in the concerted action and remaining active on the market take account of the information exchanged with their competitors in determining their conduct on that market. In particular, the Court has concluded that such a concerted practice is caught by Article 81(1) EC, even in the absence of anticompetitive effects on the market (judgment in *T-Mobile Netherlands and Others*, …, paragraph 51 and the case-law cited).' In this case it has been established that bilateral pre-pricing communications on quotation pricing were exchanged between the Dole and its competitors, that this information was relevant and served as market signals and indications as to intended development of banana prices, and that employees involved in the pre-pricing communications participated in Dole Food's internal pricing meetings. (paras 127, 128–33)

Comment

The judgment echoes the *T-Mobile* approach, according to which an exchange of price-related information constitutes an infringement of competition by object. The Court emphasised that finding of object does not necessitate the presence of a direct connection between the information exchanged and prices. Consequently, it held that pre-pricing quotation signalling at employee level infringed Article 101 TFEU. The judgment provides further support to the formal object approach toward price-related information exchange.

The Court rejected the argument that the employees involved in the exchange of information were not themselves responsible for the setting of quotations. It noted that Dole employees involved in the pre-pricing communications also participated in the internal pricing meetings. In her opinion, AG Kokott noted that even if 'the employee of an undertaking does not personally determine that undertaking's quotation prices, he may still be in possession of the underlying internal information, exchange that information with his contacts from other undertakings and thereby contribute to removing uncertainty as to the operation of the market which would normally exist in a competitive environment. The general principle is that an employee who does not have the power internally to make decisions about an undertaking's commercial policy and prices may still be involved externally in infringements of competition law.' (para 101, AG opinion)

Tesco v Office of Fair Trading **Hub and Spoke**
Case 1188/1/1/11 A-B-C Information Exchange
Competition Appeal Tribunal, [2012] CAT 31

Facts

An appeal on a UK Office of Fair Trading (OFT) decision in which a number of competing undertakings, including Tesco, were found to indirectly exchange their future retail pricing intentions in respect of British-produced cheese, via their common suppliers. In its judgment, the Competition Appeal Tribunal considered the conditions for establishing concerted practice through indirect information exchange.

Held

Indirect information exchange through a third party will amount to a concerted practice, having as its object the restriction of competition, where two phases are present:

[Phase I] Retailer A discloses to supplier B its future pricing, with the intention that B will pass that information to other retailers in order to influence market conditions.

[Phase II] C receives the information from B, knowing the circumstances in which it was disclosed by A to B; and makes use of that information in determining its own future pricing intentions. (paras 57, 58)

Phase I—Disclosures of actual or likely retail prices by a customer to its supplier are often part of normal commercial dialogue, and are permissible. However, competition concerns may arise where retailer A discloses such pricing information to its supplier B, which uses it for anti-competitive purposes such as by disclosing it to C. The state of mind of retailer A when disclosing the information to B, may be inferred from the acts of its employees and the circumstances surrounding the exchange. (paras 59–74)

Phase II—Supplier B must be shown, as a matter of fact, to have transmitted retailer A's future pricing intentions to retailer C. The Court should then consider whether retailer C may be taken to have known the circumstances in which the information was disclosed by A to B. Following this, one needs to establish that retailer C did, in fact, take into account retailer A's future pricing intentions in determining its own future pricing intentions. Unless proven otherwise, the Court may rely on the *Anic* presumption, and assume that C cannot fail to take that information into account. (paras 75–86)

Comment

The analysis of A–B–C information exchange is divided to two phases, each comprising a conduct element and a mental element. The Competition Appeal Tribunal reviewed different hub-and-spoke exchanges in which Tesco was accused of taking part. It partially accepted Tesco's appeal regarding some of the exchanges.

In considering Phase II the Court relied on the '*Anic* presumption' on the usage of information exchanged (paras 49, 86). That presumption originated in Case C-49/92P *Commission v Anic Partecipazioni* where the Court of Justice held that: '[S]ubject to proof to the contrary, which it is for the economic operators concerned to adduce, there must be a presumption that the undertakings participating in concerting arrangements and remaining active on the market take account of the information exchanged with their competitors when determining their conduct on that market, particularly when they concert together on a regular basis over a long period.' (para 121)

In Case C-8/08 *T-Mobile Netherlands BV* (page 162 above) the Court of Justice referred to the *Anic* presumption and held that subject to the market structure, it may not be ruled out that a single meeting between competitors could be sufficient to establish concerted practice. It would then be for the undertakings to adduce evidence that the concerted action did not have any effect on their conduct. (paras 59–61, cited in para 50)

On hub-and-spoke, also note the English Court of Appeal judgment in *Argos Ltd and another v Office of Fair Trading* [2006] EWCA Civ 1318 (19 October 2006).

Eturas and others	**Hub and Spoke**
C-74/14	A–B–C Information Exchange
Court of Justice, not yet published	Presumption of Innocence

Facts

A preliminary reference from the Lithuanian Supreme Administrative Court concerning a possible hub-and-spoke conspiracy facilitated by an online system. The administrator of an online travel booking system posted a notice on its system declaring a newly implemented technical restriction that affected discount rates offered by travel agents using the system. One contentious issue in this case was whether the mere dispatch of a message through the system constituted sufficient evidence to establish that its addressees were aware, or ought to have been aware, of its content.

Held

Each economic operator must determine independently the policy it intends to adopt on the common market. In addition, 'passive modes of participation in the infringement, such as the presence of an undertaking in meetings at which anticompetitive agreements were concluded, without that undertaking clearly opposing them, are indicative of collusion capable of rendering the undertaking liable under Article 101 TFEU, since a party which tacitly approves of an unlawful initiative, without publicly distancing itself from its content or reporting it to the administrative authorities, encourages the continuation of the infringement and compromises its discovery (… *AC-Treuhand v Commission* …).' (para 28)

The national court asks whether the mere dispatch of a message constitute sufficient evidence to establish the awareness of its addressees. That question 'must be regarded as relating to the assessment of evidence and to the standard of proof, with the result that it is governed—in accordance with the principle of procedural autonomy and subject to the principles of equivalence and effectiveness—by national law.' (para 34)

'The principle of effectiveness requires however that national rules governing the assessment of evidence and the standard of proof must not render the implementation of EU competition rules impossible or excessively difficult and, in particular, must not jeopardise the effective application of Articles 101 TFEU and 102 TFEU (see, to that effect, judgment in *Pfleiderer* C-360/09, EU:C:2011:389, point 24).' (para 35)

'In that respect, it must be recalled that, according to the case-law of the Court, in most cases the existence of a concerted practice or an agreement must be inferred from a number of coincidences and indicia which, taken together, may, in the absence of another plausible explanation, constitute evidence of an infringement of the competition rules (see, to that effect, judgment in Total Marketing Services v Commission, C-634/13 P, EU:C:2015:614, paragraph 26 and the case-law cited).' (para 36)

'Consequently, the principle of effectiveness requires that an infringement of EU competition law may be proven not only by direct evidence, but also through indicia, provided that they are objective and consistent.' (para 37)

'In so far as the referring court has doubts as to the possibility, in view of the presumption of innocence, of finding that the travel agencies were aware, or ought to have been aware, of the message at issue in the main proceedings, it must be recalled that the presumption of innocence constitutes a general principle of EU law, now enshrined in Article 48(1) of the Charter of Fundamental Rights of the European Union (see, to that effect, judgment in *E.ON Energie v Commission*, C-89/11 P, EU:C:2012:738, paragraph 72), which the Member States are required to observe when they implement EU competition law (… *VEBIC*, C-439/08, …, paragraph 63, and *N*, C-604/12, …, paragraph 41).' (para 38)

'The presumption of innocence precludes the referring court from inferring from the mere dispatch of the message at issue in the main proceedings that the travel agencies concerned ought to have been aware of the content of that message.' (para 39)

'However, the presumption of innocence does not preclude the referring court from considering that the dispatch of the message at issue in the main proceedings may, in the light of other objective and consistent indicia, justify the presumption that the travel agencies concerned were aware of the content of that message as from the date of its dispatch, provided that those agencies still have the opportunity to rebut it.' (para 40)

As regards the participation of the travel agency in a concerted practice: to the extent that the economic operators were aware of that message they tacitly assented to a common anticompetitive practice and may be presumed to have participated in a concerted practice. However, that will not be the case if the economic operators show that they publicly distanced themselves from that practice, for instance by sending a clear and express objection to the administrator of the E-TURAS system. The Court accepts that public distancing in this case cannot require a declaration by a travel agency of its intention to distance itself to be made to all of the competitors which were the addressees of the message, since that agency is not in fact in a position to know who those addressees are. Other means to rebut the presumption may include reporting the communication to the administrative authorities or providing evidence of a systematic application of a discount exceeding the cap in question. (paras 41–50)

Importantly, 'if it cannot be established that a travel agency was aware of that message, its participation in a concertation cannot be inferred from the mere existence of a technical restriction implemented in the system at issue in the main proceedings, unless it is established on the basis of other objective and consistent indicia that it tacitly assented to an anticompetitive action.' (para 45)

Comment

The Court held that the 'awareness' of the operators to the message is to be established based on the standard of proof as set by national law and the evidence in this case. The Court noted that the presumption of innocence constitutes a general principle of EU law and precludes the referring court from inferring 'awareness' from the mere dispatch of the message, absent other objective and consistent indicia.

The Court further held that when awareness has been established, travel agents who knew the content of the message sent via the system could be presumed to have participated in an illegal collusion, unless they publicly distanced themselves from that message or reported it to the administrative authorities. Importantly, the finding of concerted practice is conditional on establishing awareness to the communication.

The use of an administrator and online system to communicate the message meant that parties that wish to distance themselves from the message will not be able to inform all other recipients of the message—as they may not be in a position to know who those addressees are. Accordingly, distancing may be done by informing the administrator of the system. This proposed practice raises interesting questions as to the responsibility of the administrator and the action it should take following such communication.

In the US Interstate Circuit case (*Interstate Circuit v United States*, 306 US 208, 227 (1939)), a movie theatre owner approached each movie distributor individually, told each movie distributor of the contemplated conspiracy, told each movie distributor that the other movie distributors would be invited to join the conspiracy, and said that cooperation of all eight distributors was essential for the conspiracy to work. By giving their adherence to the conspiracy and agreeing to participate in it, both the movie theatre owner (the hub) and the eight movie distributors (spokes) were liable. In its judgment the US Supreme Court held that 'an unlawful conspiracy may be and often is formed without simultaneous action or agreement on the part of the conspirators'.

The European Commission condemned such active support and enabling practice, as part of its investigation into the manipulation of LIBOR. The Commission fined the UK-based broker ICAP for its participation in the cartel. It found that ICAP contributed to the cartel's objectives by, among other things, serving as a communications channel between Citigroup and RBS and thereby enabling the anticompetitive practices between the traders. (Case AT.39861—*Yen Interest Rate Derivatives* COM(2015) 432 final) Appeal pending; Case T-180/15 *Icap ao v Commission*)

Also note *AC-Treuhand AG v Commission* and the discussion on cartel facilitators in pages 157 and 158 above.

Miller International Schallplatten GmbH v Commission	**Vertical Agreements**
Case 19/77	Export Ban
Court of Justice, [1978] ECR 131, [1978] 2 CMLR 334	

Facts

Miller International Schallplatten GmbH (Miller) produced sound recordings (records, cassettes and tapes) which were sold chiefly on the German market. As part of its distribution strategy, Miller required its distributors to refrain from exporting its products outside their allocated territory. These restrictions allowed Miller to charge its German customers prices differing sharply from the export prices, the latter being lower than the prices charged to wholesalers and department stores.

Held

'[B]y its very nature, a clause prohibiting exports constitutes a restriction on competition, whether it is adopted at the instigation of the supplier or of the customer since the agreed purpose of the contracting parties is the endeavour to isolate a part of the market. Thus the fact that the supplier is not strict in enforcing such prohibitions cannot establish that they had no effect since their very existence may create a "visual and psychological" background which satisfies customers and contributes to a more or less rigorous division of the markets. The market strategy adopted by a producer is frequently adapted to the more or less general preferences of his customers ...' (para 7)

'Miller continues to maintain that neither its German customers nor its exporters or foreign customers were interested in intra-[Union] trade, so that the prohibitions on exports did not interfere with their freedom of competition. Furthermore, the higher prices charged to resellers resident in the Federal Republic of Germany in themselves rendered exports to the other Member States unprofitable.' (para 13)

'Arguments based on the current situation cannot sufficiently establish that clauses prohibiting exports are not such as to affect trade between Member States ... Furthermore, as has already been observed above, the fact that resellers, as customers of the applicant, prefer to limit their commercial operations to more restricted markets, whether regional or national, cannot justify the formal adoption of clauses prohibiting exports, either in particular contracts or in conditions of sale, any more than the desire of the producer to wall off sections of the [internal] market. Finally, the existence of the clauses in dispute has at least assisted Miller in maintaining its policy of lowering export prices.' (para 14)

Comment

The export ban was regarded as an activity which by its very nature constituted a restriction on competition. Subsequently, the analysis did not include an examination of the market and the effects of the provisions on competition.

In Case 56/64 etc *Consten & Grundig v Commission* the Court of Justice held that 'an agreement between producer and distributor which might tend to restore the national divisions in trade between Member States might be such as to frustrate the most fundamental objections of the [Union]' (p. 340). The agreement in this case lead to absolute territorial protection and was found to have the object of restricting competition. For a full analysis of this case see page 93 above, Chapter 3.

Note also Case C-279/87 *Tipp-Ex v Commission* [1990] ECR I-261, where the court held that 'the absolute territorial protection granted to a distributor under an exclusive distribution agreement, designed to enable parallel imports to be controlled and hindered, leads to separate national markets being maintained artificially, contrary to the Treaty, and is therefore such as to infringe [Article 101 TFEU].' This case, together with Case 19/77 *Miller v Commission*, were referred to in Case C-306/96 *Javico v Yves St Laurent* [1998] ECR I-1983 to support a conclusion that an 'agreement which requires a reseller not to resell contractual products outside the contractual territory has as its object the exclusion of parallel imports within the [Union] and consequently restriction of competition in the [internal] market'. (para 14)

In case COMP/35.587 *PO Video Games (Nintendo)* [2003] OJ L255/33 the Commission found Nintendo and seven of its distributors to have infringed Article 101 TFEU by colluding to maintain artificially high price differences for game consoles and games in the EU. According to the arrangements, distributors prevented parallel trade from their territories thus hindering exports to high-priced territories from low-priced territories. Nintendo and its distributors combated parallel trade by, among other things, establishing a system of information exchange and practical collaboration that enabled it to locate deviations from the restriction. The system facilitated tracing sources of parallel trade and restricting them. Although export bans only need to be enforced in low-price territories and not in high-price territories, the Commission held that all distributors who took part in this scheme were jointly responsible for the infringement. It noted that 'even if certain distributors did not have to take steps to prevent exports from their territories they were fundamental to the infringement's efficient operation, as they regularly warned [Nintendo] that parallel imports were taking place into their respective territories.' (para 282) On the liability of an undertaking which takes part in a multiform infringement to the conduct of others see *Sigma v Commission*, page 155 above and *AC-Treuhand AG v Commission*, page 157 above.

In Case C-468/06 etc *Sot Lélos kai Sia EE and others v GlaxoSmithKline AEVE* [2008] ECR I-7139, the Court of Justice held that 'an agreement between producer and distributor which might tend to restore the national divisions in trade between Member States might be such as to frustrate the objective of the Treaty to achieve the integration of national markets through the establishment of a single market. Thus on a number of occasions the Court has held agreements aimed at partitioning national markets according to national borders or making the interpenetration of national markets more difficult, in particular those aimed at preventing or restricting parallel exports, to be agreements whose object is to restrict competition within the meaning of that Treaty article. (see, for example, Joined Cases 96/82 to 102/82, 104/82, 105/82, 108/82 and 110/82 *IAZ International Belgium and Others v Commission* [1983] ECR 3369, paragraphs 23 to 27; Case C-306/96 *Javico* [1998] ECR I-1983, paragraphs 13 and 14; and Case C-551/03 P *General Motors v Commission* [2006] ECR I-3173, paragraphs 67 to 69).' (para 65)

In Joined Cases C-501/06P etc *GlaxoSmithKline Services Unlimited v Commission*, page 103 above, the Court of Justice confirmed that agreements aimed at prohibiting or limiting parallel trade have as their object the prevention of competition. In doing so it rejected the General Court's approach and held that it erred in law when it held that 'while it is accepted that an agreement intended to limit parallel trade must in principle be considered to have as its object the restriction of competition, that applies in so far as the agreement may be presumed to deprive final consumers of those advantages.' (para 121, Case T-168/01)

Also note Case C-306/96 *Javico v Yves St Laurent* [1998] ECR I-1983 where the Court of Justice considered whether an export ban which prohibits a European supplier entrusted with the distribution of products in a territory outside the Union from making any sales in a territory other than the contractual territory, including the territory of the Union, would infringe Article 101 TFEU. In a preliminary ruling the Court of Justice held that such agreement 'must be construed not as being intended to exclude parallel imports and marketing of the contractual product within the [Union] but as being designed to enable the producer to penetrate a market outside the [Union] by supplying a sufficient quantity of contractual products to that market. That interpretation is supported by the fact that, in the agreements at issue, the prohibition of selling outside the contractual territory also covers all other non-member countries. It follows that an agreement in which the reseller gives to the producer an undertaking that he will sell the contractual products on a market outside the [Union] cannot be regarded as having the object of appreciably restricting competition within the [internal] market or as being capable of affecting, as such, trade between Member States.' (paras 19, 20)

Note the hardcore restriction set out in Article 4(b) of the Vertical Block Exemption concerning market partitioning by territory or by customer. Also note paragraphs 47–59, 151–73, Vertical Guidelines.

ETA Fabriques d'Ebauches v SA DK Investment and others	**Vertical Agreements**
Case 31/85	Exclusive Distribution
Court of Justice, [1985] ECR 3933, [1986] 2 CMLR 674	Restrictions on Parallel Trade

Facts

Eta Fabriques d'Ebauches SA (Eta), a mass-producer of inexpensive 'Swatch' quartz watches, used a network of exclusive distributors to market its watches. In Belgium it assigned the exclusive distribution of 'Swatch' watches to an authorised dealer and undertook not to offer or sell its products in that territory to anyone but the dealer and to pass on to him any order relating to that territory. For his part, the authorised dealer undertook not to buy the products otherwise than from Eta, not to sell them, either directly or indirectly, outside the territory allotted and to pass on to Eta any order relating to the distribution of the products outside that territory. The watches sold by Eta were covered by a guarantee against technical defects for a period of 12 months after sale to the consumer, subject to a maximum of 18 months following delivery to the dealer. The defendants in the main proceedings sold 'Swatch' watches which they obtained by way of parallel imports, together with the guarantee certificate which referred to the 'Swatch' repair service in Switzerland. Eta applied to the Tribunal de Commerce, Brussels, for an injunction restraining the defendants from selling 'Swatch' watches with the guarantee granted by Eta to its authorised dealers by virtue of its contractual relationship with them. It argued that the guarantee provided is contractual in nature and is binding upon it only as against the recognised distributors. In a preliminary reference the Court of Justice considered the legality of the practice of not extending the guarantee to parallel imports.

Held

'The crucial element to be taken into consideration … is the actual or potential effect of withholding the guarantee on the competitive position of parallel distributors. In that connection it is necessary to consider whether parallel imports may be hindered, or whether opportunities for marketing such products may be restricted, regard being had in particular to the reaction of consumers and to the importance of the guarantee as an incentive to buy the products.' (para 12)

'A guarantee scheme under which a supplier of goods restricts the guarantee to customers of his exclusive distributor places the latter and the retailers to whom he sells in a privileged position as against parallel importers and distributors and must therefore be regarded as having the object or effect of restricting competition within the meaning of [Article 101(1) TFEU].' (para 14)

'The refusal to grant the guarantee cannot be justified by the need to ensure observance of the maximum storage period. The watches in question do not belong to a category of products in respect of which it is necessary to accept certain restrictions which are an inherent feature of a selective distribution system and are motivated by the desire to maintain a network of specialized dealers able to provide specific services for technically sophisticated, high-quality products. The battery is expressly excluded from the guarantee, its replacement does not pose any particular technical difficulties and, by its own admission, Eta honours the guarantee within the official distribution network beyond the six-month storage period, should the battery need to be replaced. The fact that, according to the parties, a defective watch cannot be repaired but can only be replaced is not without relevance in this regard.' (para 16)

Comment

The practice of not extending the guarantee to parallel imports indirectly hindered the imports of 'Swatch' watches and distorted competition and trade between Member States.

See comments on export bans, pages 179, 180 above.

Sarl Kitch Moto v SA Suzuki France	**Vertical Agreements**
Court of Appeal, Paris,	Exclusive Distribution
[2006] ECC 2 C d'A (Paris)	

Facts

An appeal on a decision from the Tribunal de Commerce (Paris). Sarl Kitch Moto (the distributor) was an authorised distributor of SA Suzuki France (the manufacturer). A new distribution contract between the two parties was agreed in 2001 with the aim of bringing the parties' relations into line with the Vertical Block Exemption (Regulation 2790/99 (later superseded by Regulation 330/2010)). Article 2 of the contract stipulated that 'The distributor is prohibited from selling actively or passively from any establishment not approved by Suzuki France. It is prohibited from selling to any unauthorised resellers. Any sales to resellers not authorised by Suzuki in the European Union shall be regarded as unlawful. Where a sale is made to another reseller, the distributor shall be obliged to establish that the purchaser is a distributor approved by Suzuki in the European Union.' Following a few incidents in which the distributor sold motorcycles outside its own territory, the manufacturer terminated the distribution agreement. The distributor brought an action in the Paris Commercial Court, complaining of the excessive and unjustified nature of the termination. On appeal to the Paris court of Appeal the court commented on the legality of Article 2 of the contract.

Held

Kitch Moto, in invoking EC Regulation 2790/1999 on the application of Article 101(3) TFEU to categories of vertical agreements and concerted practices in order to argue that the prohibition of passive sales referred to in Article 2 of the distribution contract was unlawful, and in relying on Article 4(b) of that Regulation prohibiting restriction of: 'the territory into which, or of the customers to whom, the [distributor] may sell the contract goods … except the restriction of active sales into the exclusive territory, or to an exclusive customer group reserved to the supplier or allocated by the supplier to another [distributor], where such a restriction does not limit sales by the customers of the [distributor]' to argue that 'only active sales outside the network may be prohibited' and to ask the court to declare Art 2 of the distribution contract void, fails to observe, first, that the appellant does not show how the clauses criticised might restrict sales by its customers, and secondly, that the territorial clause set out in this article is not contrary to the provisions of Art 4(c) of the above-mentioned Regulation, which permit the supplier to prohibit 'a member of the system from operating out of an unauthorised place of establishment'. (para 8)

Comment

Note that a provision in a vertical agreement which does not satisfy the conditions of the Vertical Block Exemption is not necessarily void. The Block Exemption lists restrictions which do not benefit from an outright exemption (see Article 4 (hard core), Article 5 (no compete)). Such provisions, although not benefiting from the Block Exemption may still benefit from an individual exemption, or be found not to infringe Article 101 TFEU.

In order to succeed in its claim, it was for the distributor (Sarl Kitch Moto) to show that Article 2 of the distribution agreement infringed Article 101(1) TFEU by its object or effect. This would have shifted the burden of proof to the manufacturer (SA Suzuki France) which would then have to prove that despite infringing Article 101 (1) TFEU the agreement benefits from an exemption under Article 101(3) TFEU.

In this case, the Court of Appeal seemed to suggest that the agreement benefited from the safe heaven of the Vertical Block Exemption since the article in question did not infringe the provisions of Article 4(c) of the Block Exemption.

Note Case 56/65 *Société Technique Minière v Maschinenbau Ulm GmbH* (page 96 above) and Case 23/67 *SA Brasserie de Haecht v Consorts Wilkin-Janssen* (page 96 above), where the Court considered the legality of exclusive distribution agreements. Also note Case 56/64 etc *Consten & Grundig v Commission* (page 93 above), where absolute territorial protection was found to have the object of restricting competition.

Metro SB-Großmärkte GmbH & Co KG v Commission	**Vertical Agreements**
Case 26/76	Selective Distribution
Court of Justice, [1977] ECR 1875, [1978] 2 CMLR 1	

Facts

Following a complaint submitted by Metro the Commission started an investigation into a selective distribution system for electric goods, operated by SABA. The Commission found that the conditions of sale for the domestic market as laid down in the distribution system did not fall within the prohibition in Article 101(1) TFEU and that the other provisions in the distribution agreement qualify for an exemption under Article 101(3) TFEU. Metro applied for an annulment of the Commission decision. On appeal the Court of Justice considered, among other things, the characteristics of selective distribution systems. The Application was dismissed.

Held

'The requirement contained in [Article 3(1) EC (now repealed)] and [Article 101 TFEU] that competition shall not be distorted implies the existence on the market of workable competition, that is to say the degree of competition necessary to ensure the observance of the basic requirements and the attainment of the objectives of the Treaty, in particular the creation of a single market achieving conditions similar to those of a domestic market. In accordance with this requirement the nature and intensiveness of competition may vary to an extent dictated by the products or services in question and the economic structure of the relevant market sectors. In the sector covering the production of high quality and technically advanced consumer durables, where a relatively small number of large- and medium-scale producers offer a varied range of items which, or so consumers may consider, are readily interchangeable, the structure of the market does not preclude the existence of a variety of channels of distribution adapted to the peculiar characteristics of the various producers and to the requirements of the various categories of consumers. On this view the Commission was justified in recognizing that selective distribution systems constituted, together with others, an aspect of competition which accords with [Article 101(1) TFEU], provided that resellers are chosen on the basis of objective criteria of a qualitative nature relating to the technical qualifications of the reseller and his staff and the suitability of his trading premises and that such conditions are laid down uniformly for all potential resellers and are not applied in a discriminatory fashion.' (para 20)

'It is true that in such systems of distribution price competition is not generally emphasized either as an exclusive or indeed as a principal factor. This is particularly so when, as in the present case, access to the distribution network is subject to conditions exceeding the requirements of an appropriate distribution of the products. However, although price competition is so important that it can never be eliminated it does not constitute the only effective form of competition or that to which absolute priority must in all circumstances be accorded. The powers conferred upon the Commission under [Article 101(3) TFEU] show that the requirements for the maintenance of workable competition may be reconciled with the safeguarding of objectives of a different nature and that to this end certain restrictions on competition are permissible, provided that they are essential to the attainment of those objectives and that they do not result in the elimination of competition for a substantial part of the [internal] market. For specialist wholesalers and retailers the desire to maintain a certain price level, which corresponds to the desire to preserve, in the interests of consumers, the possibility of the continued existence of this channel of distribution in conjunction with new methods of distribution based on a different type of competition policy, forms one of the objectives which may be pursued without necessarily falling under the prohibition contained in [Article 101(1) TFEU], and, if it does fall thereunder, either wholly or in part, coming within the framework of [Article 101(3) TFEU]. This argument is strengthened if, in addition, such conditions promote improved competition inasmuch as it relates to factors other than prices.' (para 21)

Comment

'To assess the possible anti-competitive effects of selective distribution under Article 101(1), a distinction needs to be made between purely qualitative selective distribution and quantitative selective distribution. Purely qualitative selective distribution selects dealers only on the basis of objective criteria required by the nature of the product such as training of sales personnel, the service provided at the point of sale, a certain range of the products being sold etc. The application of such criteria does not put a direct limit on the number of dealers. Purely qualitative selective distribution is in general considered to fall outside Article 101(1) for lack of anti-competitive effects, provided that three conditions are satisfied. First, the nature of the product in question must necessitate a selective distribution system, in the sense that such a system must constitute a legitimate requirement, having regard to the nature of the product concerned, to preserve its quality and ensure its proper use. Secondly, resellers must be chosen on the basis of objective criteria of a qualitative nature which are laid down uniformly for all potential resellers and are not applied in a discriminatory manner. Thirdly, the criteria laid down must not go beyond what is necessary. Quantitative selective distribution adds further criteria for selection that more directly limits the potential number of dealers by, for instance, requiring minimum or maximum sales, by fixing the number of dealers, etc.' (Vertical Guidelines, para 175)

The product in question must necessitate a selective distribution system. For example:

(a)   In case T-88/92 *Groupement d'achat Edouard Leclerc v Commission* [1996] ECR II-1961, (appeal by a third party on the Commission's decision to grant exemption to the Givenchy distribution system (Case IV/33.542 *Parfums Givenchy* system of selective distribution)) the General Court held that luxury cosmetics are sophisticated and high-quality products with a distinctive luxury image which is important in the eyes of consumers. 'In the luxury cosmetics sector, qualitative criteria for the selection of retailers which do not go beyond what is necessary to ensure that those products are suitably presented for sale are in principle not covered by [Article 101(1) TFEU], in so far as they are objective, laid down uniformly for all potential retailers and not applied in a discriminatory fashion.' (para 117)

(b)   In Case 31/85 *ETA Fabriques d'Ebauches v SA DK Investment and others* (page 181 above), mass produced 'Swatch' watches were considered not to belong to a category of products which require a selective distribution system. On the other hand, in Case IV/5715 *Junghans* [1977] OJ L30/10, quality, sophisticated watches were found to justify conditions in a selective distribution system relating to the technical qualification of dealers and specialist knowledge of their staff.

(c)   In Case 243/83 *SA Binon & Cie v SA Agence et Messageries de la Presse* (page 192 below) the special characteristics of newspapers and periodicals distribution were held to justify a system of selective distribution.

When the selective distribution agreement is part of a wider network of selective distribution, a 'simple' selective distribution system may give rise to competitive concerns. In Metro II, Case 75/84 *Metro SB-Großmärkte GmbH & Co KG v Commission* [1986] ECR 3021, [1987] 1 CMLR 118, the Court held that 'although the court has held in previous Decisions that "simple" selective distribution systems are capable of constituting an aspect of competition compatible with [Article 101(1) TFEU], there may nevertheless be a restriction or elimination of competition where the existence of a certain number of such systems does not leave any room for other forms of distribution based on a different type of competition policy or results in a rigidity in price structure which is not counterbalanced by other aspects of competition between products of the same brand and by the existence of effective competition between different brands.' (para 40)

In Case 107/82 *AEG v Commission* the Court of Justice held that selective distribution systems may include acceptable limitations to attain legitimate goals such as the maintenance of a specialist trade capable of providing specific services as regards high-quality and high-technology products. Such limitations lead to a reduction of price competition in favour of competition relating to factors other than price. For detailed analysis see page 65, Chapter 3 above.

Pierre Fabre v Président de l'Autorité de la concurrence	**Vertical agreements**
Case C-439/09	Selective Distribution
Court of Justice, [2011] 5 CMLR 31	Ban on Internet Sales

Facts

Pierre Fabre Dermo-Cosmétique is a manufacture of cosmetics products which are not classified as medicines. The distribution contracts for those products prohibited online sales and stipulated that sales must be made exclusively in a physical space in which a qualified pharmacist is present. The French Competition Authority found the provisions to be contrary to Article 101 TFEU. Pierre Fabre brought an action for annulment of the decision at the French court. In a reference for a preliminary ruling the Court of Justice was asked whether the general and absolute ban on internet sales constitutes a 'hardcore' restriction of competition by object for the purposes of Article 101(1) TFEU.

Held

'For the purposes of assessing whether the contractual clause at issue involves a restriction of competition "by object", regard must be had to the content of the clause, the objectives it seeks to attain and the economic and legal context of which it forms a part (see *GlaxoSmithKline and Others* v *Commission and Others*, paragraph 58 and the case law cited).' (para 35)

'As regards agreements constituting a selective distribution system, the Court has already stated that such agreements necessarily affect competition in the common market (Case 107/82 *AEG-Telefunken v Commission* [1983] ECR 3151, paragraph 33). Such agreements are to be considered, in the absence of objective justification, as "restrictions by object2. However, it has always been recognised in the case-law of the Court that there are legitimate requirements, such as the maintenance of a specialist trade capable of providing specific services as regards high-quality and high-technology products, which may justify a reduction of price competition in favour of competition relating to factors other than price. Systems of selective distribution, in so far as they aim at the attainment of a legitimate goal capable of improving competition in relation to factors other than price, therefore constitute an element of competition which is in conformity with Article 101(1) TFEU (*AEG-Telefunken v Commission*, paragraph 33).' (paras 39, 40)

'In that regard, the Court has already pointed out that the organisation of such a network is not prohibited by Article 101(1) TFEU, to the extent that resellers are chosen on the basis of objective criteria of a qualitative nature, laid down uniformly for all potential resellers and not applied in a discriminatory fashion, that the characteristics of the product in question necessitate such a network in order to preserve its quality and ensure its proper use and, finally, that the criteria laid down do not go beyond what is necessary (Case 26/76 *Metro SB-Großmärkte v Commission* [1977] ECR 1875, paragraph 20, and Case 31/80 *L'Oréal* [1980] ECR 3775, paragraphs 15 and 16).' (para 41)

It should be noted that in the past the Court has not accepted 'arguments relating to the need to provide individual advice to the customer and to ensure his protection against the incorrect use of products, in the context of non-prescription medicines and contact lenses, to justify a ban on internet sales (see, to that effect, *Deutscher Apothekerverband*, …, and Case C-108/09 *Ker-Optika* …).' In addition, the aim of maintaining a prestigious image is not a legitimate aim for restricting competition. (paras 44–6)

Accordingly, the contractual clause in the selective distribution system which results in a ban on the use of the internet for sales is not objectively justified, amounts to a restriction by object and infringes Article 101(1) TFEU. (para 47)

Such contractual clause may benefit from an individual exemption under Article 101(3) TFEU. However, in this instance, the Court does not have sufficient information before it to assess whether the contract satisfies the conditions in Article 101(3) TFEU. (paras 48–50)

A contractual clause may benefit from the vertical block exemption. Yet, it follows from Article 4(c) of the Vertical Block Exemption that the exemption does not apply to agreements which 'directly or indirectly, in isolation or in combination with other factors under the control of the parties, have as their object the restriction of active or passive sales to end users by members of a selective distribution system operating at the retail level of trade, without prejudice to the possibility of prohibiting a member of the system from operating out of an unauthorised place of establishment.' (paras 51–3)

'A contractual clause such as the one at issue in the main proceedings, prohibiting *de facto* the internet as a method of marketing, at the very least has as its object the restriction of passive sales to end users wishing to purchase online and located outside the physical trading area of the relevant member of the selective distribution system.' (para 54)

Comment

The absolute ban on internet sales was not objectively justified, fell within the scope of Article 101 TFEU and amounted to violation by object. The Court noted that, in the context of non-prescription medicines, the need to provide individual advice, the desire to ensure protection against incorrect use of products, or to maintain prestigious image, are not legitimate aims for restricting competition and do not form an objective justification.

In his opinion the AG Mazák took a less restrictive approach and considered it 'conceivable that there may be circumstances where the sale of certain goods via the internet may undermine inter alia the image and thus the quality of those goods thereby justifying a general and absolute ban on internet sales.' (para 54)

AG Mazák noted that 'in certain exceptional circumstances, private voluntary measures limiting the sale of goods or services via the internet could be objectively justified, by reason of the nature of those goods or services or the customers to whom they are sold … there may exist other situations where the ban on internet sales is objectively justified even in the absence of national or Community regulation. Private voluntary measures, if included in an agreement, may fall outside the scope of [Article 101(1) TFEU] provided the limitations imposed are appropriate in the light of the legitimate objective sought and do not go beyond what is necessary in accordance with the principle of proportionality. In my view, the legitimate objective sought must be of a public law nature and therefore aimed at protecting a public good and extend beyond the protection of the image of the products concerned or the manner in which an undertaking wishes to market its products.' (para 35)

The restriction in this case on both active and passive sales meant that the Vertical Block Exemption was not applicable to the selective distribution agreement.

Pierre Fabre argued that the ban on selling products via the internet is equivalent to a prohibition on operating out of an unauthorised establishment and that subsequently the agreement could benefit from the vertical block exemption. The Court rejected this argument and noted that by referring to 'a place of establishment', Article 4(c) of of the Vertical Block Exemption concerns only outlets where direct sales take place. The Court added the possibility for an undertaking to argue for an individual exemption justify a narrow interpretation to the provisions which bring agreements or practices within the block exemption.

The European Commission Guidelines on Vertical Restraints [2010] OJ C130/01, elaborate on the role of internet sales in competition. 'The internet is a powerful tool to reach a greater number and variety of customers than by more traditional sales methods, which explains why certain restrictions on the use of the internet are dealt with as (re)sales restrictions. In principle, every distributor must be allowed to use the internet to sell products. In general, where a distributor uses a website to sell products that is considered a form of passive selling, since it is a reasonable way to allow customers to reach the distributor.' (para 52) The Commission further elaborates on the instances in which restriction on internet sales will amount to hardcore restrictions of passive selling. (paras 50–4)

PO/Yamaha	**Vertical agreements**
Case COMP/37.975	Distribution Agreement
European Commission	Ban on Internet Sales

Facts

The European Commission opened an investigation into the business practices of Yamaha Group and the agreements governing the distribution of its musical instruments. Most Yamaha products are distributed by authorised dealers under a selective distribution system throughout Europe. The distribution system was designed to enhance Yamaha's brand image through personalised customer advice. At the end of its investigation the Commission concluded that Yamaha Group has infringed Article 101 TFEU by entering into agreements with authorised dealers, containing a number of restrictions on competition. Among other things the Commission condemned some of the agreements for including obligations on official dealers to contact Yamaha before exporting via the internet.

Held

Yamaha's distribution agreements in Austria, Belgium and Germany included a provision obliging the dealer to contact Yamaha before exporting goods via the internet because of divergent security standards, such as standards for the protection of radio frequencies, the dangerous materials regulation and technical standards. That obligation discouraged dealers from exporting via the internet and reinforced market partitioning. It constitutes an infringement of Article 101 TFEU. (para 107)

'Although the object of the agreement may not have been to directly restrict exports, it clearly had the potential effect of discouraging dealers from exporting products to other Member States. According to the settled case-law of the Court, in order to determine whether an agreement is to be considered to be prohibited by reason of the distortion of competition which is its effect, the competition in question should be assessed within the actual context in which it would occur in the absence of the agreement in dispute. However, Article 81(1) does not restrict such an assessment to actual effects alone; it must also take account of the agreement's potential effects on competition within the common market. As far as the products concerned are musical instruments, it seems indeed excessive to invoke the security norms and the clause on dangerous products before exportation. Indeed, such limitations existed only for exports arranged via the internet, and there is no reason why they should be limited to such situations if concerns were really related to security norms.' (para 109)

Comment

In its Vertical Guidelines the Commission elaborates on its approach to online sales. Every distributor should be free to use the internet to advertise and sell products. That use is generally regarded as passive selling and can only be banned in exceptional cases when it is objectively justified. (paras 50–5)

In the case of *B&W Loudspeakers distribution system* the agreements in questions were notified to the Commission and contained several 'hard-core' restrictions of competition, including a prohibition on distant sales including through the internet. Following the opening of these formal proceedings, B&W Loudspeakers undertook to delete the restrictions on pricing, cross-supplies and distance selling from its agreements. Retailers could subsequently request B&W Loudspeakers to engage in distant selling. B&W Loudspeakers can only refuse such requests in writing and on criteria that concern the need to maintain the brand image and reputation of the products. The criteria must be applied indiscriminately and must be comparable to those for sales from a traditional retail outlet. Press release IP/02/916, dated 24/06/2002.

Van den Bergh Foods Ltd v Commission	**Vertical Agreements**
Case T-65/98	Single Branding
General Court, [2003] ECR II-4653, [2004] 4 CMLR 1	Cabinet Exclusivity

Facts

Van den Bergh Foods (formerly HB Ice Cream), supplied ice-cream retailers with freezer cabinets free of charge or at a nominal rent, provided that they were used exclusively for HB ice creams. The Commission found HB's exclusive cabinet distribution agreements incompatible with Articles 101 and 102 TFEU. HB applied for the annulment of the Commission Decision arguing that freezer-cabinet exclusivity was not to be regarded as outlet exclusivity since retailers were entitled to terminate the contract with HB or to install other freezers not belonging to HB. According to HB, the retailers' freedom of choice contradicted any conclusion that the agreements foreclosed the market. Additionally HB challenged the Commission's finding that 40 per cent of sales outlets in Ireland were *de facto* tied to HB by the exclusivity clause. The Application was dismissed.

Held

The cabinet exclusivity clause was not, in formal terms, an exclusive purchasing obligation whose object was to restrict competition. The Commission was therefore required to prove that the effect of such a clause would be to lead to a sufficiently high degree of foreclosure as to constitute an infringement of Article 101(1) TFEU. (para 80) Such an inquiry would rely on the specific economic context in which the agreements operated. (para 84)

The nature of the product market, the limited space in outlets and the popularity of HB's product range would have led retailers bound by the agreement to stock HB ice-cream and to refrain from stocking a second range of impulse ice-cream. The cabinet exclusivity clause would have motivated rational retailers in small outlets to favour HB's products over products of other ice-cream manufacturers, regardless of their popularity on the market. (para 97)

Despite the fact that it was theoretically possible for retailers who only had an HB freezer cabinet to sell the ice-creams of other manufacturers, the practical effect of HB's network of distribution agreements and exclusivity clause was to restrict the commercial freedom of retailers to choose the products they wished to sell. (paras 99, 101)

The retailers' right to terminate their distribution agreements with HB at any time was not often exercised and did not operate *de facto* to reduce the degree of foreclosure of the relevant market. (para 105)

Although freezer-cabinet exclusivity may be a standard practice in the market and is part of an agreement concluded in the interests of both the retailers and HB, it constituted in the present market conditions an abuse when engaged by a dominant undertaking. (paras 159, 160)

Comment

The market in this case displays unique characteristics. The cost of freezer cabinets, cost of maintenance and cost of space in outlets, would lead a rational retailer to favour the dominant undertaking over competitors. Optimal allocation of space in small outlets would make it unprofitable to stock additional brands in a second freezer unless the profit generated is greater than the potential profit generated from using this space for displaying other goods. These unique characteristics created a strong disincentive for retailers to allow a new competitor into the outlet either instead of HB freezers or in addition to them. In other words, the retailers' legal right to terminate an agreement was of no consequence as they lacked the incentive to do so. Subsequently, freezer exclusivity transformed into outlet exclusivity in the circumstances of this case.

Note Case T-7/93 *Langnese-Iglo v EC Commission*, [1995] ECR II-1533, [1995] 5 CMLR 602 (upheld on appeal to the Court of Justice: Case C-279/95, [1998] ECR I-5609, [1998] 5 CMLR 933). There the Court considered the legality of a distribution agreement in the German market for impulse ice-cream. The agreement included an exclusive purchase obligation which required distributors of 'Scholler Lebensmittel GmbH & Co

KG' (Scholler) to obtain their ice-cream supply solely from Scholler. These provisions included freezer exclusivity but were wider as they also referred to the outlet as a whole. The Court noted that in order to determine whether the 'exclusive purchasing agreements fall within the prohibition contained in [Article 101(1) TFEU], it is appropriate, according to the case-law, to consider whether, taken together, all the similar agreements entered into in the relevant market and the other features of the economic and legal context of the agreements at issue show that those agreements cumulatively have the effect of denying access to that market for new domestic and foreign competitors. If, on examination, that is found not to be the case, the individual agreements making up the bundle of agreements as a whole cannot undermine competition within the meaning of [Article 101(1) TFEU]. If, on the other hand, such examination reveals that it is difficult to gain access to the market, it is necessary to assess the extent to which the contested agreements contribute to the cumulative effect produced, on the basis that only agreements which make a significant contribution to any partitioning of the market are prohibited (*Delimitis*, paragraphs 23 and 24).' (para 99) The court agreed with the Commission's conclusions that access to the market for new competitors was made difficult by the existence of a system under which a large number of freezer cabinets were lent by Scholler to retailers and retailers were obliged to use them exclusively for the applicant's products. 'The necessary consequence of that situation is that any new competitor entering the market must either persuade the retailer to exchange the freezer cabinet installed by [Scholler] for another, which involves giving up the turnover in the products from the previous supplier, or to persuade the retailer to install an additional freezer cabinet, which may prove impossible, particularly because of lack of space in small sales outlets. Moreover, if the new competitor is able to offer only a limited range of products, as in the case of the intervener, it may prove difficult for it to persuade the retailer to terminate its agreement with the previous supplier.' (para 108) The court upheld the Commission decision finding the agreements to give rise to an appreciable restriction of competition on the relevant market.

In Case C-234/89 *Stergios Delimitis v Henninger Bräu AG* [1991] ECR I-935, the Court of Justice, in a preliminary reference, held that in order to assess the effects of a single branding agreement (beer supply agreement) the national court should analyse its effects, 'taken together with other contracts of the same type, on the opportunities of national competitors or those from other Member States, to gain access to the market for beer consumption or to increase their market share and, accordingly, the effects on the range of products offered to consumers.' (para 15) In order to do so the relevant market needs to be defined and the agreements on this market examined in their totality, to conclude whether the network of agreements forecloses the market. For a detailed analysis of this case see page 98, Chapter 3 above.

The Vertical Guidelines (paras 129–50) outline the possible anticompetitive effects of non-compete obligations and the variables relevant in the assessment of such agreements under Article 101 TFEU.

Non-compete obligations (single branding agreements) are exempted under the Vertical Block Exemption when (1) the market share held by the supplier does not exceed 30 per cent of the relevant market on which it sells the contract goods or services, and (2) the market share held by the buyer does not exceed 30 per cent of the relevant market on which it purchases the contract goods or services, and (3) subject to a limitation in time of five years for the non-compete obligation.

Pronuptia de Paris GmbH v Pronuptia de Paris Irmgard Schillgallis	**Vertical Agreements**
Case 161/84	Franchise Agreements
Court of Justice, [1986] ECR 353, [1986] 1 CMLR 414	

Facts

A reference for a preliminary ruling from the German Federal Court of Justice concerning the application of Article 101 TFEU to franchise agreements. The questions arose in proceedings between Pronuptia de Paris GmbH (the franchisor), a distributor of wedding dresses which was a subsidiary of the French company of the same name, and Mrs Schillgalis, an independent retailer who acted as the franchisee in Hamburg, Oldenburg and Hanover.

Held

'[A] distinction must be drawn between different varieties of franchise agreements. In particular, it is necessary to distinguish between (i) service franchises, under which the franchisee offers a service under the business name or symbol and sometimes the trade-mark of the franchisor, in accordance with the franchisor's instructions, (ii) production franchises, under which the franchisee manufactures products according to the instructions of the franchisor and sells them under the franchisor's trade-mark, and (iii) distribution franchises, under which the franchisee simply sells certain products in a shop which bears the franchisor's business name or symbol. In this judgment the court is concerned only with this third type of contract, to which the questions asked by the national court expressly refer.' (para 13)

In a system of distribution franchises, the franchisor which has established itself in a given market grants independent traders, for a fee, the right to establish themselves in other markets using its business name and the business methods that have made it successful. The system allows the franchisor to expand without investing its own capital and the franchisee to benefit from the reputation and experience of the franchisor. 'In order for the system to work two conditions must be met. First, the franchisor must be able to communicate his know-how to the franchisees and provide them with the necessary assistance in order to enable them to apply his methods, without running the risk that that know-how and assistance might benefit competitors, even indirectly. It follows that provisions which are essential in order to avoid that risk do not constitute restrictions on competition for the purposes of [Article 101(1) TFEU]. That is also true of a clause prohibiting the franchisee, during the period of validity of the contract and for a reasonable period after its expiry, from opening a shop of the same or a similar nature in an area where he may compete with a member of the network. The same may be said of the franchisee's obligation not to transfer his shop to another party without the prior approval of the franchisor; that provision is intended to prevent competitors from indirectly benefiting from the know-how and assistance provided. Secondly, the franchisor must be able to take the measures necessary for maintaining the identity and reputation of the network bearing his business name or symbol. It follows that provisions which establish the means of control necessary for that purpose do not constitute restrictions on competition for the purposes of [Article 101(1) TFEU].' (paras 15–17)

'The same is true of the franchisee's obligation to apply the business methods developed by the franchisor and to use the know-how provided. That is also the case with regard to the franchisee's obligation to sell the goods covered by the contract only in premises laid out and decorated according to the franchisor's instructions, which is intended to ensure uniform presentation in conformity with certain requirements. The same requirements apply to the location of the shop, the choice of which is also likely to affect the network's reputation. It is thus understandable that the franchisee cannot transfer his shop to another location without the franchisor's approval. The prohibition of the assignment by the franchisee of his rights and obligations under the contract without the franchisor's approval protects the latter's right freely to choose the franchisees, on whose business qualifications the establishment and maintenance of the network's reputation depend.' (paras 18–20)

The control exerted by the franchisor on the selection of goods offered by the franchisee enables the public to obtain goods of the same quality from each franchisee and is necessary for the protection of the network's reputation. Such control should not prevent the franchisee from obtaining those goods from other franchisees. (para 21)

A provision requiring the franchisee to obtain the franchisor's approval for all advertising is essential for the maintenance of the network's identity, so long as it concerns only the nature of the advertising. (para 22)

Certain provisions may restrict competition between the members of the network and may lead to the sharing of the market. 'In that regard the attention of the national court should be drawn to the provision which obliges the franchisee to sell goods covered by the contract only in the premises specified therein. That provision prohibits the franchisee from opening a second shop. Its real effect becomes clear if it is examined in conjunction with the franchisor's undertaking to ensure that the franchisee has the exclusive use of his business name or symbol in a given territory. In order to comply with that undertaking the franchisor must not only refrain from establishing himself within that territory but also require other franchisees to give an undertaking not to open a second shop outside their own territory. A combination of provisions of that kind results in a sharing of markets between the franchisor and the franchisees or between franchisees and thus restricts competition within the network. As is clear from [Joined cases 56, 58/64 *Consten and Grundig v Commission* (1966) ECR 299)], a restriction of that kind constitutes a limitation of competition for the purposes of [Article 101(1) TFEU] if it concerns a business name or symbol which is already well-known. It is of course possible that a prospective franchisee would not take the risk of becoming part of the chain, investing his own money, paying a relatively high entry fee and undertaking to pay a substantial annual royalty, unless he could hope, thanks to a degree of protection against competition on the part of the franchisor and other franchisees, that his business would be profitable. That consideration, however, is relevant only to an examination of the agreement in the light of the conditions laid down in [Article 101(3) TFEU].' (paras 24, 26)

The franchisor may provide the franchisee with price guidelines as long as these do not impair the franchisee's freedom to determine its own prices, and so long as there is no concerted practice between the franchisor and franchisees or between the franchisees themselves for the actual application of such prices. (para 25)

Comment

The provisions of the franchise agreement were analysed as ancillary restraints. The court considered whether they were necessary for achieving the objectives of the franchise system. It considered provisions protecting know-how, branding advertising and product choice to be necessary in this respect. On the other hand a franchising agreement which leads to market sharing was held to restrict competition. (para 24)

A combination of exclusivity and territorial allocation (para 24) led to absolute territorial protection and, in line with *Consten and Grundig v Commission*, was found to restrict competition.

The Commission noted in several cases that clauses which are essential to prevent the know-how supplied and assistance provided by the franchisor from benefiting competitors and clauses which provide for the control that is essential for preserving the common identity and reputation of the network do not constitute restrictions of competition within the meaning of Article 101(1) TFEU. See, for example, Commission decision granting exemption under Article 101(3) in Case IV/31.697 *Charles Jourdan* [1989] OJ L35/31, and Commission decision in Cases IV/31.428 to 31.432 *Yves Rocher* [1987] OJ L8/49.

The Commission Guidelines on Vertical Restraints [2000] OJ C291 consider the analysis of franchise agreements (paras 189–91) as well as the transfer of know-how and licensing of intellectual property rights (paras 31–45).

SA Binon & Cie v SA Agence et Messageries de la Presse	**Vertical Agreements**
Case 243/83	Resale Price
Court of Justice, [1985] ECR 2015, [1985] 3 CMLR 800	Maintenance

Facts

SA Agence et Messageries de la Presse (AMP) operated a selective distribution system for newspapers and periodicals in Belgium and was responsible for close to 70 per cent of the distribution of Belgian newspapers and periodicals. AMP refused to supply newspapers to SA Binon & Cie (Binon). The dispute between the two companies reached the Brussels Commercial Court. The court, in a preliminary reference referred to the Court of Justice several questions, one of which concerned the legality of a clause in AMP's selective distribution system according to which the distributor reserved the right to fix prices and compel retailers to respect those prices.

Held (on the fixing of prices)

'Finally, the third question is concerned with the problem whether the fact that, within the framework of a selective distribution system of newspapers and periodicals, fixed prices must be observed renders the system incompatible with the prohibition laid down in [Article 101 TFEU]. AMP contends in that regard that the prices of newspapers and periodicals are fixed by the publishers and not, as the national court seems to think, by the distribution agency. Observance by retailers of the prices fixed by publishers arises from the aforementioned special characteristics of the distribution of newspapers and periodicals.' (paras 39–40)

'The government of the Federal Republic of Germany, which took part in the proceedings solely in order to submit observations with regard to the third question, considers that the freedom of the press, as a fundamental right protected by the constitutional law of the Member States and by the court's case-law, entails the freedom to contribute to the formation of public opinion. For that reason newspapers and periodicals as well as their distribution have special characteristics. The nature of newspapers and periodicals requires an extremely rapid system for their distribution in view of the very limited period during which they can be sold before they are out of date; at the end of that period, the length of which varies according to the specific publication in question, newspapers and periodicals have practically no value. To those factors must be added the heterogeneity of newspapers and periodicals and the lack of elasticity in demand since each newspaper or periodical has more or less its own body of customers.' (para 41)

'The German government concludes that, from the point of view of competition, the position of the market in newspapers and periodicals is so special that it is not possible to apply to it without modification principles which have been developed in completely different contexts. If the possibility of fixing prices for newspapers and periodicals is not accepted any effective distribution system for such products would be incompatible with the rules on competition and the effect on the diversity and freedom of the press would be disastrous. From that point of view it is not unimportant to note that systems of fixed prices in relation to the distribution of newspapers and periodicals are accepted under the legislation of most Member States or are operated without encountering any difficulties.' (para 42)

'In the Commission's opinion any price-fixing agreement constitutes, of itself, a restriction on competition and is, as such, prohibited by [Article 101(3) TFEU]. The Commission does not deny that newspapers and periodicals and the way they are distributed have special characteristics but considers that these cannot lead to an exclusion of such products and their distribution from the scope of [Article 81(3) EC]. On the contrary, those characteristics should be put forward by the undertakings relying upon them in the context of an application for exemption under [Article 101(3) TFEU].' (para 43) 'It should be observed in the first place that provisions which fix the prices to be observed in contracts with third parties constitute, of themselves, a restriction on competition within the meaning of [Article 101(1) TFEU] which refers to agreements which fix selling prices as an example of an agreement prohibited by the Treaty.' (para 44)

Such agreement may benefit from an exemption under Article 101(3) TFEU. In considering the availability of exemption account should be taken of the possibility that the fixing of the retail price by publishers constitutes the sole means of supporting the financial burden resulting from the taking back of unsold copies and the possibility that the latter practice constitutes the sole method by which a wide selection of newspapers and periodicals can be made available to readers. (para 46)

Comment

In Case 161/84 *Pronuptia de Paris GmbH v Pronuptia de Paris Irmgard Schillgallis* (page 190 above) the Court of Justice held that 'provisions which impair the franchisee's freedom to determine his own prices are restrictive of competition'. On the other hand it noted that would not be the case 'where the franchisor simply provides franchisees with price guidelines, so long as there is no concerted practice between the franchisor and the franchisees or between the franchisees themselves for the actual application of such prices.' (para 25)

Note also Case 26/76 *Metro SB-Großmärkte GmbH & Co KG v Commission* (page 184 above), where the Court of Justice commented in the context of selective distribution systems that 'it is true that in such systems of distribution price competition is not generally emphasized either as an exclusive or indeed as a principal factor. … However, although price competition is so important that it can never be eliminated it does not constitute the only effective form of competition or that to which absolute priority must in all circumstances be accorded …' (para 21)

Also note the Commission decision in Case IV/30.658 *Polistil/Arbois* [1984] OJ L136/9, where a clause in a distribution agreement was held to restrict 'Polistil's freedom to set its prices to Arbois according to conditions on the relevant market, the quantities supplied and its own commercial policy.' (para 45)

The restrictive approach to RPM has led businesses, in some instances, to use agency agreements to evade the application of Article 101 TFEU to RPM. Note, however, that to be regarded as an agent, the agent cannot accept the financial risks of the sales. See *DaimlerChrysler AG v Commission*, below, page 198.

The EU Commission Vertical Guidelines note that despite the hardcore nature of resale price maintenance, undertakings may plead an efficiency defence under Article 101(3) TFEU (paras 223–9).

Note the United States Supreme Court decision in *Leegin Creative Leather Products, Inc v PSKS, Inc*, 127 S Ct 2705 US (2007). The US Supreme Court overruled the Court's longstanding decision in *Dr Miles Medical Co v John D Park & Sons Co*, 220 US 373 (1911) and held that the 'application of per se rule, under which category of restraint of trade is deemed necessarily illegal under Sherman Act, is unwarranted as to vertical agreements to fix minimum resale prices … [since] it cannot be stated with confidence that such agreements always or almost always tend to restrict competition and decrease output.' 'Economics literature is replete with procompetitive justifications for a manufacturer's use of resale price maintenance, and the few recent studies on the subject also cast doubt on the conclusion that the practice meets the criteria for a per se rule. The justifications for vertical price restraints are similar to those for other vertical restraints. Minimum resale price maintenance can stimulate interbrand competition among manufacturers selling different brands of the same type of product by reducing intrabrand competition among retailers selling the same brand. This is important because the antitrust laws' "primary purpose … is to protect interbrand competition" … A single manufacturer's use of vertical price restraints tends to eliminate intrabrand price competition; this in turn encourages retailers to invest in services or promotional efforts that aid the manufacturer's position as against rival manufacturers. Resale price maintenance may also give consumers more options to choose among low-price, low-service brands; high-price, high-service brands; and brands falling in between. Absent vertical price restraints, retail services that enhance interbrand competition might be underprovided because discounting retailers can free ride on retailers who furnish services and then capture some of the demand those services generate. Retail price maintenance can also increase interbrand competition by facilitating market entry for new firms and brands and by encouraging retailer services that would not be provided even absent free riding.' 'Setting minimum resale prices may also have anticompetitive effects; and unlawful price fixing, designed solely to obtain monopoly profits, is an ever present temptation. Resale price maintenance may, for example, facilitate a manufacturer cartel or be used to organize retail cartels. It can also be abused by a powerful manufacturer or retailer. Thus, the potential anticompetitive consequences of vertical price restraints must not be ignored or underestimated.' (pages 2714–18)

HRS-Hotel Reservation Service v Bundeskartellamt VI—Kart 1 /14 (V) Higher Regional Court of Düsseldorf	**Most-favoured Nation Clause** Wide MFN

Facts

In 2013, the German Competition Agency (Bundeskartellamt) reached a decision concerning the use of broad parity clauses by the hotel portal HRS. The broad parity clauses in question required hotel partners to guarantee that the price offered on the HRS website was no greater than the cheapest rate offered on other online booking and travel platforms, or on the hotel's own web pages and offline sale channels. In addition, the agreements in question governed room availability, booking conditions and mobile applications. The Bundeskartellamt held that the wide MFNs directly restricted the price-setting freedom of hotels, removed the economic incentive for online travel agents (OTAs) to lower commissions they charge and made market entry difficult. Commitments offered by HRS to refrain from applying the wide parity clause for a five-year period were rejected as insufficient. HRS appealed the decision to the Düsseldorf Higher Regional Court.

Held

The Bundeskartellamt rightly concluded that the agreement of a best-price clause reduces the economic incentive for online portals to offer hotel companies lower agency commission, and that it leads to foreclosure effects, since it hinders the entry of new hotel portals into the market. The best-price clause constitutes an appreciable restriction on competition which does not meet the conditions for an individual exemption pursuant to Article 101 (3) TFEU (paras 100–72).

The argument made by HRS that the MFN: is necessary in order to solve the free-rider problem; increases the quality of the offering on the platform; and reduce transaction clauses, is not convincing. Even if HRS will experience a drop in sales due to the abolition of the MFN clause, its incentive to invest in the quality of the portal will not reduce. On the contrary, a reduction in sales will incentivise it to invest further in making its portal more attractive, through special offers, promotional activities and favourable hotel room prices (paras 178–82).

Comment

The Court upheld the Bundeskartellamt decision and condemned the restrictive effect that the parity clause had had on the hotel companies' freedom to act. While the Court's condemnation of the wide parity is convincing, its overreaching statement, which ignores the risk of free-riding, is intriguing (paras 178–82). No doubt, free-riding will pose a dilemma for the PCW as it will have to continue investing in services to maintain traffic and a user-friendly interface. Yet, over time, it seems reasonable to expect that under the existing agency model, such free-riding would undermine the PCW's profitability and subsequently its investment downstream.

The Court therefore did not accept a wide MFN as necessary in order to prevent a *vertical externality* between the upstream supplier and the downstream retailer, and a horizontal externality between platforms which would undermine the PCW's incentive to invest.

One can outline four core exclusionary and collusive anticompetitive effects commonly associated with agency-model wide MFNs. (1) *Excessive intermediation*—the price comparison website may be incentivised to increase its fees when the wide MFN protects it from the risk that a supplier will react to an increase in the commission it has to pay, by increasing the product price on that platform only. Competition between online platforms would not necessarily reduce excessive intermediation as the PCW does not face a reduction in demand as it raises its fees to sellers. (2) *Limits on low-cost entry to the downstream market* when a new platform wishes to adopt a low-cost model, yet is unable to secure lower prices from distributors who are already committed under an existing wide parity agency model. (3) Industry-wide price uniformity may result from the imposition of wide MFNs by leading platforms. (4) *Limits on innovation and investment* since, absent wide MFNs, a downstream PCW may be incentivised to invest in demand-enhancing features and other efficient measures which would increase its appeal to upstream suppliers. This theory is the least convincing of all four, as it ignores other parameters of competition—namely quality and service. It could, however, play a role when a given investment would benefit the upstream supplier but have no beneficial effect on the PCWs or its customers.

In its e-book investigation, the European Commission raised concerns as to the effects of the wide MFN and agency model used by Apple and the publishers. It noted that 'the retail price MFN clause acted as a joint "commitment device" whereby each of the Five Publishers was in a position to force Amazon to accept changes to the agency model or otherwise face the risk of being denied access to the e-books of each of the Five Publishers.' (Case *COMP/AT-39.847-E-Books*, Commission Decision of 25 July 2013) The Commission accepted commitments offered by Apple and the publishers, which included the termination of the agency agreements, a two-year ban on the publishers' ability to obstruct e-book retailers from setting their own prices or offering discounts, and a five-year ban on MFNs.

In the US, the Department of Justice also raised concerns regarding the wide MFN clauses and agency models used in agreements between Apple Inc and leading publishers. It argued that the agreements were strategically designed to increase e-book prices and, in particular, the price of new releases and *New York Times* best-sellers. The agreements pressurised Amazon to switch from a wholesale model—in which it controlled the price of e-books and heavily discounted them—to an agency model. (*United States v Apple Inc*, 952 F Supp 2d 638, 15 647 (SDNY 2013)) On appeal, the Second Circuit considered the unique economic incentives created by the introduction of a wide MFN in this case: 'The MFN Clause changed the situation by making it imperative, not merely desirable, that the publishers wrest control over pricing from ebook retailers generally. … The publishers recognized that, as a practical matter, this meant that the MFN Clause would force them to move Amazon to an agency relationship.' (*United States v Apple Inc*, No 13-3741-cv (2d Cir 2015), page 28) It is important to note the unique characteristic of this case. The agency agreement and the parity clauses were used as part of a wider illegal collusive strategy orchestrated by Apple to force collective action by the publishers. Indeed, the court condemned the agreements 'not because those [MFNs and agency] contracts themselves were independently unlawful, but because, in context, they provide strong evidence that Apple consciously orchestrated a conspiracy among the Publisher Defendants.' (page 58)

Another noteworthy case concerning wide MFN is the US Department of Justice antitrust lawsuit against the insurer, Blue Cross Blue Shield of Michigan (BCBSM) (*United States v Blue Cross Blue Shield of Michigan*, 809 F Supp 2d 665 (ED Mich 2011). The case concerned BCBSM's use of wide MFNs in its agreements with health providers. The MFNs required contracted hospitals either to charge BCBSM no more than they charge its competitors, or to charge the competitors a specified percentage more than they charge BCBSM. The DoJ found the MFNs to stifle competition and result in higher health insurance prices for Michigan consumers. As a result, the DoJ alleged that BCBSM's MFNs led hospitals to increase their prices to BCBSM's competitors and insulated BCBSM from competition. Following legislation by the State of Michigan, which prohibited health insurers from using MFNs in contracts with healthcare providers, the DoJ dismissed its antitrust lawsuit. A class action launched by small businesses and individuals against BCBSM alleging violation of antitrust laws was settled in April 2015.

Booking.com BV	**Most-favoured Nation Clause**
Decision No 596/2013 (15 April 2015)	Narrow MFN
Swedish Competition Authority	Commitment Decision

Facts

Booking.Com is an online travel agent that operates in a large number of countries. The website www.booking.com is available in over 40 languages and offers accommodation in 200 countries. The Swedish competition authority opened an investigation into the use of wide parity clauses by Booking.com in its agreements with hotels. The wide MFN established parity in price, availability and booking conditions with respect to upstream hotels and to other online travel agents (price comparison websites). Following the investigation, Booking.com offered to narrow the scope of MFN clauses and only establish a price and term parity with each hotel's own direct website but not with other PCWs. Under these commitments, the hotels retained the freedom to determine the price offline and to offer discounts to select groups of customers (such as members of the hotel's loyalty scheme and former customers). The investigating agency considered the narrowing of the parity clauses to provide a successful balancing formula sufficient to resolve their concerns while reducing the risk that hotels free-ride on investments made by Booking.com.

Held

'The Competition Authority's investigation has shown that hotels enlist on online travel agencies with the aim of reaching consumers which the hotels themselves have difficulty reaching. Online travel agencies thus make hotel rooms available to consumers on behalf of hotels, which in turn provide online travel agencies with the rooms consumers are able to book. In addition, online travel agencies offer consumers a search and comparison function that individual hotels are unable to offer. In view of this, the Competition Authority concludes that hotels and online travel agencies do not operate on the same relevant market.' (para 16)

In its commitments Booking.com undertakes to 'not apply the parity terms regarding price and other conditions in relation to Booking.com's competitors. Booking.com also undertakes to not apply parity terms with respect to the number and type of available rooms. With respect to hotels' own sales, Booking.com undertakes to not require parity with respect to room prices or other conditions as regards offline sales. Further, Booking.com undertakes to not require parity regarding such room prices or other conditions that are not available online to the general public, but that are offered by the hotels only to certain customers or groups of customers.' (para 40)

'The results of the analyses carried out by the Competition Authority support the conclusion that hotels will have incentives to offer lower room prices in exchange for lower commission rates. An important motivation for the hotels in this context will be the competition between hotels for room bookings. The investigation has also shown that hotels' incentives to offer a lower price via an online travel agency than in the hotel´s own channel increase if the share of sales not covered by price parity decreases. … The Competition Authority's investigation shows that the commitments reintroduce room prices as a competition parameter in the relationship between Booking.com and other online travel agencies. Thereby, the commitments remove the risk that price parity between online travel agencies will continue to apply in practice.' (paras 47–8)

Comment

The Investigation by the Swedish competition authority was conducted alongside an investigation by the French and Italian competition agencies, each considering its own market reality. The narrow MFN commitments were accepted by the three authorities. Booking.com subsequently applied the commitments in all EU Member States. The commitments were publically accepted or tacitly endorsed by the majority of competition agencies across Europe.

The decision reflects the understanding that in contrast to wide MFNs, narrow MFNs constitute a less intrusive restriction on pricing or terms that only concern the relationship between a single PCW and a single supplier, and do not govern the relationship between that supplier and other PCWs. Narrow parity does not give rise to many of the concerns linked to the wide-parity multivector net. First and foremost, under the limited protection offered by narrow MFNs, the web-aggregator has no guarantee that an increase in its commission would not result in a competitive disadvantage. On the contrary, each web-aggregator is incentivised to offer more competitive terms in its negotiations with suppliers. After all, under an agency model, a lower commission will incentivise suppliers to lower their prices on that PCW. Since under narrow parity, the supplier is not required to match its best price and offer it elsewhere, lower prices can be offered in exchange for lower commission. This benefits both the supplier and the PCW, as it increases the volume of business through the platform. Further, this competitive dynamic enhances competition between PCWs downstream—each competing to provide better demand-enhancing features and lower commissions. Similarly, it enhances intra-brand competition upstream, as suppliers are able to offer lower prices on different platforms. Similarly, inter-brand competition is intensified. Importantly, the narrow parity and absence of availability parity that make these competitive effects possible are not likely to undermine investment downstream. PCWs still retain protection against direct free-riding by their supplier and are thus incentivised to offer demand-enhancing features. Further, as they compete horizontally against other PCWs, they are incentivised to improve the scope and quality of their services.

In contrast to the approach taken by the French, Swedish and Italian competition agencies and by other EU competition agencies, the German Competition Authority (Bundeskartellamt) took a harsher, albeit isolated line, declining to accept the commitments offered by Booking.com and issuing a prohibition decision. The Bundeskartellamt opined that the Düsseldorf Higher Regional Court's holding in *HRS* (page 194 above) supported a complete ban on MFNs. Accordingly, since in that case the Bundeskartellamt rejected an absolute, yet temporary, ban on MFNs, the less extensive commitments offered by Booking.com were deemed unacceptable. On this point it is interesting to note that the judgment of the Düsseldorf Higher Regional Court focused, from start to finish, on the wide parity clause used by HRS and the proposal to remove it for a period of five years. As the decision under review focused solely on wide parity, the Court did not engage in an analysis of likely effects of narrow MFNs; and did not consider a proposal for an alternative narrow parity on a permanent basis. Its ruling was driven by the facts of the case and the need for clarity as to the legality of wide MFNs. With that in mind, one may argue that the Bundeskartellamt's reading of the judgment seems overly wide.

In its Private Motor Insurance Market Investigation, the UK Competition and Market Authority (CMA) explored the possibility that a narrow MFN will reduce vertical competition between the PCW and the upstream supplier. The CMA found that 'in general, attracting customers through PCWs was cheaper for PMI providers than direct customer acquisition'. This led the CMA to conclude that PCWs had the overall effect of lowering costs for insurance providers. The CMA further considered the price elasticity of demand exhibited through different sales channels. It found that customers' ability to 'compare directly the prices of different policies on PCWs was likely to be a major driver of inter-brand competition', adding that 'whilst narrow MFNs limited competition between the own website and the PCW, this was unlikely to have much of an impact on competition between brands'. It concluded that the restriction on competition imposed by narrow MFNs was unlikely to be significant. (UK Competition and Markets Authority (CMA), Private Motor Insurance Market Investigation: Final Report (CMA Report, September 2014) 8.56, 8.62, 8.63)

Facts

An appeal on Commission decision (Case COMP/36.264—*MercedesBenz*) ([2002], OJ L257/1), in which the Commission found that Mercedes-Benz (MB) had itself or through its subsidiaries infringed Article 101(1) TFEU by restricting the export of MB passenger cars. The Commission rejected MB's argument that the agreements at issue were concluded with its German agents and were thus not subject to Article 101 TFEU. It found that the agents took on a considerable share of the commercial risk associated with the sale and transport of vehicles and used their own financial resources for sale promotions. Since those risks were not typical of those borne by a true commercial agents, the agreements between MB and its German agents were subject to Article 101 TFEU and were found to infringe Article 101 TFEU. MB appealed the decision, contesting, among other things, the finding concerning the commercial agent.

Held

'[I]n competition law the term "undertaking" must be understood as designating an economic unit for the purpose of the subject-matter of the agreement in question, even if in law that unit consists of several persons, natural or legal (Case 170/83 *Hydrotherm* [1984] ECR 2999, paragraph 11, and Case T-234/95 *DSG v Commission* [2000] ECR II-2603, paragraph 124). The Court of Justice has emphasised that, for the purposes of applying the competition rules, formal separation of two companies resulting from their having distinct legal identity, is not decisive. The test is whether or not there is unity in their conduct on the market. Thus, it may be necessary to establish whether two companies that have distinct legal identities form, or fall within, one and the same undertaking or economic entity adopting the same course of conduct on the market (see, to that effect, Case 48/69 *ICI v Commission* [1972] ECR 619, paragraph 140).' (para 85)

'The case-law shows that this sort of situation arises not only in cases where the relationship between the companies in question is that of parent and subsidiary. It may also occur, in certain circumstances, in relationships between a company and its commercial representative or between a principal and its agent. In so far as application of [Article 101 TFEU] is concerned, the question whether a principal and its agent or commercial representative form a single economic unit, the agent being an auxiliary body forming part of the principal's undertaking, is an important one for the purposes of establishing whether given conduct falls within the scope of that article. Thus, it has been held that if … an agent works for the benefit of his principal he may in principle be treated as an auxiliary organ forming an integral part of the latter's undertaking, who must carry out his principal's instructions and thus, like a commercial employee, forms an economic unit with this undertaking [Case 40/73 etc *Suiker Unie and others v Commission*, [1975] ECR 1663, para 480].' (para 86)

'The position is otherwise if the agreements entered into between the principal and its agents confer upon the agent or allow him to perform duties which from an economic point of view are approximately the same as those carried out by an independent dealer, because they provide for the agent accepting the financial risks of selling or of the performance of the contracts entered into with third parties (see, to that effect, *Suiker Unie and others v Commission* … at paragraph 541). It has therefore been held that an agent can lose his character as independent economic operator only if he does not bear any of the risks resulting from the contracts negotiated on behalf of the principal and he operates as an auxiliary organ forming an integral part of the principal's undertaking (see, to that effect, Case C-266/93 *Volkswagen and VAG Leasing*, [1995] ECR I-3477, at paragraph 19).' (para 87)

'Accordingly, where an agent, although having separate legal personality, does not independently determine his own conduct on the market, but carries out the instructions given to him by his principal, the prohibitions laid down under [Article 101(1) TFEU] do not apply to the relationship between the agent and the principal with which he forms an economic unit.' (para 88)

In this case it is not the agent but MB which determines the conditions applying to car sales and sale price, and which bears the principal risks associated with that activity. The German agent is prevented by the terms of the agency agreement from purchasing and holding stocks of vehicles for sale. In those circumstances, the agents should be treated in the same way as employees and considered as integrated in that undertaking and thus forming an economic unit with it. It follows that, in carrying on business on the market in question, the German MB agent does not himself constitute an 'undertaking' for the purposes of Article 101 TFEU. It follows that the Commission did not establish the existence of an agreement between undertakings for the purposes of Article 101(1) TFEU. (paras 89–119)

Comment

In Joined Cases 40/73 etc *Suiker Unie and others v Commission* [1975] ECR 1663, the Court of Justice held that an agent may be regarded as an auxiliary organ forming an integral part of the principal when it works for the benefit of his principal and is required to carry out his principal's instructions without accepting the financial risks of the sales or of the performance of contracts entered into with third parties.

In Case C-266/93 *Bundeskartellamt v Volkswagen AG and VAG Leasing GmbH* [1995] ECR I-3477, Volkswagen AG (VAG) and VAG Leasing GmbH (VAG Leasing) argued that the relationship between VAG and its dealers, which was governed by a distribution agreement, was not subjected to Article 101 TFEU as the distributors were commercial agents which formed one economic unit with VAG and VAG Leasing. In a preliminary reference, the Court of Justice held that 'That argument must be rejected. Representatives can lose their character as independent traders only if they do not bear any of the risks resulting from the contracts negotiated on behalf of the principal and they operate as auxiliary organs forming an integral part of the principal's undertaking (see Joined Cases 40/73 … *Suiker Unie and others v Commission* [1975] ECR 1663, paragraph 539). However, the German VAG dealers assume, at least in part, the financial risks linked to the transactions concluded on behalf of VAG Leasing, in so far as they repurchase the vehicles from it upon the expiry of the leasing contracts. Furthermore, their principal business of sales and after-sales services is carried on, largely independently, in their own name and for their own account.' (para 19)

The Commission Vertical Guidelines (paras 12–21) outline the distinction between genuine and non-genuine agency agreements. Note in particular the impact risk allocation has on the classification of an agency agreement; 'The determining factor in defining an agency agreement for the application of Article 101(1) is the financial or commercial risk borne by the agent in relation to the activities for which he has been appointed as an agent by the principal. In this respect it is not material for the assessment whether the agent acts for one or several principals. Neither is material for this assessment the qualification given to their agreement by the parties or national legislation. There are three types of financial or commercial risk that are material to the definition of an agency agreement for the application of Article 101(1). First there are the contract-specific risks which are directly related to the contracts concluded and/or negotiated by the agent on behalf of the principal, such as financing of stocks. Secondly, there are the risks related to market-specific investments. These are investments specifically required for the type of activity for which the agent has been appointed by the principal, i.e. which are required to enable the agent to conclude and/or negotiate this type of contract. Such investments are usually sunk, which means that upon leaving that particular field of activity the investment cannot be used for other activities or sold other than at a significant loss. Thirdly, there are the risks related to other activities undertaken in the same product market, to the extent that the principal requires the agent to undertake such activities, but not as an agent on behalf of the principal but for its own risk. For the purposes of applying Article 101(1) the agreement will be qualified as an agency agreement if the agent does not bear any, or bears only insignificant, risks in relation to the contracts concluded and/or negotiated on behalf of the principal, in relation to market-specific investments for that field of activity, and in relation to other activities required by the principal to be undertaken in the same product market. However, risks that are related to the activity of providing agency services in general, such as the risk of the agent's income being dependent upon his success as an agent or general investments in for instance premises or personnel, are not material to this assessment.' (paras 13–15, Vertical Guidelines)

Confederación Española de Empresarios de Staciones de Servicio v Compañía de Petróleos SA **Agency Agreements**
Case C-217/05
Court of Justice, [2006] ECR 11987, [2007] 4 CMLR 181

Facts

A reference for a preliminary ruling from the Tribunal Supremo (Spain), concerning the interpretation and application of Article 101(3) TFEU to categories of exclusive fuel distribution agreements. In its decision the Court of Justice considered whether the vertical agreements at issue constitute 'agreements between undertakings' within the meaning of Article 101(1) TFEU, or form agency agreements which may fall outside the realm of Article 101 TFEU.

Held

'[A]gents can lose their character as independent traders only if they do not bear any of the risks resulting from the contracts negotiated on behalf of the principal and they operate as auxiliary organs forming an integral part of the principal's undertaking (... *Volkswagen and VAG Leasing*, paragraph 19).' (para 43)

Article 101 TFEU is not applicable where a service-station operator, while having separate legal personality, does not independently determine his conduct and does not bear the financial and commercial risks as regards the economic activity concerned. On the other hand, when under the agreement the intermediaries assume the financial and commercial risks involved, such intermediaries cannot be regarded as auxiliary organs forming an integral part of the principal's undertaking. In such circumstances the agreement between them may constitute an agreement between undertakings for the purposes of Article 101 TFEU. (paras 44, 45)

'It follows that the decisive factor for the purposes of determining whether a service-station operator is an independent economic operator is to be found in the agreement concluded with the principal and, in particular, in the clauses of that agreement, implied or express, relating to the assumption of the financial and commercial risks linked to sales of goods to third parties. As the Commission rightly submitted in its observations, the question of risk must be analysed on a case-by-case basis, taking account of the real economic situation rather than the legal classification of the contractual relationship in national law.' (para 46)

The criteria enabling an assessment to be made as to the actual allocation of the financial and commercial risks between service-station operators and the fuel supplier for the purposes of determining whether Article 101 TFEU is applicable include first 'the risks linked to the sale of the goods, such as the financing of fuel stocks and, second, of the risks linked to investments specific to the market, namely those required to enable the service-station operator to negotiate or conclude contracts with third parties.' (paras 50, 51)

'First, as regards the risks linked to the sale of the goods, it is likely that the service-station operator assumes those risks when he takes possession of the goods at the time he receives them from the supplier, that is to say, prior to selling them on to a third party.' (para 52) 'Likewise, the service-station operator who assumes, directly or indirectly, the costs linked to the distribution of those goods, particularly the transport costs, should be regarded as thereby assuming part of the risk linked to the sale of the goods.' (para 53) 'The fact that the service-station operator maintains stocks at his own expense could also be an indication that the risks linked to the sale of the goods are transferred to him.' (para 54)

'Furthermore, the national court should determine who assumes responsibility for any damage caused to the goods, such as loss or deterioration, and for damage caused by the goods sold to third parties. If the service-station operator were responsible for such damage, irrespective of whether or not he had complied with the obligation to keep the goods in the conditions necessary to ensure that they undergo no loss or deterioration, the risk would have to be regarded as having been transferred to him.' (para 55)

'It is also necessary to assess the allocation of the financial risk linked to the goods, in particular as regards payment for the fuel should the service-station operator not find a purchaser, or where payment is deferred as a result of payment by credit card, on the basis of the rules or practices relating to the payment system for fuel.' (para 56)

'In that connection, it is apparent from the order for reference that the service-station operator is required to pay CEPSA the amount corresponding to the sale price of the fuel nine days after the date of delivery and that, by the same date, the service-station operator receives commission from CEPSA, in an amount corresponding to the quantity of fuel delivered.' (para 57)

'In those circumstances, it is for the national court to ascertain whether the payment to the supplier of the amount corresponding to the sale price of the fuel depends on the quantity actually sold by that date and, as regards the turnover period for the goods in the service-station, whether the fuel delivered by the supplier is always sold within a period of nine days. If the answer is in the affirmative it would have to be concluded that the commercial risk is borne by the supplier.' (para 58)

'As regards the risks linked to investments specific to the market, if the service-station operator makes investments specifically linked to the sale of the goods, such as premises or equipment such as a fuel tank, or commits himself to investing in advertising campaigns, such risks are transferred to the operator.' (para 59)

'It follows from the foregoing that, in order to determine whether [Article 101 TFEU] is applicable, the allocation of the financial and commercial risks between the service-station operator and the supplier of fuel must be analysed on the basis of criteria such as ownership of the goods, the contribution to the costs linked to their distribution, their safe-keeping, liability for any damage caused to the goods or by the goods to third parties, and the making of investments specific to the sale of those goods.' (para 60)

'However, as the Commission rightly submits, the fact that the intermediary bears only a negligible share of the risks does not render [Article 101 TFEU] applicable. Nevertheless, it must be pointed out that, in such a case, only the obligations imposed on the intermediary in the context of the sale of the goods to third parties on behalf of the principal fall outside the scope of that article … an agency contract may contain clauses concerning the relationship between the agent and the principal to which that article applies, such as exclusivity and non-competition clauses. In that connection it must be considered that, in the context of such relationships, agents are, in principle, independent economic operators and such clauses are capable of infringing the competition rules in so far as they entail locking up the market concerned.' (paras 61, 62)

Comment

Article 101 TFEU applies to an agreement concluded between a principal and operator where that operator assumes, to a non-negligible extent, one or more financial and commercial risks linked to the sale to third parties.

Indicative factors to determine whether an entity is an independent economic operator may be found in the agreement between the parties and include, among other things, the risks linked to the sale of the goods, the risks linked to the possession and stocking of goods received from the principal, the risk and costs linked to the distribution of those goods, the possible loss and damage to goods, financial risk linked to the goods, and the risks linked to market specific investments to support sale or advertising. See para 60 above.

'[F]ormalistic approach which has regard to the designation of the intermediary as an agent, a commission agent, an independent dealer or a dealer is less decisive than an economic analysis of his role in the actual business relationship. Accordingly, the Court cannot provide the national court with an exhaustive list of criteria and can only identify factors which in a case such as the present permit conclusions to be drawn as to how risk is allocated between the parties.' (opinion of AG Kokott, para 53)

5

Article 102 TFEU

> **Article 102 TFEU:**
>
> Any abuse by one or more undertakings of a dominant position within the internal market or in a substantial part of it shall be prohibited as incompatible with the internal market insofar as it may affect trade between Member States. Such abuse may, in particular, consist in:
>
> (a) directly or indirectly imposing unfair purchase or selling prices or other unfair trading conditions;
>
> (b) limiting production, markets or technical development to the prejudice of consumers;
>
> (c) applying dissimilar conditions to equivalent transactions with other trading parties, thereby placing them at a competitive disadvantage;
>
> (d) making the conclusion of contracts subject to acceptance by the other parties of supplementary obligations which, by their nature or according to commercial usage, have no connection with the subject of such contracts.

For ease of analysis Article 102 TFEU may be divided into four main questions:

1. Is there a dominant undertaking or a group of undertakings?
2. Is this dominant position within the Internal Market or in a substantial part of it?
3. Is this dominant position being abused?
4. Could this abuse of a dominant position affect trade between Member States?

Although Article 102 TFEU does not include an exempting provision similar to Article 101(3) TFEU, conduct which is regarded as abusive may escape the prohibition in Article 102 TFEU if the dominant undertaking can objectively justify it or show that the actions generate efficiencies which outweigh the anticompetitive effects. One can therefore qualify the third question by asking whether the undertaking's conduct can be objectively justified.

The analysis of Article 102 TFEU through these questions is illustrated below.

Dominant Position

Dominance is a position of economic strength enjoyed by an undertaking which enables it to prevent effective competition being maintained in the relevant market, by affording it the power to behave to an appreciable extent independently of its competitors, customers and its consumers. The concept of dominance reflects the notion of market power and requires a preliminary consideration of the relevant market and its characteristics.

The process involves two distinct steps. First the boundaries of competition need be identified by defining the relevant product and geographic markets (see discussion in Chapter 2 above). Once the market has been defined, it is possible to proceed to the next step and assess whether the undertaking enjoys a position of dominance in that market. The analysis is based on, among other things, the market shares of the undertaking and its competitors, barriers to expansion and entry, and the market position of buyers. The following cases illustrate the process of establishing dominance and the weight attributed to market shares and to other market characteristics:

27/76	*United Brands v Commission*	213
85/76	*Hoffmann-La Roche v Commission*	215
C-62/86	*AKZO Chemie BV v Commission*	216
22/78	*Hugin v Commission*	217
322/81	*Nederlandsche Banden Industrie Michelin v Commission*	218
IV/33.384	*Soda Ash-Solvay*	219
IV/30.787	*Eurofix-Bauco/Hilti*	220
77/77	*BP and others v Commission*	221
T-125/97	*The Coca-Cola Company v Commission*	222

See also summary references to:

T-340/03	*France Télécom v Commission*	215
COMP/34.780	*Virgin/British Airways*	216
27/76	*United Brands v Commission*	216
COMP/M.6281	*Microsoft/Skype*	216
T-79/12	*Cisco Systems Inc. and Messagenet SpA v Commission*	216
C-68/94	*France v Commission*	216
T-170/06	*Alrosa Company Ltd v Commission*	218
IV/M.190	*Nestlé/Perrier*	219

The Guidance on the Commission's enforcement priorities in applying [Article 102 TFEU] to abusive exclusionary conduct by dominant undertakings [C (2009) 864 final, [2009] OJ C45/7] (hereafter 'Guidance Paper') elaborates on the Commission's approach to establishing dominance (paras 9–18). In addition, note the Commission's earlier 2005 Discussion Paper on the Application of [Article 102 TFEU] to Exclusionary Abuses (hereafter 'Discussion Paper'). The paper provides a useful overview of the relevant case-law and the process of establishing dominance. Note in particular paragraphs 20–42 which outline the methodology for establishing dominance. The paper may be accessed through the European Commission website: http://ec.europa.eu/comm/competition/index_en.html.

Dominant Position within the Internal Market or in a Substantial Part of It

After establishing the existence of a dominant or collective dominant position and before moving to consider the question of abuse, it is necessary to consider whether this position of power is held within the Internal Market or in a substantial part of it. This requirement acts as a threshold which ensures that Article 102 TFEU will only be applicable to dominant positions which occupy at least a substantial part of the Internal Market. See:

40/73 etc	*Suiker Unie and others v Commission*	223
IV/34.689	*Sea Containers v Stena Sealink*	224
IV/35.703	*Portuguese Airports*	224

Abuse and the Goals of Article 102 TFEU

Dominance in and of itself is not prohibited under Article 102 TFEU. Rather, the Article targets the abuse of a dominant (or collective dominant) position. 'The concept of abuse is an objective concept relating to the behaviour of an undertaking in a dominant position, which is such as to influence the structure of a market, where, as a result of the very presence of the undertaking in question, the degree of competition is weakened and which, through recourse to methods different from those which condition normal competition in products or services on the basis of the transactions of commercial operators, has the effect of hindering the maintenance of the degree of competition still existing in the market or the growth of that competition.' (Case 85/76 *Hoffmann-La Roche v Commission*)

The realm and reach of the concept of abuse has been influenced by the relatively broad goals of Article 102 TFEU, which have been laid down by the Court of Justice. See for example:

The following sections outline different categories of abusive behaviour.

Predatory and Below Cost Pricing

Aggressive price rivalry is central to a healthy competitive market as it ensures that firms sell their products at the lowest profitable price. Yet, under certain circumstances price competition may harm consumers rather than benefit them. Such is the case when a dominant firm abuses its dominant position by engaging in predatory pricing. The practice involves the deliberate lowering of prices by the dominant undertaking in the short term to a loss-making level, in an attempt to drive competitors out of the market or to prevent competitors from entering the market. Then, having eliminated the competition through predation, the dominant undertaking is capable of raising prices above competitive levels, ultimately harming future consumers by charging higher prices.

The following cases illustrate the analysis of predation and below cost pricing:

See also summary references to:

Selective Price Cuts above ATC

Whereas healthy price competition may drive less-efficient undertakings out of the market, selective price cuts enable the dominant undertaking to eliminate an equally efficient competitor from the market. Selective price cuts may be abusive when the dominant undertaking selectively cuts its prices with the aim of driving out a competitor from the market. Contrary to predation cases, the analysis does not focus on the cost structure or profitability, but rather on the selectiveness aimed at excluding a competitor.

C-395/96 etc	*Compagnie Maritime Belge Transports v Commission*	238

See also summary references to:

No 92-466	*Brooke Group Ltd v Brown & Williamson Tobacco Corp*	238
IV/30.787 etc	*Eurofix-Bauco v Hilti*	238
T-228/97	*Irish Sugar v Commission*	238

Price Alignment

Dominant companies have a right to align their prices in good faith with prices charged by a competitor. In doing so they can 'meet' the competition but are prohibited from strengthening their dominant position and abusing it (for example, by engaging in predatory pricing).

IP/97/868	*Digital Equipment Corporation*	239
T-228/97	*Irish Sugar v Commission*	306

See also summary references to:

27/76	*United Brands v Commission*	239
T-228/97	*Irish Sugar v Commission*	239
T-340/03	*France Télécom SA v Commission*	239

Price Discrimination

Article 102(c) TFEU stipulates that an abuse may consist in 'applying dissimilar conditions to equivalent transactions with other trading parties, thereby placing them at a competitive disadvantage'. The provision, which covers price discrimination, should be applied with caution, as it is generally accepted that price discrimination may at times increase welfare. This will be the case where, by engaging in 'price differentiation', the undertaking is able to increase output. For example, by charging higher prices for peak-time rail travellers or lower prices for last-minute air travellers.

Article 102(c) TFEU has often been used in cases concerning abusive discount strategies. These are detailed below under 'Rebates'. On its use to target geographic price discrimination, see:

27/76	*United Brands v Commission*	240
T-301/04	*Clearstream v Commission*	242
T-229/94	*Deutsche Bahn AG v Commission*	243
C-82/01P	*Aéroports de Paris v Commission*	243

See also summary references to:

C-18/93	*Corsica Ferries Italia Srl v Corpo dei Piloti del Porto di Genova*	241
C-95/04P	*British Airways v Commission*	242
C-209/10	*Post Danmark A/S v Konkurrencerådet*	242

Note that charging different customers or different classes of customers different prices for goods or services whose costs are the same, or, conversely, charging a single price to customers for whom supply costs differ, cannot of itself suggest that there exists an exclusionary abuse:

| C-209/10 | *Post Danmark A/S v Konkurrencerådet* | 236 |

Rebates

The European law concerning rebates generally distinguishes between quantity discounts, which are linked solely to the volume of purchases from the manufacturer concerned, and loyalty-inducing rebates. Whereas the former are considered valuable and acceptable components of price competition, the latter are held to be abusive. The traditional analysis of loyalty rebates, as evident from the cases below, has been criticised as too formalistic, failing to take into account the effects different discount schemes have on competition. In its Guidance Paper, the European Commission has advanced a more nuanced 'effects-based approach'. That approach was manifested, to some extent, in the Commission's decisions in *Prokent/Tomra* and *Intel Corporation* but received limited endorsement on appeal. In *Post Danmark II* the Court of Justice provided a more positive support to an 'effects-based analysis'.

85/76	*Hoffmann-La Roche & Co v Commission*	244
322/81	*Nederlandsche Banden Industrie Michelin v Commission*	246
T-203/01	*Manufacture Française des Pneumatiques Michelin v Commission*	248
T-219/99	*British Airways v Commission*	251
C-95/04	*British Airways v Commission*	253
C-549/10P	*Tomra Systems and Others v Commission*	255
COMP/C-3/37.990	*Intel Corporation*	257
T-66/01	*Imperial Chemical Industries Ltd v Commission*	260
C-23/14	*Post Danmark A/S v Konkurrencerådet (Post Danmark II)*	261

See also summary references to:

C-163/99	*Portuguese Republic v Commission*	245
T-228/97	*Irish Sugar plc v Commission*	247
27/76	*United Brands v Commission*	254
C-18/93	*Corsica Ferries Italia Srl v Corpo dei Piloti del Porto di Genova*	254
COMP/E-1/38.113	*Prokent/Tomra*	255
T-155/06	*Tomra Systems and others v Commission*	255
T-57/01	*Solvay SA v Commission*	260
HC-2013-90	*Streetmap v Google*	263

The Commission Guidance Paper elaborates on the treatment of conditional rebates in paras 37–46. Also note the Commission's earlier Discussion Paper which provides a more detailed overview of conditional rebates and their effects (paras 151–76).

Margin Squeeze

Margin squeeze (also known as price squeeze) refers to a situation where a vertically integrated dominant undertaking engages in a strategy which aims to favour its own downstream operations. The strategy may, for example, take place when the dominant undertaking supplies input both to its own downstream operation and to other competitors in the downstream market and increases the price charged to competitors, to squeeze their profit and improve the position of its own downstream operation.

See also summary references to:

Excessive Pricing

A dominant undertaking may choose to take advantage of its market power and increase the price of its products above competitive levels. Such practice may amount to an abuse of a dominant position when it involves the imposition of unfair purchase or selling prices or the application of dissimilar conditions to equivalent transactions.

Excessive prices may be analysed using two of the subsections in Article 102 TFEU. Under Article 102(a) TFEU they may be challenged when they consist of: 'directly or indirectly imposing unfair purchase or selling prices or other unfair trading conditions'. Under Article 102(c) TFEU they may be objected to when they result in a discriminatory practice. The following cases provide an illustration of the Commission's and European courts' approach to excessive prices:

See also summary references to:

Refusal to Supply

The finding of dominance imposes responsibility on the dominant undertaking not to allow its behaviour to impair effective competition. In some cases, this responsibility may lead to restrictions on the dominant undertaking's freedom to choose its trading partners and to refuse to supply others with services or goods. Such will be the case when a dominant undertaking operates at both the upstream and downstream levels and refuses to supply a competitor which operates at the downstream level. Such refusal to supply is contrary to Article 102 TFEU when it eliminates competition in the downstream market (Case 6/73 below). Another form of refusal to supply that is objectionable occurs when a dominant undertaking controls the provision of an essential infrastructure, uses that essential facility, but refuses other companies access to that facility, with no objective justification for doing so (Case IV/34.689 below). In other cases a refusal to supply may involve a refusal to licence intellectual property rights (Cases C-241/91P, T-504/93, C-418/01 below).

The analysis of refusal to supply is traditionally based on the finding of two markets: an upstream market dominated by the undertaking and a downstream market in which that undertaking competes with others. To improve its position downstream, the dominant undertaking refuses to supply the competing downstream operators. However, the requirement for two markets has been relaxed in some instances (Case C-418/01 below).

6/73	*Commercial Solvents v Commission*	279
77/77	*BP and others v Commission*	280
IV/32.279	*BBI and others v Boosey & Hawkes plc*	281
IV/34.689	*Sea Containers Ltd/Stena Sealink*	282
C-241/91P etc	*RTE & ITP v Commission (The Magill case)*	283
C-7/97	*Oscar Bronner GmbH Co KG v Mediaprint*	284
T-504/93	*Tiercé Ladbroke SA v Commission*	285
C-418/01	*IMS Health GmbH & Co OHG v NDC Health GmbH KG*	286
A3/2002/1380 etc	*Intel Corp v Via Technologies Inc*	288
T-201/04	*Microsoft Corp v Commission*	289
C-468/06 etc	*Sot Lélos kai Sia and others v GlaxoSmithKline AEVE*	292
T-301/04	*Clearstream v Commission*	295
HC10C02364	*Purple Parking Ltd & Anor v Heathrow Airport Ltd*	297

See also summary references to:

311/84	*Télémarketing*	279
IV/34.174	*Sealink/B&I Holyhead*	282
No 02–682	*Verizon Communications Inc v Trinko LLP*	287
T-201/04	*Microsoft Corp v Commission*	287
C-241/91P etc	*RTE & ITP v Commission (Magill)*	287

Tying and Bundling

Tying and bundling commonly refer to a situation where a dominant undertaking links the sale of separate products requiring customers who wish to purchase one product to purchase the other as well. Such practice enables the dominant firm to leverage its market power from the market where it enjoys a dominant position to the tied product's market where it faces competition. This may be done by contractual arrangements, through discounts or other incentives. The practice may involve pure bundling, where the products are only offered together and cannot be purchased separately. Alternatively it may involve mixed bundling, where products are available separately outside the bundled package, but are offered at a discounted price when purchased as a bundle. Article 102(d) TFEU makes direct reference to these practices and treats as abusive 'making the conclusion of contracts subject to acceptance by the other parties of supplementary obligations which, by their nature or according to commercial usage, have no connection with the subject of such contracts.'

C-333/94P	*Tetra Pak International SA v Commission*	298
T-201/04	*Microsoft Corp v Commission*	299
COMP/C-3/39.530	*Microsoft (Tying)*	302

See also summary reference to:

T-30/89	*Hilti AG v Commission*	298

Two lines of defence are noteworthy when considering claims of tying. The first stems from the need to identify the existence of two products or two markets in order to establish tying. Consequently, the dominant undertaking will often attempt to establish that the two products actually comprise one and therefore by their nature and characteristics should be sold together. Another common, yet rather more general, line of defence addresses the objective justifications, such as economies of scale, efficiencies and safety considerations which may justify tying the products. See the discussion on objective justification, below.

Other Forms of Exclusion

Practices such as refusal to supply, and exclusive dealing through contracts, tying or rebates, enable the dominant undertaking to strengthen its position while excluding competitors from the market. As stipulated in Article 102(b) TFEU they may consist of the limiting of production, markets or technical development to the prejudice of consumers. In addition, they may, for example, involve the acquisition and subsequent use of a patent (Case 24/67, Case T-51/89), the use of intellectual property rights to obstruct the operation of competing undertakings (below, Case T-151/01), prevent the development of a new product (above, Case T-201/04), or limiting the developments of new markets (for example, above, Case C-241/91P).

C-385/07	*Der Grüne Punkt—DSD v Commission*	303
24/67	*Parke, Davis & Co v Probel*	304

See also summary reference to:

T-151/01	*Duales System Deutschland v Commission*	303
T-51/89	*Tetra Pak Rausing v Commission*	304

Such practices, even when done at the request of the customer, risk foreclosing the market and may constitute an abuse under Article 102 TFEU (see above Case 85/76). For the economic implications of practices such as single branding and the application of Article 101 TFEU to these practices, see above Case T-65/98:

85/76	*Hoffmann-La Roche & Co v Commission*	244
T-65/98	*Van den Bergh Foods Ltd v Commission*	188

At times, the abuse of regulatory or legal procedures by a dominant firm may be used to exclude competitors from the market or create a barrier to entry. See for example:

T-111/96	*ITT Promedia NV v Commission*	305
T-321/05	*AstraZeneca AB v Commission*	305

Objective Justification and Efficiency Defence

Article 102 TFEU does not include an exempting provision similar to Article 101(3) TFEU. Nonetheless, seemingly abusive conduct may escape prohibition under Article 102 TFEU if the dominant undertaking can provide an objective justification for its actions or show that the actions generate efficiencies which outweigh the anticompetitive effects. These defence claims are difficult to prove and have commonly been rejected by the Commission and courts. The Commission's proposed effects based approach to Article 102 TFEU may open the way for greater consideration of these claims.

T-228/97	*Irish Sugar v Commission*	306
T-30/89	*Hilti v Commission*	308
T-191/98	*Atlantic Container Line AB and others v Commission*	309

T-340/03	*France Télécom SA v Commission*	309
C-95/04P	*British Airways v Commission*	309
T-228/97	*Irish Sugar plc v Commission*	309
COMP/37.990	*Intel Corporation*	309
C-209/10	*Post Danmark A/S v Konkurrencerådet*	310
HC-2013-90	*Streetmap v Google*	310

See also summary references to:

T-83/91	*Tetra Pak International SA v Commission*	307
27/76	*United Brands v Commission*	307
T-201/04	*Microsoft Corp v Commission*	307
193/83	*Windsurfing International v Commission*	308
226/84	*British Leyland v Commission*	308
IV/30.787	*Eurofix-Bauco v Hilti*	308

On objective justification and efficiency defence, see further the Guidance Paper and the 2005 Discussion Paper.

Appreciable Effect on Trade between Member States

Article 102 TFEU applies only to abuse which may appreciably affect trade between Member States. To fulfill the conditions for 'effect on trade between Member States' it is sufficient to establish that the conduct is capable of having that effect. On the effect on trade between Member States, see Commission Guidelines on the Effect on Trade Concept Contained in [Articles 101 and 102 TFEU], [2004] OJ C101/81. For illustration, also note the following cases:

T-228/97	*Irish Sugar v Commission*	311
322/81	*Nederlandsche Banden Industrie Michelin v Commission*	311
C-241/91P etc	*RTE & ITP v Commission ('Magill')*	311
T-24/93	*Compagnie Maritime Belge v Commission*	311

Intention

The concept of abuse is objective in nature and does not require proof of intention. Nonetheless, the intention of the dominant undertaking may be taken into account in determining abuse.

| C-549/10 P | *Tomra Systems and Others v Commission* | 312 |

Note, however, the unique analysis in *Akzo* where intention could play a role in the case of predatory pricing, above AVC and below ATC.

| C-62/86 | *AKZO Chemie BV v Commission* | 229 |

Nullity and Severance

Although Article 102 TFEU does not include a declaration of nullity equivalent to Article 101(2) TFEU, it arguably generates a similar effect when an undertaking is found to abuse its dominant position. See the following judgment from the English court:

| 2006/1338 | *English Welsh & Scottish Railway Limited v E.ON UK plc* | 313 |

An Economic Approach to Article 102 TFEU

The traditional approach to Article 102 TFEU described earlier encompasses two distinct steps: first, dominance needs to be established, following which the abuse of dominance is assessed.

In July 2005 the Commission published a consultation paper titled 'An Economic Approach to [Article 102 TFEU]' in which the Economic Advisory Group for Competition Policy (EAGCP) questioned the merit of this traditional approach. The paper advocates an effects-based approach focusing on competitive harm, and refrains from categorising certain behaviours as abusive. It stems from the understanding that the same types of actions may result in different effects on the market, some abusive and others not. Similarly, different types of actions may lead to the same anticompetitive effect. It is important to note that the paper has no binding power, yet it has stimulated the debate over the realm of Article 102 TFEU and raised important questions as to its past and present application.

In December 2005 the Commission published its 'Discussion paper on the application of [Article 102 TFEU] to exclusionary abuses' ('the 2005 Discussion Paper'). The paper outlined the traditional analysis of under Article 102 TFEU while injecting a more economically inspired approach to the assessment of abuse.

The 'Guidance on the Commission's enforcement priorities in applying [Article 102 TFEU] to abusive exclusionary conduct by dominant undertakings' was published in late 2008 ('the Guidance Paper'). This was the final phase of a lengthy consultation process in which the Commission reviewed its approach to dominance and the abuse of dominance under Article 102 TFEU. The Guidance Paper lays down the Commission's modern approach to Article 102 TFEU cases and delivers several of the innovative elements which were aired in the Commission's earlier 2005 Discussion Paper.

The Guidance Paper does more than merely summarising existing case-law on Article 102 TFEU; it seeks to influence its interpretation and widen its analytical scope. Achieving this aim, however, may be hampered by the institutional division within Europe.

Under EU law the Commission is limited in its ability to widen the analytical framework of Article 102 TFEU. Indeed the Guidance Paper stipulates that 'it is not intended to constitute a statement of the law and is without prejudice to the interpretation of [Article 102 TFEU] by the [Court of Justice and the General Court]'. (para 3)

Nonetheless, the Guidance Paper embodies some of the effect-based spirit which dominated the consultation on Article 102 TFEU. Most striking is the Commission's attempt to introduce a new efficiency defence under Article 102. This has been favoured by the Commission for some time and would be structured in the same way as Article 101(3) TFEU, which provides the mechanism for saving agreements between undertakings which would be anticompetitive, but for the efficiencies provided.

One would expect these concepts to mature through decision making. For example, in the area of rebates, noteworthy are the Commission decisions in COMP/E-1/38.113 *Prokent/Tomra* (page 255 below) and COMP/37.990 *Intel Corporation* (page 257 below). In both cases the Commission considered 'actual effect' in line with its recent effect-based agenda.

Interestingly, while the Commission is introducing effect-based variants into its analysis, the European Court has retained a rather reserved approach. See for example: *France Télécom SA v Commission* (pages 232, 235 below), *British Airways v Commission* (pages 251, 253 below), *Microsoft Corp v Commission* (page 289 below), and *Clearstream v Commission* (page 295 below). Note, however, the effects based analysis from the Court of Justice in *Post Danmark A/S v Konkurrencerådet* (page 261 below).

Of interest is the judgment of the General Court in Case T-286/09 *Intel Corporation v Commission* (page 257 below). In a formalistic judgment, the Court upheld the Commission's decision. It held that there is no need to examine the actual effects of the rebates. The Commission is only required to establish that the rebate is capable of restricting competition. Foreclosure occurs not only where access to the market is impossible, but also where that access is made more difficult.

Also noteworthy is the Courts judgment in *Tomra Systems and Others v Commission* (page 255 below) where the Court of Justice and General Court reaffirmed the 'formalistic' approach manifested in the case law and confirmed that the Commission was not required to engage in the examination of actual effects. A more positive approach may be found in *Post Danmark II* where the Court of Justice provided a more positive support to an 'effects-based analysis' (page 261).

United Brands v Commission	**Article 102 TFEU**
Case 27/76	Dominant Position
Court of Justice, [1978] ECR 207, [1978] 1 CMLR 429	

Facts

In a Commission decision United Brands (UBC) was found to have infringed Article 102 TFEU by abusing its dominant position in the market for bananas. UBC appealed to the Court of Justice and challenged the Commission's conclusions with respect to the market definition, the dominant position and the abuse of the dominant position.

Held

In order to determine whether UBC has a dominant position in the market for bananas it is necessary to define the relevant product and geographical markets. The market in this case, as defined by the Commission, is the market for bananas in a substantial part of the internal market. (paras 10–57)

Dominant position in Article 102 TFEU is 'a position of economic strength enjoyed by an undertaking which enables it to prevent effective competition being maintained on the market by giving it the power to behave to an appreciable extent independently of its competitors, customers and ultimately its consumers.' (para 65)

'In order to find out whether UBC is an undertaking in a dominant position on the relevant market it is necessary first of all to examine its structure and then the situation on the said market as far as competition is concerned. In doing so it may be advisable to take account if need be of the facts put forward as acts amounting to abuses without necessarily having to acknowledge that they are abuses.' (paras 67, 68)

UBC resources for and methods of producing, packaging, transporting, selling and displaying its product should be examined.

UBC is vertically integrated to a high degree. This integration is evident at each of the stages from the plantation to the loading in the ports and after those stages, as far as ripening and sale prices are concerned. At the production stage UBC can supplement its own production when needed by obtaining supplies from independent planters. Additionally some independent planters grow the varieties of bananas which UBC has advised them to adopt. UBC plantations are spread over a wide geographic area, a fact which enables it to cope with regional natural disasters and comply with all the requests which it receives. At the packaging and distribution stages, UBC has at its disposal factories, manpower, plant and material which enable it to handle the goods independently. It uses its own transport means to deliver products from plantation to port and is the only undertaking of its kind which is capable of carrying two-thirds of its exports by means of its own banana fleet. UBC is able to transport regularly to Europe and to ensure, using its own ships, that three regular consignments reach Europe each week. This capacity guarantees its commercial stability and well-being. In the field of technical knowledge UBC keeps on improving the productivity and yield of its plantations and perfecting new ripening methods. Competing companies are unable to develop research at a comparable level and are in this respect at a disadvantage compared with UBC. (paras 70–84)

UBC has made its product distinctive by large-scale repeated advertising and promotion campaigns which have induced the consumer to show a preference for it in spite of price differences between the price of labelled and unlabelled bananas. It has revolutionized the commercial exploitation of the banana and made its brand name 'Chiquita' the premier brand name with the result that distributors cannot afford not to offer it to the consumer. (paras 91–3)

UBC is the largest banana group having accounted in 1974 for 35 per cent of all banana exports on the world market. Without going into a discussion about percentages, which when fixed are bound to be to some extent approximations, it can be considered to be an established fact that UBC's share of the relevant market is more than 40 per cent and nearly 45 per cent. (paras 97–108)

UBC's market share does not, however, permit the conclusion that UBC automatically controls the market. Dominance must be determined having regard to the strength and number of the competitors operating in the market. UBC's market share is several times greater than that of its competitor, Castle and Cooke, which is the best placed of all the competitors, the others lagging far behind. This fact, together with the others to which attention has already been drawn, may be regarded as a factor which affords evidence of UBC's preponderant strength. (paras 109–12)

An undertaking does not have to have eliminated all opportunity for competition in order to be in a dominant position. The market for bananas displayed lively competition struggles which on several occasions included large-scale promotion campaigns and price reduction. These periods of competition were, however, limited in time and did not cover the whole of the relevant geographical market. In spite of these efforts made by competitors, they have not succeeded in appreciably increasing their market share in the national markets where they launched their attacks. (paras 113–20)

Barriers to entry to the market include 'the exceptionally large capital investments required for the creation and running of banana plantations, the need to increase sources of supply in order to avoid the effects of fruit diseases and bad weather (hurricanes, floods), the introduction of an essential system of logistics which the distribution of a very perishable product makes necessary, economies of scale from which newcomers to the market cannot derive any immediate benefit and the actual cost of entry made up, inter alia, of all the general expenses incurred in penetrating the market such as the setting up of an adequate commercial network, the mounting of very large-scale advertising campaigns, all those financial risks, the costs of which are irrecoverable if the attempt fails.' (para 122)

Although competitors are able to use the same methods of production and distribution as UBC, they come up against almost insuperable practical and financial obstacles. That is another factor peculiar to a dominant position. (paras 123, 124)

'An undertaking's economic strength is not measured by its profitability; a reduced profit margin or even losses for a time are not incompatible with a dominant position, just as large profits may be compatible with a situation where there is effective competition. The fact that UBC's profitability is for a time moderate or non-existent must be considered in the light of the whole of its operations.' (paras 126, 127)

'The finding that, whatever losses UBC may make, the customers continue to buy more goods from UBC which is the dearest vendor, is more significant and this fact is a particular feature of the dominant position and its verification is determinative in this case.' (para 128)

The cumulative effect of all the advantages enjoyed by UBC thus ensures that is has a dominant position on the relevant market.

Comment

The finding of dominance stemmed from the Commission's finding that the relevant product market was the market for bananas. See detailed analysis of the market definition on page 36 above.

Dominance was referred to as the ability to behave to an appreciable extent independently of competitors, customers and ultimately consumers. (para 62) This is a relatively wide concept, which is not purely economic in nature. The Court of Justice later elaborated that an undertaking does not have to have eliminated all opportunity for competition in order to be in a dominant position. (para 113) In Case 85/76 *Hoffmann-La Roche* (page 215 below) the Court of Justice appeared to further relax this benchmark by holding that 'Such a position does not preclude some competition, which it does where there is a monopoly or quasi-monopoly, but enables the undertaking … if not to determine, at least to have an appreciable influence on the conditions under which that competition will develop, and in any case to act largely in disregard of it, so long that such conduct does not operate to its detriment.' (para 39)

Hoffmann-La Roche & Co v Commission	**Article 102 TFEU**
Case 85/76	Dominant Position
Court of Justice, [1979] ECR 461, [1979] 3 CMLR 211	

Facts

Hoffmann-La Roche (Roche) applied for the annulment of a Commission Decision IV/29.020—*Vitamins*, which found Roche to have abused its dominant position in the market for vitamins A, B2, B3, B6, C, E and H. Roche challenged the decision on several points, including the finding of dominance and abuse.

Held

A dominant position enables an undertaking 'to prevent effective competition being maintained on the relevant market by affording it the power to behave to an appreciable extent independently of its competitors, its customers and ultimately of the consumers.' (para 38)

'Such a position does not preclude some competition, which it does where there is a monopoly or a quasi-monopoly, but enables the undertaking which profits by it, if not to determine, at least to have an appreciable influence on the conditions under which that competition will develop, and in any case to act largely in disregard of it so long as such conduct does not operate to its detriment.' (para 39)

Very large market shares which are sustained for some time are in themselves, and save in exceptional circumstances, evidence of dominance. (para 41)

Retention of market share may result from effective competition and is not—by itself—an indicator of dominance. However, when dominance is established, retention of market share supports a conclusion that the position of dominance has been maintained. (para 44) The facts that Roche produced a far wider range of vitamins than its competitors and that its turnover exceeded that of all the other competitors, were held to be immaterial to the finding of dominance. (paras 45–7)

Other factors indicating dominance include the disparity between the market share of the leading undertaking and the next largest competitor, the technological lead of an undertaking over its competitors, the existence of a highly developed sales network, barriers to entry and the absence of potential competition. (para 48)

The existence of lively competition on a particular market does not exclude the possibility that a dominant position exists on that market. In this case, price variation in the market did not lead to competitive pressure which was likely to jeopardise the marked degree of independence enjoyed by Roche. (paras 49–78)

The Commission was right to find dominance in the market for vitamins A, B2, B6, C, E and H.

The Commission was wrong in its finding of dominance in the vitamin B3 market.

Comment

Note that the two-stage analysis relies heavily on market definition, and subsequently market characteristics. Market share is only one of the indicators of dominance and should be analysed accordingly, bearing in mind the other market characteristics. Note especially that large market shares must exist 'for some time' and that in 'exceptional circumstances' they may not establish dominance. On market definition in this case see page 38 above. On the finding of abuse see page 225 below.

The reference to 'appreciable influence' in paragraph 39 lowers the threshold for establishing dominance, in comparison to that used in Case 27/76 *United Brands* (page 213 above).

Note Case T-340/03 *France Télécom* where the Court held that 'Even the existence of lively competition on a particular market does not rule out the possibility that there is a dominant position on that market, since the predominant feature of such a position is the ability of the undertaking concerned to act without having to take account of this competition in its market strategy and without for that reason suffering detrimental effects from such behaviour.' (para 101) (on the finding of abuse see page 226 below)

AKZO Chemie BV v Commission	**Article 102 TFEU**
Case C-62/86	Dominant Position
Court of Justice, [1991] ECR I-3359, 1993 5 CMLR 215	

Facts

AKZO Chemie (Akzo) applied for the annulment of a Commission decision (IV/30.698 *ECS/AKZO Chemie*) in which the Commission found that Akzo had abused its dominant position in the organic peroxides market, by pursuing against one of its competitors a course of conduct intended to damage its business and secure its withdrawal from the market. Akzo challenged the decision on several grounds, one of them being the finding of dominance.

Held

'With regard to market shares the Court has held that very large shares are in themselves, and save in exceptional circumstances, evidence of the existence of a dominant position. ... That is the situation where there is a market share of 50% such as that found to exist in this case.' (para 60)

'Moreover, the Commission rightly pointed out that other factors confirmed AKZO's predominance in the market. In addition to the fact that AKZO regards itself as the world leader in the peroxides market, it should be observed that, as AKZO itself admits, it has the most highly developed marketing organization, both commercially and technically, and wider knowledge than that of their competitors with regard to safety and toxicology.' (para 61)

Comment

The Court referred to Case 85/76 *Hoffmann-La Roche & Co v Commission* (page 215 above) and held that a market share of 50 per cent is indicative of dominance. It thus established a rebuttable presumption of dominance in market shares of 50 per cent and above.

This rebuttable presumption shifts the burden of proof to the alleged dominant undertaking which has to establish that it is not dominant despite holding a market share of 50 per cent or more. The likelihood of successfully invalidating this presumption is eroded the larger the market share is.

Market share serves as only one of several factors indicating the existence or lack of dominance. Accordingly, large market shares do not necessarily indicate a position of market power. This may be the case in dynamic fast growing markets. Note, for example, Skype and Microsoft's market share of between 80 and 90 per cent in video calls made on Windows-based PCs which was held not to be indicative of competitive strength (Case No COMP/M.6281 *Microsoft/Skype*, Case T-79/12 *Cisco Systems Inc and Messagenet SpA v Commission* (page 450 below).

Note that dominance can be found below the threshold of 50 per cent market share. See, for example, *Virgin/British Airways* (COMP/34.780, para 88), where the Commission found British Airways to dominate the market with a market share of 39.7 per cent. Also note *United Brands* (page 213 above) where a market share of 40–45 per cent supported a conclusion of dominance.

The Akzo presumption applies only to single firm dominance and not to collective dominance. See Chapter 6 herein and in particular *France v Commission (Kali und Salz)* (para 226) (C-68/94, [1998] ECR I-1375).

On single dominance, see also paragraphs 28–42, DG Competition Discussion Paper on the Application of [Article 102 TFEU] to Exclusionary Abuses (December 2005).

Hugin v Commission	**Article 102 TFEU**
Case 22/78	Dominant Position
Court of Justice, [1979] ECR 1869, [1979] 3 CMLR 345	

Facts

Hugin was fined by the European Commission for refusing to supply spare parts for its cash registers to Liptons, a company which was not part of the Hugin distribution system. The Commission found Hugin's refusal to supply to constitute an abuse of a dominant position (Case IV/29.132 *Hugin/Liptons*). On appeal to the Court of Justice, Hugin contested, among other things, the finding of dominance.

Held

The definition of the market in question should take account of the fact that the conduct alleged against Hugin consists in the refusal to supply spare parts to independent undertakings outside its distribution network. 'The question is, therefore, whether the supply of spare parts constitutes a specific market or whether it forms part of a wider market. To answer that question it is necessary to determine the category of clients who require such parts.' (para 5)

Cash registers are of such a technical nature that the user cannot fit the spare parts into the machine but requires the services of a specialised technician. That being the case, users of cash registers do not operate on the market as purchasers of spare parts but require the service of undertakings engaged in maintenance and repair work. While there certainly exists amongst users a market for maintenance and repairs which is distinct from the market in new cash registers, it is essentially a market for the provision of services and not for the sale of a product such as spare parts, the refusal to supply which forms the subject-matter of the Commission's Decision. (para 6)

However, a separate market for Hugin spare parts does exist at the level of independent undertakings which specialise in the maintenance and repair of cash registers. Hugin spare parts are not interchangeable with spare parts for cash registers of other makes. Consequently, there is a specific demand for Hugin's spare parts from independent undertakings engaged in the activities of maintenance service and repairs of Hugin cash registers. It flows from this that the market constituted by Hugin spare parts required by independent undertakings must be regarded as the relevant market for the purposes of the application of Article 102 TFEU. This is also the market on which the alleged abuse was committed. (paras 7, 8)

It is necessary to examine next whether Hugin occupies a dominant position on that market. Hugin controls most, if not all, of the production and supply of spare parts which could be used in Hugin cash registers. Therefore, Hugin occupies a dominant position on the market for its own spare parts and enjoys a position which enables it to determine its conduct without taking account of competing sources of supply. (paras 9, 10)

Comment

This decision highlights the impact market definition has on the conclusion of dominance. Although Hugin was a relatively small undertaking which occupied a small share of the general market for cash registers, the definition of the market as the market for its own spare parts led to finding of dominance. In other words, despite its lack of market power on the primary product (cash registers) it was found to dominate the narrow market for the complementary product (spare parts).

After establishing dominance the Court of Justice considered whether the Commission was successful in finding all the other conditions of Article 102 TFEU. The Court of Justice found that Hugin's conduct was not capable of affecting trade between Member States and consequently annulled the Commission's decision. (paras 15–26)

Nederlandsche Banden Industrie Michelin v Commission Case 322/81 Court of Justice, [1983] ECR 3461, [1985] 1 CMLR 282	**Article 102 TFEU** Dominant Position

Facts

Michelin NV was responsible for the production and sale of Michelin tyres in the Netherlands. The Commission found that Michelin abused its dominant position on the market for new replacement tyres for lorries, buses and similar vehicles by operating anticompetitive target-based discount schemes (Case IV/29.491). On appeal to the Court of Justice Michelin contested, among other things, the Commission's finding of a dominant position. To establish the existence of a dominant position the Court considered Michelin's share of the relevant product market as well as its position in relation to its competitors, customers and consumers.

Held

Michelin NV's share of the market in new replacement tyres for lorries, buses and similar vehicles in the Netherlands was between 57 and 65 per cent, whereas the market share of its main competitors was only 4–8 per cent. This market share constitutes a valid indication of Michelin's comparative strength. (paras 22–52)

'In order to assess the relative economic strength of Michelin NV and its competitors on the Netherlands market the advantages which those undertakings may derive from belonging to groups of undertakings operating throughout Europe or even the world must be taken into consideration. Amongst those advantages, the lead which the Michelin group has over its competitors in the matters of investment and research and the special extent of its range of products, to which the Commission referred in its Decision, have not been denied. In fact in the case of certain types of tyre the Michelin group is the only supplier on the market to offer them in its range.' (para 55)

'That situation ensures that on the Netherlands market a large number of users of heavy-vehicle tyres have a strong preference for Michelin tyres. As the purchase of tyres represents a considerable investment for a transport undertaking and since much time is required in order to ascertain in practice the cost-effectiveness of a type or brand of tyre, Michelin NV therefore enjoys a position which renders it largely immune to competition.' (para 56)

Michelin NV's large network of commercial representatives is not matched by its competitors, and gives Michelin NV direct access to tyre users at all times. This, and the standard of service which the network can give them, enables Michelin NV to maintain and strengthen its position on the market and to protect itself more effectively against competition. (para 58)

The existence of a dominant position in this case is not disproved by temporary unprofitability or losses. By the same token, the fact that the prices charged by Michelin NV do not constitute an abuse and are not particularly high is not inconsistent with the existence of a dominant position. (para 59) The finding of dominance simply means that the undertaking concerned has a special responsibility not to allow its conduct to impair genuine undistorted competition on the Internal Market. (para 57)

Comment

In Case T-170/06, *Alrosa Company Ltd v Commission*, [2007] ECR II-2601, the General Court commented on the concept of special responsibility: 'Since the object of [Article 102 TFEU] is not to prohibit the holding of dominant positions but solely to put an end to their abuse, the Commission cannot require an undertaking in a dominant position to refrain from making purchases which allow it to maintain or to strengthen its position on the market, if that undertaking does not, in so doing, resort to methods which are incompatible with the competition rules. While special responsibilities are incumbent on an undertaking which occupies such a position (*Michelin v Commission*, paragraph 57), they cannot amount to a requirement that the very existence of the dominant position be called into question.' (para 146)

Soda Ash-Solvay	**Article 102 TFEU**
Cases IV/33.384 and IV/33.378	Dominant Position
European Commission, [1992] OJ L326/31	Other Factors Indicating Dominance

Facts

The Commission found Solvay SA to have infringed Article 102 TFEU and abused its dominant position in the market for sodium carbonate (soda ash), by applying to its major customers a system of loyalty rebates aimed at excluding or severely limiting competition.

Held

Dominance is the power to hinder effective competition. 'Such power may involve the ability to eliminate or seriously weaken existing competition or to prevent potential competitors from entering the market. As the Court stated, the existence of a dominant position does not however require the producer enjoying it to have eliminated all possibility of competition (see also Case 27/76 "*United Brands v Commission*", paragraph 113(10)). ... The existence of a dominant position may depend upon a combination of factors, where no single one is necessarily decisive.' (paras 127, 128)

The consideration of market power follows the definition of the relevant market. According to Solvay's own documentation it held a market share of some 70 per cent in continental western Europe. 'Market share, while important, is only one of the indicators from which the existence of a dominant position may be inferred. Its significance may vary from case to case according to the characteristics of the relevant market.' (paras 137, 129–37)

To assess Solvay's market power the Commission took into account, among other things, the company's position as the only soda ash producer operating throughout the Union, its manufacturing strength across Europe, its high market share in several of the member states and its near-monopoly position in Italy, Spain and Portugal, it being the largest producer of salt in the EU, the fact that it has excellent market coverage as the exclusive or near-exclusive supplier to almost all the major customers in the Union, the absence of any competition from the only other EU producer of comparable market strength to Solvay, the reluctance of competitors to challenge its dominant position and compete aggressively for Solvay's traditional customers, and the improbability of any new entry to the market. (para 138)

'In assessing the extent of Solvay's market power, the Commission took account of the possible substitutability of caustic soda for soda ash. ... In practice however the possible availability of caustic soda did not constitute a substantial limitation on Solvay's market power in the [Union].' (para 139)

The Commission subsequently found Solvay to have abused its dominant position. (paras 149–85)

Comment

On market power and barriers to entry also note the Commission decision in Case No IV/M.190—*Nestlé/ Perrier* ([1992] OJ L356/1). While appraising the proposed concentration between the two companies the Commission referred to the characteristics of the French water market. It noted that the reputation of the established brands Nestlé, Perrier and BSN creates a key problem of access and grants the incumbents a long-term advantage over any local supplier or newcomer. (para 96) It noted that heavy advertising further strengthens the incumbents' market power and deters entry. 'Advertising and promotion are sunk costs which are not recoverable in the case of failure in the market.' (para 97) In addition, high market concentration 'in itself is a barrier to entry because it increases the likelihood and the efficiency of single or concerted reaction by the established firms against newcomers with a view to defending the acquired market positions and profitability.' (para 98)

Eurofix-Bauco/Hilti	**Article 102 TFEU**
Cases IV/30.787 and 31.488	Dominance
European Commission, [1988] OJ L65/19, [1989] 4 CMLR 677	

Facts

Hilti AG specialises in the manufacture and distribution of a variety of fastening systems and is recognised as a world leader in the field of nail guns and consumables for use therein. The Commission fined Hilti AG for the abuse of its dominant position in the market for nail guns and for the nails and cartridge strips for those guns. The abusive behaviour included the tying of the sale of nails to the sale of cartridge strips, a practice which excluded competitors from the market and was aimed at increasing Hilti's market power.

Held

The two separate relevant markets in question include the market for Hilti-compatible cartridge strips and for Hilti-compatible nails in the Union. (para 66)

Hilti's cartridge strips enjoy patent protection and it is therefore impossible for any cartridge strip producer to enter the market for Hilti-compatible cartridge strips. Subsequently Hilti sells virtually all the cartridges consumed in its own guns. Hilti's market share in the market for Hilti-compatible nails in the Union is not 'as high as that which it enjoys in the market for Hilti-compatible consumables. This is because independent nail makers have had more, albeit still very limited, success than independent cartridge strip makers at penetrating the market for Hilti-compatible consumables. Nevertheless these other competitors, principally the complainants, have small market shares and to date their sales have been limited to the UK. ... There are apparently no effective patents for nails.' (para 67)

In addition to the strength derived from its market share, Hilti benefits from other advantages that reinforce its position in the nail gun market. These include the novel technology used in its nail gun, the patent protection for its cartridge strips, its strong research and development position and its strong distribution system. Moreover the maturity of the market for nail guns may discourage new entrants as sales or market shares can only be obtained at the expense of existing competitors. (para 69)

'Hilti's market power and dominance stem principally from its large share of the sales of nail guns coupled with the patent protection for its cartridge strips. The economic position it enjoys is such that it enables it to prevent effective competition being maintained on the relevant markets for Hilti-compatible nails and cartridge strips. In fact Hilti's commercial behaviour, which has been described above and is analysed below, is witness to its ability to act independently of, and without due regard to, either competitors or customers on the relevant markets in question. In addition, Hilti's pricing policy also described above reflects its ability to determine, or at least to have an appreciable influence on the conditions under which competition will develop. This behaviour and its economic consequences would not normally be seen where a company was facing real competitive pressure. Therefore the Commission considers that Hilti holds a dominant position in the two separate relevant markets for Hilti-compatible nails and cartridge strips.' (para 71)

Comment

The Guidance Paper stipulates that 'The Commission considers that an undertaking which is capable of profitably increasing prices above the competitive level for a significant period of time does not face sufficiently effective competitive constraints and can thus generally be regarded as dominant.' (para 11) The assessment of dominance will take into account the competitive structure of the market, and constraints imposed by the existing supplies and competitors, constraints imposed by the credible threat of future expansion by actual competitors or entry by potential competitors and constraints imposed by the bargaining strength of the undertaking's customers. (para 12)

BP and others v Commission Case 77/77 Court of Justice, [1978] ECR 1511	**Article 102 TFEU** Dominance Transitory Market Power

Facts

The origin of the case lies in the oil 'crisis' that occurred in 1973–74 as a result of the decision of certain major oil-producing countries to sharply increase their prices for crude oil and, at the same time, to reduce their production. In Case IV/28.841—*ABG Oil*, the Commission found British Petroleum Maatschappij BV (BP) had abused its dominant position by reducing the supply of motor spirit to ABG Oil.

The Commission established its finding of dominance on the fact that during the crisis period in question the sudden reduction in supplies of oil substantially altered existing commercial relations between suppliers and their customers. 'For reasons completely outside the control of the normal suppliers, their customers can become completely dependent on them for the supply of scarce products. Thus, while the situation continues, the suppliers are placed in a dominant position in respect of their normal customers.' On appeal the court annulled the decision for lack of abuse. It did not consider in detail the question of dominance and only briefly mentioned the Commission's analysis on this point. In doing so it ignored the fact that the position of market strength was temporary and as such might not have given rise to true position of dominance.

Held

The reasons given by the Commission for the finding of dominance 'are based essentially on considerations of a general nature relating to the conditions of the whole of the Netherlands market during the crisis as regards the supply of petroleum products and the state of commercial relations, which, in a market such as this one, inevitably arise between "suppliers who have a substantial share of the market and quantities available and their customers". The first question to be examined is whether, on the supposition that special market conditions such as those in this case did in fact ensure a dominant position in the Netherlands for the large oil companies established there as against their respective customers, the factual and legal circumstances on which the Commission relies to characterize in particular the individual conduct of BP during the crisis make it possible to consider that conduct as an abuse.' (paras 17–18)

Comment

It is questionable whether BP held a position of dominance during the crisis period in question. The Court chose to ignore this issue and annulled the decision on lack of abuse. (see page 280 below)

In his opinion Advocate General JP Warner criticised the Commission's finding of dominance. He noted that 'In the first place the concept of a dominant position in [Article 102 TFEU] connotes, as the Court has said many times, most recently in Case 27/76 *United Brands v. Commission* … that the undertaking concerned has a position of such economic strength as to have power, at least, to behave to an appreciable extent independently of its competitors and customers. The Commission itself, in its Decision in the present case (at p 8), defines a dominant position as one in which the firm concerned may conduct its business 'without regard for the reactions of competitors and customers'. In a temporary emergency of the kind here in question, however, a trader cannot distribute his scarce supplies regardless of the attitude of his customers. He must have it in mind that, once the emergency is over, they will have memories of the way in which they were treated by him during the period of scarcity. Contractual customers will expect the favourable treatment to which their contracts entitle them, both as a matter of law and as a matter of commercial honour—as BP pointed out. Non-contractual but regular customers will expect the loyalty shown by them in normal competitive times to be repaid by loyalty to them on the part of their supplier in the period of scarcity. A supplier can disregard those considerations only at the peril of losing customers to his competitors after the emergency is over. So I do not think that he is, during the emergency, in a dominant position in the sense in which that expression is used in [Article 102 TFEU].' (AG opinion, para 59)

The Coca-Cola Company v Commission	**Article 102 TFEU**
Case T-125/97	Dominant Position
General Court, [2000] ECR II-1733, [2000] 5 CMLR 467	The Requirement for 'Fresh Analysis'

Facts

The Coca-Cola Company and Cadbury Schweppes plc operated in the UK partly through their subsidiary, Coca-Cola & Schweppes Beverages Ltd (CCSB). CCSB handled the bottling, distribution, promotion and marketing of beverages of the two companies. The Commission, in proceedings under the European Merger Regulation (Case IV/M.794—*Coca-Cola/Amalgamated Beverages GB*) found, inter alia, that CCSB held a dominant position on the British cola market. However the Commission declared the notified operation compatible with the internal market. On appeal, the companies challenged the Commission's finding of dominance.

Held

'It is settled case-law that any measure which produces binding legal effects such as to affect the interests of an applicant by bringing about a distinct change in his legal position is an act or decision which may be the subject of an action under [Article 263 TFEU] for a declaration that it is void (*IBM v Commission*, cited above, paragraph 9, Joined Cases C-68/94 and C-30/95 *France and others v Commission* [1998] ECR I-1375, paragraph 62, and Case T-87/96 *Assicurazioni Generali and Unicredito v Commission* [1999] ECR II-203, paragraph 37).' (para 77)

'[A] finding of a dominant position by the Commission, even if likely in practice to influence the policy and future commercial strategy of the undertaking concerned, does not have binding legal effects as referred to in the IBM judgment. Such a finding is the outcome of an analysis of the structure of the market and of competition prevailing at the time the Commission adopts each decision. The conduct which the undertaking held to be in a dominant position subsequently comes to adopt in order to prevent a possible infringement of [Article 102 TFEU] is thus shaped by the parameters which reflect the conditions of competition on the market at a given time.' (para 81)

'Moreover, in the course of any decision applying [Article 102 TFEU], the Commission must define the relevant market again and make a fresh analysis of the conditions of competition which will not necessarily be based on the same considerations as those underlying the previous finding of a dominant position.' (para 82)

'A national court which has to assess action taken by CCSB after the contested decision in the context of a dispute between CCSB and a third party is not bound by previous findings of the Commission. There is nothing to prevent it from concluding that CCSB is no longer in a dominant position, contrary to the Commission's finding at the time when the contested decision was adopted.' (para 85)

'It is clear from the foregoing considerations that the mere finding in the contested decision that CCSB holds a dominant position has no binding legal effects so that the applicants' challenge to its merits is not admissible.' (para 92)

Comment

Market definition and the finding of dominance provide an indication of the boundaries of competition and the market power of the undertakings involved, in a given time and with respect to a given product. As such, the empirical analysis cannot bind a future analysis of another product or alleged abuse at a later stage.

Suiker Unie and others v Commission	**Article 102 TFEU**
Joined Cases 40–48, 50, 54–56, 111, 113, 114/73	Substantial Part of the Internal Market
Court of Justice, [1975] ECR 1663, [1976] 1 CMLR 295	

Facts

Joint appeal on the Commission decision in Case IV/26.918—*European Sugar Industry*, in which the Commission found a number of undertakings to engage in concerted actions contrary to Article 101 TFEU with the aim of protecting national markets and eliminating interstate trade. In addition, the Commission accused some of the undertakings of abusing their dominant position by bringing economic pressure to bear on importers with the object of compelling them to restrict their imports. As part of its decision the Court of Justice considered whether the markets in question constituted a substantial part of the Internal Market.

Held

'For the purpose of determining whether a specific territory is large enough to amount to "a substantial part of the [internal] market" within the meaning of [Article 102 TFEU] the pattern and volume of the production and consumption of the said product as well as the habits and economic opportunities of vendors and purchasers must be considered.' (para 371)

'So far as sugar in particular is concerned it is advisable to take into consideration in addition to the high freight rates in relation to the price of the product and the habits of the processing industries and consumers, the fact that [Union] rules have consolidated most of the special features of the former national markets.' (para 372)

'From 1968/69 to 1971/72 Belgian production and total [EU] production increased respectively from 530,000 to 770,000 metric tons and from 6,800,000 to 8,100,000 metric tons. … During these marketing years Belgian consumption was approximately 350,000 metric tons whereas [Union] consumption increased from 5,900,000 to 6,500,000 metric tons.' (paras 373, 374)

'If the other criteria mentioned above are taken into account these market shares are sufficiently large for the area covered by Belgium and Luxembourg to be considered, so far as sugar is concerned, as a substantial part of the [internal] market in this product.' (para 375)

Comment

The relative size of Belgian sugar production in comparison to the wider EU production levels led to a finding that the area covered by Belgium and Luxembourg constituted a substantial part of the internal market. Note that when assessing whether the market was 'substantial' the court did not limit itself to the size of the geography but considered the pattern and volume of the production and consumption.

The requirement for a 'substantial part of the internal market' acts as a de minimis threshold. The finding of 'substantial part' should not be confused with the additional requirement of finding an effect on trade between Member States.

Sea Containers v Stena Sealink	**Article 102 TFEU**
Case IV/34.689, Interim Measures	Substantial Part of the Internal Market
European Commission [1994] OJ L15/8, [1995] CMLR 84	

'The complaint relates to access to a port whose geographic market constitutes a substantial part of the [internal] market because that port provides one of the main links between two Member States, the United Kingdom and Ireland, and is the only port providing a direct link between Great Britain and the capital city of Ireland. The refusal to offer SC access on a reasonable and non-discriminatory basis to port facilities at Holyhead so as to enable it to commence a ferry service, and any consequential effect that this has upon the competition situation on the maritime transport market on the Irish Sea, would have a direct effect on trade between Member States.' (para 77)

Portuguese Airports	**Article 102 TFEU**
European Commission, Case IV/35.703	Substantial Part of the Internal Market
[1999] OJ L69/31, [1999] 5 CMLR 103	

In its decision the European Commission assessed the legality of charges imposed by some of the Portuguese Airports (*The Community v Aeroportos E Navegacao Aerea—Empresa Publica (ANA)*). On the question of whether the airports' concerns can be regarded as a substantial part of the internal market the Commission noted that:

'Taken together, therefore, the airports which operate intra-[Union] services can be regarded as a substantial part of the [internal] market, if one applies the reasoning adopted by the Court in the *Crespelle* [Case C-323/93, *Crespelle*, [1994] ECR I-5077] and *Almelo* [Case C-393/92, *Almelo*, [1994] ECR I-1477] judgments to the case in hand. In the Crespelle judgment, the Court stated that: "by thus establishing, in favour of those undertakings, a contiguous series of monopolies territorially limited but together covering the entire territory of a Member State, those national provisions create a dominant position, within the meaning of [Article 102 TFEU], in a substantial part of the [internal] market" [para 17]' (para 21)

'A fortiori, a contiguous series of monopolies controlled by the same undertaking (ANA) may represent a substantial part of the [internal] market.' (para 22)

Konkurrensverket v TeliaSonera Sverige AB	**Article 102 TFEU**
Case C-52/09	The Goals of Article 102 TFEU
Court of Justice, [2011] ECR I-527, [2011] 4 CMLR 18	Abuse

'Article 3(3) TEU states that the European Union is to establish an internal market, which, in accordance with Protocol No 27 on the internal market and competition, annexed to the Treaty of Lisbon (OJ 2010 C83, p 309), is to include a system ensuring that competition is not distorted. Article 102 TFEU is one of the competition rules referred to in Article 3(1)(b) TFEU which are necessary for the functioning of that internal market.' (paras 20, 21)

'The function of those rules is precisely to prevent competition from being distorted to the detriment of the public interest, individual undertakings and consumers, thereby ensuring the well-being of the European Union (see, to that effect, Case C-94/00 *Roquette Frères* [2002] ECR I-9011, paragraph 42).' (para 22)

'In that context, the dominant position referred to in Article 102 TFEU relates to a position of economic strength enjoyed by an undertaking which enables it to prevent effective competition being maintained on the relevant market by affording it the power to behave to an appreciable extent independently of its competitors, its customers and ultimately of consumers (Case 85/76 *Hoffmann-La Roche v Commission* [1979] ECR 461, paragraph 38, and Case C-280/08P *Deutsche Telekom v Commission* [2010] ECR I-0000, paragraph 170).' (para 23)

'Accordingly, Article 102 TFEU must be interpreted as referring not only to practices which may cause damage to consumers directly (see, to that effect, Joined Cases C-468/06 to C-478/06 *Sot Lélos kai Sia and Other s* [2008] ECR I-7139, paragraph 68, and *Deutsche Telekom v Commission*, paragraph 176), but also to those which are detrimental to them through their impact on competition. Whilst Article 102 TFEU does not prohibit an undertaking from acquiring, on its own merits, the dominant position in a market, and while, a fortiori, a finding that an undertaking has a dominant position is not in itself a ground of criticism of the undertaking concerned (see, to that effect, Case 322/81 *Nederlandsche Banden-Industrie-Michelin v Commission* [1983] ECR 3461, paragraph 57, and Joined Cases C-395/96P and C-396/96P *Compagnie maritime belge transports and Others v Commission* [2000] ECR I-1365, paragraph 37), it remains the case that, in accordance with settled case-law, an undertaking which holds a dominant position has a special responsibility not to allow its conduct to impair genuine undistorted competition in the internal market (see, to that effect, Case C-202/07P *France Télécom v Commissio n* [2009] ECR I-2369, paragraph 105 and case-law cited).' (para 24)

Sot Lélos kai Sia EE and others v GlaxoSmithKline AEVE	**Article 102 TFEU**
Joined Cases C-468/06 to C-478/06	The Goals of Article 102 TFEU
Court of Justice, [2008] ECR I-7139	Abuse

In light of the Treaty objectives 'there can be no escape from the prohibition laid down in [Article 102 TFEU] for the practices of an undertaking in a dominant position which are aimed at avoiding all parallel exports from a Member State to other Member States, practices which, by partitioning the national markets, neutralise the benefits of effective competition in terms of the supply and the prices that those exports would obtain for final consumers in the other Member States.' (para 66)

'Furthermore, in the light of the Treaty objectives to protect consumers by means of undistorted competition and the integration of national markets, the [Union] rules on competition are also incapable of being interpreted in such a way that, in order to defend its own commercial interests, the only choice left for a pharmaceuticals company in a dominant position is not to place its medicines on the market at all in a Member State where the prices of those products are set at a relatively low level.' (para 68)

Oscar Bronner v Mediaprint	**Article 102 TFEU**
Case C-7/97	The Goals of Article 102 TFEU
Opinion of AG Jacobs, [1998] ECR I-7791;[1999] 4 CMLR 112	Long-term Consumer Welfare

'[T]he justification in terms of competition policy for interfering with a dominant undertaking's freedom to contract often requires a careful balancing of conflicting considerations. In the long term it is generally pro-competitive and in the interest of consumers to allow a company to retain for its own use facilities which it has developed for the purpose of its business. For example, if access to a production, purchasing or distribution facility were allowed too easily there would be no incentive for a competitor to develop competing facilities. Thus while competition was increased in the short term it would be reduced in the long term. Moreover, the incentive for a dominant undertaking to invest in efficient facilities would be reduced if its competitors were, upon request, able to share the benefits. Thus the mere fact that by retaining a facility for its own use a dominant undertaking retains an advantage over a competitor cannot justify requiring access to it.' (para 57, AG Jacobs opinion)

British Airways Plc v Commission	**Article 102 TFEU**
Case C-95/04	The Goals of Article 102 TFEU
Court of Justice, [2007] ECR I-2331; [2007] 4 CMLR 22	Exclusionary Abuse

'[A]s the Court has already held in paragraph 26 of its judgment in *Europemballage and Continental Can*, [Article 102 TFEU] is aimed not only at practices which may cause prejudice to consumers directly, but also at those which are detrimental to them through their impact on an effective competition structure.' (para 106)

'The Court of First Instance was therefore entitled, without committing any error of law, not to examine whether BA's conduct had caused prejudice to consumers within the meaning of subparagraph (b) of the second paragraph of [Article 102 TFEU], but to examine … whether the bonus schemes at issue had a restrictive effect on competition and to conclude that the existence of such an effect had been demonstrated by the Commission in the contested decision.' (para 107)

France Telecom SA v Commission	**Article 102 TFEU**
Case T-340/03	The Goals of Article 102 TFEU
General Court, [2007] ECR II-107; [2008] All ER (EC) 677	Exclusionary Abuse

'As regards WIN's argument that consumers were not harmed by its pricing but, on the contrary, benefited from it, it should be recalled that the Court of Justice has held that [Article 102 TFEU] is not only aimed at practices which may cause damage to consumers directly, but also at those which are detrimental to them through their impact on an effective competition structure (*Europemballage and Continental Can v Commission…*).' (para 266)

National Grid Plc v Gas and Electricity Markets Authority	**Article 102 TFEU**
Court of Appeal	The Goals of Article 102 TFEU
[2010] EWCA Civ 114; [2010] UKCLR 386	Exclusionary Abuse

'It is common ground that in order to find an abuse it is not necessary to prove direct harm to consumers. The competition rules promote consumer welfare indirectly by their effect on market structure and the promotion of competition. As the Court of Justice said in British Airways … "[Article 102 TFEU] is aimed not only at practices which may cause prejudice to consumers directly, but also at those which are detrimental to them through their impact on the competition structure".' (para 85)

Sot Lélos kai Sia EE and Others v GlaxoSmithKline	**Article 102 TFEU**
Joined Cases 468/06 to C-478/06	The Goals of Article 102 TFEU
Court of Justice, [2008] ECR I-7139	Market Integration v Consumer Welfare

'Accordingly, without it being necessary for the Court to rule on the question whether it is for an undertaking in a dominant position to assess whether its conduct vis-à-vis a trading party constitutes abuse in the light of the degree to which that party's activities offer advantages to the final consumers, it is clear that, in the circumstances of the main proceedings, such an undertaking cannot base its arguments on the premiss that the parallel exports which it seeks to limit are of only minimal benefit to the final consumers.' (para 57)

SYFAIT v GlaxoSmithKline Plc	**Article 102 TFEU**
Case C-53/03	The Goals of Article 102 TFEU
Opinion of AG Jacobs, [2005] ECR I-4609	Market Integration v Consumer Welfare

'I consider that a restriction of supply by a dominant pharmaceutical undertaking in order to limit parallel trade is capable of justification as a reasonable and proportionate measure in defence of that undertaking's commercial interests. Such a restriction does not protect price disparities which are of the undertaking's own making, nor does it directly impede trade, which is rather blocked by public service obligations imposed by the Member States. To require the undertaking to supply all export orders placed with it would in many cases impose a disproportionate burden given the moral and legal obligations on it to maintain supplies in all Member States. Given the specific economic characteristics of the pharmaceutical industry, a requirement to supply would not necessarily promote either free movement or competition, and might harm the incentive for pharmaceutical undertakings to innovate. Moreover, it cannot be assumed that parallel trade would in fact benefit either the ultimate consumers of pharmaceutical products or the Member States, as primary purchasers of such products.' (para 100)

'However, I regard the conclusion which I have reached here as highly specific to the pharmaceutical industry in its current condition and to the particular type of conduct at issue in the present proceedings.' (para 101)

United Brands Co v Commission	**Article 102 TFEU**
Case 27/76	The Goals of Article 102 TFEU
Court of Justice, [1978] ECR 207	Market Separation

'These discriminatory prices, which varied according to the circumstances of the Member States, were just so many obstacles to the free movement of goods and their effect was intensified by the clause forbidding the resale of bananas while still green and by reducing the deliveries of the quantities ordered.' (para 232)

'A rigid partitioning of national markets was thus created at price levels, which were artificially different, placing certain distributor/ripeners at a competitive disadvantage, since compared with what it should have been competition had thereby been distorted.' (para 233)

Sot Lélos kai Sia EE and Others v GlaxoSmithKline Joined Cases 468/06 to C-478/06 Court of Justice, [2008] ECR I-7139	**Article 102 TFEU** Articles 101 and 102 TFEU Market Separation

'In respect of sectors other than that of pharmaceutical products, the Court has held that a practice by which an undertaking in a dominant position aims to restrict parallel trade in the products that it puts on the market constitutes abuse of that dominant position, particularly when such a practice has the effect of curbing parallel imports by neutralising the more favourable level of prices which may apply in other sales areas in the Community (see, to that effect, Case 26/75 *General Motors Continental v Commission* [1975] ECR 1367, paragraph 12) or when it aims to create barriers to re-importations which come into competition with the distribution network of that undertaking (Case 226/84 *British Leyland v Commission* [1986] ECR 3263, paragraph 24). Indeed, parallel imports enjoy a certain amount of protection in Community law because they encourage trade and help reinforce competition (Case C-373/90 *X* [1992] ECR I-131, paragraph 12).' (para 27)

'In relation to the application of [Article 101 TFEU], the Court has held that an agreement between producer and distributor which might tend to restore the national divisions in trade between Member States might be such as to frustrate the objective of the Treaty to achieve the integration of national markets through the establishment of a single market. Thus on a number of occasions the Court has held agreements aimed at partitioning national markets according to national borders or making the interpenetration of national markets more difficult, in particular those aimed at preventing or restricting parallel exports, to be agreements whose object is to restrict competition within the meaning of that Treaty article (see, for example, Joined Cases 96/82 to 102/82, 104/82, 105/82, 108/82 and 110/82 *IAZ International Belgium and Others v Commission* [1983] ECR 3369, paragraphs 23 to 27; Case C-306/96 *Javico* [1998] ECR I-1983, paragraphs 13 and 14; and Case C-551/03 P *General Motors v Commission* [2006] ECR I-3173, paragraphs 67 to 69).' (para 65)

'In the light of the abovementioned Treaty objective as well as that of ensuring that competition in the internal market is not distorted, there can be no escape from the prohibition laid down in Article 82 EC for the practices of an undertaking in a dominant position which are aimed at avoiding all parallel exports from a Member State to other Member States, practices which, by partitioning the national markets, neutralise the benefits of effective competition in terms of the supply and the prices that those exports would obtain for final consumers in the other Member States.' (para 66)

Hilti AG v Commission Case T-30/89 Court of First Instance, [1991] ECR II-1439	**Article 102 TFEU** The Goals of Article 102 TFEU Safety Considerations

'As the Commission has established, there are laws in the United Kingdom attaching penalties to the sale of dangerous products and to the use of misleading claims as to the characteristics of any product. There are also authorities vested with powers to enforce those laws. In those circumstances it is clearly not the task of an undertaking in a dominant position to take steps on its own initiative to eliminate products which, rightly or wrongly, it regards as dangerous or at least as inferior in quality to its own products.' (para 118)

'It must further be held in this connection that the effectiveness of the Community rules on competition would be jeopardized if the interpretation by an undertaking of the laws of the various Member States regarding product liability were to take precedence over those rules. Hilti's argument based on its alleged duty of care cannot therefore be upheld.' (para 119)

AKZO Chemie BV v Commission	**Article 102 TFEU**
Case C-62/86	Abuse
Court of Justice, [1991] ECR I-3359, [1993] 5 CMLR 215	Predatory Pricing

Facts

AKZO Chemie (Akzo) applied for the annulment of a Commission decision (IV/30.698—*ECS/AKZO Chemie*) which found that Akzo had abused its dominant position in the organic peroxides market by endeavouring to eliminate one of its competitors (ECS) from the market mainly by massive and prolonged price-cutting in the flour additives sector. Akzo contested the Commission finding of pricing below average variable cost (AVC) and argued that it priced above AVC and therefore did not engage in predatory pricing.

Held

Article 102 TFEU prohibits a dominant undertaking from eliminating a competitor and thereby strengthening its position by using methods other than those which come within the scope of competition on the basis of quality. 'Prices below average variable costs (that is to say, those which vary depending on the quantities produced) by means of which a dominant undertaking seeks to eliminate a competitor must be regarded as abusive. A dominant undertaking has no interest in applying such prices except that of eliminating competitors so as to enable it subsequently to raise its prices by taking advantage of its monopolistic position, since each sale generates a loss, namely the total amount of the fixed costs (that is to say, those which remain constant regardless of the quantities produced) and, at least, part of the variable costs relating to the unit produced.' (paras 70, 71)

'Moreover, prices below average total costs, that is to say, fixed costs plus variable costs, but above average variable costs, must be regarded as abusive if they are determined as part of a plan for eliminating a competitor. Such prices can drive from the market undertakings which are perhaps as efficient as the dominant undertaking but which, because of their smaller financial resources, are incapable of withstanding the competition waged against them.' (para 72)

In this case AKZO directly threatened ECS that it would drop its prices in the flour additives sector if ECS continued to sell benzoyl peroxide in the plastics sector. The threats were aimed at convincing ECS to withdraw from the market. (paras 75–80)

AKZO's pricing strategy led to unreasonably low prices with the aim of damaging ECS's viability. AKZO maintained, as part of this strategy, the prices of some of its products at an artificially low level over a prolonged period without any objective justification. Akzo survived this pricing strategy because of its superior financial resources compared to those of ECS. (paras 83–109, 131–40)

Comment

In order to distinguish between permissible price competition and abusive predation, consideration needs to be given to the economics at the base of the pricing policies. In principle, competition law is not concerned with price competition which drives less-efficient undertakings out of the market; however, predation strategy enables the dominant undertaking to eliminate equally efficient competitors from the market and is therefore held abusive.

The evaluation of predation is predominantly based on cost. Two cost benchmarks were referred to in Akzo: (1) Average total costs (ATC), which reflects the total cost of production of one unit of output. This cost is calculated by taking both fixed and variable costs and dividing them by the number of units produced. (2) Average variable costs (AVC), which is the variable cost of production of one unit of output. This cost is calculated by dividing the variable costs (but not the fixed costs) by the number of units produced. This parameter ignores the fixed costs which were already incurred by the undertaking and measures the real cost of producing one unit of output.

Two other cost benchmarks, not referred to in this case but used by competition enforcers, are average avoidable costs (AAC) and long-run average incremental costs (LRAIC). AAC reflects the cost avoided by not producing a unit of product. It reflects avoidable losses and may differ from AVC when the undertaking had to make a specific investment in order to be able to predate. LRAIC is the average of all the costs the company incurs in the production of a product. LRAIC is usually above AAC as it includes not only fixed costs incurred in the period under examination, but also earlier product specific fixed costs.

Following the *AKZO* judgment, predation is presumed where undertakings price products below AVC (or AAC). This is the case as the undertaking is losing money by producing the product and therefore the practice has no commercial justification. When prices are above AVC (and AAC) but below ATC the conduct may be held abusive when the undertaking intended to eliminate a competitor. At this level although the undertaking fails to cover its fixed costs it is able to sell above its variable costs and therefore can still benefit from the production of additional units. Above ATC, the undertaking is making profits and there is no indication of predation.

It is important to note that the presumption of predation below AVC is a rebuttable one. Such price policy can in some instances be objectively justifiable, for example when an undertaking engages in short-term promotion or has entered a market based on false assumptions of profitability.

Note that although abuse is an objective concept, when considering predation the party's intention to eliminate a competitor plays a role. Accordingly, predation may be established when pricing above AVC but below ATC with the intention of eliminating competition. See para 71 above.

The Commission's Guidance Paper outlines the Commission's approach to predation in paras 63–74. It is interesting to note that according to the Commission, it may 'also pursue predatory practices by dominant undertakings on secondary markets on which they are not yet dominant. In particular, the Commission will be more likely to find such an abuse in sectors where activities are protected by a legal monopoly. While the dominant undertaking does not need to engage in predatory conduct to protect its dominant position in the market protected by legal monopoly, it may use the profits gained in the monopoly market to cross-subsidize its activities in another market and thereby threaten to eliminate effective competition in that other market.' (footnote 39, Guidance Paper) Note that the reference to a secondary market in which the undertaking is not dominant is worded more loosely than the test as set in *Tetra Pak* (below, page 231) where the Court considered interlinked markets. This raises an interesting and challenging question as to the extent to which markets ought to be linked, to establish predation on the secondary market (where the dominant undertaking does not benefit from market power).

Note on this point the Court of Justice judgment in *Post Danmark* (page 236 below) where it stated that when the dominant position has its origins in a former legal monopoly, that fact has to be taken into account in consideration of the undertaking's special responsibility not to distort competition. (para 23)

In the US in order to establish predation it is necessary to show that the monopolist is able to recoup its short-run losses in the long run. The rationale behind this condition is that in the absence of recoupment, a rational undertaking will not engage in predation. The Court of Justice did not consider recoupment as a necessary condition in its Akzo decision. On recoupment, note Case C-333/94P *Tetra Pak v Commission*, page 231 below, and Case T-340/03 *France Télécom SA v Commission*, page 232 below.

Tetra Pak International SA v Commission	**Article 102 TFEU**
Case C-333/94P	Abuse
Court of Justice, [1996] ECR I-5951, [1997] 4 CMLR 662	Predatory Pricing—Recoupment

Facts

Tetra Pak International SA (Tetra Pak) specialises in equipment for the packaging of liquid or semi-liquid food products in cartons. The Commission found Tetra Pak to have abused its dominant position by, among other things, tying the sales of machinery for packaging with the sales of cartons, and by engaging in predatory pricing (IV/31.043—*Tetra Pak II*). The General Court dismissed Tetra Pak's application for annulment of the Commission's decision. Tetra Pak appealed to the Court of Justice, asking it to quash the General Court judgment. On the issue of predatory pricing Tetra Pak argued that the General Court erred in its judgment when it failed to consider the prospect of recouping losses as part of the analysis of predation.

Held

In the judgment under appeal, the General Court carried out the examination of predation in line with the criteria set by the Court of Justice in the *Akzo* judgment. Accordingly, the General Court considered the prices of non-aseptic cartons in Italy between 1976 and 1981 and found that these were considerably lower than average variable costs. As indicated in *Akzo*, prices below average variable costs result in a loss for each item produced and sold. Such a pricing strategy must always be considered abusive as there is no conceivable economic purpose for it other than the elimination of a competitor. Proof of intention to eliminate competitors is not necessary when pricing below AVC. (paras 41, 42)

'It would not be appropriate, in the circumstances of the present case, to require in addition proof that Tetra Pak had a realistic chance of recouping its losses. It must be possible to penalize predatory pricing whenever there is a risk that competitors will be eliminated. The [General Court] found, at paragraphs 151 and 191 of its judgment, that there was such a risk in this case. The aim pursued, which is to maintain undistorted competition, rules out waiting until such a strategy leads to the actual elimination of competitors.' (para 44)

Comment

Note that the predatory practice took place in a market other than the one in which Tetra Pak held a dominant position. In paragraph 30 of its judgment the Court of Justice held that the associative links between the non-aseptic and aseptic markets meant that the Commission was not required to show that Tetra Pak was dominant on the non-aseptic markets where it engaged in predatory pricing. For an example of weaker associated links between markets which led to a conclusion on predation, see the French Competition Council decision concerning GlaxoSmithKline (GSK). There, associative links between the 'Zinnat' and 'Zovirax' markets were established, leading to a finding that GSK abused its dominant position in the Zovirax market by engaging in predatory pricing in the Zinnat market. (Décision No 07-D-09 du 14 Mars 2007 relative à des pratiques mises en oeuvre par le laboratoire GlaxoSmithKline France) Note the Commission's Guidance Paper which stipulates that the Commission may 'also pursue predatory practices by dominant undertakings on secondary markets on which they are not yet dominant.' (footnote 39, Guidance Paper)

The Commission's 2005 Discussion Paper on the Application of [Article 102 TFEU] to Exclusionary Abuses suggests that recoupment may be presumed in most cases. 'It will in general be sufficient to show the likelihood of recoupment by investigating the entry barriers to the market, the (strengthened) position of the company and foreseeable changes to the future structure of the market. As dominance is already established this normally means that entry barriers are sufficiently high to presume the possibility to recoup.' (para 122)

In Case T-340/03 *France Télécom SA v Commission* (page 232 below) the General Court, referring to the *Akzo* and *Tetra Pak* judgments, held that when proving predation it is not necessary to establish that the undertaking had a realistic chance of recouping its losses. (para 227) On recoupment, see also comments on page 234 below.

France Télécom SA v Commission	**Article 102 TFEU**
Case T-340/03	Abuse
General Court, [2007] ECR II-107, [2007] 4 CMLR 21	Predatory Pricing and Price Alignment

Facts

Wanadoo Interactive (Wanadoo), a subsidiary of France Télécom, was fined by the Commission for abusing its dominant position in the market for ADSL-based Internet access services for the general public by charging predatory prices for its Pack eXtense and Wanadoo ADSL services. The Commission found that this deliberate strategy restricted market entry and development potential for competitors in the market and was part of a plan aimed at pre-empting the market for high-output Internet access services. (Case COMP/38.233 *Wanadoo Interactive*)

In its analysis the Commission made adjustments to the application of the Akzo predation test. This was done in order to reflect the industry characteristics and the features specific to the launching of a new product. Accordingly, instead of simply examining costs and revenue as suggested in the *AKZO* judgment, the Commission had spread customer acquisition costs over 48 months, treating as it were these costs as a commercial investment to be written off over a customer's realistic lifetime. Moreover, in its assessment of the revenue generated by subscriptions, the Commission had taken into account a theoretical, nominal subscription revenue, and not the average revenue actually observed. The combined effect of these two corrections was to improve the cost recovery rates used in this decision compared with what they would have been had they simply been based on the unadjusted accounting data (*AKZO*). The Commission has also ignored the cost of capital in its analysis. These adjustments enabled the Commission to assess whether Wanadoo would be able to secure a return on its investment within a reasonable time, rather than to recover all its costs at once. (Commission Decision, paras 39–109, 257–70)

'The Commission considers that the legal precedents do not cover every possible predation scenario. Predation can take forms other than the radical elimination and wholesale ousting of competitors from the market. More generally, predation may simply consist in dictating or inhibiting the competitive behaviour of an existing or potential rival. Here, a predatory price is simply one which leads to a maximization of profits through its exclusionary or other anticompetitive effects.' (Commission Decision, para 266)

The Commission considered that proof of recoupment of losses is not a precondition for a finding of abuse through predatory pricing. 'While the recoupment of losses initially incurred may constitute a rational objective associated with predation, other scenarios are perfectly conceivable. In certain specific cases, the undertaking may embark upon a strategy of predation with aims other than the achievement of operating margins higher than those which would prevail in a competitive context. For example, in certain highly specific share ownership scenarios, the undertaking may attach only secondary importance to recoupment of its losses. It may also abandon the idea of recouping all its initial losses and concentrate instead on balancing its future costs and revenues. Lastly, it may aim at recoupment in the long term by means other than its operating results.' (Commission Decision, paras 333–9)

Wanadoo appealed to the General Court for the annulment of the Commission's decision, arguing that, among other things, the Commission committed serious errors of law and assessment, in formulating and implementing the test for predatory pricing that it used, and by failing to take account of the highly competitive market context.

Held

'It is clear from the case-law on predatory pricing that, first, prices below average variable costs give grounds for assuming that a pricing practice is eliminatory and that, if the prices are below average total costs but above average variable costs, those prices must be regarded as abusive if they are determined as part of a plan for eliminating a competitor (*AKZO v Commission* … *Tetra Pak v Commission* …).' (para 130)

It is clear from the Commission's decision that the application of the accounting method used in *AKZO* and *Tetra Pak*, which takes into account the costs simply as they appear in the undertaking's accounts, leads in the present case to very low rates of recovery. The Commission therefore corrected the data recorded on Wanadoo's accounts, in favour of Wanadoo, to take account of the particular context of the market. In doing so the Commission did not apply an unlawful test of recovery of costs. (paras 131–54)

Price alignment

'It must be pointed out, first of all, that the Commission is in no way disputing the right of an operator to align its prices on those previously charged by a competitor. It states in recital 315 of the decision that "[w]hilst it is true that the dominant operator is not strictly speaking prohibited from aligning its prices on those of competitors, this option is not open to it where it would result in its not recovering the costs of the service in question". (para 176)

In *AKZO v Commission* the conferral on a dominant undertaking of a right to align its conduct was limited. That observation applies both to the Commission Decision 83/462 making an order for interim measures and the subsequent judgment of the Court of Justice (*AKZO v Commission* … paragraph 134). (para 178)

'Indeed, in Decision 83/462, the Commission did not permit AKZO to align its prices generally on those of its competitors but only, in respect of a particular customer, to align its prices on those of another supplier ready and able to supply to that customer. In addition, that authorisation to align prices in very precise circumstances was not contained in the final decision adopted in that case (Commission Decision 85/609/EEC of 14 December 1985 relating to a proceeding under [Article 102 TFEU] (IV/30.698—*ECS/AKZO Chemie*); [1985] OJ L374, p 1).' (para 179)

'It should be recalled that, according to established case-law, although the fact that an undertaking is in a dominant position cannot deprive it of the right to protect its own commercial interests if they are attacked and such an undertaking must be allowed the right to take such reasonable steps as it deems appropriate to protect those interests, such behaviour cannot be countenanced if its actual purpose is to strengthen this dominant position and abuse it (*United Brands v Commission* … paragraph 189; Case T-65/89 *BPB Industries and British Gypsum v Commission* [1993] ECR II-389, paragraph 117; and *Compagnie Maritime Belge Transports and others v Commission* … paragraph 146).' (para 185)

'[Wanadoo] cannot therefore rely on an absolute right to align its prices on those of its competitors in order to justify its conduct. Even if alignment of prices by a dominant undertaking on those of its competitors is not in itself abusive or objectionable, it might become so where it is aimed not only at protecting its interests but also at strengthening and abusing its dominant position.' (para 187)

No need to prove effect of eliminating competition

'As regards the conditions for the application of [Article 102 TFEU] and the distinction between the object and effect of the abuse, it should be pointed out that, for the purposes of applying that article, showing an anti-competitive object and an anti-competitive effect may, in some cases, be one and the same thing. If it is shown that the object pursued by the conduct of an undertaking in a dominant position is to restrict competition, that conduct will also be liable to have such an effect. Thus, with regard to the practices concerning prices, the Court of Justice held in *AKZO v Commission*, paragraph 100 above, that prices below average variable costs applied by an undertaking in a dominant position are regarded as abusive in themselves because the only interest which the undertaking may have in applying such prices is that of eliminating competitors, and that prices below average total costs but above average variable costs are abusive if they are determined as part of a plan for eliminating a competitor. In that case, the Court did not require any demonstration of the actual effects of the practices in question (see, to that effect, Case T-203/01 *Michelin v Commission* [2003] ECR II-4071, paragraphs 241 and 242).' (para 195)

'Furthermore, it should be added that, where an undertaking in a dominant position actually implements a practice whose object is to oust a competitor, the fact that the result hoped for is not achieved is not sufficient to prevent that being an abuse of a dominant position within the meaning of [Article 102 TFEU] (*Compagnie Maritime Belge Transports and others v Commission*, paragraph 104 above, paragraph 149, and Case T-228/97 *Irish Sugar v Commission* [1999] ECR II-2969, paragraph 191).' (para 196)

'It is clear therefore that, in the case of predatory pricing, the first element of the abuse applied by the dominant undertaking comprises non-recovery of costs. In the case of non-recovery of variable costs, the second element, that is, predatory intent, is presumed, whereas, in relation to prices below average full costs, the existence of a plan to eliminate competition must be proved. According to Case T-83/91 *Tetra Pak v Commission*, paragraph 130 above, paragraph 151, that intention to eliminate competition must be established on the basis of sound and consistent evidence.' (para 197)

Recoupment of losses

'In line with [Union] case-law, the Commission was … able to regard, as abusive, prices below average variable costs. In that case, the eliminatory nature of such pricing is presumed (see, to that effect, Case T-83/91 *Tetra Pak v Commission* … paragraph 148). In relation to full costs, the Commission had also to provide evidence that [Wanadoo's] predatory pricing formed part of a plan to pre-empt the market. In the two situations, it was not necessary to establish in addition proof that [Wanadoo] had a realistic chance of recouping its losses.' (paras 227, 224–8)

Action dismissed.

Comment

The General Court favoured a form-based approach to establishing predation. It rejected arguments concerning the need to demonstrate the actual effects of the practice (paras 195–7) and held that recoupment is not necessary when establishing predation.

In its Guidance Paper the Commission notes that it 'does not consider that it is necessary to show that competitors have exited the market in order to show that there has been anti-competitive foreclosure. The possibility cannot be excluded that the dominant undertaking may prefer to prevent the competitor from competing vigorously and have it follow the dominant undertaking's pricing, rather than eliminate it from the market altogether.' (para 69)

Contrast the General Court's approach with the requirement to show likelihood of recoupment under US law. See in particular the US Supreme Court decision in *Brooke Group Ltd v Brown & Williamson Tobacco Corp* 509 US 940 (1993). Also note the Supreme Court decision in *Weyerhaeuser Co v Ross-Simmons Hardwood Lumber Co Inc* 127 S Ct 1069 (2007), dealing with predatory bidding.

Note also the UK Competition Commission's approach according to which 'in order to prove that an instance of below-cost selling is a predatory strategy, it is necessary to show that there is a strong likelihood that the predator will recoup the profit it has initially sacrificed. If the predator is unlikely to recoup its lost profit, then setting low prices is unlikely to be part of a predatory strategy. Recoupment is more likely the less profit is sacrificed and the greater the added market power the predator gains from excluding the target. Added market power from excluding the target is greater, the closer the target is as a competitor (i.e. the greater the constraint it exerts over the behaviour of the predator, while no other rivals maintain the same degree of competitive pressure) and the greater the barriers to entry and re-entry.' The AKZO test, which presumes predation if costs are below average variable cost, 'may be too rigid a test because of its apparent failure to acknowledge that prices below average variable cost may be set pro-competitively.' (UK Competition Commission 2007 'Pricing Practices Working Paper' (Groceries market inquiry) pages 6, 7). The UK Competition Commission closed on 1 April 2014. Its functions have transferred to the UK Competition and Markets Authority (CMA).

On meeting the competition, note the General Court comments (paras 176–87) in which it held that predatory pricing cannot be justified by an alignment (meeting the competition) argument.

France Télécom SA v Commission	**Article 102 TFEU**
Case C-202/07P	Abuse
Court of Justice [2009] ECR I-2369, [2009] 4 CMLR 25	Predatory Pricing and Recoupment

Facts

An appeal on the General Court judgment in Case T-340/03 (page 208 above) which upheld the Commission decision in which France Télécom was found to have abused its dominant position, among other things, through the charging of predatory prices. On this point, France Télécom argued in its appeal to the Court of Justice that the General Court failed to provide reasoning to support its conclusion that the approach adopted in *Tetra Pak v Commission*, according to which there is no need to prove the possibility of recouping the losses in order to establish predation, applied to this present case. The Court of Justice dismissed the appeal.

Held

The requirement that the General Court give reasons for its decisions does not oblige it to respond in detail to every single argument advanced by a party, especially when such argument was not sufficiently clear and not adequately supported by evidence. In the present case the General Court judgment sets out sufficiently clearly the reasons which led it to find that there is no need to prove recoupment. The General Court made reference to the *AKZO v Commission* and *Tetra Pak v Commission* judgments and applied the reasoning followed by the Court of Justice in *Tetra Pak v Commission* to the present case. (paras 30–36) 'In those circumstances, it must be held that the judgment under appeal sets out sufficiently clearly the reasons which led the [General Court] to find that the circumstances giving rise to the present case, in particular the relationship between the level of prices applied by WIN and the average variable costs and average total costs borne by WIN, were analogous to those in *Tetra Pak* v *Commission*, and to find, accordingly, that proof of recoupment of losses does not constitute a necessary precondition to a finding of predatory pricing.' (para 37)

Comment

The Court of Justice conclusions stand at odds with the opinion of Advocate General Mazák. The AG was of the opinion that the General Court failed to explain why proof of the possibility of recoupment of losses was not necessary in the instant case. According to his opinion, *Tetra Pak II* was tailored to the facts of that case. (para 59) The AG was of the opinion that the case-law requires the possibility of recoupment of losses to be proven. (para 69) 'I consider that, by using the qualifying words "in the circumstances of the present case" in *Tetra Pak II*, the Court clearly intended to avoid making a general statement that would render it unnecessary to prove the possibility of recoupment in future predatory pricing cases. (para 70) 'In my view, it also follows from *AKZO* [in para 71] and *Hoffmann-La Roche* [in para 91] that proof of the possibility of recoupment is required in order to find predation pursuant to [Article 102 TFEU]. Unless there is a possibility of recoupment, the dominant undertaking is probably engaged in normal competition.' (para 73) 'In such a case, where there is no possibility of recouping losses, consumers and their interests should, in principle, not be harmed.'(para 74) 'Finally, I will take this opportunity to point out that, apart from the above case-law, the importance of proof of the possibility of recoupment was brought to the fore inter alia by the Economic Advisory Group on Competition Policy (EAGCP), the Organisation for Economic Co-operation and Development and the European Regulators Group.' (para 75) 'In my concluding remarks on the question of proof of the possibility of recoupment I would like to point out that I am not convinced by the Commission's line of argument that in Europe and under [Article 102 TFEU] recoupment is implied by the dominance, not least because the determination of dominance is often based on historical market conditions, whilst as I explained above proof of the possibility of recoupment is inherently ex ante and forward-looking, assessing the market structure as it will be in the future.' (para 76)

The Commission's Guidance Paper outlines the analytical approach to predatory conduct. (paras 63–74) In it, the Commission briefly mentions the *Tetra Pak II* judgment and that proof of actual recoupment was not required (footnote 46). In the above judgment the Court seem to accept the Commission's reading of *Tetra Pak II*.

Post Danmark A/S v Konkurrencerådet	Article 102 TFEU
Case C-209/10	Selective Price Reductions below ATC
Court of Justice, [2012] 4 CMLR 23	Exclusionary Effect

Facts

A reference for a preliminary ruling from the Danish Supreme Court concerning selective price reductions by Post Danmark A/S (Post Danmark). Post Danmark enjoyed a legal monopoly in the delivery of addressed letters through a national network. It used the same network to distribute unaddressed mail, a market in which it held a dominant position. On that market, Post Danmark approached the clients of its largest competitor, Forbruger-Kontakt, and offered them preferential prices for distribution of unaddressed mail. Post Danmark's prices did not allow it to cover its 'average total costs', but did allow it to cover its 'average incremental costs'. The Danish Competition Council found that the practice did not amount to predatory pricing (as an intention to drive a competitor from the market was not established), but held that it did form an abusive 'secondary-line price discrimination'. The case reached the Danish Supreme Court, which referred a question on the interpretation of Article 102 TFEU and its application to selective price reductions.

Held

Article 102 TFEU condemns practices that cause direct or indirect harm to consumers, through their impact on competition. The Article does not seek to prevent an undertaking from acquiring, on its own merits, a dominant position on a market. Nor does that Article seek to ensure that competitors less efficient than the undertaking with the dominant position should remain on the market. 'Thus, not every exclusionary effect is necessarily detrimental to competition. … Competition on the merits may, by definition, lead to the departure from the market or the marginalisation of competitors that are less efficient and so less attractive to consumers from the point of view of, among other things, price, choice, quality or innovation.' (paras 20–22)

Article 102 TFEU 'prohibits a dominant undertaking from, among other things, adopting pricing practices that have an exclusionary effect on competitors considered to be as efficient as it is itself and strengthening its dominant position by using methods other than those that are part of competition on the merits. Accordingly, in that light, not all competition by means of price may be regarded as legitimate (see, to that effect, *AKZO v Commission*, paragraphs 70 and 72; *France Télécom v Commission*, paragraph 106; and *Deutsche Telekom v Commission*, paragraph 177).' (para 25)

'[T]he fact that the practice of a dominant undertaking may, like the pricing policy in issue in the main proceedings, be described as "price discrimination", that is to say, charging different customers or different classes of customers different prices for goods or services whose costs are the same or, conversely, charging a single price to customers for whom supply costs differ, cannot of itself suggest that there exists an exclusionary abuse.' (para 30)

'In the present case, it emerges from the case-file that, for the purpose of carrying out a price–cost comparison, the Danish competition authorities had recourse, not to the concept of "variable costs" mentioned in the case-law stemming from *AKZO v Commission*, but to another concept, which those authorities termed "incremental costs". In this respect, it can be seen from, in particular, the written observations of the Danish Government and its written replies to the questions asked by the Court, that those authorities defined "incremental costs" as being 'those costs destined to disappear in the short or medium term (three to five years), if Post Danmark were to give up its business activity of distributing unaddressed mail'. In addition, that government stated that "average total costs" were defined as being "average incremental costs to which were added a portion, determined by estimation, of Post Danmark's common costs connected to activities other than those covered by the universal service obligation".' (para 31)

Post Danmark was using the same infrastructure and the same staff for distribution of addressed mail, as part of its universal service obligation, and distributing unaddressed mail. It was therefore relying on 'common distribution network resources' when distributing unaddressed mail. In order to approximate the true cost of that distributing, a portion of the 'common variable costs' was attributable to the activity of distributing unaddressed mail. (paras 31–4)

The analysis revealed that when distributing unaddressed mail to the Coop Group, Post Danmark priced below average total costs and above average incremental costs. That in itself does not give rise to a conclusion of abuse. To the extent 'that a dominant undertaking sets its prices at a level covering the great bulk of the costs attributable to the supply of the goods or services in question, it will, as a general rule, be possible for a competitor as efficient as that undertaking to compete with those prices without suffering losses that are unsustainable in the long term.' Indeed, in this case it appears from the documents before the Court that Forbruger-Kontakt managed to maintain its distribution network despite reduction in the volume of mail and eventually won back the Coop group and other client's custom. (paras 38, 35–9)

Accordingly, 'Article 102 TFEU must be interpreted as meaning that a policy by which a dominant undertaking charges low prices to certain major customers of a competitor may not be considered to amount to an exclusionary abuse merely because the price that undertaking charges one of those customers is lower than the average total costs attributed to the activity concerned, but higher than the average incremental costs pertaining to that activity, as estimated in the procedure giving rise to the case in the main proceedings. In order to assess the existence of anti-competitive effects in circumstances such as those of that case, it is necessary to consider whether that pricing policy, without objective justification, produces an actual or likely exclusionary effect, to the detriment of competition and, thereby, of consumers' interests.' (para 44)

Comment

In its ruling the Court supported an effect-based assessment of pricing policies. The Court made reference to the 'impact on competition' (para 20), noting that 'not every exclusionary effect is necessarily detrimental to competition' (para 22). It also considered the possible effects on an 'as efficient competitor' (para 38) and the 'actual exclusionary effect' (para 44). Interestingly, the Court noted that 'when the existence of a dominant position has its origins in a former legal monopoly, that fact has to be taken into account.' (para 33)

The Court noted that as a general rule when a dominant undertaking sets its prices at a level above average incremental cost (AIC) and covers the great bulk of the costs attributable to the supply of the goods or services, it is not likely that such pricing strategy would exclude an 'as efficient' undertaking. (para 38)

The Court held that the price discrimination cannot of itself establish exclusionary abuse. (para 30)

Akzo formula: Recall that in *Akzo*, the benchmarks used included average variable costs (AVC) and average total cost (ATC). Pricing below AVC was deemed predatory. Pricing below ATC but above AVC could be abusive if the company intended to exclude competitors. Post Danmark's pricing did not constitute predatory pricing as defined in *Akzo* since it priced above AVC and did not have an intention to exclude.

Post Danmark formula: the Court relied on the cost benchmarks used in the main proceedings and set out a complementary analytical framework to that stipulated in *Akzo*. Accordingly, price below average total cost (ATC) and above average incremental cost (AIC) may be abusive if it excludes or is likely to exclude competitors, and the practice has no objective justification.

In its Guidance Paper on Article 102 TFEU, the Commission notes that 'Long-run average incremental cost is the average of all the (variable and fixed) costs that a company incurs to produce a particular product. LRAIC and average total cost (ATC) are good proxies for each other, and are the same in the case of single product undertakings. If multi-product undertakings have economies of scope, LRAIC would be below ATC for each individual product, as true common costs are not taken into account in LRAIC. In the case of multiple products, any costs that could have been avoided by not producing a particular product or range are not considered to be common costs. In situations where common costs are significant, they may have to be taken into account when assessing the ability to foreclose equally efficient competitors.' (footnote 18)

Compagnie Maritime Belge Transports and others v Commission	**Article 102 TFEU**
Joined Cases C-395/96P, 366/96P	Abuse
Court of Justice, [2000] ECR I-1365, [2000] 4 CMLR 1076	Selective Price Cuts Above ATC

Facts

Compagnie Maritime Belge Transports SA (CMB) was found by the Commission to have abused a collective dominant position that it held with other undertakings. Together, the companies formed the membership of a liner conference and implemented a cooperation agreement which aimed, through selective price cuts, to drive an independent competitor out of the market (a practice known as 'fighting ships'). The companies were also found to infringe Article 101 TFEU by entering into a non-competition agreement. The General Court dismissed an application by CMB to annul the Commission's decision. CMB appealed the judgment.

Held

'In certain circumstances, abuse may occur if an undertaking in a dominant position strengthens that position in such a way that the degree of dominance reached substantially fetters competition.' (paras 112–13)

The conduct at issue here is that of a liner conference having a share of over 90 per cent of the market in question and only one competitor. The conference engaged in a practice known as 'fighting ships' in an attempt to eliminate its only competitor from the market. (para 119)

'Where a liner conference in a dominant position selectively cuts its prices in order deliberately to match those of a competitor, it derives a dual benefit. First, it eliminates the principal, and possibly the only, means of competition open to the competing undertaking. Second, it can continue to require its users to pay higher prices for the services which are not threatened by that competition.' (para 117)

Comment

Distinction should be made between a permissible attempt by the dominant firm to meet the competition by lowering prices in a reasonable and proportional manner (above ATC) and an anticompetitive practice of selective price cuts aimed at beating the competition.

Contrast this approach with the US Supreme Court decision in *Brooke Group Ltd v Brown & Williamson Tobacco Corp* 509 US 940 (1993) where the Court held that above-cost price which is below general market levels either reflects 'the lower costs structure of the alleged predator, and so represents competition on the merits, or is beyond the practical ability of a judicial tribunal to control without courting intolerable risks of chilling legitimate price cutting.' In this respect note the special circumstances in CMB which included a collusive action that led to the undertakings' large collective market share, their intention to eliminate all competition in the market, the unique cost structure and characteristics of the maritime transport market, and the ability of the undertakings to share the losses of revenue among themselves. See also AG Fennelly opinion paras 131–7.

See the Commission's decision in Case IV/30.787 *Eurofix-Bauco v Hilti* [1998] OJ L65/19, where it fined Hilti for abusing its dominant position by, among other things, targeting customers of its competitors and offering them especially favourable conditions. These conditions were selective and discriminatory and were not offered to existing customers. The Commission found that 'only a dominant undertaking such as Hilti could carry out such a strategy because it is able, through its market power, to maintain prices to all its other customers unaffected by its selective discriminatory discounts.' (para 80) The decision did not involve assessment of cost structure and was argued on the basis that 'selective discriminatory pricing policy by a dominant firm designed purely to damage the business of, or deter market entry by, its competitors.' (para 81)

Also note the General Court judgment in Case T-228/97 *Irish Sugar v Commission* [1999] ECR II-2969, where the General Court upheld the Commission's decision regarding the abusive nature of selective rebates to customers.

Digital Equipment Corporation	**Article 102 TFEU**
Commission Press Release IP/97/868	Abuse
European Commission (10 October 1997)	Price Alignment

Facts

Following an investigation into the commercial practices of Digital Equipment Corporation (Digital), the Commission issued a formal statement of objections in which it found Digital to have abused its dominant position by developing a commercial policy typified by discriminatory practices and tying.

To resolve the Commission's concerns, Digital offered to modify its service portfolio and pricing practices. The formal undertakings provided by Digital included commitments according to which Digital undertook to pursue a transparent and non-discriminatory discount policy. Although Digital reserved the right to grant non-standard price reductions to meet competition, it undertook to verify that all discounted prices would remain above average total costs, would be proportionate and would not prevent or distort competition. Digital acknowledged that the Commission might initiate proceedings if service prices fall below their average total costs.

Comment

The nature of the commitment regarding meeting the competition highlights the relativity of the dominant company's right to align price. Accordingly, there is no absolute right to align prices.

In Case 27/76 *United Brands v Commission* the Court held that 'although it is true ... that the fact that an undertaking is in a dominant position cannot disentitle it from protecting its own commercial interests if they are attacked, and that such an undertaking must be conceded the right to take such reasonable steps as it deems appropriate to protect its said interests, such behaviour cannot be countenanced if its actual purpose is to strengthen this dominant position and abuse it.' (para 189)

In Case T-228/97 *Irish Sugar v Commission* the General Court held that the grant by Irish Sugar of selective rebates to certain retailers established in the border area between Ireland and Northern Ireland was abusive. The General Court rejected Irish Sugar's argument that its practice was aimed at meeting the competition and was defensive in nature. The defensive nature of the practice did not alter the fact that the practice constituted an abuse for the purposes of Article 102(c) TFEU. (paras 186–7). See page 247 below.

In Case T-340/03 *France Télécom SA v Commission* the General Court held that there is no absolute right to align prices and that predatory pricing cannot be justified by alignment (meeting the competition) argument. The Court held that a dominant company can protect it commercial interests but cannot, in doing so, strengthen its dominant position and abuse it. (paras 176–87) See page 232 above.

Note the Commission's 2005 Discussion Paper where the Commission considers that a meeting-of-competition defence can only apply to individual and not to collective behaviour to meet competition. The action taken by the undertaking needs to be suitable, proportional and indispensable. In this respect, pricing below average avoidable cost (AAC) is in general neither suitable nor indispensable to minimising the dominant company's losses. (paras 81–3)

United Brands v Commission	**Article 102 TFEU**
Case 27/76	Price Discrimination
Court of Justice, [1978] ECR 207, [1978] 1 CMLR 429	

Facts

In a Commission decision, United Brands (UBC) was found to have infringed Article 102 TFEU by abusing its dominant position in the market for bananas. Among the different forms of abuse, UBC was accused of price discrimination. UBC appealed to the Court of Justice and challenged the Commission's conclusions with respect to the market definition, the dominant position and the abuse of the dominant position.

Held

The bananas marketed by UBC under the brand name 'Chiquita' have the same geographic origin, belong to the same variety and are of almost the same quality. They are unloaded in two ports, Rotterdam and Bremerhaven, where unloading costs are similar and are resold (except to Scipio and in Ireland) subject to the same terms of payment and conditions of sale. (paras 204–05)

This being so, UBC customers going to Rotterdam and Bremerhaven to obtain their supplies might be expected to be offered the same selling price for 'Chiquita' bananas. However, this is not the case. UBC's selling price differs appreciably according to the Member State where its customers are established. 'The greatest difference in price is 138% between the delivered Rotterdam price charged by UBC to its customers in Ireland and the f.o.r. Bremerhaven price charged by UBC to its customers in Denmark, that is to say the price paid by Danish customers is 2.38 times the price paid by Irish customers.' The Commission blames UBC for abusing its dominant position by applying dissimilar conditions to equivalent transactions with the other trading parties, thereby placing them at a competitive disadvantage. (paras 213, 207–14)

'The applicant states that its prices are determined by market forces and cannot therefore be discriminatory. Further … the price in any given week is calculated so as to reflect as much as possible the anticipated yellow market price in the following week for each national market. This price is fixed by the Rotterdam management after discussions and negotiations between the applicant's local representatives, and the ripener/distributors must take into account the different competitive contexts in which ripener/distributors in the different countries are operating. It finds its objective justification in the average anticipated market price. These price differences are in fact due to fluctuating market factors such as the weather, different availability of seasonal competing fruit, holidays, strikes, government measures [and] currency denominations.' (paras 215–20)

'In short the applicant has been asked by the Commission to take appropriate steps to establish a single banana market at a time when it has in fact been unable to do so.' (para 221)

'According to the applicant as long as the [Union] institutions have not set up the machinery for a single banana market and the various markets remain national and respond to their individual supply/demand situations, differences in prices between them cannot be prevented.' (para 222)

The price differences in question can reach 30 to 50 per cent in some weeks, even though products supplied under the transactions are equivalent and despite them being freighted in the same ships, and unloaded at the same cost. (paras 223–6)

'[A]lthough the responsibility for establishing the single banana market does not lie with the applicant, it can only endeavour to take 'what the market can bear' provided that it complies with the rules for the Regulation and coordination of the market laid down by the Treaty.' (para 227)

'[O]nce it can be grasped that differences in transport costs, taxation, customs duties, the wages of the labour force, the conditions of marketing, the differences in the parity of currencies, the density of competition may eventually culminate in different retail selling price levels according to the Member States, then it follows those differences are factors which UBC only has to take into account to a limited extent since it sells a product which is always the same and at the same place to ripener/distributors who—alone—bear the risks of the consumers' market.' (para 228)

'[T]he interplay of supply and demand should, owing to its nature, only be applied to each stage where it is really manifest.' (para 229)

'[T]he mechanisms of the market are adversely affected if the price is calculated by leaving out one stage of the market and taking into account the law of supply and demand as between the vendor and the ultimate consumer and not as between the vendor (UBC) and the purchaser (the ripener/distributors).' (para 230)

'[T]hus, by reason of its dominant position UBC, fed with information by its local representatives, was in fact able to impose its selling price on the intermediate purchaser. This price and also the "weekly quota allocated" is only fixed and notified to the customer four days before the vessel carrying the bananas berths.' (para 231)

'[T]hese discriminatory prices, which varied according to the circumstances of the Member States, were … obstacles to the free movement of goods and their effect was intensified by the clause forbidding the resale of bananas while still green and by reducing the deliveries of the quantities ordered.' (para 232)

'[A] rigid partitioning of national markets was thus created at price levels, which were artificially different, placing certain distributor/ripeners at a competitive disadvantage, since compared with what it should have been, competition had thereby been distorted.' (para 233) '[C]onsequently the policy of differing prices enabling UBC to apply dissimilar conditions to equivalent transactions with other trading parties, thereby placing them at a competitive disadvantage, was an abuse of a dominant position.' (para 234)

Comment

The Court accepted that different market conditions may require a supplier to charge different prices in different territories. However, in this case UBC did not operate at the downstream level and could only take these differences into account to a limited extent.

The Court of Justice judgment was criticised as being too formalistic. It ignored the fact that the demand patterns at the downstream level are not confined to that level and are manifested through the distribution channels. In addition it encouraged UBC to charge a flat rate across the EU which would have resulted in consumers in 'cheaper' territories paying more for bananas. Arguably, the judgment was primarily motivated by the Courts's desire to avoid the partitioning of the Internal Market (paras 232–3) and is not necessarily indicative of the approach to price differentiation between markets with different demand patterns.

Note that Article 102(c) TFEU targets discrimination which places other trading parties at a competitive disadvantage. This type of competitive harm is often referred to as second-line injury as it concerns competition between undertakings at the downstream level. Despite this, in *United Brands* it was applied although the distributors did not compete with each other and did not suffer a competitive disadvantage. Similarly, in Case C-18/93 *Corsica Ferries Italia Srl v Corpo dei Piloti del Porto di Genova* [1994] ECR I-1783, the Court of Justice appeared to apply Article 102(c) TFEU without establishing a 'competitive disadvantage'. Interesting in this respect is the comment made by AG Van Gerven in this case: 'It appears implicitly from the [Union] case-law, in particular the judgments in *United Brands* and in *Merci*, that the Court does not interpret [Article 102(c) TFEU] restrictively, with the result that it is not necessary, in order to apply it, that the trading partners of the undertaking responsible for the abuse should suffer a competitive disadvantage against each other or against the undertaking in the dominant position.' (para 34) Contrast these judgments and the above statement from AG Van Gerven with the Court of Justice approach in Case C-95/04 *British Airways v Commission* (page 251 below) and with the CFI's reiteration of this position in Case T-301/04 *Clearstream v Commission* (page 242 below).

Clearstream Banking AG v Commission	**Abuse**
Case T-301/04	Price Discrimination
General Court, [2009] ECR II-3155, [2009] 5 CMLR 24	Competitive Disadvantage

Facts

Clearstream Banking AG was found to abuse its dominant position by refusing to provide cross-border clearing and settlement services to Euroclear Bank SA (EB) and by applying discriminatory prices to EB. (on refusal to supply see page 295 below). Clearstream applied for annulment of the Commission decision. Action dismissed.

Held

Article 102(c) TFEU refers to abuse consisting in 'applying dissimilar conditions to equivalent transactions with other trading parties, thereby placing them at a competitive disadvantage'. 'Thus, according to the case-law, an undertaking may not apply artificial price differences such as to place its customers at a disadvantage and to distort competition (Case T-83/91 *Tetra Pak v Commission* [1994] ECR II-755, paragraph 160, and *Deutsche Bahn* v *Commission*, paragraph 65 above, paragraph 78).' (paras 169, 170)

Clearstream argued that the Commission erred when it based its finding on comparison between two different types of providers of clearing and settlement services (the central securities depository (CSD) and the international central securities depository (ICSD)). According to Clearstream, these groups differ in the nature of the services requested, differ in their business models, transaction volume, and the attributable costs. These arguments must be rejected as the applicant did not establish its claims. The ICSDs and the CSDs constitute two groups of comparable customers. As the securities issued under German law are concerned, the non-German CSDs and the ICSDs operate at the same level and require the same primary services from Clearstream. Subsequently, the Commission did not commit an error of assessment in its finding that the applicants applied discriminatory prices to EB. (paras 159–90)

The prohibition of discrimination in Article 102(c) TFEU requires not only the finding that the behaviour is discriminatory, but also that it causes a competitive disadvantage—in other words, it hinders the competitive position of some of the business partners of that undertaking in relation to the others. 'In that regard, there is nothing to prevent discrimination between business partners who are in a relationship of competition from being regarded as abusive as soon as the behaviour of the undertaking in a dominant position tends, having regard to the whole of the circumstances of the case, to lead to a distortion of competition between those business partners. In such a situation, it cannot be required in addition that proof be adduced of an actual quantifiable deterioration in the competitive position of the business partners taken individually (*British Airways* v *Commission*, ... paragraph 145).' (paras 191–3)

'In the present case, the application to a trading partner of different prices for equivalent services continuously over a period of five years and by an undertaking having a de facto monopoly on the upstream market could not fail to cause that partner a competitive disadvantage.' (para 194)

Comment

The General Court restated the Court of Justice's approach as indicated in Case C-95/04P *British Airways v Commission*, according to which one need to verify the existence of 'competitive disadvantage' under Article 102(c) TFEU. Note, however, that the list of abusive conducts in Article 102 TFEU is not exhaustive and one can target discriminatory pricing outside the realm of Article 102(c) TFEU.

Note Case C-209/10 *Post Danmark A/S v Konkurrencerådet* (page 236 above) in which the Court clarified that 'the fact that the practice of a dominant undertaking may ... be described as "price discrimination" ... cannot of itself suggest that there exists an exclusionary abuse.' (para 30)

Deutsche Bahn AG v Commission	**Article 102 TFEU**
Case T-229/94	Abuse
General Court [1997] ECR II-1689, [1998] 4 CMLR 220	Price Discrimination

'[T]he concept of abuse of a dominant position amounts to prohibiting a dominant undertaking from strengthening its position by using methods other than those which come within the scope of competition on the basis of quality (see, to that effect, Case C-62/86 *AKZO v Commission* [1991] ECR I-3359, paragraph 70). Thus, an undertaking may not apply artificial price differences such as to place its customers at a disadvantage and to distort competition (*Tetra Pak v Commission*, … paragraph 160).' (para 78)

'Furthermore, the existence of an abuse of a dominant position cannot be ruled out by the fact that the undertaking which holds the dominant position has formally entered into an agreement the object of which is the joint fixing of tariffs and which thus falls within the scope of the prohibition of restrictive agreements. The existence of such an agreement does not preclude the possibility that one of the undertakings bound by the agreement might unilaterally impose discriminatory tariffs (see, by analogy, *Ahmed Saeed Flugreisen and Silver Line Reisebüro*, … paragraphs 34 and 37).' (para 79)

'The applicant stated that the differences in price per kilometre were due to the fact that the costs of providing the services were higher on the western journeys than on the northern journeys and to the fact that carriage by rail was subject to stronger inter-modal competition on the western journeys than on the northern journeys. The Court finds, in the first place, that the difference in costs relied on by the applicant was partially created by DB itself. In particular, DB adopted several rationalization measures within the framework of the KLV-Neu tariff structure such as increasing the use of direct and block trains and concentrating on night traffic and on carriage to certain terminals operated on rationalized lines. Those measures enabled costs to be reduced, but only for traffic to and from German ports (see paragraph 83).' (paras 87, 88)

'It is clear from the foregoing considerations that the Commission has adduced sufficient evidence to substantiate its conclusions concerning DB's conduct and that it has proved to the requisite legal standard that, by its conduct, DB imposed dissimilar conditions for equivalent services, thus placing the other parties operating on the western journeys at a disadvantage in competition with itself and its subsidiary Transfracht.' (para 93)

Aéroports de Paris v Commission	**Article 102 TFEU**
Case C-82/01P	Abuse
Court of Justice, [2002] ECR I-9297, [2003] 4 CMLR 12	Discriminatory Fees

'As noted in recital 84 of the grounds of the contested decision, under subparagraph (c) of the second paragraph of [Article 102 TFEU], an undertaking holding a dominant position on the common market or a substantial part thereof may not "apply dissimilar conditions to equivalent transactions with other trading parties, thereby placing them at a competitive disadvantage".' (para 114)

'The [General Court] found, … that the providers of third-party and self-handling services receive the same management services from ADP. From that it correctly inferred, … that it is necessary to take account of both types of groundhandling services for the purpose of ascertaining whether the fees are discriminatory.' (para 115)

'Contrary to ADP's contribution, in those circumstances the [General Court] rightly considered the effects of the self-handling rate of fee on the market for third-party services. Thus, at paragraph 215 of the contested judgment, the [General Court] pointed out that the fact that self-handling is subject to a nil or very low rate of fee means that those authorised to provide both categories of services are able to write off their investments and are able to offer better terms for services provided for third parties. As the [General Court] also pointed out, that nil or very low rate of fee may encourage certain airlines to take up self-handling rather than employ the services of a third party.' (para 116)

Hoffmann-La Roche & Co v Commission	**Article 102 TFEU**
Case 85/76	Abuse
Court of Justice, [1979] ECR 461, [1979] 3 CMLR 211	Rebates

Facts

Hoffmann-La Roche (Roche) applied for the annulment of a Commission decision (IV/29.020—*Vitamins*) which found Roche to have abused its dominant position in the market for vitamins A, B2, B3, B6, C, E and H. In its decision, the Commission argued that exclusivity terms and fidelity rebates, which were part of Roche's network of agreements with large purchasers of vitamins, amounted to an abuse of a dominant position. Roche challenged the decision on several grounds, including the finding of abuse.

Held

'An undertaking which is in a dominant position on a market and ties purchasers—even if it does so on their request—by an obligation or promise on their part to obtain all or most of their requirements exclusively from the said undertaking abuses its dominant position ... whether the obligation in question is stipulated without further qualification or whether it is undertaken in consideration of a grant or rebate. The same applies if the said undertaking, without tying the purchaser by a formal obligation, applies, either under the terms of agreement concluded with these purchasers or unilaterally, a system of fidelity rebates, that is to say, discounts conditional on the customer's obtaining all or most of its requirements—whether the quantity of its purchases being large or small—from the undertaking in a dominant position.' (para 89)

'Obligations of this kind to obtain supplies exclusively from a particular undertaking, whether or not they are in consideration of rebates or of the granting of fidelity rebates intended to give the purchaser an incentive to obtain his supplies exclusively from the undertaking in a dominant position, are incompatible with the objective of undistorted competition within the [internal] market, because—unless there are exceptional circumstances which may make an agreement between undertakings in the context of [Article 101 TFEU] and in particular of paragraph (3) of that Article, permissible—they are not based on an economic transaction which justifies this burden or benefit but are designed to deprive the purchaser of or restrict his possible choices of sources of supply and to deny other producers access to the market. The fidelity rebate, unlike quantity rebates exclusively linked with the volume of purchases from the producer concerned, is designed through the grant of a financial advantage to prevent customers from obtaining their supplies from competing producers. Furthermore the effect of fidelity rebates is to apply dissimilar conditions to equivalent transactions with other trading parties in that two purchasers pay a different price for the same quantity of the same product depending on whether they obtain their supplies exclusively from the undertaking in a dominant position or have several sources of supply. Finally these practices by an undertaking in a dominant position and especially on an expanding market tend to consolidate this position by means of a form of competition which is not based on the transactions effected and is therefore distorted.' (para 90)

'The concept of abuse is an objective concept relating to the behaviour of an undertaking in a dominant position which is such as to influence the structure of a market where, as a result of the very presence of the undertaking in question, the degree of competition is weakened and which, through recourse to methods different from those which condition normal competition in products or services on the basis of the transactions of commercial operators, has the effect of hindering the maintenance of the degree of competition still existing in the market or the growth of that competition.' (para 91)

Fidelity rebates could be in the form of both fixed and progressive rates. The fidelity rebates are characterised by a case-by-case customer assessment, setting individual targets aimed at satisfying a maximum portion of the undertaking's demand for a product. On the other hand, quantitative rebates are set to increase the quantity purchased, are solely linked to the volume of purchase and apply to all purchasers. (paras 94–100)

The Commission was right to regard the contracts containing fidelity rebates as an abuse of a dominant position. An 'English clause' in a contract does not remove the discrimination resulting from the fidelity rebates.

On the contrary, such a clause had provided Roche with information about market conditions and the pricing strategies of its competitors and aggravated the exploitation of its dominant position in an abusive way. (paras 102–08)

Comment

Fidelity rebates are objectionable when they stimulate customers to tie themselves to the dominant undertaking and create de facto exclusivity. Such rebates weaken the structure of competition in the market, strengthen the market power of the already dominant undertaking and act as a barrier to entry. It is therefore irrelevant that the tied undertaking willingly entered into the agreement and is benefiting in the short term from the rebates.

The Court of Justice distinguished between a quantity (volume) rebate and a fidelity rebate which is designed to prevent customers from obtaining their supplies from competing producers. The latter was held abusive when it led purchasers to obtain all or most of their requirements exclusively from the said undertaking. (para 89) Note the form-based language used by the Court when dealing with fidelity rebates. Contrast this with the General Court's comment in *British Airways v Commission* where the General Court noted that fidelity rebates may be economically justified (para 271) and compare with its formalistic approach as evident in para 293. (page 251 below)

In Case C-163/99 *Portuguese Republic v Commission*, [2001] ECR I-2613, [2002] 4 CMLR 31, the Court of Justice held that a volume discount on landing fees which was based on landing frequency of planes was abusive because of its 'de facto' discriminatory application. In that case the volume discount scheme, based on landing frequency, gave the Portuguese companies TAP and Portugalia average discounts of 30 and 22 per cent, respectively, on all their flights, whilst companies from other Member States with fewer planes received discounts of between 1 and 8 per cent. The court held that 'an undertaking occupying a dominant position is entitled to offer its customers quantity discounts linked solely to the volume of purchases made from it. … However, the rules for calculating such discounts must not result in the application of dissimilar conditions to equivalent transactions with other trading parties within the meaning of subparagraph (c) of the second paragraph of [Article 102 TFEU].' (para 50) 'In that connection, it should be noted that it is of the very essence of a system of quantity discounts that larger purchasers of a product or users of a service enjoy lower average unit prices or—which amounts to the same—higher average reductions than those offered to smaller purchasers of that product or users of that service. It should also be noted that even where there is a linear progression in quantity discounts up to a maximum discount, initially the average discount rises (or the average price falls) mathematically in a proportion greater than the increase in purchases and subsequently in a proportion smaller than the increase in purchases, before tending to stabilise at or near the maximum discount rate. The mere fact that the result of quantity discounts is that some customers enjoy in respect of specific quantities a proportionally higher average reduction than others in relation to the difference in their respective volumes of purchase is inherent in this type of system, but it cannot be inferred from that alone that the system is discriminatory.' (para 51) 'None the less, where as a result of the thresholds of the various discount bands, and the levels of discount offered, discounts (or additional discounts) are enjoyed by only some trading parties, giving them an economic advantage which is not justified by the volume of business they bring or by any economies of scale they allow the supplier to make compared with their competitors, a system of quantity discounts leads to the application of dissimilar conditions to equivalent transactions.' (para 52) 'In the absence of any objective justification, having a high threshold in the system which can only be met by a few particularly large partners of the undertaking occupying a dominant position, or the absence of linear progression in the increase of the quantity discounts, may constitute evidence of such discriminatory treatment.' (para 53)

The Commission's Guidance Paper reviews its approach to conditional rebates in paragraphs 37–46. On loyalty rebates, note also paragraphs 151–76 of the Commission's 2005 Discussion Paper.

Nederlandsche Banden Industrie Michelin v Commission	**Article 102 TFEU**
Case 322/81 (Michelin I)	Abuse
Court of Justice, [1983] ECR 3461, [1985] 1 CMLR 282	Rebates

Facts

The Commission found Michelin NV (Michelin) to dominate the market for replacement tyres for buses and lorries. Michelin was further found to have abused this dominant position by operating a series of selective, target-based discounts, and target bonus schemes. The discount system applied by Michelin was based on the fixing of individual and selective sales targets which surpassed the target in the preceding period. The targets were discussed at the beginning of each year between the dealer and Michelin's commercial representative. The discount system and the scale of discounts were not published by Michelin and were not clearly defined in writing after the discussions. Michelin brought an action for annulment before the Court of Justice and argued, among other things, that the discounts were quantitative in nature and were legitimately aimed at inducing dealers to buy more tyres. Accordingly it submitted that the prohibition of these discounts would amount to condemning the dominant undertaking to lose ground and penalising it merely for having a dominant position.

Held

'In contrast to a quantity discount, which is linked solely to the volume of purchases from the manufacturer concerned, a loyalty rebate, which by offering customers financial advantages tends to prevent them from obtaining their supplies from competing manufacturers, amounts to an abuse.' (para 71)

'As regards the system at issue in this case, which is characterized by the use of sales targets, it must be observed that this system does not amount to a mere quantity discount linked solely to the volume of goods purchased since the progressive scale of the previous year's turnover indicates only the limits within which the system applies. Michelin NV has moreover itself pointed out that the majority of dealers who bought more than 3000 tyres a year were in any case in the group receiving the highest rebates. On the other hand, the system in question did not require dealers to enter into any exclusive dealing agreements or to obtain a specific proportion of their supplies from Michelin NV, and that this point distinguishes it from loyalty rebates of the type which the court had to consider in its judgment in *Hoffmann-La Roche*.' (para 72)

'In deciding whether Michelin NV abused its dominant position in applying its discount system it is therefore necessary to consider all the circumstances, particularly the criteria and rules for the grant of the discount, and to investigate whether, in providing an advantage not based on any economic service justifying it, the discount tends to remove or restrict the buyer's freedom to choose his sources of supply, to bar competitors from access to the market, to apply dissimilar conditions to equivalent transactions with other trading parties or to strengthen the dominant position by distorting competition.' (para 73)

The discount system in question was based on an annual reference period. This relatively long reference period has the inherent effect, at the end of that period, of increasing pressure on the buyer to reach the purchase figure needed to obtain the discount or to avoid suffering the expected loss for the entire period. In such circumstances, when the last order may affect the rate of discount over the whole year, it puts dealers under appreciable pressure since it has a significant impact on its profit. (para 81)

Michelin's large market share increased the impact of this practice. 'If a competitor wished to offer a dealer a competitive inducement for placing an order, especially at the end of the year, it had to take into account the absolute value of Michelin NV's annual target discount and fix its own discount at a percentage which, when related to the dealer's lesser quantity of purchases from that competitor, was very high. Despite the apparently low percentage of Michelin NV's discount, it was therefore very difficult for its competitors to offset the benefits or losses resulting for dealers from attaining or failing to attain Michelin NV's targets, as the case might be.' (para 82)

The lack of transparency of Michelin's discount system and the absence of written documentation of the target and discount sales created additional uncertainty and pressure. This was especially noticeable toward the end of a year, when dealers needed to attain Michelin's sales targets. (paras 83, 84)

The impact of this discount scheme was to prevent dealers from freely selecting the best available offers from the different competitors and to change suppliers accordingly. Subsequently, as it limited the dealers' choice of supplier it made access to the market more difficult for competitors. Such a discount system amounts to an abuse of Article 102 TFEU. (paras 85, 86)

Comment

The discount scheme was condemned due to the use of individual progressing sales targets, the long reference period and the lack of transparency.

On the use of individual progressing sales targets, note the General Court judgment in Case T-228/97 *Irish Sugar plc v Commission* [1999] ECR II-2969, where the Court confirmed the Commission's objection to a sale target which was based on an increase in sales in comparison to the preceding period. (para 203) Also note Case T-219/99 *British Airways v Commission* (page 251 below).

In its Guidance Paper the Commission elaborates on the foreclosure effect of conditional rebates and states: 'As with exclusive purchasing obligations, the likelihood of anti-competitive foreclosure is higher where competitors are not able to compete on equal terms for the entire demand of each individual customer. A conditional rebate granted by a dominant undertaking may enable it to use the "non contestable" portion of the demand of each customer (that is to say, the amount that would be purchased by the customer from the dominant undertaking in any event) as leverage to decrease the price to be paid for the "contestable" portion of demand (that is to say, the amount for which the customer may prefer and be able to find substitutes).' (para 39) 'In general terms, retroactive rebates may foreclose the market significantly, as they may make it less attractive for customers to switch small amounts of demand to an alternative supplier, if this would lead to loss of the retroactive rebates. The potential foreclosing effect of retroactive rebates is in principle strongest on the last purchased unit of the product before the threshold is exceeded. However, what is in the Commission's view relevant for an assessment of the loyalty enhancing effect of a rebate is not simply the effect on competition to provide the last individual unit, but the foreclosing effect of the rebate system on (actual or potential) competitors of the dominant supplier. The higher the rebate as a percentage of the total price and the higher the threshold, the greater the inducement below the threshold and, therefore, the stronger the likely foreclosure of actual or potential competitors.' (para 40) The Commission will examine whether the rebate system may hinder expansion or entry by 'as efficient competitors' by estimating 'what price a competitor would have to offer in order to compensate the customer for the loss of the conditional rebate if the latter would switch part of its demand ("the relevant range") away from the dominant undertaking. The effective price that the competitor will have to match is not the average price of the dominant undertaking, but the normal (list) price less the rebate the customer loses by switching, calculated over the relevant range of sales and in the relevant period of time. The Commission will take into account the margin of error that may be caused by the uncertainties inherent in this kind of analysis.' (para 41)

Note that while the reliance on the 'non contestable' and 'contestable' portions of demand in the Guidance Paper provides a useful measure, its practical application is challenging. One can question, for example the ability of a dominant firm to accurately assess these variables. Similar difficulties in measurement may be attributed to the Commission proposal to examine conditional rebates by estimating the price a competitor would have to offer a customer in order to compensate the customer for the loss of the conditional rebate if they switched part of their demand away from the dominant firm. Here again, lack of access to such information and the difficulty of calculating the relevant measurement makes the benchmark a suboptimal tool for guiding the conduct of dominant undertakings.

Manufacture Française des Pneumatiques Michelin v Commission	**Article 102 TFEU**
Case T-203/01 (Michelin II)	Abuse
General Court, [2003] ECR II-4071, [2004] 4 CMLR 18	Rebates

Facts

This case concerned the commercial policy pursued by Michelin in the French markets for new replacement tyres for trucks and for retreaded tyres for trucks. The Commission found Michelin to have abused its dominant position on this market via, among other things, its loyalty-inducing rebate system. An action for annulment before the General Court.

Held

A quantity rebate system linked solely to the volume of purchases made from a dominant undertaking is generally considered not to have the foreclosure effect prohibited by Article 102 TFEU. On the other hand a loyalty rebate, which is granted by a dominant undertaking in return for an undertaking by the customer to obtain his stock exclusively or almost exclusively from an undertaking in a dominant position, is contrary to Article 102 TFEU. Such a rebate is designed through the grant of financial advantage, to prevent customers from obtaining their supplies from competing producers. It thus has a foreclosure effect on the market and therefore is regarded as contrary to Article 102 TFEU. (paras 56–8)

'It follows that a rebate system in which the rate of the discount increases according to the volume purchased will not infringe [Article 102 TFEU] unless the criteria and rules for granting the rebate reveal that the system is not based on an economically justified countervailing advantage but tends, following the example of a loyalty and target rebate, to prevent customers from obtaining their supplies from competitors …' (para 59)

In assessing rebate systems it is necessary to consider in particular 'the criteria and rules governing the grant of the rebate, and to investigate whether, in providing an advantage not based on any economic service justifying it, the rebates tend to remove or restrict the buyer's freedom to choose his sources of supply, to bar competitors from access to the market, to apply dissimilar conditions to equivalent transactions with other trading parties or to strengthen the dominant position by distorting competition'. (para 60)

The mere fact that an undertaking characterises a discount system as 'quantity rebates' does not mean that the grant of such discounts is compatible with Article 102 TFEU. (para 62)

A loyalty-inducing rebate system applied by a dominant undertaking has foreclosure effects prohibited by Article 102 TFEU, irrespective of whether or not the rebate system is discriminatory. In the present case, the Commission concluded that the rebate system constitutes an infringement of Article 102 TFEU because it is unfair, it is loyalty-inducing and it has a partitioning effect. (paras 64–5)

'This Court considers that it is necessary, first, to consider whether the Commission had good reason to conclude, in the contested decision, that the quantity rebate system was loyalty-inducing or, in other words, that it sought to tie dealers to the applicant and to prevent them from obtaining supplies from the applicant's competitors. As the Commission acknowledges in its defence, moreover, the alleged unfairness of the system was closely linked to its loyalty-inducing effect. Furthermore, it must be held that a loyalty- inducing rebate system is, by its very nature, also partitioning, since it is designed to prevent the customer from obtaining supplies from other manufacturers.' (para 66)

The Quantity Rebates (these provided for an annual refund expressed as a percentage of the turnover achieved by the dealer)

Although a dominant undertaking can take reasonable steps to protect its commercial interests, not all competition on price can be regarded as legitimate. A loyalty-inducing discount system which seeks to tie dealers to a dominant undertaking by granting advantages which are not based on a countervailing economic advantage and seeks to prevent those dealers from obtaining their supplies from the undertaking's competitors infringes Article 102 TFEU. A quantity rebate system is compatible with Article 102 TFEU if the advantage conferred on dealers is economically justified by the volume of business they bring or by any economies of scale they allow the supplier to make. (paras 74–101)

'A quantity rebate system in which there is a significant variation in the discount rates between the lower and higher steps, which has a reference period of one year and in which the discount is fixed on the basis of total turnover achieved during the reference period, has the characteristics of a loyalty-inducing discount system.' (para 95)

Michelin failed to establish that the quantity rebate system, which presents the characteristics of a loyalty-inducing rebate system, was based on objective economic reasons. The fact that the rebate system was transparent does not affect this conclusion. A loyalty-inducing rebate system is contrary to Article 102 TFEU, whether it is transparent or not. (paras 107–11)

The Commission was therefore entitled to conclude, that 'the quantity rebate system at issue was designed to tie truck tyre dealers in France to the applicant by granting advantages which were not based on any economic justification. Because it was loyalty-inducing, the quantity rebate system tended to prevent dealers from being able to select freely at any time, in the light of the market situation, the most advantageous of the offers made by various competitors and to change supplier without suffering any appreciable economic disadvantage. The rebate system thus limited the dealers' choice of supplier and made access to the market more difficult for competitors, while the position of dependence in which the dealers found themselves, and which was created by the discount system in question, was not therefore based on any countervailing advantage which might be economically justified.' (para 110)

The Service Bonus (this was paid to specialist dealers, who achieved a minimum annual turnover, to improve their facilities and after-sales service)

Michelin argued that the aim of the service bonus was to encourage dealers to improve the quality of their services and the brand image of Michelin products through remuneration. This reward system was fixed annually by mutual agreement with the dealer according to the commitments entered into by him.

The Court pointed out that the fact that the service bonus remunerates services rendered by the dealer and is not formed as a discount has no relevance for the purpose of Article 102 TFEU. The question under Article 102 TFEU is whether the service bonus system was unfair and loyalty-inducing and had a tied sales effect.

'The granting of a discount by an undertaking in a dominant position to a dealer must be based on an objective economic justification. … It cannot depend on a subjective assessment by the undertaking in a dominant position of the extent to which the dealer has met his commitments and is thus entitled to a discount. As the Commission points out in the contested decision … [that] such an assessment of the extent to which the dealer has met his commitments enables the undertaking in a dominant position "to put strong pressure on the dealer … and allow[s] it, if necessary, to use the arrangement in a discriminatory manner".' (para 140)

'It follows that a discount system which is applied by an undertaking in a dominant position and which leaves that undertaking a considerable margin of discretion as to whether the dealer may obtain the discount must be considered unfair and constitutes an abuse by an undertaking of its dominant position on the market within the meaning of [Article 102 TFEU]. …Because of the subjective assessment of the criteria giving entitlement to the service bonus, dealers were left in uncertainty and on the whole could not predict with any confidence the rate of discount which they would receive by way of service bonus.' (para 141)

Analysing 'Effect'

Michelin argued that the Commission did not examine the actual economic effect of the criticised practices and that such examination would have revealed that the conduct in question did not have the effect of either reinforcing its position or limiting the degree of competition on the market. In support of its argument, Michelin referred to the consistent line of decisions which show that 'an "abuse" is an objective concept referring to the behaviour of an undertaking in a dominant position which is such as to influence the structure of a market and which has the effect of hindering the maintenance of the degree of competition still existing in the market or the growth of that competition.' (paras 236, 238)

'The Court points out that [Article 102 TFEU] prohibits, in so far as it may affect trade between Member States, any abuse of a dominant position within the [internal] market or in a substantial part thereof. Unlike [Article 101(1) TFEU, [Article 102 TFEU] contains no reference to the anti-competitive aim or anti-competitive effect of the practice referred to. However, in the light of the context of [Article 102 TFEU], conduct will be regarded as abusive only if it restricts competition.' (para 237)

The 'effect' referred to in the case-law cited by Michelin does not necessarily relate to the actual effect of the abusive conduct complained of. 'For the purposes of establishing an infringement of [Article 102 TFEU], it is sufficient to show that the abusive conduct of the undertaking in a dominant position tends to restrict competition or, in other words, that the conduct is capable of having that effect.' (para 239)

'For the purposes of applying [Article 102 TFEU], establishing the anti-competitive object and the anti-competitive effect are one and the same thing. … If it is shown that the object pursued by the conduct of an undertaking in a dominant position is to limit competition, that conduct will also be liable to have such an effect.' (para 241)

'In the contested decision, the Commission demonstrated that the purpose of the discount systems applied by the applicant was to tie the dealers to the applicant. Those practices tended to restrict competition because they sought, in particular, to make it more difficult for the applicant's competitors to enter the relevant market.' (para 244)

Comment

The General Court accepted in paragraph 59 that a rebate system based on economically justified advantages will not infringe Article 102 TFEU. However, it later favored a simplified distinction between discounts which are economically justifiable and loyalty discounts which are regarded as abusive. The rhetoric of the Court considers all loyalty-inducing discounts as abusive notwithstanding the actual effect on competition. Note especially paragraphs 237 and 239, where the Court established what may be regarded as a low threshold for proving abuse, finding that abuse could be a behaviour 'capable of limiting competition'. In the context of rebates, this low benchmark may result in a chilling effect on competition. Compare this statement with paragraph 293, *British Airways v Commission* (page 252 below).

The use of a low threshold to establish the abusive nature of rebates results in a formalistic per se restriction which does not involve an analysis of anticompetitive effects. At the practical level, this raises difficulties when dealing with borderline cases in which the company may or may not be dominant. In addition it categorically forbids discount schemes which may have efficiency justifications. At the policy level, this stands at odds to the Commission's attempt to advance an effect based approach to Article 102 TFEU.

According to the judgment, it was for Michelin to prove that the discount system was economically justifiable. The burden of proof was therefore on Michelin to show that the discounts reflect cost savings. Michelin failed to establish that the quantity rebate system, which presents the characteristics of a loyalty-inducing rebate system, was based on objective economic reasons. (paras 107–10).

With respect to the reference period, in its decision the Commission stated that the Court of Justice has ruled against the granting of quantity rebates by a dominant undertaking where the rebates exceed a reasonable period of three months on the grounds that such a practice is not in line with normal competition based on prices. The General Court rejected this proposition and noted that the Court of Justice did not expressly hold that the reference period could not exceed three months.

British Airways v Commission	**Article 102 TFEU**
Case T-219/99	Abuse
General Court, [2003] ECR II-5917, [2004] 4 CMLR 19	Rebates

Facts

British Airways (BA) operated a range of target incentives which were offered to travel agents. These commission schemes had one notable feature in common; in each case, meeting the targets for sales growth led to an increase in the commission paid on all tickets sold by the travel agent, not just on the tickets sold after the target was reached. The Commission found that this practice amounted to an abuse of BA's dominant position. More specifically, it asserted that BA's reward schemes caused discrimination between travel agents and produced an exclusionary effect in relation to competing airlines. BA brought an action for annulment before the General Court, among other things on the ground of lack of abuse.

Held

On the Finding of Discrimination

The target schemes led to an increase in the commission paid on all tickets sold during the reference period. Subsequently, two travel agents who sell different numbers of BA tickets may receive the same payments and two agents who sell the same number of BA tickets may receive different incentive payments. 'By remunerating at different levels, services that were nevertheless identical and supplied during the same reference period, those performance reward schemes distorted the level of remuneration which the parties concerned received in the form of commissions paid by BA.' The Commission was right to hold that this practice produced discriminatory effects within the network of travel agents, thereby inflicting on some of them a competitive disadvantage within the meaning of Article 102(c) TFEU. (paras 233–40)

On the Finding of Exclusionary Effect

Although an undertaking in a dominant position cannot be deprived of its entitlement to take reasonable steps to protect its commercial interests when they are attacked, such behaviour cannot be allowed if its purpose is to strengthen that dominant position and thereby abuse it. (para 243)

A fidelity rebate, granted by a dominant undertaking which has the effect of preventing customers from obtaining supplies from market competitors will be regarded as contrary to Article 102 TFEU, irrespective of whether the rebate system is discriminatory. The same applies to a 'fidelity-building' performance reward scheme practised by a purchaser in a dominant position in relation to its suppliers of services. (paras 244–9)

'In order to determine whether BA abused its dominant position by applying its performance reward schemes … it is necessary to consider the criteria and rules governing the granting of those rewards, and to investigate whether, in providing an advantage not based on any economic service justifying it, they tended to remove or restrict the agents' freedom to sell their services to the airlines of their choice and thereby hinder the access of BA's competitor airlines to the United Kingdom market for air travel agency services'. (para 270)

'It needs to be determined in this case whether the marketing agreements and the new performance reward scheme had a fidelity-building effect in relation to travel agents established in the United Kingdom and, if they did, whether those schemes were based on an economically justified consideration.' (para 271)

(i) The Fidelity-Building Character

'Concerning, first, the fidelity-building character of the schemes in question, the Court finds that, by reason of their progressive nature with a very noticeable effect at the margin, the increased commission rates were capable of rising exponentially from one reference period to another, as the number of BA tickets sold by agents during successive reference periods progressed.' (para 272)

'Conversely, the higher revenues from BA ticket sales were, the stronger was the penalty suffered by the persons concerned in the form of a disproportionate reduction in the rates of performance rewards, even in the case of a slight decrease in sales of BA tickets compared with the previous reference period. BA cannot therefore deny the fidelity-building character of the schemes in question.' (para 273)

(ii) Economically Justified Consideration

'Concerning, secondly, the question whether the performance reward schemes applied by BA were based on an economically justified consideration, it is true that the fact that an undertaking is in a dominant position cannot deprive it of its entitlement, within reason, to perform the actions which it considers appropriate in order to protect its own commercial interests when they are threatened.' (para 279)

In order for such protection to be lawful, BA's scheme must, at the very least, be based on criteria of economic efficiency. In this case, the higher rates of commission were applied on all BA tickets handled during the reference period and not only on the tickets sold once those sales targets had been met. The additional remuneration of the agents cannot be regarded as constituting the consideration for efficiency gains or cost savings. 'On the contrary, that retrospective application of increased commission rates to all BA tickets sold by a travel agent during the reference period in question must even be regarded as likely to entail the sale of certain BA tickets at a price disproportionate to the productivity gain obtained by BA from the sale of those extra tickets.' (paras 280–85)

'Contrary to what BA maintains, its performance reward schemes could not therefore constitute a mode of exercise of the normal operation of competition or allow it to reduce its costs. The opposite arguments by BA in that regard are not capable of demonstrating that its performance reward schemes had an objective economic justification.' (para 291)

'BA cannot accuse the Commission of failing to demonstrate that its practices produced an exclusionary effect. In the first place, for the purposes of establishing an infringement of [Article 102 TFEU], it is not necessary to demonstrate that the abuse in question had a concrete effect on the markets concerned. It is sufficient in that respect to demonstrate that the abusive conduct of the undertaking in a dominant position tends to restrict competition, or, in other words, that the conduct is capable of having, or likely to have, such an effect.' (para 293)

'[W]here an undertaking in a dominant position actually puts into operation a practice generating the effect of ousting its competitors, the fact that the hoped-for result is not achieved is not sufficient to prevent a finding of abuse of a dominant position within the meaning of [Article 102 TFEU].' (para 297)

'Moreover, the growth in the market shares of some of BA's airline competitors, which was modest in absolute value having regard to the small size of their original market shares, does not mean that BA's practices had no effect. In the absence of those practices, it may legitimately be considered that the market shares of those competitors would have been able to grow more significantly (see, to that effect, *Compagnie Maritime Belge Transports*, paragraph 149).' (para 298)

Comment

Most striking is the General Court's formalistic approach and the holding that the proof of effect is not required (para 293) This stands at odds with the Commission's effects-based agenda as manifested in its Guidance and in its assessment of rebates in the *Prokent/Tomra* decision (page 255 below).

Interestingly, despite the fact that BA's competitors gained market share during that period, the Court did not consider this to affect its conclusion. (para 298) The growth in market share could have been used as an indication of lack of anticompetitive effect, yet the General Court considered it possible that absent BA's discount practice the competitors' market share would have grown even faster. This might have been the case, yet it is questionable whether the fact that a competitor is not better off should be used as a proxy to consumer harm.

British Airways v Commission	**Article 102 TFEU**
Case C-95/04P	Abuse
Court of Justice, [2007] CEC 607, [2007] 4 CMLR 22	Rebates

Facts

British Airways (BA) brought an appeal on the General Court judgment in Case T-219/99 (see page 251 above) in which the General Court dismissed its action for the annulment of Commission Decision (IV/D 2/34.780—*Virgin/British Airways*). On appeal, BA argued, among other things, that the General Court erred in its analysis of the exclusionary effects and fidelity-building effects of its bonus scheme and in the application of Article 102(c) TFEU. Appeal dismissed.

Held

'In order to determine whether the undertaking in a dominant position has abused such a position by applying a system of [fidelity discounts] … the Court has held that it is necessary to consider all the circumstances, particularly the criteria and rules governing the grant of the discount, and to investigate whether, in providing an advantage not based on any economic service justifying it, the discount tends to remove or restrict the buyer's freedom to choose his sources of supply, to bar competitors from access to the market, to apply dissimilar conditions to equivalent transactions with other trading parties or to strengthen the dominant position by distorting competition (*Michelin*, paragraph 73).' (para 67)

'It then needs to be examined whether there is an objective economic justification for the discounts and bonuses granted. In accordance with the analysis carried out by the [General Court] in paragraphs 279 to 291 of the judgment under appeal, an undertaking is at liberty to demonstrate that its bonus system producing an exclusionary effect is economically justified.' (para 69)

Exclusionary Effect

Goal-related discounts or bonuses, that is to say those the granting of which is linked to the attainment of sales objectives defined individually, may give rise to an exclusionary effect. It is clear from the General Court judgment that the bonus schemes at issue were drawn up by reference to individual sales objectives, since the rate of the bonuses depended on the evolution of the turnover arising from BA ticket sales by each travel agent during a given period. (paras 70–72)

Long Reference Period

'It is also apparent from the case-law that the commitment of co-contractors toward the undertaking in a dominant position and the pressure exerted upon them, may be particularly strong where a discount or bonus does not relate solely to the growth in turnover in relation to purchases or sales of products of that undertaking made by those co-contractors during the period under consideration, but extends also to the whole of the turnover relating to those purchases or sales. In that way, relatively modest variations—whether upward or downward—in the turnover figures relating to the products of the dominant undertaking have disproportionate effects on co-contractors (see, to that effect, *Michelin*, paragraph 81).' (para 73)

The General Court found that the bonus schemes at issue gave rise to a similar situation. 'Attainment of the sales progression objectives gave rise to an increase in the commission paid on all BA tickets sold by the travel agent concerned, and not just on those sold after those objectives had been attained …' (para 74)

Objective Economic Justification

'Discounts or bonuses granted to its co-contractors by an undertaking in a dominant position are not necessarily an abuse and therefore prohibited by [Article 102 TFEU]. According to consistent case-law, only discounts or bonuses which are not based on any economic counterpart to justify them must be regarded as an abuse (see, to that effect, *Hoffmann-La Roche*, paragraph 90, and *Michelin*, paragraph 73).' (para 84)

'Assessment of the economic justification for a system of discounts or bonuses established by an undertaking in a dominant position is to be made on the basis of the whole of the circumstances of the case (see, to that effect, Michelin, paragraph 73) …' The General Court did not err in its finding that BA's bonus scheme was not based on any objective economic justification (paras 86, 86–91)

Probable Effects

'Concerning BA's argument that the [General Court] did not examine the probable effects of the bonus schemes at issue, it is sufficient to note that, in paragraphs 272 and 273 of the judgment under appeal, the [General Court] explained the mechanism of those schemes. Having emphasised the very noticeable effect at the margin, linked to the progressive nature of the increased commission rates, it described the exponential effect on those rates of an increase in the number of BA tickets sold during successive periods, and, conversely, the disproportionate reduction in those rates in the event of even a slight decrease in sales of BA tickets in comparison with the previous period. On that basis, the [General Court] was able to conclude, without committing any error of law, that the bonus schemes at issue had a fidelity-building effect. It follows that BA's plea accusing the Court of not examining the probable effects of those schemes is unfounded.' (paras 96–8)

Article 102(c) TFEU—The Findings of a Competitive Disadvantage

'The specific prohibition of discrimination in subparagraph (c) of the second paragraph of [Article 102 TFEU] forms part of the system for ensuring, in accordance with Article 3(1)(g) EC [now repealed], that competition is not distorted in the internal market. The commercial behaviour of the undertaking in a dominant position may not distort competition on an upstream or a downstream market, in other words between suppliers or customers of that undertaking. Co-contractors of that undertaking must not be favoured or disfavoured in the area of the competition which they practise amongst themselves.' (para 143)

'Therefore, in order for the conditions for applying subparagraph (c) of the second paragraph of [Article 102 TFEU] to be met, there must be a finding not only that the behaviour of an undertaking in a dominant market position is discriminatory, but also that it tends to distort that competitive relationship, in other words to hinder the competitive position of some of the business partners of that undertaking in relation to the others (see, to that effect, Suiker Unie, paragraphs 523 and 524).' (para 144)

'In that respect, there is nothing to prevent discrimination between business partners who are in a relationship of competition from being regarded as being abusive as soon as the behaviour of the undertaking in a dominant position tends, having regard to the whole of the circumstances of the case, to lead to a distortion of competition between those business partners. In such a situation, it cannot be required in addition that proof be adduced of an actual quantifiable deterioration in the competitive position of the business partners taken individually.' (para 145)

Comment

The Court of Justice upheld the General Court judgment in a relatively short and formalistic decision. It confirmed that the list of abusive behaviour in Article 102 TFEU is not exhaustive and upheld the General Court finding concerning fidelity-building effects. The Court of Justice did not accept BA's arguments concerning the examination of actual effects and consumer harm. The decision adds little to existing case law on rebates and as such stands at odds with the effect-based approach to Article 102 TFEU as manifested in recent years by the Commission.

Note the clear statement concerning Article 102(c) TFEU and the requirement for competitive disadvantage. Contrast this with *United Brands* (page 240 above) and *Corsica Ferries* (page 241 above). Note, however, that the list of abusive conduct in Article 102 TFEU is not exhaustive and abusive discrimination may be established outside the realm of Article 102(c) TFEU.

Tomra Systems and Others v Commission	**Article 102 TFEU**
Case C-549/10P	Abuse
Court of Justice, [2012] 4 CMLR 27	Rebates

Facts

Tomra group was active in the market for reverse vending machines. These machines are used in supermarkets and outlets to collect used drinks containers in return for a deposit. The Commission found that the Tomra group had abused its dominant position in the market for reverse vending machines. The abuse consisted of a system of exclusivity agreements, quantity commitments and loyalty-inducing discounts. The Commission found these activities foreclosed the market to competition. Subsequently, the Commission imposed a €24 million fine on Tomra for abusing its dominant position (*Prokent/Tomra* COMP/E-1/38.113). In its decision the Commission noted that in order to establish an abuse under Article 102 TFEU it is sufficient to show that the conduct in question tends to restrict competition. Nonetheless, the Commission completed its analysis in this case by considering the likely effects of Tomra's practices on the market (para 332).

One of the contentious issues in this case was the actual 'suction effect' generated by Tomra's discounts scheme. Tomra's economic analysis was aimed at showing that only less than a third of the rebate schemes referred to by the Commission could be considered exclusionary. It argued that the majority of rebates had no foreclosure effects and are thus permissible. The Commission rejected Tomra's *ex post* economic model. It argued that the *ex post* empirical evidence 'cannot be considered meaningful, because it relates to actual as opposed to expected demand'. It rejected Tomra's claim that its rebate threshold was set below the level of demand and thus has no foreclosure effect. The Commission was of the opinion that Tomra's economic model 'requires irrationality on the incumbents side … it is clear that the incumbent is better off setting the threshold at expected demand.' Subsequently, if the scheme satisfies customers demand, it is expected to produce a suction effect. (paras 373, 375, 364–90)

Tomra brought an action for the annulment of the decision. Case T-155/06 *Tomra Systems and others v Commission* [2011] 4 CMLR 7. The action was dismissed by the General Court. The General Court noted that 'The Commission, even though the case-law does not require it, also analysed, in the light of market conditions, the actual effects of the applicants' practices.' (para 219) The Court further noted that 'It is thus clear that the Commission did not attempt to base its finding of an infringement of [Article 102 TFEU] on that consideration of the actual effects of the applicants' practices on each of the national markets examined but that it merely complemented its finding of infringement with a brief examination of the likely effects of those practices.' It is therefore not necessary to consider whether the evidence adduced by the Commission demonstrated actual elimination of competition. (paras 288–90)

With respect to the foreclosure effect of its rebates, Tomra argued that even if the agreements in question might have had such effects, they would apply to existing customers, but competitors would remain free to seek the business of other undertakings. Accordingly, it argued that a competitor could have profitably remained on the market by serving only the contestable part of the market. This argument was rejected by the General Court. 'The foreclosure by a dominant undertaking of a substantial part of the market cannot be justified by showing that the contestable part of the market is still sufficient to accommodate a limited number of competitors. First, the customers on the foreclosed part of the market should have the opportunity to benefit from whatever degree of competition is possible on the market and competitors should be able to compete on the merits for the entire market and not just for a part of it. Second, it is not the role of the dominant undertaking to dictate how many viable competitors will be allowed to compete for the remaining contestable portion of demand.' (paras 231–42) Tomra argued that competitors would have been able to earn positive revenues from their sales and that where retroactive rebates lead to positive prices, it cannot be presumed that they will necessarily be capable of producing exclusionary effects. The General Court rejected that approach and held that the fact that the retroactive rebate schemes oblige competitors to ask 'negative prices' from customers benefiting from rebates cannot be regarded as fundamental to show that retroactive rebate schemes are capable of anti-competitive effects. (paras 247–60) Tomra appealed to the Court of Justice. Appeal dismissed.

Held

It must be recalled that the concept of abuse of a dominant position prohibited by Article 102 TFEU is an objective concept. None the less, the Commission, as part of its examination is obliged to consider all of the relevant facts surrounding that conduct. For that purpose, it is legitimate for the Commission to refer to subjective factors, namely the motives underlying the business strategy in question. (paras 17–19)

The General Court properly approved the Commission's reasoning that, by foreclosing a significant part of the market, the Tomra group had restricted entry to one or a few competitors and thus limited the intensity of competition on the market as a whole. (para 41) '[T]he General Court was correct to hold that the determination of a precise threshold of foreclosure of the market beyond which the practices at issue had to be regarded as abusive was not required for the purposes of applying Article 102 TFEU.' (para 46)

'The General Court was correct to observe, in paragraph 289 of the judgment under appeal, that, for the purposes of proving an abuse of a dominant position within the meaning of Article 102 TFEU, it is sufficient to show that the abusive conduct of the undertaking in a dominant position tends to restrict competition or that the conduct is capable of having that effect.' (para 68)

'Contrary to what is claimed by the appellants, the invoicing of "negative prices", in other words prices below cost prices, to customers is not a prerequisite of a finding that a retroactive rebates scheme operated by a dominant undertaking is abusive.' (para 73)

'The General Court was justified in ruling that the loyalty mechanism was inherent in the supplier's ability to drive out its competitors by means of the suction to itself of the contestable part of demand. When such a trading instrument exists, it is therefore unnecessary to undertake an analyse of the actual effects of the rebates on competition given that, for the purposes of establishing an infringement of Article 102 TFEU, it is sufficient to demonstrate that the conduct at issue is capable of having an effect on competition, as recalled in paragraph 68 of this judgment.' (para 79)

Comment

The Court of Justice and General Court reaffirmed the 'formalistic' approach manifested in the case law and confirmed that the Commission was not required to engage in the examination of actual effects. The Commission's analysis of actual effects only complemented the analysis of whether the rebates 'tend to restrict competition'. Subsequently, even if the Commission erred in the analysis of actual effects, that would not undermine the legality of the decision. In essence, the Court's approach reaffirms the lower form-based threshold of abuse and refrains from endorsing the Commission's novel approach which is outlined in the Guidance Paper.

This form-based threshold for finding of abuse is lower than the self-imposed 'actual effect' threshold used by the Commission and advocated in the Guidance Paper. The practical implication of the European Court's approach is that an appeal on a Commission's finding that rebates resulted in 'actual effect' which hampered the ability of an 'as efficient competitor' to operate on the market will not succeed when the Commission correctly established that the loyalty rebate was 'capable of having such effect'.

Note the opinion of AG Mazák, who supported the Commission's effects-based analysis and commented that 'Reference to negative (anti-competitive) effects should clearly not be mechanical. The (likely) existence of such exclusionary effects in a particular case should not be merely presumed, it should be assessed and demonstrated.' The AG recommended that the Court of Justice dismiss the appeal. (para 44, AG opinion, Case C-549/10P)

Intel Corporation v Commission	**Article 102 TFEU**
Case T-286/09	Abuse
General Court, [2014] 5 CMLR 9	Rebates

Facts

The European Commission imposed a fine of €1.06 billion on Intel Corporation for abusing its dominant position in the worldwide 'x86 central processing units' market (CPUs) by (1) foreclosing the market by providing hidden rebates to computer manufacturers on condition that they purchase their CPUs exclusively, or at very high percentages, from Intel, or refraining from stocking computers which do not incorporate Intel CPUs; and (2) making direct payments to computer manufacturers to prevent or delay sales of rival products and to limit the sales channels available to these products. (Commission decision COMP/C-3/37.990 [2009] OJ C227/07)

The Commission decision was based on both 'form-based' and 'effects-based' analysis. At the formal level, the Commission argued that Intel provided rebates on condition of exclusivity and engaged in naked restrictions. The Commission noted that while it is required to consider whether the discounts tend to remove or restrict a buyer's freedom to choose its sources of supply it is not required to prove actual foreclosure. Having satisfied the formal benchmark as set out in the case law, the Commission then continued to examine the effects of Intel's rebate practices. It noted that the as-efficient competitor analysis is one way of examining the capability to harm competition but that it should not be regarded as a necessary or absolute test. The Commission then engaged in an analysis similar to the framework put forward in its Guidance Paper on Article 102 TFEU, taking into account (1) the contestable share, (2) a relevant time horizon and (3) a relevant measure of viable cost (paras 1007–155, 1154).

Intel challenged the Commission's finding that the grant of a rebate was contrary to Article 102 TFEU. The General Court dismissed Intel's action for annulment and upheld the fine.

Held

Characterisation of rebates

A distinction should be drawn between three categories of rebates: (1) *Quantity rebates* linked solely to the volume of purchases made from a dominant undertaking. These rebates do not generally have the foreclosure effect prohibited by Article 102 TFEU. They reflect gains in efficiency and economies of scale which result in lower costs for the supplier. (2) *Exclusivity rebates* which are conditional on the customer obtaining all or most of its requirements from the undertaking in a dominant position. Save in exceptional circumstances, these rebates are incompatible with the objective of undistorted competition because they are designed to remove or restrict the purchaser's freedom to choose his sources of supply and to deny other producers access to the market. (3) *Third category rebates*: 'There are other rebate systems where the grant of a financial incentive is not directly linked to a condition of exclusive or quasi-exclusive supply from the undertaking in a dominant position, but where the mechanism for granting the rebate may also have a fidelity-building effect ("rebates falling within the third category"). That category of rebates includes inter alia rebate systems depending on the attainment of individual sales objectives which do not constitute exclusivity rebates, since those systems do not contain any obligation to obtain all or a given proportion of supplies from the dominant undertaking.' In examining whether the application of such a rebate constitutes an abuse of dominant position, it is necessary to consider the criteria and rules governing the grant of the rebate, and their economic justification. (paras 74–8)

The rebates granted by Intel to Dell, HP, NEC and Lenovo are rebates falling within the second category, namely exclusivity rebates. (para 79)

Legal threshold for establishing abuse in the case of exclusivity rebates

A dominant undertaking which ties purchasers, even at their request, by setting a formal obligation or by applying an informal mechanism of loyalty rebates conditional on the customer obtaining all or most of its requirements from the dominant undertaking, abuses its dominant position. (paras 72, 73, 106)

'[T]he question whether an exclusivity rebate can be categorised as abusive does not depend on an analysis of the circumstances of the case aimed at establishing a potential foreclosure effect.' (para 80)

Proof of a capacity to restrict competition in the circumstances of the case is not required. An assessment of all the circumstances of the case is only required in the case of rebates falling within the third category (see: *Michelin I* and *British Airways*). That approach can be justified by the fact that exclusivity rebates granted by a dominant undertaking are by their very nature capable of foreclosing competitors and restricting competition. A foreclosure effect occurs not only where access to the market is impossible, but also where that access is made more difficult. (paras 81–8)

An undertaking in a strong dominant position is to a large extent, an unavoidable trading partner. Its competitor is therefore not in a position to compete for the full supply of a customer, but only for the contestable share. 'If a customer of the undertaking in a dominant position obtains supplies from a competitor by failing to comply with the exclusivity or quasi-exclusivity condition, it risks losing not only the rebates for the units that it switched to that competitor, but the entire exclusivity rebate. In order to submit an attractive offer, it is not therefore sufficient for the competitor of an undertaking in a dominant position to offer attractive conditions for the units that that competitor can itself supply to the customer; it must also offer that customer compensation for the loss of the exclusivity rebate. … Thus, the grant of an exclusivity rebate by an unavoidable trading partner makes it structurally more difficult for a competitor to submit an offer at an attractive price and thus gain access to the market. (paras 91–3)

The Commission is not required to prove actual effect. It must only show that a practice is capable of restricting competition. Accordingly, the Commission is also not required to prove a causal link between the practices complained of and actual effects on the market. In addition, the Commission is not required to prove direct damage to consumers or a causal link between such damage and the practices at issue in the contested decision. (paras 102–05)

The level of the rebate and duration of supply

'[I]t is not the level of the rebates which is at issue in the contested decision but the exclusivity for which they were given. Thus, the rebate must only be capable of inducing the customer to purchase exclusively, irrespective whether the competing supplier could have compensated the customer for the loss of the rebate if that customer switched supplier.' (paras 107, 108) As for the short duration supply, 'it must be borne in mind that, in principle, any financial incentive to purchase exclusively constitutes additional interference with the structure of competition on a market and must therefore be regarded as abusive to the extent that it is implemented by an undertaking in a dominant position.' (para 111)

Customers' buying power

Even when the dominant undertaking's contracting partner is itself a powerful undertaking and the rebates are granted as a response to its requests and taking into account its buying power, there is no justification for making them subject to an exclusive supply condition. (paras 138–40)

No need to examine actual effects—no need to apply the 'as-efficient competitor' test

The contested decision conducts an economic analysis of the capability of the rebates to foreclose a hypothetical competitor as efficient as Intel. The 'as-efficient competitor' test (AEC) assumes that the dominant firm is an unavoidable trading partner and that the competitor must compensate the customer for the exclusivity rebate that it would lose if it purchased a smaller portion than that stipulated by the exclusivity or quasi-exclusivity condition. (paras 30, 141)

'A finding that an exclusivity rebate is illegal does not necessitate an examination of the circumstances of the case. … The Commission is not therefore required to demonstrate the foreclosure capability of exclusivity rebates on a case-by-case basis.' (para 143) 'Even in the case of rebates falling within the third category, for which an examination of the circumstances of the case is necessary, it is not essential to carry out an AEC. Thus, in *Michelin I* … the Court of Justice relied on the loyalty mechanism of the rebates at issue, without requiring proof, by means of a quantitative test, that competitors had been forced to sell at a loss in order to be able to compensate the rebates falling within the third category granted by the undertaking in a dominant position. Moreover, it follows from Case C-549/10P *Tomra* ... that, in order to find anti-competitive effects, it is not necessary that a rebate system force an as-efficient competitor to charge "negative" prices, that is to say prices lower than the cost price. In order to establish a potential anti-competitive effect, it is sufficient to demonstrate the existence of a loyalty mechanism.' (paras 144, 145) 'It follows that, even if an assessment of the circumstances of the case were necessary to demonstrate the potential anti-competitive effects of the exclusivity rebates, it would still not be necessary to demonstrate those effects by means of an AEC test.' Moreover, it should be borne in mind that a foreclosure effect occurs when access to the market is made more difficult and not only where access to the market is made impossible. An AEC test only makes it possible to verify the hypothesis that access to the market has been made impossible and not to rule out the possibility that it has been made more difficult. (paras 146–53)

An exclusivity rebate is abusive because it imposes a condition of exclusive or quasi-exclusive supply on the buyer, not because of the amount of the rebate. One should therefore distinguish between the analysis in cases concerned with margin squeeze or low price practices (*TeliaSonera, Deutsche Telekom, Post Danmark*) in which a key criterion is whether a competitor as efficient as the dominant undertaking could continue to compete with the dominant undertaking and between this case. In those judgments price and cost analyses are attributable to the fact that it is impossible to assess whether a price is abusive without comparing it with other prices and costs. (para 152)

Naked restrictions

The Commission characterises as abuses three practices which it called 'naked restrictions' which involved payments to the OEMs in order that the OEMs delay, cancel or restrict the marketing of certain AMD-based products. A foreclosure effect will occur also when access is difficult and not only when it is impossible. 'For the purposes of applying [Article 102 TFEU], showing an anti-competitive object and an anti-competitive effect may, in some cases, be one and the same thing. If it is shown that the object pursued by the conduct of an undertaking in a dominant position is to restrict competition, that conduct will also be liable to have such an effect.' (paras 198–203)

Comment

The General Court confirmed the finding of abuse in a formalistic judgment. Importantly, it held that there is no need to examine the actual effects of the rebates and that the use of the As Efficient Competitor (AEC) test is superfluous, and in any event does not detect instances where access to the market is made more difficult (false negative). Further, the Court distinguished between the analysis of loyalty rebates and the analysis of abuse in margin squeeze and low price cases. According to the Court, only the latter calls for an AEC test and necessitates price and cost analysis. This holding rejects the use of the AEC analysis in rebate cases, as advocated in the Commission's Guidance paper. Note however the more positive comment made by the Court in Post Danmark II (page 261 below) where it held that AEC can be regarded as one tool amongst others for the purposes of assessing the rebate scheme.

The threshold for finding abuse in rebate cases remains formalistic and low, with a requirement to establish only that the rebate is capable of restricting competition, and the holding that a foreclosure effect occurs not only where access to the market is impossible, but also where that access is made more difficult. Evidence of competition between undertakings, buyer power or an increase in the non-dominant competitor's sales, will not affect that conclusion.

The Commission's economic approach to rebates, as stipulated in its Guidance Paper, may still affect the Commission's prioritisation and decision making when pursuing a case, but is not likely to affect the outcome on appeal, where the formal legal benchmark will be championed by the Court and the Commission's legal services. Similarly, the more formal approach to rebates is likely to prevail at Member State level.

Imperial Chemical Industries Ltd v Commission	**Article 102 TFEU**
Case T-66/01	Abuse
General Court, [2010] ECR II-2631, [2011] 4 CMLR 3	Rebates and Exclusivity

Facts

The Commission found Imperial Chemical Industries Ltd (Imperial) to infringe Article 102 TFEU, among other things, by excluding and severely limiting competition through the use of substantial rebates and other financial inducements. Imperial contested the decision and argued, among other things, that the Commission erred in its analysis of rebates. The Court rejected these arguments and repeated the form-based criteria for analysing loyalty rebates.

Held

'A fidelity rebate, which is granted in return for an undertaking by the customer to obtain his stock exclusively or almost exclusively from [a dominant undertaking, is abusive] … it is sufficient to show that the abusive conduct tends to restrict competition or is capable of having, that effect' (paras 296–8)

When a rebate system is not based on an economically justified countervailing advantage but tends to prevent customers from obtaining their supplies from competitors it will infringe Article 102 TFEU. It is necessary to consider all the circumstances governing the grant of the rebate. The Commission has done so in its decision and concluded that the 'top-slice' rebates were intended to exclude effective competition. The Commission also makes reference in its decision to documents relating to the rebate scheme, under which Imperial was seeking to exclude competitors from the market. It is clear from those documents that the rebates in question did not reflect gains in efficiency and economies of scale. (paras 299–303)

'It is clear from settled case-law that an undertaking which is in a dominant position on a market and ties purchasers—even if it does so at their request—by an obligation or promise on their part to obtain all or most of their requirements exclusively from the undertaking abuses its dominant position within the meaning of [Article 102 TFEU], whether the obligation in question is stipulated without further qualification or whether it is undertaken in consideration of the grant of a rebate. The same applies if the undertaking, without tying the purchasers by a formal obligation, applies, either under the terms of agreements concluded with these purchasers or unilaterally, a system of fidelity rebates, that is to say discounts conditional on the customer's obtaining all or most of its requirements—whether the quantity of its purchases be large or small—from the undertaking in a dominant position (*Hoffmann-La Roche v Commission*, paragraph 216 above, paragraph 89). Obligations of this kind to obtain supplies exclusively from a particular undertaking, whether or not they are in consideration of rebates or of the granting of fidelity rebates intended to give the purchaser an incentive to obtain his supplies exclusively from the undertaking in a dominant position, are incompatible with the objective of undistorted competition within the common market, because they are not based on an economic transaction which justifies this burden or benefit but are designed to deprive the purchaser of or restrict its possible choices of sources of supply and to deny other producers access to the market (*Hoffmann-La Roche v Commission* … above, paragraph 90).' (para 315)

Comment

The Court recited the form-based approach according to which it is sufficient to show that the rebate tends to restrict competition. In addition, it took a strict formal view, citing *Hoffmann-La Roche*, and held that obligations to obtain supplies exclusively from the dominant undertakings will form an abuse. This categorical statement, which views any form of exclusivity as abusive, runs counter to the more recent effects-based approach advanced by the Commission. The same categorical condemnation of exclusivity was also voiced in the General Court's earlier judgment in Case T-57/01 *Solvay SA v Commission* (para 365). There, the General Court noted, in addition, that loyalty rebates are abusive and have an impact on the conditions of competition, even if the rebate levels are moderate (1.5 per cent in that case). (paras 343, 355)

Post Danmark A/S v Konkurrencerådet (Post Danmark II)	**Article 102 TFEU**
Case C-23/14	Abuse
Court of Justice, [2015] 5 CMLR 25	Rebates

Facts

The Danish Competition Council (Konkurrencerådet) found that retroactive rebates offered by Post Danmark foreclosed the market and constituted an abuse of a dominant position. The rebate scheme in question was retroactive in nature and applied to direct advertising mail. All customers were entitled to receive the same rebate on the basis of their aggregate purchases over an annual reference period. Discounts were adjusted at the end of the period to reflect the level of purchase. On appeal, the Danish Competition Appeals Tribunal upheld the decision. A subsequent appeal to the Maritime and Commercial Court led to a request for a preliminary ruling in which the referring court asked the Court of Justice to clarify the criteria used for the assessment of rebates.

Held

Rebates may take the form of: (1) a quantity discount linked solely to the volume of purchases, granted in respect of each individual order, thus corresponding to the cost savings made by the supplier. In principle, such rebates are not liable to infringe Article 102 TFEU; (2) loyalty rebates, which, by offering customers financial advantages, tend to prevent them from obtaining all or most of their requirements from competing manufacturers. Such rebates amount to an abuse of a dominant position; (3) rebates which do not fall into any of the above categories, such as the rebates in this case which were not granted in respect of each individual order, but on the basis of the aggregate orders placed over a given period, and on the other hand were 'not coupled with an obligation for, or promise by, purchasers to obtain all or a given proportion of their supplies from Post Danmark, a point which served to distinguish it from loyalty rebates.' (paras 27–8)

'In those circumstances, in order to determine whether the undertaking in a dominant position has abused that position by applying a rebate scheme such as that at issue in the main proceedings, the Court has repeatedly held that it is necessary to consider all the circumstances, particularly the criteria and rules governing the grant of the rebate, and to investigate whether, in providing an advantage not based on any economic service justifying it, the rebate tends to remove or restrict the buyer's freedom to choose his sources of supply, to bar competitors from access to the market, to apply dissimilar conditions to equivalent transactions with other trading parties or to strengthen the dominant position by distorting competition (judgments in *British Airways v Commission*, C 95/04 P, EU:C:2007:166, paragraph 67, and *Tomra Systems and Others v Commission*, C 549/10 P, EU:C:2012:221, paragraph 71).' (para 29)

The existence of a long reference period has the inherent effect, at the end of that period, of creating a suction effect—increasing the pressure on the buyer to reach the purchase figure needed to obtain the discount. In addition, the extent of the dominant position of the undertaking concerned and the particular conditions of competition prevailing on the relevant market need to be considered. Post Danmark's very large market share makes it an unavoidable trading partner and difficult for competitors to outbid it in the face of discounts based on overall sales volume. In those circumstances, even without tying customers by a formal obligation, a rebate scheme which tends to make it more difficult for customers to obtain supplies from competing undertakings would produce an anticompetitive exclusionary effect. (paras 34–42)

The fact that the rebate scheme implemented by Post Danmark applied to all customers and was not discriminatory in nature does not preclude its being regarded as capable of producing an exclusionary effect on the market. (paras 37, 38)

'The fact that the rebates applied by Post Danmark concern a large proportion of customers on the market does not, in itself, constitute evidence of abusive conduct by that undertaking.' It 'may constitute a useful indication as to the extent of that practice and its impact on the market, which may bear out the likelihood of an anti-competitive exclusionary effect.' (paras 44–6)

Even when an exclusionary effect is established, the dominant undertaking may demonstrate that anticompetitive effects may be counterbalanced, or outweighed, by efficiencies which also benefit the customers and were brought about as a result of that necessary conduct, and that the conduct 'does not eliminate effective competition, by removing all or most existing sources of actual or potential competition.' (paras 47–50)

As-efficient-competitor test

The as-efficient-competitor test has been applied to cases of selective prices, predatory prices and margin squeeze. With respect to its application to the analysis of a rebate scheme under Article 102 TFEU, 'the Court has held that the invoicing of "negative prices", that is to say, prices below cost prices, to customers is not a prerequisite of a finding that a retroactive rebate scheme operated by a dominant undertaking is abusive (judgment in *Tomra Systems and Others v Commission*, paragraph 73 [page 255, above]). In that same case, the Court specified that the absence of a comparison of prices charged with costs did not constitute an error of law (para 80). It follows that, as the Advocate General stated in points 61 and 63 of her Opinion, it is not possible to infer from [Article 102 TFEU] or the case-law of the Court that there is a legal obligation requiring a finding to the effect that a rebate scheme operated by a dominant undertaking is abusive to be based always on the as-efficient-competitor test. Nevertheless, that conclusion ought not to have the effect of excluding, on principle, recourse to the as-efficient-competitor test in cases involving a rebate scheme for the purposes of examining its compatibility with [Article 102 TFEU].' (paras 51–8)

'On the other hand, in a situation such as that in the main proceedings, characterised by the holding by the dominant undertaking of a very large market share and by structural advantages conferred, inter alia, by that undertaking's statutory monopoly, which applied to 70% of mail on the relevant market, applying the as-efficient-competitor test is of no relevance inasmuch as the structure of the market makes the emergence of an as-efficient competitor practically impossible. Furthermore, in a market such as that at issue in the main proceedings, access to which is protected by high barriers, the presence of a less efficient competitor might contribute to intensifying the competitive pressure on that market and, therefore, to exerting a constraint on the conduct of the dominant undertaking.' (paras 59–60)

'The as-efficient-competitor test must thus be regarded as one tool amongst others for the purposes of assessing whether there is an abuse of a dominant position in the context of a rebate scheme.' (para 61)

Appreciability and Probability of the anticompetitive effect of a rebate scheme

'[I]n order to determine whether a dominant undertaking has abused its position by operating a rebate scheme, it is necessary, inter alia, to examine whether that rebate tends to remove or restrict the buyer's freedom to choose his sources of supply, to bar competitors from access to the market, to apply dissimilar conditions to equivalent transactions with other trading parties or to strengthen the dominant position by distorting competition. In that regard, and as the Advocate General stated in point 80 of her Opinion, the anti-competitive effect of a particular practice must not be of purely hypothetical. The Court has also held that, in order to establish whether such a practice is abusive, that practice must have an anti-competitive effect on the market, but the effect does not necessarily have to be concrete, and it is sufficient to demonstrate that there is an anti-competitive effect which may potentially exclude competitors who are at least as efficient as the dominant undertaking (judgment in *TeliaSonera Sverige*, C-52/09, EU:C:2011:83, paragraph 64).' (paras 64–6)

'It follows that only dominant undertakings whose conduct is likely to have an anti-competitive effect on the market fall within the scope of [Article 102 TFEU].' (para 67)

'[I]n order to fall within the scope of that article, the anti-competitive effect of a rebate scheme operated by a dominant undertaking must be probable, there being no need to show that it is of a serious or appreciable nature.' (para 74)

Comment

The Court classified rebates to: (1) pure quality rebates, (2) clear loyalty rebates (which include an obligation to obtain all or part of the supply from the dominant undertakings) and (3) other rebates, like the ones in this case, which do not fall under either of the first categories. The assessment of these rebates necessitates consideration of 'all the circumstances' (para 29)—namely the market conditions and the criteria governing the grant of the rebate.

The Court noted that a price/cost test (the 'as-efficient-competitor test') is not a required test for the assessment of a rebate scheme, but may play a complementary role in the analysis as one tool amongst others. In her opinion, AG Kokott downplayed the significance of the test and noted that the 'case-law does not support the inference of an absolute requirement always to carry out an AEC test for the purposes of assessing price-based exclusionary conduct from the point of view of competition law. On the one hand, that case-law is specifically concerned with pricing practices by dominant undertakings, such as a low-pricing policy (loss leader pricing, for example) or margin squeezing through the reduction of the cost-price ratio, which are by their very nature closely related to the cost structure of the undertakings in question. On the other hand, the form of words chosen by the Court, "among other things" … makes it clear that it cannot always be assumed that an abuse of a dominant position exists only where the exclusionary effect is felt by undertakings which are as efficient as the dominant undertaking.' (para 63) She further noted that the relevant circumstances of the individual case in question 'must not be confined to an examination of price and cost components alone. On the contrary, there are many other factors, such as the specific modus operandi of a rebate scheme and certain characteristics of the market on which the dominant undertaking operates, that may also be relevant to a finding of abuse. In fact, they may be much more informative than a price/cost analysis.' (para 68)

The court held that only when the conduct is *likely* to have an anti-competitive effect on the market it will constitute an abuse. (para 67) Further, the court clarified that once likelihood is established, one need not establish the appreciability of the anti-competitive effect. This holding confirms that no de-minimis threshold applies to the alleged abuse in this case. The anti-competitive effect does not have to be concrete and it is sufficient to demonstrate the potential exclusionary effect.

Interestingly, in *Streetmap v Google* Justice Roth distinguished this holding, as to lack of de-minimis 'threshold' from that required in cases where an abuse takes place on a related market. In that case Streetmap accused Google of abusing its dominant position by foreclosing competitors of Google Maps in the market for online maps. Streetmap submitted that there is no de minimis principle applicable to abuse of dominance and therefore no need to show that the likely anticompetitive effect is of a serious or appreciable nature. Mr Justice Roth noted on this point that: 'Both Hoffmann-La Roche and Post Danmark II concerned rebate schemes operated by the dominant undertaking, where the potential anti-competitive effect was on the market where it was dominant. The same consideration applies to the loyalty scheme condemned in Case T-286/09 *Intel v Commission* … where the General Court expressed itself in similar terms (see at para 116). That feature underlies the reasoning of the European Courts in this regard, with their express reference to an effect on the market where competition is already weakened by the presence of the dominant undertaking. In my view, it does not follow that conduct will constitute an abuse where the effect is on a separate market where the undertaking is not dominant, if that effect is not serious or appreciable. On the contrary, it must always be borne in mind that the purpose of competition law is to prevent arrangements or practices which distort competition and to safeguard the interests of consumers. That applies no less to Article 102 than to Article 101: see the observations of Jacobs AG in Case C-7/97 *Bronner v Mediaprint* … at para 58. And in the jurisprudence under Article 101, it is well-established that an agreement or arrangement will not be prohibited unless it may have an appreciable effect. That is logical, since for Article 101 to be engaged there is no requirement of dominance. Accordingly, I do not regard the pronouncements of the ECJ to which I have referred as precluding me from holding that where the likely effect relied on is on a non-dominated market, a de minimis threshold applies and that to constitute an abuse the effect must therefore be appreciable.' (paras 95–7) [2016] EWHC 253 (England and Wales High Court (Chancery Division)

Deutsche Telekom AG v Commission	**Article 102 TFEU**
Case C-280/08P	Abuse
Court of Justice, [2010] 5 CMLR 27	Margin Squeeze

Facts

The Commission found Deutsche Telekom AG ('DT') to have dominated the German markets of broadband access to local fixed networks and to have abused this position by charging its competitors more for unbundled access at wholesale level than it charged its subscribers for access at the retail level. This constituted a margin squeeze as the charges to be paid to DT for wholesale access were so expensive that competitors were forced to charge their end-users prices higher than the prices DT charges its own end-users for similar services. In order to establish the existence of a margin squeeze, the Commission compared wholesale and retail access services. In order to achieve a coherent comparison, it used a weighted approach taking into account the numbers of DT's retail customers for the different access services at the retail level.

DT brought an action for annulment to the General Court (Case T-271/03 *Deutsche Telekom AG v Commission* [2008] ECR II-477). The General Court dismissed the appeal, making the following main points:

Competition law and regulation

The fact that DT's retail charges had to be approved by the German regulatory authority for telecommunications and post ('RegTP') does not absolve it from responsibility under Article 102 TFEU. (para 107)

That conclusion is not affected by the fact that the RegTP checks the compatibility of its charges with Article 102 TFEU beforehand. (paras 108–20)

In addition, DT had sufficient scope to fix its charges at a level that would have enabled it to end or reduce the margin squeeze at issue. (paras 120–51)

The method used by the Commission to establish a margin squeeze

The abusive nature of DT's conduct is connected with the unfairness of the spread between its prices for wholesale access and its retail prices. Contrary to DT's claim, in order to establish margin squeeze, the Commission is not required to demonstrate that DT's retail prices were, as such, abusive. (para 167)

Effect on the market

An 'abuse' is an objective concept.

'Given that, until the entry of a first competitor on the market for retail access services, in 1998, the applicant had a monopoly on that retail market, the anti-competitive effect which the Commission is required to demonstrate relates to the possible barriers which the applicant's pricing practices could have created for the growth of competition in that market.' (para 235)

'If [DT's] retail prices are lower than its wholesale charges, or if the spread between the [DT's] wholesale and retail charges is insufficient to enable an equally efficient operator to cover its product-specific costs of supplying retail access services, a potential competitor who is just as efficient as [DT] would not be able to enter the retail access services market without suffering losses.' (para 237)

The fact that competition has developed less favourably in the other Member States does not show that DT's pricing practices had no anticompetitive effect in Germany. In addition, the state of competition should be examined on the basis of the elements of fact and of law existing at the time when the measure was adopted. Subsequent information about current competition on the market is not relevant in the context of an action for annulment. (paras 243, 244)

DT appealed. The Court of Justice dismissed the appeal and upheld the fine imposed by the Commission.

Held

Attribution of the margin squeeze to DT on the ground that it had the scope to adjust its retail prices

'According to the case-law of the Court of Justice, it is only if anti-competitive conduct is required of undertakings by national legislation, or if the latter creates a legal framework which itself eliminates any possibility of competitive activity on their part, that [Articles 101 and 102 TFEU] do not apply. In such a situation, the restriction of competition is not attributable, as those provisions implicitly require, to the autonomous conduct of the undertakings. [Articles 101 and 102 TFEU] may apply, however, if it is found that the national legislation leaves open the possibility of competition which may be prevented, restricted or distorted by the autonomous conduct of undertakings (Joined Cases C-359/95P and C-379/95P *Commission and France v Ladbroke Racing* [1997] ECR I-6265, paragraphs 33 and 34 and the case-law cited).' (para 80)

'If a national law merely encourages or makes it easier for undertakings to engage in autonomous anti-competitive conduct, those undertakings remain subject to [Articles 101 and 102 TFEU] (Joined Cases 40/73 to 48/73, 50/73, 54/73 to 56/73, 111/73, 113/73 and 114/73 *Suiker Unie and Others v Commission* [1975] ECR 1663, paragraphs 36 to 73, and *CIF*, paragraph 56). According to the case-law of the Court, dominant undertakings have a special responsibility not to allow their conduct to impair genuine undistorted competition on the common market (Case 322/81 *Nederlandsche Banden-Industrie-Michelin v Commission* [1983] ECR 3461, paragraph 57).' (paras 82, 83)

Since DT had scope to adjust its retail prices, the Court was entitled to attribute the margin squeeze to DT

Absence of negligence or intentional misconduct

'[I]t must be borne in mind, in relation to the question whether the infringements were committed intentionally or negligently and are, therefore, liable to be punished by a fine in accordance with the first subparagraph of Article 15(2) of Regulation No 17, that it follows from the case-law of the Court that that condition is satisfied where the undertaking concerned cannot be unaware of the anti-competitive nature of its conduct, whether or not it is aware that it is infringing the competition rules of the Treaty (see Joined Cases 96/82 … *IAZ International Belgium and Others v Commission* [1983] ECR 3369, paragraph 45, and *Nederlandsche Banden-Industrie-Michelin v Commission*, paragraph 107).' (para 124)

The General Court did not err in law when it took the view that that condition was satisfied, since the appellant could not have been unaware that, notwithstanding the authorisation decisions of RegTP, it had genuine scope to set its retail prices for end-user and, moreover, the margin squeeze entailed serious restrictions on competition. (paras 125, 126)

The margin squeeze test

Article 102 TFEU prohibits a dominant undertaking from adopting pricing practices which have an exclusionary effect on equally efficient actual or potential competitors. 'The anti-competitive effect which the Commission is required to demonstrate, as regards pricing practices of a dominant undertaking resulting in a margin squeeze of its equally efficient competitors, relates to the possible barriers which the appellant's pricing practices could have created for the growth of products on the retail market in end-user access services and, therefore, on the degree of competition in that market. … Such practice constitutes an abuse … if it has an exclusionary effect on competitors who are at least as efficient as the dominant undertaking itself by squeezing their margins and is capable of making market entry more difficult or impossible for those competitors, and thus of strengthening its dominant position on that market to the detriment of consumers' interests.' (paras 177, 252, 253)

'Admittedly, where a dominant undertaking actually implements a pricing practice resulting in a margin squeeze of its equally efficient competitors, with the purpose of driving them from the relevant market, the fact that the desired result is not ultimately achieved does not alter its categorisation as abuse within the meaning of [Article 102 TFEU]. However, in the absence of any effect on the competitive situation of competitors, a pricing practice such as that at issue cannot be classified as exclusionary if it does not make their market penetration any more difficult.' (para 254)

'[T]he wholesale local loop access services provided by the appellant are indispensable to its competitors' effective penetration of the retail markets for the provision of services to end-users, the General Court was entitled to hold ... that a margin squeeze resulting from the spread between wholesale prices for local loop access services and retail prices for end-user access services, in principle, hinders the growth of competition in the retail markets in services to end-users, since a competitor who is as efficient as the appellant cannot carry on his business in the retail market for end-user access services without incurring losses.' (para 255)

'[T]he mere fact that the appellant would have to increase its retail prices for end-user access services in order to avoid the margin squeeze of its competitors who are as efficient as the appellant cannot in any way, in itself, render irrelevant the test which the General Court applied in the present case for the purpose of establishing an abuse under [Article 102 TFEU].' (para 181)

Comment

The Court confirmed that margin squeeze forms a standalone abuse which stems from the unfairness of the spread between wholesale and retail prices. There is no need to establish that the retail prices are abusive.

The judgments confirmed the possible application of EU competition law to a regulated market, when under the national regulation the dominant undertaking has a margin of commercial discretion in determining its action and in avoiding or ending the abuse on its own initiative.

Contrast the ex post application of EU competition law to a market which was subjected to ex ante regulation, with the US Supreme Court non-interventionist approach as evident in *Verizon Communications Inc v Law Offices of Curtis v Trinko LLP* 540 US 398 (2004) (*Trinko*). In the *Trinko* judgment, Justice Scalia held that 'one factor of particular importance is the existence of a regulatory structure designed to deter and remedy anti-competitive harm. Where such a structure exists, the additional benefit to competition provided by antitrust enforcement will tend to be small, and it will be less plausible that the antitrust laws contemplate such additional scrutiny. ... The regulatory framework that exists in this case demonstrates how, in certain circumstances, regulation significantly diminishes the likelihood of major antitrust harm. ... Against the slight benefits of antitrust intervention here, we must weigh a realistic assessment of its costs. ... Mistaken inferences and the resulting false condemnations "are especially costly, because they chill the very conduct the antitrust laws are designed to protect ..." Even if the problem of false positives did not exist, conduct consisting of anticompetitive violations ... may be, as we have concluded with respect to above-cost predatory pricing schemes, "beyond the practical ability of a judicial tribunal to control." *Brooke Group Ltd v Brown & Williamson Tobacco Corp*, 509 US 209, 223 (1993).'

On the analysis of margin squeeze, the Court of Justice confirmed that margin squeeze is established by reference to the fairness of the spread between wholesale access and retail prices and is not dependent on the possible abusive nature of the retail price. It thus rejected DT's argument that the abusive nature of a margin squeeze can arise only from the abusive nature of retail prices.

Contrast this view with the US Supreme Court judgment in *Pacific Bell Telephone Co v linkLine Communications, Inc* 29 S Ct 1109 (2009). Chief Justice Roberts delivered the opinion of the Court and held that: 'An upstream monopolist with no duty to deal is free to charge whatever wholesale price it would like; antitrust law does not forbid lawfully obtained monopolies from charging monopoly prices. ... If both the wholesale price and the retail price are independently lawful, there is no basis for imposing antitrust liability simply because a vertically integrated firm's wholesale price happens to be greater than or equal to its retail price.'

In its Notice on the Application of Competition Rules to Access Agreements in the Telecommunication Sector ([1998] OJ C265/2) the Commission refers to margin squeeze and states that it 'could be demonstrated by showing that the dominant company's own downstream operations could not trade profitably on the basis of the upstream price charged to its competitors by the upstream operating arm of the dominant company. A loss making downstream arm could be hidden if the dominant operator has allocated costs to its access operations which should properly be allocated to the downstream operations, or has otherwise improperly determined the transfer prices within the organisation.' (para 117)

Note the Commission's decision in Case IV/30.178 *Napier Brown/British Sugar* ([1988] OJ L284/41) where British Sugar ('BS') was found to have engaged in margin squeeze. There, the margin allowed by BS between prices charged for bulk and packaged sugar did not allow its own downstream operation to trade profitably.

Genzyme Limited v Office of Fair Trading	**Article 102 TFEU**
1016/1/1/03	Abuse
Competition Appeal Tribunal, [2004] CAT 4, [2004] Comp AR 358	Margin Squeeze

Facts

Genzyme Limited appealed against a decision of the Office of Fair Trading (OFT) in which it was found to have abused its dominant position in the supply of Cerezyme, a treatment for Gaucher's disease, by bundling it with its homecare services and by engaging in margin squeeze against other providers of homecare services. The Competition Appeal Tribunal (CAT) allowed the appeal in part, accepting Genzyme's claims concerning the finding of bundling but upheld the OFT finding on margin squeeze.

Held

A 'margin squeeze' may occur where a dominant undertaking in an upstream market 'supplies an essential input to its competitors in a downstream market, on which the dominant company is also active, at a price which does not enable its competitors on the downstream market to remain competitive. ... See Case T-5/97 *Industrie des Poudres Sphériques v Commission* [2000] ECR II-3755, at paragraph 178. ... In *National Carbonising Company*, OJ 1976 L36/6 the National Coal Board supplied coking coal for the manufacture of coke both to its own subsidiary, National Smokeless Fuels, and to an independent company National Carbonising. National Smokeless Fuels and National Carbonising were competitors in the downstream market for coke, which was derived from the coal supplied by the National Coal Board. National Carbonising complained that the price it had to pay the National Coal Board for coal was too high to enable it to sell coke competitively at the price charged by National Smokeless Fuels. The Commission held, at paragraph 14 of its decision, that: "an undertaking which is in a dominant position as regards the production of a raw material ... and therefore able to control its price to independent manufacturers of derivatives ... and which is itself producing the same derivatives in competition with these manufacturers, may abuse its dominant position if it acts in such a way as to eliminate the competition from these manufacturers in the market for derivatives. From this general principle the services of the Commission deduced that the enterprise in a dominant position may have an obligation to arrange its prices so as to allow a reasonably efficient manufacturer of the derivatives a margin sufficient to enable it to survive in the long term." (para 491)

'The OFT argues that since May 2001 Genzyme has supplied Cerezyme to the NHS at the NHS list price, while supplying other homecare services providers at the same list price, £2.975 per unit. The effect of that is that other homecare service providers have no margin with which to compete with Genzyme Homecare, and are effectively eliminated from the supply of Homecare Services to Gaucher patients.' (para 478)

'In those circumstances it is likely to be wholly uneconomic for other homecare service providers to provide homecare services at no effective margin between its buying and selling price of Cerezyme. We therefore accept that Genzyme's pricing policy constitutes a margin squeeze, the effect of which is to force other providers to sustain a loss in the provision of Homecare Services to Gaucher patients. We also accept that no undertaking, regardless of how efficient it may be, could trade profitably in these circumstances in the downstream supply of homecare services. ... We share the OFT's conclusion that the effect of Genzyme's margin squeeze is to monopolise the supply of Homecare Services to Gaucher patients in favour of Genzyme, and to eliminate any competition in the supply of such services to Gaucher patients.' (paras 552, 554, 549–55) Contrary to Genzyme's claim, the margin squeeze is not objectively justified. (paras 576–623)

Comment

In *BSkyB* (BSB) the OFT considered whether BSB had impeded competition from other pay-TV distributors by engaging in margin squeeze. The OFT tested whether BSB had set its wholesale prices at a level that would prevent an equally efficient distributor from earning a normal return on the distribution of BSB's premium channels. (CA98/20/2002, OFT 623)

Konkurrensverket v TeliaSonera Sverige AB	**Article 102 TFEU**
Case C-52/09	Abuse
Court of Justice, [2011] ECR I-527, [2011] 4 CMLR 18	Margin Squeeze

Facts

A reference for a preliminary ruling concerning the interpretation of Article 102 TFEU with regard to the criteria for establishing margin squeeze as an abuse of a dominant position. The case before the National Court concerned accusations that TeliaSonera Sverige AB (TeliaSonera) engaged in abusive margin squeeze in the pricing of access to local loop.

Held

Margin squeeze exists when the 'spread between the wholesale prices for ADSL input services and the retail prices for broadband connection services to end users were either negative or insufficient to cover the specific costs of the ADSL input services which TeliaSonera has to incur in order to supply its own retail services to end users, so that that spread does not allow a competitor which is as efficient as that undertaking to compete for the supply of those services to end users. In such circumstances, although the competitors may be as efficient as the dominant undertaking, they may be able to operate on the retail market only at a loss or at artificially reduced levels of profitability.' To establish an abuse, one need not prove that the wholesale or retail prices are abusive. It is the exclusionary effect which constitutes the abuse. To assess the lawfulness of the pricing policy reference should be made to pricing criteria of the dominant undertaking itself, establishing whether it would have been sufficiently efficient to offer its retail services to end users otherwise than at a loss if it had first been obliged to pay its own wholesale prices for the intermediary services. If that undertaking would have been unable to offer its retail services otherwise than at a loss, competitors who might be excluded due to the margin squeeze, could not be considered to be less efficient than the dominant undertaking. Where the cost structure of the dominant undertaking is not precisely identifiable, the costs of its competitors on the same market may be examined. (paras 32–46)

Margin squeeze is an independent form of abuse distinct from that of refusal to supply. 'The absence of any regulatory obligation to supply the ADSL input services on the wholesale market has no effect on the question of whether the pricing practice at issue in the main proceedings is abusive.' (paras 56, 59)

In order to establish an abuse, price squeeze must have an anti-competitive effect which may potentially exclude competitors who are at least as efficient as the dominant undertaking. The fact that in a given case, margin squeeze did not result in de facto exclusion, does not affect the finding of abuse. 'However, in the absence of any effect on the competitive situation of competitors, a pricing practice such as that at issue in the main proceedings cannot be classified as an exclusionary practice where the penetration of those competitors in the market concerned is not made any more difficult by that practice.' (paras 64–6)

When assessing the effects of the margin squeeze, the question of whether the wholesale product is indispensable may be relevant. 'Where access to the supply of the wholesale product is indispensable for the sale of the retail product, competitors who are at least as efficient as the undertaking which dominates the wholesale market and who are unable to operate on the retail market other than at a loss or, in any event, with reduced profitability suffer a competitive disadvantage on that market which is such as to prevent or restrict their access to it or the growth of their activities on it. … In such circumstances, the at least potentially anti-competitive effect of a margin squeeze is probable. However, taking into account the dominant position of the undertaking concerned in the wholesale market, the possibility cannot be ruled out that, by reason simply of the fact that the wholesale product is not indispensable for the supply of the retail product, a pricing practice which causes margin squeeze may not be able to produce any anti-competitive effect, even potentially. Accordingly, it is again for the referring court to satisfy itself that, even where the wholesale product is not indispensable, the practice may be capable of having anti-competitive effects on the markets concerned.' (paras 69–72)

'Secondly, it is necessary to determine the level of margin squeeze of competitors at least as efficient as the dominant undertaking. If the margin is negative, in other words if, in the present case, the wholesale price for the ADSL input services is higher than the retail price for services to end users, an effect which is at least potentially exclusionary is probable, taking into account the fact that, in such a situation, the competitors of the dominant undertaking, even if they are as efficient, or even more efficient, compared with it, would be compelled to sell at a loss. If, on the other hand, such a margin remains positive, it must then be demonstrated that the application of that pricing practice was, by reason, for example, of reduced profitability, likely to have the consequence that it would be at least more difficult for the operators concerned to trade on the market concerned.' (paras 73, 74)

'[A]n undertaking remains at liberty to demonstrate that its pricing practice, albeit producing an exclusionary effect, is economically justified. … In that regard, it has to be determined whether the exclusionary effect arising from such a practice, which is disadvantageous for competition, may be counterbalanced, or outweighed, by advantages in terms of efficiency which also benefit the consumer.' If the exclusionary effect bears no relation to advantages for the market and consumers, or goes beyond what is necessary in order to attain those advantages, that practice must be regarded as an abuse. (paras 75, 76)

The assessment of margin squeeze is not affected by whether the practice is liable to drive out from the market existing clients of or rather new clients of the dominant undertaking. (para 95) 'Margin squeeze is the result of the spread between the prices for wholesale services and those for retail services and not of the level of those prices as such. In particular, that squeeze may be the result not only of an abnormally low price in the retail market, but also of an abnormally high price in the wholesale market. Consequently, an undertaking which engages in a pricing practice which results in a margin squeeze on its competitors does not necessarily suffer losses. The possibility that competitors may be driven from the market does not depend on either the fact that the dominant undertaking suffers losses or the fact that that undertaking may be capable of recouping its losses, but depends solely on the spread between the prices applied by the dominant undertaking on the markets concerned, the result of which may be that it is not the dominant undertaking itself which suffer losses but its competitors.' (paras 98–101)

Comment

The judgment clarifies that margin squeeze should not be treated as a constructive refusal to supply but as a stand-alone abuse and that a duty to deal is not a precondition for establishing it. It further establishes that indispensability of the wholesale product is a central but not necessary condition when establishing margin squeeze. These points are not without controversy. Most noticeably, the treatment of margin squeeze as a standalone abuse detached from the requirement of indispensability and from the analytical framework of refusal to deal stands at odds with the Commission's approach as manifested in the Guidance Paper on Article 102 TFEU, where it considers margin squeeze as a subcategory of refusal to supply. (paras 75–90) Also contrast with the US approach as manifested in *Pacific Bell v LinkLine* (page 266, 269 above).

Also note AG Mazák's opposing opinion, in which he considered that 'a margin squeeze is abusive only where the dominant undertaking has a regulatory obligation to supply the input in question or where that input is indispensable. If the dominant undertaking's input is not indispensable, for instance, if there are substitutes available, it cannot be the subject of an abusive margin squeeze, because competitors do not need to acquire it, either at the dominant undertaking's price or indeed at all.' (para 11, AG opinion)

The burden of proof is on the dominant undertaking to establish efficiency gains counterbalancing the negative effect. Note that consumer interest was considered in *Deutsche Telekom AG v Commission* (page 264 above) as part of the finding of abuse, whereas in *TeliaSonera* it was referred to as part of efficiency defence.

In its judgment the Court of Justice made reference to Protocol No 27 TFEU and noted the wide goals of the competition provisions and Article 102 TFEU which include the prevention of distorted competition to the detriment of the public interest, individual undertakings and consumers, thereby ensuring the well-being of the European Union. The Court confirmed that Article 102 TFEU also targets practices which do not cause direct damage to consumers. (paras 22, 24) See case entry on page 225 above.

Kingdom of Spain v Commission	**Article 102 TFEU**
Case T-398/07	Abuse
General Court, 29 March 2012, not yet published	Margin Squeeze

Facts

Following a complaint from Wanadoo España the Commission investigated allegations that Telefónica engaged in a margin squeeze in the Spanish broadband internet access market. Telefónica controlled Spanish broadband internet access services to consumers. As it was uneconomical to duplicate Telefónica's access network, alternative network operators relied on Telefónica's access network. The investigation revealed that in the period between September 2001 to December 2006, the margin between Telefónica's retail prices and the price for wholesale access at regional and national level was insufficient to cover the costs that an operator as efficient as Telefónica would have to incur to provide retail broadband access. The Commission concluded that Telefónica abused its dominant position by imposing unfair prices in the form of a margin squeeze in the Spanish broadband markets. (Case COMP/38.784 *Wanadoo España v Telefónica* [2008] OJ C83/05)

In its decision the Commission noted that 'a margin squeeze is a disproportion between an upstream and a downstream price. Contrary to what Telefónica claims, there is no need to demonstrate that either the wholesale price is excessive in itself or that the retail price is predatory in itself.' (para 283) The Commission added that 'a margin squeeze can be demonstrated by showing that the dominant company's own downstream operations could not trade profitably on the basis of the upstream price charged to its competitors by the upstream operating arm of the dominant company ("equally efficient competitor" test). A margin squeeze can also be demonstrated by showing that the margin between the price charged to competitors on the upstream market for access and the price which the downstream arm of the dominant operator charges in the downstream market is insufficient to allow a reasonably efficient service provider in the downstream market to obtain a normal profit ("hypothetical reasonably efficient competitor test").' (para 311) Using the 'equally efficient competitor' test the Commission considered whether Telefónica would have been able to offer downstream services without incurring a loss if, during the period under investigation, it had had to pay the upstream access price charged to competitors as an internal transfer price for its own retail operations.' (para 312) The appropriate method for the evaluation of costs in the present case was that of long-run average incremental costs ('LRAIC'). (para 318) The Commission subsequently concluded that Telefónica's conduct constituted a clear-cut abuse by an undertaking holding a virtual monopoly. (para 742) Its conduct restricted the capacity of ADSL operators to achieve sustainable growth in the retail market and had probably harmed the interests of end users. (paras 544–618)

The Commission noted the obligation imposed on Telefónica's by Spanish law to supply on fair terms wholesale access at regional and national levels, and the obligations imposed on Telefónica by the Spanish Telecommunications Market Commission (CMT) to supply the regional wholesale product. The Commission stated nonetheless, that despite the sector being regulated, Telefónica had leeway to prevent the margin squeeze. It could have increased its retail prices or lowered its wholesale charges. (paras 665–94).

Held

'[T]he applicability of the competition rules is not ruled out where the sectoral provisions concerned do not preclude undertakings from engaging in autonomous conduct which prevents, restricts or distorts competition (see Joined Cases C-359/95P and C-379/95P *Commission and France v Ladbroke Racing* [1997] ECR I-6265, 33, 34 …).' (para 50) In this case, despite being regulated by CMT, Telefónica had the leeway to prevent the margin squeeze. In its decision the Commission stated that the finding of an infringement of Article 102 TFEU in the form of a margin squeeze was not a contradiction of CMT's policy. Contrary to what is claimed by the Kingdom of Spain, it cannot be held that the contested decision impedes the regulatory work of CMT, has consequences in respect of its future activity, or affects its regulatory policy. (paras 51–57)

In order to establish whether the pricing practices amount to an abuse, 'it is necessary to consider all the circumstances and to investigate whether the practice tends to remove or restrict the buyer's freedom to choose his sources of supply, to bar competitors from access to the market, to apply dissimilar conditions to equivalent transactions with other trading parties, or to strengthen the dominant position by distorting competition.' (para 66) Margin squeeze is assessed by consideration of the spread between the wholesale and retail prices of the vertically integrated dominant undertaking and the exclusionary effect that practice may create for competitors who are at least as efficient as the dominant undertaking. (paras 67–68)

The Kingdom of Spain claimed that where a regulatory obligation to supply a wholesale product exists, the existence of a margin squeeze is conditional on demonstration that the product was indispensable to the provision of the retail product. It further argued that the Court of Justice holding in Case C-52/09 *Konkurrensverket v TeliaSonera Sverige AB*, according to which, at times, indispensability may not be relevant for the assessment of margin squeeze, only applies where the wholesale products at issue had been voluntarily placed on the market, in the absence of any regulatory obligation. These arguments as put forward by the Kingdom of Spain must be rejected. A margin squeeze, in the absence of any objective justification, is in itself capable of constituting an abuse within the meaning of Article 102 TFEU. (*TeliaSonera*, paragraph 31).' (paras 68–69)

'[Article 102 TFEU] prohibits a dominant undertaking from, inter alia, adopting pricing practices which have an exclusionary effect on its equally efficient actual or potential competitors, that is to say practices which are capable of making market entry very difficult or impossible for such competitors, and of making it more difficult or impossible for its co-contractors to choose between various sources of supply or commercial partners, thereby strengthening its dominant position by using methods other than those which come within the scope of competition on the merits. From that point of view, therefore, not all competition by means of price can be regarded as legitimate (see judgment in Case C-280/08P *Deutsche Telekom v Commission*, paragraph 177 and case-law cited). In that regard, while it is true that, in *TeliaSonera* (paragraph 69), the Court stated that the question whether the wholesale product is indispensable may be relevant when assessing the effects of the margin squeeze, it is clear, as correctly stated by the Commission, and as the Kingdom of Spain expressly confirmed at the hearing, first, that the Kingdom of Spain referred to the circumstance of the wholesale products being indispensable only to rebut the very existence of a margin squeeze contrary to [Article 102 TFEU] … and, second, that the Kingdom of Spain has not challenged the lawfulness of recitals 543 to 563 of the contested decision, in which the Commission held that Telefónica's conduct was likely to restrict competition on the relevant markets.' (paras 93–94)

The Commission decision was upheld. Action dismissed.

Comment

In its judgment the General Court followed closely the analytical approach to margin squeeze, as laid down by the Court of Justice in Case C-52/09 *Konkurrensverket v TeliaSonera Sverige AB* (page 268 above).

As for the interface between regulation and competition law, the General Court reaffirmed the approach as manifested in Case C-280/08P *Deutsche Telekom AG v Commission* (page 264 above). EU competition law may apply to regulated markets when national regulation does not restrict the dominant undertaking's discretion in determining its action and avoiding the abuse on its own initiative.

In Case T-5/97 *Industrie des Poudres Sphériques v Commission* [2000] ECR II-3755 the General Court held that 'In the absence of abusive prices being charged … for the raw material, …, or of predatory pricing for the derived product, …, the fact that the applicant cannot, seemingly because of its higher processing costs, remain competitive in the sale of the derived product cannot justify characterising PEM's pricing policy as abusive. In that regard, it must be pointed out that a producer, even in a dominant position, is not obliged to sell its products below its manufacturing costs.' (para 179) The General Court noted that in that case the applicant failed to show that the price of the raw material was such as to eliminate an efficient competitor from the market for the derived product.

General Motors Continental v Commission	Article 102 TFEU
Case 26/75	Abuse
Court of Justice, [1975] ECR 1367, [1976] 1 CMLR 95	Excessive Pricing

Facts

General Motors Continental (GMC) was found by the Commission to have abused its dominant position by charging excessive prices for producing certain documentation which was required by drivers of GM cars in Belgium. GMC appealed to the Court of Justice, contesting the Commission's finding of excessive pricing.

Held

An undertaking in a dominant position may abuse it by imposing a price which is excessive in relation to the economic value of the service it provides, and which has the effects of curbing parallel imports or unfairly exploiting customers. (paras 11, 12)

It is not disputed that on several cases GMC imposed a charge which was excessive in relation to the economic value of the service it provided. However, the question whether GMC abused its dominant position must be considered in the light of the actual circumstances in which the charge in question was imposed. In this case the charge was confined to a limited number of cases, was imposed for a limited period and once identified was reduced by GMC. Additionally, GMC reimbursed those persons who had made complaints to it, and did so before any intervention on the part of the Commission. GMC therefore did not abuse its dominant position. (paras 16–22)

Comment

Because of the simple facts in this case the finding that the charge imposed by GM was excessive in comparison to its economic value was simple to make. In this respect the case does not reflect the practical difficulty in assessing cost and economic value of products and services. The challenge of assessing cost and establishing unfairness is better illustrated in *United Brands v Commission* (page 273 below), *Deutsche Post AG* (page 274 below) and *At the Races* (page 277 below).

Although excessive pricing is an abuse that directly affects customers and impacts on their welfare, it has seldom been the subject of formal decisions. This is largely the result of practical difficulties in assessment. Practical difficulties include the complexity of assessing the cost structure of the undertaking which is then used to establish a competitive price. This also includes the difficulty in identifying the competitive price, either by reference to cost or by comparison to other markets, and the difficulty in establishing what constitutes an unfair price.

In addition to the practical difficulties, some may object to price regulation from a policy perspective, arguing that in the absence of market failures, excessive prices motivate potential competitors to enter into the market and are therefore self-correcting. Accordingly, the regulation of excessive pricing is only called for where new entry would not occur due to high barriers to entry or other market failures. Supporting this non-interventionist approach is the risk that the prohibition of excessive pricing may, in some instances, have a detrimental effect, ex ante, on the incentives to innovate and invest, especially in dynamic markets.

United Brands v Commission	**Article 102 TFEU**
Case 27/76	Abuse
Court of Justice, [1978] ECR 207, [1978] 1 CMLR 429	Excessive Pricing

Facts

In a Commission Decision, United Brands (UBC) was found to have infringed Article 102 TFEU by abusing its dominant position in the market for bananas. Among the different abuses, the Commission investigated claims that UBC charged excessive and discriminatory prices for its 'Chiquita' brand bananas to its customers in Belgium, Luxembourg, Denmark and Germany. UBC challenged the decision before the Court of Justice and argued that it had not charged discriminatory or unfair prices. The Court of Justice accepted the Commission's finding on discriminatory pricing but rejected its economic analysis of excessive pricing.

Held

Article 102 TFEU applies to excessive pricing and may result in the finding of abuse when the dominant undertaking charges a price which is excessive, having no reasonable relation to the economic value of the product supplied. (paras 248–50) 'This excess could, inter alia, be determined objectively if it were possible for it to be calculated by making a comparison between the selling price of the product in question and its cost of production, which would disclose the amount of the profit margin; however the Commission has not done this since it has not analysed UBC's costs structure. The questions therefore to be determined are whether the difference between the costs actually incurred and the price actually charged is excessive, and, if the answer to this question is in the affirmative, whether a price has been imposed which is either unfair in itself or when compared to competing products.' (paras 251–2)

Working out the production costs may raise great difficulties, yet in this particular case 'the production costs of the banana do not seem to present any insuperable problems'. The Commission was therefore expected at the very least to require UBC to produce particulars of all the constituent elements of its production costs. (paras 254–5)

The Commission's comparison between prices charged by UBC in different Member States can in principle provide the basis for a finding of excessive pricing. In this case, however, the Commission failed to conduct a proper comparison of prices while taking all circumstances into account. (paras 258–67)

Comment

The Court of Justice establishes a two-tiered test. First the Commission should engage in cost analysis. Then, after establishing an unacceptable gap between costs and price, the actual price needs to be held unfair. The Court of Justice acknowledged that economic theorists may provide additional ways to determine whether the price of a product is unfair.

The Court accepted in principle that comparing prices between different Member States may be used to establish excessive pricing. Note also Case 395/87 *Ministère Public v Jean-Louis Tournier* [1989] ECR 2521, where the Court of Justice indicated that when a dominant undertaking charges higher fees for its services in one Member State than in others, then 'where a comparison of the fee levels has been made on a consistent basis, that difference must be regarded as indicative of an abuse of a dominant position. In such a case it is for the undertaking in question to justify the difference by reference to objective dissimilarities between the situation in the Member State concerned and the situation prevailing in all the other Member States.' (para 38)

Also note Case 30/87 *Corinne Bodson v SA Pompes Funèbres des Régions Libérées* [1988] ECR 2479, where the Court of Justice assessed the fairness of the price charged by an undertaking which held an exclusive concession for funeral services in a particular area, by comparing these charges with other areas in which the undertaking did not hold a dominant position.

Deutsche Post AG	**Article 102 TFEU**
Case COMP/C-1/36.915	Abuse
European Commission, [2001] OJ L331/40	Excessive Pricing

Facts

The Commission considered a complaint made by the British Post Office against Deutsche Post AG (DPAG) which had a statutory monopoly that included, among other things, the delivery of cross-border mail in Germany. Following its investigation the Commission found that DPAG had abused its dominant position by discriminating between different customers and by refusing to supply its delivery service unless an unjustified surcharge was paid. It also found that the price charged by DPAG for the service was excessive and that its behaviour limited the development of the German market for the delivery of international mail and of the UK market for international mail bound for Germany.

In analysing the imposition of unfair selling prices, the Commission first sought to satisfy the 'economic value benchmark' as established in *General Motors v Commission*. According to this benchmark, excessive pricing may be established if the price charged by an undertaking was excessive in comparison to the economic value of the service.

The Commission noted that a 'price which is set at a level which bears no reasonable relation to the economic value of the service provided must be regarded as excessive in itself, since it has the effect of unfairly exploiting customers. In a market which is open to competition the normal test to be applied would be to compare the price of the dominant operator with the prices charged by competitors.' (para 159)

However, a price comparison analysis in this case proved impractical due to the existence of DPAG's wide-ranging monopoly. Furthermore, cost data provided by DPAG was not detailed enough to allow detailed analysis of DPAG's average costs.

The Commission resorted to an alternative benchmark to assess the fairness of the sale price. It compared DPAG's price for incoming cross-border mail with its domestic tariff. It then concluded that the price charged by DPAG for incoming cross-border mail exceeded the average economic value of that service by at least 25 per cent.

Comment

The Commission's analysis followed the comparative approach as accepted by the Court of Justice in *United Brands*. The comparative benchmark is used where cost is too difficult to ascertain. Accordingly, the price charged by the dominant undertaking is compared to prices charged in neighbouring markets for the same product. This benchmark is by no means problem-free. One notable difficulty is in attempting to import information from other markets in order to determine what the competitive market price might have been. Another clear difficulty is the possibility that this benchmark may lead to a conclusion of excessive pricing even when the dominant undertaking's profits are minimal.

The comparative benchmark has been used in a range of cases. In Case 30/87 *Corinne Bodson v SA Pompes Funèbres des Régions Libérées* [1988] ECR 2479, [1989] 4 CMLR 984, excessiveness was assessed by making comparisons with pricing in other regions where the market was competitive. In Case 110/88 *Lucazeau v SACEM* [1989] ECR 2811, a comparison of prices charged by different undertakings for the same service in different Member States was held to form a reasonable basis for establishing excessiveness of price. Note also Case 395/87 *Ministère Public v Jean-Louis Tournier* (page 273, 274 above).

British Horseracing Board v Victor Chandler International	**Article 102 TFEU**
HC05C00510	Abuse
High Court of Justice Chancery Division, [2005] EWHC 1074 (Ch)	Excessive Pricing

Facts

The British Horseracing Board (BHB) is a company which administrates British horseracing. As part of its activities, BHB compiles data related to horseracing and charges a fee for accessing this database. The claim arose out of the refusal of a bookmaking company, Victor Chandler International (VCI) to pay the charges for using data as agreed between BHB and VCI. BHB claimed damages for breach of contract against VCI. In its defence VCI alleged, among other things, that BHB infringed Article 102 TFEU by charging high prices and abusing its dominant position. BHB applied for summary judgment against that claim.

Held (The Hon Mr Justice Laddie)

On Excessive Pricing

VCI's claim that, in effect, high prices charged by a dominant undertaking are per se abusive, is unacceptable. 'This approach is based on a number of doubtful propositions. It assumes that in a competitive market prices end up covering only the cost of production plus the cost of capital. I am not convinced that that is so. Sometimes the price may be pushed much lower than this so that all traders are making a very small, if any, margin. Sometimes the desire of the customer for the product or service is so pressing that all suppliers, even if competing with one another, can charge prices which give them a much more handsome margin. In other words, even when there is competition, some markets are buyers' markets, some are sellers'. I do not see that there is any necessary correlation between the cost of production and the cost of capital and the price which can be achieved in the market place. Furthermore the question is not whether the prices are large or small compared to some stable reference point, but whether they are fair.' (paras 47, 48)

'In addition, this [approach] breaks down as soon as one applies it in the real world. What happens if there are only a few customers? Must the cost of production, including all research and development, be recovered from them? If so, does that mean that the price varies depending on the number of customers one has? Does it also mean that the price must go down once all the research and development costs have been recovered? Does it mean that traders cannot increase the price if they engage in successful advertising campaigns which whet the consumer's appetite? If Mr Turner's proposition were correct, it would mean that for most fashion products (clothes, cars, perfumes, cosmetics, electronics and so on) the prices charged would be deemed to be unfair. Indeed it must follow that if the price of a product differed significantly in a single market or between markets in different locations, one must assume that, at best, one set of customers is getting the fair price and all the ones being charged more are being charged an unfair price. This would be so, even though no trader occupies a dominant position.' (para 49)

In *United Brands v Commission* paragraph 252 the Court of Justice held that 'The questions therefore to be determined are whether the difference between the costs actually incurred and the price actually charged is excessive, and, if the answer to this question is in the affirmative, whether a price has been imposed which is either unfair in itself or when compared to competing products.' Contrary to VCI claim it appears from this paragraph that all the Court of Justice was saying was that comparing prices with costs determines the profit margin. 'Once that has been achieved it is necessary to go on to the next stage to determine whether the price is unfair. What it did not do was suggest that high prices or high margins are the same as unfair prices. Indeed, were [VCI] right, it seems to me that the law reports would be full of cases where undertakings in dominant positions would have been found guilty of abuse by simply charging high prices. As Mr Vaughan says, the reality is that there are no such cases.' (para 51)

'[W]e still live in a free market economy where traders are allowed to run their businesses without undue interference. What [Article 102 TFEU] and Section 18 of the Act are concerned with is unfair prices, not high prices. In determining whether a price is unfair it is necessary to consider the impact on the end consumer and all of the market conditions. In a case where unfair pricing is alleged, assessment of the value of the asset both to the vendor and the purchaser must be a crucial part of the assessment. VCI's approach does not take into account value at all. It simply relates prices to the cost of acquisition or creation.' (para 56)

'Here, were one to consider value, there are numerous factors which would suggest that the allegation of unfair pricing is unjustified. This is not a case of a trader making bumper profits. On the contrary, this is concerned with undertakings, and particularly the Board, whose prime function is to nurture British horseracing. It is non-profit making. Save for administration costs it feeds back all its income into the promotion and improvement of British horseracing not only for the benefit of the general public but also for the benefit of those who have a commercial interest in the sport including bookmakers like VCI.' (para 57)

On Euro Defence—Summary Judgment

'[P]articular care is to be expected of a party who pleads … an [Article 102 TFEU] offence. These are notoriously burdensome allegations, frequently leading to extensive evidence, including expert reports from economists and accountants. The recent history of cases in which such allegations have been raised illustrate that they can lead to lengthy and expensive trials. Mere assertion in a pleading will not do. Before a party has to respond to an allegation like this, it is incumbent on the party making the allegation to set out clearly and succinctly the major facts upon which it will rely.' (para 43)

'In the material before me, there is nothing to suggest that VCI have formulated a viable argument that BHB has breached either Section 18 or [Article 102 TFEU].' (para 60)

Comment

Note that the dispute arose between contracting parties and that the excessive price claim was part of a 'Euro defence'. The Court's approach to the excessive price argument is likely to have been influenced, to some extent, by this being an attempt by VCI to avoid its contractual obligations by contesting the legality of the agreement under Article 102 TFEU. On Euro defence, see Chapter 10 below.

In his comments Justice Laddie highlighted the practical difficulty of establishing what a fair price is. Even if one succeeds in accurately establishing the cost structure, it is still difficult to assess what might be a reasonable and fair profit margin.

Laddie J questioned whether in competitive markets prices should end up covering the cost of capital (paras 47, 48). Note in this respect that the undertaking's fixed costs—which are not affected by its level of production—do not affect the price charged in the marketplace. This is so since a profit-maximising undertaking supplies additional units as long as the revenue from supplying the additional unit is greater than the cost of supplying this unit. Only the costs per unit and the demand structure, and not fixed costs, affect this mechanism.

Furthermore, the price that would have prevailed under viable competition does not necessarily resemble the variable cost—the portion of costs that does depend on the level of production. Even with viable competition, competition is seldom perfect. It typically does not drive prices all the way down to the costs of supplying each unit. The main reasons are product differentiation (consumers do not see competing products as perfect substitutes) and capacity constraints (the competing firms have constraints as to the quantity they can supply, given the size of their plant, distribution and supply networks, etc). Hence, variable cost, or the cost per unit, serves as an imperfect proxy to the price that would have prevailed in a competitive market.

The unease with which the national court approached the task of establishing the unfairness of the price was echoed in *At the Races Limited v The British Horse Racing Limits and others*. There, the Court commented that excessive price claims present the Court with a range of factual and legal problems of a kind which even specialist lawyers and economists regard as very difficult (see page 277 below).

At the Races Limited v The British Horse Racing Limits and others	**Article 102 TFEU**
A3/2006/0126	Abuse
England and Wales Court of Appeal (Civil Division), 2007 EWCA Civ 38	Excessive Pricing

Facts

An appeal on a judgment handed down by Etherton J in which he held that the British Horseracing Board Limited (BHB) had abused its dominant position, by unreasonably refusing to supply to At the Races Limited (ATR) pre-race data which was in its sole possession, and by excessively and unfairly pricing the data.

Held

The claim of abuse in this case presents the Court with a range of factual and legal problems of a kind which even specialist lawyers and economists regard as very difficult. Difficulties in assessing when the price charged by the person controlling access to the information is excessive or unfair suggest that these problems may be solved 'more satisfactorily by arbitration or by a specialist body equipped with appropriate expertise and flexible powers. The adversarial procedures of an ordinary private law action, the limited scope of expertise in the ordinary courts and the restricted scope of legal remedies available are not best suited to helping the parties out of a deadlocked negotiating position or to achieving a business-like result reflecting both their respective interests and the public interest.' (paras 3–7)

In *United Brands* a fair price was held to be one which represents or reflects the economic value of the product supplied. A price which significantly exceeds that will be prima facie excessive and unfair. In the following case it is for the Court to consider what constitutes economic value. (para 204)

'There is nothing in [Article 102 TFEU] or its jurisprudence to suggest that the index of abuse is the extent of departure from a cost + criterion. It seems to us that, in general, cost + has two other roles: one is as a baseline, below which no price can ordinarily be regarded as abusive: the other is as a default calculation, where market abuse makes the existing price untenable.' (para 207)

'Exceeding cost + is a necessary, but in no way a sufficient, test of abuse of a dominant position. … As already noted, the Commission's decision in Scandlines supports the view that the exercise under [Article 102 TFEU], while it starts from a comparison of the cost of production with the price charged, is not determined by the comparison. This in itself is sufficient to exclude a cost + test as definitive of abuse.' (paras 209–13)

In this case ATR's handsome revenues from overseas bookmakers enable it to pay the high prices demanded by BHB. The charges made by BHB eats into ATR's profit and may be unfair, but this alone does not make them abusive. The principal object of [Article 102 TFEU] is the protection of consumers, not of business competitors. Since BHB's practice did not lead to the distortion of competition it cannot be regarded as abusive. (paras 214–18)

'We appreciate that this [analysis] leaves the realistic possibility of a monopoly supplier not quite killing the goose that lays the golden eggs, but coming close to throttling her. We do not exclude the possibility that this could be held to be abusive, not least because of its potential impact on the consumer. But [Article 102 TFEU], as we said earlier, is not a general provision for the regulation of prices. It seeks to prevent the abuse of dominant market positions with the object of protecting and promoting competition. The evidence and findings here do not show ATR's competitiveness to have been, or to be at risk of being, materially compromised by the terms of the arrangements with or specified by BHB.' (para 217)

The judge erred in holding that the economic value of the pre-race data was its competitive price based on cost +. 'This method of ascertaining the economic value of this product is too narrow in that it does not take account, or sufficient account, of the value of the pre-race data to ATR and in that it ties the costs allowable in cost + too closely to the costs of producing the pre-race data.' (para 281)

Comment

The Court of Appeal held that 'economic value' should be assessed while taking into account the value to the purchaser. The court rejected the 'cost +' benchmark for assessing the economic value of the compiled data and noted that it should serve as a baseline, below which no price can ordinarily be regarded as abusive or as a default calculation where market abuse makes the existing price untenable.

The judgment is particularly important for cases involving intellectual property rights. In such cases the direct cost of acquiring intellectual property rights is often considerably lower than their economic value and price on the market.

Note that the pricing strategies in this case affected ATR's profit but not the final consumers. Although possibly unfair, the pricing policy was not considered as abusive since the end consumer was not harmed and competition was not distorted.

By focusing on the value of the product to the consumer, the judgment set the bar for proving excessive pricing at a high level. The Court accepted that this approach 'leaves the realistic possibility of a monopoly supplier not quite killing the goose that lays the golden eggs, but coming close to throttling her.' (para 217) Yet it concluded that this would not amount to an abuse under Article 102 TFEU. The difficulty with the court's approach is that it opened the door for the monopolist to increase the price as long as the customer can bear it. This in many ways is exactly what a rational monopolist would do when maximising its profits.

Note the Commission's decision in Case COMP/A.36.568.D3 *Scandlines Sverige AB v Port of Helsingborg*. There, the Commission dismissed a complaint by a ferry company of excessive and discriminatory port charges by the port operator. In the decision, while assessing the pricing strategy, the Commission considered it necessary to take account not only of the costs incurred by the port in providing its services, but also additional costs and other factors, such as the benefits to customers conferred by the particular location of the port and the frequent and short distance service. These benefits were held to represent 'an intangible value in itself, which must be taken into account as part of the assessment of the economic value of the services provided.' (paras 234–5) Accordingly, the economic value of the product/service should also reflect the demand-side features of this product/service. After considering all the relevant economic factors, the Commission concluded that there was insufficient evidence to conclude that the port charges would have 'no reasonable relation to the economic value' of the services and facilities provided to the ferry-operators. (paras 234–48)

The *Scandlines Sverige AB v Port of Helsingborg* decision was challenged before the General Court in case T-399/04 *Scandlines Sverige AB v Commission* [2005] OJ C6/40. Scandlines Sverige AB argued that the Commission erred in concluding that port charges to ferry-operators were not excessive. The Court noted: 'According to the applicant the Commission's cost/price analysis established that HHAB has been making returns, on its ferry business, of over 100% the value of the equity employed in this business. The applicant argues that such returns cannot be achieved in a competitive market and are therefore excessive, unfair and abusive. It considers that in rejecting that conclusion the Commission misapplied the term "economic value" and failed to apply the principle of proportionality or the correct burden of proof. It also contends that the Commission wrongly rejected the comparison between prices charged to ferry-operators and those charged to cargo-operators as well as the comparison between prices charged at Helsingborg and those charged at Elsinore, at the other end of the same route. The applicant also challenges the Commission's finding that there was no price discrimination in the meaning of [Article 102 TFEU] between ferry and cargo operators. According to the applicant, the Commission wrongly concluded that services provided by HHAB to those two branches are not equivalent and that there was no competitive disadvantage to the ferry operators.' The case was subsequently closed.

Commercial Solvents v Commission	**Article 102 TFEU**
Case 6/73	Abuse
Court of Justice, [1974] ECR 223, [1974] 1 CMLR 309	Refusal to Supply

Facts

Commercial Solvents Corporation (CSC) was the main supplier of the chemical amino-butanol, a raw material for the production of other chemicals. One of CSC's customers, Zoja, purchased large quantities of this raw material and used it for the manufacture of another chemical, ethambutol. CSC informed Zoja that it would stop supplying it with the raw material necessary for the production of Ethambutol. This decision coincided with CSC's decision to engage in the production of ethambutol itself. The Commission found this refusal to supply to constitute an infringement of Article 82 102 TFEU. CSC applied for the annulment of the Commission's decision.

Held

It is possible to distinguish the market in a raw material necessary for the manufacture of a product from the market on which the product is sold. An abuse of a dominant position on the market in the raw material may restrict competition in the market on which the derivatives of the raw material are sold. (para 22)

'An undertaking being in a dominant position as regards the production of raw material and therefore able to control the supply to manufacturers of derivatives, cannot, just because it decides to start manufacturing these derivatives (in competition with its former customers) act in such a way as to eliminate their competition which in the case in question, would amount to eliminating one of the principal manufacturers of Ethambutol in the [internal] market. Since such conduct is contrary to the objectives expressed in [Article 3(g) EC (now repealed)] and set out in greater detail in [Articles 101 and 102 TFEU], it follows that an undertaking which has a dominant position in the market in raw materials and which, with the object of reserving such raw materials for manufacturing its own derivatives, refuses to supply a customer, which is itself a manufacturer of these derivatives, and therefore risks eliminating all competition on the part of this customer, is abusing its dominant position within the meaning of [Article 102 TFEU]. In this context it does not matter that the undertaking ceased to supply in the spring of 1970 because of the cancellation of the purchases by Zoja, because it appears from the applicants' own statement that, when the supplies provided for in the contract had been completed, the sale of Amino-butanol would have stopped in any case.' (para 25)

Comment

Note that in this case the Court identified an upstream and downstream market. The undertaking dominated the upstream market and also operated at the downstream market. The refusal to supply a competitor at the downstream market would have eliminated the main competitor in this market and allowed the dominant undertaking to increase its holding in this market.

In Case 311/84 *Télémarketing* [1985] ECR 3261 the Court of Justice referred to the *Commercial Solvents* judgment and held that 'that ruling also applies to the case of an undertaking holding a dominant position on the market in a service which is indispensable for the activities of another undertaking on another market. If … telemarketing activities constitute a separate market from that of the chosen advertising medium, … [T]o subject the sale of broadcasting time to the condition that the telephone lines of an advertising agent belonging to the same group as the television station should be used amounts in practice to a refusal to supply the services of that station to any other telemarketing undertaking. If, further, that refusal is not justified by technical or commercial requirements relating to the nature of the television, but is intended to reserve to the agent any telemarketing operation broadcast by the said station, with the possibility of eliminating all competition from another undertaking such conduct amounts to an abuse.' (para 26)

In subsequent cases the requirement for two distinct markets was relaxed. See in particular *IMS Health* (page 286 below) in which the Court of Justice satisfied itself with the existence of a hypothetical upstream market.

BP and others v Commission	**Article 102 TFEU**
Case 77/77	Abuse
Court of Justice, [1978] ECR 1511	Refusal to Supply

Facts

The origin of the case lies in the oil 'crisis' that occurred in 1973–74 as a result of the decision of certain major oil-producing countries to sharply increase their prices for crude oil and, at the same time, to reduce production. In Case IV/28.841—*ABG Oil*, the Commission found British Petroleum Maatschappij BV ('BP') and other undertakings to have abused their dominant position by reducing their deliveries of motor spirit intended for a customer established in the Netherlands during the period of shortage by a percentage significantly greater than that applied to other customers.

Held

In its decision the Commission stated that to avoid abusing a dominant position an undertaking in BP's position must distribute 'fairly' the quantities available amongst all its customers. Accordingly, in the event of a generalised supply crisis 'all the independent companies are bound to deal in the first place with their habitual suppliers and that reductions in the supplies to purchasers in a period of shortage must be carried out on the basis of a reference period fixed in the year before the crisis.' (paras 21–22)

It is common ground that BP had already terminated its agreement with ABG in 1972. 'It emerges from the contested decision that the fact that BP in November 1972 terminated its commercial relations with ABG was connected with the regrouping of BP's operational activities which was made necessary by the nationalization of a large part of that company's interests in the production sector and by the participation of the producer countries in its extracting activities and is thus explained by considerations which have nothing to do with its relations with ABG. It therefore follows that at the time of the crisis and even from November 1972, ABG's position in relation to BP was no longer, as regards the supply of motor spirit, that of a contractual customer but that of an occasional customer.' (paras 28–29)

'The principle laid down by the contested decision that reductions in supplies ought to have been carried out on the basis of a reference period fixed in the year before the crisis, although it may be explicable in cases in which a continued supply relationship has been maintained, during that period, between seller and purchaser, cannot be applied when the supplier ceased during the course of that same period to carry on such relations with its customer, regard being had in particular to the fact that the plans of any undertaking are normally based on reasonable forecasts.' (para 30)

'For all these reasons, since ABG's position in relation to BP had been, for several months before the crisis occurred, that of an occasional customer, BP cannot be accused of having applied to it during the crisis less favourable treatment than that which it reserved for its traditional customer.' (para 32)

Decision annulled.

Comment

In his opinion, Advocate General JP Warner questioned whether Article 102 TFEU is applicable to a situation in which, owing to an emergency causing a temporary scarcity of supplies of a particular commodity, the customers becomes dependent on a supplier. He considered the function of allocating supplies in a time of scarcity to be a function of government. He subsequently argued the case falls outside the ambit of Article 102 TFEU.

On the Commission's approach to refusal to supply, note the Commission Guidance Paper, paras 75–90.

BBI and others v Boosey & Hawkes plc	**Article 102 TFEU**
Interim Measures, Case IV/32.279	Abuse
European Commission, [1987] OJ L286/36, [1988] 4 CMLR 67	Refusal to Supply

Facts

Brass Band Instruments Ltd (BBI) was established by two companies, RCN and GHH, for the purpose of manufacturing and marketing a broad range of instruments for brass bands. It was intended to compete on that market against Boosey & Hawkes plc (B&H), one of the world's largest manufacturers of musical instruments, which supplied such instruments to RCN and GHH. BBI, RCN and GHH complained to the Commission that B&H, in an attempt to protect its position on that upstream market, took abusive actions to eliminate the BBI manufacturing venture. One of the main forms of abuse was the abrupt termination of its downstream supply relation with RCN and GHH. B&H closed the RCN and GHH account without notice and refused to supply them with instruments and spare parts.

Held

'A course of conduct adopted by a dominant undertaking with a view to excluding a competitor from the market by means other than legitimate competition on the merits may constitute an infringement of [Article 102 TFEU]. In the present case the documentary evidence indicates that B&H embarked on a course of conduct intended to remove the competitive threat from BBI, and that its withdrawal of supplies from GHH and RCN was part of that plan. It is well established that refusal of supplies by a dominant producer to an established customer without objective justification may constitute an abuse under [Article 102 TFEU] (Case 27/76 *United Brands v Commission*; Cases 6/73 and 7/73 *Commercial Solvents*'. On the facts of the present case, the dependence of GHH and RCN on B&H products is such that there was a substantial likelihood of their going out of business as a result of the withholding of supplies. The injury to competition would be aggravated where (as is alleged here) the stated purpose of the action is indirectly to prevent the entry into the market of a potential competitor to the dominant producer. A dominant undertaking may always take reasonable steps to protect its commercial interests, but such measures must be fair and proportional to the threat.

'The fact that a customer of a dominant producer becomes associated with a competitor or a potential competitor of that manufacturer does not normally entitle the dominant producer to withdraw all supplies immediately or to take reprisals against that customer. There is no obligation placed on a dominant producer to subsidize competition to itself. In the case where a customer transfers its central activity to the promotion of a competing brand it may be that even a dominant producer is entitled to review its commercial relations with that customer and on giving adequate notice terminate any special relationship. However, the refusal of all supplies to GHH and RCN, and the other actions B&H has taken against them as part of its reaction to the perceived threat of BBI, would appear in the circumstances of the present case to go beyond the legitimate defence of B&H's commercial interests.' (para 19)

'On the documentary evidence currently available, the Commission considers that a sufficient prima facie case of abuse under [Article 102 TFEU] has been established for it to order limited interim measures.' (para 21)

Comment

Note that the refusal to supply in this case was intended to protect the upstream market where the company enjoyed a dominant position. As such it differs from cases such as *Commercial Solvents v Commission* (page 279 above) in which the dominant undertaking refuse to supply the downstream player so to improve its position on that market.

Sea Containers Ltd/Stena Sealink	**Article 102 TFEU**
Case IV/34.689, (Interim measures)	Abuse
European Commission, [1994] OJ L15/8	Refusal to Supply

Facts

Sealink was the owner and operator of the port of Holyhead in Anglesey, Wales, and operated ferry services between the United Kingdom, Ireland and France. Sea Containers Ltd (SC) operated passenger, car and freight ferry services and was looking to expand its ferry services. It entered into negotiations with Sealink in order to expand its access rights to the port of Holyhead. When Sealink refused to allow adequate access, SC complained to the Commission and argued that Sealink was abusing its dominant position by failing to allow SC access on a reasonable basis to an essential facility. After the complaint was made, but before the Commission's decision, the parties reached an agreement on schedule and access rights. Despite this, the Commission considered that there remains sufficient public interest in this case and issued a formal decision.

Decision

After establishing Sealink's dominant position in the market for the provision of port facilities for car and passenger ferry operations on the central corridor route between the United Kingdom and Ireland, the Commission considered the question of abuse.

'An undertaking which occupies a dominant position in the provision of an essential facility and itself uses that facility (i.e. a facility or infrastructure, without access to which competitors cannot provide services to their customers), and which refuses other companies access to that facility without objective justification or grants access to competitors only on terms less favourable than those which it gives its own services, infringes [Article 102 TFEU] if the other conditions of that Article are met. An undertaking in a dominant position may not discriminate in favour of its own activities in a related market. The owner of an essential facility which uses its power in one market in order to protect or strengthen its position in another related market, in particular, by refusing to grant access to a competitor, or by granting access on less favourable terms than those of its own services, and thus imposing a competitive disadvantage on its competitor, infringes [Article 102 TFEU].' (para 66)

Where the operator of an essential facility is required to provide access on non-discriminatory terms, interim measures to enable a new competitor to enter a market require stronger justification than measures maintaining the situation of an already established competitor. (paras 57, 67) In this case Sealink treated the request by SC in a discriminatory manner. It consistently delayed and raised difficulties concerning SC's possible use of existing facilities while rapidly approving its own fast ferry service. (paras 70–4)

'It is the Commission's view that in the circumstances of the present case an independent harbour authority, which would of course have had an interest in increasing revenue at the port, would at least have considered whether the interests of existing and proposed users of the port could best be reconciled by a solution involving modest changes in the allocated slot times or in any plans for the development of the harbour. In situations such as the present one, unless a solution is considered fully and discussed with all the interests involved, it is likely that a port authority which is not independent will prefer an arrangement which minimizes inconvenience to itself (especially in relation to its own operations as a user) but which does not necessarily provide non-discriminatory access to the new entrant. If Sealink, in drawing up the various versions of its redevelopment plan for the east side, had always duly consulted SC … it might have been possible to avoid the difficulty of reconciling the plan with SC's wish for temporary facilities there.' (para 75)

Comment

Note an earlier Commission decision in *Sealink/B&I Holyhead* (Interim measures) [1992] 5 CMLR 255, which dealt with similar facts. In cases involving ferry services, a central question is whether the Commission was right in finding the port to be an essential facility. Much depends on the market definition which may result in a narrow market served by one port or a wider market served by several facilities.

RTE & ITP v Commission ('Magill')	Article 102 TFEU
Joined Cases C-241/91P and 242/91P	Abuse
Court of Justice, [1995] ECR I-743, [1995] 4 CMLR 718	Refusal to Supply

Facts

Magill TV Guide Ltd (Magill) wanted to introduce a new television publication which would provide a comprehensive weekly television guide in Ireland. To do so, it required the consent of the television stations, among them RTE and ITP, who owned the copyrights for the relevant information. Although at the time, the companies provided third parties with information on a daily basis, they refused to provide Magill with a weekly listing of programmes. The Commission found the refusal to constitute an abuse of Article 102 TFEU. RTE and ITP applied for the annulment of the Commission's decision. Following the General Court dismissal of the appeal, the companies appealed to the Court of Justice.

Held

'So far as a dominant position is concerned, it is to be remembered at the outset that mere ownership of an intellectual property right cannot confer such a position.' (para 46)

However, in this case, the television stations are the only source of information relating to the listings of their programmes and therefore hold a dominant position by reason of their de facto monopoly over the information. As such they are in a position to prevent effective competition on the market in weekly television magazines in the areas concerned. (para 47)

A refusal to grant a licence, even if it is the act of an undertaking holding a dominant position, cannot in itself constitute abuse of a dominant position. Nonetheless, the exercise of an exclusive right by the proprietor may, in exceptional circumstances, involve abusive conduct. (paras 49, 50)

In the present case, the refusal to provide information by relying on national copyright provisions prevented the appearance of a new product, a comprehensive weekly guide to television programmes, which the television companies did not offer and for which there was a potential consumer demand. There was no justification for such refusal which constitutes an abuse under Article 102(2)(b) TFEU. (paras 51–5)

By their conduct, the television companies reserved to themselves the secondary market of weekly television guides by excluding all competition on that market. (para 56) The General Court did not err in law in holding that the appellants' conduct was an abuse of a dominant position.

Comment

The case demonstrates the possible tension between the protection granted to intellectual property rights and competition law. Note that mere ownership of an intellectual property right does not necessarily establish the existence of a dominant position.

The special circumstances in Magill which swung the balance in favour of an obligation to license were highlighted in Case C-7/97 *Oscar Bronner* (page 284 below): (1) the refusal in question concerned a product the supply of which was indispensable for carrying on the business in question; (2) such refusal prevented the appearance of a new product for which there was a potential consumer demand; (3) the refusal was likely to exclude all competition in the secondary market of television guides; and (4) it was not justified by objective considerations. (*Oscar Bronner*, paras 39–41)

Note that the case involved a 'weak copyright' concerning lists of television and radio programmes. The doubts raised as to the justification of the copyright protection in this case to 'compilation of banal information' may have played a role in the Court's decision. Also note the secondary role played by this information and the limited impact the finding of abuse might have had on innovation and investment.

Oscar Bronner GmbH Co KG v Mediaprint	**Article 102 TFEU**
Case C-7/97	Abuse
Court of Justice, [1998] ECR I-7791, [1999] 4 CMLR 112	Refusal to Supply

Facts

Oscar Bronner GmbH & Co KG (Bronner) was the publisher of the Austrian daily newspaper *Der Standard*. Bronner wanted to use the nationwide home-delivery service for daily newspapers which was owned by the Mediaprint group and operated for the distribution of its own newspapers. Although there were a number of regional or local networks, Mediaprint's network was the only nationwide network in Austria. Mediaprint refused to provide Bronner with access to its delivery system. Bronner applied to the national Austrian court for an order requiring Mediaprint to refrain from abusing its alleged dominant position on the market and to allow Bronner access to its nationwide home-delivery service for daily newspapers. A preliminary reference from the Austrian court.

Held

In order to assess whether the refusal by Mediaprint to allow access to the single nationwide home-delivery scheme in Austria constitutes an abuse of a dominant position, one needs to consider the indispensability of this scheme for the distribution of newspapers. It is undisputed that other methods of distributing daily newspapers, although maybe less advantageous for the distribution of certain newspapers, exist. These include distribution by post and through sale in shops and at kiosks. (paras 42–4)

Moreover, it does not appear that there are any technical, legal or even economic obstacles which prevent other publishers of daily newspapers from establishing a second nationwide home-delivery scheme. The fact that the small circulation prevents a publisher from setting up, alone or with others, a second nationwide home-delivery scheme does not make the access to existing nationwide home-delivery scheme indispensable. For this to be considered indispensable it is necessary to establish at the very least that that the creation of a second nationwide home-delivery scheme with a circulation comparable to that of the daily newspapers distributed by the existing scheme is not economically viable. (paras 45, 46)

Comment

The Court distinguished the facts in this case from the circumstances in *Commercial Solvents v Commission* where the refusal to supply would have eliminated all competition from the rival's business. (para 38)

The Court referred to the exceptional circumstances in *Magill* (page 283 above) which were not found in this case. There, (1) the refusal to supply concerned a product which was indispensable for carrying on the business in question, (2) the refusal prevented the appearance of a new product for which there was a potential consumer demand, (3) the refusal was likely to exclude all competition in the secondary market, and (4) it was not justified by objective considerations. (paras 39–41)

In his opinion, AG Jacobs commented on the careful balancing of conflicting considerations which is required before interfering with a dominant undertaking's freedom to contract: 'In the long term it is generally pro-competitive and in the interest of consumers to allow a company to retain for its own use facilities which it has developed for the purpose of its business. … the incentive for a dominant undertaking to invest in efficient facilities would be reduced if its competitors were, upon request, able to share the benefits. Thus the mere fact that by retaining a facility for its own use a dominant undertaking retains an advantage over a competitor cannot justify requiring access to it. … It is on the other hand clear that refusal of access may in some cases entail elimination or substantial reduction of competition to the detriment of consumers in both the short and the long term. … In assessing such conflicting interests, particular care is required where the goods or services or facilities to which access is demanded represent the fruit of substantial investment. That may be true in particular in relation to refusal to license intellectual property rights.' (paras 57, 61, 62)

Tiercé Ladbroke SA v Commission	**Article 102 TFEU**
Case T-504/93	Abuse
General Court, [1995] ECR II-923, [1997] 5 CMLR 309	Refusal to Supply, Discrimination

Facts

Tiercé Ladbroke SA (Ladbroke) operated betting shops in Belgium. It approached the French Horse-Racing Associations and their affiliated companies (the Associations), and asked them to grant it the right to retransmit televised pictures and sound commentaries of French races in its betting outlets in Belgium. Following the Associations' refusal to grant the rights, Ladbroke lodged a complaint with the Commission alleging, among other things, that this refusal to supply constituted an abuse of a dominant position. The Commission rejected the complaint. Ladbroke brought an action for annulment before the General Court.

Held

The relevant geographical market in this case is national and comprises Belgium. Consequently, the arbitrariness of the refusal of the Associations to supply French sound and pictures to Ladbroke cannot be assessed in light of the policy followed by the Associations on other, geographically distinct, markets. In other words the practice involves no discrimination as between operators on the same market. The fact that Ladbroke is prepared to pay an appropriate fee for the licence to transmit French races does not constitute sufficient evidence of an abuse in the absence of discrimination against it by the Associations in the relevant geographical market. (paras 126–9)

'The applicant cannot rely on the *Magill* judgment to demonstrate the existence of the alleged abuse, since that decision is not in point. In contrast to the position in *Magill*, where the refusal to grant a licence to the applicant prevented it from entering the market in comprehensive television guides, in this case the applicant is not only present in, but has the largest share of, the main betting market on which the product in question, namely sound and pictures, is offered to consumers whilst the [Associations], the owners of the intellectual property rights, are not present on that market. Accordingly, in the absence of direct or indirect exploitation by the [Associations] of their intellectual property rights on the Belgian market, their refusal to supply cannot be regarded as involving any restriction of competition on the Belgian market.' (para 130)

Moreover, the refusal to supply Ladbroke could not fall within the Article 102 TFEU prohibition unless it concerned a product or service which was either essential for the exercise of the activity in question, in that there was no real or potential substitute, or was a new product whose introduction might be prevented, despite specific, constant and regular potential demand from consumers. In the present case the televised broadcasting of horse races, although constituting an additional service for bettors, is not in itself indispensable for the exercise of Ladbroke's main activity on the Belgian betting market. (paras 131, 132)

For the same reasons, Ladbroke cannot rely on the *London European v Sabena* decision in which the action taken to exclude a competitor related to a market in which both Sabena and that competitor, London European, were operating, whereas in this case the Associations are not present on the Belgian market. The same applies to *ICI and Commercial Solvents v Commission*, where Commercial Solvents, like its customers, was present on the downstream market, namely the market in derivatives. (para 133)

Comment

The Court distinguished between the circumstances in *Magill* and those in this case. (para 130) In para 131 the Court noted that the refusal to supply 'could not fall within the prohibition laid down by [Article 102 TFEU] unless it concerned a product or service which was either essential for the exercise of the activity in question … or was a new product whose introduction might be prevented …' In doing so, the court widened the scope of the doctrine by treating conditions (1) and (2) in *Magill* as alternatives rather than cumulative conditions. For another example of a wide reading of the *Magill* conditions, see *Intel v Via* (page 288 below).

IMS Health GmbH & Co OHG v NDC Health GmbH & Co KG Case C-418/01 Court of Justice, [2000] ECR I-5039, [2004] 4 CMLR 28	**Article 102 TFEU** Abuse Refusal to Supply

Facts

A reference from the German court concerning a dispute between IMS and NDC regarding the use of IMS's '1,860 brick structure' by NDC. The system, owned by IMS, provided data on regional sales of pharmaceutical products in Germany according to a brick structure consisting of 1,860 bricks and a derived structure consisting of 2,847 bricks. IMS marketed its brick structures and also distributed them free of charge to pharmacies and doctors' surgeries. That practice helped those structures to become the normal industry standard to which its clients adapted their information and distribution systems. NDC (formerly PII), whose activity also consisted in marketing regional data on pharmaceutical products in Germany, designed a brick structure which was very similar to the IMS product. IMS applied to the German court for an interlocutory order prohibiting PII (NDC) from using any brick structure derived from the IMS 1,860 brick structure. The German court granted the order and based its decision on the finding that the brick structure used by IMS is a database which may be protected by copyright. The German court stayed the proceedings and referred three questions to the Court of Justice, the central one being whether the refusal by a dominant undertaking to grant a licence to use a brick structure for which it has an intellectual property right, to another undertaking which wishes to provide such data in the same market and due to market characteristics has to use the same brick structure, constitutes an abuse of a dominant position.

Held

The question submitted by the German court is based on the premise, whose validity it is for the national court to ascertain, that the use of the 1,860 brick structure protected by an intellectual property right is indispensable in order to allow a potential competitor to have access to the market in which the undertaking which owns the right occupies a dominant position. In order to determine this indispensability the national court needs to consider whether there are products or services which constitute alternative solutions, even if they are less advantageous, and whether there are technical, legal or economic obstacles capable of making it impossible or at least unreasonably difficult to create the alternative products or services. As highlighted in paragraph 46 of the Court of Justice judgment in *Bronner*, in order to accept the existence of economic obstacles, it must be established, at the very least, that the creation of those products or services is not economically viable for production on a scale comparable to that of the undertaking which controls the existing product or service. (paras 22, 28)

A refusal to grant a licence, even if it is the act of an undertaking holding a dominant position, cannot in itself constitute abuse of a dominant position. However, the exercise of an exclusive right by the owner may, in exceptional circumstances, involve abusive conduct. (paras 34, 35)

Such exceptional circumstances were present in the case giving rise to the judgment in *Magill* which was later referred to in *Bronner*. There, the Court indicated that the exceptional circumstances in *Magill* were constituted by the fact that the refusal in question concerned a product the supply of which was indispensable for carrying on the business in question, the refusal prevented the emergence of a new product for which there was a potential consumer demand, the fact that it was not justified by objective considerations, and was likely to exclude all competition in the secondary market. (paras 36–8)

It is clear from that case-law that in order for the refusal by an undertaking which owns a copyright to give access to a product or service indispensable for carrying on a particular businesss to be treated as abusive, three cumulative conditions need to be satisfied: (1) the refusal is preventing the emergence of a new product for which there is a potential consumer demand; (2) the refusal is not justified by objective considerations; and (3) the refusal will exclude any competition on a secondary market. (paras 38, 52)

As for the first condition concerning the emergence of a new product, in balancing the interest in protection of the intellectual property right and the economic freedom of its owner, against the interest in protection of free competition, the latter can prevail only where refusal by the dominant undertaking to grant a licence to an indispensable product prevents the development of the secondary market to the detriment of consumers. Therefore, such refusal may be regarded as abusive only where the undertaking requesting the licence does not intend to limit itself to duplicating the goods or services already offered on the secondary market by the owner of the intellectual property right, but intends to produce new goods or services not offered by the owner of the right and for which there is a potential consumer demand. (paras 48, 49)

With respect to the second condition, relating to whether the refusal was unjustified, it is for the national court to examine whether the refusal is justified by objective considerations. (para 51)

With respect to the third condition, concerning the likelihood of excluding all competition on a secondary market, one needs to identify an upstream market, constituted by the product or service, and a secondary downstream market, on which the product or service in question is used for the production of another product or the supply of another service. The fact that the upstream product is not marketed separately does not preclude, from the outset, the possibility of identifying two separate markets. Such was the situation in Case C-7/97 *Bronner* where the home-delivery service was not marketed separately. (paras 40–43)

'For the purposes of the application of the earlier case-law, it is sufficient that a potential market or even a hypothetical market can be identified. Such is the case where the products or services are indispensable in order to carry on a particular business and where there is an actual demand for them on the part of undertakings which seek to carry on the business for which they are indispensable.' (para 44)

'Accordingly, it is determinative that two different stages of production may be identified and that they are interconnected, inasmuch as the upstream product is indispensable for the supply of the downstream product. Transposed to the facts of the case in the main proceedings, that approach prompts consideration as to whether the 1,860 brick structure constitutes, upstream, an indispensable factor in the downstream supply of German regional sales data for pharmaceutical products.' (paras 45, 46)

Comment

In paragraphs 44–6 the Court held that the finding of 'a potential market or even hypothetical market' would suffice. This proposition undermines the distinction between upstream and downstream markets. Note that the finding of a fictional upstream market may result in compulsory licensing from a dominant undertaking to its competitor. Contrast this approach with the US approach as evident in *Verizon Communications Inc v Trinko LLP*, 540 US 398. There the US Supreme Court considered the absence of two distinct markets as a relevant factor in its decision not to condemn a refusal to supply (para 5).

Arguably, by widening the breadth of the doctrine, the ruling risked undermining companies' incentive to invest and innovate. Moreover, by stripping the dominant undertaking of its main asset, the doctrine challenges not only the alleged abuse but also the position of dominance.

Similar to the *Magill* case, it is possible to question the justification of the copyright protection afforded in this case. Since IMS developed the brick structure in collaboration with pharmaceutical companies and it became the de facto industry standard, one might argue that competition law was used here to remedy unjustified over protection by the intellectual property laws.

Note that prior to the reference from the national court, the Commission also addressed the issue following a complaint made by NDC. In an interim decision the Commission, noting the *Ladbroke* decision, held that refusal to supply will be objectionable even without it preventing the emergence of a new product. On appeal the president of the General Court suspended the operation of the decision.

In Case T-201/04 *Microsoft Corp v Commission* the General Court reaffirmed its ruling in *IMS* (para 43 above) that an actual second market was not necessary. (para 335)

Intel Corporation v Via Technologies Inc	**Article 102 TFEU**
Cases No A3/2002/1380 and A3/2002/1381	Abuse
English Court of Appeal, [2002] EWCA Civ 1905	Refusal to Supply

Facts

Two patent infringement actions brought by Intel Corporation (Intel) in the patent court against Via Technologies (Via), alleging that Via infringed five of Intel's patents. Via's defence in the patent court was based on, among other things, the claim that Intel's actions infringed Articles 101 and 102 TFEU. The Court awarded Intel summary judgment. Via appealed the summary judgment. On appeal the Court considered, among other things, whether Intel's refusal to licence a patent on reasonable terms may amount to an abuse of a dominant position. The Court made reference to the 'exceptional circumstances' benchmark in Magill (*RTE and others v European Commission*) and its interpretation in *IMS Health Inc v European Commission* and considered whether Via has pleaded facts which are capable of constituting such exceptional circumstances.

Held

The Court does not accept Intel's argument that *IMS* and *Magill* show that there can only be exceptional circumstances within the *Magill* test if all the conditions in either *Magill* or *IMS* are satisfied. Thus, the result of the refusal must be to exclude an entirely new product from the market (*Magill*) or all competition to the patentee (*IMS*).

'*Magill* and *IMS* indicate the circumstances which the Court of Justice and the President of the [General Court] respectively regarded as exceptional in the cases before them. It does not follow that other circumstances in other cases will not be regarded as exceptional. In particular it is at least arguable, as the President recognised in *IMS*, that the Court of Justice will assimilate its jurisprudence under [Article 102 TFEU] more closely with that of the essential facilities doctrine applied in the United States. In that event there could be a breach of [Article 102 TFEU] without the exclusion of a wholly new product or all competition. This approach seems to me to be warranted by the width of the descriptions of abuse contained in [Article 102 TFEU] itself.' (paras 47, 48)

Accordingly the Court finds it arguable that the range of 'exceptional circumstances' which may give rise to an abuse by the owner of an intellectual property right of his dominant position can extend to the facts pleaded by Via.

Comment

In these proceedings the Appeal Court considered whether Via's defences under Articles 101 and 102 TFEU have real prospects of success. The Court therefore did not have to reach a final decision on the issues at stake but rather to consider whether these provide a sufficient basis meriting permission to appeal. Permission was granted.

The Court adopted a wide interpretation and held that a patent holder may be restricted from exercising his Intellectual Property Rights in circumstances which differ from those identified in *Magill* and *IMS*. In doing so, the summary judgment widens the instances in which compulsory licensing may be granted and narrows the requirement for a new product and exclusion of all competition. One should treat such approach with caution, taking into account the impact it may have on investment in innovation. This is so in particular when applying the doctrine to 'strong' Intellectual Property Rights such as patents.

The Court considered the potential effect US jurisprudence might have on the scope of abuse. It made reference to the opinion of Advocate-General Jacobs in *Oscar Bronner v Mediaprint* where the AG referred to the increasing similarities between the doctrine of essential facilities as applied in the United States and the practice of the European Commission (paras 45–51, AG opinion).

Microsoft Corp v Commission	**Article 102 TFEU**
Case T-201/04	Abuse
General Court, [2007] ECR II-3601, [2007] 5 CMLR 11	Refusal to Supply

Facts

An action for annulment of Commission decision Comp/C-3/37.792 in which the Commission found Microsoft to have infringed Article 102 TFEU by refusing to supply interoperability information to its competitors and by tying its Windows Media Player to its operating system. (On tying see page 302 below.) The Commission found Microsoft's refusal to supply to infringe Article 102(b) TFEU by limiting technical development to the prejudice of consumers. The Commission ordered Microsoft to license on reasonable and non-discriminatory terms the relevant interoperability information to its competitors. It noted that, on balance, the possible negative impact of an order to supply on Microsoft's incentives to innovate is outweighed by its positive impact on the level of innovation of the whole industry (including Microsoft). Microsoft appealed the decision and argued, among other things, that refusal to supply interoperability information cannot constitute an abuse of a dominant position within the meaning of Article 102 TFEU because (i) the information is protected by intellectual property rights (or constitutes trade secrets), and (ii) the criteria established in the case-law which determine when an undertaking in a dominant position can be required to grant a license to a third party are not satisfied in this case.

Held

It follows from the *Magill*, *IMS Health* and *Bronner* judgments that a refusal by a dominant undertaking 'to license a third party to use a product covered by an intellectual property right cannot in itself constitute an abuse of a dominant position within the meaning of [Article 102 TFEU]. It is only in exceptional circumstances that the exercise of the exclusive right by the owner of the intellectual property right may give rise to such an abuse.' (paras 331, 131–331)

'It also follows from that case-law that the following circumstances, in particular, must be considered to be exceptional: in the first place, the refusal relates to a product or service indispensable to the exercise of a particular activity on a neighboring market; in the second place, the refusal is of such a kind as to exclude any effective competition on that neighboring market; in the third place, the refusal prevents the appearance of a new product for which there is potential consumer demand.' (para 332)

Indispensability

The Commission was right to conclude that in order to be able to compete viably with Windows workgroup server operating systems, competitors' operating systems must be able to interoperate with the Windows domain architecture on an equal footing with those Windows systems. The Commission did not err in its analysis when it found that the information concerning the interoperability with the Windows domain architecture was indispensable. (paras 369–436)

Elimination of all effective competition

'In the contested decision, the Commission considered whether the refusal at issue gave rise to a "risk" of the elimination of competition on the work group server operating systems market. Microsoft contends that that criterion is not sufficiently strict, since according to the case-law on the exercise of an intellectual property right the Commission must demonstrate that the refusal to license an intellectual property right to a third party is "likely to eliminate all competition", or, in other words, that there is a "high probability" that the conduct in question will have such a result. The Court finds that Microsoft's complaint is purely one of terminology and is wholly irrelevant. The expressions "risk of elimination of competition" and "likely to eliminate competition" are used without distinction by the [Union] judicature to reflect the same idea, namely that [Article 102 TFEU] does not apply only from the time when there is no more, or practically no more, competition on the market. If the Commission were required to wait until competitors were eliminated from the market, or until their elimination was sufficiently imminent, before being able to take action under

[Article 102 TFEU], that would clearly run counter to the objective of that provision, which is to maintain undistorted competition in the common market and, in particular, to safeguard the competition that still exists on the relevant market. In this case, the Commission had all the more reason to apply [Article 102 TFEU] before the elimination of competition on the work group server operating systems market had become a reality because that market is characterised by significant network effects and because the elimination of competition would therefore be difficult to reverse. ... Nor is it necessary to demonstrate that all competition on the market would be eliminated. What matters, for the purpose of establishing an infringement of [Article 102 TFEU], is that the refusal at issue is liable to, or is likely to, eliminate all effective competition on the market. It must be made clear that the fact that the competitors of the dominant undertaking retain a marginal presence in certain niches on the market cannot suffice to substantiate the existence of such competition.' (paras 560–63)

Preventing the appearance of a new product

'It must be emphasised that the fact that the applicant's conduct prevents the appearance of a new product on the market falls to be considered under [Article 102(b) TFEU], which prohibits abusive practices which consist in "limiting production, markets or technical developments to the ... prejudice of consumers".' (para 643)

'The circumstance relating to the appearance of a new product, as envisaged in *Magill* and *IMS Health* ... cannot be the only parameter which determines whether a refusal to license an intellectual property right is capable of causing prejudice to consumers within the meaning of [Article 102(b) TFEU]. As that provision states, such prejudice may arise where there is a limitation not only of production or markets, but also of technical development.' (para 647)

'It was on that last hypothesis that the Commission based its finding in the contested decision. Thus, the Commission considered that Microsoft's refusal to supply the relevant information limited technical development to the prejudice of consumers within the meaning of [Article 102(b) TFEU] (recitals 693 to 701 and 782 to the contested decision) and it rejected Microsoft's assertion that it had not been demonstrated that its refusal caused prejudice to consumers (recitals 702 to 708 to the contested decision).' (para 648)

'The Court finds that the Commission's findings at the recitals referred to in the preceding paragraph are not manifestly incorrect.' (para 649)

'Thus, the contested decision rests on the concept that, once the obstacle represented for Microsoft's competitors by the insufficient degree of interoperability with the Windows domain architecture has been removed, those competitors will be able to offer work group server operating systems which, far from merely reproducing the Windows systems already on the market, will be distinguished from those systems with respect to parameters which consumers consider important ...' (para 656)

'It must be borne in mind, in that regard, that Microsoft's competitors would not be able to clone or reproduce its products solely by having access to the interoperability information covered by the contested decision. Apart from the fact that Microsoft itself acknowledges in its pleadings that the remedy prescribed by Article 5 of the contested decision would not allow such a result to be achieved ... it is appropriate to repeat that the information at issue does not extend to implementation details or to other features of Microsoft's source code. ... The Court also notes that the protocols whose specifications Microsoft is required to disclose in application of the contested decision represent only a minimum part of the entire set of protocols implemented in Windows work group server operating systems.' (para 657)

'Nor would Microsoft's competitors have any interest in merely reproducing Windows work group server operating systems. Once they are able to use the information communicated to them to develop systems that are sufficiently interoperable with the Windows domain architecture, they will have no other choice, if they wish to take advantage of a competitive advantage over Microsoft and maintain a profitable presence on the market, than to differentiate their products from Microsoft's products with respect to certain parameters and certain features. It must be borne in mind that, as the Commission explains at recitals 719 to 721 to the contested decision, the implementation of specifications is a difficult task which requires significant investment in money and time.' (para 658)

Microsoft's assertion that its refusal did not cause prejudice to consumers is unfounded. 'It is settled case-law that [Article 102 TFEU] covers not only practices which may prejudice consumers directly but also those which indirectly prejudice them by impairing an effective competitive structure (Case 85/76 *Hoffmann-La Roche v Commission* [1979] ECR 461, paragraph 125, and *Irish Sugar v Commission*, paragraph 229 above, paragraph 232). In this case, Microsoft impaired the effective competitive structure on the work group server operating systems market by acquiring a significant market share on that market.' (paras 664, 660–5)

The absence of objective justification

Microsoft relied as justification for its conduct solely on the fact that the technology concerned was covered by intellectual property rights. This argument cannot be accepted. The protection of the technology by intellectual property rights cannot constitute objective justification within the meaning of *Magill* and *IMS Health*. Microsoft did not sufficiently establish that if it were required to disclose the interoperability information that would have a significant negative impact on its incentives to innovate. (paras 688–711)

Comment

The General Court upheld the Commission's finding that Microsoft abused its dominant position by refusing to provide interoperability information. At three distinct levels, the judgment eroded the threshold for intervention that was established in previous cases:

[1] The Court held that the circumstances relating to the appearance of a new product, as envisaged in *Magill* and *IMS Health*, 'cannot be the only parameter which determines whether a refusal to license an intellectual property right is capable of causing prejudice to consumers within the meaning of [Article 102(b) TFEU].' (para 647) It thus used Article 102(b) TFEU to 'import' innovation into the equation. This 'internal' expansion tips the balance of the carefully crafted list of exceptional circumstances in the Magill and IMS cases and lowers the threshold for finding an abusive refusal to licence.

[2] The Court widened the notion of *indispensability*. Earlier cases were based on the absence of a potential or actual substitute which was objectively indispensible. Yet, in *Microsoft*, although access to the market might have been technically possible, the Court found that Microsoft's refusal eliminated the economic viability of such entry. It thus broadened the concept of *indispensability* to take account of economic viability.

[3] The Court lowered the threshold for intervention by eroding the requirement for elimination of *all* competition in the secondary market. In para 563 it held that it is not 'necessary to demonstrate that all competition on the market would be eliminated. What matters … is that the refusal at issue is liable to, or is likely to, eliminate all effective competition on the market.'

More generally note the General Court's findings in para 664 where as part of the assessment of consumer harm, the General Court held that Microsoft impaired competition by acquiring a significant market share. This statement controversially treats the mere attainment of significant market share as anticompetitive and stands at odds with an effects-based approach.

In its Guidance Paper the Commission makes reference to the Microsoft judgment and states that: 'The Commission considers that consumer harm may, for instance, arise where the competitors that the dominant undertaking forecloses are, as a result of the refusal, prevented from bringing innovative goods or services to market and/or where follow-on innovation is likely to be stifled.' (para 87)

With respect to objective justification the General Court made it clear that protection of the technology by intellectual property rights cannot constitute objective justification. The Court explained that if the mere fact of holding intellectual property rights could in itself constitute objective justification, the refusal to license could never be considered to constitute an infringement of Article 102 TFEU. (para 690)

Sot Lélos kai Sia EE and others v GlaxoSmithKline AEVE	**Article 102 TFEU**
Joined Cases C-468/06 to C-478/06	Abuse
Court of Justice, [2008] ECR I-7139	Refusal to Supply

Facts

A preliminary reference from the Greek court made in proceedings brought against GlaxoSmithKline AEVE (GSK AEVE) in respect of its refusal to meet wholesalers' orders for certain medicinal products. The Court of Justice was asked, among other things, whether a refusal of a dominant undertaking to meet orders sent to it by pharmaceuticals wholesalers, on account of the fact that those wholesalers are involved in parallel exports of those products to other Member States, constitutes per se an abuse.

Held

'The established case-law of the Court shows that the refusal by an undertaking occupying a dominant position on the market of a given product to meet the orders of an existing customer constitutes abuse of that dominant position under [Article 102 TFEU] where, without any objective justification, that conduct is liable to eliminate a trading party as a competitor (see, to that effect, Joined Cases 6/73 and 7/73 *Istituto Chemioterapico Italiano and Commercial Solvents v Commission* [1974] ECR 223, paragraph 25, and Case 27/76 *United Brands v Commission* [1978] ECR 207, paragraph 183).' (para 34)

'With regard to a refusal by an undertaking to deliver its products in one Member State to wholesalers which export those products to other Member States, such an effect on competition may exist not only if the refusal impedes the activities of those wholesalers in that first Member State, but equally if it leads to the elimination of effective competition from them in the distribution of the products on the markets of the other Member States.' (para 35)

'In this case it is common ground between the parties in the main proceedings that, by refusing to meet the Greek wholesalers' orders, GSK AEVE aims to limit parallel exports by those wholesalers to the markets of other Member States in which the selling prices of the medicinal products in dispute are higher.' (para 36)

'In respect of sectors other than that of pharmaceutical products, the Court has held that a practice by which an undertaking in a dominant position aims to restrict parallel trade in the products that it puts on the market constitutes abuse of that dominant position, particularly when such a practice has the effect of curbing parallel imports by neutralising the more favourable level of prices which may apply in other sales areas in the [Union] (see, to that effect, Case 26/75 *General Motors Continental v Commission* [1975] ECR 1367, paragraph 12) or when it aims to create barriers to re-importations which come into competition with the distribution network of that undertaking (Case 226/84 *British Leyland v Commission* [1986] ECR 3263, paragraph 24). Indeed, parallel imports enjoy a certain amount of protection in [Union] law because they encourage trade and help reinforce competition (Case C-373/90, [1992] ECR I-131, paragraph 12).' (para 37)

GSK AEVE argued that parallel exports of medicinal products bring only few financial benefits to the ultimate consumers. According to GSK, such may be the case when the wholesalers carrying out the exports will themselves make a profit from that parallel trade. Even so, parallel exports of medicinal products to a Member State in which prices are high opens up an alternative source of supply to buyers and is capable of offering the same products on the market of that Member State at lower prices than those applied on the same market by the pharmaceuticals companies. (paras 52–55)

'As a result, even in the Member States where the prices of medicines are subject to State regulation, parallel trade is liable to exert pressure on prices and, consequently, to create financial benefits not only for the social health insurance funds, but equally for the patients concerned, for whom the proportion of the price of medicines for which they are responsible will be lower. At the same time, as the Commission notes, parallel trade in medicines from one Member State to another is likely to increase the choice available to entities in the latter Member State which obtain supplies of medicines by means of a public procurement procedure, in which the parallel importers can offer medicines at lower prices.' (para 56)

'Accordingly, without it being necessary for the Court to rule on the question whether it is for an undertaking in a dominant position to assess whether its conduct vis- à-vis a trading party constitutes abuse in the light of the degree to which that party's activities offer advantages to the final consumers, it is clear that, in the circumstances of the main proceedings, such an undertaking cannot base its arguments on the premiss that the parallel exports which it seeks to limit are of only minimal benefit to the final consumers.' (para 57)

In the majority of Member States, medicines are subject to regulation aimed at setting selling prices for those medicines and the scales of reimbursement of the cost of prescription medicines by the relevant social health insurance systems. Such state regulation of the prices of medicinal products cannot preclude the EU rules on competition from applying. However, when assessing whether the refusal to supply medicines to wholesalers involved in parallel exports constitutes abuse, it cannot be ignored that such state regulation of the prices is one of the factors liable to create opportunities for parallel trade. (paras 58–67)

In light of the Treaty objectives 'there can be no escape from the prohibition laid down in [Article 102 TFEU] for the practices of an undertaking in a dominant position which are aimed at avoiding all parallel exports from a Member State to other Member States, practices which, by partitioning the national markets, neutralise the benefits of effective competition in terms of the supply and the prices that those exports would obtain for final consumers in the other Member States.' (para 66)

'Furthermore, in the light of the Treaty objectives to protect consumers by means of undistorted competition and the integration of national markets, the [Union] rules on competition are also incapable of being interpreted in such a way that, in order to defend its own commercial interests, the only choice left for a pharmaceuticals company in a dominant position is not to place its medicines on the market at all in a Member State where the prices of those products are set at a relatively low level.' (para 68)

'It follows that, even if the degree of regulation regarding the price of medicines cannot prevent any refusal by a pharmaceuticals company in a dominant position to meet orders sent to it by wholesalers involved in parallel exports from constituting an abuse, such a company must nevertheless be in a position to take steps that are reasonable and in proportion to the need to protect its own commercial interests.' (para 69)

'In order to appraise whether the refusal by a pharmaceuticals company to supply wholesalers involved in parallel exports constitutes a reasonable and proportionate measure in relation to the threat that those exports represent to its legitimate commercial interests, it must be ascertained whether the orders of the wholesalers are out of the ordinary (see, to that effect, *United Brands and United Brands Continental v Commission*, paragraph 182).' (para 70)

'Thus, although a pharmaceuticals company in a dominant position, in a Member State where prices are relatively low, cannot be allowed to cease to honour the ordinary orders of an existing customer for the sole reason that that customer, in addition to supplying the market in that Member State, exports part of the quantities ordered to other Member States with higher prices, it is none the less permissible for that company to counter in a reasonable and proportionate way the threat to its own commercial interests potentially posed by the activities of an undertaking which wishes to be supplied in the first Member State with significant quantities of products that are essentially destined for parallel export.' (para 71)

A producer of pharmaceutical products must be in a position to protect its own commercial interests if it is confronted with orders that are out of the ordinary in terms of quantity. It is for the national court to ascertain whether the orders are ordinary in the light of their size in relation to the requirements of the national market and in the light of the previous business relations between that undertaking and the wholesalers concerned. (paras 72–77)

Comment

In paragraph 66 the Court made reference to the Treaty objectives and the need to ensure that competition is not distorted. In this context it noted that 'there can be no escape from the prohibition laid down in [Article 102 TFEU] for the practices of an undertaking in a dominant position which are aimed at avoiding all parallel exports from a Member State to other Member States.'

The Court did not address directly the question of whether the refusal to supply constitutes, per se, an abuse. It recognised that restrictions on parallel trade would generate negative effects on consumers. (para 57) Such restrictions, however, may be justified when the dominant undertaking is taking reasonable and proportionate steps to protect its commercial interests. (para 69)

In his opinion, Advocate General Colomer argued that a formalistic approach to the question of abuse may fail to recognise activities which are of benefit to consumers. Accordingly, certain conduct cannot be deemed abusive even when the circumstances of the case make the undertaking's intention clear (AG opinion, para 123). Subsequently the real effect of the activities can only be recognised while comparing positive and negative consequences of the activity (AG opinion, paras 73–5). The opinion clearly moves away from a formalistic 'per se' analysis into an effect-based one, in which the positive effects of the conduct are examined. As such it provides valuable support for the effect-based approach to Article 102 TFEU. Unfortunately the effect-based analysis advocated in the AG opinion could not counter the court's formalistic approach. The Court of Justice did not incorporate the AG comments on the analysis of effect and reverted to formalistic reasoning—focusing on the abuse and opening the door to objective justification (Court of Justice judgment, paras 68–70 and 78–122). In doing so, the court did not comment on either the effect-based approach or the suggested framework laid out by the Advocate General.

Note in particular the following extracts from the AG opinion:

'In the first place, to accept the idea of abuses per se of a dominant position would run counter to the proposition that it is necessary to examine each case within the economic and legal context in which it arose.' (para 71)

'Secondly, from a purely economic perspective, the approach per se is too form-based, a defect criticised by some very informed commentators who advocate an alternative approach to [Article 102 TFEU], which would focus on the effects of each abuse and involve a consideration of the specific circumstances by applying an "analysis of the merits" (or a "rule of reason").' (para 72)

'Allowing preconceived and formalistic ideas on abuse of a dominant position to prevail would mask the fact that sometimes dominance can benefit consumers. This is the case when the strength of one operator reduces competition in a particular market, given that [Article 102 TFEU] does not include any provision whereby such operators can successfully defend themselves against the accusation of abuse by demonstrating the economic efficiency of their conduct, an absence which has been justly criticised.' (para 73)

'Thirdly and lastly, if, as has been said, it is common to divide the circumstances in which [Article 102 TFEU] applies into two categories, namely those that harm consumers (exploitative abuses) and those that harm actual or potential competitors (exclusionary abuses), so that any anti-competitive conduct of a dominant undertaking is capable of constituting an abuse, as there is no indication of the relative importance of these two aspects of [Article 102 TFEU], a defence of the dominant company based on economic results obtained might be advocated.' (para 74)

'A mere comparison of the positive and negative consequences for consumers and for other operators in the same market provides sufficient information to draw the relevant conclusions.' (para 75)

'I therefore recommend that the Court make an unambiguous declaration to the effect that [Article 102 TFEU] does not provide a basis for attributing abusive conduct per se to undertakings in a dominant position, even when it is clear from the circumstances of the case that there is both intent and an anti-competitive effect.' (para 76)

Clearstream v Commission	**Abuse**
Case T-301/04	Refusal to Supply
General Court, [2009] ECR II-3155; [2009] 5 CMLR 24	Discriminatory Prices

Facts

Clearstream Banking AG and its parent company, Clearstream International SA (Clearstream) provide clearing, settlement and custody services in relation to securities and are the only international central securities depositories operating in the European Union. The European Commission found Clearstream to have abused its dominant position by refusing to provide cross-border clearing and settlement services to Euroclear Bank SA (EB) for almost two years, and by applying discriminatory prices to EB (on discriminatory pricing see page 218 above). According to the Commission, the refusal to supply lasted over an unreasonable period of time and harmed innovation and competition in the provision of cross-border secondary clearing and settlement services. Clearstream applied for annulment of the Commission decision and contested the finding of abuse. The General Court dismissed the action.

Held

'[W]hilst the finding that a dominant position exists does not in itself imply any reproach to the undertaking concerned, it has a special responsibility, irrespective of the causes of that position, not to allow its conduct to impair genuine undistorted competition on the [internal] market. … Similarly, whilst the fact that an undertaking is in a dominant position cannot deprive it of its entitlement to protect its own commercial interests when they are attacked, and whilst such an undertaking must be allowed the right to take such reasonable steps as it deems appropriate to protect those interests, such behaviour cannot be allowed if its purpose is to strengthen that dominant position and thereby abuse it (Case T-203/01 *Michelin v Commission* [2003] ECR II-4071, paragraph 55, and the case-law cited).' (para 132)

'It therefore follows from the nature of the obligations imposed by [Article 102 TFEU] that, in specific circumstances, undertakings in a dominant position may be deprived of the right to adopt a course of conduct or take measures which are not in themselves abuses and which would even be unobjectionable if adopted or taken by non-dominant undertakings (Case T-111/96 *ITT Promedia v Commission* [1998] ECR II-2937, paragraph 139).' (para 133)

The concept of abuse is an objective concept. The conduct of an undertaking in a dominant position may be regarded as abusive even in the absence of any fault (Case T-65/89 *BPB Industries and British Gypsum v Commission* [1993] ECR II-389, paragraph 70). 'Consequently, the applicants' argument that they did not pursue an anti-competitive objective is irrelevant to the legal characterisation of the facts. In that context, proving that it was the applicants' objective to postpone the grant of access in order to prevent a customer and competitor of the Clearstream group from providing its services effectively may reinforce the conclusion that there is an abuse of a dominant position but is not a condition for such a finding.' (paras 140–42)

The effect referred to in paragraph 140 does not necessarily relate to the actual effect. For the purposes of establishing an infringement of Article 102 TFEU, it is sufficient to show that the abusive conduct of the undertaking in a dominant position tends to restrict competition or, in other words, that the conduct is capable of having that effect (Case T-203/01 *Michelin v Commission*, paragraph 239). (para 144)

In order to find the existence of an abuse within the meaning of Article 102 TFEU, 'the refusal of the service in question must be likely to eliminate all competition on the market on the part of the person requesting the service, such refusal must not be capable of being objectively justified, and the service must in itself be indispensable to carrying on that person's business (Case C-7/97 *Bronner* [1998] ECR I-7791, paragraph 41). According to settled case-law, a product or service is considered necessary or essential if there is no real or potential substitute (see Joined Cases T-374/94, T-375/94, T-384/94 and T-388/94 *European Night Services and Others v Commission* [1998] ECR II-3141, paragraph 208, and the case-law cited).' (para 147)

'With regard to the condition of elimination of all competition, it is not necessary, in order to establish an infringement of [Article 102 TFEU], to demonstrate that all competition on the market would be eliminated, but what matters is that the refusal at issue is liable to, or is likely to, eliminate all effective competition on the market. It is for the Commission to establish such a risk of the elimination of all effective competition (*Microsoft v Commission*, paragraph 47 above, paragraphs 563 and 564).' (para 148)

In the present case, the Commission decided that the applicants had a de facto monopoly with regard to the provision of primary clearing and settlement services on the relevant market and that EB could not duplicate the services which it was requesting. Furthermore it found that EB offered its customers a single point of access to a large number of securities markets and therefore an innovative secondary clearing and settlement service, on a European scale. According to the Commission, access to CBF was indispensable to EB in order to be able to provide those cross-border secondary clearing and settlement services, and the applicants' refusal to provide it with primary clearing and settlement services for registered shares hindered EB's capacity to provide comprehensive, pan-European and innovative services. Alternative indirect access to central a securities depository which EB could have used was not a viable alternative as it posed a number of disadvantages in the form of longer deadlines, greater risk, higher costs and potential conflicts of interest. The long period of time in which access was refused was unreasonable and unjustifiable. (paras 149–58)

Comment

In the *Clearstream* decision (Case COMP/38.096) the European Commission set to clarify the application of competition law to the financial industry and more specifically to cross-border clearing and settlement in the EU. This was the first time that the Commission analysed the complex area of clearing and settlement services and subjected it to competition law. In doing so the Commission aimed to promote a more efficient and integrated single European capital market.

The finding of abuse, which was upheld by the General Court, brought into question the viability of some of the practices used in the industry. Subsequently, while it added little to existing case-law on abuse of dominant position, it had practical significance to the development of models of operation in the industry.

As established in case-law, the concept of abuse is an objective concept. In its decision the Commission noted that when the intention of the dominant company is found 'the demonstration of the existence of an objectively abusive behaviour is made easier.' (para 218, Commission decision) The General Court endorsed this approach in para 142. Accordingly, whereas lack of intent is irrelevant for the finding of abuse, the finding of intent may reinforce the conclusion that there was an abuse.

On the issue of refusal to supply the General Court noted, in line with its *Microsoft* judgment, that the Commission need not establish that all competition was eliminated but that all effective competition was eliminated.

The Court endorsed the Commission's finding that the long period of time required to obtain access considerably exceeded that which could be considered as reasonable and justified and amounted to an abusive refusal to provide the service in question. (para 151) The long delay in granting access, for almost two years, was sufficient to constitute a refusal to supply.

Purple Parking Ltd & Anor v Heathrow Airport Ltd	**Article 102 TFEU**
HC10C02364	Refusal to Supply
Court of Appeal, [2011] EWHC 987 (Ch)	Innovation and Investment

Facts

Purple Parking Limited and Meteor Parking, two companies which offer valet parking services at Heathrow Airport, UK, accused the airport of abusing its dominant position by forcing the two companies to relocate their operations from the forecourts at Terminals 1 and 3 to the short-stay car parks, whilst allowing its own valet parking operations to operate from the forecourts. In his judgment, Mr Justice Mann held that Heathrow abused its dominant position by discriminating between its own downstream services and the other operators. The Judge relied on discrimination grounds when reaching his decision and made reference to the relevant variables which affect an order for compulsory access.

Held

A trading entity may well be entitled to trade to the exclusion of competitors if it is using its own facilities. However, there are various cases in which a facility owner has been compelled to share the main asset with a competitor. 'In my view much less weight falls to be given to the rights of [Heathrow] as an owner because this is not a case where the creator of a facility, or the acquirer of property, is being required to share the real fruits of ownership with a competitor. By "the real fruits of ownership" I mean the essential fruits of the ownership of the particular property in question and the investment in it. [In many of the cases concerning refusal to supply, reference is made to the] care that has to be taken before requiring access to be given to a competitor [to an asset which is] the result of investment in the central aspects of the property itself. In *Bronner* it was the distribution network. In *Frankfurt* it was an aspect of the handling of aircraft—part of the essential function of the airport. In *Sea Container* it was the actual port. In each case the property owner could say … that he had paid good money to create the facility and should not be required to share it, at least until he had extracted a fair benefit. To hold otherwise… would discourage other people from innovation and developing their own products.' (para 174)

'The present case is different. The forecourts at Heathrow were not developed [to] run a meet and greet operation. … The forecourts were provided so that they could help in servicing the central purpose of Heathrow which is the provision of an airport so that aeroplanes can take off and land with passengers (and cargo). They were ancillary to that central purpose (though no doubt important). [Heathrow] could not say that it is being forced to share an investment specifically made in the forecourts in the same way as a telecommunications company which is being required to grant network access to a competitor could say it is being asked to share what it actually created and invested in.' (para 175)

'In my view that materially weakens the point that could otherwise be made about the care that has to be taken before interfering with property rights and investment. Purple and Meteor are undoubtedly seeking to have the benefit of [Heathrow's] property rights, but not in the central investment in the airport in a way that is relevant to the point currently under consideration.' (para 176)

Comment

The secondary role played by the asset which was the subject of compulsory access implies that such order would have had limited effect on investment and innovation. Similar circumstances may be found in other cases. In *Magill* (page 283 above), the information was secondary to the main broadcasting business of the dominant companies. The finding of abuse would have had limited, if any, effect on innovation, not least as the protection at national level was not in line with other European Member States. In *Microsoft* (page 289 above), the case concerned a different theory of harm and revolved around interoperability information. While valuable, this information was secondary to the main assets of Microsoft. Taking into account the competitive pressure to which Microsoft was subjected, the effect on innovation was deemed limited.

Tetra Pak International SA v Commission	**Article 102 TFEU**
Case C-333/94P	Abuse
Court of Justice, [1996] ECR I-5951, [1997] 4 CMLR 662	Tying and Bundling

Facts

Tetra Pak International SA (Tetra Pak) specialises in equipment for the packaging of liquid or semi-liquid food products in cartons. The Commission found Tetra Pak to have abused its dominant position by, among other things, tying the sales of machinery for packaging with the sales of cartons, and by engaging in predatory pricing (IV/31.043—*Tetra Pak II*). The General Court dismissed Tetra Pak's application for annulment of the Commission's decision. Tetra Pak appealed to the Court of Justice.

Held

Article 102 TFEU may apply to an act committed by an undertaking in a dominant position on a market distinct from but associated to the dominated market. (paras 24–7)

'Tetra Pak interprets [Article 102(d) TFEU] as prohibiting only the practice of making the conclusion of contracts dependent on acceptance of additional services which, by nature or according to commercial usage, have no link with the subject-matter of the contracts. It must be noted, first, that the [General Court] explicitly rejected the argument put forward by Tetra Pak to show the existence of a natural link between the machines and the cartons. In paragraph 82 of the judgment under appeal, it found: "consideration of commercial usage does not support the conclusion that the machinery for packaging a product is indivisible from the cartons. For a considerable time there have been independent manufacturers who specialize in the manufacture of non-aseptic cartons designed for use in machines manufactured by other concerns and who do not manufacture machinery themselves". That assessment, itself based on commercial usage, rules out the existence of the natural link claimed by Tetra Pak by stating that other manufacturers can produce cartons for use in Tetra Pak's machines. With regard to aseptic cartons, the [General Court] found, at paragraph 83 of its judgment, that "any independent producer is quite free, as far as [Union] competition law is concerned, to manufacture consumables intended for use in equipment manufactured by others, unless in doing so it infringes a competitor's intellectual property right". It also noted, at paragraph 138, rejecting the argument based on the alleged natural link, that it was not for Tetra Pak to impose certain measures on its own initiative on the basis of technical considerations or considerations relating to product liability, protection of public health and protection of its reputation. Those factors, taken as a whole, show that the [General Court] considered that Tetra Pak was not alone in being able to manufacture cartons for use in its machines.' (paras 35, 36)

'It must, moreover, be stressed that the list of abusive practices set out in the second paragraph of [Article 102 TFEU] is not exhaustive. Consequently, even where tied sales of two products are in accordance with commercial usage or there is a natural link between the two products in question, such sales may still constitute abuse within the meaning of [Article 102 TFEU] unless they are objectively justified. The reasoning of the [General Court] in paragraph 137 of its judgment is not … in any way defective.' (para 37)

Comment

Note that abusive tying may be established even when the tied sales of two products is in accordance with commercial usage or there is a natural link between the two products in question. Such sale may constitute an abuse unless it is objectively justified. (para 37)

In Case T-30/89 *Hilti AG v Commission*, the Commission accused Hilti of abusing its dominant position by tying the sale of nails to the sale of cartridge strips, a practice that excluded competitors from the market and aimed at increasing Hilti's market power. The General Court rejected Hilti's argument that its practice was objectively justifiable. (See detailed analysis on page 308 below.)

Microsoft Corp v Commission	**Article 102 TFEU**
Case T-201/04	Abuse
General Court, [2007] 5 CMLR 11	Tying and Bundling

Facts

An action for annulment of Commission decision Comp/C-3/37.792 in which the Commission found Microsoft to have infringed Article 102 TFEU by refusing to supply interoperability information to its competitors and by bundling its Windows Media Player with its operating system (on refusal to supply, see page 289 above). The Commission found that Microsoft had abused its market power by bundling its Windows Media Player with its Windows operating system. This conduct enabled Microsoft to anticompetitively expand its position of market power and to significantly weaken competition on the media player market by foreclosing this market and artificially reducing the incentives of media companies, software developers and content providers to develop competing media players. The Commission ordered Microsoft to provide a version of its operating system without the Windows Media Player. Microsoft appealed the decision. The General Court held that the Commission's analysis of the constituent elements of bundling was correct. The Commission was right to base its finding that there was abusive tying in the present case on the following factors (Commission Decision, Recital 794): (1) the tying and tied products are two separate products; (2) the undertaking concerned is dominant in the market for the tying product; (3) the undertaking concerned does not give customers a choice to obtain the tying product without the tied product; and (4) the practice in question forecloses competition. (paras 842–59)

Held

'It must be borne in mind that the list of abusive practices set out in the second paragraph of [Article 102 TFEU] is not exhaustive and that the practices mentioned there are merely examples of abuse of a dominant position. ... It follows that bundling by an undertaking in a dominant position may also infringe [Article 102 TFEU] where it does not correspond to the example given in [Article 102(d) TFEU]. Accordingly, in order to establish the existence of abusive bundling, the Commission was correct to rely in the contested decision on [Article 102 TFEU] in its entirety and not exclusively on [Article 102(d) TFEU].' (paras 860, 861)

The existence of two separate products

'Microsoft contends, in substance, that media functionality is not a separate product from the Windows client PC operating system but forms an integral part of that system. As a result, what is at issue is a single product, namely the Windows client PC operating system, which is constantly evolving. In Microsoft's submission, customers expect that any client PC operating system will have the functionalities which they perceive as essential, including audio and video functionalities, and that those functionalities will be constantly updated.' (para 912)

The IT and communications industry is an industry in constant and rapid evolution. In such an industry what initially appear to be separate products may subsequently be regarded as forming a single product, both from the technological aspect and from the aspect of the competition rules. The Court must assess whether the Commission was correct to find two separate products at the period of the investigation. (paras 913–16)

The distinctness of products for the purpose of an analysis under Article 102 TFEU has to be assessed by reference to customer demand. In the absence of independent demand for the allegedly tied product, there can be no question of separate products and no abusive tying. (paras 917–21)

According to the EU case-law on bundling, complementary products can constitute separate products for the purposes of Article 102 TFEU. It is possible that customers will wish to obtain the client PC operating systems and application software together, but from different sources. For example, the fact that most client PC users want their client PC operating system to come with word-processing software does not transform those separate products into a single product for the purposes of Article 102 TFEU. (paras 922–3)

The Commission correctly observed at recital 807 to the contested decision, that there exists a demand for client PC operating systems. That fact is not disputed by Microsoft. In addition, 'a series of factors based on the nature and technical features of the products concerned, the facts observed on the market, the history of the development of the products concerned and also Microsoft's commercial practice demonstrate the existence of separate consumer demand for streaming media players.' (paras 925, 924–33)

'The fact that tying takes the form of the technical integration of one product in another does not have the consequence that, for the purpose of assessing its impact on the market, that integration cannot be qualified as the bundling of two separate products.' (para 935)

'Furthermore, Microsoft's argument that the integration of Windows Media Player in the Windows operating system was dictated by technical reasons is scarcely credible in the light of the content of certain of its own internal communications … it follows from Mr Bay's email of 3 January 1999 to Mr Gates … that the integration of Windows Media Player in Windows was primarily designed to make Windows Media Player more competitive with RealPlayer by presenting it as a constituent part of Windows and not as application software that might be compared with RealPlayer.' (para 937)

'Microsoft cannot rely on the fact that vendors of competing client PC operating systems also bundle those systems with a streaming media player. On the one hand, Microsoft has not adduced any evidence that such bundling was already carried out by its competitors at the time when the abusive bundling commenced. On the other hand, moreover, it is clear that the commercial conduct of those competitors, far from invalidating the Commission's argument, corroborates it. … in any event, it is settled case-law that even when the tying of two products is consistent with commercial usage or when there is a natural link between the two products in question, it may none the less constitute abuse within the meaning of [Article 102 TFEU], unless it is objectively justified (Case C-333/94 P *Tetra Pak II* … paragraph 37).' (paras 941–2)

The Commission was correct to find that client PC operating systems and streaming media players constituted separate products. (para 944)

Dominance in the market for the tying product

It is common ground that Microsoft has a dominant position on the market for the tying product, namely client PC operating systems. (para 870)

Consumers are unable to choose to obtain the tying product without the tied product

'Microsoft contends, in essence, that the fact that it integrated Windows Media Player in the Windows client PC operating system does not entail any coercion or supplementary obligation within the meaning of [Article 102(d) TFEU]. In support of its argument, it emphasizes … that customers pay nothing extra for the media functionality of Windows; [and] that they are not obliged to use that functionality; and, in the third place, that they are not prevented from installing and using competitors' media players.' (para 960)

'The Court observes that it cannot be disputed that, in consequence of the impugned conduct, consumers are unable to acquire the Windows client PC operating system without simultaneously acquiring Windows Media Player, which means (see paragraph 864 above) that the condition that the conclusion of contracts is made subject to acceptance of supplementary obligations must be considered to be satisfied.' (para 961)

The foreclosure of competition

'As indicated at recital 841 to the contested decision, the Commission considered that, in light of the specific circumstances of the present case, it could not merely assume, as it normally does in cases of abusive tying, that the tying of a specific product and a dominant product has by its nature a foreclosure effect. The Commission therefore examined more closely the actual effects which the bundling had already had on the streaming media player market and also the way in which that market was likely to evolve.' (para 868)

'Microsoft claims, in substance, that the Commission has failed to prove that the integration of Windows Media Player in the Windows client PC operating system involved foreclosure of competition, so that the fourth constituent element of abusive tying … is not fulfilled in this case.' (para 1031)

The Commission was correct in its analysis of foreclosure. It is clear that owing to the bundling, Windows Media Player enjoyed an unparalleled presence on client PCs throughout the world, because it thereby automatically achieved a level of market penetration corresponding to that of the Windows client PC operating system. No third-party media player could achieve such a level of market penetration. As Windows Media Player cannot be removed by users from the package consisting of Windows and Windows Media Player, the third-party media player could never be the only media player on the client PC. The pre installed Media Player thus makes users less likely to use alternative media players as they already have an application which delivers media streaming and playback functionality. In addition, the presence of several media players on the same client PC creates a risk of confusion on the part of users and an increase in customer support and testing costs. (paras 1037–59)

The Commission was correct to find that 'the market for streaming media players is characterised by significant indirect network effects or, to use the expression employed by Mr Gates, on the existence of a "positive feedback loop". … That expression describes the phenomenon where, the greater the number of users of a given software platform, the more there will be invested in developing products compatible with that platform, which, in turn reinforces the popularity of that platform with users. The Court considers that the Commission was correct to find that such a phenomenon existed in the present case and to find that it was on the basis of the percentages of installation and use of media players that content providers and software developers chose the technology for which they would develop their own products …' (paras 1061–2)

The absence of objective justification

Microsoft has not demonstrated the existence of any objective justification for the abusive bundling of Windows Media Player with the Windows client PC operating system. The Court rejects Microsoft's argument that the integration of media functionality in Windows is indispensable in order for software developers and internet site creators to be able to continue to benefit from the significant advantages offered by the 'stable and well-defined' Windows platform. In its decision the Commission did not interfere with Microsoft's business model in so far as that model includes the integration of a streaming media player in its client PC operating system. The Commission expressly states that Microsoft retains the right to offer a bundle of the Windows client PC operating system and Windows Media Player as long as at the same time a version of that system without Windows Media Player is available. Additionally, Microsoft's argument that the removal of media functionality from the system would undermine standardisation, and create problems to the detriment of consumers, software and Internet site developers, cannot be accepted. (paras 1144–67)

Comment

The Court acknowledged the rapid evolution of the industry and the possibility that, with time, separate products may be regarded as forming a single product. Note that the finding of two product markets was considered at the point of time when the Commission took its decision.

Note that although the Court did not engage in a detailed analysis of consumer harm, it took notice of the impact of bundling and market foreclosure on consumer choice.

The code removal remedy, under which Microsoft was ordered to offer an unbundled version, came under criticism from the US Department of Justice which argued that it went beyond what was necessary or appropriate to protect consumers and risked protecting competitors, rather than competition.

The Commission's Guidance Paper elaborates on the analysis of tying and bundling in paras 47–62.

Microsoft (Tying)	**Article 102 TFEU**
COMP/C-3/39.530	Abuse—Tying
European Commission, [2010] C-36/06	Article 9, Regulation 1/2003—Commitment Decision

Facts

Following a complaint made by Opera Software ASA, the Commission opened an investigation into an alleged abuse of Microsoft's dominant position. It subsequently sent a Statement of Objections to Microsoft in relation to the tying of its Internet Explorer web browser with its Windows operating system. In line with the legal and economic principles of the General Court judgment in Case T-201/04 (page 299 above) the Commission argued that the tying provided Microsoft Internet Explorer with an artificial distribution advantage, distorted competition and resulted in it being available on 90 per cent of the world PCs.

To alleviate the Commission's concerns, Microsoft proposed several commitments, including the introduction of a consumer ballot screen from which costumers could install competing web browsers on the Windows operating system and, if they wish to do so, disable Internet Explorer. Microsoft has also made proposals in relation to improving the interoperability between third-party products and Windows and Windows Server. In December 2009 the Commission adopted a decision pursuant to Article 9(1) of Regulation 1/2003 declaring the commitments binding and concluding that there were no longer grounds for action in this case.

Held

'Pursuant to the Commitments, Microsoft will no longer contractually oblige [Original Equipment Manufacturers (OEMs)] to ship Internet Explorer with Windows PCs. Microsoft will also not retaliate against OEMs for installing competing web browsers. … OEMs will therefore be able to freely choose between competing offerings as regards the web browsers to be installed on the PCs which they ship. … Moreover, Microsoft will allow OEMs to turn off Internet Explorer in Windows 7 and subsequent versions of Windows and provide the technical means to do so. … Users will also be able to turn Internet Explorer off in Windows 7. … Under the Commitments, the choice screen will be presented by Microsoft to a very large number of Windows users. … Through the medium of the choice screen, those users will have a specific opportunity to choose and install competing web browsers. Importantly, the users will be able to make that choice in an informed manner and in a technically straightforward environment. … The distribution of the choice screen through Windows Update requires minimum user activity for the choice screen to reach the user and does not necessitate the involvement of third parties in distributing competing web browsers which could in and of itself jeopardize the effectiveness of the measure. The Commitments are therefore suitable for providing rival web browsers with an effective opportunity to compete on the merits with Internet Explorer and for enhancing competition on the web browser market by removing Microsoft's artificial distribution advantage and by informing users about available web browser choices. … It follows that the Commitments remove the Commission's concerns with respect to the potential artificial distribution advantage for Microsoft in the web browser market brought about by the tying of Internet Explorer to Windows. Enhanced competition in the web browser market which could result from the implementation of the Commitments would also substantially weaken the network effects that the Commission preliminarily identified in the Statement of Objections as currently favouring Internet Explorer.' (paras 99–107)

Comment

The Commitments addressed the Commission's concerns regarding potential foreclosure effects, the limitation of innovation in web development, and the potential reinforcement of Microsoft's position on the client PC operating system market. Microsoft was entrusted with monitoring its own compliance with the commitment decision. It reported to the Commission that due to a technical problem the browser choice screen was not offered in the period between May 2011 and July 2012. Subsequently, in 2013, the Commission imposed a €561 million fine on Microsoft for failing to comply with its commitments. This was the first time the Commission sanctioned a breach of an Article 9 binding commitment decision.

Der Grüne Punkt - DSD v Commission	**Article 102 TFEU**
Case C-385/07P	Abuse
Court of Justice, [2009] ECR I-6155, [2009] 5 CMLR 19	Obstructive Abuse

Facts

DSD operated a nationwide system for the collection and recovery of used sales packaging in Germany. It was the only nationwide operator which provided the services, which manufacturers had to use under the German packaging ordinance. The Commission found DSD to have abused its dominant position by limiting the ability of other operators to provide similar services (Case COMP D3/34493, *DSD*, [2001] OJ L166/01). The limitation was imposed through the charge of a fee licence levied by DSD under a Trade Mark Agreement for sales of packaging bearing the 'Green Dot trademark'. The Commission found DSD to have abused its dominant position by claiming the full fee for use of its 'Green Dot trademark' in situations where it provides no or limited service because the collection and recycling was carried out by its competitors. The Commission noted that:

'As long as DSD makes the licence fee dependent solely on the use of the mark, it is imposing unfair prices and commercial terms on undertakings which do not use the exemption service or which use it for only some of their sales packaging. An undertaking in a dominant position can obstruct its competitors by binding its customers de jure or de facto to its services and thereby prevent them from using competing suppliers. The Court has stated on this matter that "a system of undistorted competition, as laid down in the Treaty, can be guaranteed only if equality of opportunity is secured as between the various economic operators". Such equality of opportunity is particularly important for new market entrants on a market on which competition is already weakened by the presence of a dominant undertaking and other circumstances. The terms governing the fee in the Trade Mark Agreement lead in the cases described below to its being of no interest to undertakings subject to the take-back and recovery obligation to take part in a competing exemption system or a competing self-management solution because either a licence fee must be paid to DSD in addition to the remuneration made to the competitor or separate packaging and distribution channels would be necessary. In their actual effect, these terms are very close to being an exclusivity requirement. They thereby make it much more difficult for competitors to enter the market, strengthen DSD's dominant position and further weaken competition.' (paras 113–15)

DSD brought an action for annulment before the General Court (Case T-151/01 *Duales System Deutschland v Commission* [2007] ECR II-1607, [2005] 5 CMLR 300). The General Court dismissed the action and held that 'Neither the Packaging Ordinance, nor trade mark law or the specific needs of the functioning of the DSD system authorise the applicant to require undertakings which use its system to pay a fee for all packaging carrying the … logo and put into circulation in Germany, where those undertakings show that they do not use the DSD system for some of that packaging.' (paras 164, 121–63) DSD appealed to the Court of Justice.

Held

The General Court correctly held that requiring payment of a fee for all packaging bearing the DGP logo, even where customers do not use the DGP system for some or all of that packaging, must be considered to constitute an abuse. Contrary to what DSD submits, the Commission's decision did not oblige DGP to grant a licence to use its logo. It merely obliged DSD not to claim payment from its contractual partners for take-back and recovery services which it has not provided. (paras 143–7)

Comment

DSD's actions were condemned as they consisted, inter alia, of directly or indirectly imposing unfair prices or other unfair trading conditions. The actions resulted in the charge of fees which were disproportionate to the economic value of the service provided by DSD. Additionally, the practice bound DSD customers and prevented them from using competing suppliers.

Parke, Davis & Co v Probel	**Article 102 TFEU**
Case 24/67	Article 101 TFEU
Court of Justice, [1968] ECR 55, [1968] CMLR 47	Market Power—Patents

Facts

A preliminary reference to the Court of Justice, concerning the exercise of rights attached by Netherlands law to a patent. While considering the questions from the National Court, the Court of Justice commented on the application of Articles 101 and 102 TFEU to the use of one or more patents.

Held

'A patent taken by itself and independently of any agreement of which it may be the subject, … is the expression of a legal status granted by a state to products meeting certain criteria, and thus exhibits none of the elements of contract or concerted practice required by [Article 101(1) TFEU].' Nevertheless it is possible that Article 101 TFEU may apply if the use of one or more patents, in concert between undertakings, leads to the creation of a situation which comes within the concepts of agreements between undertakings, decisions of associations of undertakings or concerted practices within the meaning of Article 101(1) TFEU. (page 71)

For the prohibition in Article 102 TFEU to apply it is necessary to establish the presence together of a dominant position, the abuse of this position and the possibility that trade between Member States may be affected thereby. 'Although a patent confers on its holder a special protection at national level, it does not follow that the exercise of the rights thus conferred implies the presence together of all three elements in question. It could only do so if the use of the patent were to degenerate into an abuse of the abovementioned protection.' (page 72)

Comment

In Case T-51/89 *Tetra Pak Rausing v Commission* [1990] ECR II-309, [1991] 4 CMLR 334, the court found that the acquisition of an exclusive patent licence in that case can constituted an abuse under Article 102 TFEU. It held that 'the mere fact that an undertaking in a dominant position acquires an exclusive licence does not per se constitute abuse within the meaning of [Article 102 TFEU]. … It is plain from the reasoning and conclusions of the Decision that the infringement of [Article 102 TFEU] found by the Commission stemmed precisely from Tetra Pak's acquisition of the exclusive licence "in the specific circumstances of this case". The specific context to which the Commission refers is expressly characterized as being the fact that acquisition of the exclusivity of the licence not only "strengthened Tetra's very considerable dominance but also had the effect of preventing, or at the very least considerably delaying, the entry of a new competitor into a market where very little if any competition is found" (point 45 of the Decision; see also point 60). The decisive factor in the finding that acquisition of the exclusive licence constituted an abuse therefore lay quite specifically in the applicant's position in the relevant market and in particular, as appears from the Decision (point 27), in the fact that at the material time the right to use the process protected by the BTG licence was alone capable of giving an undertaking the means of competing effectively with the applicant in the field of the aseptic packaging of milk. The takeover of Liquipak was no more than the means—to which the Commission has attached no particular significance in applying [Article 102 TFEU]—by which the applicant acquired the exclusivity of the BTG licence, the effect of which was to deprive other undertakings of the means of competing with the applicant.' (para 23)

ITT Promedia NV v Commission	**Article 102 TFEU**
Case T-111/96	Abuse of Legal Procedure
General Court, [1998] ECR II-2937, [1998] 5 CMLR 491	

'The Commission considers that "in principle the bringing of an action, which is the expression of the fundamental right of access to a judge, cannot be characterised as an abuse" unless "an undertaking in a dominant position brings an action (i) which cannot reasonably be considered as an attempt to establish its rights and can therefore only serve to harass the opposite party, and (ii) which is conceived in the framework of a plan whose goal is to eliminate competition"...' (para 30)

'According to the Commission, under the first of the two criteria the action must, on an objective view, be manifestly unfounded. The second criterion requires that the aim of the action must be to eliminate competition. Both criteria must be fulfilled in order to establish an abuse. The fact that unmeritorious litigation is instituted does not in itself constitute an infringement of [Article 102 TFEU] unless it has an anti-competitive object. Equally, litigation which may reasonably be regarded as an attempt to assert rights vis-à-vis competitors is not abusive, irrespective of the fact that it may be part of a plan to eliminate competition.' (para 56)

'According to the first of the two cumulative criteria set out by the Commission in the contested decision, legal proceedings can be characterised as an abuse, within the meaning of [102 TFEU], only if they cannot reasonably be considered to be an attempt to assert the rights of the undertaking concerned and can therefore only serve to harass the opposing party. It is therefore the situation existing when the action in question is brought which must be taken into account in order to determine whether that criterion is satisfied.' (para 72)

'Furthermore, when applying that criterion, it is not a question of determining whether the rights which the undertaking concerned was asserting when it brought its action actually existed or whether that action was well founded, but rather of determining whether such an action was intended to assert what that undertaking could, at that moment, reasonably consider to be its rights. According to the second part of that criterion, as worded, it is satisfied solely when the action did not have that aim, that being the sole case in which it may be assumed that such action could only serve to harass the opposing party.' (para 73)

AstraZeneca AB v Commission	**Article 102 TFEU**
Case T-321/05	Abuse of Regulatory Procedure
General Court, [2010] 5 CMLR 28	Intention

Article 102 TFEU imposes on an undertaking in a dominant position the special responsibility not to impair genuine undistorted competition. 'Thus, whilst the fact that an undertaking is in a dominant position cannot deprive it of its entitlement to protect its own commercial interests when they are attacked (Case T-65/89 *BPB Industries and British Gypsum v Commission* [1993] ECR II-389, paragraph 69), it cannot use regulatory procedures in such a way as to prevent or make more difficult the entry of competitors on the market, in the absence of grounds relating to the defence of the legitimate interests of an undertaking engaged in competition on the merits or in the absence of objective justification.' (paras 671, 672)

Although an undertaking does not have to intend to cause harm to abuse its dominant position, its intention is still a relevant factor which the Commission may take into account. 'The fact, relied upon by the applicants, that the concept of abuse of a dominant position is an objective concept and implies no intention to cause harm ... does not lead to the conclusion that the intention to resort to practices falling outside the scope of competition on the merits is in all events irrelevant, since that intention can still be taken into account to support the conclusion that the undertaking concerned abused a dominant position, even if that conclusion should primarily be based on an objective finding that the abusive conduct actually took place.' (para 359)

The judgment was appealed (C-457/10P).

Irish Sugar v Commission	**Article 102 TFEU**
Case T-228/97	Objective Justification
General Court, [1999] ECR II-2969, [1999] 5 CMLR 1300	Price Alignment

Facts

Irish Sugar plc, the sole processor of sugar beet and the principal supplier of sugar in Ireland, was fined by the Commission for infringing Article 102 TFEU. The Commission's decision identified seven individual abuses by Irish Sugar on the market in granulated sugar intended for retail and for industry in Ireland. Irish Sugar was found to have abused its dominant position by granting special rebates to certain retailers established in the border area between Ireland and Northern Ireland. This practice aimed to reduce the imports of cheaper retail packets from Northern Ireland into Ireland and was unrelated to objective economic factors such as the sales volume of the customers. According to the Commission, this practice amounted to abusive selective or discriminatory pricing and meant that Irish Sugar had been applying dissimilar conditions to equivalent transactions with other trading parties, thereby placing those who did not qualify for the rebate at a competitive disadvantage. Irish Sugar brought an action for annulment of the decision before the General Court for the annulment of the decision. It contested the Commission's findings and argued that its practice was aimed at meeting the competition and was defensive in nature. Accordingly, the practice was aimed at preventing Irish Sugar from losing part of its customer base and its turnover. Moreover, the practice aimed to face the competition where it manifested itself, using the limited means available to Irish Sugar at the time. Accordingly, due to financial difficulties, Irish Sugar was financially unable to cut prices on a national scale.

Held

'[T]he applicant cannot rely on the insufficiency of the financial resources at its disposal at the time to justify the selective and discriminatory granting of those border rebates and thereby escape the application of [Article 102 TFEU], without making a dead letter of the prohibition contained in that article. The circumstances in which an undertaking in a dominant position may be led to react to the limited competition which exists on the market, especially where that undertaking holds more than 88% of the market as in this case, form part of the competitive process which [Article 102 TFEU] is precisely designed to protect. Moreover, the applicant has several times underlined the high level of retail sale prices in Ireland, explaining it by the influence of the high level of the guaranteed intervention price in the context of the common organisation of the market in sugar.' (para 186)

'[T]he defensive nature of the practice complained of in this case cannot alter the fact that it constitutes an abuse for the purposes of [Article 102(c) TFEU].' (para 187)

'In this case, the applicant has been unable to establish an objective economic justification for the rebates. They were given to certain customers in the retail sugar market by reference solely to their exposure to competition resulting from cheap imports from another Member State and, in this case, by reference to their being established along the border with Northern Ireland. It also appears, according to the applicant's own statements, that it was able to practise such price rebates owing to the particular position it held on the Irish market. Thus it states that it was unable to practice such rebates over the whole of Irish territory owing to the financial losses it was making at the time. It follows that, by the applicant's own admission, its economic capacity to offer rebates in the region along the border with Northern Ireland depended on the stability of its prices in other regions, which amounts to recognition that it financed those rebates by means of its sales in the rest of the Irish territory. By conducting itself in that way, the applicant abused its dominant position in the retail sugar market in Ireland, by preventing the development of free competition on that market and distorting its structures, in relation to both purchasers and consumers. The latter were not able to benefit, outside the region along the border with Northern Ireland, from the price reductions caused by the imports of sugar from Northern Ireland.' (para 188)

'Thus, even if the existence of a dominant position does not deprive an undertaking placed in that position of the right to protect its own commercial interests when they are threatened ... the protection of the commercial position of an undertaking in a dominant position with the characteristics of that of the applicant at the time in question must, at the very least, in order to be lawful, be based on criteria of economic efficiency and consistent with the interests of consumers. In this case, the applicant has not shown that those conditions were fulfilled.' (para 189)

Comment

The Court held that the protection of commercial interests must, at the very least, in order to be lawful, be based on criteria of economic efficiency and consistent with the interests of consumers. (para 189)

Note the Court of Justice judgment in Case 27/76 *United Brands v Commission* where in paragraphs 189–92 the court held that although the existence of a dominant position does not deprive the dominant undertaking of the right to protect its own commercial interests when they are attacked, such protection is not tolerated when its actual purpose is to strengthen the dominant position and abuse it. The protective action must be proportionate to the threat, taking into account the economic strength of the undertakings confronting each other.

See also Case T-83/91 *Tetra Pak International SA v Commission* [1994] ECR II-755, where the General Court rejected Tetra Pak's claims of objective justification on the basis of public health. The Court assessed these arguments in light of the principles enshrined in the *Hilti* judgment. It concluded that the protection of public health may be guaranteed by means other than the tying of Tetra Pak's products, and added that in any event the remedy must lie in appropriate legislation or regulations, and not in rules adopted unilaterally by manufacturers, which would amount to prohibiting independent manufacturers from conducting the essential part of their business. (paras 83–5, 138)

See case T-201/04 *Microsoft Corp v Commission* (pages 289 and 299 above) where the General Court rejected Microsoft's argument that the fact that the technology concerned was covered by intellectual property rights justified its refusal to licence. The General Court also rejected Microsoft's claim that the bundling of Windows Media Player with the Windows client PC operating system was objectively justified as it was indispensable in order for software developers and Internet site creators to be able to continue to benefit from the significant advantages offered by the 'stable and well-defined' Windows platform.

In its Guidance Paper the Commission explores the possible justifications and efficiencies which may be relevant to different types of abuse. Also note the 2005 Discussion Paper in which the Commission reviews the possible defence claims in case of a finding of abuse. These include the objective necessity defence, meeting competition defence and the efficiency defence. (see paras 77–92)

Hilti AG v Commission	**Article 102 TFEU**
Case T-30/89	Objective Justification
General Court, [1991] ECR II-1439, [1992] 4 CMLR 16	

Facts

The Commission fined Hilti AG for the abuse of its dominant position in the market for nail guns and for the nails and cartridge strips for those guns. The abusive behaviour included the tying of the sale of nails to the sale of cartridge strips, a practice that excluded competitors from the market and was aimed at increasing Hilti's market power. (IV/30.787 and 31.488—*Eurofix-Bauco v Hilti*)

Hilti brought an action of annulment before the General Court and argued that, among other things, tying the sale of nails to cartridge strips was objectively justifiable on grounds of safety. Hilti claimed that deficiencies in nails produced elsewhere rendered them incompatible with Hilti's nail guns. Additionally, it argued that the tying was justified by Hilti's duty of care as a manufacturer. (paras 102–07)

Held

Hilti's argument that its actions stem out of safety concerns cannot be accepted. 'It is common ground that at no time during the period in question did Hilti approach the competent United Kingdom authorities for a ruling that the use of the interveners' nails in Hilti tools was dangerous'. (paras 115, 115–17)

There are laws in the United Kingdom which attach penalties to the sale of dangerous products and to the use of misleading claims as to the characteristics of any product. 'In those circumstances it is clearly not the task of an undertaking in a dominant position to take steps on its own initiative to eliminate products which, rightly or wrongly, it regards as dangerous or at least as inferior in quality to its own products.' (para 118)

'It must further be held in this connection that the effectiveness of the [Union] rules on competition would be jeopardized if the interpretation by an undertaking of the laws of the various Member States regarding product liability were to take precedence over those rules. Hilti's argument based on its alleged duty of care cannot therefore be upheld.' (para 119)

Comment

In its submission to the Court the Commission referred to the Court of Justice judgments in Case 193/83 *Windsurfing International v Commission* [1986] ECR 611, and Case 226/84 *British Leyland v Commission* [1986] ECR 3263. According to the Commission both cases show that 'abuse' within the meaning of Article 102 TFEU cannot be justified by considerations of product safety and reliability. (para 109)

Also note the Commission's analysis in its decision (IV/30.787 and 31.488—*Eurofix-Bauco v Hilti* [1988] OJ L65/19) relating to Hilti's claims for objective justification. There, the Commission considered at length Hilti's claims that its practices were the results of concerns as to the reliability, operation and safety of nail guns, nails and cartridge strips. The Commission concluded that Hilti's actions reflected 'a commercial interest in stopping the penetration of the market of non-Hilti consumables since the main profit from [nail guns, nails and cartridge strips] originates from the sale of consumables, not from the sale of nail guns. This is without prejudice to the possibility that Hilti had a genuine concern about safety and reliability.' (para 90)

An appeal by Hilti before the Court of Justice was dismissed. See Case C-53/92P *Hilti v Commission* [1994] ECR I-667, paragraphs 11–16.

Atlantic Container Line AB and others v Commission	**Article 102 TFEU**
Case T-191/98	Efficiency Justification
General Court, [2003] ECR II-3275	

Because Article 102 TFEU 'does not provide for any exemption, abusive practices are prohibited regardless of the advantages which may accrue to the perpetrators of such practices or to third parties.' (para 1112)

France Télécom SA v Commission	**Article 102 TFEU**
Case T-340/03	Efficiency Justification
General Court, [2007] ECR II-107, [2007] 4 CMLR 21	

The argument advanced by Wanadoo Interactive 'as to the economies of scale and learning effects in order to justify its pricing below cost are not such as to call into question the finding made by the Court. An undertaking which charges predatory prices may enjoy economies of scale and learning effects on account of increased production precisely because of such pricing. The economies of scale and learning effects cannot therefore exempt that undertaking from liability under [Article 102 TFEU].' (para 217)

British Airways v Commission	**Article 102 TFEU**
Case C-95/04P	Efficiency Justification
Court of Justice, [2007] ECR I-2331, [2007] 4 CMLR 982	

'Assessment of the economic justification for a system of discounts or bonuses established by an undertaking in a dominant position is to be made on the basis of the whole of the circumstances of the case (see, to that effect, *Michelin*, paragraph 73). It has to be determined whether the exclusionary effect arising from such a system, which is disadvantageous for competition, may be counterbalanced, or outweighed, by advantages in terms of efficiency which also benefit the consumer. If the exclusionary effect of that system bears no relation to advantages for the market and consumers, or if it goes beyond what is necessary in order to attain those advantages, that system must be regarded as an abuse.' (para 86)

Irish Sugar plc v Commission	**Article 102 TFEU**
Case T-228/97	Efficiency Justification
General Court, [1999] ECR II-2969, [1999] 5 CMLR 1300	

'[E]ven if the existence of a dominant position does not deprive an undertaking placed in that position of the right to protect its own commercial interests when they are threatened ..., the protection of the commercial position of an undertaking in a dominant position with the characteristics of that of the applicant at the time in question must, at the very least, in order to be lawful, be based on criteria of economic efficiency and consistent with the interests of consumers. In this case, the applicant has not shown that those conditions were fulfilled.' (para 189)

Intel Corporation	**Article 102 TFEU**
COMP/37.990	Efficiency Justification
European Commission, [2009] OJ C227/07	

'In order to objectively justify its conditional rebates, Intel would have to show that there is an efficiency (or another legitimate objective other than exclusion of competitors), that the conduct is capable of achieving the legitimate goal, that it had no equally effective alternative in achieving the legitimate goal with a less restrictive or less exclusionary effect and finally that the conduct is "proportionate", in the sense that the legitimate objective pursued by Intel should not be outweighed by the exclusionary effect.' (para 1624)

Post Danmark A/S v Konkurrencerådet	**Article 102 TFEU**
Case C-209/10	Objective Justification
Court of Justice, [2012] 4 CMLR 23	Efficiency Gains

'If the court making the reference, after carrying out that assessment, should nevertheless make a finding of anti-competitive effects due to Post Danmark's actions, it should be recalled that it is open to a dominant undertaking to provide justification for behaviour that is liable to be caught by the prohibition under Article 82 EC (see, to this effect, Case 27/76 *United Brands and United Brands Continental v Commission* [1978] ECR 207, paragraph 184; Joined Cases C 241/91 P and C 242/91 P *RTE and ITP v Commission* [1995] ECR I 743, paragraphs 54 and 55; and *TeliaSonera Sverige*, paragraphs 31 and 75).' (para 40)

'In particular, such an undertaking may demonstrate, for that purpose, either that its conduct is objectively necessary (see, to that effect, Case 311/84 CBEM [1985] ECR 3261, paragraph 27), or that the exclusionary effect produced may be counterbalanced, outweighed even, by advantages in terms of efficiency that also benefit consumers (Case C 95/04 P *British Airways v Commission* [2007] ECR I 2331, paragraph 86, and *Telia-Sonera Sverige*, paragraph 76).' (para 41)

'In that last regard, it is for the dominant undertaking to show that the efficiency gains likely to result from the conduct under consideration counteract any likely negative effects on competition and consumer welfare in the affected markets, that those gains have been, or are likely to be, brought about as a result of that conduct, that such conduct is necessary for the achievement of those gains in efficiency and that it does not eliminate effective competition, by removing all or most existing sources of actual or potential competition.' (para 42)

Streetmap v Google	**Article 102 TFEU**
Case HC-2013-90	Objective Justification
England and Wales High Court (Chancery Division) [2016] EWHC 253	Efficiency gains

Justice Roth: 'There is no objective justification "defence" in the legislation, but it has long been established that if the dominant company shows that the conduct impugned was objectively justified, that conduct will not be an abuse.' (para 142)

'Although the full scope of such objective justification has not been conclusively determined, two aspects are clear: (i) it is open to the dominant undertaking to show that any exclusionary effect on the market is counter-balanced or outweighed by advantages that also benefit consumers: Case C-209/10 *Post Danmark*, EU:C:2012:172, para 41; and (ii) the conduct in question must be proportionate.' (para 143)

'Relevant efficiencies are not confined to economic considerations in terms of price or cost but may consist of technical improvements in the quality of the goods: see eg the Commission's Guidance on its enforcement priorities in applying Article [102] to abusive exclusionary conduct by dominant undertakings, OJ 2009 C45/7, at para 30. In *Microsoft*, where the CFI gave extensive consideration to the various efficiency justifications put forward by Microsoft, the Court significantly stated (at para 1159): "… the Court notes that, as the Commission observes both in the contested decision and in its pleadings, Microsoft does not show that the integration of Windows Media Player in Windows creates technical efficiencies or, in other words, that it 'lead[s] to superior technical product performance' …"' (para 145)

'As regards proportionality, the application of this principle has been stressed in the jurisprudence on abuse on many occasions. Hence the Commission Guidance, under the head of "Objective Justification", states that the Commission "will assess whether the conduct in question is indispensable and proportionate to the goal allegedly pursued by the dominant undertaking" (para 28). And under efficiencies, one of the necessary criteria is expressed as follows: "there must be no less anti-competitive alternatives to the conduct that are capable of producing the same efficiencies."' (para 146)

Irish Sugar v Commission
Case T-228/97
General Court, [1999] ECR II-2969, [1999] 5 CMLR 1300

Article 102 TFEU
Effect on Trade

'It should also be remembered that, to be capable of affecting trade between Member States, it is not necessary to demonstrate that the conduct complained of actually affected trade between Member States in a discernible way; it is sufficient to establish that the conduct is capable of having that effect. As regards abusive practices envisaged by [Article 102 TFEU], in order to assess whether trade between Member States is capable of being discernibly affected by the abuse of a dominant position, account must be taken of the consequences which result for the actual structure of competition in the [internal] market...' (para 170)

Nederlandsche Banden Industrie Michelin v Commission
Case 322/81
Court of Justice, [1983] ECR 3461, [1985] 1 CMLR 282

Article 102 TFEU
Effect on Trade

'It has not been denied in this case that important patterns of trade exist as a result of the establishment of competitors of significant size in other Member States. The effects of the discount system on the chances of Michelin NV's competitors of obtaining access to the Netherlands market have already been examined in the context of the examination of the abusive nature of Michelin NV's conduct. It must also be remembered that [Article 102 TFEU] does not require it to be proved that the abusive conduct has in fact appreciably affected trade between Member States but that it is capable of having that effect.' (para 104)

RTE & ITP v Commission ('Magill')
Joined Cases C-241/91P and 242/91P
Court of Justice, [1995] ECR I-743, [1995] 4 CMLR 718

Article 102 TFEU
Effect on Trade

'In this case, the [General Court] found that the applicant had excluded all potential competitors on the geographical market consisting of one Member State (Ireland) and part of another Member State (Northern Ireland) and had thus modified the structure of competition on that market, thereby affecting potential commercial exchanges between Ireland and the United Kingdom. From this the [General Court] drew the proper conclusion that the condition that trade between Member States must be affected had been satisfied.' (para 70)

Compagnie Maritime Belge v Commission
Case T-24/93
Court of Justice, [1996] ECR II-1201

Article 102 TFEU
Effect on Trade

'It should first be recalled that it has been consistently held that, in order that an agreement between undertakings, or moreover an abuse of a dominant position, may affect trade between Member States, it must be possible to foresee with a sufficient degree of probability and on the basis of objective factors of law or fact that it may have an influence, direct or indirect, actual or potential, on the pattern of trade between Member States, such as might prejudice the realization of the aim of a single market in all the Member States (Case C-250/92 DLG [1994] ECR I-5641, paragraph 54). Accordingly, it is not specifically necessary that the conduct in question should in fact have substantially affected trade between Member States. It is sufficient to establish that the conduct is capable of having such an effect (see, as regards [Article 102 TFEU], Joined Cases C-241/91 P and C-242/91 P *RTE and ITP v Commission* [1995] ECR I-743, paragraph 69, and, as regards [Article 101 TFEU], Case T-29/92 *SPO and others v Commission* [1995] ECR II-289).' (para 201)

Tomra Systems and Others v Commission	**Article 102 TFEU**
Case C-549/10P	Abuse
Court of Justice, [2012] 4 CMLR 27	Intention

'By their first ground of appeal, the appellants seek, in essence, to establish that the General Court was wrong to endorse an alleged finding by the Commission of anti-competitive intent on the part of the Tomra group, in particular by failing to take into account internal documents proving that the Tomra group was intent on competing on the merits.' (para 16)

'In order to assess whether this ground of appeal is well founded, it must be recalled that the concept of abuse of a dominant position prohibited by Article 102 TFEU is an objective concept relating to the conduct of a dominant undertaking which, on a market where the degree of competition is already weakened precisely because of the presence of the undertaking concerned, through recourse to methods different from those governing normal competition in products or services on the basis of the transactions of commercial operators, has the effect of hindering the maintenance of the degree of competition still existing in the market or the growth of that competition (see Case C-52/09 *TeliaSonera* [2011] ECR I-527, paragraph 27 and case-law cited).' (para 17)

'None the less, the Commission, as part of its examination of the conduct of a dominant undertaking and for the purposes of identifying any abuse of a dominant position, is obliged to consider all of the relevant facts surrounding that conduct (see, to that effect, C-95/04 P *British Airways* v *Commission* [2007] ECR I-2331, paragraph 67).' (para 18)

'It must be observed in that regard that where the Commission undertakes an assessment of the conduct of an undertaking in a dominant position, that assessment being an essential prerequisite of a finding that there is an abuse of such a position, the Commission is necessarily required to assess the business strategy pursued by that undertaking. For that purpose, it is clearly legitimate for the Commission to refer to subjective factors, namely the motives underlying the business strategy in question.' (para 19)

'Accordingly, the existence of any anti-competitive intent constitutes only one of a number of facts which may be taken into account in order to determine that a dominant position has been abused.' (para 20)

'However, the Commission is under no obligation to establish the existence of such intent on the part of the dominant undertaking in order to render [Article 102 TFEU]applicable.' (para 21)

English Welsh & Scottish Railway Limited v E.ON UK plc	**Article 102 TFEU**

English Welsh & Scottish Railway Limited v E.ON UK plc
2006/1338
High Court of Justice Queen's Bench Division, [2007] EWHC 599

Article 102 TFEU
Nullity and Severance

Facts

English Welsh & Scottish Railway Limited (EWS) is an operator of bulk rail freight services. The defendant (E.ON) is in the business of electricity generation. The two parties entered into a Coal Carriage Agreement (CCA) under which E.ON was obliged to use EWS to carry all the coal required to be moved to one of a number of specified power stations from one of a number of specified locations, subject to certain exclusions.

Following a complaint by third parties, the UK Office of Rail Regulation (ORR) issued a decision in which it found EWS to have abused its dominant position by foreclosing the 'coal haulage by rail market' through, among other things, maintaining exclusionary terms in its CCA. The ORR directed that, within 30 days, EWS and, as appropriate, the other parties to each of the contracts in question, remove or modify the exclusionary terms from the contracts in existence so as to remove their exclusionary effect and/or in the event that any new contracts are concluded to exclude from those contracts any terms capable of achieving the same or similar exclusionary effect to those identified as abusive.

EWS wrote to E.ON maintaining that the effect of the ORR's decision was to render the entire CCA void. On the other hand, E.ON took the view that the CCA would continue to bind EWS even if the exclusionary terms were removed. The dispute between the two companies reached the Commercial Court.

Held

'The Directions are somewhat infelicitously worded, but in my judgement, construed against the background of the ORR's findings in respect of the exclusionary terms and giving the word "remove" its ordinary and natural meaning, their meaning is clear. If the parties have not within 30 days agreed modifications to the exclusionary terms which remove their exclusionary effect, the parties must remove the terms from the CCA. There is no question of the parties being directed to agree to remove the terms: absent compliant modifications in the time prescribed, the terms are to go, full stop …' (para 25)

'I agree with Mr Turner's submission [for the Intervener ORR] that given: (i) the ORR's findings; (ii) Article 1.3 of Council Regulation 1/2003; and (iii) the direct effect of [Article 102 TFEU], the exclusionary terms were illegal as a matter of public law from the moment the CCA was executed. And from 1st March 2000, when Chapter II of the Act came into effect, the exclusionary terms were doubly illegal for being in breach of the Chapter II prohibition. The consequence is that from the time the CCA was executed the exclusionary terms have been void. The Directions to remove the terms are an administrative measure to ensure that the CCA is brought within the law.' (para 26)

'Where terms are void at common law for being in restraint of trade or by reason of [Article 102 TFEU] and the Chapter I prohibition, the courts apply the doctrine of severance to determine if the offending terms can be severed from the contract leaving the residue to continue to operate as an enforceable contract; see e.g. *Crehan v Courage Limited*; *Byrne v Inntreprenneur Beer Supply Co Ltd* [1999] EuLR 834 at 896. In my judgement, exactly the same approach applies where a term or terms of a contract are void by reason of being in breach of [Article 102 TFEU] and the Chapter II prohibition. It is thus not a question of whether the contract is frustrated but whether the test for severance as formulated in the cases has been satisfied.' (para 27)

'The Court of Appeal in *Crehan v Courage* rehearsed various formulations of the severance test propounded over the years without identifying which if any was to be preferred. These included: (i) whether the invalid restraint formed the whole or substantially the whole consideration for the promise; (ii) whether the contract would be so changed in its character as not to be the sort of contract that the parties intended to enter at all; (iii) whether what was unenforceable was part of the main purpose and substance, or whether the deletion altered entirely the scope and intention of the agreement or, on the contrary, left the rest of the agreement a reasonable arrangement between the parties; (iv) whether it would disappoint the main purposes of one of the main parties; and (v) whether the agreement was in substance an agreement for an invalid restraint.' (para 28)

'Mr Sharpe [QC for E.ON] conceded that if the doctrine of severance applied, the CCA without the exclusionary terms would be of a fundamentally different nature. In my judgement this concession was well made. Accordingly, subject to the true effect of clause 34 of the CCA, there can be no severance of the exclusionary terms and the whole contract is void and unenforceable. As to this latter point, the Court of Appeal in *Richard Ground Ltd v (GB) Ltd* [1997] EuLR 277 upheld the finding of the first instance judge that a clause in substantially similar words to clause 34 was ineffective to allow severance where the resulting contract would not be the sort of contract that the parties intended to enter at all. Unsurprisingly, Mr Sharpe accepted that in the light of this decision clause 34 did not allow for severance where the common law test was not satisfied.' (para 29)

'For the reasons given above, EWS is entitled to a declaration the substance of which is that the effect of the ORR's Decision issued on 17 November 2006 and the Directions contained therein is that clauses 4.2, 4.3, 5.4 and 6.1 of the CCA have from the inception of the contract been void and since those clauses cannot be severed the whole of the CCA is void and unenforceable.' (para 30)

Comment

The judge made two clear statements on the outcome of an Article 102 TFEU infringement: (1) a provision in an agreement that is in breach of Article 102 TFEU is illegal and void. In such instance the nullity takes effect from the moment the agreement is executed; (2) when a provision in breach of Article 102 TFEU cannot be severed from the rest of the contract without fundamentally changing its nature, the whole contract is void and unenforceable.

In the absence of a clear statement on the matter from the European courts, this decision provides a valuable indication that agreements that infringe Article 102 TFEU will not be enforceable.

6

Collective Dominance

The concept of collective dominance was developed under both Article 102 TFEU and the European Merger Regulation (Council Regulation (EC) No 139/2004 on the control of concentrations between undertakings, [2004] OJ L24/1).

Article 102 TFEU

Article 102 TFEU targets the 'abuse by one or more undertakings of a dominant position'. Collective dominance, i.e. a dominant position held by a number of undertakings, may be established when two or more undertakings present themselves or act together from an economic point of view, as a collective entity. Their joint policies or activities subsequently enable them together to behave to a considerable extent independently of their competitors, customers and consumers.

To establish collective dominance one needs to do more than recycle the facts constituting an infringement of Article 101 TFEU (Case T-68/89). Collective dominance may arise when the economic links between undertakings result in joint policies or activities (Case C-395/96P) even if those are not identical (Case T-228/97). It may be established even in the absence of an agreement or of other links in law, through links between the undertakings which lead them to present themselves as a collective entity on the market or on the basis of an economic assessment of the structure of the market in question. In Case C-395/96P *Compagnie Maritime Belge Transports v Commission* the Court of Justice held that 'A dominant position may be held by two or more economic entities legally independent of each other, provided that from an economic point of view they present themselves or act together on a particular market as a collective entity.' (para 36) This statement reflects the understanding that in some instances market conditions would give rise to collective dominance even absent structural links between the undertakings.

In its 2005 Discussion Paper on the Application of [Article 102 TFEU] to Exclusionary Abuses, the Commission made references to the possibility of establishing collective dominance in an oligopolistic market (paras 43–50). The more recent Commission Guidance Paper on the Commission's Enforcement Priorities in Applying [Article 102 TFEU] only relates to abuses committed by an undertaking holding a single dominant position and makes no references to collective dominance (para 4).

This area of law and economics has been developed mostly under the European Merger Regulation, although as evident from the Court of Justice judgment in *Compagnie Maritime Belge Transports v Commission*, the General Court judgment in *Laurent Piau v Commission*, and the Commission's 2005 Discussion Paper, the case-law which developed under the European Merger Regulation is directly relevant to the analysis of collective dominance under Article 102 TFEU. Of particular relevance to Article 102 TFEU analysis is the Court of Justice judgment in C-413/06P *Bertelsmann and Sony v Impala* in which the Court considered the evidence necessary to establish an existing collective dominant position.

The European Merger Regulation

Whereas the analysis under Article 102 TFEU is by its nature an *ex-post* analysis, the appraisal of concentrations under the European Merger Regulation is an *ex-ante* one. In the context of collective dominance, this difference in analysis means that cases dealing with collective dominance under the European Merger Regulation are primarily concerned with establishing that market characteristics following the merger transaction would give rise to a position of collective dominance. As indicated above, unique in this respect is Case C-413/06P *Bertelsmann and Sony v Impala* which concerns not only the creation of a collective dominant position but also the determination of the existence of a collective dominant position. Another difference in analysis between the two is that whereas Article 102 TFEU condemns the abuse of a collective dominant position (and not the position in itself), the European Merger Regulation condemns the creation or strengthening of the collective dominant position.

C-68/94 etc	*French Republic and others v Commission*	324
T-102/96	*Gencor v Commission*	325
T-324/99	*Airtours plc v Commission*	326
C-413/06P	*Bertelsmann and Sony v IMPALA*	328

See also summary references to:

92-466	*Brooke Group ltd., v. Brown & Williamson Tobacco Corporation*	327
T-464/04	*IMPALA v Commission*	328

On collective dominance under the European Merger Regulation, also note the Commission's Guidelines on the Assessment of Horizontal Mergers under the Council Regulation on the Control of Concentrations between Undertakings. (paras 39–57, [2004] OJ 31/5)

Concerted Practice vis-à-vis Tacit Collusion (Conscious Parallelism)

As evident from the case-law, tight oligopolistic markets may at times by their structure enable undertakings to sustain joint policies without communicating with each other. This phenomenon, often referred to by economists as 'tacit collusion' or 'conscious parallelism', may materialise in oligopolistic markets when (1) the market is transparent and thus enables undertakings to monitor each other's activities, and (2) undertakings are capable of punishing deviators from the tacit agreement and (3) competitive constraints do not jeopardise the implementation of the common strategy. (Case T-324/99, T-464/04 above) Tacit collusion receives different treatment under the different legal instruments:

- European Merger Regulation: the creation or strengthening of a collective dominant position (through tacit collusion) which significantly impedes effective competition is prohibited.
- Article 102 TFEU: a collective dominant position (as the result of tacit collusion or due to connecting links between the companies) is only condemned if the undertakings abuse it.
- Article 101 TFEU: parallel behaviour which is a rational reaction by the undertakings to market characteristics and does not result from concerted practice or agreement is not condemned. Parallel behaviour may amount to strong evidence of concerted practice when it leads to conditions of competition that do not correspond to the market characteristics.

On the dividing line between conscious parallelism and anticompetitive concerted practice, see:

48/69	*ICI v Commission (Dyestuffs)*	332
T-442/08	*CISAC v Commission*	332
92–466	*Brooke Group Ltd v Brown & Williamson Tobacco Corp*	332
82-914	*Monsanto Co v Spray-Rite Service Corp*	332
No 14-2301	*Aircraft Check Services Co v Verizon Wireless*	333

Società Italiana Vetro SpA and others v Commission
Joined Cases T-68, 77, 78/89 (Italian flat glass)
General Court, [1992] ECR II-1403, [1992] 5 CMLR 302

Collective Dominance
Article 102 TFEU

Facts

An action for annulment of the Commission's decision in which it found that three Italian flat-glass producers had formed a cartel agreement contrary to Article 101 TFEU. The Commission also found the practice to have infringed Article 102 TFEU. The Commission asserted that the three undertakings, as participants in a tight oligopoly, enjoyed a degree of independence from competitive pressures that enabled them to impede the maintenance of effective competition, notably by not having to take account of the behaviour of the other market participants. (point 78) It concluded that the undertakings presented themselves on the market as a single entity and not as individuals (point 79) and that their conduct constituted an abuse of a collective dominant position, because it restricted the consumers' ability to choose sources of supply, limited market outlets and distorted competition within the internal market. In its judgment, the General Court considered, among other things, the Commission's finding of a collective dominant position.

Held

'The Court notes that the very words of the first paragraph of [Article 102 TFEU] provide that "one or more undertakings" may abuse a dominant position. It has consistently been held, as indeed all the parties acknowledge, that the concept of agreement or concerted practice between undertakings does not cover agreements or concerted practices among undertakings belonging to the same group if the undertakings form an economic unit (see, for example, the judgment in Case 15/74 *Centrafarm*, [[1974] ECR 1147], paragraph 41). It follows that when [Article 101 TFEU] refers to agreements or concerted practices between "undertakings", it is referring to relations between two or more economic entities which are capable of competing with one another.' (para 357)

'The Court considers that there is no legal or economic reason to suppose that the term "undertaking" in [Article 102 TFEU] has a different meaning from the one given to it in the context of [Article 101 TFEU]. There is nothing, in principle, to prevent two or more independent economic entities from being, on a specific market, united by such economic links that, by virtue of that fact, together they hold a dominant position vis-a-vis the other operators on the same market. This could be the case, for example, where two or more independent undertakings jointly have, through agreements or licences, a technological lead affording them the power to behave to an appreciable extent independently of their competitors, their customers and ultimately of their consumers (judgment of the Court in *Hoffmann-La Roche*, [[1979] ECR 461], paragraphs 38 and 48).' (para 358)

'The Court finds support for that interpretation in the wording of Article 8 of Council Regulation (EEC) No 4056/86 of 22 December 1986 laying down detailed rules for the application of [Articles 101 and 102 TFEU] to maritime transport (Official Journal L 378, p 4). Article 8(2) provides that the conduct of a liner conference benefiting from an exemption from a prohibition laid down by [Article 101(1) TFEU] may have effects which are incompatible with [Article 102 TFEU]. A request by a conference to be exempted from the prohibition laid down by [Article 101(1) TFEU] necessarily presupposes an agreement between two or more independent economic undertakings.' (para 359)

'However, it should be pointed out that for the purposes of establishing an infringement of [Article 102 TFEU], it is not sufficient, as the Commission's agent claimed at the hearing, to "recycle" the facts constituting an infringement of [Article 101 TFEU], deducing from them the finding that the parties to an agreement or to an unlawful practice jointly hold a substantial share of the market, that by virtue of that fact alone they hold a collective dominant position, and that their unlawful behaviour constitutes an abuse of that collective dominant position. Amongst other considerations, a finding of a dominant position, which is in any case not in itself a matter of reproach, presupposes that the market in question has been defined (judgment of the Court of Justice in Case 6/72 *Continental Can*, [[1973] ECR 215], paragraph 32 Case 322/81 *Michelin v Commission*

[1983] ECR 3461, paragraph 57). The Court must therefore examine, firstly, the analysis of the market made in the decision and, secondly, the circumstances relied on in support of the finding of a collective dominant position.' (para 360)

'With regard to the definition of the market, the Court recalls that the section of the factual part of the decision entitled "The market" (points 2 to 17) is almost entirely descriptive and that, moreover, it contains a number of errors, omissions and uncertainties which have already been examined by the Court. The Court also recalls that the findings made by the Commission concerning relations between the three producers, and concerning relations between, on the one hand, the three producers, and on the other hand, the wholesalers on the non-automotive market and the manufacturers on the automotive market, are in many respects insufficiently supported. Finally, the Court points out that in the section of the legal part devoted to "The relevant market" (points 76 to 77) the decision adds nothing from the factual point of view to what was stated previously.' (para 361)

'It must therefore be determined whether the analysis of the market made in points 76 and points 77 of the decision is sufficiently well-founded and, moreover, whether that analysis is sufficient in itself to prove, as the Commission claims, that the appropriate market for the purposes of the application of [Article 102 TFEU] is, as regards the product, the flat-glass market in general and, from the geographical point of view, Italy.' (para 362)

The Commission analysis of the flat-glass market was lacking in this case. The Commission did not provide sufficient explanation as to why it considered it appropriate to divide its assessment of the undertakings' behaviour in relation, respectively, to the automotive market and the non-automotive market, while claiming that for the purposes of applying Article 102 TFEU, the flat-glass market must be considered to be a single market. 'However, the Court need not give a definitive ruling on the question whether the inadequate analysis that the Commission considered it appropriate to devote to the definition of the market is supported by satisfactory evidence, since the Commission stated … that the sentence which appears in the sixth paragraph of point 79 of the decision, "the undertakings present themselves on the market as a single entity and not as individuals", constituted an essential element of its position with regard to the application of [Article 102 TFEU], and that it was for the Commission to substantiate it. It is evident from all the foregoing that the Commission has far from substantiated that statement.' (paras 365, 363–5)

'It follows that, even supposing that the circumstances of the present case lend themselves to application of the concept of "collective dominant position" (in the sense of a position of dominance held by a number of independent undertakings), the Commission has not adduced the necessary proof. The Commission has not even attempted to gather the information necessary to weigh up the economic power of the three producers against that of Fiat, which could cancel each other out.' (para 366)

Comment

The General Court held that collective dominance cannot be established by merely recycling the facts constituting an infringement of Article 101 TFEU and deducing from them the finding that the parties to an agreement or to an unlawful practice jointly hold a substantial share of the market. (para 360)

The Commission was criticised for its analysis of the relations between the undertakings, its market definition, and its finding that together the undertakings held a collective dominant position.

In Case C-393/92 *Municipality of Almelo and others v NV Energiebedrijf Ijsselmij* [1994] ECR I-1477, the Court of Justice referred to the possibility of finding a group of undertakings to collectively occupy a dominant position. It held that 'in order for such a collective dominant position to exist, the undertakings in the group must be linked in such a way that they adopt the same conduct on the market'. (para 42) For a similar statement see also Case C-140/94 etc *DIP SpA v Comune di Bassano del Grappa* [1996] 4 CMLR 157, [1995] ECR I-3257, para 26.

Note the development of the concept in Case C-395/96P etc, page 320 below.

Compagnie Maritime Belge Transports v Commission	**Collective Dominance**
Joined Cases C-395/96P and C-396/96P	Article 102 TFEU
Court of Justice, [2000] ECR I-1365, [2000] 4 CMLR 1076	Horizontal Links

Facts

Compagnie Maritime Belge Transports SA (CMB) was found by the Commission to have abused a collective dominant position that it held with other undertakings. Together, the companies formed the membership of a liner conference and implemented a cooperation agreement which aimed, through selective price cuts, to drive an independent competitor out of the market (a practice known as 'fighting ships'). The companies were also found to have infringed Article 101 TFEU by entering into a non-compete agreement. The General Court dismissed an application by CMB to annul the Commission's decision. CMB appealed to the Court of Justice, contesting, among other things, the conclusion that it held jointly with the other members of the liner conference a collective dominant position.

Held

'A dominant position may be held by two or more economic entities legally independent of each other, provided that from an economic point of view they present themselves or act together on a particular market as a collective entity.' (para 36)

'A finding that two or more undertakings hold a collective dominant position must, in principle, proceed upon an economic assessment of the position on the relevant market of the undertakings concerned, prior to any examination of the question whether those undertakings have abused their position on the market.' (para 37)

The finding of abuse of a collective dominant position includes three elements. First, it is necessary to establish whether the undertakings concerned together constitute a collective entity vis-a-vis their competitors, their trading partners and consumers on a particular market. Secondly, where such collective entity is established, the following question is whether that entity holds a dominant position. Lastly, as under Article 102 TFEU the finding of collective dominance is not in itself grounds for criticism, one should further question whether the collective entity abused its dominant position. (paras 37–9)

'In order to establish the existence of a collective entity as defined above, it is necessary to examine the economic links or factors which give rise to a connection between the undertakings concerned (see, inter alia, Case C-393/92 *Almelo* [1994] ECR I-1477, paragraph 43, and Joined Cases C-68/94 and C-30/95 *France and Others v Commission* [1998] ECR I-1375, paragraph 221).' (para 41)

'In particular, it must be ascertained whether economic links exist between the undertakings concerned which enable them to act together independently of their competitors, their customers and consumers (see *Michelin*, cited above).' (para 42)

'The mere fact that two or more undertakings are linked by an agreement, a decision of associations of undertakings or a concerted practice within the meaning of [Article 101(1) TFEU] does not, of itself, constitute a sufficient basis for such a finding.' (para 43)

'On the other hand, an agreement, decision or concerted practice (whether or not covered by an exemption under [Article 101(3) TFEU]) may undoubtedly, where it is implemented, result in the undertakings concerned being so linked as to their conduct on a particular market that they present themselves on that market as a collective entity vis-a-vis their competitors, their trading partners and consumers.' (para 44)

'The existence of an agreement or of other links in law is not indispensable to a finding of a collective dominant position; such a finding may be based on other connecting factors and would depend on an economic assessment and, in particular, on an assessment of the structure of the market in question.' (para 45)

By its very nature and in the light of its objectives, a liner conference can be characterised as an entity which presents itself as a collective vis-à-vis both users and competitors. 'That in no way prejudges the question whether, in a given situation, a liner conference holds a dominant position on a particular market or, a fortiori, has abused that position …' (paras 49, 46–51)

The Court of Justice found the liner conference in question to hold a collective dominant position and to abuse it.

Comment

The existence of a collective dominant position flows from the nature and terms of an agreement or concerted practice between undertakings, from the way in which they are implemented and, consequently, from the links or factors which give rise to a connection between undertakings.

The judgment provides a clear indication that collective dominance may be found when the undertakings operate as a collective entity even in the absence of the existence of an agreement or of other links in law. The judgment paved the way to findings of collective dominance in later cases which are based on tacit collusion (see in particular the General Court judgment in *Airtours v Commission* on page 326 below).

Accordingly, under Article 102 TFEU when market characteristics give rise to tacit collusion, collective dominance may be established without the existence of an agreement or of other links in law (on the conditions to establish tacit collusion see *Airtours v Commission* on page 326 below). On the other hand, when the market does not give rise to tacit collusion, collective dominance can only be established if sufficient links between the undertakings are present. In this respect note Case C-309/99 *Wouters and others v Algemene Raad van de Nederlandse Orde van Advocaten* [2002] ECR I-1577, [2002] 4 CMLR 27, in which the Court of Justice held that 'the legal profession is not concentrated to any significant degree. It is highly heterogenous and is characterised by a high degree of internal competition. In the absence of sufficient structural links between them, members of the Bar cannot be regarded as occupying a collective dominant position for the purposes of [Article 102 TFEU] ...' (para 114)

In paragraph 41 the Court of Justice made references to previous decisions of collective dominance under both Article 102 TFEU and the European Merger Regulation. It therefore considered the concept to be the same under the two regulatory instruments. Under both provisions, examination of the economic links or factors which give rise to a connection between the undertakings concerned, is required, in order to establish collective dominance. Note, however, the differences between the ex-post analysis under Article 102 TFEU which condemns the abuse of a dominant (or collective dominant) position, and the ex-ante analysis under the European Merger Regulation which condemns significant impediment to effective competition, in particular, as the result of the creation or strengthening of a dominant (or collective dominant) position.

In paragraph 41 the Court referred to Cases C-68/94 and C-30/95 *French Republic and others v Commission* [1998] ECR I-1375. There in paragraph 221, the Court of Justice held with respect to collective dominance under the European Merger Regulation that 'in the case of an alleged collective dominant position, the Commission is therefore obliged to assess, using a prospective analysis of the reference market, whether the concentration which has been referred to it, leads to a situation in which effective competition in the relevant market is significantly impeded by the undertakings involved in the concentration and one or more other undertakings which together, in particular because of correlative factors which exist between them, are able to adopt a common policy on the market and act to a considerable extent independently of their competitors, their customers, and also of consumers.'

In its 2005 Discussion Paper on the Application of [Article 102 TFEU] to Exclusionary Abuses, the Commission noted that in order to establish collective dominance 'it is necessary to examine the factors that give rise to a connection between the undertakings concerned. Such factors may flow from the nature and terms of an agreement ... ownership interests and other links in law lead the undertakings concerned to co-ordinate. However, the existence of an agreement or of other links in law is not indispensable to a finding of a collective dominant position. Such a finding may be based on ... an assessment of the structure of the market in question. It follows that the structure of the market and the way in which undertakings interact on the market may give rise to a finding of collective dominance.' (paras 45, 46)

Irish Sugar plc v Commission	**Collective Dominance**
Case T-228/97	Article 102 TFEU
General Court, [1999] ECR II-2969, [1999] 5 CMLR 1300	

Facts

Irish Sugar, the sole processor of sugar beet and the principal supplier of sugar in Ireland, was fined by the Commission for infringing Article 102 TFEU. The Commission found Irish Sugar to hold a collective dominant position together with the distributor of its products, Sugar Distributors Ltd (SDL). Irish Sugar applied for annulment of the decision before the General Court and contested, among other things, the Commission's finding of a joint dominant position with SDL.

Held

'A joint dominant position consists in a number of undertakings being able together, in particular because of factors giving rise to a connection between them, to adopt a common policy on the market and act to a considerable extent independently of their competitors, their customers, and ultimately consumers.' (para 46)

The existence of economic independence between two entities does not prevent them from holding a joint dominant position. The mere independence of the economic entities in question is not sufficient to remove the possibility of their holding a joint dominant position. (para 49)

In this case the Commission identified connecting factors between Irish Sugar and SDL which show that the two economic entities had the power to adopt a common market policy. These connecting factors include, among other things, Irish Sugar's shareholding in SDL's parent company (SDH), its representation on the boards of SDH and SDL, the direct economic ties between SDL and Irish sugar, and the latter's financing of all consumer promotions and rebates offered by SDL to its customers. (paras 50-8)

The fact that the Irish Sugar and SDL are in a vertical commercial relationship does not affect the finding of joint dominant position. The case-law does not contain anything to support a claim that the concept of a joint dominant position is inapplicable to two or more undertakings in a vertical commercial relationship. As pointed out by the Commission, it cannot be accepted that undertakings in a vertical relationship, without however being integrated to the extent of constituting one and the same undertaking, should be able abusively to exploit a joint dominant position. (paras 61-3)

'Whilst the existence of a joint dominant position may be deduced from the position which the economic entities concerned together hold on the market in question, the abuse does not necessarily have to be the action of all the undertakings in question. It only has to be capable of being identified as one of the manifestations of such a joint dominant position being held. Therefore, undertakings occupying a joint dominant position may engage in joint or individual abusive conduct. It is enough for that abusive conduct to relate to the exploitation of the joint dominant position which the undertakings hold in the market.' (para 66)

Comment

The decision is interesting as it confirms the Commission's position that collective dominance may exist in a vertical setting. (para 62)

In paragraph 66 the General Court held that an abuse of the collective dominant position may be the result even if an action was taken by one of the companies and not the collective entity as a whole. Accordingly, the requirement that undertakings would present themselves on the market as a single entity does not infer identical conduct on the market in every respect. Interestingly, and somewhat controversially, the Court held that it is the abusive behaviour which may be carried out by one of the companies and not the collective entity.

In its investigation the Commission accepted Irish Sugar's argument that it did not control the management of SDL, despite holding 51 per cent of SDH's capital. In the absence of control, the Commission was unable to treat the two companies as one economic entity. However the links between the companies, although falling short of control, sufficed to establish collective dominance.

Laurent Piau v Commission
Case T-193/02
General Court, [2005] ECR II-2585, [2002] 5 CMLR 317

Facts

Mr Piau lodged a complaint to the Commission concerning the Fédération Internationale de Football Association (FIFA) Players' Agents Regulations. He alleged that the Regulations restricted access to the occupation and subsequently restricted competition. The Commission initiated an administrative procedure, following which FIFA adopted new Players' Agents Regulations. Subsequently, the Commission stated that there was no Union interest in continuing with the procedure. Mr Piau brought an action against the decision. In its judgment, the General Court considered, among other things, the application of Article 102 TFEU to a collective dominant position.

Held

Article 102 TFEU prohibits any abuse by one or more undertakings of a dominant position. The expression 'one or more undertakings' implies that a dominant position may be held by two or more legally independent economic entities, provided that from an economic point of view they present themselves or act together on a particular market as a collective entity. (paras 108–10)

'Three cumulative conditions must be met for a finding of collective dominance: first, each member of the dominant oligopoly must have the ability to know how the other members are behaving in order to monitor whether or not they are adopting the common policy; secondly, the situation of tacit co-ordination must be sustainable over time, that is to say, there must be an incentive not to depart from the common policy on the market; thirdly, the foreseeable reaction of current and future competitors, as well as of consumers, must not jeopardise the results expected from the common policy (Case T-342/99 *Airtours v Commission* [2002] ECR II–2585, paragraph 62, and Case T-374/00 *Verband der freien Rohrwerke and Others v Commission* [2003] ECR II–0000, paragraph 121).' (para 111)

The FIFA Players' Agents Regulations may, when implemented on the market for the provision of players' agents' services, result in the undertakings present themselves on that market as a collective entity vis-à-vis their competitors, their trading partners and consumers. However, the Regulations (as amended) do not give rise to an abuse of that collective dominant position. (paras 113–17)

Comment

In its decision the Commission wrongly took the view that Article 102 TFEU was not applicable, due to lack of dominance. The General Court found this to constitute an error in law. Yet, it concluded that the collective dominant position in this case did not result in abuse. Subsequently, it held that the Commission did not commit a manifest error of assessment. Mr Piau's action was dismissed.

The judgment is interesting as it is the first instance in which the Court made reference to the *Airtours* criteria in the context of Article 102 TFEU (on *Airtours* see page 326 below). Note, however, that the application of these conditions to the facts of the case was rather simplistic and did not amount to a serious attempt to establish that tacit collusion may materialise on that market. It is likely that the lack of abuse, which made the claim of collective dominance superfluous, led the Court to rush through the analysis of collective dominance. Contrast the depth of analysis with that of the Court of Justice in Case C-413/06P. (page 328 below)

Note that under Article 102 TFEU collective dominance may be established through the existence of an agreement or other links between the undertakings or, as was the case in this instance, an assessment of the structure of the market and the way in which undertakings interact on the market.

French Republic and others v Commission	**Collective Dominance**
Joined Cases C-68/94 and C-30/95 (Kali und Salz)	EU Merger Regulation
Court of Justice, [1998] ECR I-1375, [1998] 4 CMLR 829	

Facts

An appeal on a Commission's decision in which it approved, subject to conditions, a concentration between Kali und Salz AG and Mitteldeutsche Kali AG (Case No IV/M308). The decision was contested by the French government, which sought its annulment on the grounds, among other things, that the Commission erred in its analysis of collective dominance. On appeal the Court of Justice annulled the decision but confirmed in principle the application of the European Merger Regulation to collective dominance.

Held

'In the case of an alleged collective dominant position, the Commission is … obliged to assess, using a prospective analysis of the reference market, whether the concentration which has been referred to it leads to a situation in which effective competition in the relevant market is significantly impeded by the undertakings involved in the concentration and one or more other undertakings which together, in particular because of correlative factors which exist between them, are able to adopt a common policy on the market and act to a considerable extent independently of their competitors, their customers, and also of consumers.' (para 221)

'Such an approach warrants close examination in particular of the circumstances which, in each individual case, are relevant for assessing the effects of the concentration on competition in the reference market.' (para 222)

In the present case the Commission relied for its decision on a cluster of structural links which were found to be not as tight or as conclusive as it sought to make out. In addition its conclusions on the level of competition in the market post-merger were not sufficiently well founded. Subsequently, the Commission failed to establish to the necessary legal standard that the concentration would give rise to a collective dominant position. (paras 225–50)

Comment

The judgment refers to the existence of certain links as a precondition for collective dominance. However, in subsequent cases it was held that the reference to structural links was by way of example and did not lay down a requirement that such links must exist in order for a finding of collective dominance to be made. In *Gencor v Commission* the Court clarified the lose periphery of the term 'links'. (see paras 273–6)

In paragraph 221 the Court refers to the ability of the companies to adopt a common policy on the market. Note the similarity in approach to the analysis under Article 102 TFEU. See in particular paragraph 41, Case C-395/96 etc *Compagnie Maritime Belge Transports v Commission* (page 320 above).

The combined market share of the collective entity in this case was approximately 60 per cent. The Court of Justice held that such a market share 'cannot of itself point conclusively to the existence of a collective dominant position on the part of those undertakings.' (para 226) The Akzo presumption is therefore not applicable in cases of collective dominance (Case C-62/86 *AKZO Chemie BV v Commission*, page 216 above). Also note the General Court judgment in Case T-102/96 *Gencor Ltd v Commission* (page 325 below) where the Court held that 'in the context of an oligopoly, the fact that the parties to the oligopoly hold large market shares does not necessarily have the same significance, compared to the analysis of an individual dominant position, with regard to the opportunities for those parties, as a group, to act to a considerable extent independently of their competitors, their customers and, ultimately, of consumers. Nevertheless, particularly in the case of a duopoly, a large market share is, in the absence of evidence to the contrary, likewise a strong indication of the existence of a collective dominant position.' (para 206)

Gencor Ltd v Commission
Case T-102/96
General Court, [1999] ECR II-753, [1999] 4 CMLR 971

Collective Dominance
EU Merger Regulation

Facts

Gencor, a company incorporated under South African law, and Lonrho Plc (Lonrho), a company incorporated under English law, proposed to acquire joint control of Impala Platinum Holdings Ltd (Implats), a company incorporated under South African law. The transaction was cleared by the South African Competition Board. The European Commission also reviewed the transaction, and raised concerns as to its impact on the internal market. Subsequently, the Commission blocked the concentration on the ground that it would lead to the creation of a collective dominant position in the world platinum and rhodium market (Case IV/M619). Gencor unsuccessfully argued, among other things, that the Commission wrongly found that the concentration would create a collective dominant position.

Held

Although the European Merger Regulation lacks express reference to the concept of collective dominance, Article 2 of the Merger Regulation is interpreted as including this concept and therefore applies the Regulation both to the creation or strengthening of individual and collective dominant positions. (paras 124–36)

The finding of structural links is not indispensable for the establishment of collective dominance. Reference to such links in the flat-glass case (Joined Cases T-68/89 etc, *Società Italiana Vetro SpA and others v Commission*) was by way of example and did not compel that such links must exist in order for a finding of collective dominance to be made. (paras 273–5)

'Furthermore, there is no reason whatsoever in legal or economic terms to exclude from the notion of economic links the relationship of interdependence existing between the parties to a tight oligopoly within which, in a market with the appropriate characteristics, in particular in terms of market concentration, transparency and product homogeneity, those parties are in a position to anticipate one another's behaviour and are therefore strongly encouraged to align their conduct in the market, in particular in such a way as to maximise their joint profits by restricting production with a view to increasing prices. In such a context, each trader is aware that highly competitive action on its part designed to increase its market share (for example a price cut) would provoke identical action by the others, so that it would derive no benefit from its initiative. All the traders would thus be affected by the reduction in price levels.' (para 276)

'That conclusion is all the more pertinent with regard to the control of concentrations, whose objective is to prevent anti-competitive market structures from arising or being strengthened. Those structures may result from the existence of economic links in the strict sense argued by the applicant or from market structures of an oligopolistic kind where each undertaking may become aware of common interests and, in particular, cause prices to increase without having to enter into an agreement or resort to a concerted practice.' (para 277)

'The Commission was entitled to conclude, relying on the envisaged alteration in the structure of the market and on the similarity of the costs of Amplats and Implats/LPD, that the proposed transaction would create a collective dominant position and lead in actual fact to a duopoly constituted by those two undertakings.' (para 279)

Comment

Note the General Court comments on the interdependence between undertakings in a tight oligipolistic market.

Note that in this case the transaction would have led to the creation of a duopoly in the market. Contrast with the Airtours/First Choice transaction where the concentration would have reduced the number of players in the market from four to three (*Airtours plc v Commission*, page 326 below).

Airtours plc v Commission	Collective Dominance
Case T-342/99	EU Merger Regulation
General Court, [2002] ECR II-2585, [2002] 5 CMLR 7	Conscious Parallelism

Facts

An action for annulment of the Commission's decision in Case IV/M1524 *Airtours/First Choice* in which the Commission blocked a take over by Airtours plc, a UK tour operator and supplier of package holidays, of First Choice plc, one of Airtours' competitors. The Commission found that the transaction would give rise to a collective dominant position in the United Kingdom short-haul foreign package-holiday market, as a result of which competition would be significantly impeded in the internal market. Airtours applied to the General Court, alleging, among other things, that the Commission erred in its finding of a collective dominant position. It argued that in the past the market has been operating competitively as a benign oligopoly and that the Commission failed to prove that the merger would have reduced the three remaining undertakings' incentive to compete. Additionally, it claimed that in any event, the absence of retaliatory measures and the low barriers to entry and expansion in the market would curtail any attempt to collude.

Held

'A collective dominant position significantly impeding effective competition in the [internal] market or a substantial part of it may ... arise as the result of a concentration where, in view of the actual characteristics of the relevant market and of the alteration in its structure that the transaction would entail, the latter would make each member of the dominant oligopoly, as it becomes aware of common interests, consider it possible, economically rational, and hence preferable, to adopt on a lasting basis a common policy on the market with the aim of selling at above competitive prices, without having to enter into an agreement or resort to a concerted practice within the meaning of [Article 101 TFEU] ... and without any actual or potential competitors, let alone customers or consumers, being able to react effectively.' (para 61)

'Three conditions are necessary for a finding of collective dominance as defined:

– First, each member of the dominant oligopoly must have the ability to know how the other members are behaving in order to monitor whether or not they are adopting the common policy. As the Commission specifically acknowledges, it is not enough for each member of the dominant oligopoly to be aware that interdependent market conduct is profitable for all of them but each member must also have a means of knowing whether the other operators are adopting the same strategy and whether they are maintaining it. There must, therefore, be sufficient market transparency for all members of the dominant oligopoly to be aware, sufficiently precisely and quickly, of the way in which the other members' market conduct is evolving;

– Secondly, the situation of tacit co-ordination must be sustainable over time, that is to say, there must be an incentive not to depart from the common policy on the market. As the Commission observes, it is only if all the members of the dominant oligopoly maintain the parallel conduct that all can benefit. The notion of retaliation in respect of conduct deviating from the common policy is thus inherent in this condition. In this instance, the parties concur that, for a situation of collective dominance to be viable, there must be adequate deterrents to ensure that there is a long-term incentive in not departing from the common policy, which means that each member of the dominant oligopoly must be aware that highly competitive action on its part designed to increase its market share would provoke identical action by the others, so that it would derive no benefit from its initiative (see, to that effect, *Gencor v EC Commission*);

– Thirdly, to prove the existence of a collective dominant position to the requisite legal standard, the Commission must also establish that the foreseeable reaction of current and future competitors, as well as of consumers, would not jeopardise the results expected from the common policy.' (para 62)

'The prospective analysis which the Commission has to carry out in its review of concentrations involving collective dominance calls for close examination in particular of the circumstances which, in each individual case, are relevant for assessing the effects of the concentration on competition in the reference market ... Where the Commission takes the view that a merger should be prohibited because it will create a situation of collective dominance, it is incumbent upon it to produce convincing evidence thereof. The evidence must concern, in particular, factors playing a significant role in the assessment of whether a situation of collective dominance exists, such as, for example, the lack of effective competition between the operators alleged to be members of the dominant oligopoly and the weakness of any competitive pressure that might be exerted by other operators.' (para 63)

The Commission's assessment of the market characteristics in this case was incomplete and incorrect. It reached inaccurate conclusions on the level of competition, the likelihood for growth, the capacity constraints, the degree of market transparency and the existence of a credible retaliatory mechanism. (paras 66–293)

Consequently, the Commission's decision 'is vitiated by a series of errors of assessment as to factors fundamental to any assessment of whether a collective dominant position might be created. It follows that the Commission prohibited the transaction without having proven to the requisite legal standard that the concentration would give rise to a collective dominant position of the three major tour operators, of such a kind as significantly to impede effective competition in the relevant market.' (para 294)

Comment

The judgment provides an important contribution to the development of the collective dominance doctrine. While continuing the approach adopted in *Gencor v Commission*, it distills the concept of collective dominance and clarifies its realm. In the judgment the General Court brought the notion of collective dominance generally in line with the economic concept of tacit collusion (conscious parallelism). The latter rests on a three-part test under which the undertakings involved are capable of (i) reaching a tacit agreement, (ii) detecting breaches and (iii) punishing deviations from the agreement. This alignment brought to an end the somewhat blurred distinction between unilateral and coordinated effects as was evident from the Commission's decision.

In paragraph 54 of its decision, the Commission argued that 'it is not a necessary condition of collective dominance for the oligopolists always to behave as if there were one or more explicit agreements'. The General Court rejected the Commission's reliance on the unilateral behaviour of the single undertaking as an indicator for collective dominance. In doing so, it clearly limited the scope of collective dominance to cases involving coordinated effects.

The General Court held that in order to determine whether a collective dominant position would be created following the merger, the Commission should have considered the pre-merger level of competition. In holding so, the Court rejected the Commission's approach that it should only consider the existing market conditions when it suspects a strengthening of a collective dominant position, but not the creation of one. In paragraph 82 the Court held that 'the level of competition obtaining in the relevant market at the time when the transaction is notified is a decisive factor in establishing whether a collective dominant position has been created.'

Also note the General Court's comments as to the standard of proof necessary in a prospective analysis of collective dominance and the need to produce 'convincing evidence'. (paras 63, 294)

The Horizontal Merger Guidelines, published by the Commission in 2004, largely reflect the criteria set in this judgment (see paras 39–57 Guidelines on the Assessment of Horizontal Mergers under the Council Regulation on the Control of Concentrations between Undertakings [2004] OJ C31).

'Tacit collusion, sometimes called oligopolistic price coordination or conscious parallelism, describes the process, not in itself unlawful, by which firms in a concentrated market might in effect share monopoly power, setting their prices at a profit-maximizing, supracompetitive level by recognizing their shared economic interests and their interdependence with respect to price and output decisions.' (*Brooke Group Ltd v Brown & Williamson Tobacco Corporation*, 509 US 209 (1993), Supreme Court of the United States)

Bertelsmann AG and Sony Corporation of America v IMPALA	**Collective Dominance**
Case C-413/06P	EU Merger Regulation
Court of Justice, [2008] ECR I-4951; [2008] 5 CMLR 17	

Facts

An appeal on the General Court's judgment in Case T-464/04 *IMPALA v Commission* ([2006] ECR II-2289, [2006] 5 CMLR 19) in which the General Court annulled the Commission Decision in Case Comp/M.3333 *Sony/BMG*, in which the Commission cleared the transaction between Sony and BMG (the second and fifth biggest record companies in the world), which reduced the number of players in the recorded industry market from five to four. In its decision the Commission considered whether the transaction would strengthen a pre-existing collective dominant position in the market, but concluded that there was not sufficient evidence that such position exists or will be created. It subsequently cleared the transaction.

On appeal, the General Court reviewed the Commission's analysis of both the pre-existing collective dominance and the creation of collective dominance. Following its review, the General Court annulled the Commission's decision.

With respect to the creation of a collective dominant position, the General Court repeated the principles laid down in *Airtours v Commission* (page 326 above). It criticised the Commission's prospective analysis as being extremely succinct (para 525) and its observation of the market 'superficial' and 'purely formal' (para 528). It concluded that the level of analysis did not satisfy the Commission's obligation to carry out a prospective and detailed appraisal. (paras 523–9) The Court noted that:

'It must be borne in mind that when the Commission examines the risk that a collective dominant position will be created, it must "assess, using a prospective analysis of the reference market, whether the concentration which has been referred to it, leads to a situation in which effective competition in the relevant market is significantly impeded by the undertakings involved in the concentration and one or more other undertakings which together, in particular because of factors giving rise to a connection between them, are able to adopt a common policy on the market and act to a considerable extent independently of their competitors, their customers, and [ultimately] of consumers" …' (para 522)

With respect to establishing the existence of a collective dominant position, the judgment laid down a new modified test: 'It follows that, in the context of the assessment of the existence of a collective dominant position, although the three conditions defined by the [General Court] in *Airtours v Commission* … which were inferred from a theoretical analysis of the concept of a collective dominant position, are indeed also necessary, they may, however, in the appropriate circumstances, be established indirectly on the basis of what may be a very mixed series of indicia and items of evidence relating to the signs, manifestations and phenomena inherent in the presence of a collective dominant position.' (para 251) 'Thus, in particular, close alignment of prices over a long period, especially if they are above a competitive level, together with other factors typical of a collective dominant position, might, in the absence of an alternative reasonable explanation, suffice to demonstrate the existence of a collective dominant position, even where there is no firm direct evidence of strong market transparency, as such transparency may be presumed in such circumstances.' (para 252)

The new test lowered the threshold for establishing a pre-existing collective dominant position through the use of indirect analysis. In doing so it widened the *Airtours* criteria by finding that collective dominance may be established indirectly on the basis of mixed series of indicia and items of evidence relating to the signs, manifestations and phenomena inherent in the presence of a collective dominance.

In its judgment the Court also commented on the role of Statement of Objections. As part of its investigation of the Sony–BMG transaction the Commission issued a statement of objection in which it objected the transaction on the bases that it will create or strengthen a collective dominant position. In its judgment, the General Court was critical of the Commission's inability to explain its departure from its earlier finding in the statement of objections and its subsequent clearance of the transaction. In its decision the Court seemed to take a novel approach to the role of the 'statement of objections' issued by the Commission. It held that the finding set out in the decision must be compatible with the finding of facts made in the statement of objections. Accordingly, these findings, although only being preliminary and set in a preparatory document, may limit the Commission's ability to adopt a final decision which is incompatible with them.

The General Court annulled the Commission's decision which cleared the concentration. The General Court's judgment was subsequently appealed to the Court of Justice which overruled it.

Held

The statement of objections

The statement of objections is a procedural and preparatory document which delimits the scope of the administrative procedure initiated by the Commission. It is inherent in the nature of the statement of objections that it is provisional and subject to amendments. Thus, the statement of objections does not prevent the Commission from altering its standpoint. It follows that the Commission is not obliged to maintain the factual or legal assessments set forth in that document. Furthermore, the Commission is not obliged to explain any differences between its final assessments and its provisional assessments. (paras 61–6)

In several instances the General Court treated some of the conclusions set out in the statement of objections as established, whereas those conclusions could, however, only be considered as being provisional. In those circumstances, it must be held that the General Court committed an error of law when 'it treated certain elements in the statement of objections as being established, without demonstrating the reasons for which, notwithstanding the final position adopted by the Commission in the contested decision, those elements should be considered as being established beyond dispute.' (paras 76, 71–6)

The standard of proof applied to the evidence submitted in response to the statement of objections

'It follows that the [General Court] committed an error of law, first, in requiring, in essence, that the Commission apply particularly demanding requirements as regards the probative character of the evidence and arguments put forward by the notifying parties in reply to the statement of objections and, secondly, in finding that the lack of additional market investigations after communication of the statement of objections and the adoption by the Commission of the appellants' arguments in defence amounted to an unlawful delegation of the investigation to the parties to the concentration.' (para 95)

Collective dominance

'[T]he existence of an agreement or of other links in law between the undertakings concerned is not essential to a finding of a collective dominant position. Such a finding may be based on other connecting factors and would depend on an economic assessment and, in particular, on an assessment of the structure of the market in question (see Joined Cases C-395/96P and C-396/96P *Compagnie Maritime Belge transports and Others v Commission* [2000] ECR I-1365, paragraph 45).' (para 119)

'In the case of an alleged creation or strengthening of a collective dominant position, the Commission is obliged to assess, using a prospective analysis of the reference market, whether the concentration which has been referred to it will lead to a situation in which effective competition in the relevant market is significantly impeded by the undertakings which are parties to the concentration and one or more other undertakings which together, in particular because of correlative factors which exist between them, are able to adopt a common policy on the market (see *Kali & Salz*, paragraph 221) in order to profit from a situation of collective economic strength, without actual or potential competitors, let alone customers or consumers, being able to react effectively.' (para 120)

'Such correlative factors include, in particular, the relationship of interdependence existing between the parties to a tight oligopoly within which, on a market with the appropriate characteristics, in particular in terms of market concentration, transparency and product homogeneity, those parties are in a position to anticipate one another's behaviour and are therefore strongly encouraged to align their conduct on the market in such a way as to maximise their joint profits by increasing prices, reducing output, the choice or quality of goods and services, diminishing innovation or otherwise influencing parameters of competition. In such a context, each operator is aware that highly competitive action on its part would provoke a reaction on the part of the others, so that it would derive no benefit from its initiative.' (para 121)

'A collective dominant position significantly impeding effective competition in the [internal] market or a substantial part of it may thus arise as the result of a concentration where, in view of the actual characteristics of the relevant market and of the alteration to those characteristics that the concentration would entail, the latter would make each member of the oligopoly in question, as it becomes aware of common interests, consider it possible, economically rational, and hence preferable, to adopt on a lasting basis a common policy on the market with the aim of selling at above competitive prices, without having to enter into an agreement or resort to a concerted practice within the meaning of [Article 101 TFEU] and without any actual or potential competitors, let alone customers or consumers, being able to react effectively.' (para 122)

'Such tacit coordination is more likely to emerge if competitors can easily arrive at a common perception as to how the coordination should work, and, in particular, of the parameters that lend themselves to being a focal point of the proposed coordination. Unless they can form a shared tacit understanding of the terms of the coordination, competitors might resort to practices that are prohibited by [Article 101 TFEU] in order to be able to adopt a common policy on the market. Moreover, having regard to the temptation which may exist for each participant in a tacit coordination to depart from it in order to increase its short-term profit, it is necessary to determine whether such coordination is sustainable. In that regard, the coordinating undertakings must be able to monitor to a sufficient degree whether the terms of the coordination are being adhered to. There must therefore be sufficient market transparency for each undertaking concerned to be aware, sufficiently precisely and quickly, of the way in which the market conduct of each of the other participants in the coordination is evolving. Furthermore, discipline requires that there be some form of credible deterrent mechanism that can come into play if deviation is detected. In addition, the reactions of outsiders, such as current or future competitors, and also the reactions of customers, should not be such as to jeopardise the results expected from the coordination.' (para 123)

'In applying those criteria, it is necessary to avoid a mechanical approach involving the separate verification of each of those criteria taken in isolation, while taking no account of the overall economic mechanism of a hypothetical tacit coordination.' (para 125)

'In that regard, the assessment of, for example, the transparency of a particular market should not be undertaken in an isolated and abstract manner, but should be carried out using the mechanism of a hypothetical tacit coordination as a basis. It is only if such a hypothesis is taken into account that it is possible to ascertain whether any elements of transparency that may exist on a market are, in fact, capable of facilitating the reaching of a common understanding on the terms of coordination and/or of allowing the competitors concerned to monitor sufficiently whether the terms of such a common policy are being adhered to. In that last respect, it is necessary, in order to analyse the sustainability of a purported tacit coordination, to take into account the monitoring mechanisms that may be available to the participants in the alleged tacit coordination in order to ascertain whether, as a result of those mechanisms, they are in a position to be aware, sufficiently precisely and quickly, of the way in which the market conduct of each of the other participants in that coordination is evolving.' (para 126)

'As regards the present case, the appellants submit that, even though the [General Court] stated in paragraph 254 of the judgment under appeal that it was following the approach adopted in its judgment in *Airtours v Commission*, in practice, it committed an error of law in inferring the existence of a sufficient degree of transparency from a number of factors which were not, however, relevant to a finding of an existing collective dominant position. In that context, the appellants object in particular to the fact that the [General Court] indicated in paragraph 251 of the judgment under appeal that the conditions laid down in paragraph 62 of the judgment in *Airtours v Commission* could "in the appropriate circumstances, be established indirectly on the basis of what may be a very mixed series of indicia and items of evidence relating to the signs, manifestations and phenomena inherent in the presence of a collective dominant position". (para 127)

'In this regard, as the Commission observed at the hearing, objection cannot be taken to paragraph 251 of itself, since it constitutes a general statement which reflects the [General Court]'s liberty of assessment of different items of evidence. It is settled case-law that it is, in principle, for the [General Court] alone to assess the value to be attached to the items of evidence adduced before it.' (para 128)

'Similarly, the investigation of a pre-existing collective dominant position based on a series of elements normally considered to be indicative of the presence or the likelihood of tacit coordination between competitors cannot therefore be considered to be objectionable of itself. However, as is apparent from paragraph 125 of this judgment, it is essential that such an investigation be carried out with care and, above all, that it should adopt an approach based on the analysis of such plausible coordination strategies as may exist in the circumstances.' (para 129)

'In the present case, the [General Court], before which Impala raised arguments relating, in particular, to the parts of the contested decision relating to market transparency, did not carry out its analysis of those parts by having regard to a postulated monitoring mechanism forming part of a plausible theory of tacit coordination.' (para 130)

'It is true that the [General Court] referred in paragraph 420 of the judgment under appeal to the possibility of a "known set of rules" governing the grant of discounts by the majors. However—as the appellants rightly submit in the context of the second specific criticism mentioned in paragraph 113 of this judgment, which relates to the question whether certain discount variations established by the Commission in the contested decision were liable to call into question the possibility of adequate monitoring of mutual compliance with the terms of any tacit coordination there may have been—the [General Court] was content to rely, in paragraphs 427 to 429 of the judgment under appeal, on unsupported assertions relating to a hypothetical industry professional. In paragraph 428 of the judgment, the [General Court] itself acknowledged that Impala, the applicant before that court, "admittedly did not explain precisely what those various rules governing the grant of campaign discounts are".' (para 131)

'It must be pointed out in that regard that Impala represents undertakings which, even if they are not members of the oligopoly formed by the majors, are active on the same markets. In those circumstances, it is clear that the [General Court] disregarded the fact that the burden of proof was on Impala in relation to the purported qualities of such a hypothetical "industry professional".' (para 132)

'In the light of the above … it must be held that, in misconstruing the principles which should have guided its analysis of the arguments raised before it concerning market transparency in the context of an allegation of a collective dominant position, the [General Court] committed an error of law.' (para 133)

Comment

The Court of Justice overruled the General Court judgment (disregarding the recommendations made by AG Kokott to uphold that judgment). It held that the *Airtours* criteria cannot be mechanically applied. Note in this respect the General Court's limited analysis of collective dominance in Case T-193/02 *Laurent Piau v Commission*. (page 323 above)

The Court of Justice clarified that the Statement of Objections serves as a preparatory document from which the Commission can deviate. The Commission is not required to explain the difference between its final decision and its provisional assessment as stipulated in the Statement of Objections.

Interestingly, the Court of Justice held in paragraph 48 that there is no general presumption that a notified concentration is compatible with, or incompatible with, the internal market. This statement is interesting as it clarifies that there is no presumption in favour of clearance under the European Merger Regulation. The same burden and standard of proof apply to both 'clearance' and 'prohibition' decisions.

Following the General Court judgment and annulment of the Commission's decision, the parties renotified the joint venture to the Commission. In its new assessment of the transaction the Commission was able to take into account current market conditions and to evaluate the actual impact of the transaction on the market following its original clearance decision in year 2004. This meant that the Commission was not limited to a prospective analysis and could examine the present effects of the transaction. In October 2007, at the end of an in-depth investigation, the Commission cleared the transaction without conditions.

Imperial Chemical Industries (ICI) v Commission (Dyestuffs)
Case 48/69
Court of Justice, [1972] ECR 619, [1972] CMLR 557

Conscious Parallelism
Parallel Behaviour

'Although parallel behaviour may not by itself be identified with a concerted practice, it may however amount to strong evidence of such a practice if it leads to conditions of competition which do not correspond to the normal conditions of the market, having regard to the nature of the products, the size and number of the undertakings, and the volume of the said market.' (para 66)

CISAC v Commission
Cases T-442/08
General Court, [2013] 5 CMLR 15

Conscious Parallelism
Concerted and Independent Action
Parallel Behaviour

As the Commission did not establish, to the requisite legal standard, the existence of a concerted practice between the collecting societies to fix the national territorial limitations, it is necessary to examine whether the Commission provided sufficient evidence to render implausible the explanations of the collecting societies' parallel conduct, put forward by the applicant, other than the existence of concertration. (paras 132, 133)

The evidence relied on by the Commission is not sufficient to render implausible the explanation provided by the applicant according to which the national territorial limitations are the result of individual, carefully considered and rational decisions on a practical and economic level, given the specific conditions of the market, and not the result of a concerted practice. (paras 134–81)

Brooke Group Ltd v Brown & Williamson Tobacco Corporation
No 92–466
Supreme Court of the United States, 509 US 209 (1993)

Conscious Parallelism
Parallel Behaviour

'[E]ven in an oligopolistic market, when a firm drops its prices to a competitive level to demonstrate to a maverick the unprofitability of straying from the group, it would be illogical to condemn the price cut: the antitrust laws then would be an obstacle to the chain of events most conducive to a breakdown of oligopoly pricing and the onset of competition.' (page 224)

'Tacit collusion, sometimes called oligopolistic price coordination or conscious parallelism, describes the process, not in itself unlawful, by which firms in a concentrated market might in effect share monopoly power, setting their prices at a profit-maximizing, supracompetitive level by recognizing their shared economic interests and their interdependence with respect to price and output decisions. See Areeda & Turner ¶ 404; Scherer & Ross 199–208.' (page 227)

Monsanto Co v Spray-Rite Service Corp
No 82-914
Supreme Court of the United States, 465 US 752 (1984)

Conscious Parallelism
Concerted and Independent Action

'[T]here is a basic distinction between concerted and independent action—a distinction not always clearly drawn by parties and courts. Section 1 of the Sherman Act requires that there be a "contract, combination … or conspiracy" between the manufacturer and other distributors in order to establish a violation … [to prove concerted action] the correct standard is that there must be evidence that tends to exclude the possibility of independent action by the [parties]. That is, there must be direct or circumstantial evidence that reasonably tends to prove that the [parties] had a conscious commitment to a common scheme designed to achieve an unlawful objective.' (page 465)

Aircraft Check Services Co. v Verizon Wireless No 14-2301 United States Court of Appeal	**Conscious Parallelism** Concerted and Independent Action Parallel Behaviour

'[T]he Sherman Act imposes no duty on firms to compete vigorously, or for that matter at all, in price. This troubles some antitrust experts, such as Harvard Law School Professor Louis Kaplow, whose book Competition Policy and Price Fixing (2013) argues that tacit collusion should be deemed a violation of the Sherman Act. That of course is not the law, and probably shouldn't be. A seller must decide on a price; and if tacit collusion is forbidden, how does a seller in a market in which conditions (such as few sellers, many buyers, and a homogeneous product, which may preclude non price competition) favor convergence by the sellers on a joint profit-maximizing price without their actually agreeing to charge that price, decide what price to charge? If the seller charges the profit-maximizing price (and its "competitors" do so as well), and tacit collusion is illegal, it is in trouble. But how is it to avoid getting into trouble? Would it have to adopt cost-plus pricing and prove that its price just covered its costs (where cost includes a "reasonable return" to invested capital)? Such a requirement would convert antitrust law into a scheme resembling public utility price regulation, now largely abolished.'

'And might not entry into concentrated markets be deterred because an entrant who, having successfully entered such a market, charged the prevailing market price would be a tacit colluder and could be prosecuted as such, if tacit collusion were deemed to violate the Sherman Act? What could be more perverse than an antitrust doctrine that discouraged new entry into highly concentrated markets? Prices might fall if the new entrant's output increased the market's total output, but then again it might not fall; the existing firms in the market might reduce their output in order to prevent the output of the new entrant from depressing the market price. If as a result the new entrant found itself charging the same price as the incumbent firms, it would be tacitly colluding with them and likewise even if it set its price below that of those firms in order to maximize its profit from entry yet above the price that would prevail were there no tacit collusion.'

'Further illustrating the danger of the law's treating tacit collusion as if it were express collusion, suppose that the firms in an oligopolistic market don't try to sell to each other's sleepers, "sleepers" being a term for a seller's customers who out of indolence or ignorance don't shop but instead are loyal to whichever seller they've been accustomed to buy from. Each firm may be reluctant to "awaken" any of the other firms' sleepers by offering them discounts, fearing retaliation. To avoid punishment under antitrust law for such forbearance (which would be a form of tacit collusion, aimed at keeping prices high), would firms be required to raid each other's sleepers? It is one thing to prohibit competitors from agreeing not to compete; it is another to order them to compete. How is a court to decide how vigorously they must compete in order to avoid being found to have tacitly colluded in violation of antitrust law? Such liability would, to repeat, give antitrust agencies a public-utility style regulatory role.'

'Or consider the case, of which the present one may be an exemplar, in which there are four competitors and one raises its price and the others follow suit. Maybe they do that because they think the first firm—the price leader—has insights into market demand that they lack. Maybe they're afraid that though their sales will increase if they don't follow the leader up the price ladder, the increase in their sales will induce the leader to reduce his price, resulting in increased sales by him at the expense of any firm that had refused to increase its price. Or the firms might fear that the price leader had raised his price in order to finance product improvements that would enable him to hold on to his existing customers—and win over customers of the other firms. If any of these reflections persuaded the other firms—without any communication with the leader—to raise their prices, there would be no conspiracy, but merely tacit collusion, which to repeat is not illegal despite the urging of Professor Kaplow and others.'

'Competitors in concentrated markets watch each other like hawks. Think of what happens in the airline industry, where costs are to a significant degree a function of fuel prices, when those prices rise. Suppose one airline thinks of and implements a method for raising its profit margin that it expects will have a less negative impact on ticket sales than an increase in ticket prices—such as a checked-bag fee or a reservation-change fee. … The airline's competitors will monitor carefully the effects of the airline's response to the higher fuel prices afflicting the industry and may well decide to copy the response should the responder's response turn out to have increased its profits.' (pages 10–12)

Competition Law and the State

7

Article 4(3) Treaty on European Union (TEU)

Article 4(3) TEU stipulates that: 'Pursuant to the principle of sincere cooperation, the Union and the Member States shall, in full mutual respect, assist each other in carrying out tasks which flow from the Treaties. The Member States shall take any appropriate measure, general or particular, to ensure fulfilment of the obligations arising out of the Treaties or resulting from the acts of the institutions of the Union. The Member States shall facilitate the achievement of the Union's tasks and refrain from any measure which could jeopardise the attainment of the Union's objectives.'

Although Articles 101 and 102 TFEU are concerned solely with the conduct of undertakings and not with laws emanating from Member States, those Articles, read in conjunction with Article 4(3) TEU, require Member States not to introduce or maintain in force measures that may render ineffective the competition rules applicable to undertakings.

In particular, a Member State may infringe Articles 4(3) TEU and Article 101 TFEU where it requires, favours or reinforces the effects of agreements or measures contrary to Article 101 TFEU, or where it divests its own rule-making powers by delegating to private economic operators responsibility for taking decisions affecting the economic sphere.

C-94/04 etc	*Federico Cipolla v Rosaria Fazari*	337
C-198/01	*CIF v Autotità Garante della Concorrenza e del Mercato*	339

See also summary references to:

C-35/99	*Manuele Arduino*	337
136/86	*Bureau National Interprofessionel du Cognac v Aubert*	338
C-35/96	*Commission v Italy*	338
C-250/03	*Mauri v Ministero della Giustizia*	338
13/77	*INNO v ATAB*	340
C-2/91	*Meng*	340
311/85	*Vzw Vereniging van Vlaamse Reisbureaus v Vzw Sociale Dienst*	340

State Compulsion Defence

Articles 101 and 102 TFEU apply only to anti-competitive conduct engaged in by undertakings on their own initiative. If anti-competitive conduct is required of undertakings by national legislation, or if the state creates a legal framework which itself eliminates any possibility for competitive activity on the undertakings' part, the restriction of competition will not be attributed to them. Their action will be shielded from the application of Articles 101 and 102 TFEU.

C-359/95P etc	*Commission and France v Ladbroke Racing*	341
C-198/01	*CIF v Autotità Garante della Concorrenza e del Mercato*	342

See also summary references to:

In its Guidelines on the Applicability of Article 101 TFEU to Horizontal Co-operation Agreements the Commission notes that: 'In certain cases, companies are encouraged by public authorities to enter into horizontal co-operation agreements in order to attain a public policy objective by way of self-regulation. However, companies remain subject to Article 101 if a national law merely encourages or makes it easier for them to engage in autonomous anti-competitive conduct. In other words, the fact that public authorities encourage a horizontal co-operation agreement does not mean that it is permissible under Article 101. It is only if anti-competitive conduct is required of companies by national legislation, or if the latter creates a legal framework which precludes all scope for competitive activity on their part, that Article 101 does not apply. In such a situation, the restriction of competition is not attributable, as Article 101 implicitly requires, to the autonomous conduct of the companies and they are shielded from all the consequences of an infringement of that article. Each case must be assessed on its own facts according to the general principles set out in these guidelines.' (para 22)

Article 106(1) TFEU

Article 106(1) TFEU focuses on the Member States and stipulates that 'In the case of public undertakings and undertakings to which Member States grant special or exclusive rights, Member States shall neither enact nor maintain in force any measure contrary to the rules contained in the Treaties, in particular to those rules provided for in Article 18 and Articles 101 to 109.'

Accordingly, Article 106(1) TFEU must be applied alongside another Treaty rule, when the latter is, or may be, infringed.

See also summary references to:

Article 106(2) TFEU

While Article 106(1) TFEU focuses on the Member States, Article 106(2) TFEU focuses on the undertakings. In an attempt to strike a balance between the application of competition law and the State's interest in providing quality services of general interest, the Article limits the application of the former. It stipulates that 'Undertakings entrusted with the operation of services of general economic interest or having the character of a revenue-producing monopoly shall be subject to the rules contained in the Treaties, in particular to the rules on competition, insofar as the application of such rules does not obstruct the performance, in law or in fact, of the particular tasks assigned to them. The development of trade must not be affected to such an extent as would be contrary to the interests of the Union.'

C-41/90	*Klaus Höfner and Fritz Elser v Macrotron GmbH*	343
C-320/91	*Paul Corbeau*	348
C-266/96	*Corsica Ferries France SA v Porto di Genova*	353
C-475/99	*Firma Ambulanz Glöckner v Landkreis Sudwestpfalz*	354
C-67/96	*Albany Int BV v Stichting Bedrijfspensioenfonds Textielindustrie*	356
C-147/97 etc	*Deutsche Post AG*	357
C-162/06	*International Mail Spain SL v Administración del Estado and Correos*	359

See also summary references to:

188/80 etc	*France, Italy and the UK v Commission*	344
66/86	*Ahmed Saeed Flugreisen*	355
COMP/39562	*Slovenská pošta*	359

Article 106(3) TFEU

Article 106(3) TFEU empowers the Commission to specify in general terms the obligations arising under Article 106(1) and (2) TFEU by adopting directives or decisions. It stipulates that 'The Commission shall ensure the application of the provisions of this Article and shall, where necessary, address appropriate directives or decisions to Member States.'

C-202/88	*French Republic v Commission*	360

State and Public Bodies Subject to the Same Laws as Private Undertakings

The concept of 'undertaking' is central to identifying the addressees of competition law provisions. A state body may be subjected to competition law provisions when it engages in economic activity and subsequently is classified as an undertaking. See further discussion on this point in Chapter 1 above.

Federico Cipolla v Rosaria Fazari	**Competition Law and the State**
Joined Cases C-94/04 and C-202/04	Article 4(3) TEU
Court of Justice, [2006] ECR I-11421, [2007] 4 CMLR 8	

Facts

References for a preliminary ruling under Article 267 TFEU from the Italian Corte d'appello di Torino and the Tribunale di Roma. Both references emerged from proceedings between lawyers and their respective clients in respect of the payment of fees. In both procedures the national court queried, among other things, whether Article 4(3) TEU and Articles 101 and 102 TFEU preclude a Member State from adopting a legislative measure which approves, on the basis of a draft produced by a professional body of lawyers, a scale fixing a minimum fee for members of the legal profession. The scale at issue did not allow derogation in respect of either services reserved to those members or those such as out-of-court services which may also be provided by any other economic operator not subject to that scale.

Held

Although Articles 101 and 102 TFEU are concerned solely with the conduct of undertakings and not with laws emanating from Member States, those articles, read in conjunction with Article 4(3) TEU, require Member States not to introduce or maintain in force measures, even of a legislative or regulatory nature, which may render ineffective the competition rules applicable to undertakings. 'The Court has held, in particular, that Articles [4(3) TEU] and [101 TFEU] are infringed where a Member State requires or encourages the adoption of agreements, decisions or concerted practices contrary to [Article 101 TFEU] or reinforces their effects, or where it divests its own rules of the character of legislation by delegating to private economic operators responsibility for taking decisions affecting the economic sphere.' (paras 46–7)

The fact that a Member State requires a professional body of lawyers to produce a draft scale of fees does not, in the circumstances specific to these cases, appear to establish that that State has divested the scale finally adopted of its character of legislation by delegating to lawyers responsibility for taking decisions concerning them. According to the regulation in question the Italian State retains its power to make decisions of last resort or to review implementation of that scale. Additionally, the draft scale is not binding and is subjected to the Minister of Justice's approval. Moreover, in certain exceptional circumstances the Court may depart from the maximum and minimum limits fixed in the scale. (paras 48–51)

Consequently, the Italian State cannot be said to have delegated to private economic operators responsibility for taking decisions affecting the economic sphere, which would have the effect of depriving the provisions of the character of legislation. Additionally, in those circumstances nor is the Italian State open to the criticism that it required or encouraged the adoption of agreements, decisions or concerted practices contrary to Article 101 TFEU or reinforced their effects. (paras 52–3)

Comment

In its decision the Court relied on the earlier case of *Manuele Arduino* (Case C-35/99 [2002] ECR I-1529, [2002] 4 CMLR 25) which concerned similar circumstances. There, the Court held that '[Articles 4(3) TEU and 101 TFEU] do not preclude a Member State from adopting a law or regulation which approves, on the basis of a draft produced by a professional body of members of the Bar, a tariff fixing minimum and maximum fees for members of the profession, where that State measure forms part of a procedure such as that laid down in the Italian legislation.' (para 44)

In his Opinion (Joined Cases C-94/04 and C-202/04), AG Poiares Maduro provided a clear overview of the joint application of Articles 4(3) TEU and 101 TFEU and suggested that 'the case-law … must certainly be construed as meaning that it is necessary to be aware what aims the State is pursuing in order to determine when its action may be made subject to competition law.' (para 33) See in particular the following extracts from the opinion:

'31. ... According to case-law, [Articles 4(3) TEU and 101 TFEU] are regarded as having been infringed only in two cases: where a Member State requires or favours the adoption of agreements, decisions or concerted practices contrary to [Article 101 TFEU] or reinforces their effects, [Case C-198/01 *CIF* [2003] ECR I-8055, paragraph 46] or where that State divests its own rules of the character of legislation by delegating to private economic operators responsibility for taking decisions affecting the economic sphere. [Case 136/86 *Aubert* [1987] ECR 4789, paragraph 23 and Case C-35/96 *Commission v Italy* [1998] I–3851; C-35/99 *Arduino*, paragraph 35, and Order of 17 February 2005 in Case C-250/03 *Mauri* [2005] ECR I-1267, paragraph 30].'

'32. There is a clear difference between the two cases. In the first case an agreement between undertakings is in existence before the State measure which validates or reinforces it. The State's liability arises from the fact that it aggravates by its action conduct that is already anticompetitive. In the second case, in which the State delegates its authority to private entities, undertakings adopt a decision which is then codified in a legislative measure. Application of [Articles 4(3) TEU and 101 TFEU] is therefore designed to prevent a measure's form alone making it subject to competition law. In my view, that means that the concept of delegation must be interpreted in a substantive way by requiring an assessment of the decision-making process leading to the adoption of the State legislation. The following cases are covered by the concept of substantive delegation: first, delegation by the State to a private entity of the right to adopt a measure and, second, delegation of official authority to a private entity to review the decision-making process leading to the adoption of a legislative measure. A State may be regarded as having delegated its authority where its intervention is limited to the formal adoption of a measure, even though public interest requires the way in which the decisions are adopted to be taken into account. To define the concept of "delegation" as covering both those cases strengthens the requirement for consistency to which State action is subject. That principle of consistency ensures that whilst the State is acting in the public interest its intervention is subject to political and democratic review procedures, and if it delegates the pursuit of certain objectives to private operators it must make them subject to the competition rules which constitute the procedures for supervising power within the market. However, the State cannot delegate certain powers to private market operators whilst exempting them from application of the competition rules ...'

'33. This is why the case-law cited above must certainly be construed as meaning that it is necessary to be aware what aims the State is pursuing in order to determine when its action may be made subject to competition law. It is necessary to establish whether legislative action by the State is dominated by a concern to protect the public interest or, on the other hand, whether the degree to which private interests are being taken into account is likely to alter the overriding objective of the State measure, which is therefore to protect those interests. Involvement of private operators in the legislative process, at the stage at which a rule is proposed, or by their presence within a body responsible for drafting that rule, is likely to have a determining influence on the content of the rule. The danger is that a legislative provision might have the sole purpose of protecting certain private interests from the elements of competition, to the detriment of the public interest.'

'34. There is no doubt that there is no justification for making every State measure subject to [Articles 4(3) TEU and 101 TFEU]. The concerns expressed in their Opinions by Advocates General Jacobs and Léger in *Pavlov and others* and *Arduino*, respectively, are not along those lines, but follow closely the case-law. They set out two criteria for determining whether State measures are in fact under the control of private operators. In their view, the measure in question does not constitute an infringement of [Articles 4(3) TEU and 101 TFEU], first, if its adoption is justified by pursuit of a legitimate public interest and, secondly, if Member States actively supervise the involvement of private operators in the decision-making process. Those criteria are intended to establish to what extent the State is supervising delegation to private operators. Although the criteria set out are intended to be cumulative, it seems to me that the public interest criterion covers the other criterion too. It is even liable to lead the Court to assess all measures likely to reduce competition. This is perhaps the reason why the Court rejected the adoption of such a criterion.'

'35. However, in my view, the concerns underlying the Advocate Generals' suggestions are valid. It seems to me that current case-law allows them to be answered. ... Doubts remain, however, as to the way in which this criterion is assessed by the Court.'

CIF v Autorità Garante della Concorrenza e del Mercato	**Competition Law and the State**
Case C-198/01	Article 4(3) TEU
Court of Justice, [2003] ECR I-8055, [2003] 5 CMLR 16	Penalties for Infringement

Facts

Reference under Article 267 TFEU which originated from proceedings in the Italian court in which Consorzio Industrie Fiammiferi (CIF), the Italian consortium of domestic match manufacturers, challenges a decision of the Italian national competition authority which declared the legislation establishing and governing the CIF contrary to Articles 4(3) TEU and 101 TFEU and found that CIF and the undertakings comprising it infringed Article 101 TFEU through the allocation of production quotas.

Held

'[A]lthough [Articles 101 and 102 TFEU] are, in themselves, concerned solely with the conduct of undertakings and not with laws or regulations emanating from Member States, those articles, read in conjunction with [Article 4(3) TEU], which lays down a duty to cooperate, none the less require the Member States not to introduce or maintain in force measures, even of a legislative or regulatory nature, which may render ineffective the competition rules applicable to undertakings (see Case 13/77 *GB-Inno-BM* [1977] ECR 2115, paragraph 31; Case 267/86 *Van Eycke* [1988] ECR 4769, paragraph 16; Case C-185/91 *Reiff* [1993] ECR I-5801, paragraph 14; Case C-153/93 *Delta Schiffahrts-und Speditionsgesellschaft* [1994] ECR I-2517, paragraph 14; Case C-96/94 *Centro Servizi Spediporto* [1995] ECR I-2883, paragraph 20; and Case C-35/99 *Arduino* [2002] ECR I-1529, paragraph 34).' (para 45)

'The Court has held in particular that [Articles 4(3) TEU and 101 TFEU] are infringed where a Member State requires or favours the adoption of agreements, decisions or concerted practices contrary to [Article 101 TFEU] or reinforces their effects, or where it divests its own rules of the character of legislation by delegating to private economic operators responsibility for taking decisions affecting the economic sphere (see *Van Eycke*, paragraph 16; *Reiff*, paragraph 14; *Delta Schiffahrts- und Speditionsgesellschaft*, paragraph 14; *Centro Servizi Spediporto*, paragraph 21; and *Arduino*, paragraph 35).' (para 46)

'Moreover, since the Treaty of Maastricht entered into force, the EC Treaty has expressly provided that in the context of their economic policy the activities of the Member States must observe the principle of an open market economy with free competition (see Articles 3a(1) and 102a of the EC Treaty (now [Article 119(1) TFEU and Article 120 TFEU])).' (para 47)

The duty to disapply national legislation which contravenes Union law applies to national courts and other organs of the State, including administrative authorities. Article 101 TFEU in conjunction with Article 4(3) TEU, 'imposes a duty on Member States to refrain from introducing measures contrary to the [Union] competition rules, those rules would be rendered less effective if, in the course of an investigation under [Article 101 TFEU] into the conduct of undertakings, the authority were not able to declare a national measure contrary to the combined provisions of [Articles 4(3) TEU and 101 TFEU] and if, consequently, it failed to disapply it.' (paras 49–50)

However, with respect to the penalties which may be imposed on the undertakings concerned, 'if the general [Union]-law principle of legal certainty is not to be violated, the duty of national competition authorities to disapply such an anti-competitive law cannot expose the undertakings concerned to any penalties, either criminal or administrative, in respect of past conduct where the conduct was required by the law concerned. ... Once the national competition authority's decision, finding an infringement of [Article 101 TFEU] and disapplying such an anti-competitive national law, becomes definitive ... the decision becomes binding on the undertakings concerned. From that time onwards the undertakings can no longer claim that they are obliged by that law to act in breach of the [Union] competition rules. Their future conduct is therefore liable to be penalised.' (paras 52–5)

The national competition authority may impose penalties on the undertakings concerned in respect of past conduct where the conduct was merely facilitated or encouraged by the national legislation. The level of the penalty in this case may be assessed in the light of the national legal framework, which is a mitigating factor. (paras 56–8)

Comment

Articles 4(3) TEU and 101 TFEU are infringed where a Member State (1) requires; or (2) favours the adoption of agreements, decisions or concerted practices contrary to Article 101 TFEU; or (3) reinforces their effects. The appraisal of reinforcement of effects comprises two stages: first the Court needs to ascertain the prior existence of agreements, decisions or concerted practices of that kind to which the legislation refers to. Secondly, the Court needs to assess whether the national regulation has the purpose or the effect of reinforcing the effects of such agreements, decisions and concerted practices.

In Case 13/77 *INNO v ATAB* [1977] ECR 2115, [1978] 1 CMLR, the Hof van Cassatie referred to the Court of Justice a question with regard to the compatibility with the Treaty of a Belgian fiscal scheme, which set retail prices of tobacco products at a level fixed freely upstream by the manufacturer or the importer, thereby allegedly having the effect of encouraging an abuse of dominant position under Article 102 TFEU. The Court of Justice articulated the principle that Member States have a duty under Article 4(3) TEU to abstain from any measure which could jeopardise the effectiveness of the Treaty rules on competition.

In Case 311/85 *Vzw Vereniging van Vlaamse Reisbureaus v Vzw Sociale Dienst van de Plaatselijke en Gewestelijke Overheidsdiensten* [1987] ECR 3801, [1989] 4 CMLR 213, the Court of Justice was asked to provide a preliminary ruling on the lawfulness of the statutory prohibition on granting of certain rebates by Belgian travel agencies. The Court of Justice considered whether the legislation in question requires or favours the conclusion of agreements contrary to Article 101 TFEU or reinforces their effects. First the Court ascertained that in the travel business there was a network of restrictive agreements contrary to Article 101 TFEU, both between the travel agents themselves and between travel agents and tour operators, the purpose or effect of which was to compel travel agents to observe the travel prices set by tour operators and subsequently restrict competition. Secondly, the Court considered whether the national legislation was capable of reinforcing the effects of agreements concluded between travel agents and tour operators. The Court concluded that this was the case.

In Case C-2/91 *Criminal proceedings against Wolf W Meng* [1993] ECR I-5751, the Court of Justice was asked by the Higher Regional Court in Berlin to clarify the obligation of the State under Articles 4(3) TEU and 101 TFEU. The case concerned insurance regulations preventing insurance intermediaries from transferring to their clients all or part of the commission paid to them by insurance companies. Mr Meng, a professional financial adviser, was subjected to a fine for infringement of these regulations and challenged, on appeal, their lawfulness under Articles 4(3) TEU and 101 TFEU. The Court of Justice observed that 'the German rules on insurance neither require nor favour the conclusion of any unlawful agreement, decision or concerted practice by insurance intermediaries, since the prohibition which they lay down is a self-contained one.' (para 15) The Court then proceeded to determine whether the rules have the effect of reinforcing an anticompetitive agreement. The rules at issue were not preceded by any agreement in the sectors to which they relate. The Court held that it is not relevant that agreements to prohibit transfers of commission existed in other sectors of insurance, to which the legislation does not apply. 'Rules applicable to a particular branch of insurance cannot be regarded as reinforcing the effects of a pre-existing agreement, decision or concerted practice unless they simply reproduce the elements of an agreement, decision or concerted practice between economic agents in that sector.' (para 20)

Commission and France v Ladbroke Racing	Competition Law and the State
Joined Cases C-359/95P and C-379/95P	State Compulsion Defence
Court of Justice, [1997] ECR I-6265, [1998] 4 CMLR 27	

Facts

Ladbroke lodged a complaint with the Commission against France under Article 106 TFEU and against the ten main racing companies for infringing Articles 101 and 102 TFEU. The Commission rejected the complaint against the undertakings, on the ground that Articles 101 and 102 TFEU were not applicable. On appeal, the General Court accepted the application by Ladbroke to annul the Commission's decision, on the ground that it was necessary for the Commission to complete its examination of the compatibility of the French legislation with the Treaty rules on competition before it could reject the complaint concerning Articles 101 and 102 TFEU. The Commission and France appealed to the Court of Justice.

Held

'[Articles 101 and 102 TFEU] apply only to anti-competitive conduct engaged in by undertakings on their own initiative. ... If anti-competitive conduct is required of undertakings by national legislation or if the latter creates a legal framework which itself eliminates any possibility of competitive activity on their part, [Articles 101 and 102] do not apply. In such a situation, the restriction of competition is not attributable, as those provisions implicitly require, to the autonomous conduct of the undertakings (see also Joined Cases 40/73 to 48/73, 50/73, 54/73 to 56/73, 111/73, 113/73 and 114/73 *Suiker Unie and Others v Commission* [1975] ECR 1663, paragraphs 36 to 72, and more particularly paragraphs 65, 66, 71 and 72).' (para 33)

'[Articles 101 and 102 TFEU] may apply, however, if it is found that the national legislation does not preclude undertakings from engaging in autonomous conduct which prevents, restricts or distorts competition (Joined Cases 209/78 to 215/78 and 218/78 *Van Landewyck and Others v Commission* ...).' (para 34)

'When the Commission is considering the applicability of [Articles 101 and 102 TFEU] ... a prior evaluation of national legislation affecting such conduct should therefore be directed solely to ascertaining whether that legislation prevents undertakings from engaging in autonomous conduct.' (para 35)

Comment

In Case C-280/08P *Deutsche Telekom v Commission* [2010] 5 CMLR 1485, the Court of Justice confirmed that the state compulsion defence applies only if the national measure precludes any possibility for wilful exercise of competitive conduct by the undertaking. The Court of Justice confirmed that *Deutsche Telekom* had scope of autonomous conduct when adjusting its retail prices for end-user access, even though its wholesale prices were regulated. (paras 80–92)

It follows that the state measure may be in breach of EU law without that affecting the undertaking's liability under Article 101 and 102 TFEU. In those circumstances, the Commission may take action against both the undertaking and the Member State. For example, the *CNSD* case involved the setting of compulsory tariffs by a public body, the representatives of customs agents in Italy, for their services. The Commission, first, issued a decision against the undertaking under Article 101 TFEU, which was appealed before the General Court and upheld in Case T-513/93 *CNSD v Commission* [2000] ECR II-01807. Pending the appeal, the Commission initiated proceeding against Italy under Article 258 TFEU. The Court of Justice condemned Italy for failure to fulfil its obligations under Article 4(3) TEU-L (ex Article 10 TEC) in conjunction with Article 101 TFEU in Case C-35/96 *Commission v Italy* [1998] ECR I-3851, [1998] 5 CMLR 889.

In Case T-387/94 *Asia Motor France SA and others v Commission (III)* [1996] ECR II-961 the Court noted that in the absence of a binding regulatory provision imposing the conduct at issue, undertakings may still lack autonomy and subsequently be shielded from the competition provisions, when their conduct was unilaterally imposed upon them by the national authorities 'through the exercise of irresistible pressures, such as, for example, the threat to adopt State measures likely to cause them to sustain substantial losses.' (para 65)

CIF v Autorità Garante della Concorrenza e del Mercato Case C-198/01 Court of Justice, [2003] ECR I-8055, [2003] 5 CMLR 16	**Competition Law and the State** State Compulsion Defence Penalties for Infringement

Facts

Reference under Article 267 TFEU which originated from proceedings in the Italian Court in which Consorzio Industrie Fiammiferi (CIF), the Italian consortium of domestic match manufacturers, challenged a decision of the Italian national competition authority which declared the legislation establishing and governing the CIF contrary to Articles 4(3) TEU and 101 TFEU and found that CIF and the undertakings comprising it infringed Article 101 TFEU through the allocation of production quotas.

Held

'As regards ... the penalties which may be imposed on the undertakings concerned, it is appropriate to draw a two-fold distinction by reference to whether or not the national legislation precludes undertakings from engaging in autonomous conduct which might prevent, restrict or distort competition and, if it does, by reference to whether the facts at issue pre-dated or post-dated the national competition authority's decision to disapply the relevant national legislation.' (para 52)

'If the general [Union]-law principle of legal certainty is not to be violated, the duty of national competition authorities to disapply such an anti-competitive law cannot expose the undertakings concerned to any penalties, either criminal or administrative, in respect of past conduct where the conduct was required by the law concerned. ... Once the national competition authority's decision, finding an infringement of [Article 101 TFEU] and disapplying such an anti-competitive national law, becomes definitive ... the decision becomes binding on the undertakings concerned. From that time onwards the undertakings can no longer claim that they are obliged by that law to act in breach of the [Union] competition rules. Their future conduct is therefore liable to be penalised.' (paras 53–5)

The national competition authority may impose penalties on the undertakings concerned in respect of past conduct where the conduct was merely facilitated or encouraged by the national legislation. The level of the penalty in this case may be assessed in the light of the national legal framework, which is a mitigating factor. (paras 56–8)

'[I]t is for the referring court to assess whether national legislation such as that at issue in the main proceedings, under which competence to fix the retail selling prices of a product is delegated to a ministry and power to allocate production between undertakings is entrusted to a consortium to which the relevant producers are obliged to belong, may be regarded, for the purposes of [Article 101(1) TFEU], as precluding those undertakings from engaging in autonomous conduct which remains capable of preventing, restricting or distorting competition.' (para 80)

Comment

If a state compulsion defence does not succeed, Articles 101 and 102 TFEU remain applicable. However, the national legal framework is taken into account as a mitigating factor when the fines are set.

In Case C-280/08P *Deutsche Telekom v Commission*, the approval of tariffs by the German Regulatory Authority for Telecommunications and Post did not eliminate *Deutsche Telekom*'s scope of autonomous conduct but did lead to a reduction of the basic amount of the fine by 10 per cent. (paras 277–9) (page 341 above)

In the circumstances that both a state compulsion defence succeeds and the national measure is found to be in breach of EU law, and in particular of Articles 4(3) TEU and 101 or 102 TFEU, the undertaking may become exposed again to Articles 101 and 102 TFEU, once the decision to disapply the anti-competitive national law becomes definitive.

Klaus Höfner and Fritz Elser v Macrotron GmbH	**Competition Law and the State**
Case C-41/90	Article 106(1) TFEU
Court of Justice, [1991] ECR I-1979, [1993] 4 CMLR 306	Article 106(2) TFEU

Facts

The dispute surrounded a recruitment contract concluded between recruitment consultants Hofner and Elser, on the one hand, and Macrotron, on the other. As required by the contract, Höfner and Elser presented Macrotron with a candidate for the post of sales director. However, Macrotron decided not to appoint that candidate and refused to pay the fees stipulated in the contract. Höfner and Elser commenced proceedings against Macrotron before the Munich Regional Court but the court dismissed their claim. On appeal to the Munich Higher Regional Court, the court considered that the contract at issue could be void as it infringed a national regulation which entrusted, subject to certain derogations, the 'Federal Office for Employment' with an exclusive right of employment procurement in Germany. The court referred the case to the Court of Justice, asking about, among other things, the interpretation of Article 106 TFEU and the legality of the national regulation.

Held

Employment procurement activity is an economic activity which is not necessarily carried out by public entities. A public employment agency such as the 'Federal Office for Employment' engaged in the business of employment procurement is an undertaking within the meaning of Articles 101 and 102 TFEU. (paras 20–23)

'[A] public employment agency which is entrusted, under the legislation of a Member State, with the operation of services of general economic interest ... remains subject to the competition rules pursuant to [Article 106(2) TFEU] unless and to the extent to which it is shown that their application is incompatible with the discharge of its duties (see judgment in Case 155/73 *Sacchi* [1974] ECR 409).' (para 24)

'As regards the manner in which a public employment agency enjoying an exclusive right of employment procurement conducts itself in relation to executive recruitment undertaken by private recruitment consultancy companies, it must be stated that the application of [Article 102 TFEU] cannot obstruct the performance of the particular task assigned to that agency in so far as the latter is manifestly not in a position to satisfy demand in that area of the market and in fact allows its exclusive rights to be encroached on by those companies.' (para 25)

'Whilst it is true that [Article 102] concerns undertakings and may be applied within the limits laid down by [Article 106(2)] to public undertakings or undertakings vested with exclusive rights or specific rights, the fact nevertheless remains that the Treaty requires the Member States not to take or maintain in force measures which could destroy the effectiveness of that provision (see judgment in Case 13/77 *Inno* [1977] ECR 2115, paragraphs 31 and 32). [Article 106(1)] in fact provides that the Member States are not to enact or maintain in force, in the case of public undertakings and the undertakings to which they grant special or exclusive rights, any measure contrary to the rules contained in the [TFEU], in particular those provided for in [Articles 101 to 109].' (para 26)

'Consequently, any measure adopted by a Member State which maintains in force a statutory provision that creates a situation in which a public employment agency cannot avoid infringing [Article 102 TFEU] is incompatible with the rules of the Treaty.' (para 27)

'It must be remembered, first, that an undertaking vested with a legal monopoly may be regarded as occupying a dominant position within the meaning of [Article 102 TFEU] (see judgment in Case 311/84 CBEM [1985] 3261) and that the territory of a Member State, to which that monopoly extends, may constitute a substantial part of the [internal] market (judgment in Case 322/81 *Michelin* [1983] ECR 3461, paragraph 28).' (para 28)

'Secondly, the simple fact of creating a dominant position of that kind by granting an exclusive right within the meaning of [Article 106(1) TFEU] is not as such incompatible with [Article 102 TFEU] (see Case 311/84 *CBEM*, ... paragraph 17). A Member State is in breach of the prohibition contained in those two provisions only if the undertaking in question, merely by exercising the exclusive right granted to it, cannot avoid abusing its dominant position. Pursuant to [Article 102(b) TFEU], such an abuse may in particular consist in limiting the provision of a service, to the prejudice of those seeking to avail themselves of it.' (paras 29, 30)

'A Member State creates a situation in which the provision of a service is limited when the undertaking to which it grants an exclusive right extending to executive recruitment activities is manifestly not in a position to satisfy the demand prevailing on the market for activities of that kind and when the effective pursuit of such activities by private companies is rendered impossible by the maintenance in force of a statutory provision under which such activities are prohibited and non-observance of that prohibition renders the contracts concerned void.' (para 31)

'It must be observed, thirdly, that the responsibility imposed on a Member State by virtue of [Articles 102 and 106(1) TFEU] is engaged only if the abusive conduct on the part of the agency concerned is liable to affect trade between Member States ...' (para 32)

A Member State which has conferred an exclusive right to carry on that activity upon the public employment agency is in breach of Article 106(1) TFEU where it creates a situation in which that agency cannot avoid infringing Article 102 TFEU. That is the case, in particular, where: (1) the exclusive right extends to executive recruitment activities; (2) the public employment agency which enjoys exclusivity is incapable of satisfying demand for such activities, (3) the pursuit of those activities by private recruitment consultants is rendered impossible by the statutory provision, and (4) the activities in question may extend to the nationals or to the territory of other Member States. (paras 27–34)

Comment

The analysis of Article 106(1) TFEU comprises of two stages. First the existence of an undertaking is ascertained, and following this, the public nature of the undertaking is assessed (finding public undertakings or undertakings to which Member States granted special or exclusive rights).

The concept of 'public undertaking' was referred to by the Court of Justice in Case 188/80 etc *French Republic, Italian Republic and the UK v Commission* [1982] ECR 2545, [1982] 3 CMLR 144. There, the Court of Justice dismissed applications to declare void the directive on the transparency of financial relations between Member States and public undertakings that was adopted by the Commission on the basis of Article 106(3) TFEU. The Court upheld the definition of public undertaking in the directive, which encompasses 'any undertaking over which the public authorities may exercise directly or indirectly a dominant influence by virtue of their ownership of it, their financial participation therein or the rules which govern it. A dominant influence is to be presumed when the public authorities directly or indirectly hold the major part of the undertakings' subscribed capital, control the majority of the votes, or can appoint more than half of the members of its administrative, managerial or supervisory body.' (paras 25–6) Note, however, that the Court of Justice considered that the object of the definition in the directive's provision is not to define the concept of public undertakings as it appears in Article 106 TFEU, 'but to establish the necessary criteria to delimit the group of undertakings whose financial relations with the public authorities are to be subject to the duty laid down by the Directive to supply information.' (para 24)

The analysis of Article 106(1) TFEU, which addresses the Member State, and Article 106(2) TFEU, which addresses the undertaking, is closely linked in this case as the employment agency was both a 'public undertaking' within the meaning of Article 106(1) TFEU, and an 'undertaking entrusted with the operation of services of general economic interest' within the meaning of Article 106(2) TFEU.

Article 106(1) TFEU is only applied in combination with other Treaty Articles. The conferral of exclusive rights may lead to infringement of Article 106(1) TFEU, read together with Article 102 TFEU, when other surrounding factors make abuse inevitable. Note AG Jacobs' opinion and his comments on the criteria for establishing abuse. (paras 42–50)

ERT and others v DEP and others	**Competition Law and the State**
Case C-260/89	Article 106(1) TFEU
Court of Justice, [1991] ECR I-2925, [1994] 4 CMLR 540	

Facts

A reference for a preliminary ruling from the Thessaloniki Regional Court. The case concerned the exclusive rights granted by the Greek State to Elliniki Radiophonia Tileorassi (ERT), a Greek radio and television undertaking, to organise, exploit and develop radio and television. These exclusive rights were infringed by Dimotiki Etairia Pliroforissis (DEP) and the Mayor of Thessaloniki, which set up a television station. ERT brought summary proceedings before the Thessaloniki Regional Court against the two. In court, the defendants relied on the provisions of EU law and the European Convention on Human Rights. The Greek court stayed the proceedings and referred to the Court of Justice several questions on the lawfulness of the television monopoly.

Held

'In Case C-155/73 *Sacchi* [1974] ECR 409, paragraph 14, the Court held that nothing in the Treaty prevents Member States, for considerations of a non-economic nature relating to the public interest, from removing radio and television broadcasts from the field of competition by conferring on one or more establishments an exclusive right to carry them out.' (para 10)

'Nevertheless, it follows from [Article 106(1) and (2) TFEU] that the manner in which the monopoly is organized or exercised may infringe the rules of the Treaty, in particular those relating to the free movement of goods, the freedom to provide services and the rules on competition.' (para 11)

'The reply to the national court must therefore be that [Union] law does not prevent the granting of a television monopoly for considerations of a non-economic nature relating to the public interest. However, the manner in which such a monopoly is organized and exercised must not infringe the provisions of the Treaty on the free movement of goods and services or the rules on competition.' (para 12)

'The independent conduct of an undertaking must be considered with regard to the provisions of the [TFEU] applicable to undertakings, such as, in particular, [Articles 101, 102 and 106(2)].' (para 28)

Article 102 TFEU may be applicable in this case as an undertaking which has a statutory monopoly may be regarded as having a dominant position within the meaning of Article 102 TFEU. Although Article 102 TFEU does not prohibit monopolies as such, it nevertheless prohibits their abusive conduct. (paras 30–32)

'[Article 106(1) TFEU] prohibits the granting of an exclusive right to transmit and an exclusive right to retransmit television broadcasts to a single undertaking, where those rights are liable to create a situation in which that undertaking is led to infringe [Article 102 TFEU] by virtue of a discriminatory broadcasting policy which favours its own programmes, unless the application of [Article 102 TFEU] obstructs the performance of the particular tasks entrusted to it.' (para 38)

Comment

Note the difference between this case and *Höfner v Macrotron*. Whereas in *Höfner v Macrotron* (page 343 above) the abuse was inevitable due to the incapability of satisfying demand, in *ERT v DEP* the Court of Justice held that 'the manner in which the monopoly is organized or exercised may infringe the rules of the Treaty'. (para 11) This finding led the court to reach the conclusion in paragraph 38. See also Case C-179/90 *Merci v Siderurgica Gabrielli SpA*, page 346 below.

Merci v Siderurgica Gabrielli SpA	**Competition Law and the State**
Case C-179/90	Article 106(1) TFEU
Court of Justice, [1991] ECR I-5889, [1994] 4 CMLR 422	Conferral of Exclusive Rights

Facts

The questions arose in the course of proceedings in the Italian Tribunale di Genova where Siderurgica Gabrielli SpA (Siderurgica) demanded compensation from Merci Convenzionali Porto di Genova SpA (Merci) for the damage it had suffered as a result of delays in the unloading of goods in the port of Genoa. In Italy, the loading and trans-shipment of goods in ports was governed by the 'Navigation Code' and reserved by it to dock-work companies whose workers were of Italian nationality. Merci enjoyed the exclusive right to organise dock work in the Port of Genoa. On reference to the Court of Justice, the Italian court asked, among other things, whether Article 106(1) TFEU precludes rules of a Member State which confer on an undertaking established in that State, the exclusive right to organise dock work and require it, for the performance of such work, to have recourse to a dock-work company formed exclusively of nationals.

Held

'[A] dock-work undertaking enjoying the exclusive right to organize dock work for third parties, as well as a dock-work company having the exclusive right to perform dock work, must be regarded as undertakings to which exclusive rights have been granted by the State within the meaning of [Article 106(1) TFEU].' (para 9)

'[A]s to the existence of exclusive rights, it should be stated first that with regard to the interpretation of [Article 102 TFEU] the Court has consistently held that an undertaking having a statutory monopoly over a substantial part of the [internal] market may be regarded as having a dominant position within the meaning of [Article 106 TFEU] (see the judgments in Case C-41/90 *Höfner and Elser v Macrotron* [1991] ECR I-1979, paragraph 28 Case C-260/89 *ERT v DEP* [1991] ECR I-2925, paragraph 31).' (para 14)

The simple fact of creating a dominant position by granting exclusive rights within the meaning of Article 106(1) TFEU is not as such incompatible with Article 102 TFEU. However, a Member State is in breach of those two provisions if the undertaking in question, merely by exercising the exclusive rights granted to it, cannot avoid abusing its dominant position or when such rights are liable to create a situation in which that undertaking is induced to commit such abuses. (paras 16–17)

It appears that in this case the undertakings enjoying exclusive rights in accordance with the national rules are, as a result, 'induced either to demand payment for services which have not been requested, to charge disproportionate prices, to refuse to have recourse to modern technology, which involves an increase in the cost of the operations and a prolongation of the time required for their performance, or to grant price reductions to certain consumers and at the same time to offset such reductions by an increase in the charges to other consumers.' (para 19)

Comment

Similarly to *ERT v DEP* (page 345 above), the Court focused on the inability of the undertaking to avoid abusing its dominant position merely by exercising the exclusive rights granted to it (paras 16–17). This extension of the judgment in *Höfner v Macrotron* widens the application of Article 106 TFEU and makes it more likely that the conferral of exclusive rights would lead to a conclusion of potential infringement of competition rules. However, the basic principle is retained. There should be other surrounding factors, which make the abuse an inevitable result of the grant of the exclusive right.

RTT v GB-Inno-BM SA	**Competition Law and the State**
Case C-18/88	Article 106(1) TFEU
Court of Justice, [1991] ECR I-5941	

Facts

A dispute between RTT and GB-Inno-BM (GB) in the Brussels Commercial Court. Under Belgian law RTT was granted an exclusive right to supply and approve equipment connected to the national telephone network. It claimed in court that GB, which sold non-approved telephones, infringed this exclusive right. In its defence, GB contested the legality of the legislation granting RTT the exclusive right. The national court referred the case to the Court of Justice, asking it to assess the legality of the legislation.

Held

'RTT has the power to grant or withhold authorization to connect telephone equipment to the network, the power to lay down the technical standards to be met by that equipment, and the power to check whether the equipment not produced by it, is in conformity with the specifications that it has laid down.' (para 15)

'[T]he fact that an undertaking holding a monopoly in the market for the establishment and operation of the network, without any objective necessity, reserves to itself a neighbouring but separate market, in this case the market for the importation, marketing, connection, commissioning and maintenance of equipment for connection to the said network, thereby eliminating all competition from other undertakings, constitutes an infringement of [Article 102 TFEU].' (para 19)

'However, [Article 102 TFEU] applies only to anti-competitive conduct engaged in by undertakings on their own initiative ... not to measures adopted by States. As regards measures adopted by States, it is [Article 106(1) TFEU] that applies. Under that provision, Member States must not, by laws, regulations or administrative measures, put public undertakings and undertakings to which they grant special or exclusive rights in a position which the said undertakings could not themselves attain by their own conduct without infringing [Article 102 TFEU].' (para 20)

'Accordingly, where the extension of the dominant position of a public undertaking or undertaking to which the State has granted special or exclusive rights results from a State measure, such a measure constitutes an infringement of [Article 106] in conjunction with [Article 102 TFEU].' (para 21)

'[I]t is the extension of the monopoly in the establishment and operation of the telephone network to the market in telephone equipment, without any objective justification, which is prohibited as such by [Article 102 TFEU], or by [Article 106(1) TFEU] in conjunction with [Article 102 TFEU], where that extension results from a measure adopted by a State.' (para 24)

RTT's monopoly is intended to make a public telephone network available to users, and constitutes a service of general economic interest within the meaning of Article 106(2) TFEU. However the restriction of competition on the market in telephone equipment cannot be regarded as justified by a task of a public service of general economic interest within the meaning of Article 106(2) TFEU. (paras 16, 22)

Comment

In paragraph 24 the Court held that it was the extension of the monopoly by law, rather than a potential abusive action by RTT, which infringed Articles 102 and 106(1) TFEU. The State was not allowed to leverage RTT's dominant position from the telephone network to the market in telephone equipment.

In this respect note the expansive application in this case which did not require abuse. Contrast with Case C-41/90 (page 343 above) in which the Articles were applied when the abuse was inevitable due to the incapability of satisfying demand, and Case C-260/89 (page 345 above) where the monopoly was organised in a manner liable to create a situation in which the undertaking is led to abuse its dominant position.

Criminal proceedings against Paul Corbeau	**Competition Law and the State**
Case C-320/91	Article 106(1) TFEU
Court of Justice, [1993] ECR I-2533, [1995] 4 CMLR 621	Article 106(2) TFEU

Facts

Mr Corbeau provided, within the City of Liège, Belgium, a service consisting of mail collection and distribution. He was charged in court with infringing Belgian legislation which conferred on the 'Regie des Postes' an exclusive right to collect and distribute mail. In a preliminary reference the Belgian Tribunal Correctionnel de Liège asked the Court of Justice, among other things, whether the Belgian legislation establishing the postal monopoly is contrary to Article 106 TFEU.

Held

A body such as the 'Regie des Postes' which has been granted exclusive rights to collect and distribute mail must be regarded as an undertaking to which the Member State concerned has granted exclusive rights within the meaning of Article 106(1) TFEU. (para 8)

'[T]he Court has consistently held that an undertaking having a statutory monopoly over a substantial part of the [internal] market may be regarded as having a dominant position within the meaning of [Article 102 TFEU] (see the judgments in Case C-179/90 *Merci Convenzionali Porto di Genova* [1991] ECR I-5889 at paragraph 14 and in Case C-18/88 *RTT v GB-Inno-BM* [1991] ECR I-5941 at paragraph 17).' (para 9)

'However, [Article 102 TFEU] applies only to anti-competitive conduct engaged in by undertakings on their own initiative, not to measures adopted by States (*RTT v GB-Inno-BM* judgment, paragraph 20).' (para 10)

'The Court has had occasion to state in this respect, that although the mere fact that a Member State has created a dominant position by the grant of exclusive rights, is not as such incompatible with [Article 102 TFEU], none the less requires the Member States not to adopt or maintain in force any measure which might deprive those provisions of their effectiveness (see the judgment in Case C-260/89 *ERT* [1991] ECR I-2925, paragraph 35).' (para 11)

'Thus [Article 106(1) TFEU] provides that in the case of public undertakings to which Member States grant special or exclusive rights, they are neither to enact nor to maintain in force any measure contrary to the rules contained in the Treaty with regard to competition.' (para 12)

'That provision must be read in conjunction with [Article 106(2) TFEU] which provides that undertakings entrusted with the operation of services of general economic interest are to be subject to the rules on competition in so far as the application of such rules does not obstruct the performance, in law or in fact, of the particular tasks assigned to them.' (para 13)

'That latter provision thus permits the Member States to confer on undertakings to which they entrust the operation of services of general economic interest, exclusive rights which may hinder the application of the rules of the Treaty on competition in so far as restrictions on competition, or even the exclusion of all competition, by other economic operators are necessary to ensure the performance of the particular tasks assigned to the undertakings possessed of the exclusive rights.' (para 14)

As regards the services at issue in the main proceedings, the 'Regie des Postes' is entrusted with a service of general economic interest. The question to be considered is therefore 'the extent to which a restriction on competition or even the exclusion of all competition from other economic operators is necessary in order to allow the holder of the exclusive right to perform its task of general interest and in particular to have the benefit of economically acceptable conditions'. (paras 15, 16)

'The starting point of such an examination must be the premise that the obligation on the part of the undertaking entrusted with that task to perform its services in conditions of economic equilibrium presupposes that it will be possible to offset less profitable sectors against the profitable sectors and hence justifies a restriction of competition from individual undertakings where the economically profitable sectors are concerned.' (para 17)

'Indeed, to authorize individual undertakings to compete with the holder of the exclusive rights in the sectors of their choice corresponding to those rights would make it possible for them to concentrate on the economically profitable operations and to offer more advantageous tariffs than those adopted by the holders of the exclusive rights since, unlike the latter, they are not bound for economic reasons to offset losses in the unprofitable sectors against profits in the more profitable sectors.' (para 18)

'However, the exclusion of competition is not justified as regards specific services dissociable from the service of general interest which meet special needs of economic operators and which call for certain additional services not offered by the traditional postal service, such as collection from the senders' address, greater speed or reliability of distribution or the possibility of changing the destination in the course of transit, in so far as such specific services, by their nature and the conditions in which they are offered, such as the geographical area in which they are provided, do not compromise the economic equilibrium of the service of general economic interest performed by the holder of the exclusive right.' (para 19)

'The answer to the questions referred to the Court … should therefore be that it is contrary to [Article 106 TFEU] for legislation of a Member State which confers on a body such as the Regie des Postes the exclusive right to collect, carry and distribute mail, to prohibit, under threat of criminal penalties, an economic operator established in that State from offering certain specific services dissociable from the service of general interest which meet the special needs of economic operators and call for certain additional services not offered by the traditional postal service, in so far as those services do not compromise the economic equilibrium of the service of general economic interest performed by the holder of the exclusive right. It is for the national court to consider whether the services in question in the main proceedings meet those criteria.' (para 21)

Comment

Note that in *Corbeau*, as well as in *RTT v GB-Inno-BM SA* (page 348 above), the Court of Justice applied Article 106(1) TFEU in conjunction with Article 102 TFEU directly to the Member State's action without separately requiring an undertaking's abuse.

It is possible to distinguish *Corbeau* from *RTT v GB-Inno-BM SA* on the basis that the former did not require a link between Article 106(1) TFEU and the finding of abuse under Article 102 TFEU. *Corbeau* seems to suggest that in the circumstances of that case, the mere conferral of exclusive rights (i.e. creation of dominance) would lead to conclusion of infringement of the competition rules. Such wide interpretation, shifts the focus from Article 106(1) to Article 106(2) TFEU and in doing so also shifts the burden of proof.

Arguably, this shift would inevitably result in a widening of the protection offered by Article 106(2) TFEU in an attempt to counterbalance the harshness of Article 106(1) TFEU. In this respect note that in paragraph 17 the Court of Justice justified the restriction by the need to offset less profitable sectors against the profitable sectors. Note, however, the opinion of Advocate General Tesauro in which he proposes a less restrictive alternative, taking into account the possibility for the postal service to achieve financial equilibrium without harming the rapid delivery service through the creation of certain thresholds. (paras 18–19)

Société Civile Agricole du Centre d'Insémination de la Crespelle v Coopérative d'Elevage et d'Insémination Artificielle Case C-323/93 Court of Justice, [1994] ECR I-5077	**Competition Law and the State** Article 106(1) TFEU

Facts

The Mayenne Cooperative, which enjoyed exclusive rights to carry out artificial insemination of animals, brought proceedings against the Crespelle Centre for breach of those rights. According to the national law, breeders within the area covered by an insemination centre may request that centre supply them with semen from production centres of their choice, but the additional costs resulting from such a choice must be borne by the users. In a reference for a preliminary ruling the French Cour de cassation asked the Court of Justice, among other things, whether the exclusive right granted to the Mayenne Cooperative in conjunction with its right to charge the above-mentioned additional costs is contrary to Articles 106(1) TFEU and 102 TFEU.

Held

'[B]y making the operation of the insemination centres subject to authorization and providing that each center should have the exclusive right to serve a defined area, the national legislation granted those centers exclusive rights. By ... establishing, ... a contiguous series of monopolies territorially limited but together covering the entire territory of a Member State, those national provisions create a dominant position, within the meaning of [Article 102 TFEU], in a substantial part of the common market.' (para 17)

'The mere creation of such a dominant position by the granting of an exclusive right within the meaning of [Article 106 (1) TFEU] is not as such incompatible with [Article 102 TFEU]. A Member State contravenes the prohibitions contained in those two provisions only if, in merely exercising the exclusive right granted to it, the undertaking in question cannot avoid abusing its dominant position.' (para 18)

'The alleged abuse in the present case consists in the charging of exorbitant prices by the insemination centres. The question to be examined is therefore whether such a practice constituting the alleged abuse is the direct consequence of the national Law. It should be noted in this regard that the Law merely allows insemination centres to require breeders who request the centers to provide them with semen from other production centres to pay the additional costs entailed by that choice. Although it leaves to the insemination centers the task of calculating those costs, such a provision does not lead the centres to charge disproportionate costs and thereby abuse their dominant position.' (paras 19–21)

Comment

In paragraph 18 the Court seems to require a strong link between the exclusive right granted and a separate abuse by the undertaking. In this case, the Court of Justice did not find that the undertaking, in merely exercising the exclusive right, was led to charge exploitative prices. Thus, the national provisions were not in breach of Articles 106(1) TFEU and 102 TFEU. Contrast this approach with the wider approach in *Corbeau* (page 348 above). Also note the less rigorous application of the test in Case C-147/97 *Deutsche Post AG*, below page 357.

In Case C-49/07 *MOTOE v Elliniko Dimosio* [2008] ECR I-4863, the Court of Justice held that '[Articles 102 TFEU and 106 (1) TFEU] are infringed where a measure imputable to a Member State, ... gives rise to a risk of an abuse of a dominant position.' (para 50) In this case, the Greek Road Traffic Code that conferred without restrictions or obligations on a legal person which organises motorcycling events the power to give consent to applications for authorisation to organise such competitions, was found to be incompatible with Articles 106(1) TFEU and 102 TFEU, because 'such a right may ... lead the undertaking which possesses it to deny other operators access to the relevant market.' (para 51)

Commission v Dimosia Epicheirisi Ilektrismou (DEI)	**Competition Law and the State**
Case C-553/12P	Article 106(1) TFEU
Court of Justice, [2014] 5 CMLR 19	Greek Lignite

Facts

An appeal on a Judgment of the General Court in Case T-169/08 *DEI v Commission* in which the Court annulled Commission Decision (Case COMP/B-1/38.700).

The Commission decision concerned the exclusive right in favour of Dimosia Epicheirisi Ilektrismou AE (DEI)—a public undertaking belonging to the Hellenic Republic which holds 51.12% of its shares. DEI enjoyed the exclusive right to produce, transport and supply electricity in Greece and benefited from rights for the extraction of lignite—a common fuel for electricity generation in the Greek market. At the time of the decision, all Greek power stations functioning on lignite belonged to DEI. In its decision the Commission concluded that the Hellenic Republic had infringed Article 106(1) TFEU, in conjunction with Article 102 TFEU, by granting or maintaining quasi-monopolistic lignite exploration rights in favour of DEI, thereby creating inequality of opportunity between economic operators on the wholesale electricity market and reinforcing the dominant position of DEI in this market.

DEI applied for the annulment of the decision. In its judgment, the General Court held that for the application of Article 106(1) TFEU in conjunction with Article 102 TFEU, the Commission has to identify an abuse of dominant position (be it actual or potential) and cannot base its decision on the inequality of opportunities between economic operators. The court noted that: 'The impossibility, for other economic operators, of having access to the lignite deposits still available cannot be imputed to the applicant. The non-granting of lignite exploitation licences depends exclusively on the will of the Hellenic Republic. On the market for the supply of lignite, the applicant's role has been limited to exploiting deposits over which it holds rights and the Commission has not maintained that it abused its dominant position on that market as regards access to lignite.' (para 89) 'The Commission has not established that privileged access to lignite was capable of creating a situation in which, by the mere exercise of its exploitation rights, the applicant could have been able to commit abuses of a dominant position on the wholesale electricity market or was led to commit such abuses on that market. Similarly, the Commission does not accuse the applicant of having, without objective justification, extended its dominant position on the market for the supply of lignite to the wholesale electricity market.' (para 92)

The Commission appealed to the Court of Justice. The judgment of the General Court was set aside.

Held

'It should be recalled that, pursuant to [Article 106(1) TFEU], Member States are not to enact or maintain in force, in the case of public undertakings and the undertakings to which they grant special or exclusive rights, any measure contrary to the rules contained in the EC Treaty, in particular those provided for in [Article 102 [TFEU].' (para 39)

'It should be noted that, according to the case-law, a Member State is in breach of the prohibitions laid down by [Article 106(1) TFEU] in conjunction with [Article 102 TFEU] if it adopts any law, regulation or administrative provision that creates a situation in which a public undertaking or an undertaking on which it has conferred special or exclusive rights, merely by exercising the preferential rights conferred upon it, is led to abuse its dominant position or when those rights are liable to create a situation in which that undertaking is led to commit such abuses. ... In that respect, it is not necessary that any abuse should actually occur (judgments in *GB-Inno-BM*, ... paragraphs 23 to 25; *Raso and Others*, ... paragraph 31; and *MOTOE*, ... paragraph 49).' (para 41)

'Thus, a Member State will be in breach of those provisions where a measure imputable to a Member State gives rise to a risk of an abuse of a dominant position (see the judgment in MOTOE ..., paragraph 50 and the case-law cited).' (para 42)

'It is clear from the Court's case-law that a system of undistorted competition, such as that provided for by the Treaty, can be guaranteed only if equality of opportunity is secured as between the various economic operators (see the judgments in *GB-Inno-BM*, ... paragraph 25; *MOTOE*, ... paragraph 51; and *Connect Austria*, ... paragraph 83 and case-law cited).' (para 43)

'It follows that if inequality of opportunity between economic operators, and thus distorted competition, is the result of a State measure, such a measure constitutes an infringement of [Article 106(1) TFEU] read together with [Article 102 TFEU] (see the judgment in *Connect Austria*, ... paragraph 84).' (para 44)

'The Court has moreover had occasion to state in that regard that, although the mere fact that a Member State has created a dominant position by the grant of exclusive rights is not as such incompatible with [Article 102 TFEU] the EC Treaty none the less requires the Member States not to adopt or maintain in force any measure which might deprive that provision of its effectiveness (judgments in *ERT*, C-260/89 ... paragraph 35; *Corbeau*, C-320/91 ... paragraph 11; and *Deutsche Post*, C-147/97 and C-148/97... paragraph 39).' (para 45)

'It follows from the matters addressed in paragraphs 41 to 45 above that, as the Advocate General states in point 55 of his Opinion, infringement of [Article 106(1) TFEU] in conjunction with [Article 102 TFEU] may be established irrespective of whether any abuse actually exists. All that is necessary is for the Commission to identify a potential or actual anti-competitive consequence liable to result from the State measure at issue. Such an infringement may thus be established where the State measures at issue affect the structure of the market by creating unequal conditions of competition between companies, by allowing the public undertaking or the undertaking which was granted special or exclusive rights to maintain (for example by hindering new entrants to the market), strengthen or extend its dominant position over another market, thereby restricting competition, without it being necessary to prove the existence of actual abuse.' (para 46)

'In those circumstances, it follows that, contrary to the General Court's analysis in paragraphs 105 and 118 of the judgment under appeal, it is sufficient to show that that potential or actual anti-competitive consequence is liable to result from the State measure at issue; it is not necessary to identify an abuse other than that which results from the situation brought about by the State measure at issue. It also follows that the General Court erred in law in holding that the Commission, by finding that DEI, a former monopolistic undertaking, continued to maintain a dominant position on the wholesale electricity market by virtue of the advantage conferred upon it by its privileged access to lignite and that that situation created inequality of opportunity on that market between the applicant and other undertakings, had neither identified nor established to a sufficient legal standard the abuse to which, within the meaning of [Article 102 TFEU] the State measure in question had led or could have led DEI.' (para 47)

'The first ground of appeal must therefore be upheld and the judgment under appeal must be set aside, without there being any need for the Court to examine the second ground of appeal, which is put forward purely in the alternative to the first.' (para 48)

Comment

The Court held that an infringement of Article 106(1) TFEU in conjunction with Article 102 TFEU may be established irrespective of whether any abuse actually exists. All that is necessary is for the Commission to identify a potential or actual anti-competitive consequence liable to result from the state measure at issue.

In line with the opinion of Advocate General Wathelet, the Court rejected the General Court holding that there is need for the Commission to prove separate abusive behaviour in order to establish violation of Article 106(1) TFEU.

Corsica Ferries France SA v Gruppo Antichi Ormeggiatori del porto di Genova Case C-266/96 Court of Justice, [1998] ECR I-3949, [1998] 5 CMLR 402	**Competition Law and the State** Article 106(1) TFEU Article 106(2) TFEU

Facts

Reference for preliminary ruling from the Tribunale di Genova, concerning proceedings in the Italian court between Corsica Ferries France SA (Corsica Ferries) and Gruppo Antichi Ormeggiatori del Porto di Genova Coop arl (Porto di Genova). In the proceedings Corsica Ferries requested the court to order Porto di Genova and other mooring providers to return fees it paid to them for mooring services. Corsica Ferries argued, among other things, that there was no legal cause for the payments it had made and that the payments had been imposed in breach of the competition rules. Porto di Genova and the other mooring providers operated under Italian legislation which granted them exclusive rights to provide mooring services. The Court of Justice considered, among other things, the compatibility of these provisions with Article 106 TFEU.

Held

The creation of a dominant position by granting exclusive rights is not in itself incompatible with Article 102 TFEU. However, a Member State is in breach of Articles 102 and 106(1) TFEU if the undertaking in question, while exercising the exclusive rights granted to it, is led to abuse its dominant position. 'It follows that a Member State may, without infringing [Article 102 TFEU], grant exclusive rights for the supply of mooring services in its ports to local mooring groups provided those groups do not abuse their dominant position or are not led necessarily to commit such an abuse.' (paras 41, 40–41)

In order to rebut the existence of abuse, the Genoa and La Spezia mooring groups rely on Article 106(2) TFEU and maintain that the tariffs applied are indispensable if a universal mooring service is to be maintained. It must therefore be considered whether the mooring service can be regarded as a service of general economic interest within the meaning Article 106(2) TFEU, which can only be achieved through the measures stipulated in the legislation. (paras 42–4)

Mooring operations in the circumstances surrounding this case 'are of general economic interest, such interest having special characteristics, in relation to those of other economic activities, which is capable of bringing them within the scope of [Article 106(2) TFEU]. Mooring groups are obliged to provide at any time and to any user a universal mooring service, for reasons of safety in port waters. At all events, the Italian Republic could properly have considered that it was necessary, on grounds of public security, to confer on local groups of operators the exclusive right to provide a universal mooring service.' (para 45)

'In those circumstances it is not incompatible with [Articles 102 and 106(1) TFEU] to include in the price of the service a component designed to cover the cost of maintaining the universal mooring service, inasmuch as it corresponds to the supplementary cost occasioned by the special characteristics of that service, and to lay down for that service different tariffs on the basis of the particular characteristics of each port. Consequently, since the mooring groups have in fact been entrusted by the Member State with managing a service of general economic interest within the meaning of [Article 106(2) TFEU] ... legislation such as that at issue does not constitute an infringement of [Article 102 TFEU], read in conjunction with [Article 106(1) TFEU].' (paras 46–7)

Comment

According to the Commission's Communication on 'A Quality Framework for Services of General Interest in Europe' (COM/2011/900 final), Universal Service Obligations set 'the requirements designed to ensure that certain services are made available to all consumers and users in a Member State, regardless of their geographical location, at a specified quality and, taking account of specific national circumstances, at an affordable price.' (page 4)

Firma Ambulanz Glöckner v Landkreis Sudwestpfalz	**Competition Law and the State**
Case C-475/99	Article 106(1) TFEU
Court of Justice, [2001] ECR I-8089, [2002] 4 CMLR 21	Article 106(2) TFEU

Facts

Proceedings in the German court between 'Ambulanz Glöckner', a private undertaking providing non-emergency ambulance services, and the administrative district Landkreis Sudwestpfalz (Landkreis). Under regional legislation (paragraph 18(3) of the Rettungsdienstgesetz 1991), the Landkreis can refuse authorisation for the provision of ambulance transport services if this would be likely to have an adverse effect on the general interest in the operation of an effective public ambulance service. The Landkreis refused the renewal of the authorisation for Ambulanz Glockner on the basis that other 'medical aid organisations' entrusted with the public ambulance service were not being fully exploited and were operating at a loss. Ambulanz Glöckner challenged the decision in court. In a preliminary reference to the Court of Justice the compatibility of the regulation with Article 106 TFEU was considered.

Held

Entities such as 'medical aid organisations' providing emergency transport services are engaged in economic activity and may be treated as undertakings. The regulation in question reserves the patient transport services to these undertakings and confers on them special or exclusive right within the meaning of Article 106(1) TFEU. These rights affect the ability of other operators to exercise the same economic activity. (paras 18–25)

In order to assess whether the regulation is liable to create a situation in which 'medical aid organisations' are led to commit abuses of a dominant position, the national court needs to establish the existence of a dominant position and then that such position was abused, without any objective necessity. A Member State will be in breach of the prohibitions laid down in Articles 102 and 106 TFEU only if the undertaking in question, merely by exercising the special or exclusive rights conferred upon it, is led to abuse its dominant position or where such rights create a situation in which that undertaking is led to commit such abuses. (paras 30–42)

The regulation in question gave an advantage to 'medical aid organisations' that already had an exclusive right on the urgent transport market by also allowing them to provide non-emergency patient transport exclusively. The regulation therefore has the effect of limiting markets to the prejudice of consumers within the meaning of Article 102(b) TFEU. (para 43)

It is necessary to examine whether the regulation may be justified by the existence of a task of operating a service of general economic interest, within the meaning of Article 106(2) TFEU. The question to be determined is 'whether the restriction of competition is necessary to enable the holder of an exclusive right to perform its task of general interest in economically acceptable conditions. The Court has held that the starting point in making that determination must be the premise that the obligation, on the part of the undertaking entrusted with such a task, to perform its services in conditions of economic equilibrium presupposes that it will be possible to offset less profitable sectors against the profitable sectors and hence justifies a restriction of competition from individual undertakings in economically profitable sectors (*Corbeau*, paragraphs 16 and 17).' (paras 56, 57, 51–7)

'It is true that, in paragraph 19 of *Corbeau*, the Court held that the exclusion of competition is not justified in certain cases involving specific services, severable from the service of general interest in question, if those services do not compromise the economic equilibrium of the service of general economic interest performed by the holder of the exclusive rights.' (para 59)

'However, that is not the case with the two services now under consideration, for two reasons in particular. First, unlike the situation in *Corbeau*, the two types of service in question, traditionally assumed by the medical aid organisations, are so closely linked that it is difficult to sever the non-emergency transport services from the task of general economic interest constituted by the provision of the public ambulance service, with which they also have characteristics in common.' (para 60)

'Second, the extension of the medical aid organisations' exclusive rights to the non-emergency transport sector does indeed enable them to discharge their general-interest task of providing emergency transport in conditions of economic equilibrium. The possibility which would be open to private operators to concentrate, in the non-emergency sector, on more profitable journeys could affect the degree of economic viability of the service provided by the medical aid organisations and, consequently, jeopardise the quality and reliability of that service.' (para 61)

'However, as the Advocate General explains in point 188 of his Opinion, it is only if it were established that the medical aid organisations entrusted with the operation of the public ambulance service were manifestly unable to satisfy demand for emergency ambulance services and for patient transport at all times that the justification for extending their exclusive rights, based on the task of general interest, could not be accepted.' (para 62)

'It is for [the] national court to determine whether the medical aid organisations which occupy a dominant position on the markets in question are in fact able to satisfy demand and to fulfil not only their statutory obligation to provide the public emergency ambulance services in all situations and 24 hours a day but also to offer efficient patient transport services.' (para 64)

Consequently, the regulation is justified under Article 106(2) TFEU 'provided that it does not bar the grant of an authorisation to independent operators where it is established that the medical aid organisations entrusted with the operation of the public ambulance service are manifestly unable to satisfy demand in the area of emergency transport and patient transport services.' (para 65)

Comment

Services of General Economic Interest (SGEI) are defined in the Commission's Communication on 'A Quality Framework for Services of General Interest in Europe' (COM/2011/900 final) as 'economic activities which deliver outcomes in the overall public good that would not be supplied (or would be supplied under different conditions in terms of quality, safety, affordability, equal treatment or universal access) by the market without public intervention. The Public Service Obligation is imposed on the provider by way of an entrustment and on the basis of a general interest criterion which ensures that the service is provided under conditions allowing it to fulfill its mission.' (page 3) Note also the reference to SGEI in Article 1 of the new Protocol No 26 on 'Services of General Interest', annexed to the TFEU, and Article 14 TFEU. Both Articles acknowledge that the organisation, delivery and financing of such services are primarily for Member States to decide at national, regional or local level.

In Case 66/86 *Ahmed Saeed Flugreisen and others v Zentrale zur Bekämpfung unlauteren Wettbewerbs* [1989] ECR 803, the Court of Justice held that the approval by the public authority of agreements regarding airline tariffs which are contrary to Article 101 TFEU and do not benefit from exemption under Article 101(3) TFEU is contrary to Article 106(1) TFEU, despite the existence in the sector of a Council Regulation aiming at gradually increasing competition in air transport services between Member States and providing national authorities with discretion to that respect. The Court of Justice added that Article 106(2) TFEU may be applicable where air carriers are obliged by the public authorities to operate on routes that are not commercially viable but in which it is necessary to operate for reasons of the general interest. However, for this to be possible the national authorities responsible for the approval of tariffs and the courts to which disputes relating thereto are submitted must be able to determine the exact nature of the needs in question and their impact on the structure of the tariffs applied by the airlines in question. (paras 47–58)

Albany International BV v Stichting Bedrijfspensioenfonds Textielindustrie	**Competition Law and the State**
Case C-67/96	Article 106(1) TFEU
Court of Justice, [1999] ECR I-5751, [2000] 4 CMLR 446	Article 106(2) TFEU

Facts

A preliminary reference to the Court of Justice from the Netherlands Hoge Raad, before which three undertakings challenged orders issued by the 'Netherlands sectoral pension funds' demanding payment of the contributions to their respective schemes. The Court of Justice was asked to appraise, among other things, whether the sectoral pension system in the Netherlands which includes compulsory affiliation to the pension funds infringes Article 106(1) TFEU in conjunction with Article 102 TFEU.

Held

'The decision of the public authorities to make affiliation to a sectoral pension fund compulsory ... necessarily implies granting to that fund an exclusive right to collect and administer the contributions paid with a view to accruing pension rights. Such a fund must therefore be regarded as an undertaking to which exclusive rights have been granted by the public authorities, of the kind referred to in [Article 106(1) TFEU]. An undertaking which has a legal monopoly in a substantial part of the internal market may be regarded as occupying a dominant position within the meaning of [Article 102 TFEU]. Subsequently, a sectoral pension fund which has an exclusive right to manage a supplementary pension scheme in an industrial sector in a Member State may be regarded as occupying a dominant position. (paras 90–2)

The creation of a dominant position by granting exclusive rights within the meaning of Article 106(1) TFEU is incompatible with Article 102 TFEU only when the undertaking in question, merely by exercising the exclusive rights granted to it, is led to abuse its dominant position or when such rights are liable to create a situation in which that undertaking is led to commit such abuses. In the present case, 'some undertakings in the sector might wish to provide their workers with a pension scheme superior to the one offered by the Fund. However, the fact that such undertakings are unable to entrust the management of such a pension scheme to a single insurer and the resulting restriction of competition derive directly from the exclusive right conferred on the sectoral pension fund.' (paras 97, 93–7)

It is necessary to consider whether the exclusive right of the sectoral pension fund may be justified under Article 106(2) TFEU as a measure necessary for the performance of a particular social task of general interest with which that fund has been charged. Article 106(2) provides for derogations from the general rules of the Treaty and 'seeks to reconcile the Member States' interest in using certain undertakings, in particular in the public sector, as an instrument of economic or fiscal policy, with the [Union]'s interest in ensuring compliance with the rules on competition and preservation of the unity of the [internal] market. The supplementary pension scheme at issue fulfils an essential social function within the Netherlands pensions system by reason of the limited amount of the statutory pension, which is calculated on the basis of the minimum statutory wage. The removal of the exclusive right conferred on the Fund might make it impossible for it to perform the tasks of general economic interest entrusted to it under economically acceptable conditions and threaten its financial equilibrium. (paras 103, 103–11)

Comment

The Court held that the granting of the exclusive right conferred on the sectoral pension fund resulted in restriction of competition. However, it did not explore fully how the undertaking in question, merely by exercising the exclusive rights granted to it, was led to abuse its dominant position. (paras 93–7) It is possible that the Court omitted this examination since the exclusive right of the sectoral pension fund was held justified under Article 106(2) TFEU.

Deutsche Post AG v Gesellschaft für Zahlungssysteme mbH and	**Competition and the State**
Citicorp Kartenservice GmbG	Article 106(1) TFEU
Cases C-147/97 and C-148/97	Article 106(2) TFEU
Court of Justice, [2000] ECR I-825, [2000] 4 CMLR 838	

Facts

A preliminary reference from the Higher Regional Court in Frankfurt concerning, among other things, the interpretation of Article 106(1) and (2) TFEU. The main proceedings concerned a dispute between Deutsche Post AG and two other undertakings over the delivery of post from abroad. The Higher Regional Court asked the Court of Justice whether certain actions taken by Deutsche Post AG under the Universal Postal Convention (UPC) may be contrary to Article 106 TFEU, read in conjunction with Articles 102 and 56 thereof.

Held

'To reply to that question, as reformulated, it should first be noted that a body such as Deutsche Post, which has been granted exclusive rights as regards the collection, carriage and delivery of mail, must be regarded as an undertaking to which the Member State concerned has granted exclusive rights within the meaning of [Article 106(1) TFEU] (Case C-320/91 *Corbeau* [1993] ECR I-2533, paragraph 8).' (para 37)

'Also, it is settled case-law that an undertaking having a statutory monopoly over a substantial part of the [internal market] may be regarded as holding a dominant position within the meaning of [Article 102 TFEU] (see Case C-179/90 *Merci Convenzionali Porto di Genova v Siderurgica Gabrielli* [1991] ECR I-5889, paragraph 14, Case C-18/88 *RTT v GB-Inno-BM* [1991] ECR I-5941, paragraph 17, and *Corbeau*, cited above, paragraph 9).' (para 38)

'The Court has had occasion to state in this respect that although the mere fact that a Member State has created a dominant position by the grant of exclusive rights is not as such incompatible with [Article 102 TFEU], the Treaty none the less requires the Member States not to adopt or maintain in force any measure which might deprive that provision of its effectiveness (see Case C-260/89 *ERT* [1991] ECR I-2925, paragraph 35, and *Corbeau*, cited above, paragraph 11).' (para 39)

'[Article 106(1) TFEU] thus provides that in the case of undertakings to which Member States grant special or exclusive rights, they are neither to enact nor to maintain in force any measure contrary, in particular, to the rules contained in the Treaty with regard to competition (see *Corbeau*, paragraph 12). That provision must be read in conjunction with [Article 106(2) TFEU] which provides that undertakings entrusted with the operation of services of general economic interest are to be subject to the rules contained in the [Treaties] in so far as the application of such rules does not obstruct the performance, in law or in fact, of the particular tasks assigned to them.' (paras 40, 41)

'For the postal services of the Member States, performance of the obligations flowing from the UPC is thus in itself a service of general economic interest within the meaning of [Article 106(2) TFEU].' (para 44)

'The grant to a body such as Deutsche Post of the right to treat international items of mail as internal post in such cases creates a situation where that body may be led, to the detriment of users of postal services, to abuse its dominant position resulting from the exclusive right granted to it to forward and deliver those items to the relevant addressees.' (para 48)

'It is accordingly necessary to examine the extent to which exercise of such a right is necessary to enable a body of that kind to perform its task of general interest pursuant to the obligations flowing from the UPC and, in particular, to operate under economically acceptable conditions. If a body such as Deutsche Post were obliged to forward and deliver to addressees resident in Germany mail posted in large quantities by senders resident in Germany using postal services of other Member States, without any provision allowing it to be financially compensated ... the performance, in economically balanced conditions, of that task of general interest would be jeopardised.' (paras 49, 50)

'In such a case, it must be regarded as justified, for the purposes of the performance, in economically balanced conditions, of the task of general interest entrusted to Deutsche Post by the UPC, to treat cross-border mail as internal mail and, consequently, to charge internal postage. It would be otherwise if terminal dues for incoming cross-border mail within the [Union] were fixed in relation to the actual costs of processing and delivering it by agreements between the postal services concerned of the kind envisaged by Article 13 of Directive 97/67/EC of the European Parliament and of the Council of 15 December 1997 on common rules for the development of the internal market of [Union] postal services and the improvement of quality of service (OJ 1998 L 15, p 14).' (paras 52, 53)

'[Article 106(2) TFEU] therefore justifies, in the absence of an agreement between the postal services of the Member States concerned fixing terminal dues in relation to the actual costs of processing and delivering incoming trans-border mail, the grant by a Member State to its postal services of the statutory right to charge internal postage on items of mail where senders resident in that State post items, or cause them to be posted, in large quantities with the postal services of another Member State in order to send them to the first Member State.' (para 54)

'On the other hand, in so far as part of the forwarding and delivery costs is offset by terminal dues paid by the postal services of other Member States, it is not necessary, in order for a body such as Deutsche Post to fulfil the obligations flowing from the UPC, that postage be charged at the full internal rate on items posted in large quantities with those services.' (para 56)

'It follows from all the foregoing considerations that, in the absence of an agreement between the postal services of the Member States concerned fixing terminal dues in relation to the actual costs of processing and delivering incoming trans-border mail, it is not contrary to [Article 106 TFEU], read in conjunction with [Articles 102 and 56] thereof, for a body such as Deutsche Post to exercise the right provided for by Article 25(3) of the UPC, … [and charge] internal postage on items of mail posted in large quantities with the postal services of a Member State other than the Member State to which that body belongs. On the other hand, the exercise of such a right is contrary to [Article 106(1) TFEU], read in conjunction with [Article 102] thereof, in so far as the result is that such a body may demand the entire internal postage applicable in the Member State to which it belongs without deducting the terminal dues corresponding to those items of mail paid by the abovementioned postal services.' (para 61)

Comment

In paragraphs 40 and 41 the Court highlighted that, when applied to the facts of a case, Article 106(1) TFEU must be read in conjunction with Article 106(2) TFEU. The Court of Justice applied a lax test on the link between the national measure and the abuse in paragraph 48, and then considered whether the rights granted to Deutsche Post were necessary to enable it to perform its task of general interest under acceptable economic conditions in paragraphs 49 *et seq.*

Note paragraph 21 of the AG opinion in which he notes that in order for a Member State to be found to be in breach of Articles 106(1) and 102 TFEU it is necessary that the abuses are the direct consequence of the national measure in issue. In the present case the German implementing legislation 'confers a right and not an obligation on the national PPO to return items to origin or to charge postage at its internal rates. But it is hard to see why the postal administration with a monopoly, which is not exposed to commercial competition in the provision of the reserved services, would in practice refrain altogether or in part from exercising the right in question, given the clear and objective economic incentive to charge senders of postal items, in the specified circumstances, the highest price permitted under the applicable legislation. The purely theoretical nature of the possibility of waiving the right is, indeed, borne out by the facts in the main proceedings. The same conclusion would be warranted, in my view, even if the national court had not found any actual abuse to have been committed by the German postal monopoly. On these grounds, provisions such as those contained in the legislation implementing the Convention must be regarded as *per se* contrary to [Article 106(1) in conjunction with Article 102 TFEU].' (opinion of AG La Pergola (para 21))

International Mail Spain SL v Administración del Estado and Correos   **Competition Law and the State**
Case C-162/06   Article 106(2) TFEU
Court of Justice, [2007] ECR I-9911, [2008] 4 CMLR 18

Facts

A reference for a preliminary ruling concerning the interpretation of Article 7(2) of Directive 97/67 EC which establishes common rules concerning, inter alia, the provision of a universal postal service within Europe. Article 3(1) of that directive stipulates that Member States are to ensure that users enjoy the right to a universal service involving the permanent provision of a postal service of specified quality at all points in their territory at affordable prices for all users. According to Article 3(7), that universal service covers both national and cross-border services. The reference to the Court of Justice arose in proceedings at the national court regarding a decision by the Secretariat-General of Communications who penalised International Mail for providing postal services reserved to the universal postal service provider, without the latter's authorisation.

Held

'The question referred by the national court asks, in essence, whether Article 7(2) of Directive 97/67 must be interpreted as allowing Member States to reserve cross- border mail to the universal postal service provider only in so far as they establish that, in the absence of such a reservation, the financial equilibrium of that provider would be in danger, or whether other considerations relating to the general situation of the postal sector, including mere expediency, are sufficient to justify that reservation. Article 7(2) of Directive 97/67 allows Member States to reserve cross-border mail to the universal service provider, under certain limitations, to the 'extent necessary to ensure the maintenance of universal service'. The use of the word 'necessary' means that the reservation cannot be justified on the ground of mere expediency. The objective of the Article is therefore to guarantee maintenance of the universal postal service, in particular by providing the necessary resources to enable it to operate under financially balanced conditions. (paras 26, 27–31)

'[T]he condition laid down in Article 7(2) of Directive 97/67 cannot be reduced to a single financial issue, inasmuch as it cannot be ruled out that there may be other reasons for which, in accordance with [Article 106(2) TFEU], the Member States can decide to reserve cross-border mail in order to ensure that the universal postal service provider is not prevented from achieving its specific objective. Considerations, such as expediency, relating to the overall situation in the postal sector, including that linked to the degree of liberalisation of the market at the time when a decision is taken as regards cross-border mail, are not enough to justify the reservation of cross-border mail, unless, in the absence of such a reservation, the achievement of a universal postal service would be prevented, or the reservation is necessary to ensure that the universal service can be provided under acceptable economic conditions. Subsequently, it must be held that Article 7(2) precludes a decision to reserve cross-border mail to the universal postal service provider being justified on the ground of mere expediency.' (paras 40–2)

Comment

Mere expediency was held insufficient to justify reserving the service to the universal service provider. Such limitation will only be accepted when it is *necessary* to ensure the maintenance of the universal services. The necessity reasoning in *International Mail Spain SL* has been cited by the Commission in *Slovenská pošta* (COMP/39562). Action for annulment dismissed (T-556/08), appeal pending (C-293/15P).

Note that Universal Service Obligations are set at European level as an essential component of market liberalisation of service sectors, such as electronic communications, post and transport. According to the Commission's Communication on 'A Quality Framework for Services of General Interest in Europe' (COM/2011/900 final), Universal Service Obligations set 'the requirements designed to ensure that certain services are made available to all consumers and users in a Member State, regardless of their geographical location, at a specified quality and, taking account of specific national circumstances, at an affordable price.' (page 4)

French Republic v Commission	**Competition Law and the State**
Case C-202/88	Article 106(3) TFEU
Court of Justice, [1991] ECR I-1223, [1992] 5 CMLR 552	

Facts

Application brought by the French Republic for the partial annulment of Commission Directive 88/301/EEC of 16 May 1988 on 'competition in the markets in telecommunications terminal equipment' which was adopted on the basis of Article 106(3) TFEU.

Held

'Inasmuch as it makes it possible for the Commission to adopt directives, [Article 106(3) TFEU] empowers it to lay down general rules specifying the obligations arising from the Treaty which are binding on the Member States as regards the undertakings referred to in [Article 106(1) and (2)]. ... [Article 106(3) TFEU] empowers the Commission to specify in general terms the obligations arising under [Article 106(1) TFEU] by adopting directives. The Commission exercises that power where, without taking into consideration the particular situation existing in the various Member States, it defines in concrete terms the obligations imposed on them under the Treaty. In view of its very nature, such a power cannot be used to make a finding that a Member State has failed to fulfil a particular obligation under the Treaty.' (paras 14–17)

'It must ... be held that the subject-matter of the power conferred on the Commission by [Article 106(3)] is different from, and more specific than, that of the powers conferred on the Council by either [Article 114] or [Article 103] ...' (paras 25–6)

With respect to the substantive provisions of the Directive: Article 2 of the Directive relates to the abolition of special rights and exclusive rights regarding the importation, marketing and connection of terminal equipment and/or maintenance of such equipment. Those exclusive rights deprive undertakings of the possibility of having their products purchased by consumers. Additionally, due to technical complexity an undertaking with exclusive rights might not be able to satisfy demand. This in turn would restrict consumer choice and inter-state trade. Therefore, the Commission was justified in requiring the withdrawal of exclusive rights regarding the importation, marketing, connection, bringing into service of telecommunications terminal equipment and/or maintenance of such equipment. However, the Article must be declared void in so far as it requires the withdrawal of special rights, because neither the provisions of the Directive nor its preamble specify the type of rights which are actually involved and in what respect the existence of such rights is contrary to the various provisions of the Treaty. (paras 31–47)

With respect to the legality of Article 7 of the directive, this Article requires Member States to make it possible to terminate leasing or maintenance contracts which are subject to exclusive or special rights within a maximum notice period of one year. The Article aims at resolving the anticompetitive effects stemming from long-term contracts which prevented the introduction of free competition. However, there is no indication that that the conclusion of long-term contracts was compelled or encouraged by State regulations. Consequently, that Article falls outside the scope of Article 106(3) TFEU which confers powers on the Commission only in relation to State measures and not in relations to anticompetitive conduct engaged in by undertakings on their own initiative. Article 106(3) TFEU is therefore not an appropriate basis for dealing with the obstacles to competition created by the long-term contracts. (paras 53–7)

Comment

Article 106(3) TFEU allows the Commission to exercise its duty of surveillance through the specification, in general terms, of the obligations of the Member States under Article 106(1) and (2) TFEU. As such, it provides an effective alternative to the commencing of proceedings against the individual Member States under Article 258 TFEU.

8

Competition Law and Intellectual Property Rights

Introduction

The following chapter explores the relationship between competition law and intellectual property (IP) rights. The interface between these two areas of law is interesting, not least due to the fact that both aim to create fertile ground for progress and innovation, although using different means.

While competition law promotes the freedom of competition as a vehicle to advance welfare, innovation and efficient allocation of resources, IP law advances these goals by selectively limiting competition through the conferral of protection to the holders of patents, copyrights, trademarks, designs and related rights. These different mechanisms, although at times inconsistent, should not be viewed as conflicting. A better way of viewing their relationship is to consider competition law and IP rights as performing a complementary role. Intellectual property law grants the right, based on a set of criteria. Competition law may be triggered at a later stage, when the exploitation of the right, in a given case, distorts or hinders competition.

Article 101 TFEU and Licensing of Intellectual Property Rights

Licensing concerns the grant by the holder of an intellectual properly right (the licensor) of a right to a third party (the licensee) to use such IP. Agreements may concern patents, copyrights, trademarks or brand licensing. They allow the licensee to make use of the protected rights, while protecting the interests of the licensor. By their nature, these agreements may include limitations on the use of the licensed materials, either in time, application or territory. When these limitations restrict competition they may trigger the application of Article 101 TFEU.

Article 101 TFEU may apply, for example, when the exclusive licence includes assignment with absolute territorial protection (258/78, IV/32.736, C-403/08). However, at times, territorial restrictions which limit the grant of other licences may fall outside Article 101 TFEU (258/78, 27/87, 262/81). Article 101 TFEU may apply to non-territorial restrictions (193/83) and in exceptional circumstances to open exclusive licences (IV/31.043).

With summary references to:

Of major significance to licensing agreements is the Technology Transfer Block Exemption (TTBER), which provides a safe haven for a range of technology transfer agreements (Regulation 316/2014 of 21 March 2014 on the application of Article 101(3) of the Treaty on the Functioning of the European Union to categories of technology transfer agreements). The Commission elaborates on the application of the TTBER in its Guidelines on the application of [Article 101 TFEU] to technology transfer agreements ([2014] OJ C89/03).

Where the IP provisions in an agreement do not constitute its primary object, the Vertical Block Exemption may be applicable (Article 2(3), Regulation 330/2010, [2010] OJ L102/1). Note that the Vertical Block Exemption blacklists restrictions on passive sales and as such provides a more limited safe harbour. The Vertical Block Exemption does not apply to vertical agreements the subject matter of which falls within the scope of any other block exemption regulation (Article 2(5), Regulation 330/2010).

Standard-Setting Bodies, FRAND Licensing and Article 102 TFEU

Standard-setting organisations promote compatibility and interoperability in industries through the development of agreed standards. Cases in this area shed light on the borderline between IP rights and the right of companies not to license their IP to third parties, and, on the other hand, the unique instances, and conditions under which they may be obliged to do so.

Leading cases have addressed the scope and requirements under the realm of 'fair, reasonable and non-discriminatory' licensing (FRAND) (T-201/04), the right of a holder of a standard essential patent to sue for unauthorised use (C-170/13, COMP/C-3/39.939), the question of abuse in the discharge of companies' obligations to license their patents as a result of the companies' contribution to the development of standards (COMP/38.636, COMP/39.247), and the strengthening of market power as a result of IP portfolio combinations following a merger (COMP/M.3998, COMP/M.4214).

See also summary reference to:

For further discussion of Standardisation Agreements see Section 7, Guidelines on Horizontal Cooperation Agreements, [2011] OJ C11/1.

Intellectual Property Rights, Market Power and Article 102 TFEU

Article 102 TFEU has predominantly been applied in cases where the holder of an IP right refuses to licence the right. In some instances, such refusal to licence may amount to an abuse of a dominant position.

See also summary references:

Pharmaceutical Sector

A range of tactics may be used by pharmaceutical companies to delay the introduction of rival generic drugs into the market. In its Pharmaceutical Sector Inquiry, the Commission raised concerns as to the use of various patent filing strategies and litigation to extend the breadth and duration of patent protection, and the use of patent settlement agreements to transfer value between the pharmaceutical and generic companies in return for delayed entry of the generic. Also noteworthy are cases involving product hopping aimed at delaying and undermining generic entry to the market.

For illustrative decisions scrutinising practices in the industry, see:

With summary reference to

IP Rights and the Free Movement of Goods

The free movement of goods provisions in the TFEU, namely Articles 34–36, have an impact on the interpretation of IP rights because of the possibility that nationally based IP rights may hinder market integration. The key cases in this area are Case 78/70 *Deutsche Grammophon Gesellschaft mbH v Metro-SB-Großmärkte GmbH & Co KG* [1971] ECR 487, Case 15/74 *Centrafarm v Sterling* [1974] ECR 1147 and Case 187/80 *Merck & Co Inc v Stephar BV and Petrus Stephanus Exler* [1981] ECR 2063.

Nungesser v Commission (the Maize Seeds case)	**Licensing**
Case 258/78	Article 101(1) TFEU
Court of Justice, [1982] ECR 2015, [1983] 1 CMLR 278	Open Exclusive Licences

Facts

An action for the annulment of a Commission decision (Case IV/28.824, *Breeders' Rights—Maize Seed*) in which the Commission found an exclusive licence of breeders' rights to infringe Article 101(1) TFEU and rejected Mr Eisele's application for an exemption under Article 101(3) TFEU. The agreement in question concerned a 'maize seed production and sales licensing contract' which was signed between the Institut National de Recherche Agronomique (INRA) and Mr Kurt Eisele. Under the agreement Mr Kurt Eisele (and Nungesser KG) acquired exclusive rights to sell INRA's varieties of maize in Germany. The agreement stipulated that Mr Eisele was obliged to import at least two-thirds of the German market's requirements from France through the French organisation responsible for centralising and coordinating exports (SSBM, later FRASEMA); the balance, that is to say no more than one-third, may be produced by Mr Eisele himself, or produced under his responsibility, on payment of royalties; Mr Eisele undertook to enforce INRA's proprietary right in its varieties, notably by protecting them against trademark infringement and passing-off.

Held

'By this submission the applicants criticize the Commission for wrongly taking the view that an exclusive licence of breeders' rights must by its very nature be treated as an agreement prohibited by [Article 101(1) TFEU]. They submit that the Commission's opinion in that respect is unfounded in so far as the exclusive licence constitutes the sole means, as regards seeds which have been recently developed in a Member State and which have not yet penetrated the market of another Member State, of promoting competition between the new product and comparable products in that other Member State; indeed, no grower or trader would take the risk of launching the new product on a new market if he were not protected against direct competition from the holder of the breeders' rights and from his other licensees.' (para 44)

'The statement of reasons on which the decision is based refers to two sets of circumstances in order to justify the application of [Article 101(1) TFEU] to the exclusive licence in question …' (para 48)

'The *first set* of circumstances is described as follows: "By licensing a single undertaking to exploit his breeders' rights in a given territory, the licensor deprives himself for the entire duration of the contract of the ability to issue licences to other undertakings in the same territory …" "By undertaking not to produce or market the product himself in the territory covered by the contract the licensor likewise eliminates himself, as well as FRASEMA and its members, as suppliers in that territory". (para 49)

The Commission found the exclusive nature of the licence to be contrary to Article 101 TFEU insofar as it imposes an obligation upon INRA to refrain from having the relevant seeds produced or sold by other licensees in Germany or producing or selling the relevant seeds in Germany themselves. (para 50)

The *second set* of circumstances referred to in the decision is described as follows: 'The fact that third parties may not import the same seed (namely the seed under licence) from other [Union] countries into Germany, or export from Germany to other [Union] countries, leads to market sharing and deprives German farmers of any real room for negotiation since seed is supplied by one supplier and one supplier only.' (para 51)

'The Commission found this exclusive nature of the licence to be contrary to [Article 101 TFEU] insofar as it imposes an obligation to prevent third parties from exporting the relevant seeds to Germany without the licensee's authorization for use or sale there, and Mr Eisele's use of his exclusive rights to prevent all imports into Germany or exports to other Member States of the relevant seeds.' (para 52)

'It should be observed that those two sets of considerations relate to two legal situations which are not necessarily identical. The first case concerns a so-called open exclusive licence or assignment and the exclusivity of the licence relates solely to the contractual relationship between the owner of the right and the licensee, whereby the owner merely undertakes not to grant other licences in respect of the same territory and not to compete himself with the licensee on that territory. On the other hand, the second case involves an exclusive licence or assignment with absolute territorial protection, under which the parties to the contract propose, as regards the products and the territory in question, to eliminate all competition from third parties, such as parallel importers or licensees for other territories.' (para 53)

The open licence, in this case, is necessary for the protection of agricultural innovations and constitutes a means of encouraging such innovations. 'A total prohibition of every exclusive licence, even an open one, would cause the interest of undertakings in licences to fall away, which would be prejudicial to the dissemination of knowledge and techniques in the [Union].' (para 55)

'In fact, in the case of a licence of breeders' rights over hybrid maize seeds newly developed in one Member State, an undertaking established in another Member State which was not certain that it would not encounter competition from other licensees for the territory granted to it, or from the owner of the right himself, might be deterred from accepting the risk of cultivating and marketing that product; such a result would be damaging to the dissemination of a new technology and would prejudice competition in the [Union] between the new product and similar existing products.' (para 57)

'Having regard to the specific nature of the products in question, the court concludes that, in a case such as the present, the grant of an open exclusive licence, that is to say a licence which does not affect the position of third parties such as parallel importers and licensees for other territories, is not in itself incompatible with [Article 101(1) TFEU].' (para 58)

With respect to the exclusive licence, which confers absolute territorial protection, it must be examined whether such agreement may benefit from an exemption from the prohibition contained in Article 101(1) TFEU. As the seeds in the case are intended to be used by a large number of farmers, an absolute territorial protection goes beyond what is indispensable for the improvement of production or distribution or the promotion of technical progress. It thus constituted a sufficient reason for refusing to grant an exemption under Article 101(3) TFEU. (paras 76–9)

Comment

In paragraph 58 the Court of Justice distinguished between an 'open exclusive licence agreement' and an agreement which entails absolute territorial protection. The former does not affect the position of third parties, parallel importers, and licensees for other territories. It is subsequently not in itself incompatible with Article 101(1) TFEU.

The Court of Justice took notice of the nature of the product, the impact of the licensing agreement on innovation, and the agreement's role in encouraging the licensee to accept risk in marketing a new product.

In Case IV/4.204 *Velcro/Aplix* [1985] OJ L233/22, [1989] 4 CMLR 157, the Commission referred to the *Maize Seed* judgment and applied it to a licensing agreement concerning the exploitation of the Velcro patents. It found the agreement to facilitate the development of a new product, contribute to technical and economic progress, and subsequently to fall outside the scope of Article 101(1) TFEU. It noted, however, that that justification does not apply once the patent expired and the technology was no longer novel.

Tetra Pak I (BTG Licence)	**Licensing**
Case IV/31.043	Article 101(1) TFEU
European Commission, [1988] OJ L272/27, [1990] 4 CMLR 47	

Facts

The case concerned the use of patented technology which was developed by Liquipak, following its acquisition by Tetra Pak, the market leader in the production and supply of liquid food packaging. The acquisition of Liquipak enabled Tetra Pak to acquire control over the technology which up until then was used by its rival Elopak. Elopak complained to the Commission on the basis that its dominant rival had obtained this exclusive licence.

Held

'The circumstances of this case are not comparable to those involving hybrid maize seed where the Court ruled that an open exclusive licence may not fall within the scope of [Article 101(1) TFEU] if concerned with the introduction and protection of new technology in a contract territory where the technology is not known. In that case, the licensee did not previously produce the product and needed protection from the experienced licensor if he was to undertake the substantial technical and commercial risks necessary to exploit the licensed product. In the present case Tetra is a dominant company … any protection that Tetra claims is necessary to bear the technical and commercial risks associated with the dissemination of new technology is not sufficient to overcome the disadvantages created by the loss of competition. In fact, the limited extent of the commercial and technical risks born by Tetra has been described above.' (para 55)

'In addition, in the maize seed case an important element in the Court's reasoning taking the open exclusive licence outside the scope of [Article 101(1) TFEU] was the fact that such protection was necessary to stimulate both inter- and intra-brand competition. In the circumstances of the present case, where Tetra is a dominant company and the barriers to entry are particularly high, the effect of the exclusivity provision is not to encourage but rather to prevent the emergence of both inter- and intra-brand competition. Inter-brand competition is damaged because competitors to Tetra (in particular Elopak) are prevented from using the technology to enter the market. Intra-brand competition is damaged because no other licences can be granted and the licensor cannot himself produce the product which makes parallel imports impossible.' (para 56)

'Thus the very competition which the Court sought to encourage by taking open exclusive licences outside the scope of [Article 101(1) TFEU] are in fact damaged by the exclusivity provisions of this case, where the tendency is in fact to eliminate competition. Thus, in market circumstances where exclusivity is necessary to encourage competition, this exclusivity may fall outside [Article 101(1) TFEU] but in other market circumstances where it is detrimental to competition it must fall within the scope of [Article 101(1)(2) TFEU].' (para 57)

Comment

The Commission distinguished between the facts of this case and the *Maize Seeds* case (*Nungesser v Commission*, page 364 above). In the latter the licensee needed protection from the licensor to encourage it to undertake the substantial technical and commercial risks. In this case, however, that reasoning did not apply as the firm in a dominant position took over a technology and did not bear the same commercial and technical risks as a smaller undertaking.

Emphasis was placed on the market structure in this case which changed the nature of the effects of an exclusive licence on inter- and intra-brand competition. The General Court later agreed with the Commission's decision here (Case T-51/89 *Tetra Pak Rausing v Commission* [1990] 4 CMLR 334), also adding that market structure plays an important part in the competition analysis and that the acquisition of an exclusive licence is not *per se* abusive.

Erauw-Jacquery v La Hesbignonne	**Licensing**
Case 27/87	Article 101(1) TFEU
Court of Justice, [1988] ECR 1919, [1988] 4 CMLR 576	

Facts

A preliminary reference from the Commercial Court, Liege, concerning the compatibility with Article 101 TFEU of certain provisions of a licensing agreement. The agreement in question concerned the granting of a licence to propagate and sell varieties of cereal seed protected by plant breeders' rights. Under the agreement, the licensee undertook, in particular, to propagate the seeds in Belgium, not to sell or assign the seed to growers or to any other person with the exception of the propagator, and not to export it to any country. The agreement also included provisions imposing minimum prices for certified seed of any species.

Held

The national court seeks to ascertain whether a provision prohibiting the holder of the licence from selling, assigning or exporting seeds falls within Article 101(1) TFEU. (para 8)

'The Commission and the breeder maintain that the provision prohibiting the sale and exportation of "e2" basic seed, which is placed at the disposal of the growers only for the purposes of propagation, is not contrary to [Article 101(1) TFEU]. Such a provision falls within the ambit of the plant breeder's rights.' (para 9)

'In this respect, it must be pointed out that, as the court acknowledged ... in Case 258/78 *Nungesser v Commission* ... the development of the basic lines may involve considerable financial commitment. Consequently, a person who has made considerable efforts to develop varieties of basic seed which may be the subject-matter of plant breeders' rights must be allowed to protect himself against any improper handling of those varieties of seed. To that end, the breeder must be entitled to restrict propagation to the growers which he has selected as licensees. To that extent, the provision prohibiting the licensee from selling and exporting basic seed falls outside the prohibition contained in [Article 101(1) TFEU].' (para 10)

'Therefore, the answer to the first part of the question referred by the national court must be that a provision of an agreement concerning the propagation and sale of seed, in respect of which one of the parties is the holder or the agent of the holder of certain plant breeders' rights, which prohibits the licensee from selling and exporting the basic seed is compatible with [Article 101(1) TFEU] in so far as it is necessary in order to enable the breeder to select the growers who are to be licensees.' (para 11)

The provision in the agreement which obliges the grower to comply with minimum prices fixed by the other party falls within the prohibition set out in Article 101(1) TFEU when the agreement is found to affect trade between members states to an appreciable degree. (paras 12–20)

Comment

The Court of Justice noted the unique circumstances in this case which justified the protection of the licensor's financial commitment and investment.

The Court referred to its judgment in the *Maize Seeds* case (*Nungesser v Commission*, page 364 above), where it previously considered the challenges involved in the developments of varieties of seeds. There the seeds in question were held not to justify an absolute territorial protection and subsequently the agreement was found to infringe Article 101 TFEU.

Coditel v SA Cine Vog Films (Coditel II)	**Licensing**
Case 262/81	Copyright Licences
Court of Justice, [1982] ECR 3381, [1983] 1 CMLR	

Facts

A preliminary reference from the Belgian Cour de Cassation concerning the compatibility of an agreement to assign the copyright in a film with Article 101 TFEU. The Belgian court asked whether the fact that the licensing agreement in question was limited to the territory of a Member State, and that a series of such assignments might result in the partitioning of the internal market as regards the undertaking of economic activity in the film industry, should result in its prohibition.

Held

'It should be noted, by way of a preliminary observation, that [Article 36 TFEU] permits prohibitions or restrictions on trade between member states provided that they are justified on grounds inter alia of the protection of industrial and commercial property, a term which covers literary and artistic property, including copyright, whereas the main proceedings are concerned with the question of prohibitions or restrictions placed upon the free movement of services.' (para 10)

'In this regard, as the court held in its judgment of … (*Coditel v Cine-vog Films* (1980) ECR 881), the problems involved in the observance of a film producer's rights in relation to the requirements of the treaty are not the same as those which arise in connection with literary and artistic works, the placing of which at the disposal of the public is inseparable from the circulation of the material form of the works, as in the case of books or records, whereas the film belongs to the category of literary and artistic works made available to the public by performances which may be infinitely repeated and the commercial exploitation of which comes under the movement of services, no matter whether the means whereby it is shown to the public be the cinema or television. In the same judgment the court further held that the right of the owner of the copyright in a film and his assigns to require fees for any showing of that film is part of the essential function of copyright.' (paras 11, 12)

'The distinction, implicit in [Article 36 TFEU], between the existence of a right conferred by the legislation of a Member State in regard to the protection of artistic and intellectual property, which cannot be affected by the provisions of the treaty, and the exercise of such right, which might constitute a disguised restriction on trade between Member States, also applies where that right is exercised in the context of the movement of services.' (para 13)

'Just as it is conceivable that certain aspects of the manner in which the right is exercised may prove to be incompatible with [Articles 56 and 57 TFEU] it is equally conceivable that some aspects may prove to be incompatible with [Article 101 TFEU] where they serve to give effect to an agreement, decision or concerted practice which may have as its object or effect the prevention, restriction or distortion of competition within the [internal] market.' (para 14)

'However, the mere fact that the owner of the copyright in a film has granted to a sole licensee the exclusive right to exhibit that film in the territory of a Member State and, consequently, to prohibit, during a specified period, its showing by others, is not sufficient to justify the finding that such a contract must be regarded as the purpose, the means or the result of an agreement, decision or concerted practice prohibited by the Treaty.' (para 15)

'The characteristics of the cinematographic industry and of its markets in the [Union], especially those relating to dubbing and subtitling for the benefit of different language groups, to the possibilities of television broadcasts, and to the system of financing cinematographic production in Europe serve to show that an exclusive exhibition licence is not, in itself, such as to prevent, restrict or distort competition. Although copyright in a film and the right deriving from it, namely that of exhibiting the film, are not, therefore, as such subject to the prohibitions contained in [Article 101 TFEU], the exercise of those rights may, none the less, come within the said prohibitions where there are economic or legal circumstances the effect of which is to restrict film distribution to an appreciable degree or to distort competition on the cinematographic market, regard being had to the specific characteristics of that market.' (paras 16, 17)

'Since neither the question referred to the court nor the file on the case provides any information in this respect, it is for the national court to make such inquiries as may be necessary. It must therefore be stated that it is for national courts, where appropriate, to make such inquiries and in particular to establish whether or not the exercise of the exclusive right to exhibit a cinematographic film creates barriers which are artificial and unjustifiable in terms of the needs of the cinematographic industry, or the possibility of charging fees which exceed a fair return on investment, or an exclusivity the duration of which is disproportionate to those requirements, and whether or not, from a general point of view, such exercise within a given geographic area is such as to prevent, restrict or distort competition within the [Internal] Market.' (paras 18, 19)

'Accordingly, the answer to be given to the question referred to the court must be that a contract whereby the owner of the copyright in a film grants an exclusive right to exhibit that film for a specific period in the territory of a member state is not, as such, subject to the prohibitions contained in [Article 101 TFEU]. It is, however, where appropriate, for the national court to ascertain whether, in a given case, the manner in which the exclusive right conferred by that contract is exercised is subject to a situation in the economic or legal sphere the object or effect of which is to prevent or restrict the distribution of films or to distort competition within the cinematographic market, regard being had to the specific characteristics of that market.' (para 20)

Comment

Absolute territorial protection did not in itself breach Article 101 TFEU. *Coditel II* is cited in the Guidelines on the application of [Article 101 TFEU] to technology transfer agreements, [2004] OJ C101/2: 'On the other hand, the licensing of rights in performances and other rights related to copyright is considered to raise particular issues and it may not be warranted to assess such licensing on the basis of the principles developed in these guidelines. In the case of the various rights related to performances, value is created not by the reproduction and sale of copies of a product but by each individual performance of the protected work. Such exploitation can take various forms including the performance, showing or the renting of protected material such as films, music or sporting events. In the application of [Article 101 TFEU] the specificities of the work and the way in which it is exploited must be taken into account (See in this respect Case 262/81, *Coditel (II)*). For instance, resale restrictions may give rise to less competition concerns whereas particular concerns may arise where licensors impose on their licensees to extend to each of the licensors more favourable conditions obtained by one of them. The Commission will therefore not apply the TTBER and the present guidelines by way of analogy to the licensing of these other rights.' (para 52)

In Case IV/31.734 *Film Purchases by German Television Stations* [1989] OJ L284/36, the Commission considered the legality of agreements on the acquisition of television rights. In its decision it made reference to the *Coditel II* judgment and distinguished it from the facts of that case. It noted that in *Coditel II* the court held that the granting of an exclusive right to exhibit a film was not, as such, a restriction of competition. However, the exercise of such a right may result in a restriction of competition, in particular when the exercise of the right creates barriers which are artificial and unjustifiable (para 42). The Commission was of the opinion that in the case before it, the unusually large number of the licensed rights, the duration of the agreements, and the provision in the agreement which provided for right of first negotiation, constituted a restriction of competition. The Commission found these restrictions disproportionate within the meaning of the *Coditel II* judgment. However, it subsequently exempted the agreements under Article 101(3) TFEU.

Re the Agreement of Davide-Campari Milano SpA	**Licensing**
Cases IV/171, IV/856, IV/172, IV/117, IV/28.173	Trademark Licences
European Commission, [1978] OJ L70/69, [1978] 2 CMLR 397	Article 101(3) TFEU

Facts

Campari-Milano, the holder of the international trademarks 'Bitter Campari' and 'Cordial Campari', set up a network of licensees to manufacture and sell its products throughout Europe. The agreements governing this network included an exclusive right to use its trademarks for the manufacture of its aperitifs in distinct territories. Under the agreements the licensees undertook not to handle competing products, not to carry on any active sales policy or set up any branches outside their respective allotted territories, but were authorised to meet unsolicited export orders. Following the notification of the agreements to the Commission, and their subsequent amendment, the Commission exempted them under Article 101(3) TFEU.

Held

Article 101 TFEU

'The exclusive rights given to the licensees prevent Campari-Milano from granting trademark licences for its products to other parties in the Netherlands, Germany, France, Belgium, Luxembourg and Denmark and also from itself manufacturing those products in these countries. The proprietor of a trademark has the exclusive right to use the distinctive mark on first sale and to protect the product against infringement of the mark. The proprietor of the trademark may, by licence, authorise the use of the protected mark, by third parties. However, if he undertakes only to allow one single undertaking to use his trademark in a particular territory and to refrain himself from manufacturing products bearing his trademark there, he loses his freedom to respond to other requests for licences and the competitive advantage to be gained from manufacture by himself in this territory. In the case in point, the exclusive nature of the licence entails a restriction upon Campari-Milano's freedom to use its marks as well as preventing third parties, particularly manufacturers of alcoholic beverages, from using them as licensees, however much they may find it in their interests to do so.' (Part A, para 1)

'The non-competition clause … prevents the licensees from manufacturing or selling products for the whole duration of the agreements. They may not buy such products, nor acquire licences to manufacture or sell them. The effect of the restriction is appreciable, since at present all the licensees, except the French one, are already distributing a whole range of beverages other than bitter Campari and all have a substantial turnover on their total business.' (Part Ii, para 2)

'The ban preventing Campari-Milano and its licensees from engaging in an active sales policy outside their respective territories prevents the licensees and the licensor from seeking custom in the territories of the other parties. They are therefore excluded from actively competing on those territories, while benefiting from a degree of protection within their own territory, where the only imports made must be in response to unsolicited orders. This ban must be considered as having an appreciable effect, since not only Campari-Milano but also all the licensees have considerable production capacity, which would enable them to supply other markets in the [Union]. While such deliveries would primarily be of products manufactured according to the specifications in respect of alcoholic strength, bottle content, and labelling required on the manufacturer's home market, they could also be for bitter manufactured according to other specifications required on the export market, for manufacturers can buy the alcohol without being taxed, in order to export the finished product. Furthermore, they may change the alcoholic strength or presentation of the product where they judge that the size of an order or at any rate the possibility of steady sales makes the manufacture of such a product and the use of new labels or bottles profitable.' (Part Ii, para 3)

'The obligation to supply the original Italian product to diplomatic corps, ship's victuallers, foreign armed forces and generally speaking all organizations with duty-free facilities prevents the licensees from supplying bitter which they have manufactured themselves to these consumers. In view of the licensees' production capacities, this restriction also has an appreciable effect.' (Part Ii, para 4)

'The exclusive rights granted by Campari-Milano prevent Campari-Milano from granting other licences which would enable other parties to use its trademarks in the allotted territories and to export from these territories to other parts of the [internal] market. They also prevent Campari-Milano itself from manufacturing bitter in these territories and consequently from exporting from such territories. The exclusion of competing products prevents the licensees from marketing such products across borders between member states, or from making licence agreements in relation to such products with undertakings in other member states. The ban on engaging in an active sales policy outside their respective territories prevents Campari-Milano and its licensees from freely disposing throughout the [internal] market of the bitter they have manufactured, restricting them to their exclusive territories, and thus affects international trade in the product. The obligation to supply certain consumers with the original Italian product rather than that which they themselves manufacture means that the licensees have to obtain supplies of bitter Campari from Italy and thus affects international trade in the product.' (Part Ii, para B)

Article 101(3) TFEU

The restrictions on competition mentioned above satisfy the tests of Article 101(3) TFEU.

'The exclusivity granted by Campari-Milano contributes to improving the production and distribution of the products. By giving each licensee a guarantee that no other undertaking will obtain a licence within its allocated territory, and that in this territory neither Campari-Milano nor any other licensee may manufacture products bearing the licensor's trademark this commitment confers upon each licensee an advantage in its allotted territory. This territorial advantage is such as to permit a sufficient return on the investment made by each licensee for the purpose of manufacturing the product bearing the trademark under conditions acceptable to the licensor and holder of the trademark, and it enables the licensee to increase its production capacity and constantly to improve the already long established distribution network. In practice the exclusivity granted has allowed each licensee to improve its existing plant and to build new plant. It has also enabled each licensee to strengthen its efforts to promote the brand, doubling the total volume of sales in the Benelux countries and Germany over the last six years, and, by establishing a multistage distribution network, to secure a constantly increasing number of customers and thus to ensure supplies throughout the allotted territory.' (Part Iii, para 1)

'The ban on dealing in competing products also contributes to improving distribution of the licensed products by concentrating sales efforts, encouraging the build-up of stocks and shortening delivery times. The restriction on the licensees' freedom to deal in other products at the same time as the products here in question prevents the licensees from neglecting Campari in the event of conflict between the promotion of Campari sales and possible interest in another product. Although a non-competition clause in a licensing agreement concerning industrial property rights based on the result of a creative activity, such as a patent, would constitute a barrier to technical and economic progress by preventing the licensees from taking an interest in other techniques and products, this is not the case with the licensing agreements under consideration here. The aim pursued by the parties, as is clear from the agreements taken as a whole, is to decentralize manufacture within the [Union] and to rationalize the distribution system linked to it, and thus to promote the sale of Campari-Milano's bitter, manufactured from the same concentrates provided by Campari-Milano, according to the same mixing process and using the same ingredients, and bearing the same trademark, as that of the licensor. The prohibition on dealing in competing products, therefore, makes for improved distribution of the relevant product in the same way as do exclusive dealing agreements containing a similar clause, which are automatically exempted by [Regulation (EC) No 2790/1999]; a declaration that the prohibition in [Article 101(1) TFEU] is inapplicable to this clause is accordingly justified.' (Part Iii, para 2)

'Distribution will also be improved by the prohibition against the parties engaging in an active sales policy outside their respective territories. This restriction on the licensees will help to concentrate their sales efforts, and provide a better supply to consumers in their territories for which they have particular responsibility, without preventing buyers elsewhere in the [Union] from securing supplies freely from any of the licensees. Application of the same restriction to Campari-Milano encourages the efforts made by the each territory allotted; the licensees thus have the benefit of a certain protection relative to Campari-Milano's strong market position.' (Part Iii, para 3)

'The obligation on licensees to supply the original Italian product rather than that which they themselves manufacture, when selling to diplomatic corps, ships' victuallers, foreign armed forces and generally speaking all organizations with duty-free facilities also helps to promote sales of Campari-Milano's bitter. By restricting licensees' freedom to supply the products they manufacture themselves it makes sure that particular catego-ries of consumers, who are deemed to be outside the licensee's territory and are usually required to move frequently from one territory to another, can always purchase the same original product with all its traditional features as regards both composition and outward appearance. Even though quality standards are observed, it is impossible in particular to avoid differences in taste between the products of the various manufacturers. This obligation is thus designed to prevent these consumers from turning to other competing products and to ensure that they continue to buy Bitter Campari, with the facility of being able to obtain stocks from their local dealer. Further, such consumers are not prevented from freely obtaining the licensees' own products even though any such purchases would be on the normal trading conditions applicable to non-duty free pur-chasers.' (Part Iii, para 4)

'The licensing agreements have increased the quantities of Bitter Campari available to consumers and improved distribution, so that consumers benefit directly. There are other producers of bitter on the mar-ket, and effective competition will be strengthened by the growing quantities produced by Campari-Milano's licensees, so that it can be assumed that the improvements resulting from the agreements and the benefits which the licensees obtain from them are shared by consumers. As buyers may secure supplies of bitter from other territories through unsolicited orders, they are in a position to exert pressure on the prices charged by the exclusive licensee in their territory if these should be too high.' (Part Iii, para B)

'The restrictions of competition imposed on the parties involved must be considered indispensable to the attainment of the benefits set out above. None of the restrictions could be omitted without endangering the parties' object of promoting sales of bitter Campari by concentrating the activities of the licensees on this product and offering the same original product to certain customers. In particular, none of the licensees and in all probability no other undertaking in the spirituous liquors industry would have been prepared to make the investment necessary for a significant increase in sales of bitter if it were not sure of being protected from competition from other licensees or Campari-Milano itself.' (Part Iii, para C)

'The licensing agreements which are the subject of this decision do not give Campari-Milano or its licensees the possibility of eliminating competition in respect of a substantial part of the bitter products in question. In the [Union] there exists a fairly large number of other well-known brands of bitter, which are all able to compete against Bitter Campari …' (Part Iii, para D)

Comment

The case provides an illustrative example of the application of Article 101 TFEU. Several of the provisions in the agreements were found to fall outside Article 101(1). These included, among other things, a ban on exports outside the internal market, and obligation to buy secret raw materials from the licensor. Other pro-visions such as the exclusivity clause and the ban on active sales (see above extracts) were held to infringe Article 101(1). However, these provisions satisfied the conditions under Article 101(3) TFEU. Thus, overall the (modified) agreements were exempted under Article 101(3) TFEU.

Moosehead/Whitbread	**Licensing**
Case IV/32.736	Trademark Licences
European Commission, [1990] OJ L100/32	Trademark Non-challenge Clause

Facts

Moosehead Breweries Limited notified to the Commission a number of agreements concerning the manufacture of a beer in the United Kingdom which is sold by Moosehead in Canada and other countries under the trademark 'Moosehead' ('the Product'). Under the Agreements, Moosehead granted to Whitbread the sole and exclusive right to produce and promote, market, and sell the Product. It also agreed to provide Whitbread, under a confidentiality agreement, with all the relevant know-how necessary to produce the Product, and to supply it with all yeast which may be necessary. Whitbread agreed to limit its activities to the UK and refrain from active sales outside that territory. It also agreed not to produce or promote within that territory any other beer identified as a Canadian beer. The Product was to be sold only under the trademark 'Moosehead' which was exclusively licensed to Whitbread in the territory. The agreement included a trademark non-challenge clause.

Held

Article 101 TFEU

'The exclusive trademark licence for the production and marketing of the Product, the prohibition of active sales outside the Territory and the non-competition clause, ... fall under the prohibition of [Article 101(1) TFEU] since they have as their object or effect an appreciable restriction of competition within the [internal] market. In this case, the exclusive character of the licence has, as a consequence, the exclusion of third parties, namely the five other large brewers in the Territory, from the use, as licensees, of the Moosehead trademark, in spite of their potential interest and their ability to do so. Likewise, the prohibition of active sales outside the Territory by the licensee and the ban on marketing competing brands of beer are appreciable restrictions of competition since Whitbread, because of its large production capacity, would be able to supply other markets within the [Internal] Market and to distribute other Canadian brands.' (para 16.1)

'The know-how provisions ... do not fall under [Article 101(1) TFEU] because the grant of know-how is not exclusive and the obligations imposed on the licensee are simply ancillary to the grant of the trademark licence and enable the licence to take effect. In particular the exclusive purchasing obligation regarding yeast set out in paragraph (9)2, does not fall under [Article 101(1) TFEU] because it is necessary to ensure technically satisfactory exploitation of the licenced technology and a similar identity between the lager produced originally by Moosehead and the same lager produced by Whitbread.' (para 16.3)

'(a) In general terms, a trademark non-challenge clause can refer to the ownership and/or the validity of the trademark: The ownership of a trademark may, in particular, be challenged on grounds of the prior use or prior registration of an identical trademark. A clause in an exclusive trademark licence agreement obliging the licensee not to challenge the ownership of a trademark, as specified in the above paragraph, does not constitute a restriction of competition within the meaning of [Article 101(1) TFEU]. Whether or not the licensor or licensee has the ownership of the trademark, the use of it by any other party is prevented in any event, and competition would thus not be affected. The validity of a trademark may be contested on any ground under national law, and in particular on the grounds that it is generic or descriptive in nature. In such an event, should the challenge be upheld, the trademark may fall [in] the public domain and may thereafter be used without restriction by the licensee and any other party. Such a clause may constitute a restriction of competition within the meaning of [Article 101(1) TFEU], because it may contribute to the maintenance of a trademark that would be an [u]njustified barrier to entry into given market. Moreover in order for any restriction of competition to fall under [Article 101(1) TFEU], it must be appreciable. The ownership of a trademark only gives the holder the exclusive right to sell products under that name. Other parties are free to sell the product in question under a different trademark or tradename. Only where the use of a well-known trademark would be an important advantage to any company entering or competing in any given market and the absence of which therefore constitutes a significant barrier to entry, would this clause which impedes the licensee to challenge the validity of the trademark, constitute an appreciable restriction of competition within the meaning of [Article 101(1) TFEU].

(b) In the present case Whitbread is unable to challenge both the ownership and the validity of the trademark.

As far as the validity of the trademark is concerned it must be noted that the trademark is comparatively new to the lager market in the Territory. The maintenance of the "Moosehead" trademark will thus not constitute an appreciable barrier to entry for any other company entering or competing in the beer market in the United Kingdom. Accordingly, the Commission considers that the trademark non-challenge clause included in the Agreement, in so far as it concerns its validity (see the second indent of point 15.4 above), does not constitute an appreciable restriction of competition and does not fall under [Article 101(1) TFEU].

Furthermore, in so far as this clause concerns ownership, it does not constitute a restriction of competition within the meaning of [Article 101(1) TFEU].' (para 16.4)

Article 101(3) TFEU

Having considered the favourable effects for the production and marketing of beer resulting from the clauses which are restrictive of competition, and in particular the non-competition clause, the Commission considers that they are indispensable to the attainment of the objectives of Article 101(3) TFEU. (para 16.2)

Comment

The exclusive trademark and restriction on active sales were found to infringe Article 101(1) TFEU. An individual exemption was subsequently granted under Regulation 17/62.

In relation to the non-challenge clause, the Commission acknowledged that it may be caught by Article 101(1) but only when the trademark is in the public domain and is open to use by a third-party, since the prohibition could constitute a barrier to market entry. When, however, as in this case, the trademark is still exclusive, third parties cannot make use of the trademark irrespective of the existence of a no-challenge clause. Contrast this approach with *Windsurfing International Inc v Commission* (page 376 below).

Before considering individual exemption, the Commission noted that the agreements in question did not benefit from Regulation 556/89 which applied to agreements combining know-how and trademark licenses. The Commission noted that in the present case the principal interest of the parties lied in the exploitation of the trademark rather than of the know-how. Since know-how was considered ancillary to the trademark, the block exemption was not applicable. In this respect note the following extracts from the Guidelies on the application of [Article 101 TFEU] to technology transfer agreements: 'The TTBER only covers the licensing of other types of intellectual property such as trademarks and copyright, other than software copyright, to the extent that they are directly related to the exploitation of the licensed technology and do not constitute the primary object of the agreement. This condition ensures that agreements covering other types of intellectual property rights are only block exempted to the extent that these other intellectual property rights serve to enable the licensee to better exploit the licensed technology. The licensor may for instance authorise the licensee to use his trademark on the products incorporating the licensed technology. The trademark licence may allow the licensee to better exploit the licensed technology by allowing consumers to make an immediate link between the product and the characteristics imputed to it by the licensed technology. An obligation on the licensee to use the licensor's trademark may also promote the dissemination of technology by allowing the licensor to identify himself as the source of the underlying technology. However, where the value of the licensed technology to the licensee is limited because he already employs an identical or very similar technology and the main object of the agreement is the trademark, the TTBER does not apply.' (para 50)

FA Premier League and others v QC Leisure and others	**Licensing**
Case C-429/08	Exclusive Broadcasting Licence
Court of Justice, [2011] ECR I-9083, [2012] 1 CMLR 29	Absolute Territorial Exclusivity

Facts

A reference for a preliminary ruling made in proceedings involving the English Football Association Premier League Ltd (FAPL) and others, concerning exclusive licences of broadcasting rights, granted by FAPL on a territorial basis. The exclusive territorial licence was designed to achieve optimal exploitation of the copyright for the live transmission of FAPL football matches. Under the terms of the licence, broadcasters agreed not to supply their territorial-based decoding devices outside the territory covered by their licence agreement. Despite this, undertakings imported decoding cards from other territories into the UK and used them to access live transmission at a cost lower than would otherwise be charged locally in the UK. In the main proceedings the FAPL attempted to block this practice. The High Court referred several questions to the Court of Justice, among other things, asking whether the exclusive territorial licence agreement constituted an infringement of Article 101 TFEU.

Held

'In order to assess whether the object of an agreement is anti-competitive, regard must be had inter alia to the content of its provisions, the objectives it seeks to attain and the economic and legal context of which it forms a part (see, to this effect, *GlaxoSmithKline Services and Others v Commission and Others*, paragraph 58 and the case-law cited).' (para 136)

'As regards licence agreements in respect of intellectual property rights, it is apparent from the Court's case-law that the mere fact that the right holder has granted to a sole licensee the exclusive right to broadcast protected subject-matter from a Member State, and consequently to prohibit its transmission by others, during a specified period is not sufficient to justify the finding that such an agreement has an anti-competitive object (Case 262/81 *Coditel and Others* ('*Coditel II*') [1982] ECR 3381, paragraph 15).' (para 137)

However, an agreement which restores the divisions between national markets is liable to frustrate the Treaty's objective of integration through the establishment of a single market. Accordingly, where a licence agreement is designed to prohibit or limit the cross-border provision of broadcasting services, it is deemed to have as its object the restriction of competition. The obligation on the broadcasters not to supply decoding devices enabling access to the protected subject-matter with a view to their use outside the territory covered by the licence agreement results in absolute territorial exclusivity in the area covered by its licence and, thus, all competition between broadcasters in the field of those services to be eliminated. (paras 139–42)

Comment

The Court endorsed an expansive approach to what constitutes a violation by object and held that exclusive territorial licence agreement has an anticompetitive object as it granted each broadcaster with absolute territorial exclusivity. The agreements did not satisfy the conditions for exemption under Article 101(3) TFEU.

'A contractual obligation linked to a broadcasting licence requiring the broadcaster to prevent its satellite decoder cards which enable reception of the licensed programme content from being used outside the licensed territory has the same effect as agreements to prevent or restrict parallel exports. Such an obligation is intended to prevent any competition between broadcasters through a reciprocal compartmentalisation of licensed territories. Such licences with absolute territorial protection are incompatible with the internal market. There is therefore no reason to treat such agreements any differently from agreements intended to prevent parallel trade.' (AG Kokkot's opinion, para 248)

Windsurfing International Inc v Commission	**Licensing**
Case 193/83	Article 101(1) TFEU
Court of Justice, [1986] ECR 611, [1986] 3 CMLR 611	Non-territorial Restrictions

Facts

Windsurfing International Inc, a US-based company which develops and sells sailboards, brought an action for annulment before the Court of Justice against a Commission decision which found that a number of clauses in licensing agreements, concluded prior to 1981 with certain German undertakings, infringed Article 101 TFEU.

Held

The first of the clauses at issue imposed on licensees the obligation to exploit Windsurfing International Inc's invention only for the purpose of mounting its patented rig on certain types of board specified in the agreement, and the obligation to submit for the licensor's approval any new board types on which the licensees intended to use the rigs. It is clear from their wording that the agreements defined the licensed product as a complete sailboard with specified characteristics and subject any modification to a board to the licensor's approval. This limitation restricts the types of sailboards which could be manufactured by the licensees. The Commission noted on this point that 'the fact that an undertaking which has granted licences to other undertakings is the proprietor of an industrial property right does not entitle it to control the market in the products under licence. Restrictions on the field of use of the products may be acceptable but only if they relate to different products belonging to different markets. The design and quality of a product are the sole concern of the licensee. According to the Commission, standards of quality and safety may fall outside the scope of [Article 101(1) TFEU] only if they relate to a product actually covered by the patent, if they are intended to ensure no more than that the technical instructions as described in the patent are in fact carried out and if they are agreed upon in advance and on the basis of objectively verifiable criteria.' (paras 38–43)

'It is necessary to determine whether quality controls on the sailboards are covered by the specific subject-matter of the patent. As the commission rightly points out, such controls do not come within the specific subject-matter of the patent unless they relate to a product covered by the patent since their sole justification is that they ensure "that the technical instructions as described in the patent and used by the licensee may be carried into effect". In this case, however, it has been established that it may reasonably be considered that the German patent does not cover the board.' (para 45)

'However, even on the assumption that the German patent covers the complete sailboard, and therefore includes the board, it cannot be accepted without more that controls such as those provided for in the licensing agreements were compatible with [Article 101 TFEU]. Such controls must be effected according to quality and safety criteria agreed upon in advance and on the basis of objectively verifiable criteria. If it were otherwise, the discretionary nature of those controls would in effect enable a licensor to impose his own selection of models upon the licensees, which would be contrary to [Article 101 TFEU]. Windsurfing international has been unable to show that there were any objective criteria laid down in advance because no indication of the technical verifications to be carried out is contained in the agreements.' (paras 46–7)

'It must therefore be held that Windsurfing International's real interest lay in ensuring that there was sufficient product differentiation between its licensees' sailboards to cover the widest possible spectrum of market demand … The protection afforded by the patent may only be claimed in the case of copies of products manufactured by the licensor himself. In so far as the clause at issue enabled Windsurfing International to detect and prevent the slavish imitation of boards by licensees, there can be no doubt that the clause constituted a restriction on the freedom of competition.' (paras 49, 52)

The second of the clauses at issue relates to the obligation on the licensees to sell the components covered by the German patent, and in particular the rigs, only in conjunction with boards approved by the licensor, as complete sailboards. The patent in this case is confined to the rig. That being the case, it cannot be accepted that the obligation to sell the patented product in conjunction with a product outside the scope of the patent is indispensable to the exploitation of the patent. Such obligation restricts competition. (paras 54–9)

The third disputed clause relates to the obligation on the licensees to pay royalties on sales of components calculated on the basis of the net selling price of the complete product. Such a method, which bases the royalties on the net selling price of a complete sailboard, restricts competition with regard to the separate sale of boards, which were not covered by the German patent. However, with respect to the sale of rigs, the royalty levied on their sale proved not to have been higher than that laid down for the sale of separate rigs. It follows that that method of calculation did not have as its object or effect a restriction of competition in the sale of separate rigs. (paras 60–67)

The fourth of the clauses at issue relates to the obligation on the licensees to affix to boards manufactured and marketed in Germany a notice stating 'licensed by Hoyle Schweitzer' or 'licensed by Windsurfing International'. The Commission maintains that only the components covered by the patent constitute places in which such a notice may be legitimately affixed. Accordingly, a notice affixed to the board creates the false impression that the complete sailboard is the subject of the patent. Despite Windsurfing International's contention that it was not the object of the clause to distort competition but merely to convey the information, by requiring such a notice it encouraged uncertainty as to whether or not the board too was covered by the patent and thereby diminished the consumer's confidence in the licensees so as to gain a competitive advantage for itself. Such a clause is incompatible with Article 101 TFEU. (paras 68–74)

The fifth disputed clause relates to the obligation on the licensees to acknowledge Windsurfing International's trademarks. The Commission argued that the acknowledgement of a trademark's validity logically implies that no attempt will be made to establish its invalidity, and this is contrary to Article 101 TFEU (no-challenge clause in trademark law). 'Windsurfing International's interest in halting the process whereby its trade-marks were being turned into generic designations of the product could not be safeguarded by means of a clause which clearly did not come within the specific subject-matter of the patent and was imposed on the licensees in the agreements relating to the exploitation of the patent even though the subject-matter of the clause was quite different.' Such a clause restricts competition and is contrary to Article 101 TFEU. (paras 80, 75–81)

The sixth clause at issue provides for the obligation on the licensees to restrict production of the licensed product to a specific manufacturing plant in Germany, together with Windsurfing International's right to terminate the agreement should the licensees change their production site. 'Windsurfing International clearly cannot rely on the specific subject-matter of the patent in order to gain the protection afforded by the patent in a country where there is no patent protection. In so far as Windsurfing International prohibited its licensees from also manufacturing the product in a country where it had no patent protection and so marketing that product without paying a royalty, it limited freedom of competition by means of a clause which had nothing to do with the patent.' That conclusion is not affected by Windsurfing International's argument that it needed to maintain quality controls over the products of its licensees. Such controls are permissible only with regard to the patented product itself and on the basis of objective criteria laid down in advance. (paras 85, 82–6)

The seventh of the clauses which the Commission regards as incompatible with Article 101(1) TFEU relates to the obligation on the licensees not to challenge the validity of the licensed patents. 'It must be stated that such a clause clearly does not fall within the specific subject-matter of the patent, which cannot be interpreted as also affording protection against actions brought in order to challenge the patent's validity, in view of the fact that it is in the public interest to eliminate any obstacle to economic activity which may arise where a patent was granted in error.' The clauses constitute an unlawful restriction on competition between manufacturers. (paras 92, 89–93)

Since Windsurfing International did not notify these clauses for exemption according to the provisions of Regulation 17/62 it is unnecessary to ascertain whether they could be regarded as satisfying the requirements stipulated in Article 101(3) TFEU, which is in any event disputed by the Commission. (paras 98–101)

Comment

The clauses in the licensing agreements concerning quality control, tying, licensed-by notices, no-challenge clauses and royalty calculation were found to constitute infringements of Article 101 TFEU. The Court of Justice overruled one clause of the Commission decision which found the obligation to pay royalties on components on the net selling price of the product to infringe Article 101 TFEU, in so far as it applies to rigs.

Note that under Regulation 1/2003, which replaced Regulation 17/62, there is now no need to notify the Commission prior to any agreement in order to obtain an individual exemption.

With respect to the calculation of royalties (paragraph 67 above), note the Guidelines on the application of Article [101 TFEU] to technology transfer agreements ([2004] OJ C101/02) which include reference to the judgment. Article 4 of the TTBER distinguishes between agreements between competitors and agreements between non-competitors. In paragraph 81 of its guidelines the Commission notes that 'The hardcore restriction contained in Article 4(1)(a) also covers agreements whereby royalties are calculated on the basis of all product sales irrespective of whether the licensed technology is being used. Such agreements are also caught by Article 4(1)(d) according to which the licensee must not be restricted in his ability to use his own technology. … In general such agreements restrict competition since the agreement raises the cost of using the licensee's own competing technology and restricts competition that existed in the absence of the agreement [Case 193/83, *Windsurfing International*, para 67]. This is so both in the case of reciprocal and non-reciprocal arrangements. Exceptionally, however, an agreement whereby royalties are calculated on the basis of all product sales may fulfil the conditions of [Article 101(3) TFEU] in an individual case where on the basis of objective factors it can be concluded that the restriction is indispensable for pro-competitive licensing to occur. This may be the case where in the absence of the restraint it would be impossible or unduly difficult to calculate and monitor the royalty payable by the licensee, for instance because the licensor's technology leaves no visible trace on the final product and practicable alternative monitoring methods are unavailable.'

In relation to the non-challenge clause, contrast the analysis in Case IV/32.736 (page 373 above) with that conducted by the Court of Justice in this case. The Court found the clause to constitute an unlawful restriction on competition between manufacturers. It held that 'such a clause clearly does not fall within the specific subject-matter of the patent, which cannot be interpreted as also affording protection against actions brought in order to challenge the patent's validity, in view of the fact that it is in the public interest to eliminate any obstacle to economic activity which may arise where a patent was granted in error.' (para 92)

Facts

An appeal against a Commission Decision which found Microsoft to have infringed Article 102 TFEU by refusing to supply interoperability information to its competitors and by tying its Windows media player with its operating system. With respect to the refusal to supply, the Commission found this to have infringed Article 102(b) TFEU by limiting technical development to the prejudice of consumers (see page 379 above).

The Commission ordered Microsoft to license on 'reasonable and non-discriminatory' (RAND) terms the relevant interoperability information to its competitors. It noted that on balance, the possible negative impact of an order to supply on Microsoft's incentives to innovate is outweighed by its positive impact on the level of innovation of the whole industry (including Microsoft). On appeal, the General Court commented on the requirement to licence on a RAND basis.

Held

According to the Commission's decision, Microsoft is required to give access to the interoperability information to undertakings wishing to develop and implement work group server operating systems. (paras 808, 809)

'[T]here is nothing to prevent Microsoft, where the interoperability information sought by a given undertaking relates to a technology covered by a patent (or by another form of intellectual property right), from giving access to and authorising the use of that information by granting a licence, subject to the application of reasonable and non-discriminatory conditions.' (para 810)

'The mere fact that the contested decision requires that the conditions to which any licences are subject be reasonable and non-discriminatory does not mean that Microsoft must impose the same conditions on every undertaking seeking such licences. It is not precluded that the conditions may be adapted to the specific situation of each of those undertakings and vary, for example, according to the extent of the information to which they seek access or the type of products in which they intend to implement the information.' (para 811)

Comment

The General Court backed the Commission's requirement that Microsoft license on a RAND basis. The General Court did not seek to add conditions or limitation of the RAND benchmark and retained its flexibility to enable its application on a case-by-case basis in consideration of market realities.

In its decision of 27 February 2008 (Case COMP/C-3/34.792 'Fixation of Penalty Payments to comply with Commission's Decisions' C (2008) 764 final) the Commission fined Microsoft for failure to comply with the terms of its first Decision. In that Decision the Commission considered the RAND commitments and noted that:

'in order for it to be reasonable, any remuneration charged by Microsoft for access to or use of the Interoperability Information should be justified by showing that it allows competitors to viably compete with Microsoft's work group server operating system and that it represents a fair compensation for the value of the technology that is transferred by Microsoft to recipients of the Interoperability Information beyond the mere ability to interoperate, namely excluding the "strategic value" stemming from Microsoft's market power in the client PC and work group server operating system markets.' (para 107)

Huawei Technologies Co Ltd v ZTE Corp	**Standard essential patents**
Case C-170/13	FRAND
Court of Justice, [2015] 5 CMLR 14	Abuse of Dominance

Facts

Huawei Technologies, a company active in the telecommunications sector, was the proprietor of a patent that was essential to a standard established by a standardisation body—the European Telecommunications Standards Institute (ETSI). Huawei Technologies notified this Standard Essential patent (SEP) to ETSI and undertook to grant licences to third parties on FRAND terms. The company later brought an action for infringement in the Düsseldorf Court against ZTE which had negotiated a possible license agreement with Huawei Technologies but eventually used the patent without paying a royalty. The Court considered that the outcome of the proceedings would depend on whether the action brought by Huawei Technologies constituted an abuse of its dominant position. The Court noted the judgment of the German Federal Court of Justice in *Orange Book*, according to which the proprietor of a patent that seeks a prohibitory injunction would abuse its dominant position only when the defendant has made the applicant an unconditional offer to conclude a licensing agreement not limited exclusively to cases of infringement, and uses the patent before the applicant accepts such an offer. The Düsseldorf Court subsequently stayed the proceedings and referred to the European Court of Justice questions about the duties of a proprietor of a SEP which agrees with a standardisation body to FRAND conditions, and the possibility that it may abuse its dominant market position if it brings an action against a patent infringer that is willing to negotiate a licence.

Held

The right to bring an action for infringement forms part of the rights of the proprietor of an intellectual-property right. Only in exceptional circumstances would the exercise of an exclusive right linked to an intellectual-property right by a dominant proprietor involve abusive conduct for the purposes of Article 102 TFEU. (paras 46–7)

The facts in this case are distinguishable from those in earlier cases (such as *Magill*, page 388 above; *IMS Health*, page 387 above). In this case: (1) the patent at issue is essential to a standard, rendering its use indispensable to all competitors that comply with that standard; (2) the patent at issue obtained SEP status only in return for the proprietor's irrevocable undertaking to grant licences on FRAND terms. (paras 48–51)

'Although the proprietor of the essential patent at issue has the right to bring an action for a prohibitory injunction or for the recall of products, the fact that that patent has obtained SEP status means that its proprietor can prevent products manufactured by competitors from appearing or remaining on the market and, thereby, reserve to itself the manufacture of the products in question.' (para 52)

'In those circumstances, and having regard to the fact that an undertaking to grant licences on FRAND terms creates legitimate expectations on the part of third parties that the proprietor of the SEP will in fact grant licences on such terms, a refusal by the proprietor of the SEP to grant a licence on those terms may, in principle, constitute an abuse within the meaning of Article 102 TFEU.' (para 53)

'The proprietor of the patent is obliged only to grant a licence on FRAND terms. In the case in the main proceedings, the parties are not in agreement as to what is required by FRAND terms. … In such a situation, in order to prevent an action for a prohibitory injunction or for the recall of products from being regarded as abusive, the proprietor of an SEP must comply with conditions which seek to ensure a fair balance between the interests concerned. … This need for a high level of protection for intellectual-property rights means that, in principle, the proprietor may not be deprived of the right to have recourse to legal proceedings to ensure effective enforcement of his exclusive rights, and that, in principle, the user of those rights, if he is not the proprietor, is required to obtain a licence prior to any use.' (paras 54–5)

'Accordingly, the proprietor of an SEP which considers that that SEP is the subject of an infringement cannot, without infringing Article 102 TFEU, bring an action for a prohibitory injunction or for the recall of products against the alleged infringer without notice or prior consultation with the alleged infringer, even if the SEP has already been used by the alleged infringer.' (para 60)

'Secondly, after the alleged infringer has expressed its willingness to conclude a licensing agreement on FRAND terms, it is for the proprietor of the SEP to present to that alleged infringer a specific, written offer for a licence on FRAND terms, in accordance with the undertaking given to the standardisation body, specifying, in particular, the amount of the royalty and the way in which that royalty is to be calculated.' (para 63)

'[I]t is for the alleged infringer diligently to respond to that offer, in accordance with recognised commercial practices in the field and in good faith, a point which must be established on the basis of objective factors and which implies, in particular, that there are no delaying tactics.' (para 65)

'Should the alleged infringer not accept the offer made to it, it may rely on the abusive nature of an action for a prohibitory injunction or for the recall of products only if it has submitted to the proprietor of the SEP in question, promptly and in writing, a specific counter-offer that corresponds to FRAND terms.' (para 66)

Where the alleged infringer is using the SEP before a licensing agreement has been concluded, it needs to provide appropriate security (such as bank guarantee or deposit), from the point at which its counter-offer is rejected. When no agreement is reached following the counter offer, the parties may, by common agreement, request that the amount of the royalty is determined by an independent third party. (paras 67–8)

'Lastly, having regard, first, to the fact that a standardisation body such as that which developed the standard at issue in the main proceedings does not check whether patents are valid or essential to the standard in which they are included during the standardisation procedure, and, secondly, to the right to effective judicial protection guaranteed by Article 47 of the Charter, an alleged infringer cannot be criticised either for challenging, in parallel to the negotiations relating to the grant of licences, the validity of those patents and/or the essential nature of those patents to the standard in which they are included and/or their actual use, or for reserving the right to do so in the future.' (para 69)

Comment

The Court reaffirmed the rights of the proprietor of an intellectual-property right, while noting the responsibility which emerges when dealing with SEP.

The proprietor of a SEP, which was agreed to be licensed on FRAND terms, is required to alert the alleged infringer and present it with a specific, written offer for a licence on FRAND terms, prior to bringing an action for infringement. Failure to do so will give rise to an abuse of a dominant position.

In its judgment the Court balanced the interests of the proprietor and the user of a SEP. On one hand the proprietor cannot engage in patent hold-up (charging above market rate). On the other hand, the Court acknowledged the proprietor's right to bring an action for infringement, thus preventing the implementer from reverse hold-up (also known as hold-out), ie refusing payment or insisting on below-market rates. The balancing formula supports a competitive environment and access to the SEP while retaining the incentive to innovate and contribute to standard development.

The Court stipulated that when an agreement regarding FRAND cannot be reached, the proprietor and implementer can agree to approach an independent third party who will determine the level of royalty. Such mechanism resembles the Commission's use of 'safe harbour' in its *Motorola* and *Samsung* decisions (page 382 below).

Motorola—Enforcement of GPRS Standard Essential Patents
CASE AT.39985
European Commission, [2014] OJ C 344/6

Standard essential patents
SEP-based Injunction
'Safe Harbour'

Facts

The Commission found that Motorola had abused its dominant position by seeking and enforcing an injunction against Apple on the basis of a standard essential patent (SEP) which it had committed to license on FRAND terms, and where Apple had agreed to be bound by a determination of the FRAND royalties by the relevant German court. In its decision, the Commission established a 'safe harbour' for potential licensees of the relevant SEP, protecting them against SEP-based injunctions.

Held

'In view of the standardisation process that led to the adoption of the GPRS standard and Motorola's voluntary commitment to license the Cudak SEP on FRAND terms and conditions, implementers of the GPRS standard have a legitimate expectation that Motorola will grant them a licence over that SEP, provided they are not unwilling to enter into a licence on FRAND terms and conditions.' (para 417)

As part of the licensing negotiations between Motorola and Apple, Apple first proposed that FRAND terms will be reviewed by the competent court (First Orange Book Offer). Apple subsequently made another offer according to which Motorola will set the royalties according to the 'FRAND standard in the industry'. This proposal allowed for a 'full judicial review of the amount of FRAND royalties, whereby both Motorola and Apple could submit their own evaluations, calculations and reasoning for consideration to the competent court' (Second Orange Book Offer). (paras 301–7)

'A SEP holder is entitled to appropriate remuneration and as such should be entitled to seek injunctions against a potential licensee who is unwilling to enter into a licence on FRAND terms and conditions. However, … Apple's Second Orange Book Offer provided a clear indication that Apple was not unwilling to enter into a licence agreement on FRAND terms and conditions as determined by a court of competent jurisdiction. Therefore, at least as of that Second Orange Book Offer, there was no need for Motorola to have recourse to an injunction in order to be appropriately remunerated for the use of its SEPs.' (para 495)

Comment

The decision established a safe harbour from SEP injunction when the licensee is willing to enter into negotiations on FRAND terms and for a court to determine them in case of failure to reach an agreement. The Commission did not elaborate on the level of 'willingness' that needed to be established.

In Case COMP/C-3/39.939 *Samsung Electronics*, the Commission raised concerns as to the competitive effects stemming from Samsung's action for a prohibitory injunction against one of its competitors for unauthorised implementation of Samsung's SEP. The Commission opined that 'the seeking of an injunction based on SEPs may constitute an abuse of a dominant position if a SEP holder has given a voluntary commitment to license its SEPs on FRAND terms and where the company against which an injunction is sought is willing to enter into a licence agreement on such FRAND terms. Since injunctions generally involve a prohibition of the product infringing the patent being sold, seeking SEP-based injunctions against a willing licensee could risk excluding products from the market. Such a threat can therefore distort licensing negotiations and lead to anticompetitive licensing terms that the licensee of the SEP would not have accepted absent the seeking of the injunction. Such an anticompetitive outcome would be detrimental to innovation and could harm consumers.' (Commission Press release, 29 April 2014) To remedy these concerns Samsung agreed not seek injunctions against licensees who sign up to a specified licensing framework. The commitments established a 'safe harbour' for potential licensees of the relevant Samsung SEPs. Any dispute over the FRAND terms for the SEPs in question will be determined by a court or arbitrator.

Rambus	**FRAND**
COMP/38.636	Abuse
European Commission, [2010] OJ C30/17	Patent Ambush

Facts

The Commission opened an investigation into the activities of Rambus, a small US company active in the market for high-bandwidth chip connection technologies which had allegedly infringed Article 102 TFEU by claiming unreasonable royalties for the use of certain patents for 'Dynamic Random Access Memory' (DRAM) chips.

Rambus was accused of engaging in 'patent ambush' by withholding information while participating in the development of the standard as part of a US standards-setting organisation for the semiconductor industry. During the development of the standard, Rambus failed to disclose the existence of its patents, leading to its technology being embedded in the standard. Subsequently, companies wishing to use the standard had to either acquire a licence from Rambus or litigate its asserted patent rights. Rambus, it was alleged, abused its dominant market position by claiming unreasonable royalties for the use of those relevant patents.

In reply to the Statement of Objections issued by the Commission, Rambus offered commitments which included, among other things, the imposition of a cap on its royalty rates, at less than half of their level at the time, for a five-year duration. The cap included a 'Most-Favoured-Customer' clause which would ensure any future rate reductions would benefit the whole market. Rambus's undertakings satisfied the Commission and it ended its investigation in a Commission decision rendering Rambus's undertakings legally binding.

Comment

The alleged deception of the memory standards-setting group enabled Rambus to embed its IP-protected technology in the standard. The Commission argued that Rambus gained market power once its technology was included in the standard and users of the standard were locked into the technology and thus forced to pay royalty fees. Despite its relatively small size, the company enjoyed market power over those users who adopted the standard. The alleged abuse concerned the artificially inflated prices charged by Rambus for the use of its IP rights.

'The Commission considers that an effective standard setting process should take place in a non-discriminatory, open and transparent way to ensure competition on the merits and to allow consumers to benefit from technical development and innovation. Standards bodies should be encouraged to design clear rules respecting these principles. However, in a specific case where there appear to be competition concerns, the Commission will investigate and intervene as appropriate.' (Commission Commitments Memo 09/273)

In parallel proceedings in the US, the Federal Trade Commission (FTC) found that Rambus had engaged in illegal monopolisation. Specifically, the FTC held that section 2 of the Sherman Act applied and that failing to disclose patents and demanding high royalties amounted to deceptive conduct giving it monopoly power and harming competition. The FTC argued that, absent the deception, the standards-setting organisation would have considered alternative technologies or would have agreed in advance on a cap on future royalties. On appeal, the District Court overturned the FTC orders, holding that the FTC had failed in sustaining its action against Rambus and establishing that its practice was exclusionary and that the higher royalty rates charged by Rambus resulted in a less competitive market. The US Supreme Court denied the FTC request for further appeal and let the District Court ruling stand.

The Commission's commitment decision in this case was challenged before the General Court in Cases T-148/10 and T-149/10 *Hynix Semiconductor v Commission*. Action withdrawn following reports of a settlement between the parties.

Texas Instruments/Qualcomm	**FRAND**
COMP/39.247	Abuse
European Commission, Memo/09/516	Patent Hold-up

Facts

The Commission opened proceedings against Qualcomm, a US chipset manufacturer, concerning an alleged abuse of its dominant position. Qualcomm was accused of claiming unreasonable royalties for the use of its IP rights in the CDMA and WCDMA standards for mobile telephones.

The Commission investigation followed complaints lodged by Ericsson, Nokia, Texas Instruments, Broadcom, NEC and Panasonic, all manufacturers mobile phone and/or chipsets that accused Qualcomm of abusing its dominant position by imposing licensing terms that were not fair, reasonable and non-discriminatory (FRAND).

The complaining companies argued that the economic principle underlying FRAND commitments is that essential patent holders should not be able to exploit the extra power they have gained as a result of having technology based on their patent incorporated in the standard. They argued that failing to observe this principle could lead to final consumers paying higher handset prices and have an adverse impact on the development of the 3G and future standards and on economic efficiency.

In November 2009 the Commission reached a decision to close its formal proceedings against Qualcomm. In a memo the Commission stated that: 'The Qualcomm case has raised important issues about the pricing of technology after its adoption as part of an industry standard. In practice, such assessments may be very complex, and any antitrust enforcer has to be careful about overturning commercial agreements … All complainants have now withdrawn or indicated their intention to withdraw their complaints, and the Commission has therefore to decide where best to focus its resources and priorities. In view of this, the Commission does not consider it appropriate to invest further resources in this case.' (MEMO/09/516)

Comment

Two of the complainants, Nokia and Broadcom, were reported to have reached settlement agreements with Qualcomm and subsequently withdrew their complaints. The other complainants reportedly withdrew their complaints in light of the slow progress of the investigation in Europe and, on the other hand, developments in other jurisdictions outside Europe. Note in particular the decisions of the South Korean and Japanese competition agencies which found Qualcomm to have infringed the competition provisions and subjected it to a hefty fine.

The case raises interesting questions as to the role of competition law enforcement in this area. On one hand one may argue that these disputes should be treated as commercial disputes which are not suitable for ex-post antitrust intervention. This is particularly so because of the difficulty in determining the 'excessiveness' of the royalty, an exercise which carries with it complexity and uncertainty. On the other hand, one may argue that current standard-setting procedures are open to manipulation as they allow opportunistic holders of IP rights embedded in a standard to extract excessive royalties from their licensees, using practices such as 'patent hold-up' and 'patent ambush'. Competition law may thus be used to enhance the enforceability of FRAND commitments and provide a deterrent which would facilitate (settlement) agreements.

Facts

The European Commission reviewed under the European Merger Regulation a proposed transaction between two companies active in the market for the administration and services of payment/smart plastic cards. When considering the likely effect of the transaction on competition the Commission assessed the probable effect of the combined IP portfolio of the merged entity. The parties argued on this point that 'intellectual property rights would not be a barrier to entry as they are accessible and the vast majority of any secure plastic card's functionality is based on technology that is either in the public domain or that is covered by patents that have been incorporated in one or more international standards (and therefore subject to fair, reasonable and non-discriminatory ("FRAND") licensing commitments).' (para 43)

Held

'In the information notified to the Commission, the parties have downplayed the importance of IP rights in the industry as, according to them, the bulk of their IP rights would be in the public domain and/or readily accessible, and the "essential" patents would be licensed under fair reasonable and non-discriminatory (FRAND) conditions. However, many competitors have expressed concerns in relation to the substantial strength stemming from the combined patent portfolio. ... In practice, Axalto and Gemplus exploit their ... IP rights in the following way: they resort to reverse engineering of their competitor's products to determine whether these products are built on technologies at least partially covered by the parties' portfolio. If this is the case, the parties let these competitors know about the alleged patent infringement(s) and urge them to agree [to license] the patent families that would spare them a legal challenge.' (paras 57–9)

'The fact that, after the merger, this type of strategy would be underpinned by a formidable IP portfolio raises serious questions [as to] whether the parties' competitors will be ... able to exert a constraint of any sort on the new entity on any smart card market. ... Furthermore, it cannot be excluded that the new entity would switch from the current offensive strategies that fetch royalties to aggressive strategies by refusing the licensing of its patents to "small" competitors with no or few patents to offer.' (para 63)

There is a very high likelihood that following the transaction the new entity will be in a position to marginalise competitors with its combined IP portfolio. To resolve these concerns the parties have offered some commitments. Subsequently the Commission has decided not to oppose the notified operation. (paras 64–96)

Comment

The proposition that the merged entity would provide access to its IP on FRAND terms was not sufficient to alleviate the concerns raised by the Commission. On the limitations of FRAND see pages 349–51 above.

Contrast with the merger decision in Case COMP/M.4214 *Alcatel/Lucent Technologies* where the Commission noted with respect to the Telecommunications sector, that 'it is essential for suppliers that their products remain interoperable with those of other suppliers. In fact, all major suppliers participate in the standardisation process. Moreover, network operators are also members of the main Standard Defining Organizations ("SDOs") and any attempt by the parties to dominate the standardisation process in order to obtain market power in a certain technology would—if undesired—meet opposition from these customers. ... In this respect, the market investigation has not indicated that access to relevant patents is generally hindered in the industry; due to requirements of the standardisation bodies regarding fair, reasonable and non-discriminatory licensing, the required licenses can usually be obtained.' (paras 62, 63)

Parke, Davis & Co v Probel	**IP Rights**
Case 24/67	Market Power
Court of Justice, [1968] ECR 55, [1968] CMLR 47	Patents

A preliminary reference to the Court of Justice, concerning the exercise of rights attached by Netherlands law to a patent. In its judgment the Court of Justice commented on the application of Article 102 TFEU to the possible use of one or more patents, and noted that for the prohibition in Article 102 TFEU to apply it is necessary to establish the presence together of a dominant position, the abuse of this position and the possibility that trade between Member States may be affected thereby.

'Although a patent confers on its holder a special protection at national level, it does not follow that the exercise of the rights thus conferred implies the presence together of all three elements in question. It could only do so if the use of the patent were to degenerate into an abuse of the abovementioned protection.' (page 72)

Tetra Pak Rausing v Commission	**IP Rights**
Case T-51/89	Market Power
General Court, [1990] ECR II-309, [1991] 4 CLMR 334	Acquisition of Exclusive Licence

'The mere fact that an undertaking in a dominant position acquires an exclusive licence does not per se constitute abuse within the meaning of [Article 102 TFEU]. ... It is plain from the reasoning and conclusions of the Decision that the infringement of [Article 102 TFEU] found by the Commission stemmed precisely from Tetra Pak's acquisition of the exclusive licence "in the specific circumstances of this case". The specific context to which the Commission refers is expressly characterized as being the fact that acquisition of the exclusivity of the licence not only "strengthened Tetra's very considerable dominance but also had the effect of preventing, or at the very least considerably delaying, the entry of a new competitor into a market where very little if any competition is found" (point 45 of the Decision; see also point 60). The decisive factor in the finding that acquisition of the exclusive licence constituted an abuse therefore lay quite specifically in the applicant's position in the relevant market and in particular, as appears from the Decision (point 27), in the fact that at the material time the right to use the process protected by the BTG licence was alone capable of giving an undertaking the means of competing effectively with the applicant in the field of the aseptic packaging of milk. The takeover of Liquipak was no more than the means—to which the Commission has attached no particular significance in applying [Article 102 TFEU]—by which the applicant acquired the exclusivity of the BTG licence, the effect of which was to deprive other undertakings of the means of competing with the applicant.' (para 23)

IMS Health GmbH & Co OHG v NDC Health GmbH & Co KG Case C-418/01 Court of Justice, [2000] ECR I-5039, [2004] 4 CMLR 28	**Article 102 TFEU** Abuse Refusal to License

Facts

A reference from the German court concerning a dispute between IMS and NDC regarding the use of IMS's '1860 brick structure' by NDC. The system, owned by IMS, provided data on regional sales of pharmaceutical products in Germany according to a brick structure consisting of 1,860 bricks and a derived structure consisting of 2,847 bricks. IMS marketed its brick structures and also distributed them free of charge to pharmacies and doctors' surgeries. That practice helped those structures to become the normal industry standard to which its clients adapted their information and distribution systems. NDC (formerly PII), whose activity also consisted in marketing regional data on pharmaceutical products in Germany, designed a brick structure that was very similar to the IMS product. IMS applied to the German court for an interlocutory order prohibiting PII (NDC) from using any brick structure derived from the IMS 1,860 brick structure. The German court granted the order and based its decision on the finding that the brick structure used by IMS is a database which may be protected by copyright. As part of the main proceedings concerning this case, the German court stayed the proceedings and referred to the Court of Justice three questions, the central one being whether the refusal by a dominant undertaking to grant a licence to use a brick structure for which it has an IP right, to another undertaking which wishes to provide such data in the same market and due to market characteristics has to use the same brick structure, constitutes an abuse of a dominant position.

Held

The question submitted by the German court is based on the premise, the validity of which it is for the national court to ascertain, that the use of the 1,860 brick structure protected by an IP right is indispensable in order to allow a potential competitor to have access to the market in which the undertaking which owns the right occupies a dominant position. In order to determine this indispensability the national court needs to consider whether there are products or services which constitute alternative solutions, even if they are less advantageous, and whether there are technical, legal or economic obstacles capable of making it impossible or at least unreasonably difficult to create the alternative products or services. As highlighted in paragraph 46 of the Court of Justice judgment in *Bronner*, in order to accept the existence of economic obstacles, it must be established, at the very least, that the creation of those products or services is not economically viable for production on a scale comparable to that of the undertaking which controls the existing product or service. (paras 22, 28)

A refusal to grant a licence, even if it is the act of an undertaking holding a dominant position, cannot in itself constitute abuse of a dominant position. However, the exercise of an exclusive right by the owner may, in exceptional circumstances, involve abusive conduct. (paras 34, 35)

Such exceptional circumstances were present in the case giving rise to the judgment in *Magill* which was later referred to in *Bronner*. There, the court indicated that the exceptional circumstances in *Magill* were constituted by the fact that the refusal in question concerned a product, the supply of which was indispensable for carrying on the business in question, the refusal prevented the emergence of a new product for which there was a potential consumer demand, the fact that it was not justified by objective considerations, and was likely to exclude all competition in the secondary market. (paras 36–8)

It is clear from that case-law that in order for the refusal by an undertaking which owns a copyright to give access to a product or service indispensable for carrying on a particular businesss, to be treated as abusive, three cumulative conditions need to be satisfied: (1) the refusal is preventing the emergence of a new product for which there is a potential consumer demand; (2) the refusal is not justified by objective considerations; and (3) the refusal will exclude any competition on a secondary market. (paras 38, 52)

As for the first condition concerning the emergence of a new product, in the balancing of the interest in protection of the IP right and the economic freedom of its owner, against the interest in protection of free competition, the latter can prevail only where refusal by the dominant undertaking to grant a licence to an indispensable product prevents the development of the secondary market to the detriment of consumers. Therefore, such refusal may be regarded as abusive only where the undertaking requesting the licence does not intend to limit itself to duplicating the goods or services already offered on the secondary market by the owner of the IP right, but intends to produce new goods or services not offered by the owner of the right and for which there is a potential consumer demand. (paras 48, 49)

With respect to the second condition, relating to whether the refusal was unjustified, it is for the national court to examine whether the refusal is justified by objective considerations. (para 51)

With respect to the third condition, concerning the likelihood of excluding all competition on a secondary market, one needs to identify an upstream market, constituted by the product or service, and a secondary downstream market, on which the product or service in question is used for the production of another product or the supply of another service. The fact that the upstream product is not marketed separately does not preclude, from the outset, the possibility of identifying two separate markets. Such was the situation in Case C-7/97 *Bronner* where the home-delivery service was not marketed separately. (paras 40–43)

'For the purposes of the application of the earlier case-law, it is sufficient that a potential market or even a hypothetical market can be identified. Such is the case where the products or services are indispensable in order to carry on a particular business and where there is an actual demand for them on the part of undertakings which seek to carry on the business for which they are indispensable.' (para 44)

'Accordingly, it is determinative that two different stages of production may be identified and that they are interconnected, inasmuch as the upstream product is indispensable for the supply of the downstream product. Transposed to the facts of the case in the main proceedings, that approach prompts consideration as to whether the 1,860 brick structure constitutes, upstream, an indispensable factor in the downstream supply of German regional sales data for pharmaceutical products.' (paras 45, 46)

Comment

The *IMS* judgment builds on previous cases which establish the doctrine on refusal to supply. As such it makes reference to the landmark judgment in *Magill* (Case C-241/91P etc *RTE & ITP v Commission*, page 256 above) as later interpreted in the Court of Justice judgment in *Oscar Bronner GmbH Co KG v Mediaprint* (Case C-7/97, page 257 above). Accordingly, a refusal to grant a licence, even if it is the act of an undertaking holding a dominant position, cannot in itself constitute abuse of a dominant position. However, in exceptional circumstances such refusal may constitute an abuse. This will be the case where 'the refusal in question concerned a product the supply of which was indispensable for carrying on the business in question, the refusal prevented the emergence of a new product for which there was a potential consumer demand, the fact that it was not justified by objective considerations, and was likely to exclude all competition in the secondary market.' (paras 36–8)

In Case T-504/93 *Tierce Ladbroke SA v Commission* (page 285 above) the Court widened the scope of the doctrine by treating the 'indispensability' and the 'appearance of a new product' as alternatives rather than cumulative conditions.

The *IMS* judgment further widens the *Magill* conditions by holding, in paragraphs 44–6, that the finding of 'a potential market or even hypothetical market' would suffice. Such a proposition undermines the distinction between upstream and downstream markets. Note that the finding of a fictional downstream market may result in compulsory licensing from a dominant undertaking to its competitor. Contrast this approach with the US approach as evident in *Verizon Communications Inc v Trinko LLP*, 540 US 398. There the US Supreme Court considered the absence of two distinct markets as a relevant factor in its decision not to condemn a refusal to supply (para 5). Arguably, by widening the breadth of the doctrine, the ruling risked undermining companies' incentive to innovate. However, similar to the *Magill* case, it is possible to raise doubts as to the justification of the copyright protection in this case since IMS developed the brick structure in collaboration with pharmaceutical companies and it became the de facto industry standard. One might argue that competition law was used here to remedy an unjustified over protection of the IP laws.

In *Intel Corporation v Via Technologies Inc*, Case No A3/2002/1380, A3/2002/1381 (page 288 above) the English Court of Appeal adopted a wide interpretation and held that a patent holder may be restricted from exercising his IP rights in circumstances which differ from those identified in *Magill* and *IMS*. In doing so, the summary judgment widens the instances in which compulsory licensing may be granted and narrows the requirement for a new product and exclusion of all competition. One should treat such approach with caution, taking into account the impact it may have on investment and innovation. However, note that as patent protection is granted for a finite period, the true effect of sporadic decisions in this area is relatively limited.

In Case T-201/04 *Microsoft Corp v Commission* (page 289 above) the General Court considered Microsoft's refusal to supply interoperability information to a competitor. The court held that the circumstances relating to the appearance of a new product, as envisaged in *Magill* and *IMS Health*, 'cannot be the only parameter which determines whether a refusal to license an intellectual property right is capable of causing prejudice to consumers within the meaning of [Article 102(b) TFEU].' (para 647) It thus used Article 102(b) to 'import' innovation into the equation. This 'internal' expansion tips the balance of the carefully crafted list of exceptional circumstances in the *Magill* and *IMS* cases and lowers the threshold for finding of an abusive refusal to licence. Subsequently, following the *Microsoft* judgment, an undertaking may challenge refusal to license on the basis of the lower benchmark of 'economic indispensability'. This benchmark, which focuses on innovation, is more abstract and carries with it legal uncertainty to the holder of the IP right.

Also in the *Microsoft* judgment the General Court considered the availability of objective justification and held on this point that the protection of the technology by IP rights cannot constitute objective justification. The court explained that if the mere fact of holding IP rights could in itself constitute objective justification for the refusal to grant a licence, the refusal to license could never be considered to constitute an infringement of Article 102 TFEU even though in *Magill* and *IMS Health* the Court of Justice specifically stated the contrary. (para 690) The General Court also rejected Microsoft's argument that the compulsory licensing would eliminate its future incentives to invest in innovation and the creation of more IP.

Observing the development of case-law, one can note the widening of the breath of the refusal to supply doctrine on account of the protection granted by IPR. As such, the carefully structured conditions as set out in *Oscar Bronner* have become vague and have lost their clarity. The *Microsoft* judgment is carefully structured around the facts of the case and as such leaves the IP rights holder with little certainty as to the threshold for intervention and the principles which may govern it.

In its Guidance on the enforcement priorities in applying Article 102 TFEU, the Commission elaborates on its approach to refusal to supply (and license). (paras 75–90)

AstraZeneca v Commission	**Pharmaceutical Industry**
Case C-457/10P	Intention to Abuse
Court of Justice [2013] 4 CMLR 7	Product Hopping

Facts

The Commission found AstraZeneca (Sweden and UK) (AZ) to infringe Article 102 TFEU by abusing its dominant position in several national markets for prescribed 'proton pump inhibitors' which are used for gastro-intestinal acid related diseases, by [1] engaging in deliberate misrepresentation to patent attorneys, national courts and patent offices in order to obtain supplementary protection certificates for its patented product 'omeprazole', and [2] unfairly restricting competition from generics and parallel imports. (COMP/A.37.507/F3 *Generics/Astra Zeneca*)

AstraZeneca challenged the Commission's decision (Case T-321/05, General Court, [2010] 5 CMLR 28), arguing that the Commission mistakenly defined the relevant market and erred in its finding of dominance and abuse. The General Court largely upheld the Commission's decision and confirmed that the misuse of the patent process amounted to a violation of Article 102 TFEU.

The General Court held that the submission to the public authorities of misleading information liable to lead them into error and make possible the grant of an exclusive right to which AZ was not entitled, constituted a practice falling outside the scope of competition on the merits, and was not in keeping with the special responsibility of a dominant undertaking. The Court noted that although proof of the deliberate nature of the conduct is not necessary for the purposes of establishing an abuse of a dominant position, intention does constitutes a relevant factor which may be taken into consideration by the Commission to support the conclusion that the undertaking concerned abused a dominant position.

With respect to the deregistration of the Losec capsules the General Court held that AZ developed a strategy to confront the threat of generic products' entry. That strategy centred around three elements: (1) Losec line extenders including Losec MUPS, (2) the raising of technical and legal barriers designed to delay the market entry of generic products, and (3) the introduction of a new-generation product, which was supposed to distinguish itself from the generic product. The Court noted that while a dominant undertaking may put a strategy in place to protect its investment and minimise erosion of its sales due to competition from generic products, such strategy should not depart from practices coming within the scope of competition on the merits, which is such as to benefit consumers. In this case the deregistration of the Losec capsule amounted to an abuse. Commission decision upheld.

AZ appealed to the Court of Justice.

Held

Misrepresentation

'[Article 102 TFEU] prohibits a dominant undertaking from eliminating a competitor and thereby strengthening its position by using methods other than those which come within the scope of competition on the merits (*AKZO v Commission*, paragraph 70, and Case C-202/07P *France Télécom v Commission* [2009] ECR I-2369, paragraph 106).' (para 75)

AZ's conduct, which was characterised by misleading representations to the patent offices and by a manifest lack of transparency, 'inter alia as regards the existence of the French technical authorisation, and by which AZ deliberately attempted to mislead the patent offices and judicial authorities in order to keep for as long as possible its monopoly on the PPI market, fell outside the scope of competition on the merits.' (para 93)

Contrary to the submission of the European Federation of Pharmaceutical Industries and Associations (EFPIA), which supported AZ's appeal, 'the General Court did not hold that undertakings in a dominant position had to be infallible in their dealings with regulatory authorities and that each objectively wrong representation made by such an undertaking constituted an abuse of that position, even where the error was made unintentionally and immediately rectified. It is sufficient to note in this connection that, first, that example is radically different from AZ's conduct in the present case, and that, secondly, the General Court pointed out, at paragraphs 357 and 361 of the judgment under appeal, that the assessment of whether representations made to public authorities for the purposes of improperly obtaining exclusive rights are misleading must be made in concreto and may vary according to the specific circumstances of each case. It thus cannot be inferred from that judgment that any patent application made by such an undertaking which is rejected on the ground that it does not satisfy the patentability criteria automatically gives rise to liability under Article [102 TFEU].' (para 99)

Deregistration

'As a preliminary point it must be stated that, as the General Court observed at paragraph 804 of the judgment under appeal, the preparation by an undertaking, even in a dominant position, of a strategy whose object it is to minimise the erosion of its sales and to enable it to deal with competition from generic products is legitimate and is part of the normal competitive process, provided that the conduct envisaged does not depart from practices coming within the scope of competition on the merits, which is such as to benefit consumers.' (para 129)

Conduct consisting of deregistration, without objective justification, and after the expiry of the exclusive right under the marketing authorisations for Losec capsules in Denmark, Sweden and Norway, does not come within the scope of competition on the merits. The fact that AZ was entitled to request the withdrawal of its marketing authorisations for Losec capsules in no way causes that conduct to escape the prohibition laid down in Article 102 TFEU. The illegality of abusive conduct under Article 102 TFEU is unrelated to its compliance or non-compliance with other legal rules. (paras 130–2)

'It is important to point out, in this context, that an undertaking which holds a dominant position has a special responsibility in that latter regard (see Case C-202/07P *France Télécom v Commission* [2009] ECR I-2369, paragraph 105) and that, as the General Court held at paragraphs 672 and 817 of the judgment under appeal, it cannot therefore use regulatory procedures in such a way as to prevent or make more difficult the entry of competitors on the market, in the absence of grounds relating to the defence of the legitimate interests of an undertaking engaged in competition on the merits or in the absence of objective justification.' (para 134)

Appeal dismissed.

Comment

The supply of incorrect and misleading information to the Patent Office in order to obtain patent protection amounted to an abuse of a dominant position.

The Court held that although intent is not a necessary element to identify abuse, it may support a finding of abuse. Arguably, intent to win competition (and drive out competitors) is inherent to all business activity and should not be relied upon when establishing abuse.

The Court noted that the illegality of abusive conduct under Article 102 TFEU is unrelated to its compliance or non-compliance with other legal rules. (para 132)

The deregistration of Losec capsules allowed AZ to delay the generic entry, by switching one version of the drug to another with the aim of shifting demand to the new patent-protected version, thus undermining generic entry which is based on the earlier version. This practice which was found abusive, is also known as product hopping and involves the introduction by the originator of new versions of the existing drugs and the discontinuing of older versions in an attempt to thwart generic competition. Such strategy makes the entry of the generic version more difficult. This occurs because the pharmacists cannot fill the prescription of the new branded drug with a generic substitute, which is not bioequivalent. To the extent that doctors become accustomed to prescribe the new version, the generic entry will be curtailed.

Noteworthy is the US Court of Appeals for the Second Circuit judgment in *Namenda (State of New York v Actavis plc (Namenda)* No 14-4624, 2014 WL 7015198), which explored the legality of such practice. The case concerned the change of a drug used by Alzheimer's patients from twice-daily Namenda to a once-daily formulation. The State of New York brought an antitrust action against Actavis, arguing that the company decided to withdraw the old version of Namenda in order to force Alzheimer's patients who depend on the drug to switch to the new version before a generic version became available. The company heavily marketed the new version (Namenda XR), offering it at significant discounts, and intended to withdraw its older version (Namenda IR) from the market completely. The Court accepted that this strategy would have enabled the pharmaceutical company to limit the entry of generic equivalents to the old version. It subsequently issued a preliminary injunction compelling Actavis to produce the older version for seven months. Actavis appealed to the Second Circuit, which upheld the preliminary injunction. In its judgment the appellant court held:

'Certainly, neither product withdrawal nor product improvement alone is anticompetitive. But under *Berkey Photo*, when a monopolist *combines* product withdrawal with some other conduct, the overall effect of which is to coerce consumers rather than persuade them on the merits …, its actions are anticompetitive under the Sherman Act. Defendants' hard switch crosses the line from persuasion to coercion and is anticompetitive. As long as Defendants sought to persuade patients and their doctors to switch from Namenda IR to Namenda XR while both were on the market (the soft switch) and with generic IR drugs on the horizon, patients and doctors could evaluate the products and their generics on the merits in furtherance of competitive objectives. By effectively withdrawing Namenda IR prior to generic entry, Defendants forced patients to switch. … In fact, the district court found that Defendants devised the hard switch because they projected that only 30% of … patients would voluntarily switch to Namenda XR prior to generic entry. … Defendants' hard switch was expected to transition 80 to 100% of Namenda IR patients to XR prior to generic entry, … and thereby impede generic competition. … Defendants argue that courts should not distinguish between hard and soft switches. But this argument ignores one of *Berkey Photo*'s basic tenets: the market can determine whether one product is superior to another only "so long as the free choice of consumers is preserved." … Had Defendants allowed Namenda IR to remain available until generic entry, doctors and Alzheimer's patients could have decided whether the benefits of switching to once-daily Namenda XR would outweigh the benefits of adhering to twice-daily therapy using less-expensive generic IR (or perhaps lower-priced Namenda IR). By removing Namenda IR from the market prior to generic IR entry, Defendants sought to deprive consumers of that choice. In this way, Defendants could avoid competing against lower-cost generics based on the merits of their redesigned drug by forcing Alzheimer's patients to take XR with the knowledge that transaction costs would make the reverse commute by patients from XR to generic IR highly unlikely.' (pages 35–9) The Court affirmed the District Court's order granting New York's motion for a preliminary injunction.

Reckitt Benckiser Healthcare (UK)	**Pharmaceutical Industry**
Case CE/8931/08	Intention to Abuse
UK OFT, Decision CA98/02/2011, 12 April 2011	Product Hopping

Facts

Reckitt Benckiser (RB) was found by the OFT to abuse its dominant position by withdrawing NHS packs of its Gaviscon Original Liquid medicine, after the product's patent had expired but before the publication of the generic name for it, and the introduction of an alternative product, Gaviscon Advance Liquid. The practice, also known as product hopping, intended to limit competition from suppliers of generic medicines, by shifting demand to the new patented medicine which has no generic equivalent.

Held

After the patent on a branded medicine has expired, manufacturers of generic medicines have the opportunity to produce generic equivalents of the branded medicine. The existence of a generic alternative can materially impact upon the choices afforded to doctors and pharmacies. The effectiveness of generic competition will depend on whether a generic name has been issued that applies to both the generic medicine and the branded originator medicine. Doctors are encouraged to prescribe generically where possible, and pharmacies are typically incentivised to dispense the cheapest applicable medicine. Where no generic name exists, the doctor will prescribe using a brand name and the pharmacies are obliged to dispense the named product. (paras 2.79–83)

The withdrawal of Gaviscon Original Liquid medicine constitutes an abuse of dominant position. 'In particular: The OFT finds that the withdrawal was motivated by a desire to hinder the development of full generic competition in the relevant market. Moreover, the OFT finds that the withdrawal would have been commercially irrational were it not for the anticipated benefits to RB of hindering the development of full generic competition.' The withdrawal cannot be regarded as 'normal competition' or 'competition on the merits'. The OFT finds that, at the time of the withdrawal, it was reasonable to expect that it would restrict competition, hindering the development of the full generic competition that would have been expected to emerge had the Gaviscon Original Liquid medicine been retained. The OFT therefore considers that the withdrawal tended to restrict competition or was capable of having that effect. (paras 61, 6.162, 6.163)

Comment

By engaging in product hopping, RB attempted to prevent generic substitution to its branded medicine. In its decision the OFT referred to RB's internal communications which outlined RB's objective to delay, for as long as possible, the introduction of a generic name. (para 2.136) The OFT referred to Case T-321/05 *AstraZeneca v Commission* (paragraph 356) (page 390 above) and noted that while the establishment of an abuse does not require the finding of intent, intent could serve a useful role in confirming the abusive nature of the conduct. (paras 3.45–3.48)

In its final report on the Pharmaceutical Sector Inquiry (8 July 2009), the European Commission noted that: 'Once the period of protection of the invention has expired, anyone may, in principle, use the invention commercially without the authorisation of the original patent holder. It is at this stage that, after having obtained a marketing authorisation from the national authorities, producers of generic medicines will normally enter the market with generic versions of the previously patented active ingredient, thus creating competition for essentially the same medicine. At that point, competition will no longer take place exclusively within the originator industry. There will now also be competition between the originator company whose product is no longer covered by patent protection and its generic competitors. This type of competition will be based mainly on price and marketing effort. Indeed, competition may now even arise between the generic versions of the off-patent medicine and other medicines still under patent protection for the same therapeutic use.' (para 256)

Lundbeck	**Pharmaceutical Industry**
Case COMP/39226	Pay-for-Delay
European Commission, [2015] OJ C80/07	

Facts

Lundbeck, an originator pharmaceutical undertaking, develops and produces medicines targeted at depression, anxiety, Alzheimer's and Parkinson's disease. One of its best-selling products, Citalopram, an antidepressant drug, was nearing the end of its lifecycle in 2002. As the patent protection for the molecule had lapsed and the remaining patent protection was limited to certain manufacturing processes, generic manufacturers were in the position to enter the market. The Commission challenged Lundbeck's attempts to delay the competition from the generic companies. It found that the company infringed Article 101 TFEU, by entering into anticompetitive agreements with generic companies in order to delay their entry to the Citalopram market. Under the agreement Lundbeck paid the generic companies the equivalent of what they would have earned if they had entered the market. As a result, it was able to maintain its position on the market and continue charging monopoly prices for its medicine, to the detriment of consumers. Lundbeck applied for the annulment of the Commission decision. Judgment pending (Case T-472/13).

Held

'[I]f a generic undertaking is paid by an originator undertaking to cease its independent efforts to enter the market with a potentially infringing product, the situation to be analysed under competition law is very different from that if the originator undertaking had succeeded in obtaining an infringement ruling from a court. If infringement is established by a court, the means used to achieve exclusion are the right to oppose based on the objective strength of the patent. Such means fall within the specific subject matter of the patent. If a settlement is agreed without any transfer of value, such an agreement is subject to the scrutiny of competition law, but is likely to be found in compliance therewith as long as the agreement has been reached based on each party's competing assessment of the patent situation. But when the generic undertaking's incentives to seek market entry are reduced or eliminated because of a transfer of value by the originator undertaking, the generic undertaking may willingly accept market exclusion which it would not accept without the inducement, and the result of market exclusion is therefore not achieved by the strength of the patent, but by the amount of the value transfer. This remains true whether or not the same exclusion might have been achieved if the originator undertaking had gone to court. By paying the generic undertaking to give up its competitive challenge, the originator undertaking obtains certainty that the generic undertaking will not enter the market for the period of the agreement, and, because the generic undertaking will no longer have the incentive to try to enter or litigate given that it cannot sell, there is a high probability that the generic undertaking will not seek a ruling of non-infringement or a ruling of invalidity of the invoked patent, even without any non-challenge clause in the agreement. From the perspective of the originator undertaking, it is the uncertainty of possible generic market entry, including through patent litigation, which reflects potential competition. This potential competition is eliminated through the transfer of value and transformed into the certainty of no competition. This is in particular the case when the amount of the value transfer matches the profit that the generic producer would have made if it had entered the market.' (para 604)

'Patent litigation, which is very common when new generic products become available through expiry of exclusivity on originator medicines, is in fact an expression of the independent efforts of generic undertakings to enter the market and therefore a form of competition in the pharmaceutical sector. Likewise, patent litigation is also an expression of competition from the side of the originator undertaking, which in this way is trying to defend its market position against generic competition.' (para 625)

'In the pharmaceutical sector, patent challenges are an essential part of the competitive process between generic companies seeking market entry for compounds that are no longer patent-protected and originator companies that invoke process patents or other process patents against such market entry.' (para 626)

The legal assessment of agreements concluded between generic undertakings and Lundbeck takes into account the economic and legal context. 'This analysis will, in particular, allow a conclusion on whether Lundbeck and the generic undertaking in question were at least potential competitors at the time when they concluded the agreement. In a second step, the actual content and objectives of the agreement will be examined. This analysis will in particular identify the commitments the generic undertaking accepted and whether the agreement was related to a transfer of value from the originator undertaking to the generic undertaking. To the extent that the implementation of the agreement throws any further light on these questions, this will also be mentioned. Finally, in a third step, each party's subjective intentions regarding the agreement will be examined to see whether they match the analysis of the objective elements of the first two steps. On this basis, the analysis will permit the conclusion for each agreement that it constituted a restriction by object. Specific arguments of the parties relating to this analysis will be taken up in the assessment of each agreement.' (para 735)

'Whilst there may not be any established precedents specifically in relation to reverse payment agreements, the notion that agreements aimed at market exclusion in exchange for a payment are likely to constitute a restriction by object under Article 101 of the Treaty is one that is well established and therefore enshrined in the Treaty. Moreover, internal evidence shows that Lundbeck and its counterparts had no doubt about the aim of their agreements, namely money in exchange for the generic producer not to compete with Lundbeck. Lundbeck also thought that such a deal would be "difficult—antitrust wise". Lundbeck was aware that "it is illegal to block competition". Nevertheless, Lundbeck proceeded. Moreover, NM Parma warned Lundbeck against antitrust issues.' (para 1309)

Comment

While companies have the right to settle their patent disputes, they cannot do so in violation of the competition laws, as a means to delay entry and exclude competition. In a public statement, Mr Joaquín Almunia, Vice President of the European Commission responsible for Competition Policy, noted that: 'The practices we are sanctioning are simply unacceptable. By today's decision we are confirming that these so-called "pay-for-delay" deals constitute severe infringements of EU competition law. They may cause severe harm to patients and taxpayers and must be sanctioned accordingly.' Brussels, 19 June 2013 (Speech/13/553)

In *Federal Trade Commission v Actavis, Inc*, No 12-416 (570 US (2013), the US Supreme Court considered the legality of 'pay-for-delay' agreements. The Court rejected the lower courts' approach which had analysed the payment settlement under the 'scope of the patent' approach. It held that in the context of the anti-trust assessment, there is no need to determine the patent's validity to determine the competitive effects. In other words, the focus of the inquiry is the payment, not the patent. The Court held that such agreement may violate the antitrust laws even where the agreements' anticompetitive effects fall within the scope of the patent. The Court noted that payments for staying out of the market keep prices at patentee-set levels and divide the benefit between the patentee and the generic, while the consumer loses. 'Although the parties may have reasons to prefer settlements that include reverse payments, the relevant antitrust question is: What are those reasons? If the basic reason is a desire to maintain and to share patent-generated monopoly profits, then, in the absence of some other justification, the antitrust laws are likely to forbid the arrangement.' (page 2237) The Court declined to accept the FTC's view and to hold that reverse payment settlement agreements are presumptively unlawful. It held that courts reviewing such agreements should proceed by applying the 'rule of reason,' rather than under a 'quick look' approach. The Court held on this point: 'The likelihood of a reverse payment bringing about anticompetitive effects depends upon its size, its scale in relation to the payor's anticipated future litigation costs, its independence from other services for which it might represent payment, and the lack of any other convincing justification. The existence and degree of any anticompetitive consequence may also vary as among industries. These complexities lead us to conclude that the FTC must prove its case as in other rule-of-reason [cases]. To say this is not to require the courts to insist, contrary to what we have said, that the Commission need litigate the patent's validity, empirically demonstrate the virtues or vices of the patent system, present every possible supporting fact or refute every possible pro-defense theory.' (page 2021) In *Loestrin* (page 397 below) the *Actavis* ruling has been applied to non-cash transfers.

Paroxetine Investigation	**Pharmaceutical Industry**
Case CE/9531-11	Pay-for-Delay
UK Competition and Market Authority, 12 February 2016	Curbing Entry to Market

Facts

The UK Competition and Market Authority (CMA) issued an infringement decision to a number of companies, including GlaxoSmithKline plc (GSK), finding that these companies had infringed the competition rules by concluding 'pay-for-delay' agreements over the supply of paroxetine in the UK. The agreements in questions had the object and effect of restricting competition. In addition, the practice amounted to an abuse of GSK's dominant position in the market for the supply of paroxetine in the UK.

Paroxetine was a 'blockbuster' medicine produced by the pharmaceutical company GSK and protected by various patents. The primary molecule patent expired in 1999, yet other patents, concerning process, remained for a number of years. In 2001 a number of generic companies took steps to enter the UK market for paroxetine with a generic version. GSK challenged the attempted entry alleging that it would infringe its patents. Following patent disputes, the companies reached settlement agreements which included payments and other value transfers such as 'promotional allowances' from GSK to the generic companies.

In late 2003, a generic company which did not enter into an agreement with GSK successfully entered the UK market for paroxetine. That entry led to a price drop by 70% over 2 years.

The CMA considered the value transfers to serve as an agreed mechanism to delay the potential entry of generic competitors into the UK market for paroxetine. It found that these value transfers could not be explained on the basis of the stated purposes of the agreements, such as promotion, marketing and discounts.

In a press release, the agency noted: 'These "pay-for-delay" agreements deferred the competition that the threat of independent generic entry could offer, and potentially deprived the National Health Service of the significant price falls that generally result from generic competition. In this case, when independent generic entry eventually took place at the end of 2003, average paroxetine prices dropped by over 70% in 2 years. The CMA has found that GSK's agreements … infringed the competition law prohibition on anti-competitive agreements. The CMA has also found that GSK's conduct, in making payments to … induce them to delay their efforts to enter the UK paroxetine market independently of GSK, infringed the competition law prohibition on abuse of a dominant position. The CMA has imposed fines totaling £44.99 million on the companies directly involved in the infringements.' (CMA Press release 12 February 2016)

Comment

The CMA found the reverse payments to constitute anticompetitive agreements with the object and effect or restricting competition and an abuse of the dominant position held by GSK.

As with other pay-for-delay agreements, the competitive harm in this case resulted from the delayed availability of cheaper generic versions of paroxetine. The out-of-court settlements removed the threat of entry and the possible challenge to the validity of the patents. It enabled the generic company to share the pharmaceutical company's rents (profits) from the sale of the drug at monopoly prices.

The transfer of value in this case was significant and amounted to £50 million. That transfer of value could not be explained by the stated aim of the agreements signed between GSK and the generic companies. Note in this respect comments made by the US Supreme Court in its *Actavis* judgment (page 395 above). There, the Court referred to the presence of large and unjustified payments as the core issue. The Court distinguished such payments from acceptable traditional settlement: 'Where a reverse payment reflects traditional settlement considerations, such as avoided litigation costs or fair value for services, there is not the same concern that a patentee is using its monopoly profits to avoid the risk of patent invalidation or a finding of non-infringement.' (2236)

In the Servier case (Case COMP/AT.39612 *Perindopril (Servier)*) the EU Commission fined the pharmaceutical company Servier and five other generic companies for reaching agreements to delay entry of a cheaper version of Servier's blood pressure medicine. In one case, the settlement did not involve payment for delay but was rather based on a market-sharing arrangement according to which the generic company was licensed in some markets and agreed not to challenge Servier's position in others. In addition to these practices, Servier also engaged in technology acquisitions which limited the availability of non-protected technology and further delayed possible entry. The technology purchased by Servier was never put to use and formed part of a defence tactic aimed at depriving generic companies of the necessary technology.

In the *Johnson & Johnson and Novartis* case (Case COMP/AT.39685 *Fentanyl*) the Commission condemned an agreement to delay the market entry of a cheaper generic version of the painkiller fentanyl in the Netherlands. The practice in this case was made possible through the creation of a 'co-promotion agreement' between the companies which put in place monthly payments from the originator to the generic company at sums which exceeded the profits that Novartis' Dutch subsidiary, Sandoz, expected to obtain from entering the market with its generic product. The agreement came to an end when another generic company entered the market.

In *Loestrin 24 FE Antitrust Litigation* (Case No 14-2071) the US Court of Appeals for the First Circuit held that reverse payment settlements agreed in drug patent litigation need not be in cash to raise antitrust concerns. In held that following *Actavis*, such settlement agreements are subject to federal antitrust scrutiny where they involve both pure cash and non-cash reverse payments. The Court referred to the *Actavis* judgment and noted while a non-cash payment raises difficulties in appraising the value of the reverse payment, and subsequently makes the determination of illegality challenging, it is nonetheless subject to antitrust scrutiny. The Court held that: 'Although the value of non-cash reverse payments may be much more difficult to compute than that of their cash counterparts, antitrust litigation often requires an "elaborate inquiry into the reasonableness of a challenged business practice" and, as a result, is "extensive and complex." *Maricopa Cty Med Soc'y*, 457 US at 343. In other words, antitrust litigation already requires courts to make intricate and complex judgments about market practices. We agree with those courts that, rather than rejecting wholesale Actavis's applicability to non-cash payments, have required that the plaintiffs plead information sufficient 'to estimate the value of the term, at least to the extent of determining whether it is "large" and "unjustified."' (page 31)

9

Mergers and Acquisitions

The European Merger Regulation

Mergers and acquisitions provide for a company's external growth, enabling it to obtain a range of benefits, such as economies of scope and scale, access to information, licences, patents, and a greater customer base.

These transactions often derive many benefits for the market in the form of low prices, high-quality products, a wide selection of goods and services, enhanced efficiency, innovation, and an increase in consumer welfare. On the other hand, some transactions may weaken competition by providing a vehicle to segment markets or to achieve significant market power. They subsequently may result in increased concentration, decreased economic efficiency, decreased innovation, higher prices, lower quality and decreased consumer welfare.

Merger control aims to distinguish between harmful and pro-competitive transactions and either to block or modify the former. To achieve this monitoring effect, the main vehicle used in the European Union is the European Merger Regulation (Council Regulation (EC) No 139/2004 of 20 January 2004 on the control of concentrations between undertakings (the ECMR) [2004] OJ L24, 1–22).

The European Merger Regulation refers to the control of a 'concentration', which includes, inter alia, mergers, joint ventures and share acquisitions which lead to acquiring control over the target company. These concentrations are subject to the exclusive jurisdiction of the European Merger Regulation when they are found to have a Community (Union) Dimension.

Concentrations

The concept of concentration is defined in Article 3(1) of the Merger Regulation and covers two types of situation. Article 3(1)(a) covers mergers between previously independent undertakings. This includes classic mergers and mergers by absorption. Article 3(1)(b) covers operations bringing about a lasting change in the control of the undertakings concerned. Section 2 of Article 3 elaborates on the meaning of control, defining it as rights, contracts or any other means which, either separately or in combination, confer the possibility of exercising decisive influence on an undertaking.

The Commission's Consolidated Jurisdictional Notice details the various forms of sole and joint control which may lead to a finding of concentration (Commission Consolidated Jurisdictional Notice under Council Regulation (EC) No 139/2004 on the control of concentrations between undertakings). Control may be established through the acquisition of property rights, shareholders' agreements or economic relationships leading to control on a factual basis.

The finding of sole and joint control may at times be possible at relatively low levels of holdings. Control may be established through a qualified minority where specific rights are attached to the minority shareholding, where a minority shareholder has the right to manage the activities of the company or where collective choice problems result in de facto control.

One of the noticeable difficulties in establishing the existence of a concentration is in cases where there is some ambiguity as to the acquisition of sole or joint control. The analysis is qualitative rather than quantitative in nature. The following decisions serve as illustrative examples of the assessment of control in borderline cases.

See also summary references to:

In the case of joint control, decisive influence is typically established through deadlock situations where actions determining the strategic commercial behaviour of an undertaking may be blocked by a minority shareholder. In exceptional cases the Commission can establish joint control on a de facto basis where strong common interests exist between minority shareholders.

See also summary references to:

Share acquisitions and other transactions which do not give rise to control are not subjected to the Merger Regulation. These transactions, often referred to as passive investments, may be subject to the application of Article 101 TFEU and Article 102 TFEU. On the application of European competition law to passive investments, see further discussion below.

Community (Union) Dimension

Only concentrations having a 'Community Dimension' fall within the exclusive scope of the Merger Regulation. A Community Dimension is established where a transaction reaches the turnover thresholds set in Article 1. In general, aggregated turnover shall comprise the amounts derived by the undertakings concerned in the preceding financial year from the sale of products and the provision of services falling within the undertakings' ordinary activities after deduction of taxes directly related to turnover. The 'undertakings concerned' for the purpose of aggregating turnover are the undertaking (or undertakings) acquiring control and the undertaking over which control is being acquired. The turnover of these 'undertakings concerned' includes that of the group of undertakings to which they belong.

Mandatory notification and suspension

Mergers are more efficiently dealt with prior to their occurrence. The Merger Regulation therefore establishes a mandatory ex-ante notification mechanism. Under Article 4 of the Merger Regulation undertakings are required to notify concentrations with a Community Dimension to the Commission prior to their implementation. Notification should accord with the requirements of Form CO as detailed in the Implementing Regulation on the control of concentrations between undertakings. Article 14(1) of the Merger Regulation provides for the imposition of fines of up to 1 per cent of the aggregate turnover of the undertakings concerned where they, inter alia, intentionally or negligently supply incorrect or misleading information on Form CO or other submissions or fail to respond or produce required records in an investigation.

The concentration shall not be implemented either before its notification or until it has been declared compatible with the internal market pursuant to a Commission Decision (Article 7, Merger Regulation). Article 14(2) of the Merger Regulation provides for the imposition of fines of up to 10 per cent of the aggregate turnover of the undertaking(s) concerned where they, inter alia, fail to notify a concentration prior to its implementation. On the exposure to fines, see for example:

IV/M.920	*Samsung/AST Research Inc*	422
IV/M.969	*AP Møller*	424
COMP/M.2624	*Deutsch BP/Erdölchemie*	425

Including references to:

IV/M.1157	*Skanska/Scancem*	424
IV/M.993	*Bertelsmann/Kirch/Premiere*	424
IV/M.4994	*Electrabel/CNR*	424
T-332/09	*Electrabel v Commission*	424
C-84/13P	*Electrabel v Commission*	424
COMP/M.7184	*Marine Harvest/Morpol*	424
COMP/M.6850	*Marine Harvest/Morpol*	424
T-704/14	*Marine Harvest v Commission*	424

Article 7 of the Merger Regulation stipulates that under certain conditions the requirement for suspension shall not prevent the implementation of a public bid. In addition, the Commission may grant derogation from the obligations to suspend.

Referrals to and from Member States

Once notified, a concentration with a Community (Union) Dimension will be subjected to the sole application of the Merger Regulation (Article 21). Accordingly, national merger regimes, Regulation 1/2003, and Articles 101 and 102 TFEU will not be applicable to the transaction. This principle ensures the one-stop-shop objective—granting the Commission exclusive jurisdiction to review concentrations with a Community dimension. The one-stop shop reduces the uncertainty created from the need to comply with different legal systems. It is subjected, however, to the possibility of referrals of cases from the Commission to Member States and vice versa.

Article 9, Merger Regulation creates a mechanism under which the Commission is able to refer a concentration with a Community dimension for appraisal by one of the competition authorities of the Member States. Such a referral may take place when the notified concentration threatens to significantly affect competition in a distinct market within a specific Member State.

Article 22 Merger Regulation provides for a referral from a Member State to the Commission of concentrations which do not have a Community dimension but which affect trade between Member States. In addition note Article 21(4) Merger Regulation which provides Member States with the authority to take appropriate measures and appraise a transaction in order to protect legitimate interests other than those taken into consideration by the Merger Regulation. Such interests may include public security, plurality of the media and prudential rules.

The third mechanism which allows referrals may be found in Article 4 of the Merger Regulation. This provision enables the undertakings, rather than Member States, to request that the Commission or Member State reviews a concentration.

Under Article 4(4), undertakings may make a 'Reasoned Submission' and ask the Commission to refer a concentration with a Community dimension to a Member State. Such requests will be appropriate when the concentration may significantly affect competition in a market within a Member State which presents all the characteristics of a distinct market. The provision enables undertakings to flag issues of concern at an early stage and influence the reallocation of the case with no delay. Under Article 4(5), undertakings may ask the Commission to appraise a concentration with no Community dimension when such concentration is capable of being reviewed under the national competition laws of at least three Member States. The provision enables the undertakings to avoid multiple notifications and request a single notification under the Merger Regulation. The Commission will consider requests from undertakings on the same basis as which it would make decisions under Articles 9 and 21.

For an illustration of the application of the referral mechanisms see:

M.2698	*Promatech/Sulzer*	427
M.2738	*GE/Unison*	427
M.3136	*GE/AGFA NDT*	427
T-119/02	*Royal Philips Electronics NV v Commission*	428
IV/M.423	*Newspaper Publishing*	430

Including references to:

M.7612	*Hutchison 3G UK/ Telefonica UK*	429
IV/M.567	*Lyonnaise des Eaux SA/Northumbrian Water Group*	430
M.1346	*EDF/London Electricity*	430

Also note the Commission Notice on Case Referral in respect of concentrations ([2005] OJ C56/02) which outlines the rationale underlying the case referral system.

Investigation

Once a concentration has been notified, the Commission will start its Phase I Investigation. At the end of this phase the concentration may be held to fall outside the jurisdiction of the Merger Regulation, cleared or cleared with conditions under Article 6.

When the concentration raises concerns, it will be subjected to a Phase II Investigation. This stage involves a more detailed investigation and operates with longer time limits. At the end of the second phase the transaction may be cleared, cleared with conditions or prohibited if it is incompatible with the internal market.

Overall, the Merger Regulation allows in most cases for a swift appraisal of concentrations. In the period between 1990 and 31 March 2014, 5,486 concentrations were notified to the Commission: 194 notified concentrations were found to fall outside the scope of the Merger Regulation, 4,818 concentrations were found compatible and 230 found compatible subject to commitments at the end of the first phase investigation. Only 220 notified concentrations were not cleared at the 'first stage' and have subsequently progressed to the 'second stage'. Twenty-four of these concentrations have been prohibited.

The Merger Regulation includes a 'stop the clock' provision which enables the extension of the timeframe for review. The mechanism is particularly beneficial to allow the undertakings and Commission additional time to reach an agreement on commitments.

With summary references to

The Substantive Test—Significant Impediment to Effective Competition

The substantive test against which concentrations are assessed is laid down in Article 2(2) of the Merger Regulation and focuses on whether the concentration would 'significantly impede effective competition in the [internal] market or in a substantial part of it, in particular as a result of the creation or strengthening of a dominant position' (the SIEC test). The Article should be read in conjunction with Recitals 25–9 of the Merger Regulation which elaborate on its applicability.

The assessment of the competitive impact under the Merger Regulation involves a two-step analysis. First, the relevant market will be defined, and, secondly, an assessment of the way in which the concentration may affect competition in the relevant market will be undertaken.

Article 2(1) requires the Commission to take into account the following factors when appraising a concentration: (a) the need to maintain and develop effective competition within the [internal market] in view of, among other things, the structure of all the markets concerned and the actual or potential competition from undertakings located either within or outwith the [Union]; (b) the market position of the undertakings concerned and their economic and financial power, the alternatives available to suppliers and users, their access to supplies or markets, any legal or other barriers to entry, supply and demand trends for the relevant goods and services, the interests of the intermediate and ultimate consumers, and the development of technical and economic progress provided that it is to consumers' advantage and does not form an obstacle to competition.

Market shares and concentration levels provide useful first indications of the market structure and of the competitive importance of both the merging parties and their competitors. The Commission Guidelines on the Assessment of Horizontal Mergers detail the weight attributed by the Commission to different market shares and to market concentration. The case-law on dominant positions and collective dominance, which is analysed fully in Chapters 5 and 6, is applicable under the Merger Regulation in assessing whether a concentration creates or strengthens a dominant position.

The substantive test applies to both unilateral (non-coordinated) and coordinated effects. To illustrate the realm of this substantive test, three anticompetitive scenarios should be noted.

The first scenario involves a significant impediment to effective competition, through non-coordinated effects, which results from the creation or strengthening of a dominant position.

The second scenario concerns a significant impediment to effective competition resulting from the non-dominant position of the merged entity on the market concerned. In other words, it concerns non-coordinated effects that may exist even absent dominance or collective dominance.

The third scenario involves a significant impediment to effective competition which results from coordinated effects—the creation or strengthening of a collective dominant position (which is discussed in detail in Chapter 6).

Concentrations are conventionally categorised according to the market relationship of the undertakings concerned. Under this classification we identify the following three types of concentrations: horizontal, vertical and conglomerate transactions. The following discussion focuses on non-coordinated effects in each of these categories.

Horizontal Mergers

These mergers, involving undertakings on the same market level, are generally of greatest concern for competition law. In a horizontal merger the number of companies present in the relevant market is reduced, leading to an increase in concentration and a reduction in competition. Non-coordinated effects may result from the concentration, creating a single company with sufficient market power which could weaken competition.

See also summary references to:

Horizontal transactions may also raise concerns when a concentration in a non-collusive oligopoly eliminates important competitive constraints that the merging parties previously exerted upon each other and reduce competition, despite the transaction not creating or strengthening a dominant position:

With summary references to:

For a thorough review of the appraisal of horizontal mergers see the Commission's Guidelines on the Assessment of Horizontal Mergers under the Council Regulation on the Control of Concentrations between Undertakings, [2004] OJ C31/55.

Vertical Mergers

Vertical mergers involve companies that operate at different levels in the chain of production and distribution. The impact of vertical mergers on competition is more controversial than in the case of horizontal mergers. Vertical relationships can be potentially anticompetitive if, for example, they foreclose the competitive opportunities of other market participants. Such vertical foreclosure will tend to occur when there is horizontal market power in one or more of the levels in which the merging companies operate. The Commission's appraisal of these transactions is outlined in the Non-horizontal Merger Guidelines (Guidelines on the assessment of non-horizontal mergers under the Council Regulation on the control of concentrations between undertakings, [2008]OJ C265/6) The following leading cases provide examples of the assessment of vertical effects:

See also summary references to:

Conglomerate Mergers

Conglomerate mergers may be categorised as transactions which are neither horizontal nor vertical and take place between companies that are active in unrelated industries. Such transactions may give rise to competitive concerns only in limited cases. The Commission's approach to these mergers is outlined in the Guidelines on the Assessment of Non-horizontal Mergers. The following leading cases provide examples of the assessment of conglomerate effects:

See also summary references to:

| COMP/M.6281 | *Microsoft/Skype* | 450 |
| COMP/M.2608 | *INA/FAG* | 467 |

Coordinated Effects

As with dominance, the concept of collective dominance may play an important role in finding a concentration to significantly impede effective competition in the internal market. Collective dominance under the Merger Regulation may stem from the interdependence between the parties to a tight oligopoly. Indeed, 'in some markets the structure may be such that firms would consider it possible, economically rational, and hence preferable, to adopt on a sustainable basis a course of action on the market aimed at selling at increased prices. A merger in a concentrated market may significantly impede effective competition, through the creation or the strengthening of a collective dominant position, because it increases the likelihood that firms are able to coordinate their behaviour in this way and raise prices, even without entering into an agreement or resorting to a concerted practice within the meaning of [Article 101 TFEU].' (para 39, Guidelines on the Assessment of Horizontal Mergers)

In *Airtours v Commission*, the General Court held that three conditions are necessary for a finding of collective dominance under the Merger Regulation. First, each member of the dominant oligopoly must have the ability to know how the other members are behaving in order to monitor whether or not they are adopting the common policy. Secondly, the situation of tacit coordination must be sustainable over time, that is to say, there must be an incentive not to depart from the common policy on the market. Thirdly, to prove the existence of a collective dominant position to the requisite legal standard, the Commission must also establish that the foreseeable reaction of current and future competitors, as well as of consumers, would not jeopardise the results expected from the common policy. On a finding of collective dominance under the Merger Regulation, see Chapter 6.

Buyer Power

The examination of buyer power in merger control may relate to one of two forms of power. It may relate to the merging parties' ability to exercise buyer power to the detriment of consumers. Alternatively, it may relate to the presence of countervailing buyer power that can relax some of the effects generated by an upstream transaction. With respect to the former, the Commission has rarely taken the view that buyer power would significantly impede effective competition. Most of the instances that have given rise to buyer power considerations concerned procurement markets of consumer goods. See for example:

| IV/M.1221 | *Rewe/Meinl* | 476 |

See also summary references to:

IV/M.784	*Kesko/Tuko*	477
T-22/97	*Kesko v Commission*	477
COMP/M.5046	*Friesland Foods/Campina*	477

Countervailing Buyer Power

Countervailing buyer power arguments have often been raised by merging parties in their attempt to show that the possible market power of the merged entity, on the upstream or midstream market, will be constrained by an existing powerful downstream purchaser.

The Commission's approach to countervailing buyer power is outlined in its Guidelines on Horizontal Mergers. The Commission will consider the parties' market shares, concentration levels and the anticompetitive effects of the merger before moving on to examine countervailing factors, such as countervailing buyer power, possible entry and efficiencies (paras 51, 76, 114).

The following cases illustrate the Commission's approach to countervailing buyer power:

IV/M.1225	Enso/Stora	478

See also summary references to:

T-282/06	Sun Chemical Group	479
COMP/M.6458	Universal Music Group/EMI Music,	479
M.3732	Procter & Gamble/Gillette	479
M.5658	Unilever/Sara Lee	480
COMP/M.2220	General Electric/Honeywell	480
COMP/M.5046	Friesland Foods/Campina	480

Efficiencies

The Commission will consider any substantiated efficiency claim in the overall assessment of the merger. When making its appraisal, the Commission will take into account 'the factors mentioned in Article 2(1), including the development of technical and economic progress provided that it is to the consumers' advantage and does not form an obstacle to competition'. (para 76, Guidelines on the Assessment of Horizontal Mergers) It will consider, among other things, whether 'the efficiencies generated by the merger are likely to enhance the ability and incentive of the merged entity to act pro-competitively for the benefit of consumers, thereby counteracting the adverse effects on competition which the merger might otherwise have'. (para 77) Efficiencies must be to the consumers' advantage and should not form an obstacle to competition.

In its Guidelines on the Assessment of Horizontal Mergers the Commission stipulates that, for it to take account of efficiency claims in its assessment of the merger, the efficiencies have to benefit consumers, be merger specific and be verifiable. On the assessment of efficiencies note the following cases:

COMP/M.4854	TomTom/Tele Atlas	464
COMP/M.4000	Inco/Falconbridge	481
COMP/M.4057	Korsnäs/AssiDomän Cartonboard	483
T-342/07	Ryanair Holdings plc v Commission	484
M.6570	UPS/TNT	485

Failing Firm Defence

The Commission may decide that an otherwise anticompetitive merger is nevertheless compatible with the internal market if one of the merging parties is a 'failing firm'. In its Guidelines on the Assessment of Horizontal Mergers the Commission notes that three criteria are especially relevant for the application of a 'failing firm defence'. First, the allegedly failing firm would in the near future be forced out of the market because of financial difficulties if not taken over by another undertaking. Second, there is no less anticompetitive alternative transaction than the notified merger. Third, in the absence of a merger, the assets of the failing firm would inevitably exit the market. See:

C-68/94 etc	*French Republic and others v Commission (Kali und Salz)*	486
IV/M.2314	*BASF/Pantochim/Eurodiol*	488
IV/M.2876	*Newscorp/Telepiù*	489
M.6796	*Aegean/Olympic II*	491

See also summary reference to:

M.6360	*Nynas/Shell/Harburg Refinery*	491

Remedies

Article 8(2) of the Merger Regulation authorises the Commission to accept commitments from the parties that modify their proposed concentration to make it compatible with the internal market. Such remedies may be offered either in the Phase I or Phase II investigation. In practice, the majority of remedies are adopted at the end of Phase I investigation, allowing the Commission to clear the transaction with commitments. The Merger Regulation states generally in Recital 30 that commitments should be proportionate to the competition concern and be capable of eliminating it.

The Commission Notice on Remedies sheds light on the commitments accepted by the Commission at the end of each phase of investigation. At the end of a Phase I investigation, the remedy is expected to provide a straightforward answer to the competition concern and to 'remove the grounds for serious doubts'. Failure by the parties to remove the serious doubts will lead to Phase II proceedings. Commitments submitted by the parties in a Phase II proceeding have to 'remove the competition concerns' identified by the Commission. The Notice lays down criteria for the Commission's assessment of remedies. These include the type, scale and scope of the remedy, and the likelihood of its successful, full and timely implementation. Additionally, to ensure an effective remedy, the commitments should be capable of being implemented within a short period and should not require additional monitoring post implementation. Only in exceptional cases will the Commission accept commitments which require further monitoring.

The Notice makes a basic distinction between structural remedies which are largely based on divestitures and 'other remedies'. Further, the Notice indicates that the Commission has a clear preference for structural remedies but will also consider quasi-behavioural remedies which include the termination of existing contractual agreements, remedies facilitating market entry and licensing agreements. On the Commission's appraisal of remedies, see:

IV/M.6570	*UPS/TNT*	485
T-210/01	*General Electric v Commission*	492
T-87/05	*EDP v Commission*	494
T-177/04	*easyJet v Commission*	496
T-102/96	*Gencor v Commission*	498
C-12/03P	*Commission v Tetra Laval BV*	499
T-119/02	*Royal Philips Electronics NV v Commission*	502

See also summary references to:

Trustee

The trustee is appointed to monitor the implementation of the commitments and/or execute divestitures. The Commission Notice on Remedies [2008] OJ C267/1, stipulates that: 'The parties shall propose one or several potential trustees to the Commission, including the full terms of the mandate and an outline of a work-plan. It is of the essence that the monitoring trustee is in place immediately after the Commission decision. ... The appointment and the mandate will be subject to the approval by the Commission which will have discretion in the selection of the trustee and will assess whether the proposed candidate is suitable for the tasks in the specific case. The trustee shall be independent of the parties, possess the necessary qualifications to carry out its mandate and shall not be, or become, exposed to a conflict of interests.' (paras 123, 124)

See also summary reference to:

Full Function Joint Ventures

Article 3(4) of the Merger Regulation provides that the Merger Regulation applies to joint ventures which perform on a lasting basis all the functions of an autonomous economic entity. These joint ventures, referred to as 'full function joint ventures' (FFJVs) constitute a concentration within the meaning of the Merger Regulation.

In its Consolidated Jurisdictional Notice the Commission details the characteristics of a FFJV. To qualify as a FFJV the entity should have the financial resources, staff and assets necessary to operate a business on a lasting basis. It must be able to perform all the functions of an autonomous economic entity. A joint venture is not full function if it only takes over one specific function within the parent companies' business activities without its own access to, or presence on, the market. By their nature, FFJVs have a structural impact similar to fully fledged mergers, regardless of whether or not the parents remain in the same or in a related market. This serves as the rationale which justifies their treatment as concentrations. FFJVs are therefore subjected to the same mandatory notification regime as other concentrations and will be assessed, ex ante, by the Commission.

With summary references to:

A FFJV is dealt with solely by using the Merger Regulation provisions. However, under Article 2(4) of the Merger Regulation, when the FFJV is found to have as its object or effect the coordination of the competitive behaviour of undertakings that remain independent, such coordination shall be appraised in accordance with the criteria of Article 101 TFEU. Accordingly, cooperation between the parent companies will be dealt with under Article 101 TFEU through the procedural regime of the Merger Regulation.

JV.15	*BT/AT&T*	508
COMP/M.3099	*Areva/Urenco/ETC JV*	509

Joint ventures which do not constitute a FFJV do not form a concentration. As such these are not subjected to the Merger Regulation and may be subjected to Articles 101 and 102 TFEU.

Judicial Review

Commission merger decisions may be challenged on appeal to the General Court under Article 263 TFEU, by any natural or legal person. The standard of review is often referred to as the 'manifest error' rule. When hearing appeals on the Commission decision it is not for the General Court to substitute its own assessment for that of the Commission.

C-12/03	*Commission v Tetra Laval*	510
T-282/06	*Sun Chemical Group BV and others v Commission*	510

The Commission may be 'non-contractually' liable for its decisions under the Merger Regulation when it is established that the decision seriously breached a rule of law and subsequently resulted in a loss to the recipients of the decision. See:

C-440/07P	*Commission v Schneider Electric SA*	511

With summary references to:

T-212/03	*MyTravel Group plc v Commission*	512

Transactions falling short of concentration—minority shareholdings

The Merger Regulation will only apply to a Concentration with a Community (Union) Dimension. In cases which involve minority shareholding and which fall short of establishing a concentration, Articles 101 TFEU and 102 TFEU may be applicable to the transaction.

142/84 etc	*British American Tobacco Company Limited and RJ Reynolds Industries Inc v Commission*	513
IV/33.440	*Warner-Lambert/Gillette and Others*	516

With summary references to:

IV/34.857	*BT/MCI*	514
T-411/07	*Aer Lingus Group plc v Commission*	514
1219/4/8/13	*Ryanair Holdings plc v Competition Commission*	514
COMP/M.6663	*Ryanair/Aer Lingus III*	514

In 2014 the European Commission launched a public consultation which explored, among other things, the possible application of the EUMR to non-controlling minority shareholdings. In its consultation paper, the Commission recognises that at times, the acquisitions of non-controlling minority shareholdings (referred to, by the Commission, as 'structural links') may lead to anticompetitive effects. The Commission notes in its paper that it 'does not seem to have the tools to systematically prevent anti-competitive effects deriving from such structural links'. This view suggests the existence of a regulatory lacuna which should be remedied by amending the scope of the Merger Regulation to cover minority shareholdings.

The proposal to expand the scope of the Merger regulation reflects an understanding that at times, passive investments may trigger anticompetitive effects. Generally, minority shareholdings among competitors may cause anticompetitive effects when the relevant market is concentrated, the parties involved are strategic players in this market and the magnitude of passive investment is large enough. In these cases, a minority shareholding may enable firms to unilaterally raise prices even absent collusion (resulting in unilateral effects). For example, a firm with a minority share in a competitor will be compensated if some of its customers switch to the competitor following a price increase by that firm. Such price increase may also induce the competitor and other rivals to raise prices. Additionally, minority shareholdings may facilitate tacit or explicit collusion between competing undertakings (resulting in coordinated effects). For example, when a firm invests in a rival in an oligopolistic industry, the investing firm may become less eager to price-cut on a collusive price. This is because it would absorb a portion of the rival's losses from this price-cut.

No changes to the scope of the merger Regulation have been implemented since the public consultation on the matter.

Chevron/Texas	**Concentration**
Case M.2208	Article 3(1)(a)
European Commission, [2001] OJ C128/2	Merger

Facts

The Commission received notification of a proposed concentration by which the US undertaking Chevron Corporation (Chevron) entered into a full merger within the meaning of Article 3(1)(a) of the Merger Regulation with the US undertaking Texaco Inc (Texaco). This case provides an example of a classic merger between previously independent undertakings, as defined in Article 3(1)(a) of the Merger Regulation.

Held

'Both Chevron and Texaco are fully integrated oil companies, active world-wide in exploration and production of mineral oil and gas, the operation of refineries, and the manufacture, supply and distribution of refined petroleum products and lubricants. In addition, Chevron is active in coal and chemicals, including a variety of additives used for fuels and lubricants.' (para 3)

'On 15 October 2000, Texaco, Chevron and Keepep executed an Agreement and Plan of Merger (the "Merger Agreement"). By virtue of the Merger Agreement, on the date of the merger, Keepep, a new wholly owned subsidiary of Chevron, will merge into and with Texaco. Thereupon, the separate existence of Keepep will cease and Texaco will be the surviving corporation and become a wholly owned subsidiary of Chevron. On the date of the merger, Chevron Corporation will be re-named as ChevronTexaco Corporation. Therefore, the notified transaction is a full legal merger and a concentration within the meaning of Article 3(1)(a) of the Merger Regulation.' (para 4)

Comment

The merger in this case involved two independent undertakings which amalgamated into a new undertaking, ceasing to exist as separate entities. After establishing that the concentration had a Community (Union) Dimension, the Commission considered its effect on competition. It subsequently cleared the transaction with no conditions.

The Commission Consolidated Jurisdictional Notice stipulates that a merger within the meaning of Article 3(1)(a) may also occur when an undertaking is absorbed by another and ceases to exist as a legal entity or even in the absence of a legal merger by combining the activities of previously independent undertakings, for example by establishing a common economic management, thus creating a single economic unit. (paras 9, 10)

Note, however, that a merger will not come within the meaning of Article 3(1)(a) if a target company is merged with a subsidiary of the acquiring company to the effect that the parent company acquires control of the target undertaking. Such a transaction would constitute an acquisition of control as stipulated in Article 3(1)(b). (See fn 8, Commission Consolidated Jurisdictional Notice) On this point see for example Case No IV/M.2510 *Cendant/Galileo*, [2001] OJ C321/8, in which Galaxy Acquisition Corp, a wholly owned subsidiary of Cendant, merged into Galileo, the latter being the surviving corporation in the merger which then became a wholly owned subsidiary of Cendant. (para 5)

A merger may also occur despite the absence of a legal merger, with a de facto combination of the activities of previously independent undertakings and the creation of a single entity. 'In determining the previous independence of undertakings, the issue of control may be relevant as the merger might otherwise only be an internal restructuring within the group. In this specific context, the assessment of control also follows the general concept set out below and includes *de jure* as well as *de facto* control.' (fn 9, Commission Consolidated Jurisdictional Notice)

Ernst & Young/Andersen Germany	**Concentrations**
Case IV/M.2824	Article 3(1)(a)
European Commission, [2002] OJ C246/21	Single Economic Entity

Facts

A proposed concentration by which the global Ernst & Young network (Ernst & Young) through its German undertakings merged within the meaning of Article 3(1)(a) with both parts of the German entities of the Andersen network and the German undertaking Menold & Aulinger.

Held

The merger of Ernst & Young, Andersen Germany and Menold & Aulinger has to be considered as a tri-lateral merger which constitutes one concentration. (para 25)

'The new merged entity will combine Ernst & Young, Andersen Germany and Menold & Aulinger. Although the newly formed legal branch, called Luther Menold, will form a separate legal entity after the merger, it will be economically integrated into Ernst & Young and will share the same permanent economic management and financial interests.' (para 26)

Comment

Similarly, in Case IV/M.1016 *Price Waterhouse/Coopers & Lybrand* [1999] OJ L50/27, [1999] 4 CMLR 665, the Commission considered a series of transactions and contractual arrangements through which the networks of companies owned by Price Waterhouse and Coopers & Lybrand combined worldwide. Given the fact that both parties were structured as international networks of separate and autonomous national firms, it was necessary to examine whether these groups of firms can be regarded as single undertakings for the purposes of the Merger Regulation, whose combination would constitute a single concentration within the meaning of Article 3(1)(a). This was done by considering whether the combination of activities has a sufficiently high degree of concentration of decision-making and financial interests to confer on it the character of a single economic entity for the purposes of the Merger Regulation. With respect to the Price Waterhouse group of companies, the Commission noted the existence of a combined management board, agreements to pool resources between the members of the group and the existence of a 'combination contract' among the companies operating in Europe and the USA, which led to their functioning as a single economic unit. These features indicated considerable centralisation of management and led the Commission to conclude that for the purpose of the Merger Regulation the Price Waterhouse group constituted one single economic entity which is party to the transaction.

Paragraph 10 of the Commission Consolidated Jurisdictional Notice elaborates on this issue and states that 'a merger within the meaning of Article 3(1)(a) may also occur where, in the absence of a legal merger, the combining of the activities of previously independent undertakings results in the creation of a single economic unit. This may arise in particular where two or more undertakings, while retaining their individual legal personalities, establish contractually a common economic management or the structure of a dual listed company. If this leads to a *de facto* amalgamation of the undertakings concerned into a single economic unit, the operation is considered to be a merger. A prerequisite for the determination of such a *de facto* merger is the existence of a permanent, single economic management. Other relevant factors may include internal profit and loss compensation or a revenue distribution as between the various entities within the group, and their joint liability or external risk sharing. The *de facto* amalgamation may be solely based on contractual arrangements, but it can also be reinforced by cross-shareholdings between the undertakings forming the economic unit.'

Arjomari-Prioux-SA/Wiggins Teape Appleton plc	Concentrations
Case IV/M.0025	Article 3(1)(b)
European Commission, [1990] OJ C285/18	Sole Control

Facts

The notified transaction involved the transfer of 39 per cent of Wiggins Teape Appleton plc ('WTA') shares to Arjomari-Prioux SA ('Arjomari') in return for Arjomari's shareholding in its wholly owned subsidiary, Arjomari Decor. Following its notification, the Commission considered whether the transaction amounted to a 'concentration' within the meaning of Article 3(1)(b) of the Merger Regulation.

Held

'The situation after the merger has been completed will be that Arjomari will hold 39% of the shares in WTA which in turn will hold 99% of the shares in Arjomari's operating company. Arjomari will be able to exercise decisive influence on WTA because the remainder of WTA's shares are held by about 107.000 other shareholders none of whom own more than 4%, with only three shareholders having over 3% of the issued share capital. Hence Arjomari will acquire control of the undertaking within the meaning of Article 3 of the Regulation. It follows that the transaction constitutes a concentration.' (para 4)

Comment

Similarly, in Case No IV/M.754 *Anglo American Corporation (AAC)/Lonrho* [1998] OJ L145/21, the Commission established the existence of a concentration through the acquisition of control. In that case AAC acquired 27 per cent in Lonrho. The disparity of the other shareholders meant that the transaction resulted in AAC's de facto control over Lonrho. To establish this, the Commission considered evidence from polls held at Lonrho shareholders' meetings in previous years and concluded that its level of holding would suffice to establish control, thus classifying the operation as a concentration.

In Case No IV/M.613 *Jefferson Smurfit Group plc/Munksjo AB* [1995] OJ C169, the Commission repeated the same test, holding that 'where a shareholder has a substantial minority interest in an undertaking and the remaining shares are widely dispersed, and particularly where the substantial but minority shareholder de facto controls the voting at the annual meeting, that shareholder exercises decisive influence on the undertaking within Article 3(3) of the Regulation.' (para 6)

Interestingly, in Case No COMP/M.2567 *Nordbanken/Postgirot* (SG (2001) D/292080) the Commission reviewed the acquisition by Scandinavian banking group Nordea of the sole control of Sweden's Postgirot Bank AB. In order to resolve the competition concerns arising from the transaction, Nordbanken undertook to eliminate its control in a third undertaking. This supposedly remedied concerns regarding structural links and potential coordination in the market. The divestiture included, among others, a reduction of Nordbanken shareholdings in the third undertaking to no more than 10 per cent. In its press release the Commission stated that 'Nordea undertook to reduce its stake in Bankgirot to 10%, a level which will no longer give it decisive influence over the company.' Although this was part of the commitments required by the Commission, and did not form part of the examination of whether there was a concentration, the Commission's statement is interesting. It implies that the Commission is willing to 'stretch' the notion of control and establish decisive influence even in a case with relatively low shareholdings.

The level of shareholdings alone should not be interpreted as setting a definite criterion. In principle, even absent special voting and veto rights, collective choice problems could result in decisive influence at even lower levels of shareholding than described above. In Case No IV/M.159 *Mediobanca/Generali* [1991] OJ C334/23, the Commission applied a similar analysis and considered whether a holding of 12.84 per cent could establish control. The Commission analysed the level of shareholder participation in meetings and subsequently concluded that sole control could not be established with such a holding.

Electrabel v Commission	**Concentrations**
Case T-332/09	Article 3(1)(b)
General Court, not yet published	Failure to Notify Acquisition of Sole Control

Facts

Electrabel, a company active in the market for networks in the electricity and natural gas sectors, acquired shares in Compagnie Nationale du Rhône (CNR), a French public undertaking. On July 2003 Electrabel purchased 17.86 per cent of CNR's capital and 16.88 per cent of its voting rights. On December 2003 it increased its holding to 49.95 per cent of the capital and 47.92 per cent of the voting rights of CNR.

In 2008 Electrabel notified the Commission of its intention to acquire de facto sole control of CNR. The Commission did not oppose that concentration and declared it compatible with the common market. However, the Commission reached the conclusion that the acquisition of control dated back to December 2003, when Electrabel increased its holding in CNR to almost 50 per cent. Consequently, the Commission adopted Decision imposing a fine of €20 million, for putting into effect a concentration in breach of the provisions of the Merger Regulation.

The Commission based its decision on the fact that on 23 December 2003 Electrabel became by far the main shareholder in CNR and was assured of having a de facto absolute majority at the general meeting of that undertaking. The Commission noted, among other things, its high share capital and voting rights, the dispersed nature of other shareholders and Electrabel's absolute majority on CNR's management board. (Case COMP/M.4994 *Electrabel/Compagnie Nationale du Rhône*)

Held

The applicant claims that the Commission erred in considering that on 23 December 2003 it had the mathematical certainty of obtaining an absolute majority in CNR's general meetings, on the ground that it would have taken a shareholder attendance rate of 95.84 per cent to defeat its proposals. It claims that the attendance rate grew consistently by around 10 per cent at each new general meeting and that an increase from 76.6 per cent which was recorded in November 2002 to 95.84 per cent after December 2003 was not unlikely.

'It must be held that that analysis is based on a selective presentation of the facts. As the Commission contends, the applicant fails to take into account the general meetings at which shareholder attendance fell … even when shareholder attendance at the general meetings was at its highest (76.6% at the general meeting of 28 November 2002), a shareholder, such as the applicant after the end of December 2003, who held 47.92% of the voting rights was assured of having the majority of the voting rights of shareholders present or represented. Likewise, the applicant's argument that the shareholder attendance rate might increase by 20% after 2004 is unconvincing. … The Commission was entitled to consider, … that the applicant could expect to obtain an absolute majority at future general meetings, with 47.92% of the voting rights since 23 December 2003, as a shareholder attendance rate equal to or above 95.84% was highly improbable.' (paras 60–6)

While the French state was involved in the governance of CNR, that involvement and the special legislative framework which applied to CNR's activities did not prevent Electrabel from acquiring control of CNR. (paras 80–150) Action dismissed. Electrabel appealed (C-84/13P). Appeal pending.

Comment

The Court endorsed the Commission's finding of control. While Electrabel's shareholding and voting rights were below 50 per cent, it obtained de facto control in December 2003. The Court accepted that past participation in shareholder meetings and the disperse nature of other shareholders would lead to an absolute majority at general meetings and constitute a notifiable concentration.

Air France v Commission	**Concentration**
Case T-2/93	Article 3(1)(b)
General Court, [1994] ECR II-323	Sole and Joint Control

Facts

An application by Air France for annulment of a Commission decision clearing a concentration between British Airways and TAT European Airlines (Case IV/M.259—*British Airways/TAT*). The concentration in question concerned the acquisition by British Airways of 49.9 per cent of the share capital of TAT European Airlines ('TAT EA'), with the remaining 50.1 per cent continuing to be held by TAT SA ('TAT'). The acquisition agreement further provided for the grant to British Airways of an option to purchase the aforementioned 50.1 per cent at any time up to 1 April 1997. TAT was granted the right to require British Airways to purchase the remaining 50.1 per cent of the shares held by TAT on 1 April 1997.

The applicant contested the decision and argued, among other things, that the Commission failed to take account of the true nature of the transaction and wrongly considered it as a case of joint control rather than acknowledging that British Airways had in fact assumed sole control of TAT EA.

Held

As stipulated by Article 3(3) of the Merger Regulation, 'control shall be constituted by rights, contracts or any other means which, either separately or in combination and having regard to the considerations of fact or law involved, confer the possibility of exercising decisive influence on an undertaking'. (para 62)

The court considers that the Commission was correct in finding that there exists joint control by British Airways and TAT. This is apparent from the fact that TAT now retains 50.1 per cent of the shares in TAT EA and the fact that major decisions can only be taken by the board of TAT EA if at least one director nominated by TAT and one director nominated by British Airways vote in favour of the proposal. (paras 63, 64)

Even though British Airways exercises a substantial and growing influence in TAT EA, the latter's business plan, containing the main aspects of the policy of the joint venture, was drawn up jointly by British Airways and TAT, cannot be changed without the agreement of both undertakings. 'In the light of the foregoing, the existence of an agreement as to representation and of a system of "code-sharing" between TAT EA and British Airways is not inconsistent with British Airways' controlling TAT EA jointly with TAT, since such agreements do not in any way alter the allocation of responsibilities in the management of TAT EA, and thus the way in which control is exercised over that undertaking, nor its legal status. Such agreements are the result of negotiations between the parties and cannot be concluded without the consent of the directors of TAT EA, in accordance with the rules contained in the statutes of that company'. (para 65)

Comment

'Joint control may exist even where there is no equality between the two parent companies in votes or in representation in decision-making bodies or where there are more than two parent companies. This is the case where minority shareholders have additional rights which allow them to veto decisions which are essential for the strategic commercial behaviour of the joint venture'. (para 65 of the Consolidated Jurisdictional Notice) Note that it is crucial that these veto rights are related to strategic business decisions of the joint venture and are sufficient to allow the parent companies to exercise decisive influence. The rights must go beyond those normally afforded to minority shareholders. (paras 66–7)

In determining whether or not joint control exists, the rights must be considered as a whole and must generally relate to strategic commercial policy, the appointment of senior management or to the budget or business plan. (para 73 of the Consolidated Jurisdictional Notice)

Hutchison/RCPM/ECT	**Concentration**
Case COMP/ JV.55	Article 3(1)(b)
European Commission, [2001] OJ C39/04	Joint Control

Facts

The Commission received notification concerning a transaction in which Hutchison Ports Netherlands BV ('Hutchison') and Rotterdam Container Participatie Maatschappij BV ('RCPM') acquired part of the control in Europe Combined Terminals BV.

In its decision the Commission considered whether the transaction gave rise to joint control and amounts to a concentration as stipulated in the Merger Regulation.

Held

'Collective action can occur on a de facto basis where strong common interests exist between the minority shareholders to the effect that they would not act against each other in exercising their rights in relation to the joint venture.' (para 14)

In the present case there are strong common interests between Hutchison and RCPM such that the parties when voting will not act against each other. These include (1) a commonality of understanding between the parties established through their joint involvement in a previous transaction and the absence of any such obvious commonality as between either of these two parties and the third main shareholder, ABN. (2) The structure of the shareholdings and voting rules have been tailored in such a way as to allow the two parties to exercise joint control over ECT. Hutchison and RMPM together have 70 per cent of the shares and voting rights, with a 6 per cent majority being required for most decisions. (3) There is a high degree of mutual dependency as between the two undertakings regarding the success of their respective investments in ECT. (4) A common guarantee provided by the two undertakings for the benefit of the financial investor, ABN, ensures that the two will maintain a minimum shareholding in ECT for a period of five years following closing, and align their interests. (para 15)

'The above elements tie Hutchison and RMPM closely together and make it unlikely that either would choose to act against the other when voting.' (para 16)

Comment

The Commission found the operation to constitute a concentration within the scope of the Merger Regulation, as Hutchison and RMPM acquired joint control over ECT within the meaning of Article 3(1)(b) of the Merger Regulation. Following its investigation the Commission cleared the transaction subject to conditions.

The decision includes references to the 'Commission notice on the concept of concentration under Council Regulation (EEC) No 4064/89' (para 14). This notice was replaced by the Commission Consolidated Jurisdictional Notice under Council Regulation (EC) No 139/2004 on the Control of Concentrations between Undertakings. Paragraphs 62–82 of the Consolidated Jurisdictional Notice deal with the acquisition of joint control.

ICI/Tioxide	**Concentration**
Case IV/M.023	Article 3(1)(b)
European Commission, [1990] OJ C304/00	Change in Control

Facts

The Commission was notified of a transaction in which ICI acquired sole control of Tioxide. Prior to the transaction ICI jointly with Cookson controlled Tioxide. In its decision the Commission considered whether the change in control constitutes a concentration within the meaning of Article 3(1)(b) of the Merger Regulation.

Held

'Article 3(3) refers to control by whatever means, conferring the possibility of exercising decisive influence on an undertaking. Decisive influence exercised singly is substantially different to the decisive influence exercised jointly, since the latter has to take into account the potentially different interest of the other party or parties concerned.' (para 2)

Prior to the agreement, Cookson and ICI each owned 50 per cent of Tioxide. The agreement which governed their holdings stipulated that the two undertakings will jointly own and control Tioxide. 'The parties each appointed an equal number of directors to the Board, and they were to agree upon the appointment and conditions of service of the Chairman of the Board. None of the parties were involved with the day-to-day management of Tioxide. The parties had to agree all major medium and long term strategic decisions, including financial policies, including the provision of additional capital; business strategy and related capital programmes; levels of authority of the executive directors; and other "matters which might have a substantial interaction with one of the shareholders". (para 3)

'On these facts, ICI and Cookson are considered to have previously controlled Tioxide jointly. By changing the quality of decisive influence exercised by ICI on Tioxide, the transaction will bring about a durable change of the structure of the concerned parties. Tioxide will become a wholly owned subsidiary of ICI; and by acquiring the ownership of all assets of Tioxide as well as the uncontested influence on the composition and decisions, etc. of Tioxide, ICI will obtain full control of Tioxide within the meaning of Art 3(1)(b) in connection with Art 3(3) of the Regulation.' (para 4)

Comment

The Commission concluded that the transaction amounted to a concentration. It subsequently cleared the concentration as it did not raised serious doubts as to its compatibility with the Internal market.

'A reduction in the number of controlling shareholders constitutes a change in the quality of control and is thus to be considered as a concentration if the exit of one or more controlling shareholders results in a change from joint to sole control. Decisive influence exercised alone is substantially different from decisive influence exercised jointly, since in the latter case the jointly controlling shareholders have to take into account the potentially different interests of the other party or parties involved.' (para 89, Consolidated Jurisdictional Notice)

'Where the operation involves a reduction in the number of jointly controlling shareholders, without leading to a change from joint to sole control, the transaction will normally not lead to a notifiable concentration.' (para 90, Consolidated Jurisdictional Notice)

Cementbouw v Commission	**Concentration**
Case T-282/02	Article 3(1)(b)
General Court, [2006] ECR II-319 [2006] 4 CMLR 26	Control

Facts

On 24 January 2002 Franz Haniel & Cie GmbH (Haniel) and Cementbouw notified the Commission of a concentration, which took place in 1999 and in which they acquired joint control, for the purposes of Article 3(1)(b) of the Merger Regulation, of the Netherlands undertaking Coöperatieve Verkoop- en Produktievereniging van Kalkzandsteenproducenten (CVK).

The Commission became aware of the concentration when it examined two other concentrations notified by Haniel. The notification followed a communication from the Commission requiring the undertakings to notify the concentration.

Following an investigation, the Commission cleared the concentration subject to conditions. Cementbouw appealed the decision, arguing, among other things, that the Commission was not competent to examine the transactions in question under Article 3 of the Merger Regulation as it did not involve a change in control.

Held

'A concentration is deemed to arise, in particular, where control of one or more undertakings is acquired either by an undertaking acting on its own or by two or more undertakings acting jointly, on the understanding that, no matter what form it assumes, the taking of control, having regard to the particular circumstances of fact and of law in each case, must confer the possibility of exercising decisive influence on the activity of the acquired undertaking as a consequence of rights, contracts or any other means.' (para 41)

'As the Commission states … joint control exists where two or more undertakings or persons have the possibility of exercising decisive influence over another undertaking, that is to say, the power to block actions which determine the strategic commercial behaviour of an undertaking. Thus, joint control may result in a deadlock situation owing to the power of two or more undertakings to reject proposed strategic decisions. It follows, therefore, that those shareholders must reach understanding in determining the commercial policy of the joint venture.' (para 42)

In the present case the concentration involved two groups of transactions. The applicants asserted that CVK was jointly controlled by its three shareholders before the second group of transactions was concluded, and therefore the transaction did not bring about a change in control. (para 46)

'Having regard to the voting arrangements within the meeting of members of CVK, it would have followed, in principle, that if RAG had kept its stake in CVK, none of the three shareholders in CVK would have been able to block the adoption of decisions by that meeting, in particular the adoption of CVK's strategic decisions. That assertion is not affected by the applicant's allegation that there were significant joint interests between the shareholders, comparable to those indicated by the Commission in its Notice on the concept of concentration, so that in fact CVK was jointly controlled by the three shareholders before that transaction.' (paras 52, 53)

While decisive influence, within the meaning of Article 3(3) Merger Regulation, 'need not necessarily be exercised in order to exist, the existence of control within the meaning of Article 3 of that regulation requires that the possibility of exercising that influence be effective.' In this case the applicant did not establish that the three shareholders acquired the possibility of exercising decisive control over CVK before the second group of transactions was concluded. (para 58)

'The Court must therefore ascertain whether the conclusion of the second group of transactions entailed the taking of control of CVK by Haniel and the applicant, granting them a right to veto the strategic decisions of CVK.' (para 64)

Following the conclusion of the second group of transactions, the shareholders held equal shares in CVK's share capital and in the associated voting rights. This means, in principle, 'that each of the shareholders can block the strategic decisions of the joint undertaking, such as those relating to the appointment of the decision-making bodies of the joint undertaking, namely the managing board and the supervisory board. In order to ensure that the strategic decisions of the joint undertaking are not thus blocked, the shareholders are therefore required to cooperate permanently.' (para 67)

Although under CVK's articles the shareholders of CVK's members do not directly have voting rights in the general meeting of CVK, this does not preclude every possibility that the shareholders of the members of CVK will exercise decisive influence on CVK. Article 3(1)(b) of the Merger Regulation states that control may be acquired 'direct[ly] or indirect[ly]' by one or more persons, whereas Article 3(4)(b) of the Merger Regulation accepts that those having control may also be persons who, while not being holders of rights or entitled to rights under contracts, have the power to exercise the rights deriving therefrom. 'Since commercial companies comply in any event with the decisions of their exclusive shareholders, their majority shareholders or those jointly controlling the company and since, moreover, the member undertakings of CVK are all subsidiaries held either exclusively or jointly by the applicant and Haniel, it necessarily follows that an appointment to CVK's decision-making bodies presumes the agreement of the two shareholders. Otherwise, the members will be unable to appoint CVK's decision-making bodies and the joint undertaking will be incapable of functioning.' (paras 72, 69–74)

The Commission correctly considered that by concluding the second group of transactions, Haniel and the applicant took joint control of CVK. (para 83)

Comment

The case was appealed to the Court of Justice. The points made above were not appealed. The Court of Justice judgment focused primarily on whether changes to the proposed concentration can take away the Commission's jurisdiction where such changes would render the transaction no longer a concentration. The Court of Justice held that not to be the case. Case C-202/06P *Cementbouw v Commission* [2007] ECR I-12129 [2008] 4 CMLR 17.

Paragraph 16 of the Consolidated Jurisdictional Notice makes reference to paragraph 58 of the above judgment and notes that: 'Control is defined by Article 3(2) of the Merger Regulation as the possibility of exercising decisive influence on an undertaking. It is therefore not necessary to show that the decisive influence is or will be actually exercised. However, the possibility of exercising that influence must be effective. Article 3(2) further provides that the possibility of exercising decisive influence on an undertaking can exist on the basis of rights, contracts or any other means, either separately or in combination, and having regard to the considerations of fact and law involved. A concentration therefore may occur on a legal or a *de facto* basis, may take the form of sole or joint control, and extend to the whole or parts of one or more undertakings.'

Also note paragraph 87 of the Consolidated Jurisdictional Notice, which states that 'The entry of a new shareholder in a jointly controlled undertaking—either in addition to the already controlling shareholders or in replacement of one of them—also constitutes a notifiable concentration, although the undertaking is jointly controlled before and after the operation. First, also in this scenario there is a shareholder newly acquiring control of the joint venture. Second, the quality of control of the joint venture is determined by the identity of all controlling shareholders. It lies in the nature of joint control that, since each shareholder alone has a blocking right concerning strategic decisions, the jointly controlling shareholders have to take into account each others interests and are required to cooperate for the determination of the strategic behaviour of the joint venture.'

Cementbouw v Commission	**Community (Union) Dimension**
Case C-202/06P	
Court of Justice, [2007] ECR I-12129 [2008] 4 CMLR 17	

Facts

An appeal on the General Court judgment in case T-282/02 the facts of which are described on page 418 above. In its judgment the Court of Justice considered an argument put forward by the parties, according to which the competence of the Commission under the Merger Regulation is not determined exclusively by the concentration in the form in which it is notified, but by the concentration in the form in which it is actually put into effect.

Held

The Merger Regulation is based on the principle of a clear division of powers between the national and EU supervisory authorities in relation to concentrations. The Merger Regulation also contains provisions which restrict the length of the proceedings for investigating transactions which are the responsibility of the Commission. 'That demonstrates that the [Union] legislature intended to make a clear allocation between the interventions to be made by the national and by the [Union] authorities, and that it wished to ensure a control of mergers within deadlines compatible with both the requirements of sound administration and the requirements of the business world'. (paras 37, 35–7)

'That concern for legal certainty implies that the authority having competence to examine a concentration must be able to be identified in a way which is foreseeable. That is the reason for which the [Union] legislature laid down, ... precise and objective criteria which allow it to be determined whether a concentration has the economic size necessary for it to have a "Community dimension" and, accordingly, to fall within the exclusive competence of the Commission'. (para 38)

'[W]here the Commission has established, in relation to a particular concentration, its competence in the light of the criteria laid down under Arts 1(2) and (3) and 5 [Merger Regulation], that competence cannot be challenged at any time or be in a state of constant flux'. (para 39)

'As the Advocate General stated in point AG48 of her Opinion, it goes without saying that the Commission loses its competence to examine a concentration where the undertakings concerned completely abandon the proposed concentration'. (para 40)

'However, the position is otherwise where the parties do no more than propose partial amendments to the draft. Proposals of that kind could not have the effect of requiring the Commission to re-examine its competence, without allowing the undertakings concerned significantly to disturb the course of the proceedings and the effectiveness of the control which the legislature sought to put in place, by obliging the Commission to verify its competence on a regular basis to the detriment of the examination of the substance of the case'. (para 41)

'It follows that the competence of the Commission to make findings in relation to a concentration must be established, as regards the whole of the proceedings, at a fixed time. Having regard to the importance of the obligation of notification in the system of control put in place by the [Union] legislature, that time must necessarily be closely related to the notification of the concentration'. (para 43)

Comment

'Two sets of thresholds are set out in Article 1 to establish whether the operation has a Community dimension. Article 1(2) establishes three different criteria: The worldwide turnover threshold is intended to measure the overall dimension of the undertakings concerned; the Community turnover threshold seek to determine whether the concentration involves a minimum level of activities in the [EU]; and the two-thirds rule aims to exclude purely domestic transactions'. (para 125, Consolidated Jurisdictional Notice)

Endesa v Commission	**Community (Union) Dimension**
Case T-417/05	Article 1, Regulation 139/2004
General Court, [2006] ECR II-2533	Article 5, Regulation 139/2004

Facts

On September 5, 2005, Gas Natural SDG SA ('Gas Natural') announced its intention to launch a bid for Endesa's entire share capital. The bid was declared hostile by Endesa's administrative bodies. Gas Natural notified the Spanish competition authorities of the concentration. Endesa approached the Commission and argued that the concentration had a Community (Union) dimension within the meaning of Article 1 of the Merger Regulation and should be notified to the Commission. The Commission adopted the decision declaring the lack of Community dimension (COMP/M.3986—*Gas Natural/Endesa*). Endesa appealed the decision and argued, among other things, that the Commission should bear the burden of proof to show that that concentration does not have a Community dimension.

Held

'[W]here a concentration has a Community dimension the Commission has exclusive competence to examine it. However, it does not follow automatically that the Commission has exclusive competence to determine whether a concentration has a Community dimension.' (para 98)

'It should be noted in that regard that the Regulation provides that it is incumbent first of all on the undertakings concerned to make the initial assessment of a concentration's dimension and to determine as a result which authorities should be notified of the planned concentration. Then when, as in the present case, a concentration is notified not to the Commission but to the authorities of one or more Member States, it is for those authorities, in particular in the light of the obligation of loyal cooperation contained in [Article 4(3) TEU], and in the light of Article 21 of the Regulation, which provides that the Commission has exclusive competence to examine whether concentrations having a Community dimension are compatible with the corresponding prohibition on Member States applying their national competition law to such concentrations, to check that the concentration referred to them does not have a Community dimension. It is true that in such situations it is always possible for the Commission to decide that, contrary to the opinion of the authorities of the Member States, the concentration does have a Community dimension and falls within its exclusive competence.' (para 99)

'Moreover, the Merger Regulation makes no specific provision expressly requiring the Commission to ensure on its own initiative that any concentration which is not notified to it does not actually have a Community dimension.' (para 100)

'It follows from the above that, contrary to what the applicant contends, the Commission is not in principle required to prove that it is not competent to decide on a concentration which is not notified to it and to show that that concentration does not have a Community dimension, even if a complaint is made to it.' (para 101)

'In any event, contrary to what the applicant contends, the Commission did not merely find that Endesa had not proved that the concentration had a Community dimension, it actually examined in detail the information concerning the concentration's dimension and concluded that it did not have a Community dimension, refuting the applicant's arguments.' (para 102)

Comment

The Court dismissed the action as unfounded. The judgment also included comments on the calculation of turnover. The court noted that when calculating turnover, adjustments to the published annual accounts should only be made in exceptional circumstances. (para 209)

Samsung/AST	**Notification**
Case IV/M.920	Fines
European Commission, [1999] OJ L225/12	

Facts

The Commission received notification of a proposed concentration by which Samsung Electronics Co Ltd ('Samsung') was to acquire control of the whole of AST Research, Inc. After examination, the Commission cleared the concentration. Samsung voluntarily informed the Commission that it is possible that it breached Article 4 of the Merger Regulation in its acquisition of control over AST prior to the notification. Accordingly, Samsung failed to comply with both Article 4(1) of the Merger Regulation which established the mandatory notification requirement and Article 7(1), under which a concentration falling under the scope of the Merger Regulation should not be put into effect prior to the notification and investigation.

Held

'In January 1996 Samsung exercised its voting rights in such a way that six out of the 11 members of the AST Board were Samsung nominees. As a result of this majority, and according to the Certificate of Incorporation and the bylaws of AST, Samsung was able to determine the strategic commercial activities of AST, and consequently acquired control within the meaning of Article 3(3) of the Merger Regulation … the acquisition of control of AST by Samsung, within the meaning of Article 3(3) of the Merger Regulation, took place at least in January 1996.' (paras 7, 8)

'That acquisition constituted a concentration with Community dimension which was notifiable under Article 4(1) of the Merger Regulation. However, the operation was not notified until 22 April 1997. Samsung therefore infringed Article 4(1) and Article 7(1) of the Merger Regulation.' (para 9)

'Samsung has repeatedly described the situation as an oversight or error caused by the unfamiliarity of its local representatives in California with the [Union] definition of concentration. The Commission accepts that there was no deliberate intention to circumvent the Merger Regulation. Nonetheless, the provisions of the Merger Regulation are clear in that they cover not only intentional circumvention, but also negligent circumvention.' (para 10)

'Samsung proposed that, in deciding whether to apply Article 14(2), a distinction should be drawn between omissions arising inadvertently and omissions in bad faith. However the text of the Merger Regulation affords no basis for such a distinction, and Article 14 explicitly covers situations involving negligence. The question whether or not there was bad faith can be taken into account in the setting of the amount of the fine, since Article 14(3) requires the Commission to have regard to the nature and gravity of the infringement in setting the amount of the fine.' (para 11)

'On the basis of the foregoing, the Commission believes, that, since Samsung is a multinational company with very extensive activities in Europe, it cannot be unaware of the need to respect European merger control rules. This is likely to be true for any company of a size meeting the Community thresholds set out in Article 1 of the Merger Regulation.' (para 12)

'Samsung has also expressed the view that Article 14(2) of the Merger Regulation should only be applied when the parties to the concentration act in bad faith, or when the failure to act is the result of gross recklessness, or when the failure to file has specific and non-negligible anti-competitive consequences. Samsung considers that Article 14(1) and (2) of the Merger Regulation cannot both be relevant in a case such as this, since undertakings that intentionally or negligently fail to notify a concentration will normally complete such a transaction.' (para 13)

'The Commission does not agree that there can be such a reason for not applying Article 14(1)(a) and (2)(b). The breach of each of those subparagraphs might have a very different effect on the market. That is why the legislator envisaged the possibility of different fines for different situations.' (para 14)

'It is true that an undertaking which fails to notify, and thereby infringes Article 14(1)(a), will then normally put the operation into effect, and infringe Article 14(2)(b) as well. However, a situation could arise where only Article 14(1)(a) would be applied, for example where an undertaking which failed to notify could not put the operation into effect. Article 14(2)(b) might apply where an undertaking complied with the obligation to notify but failed to observe other provisions, for example, the requirement not to put the operation into effect within the first three weeks after the notification. In the former case, the undertaking would infringe the obligation to give prior notification of concentrations with a Community dimension, thus calling into question the ability to exercise effective merger control, for which the Merger Regulation envisages fines. … In the second case, the infringement is potentially more serious, and consequently the fine envisaged is higher: up to 10% of the turnover of the undertaking concerned. Such infringements strike at the core of the [European] merger control system, which seeks to prevent lasting damage to competition caused by the structural operations falling under its scope. In order to do this, the Commission is empowered to review mergers and acquisitions before they actually occur.' (para 15)

'Accordingly, Samsung has negligently failed to notify a concentration in breach of Article 4 of the Merger Regulation and has negligently put the concentration into effect in breach of Article 7(1) thereof.' (para 16)

'Samsung submits that the Commission should follow a policy of granting amnesty in case's of inadvertent failure to file where there are no adverse competitive consequences, and where they are voluntarily brought to the Commission's attention and corrected by the parties. Samsung considers that by imposing fines in such circumstances the Commission would send the wrong message, and undertakings would tend not to remedy failures voluntarily in order to avoid the imposition of a fine. The Commission considers that, in the circumstances described by Samsung, that is negligent failure to file with no adverse competitive consequences and no complex situation with regard to the determination of control, an undertaking has every interest in informing the Commission and notifying the operation in question, as indeed Samsung did. … Undertakings will also be aware that it will be relatively difficult for large undertakings which meet the Community dimension thresholds to avoid being caught in the future. … It follows that there is no objective need for a policy of granting amnesty in cases such as this.' (para 18)

'The Commission considers that fines must be imposed on Samsung taking into account in particular the fact that the absence of notification, and the implementation of the operation without the Commission's authorisation, lasted for a significant period (see section IV), and that for a multinational company like Samsung those failures constitute a clear case of negligence that cannot be ignored. The Commission has the duty to uphold the basic principle that undertakings should be deterred from carrying out concentrations falling within the scope of the Merger Regulation without making appropriate notifications, and it should therefore use the powers granted to it by the Council for that purpose.' (para 21)

Taking into account the duration of the infringement, mitigating factors such the lack of anticompetitive harm to competition and Samsung's cooperation, and aggravating factors such as the size of the undertaking in this case, the Commission imposed a total fine of €33,000. (paras 24–32)

Comment

The Commission stressed that the Merger Regulation explicitly foresees that fines and daily penalties will be imposed in cases where enterprises do not respect EU rules on the notification of mergers or acquisitions and the Commission will not hesitate to apply fully the penalties where applicable. The Commission argued that Samsung is an important company with significant activities in Europe and must be considered to be aware of EU merger control rules. The relatively small fine imposed was mainly explained by the fact that the operation had no damaging effect on competition and by the fact that the parties had finally notified the operation while cooperating with the Commission. Additionally, the infringement appeared not to be intentional.

AP Møller   **Notification**
Case IV/M.969   Fines
European Commission, [1992] OJ L183/29, [1994] 4 CMLR 494

Facts

AP Møller, a large Danish company with worldwide activities in shipping, oil exploration and land-based industries, failed to notify the Commission, and implemented three concentrations with a Community Dimension. Following its investigation the Commission imposed a fine of €219,000 on the undertakings.

Held

The Commission considers that the underlying principles in Article 4(1) and Article 7(1) of the Merger Regulation 'are in themselves very important and that their violation undermines the effectiveness of the merger control provisions. Indeed, the obligation of prior notification of concentrations which fall within the scope of the Merger Regulation, allows the Commission to prevent companies from carrying out a concentration before it takes a final decision, thereby avoiding irreparable and permanent damage to competition.' (para 12)

'The Commission considers that fines must be imposed on AP Møller taking into account in particular the fact that the absence of notification, and the implementation of the operation without the Commission's authorisation, lasted for a significant period, and that for a multinational company like AP Møller those failures constitute a clear case of gross negligence that cannot be ignored. The Commission has a duty to uphold the basic principle that undertakings should be deterred from carrying out concentrations falling within the scope of the Merger Regulation without making appropriate notifications, and it should therefore use the powers granted to it by the Council for that purpose. Accordingly, the Commission considers it necessary to impose fines on AP Møller pursuant to Article 14 of the Merger Regulation.' (para 22)

Comment

Recent case-law indicates a significant increase in fines imposed where undertakings fail to notify and suspend a merger. In Cases T-332/09 and C-84/13P *Electrabel v Commission* the General Court and the Court of Justice of the European Union upheld a Commission decision to fine Electrabel €20 million for acquiring control over Compagnie Nationale du Rhône without having received prior clearance under the Merger Regulation (Case IV/M.4994 *Electrabel/CNR*). The significant €20 million fine was imposed despite the fact that the undertaking's infringement was unintentional in nature and it self-reported its failure. The Commission took into account the long period of infringement and did not consider the negligent nature of the infringement and the lack of competitive harm to act as mitigating factors. Similarly, in Case COMP/M.7184 *Marine Harvest/Morpol*, the Commission fined Marine Harvest €20 million for acquiring a 48.5% stake in Morpol without receiving prior authorisation under the Merger Regulation. The undertakings challenged the decision, Case T-704/14 *Marine Harvest v Commission* (appeal pending). The Commission approved, subject to conditions, the transaction between Marine Harvest and Morpol in a separate decision (COMP/M.6850).

In Case IV/M.1157 *Skanska/Scancem* [1999] OJ L183/01 Skanska failed to notify its acquisition of additional shares in Scancem. Skanska increased its shareholding in Scancem from 33.3 per cent of the shares and votes, to 39.16 per cent of the shares and 48.06 per cent of the votes, between 9 and 14 October 1997 on the Stockholm Stock Exchange. Skanska was required, among other things, to divest itself of its shareholding in Scancem and reduce its voting rights to 33.3 per cent of the total voting rights in Scancem. The Commission considered applying Article 14 of the Merger Regulation in this case but eventually did not impose a fine, and cleared the transaction subject to conditions.

In Case IV/M.993 *Bertelsmann/Kirch/Premiere* [1999] OJ L53/01 the Commission found that the parties to the concentration had implemented part of the concentration prior to notification by jointly marketing their digital television services in Germany. The Commission found the marketing of these services to be inseparably linked with the intended concentration. Following communications from the Commission, the parties suspended its implementation.

Facts

The Commission received a notification from Deutsche BP of a proposed concentration in the chemicals industry (COMP/M.2345—*BP/Erdölchemie*), by which it acquires sole control of Erdölchemie GmbH. The notification made by Deutsche BP contained misleading and incorrect information concerning certain agreements and the affected markets.

Held

'Under Article 14(1)(b) of the Merger Regulation the Commission may by decision impose fines from €1,000 to 50,000 where, intentionally or negligently, an undertaking supplies incorrect or misleading information in a notification pursuant to Article 4.' (para 27)

'There are no indications that Deutsche BP acted intentionally. However, the Commission takes the view that the provision of the incorrect and misleading information was committed negligently. As regards the cooperation agreements, the questions in the Form CO are clear and precise. Deutsche BP must have been aware that these agreements form an important element in the assessment of the parties' position and the independence of their competitors. The availability of imports and the ability of outside competitors to put products on the market in Europe independently is an important element of the assessment, which must have been evident for Deutsche BP.' (para 35)

'The fact that the agreement with Sterling had been notified to the Commission previously under [Article 101 TFEU] according to Form A/B supports the Commission's conclusion that Deutsche BP had no intention to hide any information from the Commission. However, it does not establish that there was no negligence. The Form CO requires the parties to submit a complete and comprehensive set of information including all aspects relevant for the assessment of the concentration. The fact that some information might have been brought to the attention of the Commission in another procedure or framework does not reduce the obligation of the parties to complete all chapters of the Form CO in full. Moreover, the parties did not even include a reference to the former procedure in the notification.' (para 36)

'As regards [Acrylonitrile] ACN technology and catalyst, the definition of a vertically affected market is clearly laid out in section 6 III (b) of the Form CO. The submission of the parties that their business units involved did not consider technology licensing and catalyst as a "product market" in the sense of section 6 of the Form CO, but only considered chemicals up- or downstream of ACN, is only of limited relevance and does not establish that there was no negligence. It is well established in the Commission's case law that technology licensing can constitute a distinct product market.' (para 37)

'Finally, the Commission cannot accept Deutsche BP's argument that there was no negligence due to the sound process and organisation of BP with regard to the preparation of merger notifications and the unfortunate and exceptional character of the present case. The Commission acknowledges that so far the members of the BP group have a satisfactory record of merger notifications. However, the present case showed that the procedures applied by BP and Deutsche BP in the present case, which according to BP and Deutsche BP deviated from their usual procedures in merger notifications, failed to ensure a complete and satisfactory notification. A complete Form CO with comprehensive information is of crucial importance for the Commission's merger control procedure, inter alia due to the tight legal deadlines the Commission is required to meet in these procedures, and the notifying parties must be aware of this importance. The internal provisions set up within the notifying party for the preparation of the Form CO have to reflect this high importance of a complete notification. Consequently, the party has to organise its internal procedures with the highest care to ensure that the legal duties and requirements under the Merger Regulation are communicated to all relevant units, and that all relevant information is identified and supplied in the Form CO. The fact that in the present case information was missing in three different areas revealed imperfections in the procedures applied by BP and Deutsche BP in this instance, which led to submission of an incomplete Form CO.' (para 39)

'These omissions go beyond minor errors which might be unavoidable in view of the complexity of large multinational undertakings. The explanation provided by Deutsche BP also does not establish any extraordinary circumstances which, despite all reasonable efforts, made it impossible to provide the missing information.' (para 40)

'In terms of the degree of negligence, it has, however, to be taken into account that ACN was not the sole focus of the case. The Commission acknowledges that the present transaction affected a large number of different chemicals which had to be discussed in the notification, ACN being only one of them.' (para 41)

'Against this background, it has to be concluded that Deutsche BP acted negligently in submitting the incorrect and misleading information, and that the negligence was of a considerable degree.' (para 42)

'The Commission takes the view that the infringement is of considerable gravity. The notification is the basis and the starting point of the Commission's investigation of a merger case. It determines to a large extent the approach of the Commission towards the case and the areas and focal points of its investigation. Incorrect and misleading information creates the risk that important aspects relevant for the competitive assessment of the transaction are neither investigated nor analysed by the Commission, and its final decision consequently is based on incorrect information. In assessing mergers, the Commission is subject to extremely tight deadlines. In this framework it is essential for the Commission's work that it can focus its investigation on the relevant issues from the very beginning of the procedure, based on comprehensive and correct information provided in the notification.' (para 48)

'As regards Deutsche BP's points, the Commission's views are as follows: The absence of intention and the degree of negligence has already been dealt with in the relevant section above, which has to be taken into account in adjusting the amount of a fine. The Commission agrees that there was no intention on Deutsche BP's side, but takes the view that Deutsche BP acted negligently in a considerable degree.' (para 50)

'The fact that the omitted information did not form the basis for competition concerns which resulted in a need for remedies cannot be taken into account as a mitigating factor. The information requirements set out in the Form CO, which Article 14(1)(b) of the Merger Regulation serves to protect and enforce, do not differentiate according to the likely outcome of the competition analysis. In the present context it is only relevant that the information omitted was of importance for the proper investigation and assessment of BP's competitive position on the ACN market. ... The fact that at the end of the Commission's assessment, taking into account the information that initially was missing, the transaction did not lead to competition concerns, does not reduce the gravity of the omission. This gravity depends on the relevance of the information for the investigation and assessment, but not on the final outcome of this assessment.' (para 51)

'[T]he Commission considers it appropriate to impose a fine of €35,000 on Deutsche BP, pursuant to Article 14(1)(b) of the Merger Regulation.' (para 55)

Comment

Following the submission of new and accurate information by Deutsche BP the Commission cleared the transaction. The Commission did not consider this to reduce the gravity of the omission. (see para 51)

Paragraph 20 of the Commission's Best Practice Guidelines stipulates that 'Given that a notification is not considered effective until the information to be submitted in Form CO is complete in all material respects, the notifying parties ... should ensure that the information contained in Form CO has been carefully prepared and verified: incorrect and misleading information is considered incomplete information.'

Promatech/Sulzer	**Referrals**
Case M.2698	Article 22
European Commission, [2004] OJ L79/27	Joint Referral

A proposed acquisition of the textile division of Sulzer by Promatech SpA. The concentration did not meet the turnover thresholds set in the Merger Regulation. It fell instead under the jurisdiction of Italy, Spain, the UK, Germany, France, Portugal and Austria. The competition authorities of these Member States made a joint referral to the Commission according to Article 22 (3) of the Merger Regulation. This was the first time that several Member States made such a joint referral.

'The authorities of the referring Member States had dispatched to the Commission documentation at their disposal consisting mainly of parties' submissions and results of preliminary investigations. This information was completed thereafter by the parties to the operation.' (para 2)

Following this the Commission opened an investigation into the transaction. It was subsequently cleared after an in-depth investigation.

GE/Unison	**Referrals**
Case M.2738	Article 22
European Commission, [2002] OJ C134/2	Joint Referral

The proposed acquisition of Unison Industries by GE Engine Services Inc did not satisfy the Community (Union) Dimension criteria as set out in the Merger Regulation. It was therefore notified to several of the Member States. Portugal and Ireland granted regulatory clearance to the transaction. Six other Member States, Germany, France, Spain, Italy, the UK and Greece, decided jointly to refer the case to the Commission pursuant to Article 22 of the European Merger Regulation.

The competition authorities of the Member States dispatched to the Commission documentation at their disposal consisting mainly of parties' submissions and results of preliminary investigations. Following this the Commission opened an investigation and appraised the transaction. It subsequently cleared the proposed acquisition.

GE/Agfa NDT	**Referrals**
Case M.3136	Article 22
European Commission, [2004] OJ C66/4	Joint Referral

A proposed acquisition of Agfa's non-destructive testing (NDT) business by General Electric (GE). The transaction did not satisfy the Community (Union) dimension and was subsequently notified to seven Member States: Germany, Austria, Greece, Ireland, Spain, Portugal and Italy. These Member States referred the case to the Commission pursuant to Article 22 of the Merger Regulation. Following its appraisal, the Commission cleared the transaction subject to conditions.

Royal Philips Electronics NV v Commission	**Referrals**
T-119/02	Article 9
General Court, [2003] ECR II-1433, [2003] 5 CMLR 53	

Facts

Following the notification of a merger between SEB and Moulinex, the Commission decided to refer part of its examination to the French Competition Authority (Commission decision C (2002) 38 of 8 January 2002). The referral followed a request from the French authorities which were concerned with the effects of the transaction on several French markets for electrical household appliances. The request was based on Article 9(2)(a) of the Merger Regulation which permits such referral when a concentration significantly impedes effective competition 'on a market within that Member State, which presents all the characteristics of a distinct market'. In its decision the Commission stated, among other things, that the geographical markets for small electrical household appliances are national in dimension, that the transaction will create a new entity of unrivalled size and range of products on the relevant markets.

The French competition authorities, by decision of 8 July 2002, approved the concentration with respect to its effects on the relevant markets in France without imposing commitments, relying on the 'failing firm' doctrine. Royal Philips Electronics NV, a third party to the transaction, subsequently applied for annulment of the Commission decision to refer the transaction. The General Court dismissed the application.

Held

'The conditions for referral laid down by Article 9(2)(a) are matters of law and must be interpreted on the basis of objective factors. For that reason, the [European] judicature must, having regard both to the specific features of the case before it and the technical or complex nature of the Commission's assessments, carry out a comprehensive review as to whether a concentration falls within the scope of Article 9(2)(a).' (para 326)

'In that regard, it must be stated that, for a concentration to be the subject of a referral on the basis of Article 9(2)(a), that provision requires two cumulative conditions to be satisfied. First, the concentration must threaten to create or strengthen a dominant position as a result of which effective competition will be significantly impeded on a market within that Member State. Second, that market must present all the characteristics of a distinct market.' (para 327)

In its decision the Commission concluded that there were distinct national markets, while taking into account a range of facts, including the variation of market shares and product categories between Member States, differences in market penetration of trademarks, differences in prices, commercial and marketing policies, logistics and distribution structures between national markets. It also took notice of the very large market shares of the new entity, its unrivalled portfolio of trademarks and the distinct distribution structure for supermarket distribution in France. In view of those considerations, Philips cannot claim that the relevant markets in France are not structurally different from those in the other Member States. (paras 335–8)

'However, it must still be considered, second, whether, by actually referring the examination of the effects of the concentration on the relevant markets in France to the French competition authorities, the Commission correctly applied the first subparagraph of Article 9(3).' (para 341)

'It follows from those provisions that, although the first subparagraph of Article 9(3) of Regulation No 4064/89 confers on the Commission broad discretion as to whether or not to refer a concentration, it cannot decide to make such a referral if, when the Member State's request for a referral is examined, it is clear, on the basis of a body of precise and coherent evidence, that such a referral cannot safeguard or restore effective competition on the relevant markets.' (para 343)

The legality of the referral decision must be assessed at the time of its adoption and is not affected by the compatibility of the approval decision taken by the French authority with the decision taken by the Commission in which the concentration was approved subject to commitments relating to the Moulinex trade mark. (paras 344–7)

'Accordingly, it must be held that the Commission was reasonably entitled to take the view that the French competition authorities would, in their decision on the referral, adopt measures to safeguard or restore effective competition on the relevant markets. That is all the more the case because, contrary to what the applicant maintains, since the relevant products are sold on distinct national markets, the referral to the French competition authorities was not liable to undermine the [Commission approval decision] or the commitments entered into in it.' (para 348)

'The argument advanced by the applicant and, ... that the referral to the French competition authorities resulted in the fragmentation of the examination of the concentration, thus jeopardising a coherent assessment of it, cannot call that conclusion into question. Such fragmentation is certainly undesirable in view of the "one-stop-shop" principle on which Regulation No 4064/89 is based, by virtue of which the Commission has exclusive competence to examine concentrations with a Community dimension. It cannot be denied that the systematic referral of concentrations with a Community dimension which concern products relating to distinct national markets would rob that principle of its substance. In its defence, the Commission even stated that, where, as in the present case, each Member State constitutes a distinct national market, it might find it necessary to refer the examination of a concentration to all the Member States requesting such a referral.' (paras 349–50)

When the Merger Regulation was adopted, the Council and the Commission stated that the application of Article 9 should be confined to cases in which the interests in respect of competition of the Member State concerned could not be adequately protected in any other way. 'Those statements clearly indicate that the Council and the Commission intended that the referral conditions laid down in Article 9(2)(a) and (b) ... should be interpreted restrictively so that referrals to national authorities of concentrations with a Community dimension are limited to exceptional cases.' (paras 351–5)

'However, since, as was held above, the wording of Article 9(2) and (7) of Regulation No 4064/89 permits the Commission to refer the examination of a concentration to the national authorities where distinct national markets are concerned, the risk that concentrations with a Community dimension will, in a large number of cases, be subject to a fragmented assessment undermining the "one-stop-shop" principle is inherent in the referral procedure currently provided for in Regulation No 4064/89.' (para 355)

Comment

Following the referral, the French competition authority approved the transaction within the distinct French market based on the 'failing firm' doctrine. This decision differed from the Commission Decision with respect to the market outside France in which the Commission approved the concentration in question only after receiving commitments relating to the Moulinex trade mark. The General Court held on this point that the legality of the referral decision is not affected by the compatibility of the decision taken by the national authority with the decision taken by the Commission.

The Commission's discretion to make referrals under Article 9(a) is broad, but can only be exercised in the interests of safeguarding or restoring effective competition on the relevant markets.

Distinguish this from referrals under Article 9(2)(b) under which the Member State must show that a concentration affects competition on a market within that Member State, which presents all the characteristics of a distinct market and which does not constitute a substantial part of the internal market.

In Case M.7612 *Hutchison 3G UK/Telefonica UK*, the Commission refused a request under Article 9(2) to refer the transaction to the UK Competition and Market Authority. In a press release the Commission explained that 'given its extensive experience in assessing cases in this sector, it was better placed to deal with the transaction and ensure consistency in the application of merger control rules in the mobile telecommunications sectors across the EEA.' (4 December 2015, IP/15/6251)

Newspaper Publishing	**Referrals**
Case IV/M.423	Article 21
European Commission, [1994] OJ C85/00	Legitimate Interests

Facts

The Commission received notification of a public bid for the acquisition of joint control of Newspaper Publishing plc by three other undertakings. Following appraisal, the Commission cleared the transaction. In its decision the Commission noted the interests of the UK in protecting the plurality of the media. The Commission noted that the transaction would have to be approved by the UK Secretary of State.

Held

'Article 21(3) of the Merger Regulation provides that Member States "may take appropriate measures to protect legitimate interests other than those taken into consideration by the Regulation", such legitimate interests to include plurality of the media. The proposed transaction involves issues such as the accurate presentation of news and free expression of opinion, and the U.K. Secretary of State must grant formal consent under the relevant provisions of the UK Fair Trading Act.' (para 22)

'The notes annexed to the Merger Regulation include the following passage concerning Article 21(3): "In application of the principle of necessity or efficacy and the rule of proportionality, measures which may be taken by Member States must satisfy the criterion of appropriateness for the objective and must be limited to the minimum of action necessary to ensure protection of the legitimate interest in question. The Member States must therefore choose, where alternatives exist, the measure which is objectively the least restrictive to achieve the end pursued."'(para 23)

'In view of this, the Commission must be kept informed of any conditions which the UK authorities might deem it appropriate to attach to the transaction.' (para 24)

Comment

In Case IV/M.567 *Lyonnaise des Eaux SA/Northumbrian Water Group* [1996] OJ C11/03, [1996] 4 CMLR 614 the Commission recognised the regulation of the UK water industry as a legitimate interest. It noted that the 'control exercised by the United Kingdom authorities is aimed at ensuring that the number of independently controlled water companies is sufficient to allow the Director General of Water Services to exercise his regulatory functions. The interest pursued by the UK regulatory legislation is not one of those specifically referred to in Article 21(3) second subparagraph of the Merger Regulation. In order not to go beyond the interest pursued by the UK regulatory legislation other issues in relation to mergers between water companies can only be taken into account to the extent that they affect the control regime as set out above … By contrast, the UK authorities are not entitled to consider other matters which the Commission must take into account in assessing concentrations that have a Community dimension and which do not directly relate to the operation of the regulatory regime. Under Article 21(1) and 21(2) of the Merger Regulation these matters are the responsibility of the Commission and would be considered in the context of any notification under the Merger Regulation.' (para 5)

Contrast with Case M.1346 *EDF/London Electricity* [1999] OJ C92/10 in which a request was refused. In that instance the UK authorities submitted a request under Article 21(3) for the recognition of certain public interests as legitimate interests other than those taken into consideration by the Regulation. The Commission concluded that 'the measures described in the request were being taken pursuant to the existing system within that Member State for the ongoing regulation of the electricity industry and were not aimed at the concentration itself. Such ongoing regulatory activity was not precluded by the Regulation. It was therefore not necessary for the Commission to recognise a legitimate interest to which they related before the United Kingdom authorities could take the measures concerned.' (para 8)

Mitsubishi Heavy Industries	**Investigation**
Case COMP/M.1634	Requests for Information
European Commission, [2001] OJ L4/31	

Facts

The Commission received a notification of a proposed joint venture between the 'pulping equipment engineering businesses' of Kvaerner ASA and A Ahlström Corporation. As part of its investigation into the transaction the Commission addressed a request for information pursuant to Article 11 of the Merger Regulation, to a third party, Mitsubishi Heavy Industries Europe, Ltd ('Mitsubishi'). Mitsubishi failed to reply to the request for information on time and later provided only partial information. Subsequently, the Commission adopted a decision pursuant to Article 11(5) of the Merger Regulation, requiring Mitsubishi to supply the relevant information. Despite several reminders Mitsubishi has not provided the information.

The Commission considered the infringement committed by Mitsubishi to be a serious one, not least because the information requested from Mitsubishi had a material impact on the assessment of the substance of the case.

Held

'Under Article 11(1) of the Merger Regulation, the Commission may obtain all necessary information from undertakings in carrying out the duties assigned to it by the Merger Regulation. The information requested by the Commission from Mitsubishi was necessary, within the meaning of Article 11(1) of the Merger Regulation, for the proper assessment of the compatibility of the notified operation with the [internal] market. In particular, the information requested was necessary in order to determine the market share of the parties to the notified operation and those of the other market participants in the markets for engineering and supply of recovery boilers.' (para 14)

'Given the limited number of manufacturers of recovery boilers for the pulp and paper industry worldwide, Mitsubishi must be considered to be an important source of information concerning the functioning of this market. Following Mitsubishi's failure to supply the information requested, the Commission was forced to base its assessment of the markets for recovery boilers partly on estimates. In particular, in view of Mitsubishi's failure to supply information on prices and turnover obtained from its worldwide recovery boiler business, the Commission had no other alternative than to estimate the overall size of the market and the market shares of the market participants partly on information obtained from other market operators and customers. This increased significantly the Commission's workload and led to estimates, which cannot be considered to be as reliable as first-hand information from Mitsubishi itself.' (para 15)

'The infringement has not ceased. To date, Mitsubishi has not complied with the Commission decision of 2 July of 1999 and has not provided the information requested. However, it may be considered that Mitsubishi's obligation to provide the information became nugatory when the proceedings concerning the merger between Ahlström and Kvaerner were closed on 8 September 1999.' (para 21)

'On the basis of the above, and taking account of the circumstances in the case, the Commission considers it appropriate to impose the fine of EUR 50,000 on Mitsubishi for failing to comply with the Commission decision of 2 July 1999, pursuant to Article 14(1)(c) of the Merger Regulation.' (para 22)

Comment

The Commission also fined Mitsubishi a periodic penalty payment of €900,000 (based on a maximum daily penalty of €25,000) for not supplying the information from the period of the request for information and the date the investigation was closed.

Omya v Commission	**Investigation**
Case T-145/06	Articles 11
General Court, [2009] ECR II-145	Stop the Clock

Facts

Following a referral by the Finnish competition authority under Article 22(1) the European Commission reviewed the proposed concentration between Omya AG and JM Huber Corp. The Commission intended to authorise the concentration without issuing a statement of objections. The Commission's draft decision was circulated within the Advisory Committee on concentrations between undertakings which is made up of representatives of the Member States. Some of the Member States expressed concerns about the effects of the notified concentration and challenged the Commission's assessment. The Commission approached the parties to the transaction and proposed that the assessment timetable should be extended, by mutual agreement, by 20 working days pursuant to Article 10(3) of the Merger Regulation. Since the parties refused to agree to an extension of the timetable, the Commission adopted a decision under Article 11(3) suspending the assessment timetable to enable it to receive additional and corrected information. Following the investigation the concentration was cleared subject to conditions. Omya applied for annulment of the Commission decision among other things on the basis that the Commission failed to comply with the conditions for adopting a decision under Article 11(3) of Regulation No 139/2004.

Held

'The Commission may exercise the powers conferred on it by Article 11 of Regulation No 139/2004 only to the extent that it considers that it is not in possession of all the information necessary to enable it to decide on the compatibility of the concentration concerned.' (para 28)

'In that connection, it must be recalled that, for the purposes of adopting a decision on a concentration, the Commission must examine, pursuant in particular to Article 2 of Regulation No 139/2004, the effects of the concentration concerned on all the markets for which there is a risk that effective competition would be significantly impeded in the [internal] market or in a substantial part of it.' (para 29)

'In addition, the fact that the requirement that information must be necessary is to be interpreted by reference to the decision on the compatibility of the concentration with the [internal] market implies that the need for the information covered by a request under Article 11 of Regulation No 139/2004 must be assessed by reference to the view that the Commission could reasonably have held, at the time the request in question was made, of the extent of the information necessary to examine the concentration. Accordingly, that assessment cannot be based on the actual need for the information in the subsequent procedure before the Commission; that need is dependent on many factors and cannot therefore be determined with certainty at the time the request for information is made.' (para 30)

'As regards the specific case of the need to correct information already communicated which proves to be incorrect, the Court considers that the criterion of the material nature of the errors identified, on which the parties moreover agree, is appropriate in the light of the wording and scheme of Regulation No 139/2004 and in particular Articles 2 and 11 thereof. Accordingly, it must be held that the Commission is entitled to request the correction of information communicated by a party which is identified as erroneous if there is a risk that the errors identified could have a significant impact on its assessment of whether the concentration at issue is compatible with the [internal] market.' (para 31)

'As regards the review of the application of the abovementioned criteria, it must be stated, first, that their application involves complex economic assessments. Accordingly, the Commission has a discretion in this respect and any review by the [European] judicature is necessarily limited to verifying whether the relevant rules on procedure and on the statement of reasons have been complied with, whether the facts have been accurately stated and whether there has been any manifest error of appraisal or a misuse of powers. However, that does not mean that the [European] judicature must refrain from reviewing the Commission's interpretation of information of an economic nature (Case C-12/03 P *Commission v Tetra Laval* [2005] ECR I-987, paragraphs 38 and 39) and, in particular, its assessment of the need for the information requested pursuant to Article 11 of Regulation No 139/2004 and the material nature of the errors by which that information is allegedly affected.' (para 32)

'Second, contrary to what the applicant submits, it is not necessary to interpret the abovementioned criteria strictly. The requirement for speed which characterises the general scheme of Regulation No 139/2004 (see, as regards Regulation No 4064/89, Case T-221/95 *Endemol v Commission* [1999] ECR II-1299, paragraph 84) must be reconciled with the objective of effective review of the compatibility of concentrations with the [internal] market, which the Commission must carry out with great care (*Commission v Tetra Laval*, paragraph 42) and which requires that it obtains complete and correct information.' (para 33)

'Lastly, it is true that the exercise by the Commission of the powers conferred on it by Article 11 of Regulation No 139/2004 is subject to compliance with the principle of proportionality, which requires measures adopted by [Union] institutions not to exceed the limits of what is appropriate and necessary in order to attain the objectives pursued (Case T-177/04 *easyJet v Commission* [2006] ECR II-1931, paragraph 133). In particular, it is necessary that an obligation imposed on an undertaking to supply an item of information should not constitute a burden on that undertaking which is disproportionate to the requirements of the inquiry (see, by analogy, Case T-39/90 *SEP v Commission* [1991] ECR II-1497, paragraph 51). However, since the period of the suspension of the time-limits set in Article 10 of Regulation No 139/2004 resulting from the adoption of a decision under Article 11 of that regulation depends on the date on which the necessary information is communicated, the Commission does not infringe the principle of proportionality by suspending the procedure until such information has been communicated to it.' (para 34)

On the facts of the case the appellant did not establish that the information, correction of which was requested by the Commission, could not be considered by it, when the request for information was made, to be necessary within the meaning of Article 11 of Regulation No 139/2004. Action dismissed. (paras 35–50)

Comment

The decision to stop the clock was upheld as the Commission reasonably believed the information to be necessary, there was a reasonable prospect that the corrected information would impact on the substantive assessment and the request was proportionate to the impact on the undertaking. The judgment confirms the Commission's right to insist on receiving accurate and complete information from the undertakings.

Article 11(3) of the Merger Regulations stipulates that 'where the Commission requires a person, an undertaking or an association of undertakings to supply information by decision, it shall state the legal basis and the purpose of the request, specify what information is required and fix the time limit within which it is to be provided. It shall also indicate the penalties provided for in Article 14 and indicate or impose the penalties provided for in Article 15. It shall further indicate the right to have the decision reviewed by the Court of Justice.'

Article 10(4) of the Merger Regulation stipulates that 'the periods set by paragraphs 1 and 3 shall exceptionally be suspended where, owing to circumstances for which one of the undertakings involved in the concentration is responsible, the Commission has had to request information by decision pursuant to Article 11 or to order an inspection by decision pursuant to Article 13.'

In Case M.3216 *Oracle/People Soft* [2007] OJ L72/24 the Commission stopped the clock due to a failure by Oracle to provide information. In that case the Commission issued a request for information under Article 11 of the Merger Regulation. In the absence of a reply from Oracle within the time limit set by the Commission, the periods laid down in Articles 10(1) and 10(3) of the Merger Regulation were suspended. Following Oracle's submission in response to the Commission's request for information, the timetable in that procedure resumed again.

Lagardère SCA v Commission	**Investigation**
T-251/00	Article 6
General Court, [2002] ECR II-4825, [2003] 4 CMLR 20	Retrospective Revocation

Facts

The Commission retrospectively amended parts of its decision which declared a concentration to be compatible with the internal market. The Commission argued that the partial withdrawal of its decision was necessary because the original decision was illegal and inconsistent with its own previous decision making practice.

Held

The Merger Regulation 'provides for the revocation of a decision approving a concentration pursuant to Article 6(1) of the Regulation only where the decision is based on incorrect information, or where it was obtained by deceit, or where the parties concerned commit a breach of an obligation attached to the decision. … However, it is common ground that none of those situations arises in the present case.' (para 129)

'It must observed nevertheless that Regulation No 4064/89 gave the Commission power to adopt in a general way decisions relating to concentrations with a Community dimension and, in particular, decisions that they are compatible with the [internal] market. Therefore, in accordance with a general principle of law that, in principle, a body which has power to adopt a particular legal measure also has power to abrogate or amend it by adopting an actus contrarius, unless such power is expressly conferred upon another body, it must be found that, in theory, the Commission had power to adopt the contested decision.' (para 130)

'If the retrospective withdrawal of illegal administrative acts is to be accepted, it is subject to very strict conditions. It has consistently been held that the retroactive withdrawal of an unlawful measure is permissible provided that the withdrawal occurs within a reasonable time and provided that the institution from which it emanates has had sufficient regard to how far the applicant might have been led to rely on the lawfulness of the measure.' (para 140)

'It has been held that the institution responsible for the act has the burden of proving the illegality of the withdrawn act. … Likewise it must be presumed that it is for that institution to prove that the other conditions for retrospective withdrawal are fulfilled.' (para 141)

In this case the Commission claimed that errors of substantive law had crept into the decision and had to be corrected in the interest of developing a consistent theory of ancillary restrictions. The Commission did not prove in what way its original decision was illegal. Having failed to prove the illegality of the act, the Commission is precluded from withdrawing its decision with retrospective effect. The need to preserve the consistency of legal theory concerning ancillary restrictions does not justify in this case the retrospective withdrawal. (paras 142–50)

Comment

In Case M.1397 *Sanofi/Synthélabo* (22 April 1999) the Commission exercised its powers under Article 6(3)(a) to revoke its decision because it was based on incorrect and incomplete information provided by the parties in their notification.

Gencor v Commission	**Horizontal Mergers**
Case T-102/96	Dominance and Market Shares
General Court, [1999] ECR II-753, [1999] 4 CMLR 971	Prospective Analysis

Facts

Gencor, a company incorporated under South African law and Lonrho plc ('Lonrho') a company incorporated under English law, proposed to acquire joint control of Impala Platinum Holdings Ltd ('Implats') a company incorporated under South African law. Following the appraisal of the concentration the Commission blocked it, declaring it incompatible with the internal market because it would have led to the creation of a dominant duopoly position in the world platinum and rhodium market as a result of which effective competition would have been significantly impeded in the internal market.

Held

Dominance and market shares

Article 2(3) of the Regulation relates to concentrations which create or strengthen a dominant position as a result of which effective competition would be significantly impeded in the internal market or in a substantial part of it. (para 199)

'The dominant position referred to is concerned with a situation where one or more undertakings wield economic power which would enable them to prevent effective competition from being maintained in the relevant market by giving them the opportunity to act to a considerable extent independently of their competitors, their customers and, ultimately, of consumers.' (para 200)

'The existence of a dominant position may derive from several factors which, taken separately, are not necessarily decisive. Among those factors, the existence of very large market shares is highly important. Nevertheless, a substantial market share as evidence of the existence of a dominant position is not a constant factor. Its importance varies from market to market according to the structure of those markets, especially so far as production, supply and demand are concerned (*Hoffmann-La Roche*, ... paragraphs 39 and 40).' (para 201)

'In addition, the relationship between the market shares of the undertakings involved in the concentration and their competitors, especially those of the next largest, is relevant evidence of the existence of a dominant position. That factor enables the competitive strength of the competitors of the undertaking in question to be assessed (*Hoffmann-La Roche*, paragraph 48).' (para 202)

'Accordingly, the fact that the Commission has relied in other concentration cases on higher or lower market shares in support of its assessment as to whether a collective dominant position might be created or strengthened cannot bind it in its assessment of other cases concerning, in particular, markets in which the structure of supply and demand and the conditions of competition are different.' (para 203)

'Furthermore, although the importance of the market shares may vary from one market to another, the view may legitimately be taken that very large market shares are in themselves, save in exceptional circumstances, evidence of the existence of a dominant position.' (para 205)

Foreseeable impact of a concentration

'So far as concerns the applicant's argument that the Commission did not properly assess what would have happened to prices if none of the factors relied on by the applicant had existed, suffice it to note that when the Commission assesses the foreseeable impact of a concentration on the market it is not required to consider what would have happened to the market in the past in the absence of one or other competitive factor. In its assessment, the Commission is required only to establish whether, by reason of, inter alia, previous developments in the conditions of competition in the market in question, the concentration may lead to the creation of a position of economic power for one or more undertakings, thereby enabling them to engage in abuses, particularly abuses involving price increases.' (para 262)

Comment

Much of the discussion in this case surrounded the conditions for establishing collective dominance. A detailed account of this discussion is found on page 325, Chapter 6, above.

The above extracts elaborate on the concept of dominance and market shares. Note in this respect the alignment of the conditions for dominance under Article 102 TFEU and under the Merger Regulation (paras 200–05).

The Guidelines on the Assessment of Horizontal Mergers further elaborate on the appraisal of concentrations and market shares: 'In assessing the competitive effects of a merger, the Commission compares the competitive conditions that would result from the notified merger with the conditions that would have prevailed without the merger. In most cases the competitive conditions existing at the time of the merger constitute the relevant comparison for evaluating the effects of a merger. However, in some circumstances, the Commission may take into account future changes to the market that can reasonably be predicted. It may, in particular, take account of the likely entry or exit of firms if the merger did not take place when considering what constitutes the relevant comparison. (para 9) 'Normally, the Commission uses current market shares in its competitive analysis. However, current market shares may be adjusted to reflect reasonably certain future changes, for instance in the light of exit, entry or expansion. Post-merger market shares are calculated on the assumption that the post-merger combined market share of the merging parties is the sum of their pre-merger market shares. Historic data may be used if market shares have been volatile, for instance when the market is characterised by large, lumpy orders. Changes in historic market shares may provide useful information about the competitive process and the likely future importance of the various competitors, for instance, by indicating whether firms have been gaining or losing market shares. In any event, the Commission interprets market shares in the light of likely market conditions, for instance, if the market is highly dynamic in character and if the market structure is unstable due to innovation or growth.' (para 15)

The prospective analysis embeds assumptions as to foreseeable changes in the market. In Case COMP/M.1806 *Astra Zeneca/Novartis* [2002] OJ C102/30 the Commission adjusted the market shares of the parties to reflect future changes in the market. In noted that: 'The parties' already strong position could be further strengthened as a result of regulatory pressure on the cheap active ingredient diuron. While there apparently are no concrete plans to prohibit the use of diuron in France, the permitted use rate has been reduced and could be further reduced. ... The main reason for concern in the French market is, however, the recent introduction of AstraZeneca's products, Katana/Mission, based on the active ingredient flazasulfuron.' (paras 413, 414)

In Case IV/M.1846 *Glaxo Wellcome/SmithKline Beecham* [2000] OJ C170/06 which concerned the pharmaceuticals industry, the Commission considered possible entry of future (pipeline) products. It noted that 'a full assessment of the competitive situation requires examination of the products which are not yet on the market but which are at an advanced stage of development (normally after large sums of money have been invested). ... The Commission has to look at R&D potential in terms of its importance for existing markets, but also for future market situations. In so far as research and development must be assessed in terms of its importance for future markets, the relevant product market can, in the nature of things, be defined in a less clear cut manner than in the case of existing markets. Market definition can be based either on the existing ATC classes or it can be guided primarily by the characteristics of future products as well as by the indications to which they are to be applied.' (paras 70–72)

Ryanair Holdings plc v Commission	**Horizontal Mergers**
T-342/07	Market Shares as Indicator
General Court, [2011] 4 CMLR 4	Air Transport Sector

Facts

In 2006 Ryanair launched a public bid for the entire share capital of Aer Lingus Group. The Commission blocked the transaction after raising serious doubts as to its competitive effect on the market (Case COMP/M.4439—*Ryanair/Aer Lingus*). Ryanair appealed the decision, arguing, among other things, that the Commission wrongly treated Ryanair and Aer Lingus as 'like-for-like' carriers, an approach which led it 'automatically' to conclude that the combined market shares of the carriers would significantly impede effective competition. It further claimed that the services offered by Ryanair and Aer Lingus are highly differentiated and focus on separate categories of passengers. Accordingly, the companies' market shares do not in themselves indicate the extent to which they exert a competitive constraint on each other.

Held

'Although the importance of market shares may vary from one market to another, the view may legitimately be taken that very large market shares are in themselves, save in exceptional circumstances, evidence of the existence of a dominant position.' The Commission did not 'automatically' infer from the high market shares that the concentration would significantly impede effective competition. On the contrary, the Commission expressly stated that market shares and concentration levels provided 'useful first indications' of the market structure and of the competitive importance of both the parties to the concentration and their competitors. It then carried out an in-depth analysis of the conditions of competition on each of the relevant routes on which both airlines operate and considered the effects on customers and competitors. (paras 41, 42)

It cannot be claimed that the decision is based on findings related solely to the combined market share of the merged entity. 'The Commission examined, simultaneously, the statistics illustrating the situation on the markets affected by the concentration at a given point in time, and dynamic data indicating the likely evolution of those markets if the concentration were to be implemented.' (para 43)

In its assessment the Commission could not ignore the importance to be attached to extremely high market shares as initial indicators. The Commission identified 35 routes on which the activities of the parties to the concentration overlap. The transaction would have created a monopoly on 22 of those routes and significant market shares on other routes. In the light of those findings the Commission was rightly able to find that the acquisition of very high market shares as a result of both the implementation of the concentration and the concentration level associated with it were relevant indicators of the market power which would have been acquired by Ryanair–Aer Lingus combined. Those findings had to be duly taken into account by the Commission and constitute, as such, elements enabling the finding that, save in exceptional circumstances, those extremely high market shares constituted, in themselves, evidence of the existence of a dominant position. (paras 45–54)

Comment

Very high market shares provide 'useful first indication'. When not contradicted by other evidence, they form a relevant indicator of the market power enjoyed by the merged entity.

In case Comp/M.5830 *Olympic Air/Aegean Airlines* the European Commission blocked a proposed transaction between the two airlines, which would have resulted in a quasi-monopoly on some of the main routes on the Greek air transport market. The Commission analysed the combined effects of the proposed merger on the individual routes on which both companies operate. It concluded that the merged entity would have controlled over 90 per cent of the Greek domestic air transport. Access to slots commitments offered by the parties were found insufficient to resolve the competitive concerns. Prior notification published [2010] OJ C174/16.

Sun Chemical Group BV and others v Commission	**Horizontal Mergers**
Case T-282/06	Market Shares and HHI Levels
General Court, [2007] ECR II-2149, [2007] 5 CMLR 438	Horizontal Merger Guidelines

Facts

The Commission appraised a proposed concentration by which Hexion Speciality Chemicals, Inc, was to acquire control of Akzo Nobel's Inks and Adhesive Resins business by way of purchase of shares and assets. On 29 May 2006, the Commission cleared the transaction declaring it to be compatible with the internal market (Case COMP/M.4071—*Apollo/Akzo Nobel IAR*). Sun Chemical Group BV and two other undertakings challenged the decision and applied for its annulment. They argued, among other things that the Commission did not conduct a detailed appraisal of the concentration levels and market shares. The General Court dismissed the action.

Held

Guidelines

'[T]he Commission is bound by notices which it issues in the area of supervision of concentrations, provided they do not depart from the rules in the Treaty and from the Merger Regulation (Case T-114/02 *BaByliss v Commission* [2003] ECR II-1279, paragraph 143, and Case T-119/02 *Royal Philips Electronics v Commission* [2003] ECR II-1433, paragraph 242).' (para 55)

The Guidelines on the assessment of horizontal mergers describe the analytical approach which the Commission aims to follow in its appraisal of horizontal mergers. They do not form a 'checklist' to be mechanically applied in each and every case; rather, the competitive analysis in a particular case is based on an overall assessment of the foreseeable impact of the merger in the light of the relevant factors and conditions. The Commission enjoys a discretion in the application of the Guidelines and is not required to examine of all the factors mentioned in them in every case. (paras 56–7)

Market shares

In its decision the Commission estimated the market shares of the merging parties and of their competitors. However it 'did not assess those market shares according to the criteria stated in paragraph 17 of the Guidelines nor did it make a Herfindahl-Hirschmann index ("HHI") calculation for the purposes of comparison with the thresholds laid down in paragraphs 19 to 21 of the Guidelines.' (para 133)

'As regards, first of all, the market shares, it must be borne in mind that, according to paragraph 17 of the Guidelines, only very large market shares of 50% or more may in themselves be evidence of the existence of a dominant market position. According to the same paragraph of the Guidelines, in the case of a smaller market share, the transaction may raise competition concerns in view of other factors such as the strength and number of competitors, the presence of capacity constraints or the extent to which the products of the merging parties are close substitutes. It follows that, in the present case, the analysis of market shares would not in itself have shown the existence of dominance, since the merged entity only held [40–50]% of the market. Therefore, the analysis of the other factors set out in paragraph 17 of the Guidelines is necessary to establish whether, overall, there is evidence of a dominant position.' (para 135)

Concentration levels

'With regard, secondly, to concentration levels, it must be pointed out that paragraphs 19 to 21 of the Guidelines set out, essentially, the HHI thresholds below which a merger is unlikely to raise competition problems. Thus, the Commission considers, in particular, that a merger is unlikely to raise horizontal competition concerns in a market with a post-merger HHI between 1000 and 2000 and a delta below 250, or where a post-merger HHI is above 2000 and the delta below 150, save in exceptional circumstances. According to paragraph 16 of the Guidelines, the HHI is equal to the sum of the squares of the individual market shares of each of the firms in the market.' (para 137)

'Those values indicate that the effects of the merger on the market exceed the HHI thresholds below which the merger does not, in principle, raise any competition concerns. However, the second sentence of paragraph 21 of the Guidelines states that exceeding those thresholds does not give rise to a presumption of the existence of competition concerns. It must be observed, however, that the greater the margin by which those thresholds are exceeded, the more the HHI values will be indicative of competition concerns.' (para 138)

'It follows that the post-merger HHI value does not provide any clear indication of the existence of competition problems in the present case, since it does not significantly exceed the HHI threshold of 2000. In fact, only the delta significantly exceeds the corresponding HHI threshold. However, that value is the only one likely to indicate competition problems, while neither the market shares nor the factors examined in the context of the second and third parts of this plea are indicative of such problems. In those circumstances, the Commission cannot be accused of disregarding the Guidelines in considering that there was no need to assess the concentration levels in the contested decision.' (para 139)

Comment

Market shares and HHI levels provide useful first indications of the market structure and of the competitive importance of both the merging parties and their competitors, but the Commission is not required to assess those factors in every decision. (Commission's Guidelines on the Assessment of Horizontal Mergers, para 14, General Court judgment para 140) The Commission will normally use current market shares in its analysis but may also adjust these to reflect future changes. (See Guidelines, para 15, cited on page 436 above)

'The overall concentration level in a market may also provide useful information about the competitive situation. In order to measure concentration levels, the Commission often applies the Herfindahl–Hirschman Index (HHI). The HHI is calculated by summing the squares of the individual market shares of all the firms in the market. The HHI gives proportionately greater weight to the market shares of the larger firms. Although it is best to include all firms in the calculation, lack of information about very small firms may not be important because such firms do not affect the HHI significantly. While the absolute level of the HHI can give an initial indication of the competitive pressure in the market post-merger, the change in the HHI (known as the "delta") is a useful proxy for the change in concentration directly brought about by the merger.' (Guidelines, para 16)

Generally, the Commission is unlikely to identify horizontal competition concerns in a market with a post-merger HHI below 1,000 or in a merger with a post-merger HHI between 1,000 and 2,000 and a delta below 250, or a merger with a post-merger HHI above 2,000 and a delta below 150, except where special circumstances are present. Such circumstances may include a merger involving a potential or recent entrant, important innovator, a maverick firm or a company with a pre-merger market share of 50 per cent of more. They may also involve cases where there are significant cross-shareholdings among the market participants or indication of coordination between them. (paras 19–20, Guidelines on the Assessment of Horizontal Mergers)

On modification of the HHI as a result of cross-shareholdings note Case IV/M.1383—*Exxon/Mobil* (cited in the Guidelines, para 20). There the Commission noted the commonality of interest between Exxon and Shell in the European gas production and in gas wholesaling in the Netherlands and Germany. This raised concerns that following the transaction only BP would need to be convinced to align itself with common Exxon/Mobil and Shell interests. To reflect the level of concentration in this market pre-merger and the impact of the transaction the Commission has estimated HHI indices that took into account the existence of cross shareholdings among most of the players in that market.

Aerospatiale-Alenia/de Havilland	**Horizontal Mergers**
Case IV/M.53	Non-coordinated Effects
European Commission, [1991] OJ L334/42	

Facts

The Commission received notification of a joint acquisition by Aerospatiale SNI (Aerospatiale) and Alenia-Aeritalia e Selenia SpA (Alenia) of the assets of the de Havilland division (de Havilland) from Boeing Company (Boeing). After establishing that the proposed joint venture had a Community (Union) dimension, the Commission assessed it in accordance with Article 2 of the Merger Regulation. Following its appraisal, the Commission declared the concentration incompatible with the internal market.

Held

'The operation has as its effect that Aerospatiale and Alenia, which control the world and European leading manufacturer of regional aircraft (ATR), acquire the world and European number two (de Havilland) as explained below. Regional aircraft (commuters) are aircraft in a range of between 20 and 70 seats intended for regional carriers and have an average flight duration of approximately one hour. The regional transport market is mainly characterized by low density traffic where turbo-prop engined aircraft are, as a general rule, less expensive to operate than jet aircraft. Although the market has for the time being and will have until the mid-90s a relatively high growth rate, the commuter market is comparatively small in terms of aerospace markets generally.' (para 7)

'The proposed concentration would significantly strengthen ATR's position on the commuter markets, for the following reasons in particular: high combined market share on the 40 to 59 seat market, and of the overall commuter market; elimination of de Havilland as a competitor; coverage of the whole range of commuter aircraft; considerable extension of the customer base.' (para 27)

'The proposed concentration would lead to an increase in market shares for ATR in the world market for commuters between 40 to 59 seats from 46% to 63%. The nearest competitor (Fokker) would have 22%. This market, together with the larger market of 60 seats and above where ATR has a world market share of 76%, is of particular importance in the commuter industry since there is a general trend towards larger aircraft.' (para 28)

'ATR would increase its share of the overall worldwide commuter market of 20 to 70 seats from around 30% to around 50%. The nearest competitor (Saab) would only have around 19%. On the basis of this the new entity would have half the overall world market and more than two and a half times the share of its nearest competitor.' (para 29)

'The combined market share may further increase after the concentration. The higher market share could give ATR more flexibility to compete on price (including financing) than its smaller competitors. ATR would be able to react with more flexibility to initiatives of competitors in the market place. Following a concentration between ATR and de Havilland, the competitors would be faced with the combined strength of two large companies. This would mean that where an airline was considering placing a new order, the competitors would be in competition with the combined product range of ATR and de Havilland.' (para 30)

The concentration would lead to the elimination of de Havilland as a competitor of ATR. (para 31)

The new entity ATR/de Havilland would be the only commuter aircraft manufacturer present in all the various commuter aircraft markets. It will allow ATR to significantly broaden its customer base thus strengthening its market power, especially once customers have made a commitment to ATR as a manufacturer and would face additional costs if they chose to place orders with another manufacturer. (paras 32–3)

The current and expected future strength of the remaining competitors is limited and it is questionable whether, outside the market of 20- to 39-seat commuters, competitors could provide effective competition in the medium to long term. (paras 34–42)

As for the position of customers in the commuter markets it appears that for most established airlines a direct negative effect from the proposed concentration would only appear over time. New airlines entering the market are likely to feel a more immediate impact. (paras 43–50)

'In general terms, a concentration which leads to the creation of a dominant position may however be compatible with the [internal] market within the meaning of Article 2(2) of the Merger Regulation if there exists strong evidence that this position is only temporary and would be quickly eroded because of high probability of strong market entry. With such market entry the dominant position is not likely to significantly impede effective competition. … In order to assess whether the dominant position of ATR/de Havilland is likely to significantly impede effective competition therefore, it is necessary to assess the likelihood of new entry into the market.' (para 53)

'Any theoretical attractiveness of entry into the commuter market by a new player must be put into perspective taking into account the forecast demand and the time and cost considerations to enter the market … in terms of increase in annual deliveries the market appears to have therefore already reached maturity. Even for a company currently active in a related industry not already present on the commuter market—in practice this would seem to be limited to large jet aircraft manufacturers—it would be very expensive to develop a new commuter from scratch. According to the study submitted by the parties, there are high sunk initial costs of entering the regional aircraft market and delays in designing, testing and gaining regulatory approval to sell the aircraft. These are important for several reasons. The critical point is that with substantial fixed and sunk costs of entering the industry, these markets will be viable only for a limited number of producers. Furthermore, once a manufacturer is committed to the design and production of an aircraft, it is extremely costly and lengthy to adjust that design and production to unanticipated changes in market demand for aircraft. … In terms of time, the study states that it takes approximately two to three years of marketing research to determine which plane is required to meet the anticipated needs of the market. … The study concludes that there is no doubt that the presence of substantial and fixed entry costs significantly reduces the entry response by others to any successful aircraft by one manufacturer. … It follows from the above that a new entrant into the market would face high risk. Furthermore, given the time necessary to develop a new aircraft and the foreseeable development of the market as described above, a new manufacturer may come too late into the market to catch the expected period of relatively high demand.' (paras 53–6)

The proposed concentration would allow the parties to the concentration to act to a significant extent independently of their competitors and customers. The dominant position created by the transaction is not merely temporary and will therefore significantly impede effective competition. (para 72)

Comment

In its decision the Commission noted how, once customers have made a commitment to ATR and purchased from it, they would be exposed to additional costs associated with purchasing products from another manufacturer.

In Case IV/M.986 *Agfa Gevaert/DuPont* [1998] OJ L211/22 the Commission considered the impact of locked-in customers who are unable to switch suppliers. It noted that the majority of end-users and dealers had difficulties in switching suppliers of negative plates. Although switching between products was theoretically possible, it was limited in practice. This undermined the ability of other competitors to challenge the market position of the merged entity. (paras 63–71) The Commission concluded on this point that 'not only the disruptive effect of switching suppliers for end-users but also the practice of tying sales of consumables to sales of equipment, and the exclusivity arrangements with dealers, are factors which limit the possibilities for current competitors to challenge the position of the new entity. As regards package deals, such competitors would either have to be able to provide financing for the existing equipment and take over any (financial) obligations entered into, and/or be able to offer a similar package to the end-user. The relative stability of market shares illustrates that under the present conditions, longstanding competitors who have sufficient market experience, will not be able to do so.' (para 71)

The following extracts from the Guidelines on the assessment of horizontal mergers shed further light on the appraisal process:

'The larger the market share, the more likely a firm is to possess market power. And the larger the addition of market share, the more likely it is that a merger will lead to a significant increase in market power. The larger the increase in the sales base on which to enjoy higher margins after a price increase, the more likely it is that the merging firms will find such a price increase profitable despite the accompanying reduction in output. Although market shares and additions of market shares only provide first indications of market power and increases in market power, they are normally important factors in the assessment.' (para 27)

'Products may be differentiated within a relevant market such that some products are closer substitutes than others. The higher the degree of substitutability between the merging firms' products, the more likely it is that the merging firms will raise prices significantly. For example, a merger between two producers offering products which a substantial number of customers regard as their first and second choices could generate a significant price increase. Thus, the fact that rivalry between the parties has been an important source of competition on the market may be a central factor in the analysis. High pre-merger margins may also make significant price increases more likely. The merging firms' incentive to raise prices is more likely to be constrained when rival firms produce close substitutes to the products of the merging firms than when they offer less close substitutes. It is therefore less likely that a merger will significantly impede effective competition, in particular through the creation or strengthening of a dominant position, when there is a high degree of substitutability between the products of the merging firms and those supplied by rival producers.' (para 28)

'When data are available, the degree of substitutability may be evaluated through customer preference surveys, analysis of purchasing patterns, estimation of the cross-price elasticities of the products involved, or diversion ratios. In bidding markets it may be possible to measure whether historically the submitted bids by one of the merging parties have been constrained by the presence of the other merging party.' (para 29)

'In some markets it may be relatively easy and not too costly for the active firms to reposition their products or extend their product portfolio. In particular, the Commission examines whether the possibility of repositioning or product line extension by competitors or the merging parties may influence the incentive of the merged entity to raise prices. However, product repositioning or product line extension often entails risks and large sunk costs and may be less profitable than the current line.' (para 30)

'Customers of the merging parties may have difficulties switching to other suppliers because there are few alternative suppliers or because they face substantial switching costs. Such customers are particularly vulnerable to price increases. The merger may affect these customers' ability to protect themselves against price increases. In particular, this may be the case for customers that have used dual sourcing from the two merging firms as a means of obtaining competitive prices. Evidence of past customer switching patterns and reactions to price changes may provide important information in this respect.' (para 31)

CVC/Lenzing	**Horizontal Mergers**
Case COMP/M.2187	Non-coordinated Effects
European Commission, [2004] OJ L82/20	Response of Rivals

Facts

The Commission received notification of a proposed concentration by which CVC Capital Partners Group Ltd ('CVC') indirectly acquired sole control of the Austrian undertaking Lenzing AG ('Lenzing') by way of a purchase of shares.

CVC provides consultancy services to investment funds and has a controlling interest in over 70 companies. One of these is the Acordis group, which is active in man-made fibres and speciality materials for industrial, textile, medical and hygienic applications. The target company, Lenzing, is active in the manufacturing and marketing of man-made cellulose-based fibres for textile and non-textile applications, engineering, plastic films and paper production. Following the appraisal of the concentration, the Commission concluded that the combination of the two companies would impede effective competition as a result of the creation or strengthening of a dominant position.

Held

The proposed transaction will eliminate competition between the two main competitors in the market, Lenzing and the Acordis group. Subsequently, the new entity will be able to behave independently of competition and consumers. It will be able to control production capacity and have an incentive to create shortage of supply in order to keep prices high. (paras 160–2)

'It should, however, be noted that the acquisition of the Lenzing plant opens an alternative strategic option for CVC which can complement the abovementioned strategy if need be. Indeed, as stated before, Lenzing had been the only European VSF manufacturer who actually raised its production capacity, against the common trend of capacity reductions. Especially in times of low demand, Lenzing had acted as a price-breaker and gained market share. This strategy to sacrifice margin for volume reflects the unique cost structure of Lenzing's business.' (para 163)

The new entity will thus have two strategic options. 'It could decide either to keep its sales volume high, reduce its margins and gain market share … or to reduce its sales volume and keep prices high. Competitors would not be in the position to match the first, and would be encouraged to support the second.' (para 165)

Under both scenarios the new entity will have the possibility to act independently of its competitors and customers as it faces insufficient competitive constraints and countervailing buying power. This is in particular as competitors have at best very limited possibilities for increasing their capacity in the next two years and are likely to act as 'price takers'. Additionally new entry into the market or increase in imports in the short to medium term is unlikely to occur. (paras 169–98)

Comment

The inability of competitors to effectively react to the market power and strategies of the new entity was a decisive factor in this decision.

On this point the Guidelines on the assessment of horizontal mergers note that:

'When market conditions are such that the competitors of the merging parties are unlikely to increase their supply substantially if prices increase, the merging firms may have an incentive to reduce output below the combined pre-merger levels, thereby raising market prices. The merger increases the incentive to reduce output by giving the merged firm a larger base of sales on which to enjoy the higher margins resulting from an increase in prices induced by the output reduction.' (para 32)

'Conversely, when market conditions are such that rival firms have enough capacity and find it profitable to expand output sufficiently, the Commission is unlikely to find that the merger will create or strengthen a dominant position or otherwise significantly impede effective competition.' (para 33)

'Such output expansion is, in particular, unlikely when competitors face binding capacity constraints and the expansion of capacity is costly or if existing excess capacity is significantly more costly to operate than capacity currently in use.' (para 34)

'Although capacity constraints are more likely to be important when goods are relatively homogeneous, they may also be important where firms offer differentiated products.' (para 35)

'Some proposed mergers would, if allowed to proceed, significantly impede effective competition by leaving the merged firm in a position where it would have the ability and incentive to make the expansion of smaller firms and potential competitors more difficult or otherwise restrict the ability of rival firms to compete. In such a case, competitors may not, either individually or in the aggregate, be in a position to constrain the merged entity to such a degree that it would not increase prices or take other actions detrimental to competition. For instance, the merged entity may have such a degree of control, or influence over, the supply of inputs or distribution possibilities that expansion or entry by rival firms may be more costly. Similarly, the merged entity's control over patents or other types of intellectual property (eg brands may make expansion or entry by rivals more difficult). In markets where interoperability between different infrastructures or platforms is important, a merger may give the merged entity the ability and incentive to raise the costs or decrease the quality of service of its rivals. In making this assessment the Commission may take into account, inter alia, the financial strength of the merged entity relative to its rivals.' (para 36)

On the ability of the merged entity to hinder the expansion of competitors note Case IV/M.784 *Kesko/Tuko* [1997] OJ L100 (on appeal T-22/97 *Kesko v Commission* [1999] ECR II-3775). In its decision, the Commission analysed the Finnish retail market and noted how Kesko and Tuko may impact on competition on the market. In its decision the Commission considered a range of variables. These included, among other things, the contracts binding the retailers to Kesko; the fact that the retailers are required to use the Kesko logotypes and the support services provided by Kesko; the bonuses and rebates providing an incentive for retailers to remain loyal to the Kesko group strategy; the control mechanisms by which Kesko ensures that each retailer adheres to the common objectives; the fact that the suppliers perceived Kesko and its retailers as an integrated entity, on account, in particular, of Kesko's invoicing system. The Commission pointed out that following completion of the concentration, Kesko will be able to organise the Tuko retailers in the same way as the Kesko retailers. (See the General Court judgment on appeal, paras 144–6)

Similarly, in case COMP/M.2621 *SEB/Moulinex* OJ C49 (on appeal Case T-114/02 *Babyliss SA v Commission* [2003] ECR II-1279), the Commission considered the effect of the merged entity on the expansion of competitors. It noted that the strength of the combined entity was accentuated by a unique portfolio of brands and by a strong presence on numerous markets. This was in contrast to the position of its competitors which had only a limited portfolio with a single brand. Subsequently, the Commission was of the opinion that in view of the importance of brands in that market and the new entity's product range and brand portfolio, 'it is unlikely that competitors will be able to challenge the parties' positions and bring to bear sufficient competition pressure on the new entity … the brand portfolio and the uniformly strong presence of the new entity in all the relevant product markets will be such that the new entity will be able to deter retailers from resisting a price rise, for example, by the threat of de-listing brands of the new entity … the predominant position of the SEB and Moulinex brands will make it difficult for a retailer to dispense with them on its shelves.' (paras 52, 53 of the Commission's decision)

Air Liquide/BOC	**Horizontal Mergers**
Case IV/M.1630	Merger with a Potential Competitor
European Commission, [2004] OJ L92/01	

Facts

The Commission received notification of a proposed concentration whereby Air Liquide SA ('Air Liquide'), an international group active in the field of industrial gases, acquired by way of a public bid control of parts of the BOC Group plc ('BOC'), which was involved in the production and distribution of industrial gases. In its investigation the Commission raised concerns as to the elimination of potential competition in the markets for cylinder and bulk gases.

Held

'Air Liquide represents one of the strongest potential entrants in BOC's national home markets. Competitors have stressed that Air Liquide would have been best placed amongst all industrial gases companies to make inroads into the United Kingdom market. Once the parties have merged, this competitive pressure would be lost. This would be true irrespective of whether or not Air Liquide was already active in BOC's home market.' (para 201)

'Air Liquide argues that its qualification as a potential competitor is purely theoretical because it has never tried to penetrate the United Kingdom market and is less likely to do so now that others have entered the market. However, a project study submitted to the Commission shows that Air Liquide has contemplated supplying bulk and cylinder gases in the United Kingdom when consulted by a customer. Moreover, Air Liquide concedes that Messer has been able to overcome the entry barriers to the United Kingdom bulk and cylinder markets, without however offering reasons why Air Liquide should not realistically be able to enter the United Kingdom market itself. Indeed, Air Liquide has the most successful history in entering other European markets of all industrial gases companies. By stating at the oral hearing that its absence from the United Kingdom is a business decision, Air Liquide has acknowledged that no objective factors would have prevented it from entering the United Kingdom market.' (para 203)

'The analysis of Air Liquide's specific competitive strengths confirms that Air Liquide is well placed to enter the United Kingdom cylinder and bulk markets. Furthermore Air Liquide is better placed than any other competitor to successfully sustain such market entry.' (para 219)

'In conclusion, potential competition in the markets for cylinder and bulk gases in the United Kingdom and Ireland largely depends on Air Liquide's continuing presence as an independent competitor. Once the incumbent (BOC) and the strongest potential entrant (Air Liquide) were merged, this competitive pressure would be lost.' (para 220)

'It should be stressed that the Commission's objections are not directed against Air Liquide's business strategy to date which may have been to not (yet) launch substantial activities in the United Kingdom and Ireland. Rather, the specific competition concerns arising from the proposed concentration relate to the elimination of the most credible potential competitor in the markets concerned. Irrespective of whether the competitor concerned has previously been willing to launch effective competition, the proposed concentration would permanently remove the possibility of such competition taking place. The proposed concentration would thus permanently eliminate potential competition and thereby strengthen BOC's existing dominant position in the markets concerned. The likely result would be that the combined entity (Air Liquide/BOC) would be able to perpetually dominate the markets for cylinder and bulk gases in the United Kingdom and Ireland.' (para 222)

Comment

The parties submitted commitments in order to remove the competition concerns identified by the Commission. Subsequently, the Commission declared the concentration compatible with the internal market.

In Case IV/M.1439 *Telia/Telenor* [2001] OJ L40/01, the Commission similarly considered the effect of a proposed transaction on potential competition. The Commission was concerned that the concentration would remove Telia, the largest telecommunications operator in Sweden, as a potential competitor in 'direct-to-home' (DTH) market. It noted that 'prior to the announcement of the proposed concentration, Telia had positioned itself to enter the DTH segment. In 1997, when Telia took the decision to make the investment to enter into a [long-term] lease for satellite transponder capacity from NSAB, it had plans to launch DTH distribution activities in competition with Telenor (and Netcom/MTG). Telia has argued that its decision not to go ahead with any DTH activities was adopted independently of the plans to merge with Telenor, and that the concentration therefore does not result in the removal of potential competition. Telia has, without providing any supporting evidence, argued that its abandoning of the DTH plans was due to its inability to convince broadcasters to grant it distribution rights for DTH. Apart from being unsupported by any evidence, this explanation therefore implies that Telia, after several years of contacts with broadcasters, would enter into a massive long-term investment in satellite capacity, without having ascertained that broadcasters could be convinced to provide it with the DTH rights needed to start the business. It is difficult to attach any importance to this explanation.' (para 331)

The Commission's Guidelines on the Assessment of Horizontal Mergers elaborate on the treatment of a concentration with a potential competitor:

'Concentrations where an undertaking already active on a relevant market merges with a potential competitor in this market can have similar anti-competitive effects to mergers between two undertakings already active on the same relevant market and, thus, significantly impede effective competition, in particular through the creation or the strengthening of a dominant position.' (para 58)

'A merger with a potential competitor can generate horizontal anti-competitive effects, whether coordinated or non-coordinated, if the potential competitor significantly constrains the behaviour of the firms active in the market. This is the case if the potential competitor possesses assets that could easily be used to enter the market without incurring significant sunk costs. Anticompetitive effects may also occur where the merging partner is very likely to incur the necessary sunk costs to enter the market in a relatively short period of time after which this company would constrain the behaviour of the firms currently active in the market.' (para 59)

'For a merger with a potential competitor to have significant anti-competitive effects, two basic conditions must be fulfilled. First, the potential competitor must already exert a significant constraining influence or there must be a significant likelihood that it would grow into an effective competitive force. Evidence that a potential competitor has plans to enter a market in a significant way could help the Commission to reach such a conclusion. Second, there must not be a sufficient number of other potential competitors, which could maintain sufficient competitive pressure after the merger.' (para 60)

The Coca-Cola Company/Carlsberg A/S	**Horizontal Mergers**
Case IV/M.833	Barriers to Entry
European Commission, [1998] OJ L145/41	Countervailing Buyer Power

Facts

The Commission received a notification of a proposed concentration by which the Coca-Cola Company (TCCC) and Carlsberg A/S (Carlsberg) would set up a jointly owned company, Coca-Cola Nordic Beverages (CCNB). The proposed joint venture was to own interests in various soft drink entities in the Nordic region, including certain assets that were to be transferred from Carlsberg to TCCC pursuant to a licence agreement. The Commission cleared the transaction subject to conditions. In its decision the Commission reviewed the barriers to entry to potential competition in the carbonated soft drinks market.

Held

'The main barriers to entry to the [carbonated soft drinks (CSD) market] are access to brands and to a distribution network, as well as to shelf space, a sales and service network, brand image and loyalty and advertising sunk costs. TCCC, PepsiCo and Cadbury Schweppes are the only international brand owners. In view of the risks, costs and the time needed to launch an international brand it is likely that only the existing three international brand owners would be able to launch new international CSD brands in any country. On the Danish market only Carlsberg and Bryggerigruppen have, in the past, been able to launch national premium brands. Therefore, it appears that only the existing brand owners in Denmark would be able to launch new brands.' (para 72)

'CSDs rely heavily on brand image to drive sales, and companies like TCCC and PepsiCo have established brand loyalty through heavy investments to maintain the high profile of their brands. The introduction of a new brand would thus require heavy expenditure on advertising and promotion in order to persuade brand-loyal consumers to switch away from their usual CSD brand. Moreover, consumer loyalty to the established brands would make it difficult for a new supplier to persuade retail customers to change suppliers and would thus further hinder entry. Such advertising and promotion expenditures are sunk costs and add substantially to the risk of entry.' (para 73)

'In addition, any potential entrant would also be hindered by the need for access to bottling and to a distribution system. Each of the major brewers in Denmark has its own distribution system, meaning that any new entrant would have to either incur the significant cost of setting up its own system or negotiate with a competitor for the use of their system. It is unlikely that a new entrant would find it economically viable to set up a new distribution operation, since the entrant would have to include beers and packaged waters in its system in order to achieve a sufficient volume of distribution. The brewers' power in this field is reinforced by the fact that CSDs are distributed in refillable containers and any new entrant's bottles would have to comply with the relevant standards. Therefore, a new entrant's products would have to be distributed by one of the existing brewers as is today the case for TCCC and Cadbury Schweppes products, which are distributed by Carlsberg, and PepsiCo brands, which are distributed by Bryggerigruppen. However, as the existing brewers are well established, and have their own line of soft drinks, it would be difficult for a new entrant to find distribution. Moreover, Carlsberg's holdings in several other Danish brewers makes it less likely that any potential entrant would be able to cooperate or otherwise form an alliance with a Danish brewing company. Furthermore, as mentioned above, it should be noted that Carlsberg has by far the best and most wide-ranging distribution system on the Danish market. For a new entrant the most efficient way to enter the Danish market would be to be distributed by Carlsberg.' (para 74)

'Finally, even if a new entrant were to obtain access to an adequate distribution network, the firm would still have to obtain shelf space and incur the expenses of supporting a sales and service network in order to ensure that its products were properly stocked and positioned.' (para 75)

Entry may be possible on a smaller scale, for example by deliveries directly to a supermarket chain with distribution completed through the supermarket chain's distribution system. This strategy does not involve heavy advertising costs or major investment in a distribution system. In addition, limited success and entry has been achieved by discount brands. However, overall there are no potential competitors who would or could enter the Danish CSD markets at either a brand or a bottling level. (paras 76–8)

Countervailing buyer power

Although big supermarket chains have more negotiating power than smaller retailers and are able to negotiate discounts which are not available to smaller retailers, they do not present sufficient countervailing buyer power to neutralise the market power of the parties. This stems from the fact that major retail chains need to stock leading brands such as those owned by TCCC and Carlsberg, as these are fast-moving consumer goods that 'build traffic'. The Coca-Cola brand, in particular, is considered a 'must stock' brand. Therefore, it appears that little, if any, countervailing buyer power arises between the customer and either the brand owner or bottler. (paras 79–81)

Comment

'The countervailing buyer power defence rests on the presumption that powerful buyers will be able to protect themselves—and thus, ultimately, also final consumers—against adverse changes in the terms of supply following the notified merger.' (Case COMP/M.5046 *Friesland Foods/Campina*, para 274)

In Case IV/M.1157 *Skanska/Scancem* [1999] OJ L183/01, the Commission noted that when assessing barriers to entry the relevant question is not only whether new entry is possible, but also whether it is likely to be on a scale sufficient to restrict the merged entity from behaving largely independently of its competitors following the concentration. (para 184)

In *Aerospatiale-Alenia/de Havilland* (above page 440) the Commission noted that the attractiveness of new entry has to be put into perspective taking into account the forecast demand and the time and cost considerations to enter the market. It then observed the substantial fixed and sunk costs of entering the industry, the high risk, the delays in designing, testing and gaining regulatory approval to sell aircrafts and the high switching costs for customers. (paras 54–6)

In Case IV/M.774 *Saint-Gobain/Wacker-Chemie* [1997] OJ L247/01 the Commission noted the high sunk costs and know-how involved in the construction of a green-field medium-sized SiC processing plant for macro grains, in addition to other barriers to entry, which reduced the likelihood for successful entrance. (paras 184–7)

The Commission's Guidelines on the Assessment of Horizontal Mergers elaborate on the examination of barriers to entry in paragraphs 68–75. Generally, 'When entering a market is sufficiently easy, a merger is unlikely to pose any significant anti-competitive risk. Therefore, entry analysis constitutes an important element of the overall competitive assessment. For entry to be considered a sufficient competitive constraint on the merging parties, it must be shown to be likely, timely and sufficient to deter or defeat any potential anti-competitive effects of the merger.' (para 68) 'The Commission examines whether entry is likely or whether potential entry is likely to constrain the behaviour of incumbents post-merger. For entry to be likely, it must be sufficiently profitable taking into account the price effects of injecting additional output into the market and the potential responses of the incumbents. Entry is thus less likely if it would only be economically viable on a large scale, thereby resulting in significantly depressed price levels. And entry is likely to be more difficult if the incumbents are able to protect their market shares by offering long-term contracts or giving targeted pre-emptive price reductions to those customers that the entrant is trying to acquire. Furthermore, high risk and costs of failed entry may make entry less likely. The costs of failed entry will be higher, the higher is the level of sunk cost associated with entry.' (para 69)

Deutsche Börse/NYSE Euronext	**Horizontal Mergers**
Case COMP/M.6166	Actual and Potential Competition
European Commission, [2011] OJ C199/9	Market Definition

Facts

The European Commission prohibited a proposed transaction between Deutsche Börse and NYSE Euronext due to its harmful effect on the sub-market for European financial derivatives (contracts traded on financial markets which are used to transfer risk). The two companies operate the two largest exchanges for financial derivatives in the world (Eurex and Liffe). The Commission found that the proposed merger would have resulted in a quasi-monopoly in the area of European financial derivatives traded globally on exchanges, leading to significant harm to derivatives users and the European economy. It is on this sub-market that the companies held a significant market share.

The finding of dominance was triggered by the Commission's narrow market definition in this case. According to the Commission, over-the-counter (OTC) trades do not compete with exchange-traded derivatives (ETDs). Subsequently, the merged entity will occupy a significant market share (90 per cent) on the ETD market. The Commission found that derivatives traded on-exchange and OTC derivatives are products with different characteristics. While Exchange-traded derivatives are fully standardised are typically around €100,000 per trade, OTC derivatives are customised to meet buyer and seller requirements, are around €200,000,000 per trade, and more expensive to execute.

The Commission rejected the argument that Deutsche Börse and NYSE Euronext specialise in the offering of different types of derivatives (short-term and long-term) on that market. While it is true that each of the exchanges focuses predominantly on short-term or long-term derivatives, the boundaries between the two are becoming blurred. The two undertakings compete with each other both as actual and potential competitors. This competition has resulted in fee cuts in the past and would be eliminated by the merger.

The Commission also considered there to be a limited likelihood for new entry or expansion which could counterbalance the market power of the merged entity. While the exchange industry is a global one, the Commission considered it unlikely that competition from the very large US-based CME Group would be sufficiently strong. That was because that company had a very limited presence on the European financial derivatives market and thus was not sufficiently established on that market to alleviate concerns as to the anticompetitive effects.

Commitments offered by the companies included (1) the sale of assets (including Liffe's European single stock equity derivatives products where these compete with Eurex) which were found by the Commission to be too small and not viable on a stand-alone basis, and (2) the provision of access to the companies' clearing-house, which the Commission considered insufficient.

Comment

The finding of impediment to competition was triggered by the narrow market definition. The Commission considered that the merger would have eliminated constraints on pricing and competition on product and innovation. These effects were not counterbalanced by efficiencies or by existing, or potential competition.

The Commission did not consider it likely that the merger will incentivise expansion or new entry to the market. In particular it did not consider it likely that the well-established US CME Group will form a viable competitor on the narrow market, as defined. This was because the company would face considerable obstacles owing to its different product portfolio and its inability to offer collateral savings comparable to those offered by the parties individually or by the merged entity.

Cisco Systems Inc and Messagenet SpA v Commission	Horizontal Effects
Case T-79/12	Conglomerate Effects
General Court, [2014] 4 CMLR 20	Standard of Proof

Facts

An appeal on the Commission decision in Case COMP/M.6281 *Microsoft/Skype*, concerning the sole acquisition by Microsoft of Skype, a provider of internet-based communications services and software. In its decision the Commission found that in the area of consumer communications, Microsoft and Skype's activities mainly overlap for video communications, where Microsoft was active pre-merger through Windows Live Messenger.

In its decision, the Commission distinguished between internet-based communications services aimed at the general public ('consumer communications') and those aimed at undertakings ('enterprise communications'). The Commission examined the impact of the concentration on those two markets. The Commission considered the horizontal effects the transaction would have on instant messaging, voice calls and video calls on personal computers functioning on the Windows operating system. It also considered horizontal effects on the enterprise communications markets. These effects did not raise concerns as to the effects of the transaction. The Commission further considered the possible conglomerate effects the transaction would have on the consumer communications market. The Commission held that the new entity had the ability, but not the incentive, to use Microsoft's strong position to distort competition in favour of Skype and Microsoft. It further held that anticompetitive effects would be limited or even non-existent, even if the new entity attempted to foreclose the market, by resorting to bundling, tying or undermining interoperability between products. Similarly, the Commission did not find there to be a risk of conglomerate effects on the enterprise communications market.

In October 2011, the Commission cleared the transaction. Cisco Systems Inc and Messagenet SpA, two competitors of Microsoft, applied for annulment of the Commission's decision. Action dismissed.

Held

Horizontal effects on the consumer communications market

Skype and Microsoft's activities in the field of consumer communications overlap, in particular with respect to video calls made on Windows-based PCs. On that market the combined entity would have a market share of between 80 and 90 per cent. However, the Commission took the view that that the high market shares are not particularly indicative of competitive strength in the fast-growing market of video communications. On that market services are provided freely, innovation is a key and competition is likely from potential competitors and existing operators, including Google and Facebook. The Commission also noted that the network effects which the concentration might give rise to would be diluted by the fact that users tend to communicate in small restricted circles and use a range of operators. (paras 51–2)

According to the Guidelines on horizontal mergers, increased market power would restrict competition if it enables the merged entity profitably to increase prices, decrease output, restrict choice, reduce quality of goods and services offered or diminish innovation, or if that power enables it to influence other parameters of competition. The burden of proving such harm lies with the Commission. (paras 61–3)

Very high market shares are liable to constitute serious evidence of the existence of a dominant position. However, it should be made clear that market shares as well as HHI are not indicative of a degree of market power which would enable the new entity to significantly impede effective competition in the internal market. '[T]he consumer communications sector is a recent and fast-growing sector which is characterised by short innovation cycles in which large market shares may turn out to be ephemeral. In such a dynamic context, high market shares are not necessarily indicative of market power and, therefore, of lasting damage to competition which Regulation No 139/2004 seeks to prevent.' (paras 65–74)

Network effects will not necessarily procure a competitive advantage for the merged entity or create a barrier to entry. Competing operators have sufficiently large market shares to constitute alternative networks. Switching between programmes is easy with no technical or economic constraints and many users will rely on more than one programme. In addition, future growth in demand for consumer video communications will to a large extent concern platforms such as tablets and smartphones and not PCs. (paras 75–84)

Competitive harm is unlikely, even if the concentration were to increase the merged entity's market power, as the bulk of video communications services are provided free of charge. As for price of advertising, it is noted that there is no evidence of a narrow advertising market aimed specifically at consumer video communications on Windows-based PCs. 'In the absence of such a market, advertisers can easily avoid any attempt to increase prices by redirecting their advertising expenditure towards other media, whether on the internet or elsewhere.' (paras 85–90)

The applicants have failed to demonstrate that the Commission erred in finding that the concentration will not harm competition on the consumer communications market. (paras 94–6)

Conglomerate effects on the enterprise communications market

'In the applicants' opinion, the Commission failed to take account of the conglomerate effects resulting from the concentration. In particular, the Commission failed to have regard to the ability of and the incentives for the new entity to use its position on the consumer communications market as leverage to distort competition on the enterprise communications market.' (para 107)

In its decision the Commission addressed the conglomerate arguments in a concise manner. The applicants incorrectly claimed that in doing so the Commission breached the requirements of Article 296 TFEU. It should be noted that the conglomerate effects theory advanced by Cisco was complex and abstract and that conglomerate mergers do not usually generate competition concerns. In such circumstances, it would be excessive to require a more detailed description of each aspect underpinning the analysis of the theory of conglomerate effects in the contested decision. (paras 110–13)

A conglomerate merger may give rise to competition concerns, among other things, where it enables the new entity to pursue a market foreclosure strategy. According to non-horizontal merger Guidelines, market foreclosure may occur if the combination of products in related markets confers on the merged entity the ability and incentive to leverage a strong market position on one market to foreclose competition on another market. The foreclosure effects feared by the applicants are too uncertain to be considered a direct and immediate effect of the concentration. (paras 116–22)

Comment

The Court endorsed the Commission's view that very high market shares and concentration levels do not necessarily indicate market power in the innovative and fast-growing video communications market. Any attempt by the parties to increase prices of PC communications is likely to trigger new entry or substitution in a market in which most products are offered free of charge.

The Court rejected the conglomerate argument as speculative. It noted that a concentration may be declared incompatible with the internal market only if it harms competition in a direct and immediate manner.

With reference to dynamic technology markets, the Court noted the possible irrelevance of large market shares. (paras 65–74) On this point, it is interesting to contrast the Commission's and the Court's assessment of market power in this case and in the *Microsoft* abuse case (concerning refusal to supply, page 289 above), where the Court noted that Microsoft impaired competition by acquiring significant market power (para 664).

Also interesting is the limited weight attributed to network effects in this dynamic market. (paras 75–84) In its Guidelines on the Assessment of Horizontal Mergers the Commission notes that '[t]he expected evolution of the market should be taken into account when assessing whether or not entry would be profitable. Entry is more likely to be profitable in a market that is expected to experience high growth in the future than in a market that is mature or expected to decline. Scale economies or network effects may make entry unprofitable unless the entrant can obtain a sufficiently large market share.' (para 72)

Facebook/WhatsApp Inc	**Horizontal mergers**
Case COMP/M.7217	Big Data and Network Effects
European Commission, C(2014) 7239 final	Consumer Communications Apps

Facts

Facebook and WhatsApp both offer communication applications for smartphones which allow text, photo, voice and video messages. The Commission found that two are not close competitors and cleared the transaction.

Held

Consumer communications services

The transaction concerns consumer communications services. These services were originally developed for personal computers and since then have shifted to smart mobile devices such as smartphones and tablets. 'Consumer communications services can be offered as a stand-alone app (for example, WhatsApp, Viber, Facebook Messenger and Skype), or as functionality that is part of a broader offering such as a social networking platform (for example, Facebook or LinkedIn). Consumer communications services can be differentiated on the basis of various elements' such as functionality, availability on operating systems and availability on different platforms. In the present case, of significance is the segmentation based on platforms, since WhatsApp is offered only for smartphones. The Commission will therefore appraise the transaction with reference to the market for consumer communications apps for smartphones. (paras 13–34)

The parties operate two consumer communications apps, Facebook Messenger and WhatsApp. A large number of other players provide consumer communications apps in competition with the parties. These include, among others, iMessage, BBM, ChatON, Google Hangouts and Skype. Consumer communications customers have a broad range of choices and many of them 'multi home'—use more than one consumer communications app simultaneously depending on their specific needs. The different apps compete against each other by attempting to offer the best and most reliable communication experience. (paras 84–7)

Facebook Messenger and WhatsApp are not close competitors. 'The Parties' offerings in consumer communications apps are different in several respects. These differences are mainly the result of Facebook Messenger being a stand-alone app which has been developed from functionalities originally offered by the Facebook social network. These differences relate to: (i) the identifiers used to access the services (phone numbers for WhatsApp, Facebook ID for Facebook Messenger); (ii) the source of the contacts (the user handset's address book for WhatsApp, all Facebook users in Facebook Messenger); (iii) the user experience (which is richer in Facebook Messenger given the integration with the core aspects of Facebook social network); (iv) the privacy policy (contrary to WhatsApp, Facebook Messenger enables Facebook to collect data regarding its users that it uses for the purposes of its advertising activities); 49 and (v) the intensity with which the apps are used.' (paras 101–02)

The users of consumer communications apps tend to be very price-sensitive and expect communications apps to be provided for free. Many customers multi-home and can easily switch between applications. The transaction is unlikely to increase switching costs. (paras 90, 108–13)

The consumer communications apps market has been characterised by disruptive innovation and no significant 'traditional' barriers to entry and expansion. The market is dynamic and fast-growing. Launching a consumer communications app does not require significant investment and there are no known patents, know-how or IPRs that would constitute barriers to entry. 'The Transaction is unlikely to give rise to an increase in entry barriers, as the Parties do not have control over any element influencing entry.' (paras 114–25)

'Network effects arise when the value of a product/service to its users increases with the number of other users of the product/service. The Commission notes that, in the present case, both Parties have large networks of users. ... The existence of network effects as such does not a priori indicate a competition problem in the market affected by a merger. Such effects may however raise competition concerns in particular if they allow the merged entity to foreclose competitors and make more difficult for competing providers to expand their customer base. Network effects have to be assessed on a case-by-case basis. In the present case, there are a number of factors which mitigate the role of network effects in impeding entry or expansion. First, ... consumer communications apps are a fast moving sector, where customers' switching costs and barriers to entry/expansion are low. ... Second, the use of one consumer communications app (for example, of the merged entity) does not exclude the use of competing consumer communications apps by the same user. ... Third, ... the Parties do not control any essential parts of the network or any mobile operating system. Users of consumer communications apps are not locked-in to any particular physical network, hardware solution or anything else that needs to be replaced in order to use competing products. ... Lastly, ... neither Facebook Messenger nor WhatsApp are pre-installed on a large base of handsets, and therefore there is no 'status quo bias' potentially affecting consumers' choices. Therefore, the Commission considers that, while network effects exist in the market for consumer communications apps, in the present case, on balance, they are unlikely to shield the merged entity from competition from new and existing consumer communications apps.' (paras 127–35)

Social networking services

Facebook operates the world's largest social network which connects over 1.3 billion users worldwide. Its services differ from consumer communications services as they tend to offer a richer social experience compared to consumer communications apps, they provide better functionality and involve more public communications and information sharing. (paras 45–61)

During the investigation, several third parties argued that absent the transaction WhatsApp would become a provider of social networking services in competition with Facebook. The Commission found no indication that WhatsApp was planning to become a social network which would have competed with Facebook absent the merger. (para 144) Further, due to the considerable differences between the functionalities and focus of WhatsApp and Facebook, the two are not close competitors in the potential market for social networking services. (para 158)

Online advertising services

'Since only Facebook, and not WhatsApp, is active in the provision of online advertising services, the Transaction does not give rise to any horizontal overlaps in the market for online advertising or in any sub-segment thereof. Moreover, WhatsApp does not currently collect data about its users concerning age, verified name, gender, social group, activities, consuming habits or other characteristics that are valuable for advertising purposes. Also, WhatsApp does not store messages once they are delivered, and a message is sent only to and from the handsets that are associated with the mobile phone numbers used. Once a user's message has been delivered WhatsApp has no record of the content of that message. Therefore, since WhatsApp does not currently collect any user data that are valuable for advertising purposes, the Transaction does not increase the amount of data potentially available to Facebook for advertising purposes.' (para 165–7)

The Commission also considered whether the transaction would strengthen Facebook's position in the online advertising market. Two possible theories of harm were considered: (1) the possible introduction of advertising on WhatsApp; and/or (2) using WhatsApp as a potential source of user data for the purpose of improving the targeting of Facebook's advertising activities outside WhatsApp. The Commission investigation into these two theories of harm did not give rise to concerns as to the compatibility of the transaction with the internal market. The Commission noted that: (1) while Facebook may be able to introduce ads on WhatsApp it would not have the incentive to do so, partly as customers will be able easily to switch to other ad free providers; (2) there are a significant number of market participants that collect user data alongside Facebook. Accordingly, even if Facebook was to use WhatsApp users' data, it will not strengthen its position in advertising services. (paras 168–91)

'Any privacy-related concerns flowing from the increased concentration of data within the control of Facebook as a result of the Transaction do not fall within the scope of the EU competition law rules but within the scope of the EU data protection rules.' (para 164)

Comment

The Commission concluded that the concentration between Facebook and WhatsApp will not give rise to concerns. The transaction was also reviewed by the US Federal Trade Commission (FTC). The FTC closed its investigation, without publicly commenting on the merger's antitrust implications. The Director of the FTC's Bureau of Consumer Protection noted in a letter to the merging parties that WhatsApp should continue to honour its privacy promises to consumers and that any usage of information which is inconsistent with the promises WhatsApp made when the data was collected would require consumers' affirmative consent.

Opponents of the transaction raised concerns as to the possible use of data following the concentration. While data, in itself, is neither good nor bad, its usage and control may undermine competition and give rise to other concerns including privacy and consumer protection. Following the transaction Facebook will benefit from distinct velocity of data collection and ability for real-time analysis. This, it has been argued, is likely to enable it to gain an advantage over competitors in advertising. While other companies, as the Commission noted, collect data alongside Facebook, the real value of data depends on timely availability, context and use. Arguably, the Commission (and the FTC) may have underestimated the true value of data in this case. One possible indication of the true value of (real-time) data may be found in the purchase price of US$19 billion, paid by Facebook to acquire WhatsApp—a company that had reported millions in net losses. Could it be that the true value of the transaction lies in the merged entity's ability to gather real-time quality data at high velocity which is not replicable through other sources?

In earlier cases involving data-related transactions the Commission took a similar view as in *Facebook/WhatsApp* and did not consider the amalgamation of data through a transaction to give rise to serious concerns, when such data does not provide a unique, non-replicable advantage and can be obtained by competitors through other means—either directly or through data brokers. For instance, in Case M.4731 *Google/DoubleClick* the Commission noted that 'the merged entity, let alone DoubleClick alone, would not have access to unique, non-replicable data because the type of information collected by DoubleClick is relatively narrow in scope. Other companies active in online advertising have the ability to collect large amounts of more or less similar information that is potentially useful for advertisement targeting.' (para 269) Similarly, in Case M.7023 *Publicis/Omnicom* the parties indicated that one of the rationales of the transaction was to develop 'big data' analytics—the ability to examine large amounts of data, and to uncover patterns, correlations and other information. In its analysis the Commission noted that a large majority of competitors 'are at least similarly placed to the merged entity to get access to big data analytics.' (para 628) It noted that competitors indicated that 'if the merged entity develops post-Transaction its own big data analytics platform and does not allow access to it, the impact will be limited as they are currently using their own data analytics platform or one from third parties.' (para 629) The Commission subsequently concluded that no serious doubts arise from the transaction in relation to 'big data'.

In Case M.5727 *Microsoft/Yahoo! Search Business*, the Commission considered 'big data' to form a competitive asset in online search and search advertising. An increase in data velocity, the Commission noted, allows more experimentation, increases the quality of search products and supports better ad matching and higher conversion rates. (para 192) The Commission acknowledged, however, the limits of scale as the 'value of incremental data decreases as the amount of data increases'. (para 174)

T-Mobile/tele.ring	**Horizontal Mergers**
Case M.3916	Non-coordinated Effects
European Commission, [2007] OJ L 88/44	Maverick

Facts

The Commission received notification of a proposed concentration whereby T-Mobile Austria GmbH acquired control over tele.ring. The Commission's appraisal reveals concerns as to the impact of the transaction on the Austrian market for the provision of mobile telephony services to final consumers. In its decision the Commission identified tele.ring as a maverick which has a much greater influence on the competitive process than its market share would suggest. The transaction was eventually cleared subject to commitments to divest part of tele.ring's business activity (UMTS frequencies and mobile telephony sites) to operators with lower market shares.

Held

'The Commission's market investigation leads it to conclude that the elimination of tele.ring as an independent network operator and the emergence of a market structure with two large network operators of similar size (Mobilkom and T-Mobile), a far smaller operator (ONE) and a very small operator (H3G) will give rise to non-coordinated effects, even though T-Mobile will not have the largest market share after the merger.' (para 40)

From 2002 to 2005 tele.ring was the most active player in the market. It 'exerts considerable competitive pressure on T-Mobile and Mobilkom in particular and plays a crucial role in restricting their freedom on pricing. The price analysis therefore suggests that tele.ring's role in the market has been that of a maverick.' (para 72)

Tele.ring's market share understates its significance in terms of competition. '[I]n view of tele.ring's target groups, customers who switched to tele.ring probably have very little incentive to return to the established providers purely on price grounds, since they probably charge higher prices.' (para 73)

'In the light of the preceding analysis, and especially with the elimination of the maverick in the market and the simultaneous creation of a market structure with two leading, symmetrical network operators, it is likely that the planned transaction will produce non-coordinated effects and significantly impede effective competition in a substantial part of the [internal] market. It is therefore probable that the proposed merger will have a tangible effect on prices in the Austrian end-customer market for mobile telephony services. Even if prices do not rise in the short term, the weakening of competitive pressure as a result of tele.ring's elimination from the market makes it unlikely that prices will continue to fall significantly as in the past.' (para 125)

'This conclusion is consistent with the [Commission's Guidelines on the Assessment of Horizontal Mergers]. These state that some firms have more of an influence on the competitive process than their market shares would suggest. A merger involving such a firm could change the competitive dynamics in a significant anti-competitive way, in particular when the market is already concentrated. This is precisely the case here. As noted ... the Austrian market for mobile telecommunications for end customers is highly concentrated. As has also been indicated, tele.ring, as a maverick, has a much greater influence on the competitive process in this market than its market share would suggest.' (para 126)

Comment

On the basis of an analysis of the switching behaviour of customers and of price comparisons, the Commission's appraisal indicated that that tele.ring's role in the market has been that of a maverick. It has exerted considerable competitive pressure, in particular on the two largest operators, Mobilkom and T-Mobile Austria. Subsequently, although T-Mobile would not have become the market leader in Austria following the proposed original transaction, the concentration would have significantly impeded effective competition on the Austrian market for the provision of mobile telephony services to final consumers. The commitments accepted by the Commission remedied these concerns.

In principle, a concentration may significantly impede effective competition when it results in one of the following effects: (1) a significant impediment to effective competition which results from the creation or strengthening of a dominant position (Non-coordinated effects); (2) a significant impediment to effective competition resulting from the non-coordinated behaviour of undertakings which would not have a dominant position (Non-coordinated effects); (3) a significant impediment to effective competition which results from the creation or strengthening of a collective dominant position (Coordinated effects).

The second category of non-coordinated effects concerns anticompetitive effects which may exist even absent dominance or collective dominance. Recital 25 of the Merger Regulation elaborates: '[U]nder certain circumstances, concentrations involving the elimination of important competitive constraints that the merging parties had exerted upon each other, as well as a reduction of competitive pressure on the remaining competitors, may, even in the absence of a likelihood of coordination between the members of the oligopoly, result in a significant impediment to effective competition. ... The notion of "significant impediment to effective competition" in Article 2(2) and (3) should be interpreted as extending, beyond the concept of dominance, only to the anti-competitive effects of a concentration resulting from the non-coordinated behaviour of undertakings which would not have a dominant position on the market concerned.'

The Guidelines on the Assessment of Horizontal Mergers further elaborate on the treatment of a transaction which would eliminate an important competitive force:

'Some firms have more of an influence on the competitive process greater than their market shares or similar measures would suggest. A merger involving such a firm may change the competitive dynamics in a significant, anticompetitive way, in particular when the market is already concentrated. For instance, a firm may be a recent entrant that is expected to exert significant competitive pressure in the future on the other firms in the market.' (para 37)

'In markets where innovation is an important competitive force, a merger may increase the firms' ability and incentive to bring new innovations to the market and, thereby, the competitive pressure on rivals to innovate in that market. Alternatively, effective competition may be significantly impeded by a merger between two important innovators, for instance between two companies with "pipeline" products related to a specific product market. Similarly, a firm with a relatively small market share may nevertheless be an important competitive force if it has promising pipeline products.' (para 38)

In Case M.877 *Boeing/McDonnell Douglas* ([1997] OJ L336/16), the Commission noted that the competitive influence of McDonnell Douglas Corporation (MDC) was greater than reflected by its market share: 'Although ... the market share of MDC has been continuously declining, it appears that the impact of MDC on the conditions of competition in the market for large commercial aircraft was higher than reflected by its market share in 1996. ... This is confirmed by a study ... in which 52 aircraft-supply competitions between 1994 and 1996 were analysed, comparing those in which MDC participated with those in which it did not participate. In this study, it was found that the MDC presence led to a reduction of over 7% in the realized price as compared with the list price as far as orders placed with Airbus were concerned.' (para 58)

Hutchison 3G Austria/Orange Austria	**Horizontal Mergers**
Case M.6497	Non-coordinated Effects
European Commission, [2013] OJ C224/06	Non-collusive Oligopoly

Facts

The Commission approved, subject to conditions, the acquisition of Orange's mobile telephony business in Austria by Hutchison 3G. The transaction changed the number of operators on the market from four to three, with the new entity having a smaller market share than its two remaining competitors. The Commission opined that the market power of the merging parties would have been higher than what their market shares suggested and considered possible non-coordinated effects in a non-collusive oligopoly, notwithstanding the absence of the creation or strengthening of dominance.

Held

'Often, a merger giving rise to … non-coordinated effects would significantly impede effective competition by creating or strengthening the dominant position of a single firm, which, typically, would have an appreciably larger market share than the next competitor post-merger. However, as set out in recital 25 in the preamble to the Merger Regulation, mergers in oligopolistic markets, involving the elimination of important competitive constraints that the Parties previously exerted upon each other together with a reduction of competitive pressure on the remaining competitors may, even where there is little likelihood of coordination between the members of the oligopoly, also result in a significant impediment to effective competition notwithstanding that they do not give rise to or strengthen a dominant position.' (paras 87–9)

Such non-coordinated effects may give rise to competitive concerns even when the combined market share of the parties is low. The Commission notes that no legal presumption exists according to which undertakings concerned may not be liable to impede effective competition if their market shares do not exceed 25%. (paras 90–2)

Comment

In its analysis the Commission took into account: the market position of the merging firms; them being close competitors; the merger eliminating an important competitive force; the limited ability of competitors to react to price increases by an increase of supplies or through price reductions; the limited likelihood of entry; and the lack of countervailing buyer power. It concluded that the reduction of operators from four to three would significantly impede effective competition by means of non-coordinated effects. It subsequently approved the transaction subject to conditions.

In its decision, the Commission noted earlier cases in which concentrations gave rise to concerns despite not leading to a dominant position. Among these cases: Case M.3916 *T-Mobile/tele.ring* (page 455 above) and Case M.5224 *EDF/Segebel* ([2010] OJ 57/0), where the market shares of the parties were smaller and the main competitor was stronger than in the Hutchison 3G Austria transaction.

Similarly, in Case M.7421 *Orange/Jazztel* ([2015] OJ C407/18), the Commission noted that 'the Merger Regulation explicitly recognises that mergers in oligopolistic markets involving the elimination of important competitive constraints that the merging parties previously exerted upon each other together with a reduction of competitive pressure on the remaining competitors, could, even if there is little likelihood of coordination between the members of the oligopoly, also result in a significant impediment to effective competition.' (para 188)

The increased reliance by the Commission on Recital 25 in the preamble to the Merger Regulation supports intervention and remedies below levels of dominance. The limits of this expansive theory of harm are yet to be reviewed by the European Court.

UPS/TNT	**Horizontal Mergers**
Case M.6570	Non-coordinated Effects
European Commission, [2014] OJ C187/14	Non-collusive Oligopoly/Maverick

Facts

The Commission prohibited the proposed acquisition of TNT Express by UPS. The Commission was concerned with the elimination of TNT, a maverick on the market for international express deliveries of small packages. The Commission opined that although UPS would not have been dominant following the transaction, competition on the market would nevertheless be significantly reduced.

Held

'In assessing whether the loss of direct competition as a result of the merger would significantly impede effective competition in the market and lead to consumer harm, the Commission takes into account, on the one hand, the likelihood that the merger will produce anticompetitive effects in the absence of efficiencies and other countervailing factors and, on the other hand, the likelihood that the anticompetitive effects would be offset by such countervailing factors (such as buyer power or entry).' (para 721)

'As regards the likelihood that the merger would lead to higher prices in the absence of offsetting efficiency gains, static economic models of oligopolistic competition predict that in mergers between companies producing imperfect substitutes the merged firm would have an incentive to increase prices post merger. This incentive arises from the ability of the merged firm to recapture, through the sales of the merger partner's product, some of the sales that would otherwise be lost as a result of such price increase. This effect is stronger if the merger brings together close competitors and/or if the concentration on the market is already high (that is if there will be few remaining rivals). … The incentive of the merging parties to increase prices also limits the competitive pressure on the other firms in the market. In general, these models predict that the equilibrium effect on the market involves higher prices and lower output, though the magnitude of the effect would depend on the nature of competition.' (para 722)

'Indeed, the Horizontal Merger Guidelines specify that "mergers in oligopolistic markets involving the elimination of important competitive constraints that the merging parties previously exerted upon each other together with a reduction of competitive pressure on the remaining competitors may, even where there is little likelihood of coordination between the members of the oligopoly, also result in a significant impediment to competition. The Merger Regulation clarifies that all mergers giving rise to such non coordinated effects shall also be declared incompatible with the common market. Paragraph 25 of the Merger Regulation No 139/2004 further clarifies that: "The notion of 'significant impediment to effective competition' in Article 2(2) and (3) should be interpreted as extending, beyond the concept of dominance, only to the anti-competitive effects of a concentration resulting from the non-coordinated behaviour of undertakings which would not have a dominant position on the market concerned". Indeed, the Transaction would eliminate an important competitive force on the market, and would relax competition which existed before between TNT and UPS. In addition, as stated in the Horizontal Merger Guidelines, non-merging firms, in particular DHL, can also benefit from the reduction of competitive pressure that results from the merger, since the merged firms' price increase may switch some demand to the rival firms, which in turn may find it profitable to increase their prices, leading to higher overall prices for intra-EEA express deliveries after the takeover of TNT by UPS.' (para 723)

Comment

To remedy the Commission's concerns, the Commission insisted that UPS commit to including an upfront buyer or fix-it-first solution. UPS's failure to comply with this request subsequently led to the prohibition of the transaction. See page 485 below for further discussion of other aspects of the transaction.

UPS has challenged the decision: Case T-194/13 *United Parcel Service v Commission* (appeal pending).

Thales/Finmeccanica/Alcatel Alenia Space/Telespazio   **Vertical Effects**
Case COMP/M.4403   Input Foreclosure
European Commission, [2009] OJ C34/05

Facts

The Commission received a notification of a proposed concentration by which Thales will acquire Alcatel's shareholdings in AAS, a French company jointly controlled by Alcatel and Finmeccanica, which is active in the design and manufacture of ground and space systems. Post-merger Thales and Finmeccanica will jointly control AAS. In its decision the Commission considered the impact of the transaction on the worldwide market of commercial telecommunications satellites, and the specific satellites subsystems for telecommunications satellites. In its investigation the Commission considered whether Thales, as the new parent company of AAS, would be likely to foreclose entry of competitors at the downstream market. More specifically, the Commission investigated whether the new entity would have the ability and incentive to discriminate in the supply of travelling wave tubes (TWTs) to rival travelling wave tube amplifier (TWTA) producers so as to favour its downstream activities on the TWTA market.

TWTs are electronic components used to amplify microwave signals received by satellites before the signals are retransmitted to the earth. They are integrated to form TWTA which is the main transmitter on a satellite, used to amplify the microwave signal before it is broadcast back to earth.

Held

'The issue raised by the proposed operation is whether or not the notified operation will give the new entity the ability and incentive to engage in input foreclosure and significantly impede effective competition downstream, that is to say whether Thales, as the new parent company of AAS, would be likely in the foreseeable future to foreclose AAS' downstream rivals on the market for TWTAs.' (para 253)

'The investigation has not focused on foreclosure strategies whereby the new entity Thales/AAS would refuse to supply TED TWTs to a rival integrator such as Tesat or to rival satellite manufacturers, as third-party complainants broadly admit that an outright refusal to supply would be unlikely. Rather, what has been investigated is whether the new entity would discriminate against Tesat, so as to favour its integrated activities downstream on the market for TWTAs, and/or against satellite manufacturers so as to favour its activities on the market for telecommunications satellite prime contracting.' (para 254)

'During its investigation, the Commission examined whether the new entity would be in a position to adopt various subtle cost-raising strategies ..., as this procurement process requires back-and forth interaction between the supplier and the customer. Such strategies could consist in not reacting in time to the integrator's or the satellite manufacturer's requests for price quotations and technical information, offering an unfavourable price, offering a less favourable delivery schedule for the TWTs, or offering a less favourable compliance list for the technical performance of the TWTs. This type of foreclosure behaviour was alleged by third parties to be particularly difficult to detect.' (para 256)

'As regards replies to requests for quotation, it was alleged that TED [a wholly owned subsidiary of Thales] would delay its replies to requests for technical information from Tesat or rival satellite manufacturers. By so doing, it would impair the ability of the new entity's rivals to participate in the back-and-forth negotiations and therefore reduce their potential to win the bid.' (para 257)

'Finally, with regard to pricing, TWTs are complex products which are customised and project-specific. As such, it has been alleged that TED could offer the same contractual conditions to the new entity and third parties, but provide for more favourable unwritten conditions for the new entity.' (para 260)

In principle, successful foreclosure strategies would allow Thales/AAS to develop its activities as TWTA integrator, to gain market share, and incentivise it to further integrate downstream in the market for TWTAs. However, the new entity's ability and incentive to foreclose rival integrators would be seriously constrained as it has limited access to production capacity of electronic power conditioners, which are required for such expansion. Additionally, the new entity will find it difficult to convince prime contractors and satellite operators to switch suppliers and in any way might lack incentive to enter into this market as margins are considerably lower at the TWTA level which is characterised by more competitive pressure than at the TWT level. (paras 262–8)

Comment

Input foreclosure may take the form of subtle strategies and need not amount to a refusal to supply. The likelihood of the new entity engaging in input foreclosure required a detailed analysis following which the Commission concluded that the new entity lacked incentive and ability to do so. The Commission therefore concluded that the concentration does not lead to a significant impediment to competition on the TWTA market.

In Case COMP/M.4300 *Philips/Intermagnetics* the notifying parties argued that input foreclosure as a result of the transaction was unlikely as it would not make economic sense for the new entity to stop selling coils to original equipment producers and third party customers. The Commission accepted that the cost and profit margins, the contractual arrangements surrounding the supply of these systems and the ability of MRI system manufacturers to switch suppliers in a reasonable period of time suggest that any foreclosure by the new entity—provided it would have the ability to do so—would have short-lived benefits (if any) and would harm the new entity's profitability on the longer run. (paras 53–64)

The Commission's Guidelines on the assessment of non-horizontal mergers add on this point:

'In assessing the likelihood of an anticompetitive input foreclosure scenario, the Commission examines, first, whether the merged entity would have, post-merger, the ability to substantially foreclose access to inputs, second, whether it would have the incentive to do so, and third, whether a foreclosure strategy would have a significant detrimental effect on competition downstream. In practice, these factors are often examined together since they are closely intertwined.' (para 32)

'Input foreclosure may occur in various forms. The merged entity may decide not to deal with its actual or potential competitors in the vertically related market. Alternatively, the merged firm may decide to restrict supplies and/or to raise the price it charges when supplying competitors and/or to otherwise make the conditions of supply less favourable than they would have been absent the merger. Further, the merged entity may opt for a specific choice of technology within the new firm which is not compatible with the technologies chosen by rival firms. Foreclosure may also take more subtle forms, such as the degradation of the quality of input supplied. In its assessment, the Commission may consider a series of alternative or complementary possible strategies.' (para 33)

'Input foreclosure may raise competition problems only if it concerns an important input for the downstream product. This is the case, for example, when the input concerned represents a significant cost factor relative to the price of the downstream product. Irrespective of its cost, an input may also be sufficiently important for other reasons. For instance, the input may be a critical component without which the downstream product could not be manufactured or effectively sold on the market, or it may represent a significant source of product differentiation for the downstream product. It may also be that the cost of switching to alternative inputs is relatively high.' (para 34)

'For input foreclosure to be a concern, the vertically integrated firm resulting from the merger must have a significant degree of market power in the upstream market. It is only in these circumstances that the merged firm can be expected to have a significant influence on the conditions of competition in the upstream market and thus, possibly, on prices and supply conditions in the downstream market.' (para 35)

Facts

The Commission received a notification of the acquisition of sole control by the American private equity investment fund WLR of the German company BST Safety Textiles Holding GmbH ('BST'). BST and Safety Components International Inc ('SCI') are both active in the EEA in the supply of automotive airbag components. BST is a supplier of flat fabrics for use in the manufacture of automotive airbag cushions, whilst SCI, controlled by WLR, produces airbag cushions. The sector involved in the transaction is the manufacture of components for automotive airbag modules, which provide passenger protection in the event of a collision. The Commission found that the new entity would not enjoy market power over its customers, who themselves have extensive in-house airbag cushion production facilities, and are thereby in a strong bargaining position when contracting out-sourced supply. The Commission also concluded that the transaction would not lead to a significant loss of customers for the merged entity's fabric competitors.

Held

The merged entity would not be able to foreclose access to a sufficient cut and sewn airbag cushion (CSC) customer base and foreclose competitors on the fabric market, for a number of reasons: (1) it is difficult for a CSC producer to switch a fabric supplier quickly; (2) only one competitor of BST currently depends for more than 10 per cent of its flat fabric turnover on SCI; (3) most of BST's main competitors are large diversified companies; (4) BST's weaving capacity is currently fully utilised, and could not be increased economically in the short term; (5) SCI's purchases of flat airbag fabrics currently represent only 15–25 per cent of total Union demand for flat airbag fabrics. Subsequently BST's competitors would still have access to a substantial customer base; (6) the transparency of the fabric/CSC production chain would not allow the merged entity to cut prices of CSCs in order to expand its share of the CSC market, without facing demands for similar price cuts from other producers. (paras 31–8)

Comment

The Commission declared the transaction compatible with the internal market.

In Case COMP/M.1879 *Boeing/Hughes* [2004] OJ L63/53 the Commission considered a transaction which combined the parties' satellite manufacturing activities and resulted in vertical integration between Hughes' satellite operations and Boeing's launch activities. Among other things, the Commission examined whether Hughes could induce its customers to choose Boeing as a launch service operator for Hughes' satellites. Given that satellite manufacturing and launch services are complementary goods such behaviour could substantially affect the competitiveness of other launch service operators and thus possibly create a dominant position by Boeing on the launch service markets. Following its investigation, the Commission concluded that the parties would not have an incentive to engage in such behaviour as they would risk losing satellite sales. In addition the Commission questioned their ability to engage in such behaviour and the extent to which the launch service sector could be monopolised by them. It subsequently cleared the transaction. (paras 81–103)

Customer foreclosure may occur when a supplier integrates with an important customer in the downstream market. 'In assessing the likelihood of an anticompetitive customer foreclosure scenario, the Commission examines, first, whether the merged entity would have the ability to foreclose access to downstream markets by reducing its purchases from its upstream rivals, second, whether it would have the incentive to reduce its purchases upstream, and third, whether a foreclosure strategy would have a significant detrimental effect on consumers in the downstream market.' (para 59, Guidelines on the assessment of non-horizontal mergers)

AOL/Time Warner   **Vertical Mergers**
Case COMP/M.1845
European Commission, [2001] OJ L268/28

Facts

The Commission received a notification of a proposed concentration by which America Online, Inc ('AOL'), the largest Internet access and service provider in the world, would merge with Time Warner, Inc ('Time Warner'), one of the world's largest recording and music publishing companies, creating a new entity AOL Time Warner. In the investigation, the Commission considered the effects of the vertical integration of Time Warner content with AOL online services, especially in light of AOL's joint promotion, distribution and sales agreement with Bertelsmann, the German music recording, publishing and broadcasting group. The Commission raised concerns that strength of the music catalogue to which AOL would have access following the transaction would enable it to act as gatekeeper, dictate the technical standards for delivering music over the Internet and monopolise the music player software. The transaction was cleared subject to conditions.

Held

Online music

The Commission considers that the new entity would become dominant in the market for on-line music.

AOL/Time Warner will control Time Warner publishing rights. AOL will additionally have access to Bertelsmann's music library and corresponding rights. As a result AOL will secure access to the leading source of music publishing rights. 'One entity controlling such a sizeable music catalogue could exercise substantial market power, by refusing to license its rights, or threatening not to license them, or imposing high or discriminatory prices and other unfair commercial conditions on its customers wishing to acquire such rights (such as Internet retailers offering music downloads and streaming).' (paras 46, 47)

The combined entity would be in a position to dictate the technical standards for delivering music over the Internet. By releasing all its music on proprietary codes or formats, the new entity could prevent its music content from being downloaded or streamed through competing technologies. Because of the breadth of Time Warner and Bertelsmann publishing rights, the new entity would be in a position to impose its technology or formatting language as the industry standard. 'For example, the new entity, by threatening not to license its technology, could force developers of music players not to support competing technologies. Competing record companies wishing to distribute their music on-line would then be required to format their music using the new entity's technology. Because of its control over the relevant technology the new entity would be in a position to control downloadable music and streaming over the Internet and raise competitors' costs through excessive license fees.' (paras 55, 56)

Music player

The Commission considers that the new entity would become dominant in the market for music software.

The combined entity could decide to format Time Warner music to make it compatible only with AOL's Winamp, which would become the only music player which could be used to play its music. AOL has also the right to reformat Bertelsmann's music to make it compatible with Winamp. Winamp could support the other formats and technologies, with which competing record companies release their music. As a result, Winamp would become the only music player in the world able to play virtually all the music available on the Internet. As a result of the transaction the new entity will control the dominant player software and could charge supracompetitive prices for it. (para 60–5)

Internet access (US)

'AOL's service has also been described as a "walled garden" or a "one-stop shop", where the generality of Internet users would have the impression they can find whatever they want. This would appear to mean that a large number of services and content are offered on the AOL homepage. Many of these are exclusive to AOL. Once the user clicks on these hyperlinks he enters a cul de sac from which he can only access other affiliated services and certain key external content. ... The breadth of AOL services and content could give rise to considerable switching inertia as users may tend to identify AOL with the Internet and not look for competing sites. Therefore, the more content AOL acquires and the bigger its community of users, the less reason for a subscriber to abandon AOL's walled garden, and the more reason for potential Internet users to join AOL. In this context, a distinction has to be drawn between passive and active Internet users. The former are inexperienced users who tend to stay with AOL, clicking on the hyperlinks as displayed by AOL. In contrast, active Internet users are experienced users, who look for specific pieces of information and are able to find their own way through the Internet. According to a presentation by ... OL's chief executive officer, evidence shows that AOL's subscribers spend (a considerable amount) of their surfing time within AOL. ... This shows that passive users represent the majority of AOL's customers.' (para 70)

'The Commission considers that the vertical integration of Time Warner content with AOL Internet services will change AOL's incentive in setting access prices to unaffiliated content providers. After the merger AOL will take into account, in its dealing with third party content providers, the impact of competition on Time Warner's profitability. Therefore, AOL will have an incentive to toughen the terms of trade and increase the price of access in order to protect Time Warner's profitability and compensate for Time Warner's reduced revenues because of competition.' (para 74)

Broadband content and access

'The new entity will be the first vertically integrated broad-band content provider. The Commission is of the opinion that a company able to bundle broad-band Internet access with a vast array of attractive broad-band content (and music) will have a considerable competitive advantage over non-integrated content providers or firms able to supply a more limited range of content.' (para 88)

Although the new entity could lever Time Warner's broad-band content into the emerging high-speed Internet access market in Europe, the Commission, after examination, considers that there is no credible basis for concluding that, in the foreseeable future, the new entity will dominate the emerging broad-band market in the EEA. (paras 93–5)

Comment

The transaction was also subjected to merger control in the US where the FTC cleared it subject to conditions.

The conditional clearance of the transaction in both jurisdictions reflected the notion that it would yield efficiencies in distribution, combining each of the companies' relative strengths in content development and distribution, and meld old media with new.

Interestingly, in December 2009, almost ten years after the transaction took place, the merged entity split its activity and demerged back to two companies. The move reflected the limited value which was achieved from the combination of the two entities and the failure to transform it into a powerhouse which would transform the landscape of media and internet markets. Faced with ongoing difficulties to materialise synergies between the two companies and AOL's declining role in Internet access, each company was set to focus on its core business.

TomTom/Tele Atlas	**Vertical Mergers**
Case COMP/M.4854	Foreclosure
European Commission, [2008] OJ C237/8	Efficiencies

Facts

Following a Phase II investigation, the Commission cleared, with no conditions, a proposed vertical transaction in which TomTom, the largest supplier of portable navigation devices (PNDs) in Europe, acquired Tele Atlas, a producer of navigable digital map databases. The Commission's appraisal centred on possible foreclosure effects which may result from input foreclosure in the downstream navigation markets or due to misuse of confidential information by the merged entity.

Held

Foreclosure

'The Non-Horizontal Merger Guidelines point to three conditions which are necessary for the merged entity to have the ability to foreclose its downstream competition, namely the existence of a significant degree of market power, the importance of the input and the absence of timely and effective counter-strategies.' (para 194)

'Post-merger, TomTom/Tele Atlas will take into account how the sales of map databases to TomTom's competitors will affect its profits not only upstream but also on the downstream market. Therefore, when considering the profitability of an input foreclosure strategy, the merged entity faces a trade-off between the profit lost in the upstream market due to a reduction of input sales and the profit gained on the downstream market by raising its rivals' costs. This trade-off depends on the level of profits that the merged entity obtains upstream and downstream.' (paras 211, 212)

The Commission's analysis reveals that while the merged entity has the ability to foreclose, it will lack the incentive to do so. Any significant price increase would not be profitable for the merged entity as the downstream gains would not be sufficient to compensate upstream losses. Accordingly, the merged entity would have no incentive to increase prices in a manner which would lead to anticompetitive effects downstream. (paras 190–230)

Effects in the downstream market—input foreclosure

'The overall effects of the vertical integration of TomTom and Tele Atlas have to be assessed in the downstream market. As mentioned in paragraph 47 of the Non-Horizontal Merger Guidelines, "a merger will raise competition concerns because of input foreclosure when it would lead to increased prices in the downstream …" the Non-Horizontal Merger Guidelines state that "if there remain sufficient credible downstream competitors whose costs are not likely to be raised, for example because they are themselves vertically integrated or they are capable of switching to adequate alternative inputs, competition from those firms may constitute a sufficient constraint on the merged entity and therefore prevent output prices from rising above pre-merger levels." Such a situation limiting the possible effects of foreclosure is present in this case. … It is important to note that this finding does not rely on the fact that the vertical integration will give an incentive for the merged entity to decrease prices since it eliminates double mark-ups.' (paras 231–7)

Efficiencies

'The overall impact of the transaction however will also be affected by the likely efficiencies that are brought about by the merger and substantiated by the parties. While there is a lack of anti-competitive effects irrespective of efficiencies, these efficiencies form a part of the overall competitive assessment.' (para 238)

'As set out in the Non-Horizontal Merger Guidelines, "a vertical merger allows the merged entity to internalise any pre-existing double mark-ups resulting from both parties setting their prices independently pre-merger." In this case, the problem of double mark-ups can not be discarded since the marginal cost of map databases [is close to zero and consequently gross margins on map databases are high].' (para 239)

'The impact of the elimination of double mark-ups may be illustrated in the following manner. Suppose the map database represents 5% of the price of the PND. ... Post-merger, the integrated company will realize that the true cost it has for an additional map database is not 5% of the PND price, but a small fraction of this amount. As a result, the merged entity will have an incentive to expand sales to take advantage of the higher profits it makes on the sale of a PND. If it is assumed that 50% of the cost decrease is passed on, one finds that the price of TomTom's PND would decrease by [0–5%], which represents approximately a [0–5%] decrease in the average market PND price (disregarding changes in market shares due to switching towards TomTom's PND as they have become cheaper).' (para 240)

'The elimination of the double marginalization should therefore be considered, to a large extent, as merger-specific.' (para 242)

In addition to the elimination of the double marginalisation, the transaction is likely to create other efficiencies. The Non-Horizontal Merger Guidelines indicate that vertical mergers 'may align the incentives of the parties with regard to investments in new products, new production processes and in the marketing of products. In this case, the parties state that the rationale of the merger is to allow the merged entity to produce "better maps—faster". In accordance with the guidelines, the Commission examined in its competitive assessment whether the alleged efficiencies would benefit customers and whether they are verifiable and merger specific. ... Although end-customers would certainly benefit from the more frequent and comprehensive map database updates made possible by the merger, these efficiencies are difficult to quantify and the estimates provided by the parties are not particularly convincing. ... The Commission also examined whether these efficiencies should be considered merger specific. Although part of the efficiencies put forward by the parties could potentially be achieved through contract, both parties are unlikely to pursue investments of the same order of magnitude as the integrated company. Such investments are risky for the non-integrated company since they are very specific to the particular relationship and hence subject to a so-called hold-up problem. ... In any case, it is not necessary to precisely estimate the magnitude of these likely efficiencies given the proposed transaction's lack of anti-competitive effect irrespective of efficiencies.' (paras 244–50)

Foreclosure as a Result of Access to Confidential Information

'According to Paragraph 78 of the Non-Horizontal Merger Guidelines, a vertical merger may give the merged entity access to commercially sensitive information regarding the downstream activity of rivals. For instance, by becoming a supplier to its downstream competitors the merged entity may obtain critical information, which could allow it to compete less aggressively or could put competitors at a competitive disadvantage making entry and expansion less attractive.' (para 252)

The Commission examined the nature of information exchanged between Tele Atlas and its customers and considered whether such information flows could be limited without harming consumers. It further considered whether the merged entity would have the incentives to continue protecting its customers' confidential information post-merger. Subsequently, the Commission finds it unlikely that confidentiality issues will lead to a significant impediment of effective competition. (paras 254–76)

Comment

The Commission concluded that it is unlikely that the transaction would significantly impede competition in the common market or in a substantial part of it. That conclusion was strengthened further once efficiencies were taken into account.

Guinness/Grand Metropolitan   **Portfolio Effect**
Case IV/M.938
European Commission, [1998] OJ L288/24

Facts

The Commission received notification of a merger between Guinness, a producer and distributor of spirits and the brewing of beer, and GrandMet, whose principal activities are the production and worldwide distribution of spirits, food manufacturing and ownership of fast-food restaurants. The Commission concerns focused on the overlap in activities of the parties in the supply of spirits throughout the world. The transaction combined the activities of the two largest spirits suppliers in the world, creating a company approximately twice the size of its nearest rival. In addition to horizontal overlaps between the parties in some of the markets, a key result of the merger was that it combined the two parties' ranges or portfolios of products and brands. The Commission reviewed the effects of the transaction is all national markets. The following discussing focuses solely on the Greek market in which portfolio effect was identified.

Held

The product market in this case constitute the individual internationally recognised main spirit types (whiskey, gin, vodka, rum, etc) and for each liqueur. Narrower definitions may, however, be appropriate to specific product or geographic areas. Due to differences in taxation between Member States and the national distribution organisation, the geographic markets are national in scope. (paras 8–29)

Although the transaction will combine the activities of the two largest spirits suppliers in the world, the competition takes place within each different spirit type, and at national level. Subsequently, the Commission's analysis focused on those markets where the merger produces significant market shares or the possibility of a 'portfolio effect'. (paras 30–1)

'One competitor remarked that "In short the market power deriving from a portfolio of brands exceeds the sum of its parts".' (para 38)

'The holder of a portfolio of leading spirit brands may enjoy a number of advantages. In particular, his position in relation to his customers is stronger since he is able to provide a range of products and will account for a greater proportion of their business, he will have greater flexibility to structure his prices, promotions and discounts, he will have greater potential for tying, and he will be able to realise economies of scale and scope in his sales and marketing activities. Finally the implicit (or explicit) threat of a refusal to supply is more potent.' (para 40)

'The strength of these advantages, and their potential effect on the competitive structure of the market, depends on a number of factors, including: whether the holder of the portfolio has the brand leader or one or more leading brands in a particular market; the market shares of the various brands, particularly in relation to the shares of competitors; the relative importance of the individual markets in which the parties have significant shares and brands across the range of product markets in which the portfolio is held; and/or the number of markets in which the portfolio holder has a brand leader or leading brand.' (para 41)

'The parties have said that consumers buy brands and not portfolios. That is true. However, the parties do not sell their products to the final consumers. They sell them to intermediaries, multiple retailers, wholesalers and others. Those customers would buy a range of products from GMG, and the fact that GMG would be able to offer in many national markets a wide and deep portfolio of leading brands would give the combined entity advantages in dealing with its clients. The strength of any portfolio effect will vary from geographic market to geographic market. In the present case, the only market in which it has been considered to be a significant feature in the context of the assessment is Greece.' (para 46)

In the Greek market horizontal overlap was found in the market for whiskey in which the combined entity will have a market share of 45–55 per cent. In other categories there is no horizontal overlap, yet the merger will bring together the existing high market shares of the parties in gin, brandy and rum. (paras 89–92)

'The issue of portfolio power is of particular relevance in the assessment of the operation with regard to the Greek market. This is mainly due to the fact that the combined entity will be present across the major categories of spirits, that is whiskey, gin, rum and brandy, where it will be able to supply the leading brands, with the exception of vodka.' (para 94)

'More particularly, a deep portfolio of whiskey brands, spread out across the various quality and price segments, confers considerable price flexibility and marketing opportunities. Therefore, the supplier is shielded from market pressures, as he is able to face price competition from other suppliers' brands by positioning and pricing his various brands within the category. For instance, with its secure high market performance of the best-selling whiskey brands, GMG will be able to devote as many resources as necessary in order to maintain its secondary brands in their position or to reposition the weaker brands upwards by expanding their share at the expense of competing brands, or in order to counter eventual competitive pressure coming from those brands. The parties have argued that such "pull-through" has not occurred in the past and is accordingly unlikely to occur in the future. However, this argument ignores the substantial increase in the parties' market shares and resources that the merger will create.' (para 99)

The wide portfolio of categories confers major marketing advantages and enables GMG the possibility of bundling sales or increasing the sales volume through tying. Existing competitors do not have such a portfolio of brands that they would be able to constrain GMG's market power. (para 100–16)

Comment

The transaction was declared compatible with the internal market, subject to conditions.

In its decision the Commission noted that portfolio power can be seen, in part, as a barrier to entry. (para 47) This, together with the other references to portfolio power, seems to take little notice of the economies of scale and scope which a wider portfolio entails, to the benefit of consumers. Note, however, the reference in the Guidelines on the assessment of non-horizontal mergers ([2008] OJ C265) to portfolio power. There, the Commission states that: 'Customers may have a strong incentive to buy the range of products concerned from a single source (one-stop-shopping) rather than from many suppliers, eg because it saves on transaction costs. The fact that the merged entity will have a broad range or portfolio of products does not, as such, raise competition concerns.' (para 104)

Also note Case COMP/M.2608 *INA/FAG* in which the Commission weighed the possible negative effects of the wider portfolio against the economies of scale: '[I]t is obvious that in this industry economies of scale may be gained especially through specialization. Furthermore, even following the proposed transaction, INA would not be the only full range supplier as for example NSK and Koyo already sell the entire range of bearings. Torrington and NTN also sell the entire range of bearings with the exception of water pump bearings. However, the potential range effects resulting from the combination of the two firms' product portfolios would have to be weighed against the economies of scale generated by product specialists that produce a limited number of products in high quantities. Such a strategy would be supported by the specific economics of the industry, that is, economies of scale primarily at the plant level and low transport costs enabling global supplies from a small number of production plants. Customers have, in addition, stated that INA/ FAG's market position is not strong enough in any of the various product segments for a tying strategy to be a viable option.' (para 34)

GE/Amersham	**Conglomerate Effects**
Case COMP/M.3304	Commercial Bundling
European Commission, [2004] OJ C74/05	Technical Tying

Facts

The Commission received a notification of a proposed concentration caused by the General Electric Company (GE) acquiring sole control of the UK diagnostic pharmaceuticals and biosciences company, Amersham plc (Amersham). The proposed acquisition did not lead to horizontal overlaps but did raise questions as to possible conglomerate effects arising from the combination of GE Medical Systems (a subsidiary of GE specialising in medical diagnostic imaging technology) with Amersham's activities.

Held

The products of GE and Amersham may be viewed as complements, in that hospitals need to procure both of them in order to provide an imaging medical service to patients. The investigation explored, firstly, whether the merged entity would be able to foreclose competition through price reductions on the product bundle; and secondly, through technical tying, thereby making its products work most optimally or exclusively with one another at the exclusion of competing products. (para 31)

Commercial bundling

Following the transaction, GE will have the ability to offer its customers a complete diagnostic imaging (DI) solution, comprising both the GE's DI equipment and the Amersham's diagnostic pharmaceuticals (DPs) (which enhances the clarity of the image produced by DI equipment). Subsequently it could attract customers by proposing a bundle of DI equipment and DPs at a lower price than the sum of the components purchased on a stand-alone basis. 'Some of Amersham's competitors have indicated that the merged entity could decide to discount the prices of equipment maintenance services in order to lure hospitals that are already equipped with GE technology into buying Amersham's DPs or to discount DPs pricing through cross-subsidisation. These third parties alleged that the result of these commercial bundling strategies would be an increase in pricing pressure, which would then reduce their revenues streams and thus their ability and incentive to invest in R&D. This, possibly in combination with other exclusionary strategies, might gradually marginalise them up to the point that they would be forced to exit the market.' (paras 33, 34)

'In contrast to these claims, other competitors of the parties as well as the vast majority of customers have seriously questioned the feasibility of such a strategy, pointing to the fact that combined offers of DI equipment and DPs are generally uncommon in this industry. They explained that there exist significant differences in the procurement procedures and supply chains for DI equipment and DPs, as well as completely different procurement timelines. For instance, DI equipment has a long lifecycle of a minimum of 10 years, it is therefore purchased infrequently and represents a one-off major capital expenditure. DPs, being consumables, are purchased more frequently and in much smaller volumes and thus represent a smaller-scale purchasing decision taken regularly throughout the lifecycle of the corresponding DI equipment. Respondents said that whilst the above differences do not exclude commercial bundling from taking place, they however complicate its successful implementation.' (para 35)

'In assessing commercial bundling, the Commission examined whether or not each one of the various conditions that would render it anti-competitive are met in the present case. Indeed, for commercial bundling to result in foreclosure of competition it is necessary that the merged entity is able to leverage its pre-merger dominance in one product to another complementary product. In addition, for such strategy to be profitable, there must be a reasonable expectation that rivals will not be able to propose a competitive response, and that their resulting marginalisation will force them to exit the market. Finally, once rivals have exited the market, the merged firm must be able to implement unilateral price increases and such increases need to be sustainable in the long term, without being challenged by the likelihood of new rivals entering the market or previously marginalised ones re-entering the market.' (para 37)

'Concerning the response of rivals, the market investigation has revealed that there exist a sufficient number of viable and resourceful rivals in DI equipment and DPs, who would be able to respond to the merged entity's commercial bundling through various counter-strategies, such as for instance price reductions, similar bundles (through teaming or counter-mergers) and technological leapfrogging as a result of innovation. For instance, GE/Amersham will not be the first combined supplier of DI equipment and DPs; Esaote, the Italian DI equipment manufacturer, has become a full subsidiary of Bracco, a competitor of Amersham, and is in theory in a position to offer both DI equipment and DPs.' (para 39)

Technical Tying

While at present all DI equipment works with all available DPs, concerns were raised about the new entity's incentive to transform the current open-system environment into a closed one. Such behaviour would impact on the introduction of new products and could occur through technical tying which would foreclose rivals as a result of (1) the lack of interconnectivity or (2) as a result of a so-called time-to-market advantage that the merged company would gain by internalising the knowledge on development plans in DI equipment and DPs carried out by each one of the merging parties. (paras 45, 46)

However, the above scenario was not confirmed by the market investigation. In their reply to the market investigation, 'both customers and competitors have stated that currently there are no interoperability issues with existing products and that no interoperability issues can be foreseen for future products, unless Amersham would develop breakthrough DP products that no other competitor is able to replicate without the parties' cooperation and which cannot be used on other DI equipment (so called "smart" DPs) than GE's. Technically speaking and according to a third party, such a development would be, if at all possible, most likely to take place in the field of nuclear imaging, and in particular PET.' (para 49)

'Finally, the Commission examined the economic incentives underlying a possible technical tying strategy and concluded that this would not be a profit-maximising strategy. Making Amersham's products work exclusively or most optimally with GE-only equipment, eg, by withholding competitors from access to data, would deny the merged entity significant sales of Amersham's products to the installed base of competing DI equipment.' (para 59)

Comment

Paragraphs 95–104 of the Guidelines on the assessment of non-horizontal mergers focus on the evaluation of the 'ability to foreclose'. They highlight that 'the most immediate way in which the merged entity may be able to use its market power in one market to foreclose competitors in another is by conditioning sales in a way that links the products in the separate markets together. This is done most directly either by tying or bundling.' (para 95) 'The specific characteristics of the products may be relevant for determining whether any of these means of linking sales between separate markets are available to the merged entity. For instance, pure bundling is very unlikely to be possible if products are not bought simultaneously or by the same customers. Similarly, technical tying is only an option in certain industries.' (para 98) 'In order to be able to foreclose competitors, the new entity must have a significant degree of market power, which does not necessarily amount to dominance, in one of the markets concerned. The effects of bundling or tying can only be expected to be substantial when at least one of the merging parties' products is viewed by many customers as particularly important and there are few relevant alternatives for that product.' (para 99) 'The more customers tend to buy both products (instead of only one of the products), the more demand for the individual products may be affected through bundling or tying.' (para 100) 'The foreclosure effects of bundling and tying are likely to be more pronounced in industries where there are economies of scale and the demand pattern at any given point in time has dynamic implications for the conditions of supply in the market in the future.' (para 101) '[T]he scope for foreclosure tends to be smaller where the merging parties cannot commit to making their tying or bundling strategy a lasting one.' (para 102)

Commission v Tetra Laval BV	**Conglomerate Effects**
Case C-12/03 P	Leveraging
Court of Justice, [2005] ECR I-987	Illegality under Article 102 TFEU

Facts

An appeal by the Commission on the General Court judgment in Case T-5/02 *Tetra Laval v Commission* [2002] ECR II-4381, in which the General Court annulled a Commission decision declaring the acquisition of Sidel SA by Tetra Laval BV to be incompatible with the internal market (Case No COMP/M.2416—*Tetra Laval/Sidel*) ([2004] OJ L43/13).

In its decision the Commission was concerned that the merged entity would be capable of exploiting Tetra's dominant position on the market for aseptic cartons and leveraging existing market power with a view to attaining a dominant position on the market for SBM machines (Sidel's equipment).

On appeal, the General Court observed that 'a merger between undertakings which are active on distinct markets is not usually of such a nature as immediately to create or strengthen a dominant position due to the combination of the market shares held by the parties to the merger.' (para 150) It criticised the Commission finding that the notified concentration would have anticompetitive conglomerate effects and give the merged entity the capacity and incentive to engage in leveraging. The General Court distinguished between a situation where a merger having conglomerate effects immediately changes the conditions of competition on the second market and results in the creation or strengthening of a dominant position on that market due to the dominant position already held on the first market and, on the other hand, a situation where the creation or strengthening of a dominant position on the second market does not immediately result from the merger, but will occur, in those circumstances, only after a certain time and will result from conduct engaged in by the merged entity on the first market where it already holds a dominant position. In this latter case, it is not the structure resulting from the merger transaction itself which creates or strengthens a dominant position within the meaning of Article 2(3) of the Regulation, but rather the future conduct in question. It noted that in this case the Commission itself had taken the view that a dominant position would not arise from the merger itself but rather from the foreseeable conduct of the merged entity. However, it held that, where the Commission takes the view that a merger should be prohibited because it will create or strengthen a dominant position within a foreseeable period, it is incumbent upon it to produce convincing evidence thereof. In addition, the General Court noted that the supposed leveraging could constitute an abuse of Tetra's pre-existing dominant position. Subsequently, when examining the likelihood of the adoption of anticompetitive conduct, the Commission should have considered not only the incentives to adopt such conduct but also 'the extent to which those incentives would be reduced, or even eliminated, owing to the illegality of the conduct in question, the likelihood of its detection, action taken by the competent authorities, both at [EU] and national level, and the financial penalties which could ensue.' (General Court, para 159)

Held

Proof of anticompetitive conglomerate effects

'Although the [General Court] stated … that proof of anti-competitive conglomerate effects of a merger of the kind notified calls for a precise examination, supported by convincing evidence, of the circumstances which allegedly produce those effects, it by no means added a condition relating to the requisite standard of proof but merely drew attention to the essential function of evidence, which is to establish convincingly the merits of an argument or, as in the present case, of a decision on a merger.' (para 41)

A prospective analysis of the kind necessary in merger control must be carried out with great care since it entails a prediction of events which are more or less likely to occur in future. The prospective analysis consists of an examination of how a concentration might alter the factors determining the state of competition in order to establish whether it would give rise to a serious impediment to effective competition. 'Such an analysis makes it necessary to envisage various chains of cause and effect with a view to ascertaining which of them are the most likely.' (paras 42, 43)

'The analysis of a conglomerate-type concentration is a prospective analysis in which, first, the consideration of a lengthy period of time in the future and, secondly, the leveraging necessary to give rise to a significant impediment to effective competition mean that the chains of cause and effect are dimly discernible, uncertain and difficult to establish. That being so, the quality of the evidence produced by the Commission in order to establish that it is necessary to adopt a decision declaring the concentration incompatible with the [internal] market is particularly important, since that evidence must support the Commission's conclusion that, if such a decision were not adopted, the economic development envisaged by it would be plausible.' (para 44)

Unlawful leveraging

The General Court was right to hold that the likelihood of the new entity's leveraging of its dominant position is aseptic cartons must be examined comprehensively, while taking account, both of the incentives to adopt such conduct and the factors liable to reduce, or even eliminate, those incentives, including the possibility that the conduct is unlawful. (para 74)

However, it would run counter to the Regulation's purpose of prevention to require the Commission, as was held in paragraph 159 of the judgment under appeal, to examine, for each proposed merger, the extent to which the incentives to adopt anticompetitive conduct would be reduced or eliminated as a result of the unlawfulness of the conduct, the likelihood of its detection, the competition enforcement action, and the financial penalties which could ensue. An assessment such as that required by the General Court 'would make it necessary to carry out an exhaustive and detailed examination of the rules of the various legal orders which might be applicable and of the enforcement policy practised in them. Moreover, if it is to be relevant, such an assessment calls for a high probability of the occurrence of the acts envisaged as capable of giving rise to objections on the ground that they are part of anti-competitive conduct. It follows that at the stage of assessing a proposed merger, an assessment intended to establish whether an infringement of [Article 102] is likely and to ascertain that it will be penalised in several legal orders would be too speculative and would not allow the Commission to base its assessment on all of the relevant facts with a view to establishing whether they support an economic scenario in which a development such as leveraging will occur.' (paras 75–7)

'The [General Court] erred in law in rejecting the Commission's conclusions as to the adoption by the merged entity of anti-competitive conduct capable of resulting in leveraging on the sole ground that the Commission had, when assessing the likelihood that such conduct might be adopted, failed to take account of the unlawfulness of that conduct and, consequently, of the likelihood of its detection, of action by the competent authorities, both at [EU] and national level, and of the financial penalties which might ensue. Nevertheless, since the judgment under appeal is also based on the failure to take account of the commitments offered by Tetra, it is necessary to continue the examination of the second ground of appeal.' (para 78)

Potential competition

'As is clear from Article 2(1) of the Regulation, the Commission, when assessing the compatibility of a concentration with the [internal] market, must take account of a number of factors, such as the structure of the relevant markets, actual or potential competition from undertakings, the position of the undertakings concerned and their economic and financial power, possible options available to suppliers and users, any barriers to entry and trends in supply and demand.' (para 125)

The General Court was therefore right to point out that 'the mere fact that the acquiring undertaking already holds a clear dominant position on the relevant market does not in itself suffice to justify a finding that a reduction in the potential competition which that undertaking must face constitutes a strengthening of its position.' (para 126)

'The potential competition represented by a producer of substitute products on a segment of the relevant market (namely in the present case the competition, in relation to aseptic carton packaging, from Sidel, as a supplier of PET packaging, on the market segment for sensitive products) is only one of the set of factors which must be taken into account when assessing whether there is a risk that a concentration might strengthen a dominant position. It cannot be ruled out that a reduction in that potential competition might be compensated by other factors, with the result that the competitive position of the already dominant undertaking remains unchanged.' (para 127)

The General Court was right to state that the Commission has to show that, 'if there is a reduction in potential competition, this will tend to strengthen Tetra's dominant position in relation to its competitors on the aseptic carton markets.' (para 128)

Comment

Appeal dismissed.

Following the General Court's judgment annulling the Commission's prohibition decision, the Commission was required to re-examine the concentration. The Commission's second investigation of the Tetra Laval/Sidel transaction focused on addressing the various points raised in the General Court's judgment, which required further investigation. The transaction was subsequently cleared subject to conditions.

The Court of Justice and General Court judgments considered the extent to which the future illegality under Article 102 TFEU of leveraging activities should play a role in the ex-ante assessment under the Merger Regulation. While the Court of Justice endorsed the General Court's comments on the need to evaluate the likelihood of the new entity's leveraging it disapproved of the depth of such examination, as suggested by the General Court. It held that 'at the stage of assessing a proposed merger, an assessment intended to establish whether an infringement of [Article 102 TFEU] is likely and to ascertain that it will be penalised in several legal orders would be too speculative.' (Court of Justice para 77)

The Court of Justice's holding on this point is echoed in the Guidelines on the assessment of non-horizontal mergers: '[W]hen the adoption of a specific course of conduct by the merged entity is an essential step in foreclosure, the Commission examines both the incentives to adopt such conduct and the factors liable to reduce, or even eliminate, those incentives, including the possibility that the conduct is unlawful. Conduct may be unlawful inter alia because of competition rules or sector-specific rules at the EU or national levels. This appraisal, however, does not require an exhaustive and detailed examination of the rules of the various legal orders which might be applicable and of the enforcement policy practised within them. Moreover, the illegality of a conduct may be likely to provide significant disincentives for the merged entity to engage in such conduct only in certain circumstances. In particular, the Commission will consider, on the basis of a summary analysis: (i) the likelihood that this conduct would be clearly, or highly probably, unlawful under [EU] law, (ii) the likelihood that this illegal conduct could be detected, and (iii) the penalties which could be imposed.' (para 46)

In Case T-210/01 *General Electric v Commission* [2005] ECR II-5575, the General Court noted on this point that 'the Commission must, in principle, take into account the potentially unlawful, and thus sanctionable, nature of certain conduct as a factor which might diminish, or even eliminate, incentives for an undertaking to engage in particular conduct. That appraisal does not, however, require an exhaustive and detailed examination of the rules of the various legal orders which might be applicable and of the enforcement policy practised within them, given that an assessment intended to establish whether an infringement is likely and to ascertain that it will be penalised in several legal orders would be too speculative. Thus, where the Commission, without undertaking a specific and detailed investigation into the matter, can identify the unlawful nature of the conduct in question, in the light of [Article 102 TFEU] or of other provisions of [EU] law which it is competent to enforce, it is its responsibility to make a finding to that effect and take account of it in its assessment of the likelihood that the merged entity will engage in such conduct.' (paras 73–4) See page 473 below.

General Electric v Commission	**Conglomerate Effects**
Case T-210/01	Portfolio Effect
General Court, [2005] ECR II-5575	

Facts

An appeal on a Commission decision in which the Commission prohibited the General Electric Co's (GE) proposed US$42bn acquisition of Honeywell Inc. The Commission asserted that the merger would have severely reduced competition in the aerospace industry. Among other things, the Commission was concerned with 'conglomerate effects' including (1) 'share shifting' which would consist of the extension of the financial power of GE Capital, and GE Capital Aviation Services (GECAS) to Honeywell's activities; and (2) bundling practices—pure, technical and mixed—through offers incorporating both aircraft engines from GE, and avionics products and non-avionics products from Honeywell. In addition, the Commission was also concerned with the 'vertical effects' of the merger—the combination of GE's dominant position on the worldwide market for large commercial jet aircraft engines with Honeywell's activity as a manufacturer of starters for those engines.

Held

Financial strength and vertical integration

While the Commission was correct in holding that GECAS's activities and GE Capital's financial position contributed to GE's pre-merger dominance on the market for large commercial jet aircraft engines, it does not necessarily follow that after the merger the merged entity would employ the same practices as those it employed on the market for large commercial jet aircraft engines in order to promote its avionics and non-avionics products. (paras 325–6)

In accordance with the judgment in *Tetra Laval v Commission*, '[I]t was for the Commission to establish not only that the merged entity had the ability to transfer those practices to the markets for avionics and non-avionics products but also, on the basis of convincing evidence, that it was likely that the merged entity would engage in such conduct. Furthermore, the Commission was required to establish that those practices would have created, in the relatively near future, a dominant position, at the very least on some of the markets for the avionics and non-avionics products concerned.' (para 327)

With respect to the likelihood of the future conduct foreseen by the Commission, the Commission has not sufficiently established that possible practices which could have been put into effect by the merged entity would have created a dominant position. (paras 328–64)

'It follows from the foregoing that the Commission has not established to a sufficient degree of probability that, following the merger, the merged entity would have extended to the markets for avionics and non-avionics products the practices found by the Commission on the market for large commercial jet aircraft engines, by which the applicant exploited the financial strength of the GE group attributable to GE Capital and the commercial lever represented by GECAS's aircraft purchases in order to promote sales of its products. In any event, the Commission has not adequately established that those practices, assuming that they had been put into effect, would have been likely to create dominant positions on the various avionics and non-avionics markets concerned. Consequently, the Commission made a manifest error of assessment in holding that the financial strength and vertical integration of the merged entity would bring about the creation or strengthening of dominant positions on the markets for avionics or non-avionics products.' (para 364)

Bundling

In the contested decision the Commission stated that the merged entity would have the ability and incentive, unlike its competitors, to offer its customers packages for large commercial aircraft, large regional aircraft and corporate aircraft, encompassing both engines and avionics and non-avionics products. As a consequence, a dominant position would have been created for Honeywell on the markets for avionics and non-avionics products and GE's dominant positions would have been strengthened, particularly on the market for large commercial jet aircraft engines. The Commission's case is based on the complementary nature of jet engines, avionics and non-avionics products. (paras 399–400)

'It should be noted, as a preliminary point, that the way it is predicted that the merged entity will behave in the future is a vital aspect of the Commission's analysis of bundling in the present case. It follows from the fact that the applicant had no presence on the markets for avionics and non-avionics products prior to the merger, together with the fact that Honeywell had no presence on the market for large commercial jet aircraft engines before the merger, that the merger would have had no horizontal anti-competitive effect on those markets. Thus, the merger would, prima facie, have had no effect whatsoever on those markets.' (para 401)

'The Commission held in the contested decision that each avionics product for regional and corporate aircraft constitutes a market in itself and that there is a market for each non-avionics product for all types of aircraft, including large commercial aircraft. Accordingly, its reasoning with regard to the creation, by means of bundling, of dominant positions on the markets for the different avionics products cannot be accepted in relation to the markets for each of the various avionics products for corporate and regional aircraft. Indeed, on the assumption that it actually becomes a reality after the transaction, any bundling attributable to the merger will affect only one segment of those markets, the large regional aircraft segment. In the same way, the Commission's reasoning is undermined (albeit to a lesser degree) in relation to non-avionics products, for which the Commission defined an individual market for each specific product, irrespective of the size and other features of the aircraft equipped.' (para 403)

It is only in the sector for large commercial aircrafts, for which the Commission has defined distinct markets both for jet engines and for each avionics product, that the Commission's case on bundling could conceivably be sustained. In these markets the Commission should have established that the merged entity would not only have the capability to engage in the bundling practices but also, on the basis of convincing evidence, that it would have been likely to engage in those practices after the merger and that, in consequence, a dominant position would have been created or strengthened on one or more of the relevant markets in the relatively near future (*Tetra Laval v Commission*, paras 146–62). However, in its decision the Commission has not sufficiently established the above. The mere fact that the merged entity would have had a wider range of products than its competitors is not sufficient to justify the conclusion that dominant positions would have been created or strengthened for it on the different markets concerned. (paras 404–70)

Comment

The Court heavily criticised the Commission's analysis of the conglomerate effects. Despite this, it did not annul the decision since these errors did not affect the rest of the Commission analysis which prohibited the transaction due to the merged undertakings' competing products and services.

The Commission's decision contrasted with the conclusion of the US Department of Justice (DOJ), which had cleared the merger earlier that year, requiring only minimal disposals. This was, and still is, the only case of the European Union blocking a merger already approved by US authorities.

In its investigation the DOJ determined that the merger, as modified by the remedies insisted upon, would have been pro-competitive and beneficial to consumers. In doing so it focused predominantly on the short-term efficiencies and the expected positive effects on consumers. On the other hand the Commission's main concern was that in the long-term, the post-merger price reductions would force competitors to exit the industry, eventually leading prices to rise above pre-merger levels.

Commenting on the Commission's *GE/Honeywell* decision, Charles A James, then Assistant Attorney General for the US DOJ Antitrust Division, issued a statement backing the DOJ decision, stating that clear and longstanding US antitrust policy holds that antitrust laws protect competition, not competitors, thus implying that the Commission's decision reflected a significant point of divergence. Carl Shapiro, then Chief Economist for the US DOJ, noted that: 'In North America, mergers expected to lead to lower prices are regarded as pro-competitive; in the EU, such mergers can be branded anticompetitive based on the fear that added pressure on rivals will ultimately cause them to exit the market. We believe the EU approach is unsound as a matter of competition policy, and that it is more accurately regarded as a form of industrial policy.'

Intel/McAfee	Conglomerate Effects

COMP/M.5984
European Commission, C(2011) 529 final

Facts

A proposed concentration between Intel, a leading producer of central processing units (CPUs) and chipsets, and McAfee, a security technology company. The two companies operated in closely related and complementary markets. In its analysis, the Commission considered possible conglomerate effects which may stem from the fact that Intel would have had the ability to offer both hardware and security solutions.

Held

'In most circumstances, conglomerate mergers do not give rise to competition problems. In some cases, in particular where as in the present case the merged entity enjoys strong market power in at least one of the markets concerned, a conglomerate merger may however create possibilities for exclusionary bundling or tying practices that could disadvantage or foreclose competitors and ultimately lead to them exiting the market, or otherwise significantly impede competition in the markets concerned.' (para 121)

The merged entity might engage in three main types of practices which should be considered:

(1) Degradation of interoperability between Intel's hardware and security solutions, and the products of competitors—Intel could keep undisclosed certain parameters and reserve those for exclusive use by McAfee. This would allow McAfee to develop better security solutions within less time than its competitors. Moreover, Intel could optimise the interfaces between its chipsets/CPUs and McAfee's security solutions. The Commission considers it likely that Intel has incentives to degrade interoperability of its hardware with other security solutions than McAfee's products and that customers would not be in a position to exert pressure on Intel to maintain interoperability. A degradation of the interoperability between the parties' products and those of the parties' competitors would lead to foreclosure of McAfee's competitors in the endpoint security markets and thereby possibly strengthen the current dominant position of Intel in the chipset and CPU markets. (paras 123–74)

(2) Technical bundling/tying—Technical tying consists in the technical combination of products of both parties, for example, by embedding McAfee security solutions in Intel's CPU and chipset platforms. The Commission's analysis suggests that Intel has the ability and incentive to engage in technical tying and that the negative effects of such a practice would be significant. It is likely that the conglomerate effects resulting from a technical tie between the parties' products would lead to the foreclosure of McAfee's competitors in the endpoint security markets and thereby possibly to the strengthening of the current dominant position of Intel in the chipset and CPU markets.' (paras 175–221)

(3) Commercial bundling strategies (pure and mixed bundling)—'In the present case, pure bundling would imply that CPUs and security software are sold exclusively together while mixed bundling would imply that either the CPUs or the security software would be offered at a discount when customers buy both products from Intel/McAfee.' (para 222) The Commission analysis suggests that Intel is able to commercially bundle hardware and security software products but that it would have limited incentive to do so. 'The market investigation also suggests that possible antitrust enforcement would have a certain deterrent effect. Finally, foreseeable effects of such a strategy would also probably remain limited.' (para 289)

Comment

Transaction cleared subject to commitments. In order to address the Commission's concerns, Intel committed to ensure interoperability and that vendors of rival security solutions will have access to necessary information in the same way as McAfee. Intel also committed not to actively impede competitors' security solutions from running on Intel CPUs or chipsets and to ensure that McAfee's security solutions will run on CPUs or chipsets sold by Intel's competitors.

Rewe/Meinl	**Buyer Power**
Case IV/M.1221	Significant Impediment to Effective Competition
European Commission, [1999] OJ L274/1	Retail Trade

Facts

The Commission appraised a proposed concentration in which Rewe, an undertaking active in the food-retailing sector, would acquire all the shares in Meinl, a trading group active in the food-retailing sector in Austria. In its assessment, the Commission considered the effects of the transaction on (1) the distribution market, in which food retailers act as suppliers to final consumers; and on (2) the procurement market, in which retailers act as buyers vis-à-vis producers of products forming part of the food-retailing trade's range. With respect to the former, the Commission found that the transaction would place the new entity in a dominant position in the food-retailing market in Austria. With respect to the latter, it held that the concentration would lead to a dominant position in the procurement markets for dairy products, bread, drinks and other consumables. To address the concerns raised by the Commission, the parties undertook, for an unlimited period, to remain independent of one another in the distribution and procurement markets. Subsequently, the Commission cleared the transaction.

Held

'The exercise of buyer power which leads to the securing of more favourable purchase deal is not to be considered per se detrimental to the economy as a whole. Especially where the supplier side is itself highly concentrated and powerful, buyers are faced with effective competition in their own selling market and hence are compelled to pass on any savings to their own customers, buyer power can prevent monopoly or oligopoly profits from being earned on the supply side. However, if the powerful buyer himself occupies in his selling market a strong position which is no longer kept sufficiently in check by the competition, any savings can no longer be expected to be passed on to customers.' (para 71)

'In the retail trade there is a close interdependence between the distribution market and the procurement market. Retailers' shares of the distribution market determine their procurement volume: the bigger the retailer's share of the distribution market, the larger the procurement volume. And the larger the procurement volume, the more favourable as a rule are the buying conditions which the trader obtains from his suppliers. Favourable buying conditions can in turn be used in various ways to improve one's position in the distribution market (sometimes through internal or external growth, but also through low-price strategies targeted at competitors). The improved position in the distribution market is itself reflected in a further improvement in buying conditions, and so on.' (para 72)

'The spiral described above leads to ever-higher concentration both in distribution markets and in procurement markets. In the short term, final consumers may benefit from the process, as there may be a period of intense (predatory) competition in the distribution market during which the powerful buyer/trader is forced to pass on his savings to consumers. But this will last only until such time as a structure (as in this case, an individual dominant position) is arrived at in the distribution market which leads to a clear reduction in competitive intensity. At this stage, any consideration for the final consumer goes by the board, as he is left with few alternatives.' (para 73)

'Buyer power also gives a trader considerable influence over the choice of products which come to market and hence are obtainable by consumers. Products which are not bought by a dominant buyer have practically no chance of reaching the final consumer as the supplier lacks alternative outlets. Lastly, the dominant buyer determines the success or otherwise of product innovations.' (para 74)

Comment

The Commission found that the supply side of the Austrian procurement market is significantly less concentrated than the demand side. It noted the significance of food-retailing trade channels for food suppliers and the difficulty of switching between suppliers. Further, it concluded that there are no 'must-stock' items that could curtail the buying power of the merged entity. To address the concerns raised by the Commission, the parties undertook, for an unlimited period, to remain independent of one another in the distribution and procurement markets.

In *Kesko/Tuko* (Case IV/M.784), the Commission considered a transaction between the two largest wholesale and retail groups in Finland. The Commission examined and blocked the transaction following a referral by the Finnish Office of Free Competition. Kesko unsuccessfully challenged the Commission's decision before the General Court (Case T-22/97 *Kesko v Commission* [1999] ECR II-3775). With regards to the buying power of Kesko/Tuko, the Commission took account of access to shelf space and the success of Kesko/Tuko's private labels range. The Commission's prime concern was that the merged entity's buyer power would allow it to obtain lower prices from suppliers that could not be matched by any of its competitors, thereby driving them out of the market and raising barriers to entry. The Commission considered the dependency of different suppliers and the difficulty of switching distribution channels. In addition, it took into account the popularity of Kesko/Tuko private labels and its loyalty cards scheme, which allowed increased access to consumer information, and further enhanced its buyer power.

In *Friesland Foods/Campina* (Case COMP/M.5046) the Commission appraised a merger between the two largest dairy cooperatives in the Netherlands. One of the affected markets was the market for the procurement of conventional raw milk in the Netherlands. The Commission concluded that the merged entity will benefit from very large market shares and will be able to exercise buyer power when dealing with the fragmented upstream suppliers. The Commission noted that: 'When assessing the impact of a concentration in an upstream market such as the procurement of raw milk, it is necessary to first analyse whether the increase of buyer power in upstream markets may significantly impede effective competition, as it appears to be the case here, by creating or strengthening a dominant position. It should be clarified whether the increased buying power of the notifying parties could have a detrimental effect on competition, by enabling the new entity to obtain lower prices from farmers by reducing its purchase of raw milk, which would in turn lead to lower output also in the downstream markets and thus harm consumer welfare.' (para 98) The transaction was approved subject to conditions.

Two main theories are commonly used to examine buyer power and appraise its effects:

(1) The Monopsony model generally refers to a single purchaser of an input that faces perfectly competitive sellers. A monopsonist can artificially withhold demand and procure input at a price below competitive levels. Under the monopsony model, the distortion which stems from monopsony power is assumed to lead to higher production costs and possible wasteful expenditure. The restrictive assumptions at the base of this model limit its application in practice.

(2) Bargaining theory provides a more applicable model for the analysis of buyer power. According to the model, lower prices are obtained through the threat of shifting demand, rather than the actual withholding of demand. Price is negotiated bilaterally and applies to the parties to the agreement rather than to the whole market. Unlike monopsony power, the effects of bargaining power on welfare are less certain and vary depending on market realities.

The two theories—the monopsony model and bargaining theory—provide an imperfect analytical tool for enforcement authorities. The former is limited by its restrictive base assumption. The latter is limited due to the uncertain nature of the predicted effects. As a result, the assessment of buyer power raises challenging questions of policy and enforcement.

Enso/Stora	**Countervailing Buyer Power**
Case IV/M.1225	Non-coordinated Effects
European Commission, [1999] OJ L254/9	

Facts

The Commission received a notification of a proposed concentration by which Enso Oyj ('Enso'), a Finnish paper and board company, merged with Stora Kopparbergs Bergslags AB ('Stora'), a Swedish paper and board manufacturer. The Commission opened an in-depth inquiry to examine the effects of the concentration in the markets for the supply of board for packaging of liquids, newsprint and magazine papers. Following an in-depth investigation, the transaction was cleared subject to conditions.

With respect to the effects of the transaction on the liquid packaging board market, the Commission's analysis revealed a two-sided oligopoly where, following the transaction, the number and the relative size of the producers would match that of the buyers. The Commission noted that the merged entity would face countervailing buyer power from packaging materials producers. It concluded that although the new entity will benefit from a large market position on the market for liquid packaging board, its market power will be constrained by the countervailing buyer power of the main buyers, in particular Tetra Pak.

Held

'The liquid packaging board market is characterised by few large producers and few large buyers. In addition to Stora and Enso, the producers of liquid packaging board in Europe include only Korsnäs and AssiDomän. Buyers of liquid packaging board are few and the market is dominated by Tetra Pak … After the merger the structure of the supply-side will mirror the structure of the demand-side of the market for liquid packaging board, with one large supplier and two smaller suppliers facing one large buyer and two smaller buyers.' (para 84)

'The investigation showed that the relationship between the suppliers and the customers is one of mutual dependency. In the liquid packaging board market the relationships between suppliers and buyer are of a long-term nature and switching supplier of liquid packaging board is rare. The customers have indicated that switching the supplier would lead to delays, is costly and technically demanding due to the fact that the evaluation process for liquid packaging board is complex and time-consuming. In particular, the investigation showed that to become a supplier for a specific type of liquid packaging board requires considerable investment from both the producer and the customer in terms of machinery, technical support production and product trials as well as human resources.' (para 86)

An examination of each of the main buyers confirms that the demand-side has countervailing buyer power. Tetra Pak has countervailing buyer power to such an extent that it will neutralise any potential increase in market power of the merger between Stora and Enso. This is so since the parties to the transaction cannot easily replace it and find another buyer which would require such large supplies. In addition, Tetra Pak would have the option of developing new capacity with other existing or new suppliers, should the parties to the transaction attempt to exercise market power. In addition, Tetra Pak, through close cooperation with the producers of liquid packaging board, has an intimate knowledge of the cost structure of the parties. (paras 88–92)

Elopak and SIG Combibloc buy much smaller volumes of liquid packaging board than Tetra Pak. However, both companies place orders large enough to fill the capacity of a board machine. This makes it difficult for them to switch a significant proportion of volumes to alternative suppliers at short notice. However, it also means that should the parties to the transaction attempt to exercise market power, Elopak and SIG Combibloc can shift a large volume to alternative suppliers such as AssiDomän and Korsnäs, and could hurt Stora Enso significantly. (paras 93, 94)

'Compared to Tetra Pak, both companies are, nevertheless, in a weaker position in the short to medium term vis-à-vis Stora Enso, since they will have only one EEA supplier after the merger, whereas Tetra Pak will have three. Furthermore, Elopak and SIG Combibloc source much smaller volumes than Tetra Pak. Therefore, while it is true that Elopak and SIG Combibloc are not without any means to counter a price increase, it seems that the proposed merger will shift the balance of power towards Stora Enso in its relationship with Elopak and SIG Combibloc.' (para 95)

'In conclusion, the merger will result in a market structure with one large and two smaller suppliers facing one large and two smaller buyers. This is a rather exceptional market structure. On balance, the Commission considers that the buyers in these rather special market circumstances have sufficient countervailing buyer power to remove the possibility of the parties' exercising market power.' (para 97)

Comment

Despite large market shares and high barriers to entry, the Commission concluded that the merged entity would not be in a position to exercise market power. The demand-side in this case was as concentrated as the supply-side, and the countervailing buyer power of the main buyers, in particular Tetra Pak, meant that the merger did not raise competition concerns. The *Enso/Stora* case is unique as the relationship between suppliers and buyers was one of mutual dependency and the fact that the largest buyer, Tetra Pak, exercised considerable buyer power which could have prevented price increases on the suppliers' side. One should distinguish this case from the large array of other cases in which countervailing buyer power arguments were raised with more limited success.

In Case T-282/06 *Sun Chemical Group* [2007] ECR II-2149 the General Court considered the treatment of countervailing buyer power. While referring to the Guidelines on the assessment of horizontal mergers the General Court noted that 'even firms with very high market shares may not be in a position, post-merger, to significantly impede effective competition, if their customers possess countervailing buyer power.' (para 210) With respect to the level of analysis required from the Commission in assessing buyer power, the Court referred to the exceptional market structure in *Enso/Stora* and distinguished this from the facts in *Sun Chemical Group*. It held that 'whilst the facts in *Enso/Stora* may have required, due to an exceptional market structure, sophisticated analyses of the industry structure and strategies that buyers could undertake to curb price increases post-merger, it is clear from the foregoing that this does not apply to the present case ... the Court considers that the Commission could not be required, in the circumstances of this case, to carry out a more detailed examination of the countervailing buyer power of the merging parties' customers.' (para 216)

In Case COMP/M.6458 *Universal Music Group/EMI Music*, the Commission considered whether countervailing market power would have an across-the-board effect, or will only benefit the large buyers. While it acknowledged the bargaining power of digital distribution channels, it cited the Horizontal Merger Guidelines and noted that 'Countervailing buyer power cannot be found to sufficiently off-set potential adverse effects of a merger if it only ensures that a particular segment of customers, with particular bargaining strength, is shielded from significantly higher prices or deteriorated conditions after the merger.' (para 715) In this respect the Commission noted that smaller customers remain exposed to the larger record companies' market power. More generally, the Commission added that 'the fact that certain customers may be particularly aggressive in their commercial negotiations does not itself constitute evidence that they enjoy countervailing buyer power.' (para 716)

In Case No M.3732 *Procter & Gamble/Gillette* the Commission examined the conglomerate effects of the merger, the parties' significant portfolio of brands and their large market shares. Anticompetitive effects in this case were considered to be unlikely as significant competition with suppliers of other branded products existed, retailers enjoyed buyer power and portfolio efficiencies were present. In examining the issue of countervailing buyer power the Commission distinguished between small and large retailers. The latter enjoyed countervailing buyer power as they could threaten to integrate private label products or sponsor new entry through in store promotion. Retailers benefited from a gatekeeper position with access to price and product information and ability to control the price differentials in the outlets. While suppliers could not afford to be excluded from a large retailer, the retailers adopted a multiple sourcing strategy and were not dependent upon a single supplier. Surprisingly, the investigation in this case showed that delisting applied to P&G's must-stock brands, raising doubts as to the actual must-stock nature of these products.

In Case COMP/M.5658 *Unilever/Sara Lee* the Commission appraised a transaction on the markets for the supply of personal care products. The transaction affected differentiated product markets where the parties' customers were mainly large retailers. Illustrative is the appraisal of the deodorants market in this case. The market was characterised by high product differentiation and was dominated by leading brands. Contrary to the Commission's analysis, the parties argued that no price increases were to be expected, since retailers enjoyed countervailing buyer power resulting from their double role as customers and competitors, controlling market access and supplying their own private label products. As a result, large retailers could threaten to delist brands and could undermine the success of a brand by, for example, increasing or decreasing shelf space or by changing shelf location. The Commission rejected the parties countervailing buyer power arguments, noting Unilever's leading position as supplier of deodorants with an active role in category management and a stronger bargaining position in comparison to its competitors. Further, since the transaction would have resulted in a structural change in a market common to all retailers, retailers could have further passed on the price increase to consumers. In addition, it would be difficult for customers to integrate vertically in the deodorants market, since this market is primarily driven by branded goods and penetration of private labels is lower than in other consumer goods markets. Arguments about the possibility of delisting Unilever's products were also rejected. While accepting the distinction between regular and non-regular delisting, Unilever failed to provide evidence distinguishing delisting because of poor performance and delisting occurring during negotiations.

In Case COMP/M.2220 *General Electric/Honeywell* the Commission found that large airlines were not willing to exert buyer power since General Electric was an unavoidable trading partner. The buyer power here was limited due to the imbalance in the commercial relationship. Further, the Commission did not accept the argument that customers (airframe manufacturers and airlines) exerted their buyer power to prevent foreclosure effects. The Commission was of the opinion that customers would have only a limited interest in exercising whatever countervailing power they may have vis-à-vis the merged entity's bundled offers. Moreover, the countervailing buyer power argument was considered irrelevant in the case of bundled offers, since it would imply that customers would act irrationally and refuse to accept lower prices.

In Case COMP/M.5046 *Friesland Foods/Campina* the Commission noted that 'the countervailing buyer power defence rests on the presumption that powerful buyers will be able to protect themselves—and thus, ultimately, also final consumers—against adverse changes in the terms of supply following the notified merger.' (para 274)

The Commission's Guidelines on the Assessment of Horizontal Mergers elaborate on the treatment of countervailing buyer power: 'The competitive pressure on a supplier is not only exercised by competitors but can also come from its customers. Even firms with very high market shares may not be in a position, post-merger, to significantly impede effective competition, in particular by acting to an appreciable extent independently of their customers, if the latter possess countervailing buyer power. Countervailing buyer power in this context should be understood as the bargaining strength that the buyer has vis-à-vis the seller in commercial negotiations due to its size, its commercial significance to the seller and its ability to switch to alternative suppliers.' (para 64) 'The Commission considers, when relevant, to what extent customers will be in a position to counter the increase in market power that a merger would otherwise be likely to create. One source of countervailing buyer power would be if a customer could credibly threaten to resort, within a reasonable timeframe, to alternative sources of supply should the supplier decide to increase prices or to otherwise deteriorate quality or the conditions of delivery. This would be the case if the buyer could immediately switch to other suppliers, credibly threaten to vertically integrate into the upstream market or to sponsor upstream expansion or entry for instance by persuading a potential entrant to enter by committing to placing large orders with this company.' (para 65)

Inco/Falconbridge	**Efficiencies**
Case COMP M.4000	
European Commission, [2007] OJ L72/18	

Facts

The Commission received notification of the acquisition by Inco Ltd ('Inco') of Falconbridge Ltd ('Falconbridge'). Both companies are active worldwide in the mining, processing, refining and sale of various nickel products, copper, cobalt and precious metals. The Commission's investigation has indicated that due to the absence of any significant competitive constraint the new entity would have had the ability and incentive to increase prices on the market for the supply of nickel to the plating and electroforming industry in the Union, and on the global markets for the supply of high-purity nickel and cobalt for the production of superalloys used in safety-critical parts. The parties offered commitments to remove these concerns and subsequently the transaction was cleared by the Commission. In its investigation the Commission considered possible efficiency gains brought about by the proposed transaction.

Held

'According to the Merger Regulation and the Commission's Horizontal Guidelines, it is possible that efficiencies brought about by a merger counteract the effects on competition and in particular the potential harm to consumers that it might otherwise have. Parties to a concentration may thus detail the efficiency gains generated by the concentration that are likely to enhance the ability and the incentive of the merged entity to act pro-competitively for the benefit of consumers. Typical examples of such efficiencies include cost savings, new product introduction and service or product improvement. Efficiency claims need to be reasoned, quantified and supported by internal studies and documents if necessary. The parties have to demonstrate that such efficiencies are likely to benefit directly customers in the relevant markets where competition concerns have been identified and could not have been achieved to a similar extent by means that are less anticompetitive than the proposed concentration.' (para 530)

'According to the Horizontal Guidelines, to declare compatible with the [internal] market a transaction for which competition concerns have been identified, the Commission should be in a position to conclude that: "the efficiencies generated by the merger are likely to enhance the ability and the incentive of the merger entity to act pro-competitively for the benefit of consumers, thereby counteracting the adverse effects on competition which the merger might have otherwise".' (para 531)

'[W]hile the efficiencies presented by the parties are quantified and well-supported by several studies prepared by Inco and are likely to effectively materialize, the parties did not demonstrate to the requisite standards that the efficiencies could not have been achieved by other means and would directly benefit end customers in the markets where competition concerns have been identified so as to offset the identified competition concerns.' (para 536)

Merger specificity

'As regards the merger specificity, according to the Horizontal Guidelines, efficiencies are relevant to the competitive assessment when they are a direct consequence of the notified merger and cannot be achieved to a similar extent by less anticompetitive alternatives.' (para 537)

The Commission noted that documents presented by Inco do not mention that the synergies are calculated as the difference between the level of efficiencies obtained through a merger and the level of efficiencies obtained through a Sudbury joint venture. The data presented by Inco represents the total synergies expected from the proposed transaction and not the difference between this total and the synergies that could have been achieved through other means such as a Sudbury joint venture. The Commission considers that the creation of such joint venture would have a lesser impact on competition in the markets for the supply of finished nickel and cobalt products than the proposed transaction. A joint venture between Inco and Falconbridge in the Sudbury basin, as envisaged in the Inco internal document, would not prevent Inco and Falconbridge from competing at the refining and marketing level, while allowing for most of the operating synergies between the two companies to be realised. It would allow the parties to capture much of the potential for synergies while being a less anticompetitive outcome than a full merger between Inco and Falconbridge. (paras 538–42)

Benefit to consumers

'As regards the benefit to consumers, the parties do not provide any explanation as to why the claimed efficiencies would be passed on to end users and simply state that this would be the case in view of the competition on the market for the supply of nickel. In particular, the parties did not state nor argue that the efficiencies would benefit directly the end customers active in the three product markets where competition concerns have been identified.' (para 543)

The Commission agrees that the proposed transaction is likely to lower New Inco's cost base due to synergies in mining and processing. However, these savings are expected to be achieved at the upstream mining and processing level only. Subsequently, the Commission considers that the efficiencies will not meaningfully benefit customers for nickel end-products in the relevant markets where competition concerns have been identified. In addition it is unlikely that new the entity which is expected to acquire a position approaching that of a monopoly will have sufficient incentives to pass on these efficiency gains to end customers due to the characteristics of the relevant markets where competition concerns arise. (paras 544–6)

The significant impediment to competition likely to be brought about by the proposed transaction will not be offset to any meaningful extent by potential benefits to end customers deriving from the efficiencies brought about by the proposed transaction. (para 547)

Comment

These efficiencies were to arise at the upstream level of the nickel production chain from optimisation of the mining and processing operations of the parties. The Commission considered it unlikely that these upstream efficiencies would be passed on to consumers in the downstream markets, where the merged entity would have had an almost monopolistic position. The Commission also took the view that similar efficiencies could be achieved through less restrictive means such as a production joint venture in the Sudbury basin.

The burden of establishing efficiencies is on the undertakings. In this respect efficiencies are treated as a defence claim. One difficulty for the parties to the transaction may be to obtain the relevant information to substantiate a claim of efficiencies ex ante in transactions which involve hostile takeovers.

Recital 29 of the Merger Regulation considers the role of efficiencies in merger assessment and states that 'In order to determine the impact of a concentration on competition in the [internal] market, it is appropriate to take account of any substantiated and likely efficiencies put forward by the undertakings concerned. It is possible that the efficiencies brought about by the concentration counteract the effects on competition, and in particular the potential harm to consumers, that it might otherwise have and that, as a consequence, the concentration would not significantly impede effective competition, in the [internal] market or in a substantial part of it, in particular as a result of the creation or strengthening of a dominant position.'

The Guidelines on the assessment of horizontal mergers elaborate on the treatment of efficiencies in paras 76–88. Generally, the Commission considers any substantiated efficiency claim in the overall assessment of the merger. When the Commission is in a position to conclude that the efficiencies generated by the merger are likely to enhance the ability and incentive of the merged entity to act pro-competitively for the benefit of consumers, thereby counteracting the adverse effects on competition which the merger might otherwise have, it may decide that there are no grounds for declaring it incompatible with the internal market. (para 77)

| *Korsnäs/AssiDomän Cartonboard* | **Efficiencies** |

Korsnäs/AssiDomän Cartonboard

Efficiencies

Case No COMP/M.4057

European Commission, [2006] OJ C209/12

Facts

The Commission received a notification of a proposed concentration by which Korsnäs AB ('Korsnäs') intended to acquire control of AssiDomän Cartonboard Holding AB ('AD Cartonboard') by way of purchase of shares. The two undertakings are both active world-wide in the production of liquid carton packaging board (LPB), which is used for the production of packaging containers. The Commission cleared the transaction after it concluded that the merging parties are likely to be constrained by countervailing buyer power, existing competition and potential new entry to the market. In its appraisal the Commission also briefly considered efficiencies and synergies which would stem from the transaction.

Held

'The notifying party submits that it expects substantial synergies to arise as a result of the proposed transaction. In particular, the notifying party expects to save input cost, reduce personnel and improve production efficiencies.' (para 57)

'In addition, Korsnäs argues that it will be in a position to realise R&D efficiencies as well as benefit from implementing best practices across the two production sites. As noted above, the merged entity will have a wider portfolio range within LPB.' (para 58)

'In order to take into account efficiency claims in its assessment, the Commission must be in a position to reach the conclusion that the efficiencies are merger specific, verifiable and benefit consumers.' (para 61)

'The submission by the parties raises a lot of issues, which cannot be fully assessed within the context of a first phase investigation, in particular with respect to savings in input costs and staff reduction.' (para 62)

'Nevertheless, it appears realistic to assume that the allocation of production among the increased portfolio of machines will indeed allow the merged entity to increase overall production on the machines (for instance by running longer batches thereby reducing time spent on switching). In light of the abovementioned term sheet agreement with Tetra Pak and on the general absence of concern about the transaction among customers, the Commission considers that the parties have sufficiently established that this category of efficiencies is likely to occur and be passed on to consumers.' (para 63)

'These efficiencies are thus likely to enhance the ability and incentive of the merged entity to act pro-competitively for the benefit of consumers, and therefore strengthen the conclusion that the proposed transaction will not significantly impede effective competition.' (para 64)

Comment

In its appraisal the Commission considered whether the efficiencies were merger specific, verifiable and of benefit to consumers.

Note that the discussion of efficiencies followed a conclusion that the new entity will face countervailing buyer power, existing and potential competition which would curtail its market power. The finding of efficiencies therefore served to strengthen the earlier conclusion that the transaction will not impede effective competition. In other words, the finding of efficiencies did not serve in this case to change the story of harm, as such a story did not exist. This also explains the relatively brief discussion of efficiencies and the comment by the Commission that it cannot fully assess the parties submission within the context of a first phase investigation.

Ryanair Holdings plc v Commission	**Efficiencies**
T-342/07	Verifiability of the Efficiency Claims
General Court, [2010] ECR II-3457, [2011] 4 CMLR 4	Consumer Benefit

Facts

In 2006 Ryanair launched a public bid for the entire share capital of Aer Lingus Group. The public bid was notified to the Commission. The Commission blocked the transaction after raising serious doubts as to its competitive effect on the market. (Case COMP/M.4439 *Ryanair/Aer Lingus*). Ryanair applied for annulment of the decision, contesting, among other things the Commission's assessment of its efficiency claims and finding that these were not sufficiently verifiable, were not merger specific and would not benefit consumers.

Held

The Commission observes that, since the merger would result in a position close to a monopoly, it is highly unlikely that it could be cleared on the ground that the efficiency gains generated would counteract its potential anticompetitive effects. In any event, the efficiencies alleged by Ryanair were not verifiable or merger-specific and would not be of benefit to consumers. (para 393)

'In the contested decision, the Commission stated that Ryanair's efficiency claims were not verifiable because they were in essence based on the general claim that Ryanair would be able to transfer its business model, and in particular the related cost levels, to Aer Lingus without the offsetting of downgrades in product characteristics and revenue having been sufficiently taken into account.' (para 403)

The Commission specifically examined whether Ryanair's efficiency claims were 'verifiable', in the sense that they made it possible for it to be reasonably certain that the efficiencies were likely to materialise and be substantial enough to counteract the concentration's potential harm to consumers. The Commission stated in recital 1133 of the contested decision that, in the light of Ryanair's efficiency claims, 'the proposition that Ryanair w[ould] be able to fully transfer its business model, and in particular the related cost levels to Aer Lingus without offsetting downgrades in product characteristics and revenue appear[ed] highly optimistic'. The Commission stated that 'Ryanair present[ed] no objective or convincing evidence in this respect other than a general confidence in "Ryanair's more ruthless management style".' (para 411)

'In the absence of information proving that the expected efficiencies as a result of the transfer to Aer Lingus of Ryanair's business model took into consideration the downgrades which would be the result of giving up Aer Lingus's business model, the Commission was entitled to call into question the verifiability of the efficiency claims.' (para 413)

The Court also accepts the Commission's stand that efficiencies relating to reduction in staff costs, improved aircraft utilisation and reductions in fuel and distribution costs, were not merger specific and could also be achieved by Aer Lingus independently of the proposed concentration. In addition, efficiencies are unlikely to be passed on to consumers in view of the very high market shares of the merged entity. (paras 424–43)

Comment

The General Court accepted the Commission's view that efficiencies flowing from the business model were not sufficiently verifiable. It also accepted the view that other efficiencies were not merger specific and would not have benefited consumers.

The General Court's discussion of efficiencies was heavily reliant on the Commission's Guidelines on the Assessment of Horizontal Mergers (paras 76–88 Horizontal Guidelines). The Court used the Guidelines' framework as a benchmark when assessing whether the Commission correctly found that efficiencies were not sufficiently verifiable, were not merger specific and would not benefit consumers.

UPS/TNT	**Efficiencies**
Case M.6570	Non-coordinated Effects
European Commission, [2014] OJ C187/14	'Fix-it-First' Remedy

Facts

The European Commission prohibited a proposed acquisition of TNT Express by UPS. The Commission found that the takeover would have restricted competition in the market for international express deliveries of small packages in 15 Member States.

The concentration would have reduced the number of significant players on these markets to only two or three, at times leaving DHL as the only alternative to UPS. It would have subsequently resulted in an increase in price for delivery services.

In its decision the Commission considered possible efficiency justifications. The Commission acknowledged the significant merger specific cost-savings which would result from the combination of UPS and TNT's air networks. In addition, the Commission accepted that part of these savings would be passed on to customers. However, these efficiencies were deemed insufficient in order to outweigh the overall negative effects the concentration would have had on competition. Transaction blocked.

Comment

In its Guidelines on the assessment of horizontal mergers the Commission indicates that it will take account of efficiency claims when three cumulative conditions are satisfied: (1) Efficiencies are merger specific—a direct consequence of the notified merger (para 85); (2) Efficiencies are substantial and timely, and should, in principle, benefit consumers in the relevant markets where competition concerns would occur (paras 79–84); (3) Efficiencies are likely to materialise, and be substantial enough to counteract a merger's potential harm to consumers (paras 86–8).

In this case the Commission acknowledged conditions (1) and (2) with respect to some of the efficiencies raised by the parties. However, the efficiency gains were found not to be substantial enough to outweigh price increases in several Member States. The Commission therefore concluded that they will not counteract the merger's potential harm (condition (3)).

On 5 April 2013 UPS brought an action for annulment of the Commission's decision (Case T-194/13 *United Parcel Service v Commission*). Among other things, UPS alleged that 'by setting an arbitrary standard for verifiability of efficiencies, the Commission erred in law and diverged from the standard set by the case law. Further, the Commission erred in law and committed a manifest error of assessment in assigning insufficient or zero weight to efficiencies that it accepted in principle. Finally the Commission breached UPS' rights of defence by basing its rejection of efficiencies on objections that UPS had not been confronted with previously.' ([2013] OJ C147/30) (appeal pending)

Also noteworthy in this case is the theory of harm. The Commission was concerned that the reduction in number of major companies operating on the market would reduce the competitive pressure and thus lead to a price increase. The transaction was prohibited due to it being predicted to significantly impede effective competition. Crucially, the merged entity would not have benefited from a dominant position post-merger.

UPS offered to divest TNT's subsidiaries in 17 Member States. The remedies offered were deemed insufficient as the purchaser would need effective coverage in other Member States or a partner in these markets. Only a handful or potential purchasers would have such coverage and the Commission therefore required the parties to identify possible buyers of the divested assets upfront. The 'fix-it-first' remedy was meant to alleviate the Commission's concerns as to the viability of the proposed divestiture.

French Republic and others v Commission	**Failing Firm Defence**

French Republic and others v Commission
Joined Cases C-68/94 and 30/95 (Kali und Salz)
Court of Justice, [1998] ECR I-1375, [1998] 4 CMLR 829

Facts

The Court of Justice considered an appeal on a Commission's decision in which it approved, subject to conditions, a concentration between Kali und Salz AG and Mitteldeutsche Kali AG (Case No IV/M.308). The decision was contested by the French government which sought its annulment on the ground, among others, that the Commission incorrectly applied the 'failing company defence'. In its decision the Commission considered the 'failing company defence' and noted that a merger generally is not the cause of the deterioration of the competitive structure if it is clear that: (1) the acquired undertaking would in the near future be forced out of the market if not taken over by another undertaking, (2) the acquiring undertaking would take over the market share of the acquired undertaking if it were forced out of the market, and (3) there is no less anticompetitive alternative purchase. (para 71, Case No IV/M.308 *Kali-Salz/MdK/Treuhand* [1994] OJ L186/38)

Held

'As regards the incorrect use of the "failing company defence", the French Government notes that this defence is derived from United States antitrust legislation, under which a concentration may not be regarded as causing a dominant position to come into being or strengthening it if the following conditions are met: (a) one of the parties to the concentration is in a position such that it will be unable to meet its obligations in the near future; (b) it is unable to reorganise successfully under Chapter 11 of the Bankruptcy Act; (c) there are no other solutions which are less anticompetitive than the concentration and; (d) the failing undertaking would be forced out of the market if the concentration were not implemented.' (para 91)

'The Commission, it is submitted, referred to the "failing company defence" without taking into account all the criteria used in the United States antitrust legislation, in particular those mentioned at (a) and (b), whereas only application of the United States criteria in full ensures that a derogating mechanism is established whose application does not have the effect of aggravating a competitive situation already in decline.' (para 92)

'The Commission concedes that in the contested decision it did not adopt the American "failing company defence" in its entirety. However, it fails to see how that could affect the lawfulness of its decision. It considers, moreover, that it has shown to the necessary legal standard that the criteria it used for the application of the "failing company defence" were indeed satisfied in the present case.' (paras 100, 101)

The court observes at the outset that under Article 2(2) of the Merger Regulation if a concentration is not the cause of the creation or strengthening of a dominant position which has a significant impact on the competitive situation on the relevant market, it must be declared compatible with the internal market. (paras 109, 110)

The fact that the conditions set by the Commission do not entirely coincide with the conditions applied in connection with the US "failing company defence" is not in itself a ground of invalidity of the contested decision. 'Solely the fact that the conditions set by the Commission were not capable of excluding the possibility that a concentration might be the cause of the deterioration in the competitive structure of the market could constitute a ground of invalidity of the decision.' (para 112)

'In the present case, the French Government disputes the relevance of the criterion that it must be verified that the acquiring undertaking would in any event obtain the acquired undertaking's share of the market if the latter were to be forced out of the market.' (para 113)

'However, in the absence of that criterion, a concentration could, provided the other criteria were satisfied, be considered as not being the cause of the deterioration of the competitive structure of the market even though it appeared that, in the event of the concentration not proceeding, the acquiring undertaking would not gain the entire market share of the acquired undertaking. Thus, it would be possible to deny the existence of a causal link between the concentration and the deterioration of the competitive structure of the market even though the competitive structure of the market would deteriorate to a lesser extent if the concentration did not proceed.' (para 114)

'The introduction of that criterion is intended to ensure that the existence of a causal link between the concentration and the deterioration of the competitive structure of the market can be excluded only if the competitive structure resulting from the concentration would deteriorate in similar fashion even if the concentration did not proceed.' (para 115)

'The criterion of absorption of market shares, although not considered by the Commission as sufficient in itself to preclude any adverse effect of the concentration on competition, therefore helps to ensure the neutral effects of the concentration as regards the deterioration of the competitive structure of the market. This is consistent with the concept of causal connection set out in Article 2(2) of the Regulation.' (para 116)

'It follows from the foregoing that the absence of a causal link between the concentration and the deterioration of the competitive structure of the German market has not been effectively called into question. Accordingly, it must be held that, so far as that market is concerned, the concentration appears to satisfy the criterion referred to in Article 2(2) of the Regulation, and could thus be declared compatible with the [internal] market without being amended. Consequently, contrary to the French Government's assertion, it is not possible without contradicting that premiss to require the Commission, with respect to the German market, to attach any condition whatever to its declaration of the concentration's compatibility.' (para 124)

Comment

The Court of Justice supported the Commission's opinion that the parties need to show that the acquiring undertaking would in any event obtain the acquired undertaking's share of the market if the latter were to be forced out of the market. It noted that that criterion helps to ensure the neutral effects of the concentration as regards the deterioration of the competitive structure of the market.

Note, however, that the approach taken by the Court of Justice was wider than the criteria set out in the Commission's decision. According to paragraph 115 of the Court of Justice judgment, a merger can be regarded as a rescue merger if the competitive structure resulting from the concentration would deteriorate in similar fashion even if the concentration did not proceed, that is to say, even if the concentration was prohibited. (See Commission comments to that extent in Case IV/M.2314 *BASF/Pantochim/Eurodiol*, para 139)

The Guidelines on the Assessment of Horizontal Mergers review the Commission's assessment of a failing firm defence: 'The Commission may decide that an otherwise problematic merger is nevertheless compatible with the [internal] market if one of the merging parties is a failing firm. The basic requirement is that the deterioration of the competitive structure that follows the merger cannot be said to be caused by the merger. This will arise where the competitive structure of the market would deteriorate to at least the same extent in the absence of the merger.' (para 89) 'The Commission considers the following three criteria to be especially relevant for the application of a "failing firm defence". First, the allegedly failing firm would in the near future be forced out of the market because of financial difficulties if not taken over by another undertaking. Second, there is no less anti-competitive alternative purchase than the notified merger. Third, in the absence of a merger, the assets of the failing firm would inevitably exit the market.' (para 90) 'It is for the notifying parties to provide in due time all the relevant information necessary to demonstrate that the deterioration of the competitive structure that follows the merger is not caused by the merger.' (para 91)

Due to the economic downturn, more cases of failing firm defence have emerged in recent years. Note the following two examples from the UK in which the defence served as the underlining reason for clearance: *Long Clawson/Millway* (Competition Commission, 14 January 2009); *HMV/Zavvi* (OFT, 28 April 2009). In the latter transaction the overwhelming evidence pointing in favour of a failing firm defence led the OFT to take the decision without referral to a detailed market analysis.

BASF/Pantochim/Eurodiol   **Failing Firm Defence**
Case IV/M.2314
European Commission, [2002] OJ L132/45

Facts

The Commission received notification of a proposed concentration by which the German undertaking BASF intended to acquire control of the whole of Pantochim and Eurodiol, two Belgian undertakings active in the chemical sector. The transaction gave rise to concerns as to the creation of a dominant position. Given the financial difficulties of Eurodiol and Pantochim, and in accordance with the failing firm defence, the Commission compared the impact of the merger on the market with that caused by the disappearance of the two Belgian companies if the acquisition was not authorised. The Commission subsequently cleared the transaction.

Held

'The approach taken by the Court of Justice [in Case C-68/94 *French Republic and others v Commission*] is wider than the criteria set out in the Commission's decision in Kali+Salz. According to the Court of Justice, a merger can be regarded as a rescue merger if the competitive structure resulting from the concentration would deteriorate in similar fashion even if the concentration did not proceed, that is to say, even if the concentration was prohibited.' (para 139)

'In general terms, the concept of the "rescue merger" requires that the undertakings to be acquired can be regarded as "failing firms" and that the merger is not the cause of the deterioration of the competitive structure. Thus, for the application of the rescue merger, two conditions must be satisfied: (a) the acquired undertaking would in the near future be forced out of the market if not taken over by another undertaking; and (b) there is no less anti-competitive alternative purchase.' (para 140)

'However, the application of these two criteria does not completely rule out the possibility of a takeover by third parties of the assets of the undertakings concerned in the event of their bankruptcy. If such assets were taken over by competitors in the course of bankruptcy proceedings, the economic effects would be similar to a takeover of the failing firms themselves by an alternative purchaser. Thus it needs to be established in addition to the first two criteria, that the assets to be purchased would inevitably disappear from the market in the absence of the merger. Given this general framework, the Commission regards the following criteria as relevant for the application of the concept of the "rescue merger": (a) the acquired undertaking would in the near future be forced out of the market if not taken over by another undertaking; (b) there is no less anti-competitive alternative purchase; and (c) the assets to be acquired would inevitably exit the market if not taken over by another undertaking.' (paras 141, 142)

'In any event, the application of the concept of the "rescue merger" requires that the deterioration of the competitive structure through the merger is at least no worse than in the absence of the merger.' (para 143)

In the present case it is established that (1) in the absence of a buyer the bankruptcy of Eurodiol and Pantochim would be an unavoidable and immediate consequence. In view of the growing demand and tight capacity constraints in the market, a bankruptcy would likely cause supply shortages and price increases which would have hurt customers more than if the merger was allowed. (2) There was no less anticompetitive alternative purchase option for the two undertakings and BASF was the only company to have made a firm offer to purchase them. (3) Without the merger the production capacity of Eurodiol and Pantochim would have definitely exited the market. (paras 143–62)

Comment

It is for the notifying parties to provide all the relevant information necessary to demonstrate that the deterioration of the competitive structure that follows the merger is not caused by the merger.

Newscorp/Telepiù	**Failing Firm Defence**
Case IV/M.2876	Failing Division Defence
European Commission, [2004] OJ L110/73	

Facts

The Commission received notification of a proposed concentration by which News Corporation Limited, Australia (Newscorp) would acquire control of the whole of the Italian pay-TV companies Telepiù SpA and Stream SpA. Telepiù and Stream would then merge their activities in a combined satellite pay-TV platform. The Commission raised concerns as to the effects of the transaction in the pay-TV market. The Commission rejected Newscorp's argument that the 'failing firm defence' should apply in this case since Stream would inevitably exit the market in the event of the merger being blocked. The Commission did take account of the financial difficulties faced by Telepiù and Stream before approving the transaction subject to a comprehensive remedy package which included both structural and behavioural commitments.

Held

'To date, the Commission has only twice based a merger decision on the concept of the "rescue merger" (commonly referred to as failing company defence), in case *Kali und Salz/MKD/Treuhand* (hereinafter *Kali und Salz*) and in the *BASF/Eurodiol/Pantochim* decision. In *Kali und Salz* the criteria set by the Commission for the application of the rescue merger defence were the following: (a) the acquired company would in the near future be forced out of the market; (b) there is no less anti-competitive purchaser; (c) the acquiring undertaking would gain the market share of the acquired undertaking if it were forced out of the market.' (para 205)

'According to its judgment in *Kali und Salz* (31 March 1998), the Court of Justice found that a merger can be regarded as a rescue merger if the deterioration in the competitive structure resulting from the concentration would occur in a similar fashion even if the concentration did not proceed. According to the Court of Justice "The introduction of this criterion (the acquiring undertaking would gain the market share of the acquired undertaking) if it were forced out of the market is intended to ensure that the existence of a causal link between the concentration and the deterioration of the competitive structure of the market can be excluded only if the competitive structure resulting from the concentration would deteriorate in similar fashion even if the concentration did not proceed. The criterion of absorption of market shares, although not considered by the Commission as sufficient in itself to preclude any adverse effect of the concentration on competition, therefore helps to ensure the neutral effects of the concentration as regards the deterioration of the competitive structure of the market. This is consistent with the concept of causal connection set out in Article 2(2) of the Regulation". (para 206)

'In its Decision in *BASF/Eurodiol/Pantochim*, the Commission indicated that the approach taken by the Court of Justice is wider than the criteria set out in the Commission's Decision in *Kali und Salz*. According to the Court of Justice, the existence of a causal link between the concentration and the deterioration of the competitive structure of the market can be excluded and so a merger can be regarded as a rescue merger only if the competitive structure resulting from the concentration is expected to deteriorate in similar fashion even if the concentration were not allowed to proceed, that is to say, even if the concentration were prohibited. In general terms, according to the *BASF/Eurodiol/Pantochim* Decision, the concept of the "rescue merger" requires that the undertakings to be acquired can be regarded as "failing firms" and that the merger is not the cause of the deterioration of the competitive structure. Thus, for the application of the rescue merger, two conditions must be satisfied: (a) the acquired undertaking would in the near future be forced out of the market if not taken over by another undertaking; and (b) there is no less anti-competitive alternative purchase.' (para 207)

'However, the application of these two criteria does not completely rule out the possibility of a takeover by third parties of the assets of the undertakings concerned in the event of their bankruptcy. If such assets were taken over by competitors in the course of bankruptcy proceedings, the economic effects would be similar to a takeover of the failing firms themselves by an alternative purchaser. Thus, the Commission in that particular case decided that, in addition to the first two criteria, it was necessary to establish that: (c) the assets to be purchased would inevitably disappear or exit from the market in the absence of the merger.' (para 208)

'In any event, the application of the concept of the 'rescue merger' requires that the deterioration of the competitive structure resulting from the merger is at least no worse than that which would have occurred in the absence of the merger.' (para 209)

'In its reply to the statement of objections, Newscorp argued that the conditions for a "failing company defence" were met in this case, namely that, in the absence of the merger, Telepiù would gain a position comparable to the combined platform's after the merger and that in any event the assets of Stream would inevitably exit the market.' (para 210)

'Before examining this claim, it should be noted that Newscorp argues that Stream, currently jointly controlled by Newscorp and Telecom Italia, is the "failing firm" which would exit the market but for the merger. The present transaction is in fact a combination of a change from joint to sole control of Stream by one of its parent companies, Newscorp, and its merger with another company (Telepiù). As Stream is a separate "division" of one "company", Newscorp, this merger raises the question whether the "failing company defence" applies when the acquiring firm is financially healthy but one of its divisions, which is failing, is merging with another entity.' (para 211)

'As indicated by the Commission in its Decision in *Rewe/Meinl*, in a case of a "failing-division defence" and not of a "failing-company defence", the burden of proving lack of causality between the merger and the creation or strengthening of a dominant position falls on the companies claiming it. Otherwise, every merger involving an allegedly unprofitable division could be justified under merger control law by the declaration that, without the merger, the division would cease to operate. The case *Rewe/Meinl* involved a division of the Meinl group that was acquired by Rewe. The importance of proving lack of causality is even greater in the case of a claimed "failing division", which is actually the acquiring company. Finally, it could reasonably be argued that it is possible that the buying group might have strategic reasons to keep its failing division alive even if the merger were to be prohibited.' (para 212)

Newscorp argues that Stream is currently a 'failing firm' which will exit the market in the absence of the merger. 'In the present transaction, the acquirer of sole control of the failing company is one of its parent companies, which is also acquiring sole control of another company (Telepiù). Although Stream is a separate legal person, there seems to be no question that a whole firm (ie Newscorp) would be forced out of the market. Newscorp acts as a holding company and Stream accounts for only part of the business activities and subsidiaries of the Newscorp group. Stream's withdrawal from the Italian pay-TV market would accordingly take the form of a management decision to abandon a business activity whose development has not lived up to the expectations of the firm's managing board.' (paras 213–14)

Newscorp argues that in the absence of substantial synergies, any potential buyer would face a similar situation to Newscorp and Telecom Italia. However, its claim that there is no alternative potential buyer apart from the acquiring firm should be rejected. Stream did not actively try to find a less anticompetitive solution than the merger of the two companies. (paras 216, 217)

'Since neither of the first two conditions is met in the present case, it is not necessary to take a final position on whether the third condition (inevitable disappearance or exit from the market of the assets to be acquired) is fulfilled in the present case.' (para 220)

Comment

The case involved a claim of 'failing-division' defence by the acquiring company. The Commission emphasised the importance of proving lack of causality in such a case. (para 212)

Aegean /Olympic II	**Failing Firm Defence**

Case M.6796
European Commission, [2015] OJ C25/7

Facts

In 2013 the Commission appraised a proposed acquisition of Olympic Air by Aegean Airlines. Both Greek air carriers were active in the market for air transport of passengers. Following an in-depth investigation the Commission established that, absent the transaction, Olympic Air's financial difficulties would force it to exit the market. The Commission noted that 'Olympic is a failing firm and would go out of business soon. Olympic has never been profitable since its privatisation in 2009 and has received considerable financial support from its sole shareholder, Marfin Investment Group ("MIG"), ever since. A thorough analysis of Olympic's business prospects has confirmed that the company is highly unlikely to become profitable in the foreseeable future under any business plan. MIG had therefore decided to discontinue its support of Olympic, should it not be sold to Aegean. This would lead to Olympic's permanent shutdown in the short term. Furthermore, the market investigation has confirmed that there is no other credible purchaser other than Aegean interested in acquiring Olympic. There has also been no expression of any credible interest in the acquisition of Olympic's assets including its brand. Consequently, the most likely scenario is that absent the transaction Olympic's assets would leave the market completely. The Commission has therefore concluded that any competitive harm caused by Olympic's disappearance as an independent competitor is not caused by the merger. As a consequence, the merger is compatible with the internal market and must be authorised.' (IP/13/927, 09/10/2013)

Comment

An earlier proposed concentration between Aegean Airlines SA and Olympic Air SA (with other affiliated companies) was blocked by the Commission in 2011. In its analysis the Commission considered failing-firm defence arguments, but rejected them, stating that 'the Parties have failed to demonstrate that the deterioration of the competitive structure that follows from the transaction is not directly caused by the transaction. The three-pronged test set out in the Horizontal Merger Guidelines is not met as it has not been demonstrated that absent the transaction Olympic would be forced out of the market in the near future, that there is no less anticompetitive alternative to the transaction and that absent the transaction the assets of Olympic Air would inevitably exit the market. Instead, the evidence collected by the Commission during its in-depth market investigation indicates that the criteria for failing firm defence are not met and that the transaction would most likely deteriorate competition to a significant extent, well beyond the extent of the deterioration that could result were Olympic Air to exit the market.' (para 2120, Case No COMP/M.5830 *Olympic/Aegean Airlines*)

In its press release, the Commission noted that 'the number of routes served by both Aegean and Olympic has decreased substantially over recent years. When the Commission blocked Aegean's previous attempt to merge with Olympic in 2011, the parties provided competing services on 17 routes, nine of which raised competition concerns (see IP/11/68). Currently, Aegean and Olympic have overlaps on seven routes of which the following five domestic routes are served only by them: Athens–Chania; Athens–Mytilene; Athens–Santorini; Athens–Corfu (Aegean only operates in the summer); Athens–Kos (Aegean only operates in the summer).' (IP/13/927, 09/10/2013)

Another transaction cleared in 2013 under the failing firm (division) defence concerned the acquisition of refinery assets of Shell Deutschland Oil GmbH by Nynas AB of Sweden. Absent the transaction Shell would have stopped to operate the Harburg refinery, as it was deemed economically unsustainable. With no alternative buyers, the Commission concluded that the reduction of the number of competitors in the market would occur anyway and would not be caused by the acquisition itself. Transaction cleared. (Case M.6360 *Nynas/Shell/Harburg Refinery*)

General Electric v Commission	**Commitments**
Case T-210/01	General Principles
General Court, [2005] ECR II-5575, [2006] 4 CMLR 15	Structural and Behavioural Remedies

Facts

On 3 July 2001, the Commission prohibited the General Electric Co's (GE) proposed US$42bn acquisition of Honeywell Inc. The Commission asserted that the merger would have severely reduced competition in the aerospace industry by combining the strong position of GE in aircraft engine markets with the similarly strong position of Honeywell in avionics and non-avionics systems. This was the 15th time the Commission had blocked a merger since September 1990, when the European Merger Regulation took effect.

On appeal the GE challenged, among other things, the Commission's rejection of the structural remedies submitted by the parties and the Commission's refusal to take into account the behavioural commitments.

Held

In its statement of objections the Commission clearly set out the objections pertaining to all the anticompetitive consequences of the merger. In order to address these objections, the applicant proposed, on 14 June 2001, structural commitments which the Commission examined but rejected. The applicants submitted a second set of commitments on 28 June 2001, although this was after the last possible day on which commitments could be proposed under the Merger Regulation. 'The only differences between the two sets of commitments concern the behavioural commitments relating to GECAS and the structural commitments relating to the proposed divestment of certain of Honeywell's activities on the various markets for avionics and non-avionics products.' (paras 49–52)

'The Commission is not responsible for technical or commercial gaps in the commitments in question (which led it to conclude that they were insufficient to permit it to approve the merger at issue); nor, more specifically, can those gaps be attributed to any unwillingness on its part to accept that other commitments, of a behavioural nature, might be effective. It was for the parties to the merger to put forward commitments which were comprehensive and effective from all points of view and to do so in principle before 14 June 2001.' (para 52)

'It must be noted that under Regulation No 4064/89 the Commission has power to accept only such commitments as are capable of rendering the notified transaction compatible with the [internal] market (see, to that effect *Gencor v Commission* … paragraph 318). It must be held in that regard that structural commitments proposed by the parties will meet that condition only in so far as the Commission is able to conclude, with certainty, that it will be possible to implement them and that the new commercial structures resulting from them will be sufficiently workable and lasting to ensure that the creation or strengthening of a dominant position, or the impairment of effective competition, which the commitments are intended to prevent, will not be likely to materialise in the relatively near future.' (para 555)

'In this case, the Commission noted, at recital 519 of the contested decision, that if the divestment of Honeywell's engine-manufacturing business for large regional aircraft, proposed by the parties, could be put into practice, it would, on the face of it, be sufficient to remove the competition problem identified in relation to that market. However, it concluded that it would be difficult to put the divestiture into practice.' (paras 556, 557)

'The Commission noted in that regard, at recital 520 of the contested decision, that … and that therefore it was uncertain whether the proposed remedy was in fact capable of eliminating the competition problem identified. It also noted that the commitment did not provide for an alternative to the divestiture. At recital 522, the Commission set out, apparently in the alternative, a number of practical problems which the commitment did not in any event adequately resolve. Given that the applicant merely asserted before the Court that the difficulties to which the Commission alleged that the commitment gives rise were entirely without foundation, it must be held that the applicant has produced neither specific arguments nor evidence that could call into question the correctness of the Commission's finding as to the unworkable nature of the proposed divestment.' (paras 558, 559)

'As pointed out at paragraph 555 above, structural commitments proposed by the parties can be accepted only in so far as the Commission is able to conclude, with certainty, that it will be possible to implement them. … However, the Commission noted, at recital 518 of the contested decision, that the transfer provided for by the commitment was subject to all necessary approvals in the context of the United States export control rules. Accordingly, the Commission concluded that it could not accept the commitment in the form proposed because, if the competent United States authorities were to refuse authorisation, the commitment would have been complied with because the merged entity would have done everything that it was required to do, not-withstanding the fact that the divestiture would not have taken place.' (paras 612, 615)

Comment

With respect to the structural commitments, the General Court held that the Commission was entitled to reject the commitments proposed on the basis that they had no practical value since they was hypothetical, their realisation being wholly dependent on a decision of the authorities of a non-Member State.

With respect to the proposed behavioural remedies, as the Court of Justice rejected the limb of the Commission's reasoning relating to bundling, it did not refer to the Commission's refusal to take into account the behavioural commitments. In its decision the Commission maintained that such commitments could not constitute the basis for a clear elimination of the competitive concerns: 'The undertakings not to engage in bundling practices are submitted in relation to the concerns on the use by the merged entity of its vertical integration and financial strength and its ability to engage in product bundling. However, they are purely behavioural and as such cannot constitute the basis for a clear elimination of the said concerns.' (Commission Decision, para 530) 'The new undertakings regarding GECAS are submitted in relation to the concerns on the use by the merged entity of its vertical integration and financial strength. Although a structural component was added to the undertaking … the undertaking regarding GECAS remains purely behavioural in nature and as such cannot constitute the basis for a clear elimination of the said concerns. In addition, its scope is limited essentially to BFE products excluding engines.' (Commission Decision, para 550)

The Commission's assessment of the transaction and the consideration of its 'conglomerate effects' are detailed on page 473 above.

The Commission Notice on Remedies acceptable under the Merger Regulation echo the General Court's holding and states that: 'Under the structure of the Merger Regulation, it is the responsibility of the Commission to show that a concentration would significantly impede competition. The Commission communicates its competition concerns to the parties to allow them to formulate appropriate and corresponding remedies proposals. It is then for the parties to the concentration to put forward commitments; the Commission is not in a position to impose unilaterally any conditions to an authorisation decision, but only on the basis of the parties' commitments. The Commission will inform the parties about its preliminary assessment of remedies proposals. If, however, the parties do not validly propose remedies adequate to eliminate the competition concerns, the only option for the Commission will be to adopt a prohibition decision.' (Notice, para 6)

'Under the Merger Regulation, the Commission only has power to accept commitments that are deemed capable of rendering the concentration compatible with the [internal] market so that they will prevent a significant impediment of effective competition. The commitments have to eliminate the competition concerns entirely and have to be comprehensive and effective from all points of view. Furthermore, commitments must be capable of being implemented effectively within a short period of time as the conditions of competition on the market will not be maintained until the commitments have been fulfilled.' (Notice, para 9)

EDP v Commission	**Commitments**
Case T-87/05	Burden of Proof
General Court, [2005] ECR II-3745, [2005] 5 CMLR 23	Monitoring

Facts

An appeal on a Commission decision in which it blocked a proposed acquisition of joint control by Energias de Portugal SA ('EDP'), the incumbent electricity company in Portugal, together with ENI SpA, an Italian energy company, of Gás de Portugal SA ('GDP'), the incumbent gas company in Portugal. In its investigation the Commission raised concerns as to the impact of the proposed transaction on the gas and electricity supply markets in Portugal. It subsequently concluded that the transaction would strengthen EDP's dominant position in the electricity wholesale and retail markets in Portugal.

On appeal, the applicant argued, among other things, that the Commission wrongly relied on the presumption that it was for the parties to prove that their commitments eliminated the competition concerns identified by the Commission. Appeal dismissed.

Held

Burden of proof

'It must be borne in mind that Article 2(2) of the Merger Regulation provides that the Commission shall declare compatible with the [internal] market a concentration which does not create or strengthen a dominant position as a result of which effective competition would be significantly impeded in the [internal] market. It follows that it is for the Commission to demonstrate that a concentration cannot be declared compatible with the [internal] market.' (para 61)

'Furthermore, Article 8(2) of the Merger Regulation provides that the Commission is to adopt a decision declaring the concentration compatible with the [internal] market where it finds that a notified concentration, following modification by the undertakings concerned if necessary, fulfils the criterion laid down in Article 2(2) of the Merger Regulation. It follows that, in so far as the burden of proof is concerned, a concentration modified by commitments is subject to the same criteria as an unmodified concentration.' (para 62)

'Accordingly, first, the Commission is under an obligation to examine a concentration as modified by the commitments validly proposed by the parties to the concentration (see, to that effect, Case T-158/00 *ARD v Commission* [2003] ECR II-3825, paragraph 280) and, second, the Commission can declare the concentration incompatible with the [internal] market only where those commitments are insufficient to prevent the creation or strengthening of a dominant position having the consequence that effective competition would be significantly impeded. In that regard, it must none the less be borne in mind that, in the case of complex economic assessments, the burden of proof placed on the Commission is without prejudice to its wide discretion in that sphere (see, to that effect, Case T-342/00 *Petrolessence and SG2R v Commission* [2003] ECR II-1161, paragraph 101, and the case-law cited, and Case C-12/03 P *Commission v Tetra Laval* [2005] ECR I-0000, paragraph 38).' (para 63)

'Furthermore, the fact that paragraph 6 of the Notice on Remedies indicates that [i]t is the responsibility of the parties to show that the proposed remedies ... eliminate the creation or strengthening of ... a dominant position identified by the Commission cannot alter that legal position. Even on the assumption that the Commission thereby intended to make the parties to a notified concentration responsible for demonstrating the effectiveness of the proposed commitments, an exercise which is consistent with their interests, the Commission could not conclude that where there is doubt it must prohibit the concentration. Quite to the contrary, in the last resort, it is for the Commission to demonstrate that that concentration, as modified, where appropriate, by commitments, must be declared incompatible with the [internal] market because it still leads to the creation or the strengthening of a dominant position that significantly impedes effective competition.' (para 64)

'It follows that it is for the Commission to demonstrate that the commitments validly submitted by the parties to a concentration do not render that concentration, as modified by the commitments, compatible with the [internal] market.' (para 65)

'The fact that the Commission regards commitments which have been validly submitted, ... as insufficient constitutes an improper reversal of the burden of proof only where the Commission bases that finding of their insufficiency, not upon an assessment of the commitments based on objective and verifiable criteria, but rather upon the assertion that the parties have failed to provide sufficient evidence to carry out a substantive assessment. In the latter case, doubt does not operate in favour of the parties to the transaction and it would have to be concluded that the burden of proving that such a transaction was compatible with the [internal] market has been reversed.' (para 69)

In its decision the Commission raised doubts as to the effectiveness of the commitments. It considered the commitments to be insufficient to ensure that additional gas capacities would actually be made available for third parties. 'The Commission is entitled to reject non-binding commitments or, which amounts to the same thing, commitments the effect of which may be reduced, or even eliminated, by the parties. In doing so, the Commission did not transfer the burden of proof to the parties but denied the certain and measurable character which the commitments had to display. Last, it should be noted that, in the context of this plea, the applicant did not dispute before the [General Court] the uncertain nature of the commitments in question.' (para 72)

Monitoring

'[A]s regards the criticism that the Commission failed to take into account the possibility that the competent Portuguese authorities might carry out the monitoring necessary to ascertain whether the conditions for the early termination of the commitments in question were satisfied, it must be held, first, that, ... it was the parties themselves that expressly envisaged requesting the Commission to verify that those conditions were satisfied. The Commission was therefore not in a position, without itself modifying the proposed commitment, which it is not empowered to do, to entrust that monitoring to the national authorities. Likewise, as regards the other two commitments to which the applicant refers, the Commission had no obligation, even if had been able to do so in the discussions with the parties, to establish a particular method of monitoring, notably one delegated to the competent national authorities. It was for the parties, on the contrary, to propose commitments that were full and effective from all aspects, especially if those behavioural commitments had intrinsic weaknesses as regards their binding nature that justified ex-post monitoring.' (para 105)

Late submission

The regulations on concentrations impose no obligation on the Commission to accept commitments submitted after the deadline. However, as indicated by the Commission in the Remedies Notice, the Commission may take into account commitments which were submitted out of time subject to two cumulative (1) where it can clearly determine that such commitments, once implemented, resolve the competition concerns identified and (2) that there is sufficient time for proper consultation of the Member States on those commitments. (paras 161–3)

Comment

In Case T-282/02 *Cementbouw v Commission* the General Court noted that 'in order to be accepted by the Commission with a view to the adoption of a decision under Article 8(2) of Regulation No 4064/89, the parties' commitments must not only be proportionate to the competition problem identified by the Commission in its decision but must eliminate it entirely; and that objective was clearly not achieved in the present case by the first draft commitments proposed by the notifying parties.' (para 307)

easyJet v Commission	**Commitments**
Case T-177/04	Judicial Review
General Court, [2006] ECR II-1931, [2006] 5 CMLR 11	Divestiture of a Viable Business

Facts

An appeal by easyJet contesting a Commission decision to clear subject to commitments, the concentration between Air France and KLM (Case COMP/M.3280—*Air France/KLM*) ([2004] OJ C60, 5). The Commission cleared the transaction after the parties surrendered 94 single take-off and landing slots per day. These commitments were meant to enable rival airlines to start a service where competition would have been eliminated or significantly reduced, therefore preserving choice of carriers and competitive prices for European travellers. These commitments were reinforced by other measures favouring competition, such as a frequency freeze, interline agreements, blocked space agreements, special pro-rate agreements, access to frequent-flyer programmes, intermodal services and obligations pertaining to fares.

On appeal easyJet argued, among other things, that the accepted commitments were not sufficient to dispel the Commission's serious doubts regarding the transaction.

Held

'According to settled case-law, the Commission enjoys a broad discretion in assessing the need for commitments to be given in order to dispel the serious doubts raised by a concentration. It follows that it is not for the [General Court] to substitute its own assessment for that of the Commission: the Court's review must be limited to ascertaining that the Commission has not committed a manifest error of assessment. In particular, the alleged failure to take into consideration the commitments suggested by the applicant does not by itself prove that the contested decision is vitiated by a manifest error of assessment. Moreover, the fact that other commitments might also have been accepted, or might even have been more favourable to competition, cannot justify annulment of that decision in so far as the Commission was reasonably entitled to conclude that the commitments set out in the decision served to dispel the serious doubts (Case T-158/00 *ARD v Commission* [2003] ECR II-3825, paragraphs 328 and 329).' (para 128)

Failure to extend the commitments to non-overlapping markets

easyJet argued that to ensure the effectiveness of the commitments, these should have been extended to include routes on which the Commission had not identified competition problems because the markets concerned were not attractive.

'The Commission acknowledges in paragraph 17 of the Notice on Remedies that "in order to assure a viable business, it might be necessary to include in a divestiture those activities which are related to markets where the Commission did not raise competition concerns because this would be the only possible way to create an effective competitor in the affected markets". It explains in its pleadings that those measures must be decided in the light of the principle of proportionality.' (para 130-2)

'According to consistent case-law, the principle of proportionality requires measures adopted by [Union] institutions not to exceed the limits of what is appropriate and necessary in order to attain the objectives pursued; when there is a choice between several appropriate measures recourse must be had to the least onerous, and the disadvantages caused must not be disproportionate to the aims pursued (Case C-157/96 *National Farmers' Union and Others* [1998] ECR I-2211, paragraph 60; Case T-211/02 *Tideland Signal v Commission* [2002] ECR II-3781, paragraph 39; and Case T-2/03 *Verein für Konsumenteninformation v Commission* [2005] ECR II-0000, paragraph 99).' (para 133)

'The Court observes that during the administrative procedure the applicant appeared minded to use certain slots which were divested by the parties to the merger for markets unaffected by the merger. Accordingly, the applicant demonstrated its intention of taking advantage of the commitments given by the merged entity to increase its commercial presence in the markets in which there were no competition problems, but without showing that that use would ensure effective competition on the markets affected. It should be noted that the commitments cannot be regarded as a means of favouring, without justification on competition grounds, a potential competitor which wishes to enter a particular market. Therefore the fact that the Commission did not extend the commitments to non-overlapping markets, even though that measure might have benefited the applicant's own commercial interests on the markets not affected by the merger, in no way proves that that extension is the only way to create an effective competitor on the markets affected.' The applicant has not shown that the Commission committed a manifest error of assessment. (paras 136, 137, 139)

Inadequate divestiture which does not include a viable business

easyJet argued that the commitments reduced the barriers to entry rather than ensuring the divestiture of a viable business or of market shares to a competitor. The Commission considers that since none of the parties had a business which could easily be divested, it cannot be criticised for failing to require the divestiture of a viable business. 'According to the Notice on Remedies, the divested activities must consist of a viable business that, if operated by a suitable purchaser, can compete effectively with the merged entity on a lasting basis. Whilst divestiture is the remedy preferred by the Commission, it may accept others. There may be situations where divestiture of a business is impossible. In such circumstances, the Commission has to determine whether or not other types of remedy may have sufficient effect on the market to restore effective competition (paragraphs 14 and 26 of the Notice).' (paras 152, 154)

'The Commission has demonstrated to the requisite legal standard in this connection that the transfer of aircraft cannot effectively remedy the competition problems raised by the merger, since it is difficult, if not impossible, to check whether the purchasers of those aircraft in fact use them on the affected markets. Moreover, a potential entrant can lease or buy a second-hand aircraft, as the use or possession of an aircraft does not appear to be the most immediate barrier to entry.' (para 156)

'As the Commission has rightly demonstrated ... the main barrier to entry in the air transport sector is the lack of available slots at the large airports. Consequently, it is necessary to determine whether the Commission erred in finding that, in the present case, the divestiture of slots provided for in the commitments package could be an effective way to restore effective competition. In that context it is for the applicant to adduce evidence that the divestiture of slots as provided for by the commitments was not sufficient to remedy the competition problems raised.' The applicant has adduced no relevant evidence to sustain its a claim that the Commission erred in its assessment. (paras 166–73)

Appeal dismissed.

Comment

The Court accepted the Commission's position, as stated in the Notice on Remedies, that where divestiture of a business is impossible, alternative remedies may be sought.

A remedy would be deemed effective if it is capable of restoring effective competition. In the present case the Commission was concerned that post-merger, the limited availability of slots would form a barrier to entry in the air transport sector. The Court rejected easyJet's claim that the slot release remedies were ineffective.

In a submission to the OECD the Commission made reference to the use of slot release remedies. It stated: 'Over the last couple of years the Commission has dealt with a number of airlines mergers that have been cleared on the basis of slot release remedies characterised by the release (and, eventually, transfer) of slots without compensation. The legal standard for these remedies, confirmed by the General Court's easyJet judgment is that they must lead to actual and sufficient entry of new competitors and such entry must be timely and likely. The market test of the remedies should confirm [the] interest of competitors to enter the problematic routes. In the most recent cases, the Commission aimed at making those remedies more effective by introducing a shorter time-window and assimilating them to a transfer of slots by providing for a transfer of grandfathering rights if the slots are used regularly in a minimum period of IATA seasons.' (para 26, Remedies in Merger Cases, OECD Working Party No 3 on Cooperation and Enforcement, 28 June 2011, DAF/COMP/WP3/WD(2011)59)

Gencor v Commission	**Commitments**
Case T-102/96	Structural and Behavioural Remedies
General Court, [1999] ECR II-753, [1999] 4 CMLR 971	

Facts

Gencor, a company incorporated under South African law, and Lonrho plc (Lonrho), a company incorporated under English law, proposed to acquire joint control of Impala Platinum Holdings Ltd (Implats) a company incorporated under South African law. Following its appraisal, the Commission blocked the transaction on the ground that it would lead to the creation of a dominant duopoly position in the world platinum and rhodium market as a result of which effective competition would have been significantly impeded in the internal market. On appeal, Gencor challenged, among other things, the Commission's refusal to accept the commitments offered by the parties to the concentration, considering that they were behavioural in nature.

Held

'Since the purpose of the Regulation is to prevent the creation or strengthening of market structures which are liable to impede significantly effective competition in the [internal] market, situations of that kind cannot be allowed to come about on the basis that the undertakings concerned enter into a commitment not to abuse their dominant position, even where it is easy to check whether those commitments have been complied with. Consequently, under the Regulation the Commission has power to accept only such commitments as are capable of rendering the notified transaction compatible with the [internal] market. In other words, the commitments offered by the undertakings concerned must enable the Commission to conclude that the concentration at issue would not create or strengthen a dominant position.' (paras 317, 318)

'The categorisation of a proposed commitment as behavioural or structural is therefore immaterial. It is true that commitments which are structural in nature, such as a commitment to reduce the market share of the entity arising from a concentration by the sale of a subsidiary, are, as a rule, preferable from the point of view of the Regulation's objective, inasmuch as they prevent once and for all, or at least for some time, the emergence or strengthening of the dominant position previously identified by the Commission and do not, moreover, require medium or long-term monitoring measures. Nevertheless, the possibility cannot automatically be ruled out that commitments which prima facie are behavioural, for instance not to use a trademark for a certain period, or to make part of the production capacity of the entity arising from the concentration available to third-party competitors, or, more generally, to grant access to essential facilities on non-discriminatory terms, may themselves also be capable of preventing the emergence or strengthening of a dominant position.' (para 319)

It is thus necessary to examine on a case-by-case basis the commitments offered by the undertakings concerned. In the instant case the commitments offered were incapable of solving the question of the oligopolistic market structure created by the concentration. (paras 320–27)

Appeal dismissed.

Comment

While accepting the general superiority of structural remedies, the General Court established the capability of a remedy to remove the competitive detriment, as the relevant benchmark and not its classification. Thus, behavioural remedies can at times provide an adequate response to the competitive detriment identified by the Commission.

The General Court held that a mere commitment not to abuse the dominant position created or strengthened by the concentration cannot be accepted since the objective of the Merger Regulation is to prevent the creation or strengthening of market structures.

Commission v Tetra Laval BV	**Commitments**
Case C-12/03P	Behavioural Remedies
Court of Justice, [2005] ECR I-987, [2005] 4 CMLR 573	

Facts

An appeal by the Commission on the judgment of the General Court in Case T-5/02 *Tetra Laval v Commission* [2002] ECR II-4381, by which the General Court annulled a Commission decision declaring the acquisition of Sidel SA by Tetra Laval BV to be incompatible with the internal market (Case No COMP/M.2416—*Tetra Laval/Sidel*) ([2004] OJ L43/13). In its investigation the Commission was concerned that the merged entity would be capable of exploiting Tetra's dominant position on the market for aseptic cartons and leveraging existing market power to persuade its customers, via different tactics, to purchase Sidel's packaging equipment. In its decision the Commission rejected commitments submitted by Tetra as it did not consider them sufficient to eliminate the major competition concerns identified in the investigation. With respect to the behavioural commitments the Commission rejected proposed commitments to separate Sidel from Tetra and an undertaking not to infringe Article 102 TFEU. The Commission asserted that these commitments are purely behavioural and 'as such are not suitable to restore conditions of effective competition on a permanent basis, since they do not address the permanent change in the market structure created by the notified operation that causes these concerns.' (para 429) On the obligations not to infringe Article 102 TFEU, the Commission commented that they 'constitute pure promises not to act in a certain manner, indeed not to act in contravention of [Union] law. Such behavioural promises are in contrast with the Commission's stated policy on remedies and with the purpose of the Merger Regulation itself and are extremely difficult if not impossible to monitor effectively.' (para 431) The commitments were subsequently rejected for being both incapable of removing the competition concerns and for complexity in implementation and monitoring.

In its judgment the General Court criticised the Commission for not taking into account the implications of Tetra's commitments. The court held that the Commission ought to have taken account of the behavioural commitments entered into by Tetra.

Held

'With respect to consideration of the behavioural commitments offered by Tetra, the [General Court] was right to hold, in paragraph 161 of the judgment under appeal, that the fact that Tetra had, in the present case, offered commitments relating to its future conduct was a factor which the Commission had to take into account when assessing the likelihood that the merged entity would act in such a way as to make it possible to create a dominant position on one or more of the relevant markets for PET equipment.' (para 85)

'In that regard, the Court points to the considerations set out by the [General Court] in paragraphs 318 and 319 of the judgment in Gencor. Contrary to what the Commission claims, it is not apparent from that judgment that the [General Court] ruled out consideration of behavioural commitments. On the contrary, in paragraph 318, the [General Court] laid down the principle that the commitments offered by the undertakings concerned must enable the Commission to conclude that the concentration at issue will not create or strengthen a dominant position within the meaning of Article 2(2) and (3) of the Regulation. Then, in paragraph 319, it inferred from that principle that the categorisation of a proposed commitment as behavioural or structural is immaterial and that the possibility cannot automatically be ruled out that commitments which are prima facie behavioural, for instance a commitment not to use a trade mark for a certain period or to make part of the production capacity of the entity arising from the concentration available to third-party competitors or, more generally, to grant access to essential facilities on non-discriminatory terms, may also be capable of preventing the emergence or strengthening of a dominant position.' (para 86)

'With respect to the Commission's consideration of the behavioural commitments, the [General Court] merely found, in paragraph 161 of the judgment under appeal, that there is no indication in the contested decision that the Commission took account of the implications of those commitments when it assessed the possibility that a dominant position might be created in future through leveraging.' (para 87)

'Nevertheless, it is not apparent that the [General Court] distorted the contested decision or failed to give sufficient reasons for the judgment under appeal in that regard. It is clear from recitals 429 to 432 in the contested decision, the only ones concerning the behavioural commitments submitted by Tetra, that the Commission refused to accept such commitments, as a matter of principle, and found, in recital 429, that as such, they are not suitable to restore conditions of effective competition on a permanent basis …, since they do not address the permanent change in the market structure created by the notified operation that causes these concerns and, in recital 431, that such behavioural promises are in contrast with the Commission's stated policy on remedies and with the purpose of the Merger Regulation itself … and are extremely difficult if not impossible to monitor effectively.' (para 88)

'[A]lthough the [General Court] erred in law by rejecting the Commission's conclusions as to the adoption by the merged entity of conduct likely to result in leveraging, it was nevertheless right to hold, in paragraph 161 of the judgment under appeal, that the Commission ought to have taken account of the commitments submitted by Tetra with regard to that entity's future conduct. Accordingly, whilst the ground of appeal is well founded in part, it cannot call into question the judgment under appeal in so far as it annulled the contested decision since that annulment was based, inter alia, on the Commission's refusal to take account of those commitments.' (para 89)

Comment

The principal statement made by the Commission in its decision is controversial as it suggests that the Commission will not consider pure behavioural commitments to refrain from acting in a certain manner. The grounds for the rejection include the difficulty in monitoring, implementing and the principal approach that behavioural remedies are not suitable to restore conditions of effective competition on a permanent basis, since they do not address the permanent change in the market structure. The Commission's approach originated out of its reading of *Gencor* as reflected in the Notice (see page 498 above). The Notice on Remedies seems to narrowly interpret the General Court's comment in *Gencor*. Paragraph 9 of the Notice suggests that any promise to behave in a certain way, and not only promises not to abuse a dominant position, would not constitute an adequate remedy. This reading of *Gencor* as reflected in the Notice seems to limit the potential toolbox of remedies available to undertakings.

The Court of Justice rejected the Commission's reading of *Gencor* and reconciled between the General Court judgments in *Tetra* and *Gencor*. In *Gencor* the concentration would have led to a lasting alteration of the structure of the relevant market by creating a dominant duopoly, and thus would have made abuses possible and economically rational. On the other hand, in *Tetra* the structure of the market 'would not have been immediately and directly affected by the notified merger but it could have been so affected only as a result of leveraging and, in particular, abusive conduct by the merged entity on the carton market'. (para 83) Hence, whereas in *Gencor*, the concentration led to alteration of the market on which the Commission intended to protect competition, in *Tetra*, the concentration led to the alteration of one market which was different from the market the Commission sought to protect. In *Tetra*, competition on the market which the Commission intended to protect would have only been affected through leveraging. Commitments relating to its future conduct offered by Tetra were a factor which the 'Commission had to take into account when assessing the likelihood that the merged entity would act in such a way as to make it possible to create a dominant position on one or more of the relevant markets for PET equipment'. (para 85)

In Case COMP/M.5984 *Intel/McAfee*, the Commission cleared Intel's proposed acquisition of McAfee subject to behavioural commitments [2011] OJ C98/01. The approval of this conglomerate merger was conditional upon a set of behavioural commitments ensuring fair competition between the merged entity and its competitors in the field of computer security. Intel committed, among other things, to ensure that vendors of rival security solutions will have access to interoperability information to use functionalities of Intel's CPUs and chipsets in the same way as those functionalities used by McAfee. Intel also committed not to actively impede competitors' security solutions from running on Intel CPUs or chipsets. The Commission accepted the commitments as to the future conduct as suitable, noting that: 'In the conglomerate case at stake, remedies other than divestiture remedies appear best suited to directly address the concerns raised.' (para 306)

In a submission to the OECD Working Party No 3 on Cooperation and Enforcement, the Commission made reference to the type of cases for which it may exceptionally consider remedies related to the future behaviour of the merged entity. To illustrate its approach, the Commission made reference to two cases: Case COMP/M.5669 *Cisco/Tandberg* and Case COMP/M.5984 *Intel/McAfee*. It noted that:

'30. In *Cisco/Tandberg*, the Commission identified horizontal competition concerns arising from the transaction in the market for videoconferencing solutions. In particular, the Commission considered that the merged entity could, based on its strengthened position in this market, impose its own technology as a de facto standard for interoperability and thereby impede competitors from competing effectively as there was no industry standard available and raise barriers to entry further.

31. In order to address the Commission's concerns, Cisco committed, inter alia, to divest the rights attached to its proprietary Telepresence Interoperability Protocol to an independent industry body, ensuring that actual and potential competitors would have access to the protocol and could make their devices interoperable with the parties' devices. Within this framework all competitors will be able to participate in the future development of the protocol, making the process similar to an open standard-setting process. The Commission preferred this transfer of the IP rights to an independent body over the granting of a license as a simple licensing remedy would have kept the relevant technology under Cisco's control and Cisco could have decided on future developments of the protocol on its own.

32. In *Intel/McAfee*, the Commission identified conglomerate concerns arising from the companies being active in neighbouring and complementary markets (Intel in CPUs and chipsets and McAfee in internet security software). The Commission considered, after a Phase I investigation, that the merger would, inter alia, likely lead to the introduction of technical tying between Intel CPUs and McAfee security products and to a lack of interoperability of other security vendors with Intel CPUs since Intel might withhold the information regarding CPUs to which security vendors needed to have access for the development of new solutions. This could result in the exclusion of rival IT security products from the marketplace given Intel's strong presence in the world markets for computer chips and chipsets.

33. The commitments submitted by Intel addressed those problems and provided that the competitors of McAfee will be able to continue to run on Intel CPUs and will have access to all necessary Intel technical information to use the functionalities of Intel's CPUs and chipsets in the same way as McAfee. The commitments were therefore designed to maintain interoperability between the merged entity's products and those of their competitors, thereby ensuring competition on an equal footing between the parties and their competitors.

34. The remedies in the *Intel/McAfee* case may partly be considered to relate to the future behaviour of the merged entity, while other parts of it are more in line with traditional access remedies. Given that the concerns identified were of conglomerate nature, the Commission concluded that the commitments were suitable to remove the competition concerns identified while preserving efficiencies brought about by the merger. The commitments also fulfilled the need for an effective monitoring mechanism as they provide for rather straight-forward obligations and include a trustee as a monitoring device. In the horizontal *Cisco/Tandberg* case, however, the Commission considered a fully structural remedy, including the transfer to an independent body of the intellectual property rights needed to ensure interoperability with other providers of videoconferencing solutions, as appropriate and justified. The comparison of the two cases underlines that the Commission may consider remedies relating to the future behaviour only in circumstances where the competition concerns themselves only arise from the future behaviour—as it may be the case in with respect of competition concerns arising in conglomerate structures.' (paras 30–34, Remedies in Merger Cases, OECD Working Party No 3 on Cooperation and Enforcement, 28 June 2011, DAF/COMP/WP3/WD(2011)59)

Royal Philips Electronics NV v Commission	**Commitments**
Case T-119/02	Judicial Review
General Court, [2003] ECR II-1433, [2003] 5 CMLR 2	Phase I v Phase II Commitments

Facts

Royal Philips Electronics NV (Philips) applied for the annulment of a Commission decision to approve, subject to conditions, the concentration between SEB and Moulinex and to refer part of its examination to the French authorities. Among other things, it challenged the sufficiency of the commitments offered by SEB during the First Phase. Appeal dismissed.

Held

'Given the complex economic assessments which the Commission is required to carry out in exercising the discretion which it enjoys with respect to examining the commitments proposed by the parties to the concentration, the applicant must, in order to obtain annulment of a decision approving a concentration on the ground that the commitments are insufficient to dispel the serious doubts, show that the Commission has committed a manifest error of assessment.' (para 78)

'However, in exercising its power of judicial review, the [General Court] must take into account the specific purpose of the commitments entered into during the Phase I procedure, which, contrary to the commitments entered into during the Phase II procedure, are not intended to prevent the creation or strengthening of a dominant position but, rather, to dispel any serious doubts in that regard. It follows that the commitments entered into during the Phase I procedure must constitute a direct and sufficient response capable of clearly excluding the serious doubts expressed.' (para 79)

'Consequently, where the [General Court] is called on to consider whether, having regard to their scope and content, the commitments entered into during the Phase I procedure are such as to permit the Commission to adopt a decision of approval without initiating the Phase II procedure, it must examine whether the Commission was entitled, without committing a manifest error of assessment, to take the view that those commitments constituted a direct and sufficient response capable of clearly dispelling all serious doubts.' (para 80)

'It is in the light of those principles that the complaints and arguments put forward by the applicant in support of the present plea must be considered.' (para 81)

Comment

The Notice on Remedies state that 'Commitments in Phase I can only be accepted where the competition problem is readily identifiable and can easily be remedied. The competition problem therefore needs to be so straightforward and the remedies so clear-cut that it is not necessary to enter into an in-depth investigation and that the commitments are sufficient to clearly rule out 'serious doubts' within the meaning of Article 6(1)(c) of the Merger Regulation. Where the assessment confirms that the proposed commitments remove the grounds for serious doubts on this basis, the Commission clears the merger in Phase I.' (para 81)

The short assessment period available in a Phase I investigation may result in difficulty in assessing the commitment's ability to remove the competitive detriment. Subsequently, the proposed remedy has to provide the Commission with a clear-cut solution. This at times may result in 'over fixing' at the end of a Phase I investigation, as parties offer more to compensate over the risk associated with the short appraisal period.

Commission v Éditions Odile Jacob SAS	**Trustee**
Joined Cases C-553/10P and C-554/10P	Independence
Court of Justice, [2013] 4 CMLR 2	

Facts

In Case COMP/M.2978 *Lagardère/Natexis/VUP* the Commission approved the notified transaction subject to conditions which included sale of assets. The Commission approved Wendel Investissement as purchaser of the assets sold. Another potential purchaser, Odile Jacob, contested the decision and applied for its annulment (Case T-279/04 *Éditions Odile Jacob SAS v Commission*). Among other things, Odile Jacob argued that the Commission failed to fulfil its obligation to supervise the selection of prospective purchasers of the assets sold, and approved Wendel Investissement on the basis of a report drawn up by a trustee who was not independent of the parties.

The General Court annulled the Commission's approval of Wendel as the purchaser of the divestment assets. It held that the report which assessed the purchaser of the assets in this case (Wendel) was drawn up by a trustee who did not satisfy the required condition of independence in relation to the target assets. This illegality vitiated the lawfulness of Wendel's approval as the purchaser of the divestment assets.

The Commission appealed to the Court of Justice and argued that the General Court erred in law because it failed to examine the effect of the possible lack of independence of the trustee. According to the Commission, only if it can be established that the trustee took account in his assessment of an interest other than that of the proper exercise of his duties, can the lack of independence be of legal significance. The Commission also challenged the weight attributed to the report submitted by the trustee. It argued that even if the Commission is required to take it into account, it is not bound by the trustee's opinion and is still required to undertake the necessary investigation in order to ascertain that the purchaser does indeed satisfy the approval criteria. Appeal dismissed.

Held

The Commitments as stipulated in the Commission decision state that 'the trustee is to be independent of Lagardère and of Éditis, and is not to be exposed to any conflict of interests. The trustee is to be remunerated by Lagardère in a manner that does not compromise the proper performance of the trustee's duties or his independence. … The General Court was correct to hold that the trustee was not independent and that subsequently, the report assessing Wendel Investissement as a prospective purchaser of the assets sold was drawn up by a trustee who did not meet the condition of independence from Éditis.' (paras 41, 45)

The Commission's argument that the General Court should have examined the effect of the lack of independence must be rejected. 'Given that the General Court correctly found that the trustee was not independent of the parties, it was under no obligation to examine whether that trustee actually acted in a way which was evidence of that lack of independence.' (paras 46, 52)

Comment

The Commission Notice on Remedies [2008] OJ C267/1, stipulates that: 'The parties shall propose one or several potential trustees to the Commission, including the full terms of the mandate and an outline of a workplan. It is of the essence that the monitoring trustee is in place immediately after the Commission decision. … The appointment and the mandate will be subject to the approval by the Commission which will have discretion in the selection of the trustee and will assess whether the proposed candidate is suitable for the tasks in the specific case. The trustee shall be independent of the parties, possess the necessary qualifications to carry out its mandate and shall not be, or become, exposed to a conflict of interests.' (paras 123, 124)

Thomson CSF/Deutsche Aerospace   **FFJVs**
Case IV/M.527   Full Functionality
European Commission, [1995] OJ C65/04

Facts

The Commission received notification of a concentration which consisted of the creation of two joint ventures between Thomson CSF, a subsidiary of the French company Thomson SA (Thomson), and Deutsche Aerospace AG (DASA), a subsidiary of the German company DaimlerBenz AG. One joint venture, Thomson DASA Armament (TDA), was to be active in the field of armaments. The other joint venture, Bayern Chemie (BC), was to be active in the field of missile propulsion. Before appraising the transaction, the Commission considered whether the joint ventures constituted a concentration. It subsequently concluded that the proposed concentration did not raise competitive concerns.

Held

'Each of the joint ventures performs on a lasting basis all the functions of an autonomous economic entity. Except for provisions in the joint venture agreement in the event of deadlock the joint ventures are intended to operate on a lasting basis. They each perform functions comparable to those carried out by other undertakings operating on the same market. The parties will transfer to them all the assets necessary to carry on their business; these include the relevant intellectual property rights, which will be assigned or (if the parties have independent applications for the rights) either licensed to the joint ventures for their duration or assigned to them and then licensed back. Each joint venture will be responsible for the marketing of its own products. Each will independently fulfil its funding requirements. Each will recruit its own staff, although some of the personnel may be seconded by the parties.' (para 10)

Thomson and DaimlerBenz will retain some activities of minimal significance which are connected with armaments and missile propulsion and will not be contributed to the joint ventures. 'With the exceptions of these activities technological barriers, high investment requirements and the general reduction in defence budgets will prevent Thomson and DaimlerBenz from reentering the markets of the joint ventures. The joint venture agreement provides that if either party by acquisition obtains an armaments or missile propulsion business it will transfer it to the joint venture.' (paras 11–12)

'The operation thus involves no substantial risk of cooperative behaviour between the parties. The proposed joint ventures are therefore of a concentrative nature within Article 3(2) of the Regulation.' (para 14)

Comment

In Case IV/M.560 *EDS/Lufthansa* [1995] OJ C163/08, the European Commission considered the full functionality of a proposed joint venture, Lufthansa Systems, which was to operate as a systems house providing IT services, which are specifically tailored to the needs of the air transport sector. The Commission confirmed that the joint venture will perform on a lasting basis all the functions of an autonomous economic entity and create a structural change in the market. (para 9) The joint venture will have adequate resources to carry out its business. It has a full functioning IT division, 1,112 employees and is expected to recruit additional employees with the increase of third party business. (para 10) The Commission then noted that 'the fact that the joint venture will rely almost entirely on sales to [Lufthansa] for an initial start up period does not affect its full function character. Although initially Lufthansa business will account for a large proportion of the joint venture's work this will decrease and the parties intend that the joint venture will be geared to play an active role on the market. The substantial financial contribution made by EDS for its shareholding in the joint venture provides further evidence of this fact and serves to confirm that the joint venture cannot be considered a normal outsourcing operation. In addition competitors have confirmed that there is a substantial and growing market for IT in the air transport industry, and … although some airline companies operate their IT services in house, many others offer such services to third parties. Lufthansa Systems is likely to be a significant player in this field in the future. Furthermore the joint venture is expected to extend its services to the travel industry in general. Therefore even if [Lufthansa] remains the main customer of Lufthansa Systems in the medium term, the joint venture's dependence on its parent will only be temporary. In addition, the services provided to [Lufthansa] will be priced on an arm's length basis. Prices will be renegotiated every year and shall be determined primarily by a comparison with market conditions for comparable services. In conclusion, Lufthansa Systems will perform on a long lasting basis all the functions of an autonomous economic entity.' (paras 11, 12)

In Case M.551 *ATR/BAe* [1995] OJ C264/08, the Commission received a notification concerning the establishment of a new joint venture company combining the regional aircraft activities of Aérospatiale, British Aerospace and Finmeccanica. The joint venture agreement envisaged the merger of all new aircraft activities and to consider further integration of existing aircraft activities. After reviewing the transaction the Commission concluded that the joint venture was not a full function autonomous economic entity: 'The Joint Venture Agreement sets out three distinct stages in the development of the joint venture for the parties' activities associated with their existing aircraft. In the first stage … the joint venture will act as an agent for the sales of existing aircraft and will be paid for these services by the parent companies on the basis of its operating costs. Stage 2 envisages a limited financial integration of the parents' activities in the joint venture with target revenues, costs and working capital requirements being placed on it. The third stage of integration would be industrial integration and integration on core products. By contrast, in relation to new aircraft, the joint venture will immediately and on its own account undertake feasibility studies into the possibility of new aircraft and full financial integration on new aircraft activity (including profit and loss, working capital, sales financing and recourse). The timing of the moves to stages 2 and 3 for existing aircraft is not specified in the joint venture agreement. There is no timescale envisaged for full industrial integration.' (paras 11, 12) 'In stage 1, the activities in which the joint venture will be engaged in respect of existing aircraft are not sufficient to give it a full function nature, given the activities which the parent companies will retain. This is notwithstanding the parties' assertions that they will be reducing their combined workforce in sales and product support … and that they would lose all access to market information and that this in itself would be an irreversible shift. However, these employees will not be employed by the joint venture but will, at least initially, be seconded by the parents to it. In addition to that, in both stages 1 and 2 the joint venture will act as the sales agent of the parties in respect to existing aircraft. In stage 1 the parents will assume all the market risk. … Another significant point is the doubt about the future of the joint venture should the feasibility studies for the new large turboprop and new regional jet demonstrate that there is no demand for such aircraft. … The feasibility studies into new aircraft are a determining factor in the future of the joint venture. If no new aircraft is developed, then the joint venture is unlikely to progress beyond the stage of being a joint sales agency and after sales service provider for the existing products of the parents with the possible consequences outlined above.' (paras 16–19)

The Commission's Consolidated Jurisdictional Notice elaborates on the evaluation of the full function character of a joint venture:

'Full function character essentially means that a joint venture must operate on a market, performing the functions normally carried out by undertakings operating on the same market. In order to do so the joint venture must have a management dedicated to its day-to-day operations and access to sufficient resources including finance, staff, and assets (tangible and intangible) in order to conduct on a lasting basis its business activities within the area provided for in the joint-venture agreement. The personnel do not necessarily need to be employed by the joint venture itself. If it is standard practice in the industry where the joint venture is operating, it may be sufficient if third parties envisage the staffing under an operational agreement or if staff is assigned by an interim employment agency. The secondment of personnel by the parent companies may also be sufficient if this is done either only for a start-up period or if the joint venture deals with the parent companies in the same way as with third parties. The latter case requires that the joint venture deals with the parents at arm's length on the basis of normal commercial conditions and that the joint venture is also free to recruit its own employees or to obtain staff via third parties.' (para 94)

Energia Italia/Interpower	**FFJVs**
Case M.3003	Full Functionality
European Commission, [2003] OJ C22/5	Reliance on Parent Company

Facts

The Commission received a notification of a proposed concentration by which the Belgian undertaking Electrabel SA (Electrabel), and the Italian undertaking Energia SpA (Energia) intended to acquire joint control of the Italian company Interpower SpA (Interpower). After examination of the notification, the Commission concluded that the proposed joint venture lacked full functionality and subsequently did not fall within the scope of the Merger Regulation.

Held

'Interpower currently sells most of the electricity produced to Enel through a Power Purchase Agreement (PPA) and, to a much lesser extent, to the National Grid Operator (the "GRTN"). After the expiration of these contracts, expected in 2003, and based on the Joint Venture Agreement, most of the electricity produced by Interpower will be committed to the parties, in proportion of their shareholdings.' (para 10)

'Furthermore, Interpower will have neither its own customers nor an independent commercial strategy. It will therefore depend for the greatest part of its turnover upon the sales to its parent companies. In the light of the above ..., it can be concluded that the proposed joint-venture will not perform on a lasting basis all the functions of an autonomous economic entity within the meaning of Article 3(2) of the Merger Regulation.' (para 11)

Comment

The reliance of Interpower on its parent companies served as a decisive factor which underlined its lack of independent activity and commercial strategy.

In Case IV/M.556 *Zeneca/Vanderhave* [1996] OJ C188/10 the Commission considered the full functionality of a proposed joint venture 'Zeneca VanderHave BV' (Newco) operating in the seeds market. The Commission concluded that the notified operation fell within the scope of the Merger Regulation. It subsequently cleared the transaction. With respect to the relationship between the joint venture and the parent companies, the Commission noted that one of its parents, Suiker Unie, operates downstream of Newco in the sugar business, and is expected to continue being an important customer in the Netherlands. However, the Commission concluded that 'this relationship is not considered materially important (accounting for less than 4% of Newco's sales) for the overall joint venture operations. It presently operates on an arm's length basis vis-à-vis the seed business which is the subject of the concentration.' (para 8)

The Commission's Consolidated Jurisdictional Notice elaborates on this point: 'The strong presence of the parent companies in upstream or downstream markets is a factor to be taken into consideration in assessing the full-function character of a joint venture where this presence results in substantial sales or purchases between the parent companies and the joint venture. The fact that, for an initial start-up period only, the joint venture relies almost entirely on sales to or purchases from its parent companies does not normally affect its full-function character. Such a start-up period may be necessary in order to establish the joint venture on a market. But the period will normally not exceed a period of three years, depending on the specific conditions of the market in question.' (para 97) 'Where sales from the joint venture to the parent companies are intended to be made on a lasting basis, the essential question is whether, regardless of these sales, the joint venture is geared to play an active role on the market and can be considered economically autonomous from an operational viewpoint. In this respect the relative proportion of sales made to its parents compared with the total production of the joint venture is an important factor.' (para 98)

DaimlerChrysler/Deutsche Telekom	**FFJVs**
Case COMP/M.2903	Full Functionality
European Commission, [2003] OJ L300/62	A Lasting Basis

Facts

The Commission received notification of a proposed concentration by which DaimlerChrysler AG and Deutsche Telekom AG will jointly own a newly created joint venture Toll Collect GmbH. The new joint venture was to establish and operate a system for the collection of road toll from heavy trucks in Germany and provide telematics services. The Commission cleared the transaction subject to conditions. In its assessment the Commission considered whether a joint venture which was limited in time could be regarded as a full function joint venture which performs on a lasting basis.

Held

'Toll Collect will perform on a lasting basis all the functions of an autonomous economic entity. It has adequate financial resources, its own staff, its own technical equipment and its own management and as such will operate independently on the market and separately from its parents.' (para 11)

'The fact that the agreement concluded on 25 June 2002 with the Federal Republic of Germany on the collection of the toll for the use of motorways by heavy goods vehicles and the establishment and operation of a system for the collection of the motorway toll from heavy goods vehicles (the Operator Agreement) stipulates that the agreement is to terminate after 12 years and can be extended only for three one-year periods is not a bar to the joint venture being established on a lasting basis. First, under Article 3 of the Joint Venture Agreement, Toll Collect's existence is not subject to any time limit. Secondly, a period of 12 years is sufficient to introduce changes on a lasting basis to the structure of the notifying undertakings.' (para 12)

Comment

The Commission considered a period of 12 years to be sufficiently long to introduce changes on a lasting basis to the structure of the notifying undertakings. Subsequently it held that the proposed transaction constitutes a concentration within the meaning of Article 3(1)(b) of the Merger Regulation.

The Commission's Consolidated Jurisdictional Notice elaborates on this point:

'Furthermore, the joint venture must be intended to operate on a lasting basis. The fact that the parent companies commit to the joint venture the resources described above normally demonstrates that this is the case. In addition, agreements setting up a joint venture often provide for certain contingencies, for example, the failure of the joint venture or fundamental disagreement as between the parent companies. This may be achieved by the incorporation of provisions for the eventual dissolution of the joint venture itself or the possibility for one or more parent companies to withdraw from the joint venture. This kind of provision does not prevent the joint venture from being considered as operating on a lasting basis. The same is normally true where the agreement specifies a period for the duration of the joint venture where this period is sufficiently long in order to bring about a lasting change in the structure of the undertakings concerned, or where the agreement provides for the possible continuation of the joint venture beyond this period.' (para 103)

'By contrast, the joint venture will not be considered to operate on a lasting basis where it is established for a short finite duration. This would be the case, for example, where a joint venture is established in order to construct a specific project such as a power plant, but it will not be involved in the operation of the plant once its construction has been completed.' (para 104)

BT/AT&T	**Joint Ventures**
Case JV.15	Article 2(4)
European Commission, [1998] OJ C390/21	Spillover Effects

Facts

The Commission received notification of a proposed concentration by which British Telecommunications plc ('BT') and AT&T intended to acquire control over a newly created joint venture. The parties planned to transfer to the new joint venture their global network facilities and international gateway to gateway assets. The Commission found the joint venture to perform on a long-lasting basis all the functions of an autonomous economic entity within the meaning of Article 3 of the Merger Regulation. In its decision the Commission raised concerns as to the effect of the joint venture on the activities of the new parent company and analysed these under Article 2(4).

Held

'Pursuant to Article 2 (4) of the Merger Regulation, to the extent that the creation of a joint venture has as its object or effect the co-ordination of the competitive behaviour of undertakings that remain independent, such co-ordination is to be appraised in accordance with the criteria of [Article 101(1) and (3) TFEU]. In order to establish a restriction of competition within the sense of [Article 101(1) and (3) TFEU], it is necessary that the co-ordination of the parent companies' competitive behaviour is likely and appreciable and that it results from the creation of the joint venture, be it as its object or its effect.' (para 165)

'Candidate markets for co-ordination are those on which the joint venture and at least two parent companies are active, or closely related neighbouring markets where at least two parent companies remain active.' In this case the Commission considers the markets on which BT and AT&T (through its subsidiary ACC UK) are active to be neighbouring and closely related markets to the joint venture. (paras 167–73)

'[T]he Commission considered that, following the formation of the joint venture, each parent company would have an incentive to avoid competing directly with the companies associated with the other parent which are likely to use the joint venture to carry their traffic. As a result, each parent also would have an incentive to increase the traffic over the joint venture's network. Each parent would therefore have an incentive to ensure that its associated companies use the joint venture to carry their international traffic.' (para 174)

'Even if the market shares held by ACC UK at present are not high, with the support of AT&T those market shares could be expected to increase in the future. In any event, the market shares of BT on all the markets in which BT and ACC UK are active are considerable. ACC UK, supported by AT&T seemed likely to be one of the strongest potential competitors of BT in the United Kingdom in the areas in which ACC UK has been active. The more successful ACC UK became, and the more business it gave to the joint venture, the greater would be the incentive for ACC UK and BT to avoid competing directly with one another.' (para 175)

'Any such co-ordination would have an effect on trade between Member States.' (para 176)

Comment

To resolve the concerns raised by the Commission under Article 2(4), AT&T offered to divest itself of ACC (UK). This commitment removed the Commission's serious doubts that the creation of the joint venture could have as its effect the coordination of BT and AT&T's competitive behaviour in relation to ACC. (Commission decision, para 178)

Areva/Urenco/ETC JV	**Joint Ventures**
Case COMP/M.3099	Article 2(4)
European Commission, [2006] OJ L61/11	Firewall Remedy

Facts

The proposed operation consisted of the acquisition by Areva of a 50 per cent interest in ETC which was owned by Urenco, and which would become a joint venture between Areva and Urenco. The concentration involved two relevant product markets which were vertically related (i) the market for the supply of equipment to enrich uranium and (ii) the market for enriched uranium. In its decision the Commission's raised serious doubts as to the creation of a joint dominant position for Areva and Urenco on the Community enrichment market in the sense of Article 2(3) of the Merger Regulation, or to co-ordination in the sense of Article 2(4) of the Merger Regulation on the enrichment market in the Community or any wider market.

Held

'Pursuant to Article 2(4) of the Merger Regulation, to the extent that the creation of a joint venture constituting a concentration pursuant to Article 3 of the merger Regulation has as its object or effect the co-ordination of the competitive behaviour of undertakings that remain independent, such co-ordination is to be appraised in accordance with the criteria of [Article 101(1) and (3) TFEU], with a view to establishing whether or not the operation is compatible with the common market. A restriction of competition under [Article 101(1) TFEU] is established when the co-ordination of the parent companies' competitive behaviour is likely and appreciable and results from the creation of the joint venture.' (para 222)

'The market for enriched uranium is downstream to the activities of the joint venture, namely, the development, design and manufacture of centrifuges for uranium enrichment. There is no evidence that the joint venture would have as its object the coordination of the parties' competitive behaviour in enrichment of uranium. There is, however, the risk that the creation of the joint venture would have as its effect the coordination of the parties' competitive behaviour in uranium enrichment on either the Community or wider market.' (para 223)

'For the reasons as set out above in the assessment under Article 2(3) of the Merger Regulation, the Commission has serious doubts as to the compatibility of the operation with the common market as the creation of the joint venture will lead to a co-ordination of the parties' competitive behaviour in the market for uranium enrichment. In view of the enhanced possibilities the joint venture ETC offers the parties to co-ordinate downstream on enrichment capacity and output in the European market, any such co-ordination would be causally linked to the creation of the joint venture. Therefore, the Commission has serious doubts arising from the participation of Areva in the joint venture which is likely to appreciably restrict competition in the sense of [Article 101(1) TFEU] in conjunction with Article 2(4) of the Merger Regulation. It further cannot be concluded with sufficient certainty that the conditions for an exemption pursuant to [Article 101(3) TFEU] are fulfilled. In particular, there are no indications that any such restrictions imposed by the agreements would be likely to benefit the consumer nor that the restrictions imposed are indispensable.' (para 224)

Comment

The commitments proposed by the parties and accepted by the Commission removed the serious doubts raised by the Commission. To remove the risk of coordination between the parties in the market for uranium enrichment the parties agreed, among other things, to reinforce firewalls to prevent information flows between the parties and the joint venture, and to provide information to the Euratom Supply Agency (ESA) to enable it to monitor prices of enrichment and take corrective actions by increasing third-party imports.

Tetra Laval BV v Commission	**Judicial Review**
Case C-12/03	Standard of Review
Court of Justice, [2005] ECR I-987, [2005] 4 CMLR 573	

'It should be observed that, in paragraph 119 of the judgment under appeal, the [General Court] correctly set out the tests to be applied when carrying out judicial review of a Commission decision on a concentration as laid down in the judgment in *Kali & Salz*. In paragraphs 223 and 224 of that judgment, the Court stated that the basic provisions of the Regulation, in particular Article 2, confer on the Commission a certain discretion, especially with respect to assessments of an economic nature, and that, consequently, review by the [European] Courts of the exercise of that discretion, which is essential for defining the rules on concentrations, must take account of the margin of discretion implicit in the provisions of an economic nature which form part of the rules on concentrations.' (para 38)

'Whilst the Court recognises that the Commission has a margin of discretion with regard to economic matters, that does not mean that the [European] Courts must refrain from reviewing the Commission's interpretation of information of an economic nature. Not only must the [European] Courts, inter alia, establish whether the evidence relied on is factually accurate, reliable and consistent but also whether that evidence contains all the information which must be taken into account in order to assess a complex situation and whether it is capable of substantiating the conclusions drawn from it. Such a review is all the more necessary in the case of a prospective analysis required when examining a planned merger with conglomerate effect.' (para 39)

Sun Chemical Group BV and others v Commission	**Judicial Review**
Case T-282/06	Standard of Review
General Court, [2007] ECR II-2149, [2007] 5 CMLR 438	

'Lastly, according to settled case-law, review by the [European] judicature of complex economic assessments made by the Commission in the exercise of the power of assessment conferred on it by the Merger Regulation is limited to ascertaining compliance with the rules governing procedure and the statement of reasons, the substantive accuracy of the facts and the absence of manifest errors of assessment or misuse of powers (see Case T-342/00 *Petrolessence and SG2R v Commission* [2003] ECR II-1161, paragraph 101; Case T-87/05 *EDP v Commission* [2005] ECR II-3745, paragraph 151 and *easyJet v Commission*, paragraph 59 above, paragraph 44). In that respect, it should be borne in mind that not only must the [Union] judicature ascertain whether the evidence relied on is factually accurate, reliable and consistent but also whether that evidence contains all the information which must be taken into account in order to assess a complex situation and whether it is capable of substantiating the conclusions drawn from it (Case C-12/03 P *Commission v Tetra Laval* [2005] ECR I987, paragraph 39).' (para 60)

'It is clear from the foregoing that review by the [General Court] of the contested decision is not limited merely to establishing whether or not the Commission took into account elements mentioned in the Guidelines as relevant to the assessment of the impact of the concentration on competition. The Court must also, in the course of its review, consider whether any possible omissions on the part of the Commission are capable of calling into question its finding that the present concentration does not raise serious doubts as to its compatibility with the [internal] market (see, to that effect, Case T-201/01 *General Electric v Commission* [2005] ECR II-5575, paragraphs 42 to 44 and 48).' (para 61)

Commission v Schneider Electric SA	**Commission's Liability**
Case C-440/07P	Judicial Review
Court of Justice, [2009] ECR I-6413, [2009] 5 CMLR 16	

Facts

An appeal by the European Commission on the General Court judgment in Case T-351/03 *Schneider Electric v Commission* [2007] ECR II-2237, in which the General Court accepted a claim in damages against the Commission. The claim was launched by Schneider Electric which sued the Commission for losses it incurred as a result of the Commission decision to prohibit the *Schneider Electric/Legrand SA* transaction—a decision that was later annulled by the General Court.

In its decision the General Court noted the three conditions as established in the case-law, which need to be met in order for a 'non-contractual liability' to arise for unlawful conduct: 'the institution's conduct must be unlawful, actual damage must have been suffered and there must be a causal link between the conduct and the damage pleaded (Case 26/81 *Oleifici Mediterranei v EEC* [1982] ECR 3057, paragraph 16, and Case T-383/00 *Beamglow v Parliament and Others* [2005] ECR II-5459, paragraph 95).' (para 113) The General Court noted further that 'where, as in this case, a legal measure is relied on as a basis for an action for damages, that measure, in order to be capable of causing the [Union] to incur non-contractual liability, must constitute a sufficiently serious breach of a rule of law intended to confer rights on individuals. The decisive criterion in that regard is whether the Union institution concerned manifestly and gravely disregarded the limits on its discretion (Case C-282/05 P *Holcim (Deutschland) v Commission* [2007] ECR I-2941, paragraph 47).' (paras 114–15) The General Court subsequently ordered the European Union to make good, first, the expenses incurred by Schneider Electric SA in respect of its participation in the resumed merger control procedure and, second, two-thirds of the loss sustained by Schneider Electric as a result of the reduction in the transfer price of Legrand SA which Schneider Electric had to concede to the transferee in exchange for the postponement of the effective date of sale of Legrand.

Held

'For the non-contractual liability of the [Union] to arise, a number of conditions must be met, including, where the unlawfulness of a legal measure is at issue, the existence of a sufficiently serious breach of a rule of law intended to confer rights on individuals. As regards that condition, the decisive criterion for establishing that a breach of [EU] law is sufficiently serious is whether the [Union] institution concerned manifestly and gravely disregarded the limits on its discretion. Where that institution has only considerably reduced, or even no, discretion, the mere infringement of [EU] law may be sufficient to establish the existence of a sufficiently serious breach (Case C-282/05 P *Holcim (Deutschland) v Commission* [2007] ECR I-2941, paragraph 47 and the case-law cited).' (para 60)

'The system of rules which the Court of Justice has worked out in relation to the non-contractual liability of the [Union] takes into account, where appropriate, the complexity of the situations to be regulated (*Holcim (Deutschland) v Commission*, paragraph 50 and the case-law cited).' (para 161)

A sufficiently serious breach—lack of clarity and precision of the statement of objections

'In the present case, it is not disputed that the illegality relied on consists, as the [General Court] rightly held in paragraphs 145 to 151 of the judgment under appeal, in the breach of a rule of law intended to confer right on individuals, namely Article 18(3) of the Regulation, which requires the principle of respect for the rights of the defence to be applied. In that connection, it is appropriate to point out, first, that the statement of objections is a document which is essential for the application of that principle. In order to ensure that the rights of the defence may be exercised effectively, the statement of objections delimits the scope of the administrative procedure initiated by the Commission, thereby preventing the latter from relying on other objections in its decision terminating the procedure (*Bertelsmann and Sony Corporation of America v IMPALA*, paragraph 63).' (paras 162–4)

The Commission argues that when characterising the Commission's conduct as a sufficiently serious breach, the General Court did not take into account the complexity of the situation when criticising the insufficient clarity and precision of the statement of objections. This argument cannot be accepted. (paras 165–74)

A direct causal link

In its judgment the General Court states that it must consider whether the unlawfulness of the negative decision resulted in a reduction in the figure at which Schneider's shareholding in Legrand was valued in the sale and purchase agreement. It concluded that the breach of the rights of the defence was sufficiently directly linked to the damage suffered by Schneider as a result of the reduction in the Legrand transfer price associated with the deferral of completion of the transfer. (para 197)

However, it is apparent 'that Schneider's decision was based essentially on its fear that, on resumption of the in-depth investigation, it would not obtain, even following a proposal for corrective measures, a decision upholding the compatibility of the concentration, although: the risk of a decision of incompatibility with the [internal] market is inherent in every merger control procedure, either initially or, following the annulment of an initial incompatibility decision, where the administrative procedure is resumed; an incompatibility decision remains in any event subject to review by the [Union] judicature.' (para 203)

The consequence of annulment of the Commission's negative decision and the divestiture decision would have been the resumption of an in-depth investigation by the Commission. Such investigation could have, in principle, concluded with a finding clearing the transaction, in which case Schneider would not have been required to transfer Legrand and would thus not have been subject to the price reduction claimed. Alternatively, it could have concluded with a further incompatibility decision and divestiture decision, in which case the transfer would have been the legal consequence of the incompatibility. As such it would form part of the risks normally assumed by an undertaking which implement a concentration through a public bid before the Commission has given a decision on the transaction concerned. (para 204)

Subsequently, the General Court 'did not draw its findings to their full conclusion and made an error in the legal characterisation of the facts, since the direct cause of the damage claimed was Schneider's decision, which it was not obliged to take under the sale procedure entered into in the circumstances referred to above, to allow the transfer of Legrand to take effect on 10 December 2002.' (para 205)

The part of the judgment under appeal which ordered the EU to make good two thirds of the loss represented by the reduction in the transfer price of Legrand is set aside. (paras 218–23)

Comment

The right to compensation stems from Article 340 TFEU which provides that in a case of non-contractual liability the Union will make good any damage caused by its institutions.

The Court of Justice restated the three conditions required to establish non-contractual liability and endorsed the General Court's principal conclusion that the Commission may be liable in damages when these conditions are satisfied. However, it emphasised the need to establish a causal link between the unlawful act and the damage. Absent such link, it set aside part of the General Court judgment. On this point note also Advocate General Ruiz-Jarabo Colomer's opinion, according to which the loss on the sale was not directly, immediately and exclusively caused by the Commission's unlawful act. (para 140)

The Court of Justice's judgment highlights the risk associated with an implementation of a concentration through a public bid in accordance with Article 7 of the Merger Regulation. Note Case T-212/03 *MyTravel Group plc v Commission* in which the General Court dismissed MyTravel's claim for damages. The General Court considered that substantive errors made by the Commission in its assessment and which led to its annulment did not give rise to non-contractual liability. The court noted the complexity of the case, the time pressure on the Commission and the margin of discretion from which it benefits.

British American Tobacco Company Limited and RJ Reynolds Industries Inc v Commission Joined Cases 142/84 and 156/84 Court of Justice, [1987] ECR 4487, [1988] 4 CMLR 24	**Minority Shareholdings** Article 101 TFEU Acquisition

Facts

The case was heard before the coming into force of the Merger Regulation. The Commission cleared the acquisition in question under Article 101 TFEU. The agreement provided for the acquisition by Philip Morris of 30 per cent of Rothmans, its rival in the cigarette market, while limiting voting rights to 24.9 per cent. Additionally, the agreement included first refusal rights and did not allow Philip Morris to gain managerial influence over Rothmans. On appeal the Court of Justice upheld the Commission's decision clearing the transaction.

Held

'Although the acquisition by one company of an equity interest in a competitor does not in itself constitute conduct restricting competition, such an acquisition may nevertheless serve as an instrument for influencing the commercial conduct of the companies in question so as to restrict or distort competition on the market in which they carry on business.' (para 37)

'That will be true in particular where, by the acquisition of a shareholding or through subsidiary clauses in the agreement, the investing company obtains legal or de facto control of the commercial conduct of the other company or where the agreement provides for commercial cooperation between the companies or creates a structure likely to be used for such cooperation.' (para 38)

'That may also be the case where the agreement gives the investing company the possibility of reinforcing its position at a later stage and taking effective control of the other company. Account must be taken not only of the immediate effects of the agreement but also of its potential effects and of the possibility that the agreement may be part of a long-term plan.' (para 39)

The market for cigarettes is stagnant and oligopolistic and exhibits no real competition on prices or research. 'In such a market situation the commission must display particular vigilance. It must consider in particular whether an agreement which at first sight provides only for a passive investment in a competitor is not in fact intended to result in a take-over of that company, perhaps at a later stage, or to establish cooperation between the companies with a view to sharing the market. Nevertheless, in order for the commission to hold that an infringement of [Article 101 TFEU] has been committed, it must be able to show that the agreement has the object or effect of influencing the competitive behaviour of the companies on the relevant market.' (paras 43–5)

Comment

The court observed the potential effect that could occur in oligopolistic markets through an acquisition of a substantial shareholding, albeit a minority one, in a competing company. The court's rhetoric evolved around the concept of *control*, the potential for informal influence flowing from Philip Morris's capacity as a substantial shareholder, the potential for future reinforcement of the investor position and the economic context surrounding the acquisition. The court highlighted that what may look like a passive investment may result in a takeover of a competitor.

Before the enactment of the Merger Regulation, the Commission applied the *Philip Morris* standard to a growing number of minority acquisitions. Following the coming into force of the Merger Regulation, the role played by the ruling was minimised. Nevertheless, the ruling remains relevant in instances which fall short of a concentration (passive investments).

In Case IV/34.857 *BT/MCI* [1994] OJ L223/36, the Commission cleared the acquisition by BT of a 20 per cent stake in the share capital of MCI, referring to the *Philip Morris* ruling. In this case the acquisition did not provide BT with the possibility to seek to control over or influence MCI. Additionally, it did not give rise to coordination of the competitive behaviour of the two companies that operated in the global telecommunications market. The Commission noted in this case: 'As a general rule, both the Commission and the Court of Justice have taken the view in the past that [Article 101(1) TFEU] does not apply to agreements for the sale or purchase of shares as such. However, it might do so, given the specific contractual and market contexts of each case, if the competitive behaviour of the parties is to be *coordinated* or *influenced*.' (para 44)

In Case T-411/07 *Aer Lingus Group plc v Commission* Aer Lingus Group plc, a low-cost, low-fares international airline based in Ireland, appealed to the General Court, contesting a Commission decision which held that Ryanair's acquisition of 29.4 per cent of Air Lingus shares did not constitute a concentration and was not subjected to the Merger Regulation. Air Lingus wanted the Commission to order Ryanair to divest itself of its minority stake in Aer Lingus. It argued that Ryanair has used its shareholding to seek access to Aer Lingus' confidential strategic plans, has blocked special resolutions that would have assisted Aer Lingus in raising capital and has threatened its directors with litigation for breach of statutory duty towards it as a shareholder.

The General Court confirmed the Commission's conclusion that the acquisition in question did not amount to a concentration.

While the holding of shares did not trigger the application of the European Merger regulation, it did trigger the application of the national merger regime in the UK. The UK Office of Fair Trading referred the matter to the UK Competition Commission, which found that Ryanair's 29.8 per cent share in Aer Lingus gave it material influence and subjected it to the merger regime. It raised concerns as to the risk that the minority holding would affect Aer Lingus' commercial policy and strategy, weaken its role as a competitor on the market and affect its ability to join forces with other airlines. It subsequently concluded that the shareholding resulted in a substantial lessening of competition within the meaning of section 35 of the Enterprise Act 2002. The Competition Commission ordered Ryanair to divest itself of the majority of its holding in Aer Lingus, by reducing its stake to no more than 5 per cent. Ryanair challenged the decision on appeal to the Competition Appeal Tribunal (*Ryanair Holdings plc v Competition Commission*). Appeal dismissed.

Also note the Commission's decision concerning Ryanair's third bid for Aer Lingus Group plc. In Case COMP/M.6663 *Ryanair/Aer Lingus III* the Commission prohibited the proposed takeover of the Irish flag carrier Aer Lingus by the low-cost airline Ryanair. The Commission concluded that the merger would have created a dominant position on 46 routes where the two companies are direct competitors.

The above case raises an interesting question as to the existence of a regulatory lacuna which undermines the Commission's ability to appraise passive investments. On this point, the order issued by the President of the General Court in which he opined that such lacuna does not exist is interesting (Case T-411/07R, 18 March 2008):

'[A]s far as the existence of a regulatory lacuna is concerned, it should be pointed out that, whilst a minority shareholding of the type in question cannot, prima facie, be regulated under the Regulation, it might be envisaged that the EC Treaty provisions on competition, and in particular [Article 101 TFEU and Article 102 TFEU], can be applied by the Commission to the conduct of the undertakings involved following the acquisition of the minority shareholding. In this regard it should be recalled that under Article 7(1) of Council Regulation (EC) No 1/2003 of 16 December 2002, where it finds that an infringement of [Article 101 TFEU or of Article 102 TFEU] has taken place, the Commission has the power to impose "any behavioural or structural remedies which are proportionate to the infringement committed and necessary to bring the infringement effectively to an end". ' (para 103)

'Whilst [Article 101 TFEU] might, prima facie, be difficult to apply in cases, such as the present, in which the infringement in question arises from the acquisition of shares on the market and, therefore, the necessary meeting of minds might be difficult to establish, the applicant may ask the Commission to initiate a procedure under [Article 102 TFEU] if it believes that Ryanair enjoys a dominant position on one or more markets and is abusing that dominant position by interfering with a direct competitor's business strategy and/or by exploiting its minority shareholding in a direct competitor to weaken its position.' (para 104)

'It is also appropriate to point out that this scenario applies in cases, such as the present, in which all parties agree that no change of control has occurred for the purposes of the Regulation. However, should Ryanair, at a later stage, be found to enjoy or to have acquired control over Aer Lingus by virtue of its minority shareholding, then Article 8(4) and (5) might apply.' (para 105)

Warner-Lambert/Gillette and Others	**Minority Shareholdings**
Case IV/33.440	Acquisition
European Commission, [1993] OJ L116/21	Article 102 TFEU

Facts

In Warner Lambert/Gillette the Commission held that Gillette, the dominant undertaking in the EU market for wet-shaving products, abused its dominant position. The transaction involved a series of agreements leading to the sale by SKB AB of the Wilkinson Sword wet-shaving business in Europe and the US to Eemland (a shell company used for the buy-outs), and the sale of the business in the rest of the world to the Gillette Group. The transaction included several agreements between Gillette and Eemland. Additionally it involved an acquisition of 22 per cent of Eemland's equity by Gillette, which was also one of Eemland's major creditors. The Commission found this to increase Eemland's financial dependence on Gillette. This, coupled with other aspects of the agreement, was found by the Commission to form part of a strategy by Gillette to weaken competition in the market, and correspondingly to strengthen Gillette's own position. Gillette's involvement in the buy-out of the Wilkinson Sword business by Eemland was found to breach the special responsibility of a dominant undertaking not to allow its conduct to impair genuine undistorted competition in the internal market.

Held

'[T]he structure of the wet-shaving market in the [EU] has been changed by the creation of a link between Gillette and its leading competitor. … The change in the structure of the wet-shaving market brought about by Gillette's participation in the overall arrangement will have an adverse effect on competition in that market in the [EU] and therefore Gillette's involvement constitutes an abuse of its dominant position.' (para 23)

Comment

In its decision the Commission held that following the transaction, Gillette would have the ability to exercise 'at least some influence on Eemland's commercial policy' as a result of it becoming Eemland's major shareholder and largest creditor. (para 24) This was enough to satisfy the Commission that the threshold indicated by the Court of Justice in the *Philip Morris* case for application of Article 102 TFEU was met.

It is interesting to note that in this case the Commission established 'some influence' by referring, among other factors, to the financial dependence of the target company. The transaction did not involve granting voting rights, and influence was established based on economic reasoning. The Commission's reliance on such implicit influence may be seen as a wider test relative to the one prescribed by *Philip Morris*. The standard for 'some influence' applied in Gillette seems to provide for the application of Article 102 TFEU to small minority shareholdings when they provide an acquirer that is dominant in its market with some level of either de jure or de facto influence.

Article 102 TFEU may assist in bridging part of the gap left by the Merger Regulation and Article 101 TFEU. Yet its practical application is rather limited. First, the Article only applies to transactions involving a dominant acquiring company. Second, the mere holding of minority shares cannot itself be regarded as abusive. The cases imply that Article 102 TFEU is only applicable to circumstances where the acquisition of minority shares enables the dominant firm to indirectly influence its rival's actions.

10

Enforcement—The European Commission

Regulatory Framework

The enforcement of competition law by the European Commission is primarily governed by Council Regulation (EC) No 1/2003 on the Implementation of the Rules on Competition Laid Down in [Articles 101 and 102 TFEU] ([2004] OJ L1/1).

Several regulations, notices and guidelines provide details on different aspects of the Commission's enforcement of competition law. See in particular:

- Commission Regulation (EC) No 773/2004 of 7 April 2004 relating to the Conduct of Proceedings by the Commission Pursuant to [Articles 101 and 102 TFEU]([2004] OJ L123/18).
- Commission Notice on the Handling of Complaints by the Commission under [Articles 101 and 102 TFEU] ([2004] OJ C101/65).
- Commission Notice on the Rules for Access to the Commission File in Cases Pursuant to [Articles 101 and 102 TFEU], Articles 53, 54 and 57 of the EEA Agreement and Council Regulation (EC) No 139/2004 ([2005] OJ C325/7).
- Commission Notice on Immunity from Fines and Reduction of Fines in Cartel Cases ([2006] OJ C298/17).
- Commission Notice on Cooperation within the Network of Competition Authorities ([2004] OJ C101/43).
- Commission Notice on Informal Guidance Relating to Novel Questions Concerning [Articles 101 and 102 TFEU] that Arise in Individual Cases (guidance letters) ([2004] OJ C101/78).
- Guidelines on the Method of Setting Fines Imposed Pursuant to Article 23(2)(a) of Regulation No 1/2003 ([2006] OJ C210/2).
- Commission Notice on the Conduct of Settlement Procedures in Cartel Cases ([2008] OJ C167/1).
- Commission Notice on Best Practices for the Conduct of Proceedings Concerning Articles 101 and 102 TFEU ([2011] OJ C308/06).
- Commission Antitrust Manual Procedure for the Application of Articles 101 and 102 TFEU (March 2012).
- Explanatory note to an authorisation to conduct an inspection in execution of a Commission decision under Article 20(4) of Council Regulation No 1/2003 (2013).

Prioritisation of enforcement

The Commission is not required to conduct an investigation in every case (T-24/90, T-229/05). It is entitled to accord different weights to the complaints brought before it according to the Union interest. The discretion to prioritise is not unlimited. The Commission is required to assess in each case how serious the alleged interferences with competition are, and is under an obligation to provide precise and detailed reasons for its decision. In its assessment, the Commission may rely on previous analysis, monitoring and surveillance exercises (T-432/10).

Inspection Powers

Article 20, Regulation 1/2003 lays down the Commission's powers of inspection and authorises Commission officials to enter any premises, examine books and other records relating to business, and demand from members of staff explanations on facts and documents relating to the subject matter of the inspection. Undertakings are required to submit to the inspection ordered by a decision of the Commission. Failure to do so results in the imposition of fines as provided in Articles 23 and 24 of Regulation 1/2003. In the event that undertakings refuse to submit to an inspection as ordered, such inspection will be conducted with the assistance of the relevant Member State's enforcement authorities in accordance with national laws and when necessary following an authorisation of the judicial authority.

Article 21, Regulation 1/2003 widens the Commission's inspection powers in relation to private premises. Subject to the authorisation of the national judicial authority, the Commission may be empowered to conduct an inspection of private premises, land and means of transport. Such inspection targets business records and other documents linked to the anticompetitive cartels that are kept in the homes of the directors, managers and other members of staff.

On the Commission inspection powers, see:

Obstruction during Inspection

The Commission's powers of inspection are central to its ability to detect and curtail anticompetitive activity. Regulation 1/2003 outlines the undertakings' obligations in the course of an inspection. Failure to comply may result in the imposition of fine. Such, for example, may be the case when a seal is broken (*E.ON Energie*

AG), when an undertaking fails to block e-mail communications during the inspection (*EPH and others*), or when an undertaking refuses to answer questions (*Professional Videotapes*).

COMP/B-1/39.326	*E.ON Energie AG*	544
T-272/12	*Energetický a prumyslový and EP Investment Advisors v Commission*	545
COMP/38.432	*Professional Videotapes*	547
COMP/F/38.456	*Bitumen*	548

See also summary references to:

COMP/39.796	*Suez Environnement*	544
T-141/08	*E.ON Energie AG v Commission*	544
C-89/11	*E.ON Energie AG v Commission*	544
COMP/39.793	*EPH and others*	545
COMP/F/38.456	*Bitumen (Netherlands)*	548
T-357/06	*Koninklijke Wegenbouw Stevin BV v Commission*	548

Request for Information

Article 18, Regulation 1/2003 sets out the Commission's power to request undertakings 'to provide all necessary information'. A request for information may take the form of a 'simple request' or 'decision'. Both types of requests result in penalties where information supplied is found to be incorrect or misleading. On the Commission's power to require the disclosure of documents in connection with a request for information, see:

374/87	*Orkem v Commission*	558
T-39/90	*SEP v Commission*	550
C-247/14P	*HeidelbergCement AG v Commission*	551

See also summary reference to:

IV/30.735	*Deutsche Castrol*	550

Statement of Objections and Access to File

Where the Commission considers on the basis of the information in its possession that a competition infringement has occurred, it will inform the parties concerned in writing of the objections raised against them. The parties will reply in written submissions to the objections raised by the Commission. The Commission shall grant access to the file to the parties to whom it has addressed a statement of objections. The right of access to the file shall not extend to business secrets, other confidential information and internal documents of the Commission or of the competition authorities of the Member States (Articles 10–17, Regulation 773/2004). On statement of objections and access to file, see:

C-51/92P	*Hercules Chemicals NV v Commission*	553
C-204/00 etc	*Aalborg Portland and others v Commission*	554

See also summary references to:

142/84 etc	*BAT and Reynolds v Commission*	553
100/80 etc	*Musique Diffusion Française and others v Commission*	553
T-30/91	*Solvay SA v Commission*	555

Professional Secrecy

Article 28, Regulation 1/2003 stipulates that information collected under the Commission's powers of investigation and inspection shall only be used for the purpose for which it was acquired. The Commission and the National Competition Authorities of the Member States shall not disclose information acquired or exchanged by them of the kind covered by the obligation of professional secrecy. Article 16, Regulation 773/2004 provides further guidance on the identification and protection of confidential information. Also note generally Article 339 TFEU (ex Article 287 EC), which deals with the non-disclosure of information of the kind covered by the obligation of professional secrecy. On professional secrecy, see:

53/85	*AKZO Chemie BV and AKZO Chemie UK Ltd v Commission*	556

See also summary references to:

85/76	*Hoffmann-La Roche & Co AG v Commission*	557
C-36/92	*SEP v Commission*	557

Limited Right against Self-incrimination

The Commission is empowered to take statements and interview natural and legal persons who consent to be interviewed for the purpose of collecting information relating to the subject-matter of an investigation. When complying with a decision of the Commission, undertakings have a right of silence only to the extent that they would be compelled to provide answers which might involve an admission on their part of the existence of an agreement which it is incumbent upon the Commission to prove. However, undertakings are obliged to answer factual questions and to provide documents, even if this information may be used to establish against them, or against another undertaking, the existence of an infringement (Recital 23, Regulation 1/2003). Note also Articles 3 and 4, Regulation 773/2004, which deal with the Commission's power to take statements and ask questions during inspections. On the limited right against self-incrimination, see:

374/87	*Orkem v Commission*	549
T-112/98	*Mannesmannröhren-Werke AG v Commission*	560

See also summary references to:

C-238/99	*Limburgse Vinyl Maatschappij NV and others v Commission*	559
T-34/93	*Société Générale v Commission*	559
C-301/04P	*Commission v SGL Carbon*	560

Professional Legal Privilege

European Union law recognises the protection of written communications between lawyer and client. However, under EU law such protection does not extend to communications with in-house counsel.

155/79	*AM&S Europe Ltd v Commission*	561
T-30/89	*Hilti AG v Commission*	563
C-550/07P	*Akzo Nobel Chemicals Ltd v Commission*	564

See also summary references to:

IV/30.809	*Re John Deere Tractors*	563
IV/35.733	*Volkswagen AG and others*	563
1971/2393	*Crompton v Customs and Excise Commissioners*	565
T-125/03 etc	*Akzo Nobel Chemicals Ltd v Commission*	564

Interim Measures

Article 8, Regulation 1/2003 stipulates that 'in cases of urgency due to the risk of serious and irreparable damage to competition, the Commission, acting on its own initiative may by decision, on the basis of a prima facie finding of infringement, order interim measures.'

Prior to the coming into force of Regulation 1/2003 the Commission's power to order interim measures was acknowledged by the European courts.

T-44/90	*La Cinq v Commission*	566

See also summary reference to:

T-41/96R	*Bayer v Commission*	567

Finding and Termination of Infringement—Remedies

Article 7, Regulation 1/2003 sets out the Commission's powers to find and terminate an infringement of Articles 101 or 102 TFEU. The Commission is empowered for that purpose to impose behavioural or structural remedies which are proportionate to the infringement committed and necessary to bring the infringement effectively to an end. Structural remedies will be imposed where there is no equally effective behavioural remedy, or where an equally effective behavioural remedy is more burdensome for the undertaking concerned. Note that structural remedies would only be proportionate where there is a substantial risk of a lasting or repeated infringement that derives from the very structure of the undertaking (Recital 12, Regulation 1/2003).

The Commission may order the termination of abuse under Article 102 TFEU. Such decision may include an order to perform certain acts which have been wrongfully withheld as well as prohibiting the continuation of certain actions (Case 6/73).

The Commission may order the termination of an anticompetitive agreement under Article 101 TFEU but does not have the power to order a party to enter into contractual relations following such infringement (Case T-24/90):

T-24/90	*Automec Srl v Commission*	568

See also summary reference to:

6/73	*Istituto Chemioterapico Italiano SpA and others v Commission*	568

Commitments

Article 9, Regulation 1/2003 stipulates that 'Where the Commission intends to adopt a decision requiring that an infringement be brought to an end and the undertakings concerned offer commitments to meet the concerns expressed to them by the Commission in its preliminary assessment, the Commission may by decision make those commitments binding on the undertakings. Such a decision may be adopted for a specified period and shall conclude that there are no longer grounds for action by the Commission.' Commitment decisions are not appropriate in cases where the Commission intends to impose a fine. See, for example, the following decisions:

COMP/C-3/39.530	*Microsoft (Tying)*	302
C-441/07P	*Alrosa Company Ltd v Commission*	569
COMP/38.173	*FA Premier League*	571
COMP/39.116	*Coca-Cola*	571
COMP/39.388	*German Electricity Wholesale Market*	571

Informal Guidance and Finding of Inapplicability

Where cases give rise to uncertainty because they present novel or unresolved questions for the application of Articles 101 and 102 TFEU, individual undertakings may obtain informal guidance from the Commission (Recital 38, Regulation 1/2003). The procedure concerning such guidance is laid down in the Commission Notice on Informal Guidance ([2004] OJ C101/78).

The Commission, acting on its own initiative, may by decision find that Article 101 TFEU is not applicable to an agreement, a decision by an association of undertakings or a concerted practice, when the Union public interest relating to the application of Articles 101 and 102 TFEU so requires (Article 10, Regulation 1/2003).

Fines

Regulation 1/2003 sets the financial penalty in cases of intentional or negligent infringement of Articles 101 and 102 TFEU. In general, the fine shall not exceed 10 per cent of the undertaking's total turnover in the preceding business year. On 28 June 2006, the Commission adopted revised guidelines on the method of setting fines in cases of infringement of Articles 101 and 102 TFEU. The Guidelines introduce new methodology for the calculation of fines within the limits set by Regulation 1/2003, [2006] OJ C-210/2. More generally on the setting of fines, see:

100/80 etc	*Musique Diffusion Française SA v Commission*	572
C-189/02P etc	*Dansk Rørindustri A/S and others v Commission*	572
T-101/05 etc	*BASF AG v Commission*	581
C-681/11	*Bundeswettbewerbsbehörde and Bundeskartellanwalt v Schenker*	583

Liability of a parent company

The concept of undertaking may encompass several legal entities or natural persons which are viewed together as a single undertaking and may be held responsible for anticompetitive activity carried out by any of the entities. However, a company will not be held responsible for infringements committed independently by its subsidiaries before the date of their acquisition:

C-408/12	*YKK v Commission*	573

See also summary references to:

C-279/98 P	*Cascades SA v Commission*	574

On the liability of a parent company, also see discussion in Chapter 1, and in particular the following cases:

C-97/08	*Akzo Nobel v Commission*	26
C-628/10P	*Alliance One International and Others v Commission*	27
C-172/12P	*EI du Pont de Nemours v European Commission*	28
T-234/07	*Koninklijke Grolsch v Commission*	30
T-185/06	*L'Air Liquid and others v Commission*	30
HC09C04733	*Toshiba Carrier UK Ltd v KME Yorkshire Ltd*	31

Recovery of fine from employees and directors

An interesting question which arises in connection with fines imposed on an undertaking by the competition agency is whether the former should be able to recover the fine from employees and directors who were responsible for the anticompetitive activity.

While such claim may help target the direct infringers and disincentivise them from engaging in anticompetitive activity, it may also generate negative externalities and affect the operation of the leniency programme. On this point see the English Court of Appeal judgment which held that a company cannot sue its directors for a breach of competition law:

A3/2010/0675	*Safeway Stores Ltd & Others v Twigger & Others*	575

Limitation Periods

Article 25, Regulation 1/2003 stipulates that the Commission's power to impose penalties is subject to the following limitation periods: '(a) three years in the case of infringements of provisions concerning requests for information or the conduct of inspections; (b) five years in the case of all other infringements.'

'Time shall begin to run on the day on which the infringement is committed. However, in the case of continuing or repeated infringements, time shall begin to run on the day on which the infringement ceases. ... Any action taken by the Commission or by the competition authority of a Member State for the purpose of the investigation or proceedings in respect of an infringement shall interrupt the limitation period for the imposition of fines or periodic penalty payments. The limitation period shall be interrupted with effect from the date on which the action is notified to at least one undertaking or association of undertakings which has participated in the infringement ... Each interruption shall start time running afresh. However, the limitation period shall expire at the latest on the day on which a period equal to twice the limitation period has elapsed without the Commission having imposed a fine or a periodic penalty payment. ... The limitation period for the imposition of fines or periodic penalty payments shall be suspended for as long as the decision of the Commission is the subject of proceedings pending before the Court of Justice.'

In the area of cartel enforcement the notion of *continuing* or *repeated* infringement has been of particular significance. See for example:

T-147/09 etc	*Trelleborg Industrie SAS v Commission*	576

See also summary references to:

COMP/39.406	*Marine Hoses*	576
T-279/02	*Degussa v Commission*	576, 577
COMP/F/38.121	*Fittings*	576
COMP/IV/30.064	*Cast iron and steel rolls*	576

Full and Effective Judicial Review

Article 263 TFEU (ex Article 230 EC) establishes the framework for judicial review under which the Court of Justice of the European Union will review the legality of the actions taken by the Commission. The grounds for review under Article 263 TFEU include lack of competence, infringement of an essential procedural requirement, infringement of the Treaties or of any rule of law or misuse of powers.

On appeal, the Court undertakes a full and comprehensive review of the Commission decision making (Case C-272/09P). The principle of effective judicial protection is a general principle of EU law, which is also expressed by Article 47 of the Charter of Fundamental Rights of the European Union (endorsed by the Union in Article 6 TEU). Note, however, that when the contested Commission decision involves complex economic analysis, the European courts have generally limited their appraisal on appeal to examination of the relevance of the facts and legal circumstances on which the Commission based its decision, or to verifying that the relevant procedural rules have been complied with. (Case 42/84, Case C-7/95P). The courts have also limited their judicial review when the Commission decision involved 'complex technical appraisal' (Case T-201/04).

See also summary references to:

Leniency Programme

The European leniency programme was hailed as being tremendously successful, and generated the vast majority of cartel investigations and decisions in Europe. A 'third generation' of the leniency notice entered into force in December 2006. See Commission Notice on Immunity from Fines and Reduction of Fines in Cartel Cases ([2006] OJ C298/17). On reduction of fine following leniency application see T-101/05. On access to leniency documents see C-360/09, T-437/08, C-536/11.

See also summary references to:

Access to the Commission's Internal Documents and Evidence

Of significance is the 'Directive on Rules Governing Actions for Damages' which was formally adopted by the EU Council of Ministers on November 2014. The Directive recognizes that disclosure of evidence should not unduly detract from the effectiveness of public enforcement of competition law. It subsequently limits the access to certain documents, and in particular those obtained as part of leniency applications and settlement procedures.

The Directive stipulates that:

'In order to ensure the effective protection of the right to compensation, it is not necessary that every document relating to proceedings under Article 101 or 102 TFEU be disclosed to a claimant merely on the grounds of the claimant's intended action for damages since it is highly unlikely that the action for damages will need to be based on all the evidence in the file relating to those proceedings.' (point 22)

'An exemption should apply in respect of any disclosure that, if granted, would unduly interfere with an ongoing investigation by a competition authority concerning an infringement of Union or national competition law. Information that was prepared by a competition authority in the course of its proceedings for the enforcement of Union or national competition law and sent to the parties to those proceedings (such as a "Statement of Objections") or prepared by a party thereto (such as replies to requests for information of the competition authority or witness statements) should therefore be disclosable in actions for damages only after the competition authority has closed its proceedings,...' (point 25)

'Leniency programmes and settlement procedures are important tools for the public enforcement of Union competition law as they contribute to the detection and efficient prosecution of, and the imposition of penalties for, the most serious infringements of competition law. Furthermore, as many decisions of competition authorities in cartel cases are based on a leniency application, and damages actions in cartel cases generally follow on from those decisions, leniency programmes are also important for the effectiveness of actions for damages in cartel cases. Undertakings might be deterred from cooperating with competition authorities under leniency programmes and settlement procedures if self-incriminating statements such as leniency statements and settlement submissions, which are produced for the sole purpose of cooperating with the competition authorities, were to be disclosed. Such disclosure would pose a risk of exposing cooperating undertakings or their managing staff to civil or criminal liability under conditions worse than those of co-infringers not cooperating with the competition authorities. To ensure undertakings' continued willingness to approach competition authorities voluntarily with leniency statements or settlement submissions, such documents should be exempted from the disclosure of evidence. That exemption should also apply to verbatim quotations from leniency statements or settlement submissions included in other documents. Those limitations on the disclosure of evidence should not prevent competition authorities from publishing their decisions in accordance with the applicable Union or national law. In order to ensure that that exemption does not unduly interfere with injured parties' rights to compensation, it should be limited to those voluntary and self-incriminating leniency statements and settlement submissions.' (point 26)

See the following case law on access to documents (judgments preceding the coming into force of the Directive):

- On access to leniency documents see: C-536/11, C-360/09.
- On access to documents related to merger procedure see: C-404/10P.
- On access to documents in accordance with the Access to Documents Regulation see C-506/08P, T-437/08, T-516/11, C-404/10P.
- On access to Commission's impact assessment see: T-516/11.

C-360/09	*Pfleiderer AG v Bundeskartellamt*	584
C-506/08P	*Kingdom of Sweden v MyTravel and Commission*	586
T-437/08	*CDC Hydrogen Peroxide v Commission*	587
C-536/11	*Bundeswettbewerbsbehörde v Donau Chemie AG*	585
C-404/10P	*Commission v Éditions Odile Jacob SAS*	589
T-516/11	*MasterCard, Inc v Commission*	590

See also summary references to:

HC08C03243	*National Grid v ABB and others*	585
C-365/12P	*Commission v EnBW Energie Baden-Württemberg AG*	585

Settlement Procedure in Cartel Cases

After the initiation of proceedings pursuant to Article 11(6) of Regulation 1/2003, the Commission may set a time limit within which the parties may indicate in writing that they are prepared to engage in settlement discussions with a view to possibly introducing settlement submissions and benefit from a 10 per cent fine reduction. (Article 10a, Regulation (EC) No 773/2004 (as amended by Regulation 622/2008)

The Commission published a notice which elaborates on settlement procedures. See: Notice on the Conduct of Settlement Procedures in View of the Adoption of Decisions Pursuant to Article 7 and Article 23 of Council Regulation (EC) No 1/2003 in Cartel Cases [2008] OJ C167/1. For an example of a cartel settlement adopted in accordance with the above procedure see:

COMP/38.511	*DRAMs*	592

Cooperation with National Competition Authorities

Article 5, Regulation 1/2003 sets out the powers of the competition authorities of the Member States. Articles 11 and 12, Regulation 1/2003 set out the framework for the cooperation and exchange of information between the Commission and the competition authorities of the Member States. The cooperation framework is further elaborated upon in the Commission Notice on Cooperation within the Network of Competition Authorities.

The Decision Powers of the National Competition Authority—Uniform Application

Article 3(1) Regulation 1/2003 provides that where the National Competition Authorities apply national competition law to agreements, they will also apply Articles 101 and 102 TFEU when these are applicable. Article 5 Regulation 1/2003 establishes that the National Competition Authority shall have the power to apply Articles 101 and 102 TFEU in individual cases.

An interesting question that arises from the parallel competence of the Commission and National Competition Authorities is whether the National Authorities can reach a final decision that Article 101 or 102 TFEU were not infringed, or whether they are precluded from such conclusion and can only adopt a decision stating that that are no grounds for action. In Case C-375/09 the Court of Justice supported the latter proposition.

| C-375/09 | *Prezes Urzędu Ochrony Konkurencji i Konsumentów v Tele2 Polska* | 593 |

Ufex and others v Commission	**Public Enforcement**
Case C-119/97P	Prioritisation of Enforcement
Court of Justice, [1999] ECR I-1341, [2009] 5 CMLR 2	

Facts

An appeal on the General Court judgment in Case T-77/95 *SFEI and Others v Commission* [1997] ECR II-1, in which the General Court dismissed an application for annulment of a Commission decision in which the Commission rejected a complaint brought by SFEI and others against the French Post Office, accusing it of breaching Article 102 TFEU. The applicants argued, among other things, that the Commission failed to take account of the conditions required by the case-law for the rejection of a complaint for lack of Union interest, the probability of establishing the existence of the infringement, and the scope of the investigation required.

Held

'It should be observed, to begin with, that according to the settled case-law of this Court, the Commission must consider attentively all the matters of fact and of law which the complainants bring to its attention (Case 210/81 *Demo-Studio Schmidt v Commission* [1983] ECR 3045, paragraph 19, Case 298/83 *CICCE v Commission* [1985] ECR 1105, paragraph 18, and Joined Cases 142/84 and 156/84 *BAT and Reynolds v Commission* [1987] ECR 4487, paragraph 20). Furthermore, complainants are entitled to have the fate of their complaint settled by a decision of the Commission against which an action may be brought (Case C-282/95P *Guérin Automobiles v Commission* [1997] ECR I-1503, paragraph 36).' (para 86)

'The Commission … is responsible for defining and implementing the orientation of [Union] competition policy (Case C-234/89 *Delimitis v Henninger Bräu* [1991] ECR I-935, paragraph 44). In order to perform that task effectively, it is entitled to give differing degrees of priority to the complaints brought before it.' (para 88)

'The discretion which the Commission has for that purpose is not unlimited, however.' (para 89)

'First, the Commission is under an obligation to state reasons if it declines to continue with the examination of a complaint. Since the reasons stated must be sufficiently precise and detailed to enable the Court of First Instance effectively to review the Commission's use of its discretion to define priorities (Case C-19/93P *Rendo and Others v Commission* [1995] ECR I-3319, paragraph 27), the Commission must set out the facts justifying the decision and the legal considerations on the basis of which it was adopted (*BAT and Reynolds*, paragraph 72, and Joined Cases 43/82 and 63/82 *VBVB and VBBB v Commission* [1984] ECR 19, paragraph 22).' (paras 90, 91)

'Second, when deciding the order of priority for dealing with the complaints brought before it, the Commission may not regard as excluded in principle from its purview certain situations which come under the task entrusted to it by the Treaty. In this context, the Commission is required to assess in each case how serious the alleged interferences with competition are and how persistent their consequences are. That obligation means in particular that it must take into account the duration and extent of the infringements complained of and their effect on the competition situation in the [Union].' (paras 92, 93)

If anticompetitive effects continue after the practices which caused them have ceased, the Commission remains competent to act with a view to eliminating or neutralising them. The Commission cannot rely in its decision solely on the fact that practices have ceased, without having ascertained that anticompetitive effects no longer continue and that the complaint has no Union interest. (paras 95, 96)

'In the light of the above considerations, it must be concluded that, by holding, without ascertaining that the anti-competitive effects had been found not to persist and, if appropriate, had been found not to be such as to give the complaint a [Union] interest, that the investigation of a complaint relating to past infringements did not correspond to the task entrusted to the Commission by the Treaty but served essentially to make it easier for the complainants to show fault in order to obtain damages in the national courts, the Court of First Instance took an incorrect view of the Commission's task in the field of competition.' (para 96)

Comment

The Commission is under an obligation to provide precise and detailed reasons for its decision, to set out the facts justifying it and state the legal considerations on the basis of which it was adopted. Furthermore the Commission is required to assess *in each case* how serious the alleged interferences with competition are and how persistent their consequences are. The Commission cannot, as a matter of principle, exclude from its range of operation, situations which come under the tasks entrusted to it by the Treaty. (para 92)

The judgment limits the Commission's power to prioritise its investigation agenda, to the extent that the Commission cannot categorically state that it will not investigate certain situations which come under the tasks entrusted to it by the Treaty. In this respect it is interesting to note the Commission Guidance Paper on Article 102 TFEU. There, the Commission is setting its enforcement priorities with regard to Article 102 TFEU. Yet, to comply with the case law and operate within the boundaries of its discretion, the Guidance states in paragraph 8 that 'the Commission will take into account the specific facts and circumstances of each case'.

In Case T-229/05 *AEPI v Commission* [2007] ECR II-84 the General Court held that the Commission is responsible for defining and implementing Union competition policy and for that purpose has a measure of discretion to prioritise complaints brought before it. The court noted that the Commission can prioritise between cases by referring to the Union interest whilst taking into account the circumstances of the particular case. (paras 38–40) This decision was upheld on appeal to the Court of Justice (C-425/07P *AEPI v Commission* [2009] 5 CMLR 2).

In Case T-24/90 *Automec Srl v Commission* the General Court held that the Commission has been entrusted with an extensive and general supervisory and regulatory task in the field of competition law. It is consistent with its obligations under Union law for it to apply different degrees of priority to the cases submitted to it. The court noted that: '[I]n the case of an authority entrusted with a public service task, the power to take all the organizational measures necessary for the performance of that task, including setting priorities within the limits prescribed by the law where those priorities have not been determined by the legislature is an inherent feature of administrative activity. This must be the case in particular where an authority has been entrusted with a supervisory and regulatory task as extensive and general as that which has been assigned to the Commission in the field of competition. Consequently, the fact that the Commission applies different degrees of priority to the cases submitted to it in the field of competition is compatible with the obligations imposed on it by [Union] law.' (para 77) The General Court noted, however, that a decision to close the file on a complaint should only be taken following a careful factual and legal examination of the particulars brought to its notice by the complainant. (paras 55–98)

In Case T-99/04 *Treuhand AG v Commission* [2008] ECR II-1501, the General Court provided an illustrative account of the limited leeway available to the Commission in its interpretation of the Treaty provisions. The court noted with respect to Article 101 TFEU that 'since the interpretation of the undefined legal concept of "agreements between undertakings" ultimately falls to be determined by the [Union] judicature, the Commission does not have any leeway enabling it, where relevant, to forgo bringing an action against a consultancy firm which satisfies the criteria for shared liability. On the contrary, by virtue of its duty under [Article 101(1) TFEU], the Commission is required to ensure the application of the principles laid down in [Article 101 TFEU] and to investigate, on its own initiative, all cases of suspected infringement of those principles, as interpreted by the [Union] judicature. Accordingly, since—notwithstanding the *Italian cast glass* decision— the Commission's decision-making practice prior to the contested decision could appear to conflict with the above interpretation of [Article 101(1) TFEU], that practice was not capable of giving rise to legitimate expectations on the part of the undertakings concerned.' (para 163)

On this point note also the Commission Notice on the handling of complaints by the Commission under [Articles 101 and 102 TFEU], ([2004] OJ C101/65).

CEAHR v Commission	**Public Enforcement**
Case T-427/08	Prioritisation of Enforcement
General Court, [2011] 4 CMLR 14	Community Interest

Facts

The European confederation for watch repairer associations (CEAHR) lodged a complaint with the European Commission against several watch manufacturers, alleging the existence of anticompetitive agreements and the abuse of a dominant position resulting from their refusal to continue to supply spare parts to independent watch repairers. The Commission rejected the complaint due to insufficient Community interest based on four essential considerations: (1) the complaint concerned a market of a limited size with the result that its economic importance is also limited; (2) the Commission could not conclude, on the basis of the documents at its disposal, that there was an infringement of the competition provisions; (3) there was no infringement of Article 102 TFEU as the two after markets did not constitute separate markets (on market definition in this case see page 50 above); and (4) even if infringements could be established, the National Competition Authorities and courts are well placed to deal with it. CEAHR appealed the decision.

Held

The Commission is responsible for 'defining and implementing the competition policy of the European Union and for that purpose has a discretion as to how it deals with complaints (Case T-193/02 *Piau v Commission* [2005] ECR II-209, paragraph 80, and the judgment of 12 July 2007 in Case T-229/05 *AEPI v Commission*, not published in the ECR, paragraph 38).' (para 26)

'When, in the exercise of that discretion, the Commission decides to assign different priorities to the examination of complaints submitted to it, the Commission may not only decide on the order in which they are to be examined but also reject a complaint on the ground that there is an insufficient Community interest in further investigation of the case (Case T-62/99 *Sodima v Commission* [2001] ECR II-655, para 36 ... Case T-5/93 *Tremblay and Others v Commission* [1995] ECR II-185, para 59, 60).' (para 27)

'The Commission's discretion is not unlimited, however. It must take into consideration all the relevant matters of law and of fact in order to decide on what action to take in response to a complaint. More particularly, it must consider attentively all the matters of fact and of law which the complainant brings to its attention (Case C-450/98P *IECC v Commission* [2001] ECR I-3947, paragraph 57 ...). Similarly, it is under an obligation to state reasons if it declines to continue with the examination of a complaint, and those reasons must be sufficiently precise and detailed to enable the Court effectively to review the Commission's use of its discretion to define priorities (Case C-119/97P *Ufex and Others v Commission* [1999] ECR I-1341, paragraphs 89 to 91, and *Sodima v Commission*, cited in paragraph 27 above, paragraphs 41 and 42).' (para 28)

Limited size of the market

The complaint in this case does not concern a local market, but a wide market which possibly covers the entire EU territory. The extent of the territory concerned is necessarily relevant for the size of the markets concerned by the complaint and for the economic importance of that or those markets. In its decision the Commission failed to take note of the size of the market and its economic importance. It therefore infringed its obligation to take into consideration all the relevant matters of law and of fact and to consider attentively all the matters of fact and of law which the applicant brought to its attention. (paras 29–33)

In addition, the Commission did not provide sufficient grounds for its conclusion that the relevant market is of limited size. In its decision it gives no clear indication as to which market it is referring to, and is not supported by any figures or estimates relating to the size of the market. It therefore did not provide sufficient grounds for its statement that the complaint concerns, at most, a market of a limited size and limited economic importance. (paras 34–40)

Community interest

The Commission may refer to the Community interest in a particular case as being a criterion for determining priority in examining complaints brought before it. (para 157)

'In order to assess the Community interest in further investigation of a case, the Commission must take account of the circumstances of the case and, in particular, of the matters of law and fact set out in the complaint referred to it. In particular, it must weigh the significance of the alleged infringement as regards the functioning of the common market against the probability of its being able to establish the existence of the infringement and the extent of the investigative measures necessary in order to fulfil, under the best possible conditions, its task of ensuring the observance of Articles 81 EC and 82 EC (see, to that effect, *Automec v Commission*, cited in paragraph 157 above, paragraph 86; *Tremblay and Others v Commission*, cited in paragraph 27 above, paragraph 62; and *Sodima v Commission*, cited in paragraph 27 above, paragraph 46).' (para 158)

'In that regard, the Court must, inter alia, examine whether it is clear from the decision that the Commission weighed the significance of the impact which the alleged infringement may have on the functioning of the common market, the probability of its being able to establish the existence of the infringement and the extent of the investigative measures required for it to perform, under the best possible conditions, its task of ensuring that Articles 81 EC and 82 EC are complied with (see *Sodima v Commission*, cited in paragraph 27 above, paragraph 46 and the case-law cited).' (para 159)

In its analysis the Commission concluded that the complaint concerned only one market of limited size and economic importance and subsequently of limited Community interest. As indicated above, that consideration is vitiated by a lack of reasoning and an infringement of the duty to consider the matters of fact and of law which the applicant brought to its attention. The Commission also erred in its assessment of the relevant market, a fact which vitiate its conclusions concerning the low probability that Articles 101 and 102 TFEU were infringed. (paras 164–5)

As to the Commission's comment that the National Competition Authorities and courts are well placed to investigate possible infringements of Articles 101 and 102 TFEU, the Court needs to consider whether this, in itself, may justify the Commission's conclusion regarding the absence of sufficient Community interest. 'According to settled case-law, where the effects of the infringements alleged in a complaint are essentially confined to the territory of one Member State and where proceedings in respect of those infringements have been brought before the courts and competent administrative authorities of that Member State by the complainant, the Commission is entitled to reject the complaint for lack of Community interest, provided however that the rights of the complainant can be adequately safeguarded by the national courts, ... (Case T-458/04 *Au lys de France v Commission* ...; *Automec v Commission*, ...). ... By contrast, ... in the present case, even supposing that the national authorities and courts are well placed to address the possible infringements complained of ... that consideration alone is insufficient to support the Commission's final conclusion that there is no sufficient Community interest. The practice complained of exists in at least five Member States, or possibly in all the Member States, and is attributable to undertakings which have their head offices and places of production outside of the European Union, which suggests that action at European Union level could be more effective than various actions at national level.' (paras 173–6)

Comment

The Court annulled the Commission's decision. The Commission erred in its assessment of the size of the market and its reasoning for lack of economic importance. It erred in the definition of markets (on the Commission's analysis of after markets see page 50 above), and subsequently in its analysis of the likelihood of competition law infringement.

In Case T-432/10 *Vivendi v Commission*, the Court held that it is for the Commission to weigh the significance of the alleged infringement, the probability of establishing the violation and the extent of the investigation required. (para 24) In its assessment the Commission may rely on its own previous analysis of the activity. (para 60) In addition it may consider information derived from previous monitoring and surveillance exercises by national authorities and consider regulatory activities on the relevant market. (para 62)

Si.mobil Telekomunikacijske Storitve dd v Commission
Case T-201/11
General Court, [2015] 4 CMLR 8

Public Enforcement
Prioritisation
Network Notice

Facts

Action for annulment of the Commission's decision to reject Si.mobil's complaint of an alleged abuse by Mobitel of its dominant position on the mobile telephone market in Slovenia. In its decision, the Commission noted that the Slovenian Competition Authority had instigated proceedings into many of the practices addressed in the complaint and that in such case it may reject the complaint. (Article 13(1), Regulation 1/2003) As for the remaining practices which were not investigated at national level, the Commission noted that there was not a sufficient degree of European Union interest in conducting a further investigation of the case (Article 7(2), Regulation 773/2004). (Case COMP/39.707 *Si.mobil/Mobitel*). Si.mobil applied to the General Court for annulment of the decision, arguing that the Commission failed to ascertain if there is sufficient European interest and that it was well placed to deal with the case, in line with the Network Notice. Action dismissed.

Held

'It is apparent from the clear wording of Article 13(1) of Regulation No 1/2003 that the Commission is entitled to reject a complaint on the basis of that provision if it is satisfied that, first, a competition authority of a Member State 'is dealing with' the case that has been referred to the Commission and, second, the case relates to 'the same agreement, decision of an association or practice'... If those two conditions are fulfilled, the Commission has 'sufficient grounds' on which to reject the complaint referred to it.' (para 33)

'[P]aragraph 4 of the Network Notice states that consultations and exchanges within the network are matters between public enforcers, and, according to paragraph 31, the Notice does not create individual rights for the companies involved to have the case dealt with by a particular authority (judgment of 8 March 2007 *in France Télécom*, T-339/04, ... paragraph 83). More generally, neither Regulation No 1/2003 nor that notice create rights or expectations for an undertaking to have its case dealt with by a specific competition authority (see, to that effect, judgment in *ThyssenKrupp Liften Ascenseurs and Others v Commission*, ... paragraph 78).' (para 39)

'Accordingly, even on the assumption that the Commission had been particularly well placed to deal with the case and the [Slovenian Competition Authority] had not been well placed to do so, the applicant did not have a right to have the case dealt with by the Commission.' (para 40)

'In the second place, it is apparent from recital 18 in the preamble to Regulation No 1/2003 that the Council intended to enable the competition authority members of the European competition network to rely on a new ground for rejecting a complaint that is different from the ground based on lack of EU interest, which may justify the Commission's rejection of a complaint. The Commission was not therefore required, in implementing Article 13 of Regulation No 1/2003, to carry out a balancing test and ascertain whether the EU had an interest in the Commission conducting a further investigation of the applicant's complaint, in so far as the complaint related to the retail market.' (para 41)

Where the Commission applies Article 13(1) to an individual case, it is not required it to carry out an assessment as to whether the approach adopted by the competition authority of a Member State dealing with the case is well founded. Nor is the Commission required to verify whether the competition authority concerned has the institutional, financial and technical means to accomplish the task entrusted to it by that Regulation 1/2003. (paras 49–57)

Comment

When rejecting a complaint due to it being handled by the National Competition authority, the Commission is not required it to consider the capacity of that authority to carry the investigation.

EasyJet Airline Co Ltd v Commission	**Public Enforcement**
Case T-355/13	Prioritisation
General Court, [2015] 4 CMLR 9	Article 13(2), Regulation 1/2003

Facts

EasyJet Airline Co Ltd lodged three complaints with the Netherlands competition authority against the operator of Amsterdam-Schiphol airport. All three complaints were rejected. EasyJet then lodged a complaint with the European Commission and argued that the charges set by Schiphol airport were discriminatory and excessive and amounted to an infringement of Article 102 TFEU. The Commission rejected that complaint on the basis of Article 13(2) of Regulation 1/2003, on the ground that a competition authority of a Member State had already dealt with the case. EasyJet applied for annulment of the decision rejecting its complaint.

Held

Article 13(2) of Regulation No 1/2003 provides that '[w]here a competition authority of a Member State or the Commission has received a complaint against an agreement, decision of an association or practice which has already been dealt with by another competition authority, it may reject it'. The expression 'complaint … which has already been dealt with' is broad in scope and is capable of including all cases of complaints which have been examined by another competition authority, whatever may have been the outcome. Further, of note is Article 13(1) and Recital 18 in the preamble to Regulation 1/2003 which support this reading. That conclusion is also supported by the overall objective of Regulation 1/2003 and the wording of the Notice on cooperation within the network of competition authorities. (paras 23–9)

In its decision to reject a complaint on the basis of Article 13(2), Regulation 1/2003, the Commission may rely on the earlier decision to reject by the authority of a Member State, even if that decision was based on separate provisions of national law rather than EU law, on the condition that that national review was conducted in the light of the rules of EU competition law. (para 46)

'[T]he Commission is under an obligation to state reasons if it declines to continue with the examination of a complaint. Since the reasons stated must be sufficiently precise and detailed to enable the General Court to review effectively the Commission's use of its discretion to define priorities, the Commission must set out the facts justifying the decision and the legal considerations on the basis of which it was adopted. … In the present case, it is apparent from the contested decision that the Commission found that the likelihood of establishing an infringement of Article 102 TFEU was limited, given the conclusions reached by the [Netherlands authority] … the Commission fulfilled its obligation to state reasons by setting out, clearly and unequivocally, the factual and legal considerations which led it to conclude that the likelihood of establishing the existence of an infringement of Article 102 TFEU was no more than very limited.' (paras 60–2)

Comment

A decision to reject a complaint, taken by a national competition agency, may be used by the European Commission as justification to it rejecting that complaint as well. The expression 'complaint … which has already been dealt with' in Article 13(2), Regulation 1/2003, includes instances of rejecting a complaint.

When the national complaint is based on national law, its rejection by the national competition agency may still be relied on by the Commission under Article 13(2), Regulation 1/2003, if the national review was conducted in the light of the rules of EU competition law.

The judgment supports the Commission's wide discretion to prioritise cases, reject complaints and the notion that review at national level is no different from a qualitative perspective, than that at EU level. One may subsequently conclude that reliance on the national rejection is sufficient in order to satisfy the Commission's duty to review carefully and impartially complaints and provide precise and detailed reasons for its decision.

Hoechst AG v Commission	**Public Enforcement**
Case 46/87	Inspection Powers
Court of Justice, [1989] ECR 2859, [1991] 4 CMLR 410	Article 8(1) ECHR

Facts

The Commission suspected that several producers and suppliers of PVC and polyethylene in the EU were fixing prices and delivery quotas for those products. As part of its investigation into this alleged cartel activity, the Commission reached a decision to carry out an investigation (under Article 14(3) Regulation 17/62) into several of the undertakings involved, one of them being Hoechst AG. When the Commission's officials arrived at Hoechst AG offices, they were refused entry on the ground that the inspection constituted an unlawful search. Following two additional failed attempts to enter the premises, the Commission adopted a decision in which it imposed a periodic penalty payment on Hoechst AG. The Commission's inspection took place two months later, on 2 and 3 April 1987, following the issue of a search warrant by the national court. Hoechst AG brought an action to declare, among other things, that the Commission decision of investigation under Article 14(3) Regulation 17/62 was void.

Held

Article 14, Regulation 17/62 cannot be interpreted in a way that gives rise to results which are incompatible with the general principles of EU law and in particular with fundamental rights. (para 12)

'The Court has consistently held that fundamental rights are an integral part of the general principles of law the observance of which the Court ensures, in accordance with constitutional traditions common to the Member States, and the international treaties on which the Member States have collaborated or of which they are signatories (see, in particular, the judgment of 14 May 1974 in Case 4/73 *Nold v Commission* [1974] ECR 491). The European Convention for the Protection of Human Rights and Fundamental Freedoms of 4 November 1950 (hereinafter referred to as "the European Convention on Human Rights") is of particular significance in that regard (see, in particular, the judgment of 15 May 1986 in Case 222/84 *Johnston v Chief Constable of the Royal Ulster Constabulary* [1986] ECR 1651).' (para 13)

In interpreting Article 14 of Regulation 17/62 regard must be had in particular to the rights of defence. This is a fundamental principle that has been stressed on numerous occasions in the Court's decisions. In Case 322/81 *Michelin v Commission* [1983] ECR 3461, paragraph 7, 'the Court pointed out that the rights of the defence must be observed in administrative procedures which may lead to the imposition of penalties. But it is also necessary to prevent those rights from being irremediably impaired during preliminary inquiry procedures including, in particular, investigations which may be decisive in providing evidence of the unlawful nature of conduct engaged in by undertakings for which they may be liable.' (paras 14, 15)

'Consequently, although certain rights of the defence relate only to the contentious proceedings which follow the delivery of the statement of objections, other rights, such as the right to legal representation and the privileged nature of correspondence between lawyer and client (recognized by the Court in the judgment of 18 May 1982 in Case 155/79 *AM & S v Commission* [1982] ECR 1575) must be respected as from the preliminary-inquiry stage.' (para 16)

'Since the applicant has also relied on the requirements stemming from the fundamental right to the inviolability of the home, it should be observed that, although the existence of such a right must be recognized in the [Union] legal order as a principle common to the laws of the Member States in regard to the private dwellings of natural persons, the same is not true in regard to undertakings, because there are not inconsiderable divergences between the legal systems of the Member States in regard to the nature and degree of protection afforded to business premises against intervention by the public authorities.' (para 17)

'No other inference is to be drawn from Article 8(1) of the European Convention on Human Rights which provides that: "Everyone has the right to respect for his private and family life, his home and his correspondence". The protective scope of that article is concerned with the development of man's personal freedom and may not therefore be extended to business premises. Furthermore, it should be noted that there is no case-law of the European Court of Human Rights on that subject.' (para 18)

'None the less, in all the legal systems of the Member States, any intervention by the public authorities in the sphere of private activities of any person, whether natural or legal, must have a legal basis and be justified on the grounds laid down by law, and, consequently, those systems provide, albeit in different forms, protection against arbitrary or disproportionate intervention. The need for such protection must be recognized as a general principle of [Union] law. In that regard, it should be pointed out that the Court has held that it has the power to determine whether measures of investigation taken by the Commission under the ECSC Treaty are excessive (judgment of 14 December 1962 in Joined Cases 5 to 11 and 13 to 15/62 *San Michele and others v Commission* [1962] ECR 449).' (para 19)

The nature and scope of the Commission's powers of investigation under Article 14, Regulation 17/62 should therefore be considered in the light of the general principles set out above. The purpose of Regulation 17/62 to enable the Commission to carry out its duty under the Treaty of ensuring that the rules on competition are applied in the internal market, and the list of powers conferred on the Commission's officials by Article 14, show that the scope of investigations may be very wide. (paras 20–6)

'The right to enter any premises, land and means of transport of undertakings is of particular importance inasmuch as it is intended to permit the Commission to obtain evidence of infringements of the competition rules in the places in which such evidence is normally to be found, that is to say, on the business premises of undertakings. That right of access would serve no useful purpose if the Commission's officials could do no more than ask for documents or files which they could identify precisely in advance. On the contrary, such a right implies the power to search for various items of information which are not already known or fully identified. Without such a power, it would be impossible for the Commission to obtain the information necessary to carry out the investigation if the undertakings concerned refused to cooperate or adopted an obstructive attitude.' (paras 26–7)

The Commission's wide powers of investigation are subject to conditions serving to ensure that the rights of the undertakings concerned are respected. 'In that regard, it should be noted first that the Commission is required to specify the subject-matter and purpose of the investigation. That obligation is a fundamental requirement not merely in order to show that the investigation to be carried out on the premises of the undertakings concerned is justified, but also to enable those undertakings to assess the scope of their duty to cooperate while at the same time safeguarding the rights of the defence.' (paras 28–9)

The Commission's investigation powers vary according to the procedure the Commission has chosen, the attitude of the undertakings concerned and the intervention of the national authorities. Investigations can be carried out with the cooperation of the undertakings concerned, either voluntarily, where there is a written authorisation, or by virtue of an obligation arising under a decision ordering an investigation. In the absence of cooperation, the Commission may conduct investigation with the assistance of the national authorities, subject to the relevant procedural guarantees laid down by national law. (paras 30–6)

In this case the Commission decision does not exceed its powers under regulation 17/62 as it merely requires the applicant 'to permit officials authorized by the Commission to enter its premises during normal office hours, to produce for inspection and to permit copies to be made of business documents related to the subject-matter of the enquiry which are requested by the said officials and to provide immediately any explanations which those officials may seek'. (para 36)

Comment

The application of Article 8(1) of the European Convention for the Protection of Human Rights and Fundamental Freedoms (4 Nov 1950) was also considered in Case 136/79 *National Panasonic (UK) Limited v Commission*. See extract of this case in the comment on page 537 below.

Roquette Frères v Directeur Général de la Concurrence	**Public Enforcement**
Case C-94/00	Inspection Powers
Court of Justice, [2002] ECR I-9011, [2003] 4 CMLR 1	Authorisation—The National Court

Facts

The Commission adopted, on the basis of Article 14(3) of Regulation 17/62, a decision ordering Roquette Frères to submit to an investigation concerning its possible participation in agreements and/or concerted practices that may have constituted an infringement of Article 101 TFEU. As a precautionary measure the Commission requested the French Government to take the necessary steps to ensure that, in the event of opposition by Roquette Frères to the investigation, the national authorities would provide assistance. To provide such assistance, an authorisation of the French court was applied for and granted. Following the Commission's inspection, in which Roquette Frères cooperated, Roquette Frères appealed against the French court's authorisation order, asserting that it was not open to the court to order entry onto private premises without first satisfying itself that there were reasonable grounds for suspecting the existence of anticompetitive practices such as to justify the grant of coercive powers. On appeal, the French Cour de cassation referred to the Court of Justice under Article 267 TFEU questions concerning the scope of the review which may need to be undertaken by a national court having jurisdiction under domestic law to authorise entry onto the premises of undertakings suspected of having infringed competition rules.

Held

The national court, when considering the matter, 'may not substitute its own assessment of the need for the investigations ordered for that of the Commission, the lawfulness of whose assessments of fact and law is subject only to review by the [Union] judicature (*Hoechst*, paragraph 35).' (paras 39, 60)

'The review carried out by the competent national court, which must concern itself only with the coercive measures applied for, may not go beyond an examination, as required by [Union] law, to establish that the coercive measures in question are not arbitrary and that they are proportionate to the subject-matter of the investigation.' (para 40)

'When conducting its review to ensure that there is nothing arbitrary about a coercive measure designed to permit implementation of an investigation ordered by the Commission, the competent national court is required, in essence, to satisfy itself that there exist reasonable grounds for suspecting an infringement of the competition rules by the undertaking concerned.' (para 54)

The similarity in the nature of that review and the review which the Union judicature may be called upon to carry out for the purposes of ensuring that the investigation decision itself is in no way arbitrary, (that is to say, that it has not been adopted in the absence of facts capable of justifying the investigation), must not obscure the distinction between the objectives which those two types of review respectively seek to attain. (paras 55, 56)

'For the purposes of enabling the competent national court to satisfy itself that the coercive measures sought are not arbitrary, the Commission is required to provide that court with explanations showing, in a properly substantiated manner, that the Commission is in possession of information and evidence providing reasonable grounds for suspecting infringement of the competition rules by the undertaking concerned.' (para 61)

'On the other hand, the competent national court may not demand that it be provided with the information and evidence in the Commission's file on which the latter's suspicions are based.' (para 62)

In that regard, it is necessary to take into consideration the obligation of the Member States, to ensure that the Commission's action is effective. To ensure effective prevention of anticompetitive practices it is of crucial importance to allow the Commission to guarantee the anonymity of certain of its sources of information by not revealing certain information from its file. Similarly, in cases involving parallel investigations carried out simultaneously in more than one Member State, a duty to reveal the information in the file may have a detrimental effect on the effectiveness of the investigation. (paras 63–6)

'In the context of the allocation of competences in terms of [Article 267 TFEU], it is in principle for the competent national court to assess whether, in a given case, the explanations referred to in paragraph 61 of this judgment have been properly provided and to carry out, on that basis, the review which it is required to undertake under [Union] law. In addition, where the national court is called upon to rule on a request for assistance submitted by the Commission pursuant to Article 14(6) of Regulation No 17, it must pay even greater heed to that allocation of competences, inasmuch as a reference for a preliminary ruling—unless made, as in the present case, after the investigations have been carried out—is apt to delay the decision of that court and may bring the request for assistance into the public domain, thereby creating a risk that the Commission's action may be paralysed and that any subsequent investigation may serve no useful purpose.' (para 67)

As regards the main proceedings in the present case, the Commission gave a very precise account of the suspicions harboured by it with regard to Roquette Frères. 'Although the Commission has not indicated the nature of the evidence on which its suspicions are based ... the mere fact that no such indication is given cannot suffice to cast doubt on the existence of reasonable grounds for those suspicions where, as in the main proceedings, the detailed account of the information held by the Commission concerning the specific subject-matter of the suspected cartel is such as to enable the competent national court to establish a firm basis for its conclusion that the Commission does indeed possess such evidence.' (paras 68–9)

'As regards the need to verify that the coercive measures are proportionate to the subject-matter of the investigation ordered by the Commission, it should be noted that this involves establishing that such measures are appropriate to ensure that the investigation can be carried out. ... It is for the Commission to provide the competent national court with the explanations needed by that court to satisfy itself that, if the Commission were unable to obtain, as a precautionary measure, the requisite assistance in order to overcome any opposition on the part of the undertaking, it would be impossible, or very difficult, to establish the facts amounting to the infringement.' (paras 71–5)

It is in principle for the Commission to decide whether particular information is necessary to enable it to bring to light an infringement of the competition rules. 'Even if it already has evidence, or indeed proof, of the existence of an infringement, the Commission may legitimately take the view that it is necessary to order further investigations enabling it to better define the scope of the infringement, to determine its duration or to identify the circle of undertakings involved.' (paras 77–8)

However, the national court may refuse to grant the coercive measures applied for 'where the suspected impairment of competition is so minimal, the extent of the likely involvement of the undertaking concerned so limited, or the evidence sought so peripheral, that the intervention in the sphere of the private activities of a legal person which a search using law-enforcement authorities entails, necessarily appears manifestly disproportionate and intolerable in the light of the objectives pursued by the investigation.' (para 80)

EU law requires the Commission to ensure that the national court has at its disposal the information that it needs in order to carry out the review that it is required to undertake. In that regard, the information supplied by the Commission must in principle include: a description of the essential features of the suspected infringement, explanations concerning the manner in which the undertaking at which the coercive measures are aimed is thought to be involved in the infringement in question; detailed explanations showing that the Commission possesses solid factual information and evidence providing grounds for suspecting such infringement on the part of the undertaking concerned; indication of the evidence sought, of the matters to which the investigation must relate and of the powers conferred on the Union investigators; and in the event that the assistance is requested by the Commission as a precautionary measure, explanations enabling the national court to satisfy itself that, if authorisation for the coercive measures were not granted on precautionary grounds, it would be impossible, or very difficult, to establish the facts amounting to the infringement. (paras 90–6, 99)

Comment

Regulation No 17/62 was replaced by Regulation 1/2003. Article 20(8), Regulation 1/2003 codifies the *Roquette Frères* finding and stipulates that 'Where authorisation as referred to in paragraph 7 is applied for, the national judicial authority shall control that the Commission decision is authentic and that the coercive measures envisaged are neither arbitrary nor excessive having regard to the subject matter of the inspection. In its control of the proportionality of the coercive measures, the national judicial authority may ask the Commission, directly or through the Member State competition authority, for detailed explanations in particular on the grounds the Commission has for suspecting infringement of [Articles 101 and 102 TFEU] as well as on the seriousness of the suspected infringement and on the nature of the involvement of the undertaking concerned. However, the national judicial authority may not call into question the necessity for the inspection nor demand that it be provided with the information in the Commission's file. The lawfulness of the Commission decision shall be subject to review only by the Court of Justice.'

Note the Court's reference in paragraph 67 which concerns the allocation of competences in terms of a preliminary ruling under Article 267 TFEU and the need to avoid unnecessary delay in ruling which may paralyse the Commission's action.

Note AG Mischo's opinion and his review of the case-law of the European Court of Human Rights. (paras 29–41)

In Case 46/87 *Hoechst AG v Commission* [1989] ECR 2859, [1991] 4 CMLR 410, the Court of Justice held that 'The Commission must make sure that the competent body under national law has all that it needs to exercise its own supervisory powers. It should be pointed out that that body, whether judicial or otherwise, cannot in this respect substitute its own assessment of the need for the investigations ordered for that of the Commission's, the lawfulness of whose assessments of fact and law is subject only to review by the Court of Justice. On the other hand, it is within the powers of the national body, after satisfying itself that the decision ordering the investigation is authentic, to consider whether the measures of constraint envisaged are arbitrary or excessive having regard to the subject-matter of the investigation and to ensure that the rules of national law are complied with in the application of those measures.' (para 35)

Note Case 136/79 *National Panasonic (UK) Limited v Commission* [1980] ECR 2033, [1980] 3 CMLR 169, in which National Panasonic challenged the validity of a Commission inspection in which competition officials arrived at its offices and, after handing a Commission decision to the directors of the company, carried out an inspection without awaiting the arrival of the company's solicitor, leaving the premises with copies of several documents and notes made during the investigation. National Panasonic applied for the annulment of the Commission's decision concerning the investigation and for the return of the documents taken from its premises. The Court held that it must be borne in mind that the investigations carried out by the Commission are intended to enable it to gather the necessary documentary evidence to check the actual existence and scope of a given factual and legal situation concerning which the Commission already possesses certain information which it could have obtained from various sources, the undertakings not necessarily being one of them. (paras 13, 21) The Commission is not required to communicate with the undertakings before reaching a decision ordering an investigation. (paras 17–22) The Court also referred to the application of Article 8(1) of the European Convention for the Protection of Human Rights and Fundamental Freedoms (paras 17–22). It noted that 'Article 8(2) of the European convention, in so far as it applies to legal persons, whilst stating the principle that public authorities should not interfere with the exercise of the rights referred to in Article 8(1), acknowledges that such interference is permissible to the extent to which it "is in accordance with the law and is necessary in a democratic society in the interests of national security, public safety or the economic well-being of the country, for the prevention of disorder or crime, for the protection of health or morals, or for the protection of the rights and freedom of others".' (para 19) The Court dismissed the application.

Koninklijke Wegenbouw Stevin BV v Commission	**Inspection Powers**
Case T-357/06	Rights of Defence
General Court, not yet reported	Article 6 ECHR

Facts

An application for annulment of Commission decision in Case COMP/F/38.456 *Bitumen* (Netherlands). Among other things, the applicant contested the Commission decision to increase the cartel fine by 10 per cent, due to lack of cooperation during a Commission inspection and for denying Commission officials entry into its premises for 47 minutes. According to the applicant, it was entitled to ask the Commission not to carry out the investigations until its external lawyers arrived, in order to protect its rights of defence.

Held

'The mere exercise by an undertaking of its rights of defence cannot constitute a refusal to cooperate within the meaning of Section 2, second indent, of the Guidelines on the method of setting fines (Case T-9/99 *HFB and Others v Commission* [2002] ECR II-1487, paragraph 478 …).' (para 222)

'The European Court of Human Rights itself has recognised, in criminal cases, that, although Article 6 of the ECHR normally requires that the accused be allowed to benefit from the assistance of a lawyer already at the initial stages of police interrogation, that right may be subject to restrictions for good cause and that the question, in each case, is whether the restriction, in the light of the entirety of the proceedings, has deprived the accused of a fair hearing (see Eur Court HR, *John Murray v the United Kingdom*, 8 February 1996-I, § 63 Reports of Judgments and Decisions 1996).' (para 229)

It is necessary to ensure that observance of the rights of the defence does not impair the effectiveness of the Commission's investigations. The Court of Justice thus recognised that the powers to carry out investigations without previous notification did not constitute an infringement of the fundamental rights of undertakings (*National Panasonic v Commission*). It is therefore necessary to weigh the general principles of European Union law relating to the rights of the defence against the effectiveness of the Commission's powers of investigation and thus to prevent the possible destruction or concealment of relevant documents. (paras 230–31)

'The Court therefore takes the view that the presence of an undertaking's external or in-house lawyer is possible when the Commission carries out an investigation, but that the presence of an external or in-house lawyer cannot determine the legality of the investigation. When an undertaking so desires, and in particular when it does not have a lawyer at the investigation site, it can thus request the advice of a lawyer by telephone and ask that lawyer to go there as soon as possible. In order to ensure that the exercise of that right to legal assistance does not impair the proper conduct of the investigation, the persons charged with carrying out the investigation must be able to enter all the undertaking's premises immediately, to notify it of the inspection decision and to occupy the offices of their choice, without waiting until the undertaking has consulted its lawyer. The persons charged with carrying out the investigation must also be put in a position to control the undertaking's telephone and computer communications in order, in particular, to prevent the undertaking from contacting other undertakings which are also the subject of an investigation decision. Moreover, the time which the Commission is required to grant an undertaking to enable it to contact its lawyer before the Commission starts consulting the books and other records, taking copies, affixing seals on premises or documents or asking any representative or member of staff of the undertaking for oral explanations depends on the particular circumstances of each individual case and, in any event, can be only extremely limited and reduced to a strict minimum.' (para 232)

Comment

The Court found that by refusing to accede to the applicant's request to await the arrival of its external lawyers the Commission did not infringe its rights of defence. Note the Commission's 'Explanatory note to an authorisation to conduct an inspection in execution of a Commission decision under Article 20(4) of Council Regulation No 1/2003' which outlines the Commission's approach to inspections of premises.

Nexans France SAS and Nexans SA v Commission	**Inspection Powers**
Case T-135/09	Article 20(4) Regulation 1/2003
General Court, [2013] 4 CMLR 6	

Facts

Application for annulment of a Commission inspection decision by which Nexans, and companies it controlled, were ordered to submit to an inspection in accordance with Article 20(4) Regulation 1/2003. The undertakings argued that the Commission was too broad in setting the scope of the inspection to cover 'the supply of electric cables and material associated with such supply'. This broad and vague delimitation of the products concerned made it impossible for them to exercise their rights of defence, or to distinguish the documents which the Commission was able to consult and copy from other documents. The undertakings also argued that it was only in the high-voltage underwater cable sector that the Commission had detailed information about possible infringement and that it should have limited its inspection to that market and not engaged in a 'fishing expedition.'

Held

Article 20(4), Regulation 1/2003 requires the Commission to specify the subject matter and purpose of an inspection. That obligation is a fundamental requirement in order to show that the investigation is justified, to enable undertakings to assess the scope of their duty to cooperate, and to safeguard the rights of the defence. The Commission is not required to communicate to the recipient of an inspection decision all the information at its disposal concerning the presumed infringements, or to delimit precisely the relevant market, or to make a precise legal analysis of the infringements. The Commission must, however, clearly indicate the presumed facts which it intends to investigate, the essential characteristics of the suspected infringement and identify the sectors covered by the alleged infringement, with a degree of precision sufficient to enable the undertaking to exercise its rights of defence and limit its cooperation to its activities in the sectors in respect of which the Commission has reasonable grounds for suspecting an infringement. (paras 38–45)

In this case the inspection decision refers to all electric cables and all the material associated with those cables. While the inspection decision concerns a very large number of products, the Commission has met its obligation to define the subject-matter of its investigation. (paras 50–9)

The Commission's right to investigate implies the power to search for various items of information which are not already known or fully identified. The Commission is therefore not required to identify documents in advance in its decision. The Commission may therefore examine certain business records of the undertaking, even if it does not know whether they relate to activities covered by the decision, in order to ascertain whether that is so and to prevent the undertaking from hiding from it evidence which is relevant to the investigation, on the pretext that that evidence is not covered by the investigation. (paras 61–3)

'Nevertheless, notwithstanding the above, when the Commission carries out an inspection at the premises of an undertaking under Article 20(4) of Regulation No 1/2003, it is required to restrict its searches to the activities of that undertaking relating to the sectors indicated in the decision ordering the inspection and accordingly, once it has found, after examination, that a document or other item of information does not relate to those activities, to refrain from using that document or item of information for the purposes of its investigation.' (para 64)

'First of all, if the Commission were not subject to that restriction, it would in practice be able, every time it has indicia suggesting that an undertaking has infringed the competition rules in a specific field of its activities, to carry out an inspection covering all those activities, with the ultimate aim of detecting any infringement of those rules which might have been committed by that undertaking. That is incompatible with the protection of the sphere of private activity of legal persons, guaranteed as a fundamental right in a democratic society.' (para 65)

'Next, the obligation on the Commission to indicate the purpose and the subject-matter of the inspection in decisions taken under Article 20(4) of Regulation No 1/2003 would be a mere technicality if it were defined in the manner suggested by the Commission. The case-law according to which the purpose of that obligation is, in particular, to enable the undertakings concerned to assess the scope of their duty to cooperate would not be complied with, inasmuch as that obligation would be systematically extended to all the activities of the undertakings at issue.' (para 66)

'It must therefore be held that, in the present case, the Commission was under an obligation, in order to adopt the inspection decision, to have reasonable grounds to justify an inspection at the applicants' premises covering all the applicants' activities in relation to electric cables and the material associated with those cables.' (para 67)

The applicants claim that the underwater cable sector was the only sector in relation to which the Commission had at its disposal information concerning possible anticompetitive conduct. Based on an analysis of the information which the Commission had at its disposal at the time of the adoption of the inspection decision, it appears that the Commission had no reasonable grounds for ordering an inspection covering all electric cables and the material associated with those cables and that the information in its disposal only raised reasonable grounds for ordering an inspection covering high voltage underwater and underground electric cables and the material associated with those cables. (paras 68–94)

As for the geographical scope of the infringement, by indicating that the suspected coordination 'probably ha[s] a global reach', the Commission described it with sufficient detail. (para 97)

'The application for annulment of the inspection decision must be upheld in so far as it concerns electric cables other than high voltage underwater and underground cables and the material associated with those other cables, and rejected as to the remainder.' (para 101)

Comment

The Court held that the scope of the dawn raid was too wide, as the Commission did not have reasonable grounds to justify an inspection of all electric cables. The ruling limits the Commission's freedom to engage in 'fishing expeditions' during dawn raids. The Court did not comment on the effects of this partial annulment.

In their application for annulment, the undertakings also challenged the Commission's intermediate measures which included, among other things, the copying of computer files which had been found during the inspection. The Court held that the act of copying is not separable from the decision under which the inspection was ordered and is a measure implementing that decision. As such, the contested acts were found not to be regarded as actionable measures. Their legality can only be examined in the context of an action for annulment of the decision imposing a penalty, or in the context of an action challenging the final decision adopted by the Commission. As a result of this being an intermediate measure the Court did not comment on the legality of computer searches.

Nexans appealed to the Court of Justice (Case C-37/13P *Nexans and Nexans France v Commission*) and argued, among other things, that the General Court failed to explain adequately, at paragraph 97 of the judgment under appeal, how it had reached the conclusion that the Commission had described in sufficient detail the geographical scope of the suspected cartel by indicating that the suspected agreements and/or concerted practices 'probably have a global reach'. The Court of Justice rejected the appeal. See page 541 below.

Nexans France SAS and Nexans SA v Commission	**Inspection Powers**
Case C-37/13P	Article 20(4) Regulation 1/2003
Court of Justice, [2014] 5 CMLR 13	

Facts

An appeal on the General Court judgment in Case T-135/09 (page 539 above). On appeal Nexans argued, among other things, that the General Court failed to explain adequately how it had reached the conclusion that the Commission had described in sufficient detail the geographical scope of the suspected cartel by indicating that the suspected agreements and/or concerted practices 'probably have a global reach'.

Held

The Commission's inspection decisions must indicate the subject and the objective of the inspection. That obligation to state specific reasons constitutes a fundamental requirement. However, 'the Commission is not required to communicate to the addressee of a decision all the information at its disposal concerning the presumed infringements, or to make a precise legal analysis of those infringements, providing it clearly indicates the presumed facts which it intends to investigate.' (paras 34–5)

'Although, admittedly, the Commission is obliged to indicate as precisely as possible the evidence sought and the matters to which the investigation must relate (*Roquette Frères* ...), it is, on the other hand, not essential in a decision ordering an inspection to define precisely the relevant market, to set out the exact legal nature of the presumed infringements or to indicate the period during which those infringements were committed, provided that that inspection decision contains the essential elements set out above (... *Dow Chemical Ibérica and Others v Commission*, ..., paragraph 46, and *Roquette Frères*, ..., paragraph 82).' (para 36)

Since inspections take place at the beginning of an investigation, the Commission often lacks precise information to make a specific legal assessment. The inspection is aimed at enabling it to gather evidence relating to a suspected infringement. In the present case, the General Court did not err when it concluded that the statement of reasons in the decision at issue concerning the geographical scope of the suspected infringement was sufficient. (paras 37–9)

'Furthermore, contrary to what the appellants claim, the Commission was not, during its inspection, required to limit its investigations to documents relating to the projects which had an effect on the common market. Taking account of Commission's suspicions concerning an infringement, which probably had a global reach, involving client attribution, even documents linked to projects located outside the common market were likely to provide relevant information on the suspected infringement.' (para 40)

Comment

The preliminary nature of an inspection implies lack of precise information. With that in mind, the Commission has satisfied the requirement to state reason when making reference to a geographical market which 'probably have a global reach'.

In Joined Cases 97/87 to 99/87 *Dow Chemical Ibérica and Others v Commission*, the Court held that the Commission's right of access during of an inspection 'would serve no useful purpose if the Commission's officials could do no more than ask for documents or files which they could identify precisely in advance. On the contrary, such a right implies the power to search for various items of information which are not already known or fully identified. Without such a power, it would be impossible for the Commission to obtain the information necessary to carry out the investigation if the undertakings concerned refused to cooperate or adopted an obstructive attitude.' (para 24) The Commission's obligation to specify the subject-matter and purpose of the investigation is 'a fundamental requirement not merely in order to show that the investigation to be carried out on the premises of the undertakings concerned is justified but also to enable those undertakings to assess the scope of their duty to cooperate while at the same time safeguarding the rights of the defence.' (para 26)

Deutsche Bahn and Others v Commission	**Inspection Powers**
Case C-583/13P	Infringement of the Rights of the Defence
Court of Justice, [2015] 5 CMLR 5	Obligation to State Reasons

Facts

The Commission issued three decisions ordering Deutsche Bahn AG and other undertakings to submit to inspections in accordance with Article 20(4) of Regulation 1/2003. In its first inspection, carried in three sites, the Commission found documents which it believed suggested the existence of another anticompetitive practice not targeted under the first inspection. The Commission adopted a second inspection decision to address the new suspicions. During the second inspection the Commission received additional information about additional anticompetitive conducts. Subsequently, the Commission ordered a third inspection. The applicants applied for annulment of the three inspection decisions. Among other things, they argued that in its first inspection the Commission came across documents which were completely unrelated to the subject matter of the inspection decision. In addition, the Commission used keywords in its electronic research which went beyond the scope of investigation. This information, the applicant argued, was obtained illegally and served as the basis for the second and third inspection decisions.

The General Court dismissed the action (Case T-289/11 etc *Deutsche Bahn and Others v Commission*). It held that if the Commission comes across a document incidentally, it may take copies of it and use it to launch new procedure to explore concerns raised from that information. The undertaking's rights of defense are respected when that information was obtained during an authorized inspection. (paras 124–34) Further, the Court held that the Commission can search exhaustively the content of offices, even without clear indication that information may be found in those premises. These powers are essential as they enable the Commission to locate information which is hidden or referenced incorrectly. Note that the title and content of a document may not always indicate its subject matter and scope. (paras 139–41) As for keyword search, the Court held that the list of keywords used during an inspection may change depending on the knowledge acquired during the inspection. (paras 145–60) Finally, with respect to the scope of the inspection, the Court noted that Article 20(4) Regulation 1/2003 requires the Commission to indicate the object and purpose of the inspection ordered. That requirement serves as a fundamental guarantee of the undertakings' rights of defence. While the Commission is not required to communicate all the information at its disposal or to define precisely the relevant market, it must indicate as accurately as possible the matters to be covered by the inspection and the essential features of the suspected infringement. (paras 161–76). Deutsche Bahn AG appealed the judgment to the Court of Justice. It argued, among other things, that its rights of defence were infringed because Commission officials were made aware of another complaint made against a subsidiary of the company, DUSS. This, it argued, has led the officials to direct their attention specifically to these documents even though they did not relate to the subject-matter of the first inspection.

Held

'Article 20(4) of Regulation No 1/2003 requires the Commission to state reasons for the decision ordering an investigation by specifying its subject-matter and purpose. As the Court has held, this is a fundamental requirement, designed not merely to show that the proposed entry onto the premises of the undertakings concerned is justified but also to enable those undertakings to assess the scope of their duty to cooperate whilst at the same time safeguarding their rights of defence (… *Roquette Frères*, C-94/00, … paragraph 47, and *Nexans and Nexans France v Commission*, C-37/13 P, … paragraph 34).' (para 56)

'Moreover, under Article 28(1) of Regulation No 1/2003, information obtained during investigations must not be used for purposes other than those indicated in the inspection warrant or decision (… *Dow Benelux v Commission*, 85/87, … paragraph 17). The Court stated in that regard that such a requirement is aimed at preserving, in addition to business secrecy, expressly referred to in Article 28, undertakings' rights of defence, which Article 20(4) is intended to safeguard. Those rights would be seriously endangered if the Commission were able to rely on evidence … which was obtained during an investigation but was not related to the subject-matter or purpose thereof (… *Dow Benelux v Commission* … paragraph 18).' (paras 57–8)

'On the other hand, it cannot be concluded therefrom that the Commission is barred from initiating an inquiry in order to verify or supplement information which it happened to obtain during a previous investigation if that information indicates the existence of conduct contrary to the competition rules in the Treaty. Such a bar would go beyond what is required to safeguard professional secrecy and the rights of the defence and would thus constitute an unjustified hindrance to the Commission in the accomplishment of its task of ensuring compliance with the competition rules in the common market and identifying infringements of Articles 101 TFEU and 102 TFEU (… *Dow Benelux v Commission*, 85/87, … paragraph 19).' (para 59)

'It follows from the foregoing that, on the one hand, the Commission is required to state reasons for its decision ordering an inspection. On the other hand, if the statement of reasons for that decision circumscribes the powers conferred on the Commission's agents, a search may be made only for those documents coming within the scope of the subject-matter of the inspection.' (para 60)

In the present case, the Commission informed its agents before the first inspection was conducted, that there was another complaint against Deutsche Bahn concerning its subsidiary, DUSS. Although the efficacy of an inspection requires the Commission to have provided the agents responsible for the inspection with all relevant information, that information must nevertheless relate solely to the subject-matter of the inspection ordered by decision. The lack of reference to that complaint in the description of the subject-matter of the first inspection decision infringes the obligation to state reasons and the rights of defence of the undertaking concerned. (paras 61–4)

'Therefore, the first inspection was vitiated by irregularity since the Commission's agents, being previously in possession of information unrelated to the subject-matter of that inspection, proceeded to seize documents falling outside the scope of the inspection as circumscribed by the first contested decision.' (para 66)

The General Court erred in law in holding that the information about the existence of the complaint about DUSS before the first inspection decision was based on valid reasons for providing the officials with general background information on the case, when that information falls outside the subject-matter of the first inspection decision. Subsequently, the second and third inspection decisions should be set aside on grounds of infringement of the rights of the defence. (paras 67–71)

Comment

The judgment sharpens the distinction between incidental finding of documents and an illegitimate 'fishing expedition'. On one hand, the Commission is not required to turn a blind eye when it finds, by coincidence, documents indecently found during an inspection, even when these are unrelated to its subject-matter (Case 85/87 *Dow Benelux NV v Commission*, para 19: 'it cannot be concluded that the Commission is barred from initiating an inquiry in order to verify or supplement information which it happened to obtain during previous investigation'). On the other hand, the obligation to state reasons and the rights of defence will be infringed, if such find was not incidental, but was a result of earlier discussion with the officials, before the inspection, of information relevant to other suspicions, which is outside the subject-matter of the inspection decision.

In his opinion, Advocate General Wahl noted the lack of any clear relationship between the subject-matter of the first inspection and the suspected infringement by DUSS. He opined that the only plausible explanation to discuss the DUSS suspicions before the first inspection was so Commission staff 'could "keep their eyes peeled" for evidence related to the second complaint'. He added that 'it is by no means certain that the Commission staff—without that prior information—would have been able to understand the meaning of the DUSS documents.' (paras 77, 78, AG opinion)

Note that, in principle, it may have been possible for the Commission to widen the scope of its first inspection decision to include DUSS. But, having decided not to do so, the Commission was not at liberty to execute an informal fishing expedition. That practice undermined the undertaking's right of defence and led to the condemnation.

E.ON Energie AG	**Obstruction during Inspection**
COMP/B-1/39.326	Article 23(1), Regulation 1/2003
European Commission, [2008] OJ C240/6	Breaking a Seal

Facts

In January 2008 the Commission imposed a fine of €38m on E.ON Energie AG ('E.ON') for the removal of a seal which was affixed by the Commission during a dawn raid. This was the first case in which the Commission has fined a company under Article 23 (1), Regulation 1/2003.

On 29 May 2006 the Commission carried out an unannounced inspection at the premises of E.ON. On the evening of the first day of the inspection, the inspection team placed a large number of documents, uncopied and only partly catalogued, in a room made available to the Commission by the undertaking for that purpose. The leader of the inspection team locked the room and affixed an official Commission security seal to the door (Article 20(2)(d) Regulation 1/2003). The seals are made of plastic film. If removed, they do not tear, but show irreversible 'VOID' signs on their surface. E.ON was informed of the significance of the seal and of the possible consequences of removing it.

On the following day the inspection team found that the seal affixed the previous evening had been displaced and a 'VOID' message was clearly evident over its surface. Once the door to the room was opened, the inspection team was unable to ascertain whether the documents stored there were still complete.

E.ON argued that no unauthorised access to the building had been observed during the night. It suggested, among other things, that the possible change in the seal might have been the result of poor adhesion of the seal to the surface, vibration of the walls, the level of humidity in the building, the fact that the official guarantee period of the seal had expired, or the possible use of an aggressive cleaning product which may have affected the seal.

The Commission consulted the manufacturer of the seal and an independent expert who tested the Commission's original seals, and confirmed that the state of the seal could not be explained by any other reason than by a breach of the seal. The investigation revealed that the proper functioning of the seal had not been affected by the fact that the official guarantee period of the seal had expired. The possibility that a defective seal had led to the 'VOID' message appearing was excluded since, if anything, a defective seal would have resulted in a false negative and would show no 'VOID' message when broken.

Subsequently, the Commission concluded that the seal had been broken and that such breach had to be attributed to E.ON because of its organisational control of the relevant office building. The Commission imposed a fine of €38 million on E.ON.

Comment

Article 23(1)(e) of Regulation No 1/2003 does not require the Commission to establish that the sealed door was actually opened or that documents placed in the sealed room were removed. All the Commission has to establish is whether, intentionally or negligently, 'seals affixed in accordance with Article 20(2)(d) by officials or other accompanying persons authorised by the Commission have been broken.' In such instances the Commission may impose a fine of up to 1 per cent of the undertaking's total turnover.

On appeal, the General Court upheld the Commission's decision (Case T-141/08 *E.ON Energie AG v Commission*), holding that the fine was proportionate to the infringement and was required in order to create a sufficient deterrent effect, preventing undertakings from tampering with evidence. The Court noted that the Commission may impose fines where seals affixed by the Commission have been broken, even if that might have been the result of a negligent act. The Commission is not required to prove entry into the sealed room. (paras 85–6) It was the responsibility of E.ON to inform employees or other persons as to the significance of not tampering with the seal and prevent possible tampering with the seal and evidence. (para 208) The parties appealed to the Court of Justice. Appeal dismissed. (Case C-89/11)

See similarly case COMP/39.796 *Suez Environnement—breach of seal* [2011] OJ C251/4 in which the European Commission fined the company for the breach of a seal affixed by the Commission during an inspection. (C(2011) 3640 final)

Energetický a prumyslový v Commission	**Obstruction during Inspection**
Case T-272/12	Failure to Block Email
General Court, [2015] 4 CMLR 2	Duty to Cooperate

Facts

In November 2009 the Commission adopted a decision ordering an inspection in the premises of Energetický a průmyslový holding and EP Investment Advisors which are active in the energy sector in the Czech Republic. The decision stated that the companies are to produce for inspection books and records irrespective of the medium on which they are stored. On the first day of the inspection the companies were asked to contact their IT provider and to block email accounts of key personnel. This was done by setting a new password only known to the Commission inspectors. On the second day of the inspection the Commission inspectors discovered that the password for one account had been modified in order to allow the account holder to access the account. On the third day of the inspection, the Commission inspectors discovered that one of the employees had requested the IT department to divert emails from blocked accounts to another server. (Case COMP/39.793—*EPH and Others*)

The Commission imposed a total of €2.5 million in fines for obstructing the inspection. In its decision the Commission noted that Article 23(1)(c) Regulation 1/2003 stipulates that refusal to submit to an inspection may be committed intentionally or negligently. In this case the failure to block the email was committed negligently, while the diversion of emails was intentional. Both actions undermined the effectiveness of the inspection.

The undertakings applied to the General Court for annulment of the decision. Action dismissed.

Held

While the undertakings agree to the facts—that is, that access to an email account was made possible during the inspection, contrary to the inspectors' instructions, and that incoming e-mails were diverted, they argue that 'the Commission did not prove to the requisite legal standard that the circumstances attributed to them resulted in the business records required by the inspectors being produced in incomplete form, so that it cannot be alleged they refused to submit to the inspection.' (paras 34–5)

Negligent access to blocked emails

The fact that the undertaking negligently allowed access to a blocked e-mail account led to that account not being under the full control of the inspectors. That fact, in itself—that the inspectors did not obtain, as requested, exclusive access to the e-mail account—is sufficient to characterise the incident at issue as a refusal to submit to the inspection. The Commission has the burden of proving that access was granted to the data in the blocked e-mail account, but is not required to prove that data was manipulated or deleted. (paras 37–9)

'[T]he purpose of Article 20(4) of Regulation No 1/2003 is to enable the Commission to carry out investigations without prior warning on the premises of undertakings suspected of infringements of Articles 101 TFEU and 102 TFEU, when an inspection decision, the reasons for which have been set out, has been correctly notified to an authorised person within those undertakings, the Commission must be able to carry out investigations, without being under an obligation to inform each person concerned of his duties in the circumstances of the case. Such an obligation would delay the inspection, the duration of which is strictly limited. … It must be stated that since the inspection decision was notified to the authorised persons at the beginning of the inspection, it was for the applicants to take all the necessary measures to implement the inspectors' instructions and to ensure that the persons authorised to act on behalf of the undertakings did not impede the implementation of those instructions (see, by analogy, *E.ON Energie v Commission*, cited in paragraph 39 above, EU:T:2010:516, paragraph 260).' (para 45)

The 'Commission's power to impose a penalty on an undertaking where it has committed an infringement presumes only the unlawful action of a person who is generally authorised to act on behalf of the undertaking.' (*E.ON Energie v Commission*, para 258). The employee in question was identified to the inspectors as the person responsible for the applicants' IT services. Accordingly, the fact that he was employed by an independent company does not alter the undertaking's responsibility. (para 46)

The intentional diversion of incoming e-mails to a server

'In the first place, the Court rejects the applicants' claims that the e-mails destined for Mr J.'s account were still relayed to the server and stored on that medium, which was accessible by the inspectors at all times if they wished to examine those emails. The inspectors should, in fact, have been able to access all the e-mails normally to be found in Mr J.'s inbox, the subject of the inspection, without being obliged to gather data from other places in order to carry out their inspection ...' (para 50)

There is no dispute that contrary to the inspectors' instructions, those e-mails were diverted and that the relevant files were not produced in complete form during the inspection. It is important to point out 'that an undertaking which is subject to investigation must, if the Commission so requests, provide it with documents in its possession which relate to the subject-matter of the investigation, even if those documents could be used by the Commission in order to establish the existence of an infringement. ... The applicants cannot therefore merely allege that the inspectors could have found the data concerned elsewhere at their premises, since they were under an obligation to make Mr J.'s e-mails available to the inspectors. In addition, it is sufficient, for the purposes of applying Article 23(1)(c) of Regulation No 1/2003, for the diverted e-mails to be covered by the inspection decision, which the applicants do not deny.' The quantity or significance of the diverted e-mails is irrelevant to establishing the infringement. (paras 51–4)

The Commission did not err in finding that the diversion of the incoming e-mails to a server was intentional. (para 59)

The rights of the defence

'[I]t is appropriate to note five categories of safeguards provided to the undertakings concerned in the context of inspections: first, the statement of reasons on which inspection decisions are based; secondly, the limits imposed on the Commission during the conduct of inspections; thirdly, the impossibility for the Commission to carry out an inspection by force; fourthly, the intervention of national authorities; and, fifthly, the existence of ex post facto remedies (... *Deutsche Bahn and Others v Commission*, T-289/11, T-290/11 and T-521/11, under appeal, ECR, EU: ..., paragraph 74).' (para 68)

In this case the undertakings were clearly informed of the scope of their duty to cooperate in the context of the inspection. 'The inspectors were under no obligation to point out to the persons concerned that infringements could result in a fine. It is sufficient, in order to safeguard the rights of the defence, that the inspection decision and the explanatory note were correctly notified to the authorised persons within the applicant companies.' The explanatory note properly explain the defence rights, the principle of good administration, and the Commission's obligations. 'Inspectors must be able to assume, once they have communicated their instructions to the undertakings, that the latter will take all necessary measures to implement them, and that they will not have to repeat them'. (paras 69–78)

Comment

The judgment emphasises the responsibility of the undertaking, once being informed of an inspection, to take proactive action to avoid any lack of cooperation. It is for the undertaking to ensure that employees and third parties authorised by the undertaking do not undermine the integrity of the inspection. The inspectors are under no obligation to repeatedly state the obligations of the undertaking to cooperate or the risk of a fine.

In practice, the responsibility of the undertaking to ensure the integrity of the inspection and the possible exposure to fines highlight the significance of clear communications within the company during the inspection, the value of competition law compliance training, and the advanced preparation of dawn raid manual which ensures compliance and cooperation.

Professional Videotape	**Obstruction during Inspection**
Case COMP/38.432	Refusal to Answer Questions
European Commission, [2008] OJ C57/10	Shredding of Documents

Facts

The Commission found that Sony, Fuji and Maxell took part in a price-fixing cartel in the market for professional videotapes in Europe. Between 1999 and 2002, the undertakings met on regular basis and colluded to control the price of professional videotapes. The Commission imposed a total fine of €74 million on the three undertakings. Sony's fine was increased by 30 per cent for two incidents during on-site inspections in which the Commission's investigation was obstructed: (1) an authorised representative of Sony Europe Holding BV, who was assisted by the company's legal counsel, refused to answer any of the oral questions asked by the Commission; (2) an employee of Sony United Kingdom Limited shredded, during the investigation, documents from a file labelled 'Competitors Pricing'.

Held

'In relation to the refusal to answer the Commission's questions, Sony has argued that certain questions went beyond the Commission's powers. ... That argument cannot be accepted as all questions were aimed at obtaining explanations concerning documents found at the inspected premises, and therefore did not exceed the scope of Article 14(1)(c) of Regulation No 17. In any event, it remains that ... Sony's refusal to answer during the inspection extended to all questions without a justification being given despite the assistance of the company's legal counsel. In addition, in the course of the administrative procedure, Sony has not even attempted to substantiate objections against most of those same questions. Under these circumstances, its outright refusal to answer all questions during the inspections appears to be all the more unacceptable.' (para 225)

'As to the shredding of documents, Sony has claimed that it was done by a junior employee acting contrary to the company's policy of full compliance with antitrust laws. The Commission notes in this respect that it is the undertaking's responsibility to employ, instruct and control its employees, and to ensure that none of them obstructs or hampers the Commission's work during an inspection. Furthermore, in this case it is not contested that the relevant employee acted with precisely that intention.' (para 226)

Comment

Sony's behaviour constituted an aggravating circumstance that led to an increase of 30 per cent in the basic amount of the fine imposed on Sony.

The decision refers to Regulation 17/62 which was superseded by Regulation 1/2003. Article 20, Regulation 1/2003 stipulates that the Commission may conduct all necessary inspections of undertakings and associations of undertakings and is empowered to enter any premises of undertakings, to examine and copy books and records, to seal any business premises, and 'to ask any representative or member of staff of the undertaking or association of undertakings for explanations on facts or documents relating to the subject-matter and purpose of the inspection and to record the answers.'

In its 'Explanatory note to an authorisation to conduct an inspection in execution of a Commission decision under Article 20(4) of Council Regulation No 1/2003' the Commission notes that: 'Where any representative or member of staff of the undertaking gives, pursuant to Article 4(1) of the Commission Regulation No 773/2004, oral explanations on the spot on facts or documents relating to the subject-matter and purpose of the inspection at the request of the Inspectors, the explanations may be recorded in any form. A copy of any such recording will be made available to the undertaking concerned after the inspection pursuant to Article 4(2) of the European Commission Regulation No 773/2004.' (para 7)

Bitumen	**Obstruction During Inspection**
Case COMP/F/38.456	Refusal to Cooperate
European Commission, [2007] OJ L196/40	Refused Entry

Facts

The undertakings involved participated in a continuous infringement of Article 101 TFEU involving the fixing of prices concerning road pavement bitumen in the Netherlands. As part of its investigation the Commission carried out several surprise investigations at the premises of the undertakings involved. In one of these instances, Commission officials were refused entry into the premises of KWS BV. When setting the fine for the infringement, the Commission took account of the refusal to cooperate with or attempt to obstruct the Commission in its investigation.

Held

'KWS refused to submit to the investigation ordered by Commission Decision of 26 September 2002, as it was required to do under Article 14(3) of Regulation No 17. The Commission was not allowed to enter the undertaking's premises or to talk to a KWS employee in a management position and to serve the Decision. Pursuant to Article 14(6) of Regulation No 17, the officials authorised by the Commission to conduct the inspection had to invoke the assistance of the national authorities (national competition authority and police) to enable them to proceed with their investigation. Later during the same inspection, the officials authorised by the Commission were equally refused entry to an office of a KWS Director, thus necessitating another call for assistance of the national authorities.' (para 340)

'The Commission considers that these actions on the part of KWS constitute refusals to cooperate and/or attempts to obstruct the Commission in carrying out its investigations. They constitute for the Commission an aggravating circumstance, justifying an increase of 10% in the basic amount of the fine to be imposed on KWS.' (para 341)

Comment

Undertakings are legally obliged to submit to an inspection ordered by a decision of the Commission under Article 20(4) of Regulation 1/2003.

In Case T-357/06 *Koninklijke Wegenbouw Stevin BV v Commission*, the General Court considered an application for annulment of Commission decision in Case COMP/F/38.456—*Bitumen (Netherlands)*. Among other things, the applicant contested the Commission decision to increase the cartel fine by 10%, due to lack of cooperation during a Commission inspection and for denying Commission officials entry into its premises for 47 minutes. (paras 340, 341) According to the applicant, it was entitled to ask the Commission not to carry out the investigations until its external lawyers arrived, in order to protect its rights of defence. The General Court dismissed the appeal. It noted that the 'increase of 10% in the amount of the fine does not appear disproportionate having regard, on the one hand, to the applicant's conduct during the investigations and to the repeated nature of its attempts to obstruct the investigations on the same day and, on the other, to the importance of investigations as a necessary tool for the Commission in carrying out its role as guardian of the Treaty in competition matters.' (para 255)

In its 'Explanatory note to an authorisation to conduct an inspection in execution of a Commission decision under Article 20(4) of Council Regulation No 1/2003' the Commission notes that the Inspectors will accept only a short delay pending consultation of the lawyer. The Inspectors cannot be required to expand upon the subject-matter as set out in the decision or to justify the decision in any way. They may however explain procedural matters, particularly with regard to confidentiality, and the possible consequences of a refusal to submit to the inspection.

Orkem v Commission	**Public Enforcement**
Case 374/87	Request for Information
Court of Justice, [1989] ECR 3283, [1991] 4 CMLR 502	

Facts

An action by Orkem SA for the annulment of a Commission decision which required it to reply to questions set out in a request for information issued by the Commission. Orkem SA argued, among other things, that the request in question (under Article 11, Regulation 17/62) was unlawful and lacked proportionality as it aimed to obtain documents which the Commission could only obtain under its powers of investigation (Article 14, Regulation 17/62).

Held

'It must be stated, with respect to the Commission's right to require the disclosure of documents in connection with a request for information, that Articles 11 and 14 of Regulation No 17 establish two entirely independent procedures. The fact that an investigation under Article 14 has already taken place cannot in any way diminish the powers of investigation available to the Commission under Article 11. No consideration of a procedural nature inherent in Regulation No 17 thus prevents the Commission from requiring, for the purposes of a request for information, the disclosure of documents of which it was unable to take a copy or extract when carrying out a previous investigation.' (para 14)

'With regard to the necessity of the information requested, it must be borne in mind that Regulation No 17 confers on the Commission wide powers to make investigations and to obtain information by providing in the eighth recital in its preamble that the Commission must be empowered, throughout the [internal] market, to require such information to be supplied and to undertake such investigations as are necessary to bring to light infringements of [Articles 101 and 102 TFEU]. As the Court held in its judgment of 18 May 1982 in Case 155/79 *AM & S Europe Limited v Commission* [1982] ECR 1575, it is for the Commission to decide, for the purposes of an investigation under Article 14, whether particular information is necessary to enable it to bring to light an infringement of the competition rules. Even if it already has evidence, or indeed proof, of the existence of an infringement, the Commission may legitimately take the view that it is necessary to request further information to enable it better to define the scope of the infringement, to determine its duration or to identify the circle of undertakings involved.' (para 15)

'In the present case it does not appear that the information requested falls outside those limits or exceeds what might be regarded as necessary in the light of the purpose of the investigation.' (para 16)

Comment

Regulation 16/72 was replaced by Regulation 1/2003. The latter enables the Commission to obtain information through various means; Article 18, Regulation 1/2003 sets out the Commission's power to request undertakings 'to provide all necessary information'. A request for information may take the form of a 'simple request' or a 'decision'. Both types of requests result in penalties where information supplied is found to be incorrect or misleading. The Commission may also obtain information while inspecting the undertakings premises. (Articles 20 and 21, Regulation 1/2003)

The fact that an inspection under Articles 20 and 21, Regulation 1/2003 has already taken place does not diminish the powers of investigation available to the Commission under other provisions, such as Article Articles 18, Regulation 1/2003.

SEP v Commission	**Public Enforcement**
Case T-39/90	Request for Information
General Court, [1991] ECR II-1497, [1992] 5 CMLR 33	

Facts

An action for the annulment of Commission Decision IV/33.539—*SEP/Gasunie* in which the Commission condemned SEP for failing to comply with a request for information and required it to disclose a gas supply contract between another company, Gasunie, and SEP.

Held

'It should be noted as a preliminary point in that regard that the term "necessary information" contained in Article 11(1) [Regulation 17/62] must be interpreted according to the objectives for the achievement of which the powers of investigation in question have been conferred upon the Commission. The requirement that there must exist a correlation between the request for information and the putative infringement is satisfied, since at that stage in the proceeding the request may legitimately be regarded as having a connection with the putative infringement.' (para 29)

'That analysis is borne out by the case-law of the Court of Justice, which held in its judgments in Case 374/87 *Orkem v Commission*, cited above, paragraph 15, and Case 27/88 *Solvay v Commission* [1989] ECR 3355 (summary publication), as well as the Opinion of Mr Advocate General Darmon in the *Orkem* case, p 3301, especially p 3320 (see also the judgment in Case 136/79 *National Panasonic v Commission* [1980] ECR 2033, paragraph 13) that "Regulation No 17 confers on the Commission wide powers to make investigations and to obtain information by providing in the eighth recital in its preamble that the Commission must be empowered … to require such information to be supplied and to undertake such investigations as are necessary to bring to light infringements of [Articles 101 and 102 TFEU]. … It is for the Commission to decide … whether particular information is necessary to enable it to bring to light an infringement of the competition rules".' (para 30)

In the present case the Commission had reasonable grounds for considering that there was a correlation between the contract and the subject of investigation. (para 31)

Comment

The case focused on the interpretation of Article 11, Regulation 17/62, which states that the Commission may obtain 'all necessary information' from undertakings. Regulation 1/2003, which replaced Regulation 17/62, similarly states that 'the Commission may, by simple request or by decision, require undertakings and associations of undertakings to provide all necessary information.' (Article 18, Regulation 1/2003)

In Case IV/30.735 *Deutsche Castrol* [1983] OJ L114/26, [1983] 3 CMLR 165, the Commission requested Deutsche Castrol Vertriebsgesellschaft mbH ('Castrol') to furnish various information with a view to explore possible restrictive effects of a network of exclusive purchasing agreements. Castrol refused to reply to the request and argued that the agreements in question cannot infringe Article 101 TFEU due to lack of effect on trade between Member States. In its decision the Commission rejected Castrol's view on the legality of the request and noted that the information it requested was necessary in order to determine the applicability of Article 101 TFEU and was in accordance with Regulation 17/62.

HeidelbergCement AG v European Commission	**Public Enforcement**
Case C-247/14P	Request for Information
Court of Justice, not yet reported	Article 18(3), Regulation 1/2003

Facts

The Commission carried out a number of inspections at the premises of companies active in the cement industry. Those inspections were followed by requests for information under Article 18(2) and Article 18(3), Regulation 1/2003. (Case COMP/39.520 *Cement*) HeidelbergCement AG answered some of the questions and applied for a time extension to complete its reply. The Commission refused to grant an extension. It noted that an extension may be possible on the basis of a reasoned application relating to relevant questions. HeidelbergCement brought an action for annulment of the Commission decision. (Case T-302/11 *HeidelbergCement v Commission*) Action dismissed. The Company subsequently appealed to the Court of Justice arguing, among other things, that the statement of reasons of the decision at issue was general in nature and did not satisfy the Commission's obligation to state the legal basis and the purpose of the request.

Held

'According to settled case-law, the statement of reasons required under Article 296 TFEU for measures adopted by EU institutions must be appropriate to the measure at issue and must disclose clearly and unequivocally the reasoning followed by the institution which adopted that measure in such a way as to enable the persons concerned to ascertain the reasons for it and to enable the competent court to review its legality. The requirements to be satisfied by the statement of reasons depend on all the circumstances of each case, in particular, the content of the measure in question, the nature of the reasons given and the interest which the addressees of the measure, or other parties to whom it is of direct and individual concern, may have in obtaining explanations. It is not necessary for the reasoning to go into all the relevant facts and points of law, since the question whether the statement of reasons meets the requirements of Article 296 EC must be assessed with regard not only to its wording but also to its context and to all the legal rules governing the matter in question (judgment in *Commission v Sytraval and Brink's France*, Case C-367/95 P, EU:C:1998:154, paragraph 63, and in *Nexans and Nexans France v Commission*, C-37/13 P, EU:C:2014:2030, paragraphs 31 and 32 and the case-law cited).' (para 16)

As regards the statement of reasons for a decision requesting information, Article 18(3) provides that the Commission shall state the legal basis and the purpose of the request. 'That obligation to state specific reasons is a fundamental requirement, designed not merely to show that the request for information is justified but also to enable the undertakings concerned to assess the scope of their duty to cooperate whilst at the same time safeguarding their rights of defence. ... With respect to the obligation to state the 'purpose of the request', this relates to the Commission's obligation to indicate the subject of its investigation in its request, and therefore to identify the alleged infringement of competition rules.' The Commission is not required to communicate to the addressee of a decision requesting all the information at its disposal, or to make a precise legal analysis of those infringements, providing it clearly indicates the suspicions which it intends to investigate. (paras 17–21)

'Since the necessity of the information must be judged in relation to the purpose stated in the request for information, that purpose must be indicated with sufficient precision, otherwise it will be impossible to determine whether the information is necessary and the Court will be prevented from exercising judicial review (... *SEP v Commission*, C-36/92 P, ..., paragraph 21) ... The General Court also correctly held, in paragraph 39 of the judgment under appeal, that the adequacy of the statement of reasons of the decision at issue depends "on whether or not the putative infringements that the Commission intends to investigate are defined in sufficiently clear terms". (paras 24, 25)

In its judgment, the General Court criticised the statement of reasons of the decision at issue for being formulated in very general terms, but held that it had the minimum degree of clarity necessary to meet the requirements of Article 18(3), Regulation 1/2003. (para 26)

Having reviewed the statement of reasons in that decision, it emerges that it does not make it possible to determine with sufficient precision what are the products to which the investigation relates and what are the suspicions of infringement justifying the adoption of that decision. 'It follows that that statement of reasons does not enable the undertaking in question to check whether the requested information is necessary for the purposes of the investigation or the European Union judicature to exercise its power of review.' (paras 27–31)

Admittedly, 'the question whether the statement of reasons relating to the decision at issue meets the requirements of Article 296 TFEU must be assessed in the light not only of its wording, but also of the context in which that decision was taken, which includes … the decision to initiate proceedings. However, the statement of reasons for that decision does not offset the brevity or the vague and generic nature of the statement of reasons of the decision at issue.' (paras 32, 33)

'It is true, as noted by the Commission, that a request for information is an investigative measure that is generally used as part of the investigation phase preceding the notification of the statement of objections and that the sole purpose of the preliminary investigation procedure is to enable the Commission to obtain the information and documentation necessary to check the actual existence and scope of a specific factual and legal situation (see, to that effect, judgment in *Orkem v Commission*, 374/87, … paragraph 21).' (para 37)

'Furthermore, although the Court has held, with respect to inspection decisions, that, even though the Commission is obliged to indicate as precisely as possible what is being sought and the matters to which the investigation must relate, it is, on the other hand, not essential, in a decision ordering an inspection, to define precisely the relevant market, to set out the exact legal nature of the presumed infringements or to indicate the period during which those infringements were allegedly committed, the Court justified that finding by the fact that inspections take place at the beginning of an investigation, at a time when precise information is not yet available to the Commission (… *Nexans and Nexans France v Commission*, C-37/13 P …).' (para 38)

'However, an excessively succinct, vague and generic—and in some respects, ambiguous—statement of reasons does not fulfil the requirements of the obligation to state reasons laid down in Article 18(3) of Regulation No 1/2003 in order to justify a request for information which, as in the present case, occurred more than two years after the first inspections, and even though the Commission had already sent a number of requests for information to undertakings suspected of involvement in an infringement and several months after the decision to initiate proceedings. Given those factors, it must be stated that the decision at issue was adopted at a time when the Commission already had information that would have allowed it to present more precisely the suspicions of infringement by the companies involved.' (para 39)

Comment

The Court set aside the judgment of the General Court. It held that the limited level of precision in this case made it impossible for the undertaking to assess whether the request is justified and what is the scope of its duty to cooperate. The lack of sufficient details, two years after the first inspection, could not be justified and had undermined the undertaking's rights of defence.

In his opinion, Advocate General Wahl commented on the wide and diverse scope of information requested in this case. He noted that the questions posed to HeidelbergCement were 'extraordinarily numerous and cover very diverse types of information. It is, to my mind, extremely difficult to identify a connecting thread among questions which range from the quantity and costs of CO_2 emissions of production facilities. to the means of transport and distance travelled for shipments of the goods sold; from the type of packaging used for the shipments to the transport and insurance costs for those shipments; from statistics regarding building permits to VAT numbers of its customers; and from the technology and fuel used in the production facilities to the costs of repair and maintenance of those facilities. Moreover, some questions posed do not seem to be fully in line with what was stated in the earlier decision to initiate proceedings: for example, questions 3 and 4 (which concern a particularly significant amount of information over a 10-year period are not limited to the Member States identified as possibly concerned by the decision to initiate proceedings.' (para 46)

Hercules Chemicals NV v Commission	**Public Enforcement**
Case C-51/92P	Statement of Objections
Court of Justice, [1999] ECR I-4235, [1999] 5 CMLR 976	Access to File

Facts

The case emerged out of the Commission's *Polypropylene* decision, in which it found that Hercules Chemicals NV (Hercules) had infringed Article 101 TFEU by taking part in anticompetitive agreements and concerted practices with other producers of polypropylene (IV/31.149—*Polypropylene* ([1986] OJ L230/1)). On appeal, an action for the annulment of the decision was dismissed by the General Court (Case T-7/89 *Hercules Chemicals v Commission* [1991] ECR II-1711). Hercules appealed to the Court of Justice, arguing, among other things, that the General Court erred when it did not examine whether the Commission's refusal to allow Hercules to access the replies of the other producers to the statement of objections constituted an infringement of the rights of defence.

Held

'Access to the file in competition cases is intended in particular to enable the addressees of statements of objections to acquaint themselves with the evidence in the Commission's file so that on the basis of that evidence they can express their views effectively on the conclusions reached by the Commission in its statement of objections (Case 322/81 *Michelin v Commission*, [1983] ECR 3461, paragraph 7; Case 85/76 *Hoffmann-La Roche v Commission* [1979] ECR 461, paragraphs 9 and 11; Case C-310/93P *BPB Industries and British Gypsum v Commission* [1995] ECR I-865, paragraph 21; and Case C-185/95P *Baustahlgewebe v Commission* [1998] ECR I-8417, paragraph 89).' (para 75)

'In the case of a decision concerning infringement of the competition rules applicable to undertakings and imposing fines or penalty payments, breach of those general principles of [Union] law in the procedure prior to the adoption of the decision can, in principle, cause the decision to be annulled if the rights of defence of the undertaking concerned have been infringed.' (para 77)

'In such a case, the infringement committed is not remedied by the mere fact that access was made possible at a later stage, in particular during the judicial proceedings relating to an action in which annulment of the contested decision is sought.' (para 78)

However, such an infringement does not bring about the annulment of the decision in question unless the undertaking concerned shows that it could have used the documents to which it was denied access for its defence. The undertaking does not have to show that if it had used the documents, the Commission decision would have been different in content, but only that it would have been able to use those documents for its defence. (paras 79–81)

Hercules did not establish that the fact that it was not able to apprise itself the replies of the other producers to the statement of objections, before the Decision was adopted, had infringed its rights of defence. (para 81)

Comment

The statement of objections sets all the essential facts upon which the Commission is relying at that stage of the procedure. The Commission final decision is not necessarily required to be a replica of the Commission's statement of objections, since the statement of objections is a preparatory document containing assessments of fact and of law which are purely provisional in nature. See paragraph 67, Joined Cases C-204/00 etc *Aalborg Portland and others v Commission* (page 554 below), paragraph 70, Joined Cases 142/84 etc *BAT and Reynolds v Commission* [1987] ECR 4487, and paragraph 14, Joined Cases 100/80 etc *Musique Diffusion Française and others v Commission* [1983] ECR 1825.

Aalborg Portland and others v Commission	**Public Enforcement**
Joined Cases C-204, 5, 11, 13, 17, 19/00	Statement of Objections
Court of Justice, [2004] ECR I-123, [2005] 4 CMLR 4	Access to File

Facts

An appeal against the General Court judgment in *Cimenteries CBR and others v Commission* in which the General Court confirmed parts of the infringements found against the appellants in Commission Decision IV/33.126 and 33.322 'Cement'. In its decision the Commission found a large number of undertakings and associations active in the European cement market to have infringed Article 101 TFEU by entering into anti-competitive agreements and concerted practices. In its decision the Court of Justice referred to, among other things, the right of access to the file.

Held

'[T]he right of access to the file means that the Commission must give the undertaking concerned the opportunity to examine all the documents in the investigation file which may be relevant for its defence (see, to that effect, Case T-30/91 *Solvay v Commission* [1995] ECR II-1775, paragraph 81, and Case C-199/99P *Corus UK v Commission* [2003] ECR I-11177, paragraphs 125 to 128). Those documents include both incriminating evidence and exculpatory evidence, save where the business secrets of other undertakings, the internal documents of the Commission or other confidential information are involved (see Case 85/76 *Hoffmann-La Roche v Commission* [1979] ECR 461, paragraphs 9 and 11; Case C-51/92P *Hercules Chemicals v Commission* [1999] ECR I-4235, paragraph 75; and Joined Cases C-238/99P, C-244/99P, C-245/99P, C-247/99P, C-250/99P to C-252/99P and C-254/99P *Limburgse Vinyl Maatschappij and others v Commission* [2002] ECR I-8375, paragraph 315).' (para 68)

'It may be that the undertaking draws the Commission's attention to documents capable of providing a different economic explanation for the overall economic assessment carried out by the Commission, in particular those describing the relevant market and the importance and the conduct of the undertakings acting on that market (see, to that effect, *Solvay v Commission*, cited above, paragraphs 76 and 77).' (para 69)

'The European Court of Human Rights has none the less held that, just like observance of the other procedural safeguards enshrined in Article 6(1) of the ECHR, compliance with the adversarial principle relates only to judicial proceedings before a "tribunal" and that there is no general, abstract principle that the parties must in all instances have the opportunity to attend the interviews carried out or to receive copies of all the documents taken into account in the case of other persons (see, to that effect, Euro Court HR, the *Kerojärvi v Finland* judgment of 19 July 1995, Series A No 322, 42, and the *Mantovanelli v France* judgment of 18 March 1997, Reports of Judgments and Decisions 1997 I, 33).' (para 70)

'The failure to communicate a document constitutes a breach of the rights of the defence only if the undertaking concerned shows, first, that the Commission relied on that document to support its objection concerning the existence of an infringement (see, to that effect, Case 322/81 *Michelin v Commission* [1983] ECR 3461, paragraphs 7 and 9) and, second, that the objection could be proved only by reference to that document (see Case 107/82 *AEG v Commission* [1983] ECR 3151, paragraphs 24 to 30, and *Solvay v Commission*, cited above, paragraph 58).' (para 71)

'If there were other documentary evidence of which the parties were aware during the administrative procedure, that specifically supported the Commission's findings, the fact that an incriminating document not communicated to the person concerned was inadmissible as evidence would not affect the validity of the objections upheld in the contested decision (see, to that effect, *Musique Diffusion Française and others v Commission*, cited above, paragraph 30, and *Solvay v Commission*, cited above, paragraph 58).' (para 72)

'It is thus for the undertaking concerned to show that the result at which the Commission arrived in its decision would have been different if a document which was not communicated to that undertaking and on which the Commission relied to make a finding of infringement against it had to be disallowed as evidence. On the other hand, where an exculpatory document has not been communicated, the undertaking concerned must only establish that its non-disclosure was able to influence, to its disadvantage, the course of the proceedings and the content of the decision of the Commission.' (paras 73, 74)

'It is sufficient for the undertaking to show that it would have been able to use the exculpatory documents in its defence (see *Hercules Chemicals v Commission*, paragraph 81, and *Limburgse Vinyl Maatschappij and others v Commission*, paragraph 318), in the sense that, had it been able to rely on them during the administrative procedure, it would have been able to put forward evidence which did not agree with the findings made by the Commission at that stage and would therefore have been able to have some influence on the Commission's assessment in any decision it adopted, at least as regards the gravity and duration of the conduct of which it was accused and, accordingly, the level of the fine (see, to that effect, *Solvay v Commission*, paragraph 98). (para 75)

'The possibility that a document which was not disclosed might have influenced the course of the proceedings and the content of the Commission's decision can be established only if a provisional examination of certain evidence shows that the documents not disclosed might in the light of that evidence have had a significance which ought not to have been disregarded (see *Solvay v Commission*, paragraph 68).' (para 76)

'In the context of that provisional analysis, it is for the Court of First Instance alone to assess the value which should be attached to the evidence produced to it (see order of 17 September 1996 in Case C-19/95P *San Marco v Commission* [1996] ECR I-4435, paragraph 40). As stated at paragraph 49 of this judgment, its assessment of the facts does not, provided the evidence is not distorted, constitute a question of law which is subject, as such, to review by the Court of Justice.' (para 77)

Comment

In Case T-30/91 *Solvay SA v Commission* [1995] ECR II-1775, [1996] 5 CMLR 57, the General Court held that where difficult and complex economic appraisals are to be made, the Commission must give the advisers of the undertaking concerned the opportunity to examine documents which may be relevant so that their probative value for the defence can be assessed. In this respect, it cannot be for the Commission alone to decide which documents are of use for the defence. If the Commission were to do so, the rights of defence which the applicant enjoys during the administrative procedure would be excessively restricted in relation to the powers of the Commission, which would then act as both the authority notifying the objections and the deciding authority, while having more detailed knowledge of the case-file than the defence. (paras 81, 83) 'That is particularly true where parallel conduct is concerned, which is characterised by a set of actions that are prima facie neutral, where documents may just as easily be interpreted in a way favourable to the undertakings concerned as in an unfavourable way. The Court considers that in such circumstances any error made by the Commission's officials in categorising as "neutral" a given document which, as an item of irrelevant evidence, will not then be disclosed to the undertakings, must not be allowed to impair their defence. The opposite view, for which the Commission contends, would mean that such an error could not be discovered in time, before adoption of the Commission's decision, except in the exceptional case where the undertakings concerned cooperated spontaneously, which would present unacceptable risks for the sound administration of justice.' (para 82)

AKZO Chemie BV and AKZO Chemie UK Ltd v Commission
Case 53/85
Court of Justice, [1986] ECR 1965, [1987] 1 CMLR 231

Public Enforcement
Professional Secrecy

Facts

The Commission investigated allegations that Akzo abused its dominant position by engaging in a pricing policy aimed at eliminating its competitor, ECS, from the flour additives market (see page 205 for a description of the abuse). As part of the administrative procedure the Commission disclosed documents it obtained through the investigation to ECS, so the latter could prepare for the hearing in the case. Akzo informed the Commission that several of the documents involved were subjected to protection as business secrets. The Commission took the view that it was for it to decide whether the documents in questions were confidential or not and released to ECS some of the documents flagged by Akzo as confidential. Akzo objected the disclosure and brought an action for a declaration that the Commission's decision to transmit confidential documents to ECS was void.

Held

'[Article 339 TFEU] requires the officials and other servants of the institutions of the [Union] not to disclose information in their possession of the kind covered by the obligation of professional secrecy. Article 20 of Regulation No 17/62, which implements that provision in regard to the rules applicable to undertakings, contains in paragraph (2) a special provision worded as follows: "without prejudice to the provisions of Articles 19 and 21, the Commission and the competent authorities of the Member States, their officials and other servants shall not disclose information acquired by them as a result of the application of this Regulation and of the kind covered by the obligation of professional secrecy."' (para 26)

'The provisions of Articles 19 and 21, the application of which is thus reserved, deal with the Commission's obligations in regard to hearings and the publication of Decisions. It follows that the obligation of professional secrecy laid down in Article 20(2) is mitigated in regard to third parties on whom Article 19(2) confers the right to be heard, that is to say in regard, in particular, to a third party who has made a complaint. The Commission may communicate to such a party certain information covered by the obligation of professional secrecy in so far as it is necessary to do so for the proper conduct of the investigation.' (para 27)

'However, that power does not apply to all documents of the kind covered by the obligation of professional secrecy. Article 19(3) which provides for the publication of notices prior to the granting of negative clearance or exemptions, and Article 21 which provides for the publication of certain Decisions, both require the Commission to have regard to the legitimate interest of undertakings in the protection of their business secrets. Business secrets are thus afforded very special protection. Although they deal with particular situations, those provisions must be regarded as the expression of a general principle which applies during the course of the administrative procedure. It follows that a third party who has submitted a complaint may not in any circumstances be given access to documents containing business secrets. Any other solution would lead to the unacceptable consequence that an undertaking might be inspired to lodge a complaint with the Commission solely in order to gain access to its competitors' business secrets.' (para 28)

'It is undoubtedly for the Commission to assess whether or not a particular document contains business secrets. After giving an undertaking an opportunity to state its views, the Commission is required to adopt a Decision in that connection which contains an adequate statement of the reasons on which it is based and which must be notified to the undertaking concerned. Having regard to the extremely serious damage which could result from improper communication of documents to a competitor, the Commission must, before implementing its Decision, give the undertaking an opportunity to bring an action before the court with a view to having the assessments made reviewed by it and to preventing disclosure of the documents in question.' (para 29)

'In this case, the Commission gave the undertaking concerned an opportunity to make its position known and adopted a Decision containing an adequate statement of the reasons on which it was based and concerning both the confidential nature of the documents at issue and the possibility of communicating them. At the same time, however, by an act which cannot be severed from that Decision, the Commission decided to hand over the documents to the third party who had made the complaint even before it notified its findings to that undertaking. It thus made it impossible for the undertaking to avail itself of the means of redress provided by Article 173 in conjunction with Article 185 of the Treaty with a view to preventing the implementation of a contested Decision.' (para 30)

'That being the case, the Decision which the Commission notified to the applicant by letter of 18 December 1984 must be declared void without there being any need to determine whether the documents communicated to the intervener did in fact contain business secrets.' (para 31)

Comment

In Case 85/76 *Hoffmann-La Roche & Co AG v Commission* [1979] ECR 461, [1979] 3 CMLR 211, the Court of Justice commented that 'the said Article 20 by providing undertakings, from whom information has been obtained, with a guarantee that their interests which are closely connected with observance of professional secrecy, are not jeopardized, enables the Commission to collect on the widest possible scale the requisite data for the fulfilment of the task conferred upon it by [Articles 101 and 102 TFEU] without the undertakings being able to prevent it from doing so, but it does not nevertheless allow it to use, to the detriment of the undertakings involved in a proceeding referred to in Regulation No 17, facts, circumstances or documents which it cannot in its view disclose if such a refusal of disclosure adversely affects that undertaking's opportunity to make known effectively its views on the truth or implications of those circumstances, on those documents or again on the conclusions drawn by the Commission from them.' (para 14)

In Case C-36/92 *SEP v Commission* [1994] ECR I-1911, the Court of Justice held that when the Commission is obliged under Article 10 of Regulation 17/62 to transmit documents to the competent authorities of the Member States, that obligation may be limited by the general principle of the right of undertakings to protection of their business secrets. When an undertaking raises before the Commission the confidential nature of a document as against the competent national authorities, it is for the Commission to judge whether or not a particular document contains business secrets. The undertaking should have an opportunity to state its views before the Commission reaches a decision on the matter. If the Commission wishes to transmit a document to the national authorities notwithstanding the claim that that document is of a confidential nature with respect to those authorities, it must, before implementing its decision, give the undertaking an opportunity to bring an action before the court with a view to having the assessments made reviewed by it and to preventing the contested disclosure.

Regulation 17/62 was replaced by Regulation 1/2003. Article 28(2), Regulation 1/2003 stipulates that 'the Commission and the competition authorities of the Member States ... shall not disclose information acquired or exchanged by them pursuant to this Regulation and of the kind covered by the obligation of professional secrecy.' Also note Article 16, Regulation 773/2004, which provides further guidance on the identification and protection of confidential information.

Also note Recital 16, Regulation 1/2003, which states that the exchange of information and the use of such information in evidence should be allowed between the members of the European Competition Network even where the information is confidential.

Orkem v Commission	**Public Enforcement**
Case 374/87	Rights of Defence
Court of Justice, [1989] ECR 3283, [1991] 4 CMLR 502	Self-incrimination

Facts

An action by Orkem SA for the annulment of a Commission decision which required it to reply to questions set out in a request for information issued by the Commission. Orkem SA argued that, among other things, the request in question breached its rights of defence as it compelled it to incriminate itself by confessing to an infringement of the competition rules and to inform against other undertakings.

Held

Regulation 17/62 conferred on the Commission wide powers of investigation and imposed on undertakings the obligation to cooperate actively in the investigative measures. This obligation implies that the undertaking must make available to the Commission all information relating to the subject-matter of the investigation. The Regulation does not give an undertaking under investigation any right to evade the investigation on the ground that the results thereof might provide evidence of an infringement by it of the competition rules. (paras 20–7)

In the absence of any right to remain silent expressly embodied in Regulation 17/62, it is appropriate to consider the general principles of Union law, of which fundamental rights form an integral part. 'In general, the laws of the Member States grant the right not to give evidence against oneself only to a natural person charged with an offence in criminal proceedings. A comparative analysis of national law does not therefore indicate the existence of such a principle, common to the laws of the Member States, which may be relied upon by legal persons in relation to infringements in the economic sphere, in particular infringements of competition law.' (paras 28, 29)

'As far as Article 6 of the European Convention is concerned, although it may be relied upon by an undertaking subject to an investigation relating to competition law, it must be observed that neither the wording of that article nor the decisions of the European Court of Human Rights indicate that it upholds the right not to give evidence against oneself.' (para 30)

'Article 14 of the International Covenant, which upholds, in addition to the presumption of innocence, the right (in paragraph 3(g)) not to give evidence against oneself or to confess guilt, relates only to persons accused of a criminal offence in court proceedings and thus has no bearing on investigations in the field of competition law.' (para 31)

'It is necessary, however, to consider whether certain limitations on the Commission's powers of investigation are implied by the need to safeguard the rights of the defence which the Court has held to be a fundamental principle of the [Union] legal order (judgment of 9 November 1983 in Case 322/82 *Michelin v Commission* [1983] ECR 3461, paragraph 7).' (para 32)

'In that connection, the Court observed recently, in its judgment of 21 September 1989 in Joined Cases 46/87 and 227/88 *Hoechst v Commission* [1989] ECR 2859, paragraph 15, that whilst it is true that the rights of the defence must be observed in administrative procedures which may lead to the imposition of penalties, it is necessary to prevent those rights from being irremediably impaired during preliminary inquiry procedures which may be decisive in providing evidence of the unlawful nature of conduct engaged in by undertakings and for which they may be liable. Consequently, although certain rights of the defence relate only to contentious proceedings which follow the delivery of the statement of objections, other rights must be respected even during the preliminary inquiry.' (para 33)

'Accordingly, whilst the Commission is entitled, in order to preserve the useful effect of Article 11(2) and (5) of Regulation No 17, to compel an undertaking to provide all necessary information concerning such facts as may be known to it and to disclose to it, if necessary, such documents relating thereto as are in its possession, even if the latter may be used to establish, against it or another undertaking, the existence of anti-competitive conduct, it may not, by means of a decision calling for information, undermine the rights of defence of the undertaking concerned.' (para 34)

'Thus, the Commission may not compel an undertaking to provide it with answers which might involve an admission on its part of the existence of an infringement which it is incumbent upon the Commission to prove.' (para 35)

Comment

In Case T-34/93 *Société Générale v Commission* [1995] ECR II-545, [1996] 4 CMLR 665, the General Court held that 'whilst the Commission is entitled, in order to preserve the effectiveness of Article 11(2) and (5) of Regulation No 17, to compel an undertaking to provide all necessary information, even if that information may be used to establish, against it or another undertaking, the existence of anti-competitive conduct, it may not, by means of a request for information, undermine the rights of defence of the undertaking concerned and compel it to provide answers which might involve an admission on its part of the existence of an infringement which it is incumbent on the Commission to prove (*Orkem*, paragraphs 34 and 35, and Case 27/88 *Solvay v Commission* [1989] ECR 3355, summary publication).' (para 74)

In Case C-238/99 etc *Limburgse Vinyl Maatschappij NV and others v Commission* [2002] ECR I-8375, [2003] 4 CMLR 10, the Court of Justice considered possible infringement of the privilege against self-incrimination. It referred to the *Orkem* judgment and held that 'the *Orkem* judgment thus acknowledged as one of the general principles of [Union] law, of which fundamental rights are an integral part and in the light of which all [Union] laws must be interpreted, the right of undertakings not to be compelled by the Commission, under Article 11 of Regulation No 17, to admit their participation in an infringement (see *Orkem*, paragraphs 28, 38 in fine and 39). The protection of that right means that, in the event of a dispute as to the scope of a question, it must be determined whether an answer from the undertaking to which the question is addressed is in fact equivalent to the admission of an infringement, such as to undermine the rights of the defence.' (para 273) 'The parties agree that, since *Orkem*, there have been further developments in the case-law of the European Court of Human Rights which the [Union] judicature must take into account when interpreting the fundamental rights, as introduced by the judgment in *Funke* [Series A No 256 A], on which the appellants rely, and the judgments of 17 December 1996 in *Saunders v United Kingdom* (Reports of Judgments and Decisions 1996–VI, p 2044) and of 3 May 2001 in *JB v Switzerland* (not yet published in the Reports of Judgments and Decisions).' (para 274) 'However, both the *Orkem* judgment and the recent case-law of the European Court of Human Rights require, first, the exercise of coercion against the suspect in order to obtain information from him and, second, establishment of the existence of an actual interference with the right which they define.' (para 275) 'Examined in the light of that finding and the specific circumstances of the present case, the ground of appeal alleging infringement of the privilege against self-incrimination does not permit annulment of the contested judgment on the basis of the developments in the case-law of the European Court of Human Rights.' (para 276)

Regulation 17/62 was replaced by Regulation 1/2003. Recital 23, Regulation 1/2003 stipulates that: 'When complying with a decision of the Commission, undertakings cannot be forced to admit that they have committed an infringement, but they are in any event obliged to answer factual questions and to provide documents, even if this information may be used to establish against them or against another undertaking the existence of an infringement.' Recital 37, Regulation 1/2003 adds that 'this Regulation respects the fundamental rights and observes the principles recognised in particular by the Charter of Fundamental Rights of the European Union. Accordingly, this Regulation should be interpreted and applied with respect to those rights and principles.'

Mannesmannröhren-Werke AG v EC Commission	**Public Enforcement**
Case T-112/98	Right of Defence
General Court, [2001] ECR II-729, [2001] 5 CMLR 1	Self-incrimination

Facts

The applicant Mannesmannröhren-Werke AG (MW) refused to reply to a request for information made by the Commission under Article 11 of Regulation 17/62. The request for information was made as part of an investigation relating to the applicant and other producers of steel tubes, in the course of which the Commission carried out inspections on the premises of the undertakings involved. The Commission rejected MW's argument that it was not obliged to provide the information and adopted a decision imposing a fine on MW if it failed to provide the information. MW applied for annulment of the Commission's decision.

Held

There is no absolute right to silence in competition proceedings.

The Commission's power of investigation during a preliminary investigation is limited insofar as it cannot undermine the right of defence. Such limitation does not give rise to an absolute right to silence, but to a partial right to silence to the extent that an undertaking would not be compelled to provide answers which might involve an admission of the existence of an infringement. (paras 59–69)

MW was obliged to respond to questions of a purely factual nature and to provide the Commission with details of meetings between steel tube producers. MW was not obliged to respond to questions which did not concern exclusively factual information and might have compelled it to admit its participation in an unlawful agreement. (paras 70–3)

Answering purely factual questions cannot be regarded as undermining the right of defence as the undertaking is free to put forward its own interpretation as to the meaning of the documents produced by it. (para 78)

The contested decision was annulled in so far as it obliged MW to answer questions which might involve it in admitting that it was a party to an anticompetitive agreement.

Comment

Recital 23 of Regulation 1/2003 reasserts the above principle and states that when complying with a decision of the Commission requiring information 'undertakings cannot be forced to admit that they have committed an infringement, but they are in any event obliged to answer factual questions and to provide documents, even if this information may be used to establish against them or against another undertaking the existence of an infringement'.

The European Court of Human Rights recognised a right to remain silent in criminal cases (see additional discussion in *Orkem*, page 558 above). Consequently, the use by National Competition Authorities of information gathered under the partial right to silence rule in Regulation 1/2003 would be limited in cases involving criminal proceedings. Note Recital 37 of Regulation 1/2003, which states that the Regulation should be interpreted and applied with due regard being given to fundamental rights and principles recognised in particular by the Charter of Fundamental Rights of the European Union.

Note Case C-301/04P *Commission v SGL Carbon* [2006] ECR I-5915, in which the Court of Justice held that an undertaking is subject to an obligation to cooperate actively with the Commission. Accordingly, it must make available to the Commission all information relating to the subject matter of the investigation. (para 40)

AM&S Europe Limited v Commission	**Public Enforcement**
Case 155/79	Legal Privilege
Court of Justice, [1982] ECR 1575, [1982] 2 CMLR 264	

Facts

Commission officials arrived at the offices of AM&S to conduct an unannounced investigation under Article 14, Regulation 17/62. Following two days of inspections, the officials seized a number of documents and left a written request, asking AM&S to provide additional documents. AM&S supplied some, but not all, of the documents required, arguing that these were protected by legal privilege. The Commission adopted a decision requiring AM&S to produce for examination all the documents for which legal privilege was claimed (Commission Decision 79/760/EEC). AM&S lodged an application to declare the decision void.

Held

Articles 11 and 14 of Regulation 17/62 provide that the Commission may obtain information and undertake the necessary investigation in order to bring to an end an infringement of EU competition laws. Article 14(1) in particular empowers the Commission to require production of business records, that is to say, documents concerning the market activities of the undertaking, in particular as regards compliance with those rules. Written communications between lawyer and client fall, in so far as they have a bearing on such activities, within the category of documents referred to in Articles 11 and 14. (paras 15–7)

'However, the above rules do not exclude the possibility of recognizing, subject to certain conditions, that certain business records are of a confidential nature. [Union] law, which derives from not only the economic but also the legal interpenetration of the Member States, must take into account the principles and concepts common to the laws of those states concerning the observance of confidentiality, in particular, as regards certain communications between lawyer and client. That confidentiality serves the requirements, the importance of which is recognized in all of the Member States, that any person must be able, without constraint, to consult a lawyer whose profession entails the giving of independent legal advice to all those in need of it.' (para 18)

'As far as the protection of written communications between lawyer and client is concerned, it is apparent from the legal systems of the Member States that, although the principle of such protection is generally recognized, its scope and the criteria for applying it vary. Whilst in some of the Member States the protection against disclosure afforded to written communications between lawyer and client is based principally on a recognition of the very nature of the legal profession, inasmuch as it contributes towards the maintenance of the rule of law, in other Member States the same protection is justified by the more specific requirement (which, moreover, is also recognized in the first-mentioned states) that the rights of the defence must be respected.' (paras 19–20)

'Apart from these differences, however, there are to be found in the national laws of the Member States common criteria inasmuch as those laws protect, in similar circumstances, the confidentiality of written communications between lawyer and client provided that, on the one hand, such communications are made for the purposes and in the interests of the client's rights of defence and, on the other hand, they emanate from independent lawyers, that is to say, lawyers who are not bound to the client by a relationship of employment.' (para 21)

'Viewed in that context Regulation No 17 must be interpreted as protecting, in its turn, the confidentiality of written communications between lawyer and client subject to those two conditions, and thus incorporating such elements of that protection as are common to the laws of the Member States.' (para 22)

'As far as the first of those two conditions is concerned, in Regulation No 17 itself, in particular in the eleventh recital in its preamble and in the provisions contained in Article 19, care is taken to ensure that the rights of the defence may be exercised to the full, and the protection of the confidentiality of written communications between lawyer and client is an essential corollary to those rights. In those circumstances, such protection must, if it is to be effective, be recognized as covering all written communications exchanged after the initiation of the administrative procedure under Regulation No 17 which may lead to a Decision on the application of [Articles 101 and 102 TFEU] or to a Decision imposing a pecuniary sanction on the undertaking. It must also be possible to extend it to earlier written communications which have a relationship to the subject-matter of that procedure.' (para 23)

'As regards the second condition, it should be stated that the requirement as to the position and status as an independent lawyer, which must be fulfilled by the legal adviser from whom the written communications which may be protected emanate, is based on a conception of the lawyer's role as collaborating in the administration of justice by the courts and as being required to provide, in full independence, and in the overriding interests of that cause, such legal assistance as the client needs. The counterpart of that protection lies in the rules of professional ethics and discipline which are laid down and enforced in the general interest by institutions endowed with the requisite powers for that purpose. Such a conception reflects the legal traditions common to the Member States and is also to be found in legal order of the [Union].' (para 24)

The protection to written communications between lawyer and client must apply without distinction to any lawyer entitled to practice his profession in one of the Member States, regardless of the Member State in which the client lives. (para 25)

'In view of all these factors it must therefore be concluded that although Regulation No 17, and in particular Article 14 thereof, interpreted in the light of its wording, structure and aims, and having regard to the laws of the Member States, empowers the Commission to require, in the course of an investigation within the meaning of that Article, production of the business documents the disclosure of which it considers necessary, including written communications between lawyer and client, for proceedings in respect of any infringements of [Articles 101 and 102 TFEU], that power is, however, subject to a restriction imposed by the need to protect confidentiality, on the conditions defined above, and provided that the communications in question are exchanged between an independent lawyer, that is to say one who is not bound to his client by a relationship of employment, and his client.' (para 27)

If an undertaking which refuses, on the ground that it is entitled to protection of the confidentiality of information, to produce, written communications between itself and its lawyer, it must nevertheless provide the Commission with relevant material of such a nature as to demonstrate that the communications fulfil the conditions for being granted legal protection as defined above, although it is not bound to reveal the contents of the communications in question. Where the Commission is not satisfied that such evidence has been supplied, the solution of disputes as to the application of the protection of the confidentiality of written communications between lawyer and client may be sought only at EU level. In that case it is for the Commission to order, production of the communications in question and, if necessary, to impose on the undertaking fines or periodic penalty payments for the undertaking's refusal to supply such evidence. The undertaking will then be able to bring an action against the decision under Article 278 TFEU. Such an action does not have suspensory effect yet the interests of the undertaking concerned are safeguarded by the possibility which exists under Articles 278 and 279 TFEU, as well as under Article 83 of the Rules of procedure of the Court, of obtaining an order suspending the application of the Decision which has been taken, or any other interim measure. (paras 29–32)

Comment

See the *Hilti* judgment on page 563 below and the *Akzo* judgment on page 564 below.

Hilti AG v Commission	**Public Enforcement**
Case T-30/89	Legal Privilege
General Court, [1990] ECR II-163, [1990] 4 CMLR 602	Independent Lawyer/In-house Counsel

Facts

Hilti AG brought an action for the annulment of a Commission Decision relating to a proceeding under Article 102 TFEU (IV/30.787 *Eurofix-Bauco v Hilti*). Two other undertakings, Bauco (UK) Ltd and Profix Distribution Ltd, were granted leave to intervene in the case in support of the Commission's decision. Hilti AG requested for certain documents in its submission to be treated, vis-à-vis the interveners, as confidential. With respect to certain documents it argued that they were covered by legal professional privilege and should be treated as confidential. It submitted that the documents should not be disclosed to the interveners, even though, vis-à-vis the Commission, it waived that privilege.

Held

'The Court of Justice has held (Case 155/79 *AM&S v Commission*) that Regulation No 17 … must be interpreted as protecting the confidentiality of written communications between lawyer and client provided that, on the one hand, such communications are made for the purposes and in the interests of the client's right of defence and, on the other hand, they emanate from independent lawyers, that is to say, lawyers who are not bound to the client by a relationship of employment. In the same judgment the Court of Justice held that that protection must, in the administrative procedure before the Commission, be recognized as covering all written communications exchanged after the initiation of the administrative procedure which may lead to a decision on the application of [Articles 101 and 102 TFEU] or to a decision imposing a pecuniary sanction on the undertaking. The Court of Justice further held that that protection must be extended to earlier written communications which have a relationship to the subject-matter of that procedure.' (para 13)

'In this case the letter in point is one sent to the applicant by an independent lawyer, after the initiation of the administrative procedure before the Commission, for the purposes and in the interests of the applicant's right of defence that letter must accordingly be regarded as confidential within the meaning of Article 93(4) of the Rules of Procedure. It follows that the applicant's request must be allowed.' (para 14)

With respect to the additional documents for which confidential treatment is requested, these include internal notes distributed within the undertaking which reported the content of advice received from external legal advisers. Such legal advice would be covered by the principle of the protection of confidentiality. The principle of the protection of written communications between lawyer and client extends also to the internal notes which are confined to reporting the text or the content of those communications. (paras 15–18)

Comment

In Case IV/35.733 *Volkswagen AG and others* [1998] 5 CMLR 33, the Commission commented in its decision that 'pursuant to Article 14(1) [Regulation 17/62] the Commission may in the course of an investigation examine the undertaking's business records. "Business Records" are those which relate to the activity of the undertakings on the relevant market. Written communication between lawyer and client are in this respect "records" in the meaning of Article 14. Regulation 17 protects the confidentiality of written communications between lawyer and client, but only on condition that, on the one hand, such communications are made for the purpose and in the interest of the client's rights of defence and, on the other hand, they emanate from independent lawyers, that is to say lawyers who are not bound to the client by a relationship of employment.' (para 199)

In Case IV/30.809 *Re John Deere Tractors* [1985] 2 CMLR 554, the Commission used as evidence communication between the company and its in house counsel to establish that the undertakings knew that the conduct was contrary to EU and national competition law. (para 21) 'Deere's own in-house counsel expressed doubts as to legitimacy of such device.' (para 27)

Akzo Nobel Chemicals and Akcros Chemicals Ltd v Commission	**Public Enforcement**
Case C-550/07P	Legal Privilege
Court of Justice, [2010] 5 CMLR 19	In-house Counsel

Facts

The Commission conducted an investigation into possible infringements of EU competition law by Akzo Nobel and Akcros Chemicals. During the investigation the Commission raided Akzo's offices and obtained various documents in accordance with its investigative powers under Article 14(3), Regulation 17/62. Akzo claimed that some of the documents were protected by professional privilege. Some of the documents included internal communications for the purpose of obtaining external legal advice on competition matters. These were placed in sealed envelops titled 'Set A'. Another group of documents, classified as 'Set B', included email correspondences between Akzo's in-house counsel (titled 'competition law coordinator') who was a registered attorney at the Dutch bar, and the General Manager of Akcros Chemicals. The 'Set B' documents were not sealed in an envelope, as the Commission was of the opinion that they did not benefit from legal privilege. Akzo claimed that both sets of documents were protected by professional privilege. Following a Commission decision, in which it indicated that it intended to read the 'Set A' documents the undertakings applied for interim measures seeking suspension of the operation of the decision. The president of the General Court granted a preliminary order requiring the Commission to deposit the 'Set A' documents at the registry of the General Court. Both the Commission and Akzo/Akcros appealed the president's order.

On appeal (Cases T-125/03 and 253/03 *Akzo Nobel Chemicals Ltd and Akcros Chemicals Ltd v Commission*) the General Court held that 'In a significant number of cases, a mere cursory look by the Commission officials at the general layout, heading, title or other superficial features of the document will enable them to confirm the accuracy of the reasons invoked by the undertaking and to determine whether the document at issue was confidential, when deciding whether to put it aside. Nevertheless, on certain occasions, there would be a risk that, even with a cursory look at the document, in spite of the superficial nature of their examination, the Commission officials would gain access to information covered by legal professional privilege. That may be so, in particular, if the confidentiality of the document in question is not clear from external indications.' (para 81)

'[A]n undertaking subject to an investigation under Article 14(3) of Regulation No 17 is entitled to refuse to allow the Commission officials to take even a cursory look at one or more specific documents which it claims to be covered by [legal professional privilege], provided that the undertaking considers that such a cursory look is impossible without revealing the content of those documents and that it gives the Commission officials appropriate reasons for its view.' (para 82)

'Where the Commission and the undertakings are not in agreement as to the confidential nature of the document, Commission officials may place a copy of the document in a sealed envelope and then remove it with a view to a subsequent resolution of the dispute. This procedure enables risks of a breach of legal professional privilege to be avoided while at the same time enabling the Commission to retain a certain control over the documents forming the subject-matter of the investigation. (para 83)

'[T]he Court considers that the Commission forced the applicants to accept the cursory look at the disputed documents, even though ... the applicants' representatives claimed ... that such an examination would require the contents of those documents to be disclosed. ... Accordingly, the Court concludes that the Commission infringed the procedure for protection under legal professional privilege in this regard.' (para 95)

In the present case, 'the Set A documents do not by themselves constitute written communications with an independent lawyer or an internal note reporting the content of a communication with such a lawyer. Nor do the applicants submit that those documents were prepared in order to be sent physically to an independent lawyer.' (para 118)

Preparatory documents, even if they were not exchanged with a lawyer or were not created for the purpose of being sent physically to a lawyer, may none the less be covered by legal professional privilege, provided that they were drawn up exclusively for the purpose of seeking legal advice from a lawyer in exercise of the rights of the defence. The mere fact that a document has been discussed with a lawyer is not sufficient to give it such protection. (paras 120–24)

With respect to the protection afforded to communications with in-house lawyers, the Court of Justice in *AM&S* expressly held that the protection accorded to legal professional privilege under Union law, only applies to the extent that the lawyer is independent, that is to say, not bound to his client by a relationship of employment (paragraphs 21, 22 and 27 of the *AM&S* judgment). (para 166)

Akzo appealed the General Court's judgment to the Court of Justice. The Court dismissed the appeal as unfounded. In its judgment the Court considered the protection to communication with in-house lawyers.

Held

In Case *155/79 AM&S Europe v Commission* [1982] ECR 1575, the Court held that the confidentiality of written communications between lawyers and clients should be protected at Community level, subject to two cumulative conditions: (1) that the exchange with the lawyer must be connected to 'the client's rights of defence', and (2) that the exchange must emanate from 'independent lawyers', that is to say 'lawyers who are not bound to the client by a relationship of employment'. (paras 40, 41)

'As to the second condition, the Court observed ... that the requirement as to the position and status as an independent lawyer, which must be fulfilled by the legal adviser from whom the written communications which may be protected emanate, is based on a conception of the lawyer's role as collaborating in the administration of justice and as being required to provide, in full independence and in the overriding interests of that cause, such legal assistance as the client needs. The counterpart to that protection lies in the rules of professional ethics and discipline which are laid down and enforced in the general interest.' (para 42)

'As the Advocate General observed, ... the concept of the independence of lawyers is determined not only positively, that is by reference to professional ethical obligations, but also negatively, by the absence of an employment relationship. An in-house lawyer, despite his enrolment with a Bar or Law Society ... does not enjoy the same degree of independence from his employer as a lawyer working in an external law firm does in relation to his client. Consequently, an in-house lawyer is less able to deal effectively with any conflicts between his professional obligations and the aims of his client.' (para 45)

Notwithstanding the professional regime applicable to the in-house lawyer, he cannot be treated in the same way as an external lawyer, because being an employee, by its very nature, does not allow him to ignore the commercial strategies of his employer, and thereby affects his ability to exercise professional independence. An in-house lawyer therefore does not enjoy a level of professional independence equal to that of external lawyers. Being in a fundamentally different position from external lawyers, the General Court rightly held that there was no breach of the principle of equal treatment in this case. (paras 47–59)

In accordance with the principle of national procedural autonomy, in the absence of EU rules governing the matter, it is for the domestic legal system of each Member State to lay down the detailed procedural rules governing actions safeguarding individuals' rights. However, in the present case, the Court is called on to decide on the legality of a decision taken by the European Commission. As the Advocate General stated in her Opinion, national law is applicable in the context of investigations conducted by the European Commission only in so far as the authorities of the Member States lend their assistance. Accordingly, neither the principle of national procedural autonomy nor the principle of conferred powers may be invoked against the powers enjoyed by the Commission in the area in question. (paras 113–20)

Comment

The Court of Justice upheld the General Court's finding that under EU law legal professional privilege does not extend to communications with in-house lawyers.

Note the position in the UK where greater protection is afforded to in-house lawyers. In *Alfred Crompton Amusement Machines Ltd v Customs and Excise Commissioners* (No 2) [1972] 2 WLR 835, the High Court held that in-house lawyers 'are regarded by the law as in every respect in the same position as those who practice on their own account. The only difference is that they act for one client only, and not for several clients. They must uphold the same standards of honour and of etiquette. They are subject to the same duties to their client and to the court.'

La Cinq v Commission	**Public Enforcement**
Case T-44/90	Interim Measures
General Court, [1992] ECR II-1, [1992] 4 CMLR 449	

Facts

An action against a Commission decision which rejected a request for interim measures submitted by La Cinq in relation to complaints it had made to the Commission concerning anticompetitive activities by the European Broadcasting Union (EBU). In its decision the Commission considered that the conditions required for the grant of interim measures are: (1) the finding of a probable existence of an infringement; (2) the probability of serious and irreparable damage to the applicant if the Commission does not intervene; and (3) urgency, which must be established. The Commission based its refusal to order interim measures on the lack of probable existence of an infringement and the absence of a risk of serious and irreparable damage to the undertaking, justifying the urgent adoption of the interim measures requested.

Held

The Court therefore considers it necessary 'to determine the conditions which, according to the case-law of the Court of Justice, must be fulfilled for the Commission to be able to exercise its power to grant interim measures in the context of the application of the competition rules of the Treaty.' (para 26)

'The Court observes, firstly that the Commission's power in this sphere was recognized by the Court of Justice in its order in *Camera Care v Commission* (Case 792/79 R [1980] ECR 119), according to which it is for the Commission, in the performance of the supervisory task conferred upon it by the Treaty and Regulation No 17 in competition matters, to decide, pursuant to Article 3(1) of Regulation No 17, whether it is necessary to take interim measures when it receives a request to that effect.' (para 27)

'Moreover, it follows from the case-law of the Court of Justice (order in *Camera Care*, cited above, paragraphs 14 and 18, and the order of the President of the Court of Justice in Cases 228/82 and 229/82 R *Ford v Commission* [1982] ECR 3091, paragraph 13) that protective measures may be granted only where the practices of certain undertakings are prima facie such as to constitute a breach of the [Union] rules on competition in respect of which a penalty could be imposed by a decision of the Commission. Furthermore, such measures are to be taken only in cases of proven urgency, in order to prevent the occurrence of a situation likely to cause serious and irreparable damage to the party applying for their adoption or intolerable damage to the public interest.' (para 28)

'It follows that the condition concerning urgency, which in the decision at issue the Commission regarded as a third condition for ordering interim measures, is in reality but one aspect of the condition concerning the risk of serious and irreparable damage.' (para 29)

'It must also be observed that, since the two conditions for ordering the measures are concurrent, failure to fulfil either of them would have sufficed in this case to prevent the Commission from exercising its power in the matter.' (para 30)

In order to determine whether the Commission's conclusions were justified, the court must examine the Commission's finding regarding each of the two conditions required for the adoption of interim measures, as defined above by the Court, that is to say the probable existence of an infringement and the probability of serious and irreparable damage which establishes the urgent need to adopt the measures. (para 32)

The condition regarding the probable existence of an infringement

'As the Court of First Instance held in its judgment in Case T-23/90 *Peugeot v Commission* [1991] ECR II-653, thereby upholding the argument put forward by the Commission during the proceedings (see paragraph 59 of the judgment), in proceedings relating to the legality of a Commission decision concerning the adoption of interim measures, the requirement of a finding of a prima facie infringement cannot be placed on the same footing as the requirement of certainty that a final decision must satisfied. In the present case the reasons adopted by the Commission for the decision at issue—confirmed, moreover, during the hearing—amount to requiring that, for a grant of interim measures to be possible, the existence of a clear and flagrant infringement must already be established at the stage of the mere prima facie appraisal which has to serve as the basis for the grant of such measures.' (para 61)

'It follows that, by identifying the requirement of a "prima facie infringement" with the requirement of a finding of a "clear and flagrant infringement" at the stage of interim measures, the Commission based its reasoning on an erroneous interpretation in law of the condition relating to the probable existence of an infringement.' (para 62)

'The Court considers that the error of law committed by the Commission in interpreting the condition relating to the probable existence of an infringement is such as seriously to affect the legality and the relevance of any appraisal undertaken by the Commission regarding the question whether this first condition for ordering the interim measures requested was in fact fulfilled.' (para 63)

'It follows from the foregoing considerations that the Commission' s finding that the condition regarding the probable existence of an infringement was not fulfilled in this case was based on an erroneous interpretation in law of that condition.' (para 66)

The condition regarding the existence of a risk of serious and irreparable damage establishing the urgent need to adopt interim measures

'[I]n stating in its decision that "the only damage that can be regarded as irreparable is that which cannot be remedied by any subsequent decision", the Commission adopted a legally incorrect conception of irreparable damage the existence or risk of which could justify the adoption of interim measures.' (para 79)

'In formulating the requirement embodied in its conception of irreparable damage, the Commission went beyond what is required by the case-law of the Court of Justice, which merely refers to damage which could no longer be remedied by the decision to be adopted by the Commission upon the conclusion of the administrative procedure (order in *Camera Care*, cited above).' (para 80)

'Moreover, the Commission's interpretation would make it almost impossible to verify the fulfilment of such a condition, and this would, in practice, amount to depriving of all substance the power granted to it to adopt interim measures.' (para 81)

Commission's decision annulled.

Comment

In Case T-41/96 R *Bayer v Commission* (Applications for interim measures) [1996] ECR II-381, [1996] 5 CMLR 290, the General Court considered first the prima facie case and then the question of urgency. On the latter it held that the risk faced by the applicant must be weighed against the interests of other undertakings and stakeholders. 'Comparison of the various interests involved shows that the damage likely to be caused to the applicant by immediate implementation of the provision in question would be disproportionate in relation to the interests of wholesalers in Spain and France in increasing their exports. … It follows from the above considerations as a whole that the balance of interests weighs clearly in favour of the applicant, with the result that the risk of damage to which it would be exposed if the Court decided to refuse the requested suspension, which would be disproportionate to say the least, is sufficient to establish the urgency of adopting the measure requested.' (paras 60, 61)

Automec Srl v Commission	**Public Enforcement**
Case T-24/90	Termination of Infringement
General Court, [1992] ECR II-2223, [1992] 5 CMLR 431	

Facts

Automec Srl was in contractual relations with BMW Italia SpA which were due to expire on 31 December 1984. Prior to the expiry of the contract between the two companies, BMW Italia informed Automec of its intention not to renew the agreement. Automec brought proceedings before the Italian national court claiming that it was wrongly excluded from the distribution network, but its action was dismissed. It then made an application to the Commission under Article 3(2) of Regulation 17/62, claiming that BMW Italia and BMW AG infringed Article 101 TFEU by refusing to continue supplying it with BMW vehicles and spare parts and preventing it from using BMW trademarks. Automec requested the Commission to order BMW Italia and BMW AG to bring the alleged infringement to an end and to resume deliveries. The Commission decided not to open an investigation on the matter, among other things, on the basis that even if the distribution agreement used by BMW was contrary to Article 101 TFEU, it could at most find that there was an infringement and that the agreement was therefore void. However, under Article 101 TFEU the Commission has no power of injunction which would allow it to require BMW to deliver, in the circumstances of this case, its own products. Automec appealed to the General Court for the annulment of the decision.

Held

'As freedom of contract must remain the rule, the Commission cannot in principle be considered to have, among the powers to issue orders which are available to it for the purpose of bringing to an end infringements of [Article 101(1) TFEU], the power to order a party to enter into contractual relations, since in general the Commission has suitable remedies at its disposal for the purpose of requiring an undertaking to terminate an infringement.' (para 51)

'In particular, there cannot be held to be any justification for such a restriction on freedom of contract where several remedies exist for bringing an infringement to an end. This is true of infringements of [Article 101(1) TFEU] arising out of the application of a distribution system. Such infringements can also be eliminated by the abandonment or amendment of the distribution system. Consequently, the Commission undoubtedly has the power to find that an infringement exists and to order the parties concerned to bring it to an end, but it is not for the Commission to impose upon the parties its own choice from among all the various potential courses of action which are in conformity with the Treaty.' (para 52)

The Commission has been entrusted with an extensive and general supervisory and regulatory task in the field of competition. It is consistent with its obligations under Union law for it to apply different degrees of priority to the cases submitted to it. A decision to close the file on a complaint will only be taken following a careful factual and legal examination of the particulars brought to its notice by the complainant. (paras 55–98)

Comment

Contrast with the Commission's powers under Article 102 TFEU to bring an abuse to an end. Such decision 'may include an order to do certain acts or provide certain advantages which have been wrongfully withheld as well as prohibiting the continuation of certain action, practices or situations which are contrary to the Treaty.' Case 6/73 *Istituto Chemioterapico Italiano SpA and Commercial Solvents Corporation v Commission* [1974] ECR 223, [1974] 1 CMLR 309. (para 45)

Alrosa Company Ltd v Commission	**Public Enforcement**
Case C-441/07P	Commitments
Court of Justice, [2010] 5 CMLR 11	Article 9, Regulation 1/2003

Facts

Alrosa Company Ltd and De Beers SA, two companies active in the production and supply of rough diamonds, notified the Commission of a supply agreement between them, with a view to obtaining negative clearance or an exemption under Regulation 17/62. Following the notification, the Commission sent a statement of objections to the two undertakings in which it expressed the opinion that the notified agreement was capable of infringing Article 101 TFEU. Additionally, the Commission informed De Beers that the agreement may constitute an abuse of a dominant position. The undertakings jointly submitted commitments designed to meet the concerns which the Commission had communicated to them. The Commission requested the parties to submit further commitments and exchanged views with each of them on the matter. Following the submission of a new set of commitments by De Beers, aimed at resolving concerns under Article 102 TFEU, the Commission adopted a decision declaring the commitment binding (Case COMP/B-2/38.381—De Beers). The commitments included a permanent prohibition of transactions between De Beers and Alrosa.

Alrosa appealed to the General Court and alleged, among other things, that the commitment which included a permanent prohibition of transactions between De Beers and Alrosa was excessive in nature and that Article 9 of Regulation 1/2003 does not allow commitments to which an undertaking concerned has not voluntarily subscribed to be made binding on that undertaking (Case T-170/06). In its judgment on appeal the Court subrogates the Article 9 procedure to the same proportionality principles which apply to Article 7, Regulation 1/2003. (paras 95, 91–5) It held that the Commission cannot lawfully propose or accept commitments which go further than a decision which it could have adopted in that case under Article 7(1) of Regulation No 1/2003. (paras 111–40) It found the commitment accepted in this case to be disproportionate and that Alrosa's right to be heard was undermined. It subsequently annulled the Commission's decision. The Commission appealed the judgment. On appeal, the Court of Justice set aside the General Court's judgment and upheld the Commission's decision.

Held

The principle of proportionality

'[A]lthough Article 9, unlike Article 7 of Regulation No 1/2003, does not expressly refer to proportionality, the principle of proportionality, as a general principle of European Union law, is none the less a criterion for the lawfulness of any act of the institutions of the Union, including decisions taken by the Commission in its capacity of competition authority.' (para 36) However, as the specific characteristics of Articles 7 and 9 of Regulation No 1/2003 are different, proportionality is observed to a different extent, depending on whether it is considered in relation to the former or the latter article. (para 38) By contrast to Article 7, under Article 9 the Commission is not required to make a finding of an infringement. Its task is confined to examining, and possibly accepting, the commitments offered by the undertakings. Subsequently, application of the principle of proportionality by the Commission in the context of Article 9 'is confined to verifying that the commitments in question address the concerns it expressed to the undertakings concerned and that they have not [also] offered less onerous commitments that also address those concerns adequately. When carrying out that assessment, the Commission must, however, take into consideration the interests of third parties. Judicial review for its part relates solely to whether the Commission's assessment is manifestly incorrect.' (paras 40–2)

In its judgment, the General Court incorrectly considered that the application of the principle of proportionality has the same effect in relation to decisions taken under Article 7, as in relation to those taken under Article 9. Those two provisions pursue different objectives, one aiming to put an end to the infringement and the other aiming to address the Commission's concerns following its preliminary assessment. While both are subject to the principle of proportionality, the application of that principle differs. There is therefore no reason why the measure which could possibly be imposed in the context of Article 7 should have to serve as a reference for the purpose of assessing commitments accepted under Article 9, or why anything going beyond that measure should automatically be regarded as disproportionate. (paras 43–50)

'Since the Commission is not required itself to seek out less onerous or more moderate solutions than the commitments offered to it, … its only obligation … in relation to the proportionality of the commitments was to ascertain whether the joint commitments offered in the proceedings initiated under [Article 101 TFEU] were sufficient to address the concerns it had identified in the proceedings initiated under [Article 102 TFEU].' (para 60) 'The General Court could have held that the Commission had committed a manifest error of assessment only if it had found that the Commission's conclusion was obviously unfounded, having regard to the facts established by it. However, the General Court made no such finding. Instead it examined other less onerous solutions for the purpose of applying the principle of proportionality, … By so doing, the General Court put forward its own assessment of complex economic circumstances and thus substituted its own assessment for that of the Commission, thereby encroaching on the discretion enjoyed by the Commission instead of reviewing the lawfulness of its assessment. That error of the General Court in itself justifies setting aside the judgment under appeal.' (paras 63–7)

The right to be heard

'It must be observed here that in the present case two sets of proceedings were started by the Commission, one under [Article 101 TFEU] concerning the conduct of De Beers and Alrosa on the market in rough diamonds, and the other under [Article 102 TFEU] concerning the unilateral practices of De Beers. In those two sets of proceedings, separate statements of objections were addressed to De Beers and Alrosa. It follows that Alrosa could have had the status of 'undertaking concerned' only in the context of the proceedings brought under [Article 101 TFEU], in which no decision was taken. In that context, Alrosa could not therefore claim the procedural rights reserved to the parties to the proceedings concerning the individual commitments, since those commitments were offered by De Beers in the administrative proceedings relating to the application of [Article 102 TFEU]…' (para 88)

'As the Advocate General observes in points 176 and 177 of her Opinion, only if it transpired that the Commission without an objective reason made a single factual situation the subject of two separate sets of proceedings would Alrosa have to be accorded the rights enjoyed by an undertaking concerned in relation to the proceedings brought under [Article 102 TFEU] …' (para 89) 'That being so, it is permissible for a third-party undertaking which considers itself to be affected by a decision taken under Article 7 or Article 9 of Regulation No 1/2003 to protect its rights by bringing an action against that decision. It does not follow, however, that such an undertaking, … acquires the status of a 'party concerned' within the meaning of Article 27(2) of Regulation No 1/2003.' (para 90) 'As the Advocate General observes in point 175 of her Opinion, in the proceedings under [Article 102 TFEU] which were concluded by the contested decision, Alrosa therefore enjoyed only the less extensive rights of an interested third party.' (para 91)

In its judgment the 'General Court misinterpreted the concept of 'undertaking concerned' within the meaning of Regulation No 1/2003 by comparing the legal position of Alrosa in the proceedings relating to the individual commitments with that of De Beers and, second, the General Court based its reasoning on the incorrect proposition that the Commission was required to give reasons for rejecting the joint commitments and to suggest to Alrosa that it offer new joint commitments with De Beers.' (para 95)

Comment

The Court of Justice detached the link between Article 7 and Article 9, Regulation 1/2003, as established by the General Court. This reinstated Article 9 as a more flexible tool which enables the Commission to accept commitments which resolve the competitive concerns.

The court held that in instances which concern unilateral action (abuse of dominance), third parties which are affected by the unilateral Commitments offered by the dominant undertaking, are not to be regarded as 'undertakings concerned'. In such cases affected third parties enjoy the less extensive rights of an 'interested third party'.

Joint selling of the media rights to FA Premier League	**Public Enforcement**
COMP/C-2/38.173	Commitments
European Commission, C (2006) 868 final	Article 9, Regulation 1/2003

In June 2001 the Commission opened an investigation, under Regulation 17/62, into the arrangements surrounding the FA Premier League competition. In a statement of objection issued in December 2002, the Commission concluded that the horizontal joint-selling arrangements put in place by the football clubs in the Premier League for exploitation of media rights to Premier League matches infringed Article 101 TFEU. The Commission was concerned that the joint-selling agreement deprived media operators and British football fans of choice, led to higher prices and reduced innovation. In July 2003 the FA Premier League introduced changes to the arrangements surrounding the sale of media rights and supplemented these with a set of commitments in December 2003 which included a commitment that no single broadcaster would be allowed to buy all of the packages of live match rights from 2007 onward. These commitments were later amended and clarified following discussions with the Commission. The amended commitments provided, among other things, for more television, mobile and internet rights to be made available and ensured that these would be sold in an open and competitive bidding process subject to scrutiny by an independent Trustee. On March 2006 the FA Premier League confirmed that the commitments it submitted are to be treated as commitments under Article 9, Regulation 1/2003 (which replaced Regulation 17/62). Subsequently, the Commission adopted a decision making these commitments binding upon the FA Premier League until 30 June 2013 and finding that there are no longer grounds for action by the Commission. The Commission could impose a fine amounting to 10 per cent of the FA Premier League's total worldwide turnover if it breaks its commitments without having to prove any violation of EU competition rules. The decision does not bind National Competition Authorities or National Courts.

Coca-Cola	**Public Enforcement**
COMP/A.39.116/B2	Commitments
European Commission, [2005] OJ L253/21	Article 9, Regulation 1/2003

The commitment decision was adopted pursuant to Article 9(1) of Council Regulation 1/2003. The procedure concerned the conduct of the Coca-Cola Company and its three major bottlers in the supply of carbonated soft drinks. In a preliminary assessment, the Commission expressed concerns that practices by the undertakings, including exclusivity-related requirements, growth and target rebates, infringed Article 102 TFEU. In order to resolve these concerns the undertakings offered a range of commitments which were formally accepted by the Commission and made binding until 31 December 2010. The Commission could impose a fine amounting to 10 per cent of Coca-Cola total worldwide turnover if Coca-Cola breaks its commitments. In the commitments the undertakings agreed, among other things, to refrain from exclusivity arrangements, target or growth rebates and tying. In addition Coca-Cola committed that where it provides a free cooler to a retailer and there is no other chilled beverage capacity in the outlet to which the consumer has a direct access, it will free at least 20 per cent of the space in the cooler provided by Coca-Cola for the display and sales of competing products.

German Electricity Wholesale Market	**Public Enforcement**
COMP/39.388	Commitments
European Commission, [2009] OJ C36/8	Article 9, Regulation 1/2003

The Commission accepted commitments offered by E.ON relating to a proceeding under Article 102 TFEU. The commitments included structural changes involving the divestiture of about 5000 MW of E.ON's generation capacity on the wholesale market. In its decision the Commission noted that divested plants will help actual and potential competitors get access to new plants and to plants with technologies that they do not possess.

Musique Diffusion Française SA v Commission	**Public Enforcement**
Joined Cases 100/80 to 103/80	Fines
Court of Justice, [1983] ECR 1825, [1983] 3 CMLR 221	

'[T]he Commission's power to impose fines on undertakings which, intentionally or negligently, commit an infringement of the provisions of [Articles 101(1) or 102 TFEU] is one of the means conferred on the Commission in order to enable it to carry out the task of supervision conferred on it by [Union] law. (para 105)

'[I]n assessing the gravity of an infringement for the purpose of fixing the amount of the fine, the Commission must take into consideration not only the particular circumstances of the case but also the context in which the infringement occurs and must ensure that its action has the necessary deterrent effect, especially as regards those types of infringement which are particularly harmful to the attainment of the objectives of the [Union]. From that point of view, the Commission was right to classify as very serious infringements; prohibitions on exports and imports seeking artificially to maintain price differences between the markets of the various Member States. Such prohibitions jeopardize the freedom of intra-[Union] trade, which is a fundamental principle of the Treaty, and they prevent the attainment of one of its objectives, namely the creation of a single market.' (paras 106–7)

'It was also open to the Commission to have regard to the fact that practices of this nature, although they were established as being unlawful at the outset of [Union] competition policy, are still relatively frequent on account of the profit that certain of the undertakings concerned are able to derive from them and, consequently, it was open to the Commission to consider that it was appropriate to raise the level of fines so as to reinforce their deterrent effect. For the same reasons, the fact that the Commission, in the past, imposed fines of a certain level for certain types of infringement does not mean that it is estopped from raising that level within the limits indicated in Regulation no 17 if that is necessary to ensure the implementation of [Union] competition policy. On the contrary, the proper application of the [Union] competition rules requires that the Commission may at any time adjust the level of fines to the needs of that policy.' (paras 108–9)

Dansk Rørindustri A/S and others v Commission	**Public Enforcement**
Joined Cases C-189, 202, 205–208, 213/02P	Fines
Court of Justice, [2005] ECR I-5425, [2005] 5 CMLR 17	

'The supervisory task conferred on the Commission by [Articles 101(1) and 102 TFEU] not only includes the duty to investigate and punish individual infringements but also encompasses the duty to pursue a general policy designed to apply, in competition matters, the principles laid down by the Treaty and to guide the conduct of undertakings in the light of those principles (see *Musique Diffusion Française and others v Commission*, paragraph 105).' (para 170)

'[T]raders cannot have a legitimate expectation that an existing situation which is capable of being altered by the Commission in the exercise of its discretionary power will be maintained (Case C-350/88 *Delacre and others v Commission* [1990] ECR I-395, paragraph 33 and the case-law cited). That principle clearly applies in the field of competition policy, which is characterised by a wide discretion on the part of the Commission, in particular as regards the determination of the amount of fines.' (paras 171–2)

Opinion of AG Tizzano: '[T]he gravity of infringements has to be determined by reference to numerous factors, such as the particular circumstances of the case, its context and the dissuasive effect of fines. … Among those numerous factors for appraisal of the infringement may be included the volume and the value of the products involved in the infringement, the size and economic strength of the undertakings which committed the infringement and the influence they are able to exercise on the market, the conduct of each undertaking, the role played by each in committing the infringement, the benefit which they have obtained from such anti-competitive practices, and the economic context of the infringement, and so forth.' (paras 68–9)

YKK v Commission	**Public Enforcement**
C-408/12P	Liability of a Parent Company to a Fine
Court of Justice, [2014] 5 CMLR 26	Calculation of Fine—Corporate Group

Facts

The Commission accused several undertakings, among them YKK Stocko, of playing a role in an infringement of Article 101 TFEU between 1991 and 2001. In 1997, during the operation of the cartel, YKK Corp and YKK Holdings acquired YKK Stocko. The Commission addressed its decision to the three companies. The YKK group applied for annulment of the decision. (Case T-448/07) Action dismissed. It subsequently appealed to the Court of Justice and argued that the fine relating to the period of the infringement prior to the acquisition by YKK Holding of YKK Stocko—a period during which YKK Stocko was regarded as exclusively responsible for the infringement—was calculated on the basis of the consolidated group turnover and subsequently represents 55% of YKK Stocko's total turnover—considerably more than the 10% upper limit laid down in the second subparagraph of Article 23(2), Regulation No 1/2003.

Held

Rejection of the consolidated group turnover

Where 'an undertaking regarded by the Commission as responsible for an infringement of Article 81 EC is acquired by another undertaking within which it retains, as a subsidiary, the status of a distinct economic entity, the Commission must take account of the specific turnover of each of those economic entities in order to apply to them, where necessary, the 10% upper limit.' (para 60)

In this case, the Commission correctly divided the responsibilities of each undertaking which participated in the infringement, given that, prior to the acquisition they constituted separate economic entities. 'The Commission did not however draw from that fact the necessary conclusion as regards the application of the 10% upper limit. Consequently, the Court cannot accept the argument relied on by the Commission that there is only one and the same undertaking, its structure and financial capacity changing over time, which is at issue during the period of the infringement. Further, in this case, such a change is not the result of structural growth of the undertaking YKK Stocko, of an increase in its turnover or even the acquisition by YKK Stocko of independent undertakings during the cartel, but constitutes, on the contrary, the result of the acquisition of that undertaking by another undertaking.' (paras 61, 62)

'It must be observed, in that regard, that the objective sought by the establishment, in Article 23(2), of an upper limit of 10% of the turnover of each undertaking participating in an infringement is, inter alia, to ensure that the imposition of a fine higher in amount that that ceiling should not exceed the capacity of an undertaking to make payment at the time when it is identified as responsible for the infringement and a financial penalty is imposed on it by the Commission.' (para 63)

'[T]he Commission's argument that a single fine should have been imposed in respect of the period of the infringement cannot be accepted. As the Commission acknowledged at the hearing, as regards the part of the fine for which YKK Stocko was held to be exclusively liable, it would not be possible to enforce that part of the fine against the parent company if YKK Stocko were to default on payment. A company cannot be held to be responsible for infringements committed independently by its subsidiaries before the date of their acquisition, since the latter must themselves answer for their unlawful conduct prior to that acquisition, and the company which has acquired them cannot be held to be responsible (see the judgment in *Cascades v Commission*, C-279/98 P, ..., paragraphs 77 to 79).' (para 65)

'[I]t is clear that the findings made in paragraphs 60 to 65 of this judgment are compatible with, first, the principle of proportionality and, second, the principle of personal responsibility and the principle that penalties must be specific to the individual, as stated in the case-law of the Court.' (para 66)

The application of a deterrence multiplier

'[T]he appellants claim that the General Court erred in law by holding, in paragraph 204 of the judgment under appeal, that the Commission was entitled to take into account, in order to determine the deterrence multiplier, the size and turnover of the appellants regarded as a single economic entity in the year preceding that when the contested decision was adopted. ... It is settled case-law that the fines imposed for infringements of [Article 101 TFEU], as laid down in Article 23(2) of Regulation No 1/2003, are designed to penalise the unlawful acts of the undertakings concerned and to deter both the undertakings in question and other economic operators from infringing ... the rules of European Union competition law.' (para 84)

'Taking into consideration the size and overall resources of the undertaking in question is, primarily, justified by the impact sought on the undertaking concerned, in order to ensure that the fine has sufficient deterrent effect, as the penalty must not be negligible in the light, particularly, of its financial capacity (*Lafarge v Commission*, ..., paragraph 104).' (Para 85)

'It follows that, in order to impose a fine of an amount capable of deterring the undertakings concerned from infringing, in the future, European Union rules of competition, account must be taken of the size and overall resources of those undertakings at the time when the contested decision is adopted. Consequently, that fact that the size and overall resources of those undertakings may be smaller at an earlier stage of the infringement has no bearing on the determination of a deterrence multiplier (the judgment in *Alliance One International v Commission*, C-668/11 P..., paragraph 64).' (para 86)

'Consequently, the fact that YKK Holding and YKK Corp are not held jointly and severally liable for the infringement committed by YKK Stocko for the period prior to March 1997 has no bearing on the determination of a deterrence multiplier.' (para 87)

Comment

The Court held that a company cannot be held to be responsible for infringements committed independently by its subsidiaries before the date of their acquisition. It cited Case C-279/98P, *Cascades SA v Commission*, where the Court held that: 'It falls, in principle, to the legal or natural person managing the undertaking in question when the infringement was committed to answer for that infringement, even if, when the Decision finding the infringement was adopted, another person had assumed responsibility for operating the undertaking.' (para 78)

The Court amended the calculation of the fine imposed exclusively on YKK Stocko to represent no more than 10% of its turnover in the business year preceding the adoption of the contested decision.

In his opinion, Advocate General Wathelet noted that: '[T]he approach adopted by the Commission and the General Court in the present case runs counter to the principles of personal responsibility and the individualisation of penalties. It is clear that the Commission can order an undertaking to pay a fine only if it is in a position to prove that that undertaking committed an infringement within the meaning of [Article 101 TFEU] or participated in it. The logical and legal link between fault and liability, on the one hand, and the penalty, on the other, necessarily implies that a fine must be determined in relation to the undertaking responsible (that is to say the undertaking which participated in the infringement). ... The penalties must be individualised in the sense that they must relate to the individual conduct and specific characteristics of the undertakings concerned. Furthermore, it falls, in principle, to the legal or natural person managing the undertaking in question when the infringement was committed to answer for that infringement, even though, at the time of the decision finding the infringement, the operation of the undertaking was no longer its responsibility.' (paras 119–23, AG opinion)

As for the calculation of deterrence multiplier, the Court noted that since YKK Stocko no longer existed as an independent economic entity at the time when the contested decision was adopted, the pursuit of a deterrent effect by means of the fine had necessarily to apply to the YKK group.

Safeway Stores Ltd & Others v Twigger & Others	**Public Enforcement**
A3/2010/0675 and A3/2010/0671	Recovery of Fine
English Court of Appeal, [2010] EWCA Civ 1472	

Facts

Following an investigation by the Office of Fair Trading (OFT) into alleged cartel activity in the UK dairy sector, Safeway and other undertakings admitted their participation in the anticompetitive activity. The OFT subsequently imposed a fine on Safeway. In an attempt to recover the fine, Safeway brought proceedings for breach of contract, breach of fiduciary duties and negligence, against eleven of its former directors and employees to recover the amount of the fine and the costs incurred during the investigation. The English Court of Appeal concluded that such action will not be allowed and in doing so limited the civil liability of the former directors and employees for infringement of the competition rules.

Held

Lord Justice Longmore: 'The difficulty and novelty of the present case is that the claimant is a corporation and can only act through its human agents. If it is those human agents who have acted intentionally or negligently and have thus caused the corporation to become liable by way of penalty to the OFT, does the [*ex turpi causa maxim*] apply to preclude recovery of that penalty and its consequences from the very employees and directors whose conduct has created the corporation's liability? … At this stage it is important to recognise that the claimants' liability is not a vicarious one. They are not liable for the illegal acts of their agents or employees because … the Competition Act only imposes liability on an undertaking. … The liability to pay the penalty is thus a liability of the undertaking where it (the undertaking) has intentionally or negligently committed the infringement.' (paras 19, 20) The undertakings are personally liable to pay those penalties and it would be inconsistent with that liability for them to recover those penalties from the defendants. (para 29)

Lord Justice Lloyd: 'The central and decisive point is that it is the undertaking, the party to the agreement, decision or concerted practice which constitutes a breach of the Chapter I prohibition, that is liable to a penalty under section 36 of the 1998 Act, if the breach was committed intentionally or negligently. Only the undertaking can be so liable.' (para 36)

Lord Justice Pill: 'The claimants, as an undertaking, have breached the prohibition … of the Competition Act … and a penalty has been imposed on the basis that the infringement has been committed "intentionally or negligently by the undertaking" within the meaning of section 36 of the Act. … A penalty under section 36 was akin to a fine and that is not now disputed by the claimants. … Only the undertaking can appeal against the imposition of a penalty, or its amount, under section 46 of the 1998 Act. The defendants rely on the principle *ex turpi causa non oritur actio* to defeat the claim. I agree with Longmore LJ that the liability is personal to the claimants and that they are not entitled to pass it on to their employees.' (paras 42, 43)

Comment

The ruling is based on the distinction between undertakings' responsibility and personal liability under the competition law provisions and the individuals who are not the subject matter of these provisions. As a result, Safeway was barred from recovering the fine from its employees and directors.

It is important to note that under the laws of the Member States, individuals may be exposed to criminal sanctions when they take part in a cartel activity, or to director's disqualification orders. These sanctions directly target the individuals, and not the corporations.

The English Court of Appeal ruling resolves a possible conflict of interest between the undertaking and its employees when considering possible leniency applications. As such it safeguards the incentive of individuals to apply for leniency on behalf of the infringing undertaking.

*Trelleborg Industrie SAS v Commission (Marine Hoses_*	**Public Enforcement**
Joined cases T-147/09 and T-148/09	Limitation Periods
General Court	Single, Repeated Infringement

Facts

The Commission fined a number of companies for their participation in cartel activity in the market for marine hoses (*Marine Hoses*, Case COMP/39.406). The coordination in question lasted, with different levels of intensity, over a long period of time, from 1986 to 2007. The Commission considered it to form a single and continuous infringement of Article 101 TFEU. It noted that when there is a break in a cartel activity it is possible to view the recommencement of the activity at a later stage as part of the same single infringement: 'It would be artificial to split up such continuous conduct, characterised by a single purpose, by treating it as consisting of several separate infringements, when what was involved was a single infringement which manifested itself in a series of anti-competitive activities throughout the period of operation of the cartel. ... Even if the break were to be of a longer duration, but the participant or participants in question resumed the same cartel after the break, then it would still be possible to find that there had been a single infringement and to impose a sanction also as regards the period prior to the break, without any limitation period being applicable, pursuant to Article 25(2) of Regulation (EC) No 1/2003.' (para 283)

In its decision, the Commission made reference to the General Court judgment in Case T-279/02 *Degussa v Commission* and to two of its own decisions in which it considered 'repeated infringement'. (Case COMP/F/38.121—*Fittings*, and Case COMP/IV/30.064—*Cast Iron and Steel Rolls*)

The undertakings applied for annulment of the decision.

Held

Single, continuing infringement

According to the Court case-law, the Commission is required to prove not only the existence of a cartel but also its duration. It is accordingly necessary for the Commission to produce sufficiently precise and consistent evidence to support the firm conviction that the alleged infringement took place. However, it is not necessary for every item of evidence produced by the Commission to satisfy those criteria in relation to every aspect of the infringement. It is sufficient if the body of evidence relied on by the institution, viewed as a whole, meets that requirement. In this case, the Commission considered the infringement to be continuous, despite its view that the cartel was less active during the intermediate period. (paras 40–55)

'As regards the lack of evidence that there was an agreement during certain specific periods or, at least, the lack of evidence of its implementation by an undertaking during a given period, it should be recalled that the fact that evidence of the infringement has not been produced in relation to certain specific periods does not preclude the infringement from being regarded as established during a longer overall period than those periods, provided that such a finding is supported by objective and consistent indicia. In the context of an infringement extending over a number of years, the fact that a cartel is shown to have applied during different periods, which may be separated by longer or shorter periods, has no effect on the existence of the cartel, provided that the various actions which form part of the infringement pursue a single purpose and fall within the framework of a single and continuous infringement.' (para 59)

'The case-law therefore permits the Commission to assume that the infringement—or the participation of an undertaking in the infringement—has not been interrupted, even if it has no evidence of the infringement in relation to certain specific periods, provided that the various actions which form part of the infringement pursue a single purpose and are capable of falling within the framework of a single and continuous infringement; such a finding must be supported by objective and consistent indicia showing that an overall plan exists.' (para 61)

In this case, however, 'the Commission does not have any proof that the applicants were involved in multilateral contacts during that intermediate period, which lasted for more than two years, or that they took part in meetings which took place with the aim of re-starting the cartel, or even that they were aware of them. Accordingly, the applicants' argument that they in fact interrupted their participation appears to be sufficiently substantiated and plausible to rebut the presumption, referred to in paragraph 61 above, that they continued, even if passively, to participate in the infringement.' (paras 66–7)

Single, repeated infringement

As the infringement in this case cannot be categorised as continuing, one should consider whether it may be regarded as repeated. 'If the participation of an undertaking in the infringement may be regarded as having been interrupted and the undertaking may be regarded as having participated in the infringement prior to and after that interruption, that infringement may be categorised as repeated if … there is a single objective which it pursued both before and after the interruption, a circumstance which may be deduced from the identical nature of the objectives of the practices at issue, of the goods concerned, of the undertakings which participated in the collusion, of the main rules for its implementation, of the natural persons involved on behalf of the undertakings and, lastly, of the geographical scope of those practices. The infringement is then single and repeated and, although the Commission may impose a fine in respect of the whole of the period of the infringement, it may not do so for the period during which the infringement was interrupted.' (paras 86–8)

In the present case, applicants have admitted that they participated in an infringement prior to and after the intermediate period and did 'not dispute the identical nature of the objectives of the practices at issue, of the goods concerned, of the undertakings which participated in collusion, of the main rules for its implementation, of the natural persons involved on behalf of the undertakings and, lastly, of the geographical scope of those practices prior to May 1997 and after June 1999.' The Court must therefore hold that Trelleborg Industrie committed a single, repeated infringement from April 1986 to 13 May 1997 and from 21 June 1999 to May 2007 and that Trelleborg committed a single, repeated infringement from 28 March 1996 to 13 May 1997 and from 21 June 1999 to May 2007.' Accordingly, the period of infringement prior to 13 May 1997 is not time-barred. (paras 91–5)

Comment

The Court held that the infringement in this case cannot be categorised as continuing but can be categorised as repeated. Subsequently, the period of the early infringement was not time-barred. The Court subsequently held that there was no need to reduce the fine which was imposed by the Commission on the applicants.

Separate periods of infringement in which the same undertaking takes part, but in respect of which a common objective cannot be established, will not be categorised as a single infringement—continuing or repeated—and would constitute separate infringements. (para 89)

Article 25(2) of Regulation 1/2003 stipulates that in the calculation of limitation periods for the imposition of penalties 'time shall begin to run on the day on which the infringement is committed. However, in the case of continuing or repeated infringements, time shall begin to run on the day on which the infringement ceases.'

In Case T-279/02 *Degussa v Commission* [2006] ECR II-897, in which the General Court noted with respect to suspension of a cartel that 'Suspension of a cartel can be acknowledged only where it is established that a given infringement, although single and continuous, was disrupted for a brief period in such a way as to preclude inclusion of that period in the calculation of the total duration of the infringement, assuming, of course, that the cartel was then resumed fully. That method thus serves to reconcile the concept of a single continuous infringement with the requirements arising from the need for precise determination of the duration of the infringement and, therefore, in so far as the calculation of the amount of the fine depends inter alia on the latter criterion, from the principle of proportionality of the fine.' (para 178)

Remia BV and others v Commission	**Judicial Review**
Case 42/84	Complex Economic Analysis
Court of Justice, [1985] ECR 2545	

'Although as a general rule the court undertakes a comprehensive review of the question whether or not the conditions for the application of [Article 101(1) TFEU] are met, it is clear that in determining the permissible duration of a non-competition clause incorporated in an agreement for the transfer of an undertaking the commission has to appraise complex economic matters. the court must therefore limit its review of such an appraisal to verifying whether the relevant procedural rules have been complied with, whether the statement of the reasons for the decision is adequate, whether the facts have been accurately stated and whether there has been any manifest error of appraisal or a misuse of powers.' (para 34)

John Deere v Commission	**Judicial Review**
Case C-7/95P	Complex Economic Analysis
Court of Justice, [1998] ECR I-3111	

'[I]t is appropriate to recall the case-law of the Court of Justice (see, in particular, Case 42/84 *Remia and Others v Commission* [1985] ECR 2545, paragraph 34, and Joined Cases 142/84 and 156/84 *BAT and Reynolds v Commission* [1987] ECR 4487, paragraph 62) according to which, although as a general rule the [Union] judicature undertakes a comprehensive review of the question whether or not the conditions for the application of [Article 105(1) TFEU] are met, its review of complex economic appraisals made by the Commission is necessarily limited to verifying whether the relevant rules on procedure and on the statement of reasons have been complied with, whether the facts have been accurately stated and whether there has been any manifest error of appraisal or a misuse of powers.' (para 34)

Microsoft Corp v Commission	**Judicial Review**
Case T-201/04	Complex Technical Appraisals
General Court, [2007] ECR II-1491	

'The Court observes that it follows from consistent case-law that, although as a general rule the [Union] Courts undertake a comprehensive review of the question as to whether or not the conditions for the application of the competition rules are met, their review of complex economic appraisals made by the Commission is necessarily limited to checking whether the relevant rules on procedure and on stating reasons have been complied with, whether the facts have been accurately stated and whether there has been any manifest error of assessment or a misuse of powers (Case T-65/96 *Kish Glass v Commission* [2000] ECR II-1885, paragraph 64, upheld on appeal by order of the Court of Justice in Case C-241/00 P *Kish Glass v Commission* [2001] ECR I-7759; see also, to that effect, with respect to [Article 101 TFEU], Case 42/84 *Remia and Others v Commission* [1985] ECR 2545, paragraph 34, and Joined Cases 142/84 and 156/84 *BAT and Reynolds v Commission* [1987] ECR 4487, paragraph 62).' (para 87)

'Likewise, in so far as the Commission's decision is the result of complex technical appraisals, those appraisals are in principle subject to only limited review by the Court, which means that the [Union] Courts cannot substitute their own assessment of matters of fact for the Commission's (see, as regards a decision adopted following complex appraisals in the medico-pharmacological sphere, order of the President of the Court of Justice in Case C-459/00 P(R) *Commission v Trenker* [2001] ECR I-2823, paragraphs 82 and 83; see also, to that effect, Case C-120/97 *Upjohn* [1999] ECR I-223, paragraph 34 and the case-law cited; Case T-179/00 *A Menarini v Commission* [2002] ECR II-2879, paragraphs 44 and 45; and Case T-13/99 *Pfizer Animal Health v Council* [2002] ECR II-3305, paragraph 323).' (para 88)

KME Germany AG v Commission
Case C-272/09P
Court of Justice, [2012] OJ C32/4

Judicial Review
Full and Effective Judicial Review
EU Charter of Fundamental Rights

Facts

KME Germany AG appealed the judgment of the General Court in Case T-127/04 *KME Germany and Others v Commission* by which the General Court dismissed its application for reduction of fine or annulment of a Commission Decision in which it was found to infringe Article 101 TFEU. Among other things, KME argued that the General Court infringed its fundamental right to a full and effective judicial review by failing to examine thoroughly its arguments and by excessively deferring to the Commission's discretion.

Held

'The principle of effective judicial protection is a general principle of European Union law to which expression is now given by Article 47 of the [Charter of Fundamental Rights of the European Union]. (para 92)

'[T]he Court of Justice has held that whilst, in areas giving rise to complex economic assessments, the Commission has a margin of discretion with regard to economic matters, that does not mean that the Courts of the European Union must refrain from reviewing the Commission's interpretation of information of an economic nature. Not only must those Courts establish, among other things, whether the evidence relied on is factually accurate, reliable and consistent but also whether that evidence contains all the information which must be taken into account in order to assess a complex situation and whether it is capable of substantiating the conclusions drawn from it (see Case C-12/03P *Commission v Tetra Laval* [2005] ECR I-987, paragraph 39, and Case C-525/04P *Spain v Lenzing* [2007] ECR I-9947, paragraphs 56 and 57).' (para 94)

'[T]he Courts must carry out the review of legality incumbent upon them on the basis of the evidence adduced by the applicant in support of the pleas in law put forward. In carrying out such a review, the Courts cannot use the Commission's margin of discretion—either as regards the choice of factors taken into account in the application of the criteria mentioned in the Guidelines or as regards the assessment of those factors—as a basis for dispensing with the conduct of an in-depth review of the law and of the facts. The review of legality is supplemented by the unlimited jurisdiction which the Courts of the European Union were afforded by Article 17 of Regulation No 17 and which is now recognised by Article 31 of Regulation No 1/2003, in accordance with Article 261 TFEU. That jurisdiction empowers the Courts, in addition to carrying out a mere review of the lawfulness of the penalty, to substitute their own appraisal for the Commission's and, consequently, to cancel, reduce or increase the fine or penalty payment imposed (… C-238/99P … *Limburgse Vinyl Maatschappij and Others v Commission*, paragraph 692).' (paras 102, 103)

'The review provided for by the Treaties thus involves review by the Courts of the European Union of both the law and the facts, and means that they have the power to assess the evidence, to annul the contested decision and to alter the amount of a fine. The review of legality provided for under Article 263 TFEU, supplemented by the unlimited jurisdiction in respect of the amount of the fine, provided for under Article 31 of Regulation No 1/2003, is not therefore contrary to the requirements of the principle of effective judicial protection in Article 47 of the [Charter of Fundamental Rights of the European Union].' (para 106)

'[A]lthough the General Court repeatedly referred to the 'discretion', the 'substantial margin of discretion' or the 'wide discretion' of the Commission … such references did not prevent the General Court from carrying out the full and unrestricted review, in law and in fact, required of it.' (para 109)

Comment

The judgment confirms the requirement for a full review in competition cases. The principle of effective judicial review precludes the Court from relying on the Commission's margin of discretion as a basis for dispensing with the need for an in-depth review of the law and facts. This ruling sends a clear signal which is likely to affect the extent and depth of future judicial reviews of Commission's decisions. For a similar ruling see the Court of Justice judgment in Case C-386/10P *Chalkor AE Epexergasias Metallon v Commission*.

Article 47 of the Charter of Fundamental Rights of the European Union (the Charter), referred to by the Court of Justice in paras 92 and 106, confirms the right to an effective judicial protection, [2000] OJ C364/1. The second paragraph of Article 47 corresponds to Article 6(1) of the European Convention of Human Rights (ECHR) which stipulates that: 'In the determination of his civil rights and obligations or of any criminal charge against him, everyone is entitled to a fair and public hearing.'

In her opinion AG Sharpston noted: 'I have little difficulty in concluding that the procedure whereby a fine is imposed for breach of the prohibition on price-fixing and market-sharing agreements in [Article 101(1) TFEU] falls under the "criminal head" of Article 6 ECHR as progressively defined by the European Court of Human Rights. The prohibition and the possibility of imposing a fine are enshrined in primary and secondary legislation of general application; the offence involves engaging in conduct which is generally regarded as underhand, to the detriment of the public at large, a feature which it shares with criminal offences in general and which entails a clear stigma; a fine of up to 10% of annual turnover is undoubtedly severe, and may even put an undertaking out of business; and the intention is explicitly to punish and deter, with no element of compensation for damage. ... If the fining procedure in the present case thus falls within the criminal sphere for the purposes of the ECHR (and the Charter), I would none the less agree that, in the words of the judgment in *Jussila*, it "differ[s] from the hard core of criminal law; consequently, the criminal-head guarantees will not necessarily apply with their full stringency". That implies, in particular, that it may be compatible with Article 6(1) ECHR for criminal penalties to be imposed, in the first instance, not by an "independent and impartial tribunal established by law" but by an administrative or non-judicial body which does not itself comply with the requirements of that provision, provided that the decision of that body is subject to subsequent control by a judicial body that has full jurisdiction and does comply with those requirements. Put another way, it must be clear that the available forms of appeal make it possible to remedy any deficiencies in the proceedings at first instance. ...The issue is whether the General Court exercised "full jurisdiction" within the meaning of the case-law of the European Court of Human Rights. ... That Court has described "full jurisdiction" in that sense as including "the power to quash in all respects, on questions of fact and law, the decision of the body below". A judicial body charged with review "must in particular have jurisdiction to examine all questions of fact and law relevant to the dispute before it". The same Court has also held that, in order to determine whether a second-tier tribunal has "full jurisdiction", or provides "sufficiency of review" to remedy a lack of independence at first instance, it is necessary to have regard to such factors as "the subject-matter of the decision appealed against, the manner in which that decision was arrived at and the content of the dispute, including the desired and actual grounds of appeal". ... It seems to me that there can be little doubt that the "unlimited jurisdiction" conferred upon the General Court. ... meets those requirements as regards appeals against the amount of the fine imposed, even if it is, as the Commission submits, a different concept from the "full jurisdiction" criterion of the European Court of Human Rights, which must be taken to cover also appeals against, for example, the actual finding of an infringement. ... Here, however, we are concerned solely with an appeal against the amount of a fine, and I do not propose to extend my analysis any further.' (paras 64–70)

In *Affaire a Menarini Diagnostics srl c Italie* (Requête no 43509/08), the European Court of Human Rights confirmed the criminal character of EU competition law fines and that the administrative enforcement by the competition agency is subjected to full jurisdiction of the review court. On the facts of the case, the European Court of Human Rights rejected the claim that in this case there was not effective judicial review of the decision of the Italian Competition Autority, as the Italian appeal court could review all the relevant facts and amend the fine imposed. On one hand the judgment subjects the competition proceedings to the European Court of Human Rights and as such requires a full jurisdiction of the review court over the decision of the Competition Agency. At EU level, such an approach may call into question the EU Court's reluctance to examine complex technical and economic matters (see page 578 above). On the other hand, the European Court of Human Rights held that the requirement for effective judicial review was satisfied in this case although under Italian law the Italian court could not have replaced the judgment of the competition agency with its own. In practice, this conclusion, on the facts of the case, seems to lower the European Court of Human Rights benchmark for establishing effective review.

BASF AG v Commission	**Public Enforcement**
Joined Cases T-101/05 and T-111/05	Fines
General Court, [2007] ECR II-4949	Leniency

Facts

An appeal on Commission decision in case COMP/E-2/37.533—*Choline chloride*, in which the Commission found a number of undertakings to have infringed Article 101 TFEU by engaging, among other things, in price-fixing and market-sharing agreements. On appeal the parties challenged the level of fines imposed by the Commission, and the weight attributed to aggravating and mitigating factors.

Held

'It must be borne in mind that the object of the penalties laid down in Article 15 of Regulation No 17 and Article 23 of Regulation No 1/2003 is to suppress illegal activities and to prevent any recurrence. Deterrence is therefore one objective of the fine (Case T-15/02 *BASF v Commission* [2006] ECR II-497, '*Vitamins*', paragraphs 218 and 219).' (para 43)

'Furthermore, the deterrence of fines is one of the factors by reference to which the gravity of infringements must be determined (Case C-219/95P *Ferrière Nord v Commission* [1997] ECR I-4411, paragraph 33).' (para 45)

'As regards the stage at which the need to apply a weighting in order to ensure the deterrence of the fine must be assessed, it is sufficient to observe that the requirements of deterrence must underpin the entire process of setting the amount of the fine and not just a single stage in that process (*Vitamins*, paragraph 43 above, paragraph 238).' (para 48)

The adoption of a compliance programme by the undertaking, in order to prevent repeated infringement, does not oblige the Commission to grant a reduction in the fine on that account. (para 52)

'The Court rejects at the outset BASF's argument that a case of repeated infringement can be recognised only where the infringements relate to the same product market. It is sufficient that the Commission is dealing with infringements falling under the same provision of the [TFEU].' (para 64)

'Next, it should be observed that Article 15(2) of Regulation No 17 and Article 23(2) of Regulation No 1/2003 are the relevant legal bases on which the Commission may impose fines on undertakings and associations of undertakings for infringements of [Articles 101 and 102 TFEU]. Under those provisions, in order to determine the amount of the fine, the duration and gravity of the infringement must be taken into consideration. The gravity of the infringement is determined by reference to numerous factors, for which the Commission has a margin of discretion. The fact that aggravating circumstances are taken into account in setting the fine is consistent with the Commission's task of ensuring compliance with the competition rules (Case C-3/06 *Groupe Danone v Commission* [2007] ECR I-1331, paragraphs 24 and 25).' (para 65)

'Furthermore, the analysis of the gravity of the infringement must take any repeated infringement into account (Joined Cases C-204/00P, C-205/00P, C-211/00P, C-213/00P, C-217/00P and C-219/00P *Aalborg Portland and Others v Commission* [2004] ECR I-123, paragraph 91, and *Groupe Danone v Commission*, paragraph 65 above, paragraph 26), and such repeated infringement may justify a significant increase in the basic amount of the fine (Case T-203/01 *Michelin v Commission* [2003] ECR II-4071, paragraph 293). In the light of that case-law, the Court rejects BASF's assertions, first, that its previous infringements have no influence on the gravity of the infringement in question and, second, that there is no clear legal basis for the application of an increase for repeated infringement.' (para 66)

'As regards the objection that a time-limit must be placed on the possibility to take any repeated infringement into account, the Court finds that the fact that Regulation No 17, Regulation No. 1/2003 and the Guidelines lay down no maximum period for making a finding of repeated infringement does not breach the principle of legal certainty. The finding and the appraisal of the specific features of a repeated infringement come within the Commission's discretion in relation to the choice of factors to be taken into consideration for the purpose of determining the amount of fines. In that connection, the Commission cannot be bound by any limitation period for such a finding. In that regard, it must be borne in mind that repeated infringement is an important factor which the Commission is required to appraise, since taking repeated infringement into account is intended to provide undertakings which have shown a propensity to breach the competition rules with an incentive to change their conduct. The Commission may therefore, in each case, take into consideration the indicia which tend to confirm such a propensity, including, for example, the time which has elapsed between the infringements at issue (*Groupe Danone v Commission*, paragraph 65 above, paragraphs 37 to 39).' (para 67)

In this case account must be taken of the fact that BASF was in flagrant breach of the competition rules for approximately 13 years. It follows that the increase of the basic amount by 50 per cent due to repeated infringement is appropriate. (paras 68–72)

Section D, paragraph 2, of the 1996 Leniency Notice clearly states that the Commission has a discretion as to the reductions to be granted under that notice (Joined Cases C-189/02P, C-202/02P, C-205/02P to C-208/02P and C-213/02P *Dansk Rørindustri and Others v Commission* [2005] ECR I-5425, paragraph 394). (para 91)

'Furthermore, a reduction based on the 1996 Leniency Notice can be justified only where the information provided and, more generally, the conduct of the undertaking concerned might be considered to demonstrate genuine cooperation on its part. It is clear from the very concept of cooperation, as described in the wording of the 1996 Leniency Notice, and in particular in the introduction and at Section D, point 1, of that notice, that it is only where the conduct of the undertaking concerned shows such a spirit of cooperation that a reduction may be granted on the basis of that notice (*Dansk Rørindustri and Others v Commission*, paragraph 91 above, paragraphs 395 and 396). The conduct of an undertaking which, even though it was not required to respond to a question put by the Commission, responded in an incomplete and misleading way cannot therefore be considered to reflect such a spirit of cooperation (see, to that effect, Case C-301/04P *Commission v SGL Carbon* [2006] ECR I-5915, paragraph 69).' (para 92)

It must be borne in mind that BASF did not disclose information as to the existence of the anticompetitive agreements prior to receiving the statement of objections from the Commission. 'It was only after receiving the statement of objections that, by not substantially contesting the facts, BASF acknowledged the existence of a cartel at European level. The information in question was therefore at the very least incomplete, since it failed to mention a very significant part of the collusive action.' (para 116)

'The Commission therefore did not err in assessing the value of BASF's cooperation and granting it a reduction of 20% of the fine that would otherwise have been imposed on it.' (para 120)

Comment

The Leniency Notice sets out the framework for rewarding cooperation in the Commission investigation by undertakings which are or have been party to a cartel agreement. The first generation of Leniency Notice referred to in this case was later amended in year 2002 and in year 2006. For the 2006 leniency notice, see: Commission Notice on Immunity from fines and reduction of fines in cartel cases, [2006] OJ C298/17.

Under the Leniency Notice, the Commission will grant immunity from fines 'which would otherwise have been imposed to an undertaking disclosing its participation in an alleged cartel affecting the [Union] if that undertaking is the first to submit information and evidence which in the Commission's view will enable it to: (a) carry out a targeted inspection in connection with the alleged cartel; or (b) find an infringement of [Article 101 TFEU] in connection with the alleged cartel.' (point 8)

'An undertaking which took steps to coerce other undertakings to join the cartel or to remain in it is not eligible for immunity from fines. It may still qualify for a reduction of fines if it fulfils the relevant requirements.' (point 13)

Bundeswettbewerbsbehörde and Bundeskartellanwalt v Schenker	**Public Enforcement**
Case C-681/11	Fines, National Leniency
Court of Justice, [2013] 5 CMLR 25	Negligent Infringement

Facts

A preliminary reference from the Federal Supreme Court of Austria, made in proceedings between the Austrian Federal Competition Authority and Federal Cartel Lawyer and 31 undertakings. The National Court referred two questions to the Court of Justice. First, whether an undertaking may escape imposition of a fine, where an infringement of Article 101 TFEU was negligent and unintentional. Second, whether the competition authority may refrain from imposing a fine on an undertaking which infringed Article 101 TFEU but has participated in a national leniency programme.

Held

Negligent infringement: 'Under Article 23(2) of Regulation No 1/2003, the Commission may by decision impose fines on undertakings and associations of undertakings where, "either intentionally or negligently", they infringe Article 101 TFEU or 102 TFEU.' Article 5, Regulation 1/2003, which defines the powers of the competition authorities of the Member States, does not address the conditions relating to intention or negligence. 'However, if, in the general interest of uniform application of Articles 101 TFEU and 102 TFEU in the European Union, the Member States establish conditions relating to intention or negligence in the context of application of Article 5 of Regulation No 1/2003, those conditions should be at least as stringent as the condition laid down in Article 23 of Regulation No 1/2003 so as not to jeopardise the effectiveness of European Union law.' (paras 34–6)

An infringement of competition provisions has been committed 'where the undertaking concerned cannot be unaware of the anti-competitive nature of its conduct, whether or not it is aware that it is infringing the competition rules of the Treaty.' (para 37)

'Article 101 TFEU must be interpreted as meaning that an undertaking which has infringed that provision may not escape imposition of a fine where the infringement has resulted from that undertaking erring as to the lawfulness of its conduct on account of the terms of legal advice given by a lawyer or of the terms of a decision of a national competition authority.' (para 43)

Non-imposition of a fine: 'A decision not to impose a fine can be made under a national leniency programme only in so far as the programme is implemented in such a way as not to undermine the requirement of effective and uniform application of Article 101 TFEU. (para 47)

In the case of the European Commission's power to reduce fines under its own leniency programme, that power is justified when the undertaking's cooperation makes it easier for the Commission to carry out its task of finding an infringement. An immunity from fine can be accorded only in strictly exceptional situations, such as where an undertaking's cooperation has been decisive in detecting and actually suppressing the cartel. Accordingly, 'in the event that the existence of an infringement of Article 101 TFEU is established, the national competition authorities may by way of exception confine themselves to finding that infringement without imposing a fine where the undertaking concerned has participated in a national leniency programme.' (paras 48–50)

Comment

In paragraph 36, the Court commented on the need to unify the Union and Member States' approach to fines and reduction of fines, so as not to jeopardise the effectiveness of European Union law. The Court also commented on the exceptional circumstances, which would justify reduction or immunity from fine at Member State and Union levels.

Pfleiderer AG v Bundeskartellamt	**Public Enforcement**
Case C-360/09	Leniency
Court of Justice, [2011] 5 CMLR 7	Access to Leniency Documents

Facts

In proceedings between Pfleiderer AG and the German Competition Authority at the National Court, Pfleiderer requested the Court to order the Bundeskartellamt to allow it access to leniency documents of another company, in order to prepare a civil action for damages against that company. In a reference for a preliminary ruling the Court of Justice considered whether such access ought to be granted.

Held

European Treaties and laws do not lay down common rules on leniency or the right of access to documents relating to leniency documents. The Commission leniency notice concerning cooperation within the network of competition authorities is not binding on Member States. Accordingly, it is for Member States to establish and apply national rules on the right of access, by persons adversely affected by a cartel, to documents relating to leniency procedures. Such national rules need to be established in accordance with EU law and should not jeopardise the effective application of Articles 101 TFEU and 102 TFEU. In this respect, the effectiveness of leniency programmes could be compromised if confidential documents were disclosed to persons wishing to bring an action for damages, even if the national competition authorities were to grant to the applicant for leniency exemption from the fine which they would have imposed. Such access will curtail the incentive of a party involved in an infringement of competition law, to take the opportunity offered by such leniency programmes. (paras 20–7)

'Nevertheless, ... any individual has the right to claim damages for loss caused to him by conduct which is liable to restrict or distort competition. ... The existence of such a right strengthens the working of the Community competition rules. ... From that point of view, actions for damages before national courts can make a significant contribution to the maintenance of effective competition in the European Union ... Accordingly, in the consideration of an application for access to documents relating to a leniency programme submitted by a person who is seeking to obtain damages from another person who has taken advantage of such a leniency programme, it is necessary to ensure that the applicable national rules are not less favourable than those governing similar domestic claims and that they do not operate in such a way as to make it practically impossible or excessively difficult to obtain such compensation ... and to weigh the respective interests in favour of disclosure of the information and in favour of the protection of that information provided voluntarily by the applicant for leniency. ... That weighing exercise can be conducted by the national courts and tribunals only on a case-by-case basis, according to national law, and taking into account all the relevant factors in the case. ... The provisions of European Union law on cartels, and in particular Regulation No 1/2003, must be interpreted as not precluding a person who has been adversely affected by a [competition law infringement] and is seeking to obtain damages from being granted access to documents relating to a leniency procedure involving the perpetrator of that infringement.' (paras 28–32)

Comment

The Court of Justice held that EU law does not preclude access to leniency documents by an injured party. Despite the risk for effective leniency procedure, the Court did not distinguish between the right to access self-incriminating statements and the right to view other documentation. It held that it is for the National Court to balance between the interests at stake, on a case-by-case basis. The German Court subsequently refused access to the leniency documents to safeguard the effectiveness of cartel detection.

In his opinion, Advocate General Mazák took the view that in order to ensure the effectiveness of leniency programmes, access to voluntary self-incriminating statements made by a leniency applicant should not, in principle, be granted. This view is supported by the 2014 'Directive on Rules Governing Actions for Damages' which confirms in Article 6(6) that leniency statements shall not be disclosed. (see discussion on page 524 above)

Bundeswettbewerbsbehörde v Donau Chemie AG	Public Enforcement
Case C-536/11	Leniency
Court of Justice, [2013] 4 CMLR 19	Access to Leniency Documents

Facts

A request for a preliminary ruling from the Higher Regional Court, Vienna, concerning access to the files of the Cartel Court. The question concerned the legality of a national provision, which required the consent of all parties to the Cartel Court proceedings in order to grant third-party-prospective-damage-claimants access to documents before the Cartel Court.

Held

When considering right of access by third-party-prospective-damage-claimants, the national courts must weigh up the respective interests in favour of disclosure of the information and in favour of the protection of that information (*Pfleiderer*). That weighing-up of the interests justifying disclosure of information and the protection of that information is necessary to ensure the effective application of, inter alia, Article 101 TFEU and the rights that provision confers on individuals. (paras 30–4)

'National law must preclude the possibility for the national courts to conduct that weighing-up on a case-by-case basis.' A national law which stipulates that access to the competition court file is granted only if none of the parties to the proceedings object, undermines the National Court's ability to weigh up (1) the interests of the requesting party in obtaining access to those documents in order to prepare its action for damages, in particular in the light of other possibilities it may have; and (2) the actual harmful consequences which may result from such access, having regard to public interests, the interest of having effective leniency programmes or the legitimate interests of other parties. 'It is only if there is a risk that a given document may actually undermine the public interest relating to the effectiveness of the national leniency programme that non-disclosure of that document may be justified.' (paras 35–48)

Comment

The Court held that EU law precludes a provision of national law which conditioned access to documents concerning the application of Article 101 TFEU and to leniency documents, on the consent of all the parties to those proceedings, without leaving any possibility for the national courts to weigh up the interests involved. Note on this point the provisions of the 2014 'Directive on Rules Governing Actions for Damages' which restricts disclosure of leniency statements and settlement submissions. (see discussion on page 524 above)

In *National Grid v ABB and others* the English High Court considered an application for disclosure of leniency documents submitted to the European Commission. The request formed part of a follow-on damages claim brought by National Grid against members of the Gas Insulated Switchgear cartel. Mr Justice Roth reviewed the documents in question and ordered partial disclosure. (Case No HC08C03243 [2012] EWHC 869(Ch)) Contrast that judgment with the German Court's holding in *Pfleiderer* (page 584 above) which held that the threat to effective detection of cartel activity, through the use of the leniency programme justifies the refusal of access to the leniency documents.

In Case C-365/12P *Commission v EnBW Energie Baden-Württemberg AG* (27 February 2014) the Court of Justice denied a request for direct access to a group of documents held by the Commission. The Court established a rebuttable presumption and held that: 'for the purposes of the application of the exceptions provided for in the first and third indents of Article 4(2) of Regulation No 1049/2001, the Commission is entitled to presume, without carrying out a specific, individual examination of each of the documents in a file relating to a proceeding under [Article 101 TFEU], that disclosure of such documents will, in principle, undermine the protection of the commercial interests of the undertakings involved in such a proceeding and the protection of the purpose of the investigations relating to the proceeding …' (para 93). Contrast the use of assumption with the case-by-case approach in C-360/09 and C-536/1.

Kingdom of Sweden v MyTravel and Commission	**Public Enforcement**
Case C-506/08P	Access to Documents
Court of Justice, [2011] 5 CMLR 18	Regulation No 1049/2001

Facts

An appeal on the General Court's judgment in case T-403/05 *MyTravel v Commission* in which the Court partially rejected MyTravel's request for access to certain internal documents of the Commission which were prepared as part of the Commission's internal consultation following the General Court decision in Case T-342/99 *Airtours v Commission*. The internal documents assessed the desirability of the Commission appealing against that judgment and the implications of that judgment for future application of the European Merger Regulation. On appeal the Court of Justice considered the provisions of Regulation 1049/2001 on Access to Documents (The Regulation) and whether the Commission correctly refused access.

Held

The Regulation is intended to give the fullest possible effect to the right of public access to documents of the European institutions. That right is none the less subject to certain limitations based on grounds of public or private interest. More specifically, Article 4 of the Regulation provides that the institutions are to refuse access to a document where its disclosure would undermine the protection of one of the interests protected by that provision. Those exceptions must be interpreted and applied strictly. (paras 72–5)

With the aim of protecting the decision making of the institutions, the Regulation distinguishes between documents relating to closed or open procedures. Once a decision is adopted, the requirements for protecting the decision-making process are less acute and the exception covers only documents containing opinions for internal use as part of deliberations and preliminary consultations within the institution concerned. After the decision has been taken, Article 4(3) allows access to these documents to be refused where their disclosure would seriously undermine the decision-making process. (paras 78–82)

It is necessary to verify whether the General Court correctly applied Article 4(3) in respect of each of the documents to which MyTravel had been refused access to. It should be stressed that the administrative activity of the institutions including the Commission does not escape in any way from the scope of Regulation 1049/2001. The Regulation applies to all documents held by an institution, that is to say drawn up or received by it and in its possession, in all areas of Union activity. The General Court should have required the Commission to indicate the specific reasons why the refusal of access to the report was justified. Having failed to do so, the Court erred in law by holding that the Commission could refuse access to the whole of the report. (paras 84–90)

With regard to the remaining documents, the General Court did not make an error of law in holding that the Hearing Officer's report, the note from DG Competition to the Advisory Committee and a file note constituted opinions for internal use as part of deliberations and preliminary consultations within the Commission, within the meaning of the second subparagraph of Article 4(3) of the Regulation. However, the General Court erred when it concluded that disclosure of the three documents would have seriously undermined the Commission's decision-making process. The General Court did not adequately verify whether the Commission had supplied specific reasons why disclosure would have seriously undermined the decision-making process even though the administrative procedure to which those documents related had been closed. The General Court also erred when it held that the Commission rightly refused access to some of its notes on the basis of the exception for protecting legal advice, without first carrying out an examination of the content of those notes. (paras 91–103)

Comment

The Regulation applies to all documents held by an institution. It is for the Commission to justify why information should not be disclosed and may adversely affect its decision-making process. Note the provisions of the 2014 'Directive on Rules Governing Actions for Damages' (see discussion on page 524 above).

CDC Hydrogen Peroxide v Commission	**Public Enforcement**
T-437/08	Access to Documents
General Court, [2012] 4 CMLR 14	Regulation No 1049/2001

Facts

CDC Hydrogen Peroxide Cartel Damage Claims was a company incorporated to bring damage claims on behalf of several undertakings injured by cartel activity which was brought to an end by the Commission in its decision in case COMP/F/C.38.620—Hydrogen peroxide and perborate. To facilitate the damage claims, CDC Hydrogen Peroxide sought from the Commission full access to the statement of contents of the case file. The Commission rejected the application for access on the ground that disclosure of the statement of contents undermines protection of the purpose of the investigation activities referred to in the third indent of Article 4(2) of Regulation No 1049/2001, undermines protection of the commercial interests of the undertakings which took part in the cartel, provided for in the first indent of Article 4(2) of Regulation No 1049/2001, and undermines the institution's decision-making process, referred to in the second subparagraph of Article 4(3) of Regulation No 1049/2001. CDC Hydrogen Peroxide applied to the General Court.

Held

'It must be recalled that according to the fourth recital and Article 1 thereof, the purpose of Regulation No 1049/2001 is to give the public the fullest possible right of access to documents held by the institutions. The second recital of that regulation notes that that right of access is part of the democratic nature of the institutions. However, that right is none the less subject to certain limitations based on grounds of public or private interest. ... More specifically, and in reflection of recital 11 in the preamble thereto, Article 4 of Regulation No 1049/2001 provides that the institutions are to refuse access to a document where its disclosure would undermine the protection of one of the interests protected by that provision. Thus, if the Commission decides to refuse access to a document which it has been asked to disclose, it must, in principle, explain how disclosure of that document could specifically and effectively undermine the interest protected by the exception provided for in Article 4 of Regulation No 1049/2001 upon which it is relying.' (paras 32–5)

'Since they derogate from the principle of the widest possible public access to documents, the exceptions laid down in Article 4 of Regulation No 1049/2001 must be interpreted and applied strictly (*Sison v Council*, paragraph 33 above, paragraph 63; Case C-64/05P *Sweden v Commission* [2007] ECR I-11389, paragraph 66; and *Sweden and Turco v Council*, paragraph 35 above, paragraph 36).' (para 36)

'The statement of contents is a mere inventory of documents which, in itself, has only a very relative probative value in the context of an action for damages brought against the companies in question. Although it is true that that inventory could allow the applicant to identify the documents which could be useful to it for the purposes of such an action, it is none the less also true that the decision to order production of those documents, or not, is for the court having jurisdiction over that action. It cannot therefore be argued that disclosure of the statement of contents would, as such, affect the interests relied on by the Commission to justify its negative decision.' (para 48)

'In addition, even if the fact that actions for damages were brought against a company could undoubtedly cause high costs to be incurred, even if only in terms of legal costs, and even if the actions were subsequently dismissed as unfounded, the fact remains that the interest of a company which took part in a cartel in avoiding such actions cannot be regarded as a commercial interest and, in any event, does not constitute an interest deserving of protection, having regard, in particular, to the fact that any individual has the right to claim damages for loss caused to him by conduct which is liable to restrict or distort competition (Case C-453/99 *Courage and Crehan* [2001] ECR I-6297, paragraphs 24 and 26, and Joined Cases C-295/04 to C-298/04 *Manfredi and Others* [2006] ECR I-6619, paragraphs 59 and 61).' (para 49)

'It follows from the above that the Commission has not established, to the requisite legal standard, that access to the statement of contents is likely specifically and effectively to undermine the commercial interests of undertakings which took part in the cartel and, in particular, of Evonik Degussa.' (para 50)

The Commission argues that the investigation in Case COMP/F/38.620 must be regarded as still open inasmuch as the hydrogen peroxide decision is not yet definitive. Disclosure would endanger the Commission's task of preventing anticompetitive practices. In addition, disclosure would jeopardise cooperation of leniency applicants if the documents supplied by applicants for leniency were to be disclosed. (paras 55–6)

The aim of the exception in the third indent of Article 4(2) is not to protect the investigations as such, but rather their purpose, which, in the case of competition proceedings, is to determine whether an infringement of Article 101 or 102 TFEU has taken place. In the present case the Commission had already adopted—more than two years earlier—the hydrogen peroxide decision. The investigation must be regarded as closed once the final decision is adopted, irrespective of whether the decision might subsequently be annulled by the courts. (paras 59–66)

The Commission argues that disclosure is likely to undermine the Commission's cartel policy and, in particular, its leniency programme. 'In particular, if applicants for leniency had to fear that, as a result of the disclosure of documents which they submitted in the context of their application, that they would be the prime target of actions for damages brought by companies damaged by the cartel, they might refrain, in the future, from cooperating with the Commission, which would affect the effectiveness of the leniency programme. … However, acceptance of the interpretation proposed by the Commission would amount to permitting the latter to avoid the application of Regulation No 1049/2001, without any limit in time, to any document in a competition case merely by reference to a possible future adverse impact on its leniency programme. Moreover, the present case is an illustration of the broad application which the Commission wishes to give to that interpretation, inasmuch as it refuses here to disclose a document which was not itself submitted by an applicant for leniency and contains no information likely in itself to damage the interests of the companies which applied for leniency. In fact, the Commission merely states that certain information contained in the non-confidential version of the hydrogen peroxide decision could be put together with other information, contained in the statement of contents, so as to permit victims of anti-competitive practices to know which documents in the file could contain further evidence of the infringement. … Such a broad interpretation of the concept of investigation activities is incompatible with the principle that, by reason of the purpose of Article 1049/2001, set out in recital 4, namely, "to give the fullest possible effect to the right of public access to documents", the exceptions laid down in Article 4 of that regulation must be interpreted and applied strictly". (paras 69–71)

Comment

The Court held that the Commission's refusal to provide access to the Statement of Contents cannot be justified using the exceptions laid down in Article 4(2) Regulation 1049/2001. Commission decision annulled.

The Court held that costs which were the result of damage claims brought by injured undertakings cannot be regarded as a 'commercial interest' under the first indent of Article 4(2) of Regulation No 1049/2001, and, in any event, do not constitute an interest deserving of protection. (para 49)

The Commission's argument that disclosure of the Statement of Contents would undermine the viability of the leniency programme was not accepted. The Court held that such general argument would have the effect of disapplying Regulation 1049/2001 to any document in a competition case merely by reference to a possible future adverse impact on the European leniency programme. On this point, note the provisions of the 2014 'Directive on Rules Governing Actions for Damages' (see discussion on page 524 above).

Article 4(2) of Regulation No 1049/2001 stipulates that 'The institutions shall refuse access to a document where disclosure would undermine the protection of: commercial interests of a natural or legal person, including intellectual property, court proceedings and legal advice, the purpose of inspections, investigations and audits, unless there is an overriding public interest in disclosure.'

Commission v Éditions Odile Jacob SAS	**Public Enforcement**
Case C-404/10P	Access to File—Merger Regulation
Court of Justice, [2012] 5 CMLR 8	Regulation 1049/2001

Facts

Odile Jacob requested the Commission to allow it access to documents relating to merger procedure in Case COMP/M.2978 *Lagardère/Natexis/VUP*, with the intention of using the documents in an action for the annulment of the Commission's decision to approve that concentration. The Commission refused to disclose the documents in question. Odile Jacob applied to the General Court which instructed the Commission to provide access to some of the documents concerned (Case T-237/05 *Éditions Jacob v Commission* [2010] ECR II-2245). Both parties appealed the judgment of the Court of Justice.

Held

The present case concerns the relationship between Regulation 1049/2001 and the Merger Regulation. 'Those regulations have different objectives. The first is designed to ensure the greatest possible transparency of the decision-making process of the public authorities and the information on which they base their decisions. It is thus designed to facilitate as far as possible the exercise of the right of access to documents, and to promote good administrative practices. The second is designed to ensure compliance with the duty of professional secrecy in merger control proceedings which have a Community aspect.' (para 109)

'Those regulations do not contain a provision expressly giving one regulation primacy over the other. Accordingly, it is appropriate to ensure that each of those regulations is applied in a manner compatible with the other and which enables a coherent application of them.' (para 110)

'Although Regulation No 1049/2001 is designed to confer on the public as wide a right of access as possible to documents of the institutions, that right of access is nevertheless subject, in the light of the regime of exceptions laid down in Article 4 thereof, to certain limits based on reasons of public or private interest (see, to that effect, *Commission v Technische Glaswerke Ilmenau*, paragraph 51).' (para 111)

In the present case, the Commission refused access to the documents relying, (1) on the exception relating to the protection of the purpose of investigations, (2) the exceptions relating to the protection of commercial interests, (3) the protection of the institution's decision-making process, and (4) the protection of legal advice. (para 112)

'For the purposes of interpretation of the exceptions under the first and third indents of Article 4(2) of Regulation No 1049/2001, the General Court should have acknowledged the existence of a general presumption that disclosure of documents exchanged between the Commission and undertakings during merger control proceedings undermines, in principle, both protection of the objectives of investigation activities and that of the commercial interests of the undertakings involved in such a procedure (see, to that effect, *Commission v Technische Glaswerke Ilmenau*, paragraph 61).' (para 123)

Comment

The General Court's Judgment was set aside. The Court of Justice decided that the Commission legitimately based its refusal of access. More generally, the Court of Justice acknowledged the existence of a general presumption protecting merger documents from disclosure. (para 123) It further noted that neither the EU Access to Document Regulation nor the Merger Regulation contain a provision expressly giving one of them primacy over the other. Accordingly, each of the Regulations should be applied in a manner compatible with the other. (para 110)

On the disclosure of evidence included in the file of a competition authority, note the provisions of the 2014 'Directive on Rules Governing Actions for Damages' (see discussion on page 524 above).

MasterCard, Inc v Commission	**Public Enforcement**
Case T-516/11	Access to Impact Assessment
General Court, not yet published	Regulation 1049/2001

Facts

MasterCard group requested the Commission, on the basis of Regulation No 1049/2001, to grant it access to a number of documents supplied to the Commission by EIM Business and Policy Research (EIM). The study was commissioned as part of the drafting of a regulation capping cross-border card payments. The Commission refused to grant access. It explained that these were preliminary working documents representing various stages of the work in progress, and that their disclosure would seriously undermine its decision-making process. In addition, the Commission noted that disclosure would cause undue delay and disruption and could prompt premature comments and criticism and lead to attempts to influence and skew its decision-making process. MasterCard group applied for annulment of the Commission decision.

Held

Regulation 1049/2001 is intended to give the fullest possible effect to the right of public access to documents of the institutions. That right is subject to certain limitations based on grounds of public or private interest. When an institution is asked to disclose a document, it must assess whether in that specific case that document falls within the exceptions, having interpreted and applied them strictly. 'The mere fact that a document concerns an interest protected by an exception is not sufficient to justify application of that exception. Such application may, as a rule, be justified only if the institution has previously assessed whether access to the document could specifically and actually undermine the protected interest.' (paras 44–7, 50)

'Under the first subparagraph of Article 4(3) of Regulation No 1049/2001, access to a document, drawn up by an institution for internal use or received by an institution, which relates to a matter where the decision has not been taken by the institution, is to be refused if disclosure of the document would seriously undermine the institution's decision-making process, unless there is an overriding public interest in disclosure.' (para 49)

The Commission argues that the EIM documents were commissioned in the context of a number of ongoing anti-trust investigations. However, the invitation to tender does not support that claim. Further, the Commission's decision makes no mention of the EIM documents forming part of an ongoing investigation. The Commission's reasoning in its decision was based on the undue delay and disruption and not on the exception relating to the protection of the decision-making process in ongoing anti-trust proceedings in which the study at issue could have been used as evidence. As that new argument was not relied upon in the Commission's decision it cannot be used as justification for the refusal. (paras 51–60)

The Commission next argued that the refusal is justified under the exception relating to the protection of the decision-making process. It must be noted that in order to be covered by the exception the decision-making process would have to be 'seriously' undermined. 'That is the case, in particular, where the disclosure of the documents in question has a substantial impact on the decision-making process. The assessment of that serious nature depends on all of the circumstances of the case including, inter alia, the negative effects on the decision-making process relied on by the institution as regards disclosure of the documents in question (… Case T-144/05 *Muñiz v Commission*, …, paragraph 75).' (para 62)

The Commission infer, in its decision to refuse access that its decision-making process would be seriously undermined from the fact that disclosure of interim documents, would take place before the final report on methodology was adopted. 'However, that reasoning conflicts with the very wording of the first subparagraph of Article 4(3) of Regulation No 1049/2001, which provides that access to a document, drawn up by an institution for internal use or received by an institution, which relates to a matter where the decision has not been taken by the institution is to be refused where its disclosure would seriously undermine the institution's decision-making process, unless there is an overriding public interest in disclosure. It follows that, in order to refuse the access sought, the institution cannot simply rely on the fact that it received the documents from a third party or on the absence of a decision and thus decide that in those circumstances its decision-making process has been seriously undermined, as required by the article cited above (see, to that effect, *Borax Europe v Commission*, cited in paragraph 50 above, paragraph 92).' (paras 65–6)

The Commission also argued that disclosure would lead to attempts to influence and skew its decision-making process. That concern may be legitimate, but only if the reality of such external pressure is established with certainty and supported with evidence. In its decision, the Commission's concern is made in a vague and general manner. In addition, some of the documents were released to a number of stakeholders as part of a consultation. Having opened the door to comments from stakeholders external to the institution, the Commission cannot simply refuse to disclose on a hypothetical risk of external influence. (paras 67–77)

The Commission further argued that disclosure may be detrimental to EIM's commercial interests and that therefore the exception provided in the first indent of Article 4(2) of Regulation 1049/2001 is applicable. That is that disclosure would seriously undermine the commercial interests of a legal person. However, that argument is not supported by sufficient evidence to conclude that there was a reasonably foreseeable—and not a purely hypothetical—risk that disclosure would undermine EIM's commercial interests. (paras 78–93)

Comment

The Court annulled the Commission decision to refuse access, finding it to breach Article 4(2) of Regulation 1049/2001.

The Judgment highlights the significance of the right of public access to documents and subsequently the requirement for well-reasoned refusal to grant access that is based on evidence. An abstract refusal based on hypothetical risks would not suffice.

The consultation by the Commission of a number of stakeholders which were allowed access to the documents undermined the Commission's argument that disclosure of the documents would unduly influence its decision-making. The Court accepted that such limited disclosure to stakeholders is distinguished from giving public access. However, having given such access, the Commission could not simply refuse to disclose on the unsubstantiated basis of a risk of external influence. The Commission was expected to put forward a more robust argument which explained why such further disclosure would undermine its process.

Impact assessments are often used by the Commission to evaluate the likely outcome of new legislation. The judgment opens the door for interested parties to gain access to documents prepared as part of the process, by the Commission or external contractors.

DRAMs	**Public Enforcement**
Case COMP/38.511	Settlement
European Commission, [2011] C180/15	Cartel

Facts

Following an application for leniency, the European Commission initiated proceedings pursuant to Article 11(6) Regulation 1/2003, into a cartel agreement the object of which was to coordinate and monitor prices for dynamic random access memory chips (DRAMs). The Commission requested the parties to the anticompetitive cartel to express whether they are interested in engaging in settlement discussions in view of introducing settlement submissions at a later stage. Once all parties agreed to settlement discussions, the Commission informed the parties of the objections it had against them and disclosed the evidence in the Commission file used to establish these objections. The parties had access to the relevant file including the oral statements and other non-confidential information. At the end of the settlement discussions, all parties considered that there was a sufficient common understanding as regards the scope of the potential objections and the estimation of the range of likely fines to be imposed by the Commission and introduced formal requests to settle in the form of settlement submissions.

In their settlement submissions the parties acknowledged their respective liability for the infringement of Article 101 TFEU and described its object and scope. The Commission subsequently adopted a Statement of Objections. The parties confirmed that it corresponded to the contents of their settlement submissions and that they remained committed to follow the settlement procedure. The Commission subsequently adopted a decision outlining their participation in the cartel and imposing fines of over €330 million on the parties for breach of EU competition law.

Comment

The Notice on the Conduct of Settlement Procedures sets out the framework for rewarding cooperation in the conduct of proceedings commenced in cartel cases. 'The Commission retains a broad margin of discretion to determine which cases may be suitable to explore the parties' interest to engage in settlement discussions, as well as to decide to engage in them or discontinue them or to definitely settle. In this regard, account may be taken of the probability of reaching a common understanding regarding the scope of the potential objections with the parties involved within a reasonable timeframe, in view of factors such as number of parties involved, foreseeable conflicting positions on the attribution of liability, [and the] extent of contestation of the facts.' (point 5)

According to the Notice, 'The Commission retains the right to adopt a final position which departs from its preliminary position expressed in a statement of objections endorsing the parties' settlement submissions, either in view of the opinion provided by the Advisory Committee or for other appropriate considerations in view of the ultimate decisional autonomy of the Commission to this effect. However, should the Commission opt to follow that course, it will inform the parties and notify to them a new statement of objections in order to allow for the exercise of their rights of defence in accordance with the applicable general rules of procedure. It follows that the parties would then be entitled to have access to the file, to request an oral hearing and to reply to the statement of objections. The acknowledgments provided by the parties in the settlement submissions would be deemed to have been withdrawn and could not be used in evidence against any of the parties to the proceedings.' (point 29)

The benefit for the companies that agree to take part in the settlement procedure is a reduction in fine of 10 per cent (point 32). In return, the companies agree to cooperate as above and waive some of their rights of defence and accept a more limited access to the file.

Prezes Urzędu Ochrony Konkurencji i Konsumentów v Tele2 Polska sp z oo Case C-375/09 Court of Justice, [2011] 5 CMLR 2	**Public Enforcement** National Competition Authority Decision Powers

Facts

Reference for a preliminary ruling from the Polish court concerning proceedings initiated by the Polish competition authority against Telekomunikacja Polska SA. In its decision the Polish competition authority concluded that the undertaking did not infringe Article 102 TFEU and the equivalent national provision on abuse of dominance. Tele2 Polska contested that decision in the national court. A principal question arose in the proceedings as to whether a National Competition Authority can reach a final decision that Article 102 TFEU was not infringed, or whether Article 5, regulation 1/2003 precludes it from such conclusion and permits it only to adopt a decision stating that that are no grounds for action.

Held

Where the national competition authority applies national competition law to an abuse of dominant position which may affect trade between Member States, it must also apply Article 102 TFEU. Article 5, Regulation 1/2003 specifies that when doing so, the national competition authority can require that an infringement be brought to an end, order interim measures, accept commitments, and impose fines, periodic penalty payments or any other penalty provided for in their national law. Article 5 further stipulates that when the conditions for prohibition are not met, the national competition authority may decide that there are no grounds for action on its part. The Article therefore clearly indicates that the power of the national competition authority is limited to the adoption of a decision stating that that are no grounds for action. (paras 20–3)

'That limitation on the power of the national competition authorities is corroborated by the determination of the Commission's decision-making power where there has been no breach of Articles 101 TFEU and 102 TFEU. According to Article 10 of the Regulation, the Commission may by decision find that Articles [101 and 102 TFEU] are not applicable. Recital 14 in the preamble to the Regulation states that the Commission may adopt such a decision of a declaratory nature "in exceptional cases". The purpose of such action, according to that recital, is "to [clarify] the law and ensur[e] its consistent application throughout the [Union], in particular with regard to new types of agreements or practices that have not been settled in the existing case-law and administrative practice". (paras 24, 25)

'Furthermore, the Court has held that, in order to ensure the coherent application of the competition rules in the Member States, a cooperation mechanism between the Commission and the national competition authorities was set up by the Regulation, as part of the general principle of sincere cooperation. ... Empowerment of national competition authorities to take decisions stating that there has been no breach of Article 102 TFEU would call into question the system of cooperation established by the Regulation and would undermine the power of the Commission. Such a "negative" decision on the merits would risk undermining the uniform application of Articles 101 TFEU and 102 TFEU, which is one of the objectives of the Regulation highlighted by Recital 1 in its preamble, since such a decision might prevent the Commission from finding subsequently that the practice in question amounts to a breach of those provisions of European Union law. It is thus apparent. ... that the Commission alone is empowered to make a finding that there has been no breach of Article 102 TFEU.' (paras 26–9)

Comment

To ensure the uniform application of the EU competition provisions and to retain the European Commission's freedom of action, national competition authorities are precluded from adopting negative decisions and declaring no breach of Article 101 and/or 102 TFEU. When the conditions for prohibiting a practice under Article 101 and/or 102 TFEU are not met the national competition authority can reach a decision that there are no grounds for action on its part.

11

Enforcement—The National Courts

Regulatory Background

The enforcement of competition law in the National Courts is primarily governed by the procedural rules of each of the Member States. At the European Union level, of major importance is Council Regulation No 1/2003 on the Implementation of the Rules on Competition Laid Down in [Articles 101 and 102 TFEU], [2003] OJ L1/1. In addition, the cooperation between the Commission and the courts of the EU Member States is addressed in the 'Commission Notice on the Cooperation between the Commission and the Courts of the EU Member States in the Application of [Articles 101 and 102 TFEU]', [2004] OJ C101/54. Also noteworthy in the context of private enforcement is the Directive on Rules governing actions for damages under national law for infringements of the competition provisions of the Member States and of the European.

Direct Effect of Articles 101 and 102 TFEU

Articles 101 and 102 TFEU produce direct effects in relations between individuals, and create rights for the individuals concerned which the national courts must safeguard.

| 127/73 | *Belgische Radio en Televisie v SABAM* | 601 |

See also summary references to:

C-282/95	*Guérin Automobiles v Commission*	601
C-453/99	*Courage Ltd v Bernard Crehan*	601
C-234/89	*Stergios Delimitis v Henninger Bräu AG*	601

Relationship between Articles 101 and 102 TFEU and National Competition Laws

Article 3, Regulation 1/2003 stipulates that:

'[1] Where the competition authorities of the Member States or national courts apply national competition law to agreements, decisions by associations of undertakings or concerted practices within the meaning of [Article 101(1) TFEU] which may affect trade between Member States within the meaning of that provision, they shall also apply [Article 101 TFEU] to such agreements, decisions or concerted practices. Where the competition authorities of the Member States or national courts apply national competition law to any abuse prohibited by [Article 102 TFEU], they shall also apply [Article 102 TFEU].

'[2] The application of national competition law may not lead to the prohibition of agreements, decisions by associations of undertakings or concerted practices which may affect trade between Member States but which do not restrict competition within the meaning of [Article 101(1) TFEU], or which fulfil the conditions of [Article 101(3) TFEU] or which are covered by a Regulation for the application of [Article 101(3) TFEU]. Member States shall not under this Regulation be precluded from adopting and applying on their territory stricter national laws which prohibit or sanction unilateral conduct engaged in by undertakings.

'[3] Without prejudice to general principles and other provisions of [Union] law, paragraphs 1 and 2 do not apply when the competition authorities and the courts of the Member States apply national merger control laws nor do they preclude the application of provisions of national law that predominantly pursue an objective different from that pursued by [Articles 101 and 102 TFEU].'

Actions for Damages

Competition law may be used in the National Court in one of two ways, either as a shield or as a sword. The use of competition law as a sword commonly involves 'actions for injunctive relief' or 'actions for damages'.

Actions for damages for loss suffered as a result of an infringement of Articles 101 or 102 TFEU are commonly divided into two categories, each carrying a different 'public value'. The first category includes 'follow-on' damage actions. These originate from a public investigation and use the authorities' decision to support the claim for compensation in court. By doing so, private parties overcome part of the risk and costs associated with litigating a competition case as they rely on the already exercised investigative power of the public authority to substantiate the claim. The second category concerns 'stand-alone' damage actions. These by their nature are more complex as they require the claimant to prove not only causation and damage but also the violation of competition law.

The European right to sue in damages in competition law cases was recognised in the seminal case of *Courage v Crehan* (C-453/99). In line with the case law of the Court of Justice, Article 3 of the Directive on Damages establishes an EU right for full compensation.

C-453/99	*Courage Ltd v Bernard Crehan*	602
C-295/04 etc	*Vincenzo Manfredi v Lloyd Adriatico Assicurazioni*	604
C-242/95	*GT-Link A/S v De Danske Statsbaner*	605
C-557/12	*KONE AG and others v ÖBB-Infrastruktur AG*	606

See also summary reference to:

127/73	*BRT v SABAM*	603
C-282/95P	*Guérin Automobiles v Commission*	603
HC05C00468	*Devenish Nutrition Limited v Sanofi-Aventis SA (France)*	604

The Measure of Damages

Article 17 of the Directive on Damages establishes a rebuttable presumption that cartel infringements caused harm.

The Article Stipulates that:

'1. Member States shall ensure that neither the burden nor the standard of proof required for the quantification of harm renders the exercise of the right to damages practically impossible or excessively difficult. Member States shall ensure that the national courts are empowered, in accordance with national procedures, to estimate the amount of harm if it is established that a claimant suffered harm but it is practically impossible or excessively difficult precisely to quantify the harm suffered on the basis of the evidence available.

2. It shall be presumed that cartel infringements cause harm. The infringer shall have the right to rebut that presumption.

3. Member States shall ensure that, in proceedings relating to an action for damages, a national competition authority may, upon request of a national court, assist that national court with respect to the determination of the quantum of damages where that national competition authority considers such assistance to be appropriate' (Article 17, Quantification of harm)

On the quantification of damage, note the Commission's communication on quantifying harm in actions for damages based on breaches of Article 101 or 102 of the Treaty on the Functioning of the European Union (2013/C 167/07), and the Commission's Practical Guide on Quantifying Harm (SWD (2013) 205).

Damages may be set at compensatory levels or include exemplary or punitive elements. In the absence of European Union provisions on this point, each Member State may establish different rules to govern the level and type of damages (C-295/04, A3/2008/0080, 1178/5/7/11).

See also summary references to:

Euro Defence

Articles 101 and 102 TFEU may be used as part of a defence claim, most commonly through the application of the civil sanction of nullity of Article 101(2) TFEU against claims for breach of contract. Such claims, often referred to as the 'Euro Defence', have, on occasion, been sceptically assessed by the courts which feared that they are used as a general escape route for those wishing to avoid bad bargains.

See also summary references to:

Interim Relief

To ensure the full effectiveness of rights claimed under European Union law, national courts are empowered to grant interim relief. When the national court deems interim relief to be necessary, but is precluded from granting it under national rules, the national court is obliged to set aside that national rule.

See also summary references to:

Early Disposal of Competition Claims

Domestic procedural rules may allow for motions to strike out claims due to unlikelihood for success or lack of reasonable grounds. Motions may, for example, be based on the existence of block exemptions or the inexistence of an undertaking that would be subjected to the competition rules. See:

Burden and Standard of Proof in Competition Cases

Article 2, Regulation 1/2003 stipulates that 'In any national or [Union] proceedings for the application of [Articles 101 and 102 TFEU], the burden of proving an infringement of [Article 101(1) or of Article 102 TFEU] shall rest on the party or the authority alleging the infringement. The undertaking or association of undertakings claiming the benefit of [Article 101(3) TFEU] shall bear the burden of proving that the conditions of that paragraph are fulfilled.'

Whereas the burden of proof in all Member States is identical, the standard of proof in the different jurisdictions varies and may, for example, be based on 'balance of probabilities' or 'winning the conviction of the court'. The claimant's evidentiary burden may be alleviated to compensate for the difficulty in establishing a claim. See for example:

C-204/00 etc	*Aalborg Portland and others v Commission*	613

Standing and Passing on Defence

The Directive on Damages establishes that a defendant may invoke, as a defence in a damage claim, the fact that the overcharge was passed by the claimant to a third party. The third party—being the indirect purchaser—shall be deemed to have proven that a passing-on to him occurred when it satisfies the conditions outlined in Article 14 of the Directive on Damages, which stipulates that:

'1. Member States shall ensure that, where in an action for damages the existence of a claim for damages or the amount of compensation to be awarded depends on whether, or to what degree, an overcharge was passed on to the claimant, taking into account the commercial practice that price increases are passed on down the supply chain, the burden of proving the existence and scope of such a passing-on shall rest with the claimant, who may reasonably require disclosure from the defendant or from third parties.

2. In the situation referred to in paragraph 1, the indirect purchaser shall be deemed to have proven that a passing-on to that indirect purchaser occurred where that indirect purchaser has shown that:

(a) the defendant has committed an infringement of competition law;
(b) the infringement of competition law has resulted in an overcharge for the direct purchaser of the defendant; and
(c) the indirect purchaser has purchased the goods or services that were the object of the infringement of competition law, or has purchased goods or services derived from or containing them.

This paragraph shall not apply where the defendant can demonstrate credibly to the satisfaction of the court that the overcharge was not, or was not entirely, passed on to the indirect purchaser.' (Article 14, Indirect purchasers)

On the treatment of passed-on damages in case law, see for example:

A3/2008/0080	*Devenish Nutrition Ltd v Sanofi-Aventis SA (France) and Others*	607

See also summary reference to:

C-192/95	*Société Comateb and others v Directeur général des douanes*	608

On the closely related question of the standing of indirect purchasers, the Court of Justice held that any individual can rely on a breach of Article 101(1) TFEU before a national court and claim compensation for the harm suffered where there is a causal relationship between that harm and the prohibited agreement or practice. See:

C-453/99	*Courage Ltd v Bernard Crehan*	602
C-295/04	*Vincenzo Manfredi v Lloyd Adriatico Assicurazioni*	604

Uniform Application of Competition Laws

Article 16(1) of Regulation 1/2003 stipulates that 'when national courts rule on agreements, decisions or practices under [Article 101 or Article 102 TFEU] which are already the subject of a Commission decision, they cannot take decisions running counter to the decision adopted by the Commission'. The provision echoes the case law in this area:

C-344/98	*Masterfoods Ltd v HB Ice Cream Ltd*	614
2005–06	*Inntrepreneur Pub Company v Crehan*	616

See also summary references to:

| C-234/89 | *Stergios Delimitis v Henninger Bräu AG* | 615 |
| C-552/03P | *Unilever Bestfoods (Ireland) Ltd v Commission* | 615 |

The use of preliminary references under Article 267 TFEU also contributes to the creation of a level playing field as it enables the Court of Justice to provide guidance and clarification on points of law to National Courts and tribunals. Note that the Court of Justice only has jurisdiction to answer questions referred by national courts and tribunals, but lacks jurisdiction when referrals are made by other institutions.

| C-53/03 | *Syfait and others v GlaxoSmithKline* | 617 |

Cooperation between National Courts and Commission

Article 4(3) TEU establishes the duty of loyal cooperation between the Commission and the Member States. This duty governs also the cooperation between the Commission and the National Courts in competition cases. The extent of cooperation between the National Courts and Commission is detailed in Regulation 1/2003 and in the 'Commission Notice on the Cooperation between the Commission and the Courts of the EU Member States in the Application of [Articles 101 and 102 TFEU]', [2004] OJ C101/54. On the cooperation between National Courts and Commission, and information disclosures between them, see:

| T-353/94 | *Postbank NV v Commission* | 618 |

See also summary references to:

| C-234/89 | *Stergios Delimitis v Henninger Bräu AG* | 619 |
| C-2/88 | *J J Zwartveld and others* | 619 |

Jurisdiction and Applicable Law

The jurisdiction of the National Court to hear cases is largely governed by Council Regulation 1215/2012 (which superseded Regulation 44/2001). Under the Regulation 'persons domiciled in a Member State shall, whatever their nationality, be sued in the courts of that Member State' (Article 4(1)). Special jurisdiction may be established in matters relating to a contract, in the courts located in the place of performance of the obligation in question (Article 7(1)). In matters relating to tort, delict or quasi-delict, jurisdiction may be established in the courts for the place where the harmful event occurred or may occur (Article 7(2)). Additionally, a person domiciled in a Member State may also be sued where he is one of a number of co-defendants, in the courts of the place where any one of them is domiciled, provided the claims are so closely connected that it is expedient to hear and determine them together to avoid the risk of irreconcilable judgments arising from separate proceedings. (Article 8). On the interpretation of Council Regulation 1215/2012 (which superseded Regulation 44/2001) see:

HC06C03489	*Sandisk Corporation v Koninklijke Philips Electronics NV*	620
C-386/05	*Color Drack GmbH v Lexx International Vertriebs GmbH*	622
A3/2009/2487	*Cooper Tire and Rubber Company v Shell Chemicals UK*	624
C-352/13	*Cartel Damage Claims Hydrogen Peroxide SA*	625

On questions of jurisdiction involving the extraterritorial application of competition laws, see Chapter 12 below.

With respect to the determination of applicable law, of major significance is the Rome II Regulation on the law applicable to non-contractual obligations (Regulation 864/2007 of the European parliament and of the council). Subject to a number of exclusions, the Rome II Regulation applies, in situations involving a conflict of laws, to non-contractual obligations in civil and commercial matters.

Article 4, Rome II Regulation, lays down the general rule according which 'the law applicable to a non-contractual obligation arising out of a tort/delict shall be the law of the country in which the damage occurs irrespective of the country in which the event giving rise to the damage occurred and irrespective of the country or countries in which the indirect consequences of that event occur.'

Article 6, Rome II Regulation, specifically addresses violation of competition law and stipulates the applicable law in cases of unfair competition and acts restricting free competition:

- In cases of *unfair competition* the law applicable to a non-contractual obligation shall be the law of the country where competitive relations or the collective interests of consumers are likely to be affected. However, when the act of unfair competition affects exclusively the interests of a specific competitor, Article 4 shall apply.
- In cases of *restrictions on free competition* the law applicable to a non-contractual obligation shall be the law of the country where the market is, or is likely to be, affected. The Rome II Regulation further stipulates the relevant law in cases where the market is affected in more than one country.

The Relative Underdevelopment of Private Enforcement in Europe

The use of competition law in national courts may generate public value by supplementing public enforcement of competition law and enhancing its deterrent effect. As such, it has an important role in sustaining a competitive economy by harnessing the private parties' economic interests to ensure the full effectiveness of competition rules. In addition to its supplementary role to public enforcement, private enforcement promotes the individual rights of parties by providing a channel for corrective justice through compensation and injunctive relief. In doing so it complements the public system and safeguards the rights of private individuals.

The introduction of Council Regulation (EC) No 1/2003 led to a turning point in the division of powers and responsibilities between the Commission, National Courts and National Competition Authorities. The Regulation decentralised the enforcement of competition law in the European Union while strengthening the Commission's powers of investigation. In the context of private enforcement, noteworthy are the provisions in Article 1 which provide for the full and direct application of Articles 101 and 102 TFEU at national level, and the provisions in Article 3 which govern the relationship between national and EU competition laws. Also noteworthy are the provisions in Article 15 which refer to the cooperation between National Courts and the Commission, and those in Article 16 which ensure a uniform application of Union competition laws. Despite the removal of some of the obstacles to private enforcement, following the coming into force of Council Regulation (EC) No 1/2003, the modernisation package did not lead to a meaningful surge in competition litigation.

Three main publications shed light on the obstacles which hampered private enforcement in Europe during that period.

The Ashurst Study, published in August 2004, provided a detailed account of the state of private litigation in Europe at the time and identified the main obstacles and possible ways to overcome them (The Ashurst Study on Claims for Damages in Case of Infringement of [EU] Competition Rules, 31 August 2004). It portrayed a gloomy picture of the state of damage actions in Europe, at the time, and described it as one of 'astonishing diversity and total underdevelopment'.

In December 2005, the Commission initiated a consultation process following the publication of a *Green Paper* and *Staff Working Paper on Antitrust Damages Actions* (Green Paper, Damage Actions for Breach of the [EU] Antitrust Rules. COM(2005) 672 final; Commission Staff Working Paper—Annex to the Green Paper, published on 19 December 2005). In these papers the Commission highlighted the significance it attributes to the development of private enforcement as a means to promote vigorous competition. The papers focused on damage actions, outlining the main obstacles to these actions and the range of options that may be used to resolve them.

In April 2008, the Commission published a White Paper on Damages Actions for Breach of the [EU] Antitrust Rules. The White Paper outlined possible measures to stimulate a balanced private enforcement regime which would complement public enforcement.

In October 2014 the Directive for Damages came into force. The Directive seeks to ensure the effective enforcement of EU competition rules by optimising the interaction between the public and the private enforcement of competition law. It also establishes principles to ensure that victims can obtain full compensation for the harm they suffered. (Directive of the European Parliament and of the Council on 'Certain rules governing actions for damages under national law for infringements of the competition law provisions of the Member States and of the European Union' (2013/0185 (COD) PE-CONS 80/14))

Belgische Radio en Televisie v SV SABAM and NV Fonior (BRT I)	**Private Enforcement**
Case 127/73	Direct Effect
Court of Justice, [1974] ECR 51	

Facts

Reference for a preliminary ruling from the Tribunal de Première Instance of Brussels concerning the interpretation of Articles 102 and 106 TFEU. Before the Court of Justice considered the reference it had to deal with an appeal by SABAM against the order for reference. SABAM argued that since the Commission had initiated proceedings in respect to SABAM, the national court lacked competence under Article 9(3) of Regulation 17/62 and should have stayed the proceedings until the Commission had given its decision.

Held

The competence of the national court to apply the provisions of Union law derives from the direct effect of those provisions. (para 15)

'As the prohibitions of [Articles 101(1) and 102 TFEU] tend by their very nature to produce direct effects in relations between individuals, these Articles create direct rights in respect of the individuals concerned which the national courts must safeguard.' (para 16)

'To deny, by virtue of the aforementioned Article 9, the national courts' jurisdiction to afford this safeguard, would mean depriving individuals of rights which they hold under the Treaty itself.' (para 17)

The fact that the expression 'authorities of the Member States' appearing in Article 9(3) of Regulation 17/62 includes, in certain Member States, courts especially entrusted with the task of applying domestic legislation on competition or that of ensuring the legality of that application by the administrative authorities cannot exempt a court, before which the direct effect of Articles 101 and 102 TFEU is pleaded, from giving judgment. (paras 18–20)

Nevertheless if the Commission initiates a procedure the court may, if it considers it necessary for reasons of legal certainty, stay the proceedings before it while awaiting the outcome of the Commission's action. (para 21)

Comment

Note the Court of Justice judgment in C-282/95P *Guérin Automobiles v Commission* [1997] ECR I-1503, [1997] 5 CMLR 447, in which it held that 'it must also be noted that any undertaking which considers that it has suffered damage as a result of restrictive practices may rely before the national courts, particularly where the Commission decides not to act on a complaint, on the rights conferred on it by [Articles 101(1) and 102 TFEU], which produce direct effect in relations between individuals.' (para 39)

See similarly the Court of Justice in C-234/89 *Stergios Delimitis v Henninger Bräu AG* [1991] ECR I-935, [1992] 5 CMLR 210, and in C-453/99 *Courage Ltd v Bernard Crehan*, [2001] ECR I-6297, [2001] 5 CMLR 28: '[I]t should be borne in mind that the Court has held that [Articles 101(1) and 102 TFEU] produce direct effects in relations between individuals and create rights for the individuals concerned which the national courts must safeguard'. (para 23)

Courage Ltd v Bernard Crehan	**Private Enforcement**
Case C-453/99	Right to Damages
Court of Justice, [2001] ECR I-6297, [2001] 5 CMLR 28	Article 101 TFEU

Facts

Mr Crehan, a tenant in two Inntrepreneur pubs was obliged, as part of his lease agreement, to purchase most of his beer from the brewer, Courage. Courage sued Crehan in the English High Court for unpaid debt. Crehan, as part of his defence, contested the lawfulness of the beer tie arrangements and claimed that these infringed Article 101 TFEU. In addition, Crehan launched a counterclaim for damages arguing, in essence, that the failure of his business and his inability to pay the debts originated from the tie arrangements. His damage claim was bared by an English law according to which a party to an illegal agreement is not allowed to claim damages from the other party. When the case reached the English Court of Appeal, the court referred it to the Court of Justice, asking, among other things, whether the provision in English law which bars Mr Crehan from claiming damages is compatible with EU law. The Court of Justice commented on the existence of the EU right to damages.

Held

Articles 101 and 102 TFEU produce direct effects in relations between individuals and create rights for the individuals concerned which the national courts must safeguard. Article 101 TFEU constitutes a fundamental provision which is essential for the accomplishment of the tasks entrusted to the Union and, in particular, for the functioning of the internal market. The principle of automatic nullity in Article 101(2) TFEU can be relied on by anyone, and the courts are bound by it once the conditions for the application of Article 101(1) TFEU are met and so long as the agreement concerned does not justify the grant of an exemption under Article 101(3) TFEU. (paras 19–23)

'It follows from the foregoing considerations that any individual can rely on a breach of [Article 101(1) TFEU] before a national court even where he is a party to a contract that is liable to restrict or distort competition within the meaning of that provision.' (para 24)

'As regards the possibility of seeking compensation for loss caused by a contract or by conduct liable to restrict or distort competition, it should be remembered from the outset that, in accordance with settled case-law, the national courts whose task it is to apply the provisions of Union law in areas within their jurisdiction must ensure that those rules take full effect and must protect the rights which they confer on individuals (see inter alia the judgments in Case 106/77 *Simmenthal* [1978] ECR 629, paragraph 16, and in Case C-213/89 *Factortame* [1990] ECR I-2433, paragraph 19).' (para 25)

'The full effectiveness of [Article 101 TFEU] and, in particular, the practical effect of the prohibition laid down in [Article 101(1)] would be put at risk if it were not open to any individual to claim damages for loss caused to him by a contract or by conduct liable to restrict or distort competition.' (para 26)

'Indeed, the existence of such a right strengthens the working of the [Union] competition rules and discourages agreements or practices, which are frequently covert, which are liable to restrict or distort competition. From that point of view, actions for damages before the national courts can make a significant contribution to the maintenance of effective competition in the [Union].' (para 27)

'There should not therefore be any absolute bar to such an action being brought by a party to a contract which would be held to violate the competition rules.' (para 28)

'However, in the absence of [Union] rules governing the matter, it is for the domestic legal system of each Member State to designate the courts and tribunals having jurisdiction and to lay down the detailed procedural rules governing actions for safeguarding rights which individuals derive directly from [Union] law, provided that such rules are not less favourable than those governing similar domestic actions (principle of equivalence) and that they do not render practically impossible or excessively difficult the exercise of rights conferred by [Union] law (principle of effectiveness) (see Case C-261/95 *Palmisani* [1997] ECR I-4025, paragraph 27).' (para 29)

Provided that the principles of equivalence and effectiveness are respected, the Union right in damages is subjected both to national rules of unjust enrichment and rules which bar an undertaking that bears significant responsibility for the distortion of competition the right to obtain damages from the other contracting party. In that regard, the court should take into account the economic and legal context in which the parties find themselves and the respective bargaining power and conduct of the two parties to the contract. (paras 30–32)

'In particular, it is for the national court to ascertain whether the party who claims to have suffered loss through concluding a contract that is liable to restrict or distort competition found himself in a markedly weaker position than the other party, such as seriously to compromise or even eliminate his freedom to negotiate the terms of the contract and his capacity to avoid the loss or reduce its extent, in particular by availing himself in good time of all the legal remedies available to him.' (para 33)

'Referring to the judgments in Case 23/67 *Brasserie de Haecht* [1967] ECR 127 and Case C-234/89 *Delimitis* [1991] ECR I-935, paragraphs 14 to 26, the Commission and the United Kingdom Government also rightly point out that a contract might prove to be contrary to [Article 101(1) TFEU] for the sole reason that it is part of a network of similar contracts which have a cumulative effect on competition. In such a case, the party contracting with the person controlling the network cannot bear significant responsibility for the breach of [Article 101 TFEU], particularly where in practice the terms of the contract were imposed on him by the party controlling the network.' (para 34)

'Having regard to all the foregoing considerations, the questions referred are to be answered as follows:

– a party to a contract liable to restrict or distort competition within the meaning of [Article 101 TFEU] can rely on the breach of that article to obtain relief from the other contracting party;

– [Article 101 TFEU] precludes a rule of national law under which a party to a contract liable to restrict or distort competition within the meaning of that provision is barred from claiming damages for loss caused by performance of that contract on the sole ground that the claimant is a party to that contract;

– [Union] law does not preclude a rule of national law barring a party to a contract liable to restrict or distort competition from relying on his own unlawful actions to obtain damages where it is established that that party bears significant responsibility for the distortion of competition.' (para 35)

Comment

Reflecting on the scope of the 'significant responsibility' benchmark Advocate General Mischo commented that the responsibility to be borne is clearly significant if a party is equally responsible for the distortion of competition. On the other hand the responsibility borne is negligible if the party is in a weaker position than the other party such that it was not genuinely free to choose the terms of the contract. (paras 71–8)

In paragraph 24 the Court held that 'any individual can rely on a breach of [Article 101(1) TFEU] before a national court'. See also Case 127/73 *BRT v SABAM* [1974] ECR 51, paragraph 16, and Case C-282/95P *Guérin Automobiles v Commission* [1997] ECR I-1503, para 39, where the court held that 'any undertaking which considers that it has suffered damage as a result of restrictive practices may rely before the national courts, particularly where the Commission decides not to act on a complaint, on the rights conferred on it by [Articles 101(1) and 102 TFEU]'. These statements support the view that both direct and indirect purchasers have standing in court. On standing and passing on defence, see also the Commission Green Paper and Staff Working Paper on antitrust damages actions.

Note AG Jacobs' opinion in Case C-264/01 *AOK Bundesverband*, where he stated his opinion that the reasoning of the Courage judgment was applicable to injunctive relief as well. (para 104)

Vincenzo Manfredi v Lloyd Adriatico Assicurazioni	**Private Enforcement**
Joined Cases C-295–298/04	Right to Damages
Court of Justice, [2006] ECR I-6619, [2006] 5 CMLR 17	The Measure of Damages

Facts

The Italian court referred to the Court of Justice several questions on the interpretation of Article 101 TFEU which arose in connection with claims against insurance companies for the repayment of excessive premiums. In its judgments the Court of Justice reaffirmed, among other things, that the European right in damages extends to third parties, and commented on the availability of punitive damages in competition cases.

Held

The principle of invalidity in Article 101(2) TFEU 'can be relied on by anyone, and the courts are bound by it once the conditions for the application of [Article 101(1) TFEU] are met and so long as the agreement concerned does not justify the grant of an exemption under [Article 101(3) TFEU]. ... Since the invalidity referred to in [Article 101(2) TFEU] is absolute, an agreement which is null and void by virtue of this provision has no effect as between the contracting parties and cannot be invoked against third parties...' (paras 56–7)

The full effectiveness of Article 101 would be put at risk if it were not open to any individual to claim damages for loss caused to him by a contract or by conduct liable to restrict or distort competition. 'It follows that any individual can claim compensation for the harm suffered where there is a causal relationship between that harm and an agreement or practice prohibited under [Article 101 TFEU].' (paras 60–1)

'As to the award of damages and the possibility of an award of punitive damages, in the absence of [Union] rules governing the matter, it is for the domestic legal system of each Member State to set the criteria for determining the extent of the damages, provided that the principles of equivalence and effectiveness are observed.' (para 92)

'In accordance with the principle of equivalence, if it is possible to award specific damages, such as exemplary or punitive damages, in domestic actions similar to actions founded on the [Union] competition rules, it must also be possible to award such damages in actions founded on [Union] rules. However, [Union] law does not prevent national courts from taking steps to ensure that the protection of the rights guaranteed by [Union] law does not entail the unjust enrichment of those who enjoy them. Secondly, it follows from the principle of effectiveness ... that injured persons must be able to seek compensation not only for actual loss (damnum emergens) but also for loss of profit (lucrum cessans) plus interest.' (paras 99–100)

Comment

'[Article 101 TFEU] produces direct effects in relations between individuals and directly creates rights in respect of the individuals concerned which the national courts must safeguard. That includes the right, for individuals, to be protected from the harmful effects which an agreement which is automatically void may create. The individuals who can benefit from such protection are, of course, primarily third parties, that is to say consumers and competitors who are adversely affected by a prohibited agreement.' (opinion of AG Mischo in *Courage Ltd v Bernard Crehan*, paras 37, 38)

In *Devenish Nutrition Limited v Sanofi-Aventis SA* (page 607 below) the English Court of Appeal referred to the Manfredi judgment and concluded that Union law does not prevent the making of a restitutionary award.

GT-Link A/S v De Danske Statsbaner (DSB)	**Private Enforcement**
Case C-242/95	Right to Damages
Court of Justice, [1997] ECR I-4449, [1997] 5 CMLR 601	Article 102 TFEU

Facts

The case was referred to the Court of Justice from the Danish court which asked, among other things, whether under Article 102 TFEU the state-owned railway company which operated a harbour was liable to compensate a ferry operator which was arguably subjected to abusive charges for the use of the port. The Court of Justice clarified the duty of a dominant undertaking to compensate those who were abused by its practices.

Held

'It is for the domestic legal order of each Member State to lay down the detailed procedural rules, including those relating to the burden of proof, governing actions for safeguarding rights which individuals derive from the direct effect of [Article 102 TFEU], provided that such rules are not less favourable than those governing similar domestic actions and do not render virtually impossible or excessively difficult the exercise of rights conferred by [Union] law.' (para 27, paras 22–7)

'[W]here a public undertaking which owns and operates a commercial port occupies a dominant position in a substantial part of the [internal] market, it is contrary to [Article 101(1) TFEU] in conjunction with [Article 102 TFEU] for that undertaking to levy port duties of an unreasonable amount pursuant to regulations adopted by the Member State to which it is answerable or for it to exempt from payment of those duties its own ferry services and, reciprocally, some of its trading partners' ferry services, in so far as such exemptions entail the application of dissimilar conditions to equivalent services. It is for the national court to determine whether, having regard to the level of the duties and the economic value of the services supplied, the amount of duty is actually unfair. It is also for the national court to determine whether exempting its own ferry services, and reciprocally those of some of its trading partners, from payment of duties in fact amounts to the application of dissimilar conditions to equivalent services.' (para 46, paras 28–46)

Comment

The Court of Justice reaffirmed that Article 102 TFEU has direct effect and confers on individuals rights which the national court must protect. It further established that national procedural rules concerning the burden of proving the conditions of Article 102 TFEU should not 'render virtually impossible or excessively difficult the exercise of rights conferred by [Union] law'. (para 27)

Note also AG Jacobs' opinion (Joint Opinion [1997] ECR I-4085) in which he stated with respect to a reimbursement of a levy contrary to Article 102 TFEU that 'It is settled law that [Article 102 TFEU] creates direct rights in respect of the individuals concerned, which the national court must safeguard. [Case 127/73, *BRT v SABAM*, [1974] ECR 313] The principle set out above will accordingly apply: it is for the domestic legal system of the Member State concerned to determine the conditions governing actions to defend those rights, subject to the requirements of equivalence with actions to defend rights deriving from domestic law and of effectiveness, namely that it must be possible in fact to recover.' (para 176)

The judgment focused on a public undertaking, yet it arguably establishes a more general rule, applicable to any undertaking, that a requirement of proof which would make it impossible or excessively difficult to prove a breach of Article 102 TFEU is incompatible with Union law.

KONE AG and others v ÖBB-Infrastruktur AG	**Private Enforcement**
Case C-557/12	Damage Claim
Court of Justice, [2014] 5 CMLR 5	Umbrella Pricing

Facts

A request for a preliminary ruling from the Austrian Court in which the Court asked whether Article 101 TFEU may allow any person to claim 'umbrella damages' from members of a cartel for loss caused by an undertaking not party to the cartel, but which benefited from the protection of the increased market prices due to the cartel activity and was able subsequently to raise its own prices above pre-cartel levels. Austrian law categorically excludes such a right to 'umbrella damages' owing to the fact that, in the absence of a contractual relationship, the causal link between the loss and the cartel is considered to have been broken.

Held

While each Member State lays down the rules governing the application of the concept of the 'causal link', those rules must take into account the objectives pursued by Article 101 TFEU and ensure that EU competition law is fully effective. (paras 31, 32)

'The full effectiveness of Article 101 TFEU would be put at risk if the right of any individual to claim compensation for harm suffered were subjected by national law, categorically and regardless of the particular circumstances of the case, to the existence of a direct causal link while excluding that right because the individual concerned had no contractual links with a member of the cartel, but with an undertaking not party thereto, whose pricing policy, however, is a result of the cartel that contributed to the distortion of price formation mechanisms governing competitive markets.' (para 33)

'Consequently, the victim of umbrella pricing may obtain compensation for the loss caused by the members of a cartel, even if it did not have contractual links with them, where it is established that the cartel at issue was, in the circumstances of the case and, in particular, the specific aspects of the relevant market, liable to have the effect of umbrella pricing being applied by third parties acting independently, and that those circumstances and specific aspects could not be ignored by the members of that cartel. It is for the referring court to determine whether those conditions are satisfied.' (para 34)

Comment

The Court held that national law cannot categorically exclude the possibility of compensation for 'umbrella damages'. The Union's interest in promoting effective competition supersedes Member State law on this matter. The Court accepts the possible causal link between cartel activity and umbrella pricing. Note, however, that the judgment does not positively endorse 'umbrella damages'.

In her opinion, Advocate General Kokott discussed the foreseeability of 'umbrella damages' and the link between cartel activity and price increase. She noted that 'in a market economy, it is common business practice for undertakings to keep a close eye on market trends and to take those trends duly into consideration when making their own commercial decisions. Accordingly, the fact that persons not party to a cartel set their prices with an eye to the market behaviour of the undertakings belonging to the cartel is anything but unforeseeable or surprising, whether they are aware of the anti-competitive practices of the latter or not. Indeed, it is very much in the normal way of things ... The stronger the cartel's position is on the market concerned, the more likely it is that the cartel will have a significant impact on pricing levels ... [I]t is very important for the success of anti-competitive agreements between the members of a cartel that the prices of non-members should also rise and come close to those of the cartel members. After all, the more prices rise as a whole, the easier it is for cartel members to impose the prices they charge themselves on the market in the long run. For this reason, too, the obvious conclusion is that cartel members acting rationally and thinking their anti-competitive practices through to their logical conclusion will not be surprised by umbrella pricing. On the contrary, they must actually expect it.' (AG opinion, paras 45–84)

Devenish Nutrition Ltd v Sanofi-Aventis SA (France) and others	**Private Enforcement**
Case A3/2008/0080	Passing-on Defence
England and Wales Court of Appeal, [2008] EWCA Civ 1086	Restitutionary Award

Facts

Following the European Commission *Vitamin* decision ([2003] OJ L6/1), Devenish Nutrition Ltd brought a follow-on action in the English High Court for damages for breach of statutory duty and asked the court to make a restitutionary award (a sum of money assessed by reference to the gain that the wrongdoer has made as a result of the wrong), in place of compensatory damages (damages that compensate the claimant for loss suffered as a result of the wrongdoing). The English High Court rejected the claim for restitutionary damages. Devenish appealed the judgment. On appeal, the court held that a restitutionary award was available only in exceptional circumstances. The court also made reference to the fact that Devenish passed the overcharge to its customers. Appeal dismissed.

Held

Restitutionary award under European Union law (Lady Justice Arden)

In *Manfredi* (C-295/04) the Court of Justice held that in the absence of Union rules governing the matter, the question as to whether an award of punitive damages greater than the advantage obtained by the offending operator should be made was one for the national courts. (paras 128, 129)

'In my judgment, [Union] law does not prevent the making of a restitutionary award. I have already indicated that, if it were open to the Court to make such an award, it would be awarded only in exceptional circumstances that would not include the case such as this where a claimant in the position of Devenish (on the assumed facts) would in an appropriate case be able to prove its loss on conventional principles. There is no relevantly exceptional difficulty in this case in doing so. It is, therefore, unnecessary to go further into this [Union] law question for the purposes of this case. Provisionally, however, it seems to me that, if the award were permitted by domestic law to enable Devenish to recover profits made by the respondents where it had failed to show any harm, it would in my judgment be no more extensive a remedy than the punitive damages considered in *Manfredi*. If the award were in those circumstances available in domestic law, the principle of equivalence would apply. Since, if *Blake* applies, a restitutionary award could only be made in exceptional circumstances where the justice of the case required it, I do not consider that there is likely to arise any question of such an award offending the [Union] law principle that the claimant should not receive unjust enrichment.' (para 130)

With respect to the question of whether the availability of a restitutionary award is necessary for the purposes of the effectiveness principle of [Union] law, it is 'clear from cases such as *Manfredi* that purely compensatory damages are sufficient for the purposes of safeguarding the rights of private persons under [Article 101 TFEU]. The doctrine of effectiveness is therefore directed to ensuring sufficient remedies rather than the fullest possible remedies. An action for compensatory damages fulfils the requirements of sufficiency. Accordingly I would dismiss the appeal on this ground.' (paras 134, 135)

Passing-on (Lord Justice Longmore)

'Once one has cleared the legal ground and appreciated that the claim made in the present case is a claim that the defendants should disgorge the profit which they have made from their breach of statutory duty in operating the cartel the difficulties of the claim become apparent. No one suggests that, to the extent the claimant has in fact suffered a loss because it has paid too high a price which it has been unable (for any reason) to pass on to its own purchasers, that loss cannot be recovered. If, however, the claimant has in fact passed the excessive price on to its purchasers and not absorbed the excess price itself, there is no very obvious reason why the profit made by the defendants (albeit undeserved and wrongful) should be transferred to the claimant without the claimant being obliged to transfer it down the line to those who have actually suffered the loss. Neither the law of restitution nor the law of damages is in the business of transferring monetary gains from one undeserving recipient to another undeserving recipient even if the former has acted illegally while the latter has not.' (para 147)

Passing-on (Lord Justice Tuckey)

'Devenish's expert has been able to calculate the amount of the overcharge using methodology typical in anti-trust cases. In calculating Devenish's loss he has not taken into account any pass-on, whereas in the case of one of the other claimants, a poultry producer further down the vitamins supply chain, he has been able to calculate the pass-on upstream and downstream of the claimant. If Devenish has suffered a loss it is recoverable as damages, but if it has not I do not see how this can be a reason for saying that damages are an inadequate remedy; they are adequate for anyone who has suffered a loss. An account of profits of the kind advanced would give Devenish a windfall. I can see no justification for this. As Longmore LJ says the law is not in the business of transferring monetary gains from one undeserving recipient to another.' (para 158)

Comment

The above extracts do not include the Court's exhaustive analysis on the availability of a restitutionary award under English law. In outline, the Court concluded that such an award is only available in exceptional circumstances which were not present in this case. The Court also held that evidential difficulties in establishing the level of compensatory damages did not provide a good justification for awarding restitutionary rather than compensatory damages.

The Court noted that European Union law has left it to national courts to establish the level and nature of damages. Accordingly, Union law does not prevent the making of a restitutionary award. However, the court held that in this case, under English law, the granting of such award was not called for. If successful, the claim for restitutionary damages would have assisted Devenish in avoiding the effects of the passing-on defence. This is so since the damages would have been calculated while considering the gain which the cartel members have made rather than the loss incurred by Devenish and the other undertakings. On this point the judges noted that 'the law is not in the business of transferring monetary gains from one undeserving recipient to another' making reference to the fact that the overcharge was passed to third parties.

Noteworthy is the UK Competition Appeal Tribunal (CAT) judgments in the Cardiff Bus Case (*2 Travel Group PLC v Cardiff City Transport Services Limited*). There the Court awarded damages for loss of profit, as well as exemplary damages. It referred to *Devenish Nutrition Ltd v Sanofi-Aventis SA* and noted that 'While the purpose of an award of damages is to compensate a claimant's loss, the object of the exemplary damages is to punish and deter. … [E]xemplary damages are a "remedy of last resort", which are not to be encouraged … the Court's inherent discretion to award exemplary damages must be "cautiously exercised".' (para 448) The CAT concluded that in the case of Cardiff Bus, such damages were appropriate, as (1) the entity was not fined by the competition agency and did not benefit from leniency, and (2) its exclusionary conduct was conscious and outrageous.

On the passing of overcharge, note Chapter IV of the Directive on Damages which deals with the passing-on of the overcharge and establishes that a defendant may invoke a passing-on defence in a damage claim.

Also note the Court of Justice judgment in Case C-192/95 *Société Comateb v Directeur général des douanes et droits indirects* [1997] ECR 1165 in which the Court held in the context of repayment of a national charge levied in breach of Union law that: 'the trader may have suffered damage as a result of the very fact that he has passed on the charge levied by the administration in breach of [Union] law, because the increase in the price of the product brought about by passing on the charge has led to a decrease in sales. … In such circumstances, the trader may justly claim that, although the charge has been passed on to the purchaser, the inclusion of that charge in the cost price has, by increasing the price of the goods and reducing sales, caused him damage which excludes, in whole or in part, any unjust enrichment which would otherwise be caused by reimbursement.' (paras 31–3)

Bernard Crehan v Inntrepreneur Pub Company and another
CH 1998 C801
English High Court, [2004] EWCA Civ 637

Private Enforcement
The Award of Interest

Facts

Following the Court of Justice judgment in Case C-453/99 *Courage Ltd v Bernard Crehan*, the Crehan case was remitted to the English High Court for a full trial and was heard in 2003. Mr Justice Park dismissed Mr Crehan's damages claim, finding that Crehan had failed to establish that the Inntrepreneur beer ties were in breach of Article 101 TFEU. In his judgment he did, however, make reference to the quantification of damages and the award of interest.

Held

'I accept that the normal rule [under English Law] is that damages are assessed at the date of loss, not at the date of judgment, and that it is assumed that interest will compensate the claimant for the passage of time between the time when he suffered his loss and the time when he gets judgment in respect of it. However, I believe the legal position to be that that is not an invariable rule of law, and that if the justice of the case requires damages to be measured at the date of judgment the court may award damages on that basis instead. This can arise, for example, in times of high inflation when interest would not be any form of acceptable compensation. In my judgment, if Mr Crehan was entitled to damages at all (which, for the reason which I have given earlier, turning on Delimitis condition 1, he is not), damages measured at 4 March 1993 (The Cock Inn) and 27 September 1993 (The Phoenix) plus interest would not be adequate compensation. Any profits which he would have made on a free of tie basis by then would have been modest at best. In this context I refer to my earlier observations to the effect that, although I think on balance that Mr Crehan would have survived if he had been free of tie from the outset on both pubs, it would have been a close run thing. The early years of his occupation of the pubs were always going to be tight in terms of profitability. The financial benefits to him if all had gone well would not have arisen in the first two years, but only in later years when he had got through the early expenditures and had been able to build up the trades of the pubs. Similarly, although the two leases would have had some capital value in 1993 if everything had progressed well, the values would not have approached those which might have been expected ten years or so later ...' (para 267)

'I therefore consider that in this case the measure of damages should be ascertained at the time of judgment, not at the two dates in 1993 when Mr Crehan had to give up the agreements for lease of his two pubs ...' (para 268)

Comment

Both the interest rate and the point in time from which interest is awarded affect the level of compensation. Had the court chosen an earlier point in time, such as the date of the infringement or injury, it would have awarded higher compensation, allegedly beyond real value. Such an award would have departed from the compensatory basis and resulted in a punitive one.

Note Case C-271/91 *M Helen Marshall v Southampton and others* [1993] ECR I-4367, [1993] 3 CMLR 293, where the Court of Justice considered the award of interest in a case concerning a claim for compensation for damages sustained by Ms Marshall as a result of her dismissal by the Authority. With respect to the award of interest the court held that the 'full compensation for the loss and damage sustained as a result of discriminatory dismissal cannot leave out of account factors, such as the effluxion of time, which may in fact reduce its value. The award of interest, in accordance with the applicable national rules, must therefore be regarded as an essential component of compensation for the purposes of restoring real equality of treatment.' (para 31)

Intel Corporation v Via Technologies Inc	**Private Enforcement**
Case Nos A3/2002/1380, A3/2002/1381	Euro Defence
English Court of Appeal, [2002] EWCA Civ 1905	Summary Judgment

Facts

Two patent infringement actions brought by Intel Corporation ('Intel') in the patent court against Via Technologies ('Via'), alleging that Via infringed five of Intel's patents. Via's defence in the patent court (High Court of Justice Chancery Division) was based on, among other things, the claim that Intel's actions infringed Articles 101 and 102 EC TFEU. Intel applied for a summary judgment.

In his summary judgment, Lawrence Collins J, commented on the approach toward the 'Euro Defence' in intellectual property cases, saying that 'the ease with which a defence based on [Article 101 or 102 TFEU] may be generated on the basis of vague or imprecise allegations makes it necessary to scrutinise them with some care in order to avoid defences with no merit at all going to a lengthy trial with expert economic evidence. ... I would add that, although the burden of proof on the party asserting conduct to be unlawful under [Articles 101 and 102 TFEU] may be the normal civil standard, the penal consequences of those provisions re-enforce the need for careful scrutiny.' (para 90)

Lawrence Collins J considered two claims made by Via, namely that bringing these infringement proceedings was an abuse by Intel of the exercise of intellectual property rights and that the terms under which Intel was prepared to grant a licence would create an infringement of Article 101(1) TFEU. He then awarded Intel summary judgment on the competition issues and gave Via permission to appeal only on one part of his decision. Via appealed the decision, seeking, among other things, permission to appeal on all parts. On appeal the Court considered whether the defences under Articles 101 and 102 TFEU were ones for which Via had real prospects of success. The Court upheld the defence claims.

Held

The tests to be satisfied if summary judgment is to be given under CPR Rule 24.2 are 'that Via has no real prospect of succeeding on the Euro-defence and there is no other compelling reason why that Euro-defence should be disposed of at a trial. A real prospect is to be contrasted with one which is fanciful, *Swain v Hillman* [2001] 1 AER 91. A Euro-defence which is likely at some stage to be the subject matter of a reference is likely also to be one which for that reason should only be disposed of at a trial. In most cases it is not necessary or appropriate to refer the point to the European Court before all the relevant facts have been ascertained by the national court.' (para 35)

'In paragraph 90 of his judgment Lawrence Collins J referred to the fact that what he described as Euro-defences are not in some special category but do demand careful scrutiny so as to avoid defences without merit going to what is likely to be a long and expensive trial. He also noted that cases involving [Articles 101 and 102 TFEU] often raise questions of mixed law and fact which are not suitable for summary determination. I would endorse both those propositions, but I would add two notes of caution. First, until the patent issues ... have been determined, the extent of the exclusivity conferred by the patents in suit on Intel and of the inhibition imposed on Via, as a consequence, is unknown. Both will depend on which claims in which patents are valid. Second, where it can be seen that the jurisprudence of the European Court of Justice is in the course of development it is dangerous to assume that it is beyond argument with real prospect of success that the existing case law will not be extended or modified so as to encompass the defence being advanced.' (para 32)

Comment

This case was part of a series of lawsuits and counter lawsuits launched by both parties and involving 27 patents. In 2003 the parties reached a settlement agreement under which all pending claims were dismissed.

Sportswear SpA v Stonestyle Ltd	**Private Enforcement**
Case No A3/2005/2316	Euro Defence
Court of Appeal, (Civ Div), [2006] EWCA Civ 380	Early Disposal of a Claim

Facts

As part of a trade mark dispute at the lower court, the court struck out of the defence a number of paragraphs in which the defendants sought to allege that the plaintiffs were parties to agreements which infringe Article 101 TFEU and that for this reason they were not entitled to enforce their trade mark rights. The defendants appealed the lower court decision arguing that the court was wrong to strike out the paragraphs.

Held

One of the main points which led to the order to strike out was the lack of sufficient nexus between the breach of Article 101 TFEU and the plaintiffs' claim. Even if proven, for a breach of Article 101 TFEU to be relevant to the claim, there must be a sufficient nexus between the two. 'A breach of the Article may give rise to various consequences, including a claim for damages, but the fact that two undertakings are parties to such an agreement does not of itself debar either of them from enforcing intellectual property rights.' (paras 29, 30)

The judge was wrong to conclude that the defence was bound to fail, on the basis that there was no arguable case of an adequate nexus between the anticompetitive agreement alleged and the plaintiffs' claim. The points are sufficiently arguable for it to be wrong to strike these paragraphs out of the defence. (para 71)

Comment

While on appeal, the main claims at the lower court proceeded to trial. This created a sense of urgency as once the paragraphs in question were reinstated the issues at trial expanded considerably. On this point Lloyd LJ commented: 'I recognise the importance of the point in relation to litigation which is near to trial and, as I understand it, currently estimated for a hearing lasting three days. The introduction of an [Article 101 TFEU] defence will add to the burden on the respondents by way of disclosure, may give rise to a need for expert evidence, and may therefore drive up the costs of the litigation, and delay its resolution significantly. To hold, as I would, that the paragraphs ought not to have been struck out will mean that the trial has to be adjourned. Assuming that the remaining pleading deficiencies can be cured, it will be desirable for the future case management of the claim to address and, so far as possible, confine the additional preparation that will be necessary, by way of disclosure and evidence.' (para 72)

Note Longmore LJ's skeptical comment on the use of a Euro Defence: 'Undoubtedly it would be convenient if it were possible to hold that the [Article 101 TFEU] issue could only be used as a sword rather than a shield so that competition issues could not be used to muddy the waters of (here) a comparatively straightforward trade mark dispute. But convenience is not always the same as justice and I have been, a little reluctantly, persuaded that it is arguable that European [Union] law does not invariably allow trade mark issues and anti-competition issues to be compartmentalised and separated from one another. It may turn out at trial that the defendant will be able to rely on S 12(2) of the Trade Marks Act 1994 to defeat the claimant's claim but, as my Lord has said in para 71 above, it is not possible to be sure that the defendant's position will not be stronger if it can also establish a breach of [Article 101 TFEU]. That is something which, in my view, the European case law, at any rate arguably, entitles the defendant to do.' (para 76)

Note also the sceptical approach in *Oakdale (Richmond) Ltd v National Westminster Bank Plc* [1997] ECC 130, where the Court held that: 'It is, in my view, necessary for a domestic court, faced at an interlocutory stage with ingenious arguments based on [Article 101 TFEU], to take care that it does not do injustice to the other party by too ready an acceptance of the submission that those arguments cannot properly be evaluated until trial in circumstances in which ... reliance on the [EU Treaties] is no more than a pretext for the non payment of a debt ...' (para 60)

R v Secretary of State for Transport ex parte Factortame Ltd	**Private Enforcement**
Case C-213/89	Interim Relief
Court of Justice, [1990] ECR I-2433, [1990] 3 CMLR 1	

Facts

A preliminary reference from the House of Lords concerning the extent of the national courts' power to grant interim relief against the Crown, in order to protect a party who is claiming rights under Union law. The questions were raised in proceedings brought against the Secretary of State for Transport by UK incorporated fishing companies which challenged the Merchant Shipping Act 1988 and the Merchant Shipping (Registration of Fishing Vessels) Regulations 1988 regarding registration of fishing boats.

Held

'In accordance with the case-law of the Court, it is for the national courts, ... to ensure the legal protection which persons derive from the direct effect of provisions of [Union] law (see, ... Case 811/79 *Ariete SpA v Amministrazione delle finanze dello Stato* (1980) ECR 2545 and Case 826/79 *Mireco v Amministrazione delle finanze dello Stato* (1980) ECR 2559.' (para 19)

'The Court has also held that any provision of a national legal system and any legislative, administrative or judicial practice which might impair the effectiveness of [Union] law by withholding from the national court having jurisdiction to apply such law the power to do everything necessary at the moment of its application to set aside national legislative provisions which might prevent, even temporarily, [Union] rules from having full force and effect are incompatible with those requirements, which are the very essence of [Union] law (judgment of 9 March 1978 in *Simmenthal*, cited above, paragraphs 22 and 23).' (para 20)

'It must be added that the full effectiveness of [Union] law would be just as much impaired if a rule of national law could prevent a court seised of a dispute governed by [Union] law from granting interim relief in order to ensure the full effectiveness of the judgment to be given on the existence of the rights claimed under [Union] law. It follows that a court which in those circumstances would grant interim relief, if it were not for a rule of national law, is obliged to set aside that rule.' (para 21)

'That interpretation is reinforced by the system established by [Article 267 TFEU] whose effectiveness would be impaired if a national court, having stayed proceedings pending the reply by the Court of Justice to the question referred to it for a preliminary ruling, were not able to grant interim relief until it delivered its judgment following the reply given by the Court of Justice.' (para 22)

Comment

The Court clarified that when the national court deems interim relief to be necessary but is precluded from granting it under national law, that national law should be set aside. (para 21) The ruling raises questions as to the scope of such 'obligation' on the national court to set aside the national law. See Case C-432/05 below.

In Case C-432/05 *Unibet (London) Ltd v Justitiekanslern* [2007] ECR I-2271; [2007] 2 CMLR 30 the Court of Justice held that 'where the competent national court examines, in the context of the claim for damages, whether the [National] Law ... is compatible with [Union] law, it must be able to grant the interim relief sought, provided that such relief is necessary, which it is a matter for the national court to determine, in order to ensure the full effectiveness of the judgment to be given on the existence of the rights claimed under [Union] law. It follows from the foregoing that ... the principle of effective judicial protection of an individual's rights under [Union] law must be interpreted as requiring it to be possible in the legal order of a Member State for interim relief to be granted until the competent court has given a ruling on whether national provisions are compatible with [Union] law, where the grant of such relief is necessary to ensure the full effectiveness of the judgment to be given on the existence of such rights.' (paras 76, 77)

Aalborg Portland and others v Commission
Joined cases C-204, 5, 11, 13, 17, 19/00
Court of Justice, [2004] ECR I-123, [2005] 4 CMLR 4

Facts

An appeal against the General Court judgment in *Cimenteries CBR and others v Commission* in which the General Court confirmed parts of the infringements found in Commission Decision Cases IV/33.126 and 33.322 (*Cement*). In its decision the Commission found a large number of undertakings and associations active in the European cement market to have infringed Article 101 TFEU by entering into anticompetitive agreements and concerted practices. On appeal, the Court of Justice referred to, among other things, the burden of proof in competition cases.

Held

According to Regulation 1/2003 on the implementation of the rules on competition laid down in Articles 101 and 102 TFEU, 'it should be for the party or the authority alleging an infringement of the competition rules to prove the existence thereof and it should be for the undertaking or association of undertakings invoking the benefit of a defence against a finding of an infringement to demonstrate that the conditions for applying such defence are satisfied, so that the authority will then have to resort to other evidence.' (para 78)

'Although according to those principles the legal burden of proof is borne either by the Commission or by the undertaking or association concerned, the factual evidence on which a party relies may be of such a kind as to require the other party to provide an explanation or justification, failing which it is permissible to conclude that the burden of proof has been discharged.' (para 79)

'According to settled case-law, it is sufficient for the Commission to show that the undertaking concerned participated in meetings at which anti-competitive agreements were concluded, without manifestly opposing them, to prove to the requisite standard that the undertaking participated in the cartel. Where participation in such meetings has been established, it is for that undertaking to put forward evidence to establish that its participation in those meetings was without any anti-competitive intention by demonstrating that it had indicated to its competitors that it was participating in those meetings in a spirit that was different from theirs (see Case C-199/92P *Hüls v Commission* [1999] ECR I-4287, paragraph 155, and Case C-49/92P *Commission v Anic* [1999] ECR I-4125, paragraph 96).' (para 81)

'The principles established in the case-law cited at paragraph 81 of this judgment also apply to participation in the implementation of a single agreement. In order to establish that an undertaking has participated in such an agreement, the Commission must show that the undertaking intended to contribute by its own conduct to the common objectives pursued by all the participants and that it was aware of the actual conduct planned or put into effect by other undertakings in pursuit of the same objectives or that it could reasonably have foreseen it and that it was prepared to take the risk (*Commission v Anic*, paragraph 87).' (para 83)

Comment

The alleviation of the claimant's evidentiary burden is justified when information asymmetry prevents the plaintiff from accessing information that is in the control of the defendant.

In paragraph 79 the Court of Justice indicated that presenting factual evidence indicating an infringement of competition law may shift the burden to the defendant who will have to provide an explanation or justification to prove that the factual evidence does not constitute an infringement of competition law.

Whereas the burden of proof in all European Member States is identical, the standard of proof in the different jurisdictions varies and may, for example, be based on 'balance of probabilities' or 'winning the conviction of the court'.

Masterfoods Ltd v HB Ice Cream Ltd	**Private Enforcement**
Case C-344/98	Uniform Application of Competition Laws
Court of Justice, [2000] ECR I-11369, [2001] 4 CMLR 14	

Facts

A reference for a preliminary ruling from the Supreme Court in Ireland. The case concerned an exclusivity clause contained in agreements for the supply of freezer cabinets concluded between HB Ice Cream Ltd (HB) and retailers of impulse ice-cream. In parallel with the Irish court proceedings, Masterfoods lodged a complaint with the Commission against HB. Following an investigation, the Commission concluded that the exclusivity provisions in the agreement and HB's inducement of retailers in Ireland to enter into the agreements infringed Articles 101 and 102 TFEU (Case Nos IV/34.073, IV/34.395 and IV/35.436 *Van den Bergh Foods Limited*). HB appealed the decision to the General Court.

The Supreme Court decided to stay the proceedings and to refer the case to the Court of Justice for a preliminary ruling on several questions. The Court asked, among other things, whether the obligation of sincere cooperation with the Commission requires the Supreme Court to stay the instant proceedings pending the disposal of the appeal on the Commission's decision to the General Court and any subsequent appeal to the Court of Justice.

Held

Under the fourth paragraph of Article 288 TFEU (ex Article 249 EC) a decision adopted by the Commission 'shall be binding in its entirety upon those to whom it is addressed. The Court has held, in paragraph 47 of *Delimitis*, that in order not to breach the general principle of legal certainty, national courts must, when ruling on agreements or practices which may subsequently be the subject of a decision by the Commission, avoid giving decisions which would conflict with a decision contemplated by the Commission in the implementation of [Articles 101 and 102 TFEU].' (paras 50–51)

'It is even more important that when national courts rule on agreements or practices which are already the subject of a Commission decision they cannot take decisions running counter to that of the Commission, even if the latter's decision conflicts with a decision given by a national [General Court].' (para 52)

If a national court has doubts as to the validity or interpretation of an act of a Union institution it may, or must, in accordance with Article 267 TFEU, refer a question to the Court of Justice for a preliminary ruling. (para 54)

If, as here in the main proceedings, the addressee of a Commission decision has, within the period prescribed in the fifth paragraph of Article 263 TFEU (ex Article 230 EC), brought an action for annulment of that decision, 'it is for the national court to decide whether to stay proceedings until a definitive decision has been given in the action for annulment or in order to refer a question to the Court for a preliminary ruling.' (para 55)

'It should be borne in mind, in that connection, that application of the [Union] competition rules is based on an obligation of sincere cooperation between the national courts, on the one hand, and the Commission and the [European] Courts, on the other, in the context of which each acts on the basis of the role assigned to it by the Treaty.' (para 56)

'When the outcome of the dispute before the national court depends on the validity of the Commission decision, it follows from the obligation of sincere cooperation that the national court should, in order to avoid reaching a decision that runs counter to that of the Commission, stay its proceedings pending final judgment in the action for annulment by the [European] Courts, unless it considers that, in the circumstances of the case, a reference to the Court of Justice for a preliminary ruling on the validity of the Commission decision is warranted.' (para 57)

'If a national court stays proceedings, it is incumbent on it to examine whether it is necessary to order interim measures in order to safeguard the interests of the parties pending final judgment.' (para 58)

'In this case it appears from the order for reference that the maintenance in force of the permanent injunction granted by the High Court restraining Masterfoods from inducing retailers to store its products in freezers belonging to HB depends on the validity of Decision 98/531. It therefore follows from the obligation of sincere cooperation that the national court should stay proceedings pending final judgment in the action for annulment by the [European] Courts unless it considers that, in the circumstances of the case, a reference to the Court of Justice for a preliminary ruling on the validity of the Commission decision is warranted.' (para 59)

'The answer to Question 1 must therefore be that, where a national court is ruling on an agreement or practice, the compatibility of which with [Articles 101(1) and 102 TFEU] is already the subject of a Commission decision, it cannot take a decision running counter to that of the Commission, even if the latter's decision conflicts with a decision given by a national court of first instance. If the addressee of the Commission decision has, within the period prescribed in the fifth paragraph of [Article 263 TFEU], brought an action for annulment of that decision, it is for the national court to decide whether to stay proceedings pending final judgment in that action for annulment or in order to refer a question to the Court for a preliminary ruling.' (para 60)

Comment

Article 16(1) of Regulation 1/2003 codifies the principles laid down in the decision and states that 'When national courts rule on agreements, decisions or practices under [Article 101 or Article 102 TFEU] which are already the subject of a Commission decision, they cannot take decisions running counter to the decision adopted by the Commission. They must also avoid giving decisions which would conflict with a decision contemplated by the Commission in proceedings it has initiated. To that effect, the national court may assess whether it is necessary to stay its proceedings. This obligation is without prejudice to the rights and obligations under [Article 267 TFEU].'

Article 9 of the Directive on Damages establishes that decisions by a national competition authority or review court will have a binding effect in other Member States. In some jurisdictions, that approach, which extends the principle in Article 16(1), Regulation 1/2003 to cover decisions of national competition authorities has already been endorsed. (See for example the German 'Gesetz gegen Wettbewerbsbeschränkungen', Section 33(4).)

Note Recital 22, Regulation 1/2003, which adds in respect to the need to avoid conflicting decisions that 'Commitment decisions adopted by the Commission do not affect the power of the courts and the competition authorities of the Member States to apply [Articles 101 and 102 TFEU].'

Note Advocate General Cosmas' opinion, which clarifies that such a risk of inconsistent decisions will not arise 'where the legal and factual context of the case being examined by the Commission is not completely identical to that before the national courts. The Commission's decision may provide important indications as to the appropriate way to interpret [Articles 101(1) and 102 TFEU], but in this case there is no risk, from a purely legal point of view, of the adoption of conflicting decisions ...' (para 16)

Also note Case C-234/89 *Stergios Delimitis v Henninger Bräu AG* [1991] ECR I-935, [1992] 5 CMLR 210, in which the Court of Justice held that 'Account should here be taken of the risk of national courts taking decisions which conflict with those taken or envisaged by the Commission in the implementation of [Articles 101(1) and 102, and also of Article 101(3) TFEU]. Such conflicting decisions would be contrary to the general principle of legal certainty and must, therefore, be avoided when national courts give decisions on agreements or practices which may subsequently be the subject of a decision by the Commission.' (para 34)

Also note Case C-552/03 *Unilever Bestfoods (Ireland) Ltd v Commission* [2006] 5 CMLR 27, where the Court of Justice held that 'the [European] Courts cannot be bound by a finding of a national court that an exclusivity clause is compatible with [Union] law.' (para 128)

Inntrepreneur Pub Company (CPC) and others v Crehan	**Private Enforcement**
House of Lords (English Court), [2006] UKHL 38	Uniform Application
	Binding Effect

Facts

Following the Court of Justice judgment in Case C-453/99 *Courage Ltd v Bernard Crehan*, the case was remitted to the English High Court for a full trial and was heard in 2003. The High Court considered the damage claim but found that in this case the beer tie agreement did not make it difficult for competitors to enter the market and therefore did not infringe Article 101 TFEU. The High Court distinguished between the case at issue and an earlier Commission finding which concerned similar beer tie arrangements, on the grounds that the case involved different parties and different arrangements. Crehan appealed the decision to the Court of Appeal, arguing that the High Court was bound to accept the Commission's factual conclusions on similar beer tie agreements. The case reached the House of Lords, which considered the extent to which the Commission's factual assessment of the UK beer market binds the national court.

Held

Lord Hoffmann: Article 16, Regulation 1/2003 stipulates that 'When national courts rule on agreements, decisions or practices under [Article 101 or Article 102 TFEU] which are already the subject of a Commission decision, they cannot take decisions running counter to the decision adopted by the Commission. They must also avoid giving decisions which would conflict with a decision contemplated by the Commission in proceedings it has initiated. To that effect, the national court may assess whether it is necessary to stay its proceedings. This obligation is without prejudice to the rights and obligations under [Article 267 TFEU].' (para 63)

'This Article makes it clear that a relevant conflict exists only when the "agreements, decisions or practices" ruled on by the national court have been or are about to be the subject of a Commission decision. It does not apply to other agreements, decisions or practices in the same market.' (para 64)

The national court cannot depart from a Commission decision which concerns the same subject matters and the same parties. However, the duty to avoid conflicting decisions, as stated by the Court of Justice in the two leading cases of *Delimitis* and *Masterfoods*, has no application to the present case as the Commission decision concerns different subject matter arising between different parties. The Commission decision in this case therefore does not bind the national court but provides important and persuasive evidence. (paras 14–74)

Comment

Some may argue that the House of Lords merely acknowledged the legal position as reflected in Regulation 1/2003. Others may see the judgment as cementing a new balancing point which requires less conformity between courts and the Commission. On a practical level claimants who seek to rely on a Commission decision in comparable circumstances risk having the national court reject the Commission's analysis. Subsequently, parties may have to adduce evidence beyond the Commission's decision to support its finding. The limited reliance on the Commission's analysis might also lead to inconsistency in national courts' findings related to similar agreements in the same market. Such potential inconsistency may impact on legal and business certainty lessening the motivation to launch an 'indirect' follow-on claim in the first place.

Syfait and others v GlaxoSmithKline	**Private Enforcement**
Case C-53/03	Uniform Application
Court of Justice, [2005] ECR I-4609	Article 267 TFEU

Facts

A request from the Greek Competition Commission (Epitropi Antagonismou) for a preliminary ruling concerning the interpretation of Article 102 TFEU. Before considering the referral, the Court of Justice examined, as a preliminary point, whether the Epitropi Antagonismou is a court or tribunal within the meaning of Article 267 TFEU (ex Article 234 EC) and whether the Court of Justice has jurisdiction to make a ruling on the questions referred to it.

Held

'According to settled case-law, in order to determine whether a body making a reference is a court or tribunal for the purposes of [Article 267 TFEU], which is a question governed by [Union] law alone, the Court takes account of a number of factors, such as whether the body is established by law, whether it is permanent, whether its jurisdiction is compulsory, whether its procedure is inter partes, whether it applies rules of law and whether it is independent (see, in particular, Case C-54/96 *Dorsch Consult* [1997] ECR I-4961, paragraph 23, Joined Cases C-110/98 to C-147/98 *Gabalfrisa and Others* [2000] ECR I-1577, paragraph 33, Case C-195/98 *Österreichischer Gewerkschaftsbund* [2000] ECR I10497, paragraph 24, and Case C-516/99 *Schmid* [2002] ECR I-4573, paragraph 34). Moreover, a national court may refer a question to the Court only if there is a case pending before it and if it is called upon to give judgment in proceedings intended to lead to a decision of a judicial nature (see, in particular, Case C-134/97 *Victoria Film* [1998] ECR I-7023, paragraph 14, and *Österreichischer Gewerkschaftsbund*, paragraph 25).' (para 29)

The Epitropi Antagonismou is subject to the supervision of the Minister for Development who is empowered, within certain limits, to review the lawfulness of its decisions. In addition, whilst the members of the Epitropi Antagonismou enjoy personal and operational independence, it nevertheless remains that there are no particular safeguards in respect of their dismissal or the termination of their appointment. Subsequently, members of the Epitropi Antagonismou may be exposed to undue intervention or pressure from the executive. It should also be noted that the President of the Epitropi Antagonismou is responsible for the coordination and general policy of the secretariat, is the immediate superior of the personnel of that secretariat and exercises disciplinary power over them. Lastly, it should be noted that like other competition authorities, the Epitropi Antagonismou is required to work in close cooperation with the European Commission and may be relieved of its competence by a decision of the Commission. Whenever the Commission uses its power to relieve a national competition authority of its competence, the proceedings initiated before that authority will not lead to a decision of a judicial nature. (paras 30–6)

'It follows from the factors examined, considered as a whole, that the Epitropi Antagonismou is not a court or tribunal within the meaning of [Article 267 TFEU]. Accordingly, the Court has no jurisdiction to answer the questions referred by the Epitropi Antagonismou.' (paras 37, 38)

Comment

The Court of Justice's ruling limits the use and impact of Article 267 TFEU references. National Competition Agencies, to the extent that their activity and mandate resemble that of the Epitropi Antagonismou, are precluded from using Article 267 TFEU and making references to the Court of Justice.

Note that a possible appeal on the national competition agency's ruling will be heard by the national court or tribunal. These organs are capable of making references under Article 267 TFEU to the Court of Justice.

Postbank NV v Commission	**Private Enforcement**
Case T-353/94	Information Disclosure
General Court, [1996] ECR II-921, [1997] 4 CMLR 33	Business Secrets

Facts

The case concerned the use of documents from an administrative procedure before the Commission, in legal proceedings before the national court. The Commission disclosed to third parties a complete version of a statement of objections which it issued during its investigation into the legality of a payment and transfer agreement. The information was disclosed on condition that it would be used only in preparation for the hearing to which the third parties were invited but not 'for any other purpose, especially in legal proceedings'. The third parties who were involved in a legal dispute which reached the Amsterdam Regional Court of Appeal asked the Commission to allow them to produce the version of the statement of objections and the minutes of the hearing to the national court. In their request they noted that the Commission had no power to prohibit them from producing those documents in national legal proceedings. The Commission agreed to their request, stating that the restriction it imposed concerning the 'use in national legal proceedings of the version of the statement of objections appeared unfounded and are therefore inoperative'. Postbank NV asked the Commission to reverse its decision as it was contrary to Union law. The Commission refused and Postbank NV appealed for the annulment of the Commission decision.

Held

The principle of sincere cooperation as laid down in Article 10 EC (now repealed, and replaced in substance by Article 4(3) TEU), requires the '[European Union] institutions, and above all the Commission, which is entrusted with the task of ensuring application of the provisions of the Treaty, to give active assistance to any national judicial authority dealing with an infringement of [Union] rules. That assistance, which takes various forms, may, where appropriate, consist in disclosing to the national courts documents acquired by the institutions in the discharge of their duties.' (para 64)

'In proceedings for the application of the [Union] competition rules, this principle implies in particular, as held by the Court of Justice, that the national court is entitled to seek information from the Commission on the state of any procedure which the Commission may have set in motion and to obtain from that institution such economic and legal information as it may be able to supply to it (Case C-234/89 *Delimitis* [1991] ECR I-935, paragraph 53, and Joined Cases C-319/93, C-40/94 and C-224/94 *Dijkstra and others* [1995] ECR I-4471, paragraph 36).' (para 65)

'As far as the rights of the defence of Postbank in the national proceedings are concerned, it must be pointed out that even if production by one of the parties to those proceedings of documents containing the above-mentioned information is capable of weakening the position of the undertakings to which the information relates, it is nevertheless for the national court to guarantee, on the basis of national rules of procedure, that the rights of defence of such undertakings are protected. In that connection, in a case for example like this one, the national court may inter alia take account of the provisional nature of the opinion expressed by the Commission in the statement of objections and of the possibility of suspending the national proceedings pending adoption by the Commission of a final position. The allegedly harmful effect of transmitting certain documents to the national courts certainly cannot therefore justify an outright prohibition by the Commission of such transmission.' (para 72)

The applicants also argue that the statement of objections contained business secrets and therefore could only be disclosed to third parties after they were informed of the disclosure and given an opportunity to object to it. Accordingly, they contested that failing to do so infringed Article 339 TFEU (ex Article 287 EC) and Article 20(2) of Regulation No 17, which prohibit disclosure outside the procedure for the application of competition law initiated by the Commission and, consequently, to the transmission to national courts of information covered by professional secrecy. (paras 78, 79)

'[Article 339 TFEU] applies to "information of the kind covered by professional secrecy". It applies in particular to "information about undertakings, their business relations or their cost components". It thus expressly refers to information which, in principle, falls, by reason of its content, within the category of business secrets, as defined by the Court of Justice (Case 53/85 *Akzo Chemie v Commission* [1986] ECR 1965).' (para 86)

Article 339 cannot be interpreted as meaning that, by virtue of its obligation to observe professional secrecy, the Commission is required to prohibit undertakings from producing, in national court, documents received in the procedure before the Commission which contain confidential information and business secrets. Such an interpretation might compromise cooperation between the national judicial authorities and the Union institutions, as provided for by Article 10 EC (now repealed, and replaced in substance by Article 4(3) TEU), and above all detract from the right of economic agents to effective judicial protection. More specifically, in a case like this one, it would deprive certain undertakings of the protection, afforded by national courts, of the rights conferred on them by virtue of the direct effect of Articles 101 and 102 TFEU. (para 89, paras 87–9)

'It follows that, in this case, the Commission failed in its obligation of professional secrecy by not giving Postbank an opportunity to state its view on the production in legal proceedings of the documents in question and by failing to take any measure designed to protect the confidentiality of the information or business secrets of which, for their part, the banks concerned requested protection.' (para 96)

Comment

Although the case surrounded the provisions of Regulation 17/62, which is no longer in force, the Court's comments on the duty of loyal cooperation are based on the Treaty provisions and are just as relevant under Regulation 1/2003. Article 15(1), Regulation 1/2003 stipulates that 'In proceedings for the application of [Article 101 or Article 102 TFEU], courts of the Member States may ask the Commission to transmit to them information in its possession or its opinion on questions concerning the application of the [Union] competition rules.'

Note the Commission's Notice on Cooperation between Commission and the Courts of the Member States which contains a section (paras 21–6) on the Commission's duty to transmit information to National Courts.

In Case C-234/89 *Stergios Delimitis v Henninger Bräu AG* [1991] ECR I-935, [1992] 5 CMLR 210, the Court of Justice held that 'It should be noted in this context that it is always open to a national court, within the limits of the applicable national procedural rules and subject to [Article 339 TFEU], to seek information from the Commission on the state of any procedure which the Commission may have set in motion and as to the likelihood of its giving an official ruling on the agreement at issue. ... Under the same conditions, the national court may contact the Commission where the concrete application of [Article 101(1) or 102 TFEU] raises particular difficulties, in order to obtain the economic and legal information which that institution can supply to it. Under [Article 10 EC, now repealed and replaced in substance by Article 4(3) TEU], the Commission is bound by a duty of sincere cooperation with the judicial authorities of the Member State, who are responsible for ensuring that [Union] law is applied and respected in the national legal system.' (para 53)

With respect to business secrets, note that Article 339 TFEU stipulates that: 'The members of the institutions of the [Union], the members of committees, and the officials and other servants of the [Union] shall be required, even after their duties have ceased, not to disclose information of the kind covered by the obligation of professional secrecy, in particular information about undertakings, their business relations or their cost components.'

Note that 'the Commission may justify a refusal to produce documents to a national judicial authority on legitimate grounds connected with the protection of the rights of third parties or where the disclosure of this information would be capable of interfering with the functioning and independence of the [European Union], in particular by jeopardizing the accomplishment of the tasks entrusted to it.' (Case C-2/88 *JJ Zwartveld and others* [1990] ECR I-4405, para 11) Also note discussion on access to Commission's file in Chapter 10 above.

Sandisk Corporation v Koninklijke Philips Electronics NV	**Private Enforcement**
Case HC06C03489	Jurisdiction
English High Court of Justice, [2007] EWHC 332 (Ch)	Regulation No 44/2001

Facts

A claim for relief made by SanDisk (a US corporation) in respect of an alleged abuse of a dominant position by several companies and patentees in the market for the licensing of patents essential to the production, sale and importation into the EEA of MP3 players and MP3-compliant memory cards. The defendants, who were based in Italy, the Netherlands, France and Germany, agued that the English court had no jurisdiction to consider the claims raised by SanDisk.

Held

'The question whether and in what circumstances the English court has jurisdiction is to be determined according to the provisions of the Council Regulation (EC) 44/2001 ("the Brussels Regulation"). The basic rule, as is well-known, is that a defendant is to be sued in the courts of the Member State where that person is domiciled (Article 2). The exceptions provided for by Sections 2 to 7 of Chapter II of the Brussels Regulation constitute the only exceptions to this rule; and, so far as this case is concerned, the only relevant rule is the special jurisdiction conferred by Article 5. Before embarking on this analysis, it is worth noting that Sisvel, against whom the greatest complaint is made, can certainly and without any doubt be sued in Italy, and there is little question that the Patentees could be joined to such proceedings under Article 6(1) which provides that a person domiciled in a Member State may also be sued, where he is one of a number of defendants, in the courts for the place where any one of them is domiciled, provided the claims are so closely connected that it is expedient to hear and determine them together to avoid the risk of irreconcilable judgments resulting from separate proceedings. Because none of the Defendants are domiciled in England and Wales (see Article 60), this possibility is not open to SanDisk in this jurisdiction, who must establish that a special jurisdiction is available. The only arguable head of jurisdiction is found in Article 5(3), which provides that: A person domiciled in a Member State may, in another Member State, be sued: ... 3. in matters relating to tort, delict or quasi-delict, in the courts for the place where the harmful event occurred or may occur.' (para 12)

'If the court is to have substantive jurisdiction by virtue of Article 5(3), the harmful act either must have occurred or may occur within England and Wales. The expression "matters relating to tort, delict or quasi-delict" have an autonomous meaning and must be regarded as an independent concept covering all actions which seek to establish the liability of the defendant and which are not related to a contract within the meaning of Article 5(1). The special jurisdictions enumerated in Articles 5 and 6 of the Brussels Regulation constitute derogations from the principle that jurisdiction is vested in the courts of the state where the defendant is domiciled, and as such must be interpreted restrictively. (See generally Case 189/87 *Kalfelis* [1988] ECR 5565). The idea of "place" also has the autonomous meaning that it embraces both the place where the damage occurred and the place of the event giving rise to it—see Case 21/76 *Bier v Mines de Potasse d'Alsace SA* [1976] ECR 1735. The option conferred on a claimant by Bier's case is not as wide as it may at first appear, since in general any claimant will suffer loss at its place of business caused to it by a harmful act committed abroad. To permit the court of the place of business of the claimant assuming jurisdiction in every such case and so weakening or entirely subverting the basic jurisdictional principle of Article 2 of the regulation, to which Article 5 is, as I have indicated, an exception, it is settled that the "place of damage" connotes the place where the physical damage is done or the recoverable economic loss is actually suffered. In Case C-220/88 *Dumez* [1990] ECR I-49, the Court of Justice said this (paragraph 20): "It follows from foregoing considerations that although, by virtue of a previous judgment of the court (in [*Bier*] ...), the expression "place where the harmful event occurred" contained in Article 5(3) of the Convention may refer to the place where the damage occurred, the latter concept can be understood only as indicating the place where the event giving rise to the damage, and entailing tortious, delictual or quasi-delictual liability, directly produced its harmful effects upon the person who is the immediate victim of that event.' (para 20)

'An interesting illustration of the principle is to be found in Case C-364/93 *Marinari* [1995] ECR I-2738, in which Mr Marinari had presented promissory bank notes to the value of US $752,500,000 to the Manchester branch of Lloyds Bank, whose staff refused to return them to him. Mr Marinari sued Lloyds Bank, domiciled in England and Wales, in the Tribunale di Pisa for compensation. He failed, the court ruling that the term "place where the harmful event occurred" in Article 5(3) of the [Brussels Regulation] does not, on a proper interpretation, cover the place where the victim claims to have suffered financial damage following upon initial damage arising and suffered by him in another Member State. In paragraph 14 of the judgment, the court said this: "Whilst it has thus been recognised that the term 'place where the harmful event occurred' within the meaning of Article 5(3) of the [Brussels Regulation] may cover both the place where the damage occurred and the place of the event giving rise to it, that term cannot be construed so extensively as to encompass any place where the adverse consequences can be felt of an event which has already caused damage actually arising elsewhere."' (para 21)

'Finally, the present case is concerned with acts which are themselves difficult to localise. Thus, assuming that the offer of an objectionable licence is rightly characterised as an abuse of a dominant position, where does the offer take place? The letter may be written in one jurisdiction and received in another. It seems to be settled that, at least in two obvious cases in which a tortious act is not complete until a statement has been both made and understood, the relevant location is that where the statement was made. In the case of defamation, the place of the harmful act was held to be the place where the statement was put into circulation, the place of receipt being the place where immediate damage arose: see Case C-68/93 *Shevill* [1995] ECR I-415, paragraph 24 of the judgment. It follows from Shevill that while all damages will be recoverable in the jurisdiction where the harmful event originated, damages for the jurisdiction in which injury to reputation is suffered will determine the extent of damage in that jurisdiction only ...' (para 22)

In order for the court to possess the exceptional jurisdiction pursuant to Article 5(3) of the Brussels Regulation in the present case, it must be satisfied that either the event setting the tort in motion was in England and Wales or, alternatively, that the claimant must show that it is the immediate victim of that abuse suffering direct harm in England and Wales. In this case damages as a result of the alleged abuse accrue to SanDisk in Delaware and not to its two subsidiaries within the UK. Consequently, the alleged abuses cannot, even if established, give rise to jurisdiction under Article 5(3) in England and Wales. (paras 25–41)

According to the claimant, the English court has jurisdiction since the enforcement of patent rights by the defendant may be regarded as an abusive and anticompetitive activity throughout Europe, including the UK, which led to a loss suffered by SanDisk throughout the EU and immediate damage is suffered in every country. This argument may establish jurisdiction both under Article 5(3) and under Article 31 which permits applications for provisional, including protective, measures even if, under the Regulation, the courts of another Member State have jurisdiction as to the substance of the matter. However, Article 31 must be interpreted strictly, given that it is an exception to the basic system of jurisdiction established by the Brussels Regulation (Case C-104/03 *St Paul Dairy* [2005] ILPR 416). The granting of provisional or protective measures on the basis of Article 31 depends upon identifying a connection between the subject-matter of the provisional or protective measures sought, on the one hand, and this jurisdiction on the other. In the present case there is no such connection and therefore jurisdiction does not exist under Article 31. (paras 42–55)

Comment

The attempt to secure interim relief failed due to the lack of a real connecting link between the subject matter of the interim measure and the jurisdiction of the court. Regulation 44/2001 has been superseded by Regulation 1215/2012. The provisions of Article 5 may be found in Article 7 of the new Regulation.

'The rules of jurisdiction must be highly predictable and founded on the principle that jurisdiction is generally based on the defendant's domicile, and jurisdiction must always be available on this ground save in a few well-defined situations in which the subject-matter of the litigation or the autonomy of the parties warrants a different linking factor. ... In addition to the defendant's domicile, there should be alternative grounds of jurisdiction based on a close link between the court and the action or in order to facilitate the sound administration of justice.' (Recitals 11, 12, Council Regulation (EC) 44/2001)

Color Drack GmbH v Lexx International Vertriebs GmbH	**Private Enforcement**
Case C-386/05	Jurisdiction
Court of Justice, [2007] ILPr 35	Regulation No 44/2001

Facts

Reference for a preliminary ruling from the Oberster Gerichtshof (Austrian Court) concerning the interpretation of the first indent of Article 5(1)(b) of Council Regulation (EC) No 44/2001. The dispute in the main proceedings concerned the performance of a contract for the sale of goods under which Lexx International Vertriebs GmbH (Lexx), a company established in Germany, undertook to deliver goods to various retailers of Color Drack GmbH in Austria. Following Lexx's failure to perform some of its obligations under the agreement, Color Drack GmbH brought an action for payment before the Austrian court within whose jurisdiction its registered office is located. That court accepted jurisdiction on the basis of the first indent of Article 5(1)(b) of Regulation No 44/2001. Following an appeal by Lexx, the appeal court set aside that judgment on the ground that the first instance court did not have jurisdiction. It took the view that a single linking place, as provided for in the first indent of Article 5(1)(b) of Regulation No 44/2001, could not be determined where there were several places of delivery not only in the area of that court's jurisdiction but at different places in Austria. Color Drack appealed the decision to the Oberster Gerichtshof, which considered that an interpretation of the first indent of Article 5(1)(b) of Regulation No 44/2001 is necessary in order to resolve the question of the jurisdiction. The court stayed the proceedings and referred the case to the Court of Justice asking whether the first indent of Article 5(1)(b) of Regulation No 44/2001 applies in the case of a sale of goods involving several places of delivery within a single Member State and, if so, whether, where the claim relates to all those deliveries, the plaintiff may sue the defendant in the court of the place of delivery of its choice.

Held

'As a preliminary point, it must be stated that the considerations that follow apply solely to the case where there are several places of delivery within a single Member State and are without prejudice to the answer to be given where there are several places of delivery in a number of Member States.' (para 16)

The wording of the first indent of Article 5(1)(b) of Regulation No 44/2001 does not refer expressly to a case such as that to which the question relates. The Article must therefore be interpreted in the light of the origins, objectives and scheme of that regulation. (paras 17, 18)

Regulation No 44/2001 seeks to unify the rules of conflict of jurisdiction in civil and commercial matters and to strengthen the legal protection of persons established in the Union, by enabling the plaintiff to identify easily the court in which he may sue and the defendant reasonably to foresee before which court he may be sued. (paras 19, 20)

The principal rule in the Regulation that 'jurisdiction is generally based on the defendant's domicile is complemented, in Article 5(1), by a rule of special jurisdiction in matters relating to a contract. The reason for that rule, which reflects an objective of proximity, is the existence of a close link between the contract and the court called upon to hear and determine the case. Under that rule the defendant may also be sued in the court for the place of performance of the obligation in question, since that court is presumed to have a close link to the contract.' (paras 21–3)

'Pursuant to the first indent of Article 5(1)(b) of that regulation, the place of performance of the obligation in question is the place in a Member State where, under the contract, the goods were delivered or should have been delivered. In the context of Regulation No 44/2001, contrary to Lexx's submissions, that rule of special jurisdiction in matters relating to a contract establishes the place of delivery as the autonomous linking factor to apply to all claims founded on one and the same contract for the sale of goods rather than merely to the claims founded on the obligation of delivery itself.' (paras 25, 26)

The first indent of Article 5(1)(b) of the regulation must be regarded as applying whether there is one place of delivery or several. 'By providing for a single court to have jurisdiction and a single linking factor, the [Union] legislature did not intend generally to exclude cases where a number of courts may have jurisdiction nor those where the existence of that linking factor can be established in different places.' (paras 28, 29)

The first indent of Article 5(1)(b) of Regulation No 44/2001 is applicable where there are several places of delivery within a single Member State. This applicability complies with the Regulation's objective of predictability as parties to the contract can easily and reasonably foresee before which Member State's courts they can bring their dispute. Additionally, it complies with the objective of proximity underlying the rules of special jurisdiction in matters relating to a contract. (paras 31–6)

'With regard, secondly, to the question whether, where there are several places of delivery within a single Member State and the claim relates to all those deliveries, the plaintiff may sue the defendant in the court for the place of delivery of its choice on the basis of the first indent of Article 5(1)(b) of Regulation No 44/2001, it is necessary to point out that one court must have jurisdiction to hear all the claims arising out of the contract.' (para 38)

'In that regard, it is appropriate to take into consideration the origins of the provision under consideration. By that provision, the [Union] legislature intended, in respect of sales contracts, expressly to break with the earlier solution under which the place of performance was determined, for each of the obligations in question, in accordance with the private international rules of the court seised of the dispute. By designating autonomously as the place of performance' the place where the obligation which characterises the contract is to be performed, the [Union] legislature sought to centralise at its place of performance jurisdiction over disputes concerning all the contractual obligations and to determine sole jurisdiction for all claims arising out of the contract.' (para 39)

'In that regard it is necessary to take account of the fact that the special jurisdiction under the first indent of Article 5(1)(b) of Regulation No 44/2001 is warranted, in principle, by the existence of a particularly close linking factor between the contract and the court called upon to hear the litigation, with a view to the efficient organisation of the proceedings. It follows that, where there are several places of delivery of the goods, "place of delivery" must be understood, for the purposes of application of the provision under consideration, as the place with the closest linking factor between the contract and the court having jurisdiction. In such a case, the point of closest linking factor will, as a general rule, be at the place of the principal delivery, which must be determined on the basis of economic criteria.' (para 40)

'If it is not possible to determine the principal place of delivery, each of the places of delivery has a sufficiently close link of proximity to the material elements of the dispute and, accordingly, a significant link as regards jurisdiction. In such a case, the plaintiff may sue the defendant in the court for the place of delivery of its choice on the basis of the first indent of Article 5(1)(b) of Regulation No 44/2001.' (para 42)

Comment

Note Advocate General Bot's opinion in which he took a different view on the determination of the competent court among those in whose territorial jurisdictions deliveries were made. (AG Bot opinion, 15 February 2007, paras 95–116, 130)

Regulation 44/2001 has been superseded by Regulation 1215/2012. The provisions of Article 5, may be found in Article 7 of the new Regulation (Special Jurisdiction).

Cooper Tire and Rubber Company v Shell Chemicals UK	**Private Enforcement**
A3/2009/2487 & A3/2009/2489	Jurisdiction
English Court of Appeal, [2010] EWCA Civ 864	Regulation No 44/2001

Facts

The legal proceedings in the national court stem from the European Commission's decision in Case COMP/F/38.638—*Butadiene Rubber and Emulsion Styrene Butadiene Rubber*. In its decision the Commission found 13 companies guilty of an infringement of Article 101 TFEU. The undertakings concerned were found to commit a complex single and continuous infringement of Article 101 TFEU by agreeing price targets for their products, sharing customers by non-aggression agreements, and exchanging sensitive commercial information relating to prices, competitors and customers. Following the Commission's decision, several tyre manufacturers issued proceedings in England against 24 defendants, only three of which were domiciled in England, who were alleged to be part of the cartel. These claims, for damages for breach of statutory duty, supplemented other proceedings which took place before the Italian court. The three defendants domiciled in England were not addressees of the Commission Decision. The defendants argued that they had been selected as a tactical device ('anchor defendants') to establish jurisdiction against the other defendants pursuant to Article 6(1), Regulation 44/2001.

Held

'The primary ground on which jurisdiction was asserted against [the defendants] is that the claims against the Anchor Defendants ... and the claims against the Dow Defendants are, in the words of Article 6(1) of the Judgments Regulation, "so closely connected that it is expedient to hear and determine them together to avoid the risk of irreconcilable judgments resulting from separate proceedings". (para 27)

'It seems to us that the particulars of claim encompass both the possibility that the Anchor Defendants were parties to or aware of the anti-competitive conduct of their parent company and the other Addressees and the possibility that they were not. It is only if they were not that what we have called the *Provimi* point will arise. But it is unnecessary to decide it on this application because it is open to the claimants on the pleadings to prove that the Anchor Defendants were parties to (or aware of) the Addressees' anti-competitive conduct. The strength (or otherwise) of any such case cannot be assessed (or indeed usefully particularised) until after disclosure of documents because it is in the nature of anti-competitive arrangements that they are shrouded in secrecy.' (para 43)

'In those circumstances, it is self-evident that the claims against the Dow Defendants are sufficiently closely connected with the claims against the Anchor Defendants to make it "expedient to hear and determine them together to avoid the wish of irreconcilable judgments resulting from separate proceedings" and that there is therefore jurisdiction for the English court to determine the claims against the Dow Defendants pursuant to Article 6(1). It also follows that it is not possible to distinguish between the claims.' (para 44)

Comment

Regulation 44/2001 has been superseded by Regulation 1215/2012. The provisions of Article 6(1) are found in Article 8 of the new Regulation.

The *Provimi* point referred to in the judgment (para 43) concerns the possibility that the Anchor companies were not aware of the anticompetitive activity. The English Court of Appeal questioned whether a subsidiary should be liable for what its parent does. The Court noted that if it had been necessary to address the *Provimi* point, it would have been inclined to make a reference to the Court of Justice before coming to a conclusion on jurisdiction. For a full discussion of that point see page 24 above (Undertakings). The Court held, however, that there is no need to resolve the matter at this stage as it is open to the claimants on the pleadings to prove that the Anchor defendants were parties to, or aware of, the anticompetitive conduct.

Cartel Damage Claims Hydrogen Peroxide SA	**Private Enforcement**
Case C-352/13	Jurisdiction
Court of Justice, [2015] 5 CMLR 4	Regulation No 44/2001

Facts

A request for a preliminary ruling concerns the interpretation of Articles 5(3), 6(1) and 23 of Council Regulation 44/2001. The request has been made in proceedings initiated by Cartel Damage Claims Hydrogen Peroxide SA ('CDC')—a company domiciled in Brussels, which was established for the purpose of pursuing claims for damages on behalf of undertakings affected by a cartel. CDC brought an action for damages against six chemical undertakings for infringement of Article 101 TFEU. The National Court requested the Court of Justice to advise on the application of Regulation No 44/2001 in light of the multitude of claims and defendants in the case.

Held

Single and continuous infringement

Derogations from the principle that jurisdiction is based on the defendant's domicile must be strictly interpreted. Article 6(1) of Regulation 44/2001 provides that 'a person may, where he is one of a number of defendants, be sued in the courts for the place where any one of them is domiciled, provided the claims are so closely connected that it is expedient to hear and determine them together to avoid the risk of irreconcilable judgments resulting from separate proceedings (… *Painer*, C-145/10, … paragraph 73, and in *Sapir and Others*, C-645/11, …, paragraph 40).' (paras 16–18)

'[I]n order for Article 6(1) of Regulation No 44/2001 to apply, it is necessary to ascertain whether, between various claims brought by the same applicant against various defendants, there is a connection of such a kind that it is expedient to determine those actions together in order to avoid the risk of irreconcilable judgments resulting from separate proceedings… In that regard, in order for judgments to be regarded as irreconcilable, it is not sufficient that there be a divergence in the outcome of the dispute, but that divergence must also arise in the context of the same situation of fact and law.' (para 20)

Where, as in this case, the cartel agreement amounted to a single and continuous infringement, a separate determination of actions for damages against several undertakings in different Member States may lead to irreconcilable judgments within the meaning of Article 6(1) of Regulation 44/2001. (paras 21–5)

Use of anchor defendant

'CDC withdrew its action against the anchor defendant—Evonik Degussa. This does not affect the jurisdiction of the court. Where claims brought against various defendants are connected within the meaning of Article 6(1) of Regulation 44/2001, … the rule of jurisdiction laid down in that provision is applicable without there being any further need to establish separately that the claims were not brought with the sole object of ousting the jurisdiction of the courts of the Member State where one of the defendants is domiciled … can find that the rule of jurisdiction laid down in that provision has potentially been circumvented only where there is firm evidence to support the conclusion that the applicant artificially fulfilled, or prolonged the fulfilment of, that provision's applicability.' (paras 28–9)

Place of the harmful event

'In matters relating to tort and delict and quasi-delict, the courts for the place where the harmful event occurred or may occur are usually the most appropriate for deciding the case, in particular on the grounds of proximity and ease of taking evidence (judgment in *Melzer*, C-228/11, … paragraph 27).' (para 40)

'However, given that the jurisdiction of the court seised of the matter by virtue of the place where the loss occurred is limited to the loss suffered by the undertaking whose registered office is located in its jurisdiction, an applicant such as CDC, who has consolidated several undertakings' potential claims for damages, would therefore, in accordance with the case-law set out in paragraph 35 above, need to bring separate actions for the loss suffered by each of those undertakings before the courts with jurisdiction for their respective registered offices.' (para 55)

'In the light of the above, the answer to the second question is that Article 5(3) of Regulation No 44/2001 must be interpreted as meaning that, in the case of an action for damages brought against defendants domiciled in various Member States as a result of a single and continuous infringement of Article 101 TFEU and Article 53 of the EEA Agreement, which has been established by the Commission, in which the defendants participated in several Member States, at different times and in different places, the harmful event occurred in relation to each alleged victim on an individual basis and each of the victims can, by virtue of Article 5(3), choose to bring an action before the courts of the place in which the cartel was definitively concluded or, as the case may be, the place in which one agreement in particular was concluded which is identifiable as the sole causal event giving rise to the loss allegedly suffered, or before the courts of the place where its own registered office is located.' (para 56)

Choice of forum clause

'[B]y concluding an agreement on the choice of court under Article 17 of the Brussels Convention, the parties may derogate, not only from the general jurisdiction under Article 2 thereof, but also from the special jurisdiction laid down in Articles 5 and 6 of that convention.' (para 59)

'Given that the undertaking which suffered the loss could not reasonably foresee such litigation at the time that it agreed to the jurisdiction clause and that that undertaking had no knowledge of the unlawful cartel at that time, such litigation cannot be regarded as stemming from a contractual relationship. Such a clause would not therefore have validly derogated from the referring court's jurisdiction. By contrast, where a clause refers to disputes in connection with liability incurred as a result of an infringement of competition law and designates the courts of a Member State other than the Member State of the referring court, the latter ought to decline its own jurisdiction, even where that clause entails disregarding the special rules of jurisdiction laid down in Articles 5 and/or 6 of Regulation No 44/2001.' (paras 70–1)

Comment

When dealing with a single and continuous infringement, it is likely to be expedient to hear the claims together to avoid irreconcilable judgments within the meaning of Article 6(1) of Regulation 44/2001.

The use of anchor defendant: a withdrawal of the anchor defendant (following a settlement) should not affect jurisdiction, as long as jurisdiction was not artificially created—for instance through illicit agreement between the anchor defendant and the claimant.

Place of harmful event: Article 5(3) is not a useful benchmark for establishing jurisdiction in the case of a single and continuous infringement by numerous defendants in several Member States, since the jurisdiction of the court is limited to the loss suffered by the undertaking whose registered office is located in its jurisdiction. Article 6, and the use of anchor defendant, offer a superior jurisdictional base.

Choice of forum: a jurisdiction clause concerning contractual disputes will not be viable in the case of a competition law infringement. To have effect, such clause would need to refer specifically to disputes concerning liability incurred as a result of an infringement of competition law.

Regulation 44/2001 has been superseded by Regulation 1215/2012.

12

Extraterritoriality

Principles of Extraterritoriality

In the field of competition law an infringement can have consequences within a given territory even though the conduct that caused those consequences occurred, and may have even been completed, elsewhere. In order to protect their domestic markets, competition agencies may extend their jurisdiction beyond the boundaries of their state and apply their national laws to activities that may have been cleared by the local jurisdiction in which they took place, but nevertheless affect competition within the former.

This concept of extraterritoriality departs from the traditional 'territoriality principle' under which a country has the power to make laws to affect conduct within its territory or to regulate conduct which although initiated in another jurisdiction, is completed within its territory.

The extension of the territoriality principle in competition cases commonly relies on one of two concepts. The first extends jurisdiction where the transaction has an effect within the given territory. The second is more restricted in nature and requires 'implementation' within the given territory as a condition for extraterritorial application of domestic laws.

The Effects Doctrine—US Antitrust Law

The examination of effects was initially recognised by the Permanent Court of International Justice in the *Lotus* case, with regard to the extent of States' criminal jurisdiction over acts causing a collision in open sea (*France v Turkey*, 1927 Permanent Court of International Justice, Ser A, no 10). The Court found that international law does not contain a general prohibition on States to extend the application of their laws and the jurisdiction of their Courts to persons, property and acts outside their territory. The Court developed the objective of the territorial principle into its variation of the effects principle and stated that 'offences ... which at the moment of commission are in the territory of another State, are nevertheless to be regarded as having been committed in the national territory, if one of the constituent elements of the offence, and more especially its effects, have taken place there'. (para IV)

The effects doctrine has been particularly significant in US enforcement of antitrust law. In *United States v Aluminum Co of America*, the US Second Circuit Court asserted that: 'Any state may impose liabilities, even upon persons not within its allegiance, for conduct outside its borders, which has consequences within its borders, which State reprehends; and these liabilities other States will ordinarily recognize.' *United States v Aluminum Company of America* (Aloca) 148 F 2d 416 (2 Cir 1945).

In some of the cases which followed, such as *Timberlane Lumber Co v Bank of America* (549 F 2d at 596, 613–14 (9th Cir 1976)) and *Metro Industries Inc v Sammi Corp* (82 F 3d 839 (9th Cir 1996)), the courts applied the effects doctrine in a more restrictive way, requiring that not only should there be a direct and substantial effect within the US, but also that the respective interests of the US should be weighed against the interests of other States involved. By contrast, other cases followed a more expansive approach as laid down by the Supreme Court in the case of *Hartford Fire Insurance Co v California* (*Hartford Fire Insurance Co v California* 113 S Ct 2891 (1993)).

These cases, although different in their tone and emphasis, share the notion that under certain conditions the finding of direct and substantial effects enables the assertion of US jurisdiction.

The Implementation Doctrine

The European Court of Justice has taken a narrower approach and has refrained from a direct and clear adoption of the 'effects' doctrine. In its rulings, the Court of Justice preferred to limit itself to the extension of the territoriality principle.

In the *Wood Pulp* judgment, the Court of Justice held that jurisdiction under EU law exists over firms outside the Union if they implement a price-fixing agreement reached outside the EU by selling to purchasers within it. See:

89/85 etc	*A Ahlström Osakeyhtiö v Commission (Wood Pulp)*	630

Although the effects and implementation doctrines rely on different principles of public international law, they do provide for similar jurisdictional coverage. In other words, most anticompetitive activities would generate effects through implementation, thus satisfying both benchmarks. A noticeable activity which may result in 'effects' yet not 'implementation' is that of a boycott cartel, where undertakings refuse to supply goods to a territory, thus affecting competition without implementing the agreement in the foreign territory.

Implementation <u>and</u> immediate, foreseeable and substantial effect in the European Union

In *Gencor Limited v Commission* the General Court made reference to the implementation principle as established in *Wood Pulp* before finding that the transaction can be subjected to the European Merger Regulation. The General Court then supplemented the *Wood Pulp* test by establishing that EU competition laws are applicable if the conduct at issue has immediate, foreseeable and substantial effect in the Union.

In the *LCD Cartel* case, the Commission referred to both the *Wood Pulp* and *Gencor* judgments when applying Article 101 TFEU to foreign companies which operated the cartel. The Commission combined the implementation benchmark (*Wood Pulp*) and the 'immediate, foreseeable and substantial effect' benchmark (*Gencor*), when establishing its long arm jurisdiction.

T-102/96	*Gencor Ltd v Commission*	632
COMP/39.309	*Liquid Crystal Displays (LCD) Cartel*	634

See also summary references to:

IV/M.877	*Boeing/McDonnell Douglas*	633
COMP/M.2220	*General Electric/Honeywell*	633

Implementation <u>or</u> Immediate, foreseeable and substantial effect in the European Union

In the *Intel Corp* judgment, the General Court clarified that the *Woodpulp and Gencor* benchmarks are alternative and that there is no legal requirement to satisfy both.

T-286/09	*Intel Corp*	636

The Single Economic Entity Doctrine

Another doctrine that has been used to exert jurisdiction over foreign undertakings is the 'single economic entity' doctrine. This doctrine enables the extension of jurisdiction over corporations located outside the jurisdiction by treating the corporate group as a single economic unit and attributing the conduct of one of the group's members which is located outside the jurisdiction to other members of the group based inside the jurisdiction. This doctrine is limited in scope and application, as it requires the presence of at least one of the group's undertaking in the domestic territory and the finding of a 'single economic entity'. See:

Also note the following case entries in Chapter 1 on the concept of 'undertakings' and 'single economic entity':

A Ahlström Osakeyhtiö and others v Commission (Wood Pulp)	**Extraterritoriality**
Joined Cases 89, 104, 114, 116, 117 and 125 to 129/85	Implementation Doctrine
Court of Justice, [1988] ECR 5193, [1988] 4 CMLR 901	

Facts

In this case, the Commission had issued a decision against non-EU producers of wood pulp for various restrictive practices alleged to have restrained trade within the EU. A number of the producers had no subsidiaries or branches in the EU and one, KEA, was a US Webb–Pomerene export association. The Commission stated that Article 101 TFEU applies to restrictive practices which may affect trade between Member States even if the undertakings and associations which are parties to the restrictive practices are established outside the European Union. The foreign defendants argued, among other things, that the Commission lacked jurisdiction over them because of their location outside the EU. The Court of Justice rejected their argument and held that jurisdiction under EU law exists over firms outside it if they implement price fixing reached outside the EU by selling to purchasers within the Union.

Held

'In so far as the submission concerning the infringement of [Article 101 TFEU] itself is concerned, it should be recalled that that provision prohibits all agreements between undertakings and concerted practices which may affect trade between Member States and which have as their object or effect the restriction of competition within the [internal] market.' (para 11)

'It should be noted that the main sources of supply of wood pulp are outside the [Union], in Canada, the United States, Sweden and Finland, and that the market therefore has global dimensions. Where wood pulp producers established in those countries sell directly to purchasers established in the [Union] and engage in price competition in order to win orders from those customers, that constitutes competition within the [internal] market.' (para 12)

'It follows that where those producers concert on the prices to be charged to their customers in the [Union] and put that concertation into effect by selling at prices which are actually coordinated, they are taking part in concertation which has the object and effect of restricting competition within the [internal] market within the meaning of [Article 101 TFEU].' (para 13)

'Accordingly, it must be concluded that by applying the competition rules in the Treaty in the circumstances of this case to undertakings whose registered offices are situated outside the [Union], the Commission has not made an incorrect assessment of the territorial scope of [Article 101].' (para 14)

'The applicants have submitted that the decision is incompatible with public international law on the grounds that the application of the competition rules in this case was founded exclusively on the economic repercussions within the [internal] market of conduct restricting competition which was adopted outside the [Union].' (para 15)

'It should be observed that an infringement of [Article 101 TFEU], such as the conclusion of an agreement which has had the effect of restricting competition within the [internal] market, consists of conduct made up of two elements, the formation of the agreement, decision or concerted practice and the implementation thereof. If the applicability of prohibitions laid down under competition law were made to depend on the place where the agreement, decision or concerted practice was formed, the result would obviously be to give undertakings an easy means of evading those prohibitions. The decisive factor is therefore the place where it is implemented.' (para 16)

'The producers in this case implemented their pricing agreement within the [internal] market. It is immaterial in that respect whether or not they had recourse to subsidiaries, agents, sub-agents, or branches within the [Union] in order to make their contacts with purchasers within the [EU].' (para 17)

'Accordingly the [EU's] jurisdiction to apply its competition rules to such conduct is covered by the territoriality principle as universally recognized in public international law.' (para 18)

'As regards the argument based on the infringement of the principle of non-interference, it should be pointed out that the applicants who are members of KEA have referred to a rule according to which, where two States have jurisdiction to lay down and enforce rules and the effect of those rules is that a person finds himself subject to contradictory orders as to the conduct he must adopt, each State is obliged to exercise its jurisdiction with moderation. The applicants have concluded that by disregarding that rule in applying its competition rules the [Union] has infringed the principle of non-interference.' (para 19)

'There is no need to enquire into the existence in international law of such a rule since it suffices to observe that the conditions for its application are in any event not satisfied. There is not, in this case, any contradiction between the conduct required by the United States and that required by the [Union] since the Webb Pomerene Act merely exempts the conclusion of export cartels from the application of United States anti-trust laws but does not require such cartels to be concluded.' (para 20)

'It should further be pointed out that the United States authorities raised no objections regarding any conflict of jurisdiction when consulted by the Commission pursuant to the OECD Council Recommendation of 25 October 1979 concerning Cooperation between Member Countries on Restrictive Business Practices affecting International Trade (Acts of the Organization, Vol 19, p 376).' (para 21)

'Accordingly it must be concluded that the Commission's decision is not contrary to [Article 101 TFEU] or to the rules of public international law relied on by the applicants.' (para 23)

Comment

By referring to the implementation of the agreement (and not to its formation) and by relying on the specific facts of the case, the Court of Justice was able to establish jurisdiction using an extension of the territoriality principle. Overall, although tailored narrowly to the facts of the case, *Wood Pulp* set the basic criteria for the extraterritorial application of EU competition law while defining the implementation of an agreement as the leading benchmark for jurisdiction.

The court held that implementation is not dependent on the existence of 'subsidiaries, agents, sub-agents, or branches within the [Union]'. (para 17) The focus is therefore on the act of sale within the EU. Note in this respect the General Court judgment in Case T-102/96 *Gencor Ltd v Commission* (page 632 below) in which the court held that 'the implementation of an agreement is satisfied by mere sale within the [Union]. (para 87)

After establishing the extraterritorial jurisdiction based on the implementation doctrine, the Court considered the possible infringement of the principle of non-interference. It held that there was no contradiction between the conduct required by the United States and that required by the European Union since the Webb–Pomerene Act merely permits the conclusion of export cartels but does not require such cartels to be concluded. (paras 19–21)

In his opinion, Advocate General Darmon asserted that the wording of Article 101 TFEU offers general support for the applicability of EU competition law whenever anticompetitive effects have been produced within the territory of the Union. The Advocate General, supporting the adoption of the effects doctrine, took the view that it is 'neither the nationality nor the geographical location of the undertaking but the location of the anti-competitive effect which constitutes the criteria for the application of [Union] competition law'. (opinion of Advocate General Darmon [1988] 4 CMLR 901, 916–37)

Gencor Ltd v Commission	**Extraterritoriality**
Case T-102/96	Implementation Doctrine
General Court, [1999] ECR II-753	Immediate, Foreseeable and Substantial Effects

Facts

Gencor, a company incorporated under South African law, and Lonrho Plc (Lonrho), a company incorporated under English law, proposed to acquire joint control of Impala Platinum Holdings Ltd (Implats), a company incorporated under South African law. The transaction was cleared by the South African Competition Board. The European Commission also reviewed the transaction under the European Merger Regulation and was concerned with its impact on the internal market. Following its investigation the Commission blocked the transaction on the ground that it would lead to the creation of a dominant duopoly position in the world platinum and rhodium market as a result of which effective competition would have been significantly impeded in the internal market. Gencor applied to the General Court for annulment of the decision, and argued, among other things, that the Commission lacked jurisdiction over the transaction at issue.

Held

In contrast to the Commission's view, the mere notification of a concentration to the Commission under the procedure in the European Merger Regulation does not imply a voluntary submission by the undertaking to the Commission's jurisdiction. Such notification stems from the severe financial penalties which may be imposed under the European Merger Regulation for failure to notify the Commission of the concentration. (para 76)

The European Merger Regulation applies to all Concentrations with a Community Dimension. Article 1 of the Regulation does not require that, in order for a Concentration to be regarded as having a Community Dimension, the undertakings in question must be established in the EU or that the production activities covered by the Concentration must be carried out within Union territory. (paras 78–86)

'According to *Wood Pulp*, the criterion as to the implementation of an agreement is satisfied by mere sale within the [EU], irrespective of the location of the sources of supply and the production plant. It is not disputed that Gencor and Lonrho carried out sales in the [EU] before the concentration and would have continued to do so thereafter.' (para 87)

'Accordingly, the Commission did not err in its assessment of the territorial scope of the [European Merger Regulation] by applying it in this case to a proposed concentration notified by undertakings whose registered offices and mining and production operations are outside the [Union].' (para 88)

It is necessary to consider whether the Commission's decision is compatible with principles of public international law. In this case the concentration would have altered the competitive structure within the internal market since in would reduce the number of undertakings in the market from three to two. 'The implementation of the proposed concentration would have led to the merger not only of the parties' ... operations in South Africa but also of their marketing operations throughout the world, particularly in the [Union] where Implats and LPD achieved significant sales.' (para 89)

Application of the Regulation is justified under public international law when it is foreseeable that a proposed concentration will have an immediate, substantial and foreseeable effect in the EU. These three criteria are satisfied in this case. (paras 90–101)

It is necessary to examine next whether the EU violated a principle of non-interference or the principle of proportionality in exercising its jurisdiction. In this case there was no conflict between the course of action required by the South African Government and that required by the Commission given that the South African competition authorities simply concluded that the concentration agreement did not give rise to any competition policy concerns, without requiring that such an agreement be entered into. (paras 102–5)

Comment

After establishing that the concentration had a Community dimension, the Court made references to the implementation doctrine and held that it is satisfied by a mere sale within the EU.

After referring to the implementation of the agreement, the General Court considered its effects in the internal market. (paras 81–101) This section of the judgment created some ambiguity as to whether the General Court embraced the effects doctrine as a jurisdictional benchmark. The Court supplemented the implementation test by examining whether the conduct at issue has immediate, foreseeable and substantial effect in the Union. The relationship between these two tests was later explored in the *Intel* judgment (page 636 below).

Transactions which satisfy the requirement for concentration and Community (Union) Dimension as set in the Merger Regulation will exhibit large turnover within the EU and thus satisfy the requirement for implementation. The requirement for EU-wide turnover creates a strong nexus between the transaction and the internal market and is likely to result not only in implementation but also in substantial and foreseeable effect. In other words, in practice, the European Merger Regulation jurisdictional threshold of concentration with a Community (Union) Dimension is likely to encompass both the implementation and effects threshold.

Two noticeable Commission Decisions that highlight the potential tension such long-arm jurisdiction may result in are the *Boeing/McDonnell Douglas* and *General Electric/Honeywell* transactions.

In *Boeing/McDonnell Douglas* (Case IV/M.877), the European Commission reviewed a transaction between two corporations based in the United States. Although neither Boeing nor McDonnell Douglas had any facilities or assets in the European Union, their EU-wide and worldwide turnover met the thresholds laid down in Article 1 European Merger Regulation and brought the transaction under the Commission's jurisdiction. Before the Commission withdrew its objections to the transaction, the merger triggered a debate on the Commission's authority to assess and block the transaction. Some critics suggested that the Commission's concerns were based purely on its protectionist interest in promoting Airbus, rejecting the Commission's claim that its investigation was conducted strictly on the basis of EU law. The tension between the EU and the US authorities increased, leading to President Clinton's announcement threatening that the matter could be taken to the World Trade Organization if the EU carried out its threat to declare the merger illegal. The clearance of the merger served to silence most of these critics, but the case nevertheless illustrates the possible political clashes due to extraterritorial application of merger analysis on significant transactions close to the heart of the home jurisdiction.

In the *General Electric/Honeywell* decision (Case COMP/M.2220), the European Commission prohibited the proposed $42 billion acquisition by General Electric Co (GE) of Honeywell Inc. The Commission asserted that the merger would have severely reduced competition in the aerospace industry by combining GE's strong position in the aircraft engine markets with Honeywell's similarly strong position in avionics and non-avionics systems. The importance of the *GE/Honeywell* decision lies in the fact that the Commission's decision followed an opposite conclusion by the US Department of Justice (DOJ), which cleared the merger earlier that year, requiring only minimal disposals. The DOJ Antitrust Division reached the conclusion that the merger, as modified by the remedies insisted upon, would have been procompetitive and beneficial to consumers. The DOJ concluded that the combined firm would offer better products and services at more attractive prices than either firm could do individually. In addition to the differences in the legal approach towards the transaction, the extraterritoriality resulted in political tension between the two jurisdictions. Similar to the *Boeing/McDonnell Douglas* case, this transaction drew attention to the possibility of implementing non-competitive considerations disguised by competition analysis. The Commission was subject to accusations that it implemented such considerations in its assessment. Commissioner Monti rejected these claims, asserting that 'this is a matter of law and economics, not politics'. The Commissioner added that 'the nationality of the companies and political considerations have played and will play no role in the examination of mergers in this case and in all others'. This statement by the Commission may also be seen as a response to increased political pressure from the US, attempting to persuade the Commission to relax its opposition.

Liquid Crystal Displays (LCD) Cartel	**Extraterritoriality**
Case COMP/39.309	Implementation Doctrine
European Commission, [2011] OJ C295/8	Immediate, Foreseeable and Substantial Effects

Facts

The Commission found six foreign producers of LCD panels to infringe Article 101 TFEU by entering into a cartel agreement which harmed European buyers of television sets and computers. Members of the cartel fixed prices, and exchanged information on production planning, capacity and other commercial conditions. The cartel impacted directly on European customers who purchased LCD panels produced by the cartel members. The parties argued, among other things, that in this case the European Commission lacked jurisdiction over undertakings outside the European Union since the agreement lacked sufficient nexus with the European Union and because the principle of international comity requires the Commission to refrain from applying domestic laws when doing so would impinge on the territorial sovereignty of another state. In addition they argued that the Commission should have established that the cartel agreement had an effect on sales to direct customers established in the Union and that those effects were substantial, immediate and foreseeable.

Held

'The application by the Union of its competition rules is governed by the territoriality principle as a universally recognised principle of international law. In this respect, the Court of Justice established in the *Wood Pulp* case that the decisive factor in the determination of the applicability of Article 101 of the Treaty in cases where the participants of a cartel are seated outside the Union is whether the agreement, decision or concerted practice was implemented within the Union. More specifically, the Court of Justice observed in that case that the producers were selling directly into the Union and were engaging in price competition in order to win orders from the customers, thereby constituting competition within the Union. Therefore, stated the Court of Justice, where those producers concert on the prices to be charged to their customers in the Union and put that concertation into effect by selling at prices which are actually coordinated, they are taking part in a concertation which has the object and effect of restricting competition within the internal market within the meaning of Article 101 of the Treaty. The Court of Justice also stated that an infringement of Article 101, such as the conclusion of an agreement which has had the effect of restricting competition within the internal market, consists of conduct made up of two elements: the formation of the agreement, decision or concerted practice and the implementation thereof. If the applicability of the prohibitions laid down under Union competition law were made to depend on the place where the agreement, decision or concerted practice was formed, the result would be to give undertakings an easy means of evading those prohibitions. The decisive factor is therefore the place where the agreement, decision or concerted practice is implemented. Accordingly, the jurisdiction of the Union to apply its competition rules to such conduct is covered by the territoriality principle.' (para 230)

'The General Court supplemented [in Case T-102/96, *Gencor Ltd v Commission*] that test by establishing that the rules of Union competition law [The Merger Regulation] are applicable if the conduct at issue has immediate, foreseeable and substantial effect in the Union.' (para 231)

'In this case, it can be established that the agreements related to the world-wide sales of the LCD panels, without geographical limitations, affecting prices globally. This is clear from the fact that in most cases no such limitations were applied by the parties during their discussions on panel types and sizes in general... Within the global framework, the agreement ... also related to direct sales of panels to undertakings seated in the EEA. ... Europe was also targeted by substantial Indirect Sales, in which the parties had a very high joint market share.' (para 235)

'In line with the criteria set by the Court of Justice in the *Wood Pulp* case, the Commission has jurisdiction to establish an infringement in this case where LCD suppliers established in third countries concerted on the prices to be charged to their customers in the EEA and put that concertation into effect by selling to those customers at prices which were actually coordinated. Even if the cartel arrangements were formed outside the EEA, the cartel participants, through their direct sales into the EEA, implemented their agreements and concerted practices within such geographic area.' (para 236)

'Even if ... the main focus of the agreement was not Europe, ... contemporaneous evidence shows that beside explicitly discussing some of their main customers in Europe ... the parties were analysing and referring to the effects of the implemented agreement on the European market and therefore sought their agreement to be implemented and have effects also within the EEA. ...That implementation took place through the direct sales ... in the EEA ... even if the negotiation of the price took place outside the EEA.' (para 237)

'Based on the sale of the LCD panels to the EEA ... it can thus also be established that the infringement had foreseeable, immediate and substantial effect in the Union in the sense of the *Gencor* case law. First, the infringement immediately affected the EEA market since the agreements and concerted practices directly influenced the setting of price for LCD panels delivered directly or through transformed products to European customers. In this case the effects on the market of the price fixing agreements have been even more immediate as the monthly fixing of prices were prone to result in effects within a month or, at the latest, with the selling out of existing customer stocks. Secondly, the effect on the European market was foreseeable as the price rise or the maintenance of higher prices and the reduction of output were to have evident consequences on the conditions of competition at the downstream level for all IT and TV applications. Since the undertakings participated in a global cartel with which they intended to cover customers in Europe and which was implemented through direct sales of LCD panels and transformed products in the EEA, it is irrelevant whether the suppliers knew of the destination of specific orders, whether sales into the EEA were made to key customers actually named during the cartel meetings or whether the price negotiations with individual customers took place within or outside the EEA. The immediate and foreseeable effect on the EEA market were also present in the case of integrated suppliers like Samsung. As confirmed by the General Court in *Cartonboard* even if the higher price resulting from a cartel is not always or not in its entirety passed on to intra-group customers, the competitive advantage deriving from this positive discrimination does foreseeably influence competition on the market. Intra-group sales of LCD panels—in as far as they ended up into transformed products sold in the EEA—are therefore to be taken into account, just like intra-cartel sales in the EEA. Finally, the effect of the agreement were substantial due to the seriousness of the infringement, its long duration and the role of the parties on the European market for final and intermediate products. In this assessment sales of panels of non-IT or TV application and sales outside the EEA are not involved.' (para 238)

'As to AUO's argument concerning the low level of EEA sales as compared to its overall sales in the first years of the infringement, it should be noted that, for the purpose of establishing jurisdiction, all that matters is whether the cartel as a whole was implemented and had immediate, foreseeable and substantial effects in the EEA. It is irrelevant whether those effects were limited for a given party, in a given period of time, as compared to the world-wide effects of the cartel. In any event,... the parties had significant Direct EEA Sales and Direct EEA Sales Through Transformed Products.' (para 239)

'Concerning the arguments of AUO and LPL on the issue of international comity, the procedure of the Commission is by no means in breach of the obligations deriving from the international law principle of comity, ... The Korean competition authority was duly consulted during the administrative procedure and did not claim that any of the important interests mentioned in Article 5 of the EU-Korea agreement was affected ... As the General Court has confirmed in the *Tokai Carbon* case, the assessment of a cartel's application and effects within the EEA clearly belongs to the jurisdiction of the Commission. [Case T-236/01 etc *Tokai Carbon and others v Commission* [2004] ECR II-1181, paragraph 143.]' (paras 240–1)

Comment

The Commission concluded that it has jurisdiction to apply EU competition law to this case as the agreement was implemented (*Wood Pulp* criteria) and had immediate, foreseeable and substantial effects in the Union (*Gencor* criteria).

Intel Corp v European Commission	**Extraterritoriality**
Case T-286/09	Implementation Doctrine
General Court, [2014] 5 CMLR 9	Immediate, Foreseeable and Substantial Effects

Facts

The European Commission imposed a fine of €1,060,000,000 on Intel Corporation for abusing its dominant position in the worldwide market for 'x86 central processing units' (CPUs). Intel challenged the Commission's finding that the grant of a rebate was contrary to Article 102 TFEU. (On the analysis of abuse, see Chapter 5.) It also raised arguments with respect to the Commission's jurisdiction in this case. The General Court dismissed Intel's action for annulment and upheld the fine. The Court clarified that two alternative approaches may be used to establish extraterritorial application based on *implementation*, or alternatively on *qualified effects*.

Held

Alternative conditions

'[I]n the case-law of the Court of Justice and the General Court, two approaches have been followed in order to establish that the Commission's jurisdiction is justified under the rules of public international law. The first approach is based on the principle of territoriality. That approach was followed in Joined Cases 89/85 … *Ahlström Osakeyhtiö and Others v Commission* [1988] ECR 5193, 'Woodpulp'). In paragraph 16 of that judgment, the Court held that it was necessary to distinguish two elements of conduct, namely the formation of the agreement, decision or concerted practice and the implementation thereof. If the applicability of prohibitions laid down under competition law were made to depend on the place where the agreement, decision or concerted practice was formed, the result would obviously be to give undertakings an easy means of evading those prohibitions. The Court therefore held that the decisive factor is the place where it is implemented. The second approach is based on the qualified effects of the practices in the European Union. That approach was followed in Case T-102/96 *Gencor v Commission* [1999] ECR II-753, 'Gencor'. In paragraph 90 of that judgment, the Court held that application of Council Regulation (EEC) No 4064/89 of 21 December 1989 on the control of concentrations between undertakings (OJ 1989 L 395, p 1), as corrected (OJ 1990 L 257, p 13), is justified under public international law when it is foreseeable that a proposed concentration will have an immediate and substantial effect in the European Union.' (paras 231–3)

'[D]emonstrating the implementation of the practices at issue in the EEA or demonstrating qualified effects are alternative and not cumulative approaches for the purposes of establishing that the Commission's jurisdiction is justified under the rules of public international law.' (paras 236–7)

Substantial, direct and foreseeable effects

'The applicant claims that the Commission's failure to examine the existence of substantial, direct and foreseeable effects in the European Union is a particularly significant failing in circumstances where the Commission states, at recital 1685 of the contested decision, that it does not need "to prove the actual effects of an abuse under Article 82 [EC]".' (para 250)

'In that regard, the Court would point out that the Commission is not obliged to establish the existence of actual effects in order to justify its jurisdiction under public international law. The criteria of immediate, substantial and foreseeable effects do not mean that the effect must also be actual.' (para 251)

'Accordingly, the view cannot be taken that the Commission is required to confine itself to pursuing and punishing abuse which achieved the intended result and in respect of which the threat to the functioning of competition materialised. The Commission cannot be expected to adopt a passive position where there is a threat to the effective competition structure in the common market and may therefore intervene also in cases in which the threat did not materialise or has not yet materialised.' (para 252)

Single and continuous infringement

When considering a single and continuous infringement by an undertaking and whether the Commission's jurisdiction is justified under public international law, the undertaking's practices should viewed as a whole.

'Undertakings cannot be allowed to escape application of the competition rules by combining several practices pursuing the same objective, when each practice viewed in isolation is not liable to produce a substantial effect in the European Union but the practices, taken together, are liable to produce such an effect.' (paras 269, 270)

'In the present case, it should be recalled that the single and continuous infringement, viewed as a whole, affected on average, according to the calculations by the applicant's adviser, approximately 14% of the global market if those calculations are not limited to only the contestable share; this must be regarded as a significant share of the market (see paragraph 194 above). That is sufficient to establish that the potential effects of the applicant's practices were substantial.' (paras 271, 272)

Indirect sales and implementation

'The applicant claims that, according to case-law, direct sales into the European Union by the undertaking itself of the products covered by the conduct concerned are required to establish the Commission's jurisdiction. In the present case, the Commission has not established that each of the alleged acts of abuse encompassed direct sales of the relevant product … by Intel to purchasers in the European Union.' (paras 298–9)

The mere fact that Intel did not sell CPUs to purchasers in the European Union does not preclude implementation of the practices at issue. 'In the present case, the Commission did not refer, in the contested decision, to action initiated by the applicant itself in the territory of the EEA in order to implement the naked restriction concerning Acer. Nevertheless, the abuse of a dominant position consisted in the present case in the grant of a financial incentive in order to encourage Acer to postpone the launch of a certain notebook worldwide. The condition to which the payments granted by Intel were subject, namely the postponement of a certain AMD-based notebook, was therefore intended to be implemented worldwide by Acer, including in the EEA. In such circumstances, it would be artificial merely to take into consideration the implementation of the practices at issue by the undertaking in a dominant position itself. On the contrary, it is also necessary to take into consideration the implementation of those practices by the customer of that undertaking. In that context, the fact that the customer of the undertaking in a dominant position refrains from selling a certain computer model in the EEA for a certain period must be regarded as implementation of the naked restriction. … It follows from the foregoing that the Commission's jurisdiction was justified also on account of the implementation of the infringement in the territory of the European Union.' (paras 303–7)

Comment

The Court rejected Intel's argument that that implementation and qualified effects in the European Union should be viewed as cumulative conditions. It held that they form alternative benchmarks for jurisdiction. The Court then held that both benchmarks were successfully established in this case.

The Court held that the criteria of 'immediate, substantial and foreseeable effects' do not amount to 'actual effect'. The Commission is not obliged to establish the existence of actual effects in order to justify its jurisdiction under public international law.

Implementation may occur through the actions of a customer of a dominant undertaking which implements the dominant undertaking's strategy by refraining from selling a competitor's products in the EU.

Imperial Chemical Industries Ltd v Commission (Dyestuffs)	**Extraterritoriality**
Case C-48/69	Economic Entity Doctrine
Court of Justice, [1972] ECR 619, [1972] CMLR 557	

Facts

An application for annulment of a Commission Decision in which seventeen producers of dyestuffs established within and outside the internal market were found to have colluded with the aim of increasing the price of dyestuffs. In its decision the Commission asserted that Article 101 TFEU applies to all agreements or concerted practices which distort competition within the internal market, regardless of the location of the undertakings involved. The producers challenged the Commission's extraterritorial jurisdiction.

Held

The increased prices at issue were put into effect within the internal market. The actions for which the fine at issue has been imposed constitute practices carried on directly within that market. (paras 127, 128)

'By making use of its power to control its subsidiaries established in the [Union], the applicant was able to ensure that its [d]ecision was implemented on that market.' (para 130)

'The applicant objects that this conduct is to be imputed to its subsidiaries and not to itself.' (para 131)

'The fact that a subsidiary has separate legal personality is not sufficient to exclude the possibility of imputing its conduct to the parent company.' (para 132)

'Such may be the case in particular where the subsidiary, although having separate legal personality, does not decide independently upon its own conduct on the market, but carries out, in all material respects, the instructions given to it by the parent company.' (para 133)

'Where a subsidiary does not enjoy real autonomy in determining its course of action in the market, the prohibitions set out in [Article 101(1) TFEU] may be considered inapplicable in the relationship between it and the parent company with which it forms one economic unit.' (para 134)

'In view of the unity of the group thus formed, the actions of the subsidiaries may in certain circumstances be attributed to the parent company.' (para 135)

In this case the applicant held the majority of the shares in the subsidiaries and was able to exercise decisive influence over the policy of the subsidiaries as regards selling prices in the internal market. In fact the applicant used this power in relation to the three price increases in question. 'The formal separation between these companies, resulting from their separate legal personality, cannot outweigh the unity of their conduct on the market for the purposes of applying the rules on competition.' (paras 136–40)

Comment

In this case the Court of Justice had its first opportunity to rule on the extraterritorial application of competition law. The Court of Justice refrained from ruling directly on the existence or lack of existence of the effects doctrine under European law and relied on the economic-entity doctrine. The judgment was criticised as to the finding of a single economic entity, since it was supported by unsubstantial evidence. Note in this respect Chapter 1 and the conditions under which the separate legal personalities of companies give way to a finding of a single economic entity.

The Commission, supported by Advocate General Mayras, favoured the acceptance of the effects doctrine. It was claimed that substantial and foreseeable effects in the EU should trigger the extraterritorial application of Articles 101 and 102 TFEU.

13

State Aid

Introduction

The law of state aid restricts the grant, by a state or through the use of state resources, of a financial or other advantage to an undertaking, which could distort competition and trade in the European Union. State aid law serves as a unique EU instrument which has evolved to promote efficient use of public resources, limit competition distortion, and support a level playing field in the internal market.

Article 107(1) TFEU lays down the principal characteristics and the general prohibition on state aid:

> Save as otherwise provided in the Treaties, any aid granted by a Member State or through State resources in any form whatsoever which distorts or threatens to distort competition by favouring certain undertakings or the production of certain goods shall, in so far as it affects trade between Member States, be incompatible with the internal market.

At times, however, state aid may prove beneficial and necessary to facilitate the functioning of society and the economy. With that in mind, Article 107(2) TFEU outlines types of aid that are deemed compatible with the internal market (such as aid having a social character which is granted to individual consumers, or aid aimed at remedying damage caused by natural disasters or exceptional occurrences).

Article 107(3) TFEU further outlines aid that may be considered to be compatible with the internal market. For instance, this category may encompass aid to promote the economic development of deprived areas, aid to promote projects of common European interest, and aid to promote certain economic activities or culture and heritage.

Categorisation as state aid

For aid to be categorised as state aid within the meaning of Article 107(1) TFEU, four cumulative conditions need to be satisfied. The aid must:

1. Be granted by the state or through state resources;
2. Confer an advantage on the recipient undertaking(s);
3. Be granted on a selective basis to one or more undertaking(s); and
4. Distort or have the potential to distort competition and affect or be liable to affect trade between Member States.

The scope of these conditions has been delineated in case-law, creating an objective concept which uses 'effect' as the leading benchmark for categorisation (Case C-480/98). In what follows, these conditions are considered in detail.

Condition 1—by the state and through state resources

Article 107(1) TFEU stipulates that state aid must be granted by the state or through state resources. These two conditions were held by the Court to be cumulative in nature (Cases C-379/98, C-482/99). Accordingly, one needs to establish that: (1) the aid measure needs to be imputable to the state; and (2) and the aid needs to involve state resources.

The concept of 'state resources' has been interpreted broadly to include: the resources of public undertakings (Case C-482/99); intra-state entities such as regional or decentralised bodies; and even, at times, resources originating from private bodies or persons (Case C-206/06). Advantages granted directly or indirectly through state resources can constitute state aid.

To show imputability, the grant of an advantage must be attributable to the state. Such will be the case when the aid is granted through legislative means or directly by a public authority. At times, however, when aid is granted through either a public or private intermediary, imputability may be more difficult to ascertain. The imputability of a measure is appraised with regard to the circumstances of the case and the context in which that measure was adopted (Case C-482/99).

78/76	*Steinike und Weinlig v Federal Republic of Germany*	645
C-67/85 etc	*Van der Kooy v Commission*	646
C-72/91 etc	*Sloman Neptun Schiffahrts AG v Bodo Ziesemer*	647
C-379/98	*PreussenElektra AG*	648
C-482/99	*France v Commission (Stardust Marine)*	649
C-345/02	*Pearle BV*	651
C-206/06	*Essent Netwerk Noord BV v Aluminium Delfzijl BV*	652
C-399/10P etc	*Bouygues SA v Commission*	654

With summary references to:

C-480/98	*Spain v Commission*	645
173/73	*Italy v Commission*	645
C-379/98	*PreussenElektra*	645
C-189/91	*Petra Kirsammer-Hack*	647
C-52/97	*Epifanio Viscido*	647
173/73	*Italy v Commission*	647
C-677/11	*Doux Elevage SNC*	651
78/76	*Firma Steinike und Weinlig*	651
C-262/12	*Association Vent De Colère! Fédération nationale*	653
T-425/04	*France v Commission*	655

Condition 2—conferral of an advantage

An advantage, pursuant to Article 107(1) TFEU, may take 'any form whatsoever', and include positive benefits such as subsidies, which would not have obtained under normal market conditions. They also encompass measures that mitigate charges imposed on the undertaking, such as the use of state assets for free or below-market price or the award of tax exemptions (Case 30/59).

Article 107(1) TFEU targets measures on the basis of their effect, rather than their stated aim (Case 173/73). To appraise the effect, the Commission will consider the counterfactuals—the undertaking's financial position before and after the conferral of the alleged advantage.

In its Draft Notice on the notion of state aid, the Commission states that: 'Only the effect of the measure on the undertaking is relevant, neither the cause nor the objective of the State intervention. Whenever the financial situation of an undertaking is improved as a result of State intervention, an advantage is present. To assess this, the financial situation of the undertaking following the measure should be compared with its financial situation if the measure had not been introduced. Since only the effect of the measure on the undertaking matters, it is irrelevant whether the advantage is compulsory for the undertaking in that it could not avoid or refuse it.' (para 68)

If the advantage is provided by the state on genuinely commercial terms, then it may evade the prohibition under Article 107(1) TFEU. That may be the case when the state can show that a private investor operating on the market would have found it rational and profitable to provide a similar advantage. When such is the case, no special advantage is awarded, as the same advantage would have been obtained under normal market conditions. To establish this, a 'market economy operator test' or 'market economy investor principle' will be applied. Accordingly, one needs to compare the state's actions to those that a market economy operator would have taken in similar circumstances (Case C-142/87).

30/59	*De Gezamenlijke Steenkolenmijnen in Limburg*	656
173/73	*Italy v Commission*	657
C-142/87	*Kingdom of Belgium v Commission (Tubemeuse)*	658
C-280/00	*Altmark Trans and Regierungspräsidium Magdeburg*	659
C-446/14 P	*Federal Republic of Germany v Commission*	661
C-182/03 etc	*Kingdom of Belgium and Forum 187 v Commission*	662
C-124/10P	*Commission v Électricité de France (EDF)*	663
C-214/12P etc	*Land Burgenland and others v Commission*	665
T-461/13 etc	*Kingdom of Spain v Commission*	667

With summary references to:

| C-53/00 | *Ferring SA v Agence centrale des organismes de sécurité sociale* | 660 |
| T-268/08 etc | *Land Burgenland (Austria) v Commission* | 665 |

Condition 3—selectivity

Article 107(1) TFEU, stipulates that for state aid to exist, the measure in question must be selective and favour 'certain undertakings or the production of certain goods'. To establish selectivity, the measure needs to favour certain undertakings or the production of certain goods in comparison with other undertakings which are in a comparable legal and factual situation in light of the objective pursued by the measure in question (Case C-143/99).

Selectivity may be present with reference to a group of undertakings or economic sectors within a Member State (material selectivity) or with reference to a given region or territory in a Member State (regional selectivity) (Case C-88/03). In principle, generally applicable measures, such as a reduction of the overall tax rate, would fall outside the scope of Article 107(1) TFEU, as they are not selective in nature. However, a measure of apparent general nature may at times constitute a selective measure. Such conclusion would often follow a three-step analysis: (1) the relevant reference framework is identified; (2) the measure constitutes a derogation therefrom and is thus prima facie selective; and (3) this derogating measure can be justified by the nature or general scheme of the system of reference (Cases C-78/08 etc).

With summary references to:

Condition 4—distortion of competition and effect on trade

A selective advantage granted through state resources will constitute state aid only if it has, or could have, a distorting effect on competition which affects trade between Member States. The two conditions—distorting competition and affecting trade—are inextricably linked and often examined together in the case law (Draft Notice, p 47).

The actual or possible distortion of competition is often easily established. For instance, such may be the case when the state grants an advantage to an undertaking in a liberalised sector where there is, or could be, competition (Draft Notice, para 188).

Similarly, an effect on trade may be established with actual or possible effects. For instance, when the aid strengthens the position of the recipient as compared to other undertakings operating on the EU market (Case 730/79).

With summary references to:

Notification

When the four conditions are satisfied and the assistance in question constitutes state aid, prior notification to the Commission and suspension of the aid are called for. Failure of a Member State to notify the Commission and obtain prior approval for state aid renders the award of that aid unlawful.

However, there are a number of exceptions to mandatory notification (and/or prior approval), which may apply to any given case. These exceptions derive from a number of sources, including:

1. The De Minimis Regulation, which exempts state aid totalling no more than €200,000 over a three-year period.
2. The Services of General Economic Interest (SGEI) rules, which are constituted by the SGEI De Minimis Regulation, the SGEI Decision and Commission communications. The former generally applies to aid of up to €500,000 over a three-year period, while the latter concerns aid of up to €15,000,000 per year.

3. The General Block Exemption Regulation (GBER), which sets out a number of types of state aid that do not require individual approval (but must nonetheless be notified to the Commission within 20 working days). The GBER was substantially modified in 2014 as part of the 'State Aid Modernisation Programme' so as to encompass a wider range of state aid and to improve transparency. Examples of aid falling within the GBER include: aid to SMEs; aid for environmental protection; and aid for local infrastructure.

4. The previous approval of the aid scheme by the European Commission.

Appraisal and approval

State aid that is not exempted from notification must be notified to the European Commission. If the aid satisfies the conditions of Article 107(2) TFEU, it will be deemed compatible with the internal market and approved by the Commission. In all other instances the Commission has discretion whether to approve the state aid at issue.

Article 107(3) TFEU outlines the type of aid that may be considered to be compatible with the internal market:

(a) aid to promote the economic development of areas where the standard of living is abnormally low or where there is serious underemployment, and of the regions referred to in Article 349, in view of their structural, economic and social situation;

(b) aid to promote the execution of an important project of common European interest or to remedy a serious disturbance in the economy of a Member State;

(c) aid to facilitate the development of certain economic activities or of certain economic areas, where such aid does not adversely affect trading conditions to an extent contrary to the common interest;

(d) aid to promote culture and heritage conservation where such aid does not affect trading conditions and competition in the Union to an extent that is contrary to the common interest;

(e) such other categories of aid as may be specified by decision of the Council on a proposal from the Commission.

In its analysis, the Commission will consider whether the aid is aimed at promoting a well-defined efficiency or equality objective of common interest. Following this, it will consider whether the aid measure is well designed—being *appropriate* (provides the optimal means by which to address the failure); *proportionate* (does not go beyond the minimum necessary); *beneficial* (has an overall effect which is on balance beneficial); and *effective* (has an incentive effect, ie alters the beneficiary's behaviour). In applying these criteria, the Commission will be guided by any applicable guidelines and approved frameworks. The guidelines and frameworks are published by the Commission, and concern particular industries and categories of aid (such as regional, employment and environmental aid).

Procedure

Article 108 TFEU governs various aspects of procedure, from the requirement to notify the Commission and suspend implementation of the aid by the state, to the adoption of decisions by the Commission and the respective roles of the Court of Justice and the Council.

Article 109 TFEU authorises the Council to adopt regulations concerning state aid (and, in particular, to exempt certain forms of aid from the requirement of notification).

Two regulations serve as the main pillars which shape the procedural environment for State aid:

- The Procedural Regulation—Council Regulation (EU) 2015/1589, of 13 July 2015, laying down detailed rules for the application of Article 108 of the Treaty on the Functioning of the European Union [2015] OJ L248/9.
- The Implementing Regulation—Commission Regulation (EC) No 794/2004 of 21 April 2004, implementing Council Regulation (EC) No 659/1999 laying down detailed rules for the application of Article 93 of the EC Treaty (as amended).

Unlawful aid

The Procedural Regulation stipulates that 'in cases of unlawful aid which is not compatible with the internal market, effective competition should be restored. For this purpose it is necessary that the aid, including interest, be recovered without delay. It is appropriate that recovery be effected in accordance with the procedures of national law.' (Recital 25) Article 13 of the Procedural Regulation elaborates on the use of suspension and recovery injunctions. Article 16 concerns the recovery of aid in case of a negative decision. The Commission's power to recover aid is subject to a limitation period of 10 years (Article 17).

Commission's State Aid Modernisation programme (SAM)

The state aid regime has undergone significant changes, precipitated by the Commission's State Aid Modernisation Programme (SAM). The SAM was designed to foster growth, improve the application of state aid laws and enhance the procedure. Most notable is the impact which the SAM has had on the ambit of the General Block Exemption Regulation (GBER). The programme widened the scope of the GBER and in doing so reduced the instances in which Member States are required to seek Commission's approval for aid. The SAM reform also increased the obligations placed on Member States, putting greater emphasis upon transparency, communication, evaluation and monitoring.

Steinike und Weinlig v Federal Republic of Germany Case 78/76 Court of Justice, [1977] ECR 595	**State Aid** Condition 1—State Resources

Facts

A reference from the Frankfurt court in relation to state aid classification which arose in an action between Steinike und Weinlig, a German company importing citrus concentrates, and the Federal Republic of Germany. Steinike und Weinlig challenged the legality of a federal German law which set up a fund to promote the sale and export of products of the German agricultural and food industry. The fund was governed by public law and was financed, among other things, through federal subsidies and contributions from undertakings in the agricultural, forestry and food sectors. The national court requested clarification on whether the concept 'any aid granted through state resources' is satisfied when the state agency receives aid from the state or private undertakings.

Held

'The prohibition contained in [Article 107(1) TFEU] covers all aid granted by a Member State or through State resources without its being necessary to make a distinction whether the aid is granted directly by the State or by public or private bodies established or appointed by it to administer the aid. In applying [Article 107 TFEU] regard must primarily be had to the effects of the aid on the undertakings or producers favoured and not the status of the institutions entrusted with the distribution and administration of the aid.' (para 21)

'A measure adopted by the public authority and favouring certain undertakings or products does not lose the character of a gratuitous advantage by the fact that it is wholly or partially financed by contributions imposed by the public authority and levied on the undertakings concerned.' (para 22)

Comment

The application of Article 107 TFEU is predominantly based on the effects of the aid, not its stated aims. On this point also see Case C-480/98 *Spain v Commission*, where the Court held that 'According to settled case-law, [Article 107(1) TFEU] does not distinguish between measures of State intervention by reference to their causes or aims but defines them in relation to their effects (see, inter alia, Case 173/73 *Italy v Commission* [1974] ECR 709, paragraph 27; and Case C-241/94 *France v Commission* [1996] ECR I-4551, paragraph 20).' (para 16)

Paragraph 21 provides for the common benchmark for the application of Article 107(1) TFEU which has been cited in subsequent cases. Accordingly, the state aid prohibition applies equally to aid granted directly by the state and aid granted by private and public bodies 'established as appointed by it to administer the aid' (para 21). On the facts of this case, the aid granted by the fund was held to constitute state aid, regardless of the fact that it was financed by both the German government and through contributions from private undertakings.

It is interesting to consider the benchmark in paragraph 21 in light of the Court of Justice judgment in Case C-379/98 *PreussenElektra*. There, the scheme which appeared to involve both public and private bodies was held not to amount to state aid. The reason for that conclusion was the unique factual matrix in that case which meant that, in practice, the private entity giving the aid used its own private resources, rather than those of the state. The aid, therefore, could not have been attributed to the State. For a discussion of this case see page 648 below.

Van der Kooy v Commission	**State Aid**
Joined Cases 67, 68 & 70/85	Condition 1—State Resources
Court of Justice, [1988] ECR 219	'Attributed to the State'

Facts

An application for the annulment of a Commission decision of 13 February 1985 on the preferential tariff charged to glasshouse growers for natural gas in the Netherlands. In its decision the Commission declared that lower tariffs (which were subject to the approval of the Minister for Economic Affairs) that were charged by the Gasunie company (in which the Dutch state held 50%) constituted incompatible state aid.

In their action for annulment the applicants argued that the tariff was not imposed by the Dutch state but was rather the outcome of an agreement concluded under private law between Gasunie and two other companies to which the Dutch state was not a party. They also argued that while the Minister for Economic Affairs has a right of approval over the tariffs, its role is no more than a retrospective supervisory power which is solely concerned with whether the tariffs accord with the aims of the Netherlands' energy policy.

Held

'As the Court has held (see in particular the judgments of 22 March 1977 in Case 78/76 *Steinike* v *Germany* [1977] ECR 595 and 30 January 1985 in Case 290/83 *Commission* v *France* [1985] ECR 439), there is no necessity to draw any distinction between cases where aid is granted directly by the State and cases where it is granted by public or private bodies established or appointed by the State to administer the aid. In this instance, the documents before the Court provide considerable evidence to show that the fixing of the disputed tariff was the result of action by the Netherlands State.' (para 35)

'First of all, the shares in Gasunie are so distributed that the Netherlands State directly or indirectly holds 50% of the shares and appoints half the members of the supervisory board—a body whose powers include that of determining the tariffs to be applied. Secondly, the Minister for Economic Affairs is empowered to approve the tariffs applied by Gasunie, with the result that, regardless of how that power may be exercised, the Netherlands Government can block any tariff which does not suit it. Lastly, Gasunie and the Landbouwschap have on two occasions given effect to the Commission's representations to the Netherlands Government seeking an amendment of the horticultural tariff.' (para 36)

'Considered as a whole, these factors demonstrate that Gasunie in no way enjoys full autonomy in the fixing of gas tariffs but acts under the control and on the instructions of the public authorities. It is thus clear that Gasunie could not fix the tariff without taking account of the requirements of the public authorities. It may therefore be concluded that the fixing of the contested tariff is the result of action by the Netherlands State and thus falls within the meaning of the phrase 'aid granted by a Member State' under [Article 107 TFEU].' (paras 37, 38)

Comment

The state's holdings in Gasunie which enable it to affect the determination of tariffs, and the powers of the Minister for Economic affairs to block tariffs, led the court to conclude that Gasunie acted under the control of the state and that the fixing of tariffs was the result of action by the Dutch State.

The imputability condition was further refined in Case C-482/99 *France v Commission* (page 649 below), where the Court held that it needs to be established that the state exercised control over the undertaking and was involved in the adoption of the measure in question.

Sloman Neptun Schiffahrts AG v Bodo Ziesemer	**State Aid**
Joined Cases C-72/91, 73/91	Condition 1—State Resources
Court of Justice, [1993] ECR I-887	

Facts

A reference for a preliminary ruling from the Arbeitsgericht Bremen (Federal Republic of Germany) concerning the compatibility with the EU state aid rules of a new employment law governing shipping companies. The new law introduced the International Shipping Register (ISR) and stipulated that crew members of ships registered in the ISR, who are not EU nationals and have no permanent residence in Germany, could be employed at lower rates of pay than German EU employees and could make lower social security contributions.

Held

'As the Court held in its judgment in Case 82/77 *Openbaar Ministerie of the Netherlands v Van Tiggele* ([1978] ECR 25, paragraphs 23–25), only advantages which are granted directly or indirectly through State resources are to be regarded as State aid within the meaning of [Article 107(1) TFEU]. The wording of this provision itself and the procedural rules laid down in [Article 108 TFEU] show that advantages granted from resources other than those of the State do not fall within the scope of the provisions in question. … Therefore it is necessary to determine whether or not the advantages arising from a system such as that applicable to the ISR are to be viewed as being granted through State resources.' (paras 20–21)

'The system at issue does not seek, through its object and general structure, to create an advantage which would constitute an additional burden for the State or the abovementioned bodies, but only to alter in favour of shipping undertakings the framework within which contractual relations are formed between those undertakings and their employees. The consequences arising from this, in so far as they relate to the difference in the basis for the calculation of social security contributions, mentioned by the national court, and to the potential loss of tax revenue because of the low rates of pay, referred to by the Commission, are inherent in the system and are not a means of granting a particular advantage to the undertakings concerned. It follows that a system such as that applicable to the ISR is not a State aid within the meaning of [Article 107(1) TFEU].' (paras 21–2)

Comment

The Court of Justice concluded that the scheme in question did not amount to state aid and did not seek to create an advantage which would constitute an additional burden for the state.

A similar restrictive interpretation of the 'state resources' in employment provisions may be found in Case C-189/91 *Petra Kirsammer-Hack* where a law, which excluded small businesses from the system of protection against unfair dismissal, was held not to constitute aid within the meaning of Article 107(1) TFEU. While the law provided small businesses with a competitive advantage over other undertakings, that benefit did not entail any direct or indirect transfer of state resources. (para 17)

Similarly, in Case C-52/97 *Epifanio Viscido* the Court considered the compatibility of an Italian employment law which selectively permitted fixed-term contracts in a number of specified exceptional cases. That Court held that 'non-application of generally applicable legislation concerning fixed-term employment contracts to a single undertaking does not involve any direct or indirect transfer of State resources to that undertaking.' (para 14) Also note Case C-379/98 *PreussenElektra* (page 648 below).

PreussenElektra AG   **State Aid**
Case C-379/98   Condition 1—State Resources
Court of Justice, [2001] ECR I-2099

Facts

A referral from the Landgericht (Regional Court) Kiel, concerning the compatibility of a German law designed to promote the use of electricity from renewable energy sources with Article 107 TFEU. The law required both private and public electricity suppliers to purchase electricity produced from renewable energy sources at fixed minimum prices higher than the real economic value of that type of electricity. The financial burden from that obligation was allocated amongst electricity supply undertakings, and upstream private electricity network operators that were required to partially compensate the distribution undertakings for the additional costs caused by that purchase obligation. PreussenElektra was an upstream electricity network operator. It argued that the obligation to compensate the distribution undertakings violated Article 107 TFEU.

Held

'[O]nly advantages granted directly or indirectly through State resources are to be considered aid within the meaning of [Article 107(1) TFEU]. The distinction made in that provision between "aid granted by a Member State" and aid granted "through State resources" does not signify that all advantages granted by a State, whether financed through State resources or not, constitute aid but is intended merely to bring within that definition both advantages which are granted directly by the State and those granted by a public or private body designated or established by the State.' (para 58)

'In this case, the obligation imposed on private electricity supply undertakings to purchase electricity produced from renewable energy sources at fixed minimum prices does not involve any direct or indirect transfer of State resources to undertakings which produce that type of electricity. Therefore, the allocation of the financial burden arising from that obligation for those private electricity supply undertakings as between them and other private undertakings cannot constitute a direct or indirect transfer of State resources either.' (paras 59–60)

'In those circumstances, the fact that the purchase obligation is imposed by statute and confers an undeniable advantage on certain undertakings is not capable of conferring upon it the character of State aid within the meaning of [Article 107(1) TFEU]. That conclusion cannot be undermined by the fact, pointed out by the referring court, that the financial burden arising from the obligation to purchase at minimum prices is likely to have negative repercussions on the economic results of the undertakings subject to that obligation and therefore entail a diminution in tax receipts for the State. That consequence is an inherent feature of such a legislative provision and cannot be regarded as constituting a means of granting to producers of electricity from renewable energy sources a particular advantage at the expense of the State (see, to that effect, *Sloman Neptun*, paragraph 21, and *Ecotrade*, paragraph 36).' (paras 61–2)

Comment

The Court held that the imposition of a purchase obligation on private undertakings does not constitute a direct or indirect transfer of state resources. This qualification does not change because of the lower revenues of the undertakings subject to that obligation to purchase at minimum price, which is likely to cause a diminution in tax receipts for the state, because this consequence is an inherent feature of the measure.

In order to constitute state aid, the advantage conferred on the recipient undertaking must be: (1) granted by a Member State; and (2) through state resources. If state resources are not engaged, the measure falls outside the ambit of Article 107 TFEU.

France v Commission (Stardust Marine)	**State Aid**
Case C-482/99	Condition 1—State Resources
Court of Justice, [2002] ECR I-4397	Imputability

Facts

Following financial difficulties, the bank Crédit Lyonnais was granted state aid from the French government. The support was conditional on the bank transferring certain risks and costs to its wholly owned subsidiary, CDR. CDR purchased nearly FRF190 billion of assets from Crédit Lyonnais. Under the restructuring plan, all the assets concerned were to be transferred or sold.

As part of this transfer, Crédit Lyonnais also transferred one of its assets—Stardust Marine—a company active in the pleasure-boat market. Stardust was initially financed by loans and guarantees, and later, through conversion of debts and capital injection, came under the control of SBT and Altus Finance; subsidiaries of Crédit Lyonnais.

Once Stardust was transferred to CDR, CDR increased Stardust's capital in three stages with a total of around FRF450 million. CDR subsequently sold its holding in Stardust (which was 99.90% of its capital) to FG Marine for FRF2 million.

The European Commission found that the capital injected into Stardust Marine, first by Altus Finance and then by CDR amounted to incompatible state aid. The French government applied for annulment of the decision.

Held

'Crédit Lyonnais, Altus and SBT were under the control of the State and had to be regarded as public undertakings. ... The French authorities were indeed able, directly or indirectly, to exercise a dominant influence over those undertakings.' (para 34)

'It therefore needs to be examined whether such a situation of State control allows the financial resources of the undertakings subject to that control to be regarded as "State resources", within the meaning of [Article 107(1) TFEU]. ... In that respect, it should first be noted that, according to settled case-law, it is not necessary to establish in every case that there has been a transfer of State resources for the advantage granted to one or more undertakings to be capable of being regarded as a State aid. ... Second, it should be recalled that ... [Article 107(1) TFEU] covers all the financial means by which the public authorities may actually support undertakings, irrespective of whether or not those means are permanent assets of the public sector.' (paras 35–7)

'It follows that, by holding in the contested decision that the resources of public undertakings, such as those of Crédit Lyonnais and its subsidiaries, fell within the control of the State and were therefore at its disposal, the Commission did not misinterpret the term "State resources" in Article 87(1) EC. The State is perfectly capable, by exercising its dominant influence over such undertakings, of directing the use of their resources in order, as occasion arises, to finance specific advantages in favour of other undertakings.' (para 38)

'There is no dispute that, in the contested decision, the Commission inferred the imputability of the financial assistance granted to Stardust by Altus and SBT to the State simply from the fact that those two companies, as subsidiaries of Crédit Lyonnais, were indirectly controlled by the State.' (para 50)

'Such an interpretation of the condition that, for a measure to be capable of being classified as State aid within the meaning of [Article 107(1) TFEU], it must be imputable to the State, which infers such imputability from the mere fact that that measure was taken by a public undertaking, cannot be accepted. Even if the State is in a position to control a public undertaking and to exercise a dominant influence over its operations, actual exercise of that control in a particular case cannot be automatically presumed. A public undertaking may act with more or less independence, according to the degree of autonomy left to it by the State. That might be the situation in the case of public undertakings such as Altus and SBT. Therefore, the mere fact that a public undertaking is under State control is not sufficient for measures taken by that undertaking, such as the financial support measures in question here, to be imputed to the State. It is also necessary to examine whether the public authorities must be regarded as having been involved, in one way or another, in the adoption of those measures.' (paras 51–2)

'On that point, it cannot be demanded that it be demonstrated, on the basis of a precise inquiry, that in the particular case the public authorities specifically incited the public undertaking to take the aid measures in question. ... Moreover, it will, as a general rule, be very difficult for a third party, precisely because of the privileged relations existing between the State and a public undertaking, to demonstrate in a particular case that aid measures taken by such an undertaking were in fact adopted on the instructions of the public authorities. For those reasons, it must be accepted that the imputability to the State of an aid measure taken by a public undertaking may be inferred from a set of indicators arising from the circumstances of the case and the context in which that measure was taken. In that respect, the Court has already taken into consideration the fact that the body in question could not take the contested decision without taking account of the requirements of the public authorities (see, in particular, *Van der Kooy*, paragraph 37) or the fact that, apart from factors of an organic nature which linked the public undertakings to the State, those undertakings, through the intermediary of which aid had been granted, had to take account of directives ... (Case C-303/88 *Italy v Commission*, ... paragraphs 11 and 12; Case C-305/89 *Italy v Commission* ... paragraphs 13 and 14). Other indicators might, in certain circumstances, be relevant in concluding that an aid measure taken by a public undertaking is imputable to the State, such as, in particular, its integration into the structures of the public administration, the nature of its activities and the exercise of the latter on the market in normal conditions of competition with private operators, the legal status of the undertaking (in the sense of its being subject to public law or ordinary company law), the intensity of the supervision exercised by the public authorities over the management of the undertaking, or any other indicator showing, in the particular case, an involvement by the public authorities in the adoption of a measure or the unlikelihood of their not being involved, having regard also to the compass of the measure, its content or the conditions which it contains.' (paras 53–6)

'In this case, the Commission adopted in the contested decision, as the sole criterion, the organic criterion according to which Crédit Lyonnais, Altus and SBT, as public undertakings, were under the control of the State. In those circumstances, it must be held that that interpretation of the criterion of imputability to the State is erroneous.' (para 58)

Comment

Imputability cannot be inferred from the fact that a state controls a company. The crucial issue is whether the state was involved in the adoption of the alleged aid measure. This involvement can be inferred from a set of indicators arising from the circumstances of the case and the context in which that measure was taken.

In its 'Draft Commission Notice on the notion of State aid pursuant to Article 107(1) TFEU' the Commission heavily relies on the *Stardust Marine* judgment when it states that: 'The mere fact that a measure is taken by a public undertaking is not per se sufficient to consider it imputable to the State. However, it does not need to be demonstrated that, in a particular case, the public authorities specifically incited the public undertaking to the aid measures in question. In fact, since relations between the State and public undertakings are necessarily close, there is a real risk that State aid may be granted through the intermediary of those undertakings in a non-transparent manner and in breach of the rules on State aid laid down by the Treaty. Moreover, precisely because of the privileged relations that exist between the State and public undertakings, it will, as a general rule, be very difficult for a third party to demonstrate that aid measures taken by such an undertaking were in fact adopted on the instructions of the public authorities in a particular case.' (para 44)

Pearle BV	**State Aid**
Case C-345/02	Condition 1—State Resources
Court of Justice, [2004] ECR I-7139	Compulsory Contributions

Facts

A referral from the Supreme Court of the Netherlands concerning the compatibility with Article 107 TFEU of binding by-laws adopted by a private association of opticians which formed part of a trade association governed by public law, which imposed compulsory levies on member opticians. The levy was aimed at financing a collective advertising campaign for opticians' businesses. Pearle BV and other members of the association contested the legality of the by-laws and argued that the advertising system constituted state aid.

Held

'The Court's case-law makes it clear that where the method by which aid is financed, particularly by means of compulsory contributions, forms an integral part of the aid measure, consideration of the latter by the Commission must necessarily also take into account that method of financing the aid (Joined Cases C-261/01 and Case C-262/01 *Van Calster and Others* [2003] ECR I-0000, paragraph 49, and Joined Cases C-34/01 to C-38/01 *Enirisorse* [2003] ECR I-0000, paragraph 44).' (para 29)

'In such a case, the notification of the aid … must also cover the method of financing, so that the Commission may consider it on the basis of all the facts. If this requirement is not satisfied, it is possible that the Commission may declare that an aid measure is compatible when, if the Commission had been aware of its method of financing, it could not have been so declared (*Van Calster and Others*, paragraph 50).' (para 30)

For an advantages to be categorised as aid within the meaning of Article 107(1) TFEU, it must be granted directly or indirectly through state resources and, be imputable to the state. Even if the trade association governed by public law is a public body, it does not appear that the advertising campaign was funded by resources made available to the national authorities. On the contrary, the monies used by the association for the purpose of funding the advertising campaign were collected from its members who benefited from the campaign. Since the costs incurred by the public body for the purposes of that campaign were offset in full by the levies imposed on the undertakings benefiting therefrom, the trade association's action did not tend to create an advantage which would constitute an additional burden for the state or that body. Furthermore, the initiative for the organisation and operation of that advertising campaign was that of the private association of opticians, and not that of the public trade associations. (paras 35–7)

Comment

The Court distinguished the facts in this case from those in Case 78/76 *Steinike & Weinlig* (page 645 above) where the fund concerned was financed both by state subsidies and contributions from members. In addition, the funds served there were to implement a policy determined by the state, whereas the advertising campaign in this case was the initiative of the association of opticians.

The *Pearle* judgment may be viewed as continuing the restrictive interpretation of the concept of state resources as manifested in Case C-379/98 *PreussenElektra*'s (page 648 above). Another interesting example of such a restrictive approach may be found in Case C-677/11 *Doux Élevage SNC*. There, an agricultural trade association for poultry introduced a levy to help finance certain activities. The French government subsequently tacitly extended the levy to non-members operating in the sector. Complaints about the mandatory levy reached the national court which referred a question to the Court of Justice on its compatibility with Article 107(1) TFEU. The Court held, in line with the *Pearle* ruling, that state resources were not involved. It noted that the funds originated from private operators, the mechanism did not 'involve any direct or indirect transfer of State resources, the sums provided by the payment of those contributions do not go through the State budget or through another public body and the State does not relinquish any resources, in whatever form …, which, under national legislation, should have been paid into the State budget. The contributions remain private in nature throughout their lifecycle.' (para 32)

Essent Netwerk Noord BV v Aluminium Delfzijl BV
Case C-206/06
Court of Justice, [2008] ECR I-5497

State Aid
Condition 1—State Resources

Facts

A reference for a preliminary ruling concerning the compliance of a charge related to the generation, transmission and distribution of electricity in the Netherlands with Article 107 TFEU. The charge in question was aimed at covering earlier investments made by SEP, a statutorily-designated company, to support the market prior to its liberalisation. These investments related to non-market-compatible costs (stranded costs) which were not expected to be recovered. The charge was set up in Article 9 of the OEPS—the Transitional Law on the Electricity Generating Sector—and imposed by the state on all 'non-protected' customers.

Held

'It should be noted at the outset that a charge applied under the same conditions as regards its collection to both domestic and imported products, the revenue from which is used for the benefit of domestic products alone, so that the advantages accruing from it offset the burden borne by those products, may constitute, having regard to the use to which the revenue from that charge is put, State aid incompatible with the common market, if the conditions for the application of [Article 107 TFEU] are met (see, to that effect, Case C-17/91 *Lornoy and Others* [1992] ECR I-6523, paragraph 32, and Case C-72/92 *Scharbatke* [1993] ECR I-5509, paragraph 18).' (para 58)

'[T]he surcharge in question is a charge which is imposed on electricity, whether imported or domestic, according to an objective criterion which is the number of kWh transmitted. It is therefore with regard to the use to which the revenue from the charge is put that it must be ascertained whether that charge constitutes a charge having equivalent effect or discriminatory internal taxation.' (para 47)

As regards the first condition of Article 107 TFEU, it is necessary to ascertain whether the amounts paid to SEP constitute intervention by the state or through state resources. (para 65)

'Article 9 of the OEPS provides for the payment to the designated company, namely SEP …, for the payment of the excess of the charge received to the Minister, who must set that amount aside for the purpose of defraying the costs referred to in Article 7 of the OEPS. … In that regard, it must be borne in mind that those amounts have their origin in the price surcharge imposed by the State on purchasers of electricity under Article 9 of the OEPS, a surcharge with regard to which it has been established, in paragraph 47 of this judgment, that it constitutes a charge. Those amounts thus have their origin in a State resource.' (para 66)

'It is apparent from the provisions of the OEPS that the designated company is not entitled to use the proceeds from the charge for purposes other than those provided for by the Law. Furthermore, it is strictly monitored in carrying out its task, since Article 9(5) of the OEPS requires it to have the detailed account of the sums received and transferred certified by an auditor.' (para 69)

'It is of little account that that designated company was at one and the same time the centralising body for the tax received, the manager of the monies collected and the recipient of part of those monies. The mechanisms provided for by the Law and, more specifically, the detailed accounts certified by an auditor, make it possible to distinguish those different roles and to monitor the use of the monies. It follows that as long as that designated company did not appropriate to itself the amount of NLG 400 million, at the time when it was freely able to do so, that amount remained under public control and therefore available to the national authorities, which is sufficient for it to be categorised as State resources (see, to that effect, Case C-482/99 *France v Commission* [2002] ECR I-4397, paragraph 37).' (para 70)

'The objective of Article 9 of the OEPS appears to be that of enabling the electricity generating undertakings, through their subsidiary SEP, to recover the non-market-compatible costs which they have incurred in the past. That provision relates to the costs for 2000, whereas certain costs in respect of subsequent years are to be offset by subsidies which are to be authorised by the Commission as State aid.' (para 71)

'Those different circumstances distinguish the measure at issue in the main proceedings from that referred to in Case C-345/02 *Pearle and Others* [2004] ECR I-7139. The monies at issue in that case, which were used for an advertising campaign, had been collected by a professional body from its members who benefited from the campaign, by means of compulsory levies earmarked for the organisation of that campaign (*Pearle and Others*, paragraph 36). They were, therefore, neither revenue for the State nor monies which remained under State control, by contrast to the amount received by SEP, which has its origin in a charge and can be used for no other purpose than that provided for by the Law. Furthermore, in the case which gave rise to the judgment in *Pearle and Others*, although the monies were collected by a professional body, the advertising campaign was organised by a private association of opticians, had a purely commercial purpose and had nothing to do with a policy determined by the authorities (*Pearle and Others*, paragraphs 37 and 38). By contrast, in the case in the main proceedings, the payment of the amount of NLG 400 million to the designated company had been the subject of a decision by the legislature.' (paras 72–3)

'Likewise, the measure in question differs from that referred to in Case C-379/98 *PreussenElektra* [2001] ECR I-2099, in which the Court held, at paragraph 59, that the obligation imposed on private electricity supply undertakings to purchase electricity produced from renewable energy sources at fixed minimum prices did not involve any direct or indirect transfer of State resources to undertakings which produced that type of electricity. In the latter case, the undertakings had not been appointed by the State to manage a State resource, but were bound by an obligation to purchase by means of their own financial resources.' (para 74)

Accordingly, the amounts paid to SEP constitute intervention by the state through state resources. (para 75)

Comment

The Court distinguished the facts of the case from those in Case C-345/02 *Pearle and Others* (page 651 above), and Case C-379/98 *PreussenElektra* (page 648 above). In doing so, it emphasised that in the case at hand, the state was the one to initiate the charge (paras 72–3) and the company—SEP—had been appointed by the state to manage the 'State resource' (para 74).

In its 'Draft Commission Notice on the notion of State aid pursuant to Article 107(1) TFEU' the Commission makes reference to paragraphs 69–75 of the *Essent Netwerk* judgment and cites the case as authority for the Commission's expansive view that: '[S]urcharges imposed by law on private persons can be qualified as State resources. This is the case even where a private company is appointed by law to collect such charges on behalf of the State and to channel them to the beneficiaries, without allowing the collecting company to use the proceeds from the charges for purposes other than those provided for by the law. In this case, the sums in question remain under public control and are therefore available to the national authorities, which is sufficient reason for them to be considered State resources.' (para 66)

In Case C-262/12 *Association Vent De Colère! Fédération nationale*, the Court considered the compatibility with Article 107 TFEU of a ministerial order laying down the conditions for the purchase of electricity generated by wind-power installations at a price higher than its market value. The Court held that, 'It is clear that the offset mechanism at issue in the main proceedings was established by Law … and must therefore be regarded as attributable to the State.' (para 18) The Court noted that: 'Article 107(1) TFEU covers all the financial means by which the public authorities may actually support undertakings, irrespective of whether or not those means are permanent assets of the public sector.' (para 21) It subsequently held that where, as in this case, the charge is collected by a public body, remained under public control and determined by the Energy Minister, and where administrative sanctions were imposed for failure to pay, that mechanism constituted intervention through state resources.

Bouygues SA v Commission
Joined Cases C-399/10 P, C-340/10P
Court of Justice, [2013] 3 CMLR 6

State Aid
Condition 1—State Resources
State Guarantee

Facts

The French state, a majority shareholder in France Télécom, announced that it would take active measures to support the company in the face of financial difficulties. The government announced a proposal of a €9 billion shareholder loan, which France Télécom, however, did not accept. Nonetheless, the Commission concluded that the loan offer, in combination with the publicised statements, amounted to incompatible state aid. Following an action for annulment of that decision, the General Court held that no state resources had been committed in that case (Joined Cases T-425/04 etc). The parties appealed to the Court of Justice.

Held

'It follows that the General Court took the view that, for each State intervention measure, the Commission was obliged to examine individually whether it conferred a specific advantage through State resources. In addition, it found that only a reduction of the State budget or a sufficiently concrete economic risk of burdens on that budget, closely linked and corresponding to an advantage thus identified, would complied with the condition relating to financing through State resources, within the meaning of Article 107(1) TFEU.' (para 97)

'In that respect, it should be pointed out that, under the terms of Article 107(1) TFEU, save as otherwise provided in the Treaties, any aid granted by a Member State or through State resources in any form whatsoever which distorts or threatens to distort competition by favouring certain undertakings or the production of certain goods, in so far as it affects trade between Member States, is incompatible with the internal market.' (para 98)

'On that basis, only advantages granted directly or indirectly through State resources or constituting an additional burden on the State are to be regarded as aid within the meaning of Article 107(1) TFEU. The very wording of this provision and the procedural rules laid down in Article 108 TFEU show that advantages granted from resources other than those of the State do not fall within the scope of the provisions in question (see, to that effect, Joined Cases C-72/91 and C-73/91 *Sloman Neptun* [1993] ECR I-887, paragraph 19; Case C-200/97 *Ecotrade* [1998] ECR I-7907, paragraph 35; and Case C-379/98 *PreussenElektra* [2001] ECR I-2099, paragraph 58).' (para 99)

'It should be noted that, according to settled case-law, it is not necessary to establish in every case that there has been a transfer of State resources for the advantage granted to one or more undertakings to be capable of being regarded as a State aid within the meaning of Article 107(1) TFEU (see, to that effect, Case C-387/92 *Banco Exterior de España* [1994] ECR I-877, paragraph 14; Case C-6/97 *Italy v Commission* [1999] ECR I-2981, paragraph 16; and Case C-482/99 *France v Commission* [2002] ECR I-4397, paragraph 36).' (para 100)

'In particular, measures which, in various forms, mitigate the burdens normally included in the budget of an undertaking, and which therefore, without being subsidies in the strict meaning of the word, are similar in character and have the same effect, are considered to be aid (see, to that effect, *Banco Exterior de España*, paragraph 13; Case C-75/97 *Belgium v Commission* [1999] ECR I-3671, paragraph 23; and Case C-156/98 *Germany v Commission* [2000] ECR I-6857, paragraph 25).' (para 101)

'It is settled case-law that Article 107(1) TFEU defines measures of State intervention in relation to their effects (Case C-124/10 P *Commission v EDF and Others* [2012] ECR, paragraph 77 and the case-law cited).' (para 102)

'As State interventions take various forms and have to be assessed in relation to their effects, it cannot be excluded, as the Bouygues companies and the Commission rightly argued, that several consecutive measures of State intervention must, for the purposes of Article 107(1) TFEU, be regarded as a single intervention.' (para 103)

'That could be the case in particular where consecutive interventions, especially having regard to their chronology, their purpose and the circumstances of the undertaking at the time of those interventions, are so closely linked to each other that they are inseparable from one another (see, to that effect, Case 72/79 *Commission* v *Italy* [1980] ECR 1411, paragraph 24).' (para 104)

'It follows that, having found that it was necessary to identify a reduction of the State budget or a sufficiently concrete economic risk of burdens on that budget, closely linked and corresponding to, or having as a counterpart, a specific advantage deriving either from the announcement of 4 December 2002 or from the shareholder loan offer, the General Court erred in law by applying a test that immediately excludes those State interventions, depending on their links with one another and their effects, from being regarded as a single intervention.' (para 105)

'Next, according to the case-law of the Court, State intervention capable of both placing the undertakings which it applies to in a more favourable position than others and creating a sufficiently concrete risk of imposing an additional burden on the State in the future, may place a burden on the resources of the State (see, to that effect, *Ecotrade*, paragraph 41).' (para 106)

'In particular, the Court of Justice has had occasion to state that advantages given in the form of a State guarantee can entail an additional burden on the State (see, to that effect, *Ecotrade*, paragraph 43, and Case C-275/10 *Residex Capital IV* [2011] ECR I-13043, paragraphs 39 to 42).' (para 107)

'Furthermore, the Court has already held that, where, in economic terms, the alteration of the market conditions which gives rise to an advantage given indirectly to certain undertakings is the consequence of the public authorities' loss of revenue, even the fact that investors then take independent decisions does not mean that the connection between the loss of revenue and the advantage given to the undertakings in question has been eliminated (see, to that effect, *Germany v Commission*, paragraphs 25 to 28).' (para 108)

'Consequently, for the purposes of establishing the existence of State aid, the Commission must establish a sufficiently direct link between, on the one hand, the advantage given to the beneficiary and, on the other, a reduction of the State budget or a sufficiently concrete economic risk of burdens on that budget (see, to that effect, Case C-279/08 P *Commission v Netherlands* [2011] ECR I-7671, paragraph 111).' (para 109)

'However, contrary to what the General Court found, it is not necessary that such a reduction, or even such a risk, should correspond or be equivalent to that advantage, or that the advantage has as its counterpoint such a reduction or such a risk, or that it is of the same nature as the commitment of State resources from which it derives. It follows that the General Court erred in law, both in its review of the Commission's identification of the State intervention measure conferring State aid and in the examination of the links between the advantage identified and the commitment of State resources found by the Commission.' (paras 110–11)

Comment

The judgment clarifies that the creation of a 'sufficiently concrete economic risk' of imposing an additional burden on the state in the future, by a guarantee or by a contractual offer, is sufficient to establish the use of 'state resources' for the purposes of Article 107(1) TFEU.

'In certain cases, several consecutive measures of State intervention must, for the purposes of Article 107(1) TFEU, be regarded as a single intervention. That could be the case, in particular, where consecutive interventions are so closely linked to each other, especially having regard to their chronology, their purpose and the circumstances of the undertaking at the time of those interventions, that they are inseparable from one another.' (para 84, Commission Draft Notice on the notion of State aid, referring to the *Bouygues* judgment)

The case was referred back to the General Court, which in a subsequent judgment (T-425/04 and T-444/04 *RENV*) once again annulled the Commission's decision, albeit on the grounds that the Commission had misapplied the 'prudent private investor' test.

Facts

The case concerned the award, by the German Federal Government, of bonuses to miners and the exemption of these subsidies from income tax and social security contributions. These bonuses, it was argued, distorted competition in the market by artificially reducing the price of German coal. The case reached the Court of Justice and was considered under the framework of the European Coal and Steel Community (ECSC) Treaty. In its judgment, the Court considered the interpretation of Article 4(c) ECSC and the definition of the concepts of 'subsidies' or 'aids' granted by states found therein.

Held

'The Treaty contains no express definition of the concept of subsidy or aid referred to under Article 4(c). A subsidy is normally defined as a payment in cash or in kind made in support of an undertaking other than the payment by the purchaser or consumer for the goods or services which it produces. An aid is a very similar concept, which, however, places emphasis on its purpose and seems especially devised for a particular objective which cannot normally be achieved without outside help. The concept of aid is nevertheless wider than that of a subsidy because it embraces not only positive benefits, such as subsidies themselves, but also interventions which, in various forms, mitigate the charges which are normally included in the budget of an undertaking and which, without, therefore, being subsidies in the strict meaning of the word, are similar in character and have the same effect. ... A subsidy or aid, within the meaning of the definition given above in itself constitutes an obstacle to the most rational distribution of production at the highest possible level of productivity inasmuch as, being a payment made by someone other than the purchaser or consumer, it makes it possible to fix or maintain selling prices which are not directly related to production costs and thereby to establish, maintain and develop economic activity which does not represent the most rational distribution of production at the highest possible level of productivity.' (page 19)

The German coal industry 'believes that its output and productivity will be enhanced by an increase in the number of underground workers as a result of the increase in miners' pay produced by the shift bonus. This increase in pay is undoubtedly an element in production costs. If it is separated from it (as it is, in fact, by the financing of the shift bonus out of public funds), the coal industry pockets the saving without bearing the cost of a measure which increases both its output and its productivity. This means that production costs are not the true costs of the coal which it has actually mined. This artificial reduction in accountable production costs places the coal industry which benefits from it in a privileged competitive position compared with that of coal industries which have to pay for the whole of their production costs on their own.' (page 29)

Comment

The Court noted the absence of a definition of 'subsidies' and 'aids' in the ECSC Treaty. It therefore considered the ECSC Treaty's objects. The Court noted that: 'Among the declared aims of the Community, in Article 2 of the Treaty, is that it "shall progressively bring about conditions which will of themselves ensure the most rational distribution of production at the highest possible level of productivity, while safeguarding continuity of employment and taking care not to provoke fundamental and persistent disturbances in the economies of Member States".' (page 19) The Court subsequently found that a subsidy which covered a proportion of production costs violated the ECSC Treaty.

While this early judgment concerned the interpretation of Article 4(c) of the ECSC Treaty, rather than the state aid provisions in the TFEU, it provided a valuable analytical framework for subsequent consideration of the effects of state aid measures. This expansive interpretation of the concept of aid has later served to capture a wide range of mitigation of charges, thus widening the realm of state aid control.

Italy v Commission	**State Aid**
Case 173/73	Condition 2—Advantage
Court of Justice, [1974] ECR 709	Effects-based Doctrine

Facts

In 1971, the Italian Republic adopted a new law as part of the restructuring of the textile industry. Article 20 of the new legislation established a three-year reduction of social charges relating to family allowances. That reduction was held by the Commission to constitute state aid. In its action for annulment of the decision, Italy argued that the decision was vitiated by reason of abuse of powers and that the reduction of social charges constituted a measure of a social nature and fell outside the scope of Article 107 TFEU.

Held

'In order to ensure the progressive development and functioning of the common market, ... [the TFEU] provides for constant review of aids granted or planned by the Member States, an operation which assumes constant cooperation between these States and the Commission.' (para 7)

'The aim of [Article 107 TFEU] is to prevent trade between Member States from being affected by benefits granted by the public authorities which, in various forms, distort or threaten to distort competition by favouring certain undertakings or the production of certain goods. Accordingly, [Article 107 TFEU] does not distinguish between the measures of State intervention concerned by reference to their causes or aims but defines them in relation to their effects. Consequently, the alleged fiscal nature or social aim of the measure in issue cannot suffice to shield it from the application of [Article 107 TFEU].' (para 13)

'It must be concluded that the partial reduction of social charges pertaining to family allowances devolving upon employers in the textile sector is a measure intended partially to exempt undertakings of a particular industrial sector from the financial charges arising from the normal application of the general social security system, without there being any justification for this exemption on the basis of the nature or general scheme of this system.' (para 15)

'The argument that the contested reduction is not a "State aid", because the loss of revenue resulting from it is made good through funds accruing from contributions paid to the unemployment insurance fund, cannot be accepted. As the funds in question are financed through compulsory contributions imposed by State legislation and as, as this case shows, they are managed and apportioned in accordance with the provisions of that legislation, they must be regarded as State resources within the meaning of [Article 107 TFEU], even if they are administered by institutions distinct from the public authorities.' (para 16)

'As to the argument that the social charges devolving upon employers in the textile sector are higher in Italy than in the other Member States, it should be observed that, in the application of [Article 107(1) TFEU], the point of departure must necessarily be the competitive position existing within the common market before the adoption of the measure in issue. This position is the result of numerous factors having varying effects on production costs in the different Member States ... the unilateral modification of a particular factor of the cost of production in a given sector of the economy of a Member State may have the effect of disturbing the existing equilibrium. Consequently, there is no point in comparing the relative proportions of total production costs which a particular category of costs represents, since the decisive factor is the reduction itself and not the category of costs to which it relates.' (para 17)

Comment

The Court stressed that Article 107 TFEU does not distinguish between measures of state intervention by reference to their causes or aims but defines them in relation to their effects. With this 'effects-based doctrine' in mind, the Court subsequently held that the social aim of the measure in issue cannot shield it from state aid scrutiny.

Kingdom of Belgium v Commission (Tubemeuse)	**State Aid**
Case 142/87	Condition 2—Advantage
Court of Justice, [1990] ECR I-959	Market Economy Investor Principle

Facts

An application for the annulment of a Commission decision in which the Commission found that aid awarded by the Kingdom of Belgium to Tubemeuse, a steel pipe and tube manufacturer, was illegal. The Kingdom of Belgium acquired most of the shares in Tubemeuse, following the withdrawal of private shareholders who reacted to the company's precarious financial position and the fall in the demand for seamless tubes. The state granted the Company BFR12 billion in capital increases and through other measures. These measures were notified to the Commission but implemented prior to it reaching a decision. The Commission subsequently found the measure to be incompatible with the internal market, and ordered Belgium to recover the aid. In its action for annulment, the Belgian state argued that Article 107(1) TFEU was wrongly applied because the measures in question did not constitute aid within the meaning of that provision but rather a normal contribution by a shareholder to the company. It further argued that its support for Tubemeuse should be seen as a normal reaction of any investor whose initial investment is at risk.

Held

'[I]nvestment by the public authorities in the capital of undertakings, in whatever form, may constitute State aid where the conditions set out in Article 92 are fulfilled (see the judgments of 14 November 1984 in Case 323/82 *Intermitis v Commission* [1984] ECR 3809, and of 13 March 1985 in Joined Cases 296/82 and 318/82 *Netherlands and Leeuwarder Papierwarenfabriek v Commission* [1985] ECR 809).' (para 25)

In order to assess the nature of the measure, the relevant criterion is whether the undertaking could have obtained the amounts in question on the capital markets. In the case at hand the company had faced financial difficulties, excessively high production costs, continual operating losses, poor liquidity and heavy indebtedness which led to the withdrawal of almost all of its private shareholders. (paras 26–7)

'Moreover, it is not contested that the seamless steel tubes sector, whose production was intended principally for use in oil exploration, was in a state of crisis, marked by considerable surplus capacity in the producing countries and new production capacity in the developing and State-trading countries.' (para 28)

'Under those circumstances, there is nothing which suggests any error in the Commission's assessment that Tubemeuse's prospects of profitability were not such as to induce private investors operating under normal market economy conditions to enter into the financial transactions in question, that it was unlikely that Tubemeuse could have obtained the amounts essential for its survival on the capital markets and that, for that reason, the Belgian Government's support for Tubemeuse constituted State aid.' (para 29)

Comment

The Court noted that the market conditions at the time were so bleak that no private entity would have invested in Tubemeuse. The investment by the state did not therefore take place under normal market economy conditions. This benchmark of assessment, known as the 'market economy investor principle' led the Court to conclude that the capital injection constituted state aid.

In its 'Draft Notice on the notion of State aid', the Commission makes reference to the market economy investor principle used to identify the presence of state aid in cases of public investment: 'Economic transactions carried out by a public body or a public undertaking do not confer an advantage on its counterpart, and therefore do not constitute aid, if they are carried out in line with normal market conditions. … To determine whether a public body's investment constitutes State aid, it is necessary to assess whether, in similar circumstances, a private investor of a comparable size operating in normal conditions of a market economy could have been prompted to make the investment in question.' (para 77)

Altmark Trans and Regierungspräsidium Magdeburg Case C-280/00 Court of Justice, [2003] ECR I-7747	**State Aid** Condition 2—Advantage Service of General Economic Interest

Facts

The transport of passengers by road vehicles on scheduled services is subject in Germany to the grant of a licence. In a preliminary reference, the German administrative court requested clarifications on whether the grant of a licence to operate scheduled transport services and the award of public subsidies for operating those services infringes Article 107 TFEU. In its judgment, the Court of Justice considered whether the grant of a licence may be regarded as an advantage conferred on the recipient undertaking.

Held

'Measures which, whatever their form, are likely directly or indirectly to favour certain undertakings (Case 6/64 *Costa* [1964] ECR 585, at p 595) or are to be regarded as an economic advantage which the recipient undertaking would not have obtained under normal market conditions (Case C-39/94 *SFEI and Others* ... paragraph 60, and Case C-342/96 *Spain* v *Commission* ... paragraph 41) are regarded as aid.' (para 84)

'Mention should, however, be made of the Court's decision in a case concerning an indemnity provided for by Council Directive 75/439/EEC of 16 June 1975 on the disposal of waste oils (OJ 1975 L 194, p 23). That indemnity was able to be granted to waste oil collection and/or disposal undertakings as compensation for the collection and/or disposal obligations imposed on them by the Member State, provided that it did not exceed the annual uncovered costs actually recorded by the undertakings taking into account a reasonable profit. The Court held that an indemnity of that type did not constitute aid within the meaning of Articles 92 et seq of the Treaty, but rather consideration for the services performed by the collection or disposal undertakings (see Case 240/83 *ADBHU* [1985] ECR 531, paragraph 3 ... and paragraph 18).' (para 85)

'Similarly, the Court has held that, provided that a tax on direct sales imposed on pharmaceutical laboratories corresponds to the additional costs actually incurred by wholesale distributors in discharging their public service obligations, not assessing wholesale distributors to the tax may be regarded as compensation for the services they provide and hence not State aid within the meaning of Article 92 of the Treaty. The Court said that, provided there was the necessary equivalence between the exemption and the additional costs incurred, wholesale distributors would not be enjoying any real advantage for the purposes of Article 92(1) of the Treaty, because the only effect of the tax would be to put distributors and laboratories on an equal competitive footing (*Ferring*, paragraph 27).' (para 86)

'It follows from those judgments that, where a State measure must be regarded as compensation for the services provided by the recipient undertakings in order to discharge public service obligations, so that those undertakings do not enjoy a real financial advantage and the measure thus does not have the effect of putting them in a more favourable competitive position than the undertakings competing with them, such a measure is not caught by [Article 107(1) TFEU].' (para 87)

'However, for such compensation to escape classification as State aid in a particular case, a number of conditions must be satisfied. First, the recipient undertaking must actually have public service obligations to discharge, and the obligations must be clearly defined. In the main proceedings, the national court will therefore have to examine whether the public service obligations which were imposed on Altmark Trans are clear from the national legislation and/or the licences at issue in the main proceedings. Second, the parameters on the basis of which the compensation is calculated must be established in advance in an objective and transparent manner, to avoid it conferring an economic advantage which may favour the recipient undertaking over competing undertakings. Payment by a Member State of compensation for the loss incurred by an undertaking without the parameters of such compensation having been established beforehand, where it turns out after the event that the operation of certain services in connection with the discharge of public service obligations was not economically viable, therefore constitutes a financial measure which falls within the concept of State aid within the meaning of [Article 107(1) TFEU]. Third, the compensation cannot exceed what is necessary to cover all or part of the costs incurred in the discharge of public service obligations, taking into account the relevant receipts and a reasonable profit for discharging those obligations. Compliance with such a condition is essential to ensure that the recipient undertaking is not given any advantage which distorts or threatens to distort competition by strengthening that undertaking's competitive position. Fourth, where the undertaking which is to discharge public service obligations, in a specific case, is not chosen pursuant to a public procurement procedure which would allow for the selection of the tenderer capable of providing those services at the least cost to the community, the level of compensation needed must be determined on the basis of an analysis of the costs which a typical undertaking, well run and adequately provided with means of transport so as to be able to meet the necessary public service requirements, would have incurred in discharging those obligations, taking into account the relevant receipts and a reasonable profit for discharging the obligations.' (paras 88–93)

'The condition for the application of [Article 107(1) TFEU] that the aid must be such as to affect trade between Member States does not depend on the local or regional character of the transport services supplied or on the scale of the field of activity concerned. However, public subsidies intended to enable the operation of urban, suburban or regional scheduled transport services are not caught by that provision where such subsidies are to be regarded as compensation for the services provided by the recipient undertakings in order to discharge public service obligations.' For the purpose of applying that criterion, it is for the national court to ascertain that the four conditions in paragraphs 88–93 are satisfied. (para 95)

Comment

For compensation to escape classification as state aid, four conditions must be satisfied: (1) the recipient undertaking must have clearly defined public service obligations to discharge; (2) the parameters on the basis of which the compensation is calculated have been established beforehand in an objective and transparent manner; (3) the compensation does not exceed what is necessary to cover all or part of the costs incurred in the discharge of public service obligations, taking into account the relevant receipts and a reasonable profit; (4) where the undertaking is not chosen via a public procurement procedure, the level of compensation must be determined on the basis of cost analysis, taking into account the 'costs which a typical undertaking, well run and adequately provided with means of transport so as to be able to meet the necessary public service requirements, would have incurred in discharging those obligations, taking into account the relevant receipts and a reasonable profit for discharging the obligations.' (paras 88–93, 95) Failure to satisfy these four conditions would result in compensation for the provision of public services which confers an advantage on the recipient being classified as state aid.

The four conditions put forward by the Court provide a detailed benchmark for assessment of compensation for the provision of service of general economic interest (SGEI). Note, however, that some of the concepts referred to by the Court, such as 'reasonable profit,' 'typical' and 'well run' undertaking, provide for a wide margin of assessment. Clarification of the way the judgment affects the operation of the state and the public service provider may be found in the Commission's 'Guide on the application of the EU rules on state aid, public procurement and the internal market to services of general economic interest, and in particular to social services of general interest' (SWD) 2013 53 final/2.

Contrast the four detailed conditions set out in this case with the Court's holding in Case C-53/00 *Ferring SA v Agence centrale des organismes de sécurité social e* (page 669 below). There, the Court put forward a more succinct benchmark. The Court considered whether selective tax on sales of pharmaceuticals, which applied to direct sales by pharmaceutical laboratories but not to wholesale distributors, amounted to state aid. The Court noted that a specific public service obligation was imposed by French law on wholesale distributors which are required to stock a permanent range of medicines. Such obligation did not apply to direct distributors. The Court held that 'provided that the tax on direct sales imposed on pharmaceutical laboratories corresponds to the additional costs actually incurred by wholesale distributors in discharging their public service obligations, not assessing wholesale distributors to the tax may be regarded as compensation for the services they provide and hence not State aid within the meaning of [Article 107 TFEU]. Moreover, provided there is the necessary equivalence between the exemption and the additional costs incurred, wholesale distributors will not be enjoying any real advantage for the purposes of [Article 107(1) TFEU] because the only effect of the tax will be to put distributors and laboratories on an equal competitive footing.' (para 27)

Federal Republic of Germany v Commission	**State Aid**
Case C-446/14P	Condition 2—Advantage
Court of Justice, not yet reported	

Facts

An appeal by the Federal Republic of Germany on a judgment of the General Court which upheld a Commission decision, finding that financial contributions from several municipalities to a German public corporation for the disposal of animal carcasses constituted state aid. In its appeal, the Federal Republic of Germany argued that, contrary to what the General Court held, the four cumulative conditions set out in Case C-280/00 *Altmark Trans and Regierungspräsidium Magdeburg* to consider whether public service compensation does not constitute state aid are met in this case (see page 659 above for detailed review). In particular, it argued that the fourth condition would be satisfied regarding the requirement that, in the absence of a public procurement procedure, the level of compensation had been based on an analysis of the costs that could have been incurred by an average well-run company. Appeal dismissed.

Held

Where a state measure serves as compensation for the services provided by the recipient undertakings in order to discharge public service obligations, so that those undertakings do not enjoy a real financial advantage and the measure thus does not have the effect of putting them in a more favourable competitive position than the undertakings competing with them, such a measure is not caught by Article 107(1) TFEU. (para 24)

However, a number of cumulative conditions must be satisfied for such compensation to escape classification as state aid in a particular case, as clearly established in the *Altmark* judgment. First, the recipient undertaking must have clearly defined public service obligations to discharge. Second, the parameters on the basis of which the compensation is calculated must be established in advance in an objective and transparent manner. Third, the compensation cannot exceed what is necessary to cover all or part of the costs incurred in the discharge of public service obligations. Fourth, where the undertaking which is to discharge public service obligations, in a specific case, is not chosen pursuant to a public procurement procedure, the level of compensation needed must be determined on the basis of an analysis of the costs which a typical well run undertaking would have incurred in discharging those obligations, taking into account relevant receipts and reasonable profit for discharging the obligations. (paras 25–9)

In this case, the Commission rightly considered that the fourth condition was not satisfied. In its judgment the General Court correctly assessed the conditions and did not err in its analysis when it determined whether the fourth condition set out in *Altmark* had been properly analysed by the Commission. (paras 30–9)

Comment

After outlining the four conditions as set out in Case C-280/00 *Altmark Trans and Regierungspräsidium Magdeburg* (page 659 above), the Court of Justice confirmed the judgment of the General Court, rejecting the claim that the Court erred in its analysis and confused the requirements of the different conditions.

In its 'Draft Notice on the notion of State aid pursuant to Article 107(1) TFEU', the Commission refers to the Altmark judgment and notes that: '[W]here the undertaking which is to discharge public service obligations is not chosen following a public procurement procedure to select a tenderer capable of providing those services at the least cost to the community, the level of compensation needed must be determined on the basis of an analysis of the costs which a typical undertaking, well run and adequately provided with means to meet the public service requirements, would have incurred in discharging those obligations, taking into account the relevant receipts and a reasonable profit for discharging the obligations.' (para 72)

Facts

An action for annulment of a Commission decision in which it found that a special tax regime applicable to coordination centres in Belgium amounted to incompatible state aid. Coordination centres are undertakings created by a group of multinational companies for the purpose of providing various services to those companies. The scheme in question was fiscally advantageous to coordination centres that fulfilled the conditions as set in a national law and received authorisation to operate. Both the Kingdom of Belgium and Forum 187, the coordination centres' representative body, brought actions for annulment of the Commission's decision.

Held

'The concept of aid may cover not only positive benefits, such as subsidies, loans or the taking of shares in undertakings, but also action which, in various forms, mitigates the charges which are normally included in the budget of an undertaking and which, without therefore being subsidies in the strict meaning of the word, are similar in character and have the same effect (Case C-126/01 *Gemo* [2003] ECR I-13769, paragraph 28, and the case-law cited there).' (para 86)

'Furthermore, the Court has held that a measure by which the public authorities grant to certain undertakings a tax exemption which, although not involving a transfer of State resources, places the persons to whom it applies in a more favourable financial situation than other taxpayers constitutes State aid (Case C-387/92 *Banco Exterior de España* [1994] ECR I-877, paragraph 14).' (para 87)

The method of assessment of taxable income for coordination centres is based on the 'cost-plus method'. In order to decide whether this method confers an advantage on the coordination centres, it is necessary to compare that regime with the ordinary tax system. In this case, the exclusion of staff and financial costs from the expenditure which serves to determine the taxable income of the coordination centres does not correspond with the ordinary tax system and confers an economic advantage on the centres. (paras 94–7)

In addition, the coordination centres were: exempted from property tax on the buildings which they use in order to carry on their activities' exempted from capital duty; and exempted from withholding tax. These exemptions conferred an advantage on the coordination centres. (paras 103–18)

Comment

In its Draft Notice on the notion of state aid, the Commission notes that: 'Administrative rulings that merely contain an interpretation of the relevant tax provisions without deviating from the case law and administrative practice do not give rise to a presumption of aid. However, the absence of publication of tax rulings and the room for manoeuvre which tax authorities sometimes enjoy support the presumption of aid. This does not make Member States any less able to provide their taxpayers with legal certainty and predictability on the application of general tax rules. As a result, tax rulings should only aim to provide legal certainty to the fiscal treatment of certain transactions and should not have the effect of granting the undertakings concerned lower taxation than other undertakings in a similar legal and factual situation (but which were not granted such rulings). As demonstrated by the Commission's decisional practice, rulings allowing taxpayers to use alternative methods for calculating taxable profits, eg the use of fixed margins for a cost-plus or resale-minus method for determining an appropriate transfer pricing, may involve State aid.' (paras 175–6)

Commission v Électricité de France (EDF)	**State Aid**
Case C-124/10P	Condition 2—Advantage
Court of Justice, [2012] 3 CMLR 17	Market Economy Investor Test

Facts

As part of the liberalisation of the electricity market in France and the privatisation of Électricité de France (EDF), the French government reclassified certain grantor rights (relating to the free use of infrastructure by EDF) as capital injections without any tax being incurred. France claimed that the tax advantage was comparable to a capital injection a private investor would have granted in similar circumstances. It invoked the market economy investor test and asserted that, despite using fiscal means to support EDF, the advantage conferred on it satisfied that test. The Commission rejected this argument and found the advantage to constitute state aid. The Commission argued that the market economy investor test is inapplicable in this case, since a market operator could never conceivably hold a tax claim against an undertaking—this is solely the state's prerogative. The General Court annulled the Commission's decision, holding that the test was conceivable despite the fiscal nature of the aid measure. The Commission appealed to the Court of Justice.

Held

'[Article 107(1) TFEU] does not distinguish between measures of State intervention by reference to their causes or their aims but defines them in relation to their effects (*Comitato "Venezia vuole vivere" and Others* v *Commission*, paragraph 94 and the case-law cited).' (para 77)

'However, it is also clear from settled case-law that the conditions which a measure must meet in order to be treated as "aid" for the purposes of [Article 107 TFEU] are not met if the recipient public undertaking could, in circumstances which correspond to normal market conditions, obtain the same advantage as that which has been made available to it through State resources. In the case of public undertakings, that assessment is made by applying, in principle, the private investor test.' (para 78)

'In particular, it is clear from case-law that, in order to assess whether the same measure would have been adopted in normal market conditions by a private investor in a situation as close as possible to that of the State, only the benefits and obligations linked to the situation of the State as shareholder—to the exclusion of those linked to its situation as a public authority—are to be taken into account. ... It follows that the roles of the State as shareholder of an undertaking, on the one hand, and of the State acting as a public authority, on the other, must be distinguished.' (paras 79–80)

'The applicability of the private investor test ultimately depends, therefore, on the Member State concerned having conferred, in its capacity as shareholder and not in its capacity as public authority, an economic advantage on an undertaking belonging to it. It follows that, if a Member State relies on that test during the administrative procedure, it must, where there is doubt, establish unequivocally and on the basis of objective and verifiable evidence that the measure implemented falls to be ascribed to the State acting as shareholder. That evidence must show clearly that, before or at the same time as conferring the economic advantage (see, to that effect, *France v Commission*, paragraphs 71 and 72), the Member State concerned took the decision to make an investment, by means of the measure actually implemented, in the public undertaking. In that regard, it may be necessary to produce evidence showing that the decision is based on economic evaluations comparable to those which, in the circumstances, a rational private investor in a situation as close as possible to that of the Member State would have had carried out, before making the investment, in order to determine its future profitability.' (paras 81–4)

'By contrast, for the purposes of showing that, before or at the same time as conferring the advantage, the Member State took that decision as a shareholder, it is not enough to rely on economic evaluations made after the advantage was conferred, on a retrospective finding that the investment made by the Member State concerned was actually profitable, or on subsequent justifications of the course of action actually chosen (see, to that effect, *France v Commission*, paragraphs 71 and 72).' (para 85)

'If the Member State concerned provides the Commission with the requisite evidence, it is for the Commission to carry out a global assessment, taking into account—in addition to the evidence provided by that Member State—all other relevant evidence enabling it to determine whether the Member State took the measure in question in its capacity as shareholder or as a public authority … the nature and subject-matter of that measure are relevant in that regard, as is its context, the objective pursued and the rules to which the measure is subject.' (para 86)

'Accordingly, in the circumstances of the case, the General Court was right to hold that the objective pursued by the French State could be taken into account, in the context of the requisite global assessment, for the purposes of determining whether the State had indeed acted in its capacity as shareholder and whether, as a consequence, the private investor test was applicable in the present case.' (para 87)

'As regards the question whether the applicability of the private investor test could be ruled out in the present case simply because the means employed by the French State were fiscal, it should be recalled that, under [Article 107(1) TFEU] any aid granted through State resources—in any form whatsoever—which, in terms of its effects, distorts or threatens to distort competition is incompatible with the common market in so far as it affects trade between Member States (see Case C-156/98 *Germany v Commission*, paragraph 25 and the case-law cited). Moreover, it has been noted in paragraph 78 above that the private investor test is applied in order to determine whether, because of its effects, the economic advantage granted, in whatever form, through State resources to a public undertaking distorts or threatens to distort competition and affects trade between Member States. The intention underlying [Article 107(1) TFEU] and the private investor test is thus to prevent the recipient public undertaking from being placed, by means of State resources, in a more favourable position than that of its competitors (see, to that effect, Case C-387/92 *Banco Exterior de España* [1994] ECR I-877, paragraph 14, and Case C-6/97 *Italy v Commission*, paragraph 16).' (paras 88–90)

'[W]hen considering whether the private investor test was applicable, the General Court did not err in law by focusing its analysis, not on the fiscal nature of the means employed by the French State, but on the improvement—with a view to the opening up of the electricity market—in EDF's financial situation and on the effects of the measure in question on competition.' (para 91)

'However, in the course of considering the second ground of appeal, it has been found that, where a Member State confers an economic advantage upon an undertaking belonging to it, the fiscal nature of the process used to grant that advantage does not mean that the applicability of the private investor test can automatically be ruled out. It follows, a fortiori, that the precise *modus operandi* chosen by the Member State is irrelevant for the purposes of assessing whether that test applies.' (para 108)

Comment

The Court rejected the Commission's approach according to which a fiscal nature of an advantage—ie the waiver of tax payment—prevents the application of the private investor test, as such private investor could not hold a tax claim against an undertaking.

The Court clarified that the test concerns the substance, not the form, of the advantage. The fiscal nature of the advantage (such as tax credit) does not affect the application of the market economy investor test. The focus of the test is on the effects of the measure—the improvement—and whether the state took that decision as a shareholder.

According to the market economy operator (investor) principle, a Member State is acting as a rational private shareholder when it can show that, before or when it conferred the advantage in question, it took that decision in its capacity as a shareholder—following an economic evaluation, and motivated by financial return—and not in its capacity as a public authority concerned with public objectives. Once the state establishes that it operated as a rational market operator, it is for the Commission to carry out a global assessment, taking into account, among other things, the nature and subject-matter of that measure, its context and objectives.

Land Burgenland and others v Commission	**State Aid**
Cases C-214/12P etc	Condition 2—Advantage
Court of Justice, 24 October 2013	Private Vendor Test

Facts

The Commission found the Republic of Austria to have infringed state aid rules during the privatisation of Bank Burgenland (BB). The bank in question was wholly owned by the Province of Burgenland (Land Burgenland). Under Austrian law, Land Burgenland was liable as a deficiency guarantor for all the bank's liabilities (liability under the state performance guarantee system, known as *Ausfallhaftung*, which in itself was confirmed as permissible state aid, by the Commission in Decision COM(2003) 1329 final). Land Burgenland initiated a privatisation procedure for BB and received two bids: the first from an Austrian insurance undertaking, GRAWE, which offered €100.3 million; the second from an Austro-Ukrainian consortium, which offered €155 million. Land Burgenland awarded BB to GRAWE, despite its lower offer, taking into account, among other things, its exposure due to the *Ausfallhaftung*.

The Austro-Ukrainian consortium filed a state aid complaint with the Commission. In its decision, the Commission examined whether Land Burgenland had behaved like any seller operating in a market economy (the 'private vendor' test). The Commission opined that accepting a lower bid may be permissible under the test where: (1) the sale to the highest bidder is not realisable; and (2) factors other than the price, which a private vendor would have taken into account, dictate a sale to a lower bidder. The Commission found that Land Burgenland's decision in this case was affected by its liability as a deficiency guarantor and subsequently amounted to state aid.

Land Burgenland's applied for annulment of that decision—Joined Cases T-268/08 and T-281/08 *Land Burgenland (Austria) v Commission*. The General Court dismissed the action. In its judgment it summarised the 'private investor concept' and held that: 'It is apparent from the case-law that, when applying the private investor test, it is appropriate to draw a distinction between the obligations which the State must assume as owner of the share capital of a company and its obligations as a public authority (Joined Cases C-278/92 to C-280/92 *Spain v Commission* [1994] ECR I-4103, paragraph 22). Thus, in Case C-334/99 *Germany v Commission* ... the Court precluded various loans and guarantees, which a private investor would never have granted under the same conditions and which had to be classified as unlawful State aid, from being taken into consideration in connection with examination of whether the liquidation of Gröditzer Stahlwerke was more expensive than its privatisation at a negative price. ... What is decisive when applying the private operator test is whether the measures in question are those which a private operator in a market economy, who counts on making a profit in the shorter or longer term, could have granted. Thus, regardless of how the commitments at issue could have been classified, the fundamental question which arises is that of whether those commitments are among those which could have been entered into by a private operator in a market economy.' (paras 155–7)

Land Burgenland appealed to the Court of Justice. Appeal dismissed.

Held

The General Court correctly summarised the 'private investor concept' and correctly held that when applying the 'private investor' test, it must be determined whether the measures in question are those which such an investor, who counts on making a profit in the short or long term, could have granted. Such an investor would be liable as a deficiency guarantor. (paras 47–8)

The General Court found that *Ausfallhaftung* was not entered into on normal market conditions, given its characteristics, and therefore could not be taken into account when assessing the conduct of the Austrian authorities in the light of the private vendor test. (paras 49–50)

'Further, as regards the impact of *Commission v EDF*, it must be pointed out that that judgment was principally concerned with whether the private investor test was applicable in the circumstances of that case. ... However, in the present cases, it is undisputed that the Commission applied the private vendor test and the Province of Burgenland, the Republic of Austria and GRAWE are in actual fact challenging the General Court's approval of the manner in which the Commission applied that test.' (para 51)

'As regards the application of that test, *Commission v EDF* confirmed the case-law which emerges, in particular, from *Spain v Commission* and *Germany v Commission*, according to which, in order to assess whether the same measure would have been adopted in normal market conditions by a private vendor in a situation as close as possible to that of the State, only the benefits and obligations linked to the situation of the State as shareholder—to the exclusion of those linked to its situation as a public authority—are to be taken into account (see, to that effect, *Commission v EDF*, paragraph 79).' (para 52)

'In *Commission v EDF* judgment, the Court further made it clear that, when carrying out that assessment, the manner in which the advantage is provided and the nature of the manner by which the State intervenes are irrelevant where the Member State concerned conferred that advantage in its capacity as shareholder of the undertaking concerned (see *Commission v EDF*, paragraphs 91 and 92).' (para 53)

In its assessment, the General Court examined whether *Ausfallhaftung* had to be taken into account when implementing the private vendor test and found that a private vendor would not have entered into such a guarantee. The parties do not contest the fact that the *Ausfallhaftung* has been classified as state aid. 'In those circumstances, and since, by granting aid, a Member State pursues, by definition, objectives other than that of making a profit from the resources granted to an undertaking belonging to it, it must be held that those resources are, in principle, granted by the State exercising its prerogatives as a public authority.' (paras 54–6)

The appellants argue that the sale was nonetheless conducted with a profit-making aim. Yet, 'it must be recalled that, if a Member State relies on a test such as the private vendor test, it must, where there is doubt, establish unequivocally and on the basis of objective and verifiable evidence that the measure implemented is to be ascribed to the State acting as shareholder. ... That evidence must show clearly that, before or at the same time as conferring the economic advantage, the Member State concerned took the decision to make an investment, by means of the measure actually implemented, in the public undertaking. ... In that regard, it may be necessary to produce evidence showing that the decision is based on economic evaluations comparable to those which, in the circumstances, a rational private vendor in a situation as close as possible to that of the Member State would have had carried out, before making the investment, in order to determine its future profitability. ... It is only in cases where the Member State concerned provides the Commission with the necessary evidence that the onus is on the Commission to carry out a global assessment, taking into account—in addition to the evidence provided by that Member State—all other relevant evidence enabling it to determine whether the Member State took the measure in question in its capacity as shareholder or as a public authority (see, to that effect, *Commission v EDF*, paragraph [82–86]).' (paras 57–60)

'However, neither during the administrative procedure nor before the General Court did the Province of Burgenland, the Republic of Austria or GRAWE put forward any evidence showing that the introduction or retention of *Ausfallhaftung* was based on economic evaluations.' (para 61)

Comment

The Court endorsed the Commission's and General Court's application of the 'private vendor test'. It relied heavily on its ruling in *Commission v EDF* (page 663 above) to outline the conditions for the test.

The facts of the case are somewhat complicated by the pre-existing guarantee to BB that had been classified as state aid by the Commission before the bank's privatisation. The Court confirmed the Commission and General Court holding that the increased likelihood of the guarantee being triggered in the event that BB was sold to the highest bidder could not be taken into account in relation to the private vendor test. This is because Austria had not put forward any evidence showing that the guarantee was based on economic evaluations conducted for the purpose of establishing its profitability as a private vendor would have done. By omitting to do so, the appellants did not discharge the obligations under the *Commission v EDF* judgment.

Kingdom of Spain v Commission	**State Aid**
Cases T-461/13 etc	Condition 2—Advantage
General Court, 26 November 2015	Public Service

Facts

Between 2005 and 2009 the Spanish authorities adopted a series of measures aimed at facilitating the transition from analogue to digital television broadcasting. To facilitate the transition, the Spanish authorities made public funding available to the Spanish digital terrestrial television service (DTT) in order to support the process of digitisation. Following a complaint from a European satellite operator, the Commission adopted a decision by which it declared that the funding amounted to state aid, incompatible with the internal market. Spain applied for annulment for the decision. Among other things, it argued that the operation by DTT was a public service—fulfilling the state's desire to offer digital services to rural communities. Subsequently, the Commission erred in its holding that in absence of a clear definition of the operation of a terrestrial network as a public service, the aid to DTT should be qualified as state aid and cannot be viewed as compensation. Action dismissed.

Held

One of the conditions for classification as state aid is the conferral of an economic advantage on the recipient which it would not have obtained under normal market conditions. One therefore needs to determine whether DTT's activities fell within the exercise of public powers (by its nature, purpose and rules) as argued by Spain, or the exercise of economic activities as argued by the Commission. In that context one should recall that an entity exercising a formal mandate may operate as an undertaking when it is engaged in economic activity. (paras 33–40)

As noted by the Commission, the activity in question did not form part of the state's public power. It was offered by other operators on the market, the DTT network was not within the state's prerogatives and it was not an activity that only the state could exercise. (para 41)

One should distinguish a situation in which the state acts in exercising public authority and one in which it carries on economic activities of an industrial or commercial nature—offering goods or services on the market. In this respect, it does not matter that the state is acting directly through a body forming part of the public administration or via an entity that has granted special or exclusive rights. It is generally the case that when an activity undertaken by an entity may be exercised by a private undertaking, then that activity forms an economic activity. (para 43)

Lack of profitability cannot serve as a measure to determining whether the activity in question was of an economic nature. (para 45)

DTT, as the recipient undertaking, did not have a clearly defined public service obligation to discharge. In the absence of a clear definition of the operation of a terrestrial network as a public service, the measures should be qualified as state aid. (paras 43–7)

Comment

The Court rejected the argument of the Kingdom of Spain according to which the services offered by DTT were those of a public authority and not economic in nature. The Court noted that other operators offered these services and that by their nature these services were not unique to the state.

The finding that the operation of a terrestrial network does not form a public service meant that the aid provided by Spain could not have been viewed as compensation for carrying out a public service.

Appeal before the Court of Justice is pending. Case C-81/16P.

Adria Wien Pipeline GmbH	**State Aid**
Case C-143/99	Condition 3—Selectivity
Court of Justice, [2001] ECR I-8365	Material Selectivity Test

Facts

A reference for a preliminary ruling from the Austrian Constitutional Court concerning the compatibility of a 'law on the rebate of energy taxes' (EAVG) with Article 107(1) TFEU. The EAVG granted undertakings active in the production of goods a rebate on energy taxes charged on the supply of electricity and natural gas.

Held

'[A]n economic benefit granted by a Member State constitutes State aid only if, by displaying a degree of selectivity, it is such as to favour certain undertakings or the production of certain goods. A State measure which benefits all undertakings in national territory, without distinction, cannot therefore constitute State aid.' (paras 34–5)

'For the application of [Article 107 TFEU], it is irrelevant that the situation of the presumed beneficiary of the measure is better or worse in comparison with the situation under the law as it previously stood, or has not altered over time (see, to that effect, Case 57/86 *Greece v Commission* [1988] ECR 2855, paragraph 10). The only question to be determined is whether, under a particular statutory scheme, a State measure is such as to favour certain undertakings or the production of certain goods within the meaning of [Article 107(1) TFEU] in comparison with other undertakings which are in a legal and factual situation that is comparable in the light of the objective pursued by the measure in question (see, to that effect, Case C-75/97 *Belgium v Commission* [1999] ECR I-3671, paragraphs 28 to 31). According to the case-law of the Court, a measure which, although conferring an advantage on its recipient, is justified by the nature or general scheme of the system of which it is part does not fulfil that condition of selectivity (see Case 173/73 *Italy v Commission* [1974] ECR 709, paragraph 33, and *Belgium v Commission*, cited above, paragraph 33).' (paras 41–2)

The large number of eligible undertakings or the diversity and size of the sectors to which those undertakings belong do not provide any grounds for concluding that a state initiative constitutes a general measure of economic policy. The taxation system in this case does not include any justification for the grant of the advantages to a select group. (paras 48–9)

'[U]ndertakings supplying services may, just like undertakings manufacturing goods, be major consumers of energy and incur energy taxes. … There is nothing in the national legislation at issue to support the conclusion that the rebate scheme restricted to undertakings which primarily manufacture goods is a purely temporary measure enabling them to adapt gradually to the new scheme because they are disproportionately affected by it, as the Austrian Government maintains. … For another thing, the ecological considerations underlying the national legislation at issue do not justify treating the consumption of natural gas or electricity by undertakings supplying services differently than the consumption of such energy by undertakings manufacturing goods. Energy consumption by each of those sectors is equally damaging to the environment. … It follows from the foregoing considerations that, although objective, the criterion applied by the national legislation at issue is not justified by the nature or general scheme of that legislation, so that it cannot save the measure at issue from being in the nature of State aid. Besides, as the Commission has rightly observed, the statement of reasons for the bill which led to the enactment of the national legislation at issue indicates that the advantageous terms granted to undertakings manufacturing goods were intended to preserve the competitiveness of the manufacturing sector, in particular within the Community.' (paras 50–4)

Comment

The material selectivity test establishes a comparability exercise—considering whether other undertakings are in a comparable legal and factual situation with the beneficiary and, if yes, whether they have been treated differently. If so, the measure is prima facie selective and one should consider whether it may be justified by the nature or general scheme of the legislation.

Ferring SA	**State Aid**
Case C-53/00	Condition 3—Selectivity
Court of Justice, [2001] ECR I-9067	

Facts

The case concerned French legislation which imposed on wholesale medicine distributors a public service obligation to stock a wide range of medicines, comprising at least one-tenth of all forms of medicine sold in France. A similar obligation was not imposed on pharmaceutical laboratories that engaged in direct sales to pharmacies. To restore the competitive balance of competition between wholesale and pharmaceutical laboratories' direct distribution channels, a new tax was introduced that applied only to direct sales. In its preliminary reference, the French Tribunal des affaires de sécurité sociale de Créteil asked, among other things, whether the non-subjection of wholesale distributors to the tax constituted state aid.

Held

The French authorities have waived their right to receive tax payments from wholesale distributors, thus conferring upon them an economic advantage through the use of state resources. That advantage strengthened the position of this class of undertakings in relation to other undertakings and affected trade patterns between the Member States. Accordingly, the tax on direct sales may constitute state aid within the meaning of Article 107(1) TFEU inasmuch as it does not apply to wholesale distributors. (paras 20–2)

However, it is necessary to consider whether the public service obligations imposed only on wholesale distributors by the French system for the supply of medicines to pharmacies precludes the tax from being state aid. Discharging those public service obligations entails additional costs for wholesale distributors. Provided that the tax on direct sales imposed on pharmaceutical laboratories corresponds to the additional costs actually incurred by wholesale distributors in discharging their public service obligations, one may view the exemption from tax as compensation for the services they provide. In such case, wholesale distributors will not be enjoying any real advantage for the purposes of Article 107(1) TFEU because the only effect of the tax will be to put distributors and laboratories on an equal competitive footing. It is for the national court to decide whether that condition is satisfied. (paras 22–8)

Comment

The Court held that non-subjection to tax can amount to a selective benefit and may constitute state aid. However, such benefit will not amount to state aid if it serves as adequate compensation for public services obligation. In both *Ferring* and C-280/00 *Altmark Trans and Regierungspräsidium Magdeburg* the Court stressed that the benefit would constitute an advantage if it exceeds the undertakings' additional costs.

In Case C-526/04 *Laboratoires Boiron SA*, [2006] ECR I-7529, a pharmaceutical laboratory which produced homeopathic medicines and was liable to the tax on direct sales had argued, in line with the Court's ruling in *Ferring*, that the wholesale distributors' exemption from tax amounted to state aid. Boiron argued that the wholesalers were overcompensated and received a benefit greater than the cost associated with their public service obligations. It therefore sought repayment of sums it paid as tax on direct sales. The Court of Justice accepted that 'an economic operator such as Boiron may plead that the charge on direct sales is unlawful, for the purposes of applying for reimbursement, on the ground that it amounts to an aid measure … such reimbursement, to the extent that it is payable, is a very appropriate way of reducing the number of economic operators harmed by the measure deemed to constitute aid, and thus, of limiting the anti-competitive effects of that measure.' (paras 40–1) The Court noted the unique circumstances of the case which may justify reimbursement: 'For a tax to be regarded as forming an integral part of an aid measure, it must be hypothecated to the aid measure under the relevant national rules, in the sense that the revenue from the tax is necessarily allocated for the financing of the aid. … In the case of the tax on direct sales, a special feature is that that charge and the alleged aid measure constitute two elements of one and the same fiscal measure which are inseparable. In such a case, the charge and the aid are more closely linked than in the case of a parafiscal charge such as that forming the subject-matter of the judgment in *Van Calster*.' (paras 44–5)

Portuguese Republic v Commission (Azores)
Case C-88/03
Court of Justice, [2006] ECR I-7115

State Aid
Condition 3—Selectivity
Regional Selectivity

Facts

Action for the annulment of a Commission decision which considered tax measures adopted by the Azores region in Portugal. The measures in question reduced the income and corporation tax rate for undertakings established in the Azores. The Commission found them to constitute state aid, but declared it compatible with the internal market in view of the Azores' regional handicaps, with the exception of the reduction for under-takings carrying out financial activities of the 'intra group services' type. The Portuguese Republic challenged that decision and argued, among other things, that the reduction fell outside the scope of Article 107(1) TFEU as it was justified by the nature and general scheme of the tax system.

Held

'[I]n order to determine whether the measure at issue is selective it is appropriate to examine whether, within the context of a particular legal system, that measure constitutes an advantage for certain undertakings in comparison with others which are in a comparable legal and factual situation. The determination of the refer-ence framework has a particular importance in the case of tax measures, since the very existence of an advan-tage may be established only when compared with "normal" taxation. The "normal" tax rate is the rate in force in the geographical area constituting the reference framework.' (para 56)

'In that connection, the reference framework need not necessarily be defined within the limits of the Member State concerned, so that a measure conferring an advantage in only one part of the national territory is not selective on that ground alone for the purposes of [Article 107(1) TFEU]. It is possible that an infra-State body enjoys a legal and factual status which makes it sufficiently autonomous in relation to the central government of a Member State, with the result that, by the measures it adopts, it is that body and not the central govern-ment which plays a fundamental role in the definition of the political and economic environment in which undertakings operate. In such a case it is the area in which the infra-State body responsible for the measure exercises its powers, and not the country as a whole, that constitutes the relevant context for the assessment.' (paras 57–8)

The fact that an aid programme has been adopted by a regional authority does not prevent the application of Article 107(1) TFEU if the relevant conditions are satisfied. However, the mere fact that a measure is applica-ble only in a limited geographical area of a Member State does not lead to the conclusion that that measure is selective. (paras 59–60)

'In order to determine the selectivity of a measure adopted by an infra-State body which, like the measure at issue, seeks to establish in one part of the territory of a Member State a tax rate which is lower than the rate in force in the rest of that State it is appropriate, as stated in paragraph 58 of this judgment, to examine whether that measure was adopted by that body in the exercise of powers sufficiently autonomous vis-à-vis the central power and, if appropriate, to examine whether that measure indeed applies to all the undertakings established in or all production of goods on the territory coming within the competence of that body.' (para 62)

'In paragraph 50 et seq of his Opinion, the Advocate General specifically identified three situations in which the issue of the classification as State aid of a measure seeking to establish, in a limited geographical area, tax rates lower than the rates in force nationally may arise. In the first situation, the central government unilat-erally decides that the applicable national tax rate should be reduced within a defined geographic area. The second situation corresponds to a model for distribution of tax competences in which all the local authorities at the same level (regions, districts or others) have the autonomous power to decide, within the limit of the powers conferred on them, the tax rate applicable in the territory within their competence. The Commis-sion has recognised, as have the Portuguese and United Kingdom Governments, that a measure taken by a local authority in the second situation is not selective because it is impossible to determine a normal tax rate capable of constituting the reference framework. In the third situation described, a regional or local authority adopts, in the exercise of sufficiently autonomous powers in relation to the central power, a tax rate lower than the national rate and which is applicable only to undertakings present in the territory within its competence. In the latter situation, the legal framework appropriate to determine the selectivity of a tax measure may be limited to the geographical area concerned where the infra-State body, in particular on account of its status and powers, occupies a fundamental role in the definition of the political and economic environment in which the undertakings present on the territory within its competence operate.' (paras 63–66)

'As the Advocate General pointed out … in order that a decision taken in such circumstances can be regarded as having been adopted in the exercise of sufficiently autonomous powers, that decision must, first of all, have been taken by a regional or local authority which has, from a constitutional point of view, a political and administrative status separate from that of the central government. Next, it must have been adopted without the central government being able to directly intervene as regards its content. Finally, the financial consequences of a reduction of the national tax rate for undertakings in the region must not be offset by aid or subsidies from other regions or central government.' (para 67)

'It follows that political and fiscal independence of central government which is sufficient as regards the application of Community rules on State aid presupposes, as the United Kingdom Government submitted, that the infra-State body not only has powers in the territory within its competence to adopt measures reducing the tax rate, regardless of any considerations related to the conduct of the central State, but that in addition it assumes the political and financial consequences of such a measure.' (para 68)

The tax reduction measures in question, which favour undertakings liable for tax in the Azores, do not fulfil the requirements set out in paragraphs 67 and 68 of this judgment and are therefore selective and not general measures. (paras 69–79) Next, it is appropriate to examine whether the tax measures at issue may be justified by the nature or overall structure of the Portuguese tax system. This is for the Member State concerned to demonstrate. Yet, the Portuguese government has not shown that the adoption by the Autonomous Region of the Azores of the measures at issue was necessary for the functioning and effectiveness of the general tax system. The measures at issue apply to all economic operators in the Azores, without distinction as to their financial circumstances. They therefore cannot be regarded as ensuring that for the purpose of redistribution the criterion of ability to pay is observed. 'The mere fact that the regional tax system is conceived in such a way as to ensure the correction of such inequalities does not allow the conclusion to be drawn that every tax advantage granted by the authorities of the autonomous region concerned is justified by the nature and overall structure of the national tax system. The fact of acting on the basis of a regional development or social cohesion policy is not sufficient in itself to justify a measure adopted within the framework of that policy.' (paras 80–3)

Comment

Regional selectivity of measures adopted by infra-state authorities are examined through a three-step test aimed at establishing whether the relevant reference framework is the geographical area which the regional authority regulates or the entire territory of the Member State. When the conditions are met, the region's institutional, procedural and fiscal autonomy is established. Consequently, the relevant reference framework is the relevant set of rules applying in that geographical region. The three steps, outlined in paragraph 67, are commonly referred to as the 'Azores conditions' which examine the region's institutional, procedural and fiscal autonomy.

The 'Azores conditions' have been referred to in subsequent case law, most notably in Cases C-428/06 etc *Unión General de Trabajadores de La Rioja (UGT-Rioja)*. With respect to the institutional autonomy criterion, the Court held that it is satisfied when the region has a political and administrative status which is distinct from that of central government. As for procedural autonomy, the Court held that it 'does not preclude the establishment of a conciliation procedure in order to avoid conflicts, provided that the final decision taken at the conclusion of that procedure is adopted by the infra-State body and not by the central government.' (para 96) With regard to the economic and financial autonomy, the Court held that 'the financial consequences of a reduction of the national tax rate for undertakings in the region must not be offset by aid or subsidies from other regions or central government.' (para 123)

British Aggregates Association	**State Aid**
Case C-487/06P	Condition 3—Selectivity
Court of Justice, [2008] ECR I-10505	Environmental Considerations

Facts

Aggregates (eg sand, gravel and hard rock) were subjected to a levy (known as the AGL) in the UK. In 2002, the UK government amended the AGL and exempted certain aggregates from the levy. The purpose of the exclusion was to encourage resource efficiency and use of environmentally friendly materials extracted as by-products or waste from other processes. The Commission reviewed the AGL and decided not to object to it. It held that the levy did not comprise any elements of state aid and that its scope was justified by the logic and nature of the tax system. The British Aggregates Association (BAA) applied for the annulment of the decision. The General Court dismissed the action. BAA appealed to the Court of justice.

Held

'[T]he concept of State aid does not refer to State measures which differentiate between undertakings and which are, therefore, prima facie selective where that differentiation arises from the nature or the overall structure of the system of which they form part (see, to that effect, inter alia, *Adria-Wien Pipeline and Wietersdorfer & Peggauer Zementwerke*, paragraph 42, and *Portugal v Commission*, paragraph 52).' (para 83)

'The objective pursued by State measures is not sufficient to exclude those measures outright from classification as "aid" for the purposes of [Article 107 TFEU] … [Article 107(1) TFEU] does not distinguish between the causes or the objectives of State aid, but defines them in relation to their effects.' (paras 84–5)

'In the light of that case-law, the unavoidable conclusion is that the Court of First Instance disregarded [Article 107(1)TFEU], as interpreted by the Court of Justice, by holding … that Member States are free, in balancing the various interests involved, to set their priorities as regards the protection of the environment and, as a result, to determine which goods or services they decide to subject to an environmental levy, with the result that the fact that such a levy does not apply to all similar activities which have a comparable impact on the environment does not mean that similar activities, which are not subject to the levy, benefit from a selective advantage.' (para 86)

'[T]hat approach, which is based solely on a regard for the environmental objective being pursued, excludes a priori the possibility that the non-imposition of the AGL on operators in comparable situations in the light of the objective being pursued might constitute a "selective advantage", independently of the effects of the fiscal measure in question, even though [Article 107(1) TFEU] does not make any distinction according to the causes or objectives of State interventions, but defines them on the basis of their effects.' (para 87)

'[T]he need to take account of requirements relating to environmental protection, however legitimate, cannot justify the exclusion of selective measures, even specific ones such as environmental levies, from the scope of [Article 107(1) TFEU] (see, to that effect, inter alia Case C-409/00 *Spain v Commission*, paragraph 54), as account may in any event usefully be taken of the environmental objectives when the compatibility of the State aid measure with the common market is being assessed pursuant to [Article 107(3) TFEU].' (para 92)

Comment

The Court reaffirmed the effects-based doctrine and the principle that that non-subjection to tax can amount to a selective benefit and may constitute state aid. (See *Ferring*, page 669 above.)

The case bears similarities with Case C-279/08P *Commission v Netherlands (NOx)* where the Court held that: 'Even if environmental protection constitutes one of the essential objectives of the European Community, the need to take that objective into account does not justify the exclusion of selective measures from the scope of [Article 107(1) TFEU].' (para 75) In both cases the Court disapproved of the General Court accommodating the environmental objectives of the national measures within the selectivity test.

Ministero dell'Economia e delle Finanze v Paint Graphos	**State Aid**
Cases C-78/08 etc	Condition 3—Selectivity
Court of Justice, [2006] ECR I-7529	General Scheme Justification

Facts

A reference for a preliminary ruling in which the Italian Supreme Court asked whether an Italian law which grants total or partial exemption from various taxes to a select group of cooperative societies active in the promotion of the social function, constitutes state aid.

Held

State financing

The definition of aid in Article 107(1) TFEU 'is more general than that of a subsidy because it includes not only positive benefits, such as subsidies themselves, but also measures which, in various forms, mitigate the charges which are normally included in the budget of an undertaking and which thus, without being subsidies in the strict sense of the word, are similar in character and have the same effect. ... Consequently, a measure by which the public authorities grant certain undertakings a tax exemption which, although not involving the transfer of State resources, places the recipients of the exemption in a more favourable financial position than that of other taxpayers amounts to State aid within the meaning of [Article 107(1) TFEU]. Likewise, a measure allowing certain undertakings a tax reduction or to postpone payment of tax normally due can amount to State aid [Case C-222/04 *Cassa di Risparmio di Firenze and Others*, paras 131, 132].' (paras 45, 46)

Selectivity

Accordingly, the provision at hand involves state financing. One should next consider whether the measure is selective. 'In order to classify a domestic tax measure as "selective", it is necessary to begin by identifying and examining the common or "normal" regime applicable in the Member State concerned. It is in relation to this common or "normal" tax regime that it is necessary, secondly, to assess and determine whether any advantage granted by the tax measure at issue may be selective by demonstrating that the measure derogates from that common regime inasmuch as it differentiates between economic operators who, in light of the objective assigned to the tax system of the Member State concerned, are in a comparable factual and legal situation (see, to that effect, Case C-88/03 *Portugal v Commission* [2006] ECR I-7115, paragraph 56).' (paras 47–9)

In the case at issue, it is necessary to determine whether the tax exemptions 'are liable to favour certain undertakings or the production of certain goods by comparison with other undertakings which are in a comparable factual and legal situation, in the light of the objective pursued by the corporation tax regime, namely the taxation of company profits.' Cooperative societies conform to particular operating principles which distinguish them from other economic operators and are set in European legislation and outlined in the Commission's Communication on the promotion of cooperative societies in Europe. They operate in line with the principle of the primacy of the individual, which is reflected in the rules on membership, resignation and expulsion. Further, these societies are not managed in the interests of outside investors. These societies have no or limited access to equity markets and are therefore dependent for their development on their own capital or credit financing. Shares in cooperative societies are not listed on the stock exchange and investment in them is less advantageous—leading to their profit margins to be lower than that of capital companies, which are better able to adapt to market requirements. In the light of those special characteristics these cooperative societies cannot, in principle, be regarded as being in a comparable factual and legal situation to that of commercial companies. (paras 50–61)

When a 'cooperative' society does not have these unique characteristics normally associated with that type of society, and does not truly pursue an objective based on mutuality, it will have to be distinguished from the model described above. It is for the referring court to determine whether the producers' and workers' cooperative societies at issue in the main proceedings are a 'cooperative' society as the ones in the model described above, or in fact are comparable to profit-making companies liable to corporation tax. (paras 62, 63)

Justification by the nature or general scheme of the tax system

'If the national court concludes that, in the disputes before it, the condition set out in the preceding paragraph is in fact met, it will still be necessary to determine, in accordance with the Court's case-law, whether tax exemptions such as those at issue in the main proceedings are justified by the nature or general scheme of the system of which they form part (see, to that effect, *Adria-Wien Pipeline and Wietersdorfer & Peggauer Zementwerke*, paragraph 42).' (para 64)

'Thus, a measure which constitutes an exception to the application of the general tax system may be justified if the Member State concerned can show that that measure results directly from the basic or guiding principles of its tax system (see *Portugal v Commission*, paragraph 81).' (para 65)

'In that context, it is appropriate to provide the referring court with the following guidance with a view to enabling it to give an effective ruling in the disputes before it. First, the Court has held on numerous occasions that the objective pursued by State measures is not sufficient to exclude those measures outright from classification as "aid" for the purposes of [Article 107 TFEU]. … It should also be recalled that a measure which creates an exception to the application of the general tax system may be justified if it results directly from the basic or guiding principles of that tax system. In that context, a distinction must be made between, on the one hand, the objectives attributed to a particular tax regime and which are extrinsic to it and, on the other, the mechanisms inherent in the tax system itself which are necessary for the achievement of such objectives (see, to that effect, *Portugal v Commission*, paragraph 81). Consequently, tax exemptions which are the result of an objective that is unrelated to the tax system of which they form part cannot circumvent the requirements under [Article 107(1) TFEU]. Next, as is apparent from paragraph 25 of the notice on direct business taxation, the Commission takes the view that the nature or general scheme of the national tax system may properly be relied on as justification for the fact that cooperative societies which distribute all their profits to their members are not taxed themselves as cooperatives, provided that tax is levied on the individual members. Finally, as submitted in its written observations, the Commission also takes the view that the nature or general scheme of the tax system in question can provide no valid justification for a national measure if it provides that profits from trade with third parties who are not members of the cooperative are exempt from tax or that sums paid to such parties by way of remuneration may be deducted. Moreover, it is necessary to ensure compliance with the requirement that a benefit must be consistent not only with the inherent characteristics of the tax system in question but also as regards the manner in which that system is implemented.' (paras 66–73)

'In any event, in order for tax exemptions such as those at issue in the main proceedings to be justified by the nature or general scheme of the tax system of the Member State concerned, it is also necessary to ensure that those exemptions are consistent with the principle of proportionality and do not go beyond what is necessary, in that the legitimate objective being pursued could not be attained by less far-reaching measures.' (para 75)

Comment

The Court outlined three stages for the inquiry. First, whether the tax exemption amounts to state financing. Second, whether the measure is selective. Third, whether the selective measure can be justified as resulting directly from the basic or guiding principles of the tax system.

With respect to the consideration of selectivity, the Court outlined the characteristics of cooperative societies and the need for a comparability exercise which takes account of the real characteristics of the societies in a given case.

As for the 'nature and general scheme justification', the Court made reference to the Commission's Notice on the Application of the State Aid Rules to Measures relating to Direct Business Taxation, and noted the requirement that the Member State concerned adequately monitors the application of these exceptions. The Court also emphasised that the tax exemptions should conform with the principle of proportionality.

Commission v Government of Gibraltar	**State Aid**
Cases C-106/09P etc	Condition 3—Selectivity
Court of Justice, [2011] ECRI-11113	

Facts

The Commission initiated an investigation in respect of corporate tax reform applied in Gibraltar. The Commission found these measures to be materially and regionally selective and to constitute state aid, among other things, due to the measures favouring offshore companies, with limited or no real physical presence in Gibraltar. The General Court annulled the Commission's decision, holding that its method of determining material selectivity was flawed. The General Court focused on the proposed reform's regulatory technique—that it appears to be of a general measure with no derogating provisions. On appeal to the Court of Justice, the Court overruled the General Court, criticising its formalistic analysis.

Held

Legal background

'[T]he definition of aid is more general than that of a subsidy, given that it includes not only positive benefits, such as subsidies themselves, but also State measures which, in various forms, mitigate the charges which are normally included in the budget of an undertaking and which thus, without being subsidies in the strict sense of the word, are similar in character and have the same effect (see Case C-143/99 *Adria-Wien Pipeline and Wietersdorfer & Peggauer Zementwerke* [2001] ECR I-8365, paragraph 38, and Joined Cases C-78/08 to C-80/08 *Paint Graphos and Others* [2011] …, paragraph 45 and the case-law cited).' (para 71)

'Consequently, a measure by which the public authorities grant certain undertakings favourable tax treatment which, although not involving the transfer of State resources, places the recipients in a more favourable financial position than other taxpayers amounts to State aid within the meaning of [Article 107(1) TFEU] (see Case C-387/92 *Banco Exterior de España* [1994] ECR I-877, paragraph 14, and *Paint Graphos and Others*, paragraph 46 and the case-law cited). On the other hand, advantages resulting from a general measure applicable without distinction to all economic operators do not constitute State aid within the meaning of [Article 107 TFEU] (see, to that effect, Case C-156/98 *Germany v Commission* [2000] ECR I-6857, paragraph 22, and Joined Cases C-393/04 and C-41/05 *Air Liquide Industries Belgium* [2006] ECR I-5293, paragraph 32 and the case-law cited).' (paras 72–3)

'As regards appraisal of the condition of selectivity, it is clear from settled case-law that [Article 107(1) TFEU] requires assessment of whether, under a particular legal regime, a national measure is such as to favour 'certain undertakings or the production of certain goods' in comparison with others which, in the light of the objective pursued by that regime, are in a comparable factual and legal situation (… Case C-487/06 P *British Aggregates v Commission* [2008] ECR I-10515, paragraph 82 and the case-law cited).' (para 75)

The General Court analysis of advantages for offshore companies

'The General Court concluded, in paragraph 185 of the judgment under appeal, that there are no selective advantages for offshore companies. It found that the Commission, having failed to observe the analytical framework relating to the determination of the tax measure's selectivity … did not succeed in demonstrating that offshore companies, which by their nature have no physical presence in Gibraltar, enjoy selective advantages. That reasoning is vitiated by an error of law.' (paras 85–6)

'First, it is appropriate to recall that the Court has consistently held that [Article 107(1) TFEU] does not distinguish between measures of State intervention by reference to their causes or their aims but defines them in relation to their effects, and thus independently of the techniques used (see *British Aggregates v Commission*, paragraphs 85 and 89 and the case-law cited, and Case C-279/08 P *Commission v Netherlands* [2011] ECR I-0000, paragraph 51).' (para 87)

'The General Court's approach, based solely on a regard for the regulatory technique used by the proposed tax reform, does not allow the effects of the tax measure in question to be considered and excludes from the outset any possibility that the fact that no tax liability is incurred by offshore companies may be classified as a "selective advantage". That approach is … at variance with the case-law cited in paragraph 87 above.' (para 88)

'Secondly, the General Court's approach also disregards the case-law cited in paragraph 71 above, according to which the existence of a selective advantage for an undertaking entails mitigation of the charges which are normally included in its budget. The Court admittedly held in paragraph 56 of *Portugal v Commission* that the determination of the reference framework has a particular importance in the case of tax measures, since the very existence of an advantage may be established only when compared with "normal" taxation. However, contrary to the General Court's reasoning … that case-law does not make the classification of a tax system as "selective" conditional upon that system being designed in such a way that undertakings which might enjoy a selective advantage are, in general, liable to the same tax burden as other undertakings but benefit from derogating provisions, so that the selective advantage may be identified as being the difference between the normal tax burden and that borne by those former undertakings.' (paras 89–93)

'Thirdly, the General Court was wrong in criticising the Commission, in paragraphs 184 to 186 of the judgment under appeal, for not demonstrating the existence of a selective advantage for offshore companies, having failed to identify in the contested decision a reference framework for establishing the existence of a selective advantage. It should be noted in that respect that, contrary to what the General Court held … it is apparent … that the Commission examined the existence of selective advantages for offshore companies in the light of the tax regime at issue, which formally applies to all undertakings. It is thus apparent that the contested decision identifies that regime as a reference framework in relation to which offshore companies are, in fact, favoured.' (paras 94–5)

'Lastly, the Commission, contrary to what the General Court held, did demonstrate to the requisite legal standard in the contested decision that offshore companies enjoy, in the light of that reference framework, selective advantages within the meaning of the case-law cited in paragraph 75 above.' (para 96)

The regime at issue, even though it is founded on criteria that are in themselves of a general nature, discriminates in practice between companies which are in a comparable situation with regard to the objective of the proposed tax reform. (para 101)

'Admittedly, according to the case-law cited in paragraph 73 above, a different tax burden resulting from the application of a "general" tax regime is not sufficient on its own to establish the selectivity of taxation for the purposes of [Article 107(1) TFEU]. Thus, the criteria forming the basis of assessment which are adopted by a tax system must also, in order to be capable of being recognised as conferring selective advantages, be such as to characterise the recipient undertakings, by virtue of the properties which are specific to them, as a privileged category, thus permitting such a regime to be described as favouring "certain" undertakings or the production of "certain" goods within the meaning of [Article 107(1) TFEU]. That is specifically the case here. In that regard, it should be observed that the fact that offshore companies are not taxed is not a random consequence of the regime at issue, but the inevitable consequence of the fact that the bases of assessment are specifically designed so that offshore companies, which by their nature have no employees and do not occupy business premises, have no tax base under the bases of assessment adopted in the proposed tax reform.' (paras 103–6)

Comment

Gibraltar is one of the most important selectivity rulings of the past few years, in which the Court vigorously reaffirmed its effects-based approach to state aid assessment, noting the scheme in question de facto favoured offshore companies, and criticising the general Court's formalistic review.

In its Draft Notice on the notion of state aid, the Commission makes reference to the case and notes that: 'De facto selectivity can be established in cases where, although the formal criteria for the application of the measure are formulated in general and objective terms, the structure of the measure is such that its effects significantly favour a particular group of undertakings (as in the examples indicated above).' (para 122)

Banco Santander v Commission (Spanish Goodwill)	**State Aid**
Case T-399/11	Condition 3—Selectivity
General Court, 7 November 2014	

Facts

Application for annulment of part of a Commission decision on the Spanish tax amortisation of financial goodwill for foreign shareholding acquisitions. The contested decision declared the scheme at issue, which was introduces under Spanish corporation tax, to be incompatible with the internal market where it applies to the acquisition of shareholdings in companies established outside the European Union. Subsequently, the Commission ordered Spain to recover the aid granted. The General Court annulled the Commission decision.

Held

A measure could be held to be selective even when its application was not limited to a clearly defined sector of activity. 'Indeed, the Court of Justice recognised the existence of State aid where a measure is "essentially intended to apply" to a sector of activity, or even to several sectors (Case C-169/84 *COFAZ v Commission* [1990] ECR I-3083, paragraphs 22 and 23, and Case C-126/01 *GEMO* [2003] ECR I-13769, paragraphs 37 to 39).' (paras 39–40)

'[T]he definition of a category of undertakings which are exclusively favoured by the measure at issue is a prerequisite for recognising the existence of State aid ... Article 107(1) TFEU requires assessment of whether, under a particular statutory scheme, a State measure is such as to "favour certain undertakings or the production of certain goods" in comparison with other undertakings which are in a legal and factual situation that is comparable in the light of the objective pursued by the measure in question.' (paras 45–7)

'However, where the measure at issue, even though it constitutes a derogation from the common or "normal" tax regime, is potentially available to all undertakings, it is not possible to compare, in the light of the objective pursued by the common or "normal" regime, the legal and factual situation of undertakings which are able to benefit from the measure with that of undertakings which cannot benefit from it.' (para 48)

'It follows from the foregoing that for the condition of selectivity to be satisfied, a category of undertakings which are exclusively favoured by the measure at issue must be identified in all cases and that, in the situation referred to in paragraph 48 above, the mere finding that a derogation from the common or "normal" tax regime has been provided for cannot give rise to selectivity.' (para 49)

'Furthermore, it is for the Commission to prove that a measure creates differences between undertakings which, with regard to the objective pursued, are in a comparable factual and legal situation (Case C-279/08 P *Commission v Netherlands* [2011] ECR I-7671, paragraph 62).' (para 50)

'In *Commission v Netherlands*, cited in paragraph 50 above (paragraph 63), the Court of Justice thus noted that the Commission had adequately established in the contested decision that only a specific group of large industrial undertakings engaged in trade between the Member States enjoyed an advantage which was not available to other undertakings. The Commission therefore succeeded, in the case giving rise to that judgment, in establishing that the measure at issue applied selectively to certain undertakings or the production of certain goods. Similarly, in *Commission and Spain v Government of Gibraltar and United Kingdom*, cited in paragraph 33 above (paragraph 96), the Court of Justice found that the Commission had adequately established, in the contested decision, that certain undertakings, "offshore" companies, benefited from selective advantages.' (paras 51, 52)

'In this case, it is therefore necessary to assess whether the various reasons on which the Commission relied in the contested decision to find that the measure at issue is selective, which it restated in the legal proceedings, make it possible to establish that that measure is selective in nature.' (para 53)

In its decision, the Commission, to conclude that the measure at issue is selective, relied primarily on the existence of a derogation from a reference framework. However, 'the existence, even if it were established, of a derogation from or exception to the reference framework identified by the Commission cannot, in itself, establish that the measure at issue favours "certain undertakings or the production of certain goods" within the meaning of Article 107(1) TFEU, since that measure is available, a priori, to any undertaking.' (paras 54–6)

'It is true that, in certain cases, undertakings can effectively be excluded from the scope of a measure which is none the less presented as a general measure (see, to that effect, Joined Cases 6/69 and 11/69 *Commission v France* [1969] ECR 523, paragraphs 20 and 21, and *Commission and Spain v Government of Gibraltar and United Kingdom*, cited in paragraph 33 above, paragraphs 101 and 107).' (para 58)

'[I]t should be recalled that a measure which is to be applied regardless of the nature of the activity of undertakings is not, in principle, selective (see, to that effect, *Adria-Wien Pipeline and Wietersdorfer & Peggauer Zementwerke*, cited in paragraph 41 above, paragraph 36). Furthermore, the measure at issue does not set any minimum amount in respect of the minimum 5% shareholding threshold referred to in paragraph 57 above and therefore does not in fact restrict the undertakings which can take advantage of it to those which possess sufficient financial resources to do so, unlike the measure at issue in the case giving rise to the judgment in Joined Cases T-227/01 to T-229/01, T-265/01, T-266/01 and T-270/01 *Diputación Foral de Álava and Others v Commission* [2009] ECR II-3029, paragraphs 161 and 162.' (paras 61–2)

'Finally, the measure at issue provides that a tax advantage is to be granted on the basis of a condition linked to the purchase of particular financial assets, that is to say shareholdings in foreign companies. However, in *Germany v Commission*, cited in paragraph 42 above (paragraph 22), the Court of Justice ruled that a tax concession in favour of taxpayers who sold certain financial assets and could offset the resulting profit in the case of shareholding acquisitions in capital companies having their registered office in certain regions conferred on those taxpayers an advantage which, as a general measure applicable without distinction to all economically active persons, did not constitute aid within the meaning of the relevant provisions of the Treaty. The measure at issue therefore does not exclude, a priori, any category of undertakings from taking advantage of it.' (paras 63–5)

'As a consequence, even if the measure at issue constitutes a derogation from the reference framework used by the Commission, this would not, in any event, be a ground for establishing that that measure favours "certain undertakings or the production of certain goods" within the meaning of Article 107(1) TFEU.' (para 66)

'Secondly, the Commission stated that 'the contested measure [was] selective in that it only favour[ed] certain groups of undertakings that carr[ied] out certain investments abroad' (recital 102 of the contested decision). It argued that a measure which favoured only undertakings satisfying the conditions on which its grant was subject was selective 'by law' and that it is not necessary to ensure that that measure is likely to have the effect of conferring an advantage only on certain undertakings or the production of certain goods. However, nor does this other reason for the contested decision make it possible to establish that the measure at issue is selective in nature. According to settled case-law, Article 107(1) TFEU distinguishes between State interventions on the basis of their effects (Case 173/73 *Italy v Commission* [1974] ECR 709, paragraph 27, and Case C-159/01 *Netherlands v Commission* [2004] ECR I-4461, paragraph 51). It is therefore on the basis of the effects of the measure at issue that it is necessary to evaluate whether that measure constitutes state aid, in particular because it is selective (see, to that effect, *Commission and Spain v Government of Gibraltar and United Kingdom*, cited in paragraph 33 above, paragraphs 87 and 88).' (paras 67–9)

'Furthermore, in the judgment in Case C-417/10 *3M Italia* [2012] ECR, paragraph 42, the Court of Justice ruled that the fact that only taxpayers satisfying the conditions for the application of the measure at issue in that case could benefit from the measure could not in itself make it into a selective measure.' (para 70)

'Finally, in *Commission and Spain v Government of Gibraltar and United Kingdom*, cited in paragraph 33 above (paragraphs 103, 104 and 107), the Court of Justice ruled that not all tax differentiation involved the existence of aid and that, in order for tax differentiation to be classified as aid, it had to be possible to identify a specific category of undertakings which can be distinguished on account of their specific characteristics.' (para 71)

'However, the approach proposed by the Commission could, contrary to the case-law referred to in paragraph 71 above, lead to every tax measure the benefit of which is subject to certain conditions being found to be selective, even though the beneficiary undertakings would not share any specific characteristic distinguishing them from other undertakings, apart from the fact that they would be capable of satisfying the conditions to which the grant of the measure is subject.' (para 72)

'Thirdly, in recital 154 of the contested decision, the Commission stated that it "[considered] that … in the present case, the contested measure [wa]s intended to promote the export of capital out of Spain in order to strengthen the position of Spanish companies abroad, thereby improving the competitiveness of the beneficiaries of the scheme". In that regard, it should be recalled that a State measure which benefits all undertakings in national territory, without distinction, cannot therefore constitute State aid with regard to the criterion of selectivity (*Adria-Wien Pipeline and Wietersdorfer & Peggauer Zementwekre*, cited in paragraph 41 above, paragraph 35) … the fact that a measure treats undertakings which are taxable in one Member State more favourably than undertakings which are taxable in the other Member States, in particular because the measure facilitates acquisitions by undertakings established in a Member State of shareholdings in the capital of undertakings established abroad, does not affect the analysis of the selectivity criterion.' (paras 73–6)

'It is true that in *Commission v France*, cited in paragraph 58 above (paragraph 20), the Court of Justice ruled that an advantage granted" in favour only of national products exported and for the purpose of helping them to compete in other Member States with products originating in the latter" constituted State aid. However, that reference to products originating in other Member States concerned the condition relating to the effect on competition and trade. That interpretation of *Commission v France*, cited in paragraph 58 above, is supported by the judgment in Case 57/86 *Greece v Commission* [1988] ECR 2855, paragraph 8, in which the distinction between national products and products of other Member States does not appear in the analysis of the criteria relating to selectivity. Similarly, in the judgment in Case C-501/00 *Spain v Commission* [2004] ECR I-7617, paragraph 120, the distinction between national products and products from other Member States is not taken into account within the context of the analysis of the selectivity of the measure. It is clear from that case-law that the finding that a measure is selective is based on a difference in treatment between categories of undertakings under the legislation of a single Member State and not a difference in treatment between the undertakings of one Member State and those of other Member States.' (paras 77–9)

'Fourthly, it cannot be inferred from the case-law on which the Commission relies that the EU courts have already classified a tax measure as selective without it being established that the measure at issue favoured a particular category of undertakings or the production of certain goods, to the exclusion of other undertakings or the production of other goods.' (para 81)

Comment

The General Court held that in its decision the Commission failed to establish that the Spanish regime was selective. The Court rejected the Commission's reading of the European Courts' selectivity case-law, and held that the finding of a derogation from the relevant reference framework will not suffice to conclude that a measure is prima facie selective.

The Court held that when the measure in question constitutes a derogation from the common or 'normal' tax regime, but is potentially available to all undertakings, it does not necessarily favour 'certain undertakings or the production of certain goods' for the purposes of Article 107(1) TFEU. For the condition of selectivity to be satisfied, a category of undertakings which are exclusively favoured by the measure at issue must be identified.

The Commission has appealed the judgment to the Court of Justice, Case C-21/15P, judgment pending.

Philip Morris v Commission	**State Aid**
Case 730/79	Condition 4—Effect on Trade
Court of Justice, [1980] ECR 2671	

Facts

Philip Morris Holland BV was the Dutch subsidiary of an international tobacco manufacturer. In 1978, the Netherlands notified the Commission of its intention to grant aid to Philip Morris in accordance with its law 'on the promotion and guidance of investment'. This aid would have assisted the recipient in concentrating its production of cigarettes by closing one of its two Dutch factories down and greatly increasing the annual production capacity of the second factory. Following an in-depth investigation, the Commission decided not to approve the aid. Philip Morris brought an action for annulment against this decision before the Court of Justice. In its judgment the Court considered, among other things, whether the aid in question affected trade between Member States. Action dismissed.

Held

'When state financial aid strengthens the position of an undertaking compared with other undertakings competing in intra-Community trade the latter must be regarded as affected by that aid. In this case the aid which the Netherlands government proposed to grant was for an undertaking organized for international trade and this is proved by the high percentage of its production which it intends to export to other member states. The aid in question was to help to enlarge its production capacity and consequently to increase its capacity to maintain the flow of trade including that between member states. On the other hand the aid is said to have reduced the cost of converting the production facilities and has thereby given the applicant a competitive advantage over manufacturers who have completed or intend to complete at their own expense a similar increase in the production capacity of their plant.' (para 11)

'These circumstances, which have been mentioned in the recitals in the preamble to the disputed decision and which the applicant has not challenged, justify the Commission's deciding that the proposed aid would be likely to affect trade between member states and would threaten to distort competition between undertakings established in different member states.' (para 12)

'It follows from the foregoing considerations that the first submission must be rejected in substance and also as far as concerns the inadequacy of the statement of reasons on which the decision was based.' (para 13)

Comment

Intra-EU trade is affected when a measure strengthens the position of an undertaking compared with other undertakings competing in intra-Community trade.

Further, the Court indicated that 'effect on trade condition' is satisfied when such effect is likely (para 12) with no need to show actual effect. Similarly, when the measure threatens to distort competition, the 'competition distortion condition' is fulfilled.

In its judgment the Court also considered whether the determination of market definition is a prerequisite for consideration of effect. It held that that is not the case.

In Case 78/76 *Firma Steinike und Weinlig*, the Court held that: '[A]ny breach by a Member State of an obligation under the Treaty in connexion with the prohibition laid down in [Article 107 TFEU] cannot be justified by the fact that other Member States are also failing to fulfil this obligation. The effects of more than one distortion of competition on trade between Member States do not cancel one another out but accumulate and the damaging consequences to the common market are increased.' (para 24)

Altmark Trans and Regierungspräsidium Magdeburg	**State Aid**
Case C-280/00	Condition 4—Effect on Trade
Court of Justice, [2003] ECR I-7747	

Facts

A preliminary reference from the German Federal Administrative Court concerning the interpretation of Article 107 TFEU. The case at issue concerned a licence, granted to Altmark, in line with national law, for the transport of passengers by road vehicles on scheduled services. One of Altmark's competitors, which was unsuccessful in obtaining the licence, challenged its legality under Article 107 TFEU. Among other things, the German Court, in its reference, asked about the interpretation of the effect-on-trade condition in that article.

Held

The national court's question concerns the condition in Article 107 TFEU which states that the intervention in question must be liable to affect trade between Member States. (paras 75–6)

'In this respect, it must be observed, first, that it is not impossible that a public subsidy granted to an undertaking which provides only local or regional transport services and does not provide any transport services outside its State of origin may none the less have an effect on trade between Member States.' (para 77)

'Where a Member State grants a public subsidy to an undertaking, the supply of transport services by that undertaking may for that reason be maintained or increased with the result that undertakings established in other Member States have less chance of providing their transport services in the market in that Member State (see, to that effect, Case 102/87 *France v Commission* [1988] ECR 4067, paragraph 19; Case C-305/89 *Italy v Commission* [1991] ECR I-1603, paragraph 26; and *Spain v Commission*, paragraph 40).' (para 78)

'In the present case, that finding is not merely hypothetical, since, as appears in particular from the observations of the Commission, several Member States have since 1995 started to open certain transport markets to competition from undertakings established in other Member States, so that a number of undertakings are already offering their urban, suburban or regional transport services in Member States other than their State of origin.' (para 79)

'[A]ccording to the Court's case-law, there is no threshold or percentage below which it may be considered that trade between Member States is not affected. The relatively small amount of aid or the relatively small size of the undertaking which receives it does not as such exclude the possibility that trade between Member States might be affected (see *Tubemeuse*, paragraph 43, and *Spain* v *Commission*, paragraph 42).' (para 81)

'The second condition for the application of [Article 107(1) TFEU], namely that the aid must be capable of affecting trade between Member States, does not therefore depend on the local or regional character of the transport services supplied or on the scale of the field of activity concerned.' (para 82)

Comment

The judgment set the threshold for 'effect on trade' at a rather low level, clarifying that there is no set threshold or percentage below which it may be considered that trade between Member States is not affected. Accordingly, a purely local provision of services, which are not offered outside the region or state may nonetheless affect intra-Union trade. That is so since the aid may strengthen the recipient's position on the local market, thus making it more difficult for potential competitors to enter this market in the future.

In its 'Communication on the application of the European Union State aid rules to compensation granted for the provision of services of general economic interest' [2012] OJ C8/02, the Commission notes that: '[The] relatively small amount of aid or the relatively small size of the recipient undertaking does not a priori mean that trade between Member States may not be affected.' (para 39).

<table>
<tr><td>

Commission v Italy and Wam SpA
Case C-494/06P
Court of Justice, [2009] ECR I-3639

</td><td>

State Aid
Condition 4—Effect on Trade
Competition Distortion

</td></tr>
</table>

Facts

An appeal by the Commission to set aside the judgment of the General Court (Joined Cases T-304/04 and T-316/04 *Italy and Wam v Commission*) by which the Court annulled a Commission decision which established that an Italian law which provided financial support to exporting companies undertaking market penetration programmes in non-Member States constituted state aid. The General Court in its judgment criticised the Commission for breaching its obligation to state reasons. On appeal, the Court of Justice upheld the General Court's judgment. Among other things, it engaged in detailed review of the 'competition distortion' and 'effect-on-trade' conditions.

Held

'[F]or the purpose of categorising a national measure as State aid, it is not necessary to demonstrate that the aid has a real effect on trade between Member States and that competition is actually being distorted, but only to examine whether that aid is liable to affect such trade and distort competition (Case C-222/04 *Cassa di Risparmio di Firenze and Others* [2006] ECR I-289, paragraph 140 and the case-law cited).' (para 50)

'With regard more specifically to the condition that trade between Member States be affected, it follows from the case-law that the grant of aid by a Member State, in the form of a tax relief, to some of its taxable persons must be regarded as likely to have an effect on trade and, consequently, as meeting that condition, where those taxable persons perform an economic activity in the field of such trade or it is conceivable that they are in competition with operators established in other Member States (see *Portugal v Commission*, paragraph 91, and Case C-172/03 *Heiser* [2005] ECR I-1627, paragraph 35).' (para 51)

'Furthermore, the Court has held that, when aid granted by a Member State strengthens the position of an undertaking compared with other undertakings competing in intra-Community trade, the latter must be regarded as influenced by that aid (*Cassa di Risparmio di Firenze and Others*, paragraph 141 and the case-law cited). In that regard, the fact that an economic sector has been liberalised at Community level may serve to determine that the aid has a real or potential effect on competition and affects trade between Member States (*Cassa di Risparmio di Firenze and Others*, paragraph 142 and the case-law cited).' (paras 52–3)

'With regard to the condition of the distortion of competition, it should be borne in mind in that regard that, in principle, aid intended to release an undertaking from costs which it would normally have to bear in its day-to-day management or normal activities distorts the conditions of competition (see Case C-156/98 *Germany v Commission* [2000] ECR I-6857, paragraph 30, and *Heiser*, paragraph 55).' (para 54)

Regarding the specific circumstances of the present case, the General Court correctly stated that: '[T]he aid at issue is intended to finance, by means of loans at reduced rates, expenses for market penetration programmes in non-member States concerning the establishment of permanent structures or for trade promotion and that the grant equivalent is relatively small in amount.' Furthermore the Court 'underlined that the aid is not intended directly and immediately to support exports to outside the EU, but to finance a market penetration programme.' (para 56)

The General Court 'rightly explained that it would suffice that the Commission show correctly how the aid at issue was likely to affect trade between Member States and to distort or threaten to distort competition. The [General Court] notably stressed in that context that the Commission was not obliged to carry out an economic analysis of the actual situation of the relevant market or the patterns of the trade in question between Member States or to show the real effect of the aid at issue, in particular on the prices applied by Wam, or to examine Wam's sales on the United Kingdom market.' (para 58)

With regard to the practical implementation of those principles, the General Court was correct to hold that the Commission did not provide sufficient reasoning. The contested decision does not make it possible to understand how, in the circumstances of the present case, the aid at issue was likely to affect trade between Member States and to distort or threaten to distort competition. (paras 59–61)

'In that context, it should be noted, in particular, that although it follows from the case-law cited in paragraphs 50 and 53 of this judgment that such effects can, in principle, result from the fact that the beneficiary of an aid is active on a liberalised European market, the fact remains that in the circumstances of this case and contrary to the circumstances giving rise to those cases, the aid at issue is not directly connected to the activity of the beneficiary on that market, but is intended to finance expenditure for a non-member State market penetration programme. In those circumstances, and all the more when it involves aid, the grant equivalent of which was of relatively low value, the effect of the aid on trade and on intra-Community competition is less immediate and even less discernible and this requires a greater effort to state reasons on the part of the Commission.' (para 62)

'Finally, as to the case-law cited in paragraph 54 of this judgment, according to which, in principle, the aid which is intended to release an undertaking from costs which it would normally have had to bear in its day-to-day management or normal activities distorts the conditions of competition, it is sufficient to note that the aid at issue is not in fact intended to release Wam from such costs.' (para 63)

Comment

The Court of Justice dismissed the appeal and confirmed that the General Court had not departed from the Court's case-law, but rather applied it while taking account of the specific circumstances of the case.

The Court held that trade between Member States may be affected even if the recipient of the state aid exports all or most of its production outside the European Union. In such instance the effect on trade is less immediate and cannot be assumed from the mere fact that the market is open to competition.

On the 'competition distortion' condition, the Court reiterated its position that, in principle, aid intended to release an undertaking from costs which it would normally have to bear in its day-to-day management or normal activities distorts the conditions of competition.

In its Draft notice on State aid, the Commission notes that: 'An advantage granted to an undertaking operating in a market which is open to competition will normally be assumed to distort competition and also be liable to affect trade between Member States. Indeed, "where State financial aid strengthens the position of an undertaking as compared with other undertakings competing in intra-Community trade, the latter must be regarded as affected by the aid" [Case T-288/07 *Friulia Venezia Giulia*, [2001] ECR II-1619, paragraph 41]'. (para 191)

Public support can be considered capable to affect intra-EU trade even if the recipient is not directly involved in cross-border trade. For instance, the subsidy may make it more difficult for operators in other Member States to enter the market by maintaining or increasing local supply [Case C-280/00 *Altmark Trans* [2003] ECR I-7747, paragraph 78]'. (para 192)

'Even a public subsidy granted to an undertaking which provides only local or regional services and does not provide any services outside its State of origin may nonetheless have an effect on trade between Member States where undertakings from other Member States might provide such services (also through the right of establishment) and this possibility is not merely hypothetical. For example, where a Member State grants a public subsidy to an undertaking for supplying transport services, the supply of these services may, by virtue of the subsidy, be maintained or increased with the result that undertakings established in other Member States have less of a chance of providing their transport services in the market in that Member State. Such an effect may however be less likely where the scope of the economic activity is very small, as may be evidenced by a very low turnover.' (para 193)

Index

Peel each sticker, carefully fold along scored line to create a navigation tab, and stick at the top (or side) of the appropriate page.

Market Definition

Market Definition

Undertakings

Undertakings

Table of Cases

Table of Cases

Table of Cases

Article 101 TFEU

Article 101 TFEU

Horizontal and
Vertical Agreements

Horizontal and
Vertical Agreements

Article 102 TFEU

Article 102 TFEU

Collective
Dominance

Collective
Dominance

Competition
and the State

Competition
and the State

Competition
and IPR

Competition
and IPR

Mergers and
Acquisitions

Mergers and
Acquisitions

Enforcement—
Commission

Enforcement—
Commission

Enforcement—
National Court

Enforcement—
National Court

Extraterritoriality

Extraterritoriality

State aid

State aid

Index

Index